SAGALASSOS V

Dedicated to the memory of Hubert DEVIJVER (1936-1997),
who made the Sagalassos families speak again

and to the memory of Richard VAN STEEN (1933-1997)
member of the L. Baert-Hofman family, one of our major sponsors.

ACTA ARCHAEOLOGICA LOVANIENSIA
MONOGRAPHIAE
11/A

VOLUME I

KATHOLIEKE UNIVERSITEIT LEUVEN
AFDELING ARCHEOLOGIE
LEUVEN (BELGIUM)

SAGALASSOS V

REPORT ON THE SURVEY AND EXCAVATION CAMPAIGNS
OF 1996 AND 1997

Edited by
M. Waelkens and L. Loots

Leuven University Press
2000

Published with the financial support of the K.U. Leuven Commissie voor Publicaties.

© 2000 Universitaire Pers Leuven / Leuven University Press /
Presses Universitaires de Louvain
Blijde-Inkomststraat 5, B-3000 Leuven (Belgium)

All rights reserved. Except in those cases expressly determined
by law, no part of this publication may be multiplied, saved in
an automated data file or made public in any way whatsoever
without the express prior written consent of the publishers.

ISBN 90 5867 079 1

D/2000/1869/77

CONTENTS

VOLUME I

MARC WAELKENS
Introduction 7
Summary of research 10

PART I. THE SURVEY AND EXCAVATIONS IN 1996 AND 1997
PRELIMINARY REPORTS

MARC WAELKENS, ETIENNE PAULISSEN, HANNELORE VANHAVERBEKE, JEROEN REYNIERS, JEROEN POBLOME, ROLAND DEGEEST, WILLY VIAENE (†), JOZEF DECKERS, BEA DE CUPERE, WIM VAN NEER, HACİ ALİ EKİNCİ AND MUSTAFA ORAL ERBAY
The 1996 and 1997 Surveys in the Territory of Sagalassos 17

MARC WAELKENS, JEROEN POBLOME, ETIENE PAULISSEN, PETER TALLOEN, JULIE VAN DEN BERGH, VANESSA VANDERGINST, BURCU ARIKAN, INGE VAN DAMME, IPEK AKYEL, FEMKE MARTENS, MARLEEN MARTENS, INGE UYTTERHOEVEN, TOM DEBRUYNE, DAVID DEPRAETERE, K. BARAN, BERNARD VANDAELE, ZISSIS PARRAS, ŞAHIN YILDIRIM, SHAWN BUBEL, HANNELORE VANHAVERBEKE, CORINNE LICOPPE, FRÉDÉRIQUE LANDUYT, ROLAND DEGEEST, LUTGARDE VANDEPUT, LIEVEN LOOTS, TERESA PATRÍCIO, SEMİH ERCAN, KOENRAAD VAN BALEN, ELISABETH SMITS, FRANS DEPUYDT, LUC MOENS AND PAUL DE PAEPE
The 1996 and 1997 Excavation Seasons at Sagalassos 217

TERESA PATRÍCIO, SEMTH ERCAN AND KOENRAAD VAN BALEN
Restoration of the Late Hellenistic Fountain House: Field Works 399

MARC WAELKENS, HANDE KÖKTEN ERSOY, KENT SEVERSON, FEMKE MARTENS AND SELÇUK SENER
The Sagalassos Neon Library Mosaic and its Conservation 419

VOLUME II

PART II. PRE- AND PROTO HISTORICAL RESEARCH

PIERRE M. VERMEERSCH, ILHAME ÖZTÜRK, HACİ ALİ EKİNCİ, PATRICK DEGRYSE, BEA DE CUPERE, JEROEN POBLOME, MARC WAELKENS AND WILLY VIAENE (†)
Late Palaeolithic at the Dereköy Karain Cave 451

HANNELORE VANHAVERBEKE
How Can There Still Be Such a Degree of Uncertainty? Problems of Chronology for the Prehistoric Periods in the Territory of Sagalassos. 463

MARC WAELKENS
Sagalassos and Pisidia during the Late Bronze Age 473

PART III. HISTORICAL STUDIES

KATLIJN VANDORPE
Negotiators' Laws from Rebellious Sagalassos in an Early Hellenistic Inscription 489

SIMONE SCHEERS
Coins Found in 1996 and 1997 509

PART IV. URBANISM AND ARCHITECTURAL STUDIES

MARC WAELKENS, LUTGARDE VANDEPUT, CHRISTOF BERNS, BURCU ARIKAN, JEROEN POBLOME AND EBRU TORUN
The Northwest Heroon at Sagalassos 553

LIEVEN LOOTS, MARC WAELKENS AND FRANS DEPUYDT
The City Fortifications of Sagalasoss from the Hellenistic to the Late Roman Period 595

AN STEEGEN, KRIS CAUWENBERGHS, GERARD GOVERS, EDWIN OWENS, MARC WAELKENS AND PHILIP DESMET
The Water Supply to Sagalassos 635

KRISTOF CALLEBAUT, WILLY VIAENE (†), MARC WAELKENS, RAOUL OTTENBURGS AND JEAN NAUD
Provenance and Characterization of Raw Materials for Lime Mortars used at Sagalassos with Special Reference to the Volcanic Rocks 651

PART V. CERAMIC STUDIES

Jeroen Poblome, Haci Ali Ekinci, Ilhame Öztürk,
Patrick Degryse, Willy Viaene (†) and Marc Waelkens
An Early Byzantine Tile and Lime Kiln in the Territory of
Sagalassos   669

Lieven Loots, Marc Waelkens, Willy Clarysse,
Jeroen Poblome and Gerhild Hübner
A Catalogue of the Tile Stamps Found at Sagalassos   685

Roland Degeest, Patrick Degryse, Raoul Ottenburgs,
Willy Viaene (†) and Marc Waelkens
Miniature Jars of Sagalassos. An Analytical, Quantitative
and Typological Overview of a Series of Very Small
Pottery Vessels from Late Antiquity   697

Patrick Degryse, Roland Degeest, Jeroen Poblome,
Willy Viaene (†), Raoul Ottenburgs, Harry Kucha
and Marc Waelkens
Mineralogy and Geochemistry of Roman Common Wares
Produced at Sagalassos and their Possible Clay Sources   709

PART VI. ENVIRONMENTAL STUDIES

Kristien Donners, Marc Waelkens, David Celis,
Kris Nackaerts, Jozef Deckers, Marleen Vermoere
and Hannelore Vanhaverbeke
Towards a Land Evaluation of the Territory of Ancient
Sagalassos   723

Kristof Schroyen, Marleen Vermoere, Ireen Librecht,
Patrick Degryse, Philippe Muchez, Willy Viaene (†),
Eric Smets, Etienne Paulissen, Eric Keppens and
Marc Waelkens
Preliminary Study of Travertine Deposits in the Vicinity of
Sagalassos. Petrography, Geochemistry, Geomorphology
and Palynology   757

Gert Verstraeten, Etienne Paulissen, Ireen Librecht,
and Marc Waelkens
Limestone Platforms around Sagalassos Resulting from
Giant Mass Movements   783

Ireen Librecht, Etienne Paulissen, Gert Verstraeten
and Marc Waelkens
Implications of Environmental Changes on Slope
Evolution near Sagalassos   799

PART VII. ANTHROPOLOGICAL AND ARCHAEOZOOLOGICAL STUDIES

Els Jehaes, Marc Waelkens, Ann Muyldermans,
Jean-Jacques Cassiman, Elisabeth Smits, Jeroen
Poblome, Paul Lambrechts and Ronny Decorte
DNA Analysis of Archaeological Human Remains from
Sagalassos   821

Wim Van Neer, Ruud Wildekamp, Fahrettin Küçük,
Mustafa Ünlüsayin, Marc Waelkens and
Etienne Paulissen
Results of the 1996 Survey of the Fish Fauna of the Aksu
River (Kestros) and Some Lakes in Southwestern Anatolia,
and the Implications for Trade at Sagalassos   833

Ingrid Beuls, Bea De Cupere, Marleen Vermoere,
Leo Vanhecke, Hugues Doutrelepont, Luc Vrydaghs,
Ireen Librecht and Marc Waelkens
Modern Sheep and Goat Herding near Sagalassos and
its Revelance to the Reconstruction of Pastoral Practices in
Roman Times   847

Zissis Parras
An Experimental Approach to Understanding the Bone
Working Industry at Roman Sagalassos   863

INTRODUCTION

During our first visit to Sagalassos in 1984, we had been struck by the extraordinary state of preservation of the city, frozen at a particular moment of time by a massive earthquake, and later covered and protected by erosion material. It was immediately clear to us that excavation would yield much monumental architecture, and possibly also a rich epigraphical and sculptural harvest. But we also realised that, because the site had never been reoccupied or looted since its final decline twelve hundred years ago, its archaeological strata had to be treated as a well-documented archive for the reconstruction of the environmental history of the surrounding area. We believed that the rise, the growth and the decline of the site would never be understood without such a reconstruction and without a detailed study of climatic change, vegetation and faunal history, or without research into the exploitation by the inhabitants of Sagalassos of the raw materials of the district. As a result, beside excavations in the city, the ultimate purpose of the excavation project that was started in 1990, developed into an interdisciplinary study of all its material remains and research concerning the relationship of Sagalassos with its vast territory. From 1994 onward especially, a survey of the geology, the geomorphology, palaeo-ecology and archaeozoology of the surrounding countryside was included in the project.

We realised then that such an interdisciplinary approach would require a specific publication policy. We decided that final reports on specific buildings, certain categories of materials (fine wares, coarse wares, glass, coins, inscriptions), or certain general topics (for example, architectural decoration, settlement history of the district, urbanisation, religious life) would be published in a special series called *Studies in Eastern Mediterranean Archaeology*. Two volumes in this series on the architectural decoration of Sagalassos and the locally produced fine tablewares have been published so far. A third volume on the coarse and common wares from the site, both locally produced and imported, will appear in the fall of 2000. A fourth and fifth volume on the faunal remains of the excavation (by B. De Cupere) and the settlement patterns on the city's vast territory (by H. Vanhaverbeke) are in an advanced stage of preparation.

– L. Vandeput (1997) *The Architectural Decoration in Roman Asia Minor. Sagalassos: a Case Study* (*Studies in Eastern Mediterranean Archaeology edited by M. Waelkens*, vol. I) Brepols Publishers.
– J. Poblome (1999) *Sagalassos Red Slip Ware. Typology and Chronology* (*Studies in Eastern Mediterranean Archaeology edited by M. Waelkens*, vol. II) Brepols Publishers.
– R. Degeest (2000) *The Common Wares of Sagalassos* (*Studies in Eastern Mediterranean Archaeology edited by M. Waelkens*, vol. III) Brepols Publishers.

However, because of this interdisciplinary approach, it rapidly became clear that the preparation of final excavation reports would take a long time. We decided that preliminary reports, in the past presented in *Anatolian Studies*, should still be published within two or three years of the completion of each campaign, in order to present its results and materials (coins, inscriptions, pottery) to the scholarly world. At the same time, the publication of preliminary or partial results of the various non-archaeological or non-historical disciplines, especially those of the exact sciences, should equally not be postponed, as publication in these disciplines tends to be very immediate. It was felt to be important, however, that these results should not 'disappear' in the various scholarly journals or congress proceedings of each discipline, but should be included in the same volumes as the archaeological studies. In fact, our ultimate aim was and still is to show classical archaeologists that an interdisciplinary approach with the study of all kinds of material remains, even the smallest ones, so familiar to pre- and protohistorians, should become a must for classical archaeology.

Therefore, it was decided to create a second publication series, called *Sagalassos*, that would contain preliminary or partial results from all the disciplines involved in the project. We realised that this series, of which this is the fifth volume, would be rather heterogeneous, but we were confident that, as the project proceeded, it would become more obvious with each new volume how all these data are interlocked and linked to the archaeological fieldwork. To make this point clearer, from this volume onward, a summary of all the activities and results published in the Sagalassos volumes will be presented at the beginning of each volume. Four volumes with the results of the surveys in the years 1986-1989 and the survey and excavation seasons of the years 1990-1995 have already been published:

- M. Waelkens (ed.) (1993) *Sagalassos I. First General Report on the Survey (1986-1989) and Excavations (1990-1991)* (Acta Archaeologica Lovaniensia Monographiae 5) Leuven University Press.
- M. Waelkens and J.Poblome (eds) (1993) *Sagalassos II. Report on the Third Excavation Campaign of 1992* (Acta Archaeologica Lovaniensia Monographiae 6) Leuven University Press.
- M. Waelkens and J. Poblome (eds) (1995) *Sagalassos III. Report on the Fourth Excavation Campaign of 1993* (Acta Archaeologica Lovaniensia Monographiae 7) Leuven University Press.
- M. Waelkens and J. Poblome (eds) (1997) *Sagalassos IV. Report on the Survey and Excavation Campaigns of 1994 and 1995* (Acta Archaeologica Lovaniensia Monographiae 9) Leuven University Press.

A third category of papers, presenting more or less intermediate or completed studies of a more general nature, but too limited in length to be published as monographs (for example, on the settlement development during a specific period, seismic activities, the changing environment, cultural regionalism, etc.) are published in the various scholarly journals or congress proceedings of each discipline. Several of these studies are now in print. The next volumes will include a list of these articles or proceedings as they are published, so that they will not escape the attention of the archaeological public. In 1998-2000, the following articles in this category were published:

- B. De Cupere and M. Vermoere (1998) The antique site of Sagalassos (Turkey): Faunal results from the 1990-1994 excavation seasons, in: H. Buitenhuis, I. Bartosiewicz and A.M. Choyke (eds) *Archaeozoology in the Near East III. Proceedings of the Third International Symposium on the Archaeozoology of Southwestern Asia and Adjacent Areas*, Groningen: 276-284.
- G. Govers and J. Poesen (1998) Field experiments on the transport of rock fragments by animal trampling on scree slopes, *Geomorphology* 23, 193-203.
- J. Poblome (1998) Dionysiac oinophoroi from Sagalassos found in Egypt, in: W. Clarysse, A. Schoors and H. Willems (eds) *Egyptian Religion. The Last Thousand Years 1. Studies Dedicated to the Memory of Jan Quaegebeur* (Orientalia Lovaniensia Analecta 84) Leuven, 205-225.
- J. Poblome (1998) Sagalassos red slip ware and the ceramic tradition of sigillata, *Forum Archaeologiae. Zeitschrift für klassische Archäologie* 7, VI (only available on the internet: http://allergy.hno.akhwien.ac.al/forum/forum0698/07sagalassos.htm).
- J. Poblome and M. Waelkens (1998) Recent excavations in the Potters' Quarter of Roman Sagalassos, *Near Eastern Archaeology* 61, 129.
- J. Poblome, P. Degryse, I. Librecht and M. Waelkens (1998) Sagalassos red slip ware. The organization of a manufactory, *Münstersche Beiträge zur antiken Handelsgeschichte* 17, 52-64.
- J. Poblome, H.A. Ekinci, I. Öztürk, P. Degryse, W. Viaene and M. Waelkens (1998) An early Byzantine tile kiln in the territory of Sagalassos, *XIXth Kazı sonuçları toplantısı, Ankara 26-30 Mayış 1997*, Ankara, 507-522.
- J. Poblome, M. Schlitz and P. Degryse (1998) Recycling misfired pottery. A standard practice of the potters at ancient Sagalassos?, *Forum Archaeologiae. Zeitschrift für klassische Archäologie* 7, VII (only available on the internet: http://allergy.hno.akhwien.ac.al/forum/forum0698/07sagalassos.htm).
- H. Vanhaverbeke and M. Waelkens (1998) Lower, Middle and Upper Palaeolithic in the territory of Sagalassos (SW Turkey): problems and prospects, *Anatolia-Eski Anadolu* 6, 1-19.
- M. Vermoere and E. Smets (1998) Palynological investigations of travertine deposits in Başköy (Southwest Turkey), *Biologisch Jaarboek Dodonaea* 64, 160-175.
- M. Waelkens (1998) The survey and archaeometrical research at Sagalassos 1996, in: *XIII. Arkeometri sonuçları toplantısı. Ankara 26-30 Mayış 1997*, Ankara, 1-30.
- K. Van Balen, S. Ercan and T. Patrício (1999) Compatibility and retreatability versus reversibility: a case study at the late Hellenistic nymphaeum of Sagalassos (Turkey), *American Society for Testing and Materials. Standard Technical Publication* 1355, 105-118.
- H. Vanhaverbeke, P.M. Vermeersch and M. Waelkens (1996) [1999] Living between the river and the lake: the evolution of the prehistoric settlement pattern on the territory of Sagalassos (Pisidia, Southwestern Turkey), *Aegean Archaeology* 3, 7-25.
- M. Vermoere, P. Degryse, L. Vanhecke, Ph. Muchez, E. Paulissen, E. Smets and M. Waelkens (1999) Pollen analysis of two travertine sections in Başköy (southwestern Turkey): implications for environmental conditions during the early Holocene, *Review of Palaeobotany and Palynology* 105, 93-110.
- M. Waelkens, E. Paulissen, M. Vermoere, P. Degryse, D. Celis, K. Schroyen, B. De Cupere, I. Librecht, K. Nackaerts, H. Vanhaverbeke, W. Viaene, Ph. Muchez, R. Ottenburgs, S. Deckers, W. Van Neer, E. Smets, G. Govers, G. Verstraeten, A. Steegen and K. Cauwenberghs (1999) Man and environment on the territory of Sagalassos, a classical city in SW Turkey, *Quaternary Science Reviews* 18, 697-709.
- M. Waelkens (1999) The 1997 archaeometrical research at Sagalassos, in: *XIV. Arkeometri sonuçları toplantısı. Tarsus 25-29 Mayış 1998*, Ankara, 283-312.
- M. Waelkens (1999) Sagalassos. Religious life in a Pisidian town during the Hellenistic and Early Imperial period, in: C. Bonnet and A. Motte (eds) *Les syncrétismes religieux dans*

le monde méditerranéen antique. Actes du Colloque International en l'honneur de Franz Cumont à l'occasion du cinquantième anniversaire de sa mort; Rome, Academia Belgica, 25-27 septembre 1997, Bruxelles-Brussel-Rome, 191-226.
- R. Degeest, R. Ottenburghs, H. Kucha, W. Viaene, P. Degryse and M. Waelkens (1999) The late Roman unguentaria of Sagalassos, *Bulletin Antieke Beschaving* 74, 247-262.
- M. Waelkens, M. Sintubin, Ph. Muchez and E. Paulissen (2000) Archaeological, geomorphological and geological evidence for a major earthquake at Sagalassos (SW Turkey) around the middle of the seventh century AD, in: B. McGuire, D. Griffiths and I. Stewart (eds) *The Archaeology of Geological Catastrophes. Geological Society, London, Special Publications* 171, 373-383.

In accordance with this publication policy, the new Sagalassos volume again contains two types of article. First, there are almost completed studies on specific topics such as inventories of certain categories of objects found in 1996 and 1997. These will, at a later stage, be included more or less unchanged in a more general catalogue of all objects of this specific class. This material is included in the series so that it becomes available to the scholarly public. A second category of contributions comprises preliminary reports of the various research activities during the same two years. These topics will generally be completed and corrected by future research and their results may be altered considerably before they can be presented as a final publication. They are presented here to show the scientific community at large their importance for classical archaeology. The present volume thus contains preliminary reports of the 1996 and 1997 excavation and survey seasons.

ACKNOWLEDGEMENTS

Thanks are due to the Anıtlar ve Müzeler Genel Müdürlüğü and its General Directors, Prof. Dr. Engin Özgen and Akif Işık, of the Turkish Ministry of Culture, who gave permission for the excavations and the surveys. We wish to thank Miss Solmaz Gülsen, Miss Ümran Yüğrük, Miss Melek Yıldızturan, Mr. Mustafa Akaslan and Mr. Reyhan Körpe who acted as representatives of the Ministry during the 1996 and 1997 campaigns.

We also wish to acknowledge the kind co-operation of Erhan Tanju, governor of Burdur, of the staff of the Emniyet Müdürlüğü and of the Archaeological Museum at Burdur (especially its director Haci Ali Ekinci). Finally, we also thank all Kaymakamlık and Belediye officials at Ağlasun (and especially the mayor Mustafa Altındal) for their valuable help.

Special thanks are due to the authorities of the Catholic University of Leuven and the many 'Friends of Sagalassos' and private sponsors for their continuous support and funding.

The contents of the present volume present results of the Belgian Programme of Interuniversity Poles of Attraction (IUAP IV/12) initiated by the Belgian State, Prime Minister's Office, Federal Services for Scientific, Technical and Cultural Affairs. Our research is also supported by a Concerted Action (GOA 97/2) financed by the Flemish Government and by a project (G.2145.94) financed by the Fund for Scientific Research-Flanders. Scientific responsibility is assumed by the authors. We thank Sue Harper for having corrected the English of all contributions to this volume. A major financial contribution to this publication was made by BACOB Bank, Brussels.

Marc Waelkens
L.Baert-Hofman Professor of Archaeology
Catholic University of Leuven
11 October 1998

SUMMARY OF RESEARCH

The completion of the 'low-intensity' survey of the territory of the city has resulted in the identification of ca. 200 'sites'. We realize that this number would be considerably greater if 'intensive' surveying techniques were applied. Unfortunately, this has not been possible since detailed maps of the area or aerial photographs have not so far been available. However, we feel confident that the results are reliable enough to document certain 'trends' in the settlement patterns. These settlement trends and their changes through time in the western half of the city's territory surveyed in 1996 and 1997 are discussed by Waelkens *et al.* These survey campaigns also established the prominent role which the changing landscape and physical environment have played in the occupation history of the area.

The two campaigns of 1996 and 1997 again produced excellent results that document various activities of urban life and that cover almost the complete occupation period of the city since middle Hellenistic times. However, as was to be expected, most excavated sectors produced evidence documenting the last phase of the city's occupation (sixth and seventh centuries AD). In an appendix, Moens and De Paepe have been able to show that the marble of the second Dionysos and satyr group from the middle Antonine nymphaeum of the Upper Agora, like that of the first group already identified in the previous volume as Aphrodisian, also came from Aphrodisias.

The 1997 season saw the inauguration of Sagalassos' first two restored buildings, the late Hellenistic fountain house and the Neon Library. A paper by Patrício *et al.* deals with the 1996 anastylosis activities on the late Hellenistic fountain house. A more substantial article dealing with the final results and the philosophy of the anastylosis will appear in the next volume.

The restoration of the Neon Library also involved a thorough conservation of its well-preserved mosaic floor. The history of the erection and function of the monument and the date of its mosaics and their conservation are treated in a paper by Waelkens *et al.* The study shows that the final repair of the building dates back most probably to the reign of the emperor Julian (AD 361–363). This restoration of the building and the scene represented in the *emblema* of the mosaic pavement that was laid on that occasion, fit perfectly with a general policy of supporting Greek *paideia,* stimulated by the emperor himself and by such figures as the famous rhetor Libanios. The proposed date appears also to be consonant with the stylistic features of the mosaic. The local mosaic tradition could be identified as a mixture of Hellenistic prototypes and influences from the Italian mosaic tradition. This seems to confirm the hypothesis that the Anatolian mosaicists turned to the West rather than to the South for their inspiration. The deliberate destruction of the library during the last decades of the fourth century AD was probably a result of one of the urban riots that characterized city life during that period. The principles followed by the conservation team working on the mosaic are explained by Kökten *et al.*

More detailed research has been begun on the prehistoric occupation of the area. It has revealed a dichotomy between the western part of the city's territory, where from the Neolithic period onward villages of the *höyük* type developed, and the valleys of the eastern part, where a semi-nomadic Epipalaeolithic way of life continued right into the protohistoric period.

One of the oldest traces of this second way of life is a cave site at Karain near Dereköy in the eastern part of the Ağlasun valley. Discovered during the survey of 1995, it was excavated by Vermeersch in collaboration with the Burdur Museum as part of the 1997 season. The excavation revealed an occupation in or in front of the cave towards the end of the Late Glacial or during the Tardoglacial. The lithic material suggests a date around 12,000 BP. Unfortunately, post-depositional processes had obliterated what may have been a multi-layered settlement. In fact, the site had already been destroyed by slope evolution before the end of the Last Ice Age. Part of the cave had collapsed, probably at some point in the early Holocene. Later occupations seem to have taken place at some time between the Neolithic and protohistoric times, and during the Roman to early Byzantine period.

A paper by Vanhaverbeke evaluates the problems of trying to establish a scientifically based chronological sequence for prehistoric settlements like these on Sagalassian territory. Despite these problems, a chronological framework based upon radiocarbon dating is suggested for the successive 'cultural' sequences of prehistory.

For the protohistorical and early historical period, the apparent lack of Middle Bronze, Late Bronze and Early Iron Age sites in the territory of Sagalassos is discussed by Waelkens. Palynological evidence reveals a clear deforestation phase during this period, despite the absence of contemporary sites according to evidence provided by surface finds. Hittite sources also reveal the existence of princedoms and civic settlements in Pisidia and Lycia during this period, some of which seem to have developed into known cities of Graeco-Roman times. Sagalassos itself is most probably referred to as Salawassa during the second half of the fifteenth century BC. The most plausible explanation therefore is that around the middle of the second millennium BC, after the Luwians had settled in the area, people established themselves in well protected mountain sites, where they continued to live right into classical times, so that the expanding later settlements obliterated any older surface material.

As far as the classical period is concerned, epigraphic and numismatic evidence found during the 1996 and 1997 seasons again increased our knowledge of the history of the city. An inscription from the Upper Agora published by Vandorpe thus far represents the oldest epigraphic record ever found at Sagalassos. It was identified as an agreement enforced by an early Hellenistic ruler and negotiated between two feuding Sagalassian parties. It seems likely that the king was Antiochos I and the parties were supporters and opponents of Seleucid power at the time of the Galatian invasion of the 270s. The text is also important because it shows that Sagalassos probably had a Greek legal code already in a very early stage of its Hellenization process, perhaps as early as the late fourth-early third century BC. At the same time the inscription seems to confirm the early Hellenistic date of the fortress above the city, discussed in this volume by Loots. Finally, Vandorpe also draws attention to the fact that Sagalassos had already issued a limited autonomous coinage in the years 200-189 BC, during the reign of Antiochos III, a fact which has escaped the attention of most numismatic studies dealing with the city's coins.

The coins found during the 1996 and 1997 campaigns and discussed by Scheers confirm the picture of past seasons. Most of the few autonomous coins are city coins issued by Sagalassos itself, with Perge again in second position. This confirms once more (see *Sagalassos IV*) that there was an intense circulation between the two cities and that the Pamphylian port may probably have been the gateway for both the exports and imports of Sagalassos. However, due to the fact that the excavations have largely dealt with the late Roman-early Byzantine strata of the city, the overwhelming majority of numismatic finds are Roman Imperial coins dated to the fourth and fifth century AD. Most of these coins however come from contexts dated by pottery to the early Byzantine period (sixth-first half of the seventh century AD). They confirm the fact already discussed before (Poblome *Sagalassos III*, 185-207) that there is a difference in this respect between sherds and coins and that the latter may have had a long period of circulation, thus reducing their value as chronological indicators. In the past, the most recent numismatic evidence from stratigraphical contexts were coins of Constans II (641-668 AD) under whose reign the city seems to have been flattened by a major earthquake. The latest evidence from the 1996 and 1997 campaigns belongs to the reign of Heraclius (610-640 AD). So far, seven years of excavations have not revealed any stratigraphically sealed material, neither coins nor pottery, that could be dated after the seventh century AD, thus confirming that the seismic catastrophe of the middle of the seventh century AD eventually resulted in a (near total?) depopulation of the site. Some isolated later coins have been found, including a coin issued by either Basil II (976-1025) or Romanus III (1028-1034) published in this volume, but they all were surface finds and only document the occasional presence of visitors or of traders following the caravan route through the ruins.

The architectural studies published in this volume begin with a study by Waelkens *et al.* of the Northwest Heroon at Sagalassos, an impressive and richly decorated memorial for a private individual, built during the reign of Augustus, and characteristic of the late Hellenistic-early Imperial competition among the ruling classes of Asia Minor. Although the decoration of the Heroon fits the local building tradition fairly well, several decorative motifs clearly indicate Italian influences, most probably via Augustan colonies, perhaps especially Pisidian Antioch, in the vicinity of Sagalassos.

The defence systems around the city are described in a paper by Loots *et al.* Research has shown that the various approaches to Sagalassos were already well guarded by the early third century BC at the latest, when part of the northern defence line across the mountain ridge dominating the city already existed. During the late Hellenistic period, a new city wall with square towers seems to have replaced an older pre-Hellenistic wall for which there is only literary evidence. During the Imperial period the Hellenistic city wall was eventually dismantled. However, the instability that characterized the transition from the fourth to the fifth century AD in Pisidia forced the city's inhabitants to fortify its monumental centre. This late Roman fortification was most probably abandoned after the 518 AD earthquake that may have damaged it beyond repair.

Equally important for the survival of the city was its water supply. The architectural remains of six aqueducts had already be studied in the past from an archaeological point of view (Owens, *Sagalassos III*, 91-114). A joint geomorphological-archaeological paper by Steegen *et al.* in this volume studies the possible catchment area of these aqueducts and the gradient of their trajectory. It became clear that the upper eastern aqueduct extended much further east than previously assumed and that its discharge amounted to somewhere between 10,000 and 40,000 m^3/day. Even the lower figure represents a good water supply, bearing in mind that at some point there were at least five aqueducts providing the city with water at the same time.

The surrounding countryside not only provided Sagalassos with its water supply, but also served as an almost inexhaustible source of raw materials that could be exploited for industrial purposes. Besides the exploitation of extremely rich clay deposits creating a lively ceramic industry that also exported its ware, the immediate vicinity of the town offered also a rich supply of solid building materials. Throughout the city's history, local limestones would remain the most commonly used material for monumental architecture in Sagalassos (Viaene *et al. Sagalassos* I: 85-92). However, the rather rapid Romanization of the local elite resulted in the introduction of 'Roman' building techniques also, particularly Roman concrete and fired brick. The lack of sand in the region explains why volcanic powder was used as an alternative in local structural mortars (Viaene *et al. Sagalassos IV*: 405-422). An article in this volume by Callebaut *et al.* identifies the volcanic deposits immediately to the northwest of the site as the most likely source of these additives.

In Imperial times, the local building industry also made increasing use of fired clay products, both tiles and brick. A paper by Poblome *et al.* deals with the rescue excavation of an early Byzantine tile kiln near Taşkapı in the territory of Sagalassos.

A study by Loots *et al.* presents a catalogue of seventy tile stamps from Sagalassos. Most of them apparently refer to either the building authority or the supplier of the material. Since almost all the stamps come from early Byzantine destruction layers or fills, there is hardly any solid evidence to date them exactly. Some tiles may be recycled material of older date. However, most of them bear a stamp with the same text and were clearly produced to provide the Roman baths with new tiles, most likely during the later Roman period.

Pottery studies were also continued. This volume thus contains a study by Degeest *et al.* of a distinct group of two types of miniature vessels, a jug and a jar, that are frequently found in later contexts at Sagalassos. Chemical and mineralogical analysis showed that this ware group was certainly imported, probably because of its valuable content. Published parallels thus far seem to be limited to Constantinople, where they occur in not reliably dated Byzantine contexts. The evidence from Sagalassos, however, points to a main distribution during the first half of the sixth century AD, extending into the final years of the site's occupation around the middle of the seventh century AD.

A mineralogical and geochemical analysis of the potential clay sources in the territory of Sagalassos that could be used for manufacturing the locally produced common wares has now also provided a partial answer to the question of why the potters of Sagalassos never based themselves in the plain of Çanaklı, near the raw materials which otherwise they had to transport over a distance of 8 kilometers. A study by Degryse *et al.* published in this volume thus established that, for the mass production of the common wares, the Sagalassos potters throughout at least seven centuries of production used residual clays derived from weathered ophiolite present in the potters' quarter itself. The amount of raw material needed for these often large vessels was much more than that needed for the smaller fine wares, so that it was more practical to import the clays needed for the latter. The various types of temper that were added to the clays used for the common wares were identified as volcanic material, possibly from the Lake Gölçük area located immediately northwest of the site, as residual clays derived from flysch deposits present in the Ağlasun valley to the east of the site, and as grog recycled from Sagalassos red slip wares.

During the past years many environmental studies have been carried out in the territory of Sagalassos. Preliminary results have already been summarized by Waelkens *et al.* in *Sagalassos IV* (225-252). These results are constantly updated and completed.

One of the objectives of our environmental research is to document agricultural and forestry potential in the ancient subsistence and economy. A study by Donners *et al.* combines soil data with climatic, vegetation and geomorphologic evidence to produce a land-evaluation for antiquity and suggest an estimation of the potential crop production in the past. Cereals, most probably winter wheat, played a major role in the local subsistence and economy, and the potential of forestry activities is also documented.

The paper published by Schroyen *et al.* in this volume combines the evidence of several disciplines. A geological, geomorphological, palynological and archaeological study was undertaken of travertine deposits in the valley of Başköy some 7 km to the west of Sagalassos. Their precipitation and climatic environment was determined, while two sections were sampled for palynological analysis. Their pollen diagrams reveal a vegetation change, most probably during the historical period, from an open forest-steppe to an open needle-leaved forest that at present has disappeared as the result of overgrazing during the last centuries. This seems to confirm that Roman Sagalassos may have been located in a more heavily afforested environment than at present, a fact which had been already suggested by archaeozoological evidence (see Waelkens *et al. Sagalassos IV*: 225-252). The most recent of the two pollen diagrams also offers additional evidence for the practice of olive cultivation in the past, confirming the previous evidence of the numerous counter-weights for olive presses found in the territory of the ancient city during the surveys of the last years (see the survey article in this volume and Waelkens *et al. Sagalassos IV*: 11-103).

The geomorphological location of Sagalassos itself had already been described by Paulissen *et al.* (*Sagalassos II*: 229-248). Some of the major monuments of the city are built on limestone platforms that are isolated from the cliff of Lycian nappes that dominates the site and that carries the Hellenistic fortifications mentioned above. A geomorphological study of these platforms and of similar massifs to the east and to the west of the site identifies them as giant rock mass slides characterized by a rotational movement (Verstraeten *et al.* this volume). The lithography and the presence of faults and joints made the area very susceptible to these slides, which could be triggered by major groundwater fluctuations over short periods or by earthquakes. A sequence of several mass slides could be discerned, some of which had occurred in historic times. One may even have damaged part of the late Hellenistic (to Roman Imperial) rock-cut aqueduct that provided the city with water from the east and that is carved into the front of an older mass slide. This may explain why this section apparently had to be re-carved at a higher level to join it up again with the rest of the aqueduct.

A second geomorphological phenomenon that now characterizes the physical environment at and around the site is that of slope deposits related to still active rapid mass movements at higher levels and the presence of fossil slope deposits at lower altitudes. A study by Librecht *et al.* reveals that scree formation and slope movements were not a continuous process throughout time, but that periods of intense and of less intense activity may have alternated. Some fossil deposits could result already from cold climatic conditions and a sparse natural vegetation during the Last Glacial. Sagalassos itself probably developed during a period when the slopes were less unstable and there was more forest cover. However, human intervention (deforestation) after the abandonment of the site around the middle of the seventh century AD once more produced a degraded environment that is not caused by contemporary climatic conditions. It also caused frost weathering, especially near joints and faults in the limestone massif above the city, resulting in rapid mass movements of debris, which eventually destroyed some of the remaining approaches and aqueducts of the city.

During the past years, the excavations produced masses of bone material, mainly faunal remains, but also human bones. Jehaes *et al.* carried out DNA-analysis of a series of early Byzantine corpses, buried along the western edge of the Lower Agora. Authentic mtDNA sequence information could be obtained from ancient bone and tooth samples, though not for all twenty-four skeletons that were exposed. So far, none of these skeletons appear to have belonged to the same matrilinear family, although it cannot be excluded completely for one of the double graves.

In antiquity, fish was a small though not negligible part of the local diet. The consumption of marine fish has already been discussed in a previous volume (Van Neer *et al. Sagalassos IV*: 571-586). A further paper by the same author in this volume presents the result of a survey aimed at documenting the geographical distribution of freshwater fish in the Aksu (ancient Kestros) river system to the southeast of Sagalassos. Since this river was the only major river system in the vicinity of the city and since there were indications of a significant amount of trade from the city southwards, it was assumed that much of the freshwater fish consumed at Sagalassos might have come from that area. However, the Aksu river proved to be very poor in both the number and the species of fish. Most of the freshwater fish seem in fact to have come from localities to the north and to the west of the site, which bears out the already known existence of trade relations with those areas.

In previous years, it was established that ovicaprines played a considerable ecological role, not only in the deforestation of the area, but also in moving debris by trampling (Govers *et al. Sagalassos IV*, 541-552). Archaeozoological research has shown that flocks of sheep and goats were also an important economic asset throughout the occupation phase of Sagalassos. In order to reconstruct their role in the ancient subsistence and economy, it is necessary to determine their age at the time of slaughter and the season of slaughtering. The former is done by cementum line analysis, the latter by studying dental microwear combined with a study of plant phytoliths extracted from the teeth. However, dental microwear studies of fossil teeth can only be interpreted correctly if they can be correlated with a study of the modern diet of the animals and the dental microwear resulting from it. Therefore, over the last two years modern herding and feeding practices of sheep and goats in the Sagalassos area have been studied in detail. A paper by Beuls *et al.* reports on a first survey campaign during the month of June

1996. Dental microwear analysis from this survey is still in progress, but several herding practices known from ancient literary sources could still be recognized today.

Cattle also played an enormous role in the ancient economy, both for subsistence and as draught animals. From the very beginning of the excavations, the material from Sagalassos provided ample evidence that even bone refuse from these animals was reworked in a small-scale bone working industry, either by individuals or in workshops (De Cupere *et al.*, *Sagalassos II*: 269-278). Experimental research by Parras published in this volume now provides information about the basic technology, extracted from a comparison with excavated artefacts and refuse.

PART I

THE SURVEY AND EXCAVATIONS IN 1996 AND 1997
PRELIMINARY REPORTS

THE 1996 AND 1997 SURVEY SEASONS AT SAGALASSOS

Marc WAELKENS[1], Hannelore VANHAVERBEKE[1], Etienne PAULISSEN[2],
Jeroen POBLOME[1], Jeroen REYNIERS[2], Willy VIAENE (†)[3], Jozef DECKERS[4],
Bea DECUPERE[5], Wim VAN NEER[5], Haci Ali EKİNCİ[6] and Mustafa Oral ERBAY[6].

1 - Department of Archaeology, K.U.Leuven, Blijde Inkomststraat 21, B-3000 Leuven, Belgium
- J. Poblome is Postdoctoral Fellow of the Fund for Scientific Research Flanders
- H. Vanhaverbeke is Postdoctoral Fellow of the Fund for Scientific Research Flanders
2 - Geomorphology and Regional Geography, K.U.Leuven, Redingenstraat 16, B-3000 Leuven, Belgium
3 - Physico-chemical Geology, K.U.Leuven, Celestijnenlaan 200C, B-3001 Heverlee, Belgium
4 - Institute for Land and Water Management, K.U.Leuven, Vital Decosterstraat 102, B-3000 Leuven, Belgium
5 - Laboratory for Osteology, Royal Museum of Central Africa, B-3080 Tervuren, Belgium
6 - Archaeological Museum Burdur, Turkey

1. INTRODUCTION

The archaeological survey in the territory of Roman Sagalassos, initiated during the 1993 campaign in the immediate vicinity of the city (Waelkens 1995), was continued during the 1994 and 1995 seasons in the central and eastern part of Sagalassian held territory (Waelkens et al. 1997a). Between June the third and June the twenty-second 1996, members of the Sagalassos team, composed of the director M. Waelkens and two other archaeologists (H. Vanhaverbeke, J. Poblome), of two geomorphologists (E. Paulissen, J. Reyniers), of two archaeozoologists (W. Van Neer, B. De Cupere), of a geologist (W. Viaene) and a pedologist (J. Deckers), continued for the fourth year a survey in the remaining western part of the city's territory. Geographically, this area is composed, firstly, of the limestone mountain country around the Beşparmak Dağı, which forms the northern extension of the Kantrancık Dağı and contains the upper valleys of the Kerme or Çebiş Deresi (Waelkens et al. 1997a: 54) and of the Büğduz Çayı and its tributaries; secondly, of the infertile badlands region located immediately to the west of it, and finally of the plain to the south of Lake Burdur (see Fig. 6). This survey was done in close collaboration with Solmaz Gülsen (Anıtlar ve Müzeler Genel Müdürlüğü, Ankara) and Mustafa Akaslan (Isparta Müzesi), who acted as *temsilcis* of the Turkish Ministry of Culture. The survey was also carried out in collaboration with the Burdur Museum, represented by Mustafa Oral Erbay. In 1996, the survey team worked mainly on the sheets of the Turkish topographical maps Isparta M 23 c 3, M 24 a 1, M 24 b 1, M 24 b 4, M 24 c 1, M 24 c 4, M 24 d 1, M 24 d 2, M 24 d 3, M 24 d 4 and M 25 d 1. During this survey a total of 86 sites or isolated monuments were discovered (Fig. 1). Survey activities continued during the months of July and August 1996, in the immediate vicinity of Sagalassos, but these were carried out mostly by geologists, geomorphologists, archaeozoologists and pedologists. Some additional minor sites were then discovered, which have been incorporated into this article. The other results however, are published separately, in various articles in this volume.

This is also the case for the activities that were resumed between the ninth of July and the twenty-ninth of August 1997 and carried out by a team that was composed of non-archaeologists in close collaboration with Melek Yıldızturan (Museum of Near Eastern Civilizations, Ankara) who represented the Turkish Ministry of Culture, although within the framework of this multidisciplinary research, some archaeological surveys on a micro-scale were undertaken by J. Poblome and L. Loots. The survey carried out between 1993 and 1996 in the entire territory of the ancient town of Sagalassos, had been an extensive reconnaissance survey. Different types of sites were recognised during this project, such as farmsteads, villages, sanctuaries, or specific purpose sites. For a doctoral dissertation by Vanhaverbeke concerning the settlement history of the area, the 1997 archaeological survey selected some of these sites and studied the dispersal of artefacts at the surface. The aim of this was to recognize dispersal patterns, which could be features of specific chronological phases, characteristic of a specific function, or typical for both. Research focused on a Hellenistic-late Roman village site (Körüstan), on an early Byzantine farming site (Tepe Düzen), during which a small limestone quarry was also discovered, and on a Roman Imperial 'special purpose site', the large Roman Imperial limestone quarry of Sarıkaya, all located immediately to the southwest of ancient Sagalassos (on these sites, see Waelkens *et al.* 1997a: 41-50). The results of these micro-surveys are discussed in the above-mentioned dissertation that will be published in our *Studies in Eastern Mediterranean Archaeology* series.

During the survey, representative samples of survey finds were gathered and stored in the depots of the excavation house at Ağlasun. Afterwards, this material was studied by Vermeersch (prehistoric lithic artefacts), by Poblome (table wares) and by Degeest (coarse wares), who are responsible for its dating. Originally, it was intended to publish the rich epigraphic harvest of the 1996 survey within the scope of this article. However, the rather sudden death of our epigrapher Devijver has prevented this. Following the request of the Turkish authorities to publish the results of each campaign rather quickly, it was decided to present the archaeological and other results of the 1996 and 1997 surveys without the epigraphical material. The latter will be published shortly, together with the inscriptions copied during the 1993-1995 seasons, in a separate article.

2. PREVIOUS RESEARCH IN THE WESTERN PART OF THE TERRITORY OF SAGALASSOS

In our report of the 1994 and 1995 survey campaigns, we said that the district covered by our team during those years had hardly been surveyed by the many visitors of the past who had passed through it on their way to either Sagalassos or Kremna (Waelkens *et al.* 1997a: 11-18). This is even more the case for the geographical area studied by our team in 1996 (Fig. 2). During the late nineteenth and the twentieth century, a lot of, mostly epigraphical, surveys covered the district located immediately to the south of Sagalassian held territory, that is, the upper Lysis valley and the plain and valleys surrounding Lake Kestel. Only a few travelers ventured as far north as Burdur, many of them without really covering in detail the district located in-between. Scholars who reached Burdur from the north, the east or the southeast were mentioned in our previous report (Waelkens *et al.* 1997a).

The first visitor to that part of the city's territory that was surveyed by us in 1996, was the Reverend F.V.J. Arundell. In 1833, he visited the district between Burdur and Yarışlı (Arundell 1834: 115-117), where he copied some inscriptions (*CIG* 3956 b-c). In 1854, H. Kiepert produced a very defective map of the area (Kiepert 1854).

After this first visit by a western scholar, it was not until the later part of the century that the French travelers Duchesne and Collignon, from the second of May to the sixteenth of July 1876, ventured in the same area, on an epigraphical journey from Kibyra (Gölhisar), through the upper reaches of the Lysis valley (Eren Çayı) and along the northern shores of Lake Burdur, towards Burdur and Isparta. On this journey, they discovered the sites of Tefenni (Takina), of Eğneş (Hadrianoi), of Olbasa and of Lysinia, and also found evidence of the more rural districts of the Ormeleis and the Makropedion, all located beyond Sagalassian territory. Within this territory, they visited only Soğanlı, located near the edge of the limestone massif around Mt. Beşparmak and overlooking the infertile badlands to the west of it, but they did not describe any of the sites around it (Duchesne and Collignon 1877; Collignon 1878; Duchesne 1879). On their return from Burdur to Antalya, part of the Kestel area was studied (Collignon 1879).

In 1884, the American Sterrett made almost the same trip as Duchesne and Collignon undertook eight years before him (Sterrett 1888). His journey was mapped by Kiepert (1886). During the same year, another team composed of Ramsay and Smith, covered the same area even more intensively. They visited Yarışlı, Düğer, Hacılar and Yarıköy in the southern part of the plain of Burdur, where they discovered one of the boundary stones of Sagalassian held territory. Along the lake, they also visited the site of Ilyas on the northern shore and Burdur on the opposite site (Ramsay 1886: 130; Smith 1887: 230-231). To the east, they reached a number of other villages belonging to Sagalassos, located in the limestone hill district around Mt. Beşparmak. They visited more specifically Bereket, Gölde, Gâvur Ören and Bayındır (Ramsay 1886: 339; Smith 1887: 229, 259-262). Further south, immediately beyond the boundaries of the city's territory, they worked in the upper valley of the Lysis river and in the district around Tefenni (Ramsay 1887: 363; Smith 1887: 226-229, 235-251; Ramsay 1888). They visited also various sites located between Lake Kestel and Istanoz/Korkuteli (Smith 1887:252-257, 266-267; Ramsay 1888). Some of the inscriptions recorded during this journey were published by Ramsay in his more recent monographs (1895; 1941). Another collection of inscriptions from the same area, i.e. the district from the Upper Lysis valley towards the Kestel area and further south, was published in 1892 by Bérard (Bérard 1892). A trip in 1897 by Jüthner and Heberdey from Ephesos to the site of Olbasa in the Upper Lysis plain eventually produced some new inscriptions (Jüthner 1902). In June and July of 1910, almost all of Pisidia to the southwest of the territory of Sagalassos, from the mountain range in the north which formed the territory's southern limit (see below) to the district around Termessos and the plain of Elmalı in the south, became the subject of a survey undertaken by two members of the British School at Athens, Woodward and Ormerod, who located many prehistoric mounds and published a large number of new inscriptions. However, they never ventured into Sagalassian held territory (Woodward and Ormerod 1909-1910).

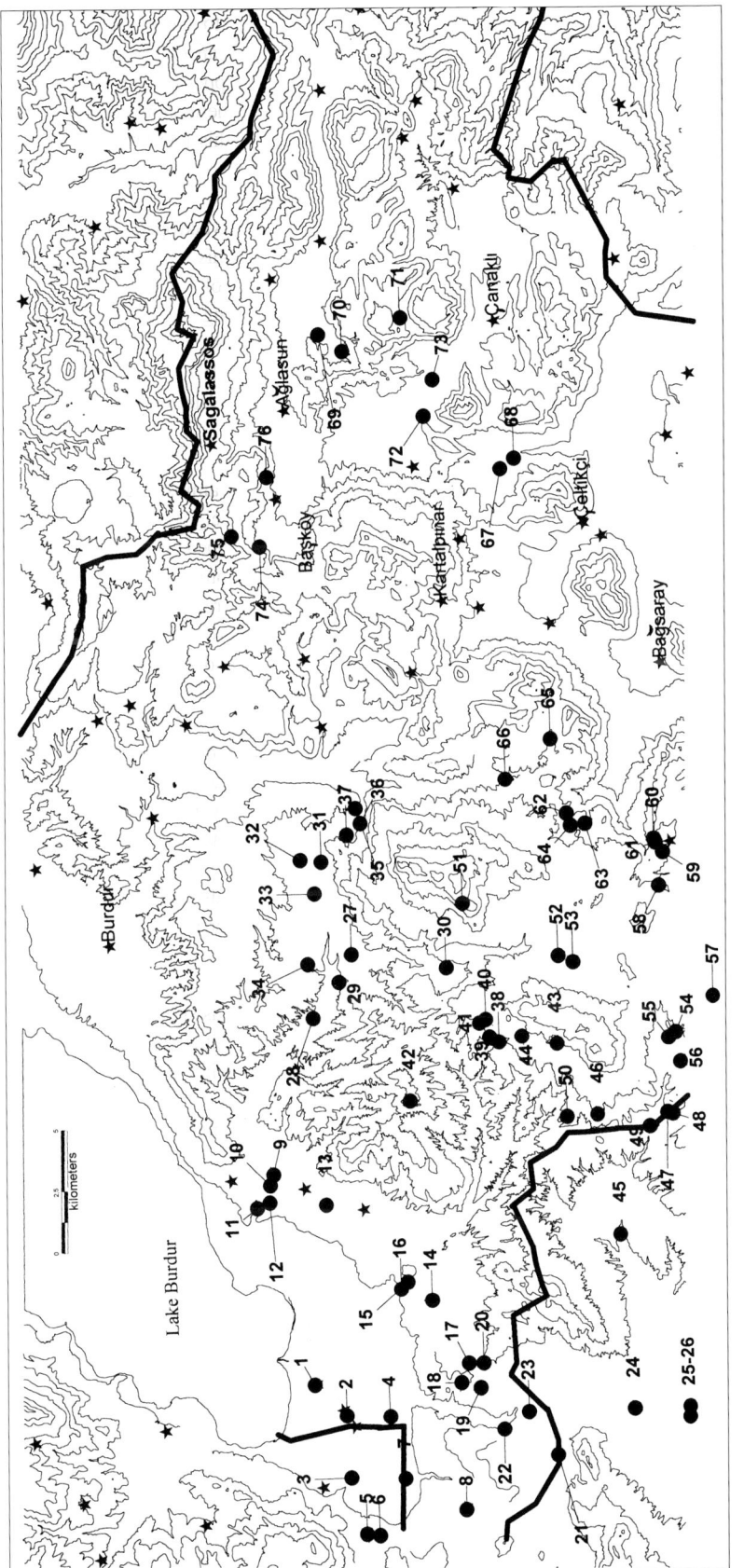

Fig. 1: Map of the sites found during the 1996 and 1997 surveys.

1. Yazıköy
2. Yarıköy
3. Gâvur Evi Tepesi (Yarıköy)
4. Kilise (Yarıköy)
5. Aşağımüslimler
6. Halı Kayası (Aşağımüslimler)
7. Borderstone (Düğer)
8. Düğer
9. Suludere
10. Ören (Suludere)
11. Eski Mezarlık (Suludere)
12. Çığırtkankaya
13. Kuruçay Höyük
14. Yassıgüme
15. Kale (Yassıgüme)
16. Kokar Pınar (Yassıgüme)
17. Hacılar
18. Öz (Hacılar II)
19. Kerit (Hacılar I, Mellaart's Hacılar)
20. Tekke (Hacılar)
21. Kozaklı/Yeni Çeşme (Karaçal)
22. Höyük (Karaçal)
23. Karaçal
24. Boğaziçi
25. Kınalı Taş (Kozluca)
26. Höyük (Kozluca)
27. Büğdüz
28. Old Büğdüz
29. Göbecik Tepesi (Büğdüz)
30. Yayla (Büğdüz)
31. Bayındır
32. Höyük (Bayındır)
33. Hamam Yıkığı (Bayındır)
34. Körüstan (Bayındır)
35. Kayaaltı/Gravgaz
36. Kocapınar (Kayaaltı)
37. Güzle (Kayaaltı)
38. Soğanlı
39. Sazak (Soğanlı)
40. Taşlı Tepe (Soğanlı)
41. Yapımca Olak
42. İlyas Tepe (Soğanlı)
43. Monastır (Soğanlı)
44. Kale (Soğanlı)
45. İğdeli
46. Karacaören
47. Gâvur Ören (Karacaören)
48. Kurukuyu (Gâvur Ören - Karacaören)
49. Dikenli Tarla (Karacaören)
50. Ören/Pazar (Karacaören)
51. Kale (Kökez)
52. Bereket
53. Kirselik (Bereket)
54. Yeşildağ/Gölde
55. Höyük (Yeşildağ)
56. Kireçocağı (Yeşildağ)
57. Kapaklı
58. Aksu
59. Kilise Yıkığı (Akyayla)
60. Kale (Akyayla)
61. Asar (Akyayla)
62. Kayış
63. Asar Tepesi (Kayış)
64. Çatal Oluk (Kayış)
65. Eski Kayaş (Kayış)
66. Fırın Yıkığı (Kayış)
67. Sülemiş (Çeltikçi)
68. Peçenek (Çeltikçi)
69. Erek (Köyünü)
70. Kilocağı (Köyünü)
71. Manastır (Çanaklı)
72. Kocadağ (Çanaklı)
73. Kör Kuyu (Çanaklı)
74. Körüstan (Başköy)
75. Sarıkaya (Başköy)
76. Tepe Düzen (Başköy)

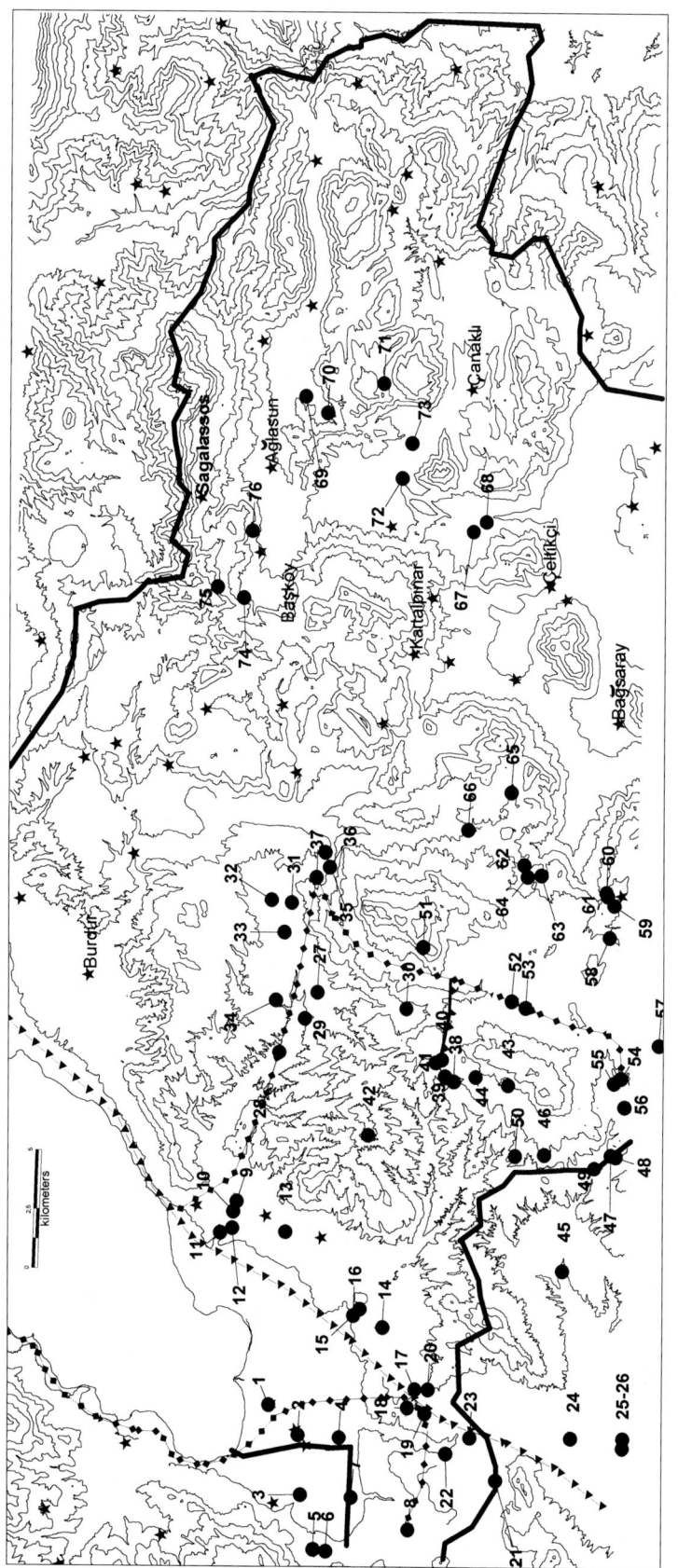

Fig. 2: Map with the journeys of earlier travellers (the thick line indicates the territorial boundaries of the city in Imperial times).

Travellers' routes

▲▲▲▲ Duchesne & Collignon 1876, Ramsay & Smith 1884, Sterrett 1884
♦♦♦♦ Ramsay & Smith 1884, Bean 1955-1957
▬▬▬ Bean 1957

After this last journey, it was almost four decades before new scientists crossed our district. In 1948, Jeanne and Louis Robert worked in northern Pisidia, including the vicinity of Lake Burdur, but they never published their complete epigraphic harvest (Robert 1948; Bean 1959: 68 n.4).

From the 1950s onwards, Pisidia became a realm of British scholars, both archaeologists and ancient historians. In 1954, Bean published a first group of inscriptions collected from municipal buildings at Burdur, at least some of which came from Sagalassian territory (Bean 1954). A year later, Levick surveyed the sites of the Augustan colonies to the north and to the south of Sagalassos, which eventually resulted in her excellent monograph (Levick 1967). From 1955, Bean began to carry out a systematic exploration, village by village, of the western half of Sagalassian held territory and of the areas further south. In 1955, he worked in the badlands zone described below (Büğduz, Bayındır, Burdur), and in 1956 along the northern (Karakent, Ilyas, Kılıç, Kavacık) and southwestern shores of Lake Burdur (Düğer, Yaraşlı), where he discovered another Sagalassian boundary stone (see below). A year later, he surveyed the southwestern part of the Plain of Burdur (Hacılar, Yarıköy), the badlands and the limestone mountains to the east of it (Soğanlı, Karacaören, Gâvür Ören, Bereket, Gölde), and some sites located immediately to the south of Sagalassos' territory (Eğneş, Boğaziçi, Akçaören, Akören). This was the most extensive survey undertaken in the area under consideration. But, since Bean was mainly looking for inscriptions, many ancient sites went unnoticed. In 1958, his attention was directed towards the sites around the plain of Lake Kestel and the valleys further south of it, as far as Melli and Hyia. Finally, in 1959, he revisited Bereket. In 1959 and 1960, the rich epigraphic harvest from these trips was published in two volumes of *Anatolian Studies* (Bean 1959, Bean 1960).

Bean was followed by three major authorities on the history and archaeology of Southwest-Anatolia, D. French, A. Hall and S. Mitchell. In 1973, Mitchell, was shown a stone which had been found *in situ* near Burdur railway station and had been brought to the Burdur Museum, by its director, K. Dörtlük. A year later, a squeeze of its inscription was taken by French. In July 1975, another squeeze was produced and the inscription was studied by French, Hall and Mitchell, and eventually published by Mitchell. It proved to be the famous edict of the emperor Tiberius' *legatus pro praetore*, Sextus Sotidius Strabo Libuscidianus, written ca. AD 13-15, concerning the organisation of requisitioned transport through the territory of Sagalassos (Mitchell 1976; French and Mitchell 1977: 216-218). It is thus far the only preserved example of a text that, according to its implication must also have been erected in other villages in this territory (Mitchell 1976: 116, 119). In any case, the edict shows that Sagalassos was responsible for the organisation of official transport through its territory, between the cities of Konana in the north and Kormasa in the south.

In 1974 and 1975, French's study of Roman roads in Anatolia also took him to our region, where he copied or recopied milestones at Akçaören, Boğaziçi, Ürkütlü, Yarışlı, Karakent, Burdur and Yarıköy (French 1976: 53; French and Mitchell 1977: 213-215; French 1978; French 1980; French 1988:101-114). During these surveys, French discovered milestones that mention the construction of the *via Sebaste* by the emperor Augustus in the year 6 BC, at Ürkütlü (Comama), at Boğaziçi in the Upper Lysis valley and at Yarı in the Burdur Plain. His investigations showed that the *via Sebaste* ran from Pisidian Antioch, Apollonia and Keçiborlu in the north to a point to the west of the site of Baris, and further south along the northern shores of Lake Burdur, towards Lysinia. From there, it headed straight southward, through the plain to the southwest of the lake, then west of the villages of Yazı and Yarı, and east of Düğer, towards Karaçal, where the road left Sagalassian territory (French and Mitchell 1977: 214 and 219, fig. 1).

In 1978, Hall also worked in the Belenli (Olbasa) area, where he discovered an important inscription dated to the Attalid period. During the same year, it was moved to the Burdur Museum and eventually published by R.A. Kearsly (Kearsly 1994).

In August 1977, as part of the preparatory work for a *R.E.C.A.M.* volume concerning the Burdur Museum, R.P. Harper noted and photographed some 150 inscriptions, all from Pisidia, that were squeezed a year later (Hall 1979: 4; French 1979: 6). During this work, he recorded two parts of an inscription, dated to 5/4 BC and coming from a sanctuary originally dedicated to Rome and Augustus near Kozluca Höyük, located just south of the lands which Sagalassos held in the Plain of Burdur. A third joining fragment had been copied already by Bean in the Boğaziçi bridge. The texts were eventually studied and published by Hall, who during an epigraphical survey in the Kibyratis in September 1985, discovered two more inscriptions from the same Sebasteion, respectively in the Boğaziçi bridge and at Çallıca (formerly Eğneş). In the latter place, he also copied a milestone (Hall 1985). The new material helped to solve some of the remaining topographical problems in the Upper Lysis valley (Hall 1986b). The 1984 and 1985 Kibyratis surveys took Hall to Karamanlı, where an imperial letter was found, and to Olbasa, where he copied a second Attalid letter (Hall 1986a).

In 1983, French's study of Roman roads and milestones in Asia Minor, brought him back to the region of Burdur, where he found evidence of the Roman Republican road built by M. Aquillius between 129 and 126 BC. He discovered part of the road section between Laodikeia ad Lycum (near Denizli) and Takina (Yarışlı). Old and new milestones near Yarışlı confirmed that the *caput viae* of the road had been Pergamon and not Ephesos (French 1984: 11; French 1991: 53-54).

In 1987, Kearsly and Horsley began to produce a catalogue of all the Greek inscriptions at Burdur, which will include many inscriptions moved there from villages in Sagalassian territory (see Horsley 1992). Work on this collection for a *R.E.C.A.M.* volume had already been started by Van Bremen during the spring of 1981 (Mitchell 1982: 6). It will be published shortly by Mitchell, Kearsly and Horsley.

In 1989, French worked once more in the province of Burdur, where this time he studied the Roman road (*via Sebaste*) between Kozluca and Ürkütlü in the Upper Lysis valley. Further north, he found evidence of another east-west road running from Acıpayam towards Burdur and studied a seventh (sic) boundary-marker, recently taken to the Burdur Museum, that was erected under Nero to define the boundary between Sagalassos and Tymbrianassos. This made him suggest that the *via Sebaste* had perhaps been used as the definite boundary between the territories (French 1990: 10-11).

Finally, during September 1993, Mitchell carried out a survey in western Pisidia and the Milyas, which extended from Korkuteli in the southwest to Bucak in the north and Kocaaliler in the east. During this survey, he identified the location of three cities located to the south of Sagalassos: Kretopolis, Panemoteichos and Kodrula (?) (Mitchell 1994).

Most of the above-mentioned survey activities had an epigraphical character, or were intended to identify classical sites. But, in the meantime, prehistoric research had also been developed in the same area. It basically started, when in 1957, J. Mellaart initiated the excavation of the world famous höyük at Hacılar, which was occupied from the aceramic Neolithic to the Early Chalcolithic period (Mellaart 1970). From 1978 to 1988, R. Duru carried out an excavation in the neighbouring Early Neolithic to Early Bronze Age site of Kuruçay (Duru 1994, 1996).

Beside these excavations, a series of very productive surveys carried out by M. Özsait in the Lake District led to the discovery of numerous Neolithic, Chalcolithic and Early Bronze Age mounds (1976-77, 1980, 1983, 1984, 1985, 1989, 1990, 1991, 1992 and 1996). In 1982, Özsait thus identified a number of Early Chalcolithic and Early Bronze Age sites in the district between Akgöl, Gökçe Göl and Yarışlı Göl, all located to the southwest of the Plain of Burdur, and in the valley of the Lysis (Boz Çayı) (Özsait 1983). The year after, he worked, among other places, on either side of Mt. Kestel, respectively at Aziziye and at Gölde (now Yeşildağ), the latter being on Sagalassian territory (Özsait 1984: 208-209). The year 1984 saw him active in the central part of this territory and in the district immediately to the south of it, as well as along the northern shores of Lake Burdur (Özsait 1996). In 1991, a number of höyüks in the plain of Çeltikçi in the central part of Sagalassian held territory and a district to the west and north of Lake Burdur were surveyed (Özsait 1992). During the 1995 season, his research focused on the Upper Lysis valley (Kozluca, Akçaören), on the plain of Kestel (Yazıpınar), both located immediately to the south of Sagalassos, but also on some sites within the latter's *chora,* such as the plain of Çeltikçi, the district around Büğduz in the badlands and Kepez Kalesi in the valley of Kuzköy (Özsait 1996).

3. ROADS AND CONNECTIONS IN THE WESTERN PART OF THE TERRITORY OF SAGALASSOS

The plain to the southwest of Lake Burdur, which in Hellenistic and Imperial times was in the western part of Sagalassian held territory, appears to have been pre-selected by nature to become a natural thoroughfare (Fig. 5). Its northern boundary is formed by the lake itself whose northern and the southern shores offer good connections towards the Phrygian plateau and the Maeander valley. Towards the south, the Burdur Plain has two natural exits: one to the west, through the plain around Lake Yarışlı, and one to the south, following the course of the Lysis river (Bozçay). As the remains of important settlements, at Yarımada (or Ada Mevkii) in Lake Yarışlı and at Kozluca Höyük in the Lysis valley show (see below), both routes must have been in use in pre-Hellenistic times. They may have been the kind of non-built, non-paved, but known and accepted tracks which in Anatolia, since pre-Hittite times, were used as lines of communications. Many of these trackways continued to exist right into the Hellenistic period, when built, engineered, but narrow roadways made their first appearance (French 1980: 705).

During the Hellenistic period, lines of communication became of vital importance for the survival of some of the developing kingdoms and were hence guarded by fortifications or well-fortified cities (Fig. 3). One such road was the one connecting the Pamphylian ports with Kelainai (near Dinar). It entered Sagalassian territory in the plain to the south of Lake Burdur and continued along the lake's northern shore (Mitchell 1994: 133 fig. 2). It was already used by Alexander in 333 BC on his march to Gordion (Arrian, *Anabasis Alexandri* I, 27; Ramsay 1890: 298; Levick 1967: 15). In 189 BC, part of this road was also followed by Cn. Manlius Vulso on his journey from Southern Pisidia towards Galatia. A more detailed description of his movements in the plain of Burdur will be given below. In winter, this road which crossed the Taurus range by means of the Döşemeboğazı (ancient Klymax) pass, was the only

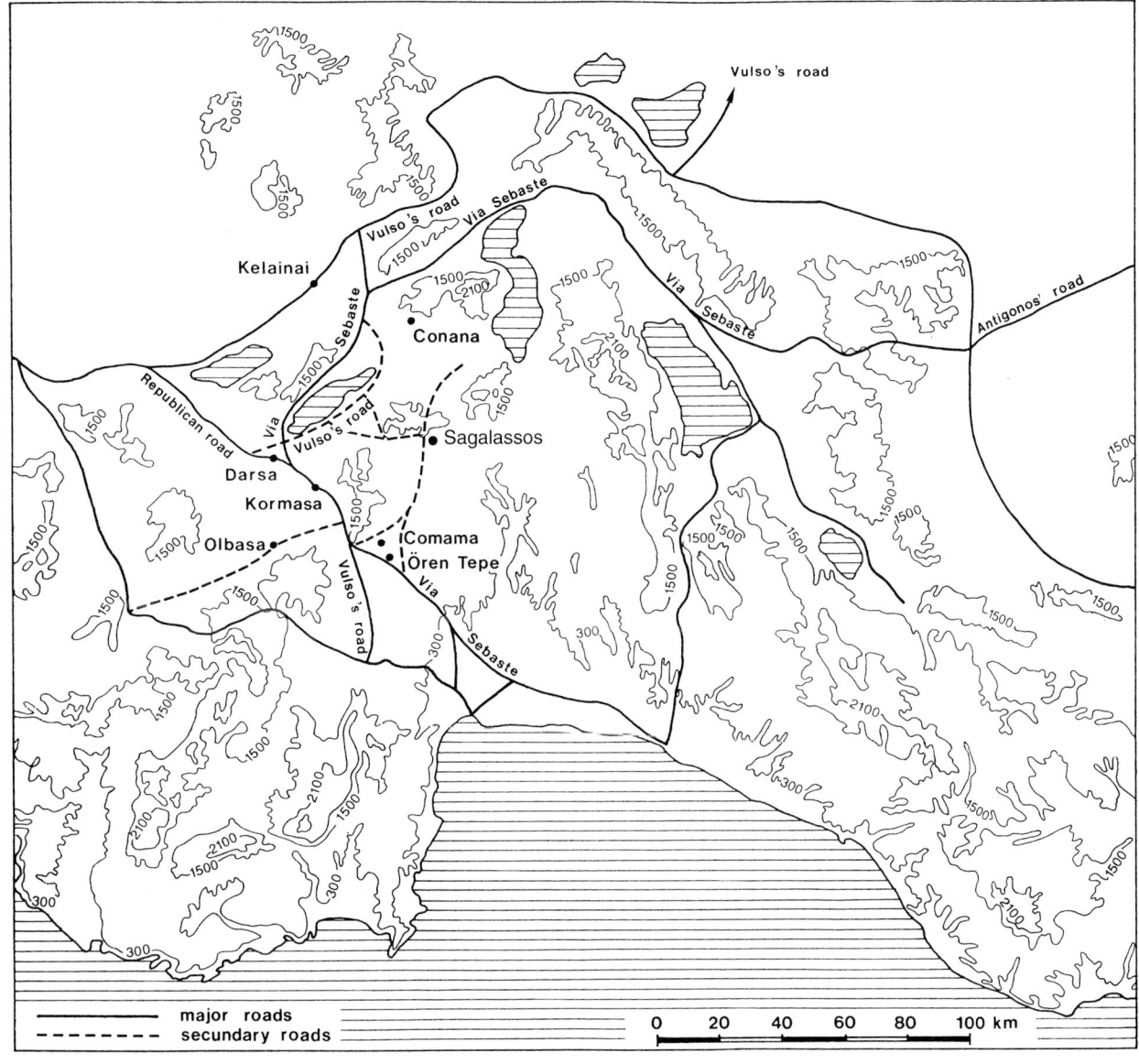

Fig. 3: Map with the major road systems in Northern Pisidia. Adapted from S.Mitchell (1994: 133 fig.2).

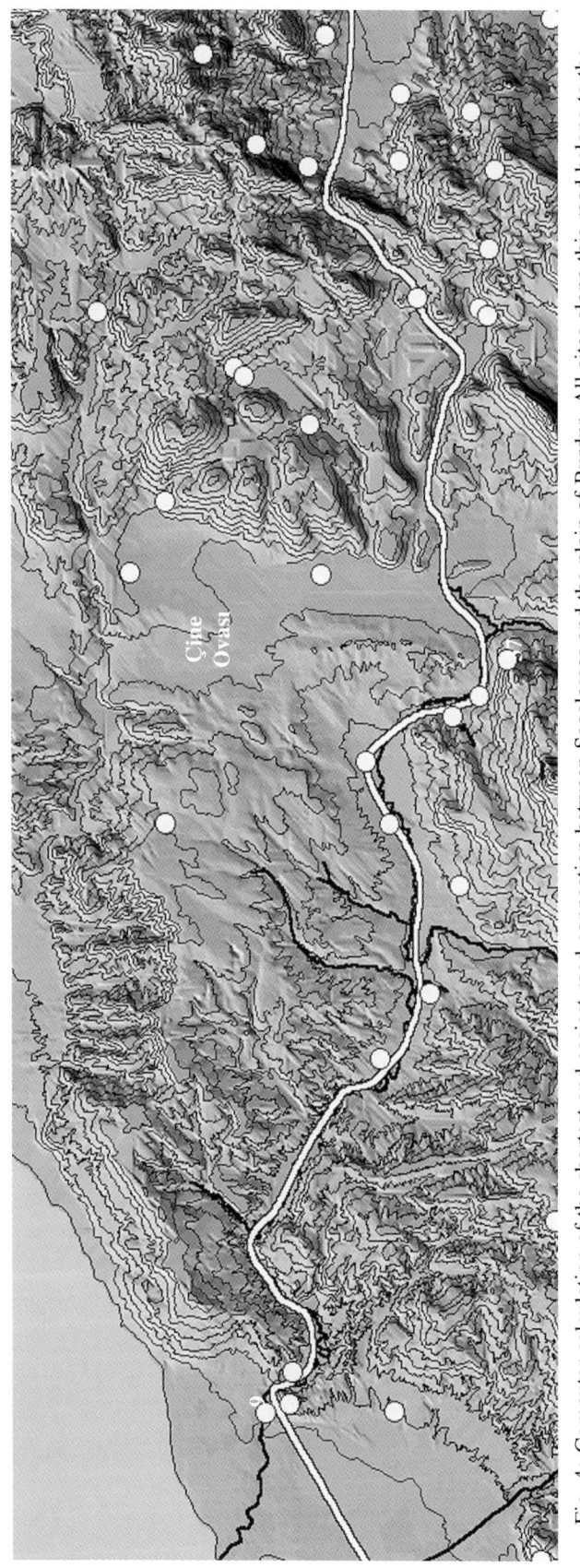

Fig. 4: Computer calculation of the shortest and easiest road connection between Sagalassos and the plain of Burdur. All sites along this road belong to the Imperial period.

connection through this mountain chain into Phrygia (Sekunda 1997: 222). Therefore, its junctions with other roads were guarded by a number of Hellenistic strongholds. As early as the late fourth century BC, Kretopolis is likely to have been founded either by Nearchos the Cretan (in 333-331 BC) or by Antigonos Monophthalmos (between 333 and 319 BC) to protect such a key strategic road junction, at the point where it connected to another road running from the Milyas through the Kestel plain towards Sagalassos and beyond its mountain pass to the north (Sekunda 1997). In 319 BC, the latter road was used by Antigonos Monophthalmos on his hasty journey from Cappadocia to Kretopolis (Mitchell 1994: 130), where he defeated Alketas and his Pisidian allies. Almost a hundred years later, in 218 BC, Achaios' general Garsyeris also camped near Kretopolis before descending on the besieged city of Pednelissos (Sekunda 1997: 218). From the Augustan period onwards, the Roman colony of Comama, seems to have adopted the former military role of Kretopolis (Mitchell 1994: 136).

Further south, a fortlet (Ören Tepe) near Panemoteichos (Boğaziçi) guarded the approach to the Klymax Pass as well as the junction with a road coming from Sagalassos through the very narrow pass north of Panemoteichos (Mitchell 1994: 144; Aydal et al. 1997: 163-172, figs. 1 and 8). It is very likely that the fortlet was built by the Attalids between 189/8 and 133 BC in order to protect the main route which connected their capital with their possessions in Pamphylia. The foundation in this region of Attaleia (Antalya) by Attalos II, between 159 and 150 BC, may also reflect the Attalid concern to protect their interests in southern Anatolia (Aydal et al. 1997: 168-169). Pergamenian military presence and the existence of Attalid garrisons in Northern Pisidia are documented also by the Attalid letter to Olbasa (Kearsly 1994; Aydal et al. 1997). It is possible that the Hellenistic fortlet near Insuyu in the Çineovası, which is the only one on Sagalassian territory located in a plain and not on a hill top, was in reality not part of the defence system of Sagalassos, as we assumed in the past (Waelkens et al. 1997a: 81), but occupied by one of these Pergamenian garrisons. Its location is clearly comparable with that of the fortlet of Ören Tepe. The strategic site at Gâvur Evi Tepesi in the northwestern part of the plain of Düğer (Figs. 140 and 208) perhaps fulfilled a similar function.

Between 129 and 126 BC, the major highway connecting the south coast with the plain of Burdur and hence with Pergamon and western Anatolia, was transformed by M. Aquillius into the first road which the Romans built in their newly created province of Asia (French 1991: 54; Aydal et al. 1997: 168). This highway was probably already a broad paved road (French 1980: 707). Three of its milestones were found to the west of the plain of Burdur in the villages of Alanköy (French 1988: 101 no. 266), Harmanlı (French 1988: 106 no. 279) and Yarışlı-Takina (French 1980: 706 map 1, 707, 714 nos. 2-3; French 1988: 111 nos. 294-295). This road continued along the southern edge of the plain of Düğer (D. French: personal communication) and, from there, followed a stretch of the Lysis valley towards the southeast (Mitchell 1994: 133 fig. 2). The function of this road was purely strategical, i.e. to control the regions where the revolt of Aristonikos had been focused after Rome had inherited the Pergamene kingdom in 133 BC (Sherwin-White 1977: 69).

In 6 BC, part of this road, i.e. from the plain of Burdur onwards towards the south, became incorporated into the *via Sebaste,* built by the governor of the province of Galatia, Cornutus Aquila, and linking Pisidian Antioch and the other Augustan colonies with one another and with the Pamphylian ports (French 1980: 707-708 map 2). During the early Imperial period, the military importance of this road system remained unchanged (Sherk 1980: 906). Well-preserved stretches of road in the Döşemeboğazı Pass (Klymax) show that it was a broad paved highway intended for the use of wheeled traffic (Mitchell 1993: 70). As we have said above, Sagalassos was responsible for official traffic along this road, between Konana and Kormasa (Mitchell 1976). To the south of Sagalassian territory (in the plain of Burdur), the *via Sebaste* crossed the Lysis most probably at Boğaziçi (near Kormasa) and passed between there and Elmacık before crossing the mountains to Aziziye on its way to Komama (Hall 1976: 148 note 41; French and Mitchell 1977: 219, map). Milestones from it have been found at Yarı in the plain of Burdur (French 1988: 112 no. 298), at Boğaziçi (French 1988: 102 no. 267) and at Ürkütlü, near Komama (French and Mitchell 1977; French 1988: 110 nos 292-293).

In the Lysis valley, another road may have branched off from the *via Sebaste* towards Kibyra. The strategic importance of this connection is shown by the foundation of the Augustan colony of Olbasa to protect the junction with a road crossing the mountains to the east (Levick 1967: 48-49). That Olbasa had a strategic role already under the Attalids is shown by a recently published inscription (Kearsly 1994; Aydal et al. 1997: 169-70).

Beside these major 'highways' (Fig. 3), the western part of Sagalassian territory must also have contained many smaller roads or tracks of local or regional importance. It is striking that the present connection between Sagalassos and Lake Burdur, which follows the valley of Taşkapı and of Gökpınar (the former Çine) towards the west as far as this last village, and from there makes a 90° turn to the north, through the Çineovası, contains almost no classical sites in the latter valley (Waelkens et al. 1997a: 80). The only major site here is the Hellenistic and late Roman fortress located near Insuyu. Taken together with a concentration of Roman settlements in the hill country to the east of the Çineovası, near the villages of Çatağıl, Halıcılar and Günalan (the former Lengüme, the ancient Magastara), this evidence seems to suggest that in Roman antiquity, the road system from Sagalassos towards the northern part of the Plain of Burdur, followed the present road linking Günalan over Halıcılar and Çatağıl towards Taşkapı. This road was also followed in 1868 by de Tchihatcheff (Waelkens *et al.* 1997a: 17 fig. 2; 84-96). On the other hand, the concentration of Roman sites and settlements in the valley of the Büğdüz Çayı around the present villages of Kayaaltı, Bayındır, and Büğdüz towards Suludere (see Fig. 4), clearly suggests that the present road from Sagalassos to Gökpınar (Çine) in antiquity continued through the valley of the Büğdüz Çayı towards the southern part of the plain of Burdur, where the city possessed its most extensive farming lands. The location of a strategic prehistoric site (Çığırtkankaya) near the place where this valley enters the Burdur Plain (see below) could suggest that the valley was already used as a prehistoric track. A computer calculation by Reyniers (Fig. 4) showed that this hypothetical road represents not only the shortest connection between both areas, but also the easiest one as far as slopes or other natural obstacles are concerned. Today, traffic makes a detour by the way of Burdur, presumably because of the growing prominence of that city from the Turkish period onwards. In the plain to the south of Lake Burdur, the Büğdüz Çayı road system seems to connect precisely with an old east-west oriented Turkish road, known as 'Sultan yolu' (Sultan's road), at the place where the latter joined the *via Sebaste* (see below). In this plain, the course of the *via Sebaste* today seems to correspond more or less with another Turkish road heading south and coming from the northern shores of Lake Burdur (Fig. 5). The latter is known as 'Deve yolu' (camel's road). The 'Sultan yolu' which branched off the Roman republican road continues to the east of this major crossroads, along the southern shores of Lake Burdur, where at Suludere it is joined by the hypothetical Büğdüz road system. It seems very likely, therefore, that this eastern extension of the 'Sultan yolu' and the Büğdüz road correspond with an ancient road offering the shortest connection to Sagalassos. Most probably, the 'Sultan yolu' itself continued along the southeastern shore of the lake towards the north. In fact, the site where the famous inscription of Libuscidianus was found (near the station of Burdur, where there was a settlement, see below), makes it very unlikely that the local inhabitants had to provide transport on the stretch of the *via Sebaste* located on the opposite side of the lake from where they lived. Mitchell has suggested that, instead, they may have provided their services on a more direct connection between Konana and Kormasa running through the territory of Sagalassos along the southern shore of Lake Burdur (Mitchell 1976: 122). Mitchell correctly stated that no traces of this road can be found on the ground. But, Livy's description of Manlius Vulso's journey (Livy XXXVIII 15, 9) seems to suggest that the Roman general followed exactly such a southern road around the lake. Otherwise, the people of Lysinia, a city located on the north side of the lake and along the stretch of the later *via Sebaste*, would probably not have sent representatives to meet Vulso at the point where he entered Sagalassian territory. In fact, a journey north of the lake would have automatically taken him through their city. In our view, the 'Sultan yolu' could therefore correspond with a southern shortcut of the Roman road system, between Konana and Kormasa (see below).

4. PHYSIOGRAPHIC SUBDIVISION OF THE WESTERN PART OF SAGALASSIAN TERRITORY

The western part of Sagalassos held territory as described in the following text can be defined as the district located to the west of the Çineovası, which forms an elongated north–south oriented plateau, located at a mean altitude of ca. 1200 m a.s.l. (Waelkens *et al.* 1997a: 79-81). Coming from Sagalassos this line marks a remarkable transition in geology, and as a result a change in land use and in landscape. These differences spring from the underlying geological structure, the geomorphological processes and the human occupation which adapted to the given potentials and restrictions. On a broad scale, the geological and geomorphological history resulted in three distinct areas (Fig. 6):

- the limestone range of Mt. Beşparmak
- the plateau landscape on neogene marl deposits of the Burdur Basin, on which the Burdur badlands developed
- the plain of Lake Burdur located between the badlands area in the east and the limestone range of Mt. Soğut in the west. The settlement and land use patterns are remarkably well adapted to this three-part landscape structure.

During the geomorphological survey all coordinates were measured with a handheld GPS Trimble Navigation system. The altitudes were measured with a precision electronic altimeter Alpin EL (Eschenbach, Germany). Each morning, the height of the altimeter was set corresponding the absolute height of a fixed point at Ağlasun. In the evening, altitudes were checked again and calibrated against the same point. Accuracy in the order of 10 m can thus be expected. Corrections of some GPS-altitudes have also been made with data from the Turkish topographical maps at scale 1:25.000 The coordinates were measured according to the WGS-84 (World Geodetic System).

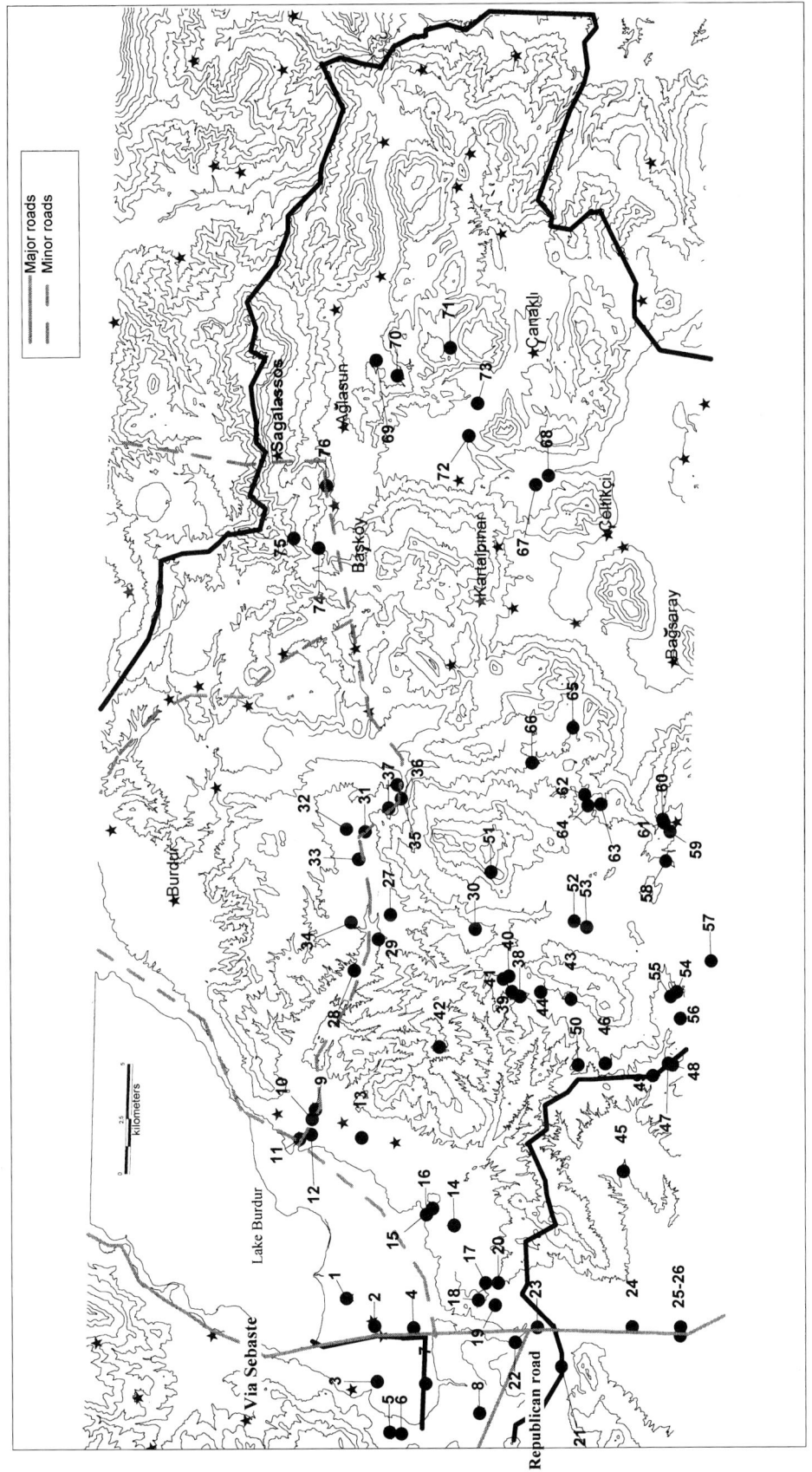

Fig. 5: Map with the ancient roads in the plain of Burdur. (The thick line indicates the territorial boundaries of the city in Imperial times).

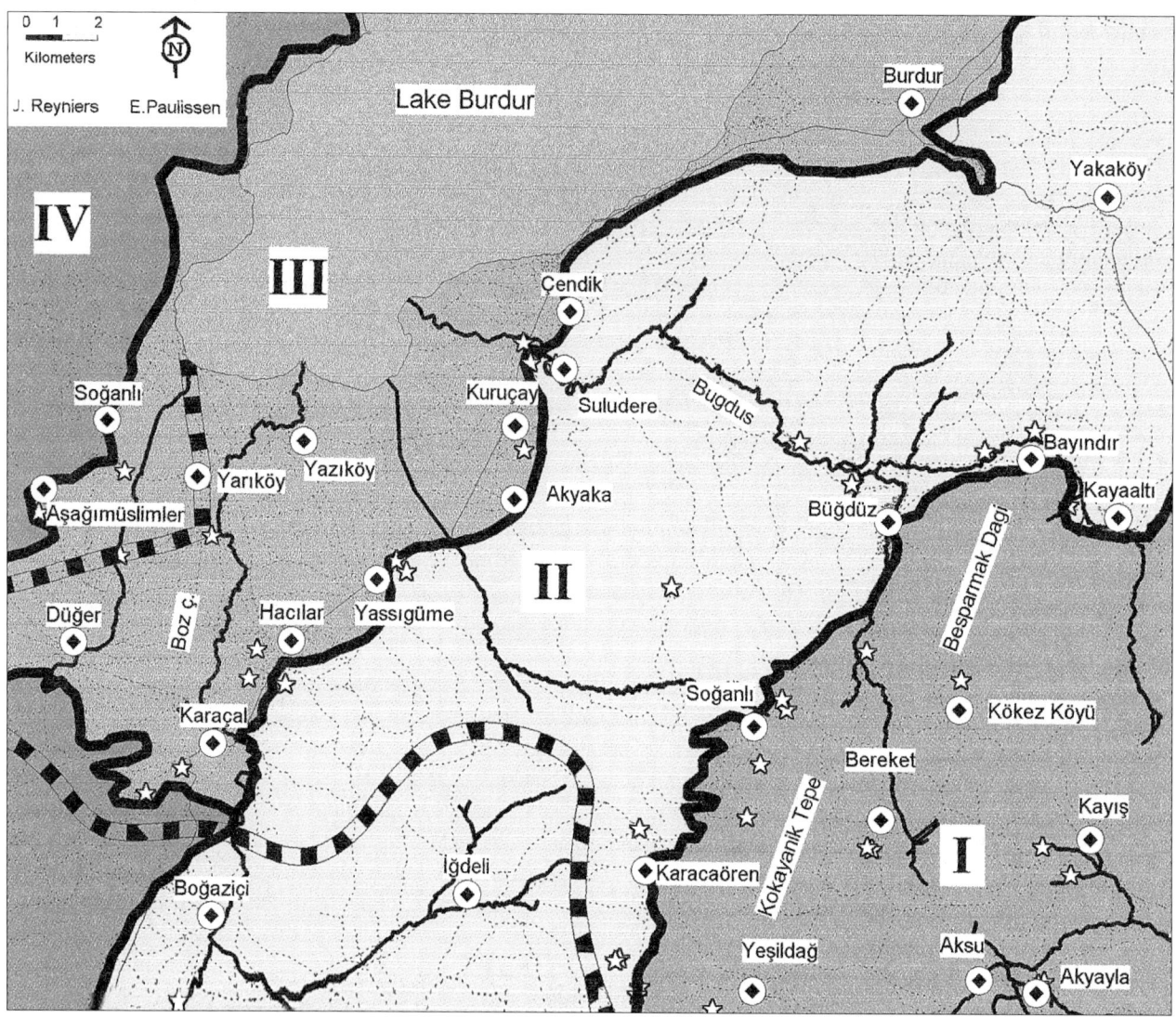

Fig. 6: The three major geographical districts in the western part of Sagalassian territory.
(thick dotted line indicates the southern boundary of the city's territory).

Fig. 6: Landscape structure of the Western Sagalassos Territory
  I   Limestone mountains of Mt. Beşparmak
  II Plateau remnants and Burdur badlands (dissected plateau) on marl deposits
  III Plain of Lake Burdur
  IV Limestone mountains of Mt. Soğut

5. THE LIMESTONE RANGE OF MT. BEŞPARMAK

Moving west from Sagalassos and from the district surveyed in previous years (Waelkens *et al.* 1997a), one first encounters the limestone area of the Beşparmak Dağı (i.e. the Five Fingered Mountain) of which two (Kale Tepe: 1928 m a.s.l.; Şişli Tepe: 2028 m a.s.l.) of the five peaks reach a height of ca. 2000 m a.s.l. (Figs 7-8). This area resembles the mountain area located to the west and southwest of Sagalassos, but the mass of the north-south oriented Beşparmak Dağı both forms an ultimate barrier for easy east-west communication between sites and represents a valuable water source for all surrounding settlements. The Beşparmak Dağı and the Kocauyanık Tepe (1833 m a.s.l.), which constitutes a southwestern extension on the other side of the Büğdüz Çayı (Fig. 6), form a limestone area of almost 100 square km in which, except for the above-mentioned river valley, road communications are very difficult. To the south of the Beşparmak Dağı, there is a lower area where we find elongated areas with good soils between the mountains that are used for agriculture and in which road systems could develop.

In the limestone district of Mt. Beşparmak, the link between springs and permanent rivers on the one hand and modern settlements or ancient sites on the other, is obvious. In fact, the mountainous limestone district contains numerous springs, many of which have a permanent character. The topographical map does not allow any distinction between the different types of spring. However, field observations suggest that most of the settlements in this area were clearly associated with permanent springs or rivers. Some sites, for instance Kayaaltı, Yayla, Bereket, Kayış, Akyayla, Soğanlı, and to a lesser extent Karacaören can even be directly linked to a permanent water supply. Büğdüz and Bayındır profit from the permanent Büğdüz Çayı river. Exceptions to this rule can be logically explained. In some cases one can suppose that, mainly as the result of recent irrigation, the water supply has changed since the occupation of the site. The area may have been more humid or the available water may have been used more economically. On the other hand, sites located at a greater distance from a permanent water supply, clearly owed their location to their great strategic importance, which factor was preferred above ecological deficiencies. This is the case with some very distinctive fortified strongholds located in the limestone mountain range and dominating the surrounding area.

On the north and west side of the Beşparmak, neogene marls cover the limestone formations between the mountain and the valleys of the Büğdüz and the Yayla rivers. In this area, up to a height of 1400 m a.s.l., badlands are formed in the marls on the lower slopes of the Beşparmak. The result is an erosive landscape with poor soil development, only fit for poor crops such as chickpeas, and with rather steep slopes. Environmentally and from a landscape point of view, this area belongs to the Beşparmak area, but geologically it has more in common with the second geographical subdivision of the western part of the Sagalassos territory, i.e. the Burdur badlands.

The Büğdüz river system and its eastern tributaries form the easiest and most natural connection between Sagalassos and its possessions in the Burdur plain. Since there is no natural boundary between this river system and that of its main southern tributary, the Çarşamba Çayı, the territory of the city must have stretched at least as far south as the basin of Bereket (see below). Between the latter and the Kestel Dağı range in the south, the basins of Yeşildağ, of Aksu and of Akyayla, are much better linked with and oriented towards the areas to the north, than those to the south of the Kestel range, so that we can suggest that they formed the southernmost extension of Sagalassian territory. There are indeed no other city sites in this area, since the major site at Gâvur Ören does not seem to have been that of an autonomous city at all (see below). We therefore believe that the southwestern boundary of Sagalassos ran along the water divide to the west of the Kuzköy and Bağsaray basins towards Akyala and from there over the crests of the Kestel range along the southern edges of the marl plateau between Lake Burdur and the limestone mountains, as far as the Lysis gorge near Karaçal (Fig. 6). Its westbound continuation will be described while discussing the plain of Burdur.

The Beşparmak limestone massif can be subdivided into the following areas:

5.1. The spring catchment area of the Kerme Deresi to the north and west of the valley of Bağsaray (formerly Arvallı)

The valley of Bağsaray was surveyed during the 1995 season. It is drained by the Kerme or Çebiş Deresi which takes its water from a large number of springs located on the western slopes. In 1995, a major site (Demirli) was found on these slopes, approximately 6 km to the northwest of Bağsaray (Waelkens *et al.* 1997a: 54, 61-64).

In this area, the Kerme Deresi is fed by both a western (Tekke Deresi) and a northern tributary, known as Usunkoz Deresi in its lower, as Asmalı Deresi in its middle and as Gümbinek Deresi in its upper reaches. Whereas the lower course with the site of Eski Kayış still belongs geographically to the Bağsarayovası and therefore during the Hellenistic period may have been part of the territory of Keraitai, the higher reaches of the river system, with the village of Kayış, are located in an intramontane basin that seems more oriented towards Akyayla from which it can be reached easily.

During the Imperial period, the fertile valley of Bağsaray had a very dense settlement pattern, both in the actual valley bottom and on the slopes that surround it (Waelkens *et al.* 1997a: 59-64). The sites of Sarız Yeri (coordinates 37° 31,4560 E; 30 22,568' N; altitude: 1048 m a.s.l.) and of Eski Kayış (coordinates 37°31,738' N; 30°22,180' E; altitude: 1171 m a.s.l.) that were surveyed in 1996, fit perfectly in this pattern.

Sarız Yeri is located in the middle of wheat fields, on a south-southwest facing slope, immediately to the east of the road to Kayış and a little to the west of Bağsaray. At the surface some traces of walls and some mostly coarse late Imperial sherds (SA 96 S 72) were seen. A small agricultural structure (or a tomb) may have been located here.

The site of Eski Kayış is located further north, on a south-facing hill slope, and surrounded by wheat fields. Most of the remains are scattered on a kind of natural terrace (ca. 40 to 50 m by 100 m). Here, the soil is covered with tiles and with fine and coarse sherds, including Sagalassos red slip wares, some dated to the early, but most to the late Roman period (SA 96 S 73). The ruins included stretches of rubble walls, a doorpost *in situ* as well as some fluted columns (Fig. 9). On a slope to the north, there is a spring (Uzun Koz) surrounded by surface sherds. At least three counter-weights for simple lever-and-weight olive presses have been found here (Fig. 10) and seem to reveal the existence of olive cultivation in this valley during classical times. This type of presses was mainly used in the production of olive oil, but to a lesser extent also in the production of wine. In both cases, the device was used during the second stage of processing, respectively after the crushing of the olives to a mash, or after the treading of the grapes to express most of the must. Yet, in the case of the grapes, most of the must had already been extracted in a previous stage, whereas in that of the olives this happened precisely during the second stage (Frankel 1994: 41, 61). Therefore, such presses were far mor important for the processing of olives and usually are identified as being connected with olive culture (see Eitam 1993; Kloner and Sagiv 1993; Frankel 1994, on these). Moreover, carbonized olive wood in charcoal found on the site of Sagalassos (Schoch 1995), as well as high percentages of olive pollen from the Gravgaz marshes in the central part of Sagalassian territory (ca. 1200 m a.s.l.) also confirm a local cultivation of these trees in Roman times at higher altitudes than is possible today (Vermoere *et al.* in press). In 1995, traces of contemporary olive cultivation could still be seen in the lower part of the valley near Bağsaray (Waelkens *et al.* 1997a: 61 fig. 60). Everything thus points to the presence of a rather rich agricultural settlement (a large farm or a small village) at Eski Kayış which flourished from early to late Imperial times.

To the northwest of Eski Kayış, there are said to be ancient remains at Çatal Pınar but the site was not visited by the survey team. The remains included a sarcophagus, inscribed and decorated stones and wall traces.

The intramontane basin of Kayış (Fig. 11) to the northwest of the Bağsaray valley, was most probably located within Sagalassian territory from Hellenistic times. In fact, it is unlikely that the territory of the small, unidentified city site at Kepez Kalesi (Waelkens *et al.* 1997a: 69-72), located in the northern part of the Kuzköy valley to the east of Kayış, ever extended beyond the steep mountain slopes which enclosed it to the west. In 1996 several traces of rather dense Hellenistic and Roman occupation were noted in this basin.

The modern village of Kayış itself (Fig. 12) is full of antiquities which seem to have been removed from the ancient sites around it. The latter must have contained at least two larger settlements (the sites belonging to Asar Tepesi and to Fırın Yıkığı), but it may also have included some smaller sites. This intramontane basin, located at an altitude of approximately 1300 m a.s.l., must have grown olives in Roman antiquity. Since olives are not cultivated nowadays above a height of 900 m a.s.l., this can only mean that climate must have been different, with very rare strong frost events that could severely damage or destroy the olive trees.

The area must already have been occupied during the late Hellenistic to early Imperial times as is shown by the pottery (see below), but also by the presence of a late Hellenistic to early Imperial ostotheca built upside down in one of the fountains of Kayış (Figs. 13-14). The coffin (ca. 0.70 by 0.46 m; pres. h.: 0.42 m) is decorated with a *patera* flanked by rosettes on the only visible long side, and with the usual door on the visible small side. The lower door panels are filled with rosettes, while the upper panels contained other motifs (a doorlock, a knocker?). The exact provenance of the stone is unknown. This is also the case for a much decorated limestone fragment (pres. h.: 0.27 m; w.: 0.47 m) built into the walls of Ferzu Kaya's house. It represents a rich vine ornament with leaves, voluted stems and bunches of grapes (Fig. 15). The fragment undoubtedly belongs to one of the vase-like ostothecae which according to a study by V. Köse (in preparation) seem to have become popular at Sagalassos during the early Imperial period. Other houses contain worked architectural blocks (for instance that of Mustafa Aykurt: two nicely worked bases in white and red limestone; elsewhere, the top of an altar). At the local school a limestone funerary stele (h.: 1.14 m; w.: 0.40 m) represents a bearded man clad in a *himation* and holding a scroll in his left hand (Fig. 16). The steep gable is decorated with plain akroteria below and a large wreath in its centre. The local mosque has re-used some ancient stones as supports for its wooden columns. Among them, there are two

Fig. 7: View of Mt. Beşparmak seen from the west (near Soğanlı).

Fig. 8: Mt. Beşparmak (in the background) seen from the plain of Burdur.

Fig. 9: View of some building remains at Eski Kayış.

Fig. 10: Counterweight for an olive press at Eski Kayış.

Fig. 11: The intramontane basin of Kayış seen from the village.

Fig. 12: View of the village of Kayış.

Fig. 13: Long side of the ostotheca built into a fountain at Kayış.

Fig. 14: Small side of the same ostotheca.

Fig. 15: Fragment of a vase-like ostotheca built into a house wall at Kayış.

Fig. 16: Funerary stele at Kayış.

Fig. 17: Funerary column drum re-used inside the mosque of Kayış.

Fig. 18: Upper moulding of a pedestal with palmette *anthemion* in the mosque of Kayış.

Fig. 19: View of the site of Asar Tepesi.

Fig. 20: View of the fields below the site of Asar Tepesi.

Fig. 21: Head in relief said to come from Asar Tepesi, at Kayış.

Fig. 22: Counterweight for a simple lever-and-weight oil press at Asar Tepesi.

Fig. 19: View of the site of Asar Tepesi.

Fig. 20: View of the fields below the site of Asar Tepesi.

Fig. 21: Head in relief said to come from Asar Tepesi, at Kayış.

Fig. 22: Counterweight for a simple lever-and-weight oil press at Asar Tepesi.

fluted column drum fragments (diameter: 0.57 m), one decorated with a *tabula ansata* with the fragment of a third century AD epitaph (Fig. 17). Another support is made from the upper moulding of a pedestal (now: 0.60 by 0.50 m; h.: 0.29 m), decorated with a probably first century AD *anthemion* (Fig. 18). The exact provenance of all these antiquities could no longer be established, but for others the villagers could still provide some information.

There is a major site at Asar Tepesi (37°32,358 N; 30°20,528E; altitude: 1360 m a.s.l.), located approximately 500 m to the southwest of Kayış (Figs. 19-20). It can be found immediately to the south of the road leading from Kayış to Bereket and got its name from the rocky outcrop to the north of it. The site contains a lot of rubble, mixed with tiles and pottery (SA 96 S 70). The coarse and fine ceramics, including Sagalassos red slip wares, could be attributed to the early and the late Roman period. Some worked stones and a fluted column drum at Kayış seem to have come from here. Villagers said that a small statue had once been uncovered at Asar Tepe. A rather primitive head (relief; h.: 0.24 m; w.: 0.12 m), reportedly from the site, is built into a wall of Mustafa Koç's house (Fig. 21). The site also held a number of counterweights for simple lever-and-weight oil presses (Fig. 22), as well as the remains of a water supply system that brought water from the site at Çatal Oluk. This means that one could deduce the presence of a farming community, practicing among other things olive cultivation. The site of Asar Tepe may have been the Roman predecessor of Kayış, which perhaps to some extent occupies the ancient settlement. Çatal Oluk (or Çay Gözü) is located near a spring, in the midst of fields (Fig. 23), to the west of the village (37°32,660' N; 30°20,107 E; altitude: 1365 m a.s.l.). The name of the site, 'Forked groove' (Çatal Oluk) or 'Eye of the stream' (Çay Gözü), undoubtedly refers to the water supply system which carried its water to Asar Tepesi and to the spring. Several stones (w.: 0.59 m to 0.60 m; h.: ca. 0.51 m to 0.65 m) with a sunken surface above and a rounded groove in the middle (w.: 0.18 m) built into the houses of Kayış (Mustafa Uçak, Veli Çelik) may have belonged to this water system. The fields around the spring contain a lot of rubble, a few tiles and a very few sherds, both ancient and modern. Some water catchment structures can be found here and there may even have been a kind of (spring?) sanctuary, since a votive altar in the house of Çelil Aykurt at Kayış is supposed to have been found there. The square altar (h.: 0.74 m; w. in middle: 0.30 m; th. in middle: 0.23 m) is broken and much weathered on all sides (Fig. 24). On top, it is decorated with a *patera* between akroteria. Its front bore a relief of a horseman waving a shield in front of him, so that it is certainly not a representation of Kakasbos, whose iconography in Western Pisidia is different (Smith 1997: 16-17). A votive inscription surrounds the relief above and below, saying that a certain Eustochos, son of Severianos, had erected the altar 'for the well-being of the *despotai*'. The left side carries the weathered representation of a standing human figure, the back has a wreath with hanging ribbons, and the right side is decorated with a worn bust.

A second site has been found at Fırın Yıkığı (the 'oven ruin'), located 2.8 km to the northeast of Kayış (37°33,894' N; 30°21,805'E; altitude: 1308 m a.s.l.). The site is located in the midst of cultivated fields (beans, chick-peas, wheat, barley, maize) in an elongated intramontane basin with gentle slopes, near a spring (Fig. 25). The fields themselves do not show any trace of tiles, stones or pottery at the surface, but the road incursion has exposed some deeper profiles which show that it had cut through a necropolis (Fig. 26). The exposed tombs, which are empty now, were delineated by rubble stone walls. In at least one case a white plaster layer covered the floor. The roof was made of large tiles, covered with smaller stones. The whole arrangement is reminiscent of that at Kapıhanı near Bağsaray (Waelkens *et al.* 1997a: 60 fig. 61). Several stones at Kayış are said to have come from here, showing that the site originally contained also some more elaborate funerary structures. Two (of which at least one funerary) columns (vis. h.: 1.18 and 1.03 m; upper diameter: ca. 0.50 m) said to have come from Fırın Yıkığı, now flank a second fountain at Kayış. One of the column drums contains a simple *tabula ansata* with a probably second century AD epitaph, saying that Solon and his wife had erected the monument during their lifetime for themselves and for their children (Fig. 27). A fluted column (pres.h.: 1.27 m; diam.: 0.50 m) and an unfinished column capital in the house of Veli Aydoğdu near the same fountain, are also said to have been brought from the same site. The settlement to which the necropolis once belonged, has not been identified yet.

During the 1996 campaign, beside surveying its northern catchment area around Kayış, the upper valley of the Kerme Deresi was also followed upstream towards the west. Beyond Demirli, the slopes become more pronounced and they are covered with black pine, juniper, plane-trees, and some stands of mulberry (Fig. 28). Most of the forest vegetation is concentrated on the slopes exposed to the north, while the southern slopes are covered with a secondary shrub vegetation (mostly kermes oak). Higher up the slopes, the juniper stands become denser, while the highest hill-tops are covered with black pine. A pass between the Salavatgediği Tepe (1496 m a.s.l.) to the north and the Göynükgedik Tepe to the south leads towards an intramontane basin occupied by the village of Akyayla (formerly Akpınar). This village, located at a mean altitude of ca. 1400 m a.s.l., contains some hundred houses. The whole basin is under cultivation (Fig. 29).

A few hundred meters to the north/northeast of the modern village, there is a hill with steep slopes towards the pass, called Kale Tepe (i.e. fortress hill) (Fig. 30), rising to an altitude of 1430 m a.s.l. (GPS coordinates: 37°30,623'N – 30° 20,216' E). This hill is located to the southeast of the valley of the Tekke Deresi, a western tributary of the Kerme Deresi, on the northwestern termination of a northwest-southeast oriented limestone mountain range. In this area, the Tekke Deresi, which drains towards the north, breaches the limestone formations, which results in a 1 km long and narrow valley with very steep walls about 100 m in height. This canyon-like feature is unique along the Tekke Deresi.

During the Hellenistic period, when the Bağsarayovası and the adjoining plain of Çeltikçi belonged to the site of Keraitai, rather than to Sagalassos (Waelkens *et al.* 1997a: 54-55), the canyon of the Tekke Deresi, and not the mountain range further west (see Waelkens *et al.* 1997a: 99) must have formed the boundary between the territories of Keraitai to the east, and Sagalassos to the west. In fact, connections with the basin of Bereket and the western part of Sagalassian territory are easier than with the Bağsarayovası and Keraitai. The road towards Bereket follows a small valley with juniper and black pine on the northern slopes, and wheat on the lower 50 to 100 m, below juniper stands, on the southern slopes.

Towards the northeast, the river valley opens and the general topography becomes lower, so that the Kale Tepe site dominates the area and controls the roads coming both from the direction of Bağsaray to the southeast and from Kayış in the north (the Göcük Yolu). It is even possible to see the ridge of Mt. Ağlasun (Fig. 31) with its fortress and watchtower above Sagalassos (Loots *et al.* 2000). The valley slopes are covered with forests of Pinus nigra, mixed with Juniperus, while the Kale Tepe is covered with Quercus calliprinos and some junipers. In the past, juniper was cut for making roof timbers, but the trees are now protected and have recently been replaced by black pine as a building material.

It is interesting to note that on the plateau-like relief to the northwest, mainly situated between 1400 and 1600 m a.s.l., the plain areas are nearly all under cultivation as arable lands.

Towards the village of Akyayla, upstream from the canyon-like section of the Tekke Deresi, the morphology becomes less pronounced and a broad, shallow and elongated basin has developed. This basin, which is less than 100 m below the hill tops, is filled with red-brown clayey materials and is nowadays fertile land (wheat, barley, maize, beans, potatoes). It is probably structurally controlled as it has a northwest-southeast orientation, which is oblique to the general direction of the Tekke Deresi, the main drainage line.

The top of the Kale Tepe is occupied by a small fortress, which on the northeast side is perched on a nearly 50 m high cliff. On that side, it is not protected by walls but, towards the west, south and east, dry stone walls surround a rectangular area of 34 m in an east-west direction and 19.50 to 22 m in a north–south direction. A square structure (4 by 4 m) is built inside the southeast corner, while a square bastion (inside dimensions 1.60 by 1.60 m) abuts on the southwest corner. The fortification wall has a width of 1.90 m throughout and still stands to a height of max. 1.40 m (Fig. 32). It is built in an *emplekton* technique with medium to large sized blocks outside and a fill of smaller rubble stones inside. The building technique resembles that of the fortifications and barrier walls above Sagalassos (Loots *et al.* 2000). Since no datable pottery could be found inside the fortified area or around it, the site was apparently only occupied for shorter periods. The wall technique indicates a date in the Hellenistic period. Most probably the fortlet on the Kale Tepe was part of the Hellenistic defence system guarding the boundaries of Sagalassian territory. In fact, the fortlet seems to have protected the approaches from Keraitai in the east, and from the unidentified city site at Kepez Kalesi (Waelkens *et al.* 1997a: 69-72) via Kayış in the northeast. At the same time, it overlooked the southern boundary of Sagalassian territory in this area, which must have been formed by the dominating and steep mountain range of the Katrancık or Kestel Dağı (2328 m a.s.l.). In fact, from the northeast to the southwest this mountain barrier separated Sagalassos from the territories of Kolbasa, the unidentified city site at Kaynar Kalesi, and Kretopolis. Kolbasa has been identified on epigraphic evidence with the ancient city site of Gâvur Ini near Kuşbaba (Bean 1960: 44-47; Mitchell 1991: 137) which possesses a fortified acropolis surrounded by a wall in rough polygonal masonry, which, according to Bean, might even be pre-Hellenistic. The site must go back at the latest to the late Bronze Age since, during the later part of the thirteenth century BC, it is already mentioned under the name Kuwalapassa in the annals of the Hittite king Hattusili III (*KUB* XXI 6 and 6a, see Waelkens 2000 and Hawkins 1995: 52 note 181; 56). Under the Roman Empire, the city of Kolbasa minted coins (Mitchell 1991: 137). Further west, the southeastern slopes of Mt. Kestel contain the ruins of a considerable, still unidentified city site, called Kaynar Kalesi, with an acropolis and a city wall. The site contained a probably late Hellenistic Doric prostyle temple and a sanctuary for Plouton and Korè. According to at least one ostotheca decorated with a Macedonian shield, it may have received Macedonian veterans as settlers during the Seleucid period (Bean 1960: 47-50; Mitchell 1991: 133). The ruins must represent one of the smaller unknown Pisidian cities that flourished during the Hellenistic period (such as Kepez Kalesi further north). A little to the south of Kaynar Kalesi, Nearchos the Cretan or Antigonos Monophthalmos, during the later fourth century BC (see above), had founded the city of Kretopolis, identified by Mitchell with a site near the modern

Fig. 23: View of the site of Çatal Oluk.

Fig. 24: Front of the votive altar from Çatal Oluk at Kayış.

Fig. 25: View of the site at Fırın Yıkığı.

Fig. 26: View of the exposed tombs at Fırın Yıkığı.

Fig. 27: Funerary column of Solon from Fırın Yıkığı at Kayış.

Fig. 28: View of the Kerme Deresi valley between Demirli and Akyayla.

Fig. 29: View of the basin of Akyayla, seen from Kale. In the background, Mt. Kestel.

Fig. 30: View of Kale near Akyayla.

Fig. 31: View from Kale towards the northeast and the fortresses on Mt.Ağlasun (arrow).

Fig. 32: The fortification walls of Kale.

Fig. 33: The site of Asar Mevkii near Akyayla.

Fig. 34: Pedestal from the columnar monument near the crossroad to the north of Aksu.

Fig. 35: The corresponding pedestal near the mosque of Aksu.

village of Yüreğil at the north end of the Bozova (Mitchell 1994: 129-136). The site commanded a key strategic road junction, guarding the meeting of the Hellenistic military road (later incorporated into the *Aquilliuś road* and the *via Sebaste*), which passes immediately to the south of the site, and another road branching off to the northeast of it, running towards Sagalassos and beyond. From the Augustan period onward, Kretopolis was eclipsed by the foundation of the Roman colony of Comama (Ürkütlü), sitting astride the *via Sebaste,* which may have taken over much of the territory previously controlled by Kretopolis (Mitchell 1994: 136). It thus is clear that the Kale Tepe may have played a key strategic role in the southern defence system of Sagalassian territory. Its position can be compared with that of the fortlet on Dikmen Tepesi further east (Waelkens *et al.* 1997a: 38-40).

Although no remains of Imperial times were recovered at Akyayla, it is evident that this fertile intramontane basin must have been occupied during this period. The absence of the characteristic counterweights of simple lever-and-weight presses in this basin might suggest that, even with a slightly warmer climate in Imperial times, olive culture was too risky at this altitude above 1400 m a.s.l. Yet, in the basin of Bereket, unless the presses there were used as part of grape processing, there are traces of olive culture at similar altitudes. Settlement in this remote area continued during the late Roman period. On the southwest side of the Kale Tepe, more precisely on the lower concave slope between the hill and the broad basin of Akyayla, a concentration of tile fragments and ceramics has been found at the surface, at an altitude of 1390-1400 m a.s.l. (co-ordinates: 37°30,600' N – 30°20,100' E). On the concave slopes the red-brown clayey materials are covered with coarse slope materials of limestone fragments. The site, known as Asar Mevkii, occupies an area of nearly 600 by 400 m and may represent a small village or larger farming site (Fig. 33). Both the sherds (SA 96 S 3) and the glass fragments, indicate a probable date during the late Roman period for this settlement. A third small site, called Kilise Yıkığı (i.e. 'Church ruin'), located in a field immediately to the northwest of the village used for the cultivation of vetch (for animals), which is full of tile fragments and undatable rough pottery, could, from its name and small size, represent the site of a church.

From Akyayla an easy road through wheat fields continues towards the basin of Bereket. A few hundred meters along this road, in full view of the Kale Tepe, there is a crossing (co-ordinates: 37°30,762' N – 30°19,045' E; altitude: 1413 m a.s.l.) with a north–south road, the south branch of which leads to the village of Aksu (formerly Hatebi). This crossing is situated just south of the point where the canyon structure of the Tekke Deresi ends, so that the roads do not have to cross the deep valley incision. The north–south road connects Kayış with Aksu and is situated on a plateau to the west of the valley of the Tekke Deresi. The west-east road coming from Bereket follows the broad fertile basin of Akyayla, crosses the road Kayış-Aksu and heads towards Bağsaray, passing below the observation hill of Kale Tepe towards the canyon of the Tekke Deresi. Near this crossroad, in the fields, there is an inscribed limestone pedestal with a column base (h.: 0.87 m; w.: 0.68 m to 0.77 m) that once supported a funerary column (Fig. 34). It formed part of a family tomb, composed of two identical columns supported by a single pedestal made up of at least two blocks. The columns may have supported a single architrave with statuary above. The second pedestal now lies near the mosque of the village of Aksu (Fig. 35). A funerary inscription running across the front of both pedestals (to be published shortly), which according to the workmanship on one side were originally placed against one another or against a third intermediary block, identifies the monument as being set up by Aur. Maronianos Meneas in memory of his father Maramoas, his mother Gè, Meneas himself, his brother Galatos and his sister Mamma. The monument probably dates from the third century AD. This type of monument is very similar to the two-columned votive monuments with statues representing family groups of the Aitolian elite that were set up at Delphi from the second to the last quarter of the third century BC (Jordan-Ruwe 1995: 21-30). Although a direct link to Delphi is hardly possible, the shape of the monument could go back to these early Hellenistic votive groups. It is known that the Lysis valley, with the cities of Olbasa and Kormasa, was already Hellenized at a very early stage, possibly as the result of Greek and Thracian settlers established there by the Seleucids during the third century BC (Kearsly 1994: 56-57). So it cannot be excluded that these settlers introduced this type of votive monument in the area, which was eventually adapted for sepulchral purposes.

Aksu itself is situated in the middle of a 1 km long elongated depression connecting two intramontane basins. According to the local villagers the Aksu pedestal would have come from the village of Kapaklı on the other side of Mt. Kestel. This last village (coordinates: 37°32,785' N – 30°16,921' E; altitude 1460 m a.s.l.), perhaps located in the territory of Kormasa (see below), is situated to the west of the limestone Kestel Dağı range of which the highest peak (Fig. 36), the Kulübe Tepe (2328 m a.s.l.), has an altitude comparable to that of the Akdağ near Sagalassos. In 1996, at the beginning of June, there were still patches of snow on the northern slopes of the mountain top. The village of Kapaklı, contains the *in situ* remains of a monumental structure of Imperial date, most probably a family tomb (ca. 5 by 10 m). It could be entered via a monumental door (Fig. 37) and was decorated with a frieze of female heads and theatre masks carrying garlands (Fig. 38). The workmanship of the heads is excellent and the whole motif very similar to that of the mask and garland frieze of a monumental tomb at Bereket (Fig 65). More architectural fragments can be found around it, built into the house walls.

The village, surrounded by wheat fields, may occupy the site of a family estate with a corresponding mausoleum. The columnar sepulchral monument from Aksu, on the other side of the mountain, most probably also belonged to such a family of wealthy landowners. Despite the fact that the connections with Kapaklı are fairly easy, it is likely that the pedestals from Aksu come from a place near the village itself and that the claimed origin of one of the pedestals is explained by the regional fame of the ruins at Kapaklı.

5.2. The basin of Yeşildağ (formerly Gölde)

The village of Yeşildağ (co-ordinates on the market place: 37°30,243' N; 30°14,704' E; altitude: 1370 m a.s.l.; ca. 150 inhabitants) occupies a small basin in the upper reaches of the valley of the Havuz Deresi (Fig. 39). This valley drains in a southwestern direction. The basin of Yeşildağ belongs to a structural low that extends in a west-east direction over more than 5 km, as far as the village of Aksu. The water divide between the Lake Burdur basin and the Kerme Deresi water catchment area is on the Gölde Boğazı pass (altitude: 1460 m a.s.l.) about 2 km east of Yeşildağ that leads towards Aksu and Bereket. The top of the pass is very windy as the western winds are funneled through a steep valley connecting the intramontane basins. The curving of the vegetation to the east on the pass, mainly consisting of *Quercus calliprinos*, is very illustrative for this phenomenon. The hills on either side of the pass are covered with black pine and juniper.

Yeşildağ is the westernmost village of the area which is still entirely surrounded by limestone mountains (top: 1800 m a.s.l.). They are covered with needle forests (mostly black pine and juniper), while the basin and the affluent flat valley bottoms (estimated surface: 30 ha) are under cultivation (Fig. 40). Today, this cultivation includes wheat, barley, oats (used to feed animals) and chickpeas. The cultivated area around Yeşildağ is part of a larger low-lying depression, which broadens towards the west and coincides with an incursion of the geologic basin of Burdur. We have provisionally named this geological structure 'the gulf of Yeşildag'. In this gulf, the top layers are marl deposits from the Burdur basin that are deposited over the underlying folded limestone formations. The marl deposits give the soils a grayish colour. Further research is needed to map the extent of these deposits which probably terminate just east of the village (see also Gâvur Ören below). The hills bounding the basin towards the west (Keziban Tepe, over 1400 m; Asar Tepe, 1487 m a.s.l.) must have separated the settlement of Kireçocağı (see below) from Gâvur Ören, the major site on the other side of the mountain. A mountain pass at a spot called Üçtepearası, to the northwest of Yeşildağ, between the Asar Tepesi (1487 m a.s.l.) and the Tilkitaş Tepesi (1554 m a.s.l.), is the best route to the village of Karacaören and the major site of Gâvur Ören. The summit of the pass offers a magnificent view of the valley of the Lysis to the southwest and of the plain of Burdur to the north (Figs. 41-42).

The fertile valley bottom apparently attracted farmers as early as the Neolithic period, continued to house farming communities throughout classical times (at least two) and provided a living to rich land-owning families as late as Ottoman times (see below). Here again, the altitude (more than 1350 m a.s.l.) was probably the deciding factor in choosing cereal cultivation rather than olives, although in the neighbouring basin of Bereket, olives were possibly cultivated. Today, the valley receives more snow in winter than in the neighbouring basins, so that small differences in the microclimate might explain different farming practices.

Apart from the Early Neolithic höyüks of Hacılar and Kuruçay, in the plain of Burdur to the west, that were still occupied in the Late Neolithic period, the basin of Yeşildağ appears to be the first district on the territory of classical Sagalassos to receive a permanent settlement. The geographical description above suggests that these settlers came from the Burdur basin. Özsait even suggested that this höyük could represent the missing link in the nearly thousand year gap between the Aceramic and the Late Neolithic occupation at Hacılar (Özsait 1989, 1991).

A mound, about 10 m high, is situated on the northern edge of the village, just behind the northern row of houses (co-ordinates: 37°30,300' N; 30°14,637' E; altitude: 1380 m a.s.l.). A steep slope separates the höyük from the valley bottom of the Havuz Deresi. At present, the mound is under cultivation (Fig. 43). The soil is marly. The mound was already identified by Özsait in 1988. Surface finds of pottery allowed him to date its occupation as early as the Late Neolithic period (Özsait 1989: 2-3, Özsait 1991: 61). Many sherds and stone tools can still be seen at the surface. Özsait did not find any traces of a later prehistoric occupation of the mound, but ascribed the wheel-made sherds that he found northeast of the höyük to the Hellenistic and Imperial age (Özsait 1984: 208). The latter is confirmed by finds of glass (SA 96 S 10) and pottery, including Sagalassos red slip wares (SA 96 S 9), made by our survey team. Immediately to the south of the mound, on the central place of the village, is a fountain with a good flow of water.

The fountain and the buildings around it contain a lot of Roman antiquities, most of which, according to the villagers, would have come from a site known as Kireçocağı (lime quarry). The site was probably named because villagers burned some of its antiquities in lime kilns.

Fig. 36: View of the Kulübe Tepe, seen from the south.

Fig. 37: Door *in situ* belonging to a mausoleum at Kapaklı.

Fig. 38: Part of the garland frieze belonging to the mausoleum at Kapaklı.

Fig. 39: View of the basin of Yeşildağ/Gölde, seen from the northwest.
The arrow indicates the location of the Neolithic mound.

Fig. 40: View of the basin of Yeşildağ, seen from the northeast. Mt. Kestel is visible in the background.

Fig. 41: View from the mountain pass to the northwest of Yeşildağ towards the southwest
(the Lysis valley in the background).

Fig. 42: View from the mountain pass to the northwest of Yeşildağ towards Lake Burdur.

Fig. 43: View of the mound near Yeşildağ.

The site of Kireçocağı (co-ordinates: 37°30,0' N; 30°14' E; altitude: 1360-1370 m a.s.l.), located at about 1 km to the west of Yeşildag, is situated in the fields on the edge of a flat area to the south and 40 m above the small valley bottom of the Havuz Deresi. The folded limestone massifs are about 500 m to the south.

The agricultural area has the characteristics of a farmed parkland. The site overlooks a nearly 1 km long valley full of winter wheat. The slopes above it exposed towards the north, are covered with juniper and black pine. The southern limit of the valley is dominated by the Kulübe Tepe, the highest spot in the Kestel range (Fig. 44). On the site itself there are several stands of corn-cockle (Fig. 45), the fruit of which is both eaten and pressed for drinks by the villagers.

Nowadays ancient remains can be seen at Kireçocağı over a surface of at least 600 by 500 m. In the centre of it, there are substantial remains, including large pillars *in situ* and fluted column fragments (Fig. 46). Some of the columns seem to have been taken to Yeşildag where they have been built into the fountain on the central square and into the walls of the mosque. At the time of our visit in 1996, we had the impression that it may have been a small shrine or sanctuary, or a mausoleum. The area around this monument is much overgrown, but covered with rubble, tile fragments and Roman Imperial coarse and fine wares (SA 96 S 12). In the woods on the slopes to the west of the site, terracotta pipes are said to carry water to the large ancient settlement of Gâvur Ören (see below). Kireçocağı must represent a fairly substantial village of the Imperial period, of which the more elaborate antiquities were taken to Yeşildağ. Whether three column drums and a beautiful Ionizing Doric capital with acanthus leaves covering the *echinus* (with an egg-and-tongue motif), that have been re-used in the mansion of Hüseyin Otan on Yeşildağ's main square (Fig. 47), came from here or from the nearby mound, can no longer be established. Most of the following antiquities were said, however, to have been found at Kireçocağı. The mosque thus contains an uninscribed first – second century AD square limestone altar (h: 1.12 m; w: 0.44 m in middle, 0.54 m below and 0.67 m above). The back is plain, but the three other sides have ram's heads, from which ribbons float down. At the front and on the right side the ram's heads support a rich fruit garland. At the front, a nice Medusa head is carved above the garland (Fig. 48).

A wall on the east side of the square contains the upper part of a funerary limestone altar and of a funerary column, as well as a plain pedestal like the ones copied at Aksu. The altar and the column were said to have been brought from 'a site to the north'. However, the epitaph on the altar had already been copied at Gölde by Ramsay and Smith in 1884 (Ramsay 1888: 265 n. 7; Ramsay 1895: 339 n. 187). It contains a dedication by Hermes, son of Loukios, to the memory of his wife Gè, daughter of Alopos, and his young son Hermes. The epitaph ends with a curse and an invocation of Helios (Fig. 49). The inscription was copied again at Gölde, in 1955, by Bean (Bean 1959: 109 no. 78), who believed that it belonged to the site of Gâvur Ören (to the west of Gölde). Since it was already at Gölde in 1884, it is almost impossible that, at the time of Bean's visit, local information concerning its origin was still reliable. It is more likely therefore that the stone came from one of the sites near Yeşildağ (either the mound, or rather Kireçocağı), and that the regional fame of the ruins at Gâvur Ören was the reason for its claimed provenance. This is probably also the case with the funerary column (pres.h.: 0.50 m; abacus w.: 0.59 m; pres.th. of abacus: 0.49 m; lower diam.: 0.38 m). The unfluted column ends in a capital of the Doric type, of which the abacus at either side is provided with a small projecting console that increased its carrying capacity. A dowel hole on the left side of the abacus shows that the capital must have supported an architrave rather than a statue socle. Most probably therefore, the column belonged, together with the nearby pedestal, to a columnar monument like the one already described at Aksu. Below the capital, the column carries an epitaph by Mennaes "dis", grandson of Mennaes, and his wife Nais, daughter of Thoas, for themselves during their lifetime (Fig. 50). That sepulchral columns were popular in this area is also shown by a fluted column fragment (Fig. 51), built into the fountain on the square (pres.h.: 0.98 m; upper diam.: 0.50 m), provided with a *tabula ansata* with faint traces of an epitaph. In house A 51 near the mosque a frieze block (vis.h.: 0.74 m; w.: 0.37 m; th.: 0.23 m) is decorated with a veiled female bust (Fig. 52).

The fine workmanship of its remains imply that the site at Kireçocağı was a wealthy settlement, deriving from the apparent fertility of the valley around it. In Ottoman times Gölde was a 'çiftlik' (a farming community). A beautiful, but largely ruined Ottoman house, on the main square (Fig. 53), which in 1996 belonged to Hüseyin Otan, who had moved to Ankara, most probably belonged to the local prominent landowner.

5.3. The river system of the Büğdüz Çayı

The main river flowing into Lake Burdur from the east is the Büğdüz Çayı (Fig. 54). This river has two major tributaries, one coming from the east (Bayındır, Kayaaltı) and one from the south (from Bereket).

In its upper reaches, the latter is called Aykırdak Deresi and has its source in the basin of Bereket. The village of Bereket is located on the western concave slope of a considerable south-north oriented intramontane basin situated within gently sloping limestone massifs which attain an altitude of more than 1600 m a.s.l. to the south (Kuzuardiç Tepesi: 1602 m a.s.l.; Almanta Tepesi; Kilimli Tepe: 1577 m a.s.l.), 1770 m a.s.l. to the west and 1620 m a.s.l. to the east (Yanık Tepe: 1625 m a.s.l.; Alaçam Tepesi: 1604 m a.s.l.; Saçılık Tepesi: 1528 m a.s.l.).To the north, some gentler slopes separate it from the village of Kökez. This basin is quite large and triangular in shape, with a base of about 1.5 km in the south and a length of 3 km. It is drained towards Lake Burdur by the Aykirdak Deresi and its affluents. The main drainage divide between Lake Burdur and the Aksu (village) basin is situated in the valley connecting the village of Bereket with Aksu, at an altitude of 1450 m a.s.l., about 2 km south of Bereket. This valley is covered with juniper and black pine on the northern slopes, whereas the south-facing slopes are cultivated below (with wheat), over a width of 50 to 100 m. Further to the west, an affluent valley forms an easy connection with Yeşildağ. The slopes of this valley are almost completely covered with juniper and kermes oak as a secondary vegetation (Fig. 55). In the valley bottom there are some isolated small wheat fields (of max. 50 m wide).

The basin of Bereket is filled with red-brown fine clayey materials containing some limestone rock fragments and is entirely cultivated (Fig. 56). The cultivated area extends into the valley bottoms between the low mountains, which are in this area about 300 m above the valley bottom. The limestone mountains have a thin soil cover and are forested. Some lower limestone hills that are not under cultivation are covered with a Juniperus woodland, probably the traditional grazing land. Higher up, there are black pines. The landscape of the arable land is a farmed parkland, a peculiar landscape with individual stands of trees, here mainly juniper, situated not only on the boundaries between the individual fields, but also within the fields. This arable land probably originated from reclaimed grazing land.

Flat bottom valleys, following geological weaknesses, probably fault lines or joints, interconnect the different intramontane basins and form elongated low-level land over considerable distances. The main road, the Devret Yolu near Bereket, follows this morphological unit.

The village of Bereket, the name of which means 'abundance', which might refer to the good farm land or the abundance of water in this highland area (37°26,819' N; 30°17,561' E; altitude: 1455 m a.s.l.), was visited by Ramsay and Smith in 1884, and by Bean in 1956, in 1957 and again in 1959.

Based on an inscription, the first visitors could already identify the site that in Roman antiquity controlled the basin as the village of Moatra or κώμη Μοατρέων (Smith 1887: 229 no. 10; Ramsay 1895: 338 no. 185).

It is most probable that this village was not located at Bereket itself, but on a low hill (37°32,500' N; 30°16,877' E; altitude: 1535 m a.s.l.) known as Kirselik, to the south of the modern settlement (Fig. 57-58). Its east-facing slope is covered with tiles and pottery (SA 96 S 5-6), including large quantities of Sagalassos red slip wares, dating from the early to the late Imperial/early Byzantine period. There is also much late coarse ware, glass and stucco fragments. Most fragments are rather small as the result of deep ploughing. According to the villagers the fields around the site also contain many skeletons and they may therefore occupy the site of a graveyard. The settlement (see also Bean 1959: 111), undoubtedly a village, must have been occupied from the beginning of the early Imperial period at the latest right into early Byzantine times.

Ramsay had published an epitaph from the village of Bereket of Apollonios, son of Menandros (Ramsay 1888: 266 no. 9). Bean described a "small sarcophagus" there, clearly an ostotheca, "showing on the front three damaged figures, on the left a door, on the right two figures, and on the back a shield crossed by sword and sheath, as often at Sagalassus". In this city, this type of bone-container is characteristic of the late Hellenistic and early Imperial period. In 1996, we discovered at Bereket the remains of a major Julio-Claudian structure. This structure was a monumental tomb located in the lower part of the valley (37°32,454' N; 30°16,877' E; altitude: ca. 1450 m a.s.l.), ca. 150 m to the east of the hill which carried the ancient settlement. At the time of Bean's visit, this structure, today called Kirselik or Giaour Taşlar ('heathen stones'), would have been still standing 4 to 5 m high. According to Bean, its dimensions were some 10 by 8 m. Unfortunately, he did not publish any photograph of the monument, which nowadays has been reduced to a single row of ashlar blocks (Fig. 57). Most probably, the structure was already then rather less well-preserved than Bean described, since it must correspond with the "heroon or some such building" of which the four lower courses were *in situ* at the time of Smith's visit in 1884 (Smith 1887: 230). The dimensions in the latter's publication (26.5 ft by 32 ft) also corresponded better with the real dimensions of the building, which are 9.70 m (east-west) by 4.70 m (north–south). Apparently, when a newly formed 'dere' (intermittent river) endangered some houses recently at Bereket, the old structure was dismantled to provide material for a dam to protect the village. Other stones now form a kind of animal pound in the village (Fig. 59), while some few ashlar blocks can still be found around the original building (Fig. 57). A third group of dismantled blocks was moved to a modern cemetery (the 'mezarlık'), further east, on the other side of the road between Bereket and Akyayla. Despite the dispersion of the material, it is still possible to get a clear picture of the whole monument. It must have been built as a *distylos in antis* temple. Three joining fluted column drums can be seen at the 'mezarlık' (Fig. 60). Their height from top to bottom is 1.36 m, 1.17 m

Fig. 44: The valley near the site of Kireçocağı. The Kestel range in the background.

Fig. 45: Corn-cockle trees at Kireçocağı.

Fig. 46: View of the site of Kireçocağı.

Fig. 47: Ionizing Doric capital in the house of H. Otan at Yeşildağ.

Fig. 48: Side view of the altar at Yeşildağ.

Fig. 49: Funerary altar of Hermes and his family.

Fig. 50: Funerary column of Menneas and family.

Fig. 51: Funerary column in the fountain on the square of Yeşildağ.

Fig. 52: Relief with female bust at Yeşildağ.

Fig. 53: Ottoman mansion at Yeşildağ.

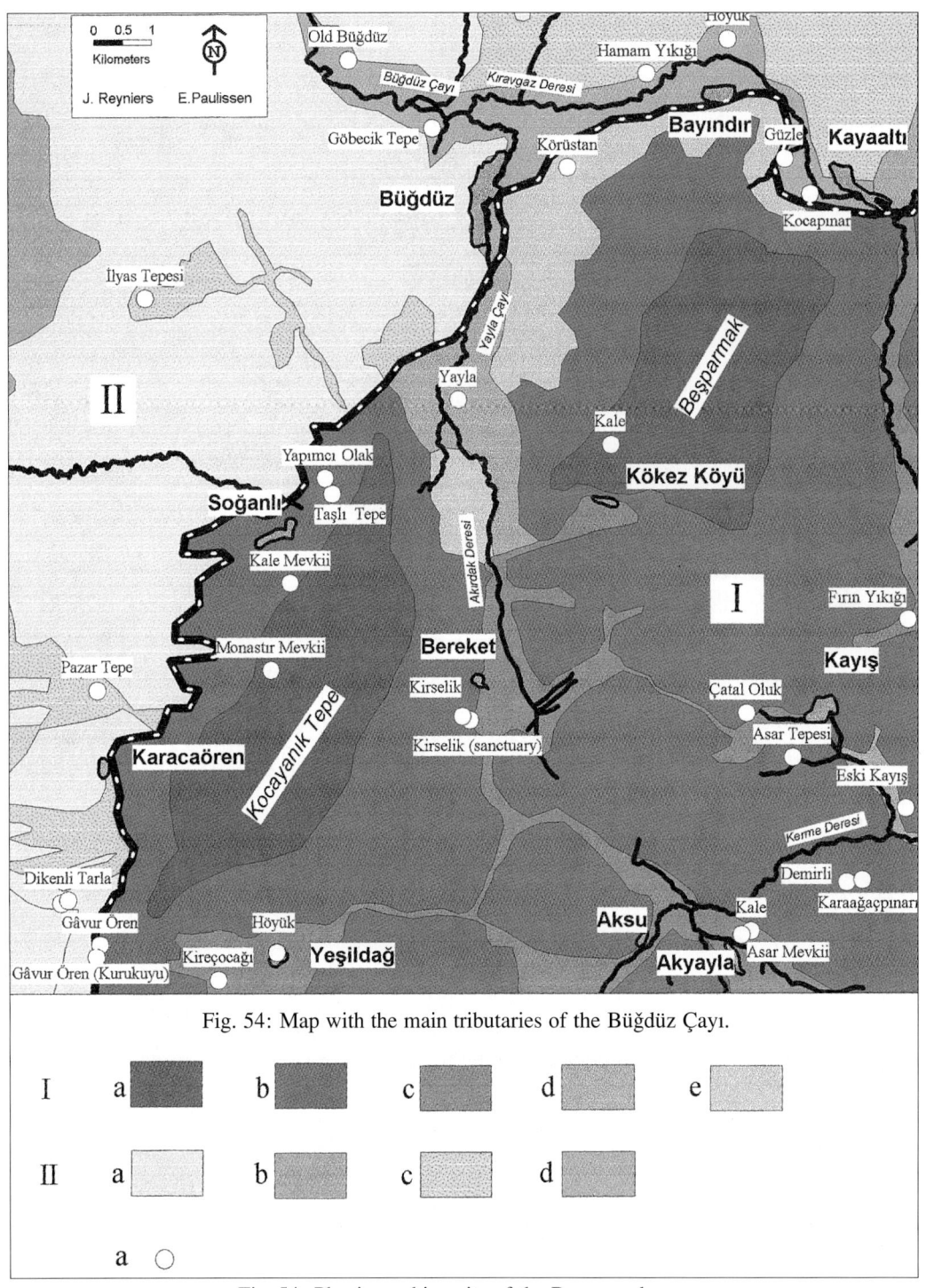

Fig. 54: Map with the main tributaries of the Büğdüz Çayı.

Fig. 54: Physiographic units of the Beşparmak area

I a High mountains of Beşparmak and Kokaayanık Tepe
I b Mountainous limestone area
I c Intramontane basins
I d Lower intramontane basins towards the Büğdüz
I e Marls on limestone with badlands development

II a Burdur badlands
II b Limestone outcrops in the Burdur badlands
II c Plateau remnants on marl with poor vegetation coverage
II d Valley of the river Büğdüz, irrigated and densely vegetated

a Site

Fig. 55: View of the southern end of the valley connecting the basin of Gölde with that of Bereket.

Fig. 56: The basin of Bereket, seen from the village. Mt. Kestel in the background.

Fig. 57: The hill with the site of Moatra (background), seen from the ruins of the monumental tomb to the east of it.

Fig. 58: The site of Kirselik (centre), seen from Bereket.

and 1.17 m. Their diameters vary from 0.43 m to 0.46 m. The lower parts of the columns were unfluted. Parts of the Ionic capitals can be found in a house at Bereket. At the corners the building possessed slightly projecting pilasters, some blocks of which still lay around the ruined monument, or can be found in the village and the cemetery. Some ashlars show that the long sides also had projecting half-pilasters in the middle of the wall. The upper wall section apparently possessed a frieze of flutes (*Pfeifenfries*) with a flat base and a semi-circular upper edge, laid out on an Egyptian throat (Fig. 61), with successive flutes separated by a thin protruding rim (h.: 0.39 m). The motif can be compared with that on two Augustan monuments at Sagalassos: the Northwest Heroon (Waelkens *et al.* 2000) and the temenos wall of the Apollo Klarios sanctuary (Vandeput 1997: 53, pl. 17,3), where it occupied the place of a real frieze. On the Northwest Heroon and on another major Pisidian monument dated to the reign of Augustus, in the Temple of Augustus at Pisidian Antioch (on this monument, see now Mitchell and Waelkens 1998: 113-173), the upper wall sections of the cella also had a frieze decoration of tendrils. These high upper wall friezes may reflect a regional north Pisidian feature (Waelkens and Vandeput in press). The entablature of the building contained an architrave with nicely carved bead-and-reels crowning the upper part of the three *fasciae* (Fig. 62). The top of the architraves of which several examples can be found in the village (h.: 0.375 m to 0.40 m; l.: 1.24 m to 1.34 m), was formed by a Lesbian cymation which did not correspond with the beads-and-reels below it (Fig. 63). It is a fully developed stirrup-framed *kyma*, in which the stem of the intermediate flower is completely free. The intermediate flowers are composed of two petals with a central third stem between them, thus creating a more elaborate floral appearance. Whereas the wall architraves had a smooth lower section, the section of the architraves between the columns and the *antae* is decorated with a small soffit (w.: 7.5 cm), filled with a guilloche made of two interwoven ribbons (Fig. 64). The bead-and-reels are very similar to those on the upper door moulding of the Augustan Northwest Heroon (Waelkens *et al.* 2000) and on the Tiberian Southwest Gate on the Lower Agora of Sagalassos (Vandeput 1997: 58-63, pls 22-23). The soffit decoration is also similar in execution to that of the Southwest Gate (Vandeput 1997, pl. 23,2). The intermediate flowers of the Lesbian kyma however, show a slightly more developed form than that on the Northwest Heroon, but may still belong to the reign of Tiberius or his immediate successors (Waelkens *et al.* 2000; Vandeput 1997: 151-152). The frieze blocks (h.: 0.42 m), now taken to the cemetery, were decorated with theatre masks and fruit garlands (Fig. 65). This motif may again have been inspired by that of the Tiberian Southwest Gate on the Lower Agora at Sagalassos (Waelkens *et al.* 1997b: 208-209; Vandeput 1997: 57-63). Its execution is also very similar to the frieze on the monumental tomb at Kapaklı (Fig. 38). Finally, the top of the entablature was a carefully executed cornice with a lower row of dentils (total h.: 0.26 m). A clearly early imperial *akroterion* (h.: 1.01 m; w. below on one side: 0.64 m) built into the corner of one of the houses near the main square of Bereket (Fig. 66), most probably once crowned the gable of the monumental structure. The date of the monument must have been the reign of Tiberius or one of his immediate successors. It is also clear that the monument was strongly influenced by the Augustan and Tiberian constructions at Sagalassos, which offer excellent parallels for its various ornaments. The quality of these is such that they may have been carved by stoneworkers from Sagalassos. The function of the building must have been a monumental tomb. In fact, Bean noticed "close by, a handsome, but damaged, marble sarcophagus lid showing three persons reclining, each with an arm over the shoulders of the next; all the heads are lost" (Bean 1959: 111). Today, two broken limestone sarcophagus lids can be found in the fields between the ruined monument and the cemetery. One is a saddle-roofed lid with *imbrices* (l.: ca. 2.20 m; vis. w.: ca 0.50 m), the second one the fragment of a klinè lid that was recently broken (max. l.: 1.40 m; max. w.: 0.97 m). Both lids may be later in date than the monument proper, but the fact that they were found near it clearly suggests a funeral function for the latter. A 'shrine' would also have occupied a more central place within the settlement and not an isolated spot located in the fields in front of it and surrounded by sarcophagi. The size of the tomb and the quality of its workmanship illustrate the wealth that the local landholding gentry might have amassed already during the Julio-Claudian period. Farming may have included both cereal growing (as today) and, even at this altitude, some olive culture, since counterweights for oil presses are found in the fields between the tomb and the village of Bereket (Fig. 67).

The settlement apparently had a rich religious life. In 1884, Ramsay and Smith could read the name of the village on the side of "a rude Herakles figure in high relief" (h.: 1.37 m). The inscriptions identified the figure as "the Herakles of the komè of the Moatreis". It was set up by Manès, son of Tatas, and by Attalos, son of Apollonios, and had been carved by Troilos, son of Arnestes, grandson of Tudes (Smith 1997: 229 no. 10; Ramsay 1895: 338 no. 185). The cult of Herakles may have been popular in this area. In fact, during our 1996 survey, a similar relief was found in the village of Kozluca, a few kilometers to the west of Bereket (see below, Fig. 249; Waelkens 1999). This also represented Herakles in a pure Greek iconography, holding a club and clad with a lion skin. There are several traces of his worship at Sagalassos and on its territory (Waelkens 1999). This is also the case for the cult of Hermes who appears to have been a very popular deity, especially in rural contexts (*ibidem*). Bean noticed at the fountain in Bereket a frieze block (or pedestal?), bearing on one side a much damaged relief of "Hermes with caduceus", and on the right return the representation of "a torch, a strung bow, a human bust, and a weird creature like a coiled snake expanding into nine fingers" (Bean 1959: 111, pl. XXc). The torch and the snakes could refer to the cult of Leto (see Bean 1959: 77), which was popular in nearby Yayla Mevkii in the Büğdüz basin, a little to the north of Bereket. On the other hand, the snake could also represent the Lerna monster and refer to the cult of Herakles. Nowadays, a small altar (h.: 0.315 m; w.: 0.17 to 0.20 m), belonging to a third cult, is built into a house wall near the main square of Bereket. On the front it shows a rather nicely carved veiled female bust, below a dedication by a person with an indigenous name "to the goddess" (Fig. 68). The style of the carving and the very fine lettering suggest a late Hellenistic to early Imperial date.

To the north of Bereket, the Akırdak Deresi cuts through a small but well-watered valley between steep hills covered with juniper and black pine. In this north–south oriented and elongated valley, the river is joined by various tributaries, fed by springs on both the western and the eastern slopes, and takes the name of Yayla Çayı (Fig. 54). The hills to the west have a height of less than 1400 m a.s.l., while those on the east reach altitudes between 1500 and 1700 m a.s.l. (Pireligedik Tepesi: 1710 m a.s.l.). The village of Kökez Köyü (altitude: ca. 1600 m a.s.l.) occupies a remote place on the eastern slopes of the valley, at the foot of the westernmost of the five 'fingers' of the Beşparmak Dağı, i.e. the Kale Tepe (altitude: 1928 m a.s.l.). The land around it is very poor. This explains why not a single antiquity could be found in the village, which seems to be completely modern. The slopes above the village do not permit any kind of farming, since they consist of completely bare limestone. Some traces of karstic activity could be distinguished.

However, immediately above and to the north of the village, the Kale Tepe (see Fig. 72) bears the remains of an ancient site, at an altitude of 1928 m a.s.l. (37°35,345' N; 30°18,659' E). The mountain consists here of two flat tops with a sparse vegetation, separated by a lower area in-between that can be used as grazing land. In this depression, some pre-Hellenistic or at the latest Hellenistic (?) pottery was found (SA 96 S 71). No remains of tiles occur. A collapsed rubble wall connected the two flat tops on the eastern side and continued around the crest of the highest, northern peak (Fig. 69). There are traces of two cisterns. The site was clearly a pre-Hellenistic, or at the latest Hellenistic, fortlet. Whereas to the north and east, its view was limited by the higher northeastern peaks of the Beşparmak, it afforded a nice view of the western parts of the territory of Sagalassos. From here, signals could be sent to or received from the watchtower at Tekke above the plain of Lake Burdur (see below), to and from the fortress at Soğanlı (see below) which overlooked the whole badlands area and part of the plain of Burdur, and to and from the fortlet at Kale near Akyayla, which guarded the southern boundary of Sagalassian territory and was within view of the fortification system on the Ağlasun Dağı proper, immediately above the city of Sagalassos. It is clear that the latter possessed a connecting system of watchtowers and fortlets which, in case of an imminent danger, could transmit fire signals to one another. The view from the Kale Tepe is superb: to the southeast it offers a view of Akyayla and its Kale fortlet, to the south it overlooks the basin of Bereket and the road to Antalya, to the southwest it watches the southwestern boundary of Sagalassos and the Lysis valley. To the west the whole plain of Lake Burdur and the fortress of Soğanlı are within full view (Fig. 70), while to the northwest the valley of Büğdüz can be seen. The fortress is probably contemporary with those above Sagalassos itself.

To the north of the Kökez valley, there is a larger basin with a north–south orientation (Fig. 54), framed between the edge of the badlands to the west (Yelekin Tepe: 1247 m a.s.l.) and the beginning of the limestone mountains to the east (Taşlı Tepe: 1483 m a.s.l.). In 1971, the village of Büğdüz was moved to the northern extremity of the valley, after a severe earthquake had destroyed the old village with the same name. Since this was located in the badlands zone further to the west, it will be described there, together with the site on the Göbecik Tepe. Old Büğdüz had been visited by Bean in 1955, who found out that nearly all the ancient stones there came from "the yayla, some two hours further up towards Bereket, where they were found among ruins of old buildings" (Bean 1959: 75). Bean did not visit the spot, but it must have been identical with the Yayla Mevkii (37°35, 290' N; 30°16,616' E; altitude: 1293 m a.s.l.) that was surveyed by our team in 1996, some 3.5 km to the south of the modern site and 6 km to the south-southeast of old Büğdüz. This yayla ('summer village') is located in an amphitheatre-like intramontane basin at the transition between the neogene marls and the limestone formations (Fig. 71). The valley bottom is framed by various tali. Some of them are cultivated, but an ancient site covers another talus to the east of the road connecting Büğdüz with Bereket, at some 30 m above the river bed (Figs. 72-73). An area of more than 2 ha stretching as far as the other side of the modern road is covered with pottery (SA 96 S 49). It contains lots of tiles, Imperial coarse wares, as well as finer Sagalassos red slip table wares, mostly of early Imperial date. There are also some dispersed worked stones. An isolated rock has traces of a *chamosorion* (Fig. 74). The site received water from a permanent spring nearby and from the river. The farming possibilities in the valley are rather restricted, but certainly good enough to feed the village settlement which must have existed here in Imperial times. As mentioned above, most of the stones remarked upon by

Fig. 59: The animal pen at Bereket, containing wall blocks from the early Imperial tomb.

Fig. 60: Column drums from the early Imperial tomb in the cemetery near Bereket.

Fig. 61: *Pfeifenfries* from the upper wall section of the tomb near Bereket.

Fig. 62: One of the architraves from the Julio-Claudian tomb at Bereket.

Fig. 63: Upper part of the architrave from the tomb.

Fig. 64: Soffit decoration on one of the architraves at Bereket.

Fig. 65: One of the frieze blocks from the early Imperial tomb.

Fig. 66: Akroterion in a house at Bereket.

Fig. 67: Counterweights for lever-and-weight oil presses in the fields near Bereket.

Fig. 68: Small votive altar built into a house wall at Bereket.

Fig. 69: View of the fortification wall surrounding the Kale Tepe at Kökez.

Fig. 70: View from Kale Tepe towards the west.

Fig. 71: View of the amphitheatre-like basin of Yayla Mevkii near Bügdüz.

Fig. 72: View from the site of Yayla Mevkii towards the southeast, with the Beşparmak and the Kale Tepe fortlet (arrow) in the background.

Fig. 73: View from the site of Yayla Mevkii towards the west, with the valley bottom in the centre.

Bean in old Büğdüz, must have come from here. After the 1971 earthquake, most of them were moved to modern Büğdüz, where they have been collected in a tea garden.

From the quality of the stones at Büğdüz, the Roman settlement at Yayla Mevkii must have been rather prosperous. Among the architectural fragments, there is again a frieze block (h.: 0.42 m; pres.l.: 1.30 m; th. above: 0.54 m) in the shape of an Egyptian throat, decorated with flutes of the *Pfeifenfries* type, each flute provided with an individual rim. The top of the frieze is decorated with an egg-and-dart motif, the darts ending in a rounded arrowhead. The shape of the egg-and-dart suggests a late second or third century AD date (Fig. 75). The frieze may have belonged to a monumental tomb or shrine. The tea garden at Büğdüz also contains two Ionic or Corinthian column drums (h.: 1.08 and diam.: 0.45 m; h.: 1.12 m and diam.: 0.48 m), bearing a Doric capital (one unfinished; the other: h.: 0.34 m; diam.: 0.35 m) which does not belong to them (Fig. 76).

Various stones show that the settlement at Yayla Mevkii housed a sanctuary for Apollo and Leto. The house of Emine Sener (Büğdüz) thus contains an unpublished stone (l.: 0.42 m; h.: 0.26 m) decorated on the front with a sunk patera flanked in a heraldic position by two zebus, their heads resting on an altar. Above the relief there is an inscribed band of two lines, while the third line continues on a stand below the zebus and below the patera. It is a votive text dedicated by Kallikles to the god Apollo (Fig. 77). Two more stones from the same sanctuary were published by Bean in 1959. The first is a rather crude rectangular altar which he had found at the 'Lycée' in Burdur, where it had been brought from Büğdüz (i.e. the old village). The front is decorated with a female figure, seated on a wide chair, with a veil over her head, a necklace and a large pendant, and holding a long sceptre upright in her left hand (Bean 1959: 77 no. 21, pl. XV, e-f). This side also bore a poorly written votive inscription, set up by a certain Hermes and his brother, sons of Troilos and grandsons of Meleager, to Leto and Apollo. Bean rightly identified the seated women as Leto. He referred to another votive relief then at Dresden but said to come from Isparta, with a dedication to the 'goddess Leto' who is represented again with a sceptre in the left hand. Another female figure, standing, with a veil over her head, a necklace and a pendant, holding in each hand a "roundish knobbly object by its narrow end" could be seen on the reverse of the Burdur altar. Most probably, she also represents Leto. Both sides are decorated with a male bust on a ledge, with a cloak over the shoulders fastened in front by a large brooch from which hang tasseled ribbons. Bean hesitated to say whether the male busts represented the two dedicators or Apollo. However, the wreath on the head of the only bust with an intact head, rather favours an identification with the god. Most probably, a similar, large but headless bust, draped in a cloak, again "fastened in front by a large medallion brooch on which is a small bust", and carrying a dedication by Thoas, son of Attalos, copied by Bean at old Büğdüz (Bean 1959: 77 no. 20), also represented Apollo. Finally, a large vessel, re-used as a 'dibektaşı' in old Büğdüz, decorated with two plain garlands, and carrying a fragmentary votive inscription (εἱερατεύσας), may have come from the same context (Bean 1959: 76 no. 18). The stone is now kept in the tea garden at new Bügdüz (Fig. 78). Bean suggested that it might be a 'λουτήρ', a vessel to hold anointing oil. In 1974, a similar vessel, identified by its inscription as a 'λουτήρ' was discovered at Sagalassos and published by Waldmann (Waldmann 1978). It was dedicated, together with "the water (supply) by [–]on, son of Makedon, who was an *archimystès*". As the author says, the word can only have meant a water vessel in this context, perhaps for ritual cleaning, placed at the entrance of a sanctuary. It may have had the same meaning and function at Yayla Mevkii. There is a strong possibility that yet another altar from Büγdüz, with reliefs on all four sides, that was published by Bean, came from the same sanctuary. The front had two standing figures, one male, one female, the left side a standing male, naked but for a cloak over the shoulders (Apollo?), the back three defaced standing figures and the right side two standing figures (both chiselled away). The front carried a probably third century AD inscription that was partly Greek, partly written in a local Pisidian dialect (Bean 1959: 76 no. 19).

At Sagalassos, the cult of Apollo was most probably introduced by the Seleucids in the third century BC, but it became very important after the construction of the Temple of Apollo Klarios in Augustan times, when the god's popularity may have been boosted by the fact that he was considered to be the patron deity of the first emperor. It is striking that the god was very popular throughout the territory of the city. His mother, Leto, was also worshipped in Northern Pisidia (Waelkens 1999). The settlement at Yayla Mevkii may have been an important cult place of this divine family. Other dedications to Apollo were found at nearby Bayındır (see below).

The necropolis of the settlement must have contained a variety of tomb types. Besides the *chamosorion*, part of a stele with an almost life-sized male head in its gable was mentioned by Bean (Bean 1959: 77-78). He also published a fluted column with an inscribed *tabula ansata*. According to the inscription it once carried a 'hydria', perhaps the name given to the round funerary urns that became popular at Sagalassos from early Imperial times onward, which contained the remains of Rhodon and his family. This text which is certainly not early Imperial in date, contains some misspellings. Together with the dialect inscription mentioned above, this might indicate that the villagers of the site had not become completely Hellenized in their speech (Bean 1959:

76 no. 17). The stone is also interesting because it shows that some of the funerary columns served as bases carrying urns or other funerary objects. It has now been moved from old Büğdüz to the tea garden in the new village (Fig. 79). The same garden also displays the small side of a garland sarcophagus, with floating ribbons and fruit garlands, from which the corner supports have been broken (h.: 0.54 m; w.: 0.68 m; th.: 0.44 m). The style of carving indicates a date in the later second or third century AD (Fig. 80).

Although the pottery at Yayla Mevkii documents the existence of a village here, at the latest from the early Imperial period, the inscriptions and other stones discussed above confirm the continuity of the settlement right into the later Imperial period. To the latter may also belong a large stone vessel with protruding handles (h.: 0.65 m; diam.: 0.47 m) kept in the house of Ahmet Türkçan at new Büğdüz (Fig. 81). It belongs to a vessel type which at Sagalassos seems to occur mainly in early Byzantine contexts (UA North; Domestic Area 1). In 1996, the survey team was also shown Byzantine and Ottoman coins which offer evidence of an even later occupation of the Büğdüz area, as well as loom weights and various vessels.

Immediately west of old Büğdüz, the Büğduz Çayı (here called Çarşamba Çayı) is joined by a tributary coming from the east and called Kıravgaz Deresi (Fig. 54). Its name is derived from the village of Gravgaz or Kıravgaz, now called Kayaaltı (37°37,192' N; 30°20,859' E; altitude: 1200 m a.s.l.). The modern village is located immediately below the northeastern peak of the Beşparmak Dağı (here: 1896 m a.s.l.), between the very steep mountain slope and the river. To the north and northeast there are sizeable gravel deposits. Behind them the hills rise to a height of over 1200 m a.s.l. (Çömlekçi Tepe: 1226 m a.s.l.; Çamlıdere Tepesi: 1266 m a.s.l.) Towards the west, in the direction of Bayındır, the badlands start. In this direction, the village of Kayaaltı is dominated by the Zırpıncak Tepesi (1258 m a.s.l.) The river bed cuts through a deep red soil that contains large boulders and the remains of large mass movements. There is evidence of similar movements along the east and southeast side of the mountain, especially to the north of Kayış. The steep slopes towards the mountain peak are covered with oaks. Kayaaltı itself is not an ancient site. The few antiquities (ashlars, a stone basin) in the village must have come from a site, ca. 500 m towards the west and called Kocapınar. It occupies a northeast-facing slope immediately above a permanent spring (Fig. 82). It contains some stones, even part of a wall, and traces of burials, and is strewn with pottery, both coarse wares, and early to middle Imperial Sagalassos red slip wares (SA 96 S 50). The approximate size of the site, which has suffered a lot from erosion, could no longer be established. The most elaborate object taken from it to Kayaaltı is a small altar (h.: 0.56 m; w.: 0.18 to 0.25 m), built into a wall of house no. 199, with a patera on top and a bunch of grapes on the only visible side (Fig. 83). In 1959, Bean had published another, hexagonal funerary altar, carrying an incomplete epitaph and some crude reliefs, which had been taken from Kıravgaz to the museum of Burdur.

A smaller 'site' occurs to the northwest of Kocapınar, at a spot called Güzle (or Köy Beleni: 37°37,475' N; 30°20,152' E; altitude: 1212 m a.s.l.). Only sherds, both coarse wares and Sagalassos red slip wares of Imperial date, could be seen at the surface (Fig. 84).

The name of one of the mountain peaks, immediately south of Kayaaltı, the Kale Tepe (altitude: 1514 m a.s.l.), which was not visited by the survey team from lack of time, may suggest the presence of another fortlet of the same type as the homonymous fortress above Kökez in the same mountain range.

Downstream, the Kıravgaz Deresi flows through the village of Bayındır. The garden of the local mosque contains some ashlar blocks, said to have been taken from a collapsed bridge. Two houses contain travertine building blocks, supposedly from a spot ca. 6 km to the north of Bayındır, the construction site of the University of Burdur. Yet, the village also contains some more elaborate architectural elements. A small tuffo capital (h.: 0.35 m; w.: 0.23 m) of Imperial date in the village, with an acanthus decoration on either side of a stemmed flower (Fig. 85), is said to have come from a ruined house near the Ulu Cami at Burdur. But this provenance seems very doubtful, since two more capitals of the same type have been built into the houses of Ali Ihşan and of Ismail Işler at Bayındır (Figs. 86-87). The latter house also contains various fragments of a cassette decoration with tendril friezes carved in the same stone (Fig. 88), and parts of pilaster capitals (?) decorated with rosettes and a Lesbian *kyma* of western type (Fig. 89). Therefore, a local provenance for all these building elements, which seem to belong to a single structure, seems more reasonable.

That this area contained 'monumental' architecture is shown also by some limestone remains in the local cemetery. Among them, various architrave blocks (h.: 0.43 m; w.: 0.61 m), one with a soffit bearing a tendril decoration (Fig. 90) and three blocks (h.: 0.44 m; vis.w.: 0.64 m), including a corner piece, with a *Pfeifenfries* on an Egyptian throat profile (Fig. 91). These may derive from a single structure (shrine or monumental tomb). This may also be the case with some column drums in the same graveyard. An alleged provenance from the site of Hamam Yıkığı (see below) could not be confirmed.

Finally, the survey team copied at the same location a funerary column with a long inscription (9 ll.) in a *tabula ansata*, mentioning three sons of Kallikles: Manes, Neon

Fig. 74: The rock with the *chamosorion* at Yayla Mevkii near Büğdüz.

Fig. 75: *Pfeifenfries* from a building at Yayla Mevkii.

Fig. 76: One of the Ionic columns with a Doric capital at Büğdüz.

Fig. 77: The votive relief for Apollo.

Fig. 78: The '*loutèr*' from Büğdüz.

Fig. 79: The funerary column which once supported a '*hydria*'.

Fig. 80: Small side of a sarcophagus at Büğdüz.

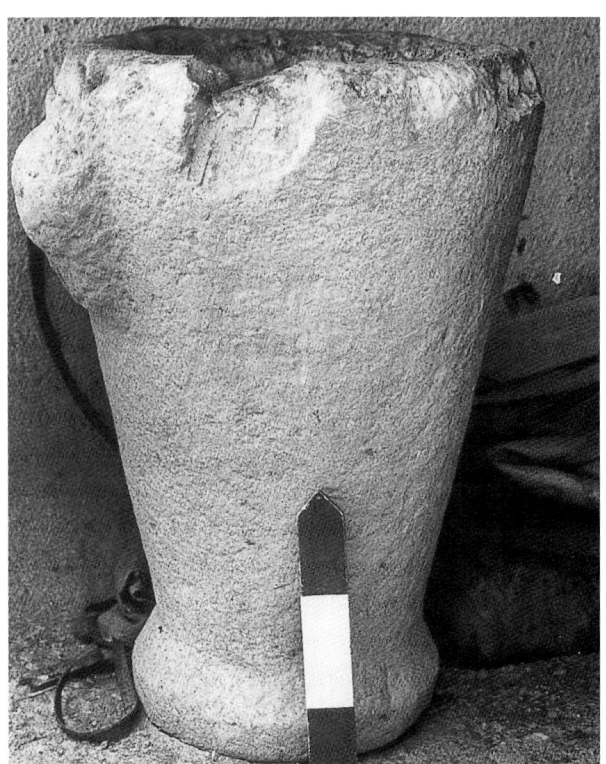

Fig. 81: Stone vessel at Büğdüz.

Fig. 82: The site of Kocapınar, to the west of Kayaaltı.

Fig. 83: Altar from Kocapınar in a house wall at Kayaaltı.

Fig. 84: The site of Güzle, to the northwest of Kayaaltı.

Fig. 85: Tuffo acanthus capital from Bayındır.

Fig. 86: Similar capital built into a house wall at Bayındır.

Fig. 87: Identical capital built into a house at Bayındır.

Fig. 84: The site of Güzle, to the northwest of Kayaaltı.

Fig. 85: Tuffo acanthus capital from Bayındır.

Fig. 86: Similar capital built into a house wall at Bayındır.

Fig. 87: Identical capital built into a house at Bayındır.

Fig. 88: House of Ismail Iğler at Bayındır, containing various fragments of a cassette decoration with tendril friezes.

Fig. 89: Fragments of pilaster capitals (?) at Bayındır.

Fig. 90: Architrave with lower soffit decoration in the cemetery of Bayındır.

Fig. 91: Corner of a frieze block from the same building.

and Attalos (Fig. 92). In 1959, Bean published two rectangular altars, then kept in the museum at Burdur, but which he had seen in 1955, in a village street and in a fountain at Bayındır respectively. Both were dedicated to Apollo, documenting once more the popularity of the god in this part of the Sagalassian territory. One altar was decorated with a loom (?) on the front, three ears of corn to the left, and a bunch of grapes to the right (Bean 1959: 70 no. 1). The second one was decorated on the left with a boukephalion, on the back with a wreath and on the right with a bunch of grapes. The decoration of the altars documents the importance of agriculture in this area as well as the fact that Apollo must also have been considered as a protector of farming. The front, according to Bean (1959: 70 no. 2, pl. XIVa), showed "a seated woman and a large object, which I do not recognise". Yet, the picture shows clearly a seated Apollo *kitharedos* with a cloak over the shoulder, to the left of a pedestal supporting his lyre.

Most, if not all of these stones probably come from one of the three sites around Bayındır (Fig. 54). The nearest one is a 3 to 4 m high elongated 'höyük' (37°38,666 N; 30°19,572 E; altitude: 1146 m a.s.l.) located ca. 800 m to the north of the village and 300 m northeast of a bridge over the river. It is surrounded on all sides by cultivated fields (Fig. 93) and to the south bounded by the Bayındır Çayı which is the local name for the Kıravgaz Deresi. In this area, the river has created an almost 50 m wide and 2 m deep immersion. The fields around it are on clayey soils.

Today, even the höyük is used for farming (chickpeas). It contains many dispersed rubble stones and boulders (Fig. 94) and, especially on its eastern extremity, over an area of 50 by 50 m, a lot of mostly coarse, but also some late Imperial Sagalassos red slip wares (SA 96 S 52). Despite the scarcity of material remains, probably the result of farming, the höyük must have housed an important village in antiquity and is the most probable provenance of the antiquities at Bayındır.

A second site, called Hamam Yıkığı (the 'bath ruin'), is located at 1.2 km to the west of Bayındır (37° 38,356' N; 30°18,645' E; altitude: 1142 m a.s.l.). The site occupies a gentle slope facing southeast, in the middle of wheat fields (Fig. 95) that are nowadays irrigated artificially. There is an undulating topography to the northwest of the site, flat fields to the east and west, the Bayındır Çayı which flows 20 m below it to the southeast, and the Kanlıkaya Tepe and the Şişli Tepe, the highest peak (2028 m a.s.l.) of the Beşparmak range, to the south. The local farmers grow potatoes, wheat, barley, oats and beets. The area also produces fruit (apples, pears, cherries, prunes, apricots and walnuts). The site contains quite a lot of pottery (SA 96 S 53) which is composed of middle to late Imperial coarse wares and late Imperial Sagalassos red slip wares, but also one green glazed sherd.

Some people of Bayındır said that in earlier days there had been a ruin on the hill near Hamam Yıkığı, which must have given its name to the site, and that the stones in the cemetery at Bayındır, came from this area. However, the man supposed to know the provenance of the Bayındır material best, could confirm this statement only for some plain blocks in the village. For the moment, the nature of the site cannot be established, but it is most likely to be a small farming site.

A fourth site was identified at Körüstan Mevkii. It is located some 3 km west of Bayındır and only 1.3 km north of modern Büğdüz (37°37,493' N; 30°17,652' E; h.: 1167 m a.s.l.). The site contains only a rock-cut tomb, called Berber Taşı (Fig. 96). A rectangular doorway (h.: 0.68 m; w.: 0.48 m) gives access to a rectangular grave chamber (h.: 1.32 m; w.: 1.08m; l.: 1.68 m). Facing the entrance, the chamber contains a plain klinè (Fig. 97). The entrance to a second rock-cut tomb is visible higher up the mountain slopes. The tombs may have belonged to local landowners. No pottery was found here, so that the tomb cannot be dated closer than to the 'classical' period.

5.1. The western slopes of the Kocayanık Tepe

Towards the west, the Büğdüz Çayı river system is bounded by a smaller limestone massif, with its highest peak in the south, the Kocayanık Tepe (1833 m a.s.l.), which is to the east of Karacaören and to the north of Yeşildağ, and stretching as far north as Büğdüz (Yelekin Tepesi: 1247 m). This range forms a transition from the limestone mountains towards the neogene marls in the west, which form the substrate for the badlands area between the limestone massif around Mt. Beşparmak and the plain of Lake Burdur (Fig. 54).

In the southern part of this district, lies the major site of Gâvur Ören (i.e. 'ruins of the heathen': from 37°30, 270' to 37°30,466' N; from 30°12,462' to 30°12,670' E). This important site of several hectares in a *Pinus nigra* forest is situated 3 km south of Karacaören on a morphological platform at about 1300-1350 m a.s.l. The platform is located on a divide between the 40 m deep valleys of two seasonal rivers, respectively the Kurukuyu Deresi to the west and the Kapız Deresi to the north (Fig. 98). The river that collects the waters of the drainage basin towards Yeşildağ and further flows westwards in the direction of Iğdeli is the Kapız Deresi. Both rivers are highly erosive in the conglomerate formations and have a braided river bed. They form barren valleys with bare and very active slopes comparable with badlands. In June of 1996 the river-beds were dry. A scarp about 50 m high with a northeast-southwest orientation, delimits the site towards the southeast. The scarp forms the prolongation of a dry waterfall along the Kurukuyu Deresi. This dry waterfall with several potholes is located on the border between the limestone formations and the conglomates. It is suggested that the scarp and the dry waterfall correspond with one of the fault lines delimiting the geologic Burdur Basin. As we did not notice any spring on this site, the river-beds must be fed by springs and must have contained water in the recent past. The actual water content of the river-beds is much modified due to irrigation works. Upstream from the dry waterfall, the traverse of the valley of the Kurukuyu Deresi is easy.

It is important to note that the site of Gâvur Ören is located in the mouth of the 'Gulf of Yeşildağ' (see above), so that here no morphological scarp separates the Burdur basin from the areas to the east. The distance to the site of Kireçocağı is only 2 km and that to Yeşildağ with its prehistoric mound 3 km, but there is no direct road connecting these sites. Nowadays, the only connection is through the pass of Uçtepearası, linking Yeşildağ with Karacaören and running immediately east of Gâvur Ören.

As we have said, this last site is located on conglomerates. These conglomerates form the lowest layers of the sub-horizontal deposits in the Burdur basin and are present also in the mouth of the 'Gulf of Yeşildağ' directly above the folded limestone formations.

The ruins of Gâvur Ören are famous throughout the district, so that it comes as no surprise that the site has attracted several scholars in the past. The first were W.M. Ramsay and A.H.M. Smith who in 1884 visited a "site to the west of Gulde Chiftlik" (i.e. the Golde farm), by which they meant the ruins of Gâvur Ören. In 1888, Ramsay identified the latter with the city of Kormasa mentioned in Livy's description of Manlius Vulso's journey in 189 BC (Ramsay 1888: 264; pl. II-III; Ramsay 1895: 326-327). At first, he mistook Kormasa also for the same settlement as Kolbasa, and thought that the Kolbaseis had been a tribe, spread over a number of villages, with a central settlement located at Gâvur Ören. Later, he changed his mind and located Kormasa closer to Lake Kestel (Ramsay 1941: 239). The site was revisited by Bean in 1957. He noticed that it does not appear to have been fortified and thought that its west slope must have been the residential area, since there were "many uncut building-blocks and much pottery, including the red and orange sigillata ware". On the southwest slope he found "the ruins of a substantial building of large well-cut blocks lying in a heap" (Bean 1959: 108). As he had found several inscriptions at and near Kozluca mentioning the name of the city of Hadrianoi, which is unknown from literary sources and from coins, but in Byzantine sources occurs frequently as a bishopric in this district, he attached the name of Hadrianoi to the major site at Gâvur Ören. The fact that this site had no good farming land close to it made him believe that its territory had extended as far west as the Lysis river and that it even included the basin of Bereket (Moatra) on the other side of the mountain range. Although the name might suggest that the city had been a completely new foundation from the time of Hadrian and despite the fact that he had not found "anything that needed to be earlier than the second century AD", Bean decided that the city had already been previously inhabited under an unknown name (Bean 1959: 109-110). In 1986, Hall made a different suggestion. He correctly identified Hadrianoi with a city site near Eğneş, and Kormasa with Kozluca Höyük. However, he did not exclude the possibility that the name of this last had been transferred later to the site at Gâvur Ören, while Kozluca Höyük would have become one of the still unidentified Pisidian cities, possibly Palaiopolis (Hall 1986b: 141-142).

Our visit to Gâvur Ören in 1996 immediately convinced us that Hall had been right in rejecting its identification with Hadrianoi, but also that it had never been a city site at all. As early as 1884, Ramsay had seen that the site had not been a real 'polis' (Ramsay 1888: 264). The remains do cover a fairly large area (ca. 300 by 300 m), but they do not include any trace of a major public ashlar building such as one would expect to find in a city site (Fig. 99). The absence of such buildings is even more striking as remains of monumental structures remain in the necropolis, so it is unlikely that only the public structures would have disappeared completely. The neighbouring villages of Karacaören, Iğdeli and even Kozluca do contain lots of antiquities that have come from Gâvur Ören, but most of them again seem to come from a necropolis and not from a civic centre. There is no reason, therefore, to place a 'city' here, which would have needed a large territory as a site catchment area. In our view, the territory of the settlement may have been confined to the highland and the mountain slopes surrounding it. The inhabitants need not to have made a living from farming alone, but may also have been active in forestry, in related activities (bee-keeping, for example) or even in the exploitation of the local conglomerates. Today, the slopes around the site are covered with black and green pines. Towards the northwest there are also some flatter zones that can be cultivated (Fig. 100). The statement of Karacaören's mayor that counterweights for olive presses have also been found at Gâvur Ören, which would indicate the practice of olive cultivation in the past, could not be confirmed during our visit to this site.

The site has plenty of rubble wall remains, as one would expect in an ancient village, and lots of pottery (SA 96 S 13-14). They include large quantities of early and late Imperial Sagalassos red slip wares, proving that the site had certainly been inhabited before the second century AD.

In 1884, Ramsay and Smith copied at Gâvur Ören among other things "two large architectural fragments" with a dedication by Menandros, son of Troilos, to Plouton and Korè (Smith 1887: 258 no. 43). The gods of the Underworld, Plouton and Korè, also had a sanctuary at Kaynar Kalesi on

Fig. 92: Funerary column in the cemetery at Bayındır.

Fig. 93: View of the fields to the west of the Bayındır Hüyük.

Fig. 94: Some traces of rubble constructions on Bayındır Höyük. In the background Mt. Beşparmak.

Fig. 95: View of the site of Hamam Yıkığı near Bayındır.

Fig. 96: Entrance of the Berber Taşı tomb between Büğdüz and Bayındır.

Fig. 97: The kline inside the grave chamber.

Fig. 98: View of the Kapız Deresi with the site of Gâvur Ören on the hill behind it, seen from the north.

Fig. 99: View of the central area of Gâvur Ören.

the other site of the Kestel mountain range (Bean 1960: 47-50; Mitchell 1991: 133). Another cult that seems to have existed at Gâvur Ören is that of Sozon, as is shown by an altar with a dedication to that divinity, copied by Bean at Karacaören (Bean 1959: 106 no. 70).

The "substantial building" which Bean had noticed on the southwest slope, is a monumental tomb located at the outskirts of a major necropolis, called Kurukuyu ('dry well': 37°30,466' N; 30°12,462' E; altitude: 1320 m a.s.l.).

The mausoleum, which faces westwards, stood on a massive terrace with an upper moulding of 6.70 by 6.65 m, still visible to a height of 1.30 m (Fig. 101). The remains of a naiskos, which it once supported, are strewn around it. The naiskos had projecting corner pilasters (w.: 0.57 m), but there are no traces of columns to be seen. It was crowned by an architrave (h.: 0.57 m), which carried a *Pfeifenfries* (Fig. 102). Various cornice blocks lay around it, including a corner of the pediment (Fig. 103). The horizontal cornice was decorated with a wave pattern, above a row of dentils. At Sagalassos, the first motif occurs only on the socle of the late Hadrianic nymphaeum located to the north of the Lower Agora, which was built by a construction team of supposedly Pamphylian origin. The wave motif itself does not have much chronological value (Vandeput 1997: 93, pl. 38, 2). The sloping cornices are decorated with egg-and-tongues above a row of dentils below, and with a nice palmette anthemion above, on which palmettes of different shape, some plain, some floral, alternate. They are placed alternately upright and pendent and are linked by S-shaped scrolls in contraposition. A good parallel is offered by various anthemia on the nymphaeum on the Upper Agora at Sagalassos, built under Marcus Aurelius (Vandeput 1997: 102 pls. 43, 1; 46,2). A middle Antonine date also seems the best suggestion for the construction date of the mausoleum at Gâvur Ören. Like the monumental tomb at Bereket, it must have belonged to a wealthy landholding family, the members of which perhaps lived, and certainly chose to be buried, on or near their estates. Remains in other settlements on the territory of the city and even beyond (for instance at Kapaklı) suggest a similar picture: social life in many rural settlements seems to have been dominated by (at least) one prominent family, which displayed its prominence through the construction of a family tomb that often became the most monumental structure of the settlement. Some of these structures were clearly inspired by contemporary architecture at Sagalassos and perhaps even completed by building teams from there. The wealth of the family which buried its dead inside the mausoleum at Gâvur Ören is evident also from the fact there must at one time have been a very expensive marble sarcophagus of the columnar type from Dokimeion (Waelkens 1982), of which only part of the klinè lid (pres.l.: 1.50 m; pres.w.: 0.75 m; pres.h.: ca. 0.60 m) remains (Fig. 104). This must have been the "apparently funerary" relief showing "two reclining figures about life-size, one behind the other" noticed by Bean (1959: 108). To the southeast lies, upside down, another klinè lid in white limestone, that was never completed (l.: 2.29 m; w.: 1.12 m; vis.h.: 0.72 m). It corresponds with the "other relief" of which Bean wrote: "it seems to be complete, but I do not understand it" (Bean 1959: 108 pl. XIX e-f). A third klinè lid, which may also be of Docimian origin and was said to come from Gâvur Ören, was seen by Bean at Kozluca (Bean 1959: 109, pl. XXd).

In the case of the settlement at Gâvur Ören, there must have been more wealthy families. To the west of the mausoleum, over a distance of at least 500 m, several traces of other built tombs (ashlar blocks) and fragments of sarcophagi, some of them rock-cut, can be found. Ramsay published an inscription on the entablature of a heroon built by Termilas, son of Attalos, for his wife and four other members of the family (Ramsay 1888: 265 no. 5). He also published the epitaph of Neon, son of Komon, with the name of the artist who had carved the gravestone, "Komon from Alastos" (see below s.v. VIII), as well as another epitaph belonging to Aur. Apollonios "dis", grandson of Kalpournios (Ramsay 1888: 265 nos 5 and 8). At the time of Bean's visit a built tomb had been dug out recently by villagers. Some funerary monuments belonging to it had been taken to the nearby village of Karacaören, to the house of Mehmet Aksu. Among them was a hexagonal pillar with the epitaph of Ainas, daughter of Kastor, as well as a headless statue and a slab with a standing figure in high relief (Bean 1959: 107, pls. XIX a-b). The house belongs now to Ibrahim Aksu, the former mayor of the village. It still contains the pillar for Ainas (Fig. 105), but except for the Ionic "late column-capital with fronds at the corners" (Bean 1959: 107, pl. XIX c), all other antiquities mentioned by Bean can no longer be seen there.

Near the eastern extremity of the necropolis, another limestone klinè lid with a reclining male figure holding a scroll (Fig. 106) can be found (pres.l.: 1.33 m; pres.w.: 1.04 m; pres.h.: 0.98 m). Ca. 60 m to the west of it, there are two sarcophagi (Fig. 107). The coffin of one of them is almost complete (l.: 2.03 m; h.: 1 m). It is decorated with a projecting ledge below and a *tabula ansata* on the front. Above it and inside the *tabula ansata,* one can still read the philosophical inscription published by Smith (1887: 258 no. 55) and Bean (AS 1959: 108 no. 75). Nearby lies a broken lid of the gable type. Next to it, there is a second coffin with a similar moulding below, that is broken above (l.: 2.07 m; w.: 1.09 m; pres.h.: 0.96 m). In the middle of its front there are three standing figures (one male, one female) (Fig. 108). Smith also published another, now lost, sepulchral relief (Smith 1887: 258 no. 44).

Besides the antiquities mentioned above, at the time of Bean's visit in 1957, several other transportable funerary monuments from the necropolis around Gâvur Ören had found their way to Karacaören. Among them was the stele which Thoas, Manès and Tatas erected for their parents Manès and Ainas. Both parents are represented inside a niche flanked by pilasters, carrying a gable decorated with an eagle (Bean 1959: 106 no. 71, pl. XVIIId). A rectangular altar decorated with human figures on three sides, with the epitaph of Aur. Attalos "dis", grandson of Menneas and his wife Amma, set up by their daughter Aur. Gè, also came from Gâvur Ören (Bean 1959: 107 no. 74).

During the 1996 survey, various new monuments, coming from this site, were copied at Karacaören in the house of Ibrahim Aksu. The exterior wall of a stable contains the lower part of a female statue in limestone (Fig. 109; h.: 0.81 m; w. below: 0.50 m). In the courtyard of the house, the owner has re-used a late second century AD cornice fragment (Fig. 110; vis.l: 0.47 m; pres.h.: 0.31 m; w.: 0.77 m), a socle base of a monument with lion feet, a rather crudely executed entablature block (l.: 2.13 m; h.: 0.66 m) that is composed of a low architrave and a fruit garland frieze suspended from weathered Medusa heads and theatre masks (Fig. 111). Most of these came probably from the mausolea in the necropolis of Gâvur Ören. A funerary column (h.: 1.85 m; diam.: ca. 0.42 m) bearing the epitaph of Mazès daughter of Trokondas has been built into the lower part of the house wall. The same house also contains an Ionic (or Corinthian) column base, a small Medusa head built into the stable wall and, above the door of the latter, an early Byzantine inscription referring to a deacon (Fig. 112). Inside the stable, a limestone pillar decorated with a Latin cross (h.: 0.93 m; w.: 0.24 to 0.26 m) bears also testimony to a Christian community at Gâvur Ören. Finally, the same stable houses a small square limestone altar, decorated on two sides with a standing male and female couple (Figs. 113-114).

Bean also noticed the presence of antiquities from Gâvur Ören at Kozluca. Beside the klinè lid discussed above, a headless female statue (h.: 1.10 m) set up in the Aşağı Mahalle would thus have come from there.

During the 1996 campaign, our survey team discovered an even more important group of antiquities from Gâvur Ören in the village of Iğdeli. This village is located in the Lysis valley, immediately to the south of Sagalassian territory and its badlands. The distance to Gâvur Ören to the east is, as the crow flies, ca. 5 km.

Some houses near the central square contain a few ashlar blocks said to come from this site and there are also an architrave lying upside down on the square and three column drums (limestone breccia) in the cemetery and in the mosque. The courtyard of the latter contains the upper part of a pilaster, with reliefs on four sides (l.: 0.75 m; w.: 0.41 m; h.: 0.35 m). The front has a Gorgoneion placed between two horse's heads turned outwards (Fig. 115). The left side has a defaced bust (Fig. 116), the right side a bust of Hermes with a *caduceus* (Fig. 117). The back is decorated with another defaced bust (perhaps with a Phrygian cap) between two similar horse's heads as those on the front (Fig. 118). The type of monument to which the pilaster once belonged can no longer be established, but it is more likely to be a religious monument (shrine) than a tomb.

However, all the other antiquities certainly have a funeral character and seem to have been removed from the necropolis of Gâvur Ören. Among them is a small unfinished altar (h.: 0.90 m; w.: 0.40 to 0.55 m) decorated with a weathered patera on one side and possibly a similar unfinished decoration on a second side (Fig. 119). The lower part of a limestone funerary stele (pres.h.: 0.60 m; w. 0.44 to 0.54 m; th.: 0.32 m) has been built into the house of Süleyman Akgül. It represents a standing figure between two pilasters (Fig. 120). Finally, the village contains four draped statues in limestone that must have been taken from the mausolea at Gâvur Ören. A similar statue, described by Bean as coming from a tomb, had already been recorded at Karacaören (see above). An unpublished monumental tomb in the southern necropolis of Sagalassos also has various statues of a similar type lying around it. The quality of the workmanship of the Iğdeli statues is rather poor. The central part of one of them (Fig. 121) is built into the wall of the tea garden at Iğdeli (pres.h.: 0.50 m; w.: 0.48 m). A headless torso (pres.h.: 0.40 m; w.: 0.65 m) can be found in the corner of the house of Ibrahim Uğur (Fig. 122). The last two statues are complete, except for the head. One (pres.h.: 1.04 m; w.: 0.40 m; th.: 0.28 m) stands in front of the house of Hasan Hüseyin Yıldırım (Fig. 123). The second one (pres.h.: 0.95 m; w.: 0.37 m; th.: 0.25 m) is built into the local fountain (Fig. 124).

All these antiquities reflect once more the picture of a very wealthy community at Gâvur Ören, of which the most important monuments were the mausolea of rich landholding families, whereas civic architecture was apparently much less grand. The crude execution of most of the funeral sculpture and reliefs is again rather typical of a major rural settlement, undoubtedly one of the most important ones in Sagalassian territory, than of an urban community. The very expensive sarcophagi and the corresponding elaborate mausoleum do not contradict such a view, since they may have belonged to one important family.

Approximately 4 km to the northeast of Karacaören and 2.4 km to the south of Soğanlı, our survey team discovered a late Roman and early Byzantine site at Monastır (i.e. 'monastery') Mevkii (37°890' N; 30°14, 617' E). The road between Karacaören and Soğanlı winds through a forest of

Fig. 100: The fields to the northwest of Gâvur Ören.

Fig. 101: The mausoleum in the southwest necropolis of Gâvur Ören.

Fig. 102: Part of the frieze from the mausoleum.

Fig. 103: Gable fragment of the mausoleum.

Fig. 104: The Docimian kline lid near the mausoleum.

Fig. 105: Pedestal of Ainas in a house at Karacaören.

Fig. 106: Kline lid near the western end of the necropolis of Gâvur Ören.

Fig. 107: Two sarcophagi in the southwestern necropolis of Gâvur Ören.

Fig. 108: Front of a sarcophagus with three standing figures at Gâvur Ören.

Fig. 109: Statue fragment from Gâvur Ören at Karacaören.

Fig. 110: Cornice fragment at Karacaören.

Fig. 111: Entablature from Gâvur Ören at Karacaören.

Fig. 112: Early Byzantine inscription at Karacaören.

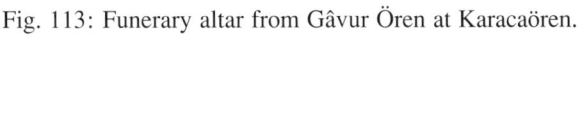
Fig. 113: Funerary altar from Gâvur Ören at Karacaören.

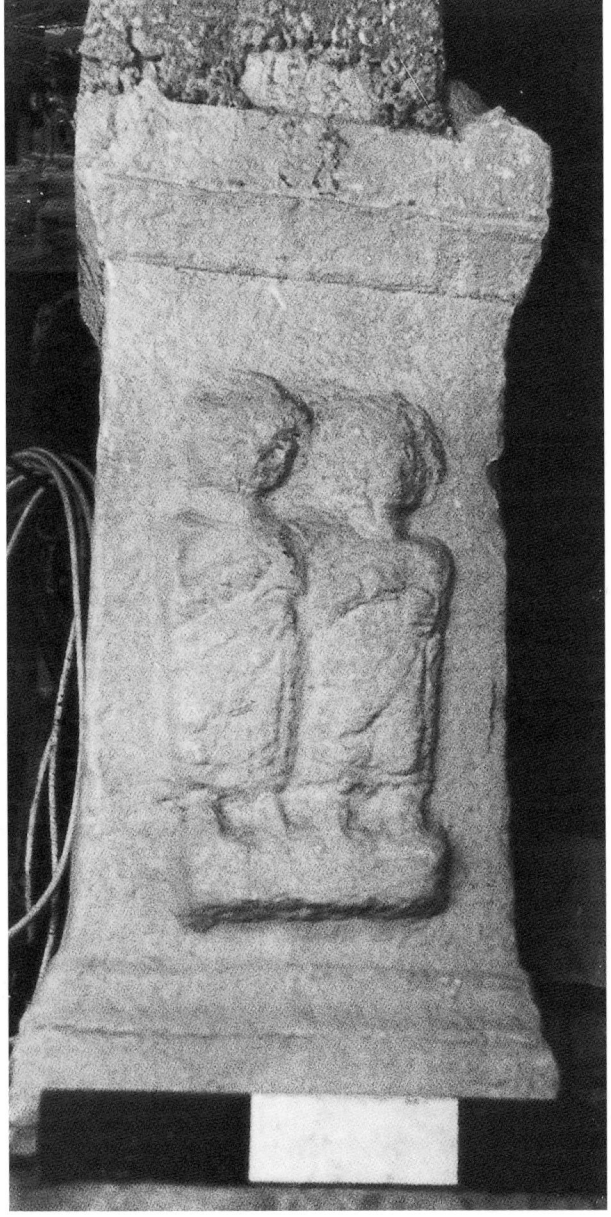

Fig. 114: Other side of the same funerary altar.

Fig. 115: Upper part of a decorated pilaster said to come from Gâvur Ören at Iğdeli.

Fig. 116: Left side of the pilaster.

Fig. 117: Hermes bust on the right side of the pilaster.

Fig. 118: Back of the pilaster at Iğdeli.

Fig. 119: Altar from Gâvur Ören at Iğdeli.

Fig. 120: Funerary stele from Gâvur Ören at Iğdeli.

Fig. 121: Central part of a funerary statue said to come from Gâvur Ören at Iğdeli.

Fig. 122: Bust from a funerary statue at Iğdeli.

black pine and juniper. Only the lower slopes of the valley are cultivated (with roses, among other crops). The site of Monastır Mevkii is located in a small, open, well watered grazing area with some juniper trees in the middle of a Pinus nigra forest and close to a permanent spring called Monastır Pınar (Fig. 125). The site, at an altitude of 1590 m a.s.l. or about 200 m above the Burdur Basin, occupies the bottom of a shallow valley downstream of the spring (Fig. 126). The valley is cut into the western slope of the limestone mountains which reach an altitude of 1770 m a.s.l. Today, the site is completely hidden from view by the rather dense vegetation around it. Together with the altitude, this may indicate that the site was deliberately selected to be hidden in the mountains. There is no possibility of arable farming in the immediate vicinity, so that the inhabitants may have lived by forestry activities or animal husbandry, unless they cultivated the fields which start a few hundred meters down the slope.

Between the juniper stands there are a lot of rubble heaps, clearly the ruins of widely dispersed simple buildings. There are only a few tile fragments and coarse wares, apparently of late Roman date or later. Occupation may have begun in the later Roman period, during a period of insecurity (the Isaurian raids of the late fourth/early fifth century or the Arab invasions of the seventh century AD?). The settlement contains an apsidal building with 1.20 m thick, mortared rubble walls (inside dimensions: 6.50 by 2.50 m), perhaps a chapel or small church (Fig. 127). From the site, there is a marvelous view towards the Lysis valley.

Another mountain site is located 900 m to the south of Soğanlı, on the Kale Tepe. As might be expected from its name, the latter is an observation spot with a Hellenistic fortification on top of a limestone hill (alt. 1555 m a.s.l.; co-ordinates: 37°33,645' N; 30°14,645' E) that stands isolated from the limestone scarp. The mountain tops to the east are at 1750 m a.s.l. The top of the hill is nearly bare, except for some isolated juniper trees. The area downhill from there is a pasture with individual stands of juniper trees. From this hill there is an open view towards the northern badland area with the Ilyas Tepe (at 5 km towards the northwest) and towards the arable land around present-day Soğanlı (Fig. 128). The view to the southwest and south is cut off by the pine forest. From a geomorphological point of view, the Kale Tepe is a nice example of a hill that has resulted from a macroslump from the limestone scarp (see Verstraeten *et al.* 2000).

To the east, the hill falls away in a very steep cliff. From the northwest, a ca. 1.10 m rock-cut road winds down towards the village. The whole hill-top is surrounded by a 1.60 m thick wall in large irregular limestone blocks (Fig. 129). On the west side, there are two rectangular towers (ca. 5 by 4 m), one of which contained a second gateway (Fig. 130). The interior space that is protected by the circuit wall is approximately 120 (north–south) by 60 m (east–west). Inside, no pottery could be found, but it is clear that the whole arrangement and wall construction technique is Hellenistic or older. The fortlet offered a very nice view of the Ilyas Tepe and of the badlands between Soğanlı and Lake Burdur. It was also within view of the fortlet on the Kale Tepe near Kökez and probably part of the same defence system.

The western slopes below the fortification walls contain the rubble remains of a settlement spread out amidst the junipers (Fig. 131). According to the mostly coarse sherds that were visible at the surface (SA 96 S 24), this settlement is of Roman Imperial date. The area of Soğanlı may however have already been occupied at an earlier date, so that the fortlet may not have been completely isolated.

Ca. 900 m to the northeast of Soğanlı, there is a kind of limestone scarp on a small divide about 50 m below the site of Taşlı Tepe. The western extremity of the scarp (37°34,590 N; 30°) 15,000 E; altitude: 1430 m a.s.l.) is full of worked stones (Fig. 132), among them a cylindrical limestone block (max. h.: 0.70 m; diam. ca: 1 m) with a hollowed out centre (diam.: 0.58 m), perhaps part of a kind of mill or press (Fig. 133). There is a similar stone higher up. The spot is called Yapımca Olak and littered with pottery, both late Imperial coarse wares and early Imperial Sagalassos red slip wares (SA 96 S 19). The scarp is surrounded by fields where wheat, barley and chickpeas are cultivated. The area has a sparse vegetation composed of juniper and of bushes (mainly kermes oak). The spot appears to be the ideal place for an isolated villa or estate and one of the owners of it was perhaps buried in a second site, some 100 m to the southwest and ca. 50 m higher up the slopes.

This site, called Taşlı Tepe ('stoney hill'), is located at an altitude of 1480 m a.s.l. on a small hill top in the upper part of the limestone scarp (co-ordinates: 37°34,472' N; 30°15,108' E). The scarp is under forest (*Pinus nigra*), while the Taşlı Tepe is completely bare. The tops of the limestone mountains are at 1600 m a.s.l. here.

Taşlı Tepe consists of an enormous heap of limestone fragments (mean diameter: 0.3-0.5 m) which is still ca. 2.50 m high (Fig. 134). They cover a circular area with a diameter of ca. 25 m. The whole site had been searched recently and looks like the remains of a burial mound made of rough, middle-sized stones. Unfortunately, the stone heap itself did not contain any kind of pottery, but this type of tumulus might be Roman at the very latest. On the lower slopes around it, some Imperial Sagalassos red slip wares and probably contemporary coarse wares were found. They may belong to the occupation of Yapımca Olak. The site affords a splendid view over the Burdur Basin (Fig. 135).

Between Yapımca Olak and Soğanlı, ca. 300 m to the northwest of the village, a spot called Sazak Mevkii (37°34,329' N; 30°14,837' E; altitude: 1455 m a.s.l.) located on a level spot at the outer border of the Burdur basin, contains a rock-cut *chamosorion* (Fig. 136; l.: 1.68 m; w.: 0.66 to 0.84 m). Its soil is already based on marl.

The village of Soğanlı itself contains a few antiquities. Most of them can be found built into the walls of a very abundant spring at the edge of the village, called Kirseli Pınar (37°34,130' N; 30°14,610 E; altitude: 1424 m a.s.l.). The present fountain fed by the spring was built in 1954. Most worked blocks around it, including a door fragment and some column drums (Fig. 137) were said to be found at this very spot. According to the villagers, the ashlar blocks that were found here were so numerous that two houses in the village were built with them. As such local statements are usually exaggerated, one may perhaps assume that Kirseli Pınar occupies the spot of an ancient fountain house or monumentalised spring. The present monument captures a considerable spring at the contact zone between the limestone and the ophiolites.

Some houses of Soğanlı do contain worked blocks in their walls, but not many. Among them are a bench with lion feet (Fig. 138) and a nicely decorated architectural piece (l.: 0.68 m; vis.w.: 0.22 m; th.: 0.21 m) from a Byzantine church (Fig. 139). These antiquities could easily come from either Yapımca Olak or from the settlement below the Kale Tepe and do not necessarily indicate the existence of an old settlement at Soğanlı proper. However, it is also possible that they were removed from 'old' Soğanlı.

In fact, Soğanlı itself is a new village. Identical to Karacaören, the old village with that name was situated in the Burdur Basin, lower down the slopes, and at a distance of a few kilometers from the mountains. According to local information, it was abandoned in 1926, due to a shortage of water (see also Bean 1959: 105 note 69), and a new village was built at the foot of the limestone scarp.

As a result, it is possible that some of the antiquities at modern Soğanlı were removed from there. The badlands extend to the outskirts of the village and just leave an uneroded surface of about 1 km².

The old village was visited by Duchesne and Collignon in 1876 (Collignon 1877: 371-372; Collignon 1879: 342), who believed that this site had in fact been an ancient town or village. Collignon's description ("un autre emplacement couvert de débris antiques; trois inscriptions, dont une funéraire, quelques fragments épars, et surtout l'aspect général des lieux montrent qu'il y eut ici une ville ou un village…") is not clear enough to distinguish whether they actually saw a ruined site here, or a village containing re-used antiquities.

In the 1950s, Bean visited the new village, where he noticed an funerary urn without an inscription and part of a semicircular altar with three busts in relief. He also discovered three funerary inscriptions that we could not find in 1996 (Bean 1959: 106 nr.67-69). One was a round cippus erected at the request of L. Firmus Frougi (genitive case), another epitaph was found inside a *tabula ansata* on a fluted funerary column and belonged to the same family of whom Collignon and Duchesne had copied a similar funerary monument at old Soğanlı (Collignon 1879: 342 nr. 16). The French team published also a second funerary column from the same village (Collignon 1879: 342 nr. 17).

6. THE BURDUR BADLANDS BETWEEN Mt. BEŞPARMAK AND THE PLAIN OF LAKE BURDUR

The second subdivision of the western Sagalassos territory is the area of neogene marls of the Burdur basin. This is a southwest-northeast oriented area of 10 km wide and 30 km long separating the limestone area of the Beşparmak from Lake Burdur and the plain around it (Figs 140-141). Some limestone hills rise out of the great synclinal marl structure forming the highest parts of the area (up to 1450 m a.s.l.). The original surface on the marl formations is a slightly undulating plateau of which only a few remnants remain visible. However, the greater part of the marl area is covered with well developed badlands (Figs 142-143). Badland formation is still a major environmental problem in the region, as could be seen during heavy rainfall at the time of the survey. The remaining plateau surfaces between the incised valleys are brought into cultivation, but they result in a poor coverage. Valley heads that are being eroded deeply, near the fields are filled with cobbles in an effort to slow down erosion.

In extreme contrast to the desertic appearance of the badlands described above, the Büğdüz River coming from the Beşparmak area cuts through like a green knife. The river has forced a connection between the limestone mountains to the east and the plain area of Lake Burdur to the west. In the heart of the barren area only one site has been found, that of Ilyas Tepe. The other sites are located on the edge of the area, either near the mountains of the Beşparmak Dağı and the Kocayanık Tepe ranges, or near the plain of Lake Burdur (Fig. 140). It is characteristic of the area that the water coming from the slopes of the nearby mountains is completely used for irrigation, so that, except for the Büğdüz Çayı, there is no permanent river system. Only heavy rainfall and direct run-off provide enough water to make rivers flow in the desert area and in this case the flow can hardly be called 'water' but is almost a mudflow because of its very high content of suspended material.

Fig. 123: Funerary statue said to come from Gâvur Ören at Iğdeli.

Fig. 124: Funerary statue said to come from Gâvur Ören in a fountain at Iğdeli.

Fig. 125: View of the forested slopes with the location of Monastır Mevkii. The arrow indicates the location of the settlement.

Fig. 126: View of the spring at Monastır Mevkii.

Fig. 127: Remains of a chapel (?) at Monastır Mevkii.

Fig. 128: View towards the north from the fortlet on the Kale Tepe near Soğanlı.

Fig. 129: Detail of the circuit wall surrounding the Kale Tepe.

Fig. 130: The entrance to the fortlet in one of the western towers.

Fig. 131: The area with the Roman settlement on the western slopes below the Kale Tepe.

Fig. 132: View of the site of Yapımca Olak (arrow) from the southeast.

Fig. 133: One of the hollowed-out stones at Yapımca Olak.

Fig. 134: View of the Taşlı Tepe near Soğanlı.

Fig. 135: View towards the basin of Burdur from the Taşlı Tepe.

Fig. 136: The *chamosorion* at Sazak Mevkii, near Soğanlı.

Fig. 137: The spring of Kirseli Pınar at Soğanlı.

Fig. 138: Bench with lion feet built into a house wall at Soğanlı.

Fig. 139: Byzantine architectural piece at Soğanlı.

It is certain that erosion in the badlands is very significant. In other areas, reafforestation tends to stabilise the slopes. The rate of badland formation and slope retreat and the consequences of this over the last thousand years on the dispersion of the sites and on the road pattern is still unknown.

In this area, road communication is very difficult, if not completely impossible. In the badlands zone, a few roads wind on very narrow and steep ridges between deeply eroded valley (Figs. 141, 143). In the eastern part of the district, near the Çineovası, the area has not yet deteriorated into badland development, so that agriculture and road systems are better developed there. The valley of the Büğdüz river also provides an ideal communication route through this desolate area, linking the village site near Suludere at the edge of the plain of Lake Burdur with the site near old Büğdüz, and further east with the sites of Göbecik Tepe, Hamam Yıkığı, Bayındır Höyük, Güzle, Kocapınar and then, around the northern peaks of the Beşparmak Dağı, with the Çineovası, the Başköy valley and Sagalassos (Fig. 4). As we have said, the location of all these contemporary sites indicates that this connection was already developed in antiquity. So the whole intermediate badlands district between the plain of Lake Burdur, where Sagalassos is known to have owned most of the valley, and Mt. Beşparmak must have belonged to the city's territory. Its southern boundary can only have corresponded with the scarps separating the southern extremity of the badlands zone from the Lysis valley, halfway between Karacaören and Gâvur Ören and Iğdeli, since that is the only geographical demarcation.

6.1. Sites along the eastern edge of the Burdur badlands

As we have said above, most of the ancient sites are located near the edges of the badlands zone, suggesting that similarly unfavourable conditions for farming may have already prevailed in antiquity.

A first site (37°30,791' N; 30°12,075' E; altitude ca. 1240 m a.s.l.) is located in the southern part of the area, ca. 1 km to the northwest of Gâvur Ören and 3 km to the south-southwest of the village of Karacaören. It is locally known as Dikenli Tarla (i.e. 'thorny field').

The site is located on a plateau remnant at about 2 km to the west of the limestone scarp. The 30 m deep affluent valleys of the Irimlicalı Deresi, belonging to the basin of Iğdeli, form large divides with gentle slopes here (Fig. 144). The whole area is under cultivation (wheat) and towards the west and south is it bordered by green and black pines (Fig. 145). In this area, the marls are covered with brown clays containing rock fragments that form the present soil surface. The amount of rock fragments in the soil increases towards the limestone scarp. These materials can therefore be seen as fan deposits of first order basins eroded in the limestone mountains.

The ruins of Dikenli Tarla (Fig. 146) are located on the finest fan deposits, at the confluence of two affluent valleys, so that the view is open over the Burdur basin towards the west, especially downstream of the valley of the Irimlicalı Deresi (Fig. 54). In 1957, the spot was visited by Bean who described "a number of built tombs or mausolea, two or three of which are quite impressive in size, now lying as heaps of blocks" and identified the site as the main necropolis of Gâvur Ören (Bean 1959: 108-109).

But the distance from Dikenli Tarla to Gâvur Ören is rather great, and the area in between does not contain sufficient remains to suggest a continuous necropolis, as one would expect. It is probably better therefore to consider Dikenli Tarla as a site on its own. Besides clear traces of ashlar-cut mausolea, a number of other buildings made of mortared rubble can be distinguished (Fig. 147). Some of them even contained re-used older blocks. A kind of water basin (outside dimensions: 2.45 by 1.15 m; interior dimensions: 1.75 by 1.05 m) had been built of these blocks (Fig. 148). Near the western edge of the plateau, a fairly substantial structure overlooking the deep valley bottom and made of rubble walls still 1.80 m high, has been illegally excavated (Fig. 149). The whole area is covered with pottery, mainly early to late Imperial Sagalassos red slip wares, and only a few coarse wares (SA 96 S 15-16). The general impression is that the site is probably an important estate or villa in a nice location that can be compared with that of Yapımıca Olak a few kilometers to the north, surrounded by the mausolea and tombs of the landholding family and other members of the household. The wheat fields around the site are extensive enough to maintain such an estate.

One of the mausolea (ca. 8.90 by 7.93 m) stood on a podium, like that of the large mausoleum in the Kurukuyu necropolis at Gâvur Ören, and could be entered via a monumental door with consoles supporting an impressive door lintel (l. below: 2.81 m; w. below: 0.60 m; h.: 0.55 m) facing west (Fig. 150). The lintel bears an extremely weathered inscription, which could still be partly read and published by Bean. It identified the tomb builder as [M]enneas (Bean 1959: 109 no. 76). Remains of an archivolt suggest the presence of an arched gable (Fig. 151). The ashlar walls made of a single row of blocks are nearly 1 m thick.

A large sarcophagus, already published by Bean (1959: 108, pl. XXa) may have belonged to the same estate. It had been recently unearthed then and stands now at the edge of the field, a few hundred meters to the north of Dikenli Tarla. Its coffin (l.: 2.24 m; w.: 1.02 m; inside dimensions: l.: 1.78 m; w.: 0.63 m; vis.h.: 1 m) is plain on three sides, except for a heavy upper and lower moulding. On the front, two winged putti hold an uninscribed *tabula ansata* (Fig. 152). A broken klinè lid with one reclining figure on a nicely decorated mattress lies

upside down near the coffin (Fig. 153). The surface is too weathered to distinguish whether it is made of white crystalline limestone or of white marble.

The funerary altar (h.: 1.21 m; w.: 0.40 to 0.46 m), for among others a man called Trokondas, that Bean found in an open field some 200 m east of the sarcophagus (Bean 1959: 109 no. 77), has now been built into a rubble wall fencing off one of the fields (Fig. 154).

Nowadays, both Gâvur Ören and Dikenli Tarla can best be reached from the village of Karacaören. The latter and the sites of Pazar Tepe and Ören Mevkii near it are situated on the contact between the higher, folded limestone mountains to the east and the lower, subhorizontal deposits to the west that belong to the geologic Burdur basin (Fig. 54). The differences in landscape between these two areas are very obvious and present one of the main geographical differences in the territory of Sagalassos.

At Karacaören (Fig. 155), this difference in altitude amounts to about 450 m: the village is located at 1370-1400 m a.s.l., while the top of the limestone mountains 2.5 km to the east reach an altitude of 1833 m a.s.l. (Kocayanık Tepe). The geological contact between the limestone mountains and the Burdur basin is formed by faults and folds. Deep layers of ophiolites, situated stratigraphically underneath the folded limestone formations, are exposed along the road from Yeşildağ towards Karacaören at altitudes below 1500 m a.s.l. Some ophiolite exposures also occur in the eastern part of the village. The contact zone between limestone and ophiolites is full of springs. The scarp with limestone overlying the ophiolite formations is intersected by spurs of giant mass movements which results in the occurrence of isolated limestone platforms downhill. Similar phenomena have been studied around Sagalassos (Verstraeten *et al.* 2000).

The village of Karacaören contains around a hundred houses and does not seem to occupy an ancient site. It was visited in 1957 by Bean, who noted that most of its antiquities had been taken from Gâvur Ören (Bean 1959: 106).

Yet other stones were moved to it from other sites located to the north of the village. It was no longer possible to determine the provenance of two stones at Karacaören, so they are included here. One is built into one of the first houses on entering the village and is part of a limestone grave stele (h.: 0.89 m; w.: 0.57 m) with the representation of a gabled recess housing the figure of a standing male (Fig. 156). A second one is an unfinished limestone altar (h.: 1.01 m; w.: 0.60 to 0.76 m), with on its front two ram's heads supporting a garland ending in a grape, below a Gorgoneion (Fig. 157). It is built into a wall near the central square of the village.

Despite the fact that most antiquities in the village seem to have come from Gâvur Ören, there is a second settlement which is even closer to Karacaören. Its southern part is known as Ören Mevkii, while the northern part has a separate name, Pazar Tepe, which was noted by Bean (1959: 106). Our survey suggests that both sites were part of a single village settlement, covering several hectares. This settlement was separated from that at Gâvur Ören by the Çalça Tepesi to the west of Karacaören and by the Kara Tepe to the southeast of it (Fig. 54).

The Ören Mevkii-Pazar Tepe settlement lies immediately north of a smaller hill, known as Afyonluk Tepesi, an isolated massif at a distance of more than 1 km from the limestone scarp. It is still located on the badlands near the westernmost slopes of the Kocayanık Tepesi. This settlement, originally at a distance of only a few kilometers from the mountains, may have disappeared and been replaced later by Karacaören because of problems with its water supply. In more recent times, the nearby village of old Soğanlı was also moved, for the same reason. All these sites, north of Karacaören, belong to the outer limit of the badland area. The soils are on marl and are gray in colour. In this area, the valleys are cut down to a depth of 100 m or more.

Ören Mevkii is located on a level area to the northwest of the Afyonluk Tepesi. The site is quite large and occupies a plain at 1340 m a.s.l., to the south of the head of a considerable badland valley and the adjacent concave slopes towards the Afyonluk Tepesi (Fig. 158). The co-ordinates of the site near the head of the valley are: 37°32,640' N; 30°12,445' E. There is a fork in the road nearby. The site, which is cultivated today, contains a few ashlar blocks, including a large doorstep. The fields around it are littered with pottery, both late Imperial coarse wares and early to late Imperial Sagalassos red slip wares (SA 96S 17). At least one counterweight for a simple lever-and-weight olive press was noticed (Fig. 159).

From the spot with the ashlar blocks at Ören Mevkii, the pottery-littered fields continue further north towards Pazar Tepesi. This spot (co-ordinates 37°327,67' N; 30°12,407' E), at an altitude of about 1330 m a.s.l., is situated on a convex surface at the divide between two badland valleys (Fig. 160) and is probably the northern extremity of the site of Ören Mevkii. This edge of the site is full of rubble stones (Fig. 161), tile fragments and sherds that are contemporary with those at Ören Mevkii. There are also some dolium fragments and larger architectural elements, such as a pedestal, a fluted column and an architrave, perhaps belonging to a more monumental tomb (Fig. 162). Most probably the handsome sarcophagus that Bean saw in 1957 in the house of Mehmet Akta at Karacaören, that had been dug up about 1952 at Pazar Tepe, came from the same spot. It had three human figures on the long side, rams' heads at the

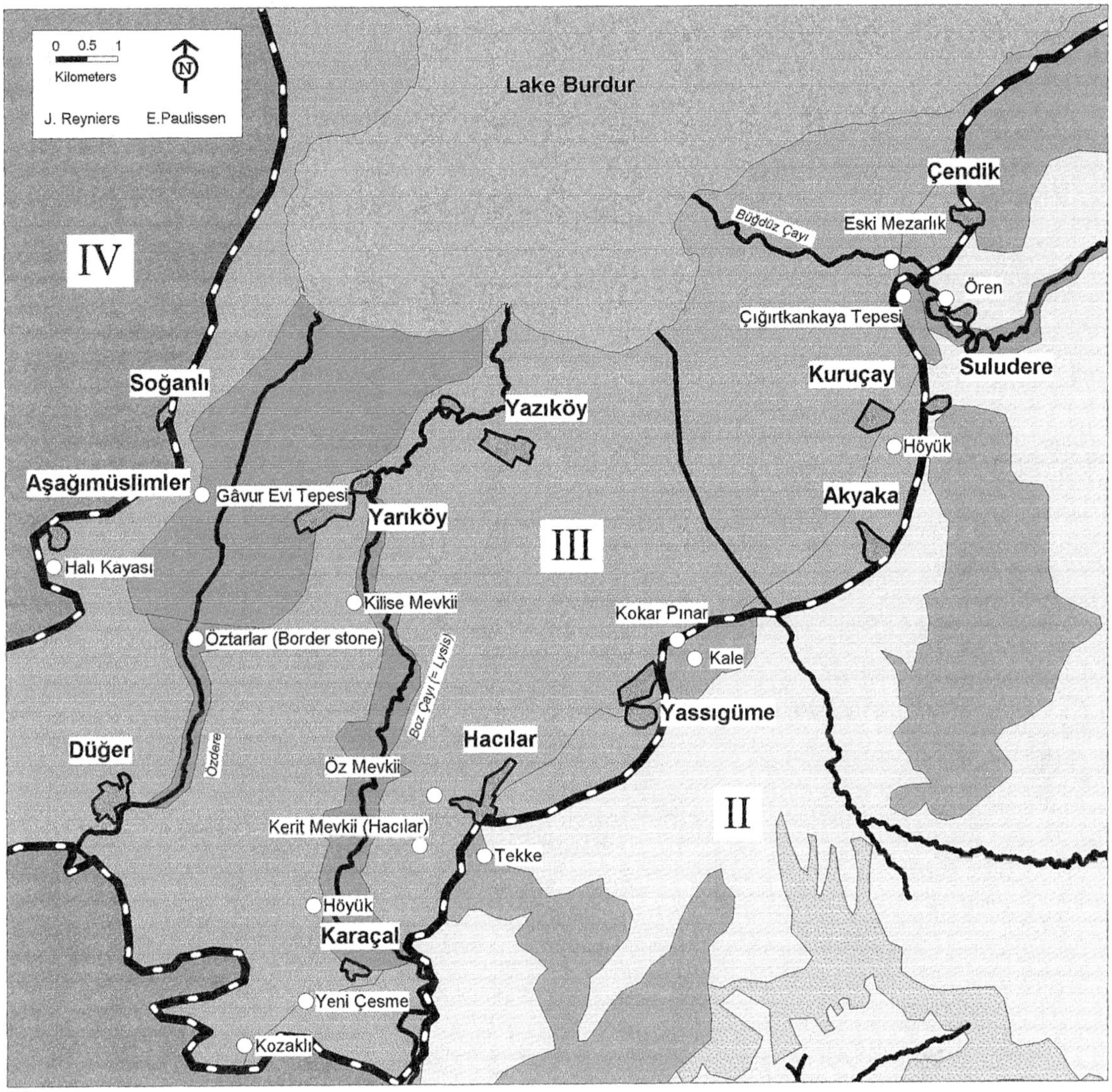

Fig. 140: Map of the plain of Burdur and adjoining badlands area.

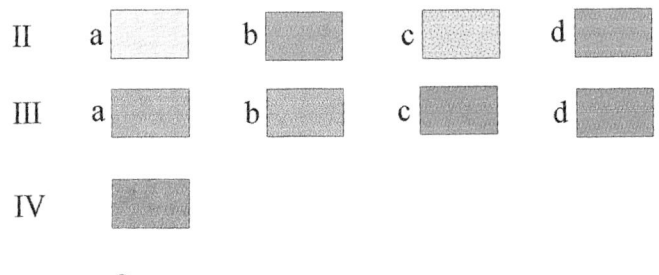

Fig. 140: Physiographic units of the Southern Lake Burdur Plain and the adjacent marl area.

II a Burdur badlands
II b Limestone outcrops in the Burdur badlands
II c Plateau remnants on marl with poor vegetation coverage
II d Valley of the river Büğdüz, irrigated and densely vegetated
IV Limestone mountains of Mt Soğut

III a Düğer plain
III b Contact zone between Lake Burdur plain and Burdur badlands.
III c Valley of the Boz Çayı (= Lysis) and the Özdere (W)
III d Swamps of Yarıkoy, nowadays mainly drained
a site

Fig. 141: View of the badlands to the west of Soğanlı.

Fig. 142: View of the badlands between Ilyas Tepe and Lake Burdur.

It is certain that erosion in the badlands is very significant. In other areas, reafforestation tends to stabilise the slopes. The rate of badland formation and slope retreat and the consequences of this over the last thousand years on the dispersion of the sites and on the road pattern is still unknown.

In this area, road communication is very difficult, if not completely impossible. In the badlands zone, a few roads wind on very narrow and steep ridges between deeply eroded valley (Figs. 141, 143). In the eastern part of the district, near the Çineovası, the area has not yet deteriorated into badland development, so that agriculture and road systems are better developed there. The valley of the Büğdüz river also provides an ideal communication route through this desolate area, linking the village site near Suludere at the edge of the plain of Lake Burdur with the site near old Büğdüz, and further east with the sites of Göbecik Tepe, Hamam Yıkığı, Bayındır Höyük, Güzle, Kocapınar and then, around the northern peaks of the Beşparmak Dağı, with the Çineovası, the Başköy valley and Sagalassos (Fig. 4). As we have said, the location of all these contemporary sites indicates that this connection was already developed in antiquity. So the whole intermediate badlands district between the plain of Lake Burdur, where Sagalassos is known to have owned most of the valley, and Mt. Beşparmak must have belonged to the city's territory. Its southern boundary can only have corresponded with the scarps separating the southern extremity of the badlands zone from the Lysis valley, halfway between Karacaören and Gâvur Ören and Iğdeli, since that is the only geographical demarcation.

6.1. Sites along the eastern edge of the Burdur badlands

As we have said above, most of the ancient sites are located near the edges of the badlands zone, suggesting that similarly unfavourable conditions for farming may have already prevailed in antiquity.

A first site (37°30,791' N; 30°12,075' E; altitude ca. 1240 m a.s.l.) is located in the southern part of the area, ca. 1 km to the northwest of Gâvur Ören and 3 km to the south-southwest of the village of Karacaören. It is locally known as Dikenli Tarla (i.e. 'thorny field').

The site is located on a plateau remnant at about 2 km to the west of the limestone scarp. The 30 m deep affluent valleys of the Irimlicalı Deresi, belonging to the basin of Iğdeli, form large divides with gentle slopes here (Fig. 144). The whole area is under cultivation (wheat) and towards the west and south is it bordered by green and black pines (Fig. 145). In this area, the marls are covered with brown clays containing rock fragments that form the present soil surface. The amount of rock fragments in the soil increases towards the limestone scarp. These materials can therefore be seen as fan deposits of first order basins eroded in the limestone mountains.

The ruins of Dikenli Tarla (Fig. 146) are located on the finest fan deposits, at the confluence of two affluent valleys, so that the view is open over the Burdur basin towards the west, especially downstream of the valley of the Irimlicalı Deresi (Fig. 54). In 1957, the spot was visited by Bean who described "a number of built tombs or mausolea, two or three of which are quite impressive in size, now lying as heaps of blocks" and identified the site as the main necropolis of Gâvur Ören (Bean 1959: 108-109).

But the distance from Dikenli Tarla to Gâvur Ören is rather great, and the area in between does not contain sufficient remains to suggest a continuous necropolis, as one would expect. It is probably better therefore to consider Dikenli Tarla as a site on its own. Besides clear traces of ashlar-cut mausolea, a number of other buildings made of mortared rubble can be distinguished (Fig. 147). Some of them even contained re-used older blocks. A kind of water basin (outside dimensions: 2.45 by 1.15 m; interior dimensions: 1.75 by 1.05 m) had been built of these blocks (Fig. 148). Near the western edge of the plateau, a fairly substantial structure overlooking the deep valley bottom and made of rubble walls still 1.80 m high, has been illegally excavated (Fig. 149). The whole area is covered with pottery, mainly early to late Imperial Sagalassos red slip wares, and only a few coarse wares (SA 96 S 15-16). The general impression is that the site is probably an important estate or villa in a nice location that can be compared with that of Yapımca Olak a few kilometers to the north, surrounded by the mausolea and tombs of the landholding family and other members of the household. The wheat fields around the site are extensive enough to maintain such an estate.

One of the mausolea (ca. 8.90 by 7.93 m) stood on a podium, like that of the large mausoleum in the Kurukuyu necropolis at Gâvur Ören, and could be entered via a monumental door with consoles supporting an impressive door lintel (l. below: 2.81 m; w.below: 0.60 m; h.: 0.55 m) facing west (Fig. 150). The lintel bears an extremely weathered inscription, which could still be partly read and published by Bean. It identified the tomb builder as [M]enneas (Bean 1959: 109 no. 76). Remains of an archivolt suggest the presence of an arched gable (Fig. 151). The ashlar walls made of a single row of blocks are nearly 1 m thick.

A large sarcophagus, already published by Bean (1959: 108, pl. XXa) may have belonged to the same estate. It had been recently unearthed then and stands now at the edge of the field, a few hundred meters to the north of Dikenli Tarla. Its coffin (l.: 2.24 m; w.: 1.02 m; inside dimensions: l.: 1.78 m; w.: 0.63 m; vis.h.: 1 m) is plain on three sides, except for a heavy upper and lower moulding. On the front, two winged putti hold an uninscribed *tabula ansata* (Fig. 152). A broken klinè lid with one reclining figure on a nicely decorated mattress lies

upside down near the coffin (Fig. 153). The surface is too weathered to distinguish whether it is made of white crystalline limestone or of white marble.

The funerary altar (h.: 1.21 m; w.: 0.40 to 0.46 m), for among others a man called Trokondas, that Bean found in an open field some 200 m east of the sarcophagus (Bean 1959: 109 no. 77), has now been built into a rubble wall fencing off one of the fields (Fig. 154).

Nowadays, both Gâvur Ören and Dikenli Tarla can best be reached from the village of Karacaören. The latter and the sites of Pazar Tepe and Ören Mevkii near it are situated on the contact between the higher, folded limestone mountains to the east and the lower, subhorizontal deposits to the west that belong to the geologic Burdur basin (Fig. 54). The differences in landscape between these two areas are very obvious and present one of the main geographical differences in the territory of Sagalassos.

At Karacaören (Fig. 155), this difference in altitude amounts to about 450 m: the village is located at 1370-1400 m a.s.l., while the top of the limestone mountains 2.5 km to the east reach an altitude of 1833 m a.s.l. (Kocayanık Tepe). The geological contact between the limestone mountains and the Burdur basin is formed by faults and folds. Deep layers of ophiolites, situated stratigraphically underneath the folded limestone formations, are exposed along the road from Yeşildağ towards Karacaören at altitudes below 1500 m a.s.l. Some ophiolite exposures also occur in the eastern part of the village. The contact zone between limestone and ophiolites is full of springs. The scarp with limestone overlying the ophiolite formations is intersected by spurs of giant mass movements which results in the occurrence of isolated limestone platforms downhill. Similar phenomena have been studied around Sagalassos (Verstraeten *et al.* 2000).

The village of Karacaören contains around a hundred houses and does not seem to occupy an ancient site. It was visited in 1957 by Bean, who noted that most of its antiquities had been taken from Gâvur Ören (Bean 1959: 106).

Yet other stones were moved to it from other sites located to the north of the village. It was no longer possible to determine the provenance of two stones at Karacaören, so they are included here. One is built into one of the first houses on entering the village and is part of a limestone grave stele (h.: 0.89 m; w.: 0.57 m) with the representation of a gabled recess housing the figure of a standing male (Fig. 156). A second one is an unfinished limestone altar (h.: 1.01 m; w.: 0.60 to 0.76 m), with on its front two ram's heads supporting a garland ending in a grape, below a Gorgoneion (Fig. 157). It is built into a wall near the central square of the village.

Despite the fact that most antiquities in the village seem to have come from Gâvur Ören, there is a second settlement which is even closer to Karacaören. Its southern part is known as Ören Mevkii, while the northern part has a separate name, Pazar Tepe, which was noted by Bean (1959: 106). Our survey suggests that both sites were part of a single village settlement, covering several hectares. This settlement was separated from that at Gâvur Ören by the Çalça Tepesi to the west of Karacaören and by the Kara Tepe to the southeast of it (Fig. 54).

The Ören Mevkii-Pazar Tepe settlement lies immediately north of a smaller hill, known as Afyonluk Tepesi, an isolated massif at a distance of more than 1 km from the limestone scarp. It is still located on the badlands near the westernmost slopes of the Kocayanık Tepesi. This settlement, originally at a distance of only a few kilometers from the mountains, may have disappeared and been replaced later by Karacaören because of problems with its water supply. In more recent times, the nearby village of old Soğanlı was also moved, for the same reason. All these sites, north of Karacaören, belong to the outer limit of the badland area. The soils are on marl and are gray in colour. In this area, the valleys are cut down to a depth of 100 m or more.

Ören Mevkii is located on a level area to the northwest of the Afyonluk Tepesi. The site is quite large and occupies a plain at 1340 m a.s.l., to the south of the head of a considerable badland valley and the adjacent concave slopes towards the Afyonluk Tepesi (Fig. 158). The co-ordinates of the site near the head of the valley are: 37°32,640' N; 30°12,445' E. There is a fork in the road nearby. The site, which is cultivated today, contains a few ashlar blocks, including a large doorstep. The fields around it are littered with pottery, both late Imperial coarse wares and early to late Imperial Sagalassos red slip wares (SA 96S 17). At least one counterweight for a simple lever-and-weight olive press was noticed (Fig. 159).

From the spot with the ashlar blocks at Ören Mevkii, the pottery-littered fields continue further north towards Pazar Tepesi. This spot (co-ordinates 37°327,67' N; 30°12,407' E), at an altitude of about 1330 m a.s.l., is situated on a convex surface at the divide between two badland valleys (Fig. 160) and is probably the northern extremity of the site of Ören Mevkii. This edge of the site is full of rubble stones (Fig. 161), tile fragments and sherds that are contemporary with those at Ören Mevkii. There are also some dolium fragments and larger architectural elements, such as a pedestal, a fluted column and an architrave, perhaps belonging to a more monumental tomb (Fig. 162). Most probably the handsome sarcophagus that Bean saw in 1957 in the house of Mehmet Akta at Karacaören, that had been dug up about 1952 at Pazar Tepe, came from the same spot. It had three human figures on the long side, rams' heads at the

It is certain that erosion in the badlands is very significant. In other areas, reafforestation tends to stabilise the slopes. The rate of badland formation and slope retreat and the consequences of this over the last thousand years on the dispersion of the sites and on the road pattern is still unknown.

In this area, road communication is very difficult, if not completely impossible. In the badlands zone, a few roads wind on very narrow and steep ridges between deeply eroded valley (Figs. 141, 143). In the eastern part of the district, near the Çineovası, the area has not yet deteriorated into badland development, so that agriculture and road systems are better developed there. The valley of the Büğdüz river also provides an ideal communication route through this desolate area, linking the village site near Suludere at the edge of the plain of Lake Burdur with the site near old Büğdüz, and further east with the sites of Göbecik Tepe, Hamam Yıkığı, Bayındır Höyük, Güzle, Kocapınar and then, around the northern peaks of the Beşparmak Dağı, with the Çineovası, the Başköy valley and Sagalassos (Fig. 4). As we have said, the location of all these contemporary sites indicates that this connection was already developed in antiquity. So the whole intermediate badlands district between the plain of Lake Burdur, where Sagalassos is known to have owned most of the valley, and Mt. Beşparmak must have belonged to the city's territory. Its southern boundary can only have corresponded with the scarps separating the southern extremity of the badlands zone from the Lysis valley, halfway between Karacaören and Gâvur Ören and Iğdeli, since that is the only geographical demarcation.

6.1. Sites along the eastern edge of the Burdur badlands

As we have said above, most of the ancient sites are located near the edges of the badlands zone, suggesting that similarly unfavourable conditions for farming may have already prevailed in antiquity.

A first site (37°30,791' N; 30°12,075' E; altitude ca. 1240 m a.s.l.) is located in the southern part of the area, ca. 1 km to the northwest of Gâvur Ören and 3 km to the south-southwest of the village of Karacaören. It is locally known as Dikenli Tarla (i.e. 'thorny field').

The site is located on a plateau remnant at about 2 km to the west of the limestone scarp. The 30 m deep affluent valleys of the Irimlicalı Deresi, belonging to the basin of Iğdeli, form large divides with gentle slopes here (Fig. 144). The whole area is under cultivation (wheat) and towards the west and south is it bordered by green and black pines (Fig. 145). In this area, the marls are covered with brown clays containing rock fragments that form the present soil surface. The amount of rock fragments in the soil increases towards the limestone scarp. These materials can therefore be seen as fan deposits of first order basins eroded in the limestone mountains.

The ruins of Dikenli Tarla (Fig. 146) are located on the finest fan deposits, at the confluence of two affluent valleys, so that the view is open over the Burdur basin towards the west, especially downstream of the valley of the Irimlicalı Deresi (Fig. 54). In 1957, the spot was visited by Bean who described "a number of built tombs or mausolea, two or three of which are quite impressive in size, now lying as heaps of blocks" and identified the site as the main necropolis of Gâvur Ören (Bean 1959: 108-109).

But the distance from Dikenli Tarla to Gâvur Ören is rather great, and the area in between does not contain sufficient remains to suggest a continuous necropolis, as one would expect. It is probably better therefore to consider Dikenli Tarla as a site on its own. Besides clear traces of ashlar-cut mausolea, a number of other buildings made of mortared rubble can be distinguished (Fig. 147). Some of them even contained re-used older blocks. A kind of water basin (outside dimensions: 2.45 by 1.15 m; interior dimensions: 1.75 by 1.05 m) had been built of these blocks (Fig. 148). Near the western edge of the plateau, a fairly substantial structure overlooking the deep valley bottom and made of rubble walls still 1.80 m high, has been illegally excavated (Fig. 149). The whole area is covered with pottery, mainly early to late Imperial Sagalassos red slip wares, and only a few coarse wares (SA 96 S 15-16). The general impression is that the site is probably an important estate or villa in a nice location that can be compared with that of Yapımca Olak a few kilometers to the north, surrounded by the mausolea and tombs of the landholding family and other members of the household. The wheat fields around the site are extensive enough to maintain such an estate.

One of the mausolea (ca. 8.90 by 7.93 m) stood on a podium, like that of the large mausoleum in the Kurukuyu necropolis at Gâvur Ören, and could be entered via a monumental door with consoles supporting an impressive door lintel (l. below: 2.81 m; w.below: 0.60 m; h.: 0.55 m) facing west (Fig. 150). The lintel bears an extremely weathered inscription, which could still be partly read and published by Bean. It identified the tomb builder as [M]enneas (Bean 1959: 109 no. 76). Remains of an archivolt suggest the presence of an arched gable (Fig. 151). The ashlar walls made of a single row of blocks are nearly 1 m thick.

A large sarcophagus, already published by Bean (1959: 108, pl. XXa) may have belonged to the same estate. It had been recently unearthed then and stands now at the edge of the field, a few hundred meters to the north of Dikenli Tarla. Its coffin (l.: 2.24 m; w.: 1.02 m; inside dimensions: l.: 1.78 m; w.: 0.63 m; vis.h.: 1 m) is plain on three sides, except for a heavy upper and lower moulding. On the front, two winged putti hold an uninscribed *tabula ansata* (Fig. 152). A broken klinè lid with one reclining figure on a nicely decorated mattress lies

upside down near the coffin (Fig. 153). The surface is too weathered to distinguish whether it is made of white crystalline limestone or of white marble.

The funerary altar (h.: 1.21 m; w.: 0.40 to 0.46 m), for among others a man called Trokondas, that Bean found in an open field some 200 m east of the sarcophagus (Bean 1959: 109 no. 77), has now been built into a rubble wall fencing off one of the fields (Fig. 154).

Nowadays, both Gâvur Ören and Dikenli Tarla can best be reached from the village of Karacaören. The latter and the sites of Pazar Tepe and Ören Mevkii near it are situated on the contact between the higher, folded limestone mountains to the east and the lower, subhorizontal deposits to the west that belong to the geologic Burdur basin (Fig. 54). The differences in landscape between these two areas are very obvious and present one of the main geographical differences in the territory of Sagalassos.

At Karacaören (Fig. 155), this difference in altitude amounts to about 450 m: the village is located at 1370-1400 m a.s.l., while the top of the limestone mountains 2.5 km to the east reach an altitude of 1833 m a.s.l. (Kocayanık Tepe). The geological contact between the limestone mountains and the Burdur basin is formed by faults and folds. Deep layers of ophiolites, situated stratigraphically underneath the folded limestone formations, are exposed along the road from Yeşildağ towards Karacaören at altitudes below 1500 m a.s.l. Some ophiolite exposures also occur in the eastern part of the village. The contact zone between limestone and ophiolites is full of springs. The scarp with limestone overlying the ophiolite formations is intersected by spurs of giant mass movements which results in the occurrence of isolated limestone platforms downhill. Similar phenomena have been studied around Sagalassos (Verstraeten *et al.* 2000).

The village of Karacaören contains around a hundred houses and does not seem to occupy an ancient site. It was visited in 1957 by Bean, who noted that most of its antiquities had been taken from Gâvur Ören (Bean 1959: 106).

Yet other stones were moved to it from other sites located to the north of the village. It was no longer possible to determine the provenance of two stones at Karacaören, so they are included here. One is built into one of the first houses on entering the village and is part of a limestone grave stele (h.: 0.89 m; w.: 0.57 m) with the representation of a gabled recess housing the figure of a standing male (Fig. 156). A second one is an unfinished limestone altar (h.: 1.01 m; w.: 0.60 to 0.76 m), with on its front two ram's heads supporting a garland ending in a grape, below a Gorgoneion (Fig. 157). It is built into a wall near the central square of the village.

Despite the fact that most antiquities in the village seem to have come from Gâvur Ören, there is a second settlement which is even closer to Karacaören. Its southern part is known as Ören Mevkii, while the northern part has a separate name, Pazar Tepe, which was noted by Bean (1959: 106). Our survey suggests that both sites were part of a single village settlement, covering several hectares. This settlement was separated from that at Gâvur Ören by the Çalca Tepesi to the west of Karacaören and by the Kara Tepe to the southeast of it (Fig. 54).

The Ören Mevkii-Pazar Tepe settlement lies immediately north of a smaller hill, known as Afyonluk Tepesi, an isolated massif at a distance of more than 1 km from the limestone scarp. It is still located on the badlands near the westernmost slopes of the Kocayanık Tepesi. This settlement, originally at a distance of only a few kilometers from the mountains, may have disappeared and been replaced later by Karacaören because of problems with its water supply. In more recent times, the nearby village of old Soğanlı was also moved, for the same reason. All these sites, north of Karacaören, belong to the outer limit of the badland area. The soils are on marl and are gray in colour. In this area, the valleys are cut down to a depth of 100 m or more.

Ören Mevkii is located on a level area to the northwest of the Afyonluk Tepesi. The site is quite large and occupies a plain at 1340 m a.s.l., to the south of the head of a considerable badland valley and the adjacent concave slopes towards the Afyonluk Tepesi (Fig. 158). The co-ordinates of the site near the head of the valley are: 37°32,640' N; 30°12,445' E. There is a fork in the road nearby. The site, which is cultivated today, contains a few ashlar blocks, including a large doorstep. The fields around it are littered with pottery, both late Imperial coarse wares and early to late Imperial Sagalassos red slip wares (SA 96S 17). At least one counterweight for a simple lever-and-weight olive press was noticed (Fig. 159).

From the spot with the ashlar blocks at Ören Mevkii, the pottery-littered fields continue further north towards Pazar Tepesi. This spot (co-ordinates 37°327,67' N; 30°12,407' E), at an altitude of about 1330 m a.s.l., is situated on a convex surface at the divide between two badland valleys (Fig. 160) and is probably the northern extremity of the site of Ören Mevkii. This edge of the site is full of rubble stones (Fig. 161), tile fragments and sherds that are contemporary with those at Ören Mevkii. There are also some dolium fragments and larger architectural elements, such as a pedestal, a fluted column and an architrave, perhaps belonging to a more monumental tomb (Fig. 162). Most probably the handsome sarcophagus that Bean saw in 1957 in the house of Mehmet Akta at Karacaören, that had been dug up about 1952 at Pazar Tepe, came from the same spot. It had three human figures on the long side, rams' heads at the

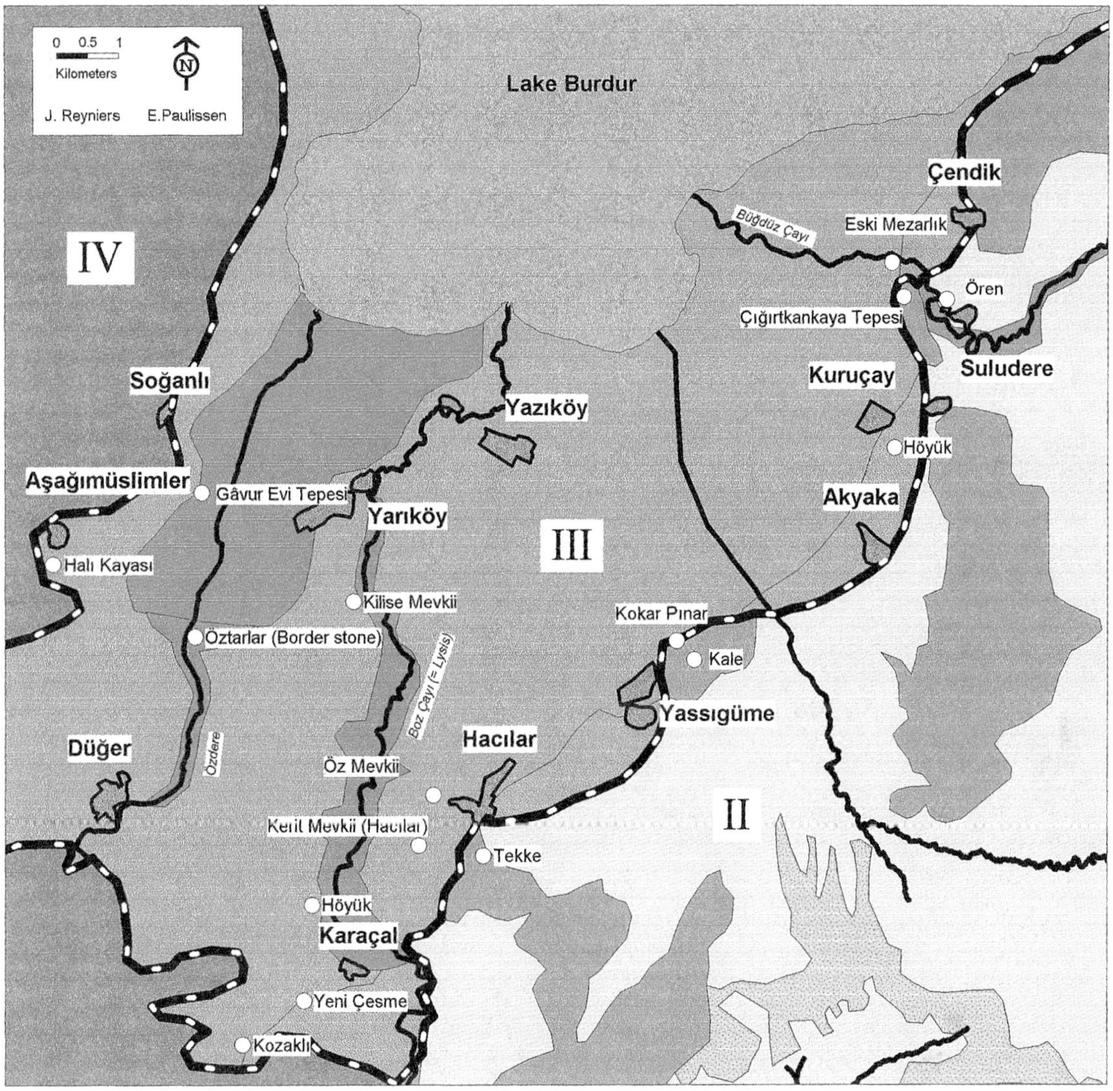

Fig. 140: Map of the plain of Burdur and adjoining badlands area.

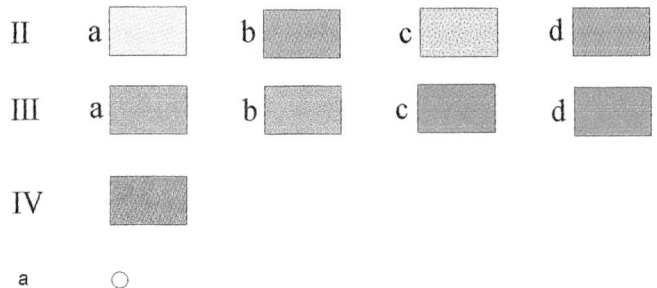

Fig. 140: Physiographic units of the Southern Lake Burdur Plain and the adjacent marl area.

II a Burdur badlands
II b Limestone outcrops in the Burdur badlands
II c Plateau remnants on marl with poor vegetation coverage
II d Valley of the river Büğdüz, irrigated and densely vegetated
IV Limestone mountains of Mt Soğut

III a Düğer plain
III b Contact zone between Lake Burdur plain and Burdur badlands.
III c Valley of the Boz Çayı (= Lysis) and the Özdere (W)
III d Swamps of Yarıkoy, nowadays mainly drained
a site

Fig. 141: View of the badlands to the west of Soğanlı.

Fig. 142: View of the badlands between Ilyas Tepe and Lake Burdur.

Fig. 143: The deeply eroded valleys in the central part of the badlands.

Fig. 144: The gentle slopes to the southwest of Karacaören, overlooking the Lysis valley and the basin of Iğdeli to the west (background).

Fig. 145: The cultivated wheat fields around Dikenli Tarla.

Fig. 146: The ruins at Dikenli Tarla.

Fig. 147: Remains of structures in mortared rubble at Dikenli Tarla.

Fig. 148: Water basin at Dikenli Tarla.

Fig. 149: Illegally excavated structure at Dikenli Tarla.

Fig. 150: Remains of a large mausoleum at Dikenli Tarla.

Fig. 151: Remains of a large mausoleum at Dikenli Tarla.

Fig. 152: Sarcophagus near Dikenli Tarla.

Fig. 153: Fragment of the klinè lid of the same sarcophagus.

Fig. 154: Funerary altar for, among others, Trokondas at Dikenli Tarla.

Fig. 155: Karacaören, seen from the northeast. In the background, the Lysis valley.

Fig. 156: Funerary stele at the entrance of the village of Karacaören.

Fig. 157: Unfinished altar in a parking lot on the square of Karacaören.

Fig. 158: The site of Ören Mevkii seen from the north with the Afyonluk Tepesi in the background.

Fig. 159: Counterweight for an olive press at Ören Mevkii.

Fig. 160: View of the deep valley at the northern edge of Pazar Tepesi.

Fig. 161: The rubble remains at Pazar Tepesi.

Fig. 162: Remains of a monumental tomb (?) at Pazar Tepesi.

front corners and goats' heads at the back corners (Bean 1959: 108, pl. XIX d). Another tombstone from here is now kept in the house of Ibrahim Aksu at Karacaören. It is a square altar (h.: 1.33; w.: 0.51 to 0.67 m) with a gable worked in the upper moulding on four sides (Fig. 163). The gable on the left side had a cross carved in it later, that on the back contains an eagle, while on the front and on the right side the gable is decorated with a head (unfinished on the right side). There is no inscription, but on the front a pair of hands has been carved, usually a symbol invoking the sun to reveal and punish those responsible for unnatural or premature deaths (Waelkens 1986: 48 note 62). Since the stone bears no inscription it may have been part of a larger complex, perhaps the mausoleum mentioned above. Here again, the picture of a rural settlement dominated by an important landholding family could apply.

At Pazar Tepesi more counterweights for olive presses were found (Fig. 164). On a small area five of them were counted, so that this district must have possessed extensive olive yards in Roman antiquity. The mayor of Karacaören told the survey team that similar stones could be found at Gâvur Ören, but at the time of our visit in 1996 none of these were seen.

6.2. The central part of the Burdur badlands

Today the central area of the badlands contains only one site, Ilyas Tepe or Oyuklar (37°36,091 N; 30°12,839 E). It can only be reached from Soğanlı and even this approach is far from easy. A track to the northwest of Soğanlı leads in a large curve to the middle of the badland area. Most of the road is located on a major divide between the basin of the Büğdüz Çayı the north and the Bodarmir Deresi to the west. In some places the width of this divide is no more than a few meters as valleys from different basins of the desert area nearly meet. The mean depth of the valleys is estimated at 100 m (see Fig. 143).

The track leads towards an undissected area located above 1400 m a.s.l. with a rectangular surface area of about 1 km² (about 1.5 km in northwest–southeast direction and 0.6 km in northeast–southwest direction). Its top located at 1450 m a.s.l. towards the southwest carries the site of Ilyas Tepesi. The Ilyas Tepesi is the highest part of the badlands area (Fig. 165). From here, there are magnificent and uninterrupted views over several kilometers, extending in all directions from Gâvur Ören in the southeast, the length of the Lysis valley, to Düğer and the southern part of the plain of Lake Burdur in the southwest (Fig. 166). Towards the west there is a good view of the mountains to the west of Lake Burdur, separating Phrygia from Pisidia (Fig. 167).

The site is based on resistant formations near the surface. The Ilyas Tepesi forms the top of a cuesta front that looks towards the southwest. The cuesta back rests on subhorizontal layers of flakey calcareous sandstone, about 20 m thick, overlying marl formations (see Fig. 165). The resistant layers dip towards the northeast, form a gentle synclinal fold and reappear 1.5 km to the east where they form another cuesta scarp. The strike of this fold is west northwest – east southeast. The Ilyas Tepesi zone is probably the area that still conserves the most recent Tertiary deposits in the Burdur Basin. Today the area suffers in all directions from severe erosion in the heads of the valleys.

The site of Ilyas Tepesi lies on the highest part of the surface, at an altitude of 1450 m a.s.l. Immediately south and below the site, on the other side of a small dere, there is a spring (Ilyas Çeşmesi). Another is located a little way to the east on the same river of the dere (Ahmet Ali Pınarı). However, the whole environment is so eroded and full of stones that only sparse grazing is possible here, and arable farming is impossible.

An area of ca. 100 by 30 m on the top of the Ilyas Tepesi is full of rubble stones and tile fragments (Fig. 168). According to the villagers at Soğanlı, loads of larger blocks have been removed by tractor from here. The area contains a lot of pottery, mostly late Imperial coarse wares.

Because of its very inhospitable environment and its nature as an excellent look-out station, we suggest that the main function of the site must have been strategic. It probably represents a late Roman military watchpost over the Lysis valley and the Lake Burdur area.

6.3. The valley of the Büğdüz Çayı

To the west of the new Büğdüz, the river with the same name forms a beautiful green valley amidst the badlands. The lower parts of the river valley are covered with poplars, while higher up wheat is cultivated. The deeply sunk valley bottom (Fig. 169) is located at an altitude of ca. 1090 m a.s.l. At either side of it, farming is only possible on the plain divides between the deeply eroded badlands.

The fertility of the valley certainly explains why it already attracted settlers in prehistoric times.

Ca. 1.2 km to the southeast of the old village of Büğdüz, lies the site of Göbecik Tepesi (37°37,700' N; 30°16,117' E; altitude: 1120 m a.s.l.). The site (Fig. 170) is located near the present transition between the cultivated valley bottom and slopes and the bare badlands higher up (Fig. 54). The slopes of the site are heavily eroded and the erosion has exposed a lot of pottery. Today, there is no water to be found in the immediate vicinity, but further to the southwest there is supposedly a source. Recently, Özsait found some Early Bronze Age pottery here (Özsait 1996: 194). The 1996 survey discovered early Imperial Sagalassos red slip wares, as well as (early) and middle to late Imperial coarse wares (SA 96 S 48). A loom weight and a black burnished prehistoric vessel shown to us at new Bügdüz were also found here. The site corresponds most probably with a prehistoric, and much later a Roman Imperial farming site.

In the same valley, ca. 3 km to the northwest of new Bügdüz, one can find the remains of the old village, that was destroyed by an earthquake in 1971 (Fig. 54; 37°38,289' N; 30°15,207' E). The village is surrounded by wheat and maize fields, and by fruit trees (prunes, apples). To the north, east and west, it is framed by low hills, towards the southeast it is completely dominated by the Beşparmak range. The only antiquity which can still be seen here is a broken, smooth column fragment (h.: 1.95 m; diam.: 0.57) built into the old school. As we said above, the village was most probably not an ancient site, and seems to have taken most of its former antiquities, now moved to new Bügdüz, from the site of Yayla Mevkii, ca. 5 km to the southeast.

Further west, the next settlements occur near Yassigüme, at the western edge of the badlands, and will be discussed in the following section.

6.4. The western edge of the Burdur badlands

Just as on the eastern edge near the transition zone to the more fertile or forested limestone area, the western scarp of the badland area overlooking the fertile plain of Lake Burdur also contains a number of sites. None of them occur on the badlands proper. Most were located on the limestone outcrops that emerge from the marl deposits in this area. Some can be found on terraces and colluvial fans on the northwest slopes along the edge of the badlands (Fig. 140).

Because of its proximity to the fertile Lake Burdur plain with its Neolithic to Early Bronze Age settlements, this part of the badlands was, not surprisingly, occupied much earlier than the areas further east.

The oldest settlement here is near Kuruçay on the northwest slope of the badlands border. The village of Kuruçay was moved to its present spot ca. 15 km to the south of Burdur and 4 km to the southeast of the lake, after its predecessor had been destroyed by an earthquake which struck the area in 1971. The old village was located near a prehistoric höyük ca. 400 m to the south-southeast of Kuruçay (37°38,048' N; 30°10,028' E; altitude: 972 m a.s.l.). The mound is surrounded by fields that today are used for the cultivation of wheat, chickpeas and grapes. It rises ca. 8 m above the fields and ca. 110 m above the lake.

The site was excavated by Duru in 1978-1988. He distinguished 15 occupation levels ranging in date from the Early Neolithic to the Early Bronze Age 2 period (Fig. 171). Occupation seems to have started around 6180-5950 calBC and ended ca. 3400-3300 calBC. Nothing is known concerning the vegetation and fauna of the earliest levels, but the presence of grindstones and pestles indicate the use of organic material. During the Late Neolithic period (ca. 5970-5780 calBC) the settlement was already fortified, but its economy does not show any trace of animal domestication. No plant remains were found. The Early Chalcolithic settlement (fourth millennium BC) formed by houses provided with internal buttresses, was destroyed by fire. The village that succeeded it in Late Chalcolithic times was again destroyed by fire, despite the fact that towards the end of its existence it had been fortified. During this phase, there is still no trace of animal domestication, but plant remains provide evidence of the cultivation of emmer, wheat and pulses. The mound was occupied a last time during the Early Bronze Age 1 and 2 periods (ca. 3000-2300/2200 calBC). The stratigraphy of this period was much disturbed, but the faunal remains still show no signs of domesticated species (Duru 1994, 1996).

The next site chronologically speaking near the edge of the badlands can be found at Çığırtkankaya Tepesi, a natural limestone hill, ca. 12 km to the southwest of Burdur and 1 km to the north of Kuruçay (Fig. 140; 37°39,331'N; 30°10,041' E; altitude: 1055 m a.s.l.). The hill rises ca. 147 m above the Burdur plain and is rather isolated from possible farming land and even from a water source. The limestone hilltop overlooks the marl badlands to the east. The site seems to have been selected because of its strategic position. In fact it offers an excellent view over the lake and the plain to the south (with a view over the prehistoric settlements at Kuruçay and Hacılar), west and north (Fig. 172), and at the same time it seems to control the green valley of the Büğdüz Çayı to the northeast, which emerges here in the plain of Lake Burdur after having crossed the badlands (Fig. 173). The site contains some sherds at the surface. Most of them are prehistoric and were dated by Özsait to the Early Chalcolithic period (Özsait 1976-77: 77-78; Özsait 1991: 62-63). Our survey team also sampled some Imperial Sagalassos red slip wares and some late Roman coarse wares (SA 96 S 67). Most probably, the site, which is located near the entrance of the most natural connection between the farm lands in the plain of Burdur and the limestone area (including Sagalassos) further east, formed by the valley of the Büğdüz Çayı, was mainly, if not exclusively, a strategic site of the early Chalcolithic period, a period when all the neighbouring sites (Hacılar, Kurucay) seem to have been fortified. It may have regained a similar strategic importance during the late Roman period, when a second strategic settlement with no obvious possibilities for agriculture arose on the Ilyas Tepesi, in the middle of the badlands (see 6.2 above).

Fig. 163: Funerary altar from Pazar Tepesi at Karacaören.

Fig. 164: One of the counterweights for oil-presses at Pazar Tepesi.

Fig. 165: The Ilyas Tepesi seen from the north.

Fig. 166: View from Ilyas Tepesi towards the south.

Fig. 167: View from Ilyas Tepesi towards the Phrygian Pisidian border.

Fig. 168: View of the remains at Ilyas Tepesi.

Fig. 169: The deeply sunk Büğdüz valley near old Büğdüz.

Fig. 170: View of the site of Göbecik Tepesi.

Fig. 171: The excavated part of Kuruçay Höyük.

Fig. 172: View from Çığırtkankaya Tepesi towards the west.

Fig. 173: View from Çığırtkankaya Tepesi over the meandering Büğdüz Çayı.

Fig. 174: View from Ören Yeri towards the village of Suludere and the Büğdüz Çayı.

Fig. 171: The excavated part of Kuruçay Höyük.

Fig. 172: View from Çığırtkankaya Tepesi towards the west.

Fig. 173: View from Çığırtkankaya Tepesi over the meandering Büğdüz Çayı.

Fig. 174: View from Ören Yeri towards the village of Suludere and the Büğdüz Çayı.

At the latest from the late Hellenistic period, a real settlement developed a little further east (37°39,353' N; 30°10,602' E; altitude: 990 m a.s.l.). This site called Ören Yeri ('ruins') is located ca. 400 m to the northwest of the village of Suludere on a south-southwest facing slope above the Bügdüz Çayı (Figs 140, 174-175). This site again occupies a strategic position and overlooks the badlands to the south, west and east, and Lake Burdur and the homonymous plain to the north. There is a spring at Suludere and the distance to arable fields (wheat, barley, tomatoes, grapes) is only 300 m. Along the river, the possibilities for farming are more restricted although there are some fruit trees (apple, prune, cherries, morello cherries, oranges and walnuts). The site occupies an area of ca. 60 by 150 m. It shows some traces of rubble walls, but supposedly some worked blocks also had been recently found and removed to build a school at Suludere. As the walls of this last are all plastered over, nothing can any longer be distinguished. Today, some tiles are visible at the surface of Ören Yeri, together with lots of pottery. The latter (SA 96 S 68) includes both late Hellenistic sherds and early Imperial Sagalassos red slip and coarse wares. This indicate a rather short occupation period.

Suludere itself contains a limestone architrave (pres.l.: 0.80 m; h.: 0.50 m; w.: 0.42 m) with a much weathered funeral inscription of Imperial date (Fig. 176), but its provenance is unknown.

Close to it, there is the counterweight of a lever-and-weight olive-press (h.: 0.63 m; l.: 0.75 m) which indicates the presence of olive groves in antiquity (Fig. 177). A similar weight was also found between Yassigüme and Kale (see below).

Since no middle or late Imperial pottery was found, it is possible that the settlement of Ören Yeri later moved further west, closer to better arable land, perhaps because of changing environmental conditions. Another site could be identified at Eski Mezarlık (the 'old graveyard'), located to the west of Suludere and to the left of the road to Burdur, in the middle of a chickpea and bean field (Figs 140, 178). The site (37°39,819' N; 30°10,062' E; altitude: 930 m a.s.l.) which is also close to Çıgırtkankaya Tepesi, contains at the surface only a very little pottery (SA 96 S 69) which could be identified however as late Imperial Sagalassos red slip ware. A small votive altar (Fig. 179), now kept in the house of Hasan Aldemir at Suludere (h.: 0.54 m; w.: 0.19 to 0.25 m), also came from here. On top, it has a patera between small acroteria. The front is decorated with a (female?) bust and carries a long votive inscription asking Demeter for a good harvest. On the left, a wreath with pendent ribbons has been carved, and on the right side there are three ears of corn (Figs 180-181). The site may have housed an estate or a small sanctuary. The cult of Demeter seems to have been popular in Northwest-Pisidia. One of the house walls of Ağlasun contains an unpublished altar for the goddess. In the district around Tefenni, to the southwest of the plain of Burdur, there are various traces of her cult (Ramsay 1887: 363; Ramsay 1895: 293, 305 nos 101-102). The nearby village of Çendik seems to be completely modern and does not contain any antiquities.

Another pre-Roman site, again with a strategic purpose, can be found in the southern part of the district under discussion here. It is located 700 m to the south and 150 m above the village of Hacılar (Fig. 182), at a place called Tekke (37°34,529' N; 30°05,668' E; altitude: 1167 m). The site can be reached through a deeply eroded intermittent riverbed in the badlands. The latter cuts through unfolded neogene marl deposits, surrounding a limestone spur. The spur can now be climbed from the south through a rock crevice (Fig. 183) and shows all over its surface traces of building activity, mostly now heaps of rubble stones (Fig. 184).

The site was described by Bean in 1959 (Bean 1959: 104-105). He noticed on the actual summit a few rather rough rock-cuttings, but just below the summit, guarding the approach, a tower of ashlar masonry "10 m square". Its real dimensions are 6.30 by 5.80 m (Fig. 185). The walls still stand 1.70 m high, much less than the height of 2.50 m recorded by Bean. The lower rows of stones are partly worked, partly rough. Bean measured one block of 2.20 by 0.75 by 1.03 m.

On the south side, close to the main road, Bean also discovered two rock-cut sarcophagi and the rock-cut base of another one. Today, more remains can be seen. The site seems to have had a rock-cut approach on the north side (Fig. 186). In the centre of the spur there are two circular rock-cut cisterns. Ca. 56 m to the north of the tower there are two rectangular constructions next to one another. The eastern one (3.60 by 4.30 m) is made of rough blocks (Fig. 187) in assembled dry masonry (h.: 0.70 m). The western one (6 by 6.50 m) is made of dry rubble walls (h.: 0.60 m).

Bean noted that around the tower and all over the slopes, almost to the bottom of the hill, there were great quantities of sherds, some of which were probably of Hellenistic date. The sherds that we sampled in 1996 (SA 96 S 62) were all coarse wares, certainly not of Imperial, but probably of Hellenistic date. Bean's assumption therefore that this is a small fortified site, "probably a permanent garrison", seems to be correct. Most probably it was part of the Hellenistic or even older defence system protecting the boundaries of Sagalassian territory. As we have said above, the site can be seen from the fortlet on the Kale Tepe near Kökez, from where signals could be transmitted to Kale near Akyayla and thence to Sagalassos itself. Moreover, Tekke seems to have overlooked the western extremity of the city's estates and guarded two southern approaches to it. One of these arrived from Yarışlı, from where M. Aquillius' road entered the plain of Burdur, and one came through the Lysis river valley with its *Via Sebaste*. The site thus formed a nice counterpart to the lookout above Günalan/Lengüme that overlooked the northern approaches to the lake (Waelkens *et al.* 1997a: 97 figs 107-108). The location is clearly strategic. To the north, the view covers the shores of Lake Burdur and the territories of the neighbouring cities of Lysinia and Baris on the other side of the lake (Fig. 188) and reaches as far as Yassıgüme to the northeast. To the west, the plain to the south of the lake is within full view (Fig. 189). To the southwest (Fig. 190), one can see the connection with the Yarışlı basin. In the south, the entrance of the Burdur plain near Karaçal is very close. Beyond it, there is a magnificent view of the whole plain of the Lysis river (Fig. 191). The view is only obstructed to the east by higher hills and mountains, but in that direction the fortlet on the Kale Tepe near Kökez remains visible.

A northwest slope with terraces and colluvial fans at the border of the badlands separates Tekke from the village of Yassıgüme, a few kilometers to the northeast (37°35,937' N; 30°07,597' E; altitude: 979 m a.s.l.).The present village of Yassıgüme, located again on a limestone outcrop at the edge of the marl area, was built here in 1983-1984. The oldest village with that name was located at a lower level, in the contact zone between the limestone and the badlands. In 1971, it was destroyed by the same earthquake that struck the villages of Kuruçay to the north and old Büğdüz further east. After this catastrophe a new village was built on a gravel deposit higher op the slopes towards the badlands. It was eventually abandoned because of its unfavourable location (too far away from the present asphalt road) and rebuilt at the present spot.

The village that was destroyed in 1971 (Fig. 192), still contains some antiquities in its ruined buildings. One of the oldest ones is a frieze block in the garden of the old 'muhtarlık' (pres.l.: 1.54 m; w.: 0.64 m; h.: 0.57 m). The frieze is broken on the left and has an upper moulding running along all other sides. The small right side is decorated with a shield in front of a sword (Fig. 193). The front carries a fruit garland with hanging ribbons that is suspended from two very weathered heads, the right one of which is a Medusa head (Fig. 194). An epitaph of three lines has been carved on the upper moulding, above and below the garland. It refers in nicely cut characters to a couple and their children. The monument seems to belong to the first – second century AD and perhaps crowned a pair of funerary columns.

A fluted column of this type (pres.h.: 0.90 m; diam.: 0.61 m) with a weathered *tabula ansata*, can be found in the garden of the old 'konak'. Another fluted column fragment (pres.h.: 0.85 m; diam.: 0.61 m) is said to have been brought from a place called Çeşme Yakası, ca. 300 m to the east of Yassıgüme (37°35,937' N; 30°07,597' E; altitude: 979 m). This site is located on a west-facing slope and, according to the villagers, was a necropolis with stone-lined tombs, pottery and decorated stones. Today, the whole site has been destroyed by illegal digging and nothing can be seen on the spot, but the stones in the old village probably came from here. The site may have served as a necropolis for the settlement on the Kokar Pınarı hill, located in the plain of Lake Burdur, just below Yassıgüme (see Fig. 140). Another inscribed slab (h.: 1.05 m; w.: 0.50 m; th.: 0.50 m), apparently re-used several times, since it has two successive lifting holes, can be seen in the garden of the old mosque and may have come from the same necropolis (Fig. 195).

The provenance of the most elaborately worked stone at old Yassıgüme can no longer be established, but it may have come from the Kale (see below) where there are traces of a Byzantine settlement. This stone, broken in two pieces (h.: 0.25 m; pres.l.: 0.82 m and 0.96 m; w.: 0.58 m), can be found inside the old wash-place of the village. It is part of the decoration of a Byzantine church (Figs 196-197).

The site of Kale is located at 1 km to the northeast of Yassıgüme (37°36,217' N; 30°07,915' E; altitude: 1075 m a.s.l.). It occupies a limestone outcrop in the marl badlands that is very steep on all sides, except for the northeast side (Figs 140, 198). The top is supposed to carry a tower that can no longer be reached. The slopes below it are covered with rubble stones, with a few tiles and with pottery. The sherds include Imperial Sagalassos red slip wares, Late Imperial and Byzantine coarse wares, and even some Ottoman sherds (SA 96 S 69). The hill seems to have been occupied by a small settlement from Roman Imperial to Byzantine times, and perhaps even as late as the Ottoman period. Whether the tower also played a role in the older defence systems of Sagalassos remains uncertain. The site affords a good view over the plain (Fig. 199) and can itself also be seen from Kale near Hacılar and from Kale near Soğanlı.

A counterweight for an olive press halfway between Yassıgüme and Kale provides evidence for the presence of olive groves in the area in antiquity (Fig. 200). The village of Akyaka, between Yassıgüme and Kuruçay, does not contain any antiquities and seems to be a completely modern settlement.

7. THE PLAIN OF LAKE BURDUR

The third and westernmost subdivision of the western part of the territory of Hellenistic and Roman Sagalassos is the plain around Lake Burdur (854 m a.s.l.), nearly 80% of

Fig. 175: The valley of the Büğdüz Çayı between Suludere and the plain of Burdur.

Fig. 176: Architrave from a funeral monument at Suludere.

Fig. 177: Counterweight for an olive press at Suludere.

Fig. 178: View of the site of Eski Mezarlık near Suludere.

Fig. 179: Altar to Demeter at Suludere from Eski Mezarlık.

Fig. 180: Left side of the same altar.

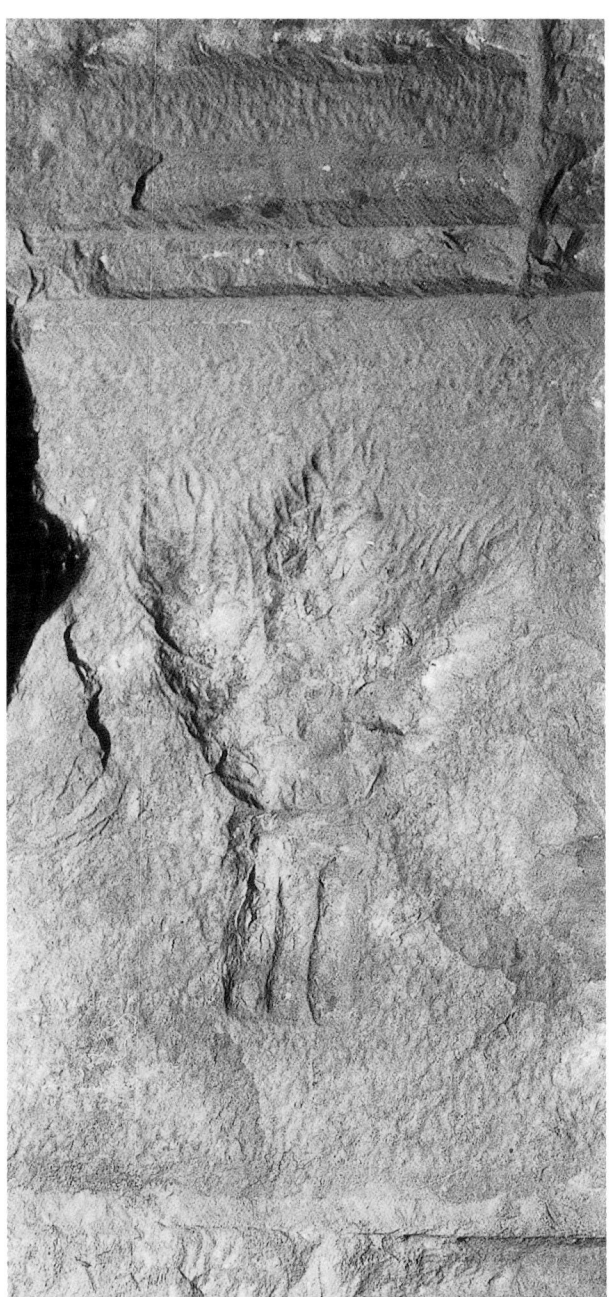

Fig. 181: Right side of the same altar.

Fig. 182: View of the spur with the watchtower of Tekke, seen from Hacılar.

Fig. 183: Rock crevice giving access to the fortress of Tekke from the south.

Fig. 184: View of the rubble walls of Tekke.

Fig. 185: The watchtower of Tekke.

Fig. 186: The rock-cut northern entrance.

Fig. 187: One of the buildings on the northern part of spur.

Fig. 188: View from Tekke towards the northwest (Lake Burdur in the background).

Fig. 189: View from Tekke towards the west.

Fig. 190: View from Tekke towards the southwest, with the entrance to the Yarışlı basin in the background.

Fig. 191: View from Tekke towards the Lysis plain.

Fig. 192: The ruins of old Yassıgüme destroyed by an earthquake in 1971.

Fig. 193: Side of the frieze slab from a funerary monument.

Fig. 194: Front of the same frieze.

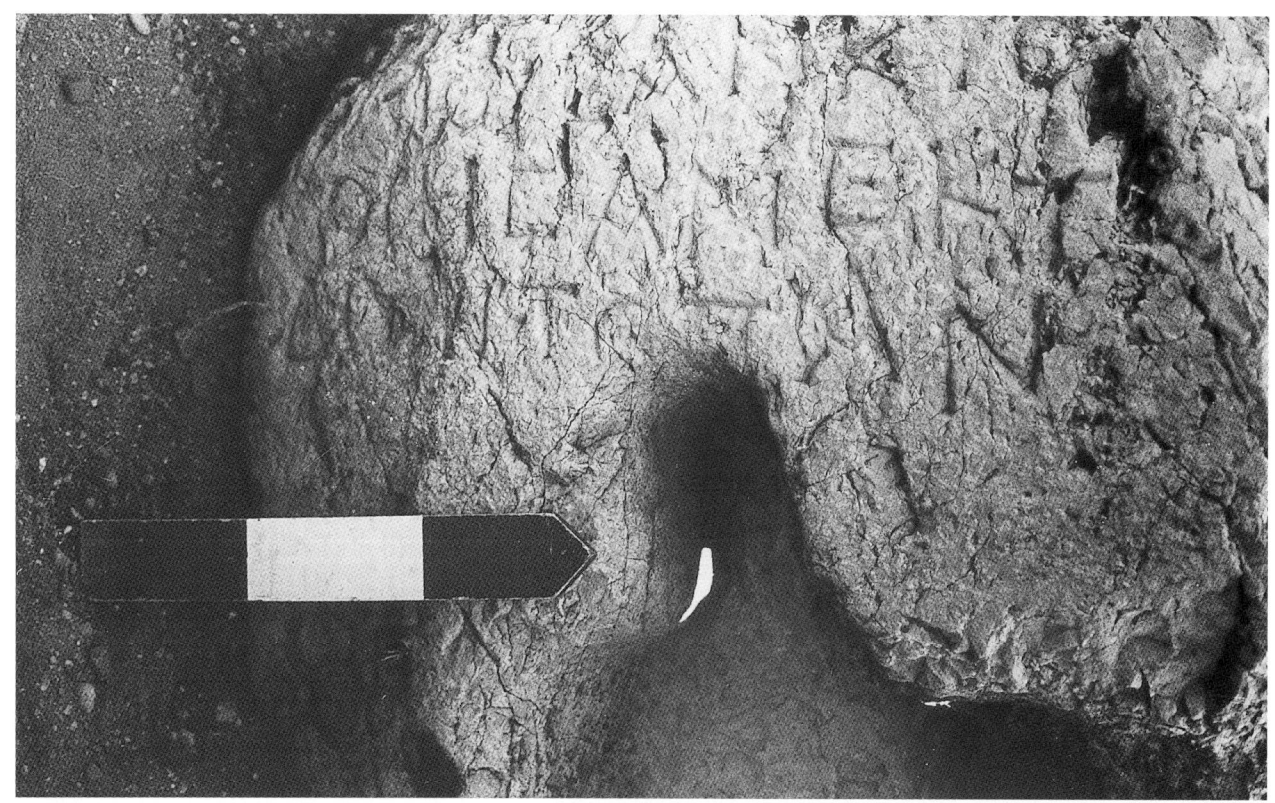

Fig. 195: Inscribed stone at Yassıgüme.

Fig. 196: Decorated part of a Byzantine church at Yassıgüme.

Fig. 197: Second part of the same architectural element.

Fig. 198: View of the site of Kale near Yassıgüme.

Fig. 199: View from the Kale site near Yassıgüme towards the plain of Burdur.

Fig. 200: Counterweight for an olive press from between Yassıgüme and Kale.

Fig. 201: The present location of the site of Hacılar I.

Fig. 197: Second part of the same architectural element.

Fig. 198: View of the site of Kale near Yassıgüme.

Fig. 199: View from the Kale site near Yassıgüme towards the plain of Burdur.

Fig. 200: Counterweight for an olive press from between Yassıgüme and Kale.

Fig. 201: The present location of the site of Hacılar I.

which is taken up by the water of the lake. Towards the badlands the plain rises to nearly 950 m a.s.l. This plain, in which Lake Burdur formed, is probably part of a 'graben' structure between two southwest-northeast running faults. In 1971 an earthquake struck the area, destroying several villages in and around the plain (Kuruçay, Yassıgüme, Yarı, Yazı). Ruins of these villages can still be seen at various spots.

In this tectonic basin, characterised by neogene deposits within the limestone mountains, one can distinguish two main morphological units: first of all, towards the southeast, the Burdur badlands (see 6 above) which are eroded marl deposits, and secondly, the plain of Lake Burdur, which encompasses the low, mostly flat areas ending in the lake. The Burdur badlands and the plain of Lake Burdur are separated from one another by a prominent scarp. Most of the ancient settlements and modern villages are situated at the foot of this scarp and near the mouth of the most important badland rivers (Fig. 140). In any case, the border of the plain seems to have been the preferred location. For the prehistoric period, this could reflect the fact that at that time the lake covered a much larger surface. There are several publications on the fluctuations of Lake Burdur during the Quaternary. For the most recent summary, one can refer to Erol (1997). The dating of the former lake levels is still largely based on radiocarbon dating of shells (Kis *et al.* 1989).

Another possible argument for the above mentioned settlement distribution, that in these locations there was apparently a good potential water supply is only clear for the sites near Suludere, but it is currently uncertain for most other locations. Today, the rivers coming from the badlands are not permanent and most of the time the water is scarcely usable because of its high concentration of sediment. Nowadays, hardly any sources can be found near the border of the plain. Along the eastern edge of the plain three limestone rocks (near Hacılar, Yassıgüme and Suludere) rise high above the surrounding badlands. As we have said above (see 6.3) all three seem to have had a strategic role.

In antiquity, the whole of the plain of Lake Burdur did not belong to Sagalassos. In the northeast, the border with the territory of the Roman colony of Baris (located at Fari near Kılıç) and/or with an Imperial estate, which together occupied the northern extremity of the plain, may have corresponded with a small limestone promontory running towards the lake, immediately to the north of the village of Gökçebağ (Waelkens *et al.* 1997a: 97). Near it, at Baladız, a boundary stone indicating the limits of an imperial estate was copied by Ramsay (1895: I, 346 no. 164; *CIL III*, 6682). The northwestern shores of the lake must have been divided between the city of Lysinia, located on a rocky hill named Üveyik Burnu ca. 3 km to the north of Karakent (Bean 1959: 78) in the west, and a second still unidentified city site located on a low hill 4 km to the east of Ilyas (Collignon 1879: 371; Duchesne 1879: 482; Bean 1959: 81-82) in the east. It is unlikely that Sagalassos had a common boundary with Lysinia, at least during the Roman Imperial period, since there seems then to have been an imperial estate with the village of Tymbrianassos in between (see below).

In contrast with the other two areas described above (5 and 6), there are no restrictions for the development of communication systems in the southern part of the Burdur basin (see 3). It is here that the so called *via Sebaste* crossed the territory of Sagalassos. The route of this once very important road can perhaps still be seen in the current road system called the 'Deve yolu'. Evidence for the existence of other roads can also be derived from the current road system and its relation to certain sites. For example, we can postulate a southwest–northeast communication route (called the 'Sultan yolu' on the topographical maps) coming from Yarışlı and reaching the badlands near Suludere (Fig. 4). As we have said above (3), the road probably continued over Burdur towards the north, but another branch must have run through the Büğdüz Çayı valley towards Sagalassos. As far as we could see this route does not seem to have been paved in antiquity, unless colluvial deposits are hiding this from view. In 1996, a border stone was found, perhaps still *in situ* along this road. Further east, near its crossing with the Deve Yolu, the site of Kilise Mevkii near Yarıköy occupied a significant location where the Sultan Yolu road crossed the river Boz Çayı (Lysis) and the *via Sebaste* (see below).

A third route, again coming from Yarışlı, followed the southern edges of the plain of Lake Burdur, immediately south of Düger, towards Karaçal. According to D. French (personal communication to be published shortly), some paved stretches of it, are still visible. This road corresponds with the Roman republican road built by M.Aquillius.

In the part of the plain of Lake Burdur that is located to the south of the lake, the northwestern boundary of Sagalassian territory, which will be discussed below, must have run in a north–south direction along the *via Sebaste* as far as its junction with the Sultan Yolu, and then have turned west along the latter as far as the small pass between the hills which separate the Burdur basin from that of Lake Yarışlı. In fact, the crest of those hills (Kara Tepe: 1205 m a.s.l.; Devedüsen Tepesi: 1274 m a.s.l.; Akalan Tepesi: 1148 m a.s.l.; Kireçocağı Tepesi: 1332 m a.s.l.; Burgulutaş Tepesi: 1196 m a.s.l.) must have formed the southern boundary of the city's possessions, only interrupted by this pass in the southwest and by the Lysis river near Karaçal in the southeast. Further east, as already suggested above, the boundary probably continued over the crest of the limestone hills to the southeast of Karaçal (Sarıyer Tepesi: 1326 m a.s.l.; Savuran Tepesi: 1248 m a.s.l.) and then along the edge of the scarp which separates the badlands from the fertile Lysis valley, until it eventually reached the western slopes of the Kestel range.

The limestone district to the east of the city of Burdur has already been described in the previous *Sagalassos* volume, so that in 1996 the survey team could concentrate on the southern part of the basin, starting from Burdur.

This part of the plain is also called the plain of Düğer, after the most important settlement near its southern extremity. The plain is rectangular in shape with a northeast–southwest orientated long axis of about 10 km and forms a natural prolongation of Lake Burdur. It is 7.5 km wide, roughly the same as the lake. The Düğer plain slopes from an altitude of about 930 m a.s.l. in the southwest to an altitude of 855 m a.s.l. near the lake shore in the northeast. The altitude of 930 m a.s.l. in the southwest part of the plain forms the actual 3 km wide divide between the hydrological basin of Lake Burdur (854 m a.s.l.) and that of Lake Yarışlı, a salt lake at an estimated altitude of 900 m a.s.l., just 2 km to the southwest of Düğer (see below).

The Düğer plain has a complex morphology and has undergone a complex development through time, neither of which has yet been studied. Apart from lake sediments, huge amounts of sediment in the Düğer plain have a fluvial origin and were deposited as fans or lacustrine deltas at the mouth of the tributary rivers, coming mainly from the Burdur badlands, but also from the limestone mountains. The complexity of such an evolution is illustrated in a paper by Kazancı and Erol (1987). Alluvial fans are still visible in the local morphology. There is, for example, the huge fan of the Buğdüz Çayı near Suludere, the fan of the Bodarmir Deresi to the south of Akyala and of the Boz Çayı (ancient Lysis) to the north of Karaçal. These fans do not coalesce but leave lower lying areas in-between. Fan-building from the badland rivers still continues today. This can be seen from the formation of small fans in Lake Burdur and from the huge amounts of sediment carried towards the plain, as was observed, for example, during a thunderstorm on 19 June 1996.

The plain of Düğer is crossed by the Boz Çayı or ancient Lysis river in the eastern, and by the Düğer Çayı or Özdere, a small stream coming from Düğer, in the western half of it (Fig. 140).

After the Epipalaeolithic sites located in the eastern part of the territory of Sagalassos (Waelkens *et al.* 1997a: Dereköy, Sandalion; Vermeersch *et al.* 2000), the Düğer plain was the first part of later Sagalassian territory to be occupied and the first to attract permanent settlers during the eighth millennium BC.

This was in the southeastern part of the plain near the present village of Hacılar, ca. 26 km to the southwest of Burdur. At 1.5 km to the southwest of that village, Mellaart in the 1950s discovered the world famous site of Hacılar I, now buried 3.50 m below the surface of the plain (Fig. 140). The site (37°34,638' N; 30°04,844' E) of Hacılar I, locally known as Kerit Mevkii, which is today, at 960 m, more than a hundred meters above the level of the lake, is completely cultivated (wheat, barley, beets, maize, onions, beans, chickpeas). Here the valley slopes very gently towards the west (Fig. 201). Today, the fields above Hacılar I rise only 1 to 2 m above the surroundings. There is still a lot of ceramics and flints to be seen at the surface (Fig. 202). In 1957-1960, the site was excavated by Mellaart. Originally, it seems to have been situated behind an embankment formed by the periodic overflow of the Boz Çayı which passes ca. 1 km to the northwest of it. Mellaart distinguished seven aceramic Early Neolithic phases, which could be dated to ca. 7920-7550 calBC. At that time, the settlement was already a well developed village, built on virgin soil. In 1985-86, however, a sondage by Duru produced some pottery on what was supposedly an aceramic floor level. For animal protein, the inhabitants seem to have been dependent on hunting, although they already had domesticated dogs. On their fields, however, they cultivated lentils, emmer and various types of barley. Some of these crops could have been local, others were certainly imported. There is a thousand year gap between this settlement and the Late Neolithic village which developed above it ca. 6550-6040 calBC. The settlement of phase VI is the most evident, whose inhabitants produced a nice, mostly monochrome, burnished pottery. For their subsistence, they were still largely dependent on hunting (possibly with domesticated cattle) and on collecting wild cereals (einkorn), although most of their cereal or plant protein intake came from domesticated plants (15% pulses such as bitter vetch, 40% wheat and 45% barley). This village was succeeded by an Early Chalcolithic settlement that was already fortified in its first phase, ca. 6170-5850 calBC, when it produced a beautiful painted pottery that is almost unparalleled during that period. In its second phase (ca. 5950-5710 calBC) it seems to have become the fortified residence of a ruler. That is also the time when the Çığırtkankaya Tepesi was used for a site with a probably strategic function and when Kuruçay was fortified. During this period, the inhabitants of Hacılar already practice irrigation farming and produced various types of grain and pulses. The only domesticated animal that we can be certain of, however, was the dog (Mellaart 1970).

During the Late Chalcolithic period, another settlement developed ca. 800 m to the west of the modern village of Hacılar, at a place known as Öz Mevkii (37°35' N; 30°

Fig. 202: View from the site of Hacılar I towards the northwest.

Fig. 203: The small hüyük occupying the site of Hacılar II.

Fig . 204: View of Karaçal Höyük (arrow), seen from the north. The Boz Çayı (Lysis r.) valley in the background.

05,107' E; altitude: 960 m a.s.l.). The site known as Hacılar II forms a small höyük (Fig. 203), slightly raised above the plain, which is here cultivated with wheat and chickpeas. There is no water on or near the site proper, but there is a good spring at the entrance of Hacılar (Özpınar Çeşmesi). The site was never excavated but, according to the surface finds (Lloyd and Mellaart 1962: 70 map 1; Birmingham 1964: 29), it was occupied from the Late Chalcolithic to the end of the Bronze Age 2 period (ca. 4500-300/2200 BC). It may have been the successor of the more famous older site. Today, there are still flints and prehistoric sherds to be found at the surface, but our survey team also sampled Imperial Sagalassos red slip wares and even some Ottoman sherds on the spot (SA 96 S 58). It is possible, therefore, that there was a smaller farming site at Hacılar II during Imperial times. The small funerary altar which Ramsay and Smith copied in a fountain in the modern village (Smith 1887; 259 no. 46), as well as a second third century AD altar discovered by Sterret in the local cemetery (Sterrett 1888: 115 no. 85), may both have belonged to it.

A contemporary Late Chalcolithic settlement can be found near the southern extremity of the plain, ca. 1 km to the north-northwest of Karaçal and a bit further to the southwest of Hacılar I (Fig. 140).

The höyük (Karaçal Höyük; 37°34,070' N; 30°03,824' E; altitude: 960 m a.s.l.) rises as a low hill above the plain (Fig. 204) to the north of the Boz Çayı which forces its way through the limestone hills to the south. The site affords a good view of the surrounding plain in all directions (Fig. 205). The lower lying slopes towards the Boz Çayı are clearly more fertile and are cultivated with wheat. The higher slopes are covered with the more drought resistant chickpeas. The höyük has a spring both to the north (now dried up) and to the east. Today, the site is rather removed from the most fertile part of the valley, but still close enough for part of it to be cultivated. The surface is littered with pottery (SA 96 S 62), mostly handmade coarse wares, which have been dated in the past to the Late Chalcolithic and Early Bronze Age 2 period (Lloyd and Mellaart 1962: 70 map 1; 196 map VI). One of the older villagers of Karaçal mentioned that in the past an ashlar building had been dismantled in the nearby fields. He also said that he had seen, ca. 45 years ago, an ancient road covered with large slabs, coming from the north, which must have been a well preserved stretch of the via Sebaste.

The höyük does not show any traces of later occupation and may have gone under during the general destruction that struck western Anatolia and our district at the end of EBA2. There is however a more recent site on a north-facing slope 1 km to the south-southwest of Karaçal. Here, the limestone hills which border the southern boundary of Sagalassian held territory (Kireçocağı Tepesi: 1332 m a.s.l. and Burgulutaş Tepesi: 1196 m a.s.l.) form a kind of promontory to the north, known as Kozaklı Tepe (1092 m a.s.l.). Its northern slope is locally known as Kozaklı Mevkii (Fig. 140). At a spot, where supposedly ashes, burnt loam and pottery were found, only a few sherds could be seen at the surface, and none in an exposed profile (37° 32,915' N; 30° 03,266' E; altitude: 1000 m a.s.l.). Lower down the same slope however (37°33,233' N; 30°03,726' E; altitude: 980 m a.s.l.), in the direction of Karaçal and near the Yeni Çeşme ('new spring'), some tiles and pottery fragments were found (SA 96 S 57) in the middle of wheat fields (Fig. 206). This may include pre- or protohistorical material, as well as possibly Hellenistic coarse wares. Most of it however, could be identified as Imperial common wares and late Imperial Sagalassos red slip wares. We can assume that a small pre- or protohistoric, and later a (Hellenistic?-late) Imperial farming site (?) existed here.

A third late Chalcolithic site is now covered by the provincial capital of Burdur, on the east shores of Lake Burdur. In the northern part of the city, near the railway station, there was a höyük, Istasyon Höyük, where Mellaart and Özsait discovered pottery dated to the Late Chalcolithic, and Early Bronze Age 1-2 periods (Mellaart 1954: 223 nr. 220, 229 no. 232; Lloyd and Mellaart 1962: 70 map I, 133 map III and 196 map VI; Özsait 1989: 10, pl. XI.1-11). This may represent a farming site, close to the lake shore. This site may have been re-occupied at the latest in Augustan times, since in the early 1970s, the famous edict of the emperor Tiberius' *legatus pro praetore*, Sextus Sotidius Strabo Libuscidianus, written ca. AD 13-15, concerning the organisation of requisitioned transport through the territory of Sagalassos (Mitchell 1976; French and Mitchell 1977: 216-218) was discovered *in situ* here. As we have said above (see 3), this must have had the purpose of regulating the traffic along the southeastern shores of the lake. Some scholars assumed that Burdur was a Turkish foundation and not an ancient site (Duchesne and Collignon 1877: 371; Collignon 1879: 333). Most however attempted to find an ancient name for it. These attempts have been discussed by Bean (1859: 78) who rightly rejected such identifications as Dyrzela, Darsa, Limobrama, Limobria (Ramsay) and Baris (Radet).

According to Bean, if it ever was an ancient site, Burdur can hardly have been more than a deme of Sagalassos. He did not exclude the possibility that the older version of the name, i.e. Buldur, might have been derived from the Greek name which the city has on a 1919 map, that is, Polydorion. This last name was also suggested (by Cl. Huart?) as a former name for Burdur in an old Islamic encyclopedia (Honigmann 1939: 654-655) and in a Greek encyclopedia dated to the year 1931 (Andriotis 1931). The latter mentioned also the name Limnórrroia as the ancient predecessor of Burdur. Honigmann was rightly very skeptical about these identifications for which there was no evidence. Instead, he proposed to identify Burdur with the Praetoria, mentioned in this area, in early fifteenth century AD annotations to Ptolemaios' *Geographia* (Honigmann 1939: 654) and Mitchell also adopted this identification (Mitchell 1976: 116 note 46). The name might suggest a former strategic role, which is understandable since Burdur is located in the narrowest part of the valley to the southeast of the lake, but at the mouth of an important affluent that gives access to the east (Fig. 6). The modern road to Antalya follows this valley.

During the Early Bronze Age I and/or II period some of the older sites continued to exist (Hacılar II, Karaçal Höyük, Burdur Istasyon Höyük), while other new sites apparently had their origin in this period.

Among them is the site of Kokar Pınar near Yassıgüme (Fig. 140). The site rises as a 10 m high hill above the plain (Fig. 207), some 700 m to the north-northeast of the modern village (37°36,386' N; 30°07,650' E; altitude: 925 m a.s.l.). It is surrounded by wheat fields and separated from the badlands to the east and north of it (with the site of Kuruçay here). The site has a good spring, which gave its name to it, immediately to the southeast of the hill. The hill is covered with lots of pottery, indicating a fairly important farming settlement. The pottery was dated to the Early Bronze Age by Özsait (1976-77: 73 note 10), but in 1996 our survey team also sampled late Roman coarse and Sagalassos red slip wares (SA 96 S 64). As we have said above, the site of Çeşme Yakası, located on the badlands ca. 300 m to the east of Yassıgüme, possibly served as a necropolis for this Roman settlement.

A last Early Bronze Age site occurs in the northwestern part of the plain of Düğer, already to the west of the western boundary of Sagalassos' territory in Imperial times (see below). The site, known as Gâvur Evi Tepesi ('the hill with the heathen house'), is located ca. 2 km to the west of the village of Yarıköy (37°37,476' N; 30°02,496' E; altitude: 918 m a.s.l.). It rises as a hill ca. 15 m above the fields (Fig. 208) and is located near the end of a southeast projecting promontory of the limestone hills which border the plain towards the west (Göbekli Tepe: 1194 m a.s.l.; Erenler Tepesi; Kirişli Tepe: 1281 m a.s.l.), a little to the southeast of the Soğanlı Mahalle. Immediately to the north of it, there is a spring (Eski Soğanlı Çeşmesi), while the Düğer Çayı flows at a small distance to the southeast. The southern shore of the lake is ca. 3 km to the northeast of the site. Mellaart collected Early Bronze Age 2-3 sherds which give evidence of the existence of a settlement during that period (Lloyd and Mellaart 1962: 196 map VI; 252 map VIII). Even today, protohistoric sherds and flints can be observed at the surface. Most of the surface sherds (SA 96 S 39), however, derive from an occupation of the hill during Hellenistic, Imperial and Ottoman times. In the southeastern part of the site are the remains of a probably Hellenistic (or even older) wall in dry masonry (Fig. 209), perhaps part of a defence system, as well as a building in Roman concrete (Figs 210-211), the walls of which still stand 1.30 m high. Besides housing a farming settlement, the site may also have had a strategic function since it is located near the place where the road system along the northern shore of Lake Burdur must have entered the plain to the south of it. The hill offers an excellent view in all directions (Fig. 212). The fortification was certainly not a part of the Hellenistic defence system protecting the boundaries of Sagalassian territory, since it is to the west of the city's territorial limits (see below). Its location in the middle of the plain is rather reminiscent of the situation of the Attalid fortlet at Örentepe near Panemoteichos and the fortlet near Insuyu on Sagalassian territory (Waelkens et al. 1997a: 78-82). As we have said, the Attalid letter to Olbasa suggests the presence of Attalid garrisons in Northern Pisidia, guarding, *inter alia*, important road connections (Aydal et al. 1997). Others may have been established in the Lysis valley by the Seleucids (see below). Such a potentially strategic function is clear in the case of Gâvur Evi Tepesi, but it may also be the case with the Insuyu fortress. In fact, this last is located halfway along the secondary road connecting Sagalassos to the plain of Burdur, through the valley of the Buğdüz Çayı. It is possible, therefore, that Gâvur Evi Tepesi was perhaps also an (Attalid or Seleucid) garrison site.

To the northeast of the site a white limestone column drum lies in the fields. A gravel quarry to the west of the hill has exposed remains of broken pithoi (protohistoric graveyard?), and is said to have produced "gold coins". The quarrying possibly destroyed a necropolis at the site.

Another late Roman to early Byzantine necropolis is located ca. 1.7 km to the southwest of Yarı, at a place called Kilise Mevkii (37° 36,812' N; 30° 04,042' E; altitude: 895 m a.s.l.). The site is completely covered with wheat fields now (Fig. 213). It is located between the Düğer Çayı to the east and the crossing of the Sultan Yolu and the Deve Yolu (*via Sebaste?*) to the west. There is abundant water in the location. Over a large surface area, remains of rubble walls can be seen. According to the villagers, at least two 'houses' have been destroyed here by tractors. An old limestone doorpost is being used as the lid of a cistern. The fields and also some exposed profiles show lots of tile fragments, pottery and human bones. Some of the latter were found inside ceramic vessels, at least according to local farmers, although the currently visible terracotta fragments rather suggest tombs covered with large tiles. The pottery that we could sample (SA 96 S 38) is composed of late Imperial coarse wares. The site was probably a fairly large necropolis that belonged to the territory of Sagalassos. Since the

Fig. 205: The Düğer plain, seen from Karaçal Höyük.

Fig. 206: View from the site of Yeni Çeşme towards the Kozaklı Tepe.

Fig. 207: The site of Kokar Pınar near Yassıgüme.

Fig. 208: View of Gâvur Evi Tepesi from the south.

location is strategically very important (junction of two road systems) it is tempting to suggest that it may be the site of a late Roman control post. Some remains from this site, as well as milestones from the roads, may have been taken to Yarıköy.

The village of Yarıköy was completely destroyed by an earthquake in 1971 (Fig. 214). A worked stone (l.: 1.40 m; h.: 0.64 m; th.: 0.42 m) can still be seen in the old cemetery. Near the old mosque various remains have been assembled. Among them, there are a fluted (l.: 1.40 m; diam.: 0.50 m) and an unfinished column (l.: 1.70 m; diam.: 0.45 m above and 0.70 m below). Other remains include an ashlar block and a counterweight for an olive press (h.: 0.60 m; l.: 0.64 m; th.: 0.60 m), showing that in antiquity the plain may also have produced olives. In 1884, Ramsay and Smith copied the epitaph of Claudia Pelagia here, which also includes the name of her husband Kalliklès, son of Kalliklès (Ramsay 1895: 336 no. 169). In 1948, J. and L. Robert copied in this village two boundary stones, which unfortunately have never been published, separating the land holdings of Sagalassos and those of Tymbrianassos. They also found a dice oracle there (Robert 1960: 596; Mitchell 1976: 118).

Another important antiquity today is a milestone for the emperor Claudius II Gothicus, set up in AD 268-270, that was copied by French. It mentions "the venerable city of Sagalassos, first of Pisidia, friend and ally of the Romans" and thus confirmed that it once stood on Sagalassian territory (French 1988: 113 no. 299; 457). In 1884, Ramsay and Smith copied another milestone in the graveyard of the village. It dates to the years AD 198-209 (Smith 1887: 259 no. 48; Ramsay 1895: 331 no. 143; French 1988: 112 no. 297; 440). In 1974-1975, French copied four more milestones at or near the village, three of them without any visible inscription. The fourth one, near the northwest corner of the old mosque, could be dated to the year 6 BC and mentions the construction of the *via Sebaste* by Cornutus Aquila. It also records a distance of XXCIIX miles towards its *caput viae* (French 1980: 727 map 2 no. 4; French 1988: 112-113 nos. 298, 300-302). This very important milestone (h.: 1.07 m; diam.: 0.54 m) has been removed now to the new village of Yarıköy, where it stands in the middle of the local tea garden (Fig. 215).

A few kilometers to the northeast, the village of Yazıköy has also been completely rebuilt after the 1971 earthquake. Near the old mosque one can see a smooth column (l.: 1.72 m; diam.: 0.50 m), with a dedication to the emperors M. Aurelius and L. Verus by the city of Sagalassos (Fig. 216). It was copied in 1884 by Ramsay (Ramsay 1895: 336 no. 166; *IGR* III, 332). As Christol and Drew-Bear have already suggested, its shape and provenance identify it as a milestone/dedication that must have been part of a road repair during the first half of the year AD 165. In fact, a milestone with the name of the proconsul, D. Fonteius Fronto, dedicated to the same emperors, was discovered by French further south at the village of Boğaziçi in the Lysis valley (French 1988, 102 no. 268; 437). Christol and Drew-Bear rightly suggested that the first milestone may have originally stood at the spot where the *via Sebaste* entered the territory of Sagalassos (Christol and Drew-Bear 1991: 406-410).

In the same village, Ramsay also copied two sepulchral altars. One of them (vis. h.: 1.05; w.: 0.50 m; th.: 0.43 m), set up by Termilas, son of Krateros, for his wife (Ramsay 1895: 336 no. 169), can still be found in the old graveyard (Fig. 217). It is decorated with a standing couple on the left side. The second one was set up by Poplios, son of Seuthès, for his brother Krateros. Ramsay assumed that the Thracian name Seuthès, might indicate the presence of a settlement of Thracian mercenaries around Lake Burdur during the Pergamene period (Ramsay 1895: 336 no. 168). Recently, the presence of Thracian settlers in the Lysis valley, immediately south of the Düğer plain, perhaps established there by the Seleucids during the third century BC, has been proved by an inscription at Kozluca (see below). If Thracian settlers were ever settled in the area around Yazıköy as well, either by the Seleucids or by the Attalids, the strategic site of Gâvur Evi Tepesi, a few km to the west of the village, may have been a suitable candidate.

In the 1950s, Bean copied an inscribed sarcophagus lid for a certain Aur(elius) Moschos in the old graveyard of the village (Bean 1959, 105 no. 65). It corresponds perhaps with the two fragments of a sarcophagus lid (pres.l.: 1.02 m and 0.70 m; pres.h.: 0.65 m; pres.w.: 0.45 to 0.60 m), decorated with *tegulae*, that are lying in the cemetery (Fig. 218).

Other remains in the cemetery seem to belong to older grave types, of Hellenistic, or at the latest early Imperial date. To this category belong a fragment of an ostotheca decorated with a shield, and a phallus stone (pres.h.: 0.65 m; diam.: 0.37 to 0.45 m), a grave marker usually placed on top of gravemounds (Fig. 219). This stone was described already by Bean (1959: 105 Pl. XVIIIe). Another, albeit much more elegant phallus stone, was copied in not too far away Lysinias on the northern shore of Lake Burdur (Bean 1959: 80 pl. XV d), so that this type of grave may have been rather common in the area. Other remains in the old graveyard include two fluted (pres.l.: 1.30 m and 0.40 m; diam.: 0.45 and 0.47 m) and one smooth column (pres.l.: 0.69 m; diam.: 0.43 m) fragments. A square socle moulding perhaps identifies the latter as a milestone, but no inscription was visible on as much of the surface as could be seen (Fig. 220). Finally, here as well, a counterweight (h.: 0.31 m; l.: 0.69 m) for a simple lever-and-weight olive-press was found (Fig. 221).

The fact that some of the inscriptions in the graveyard had already been copied there in 1884 confirms the statement of the village's elders that they have always been there. No ancient sherds could be observed at or near Yazıköy, so that the stones must have been taken there from one of the sites in the Düğer plain. The older monuments could easily have come from Gâvur Evi Tepesi, where Hellenistic and even older pottery was observed. As the site was inhabited throughout Imperial times and even later, it is possible that some if not most of the other antiquities were taken from there as well. The fact, however, that these latter include an inscription erected by the city of Sagalassos whose territory certainly did not extend as far to the northwest (see below), indicates that the villagers also gathered stones from elsewhere. The Sagalassos inscription must have stood along the *via Sebaste*. Some stones may come from the large necropolis at Kilise Mevkii near its crossing with the Sultan Yolu and from the corresponding, not yet located, settlement.

There is another classical site in the northwestern part of the plain of Düğer. Its remains are scattered over the village of Aşağımüslimler (Fig. 222), which is located on the lower bare slopes of the limestone massif to the west of Lake Burdur (co-ordinates of the graves near the house: 37°36,970' N; 30°00,820' E; altitude 950 m). The site was visited by Bean who called it Örenler (i.e. 'ruins') and rightly identified it as the location of an extensive village site. At the time of his visit, over a distance of nearly a kilometer, the ground was covered with uncut building-stones and some ashlars (Bean 1959: 88). The modern village seems to occupy the spot of an ancient necropolis. Behind the house of Şaban Karabaş, there is a rock-cut sarcophagus (exterior dimensions: 2.03 by 0.96 m; interior dimensions: 1.67 by 0.68 m; depth: 0.51 m) for Doulion, son of Eutychos and his wife Zotikè (Fig. 223). To the east of it, there is a rock-cut structure, composed of a flight of rock-steps leading to a now empty platform, which may have borne a sarcophagus. The village contains another rock-cut sarcophagus and a few sarcophagus lids. All these remains were described by Bean, who also published Doulion's epitaph (1959: 88 no. 31).

Ca. 400 m to the south of the village, a valley that is cut out of the limestone massif has built a considerable fan towards the lowest part of the Düğer plain. The fact that the fans from the limestone massif slope more steeply than the fans from the badlands is related to the coarseness of the accumulated sediments. The sediments from the limestone massifs are much coarser, so that the soil on these fans includes very many rock fragments. The fields near the apex of the fan, at an altitude of about 937 m (co-ordinates: 37°36,846' N; 30°00,914' E), are littered with fieldstones and pottery, mainly Sagalassos red slip wares dated from the early to the late Imperial period (SA 96 S 25). This certainly fits in with the site of the village itself (Fig. 224), which is surrounded by a theatre-like rock, called Halı Kayası ('the rock of the rug'; altitude 1087 m a.s.l.). Bean was told that this hill carried a fort ('kale'), but he did not have time to visit it. In 1996, our local guide, who had also taken Bean around, claimed that the latter had found 'Greek' pottery there. However, a visit to the higher slopes in 1996 did not produce any find.

The apparently *in situ* boundary stone of Sagalassos, which we discovered to the southeast of the village (see below), clearly confirms Bean's suggestion that this village site should be identified with the *komè* of Tymbrianassos, mentioned in the Sagalassian boundary stones discussed below. These boundary stones confirm that one fifth of the revenue of the village's territory had to be given to Sagalassos, while the remaining part was located on an Imperial estate, which might go back to former royal estates (of the Attalids), as was suggested by Ramsay (1886: 130). The latter located Tymbrianassos alternatively near Eğneş or at Ilyas (1895: 322; 1941: 234 ff.). The village of Tymbrianassos overlooked the Düğer plain and also offered a good view of the Beşparmak Mountains behind it (Fig. 225).

On the other side of the valley mouth that gives access to the plain of Yarışlı in the southwest, and facing Aşağımüslimler, is the village of Düğer (in older sources sometimes called Düver). This is located immediately to the north of the Kara Tepe (1205 m a.s.l.), which forms the southern boundary of the plain of Lake Burdur. Today, Düğer is a prosperous village with fertile lands (cereals, vegetables and rich fruit orchards). A considerable spring, Koca Pınar, is situated at the foot of a limestone massif (Pınartaşı Tepe), immediately to the west of the cemetery of Düğer and 1 km south of the village. This important spring, at 920 m a.s.l., is the origin of the Düğer Çayı. It forms the main water source of the area and has been completely transformed by various irrigation arrangements with major channels branching from it. Bean (1959: 87) noted that this stream did not change its volume from winter to summer, but wrongly believed that on its way to Lake Burdur it joined the Boz Çayı (Lysis r.) which runs a good hour on foot to the east of Düğer. In fact, the Düğer Çayı continues as an independent stream as far as the lake, which it enters under the name Özdere (Fig. 231). During our survey of June 1996, most of its course to the north of Düğer was dried up, probably because of the demands of irrigation.

In the village of Düğer, the river valley is already 5 m deep (Fig. 226). The depth of the valley rapidly increases and attains more than 10 m, 2 km to the north. An incised valley formation is also very obvious along the Boz Çayı with a maximum of about 25 m. It is suggested that these incisions took place in an older part of the Düğer plain.

In the past, Düğer has been visited by many scholars. Ramsay and Smith worked here in 1884. The latter copied a mile-

Fig. 209: The remains of a Hellenistic fortification (?) at Gâvur Evi Tepesi.

Fig. 210: The ruin of a Roman building at Gâvur Evi Tepesi.

Fig. 211: Detail of the walls in Roman concrete of the building.

Fig. 209: The remains of a Hellenistic fortification (?) at Gâvur Evi Tepesi.

Fig. 210: The ruin of a Roman building at Gâvur Evi Tepesi.

Fig. 211: Detail of the walls in Roman concrete of the building.

Fig. 212: View from Gâvur Evi Tepesi towards the northwest.

Fig. 213: The site of Kilise Mevkii near Yarı.

Fig. 214: The ruins of old Yarıköy.

Fig. 215: Milestone belonging to the *via Sebaste* and dated to 6 BC in the tea garden at Yarıköy.

Fig. 216: Dedication to M. Aurelius and L. Verus at Yazıköy.

Fig. 217: Funerary altar of Termilas at Yazıköy.

Fig. 218: Fragment of a sarcophagus lid in the old cemetery of Yazıköy.

Fig. 219: Phallos-shaped grave marker from Yazıköy.

Fig. 220: Milestone (?) in the old graveyard of Yazıköy.

Fig. 221: Counterweight for an olive press at Yazıköy.

Fig. 222: View of Aşağımüslimler from the east. The houses are located in the middle of the ancient necropolis.

Fig. 223: The rock-cut sarcophagus at Aşağımüslimler.

Fig. 224: View of Tymbrianassos from the north, with the Halı Kayası behind it.

Fig. 225: View from Tymbrianassos towards the east. The arrow indicates the location of the boundary stone *in situ (?)*.

Fig. 226: The Düğer Çayı in the village of Düğer.

Fig. 227: Milestone of the Tetrarchs in the mosque at Düğer.

stone/dedication to Diocletianus, Maximianus, Constantius and Galerius, dated to the years AD 293-305 and erected by the city of Sagalassos. It seems to be part of an extensive programme of road repairs at and around Sagalassos during that period (French 1998: 101 no. 264; 104 no. 273; 146 no. 383). At the time of Smith's visit, the stone was copied while it was situated in the centre of the village. Because of its size, Smith assumed that it was unlikely to have travelled far from its original position. Today, it is used as a support (Fig. 227) in the porch of the local mosque (Smith 1887: 230 no.11; Ramsay 1895: 336 no. 167; *IGR* III, 336; Ramsay 1941: 237 no. 240; French 1988: 105 no. 275). Inside the same mosque, there is second milestone copied by Bean in 1956 and dedicated to Maximinus, Constantinus and Licinius (AD 311-313), which is now hardly visible (Bean 1959: 89 no. 34; French 1988: 105 no. 276). This milestone corresponds with another period of extensive road repairs along the *via Sebaste* (French 1988: 101 no. 265; 102 no. 269; 106 no. 280; 107 no. 284). It had been carved upside down on a former sepulchral column, carrying an epitaph inside a *tabula ansata*, which announced a fine against tomb violation (Bean 1959: 89 no. 34). A second funeral column belonging to Demetrios, son of Attalos, and his wife, was also copied by Bean in the same mosque (Bean 1959: 89 no. 33). A third one (pres.h.: 0.58 m; diam.: 0.38 m), with a hardly legible inscription (1 line) inside a *tabula ansata,* now lies in a field near the mosque (Fig. 228). An ostotheca belonging to Apollodoros, son of Apollodoros (?), had been copied by Bean in house no. 22 (Bean 1959: 89 no. 32). Because of the presence of a number of tombstones, it may be that Düger is built on an ancient settlement, but no such site with pottery at the surface was shown to us during our visit in 1996. However, a second visit in 1999 produced extensive pottery finds of Roman Imperial times in a field to the south of the village. Therefore, the antiquities in the village should not necessarily have been removed from one of the sites in the Düger plain, but might be of local provenance.

By far the most important antiquities of Düger are the famous boundary stones of Sagalassos. The first one was copied by Ramsay in 1884 in the cemetery of the village, where it was seen by Bean in 1956, and published without any description of the stone (Ramsay 1886: 129; 1895: 336 no. 237; Ramsay 1941: 234; *IGR* III, 335; Bean 1959: 84 no. 30 X). In 1941, Ramsay described it as a "thick round cippus" standing about 3 feet out of the ground, a description which did not apply to the rectangular stone which Bean discovered in the cemetery. Because of pronounced similarities in the line-divisions and in the lacunae, Bean was convinced that the stone which he saw in the graveyard was the same one that Ramsay had seen there, and he ascribed the different shape in Ramsay's description to a lapse in the latter's memory after an interval of fifty years. Yet, since his guide failed to come up with another inscribed stone in the cemetery which he remembered having seen there (Bean 1959: 88 no. 44), this assumption cannot be completely taken for granted. At the time of our visit in 1996, we could no longer find any inscribed stone in the burial ground, since it was completely overgrown. The boundary-marker(s?) copied by Ramsay and by Bean say that, in accordance with a rescript of the emperor Nero, the *legatus pro praetore* Quintus Petronius Umber and the *procurator* Lucius Pupius Praesens had fixed the boundary between Sagalassian territory and that of the village of Tymbrianassos, located on an imperial estate, so that the fields "on the right" should belong to the Sagalassians, whereas those "on the left" belonged to Tymbrianassos. Bean (1959: 15-18) took Q. Petronius Umber for the legate of the province of Galatia in AD 53-54, whereas L. Pupius Praesens is also known to have been active as a procurator at Iconium in Galatia (*IGR* III, 263). Mitchell however, believed that most of Pisidia was already attached to the province of Lycia-Pamphylia as early as AD 43, so that Q. Petronius Umber would have been one of the governors of the latter province at the end of Claudius' reign. Apparently, the instructions for fixing the boundaries had been issued already by Claudius, but they were only carried out after his death, early in Nero's reign (Bean 1959: 86). Since the responsibilities of procurators sometimes extended beyond provincial boundaries, the procurators' activities at Iconium and at Sagalassos is not necessarily an obstacle to this theory (Mitchell 1993: I, 67; II, 154). In any case, a new inscription from Sagalassos shows (Devijver and Waelkens to be published in Sagalassos VI) that in (late) Flavian and Trajanic times, Sagalassos was transferred again to Asia. As Mitchell suggested, the procurator may have been directly involved in this boundary settlement, since it affected an imperial estate, for which he had specific responsibilities (Mitchell: 1993 I, 67, 157). The estate may have reverted to the Attalid royal properties (Ramsay 1886: 130), since as we have said above, their hold on Pisidia may have been much stronger than was sometimes assumed in the past. Kearsly even believed that, for example at Olbasa in the nearby Lysis valley, the Attalids, like the Seleucids elsewhere before them, may have distributed land grants to select friends who had demonstrated their loyalty to them (Kearsly 1994: 54-55). The estate of the Düger plain could have passed into the Roman *ager publicus* after 129 BC and hence into the royal estates of Amyntas, which in 25 BC became Roman property again. It is known that during the first century AD the Roman emperor also had estates on the north side of Lake Burdur, since a boundary stone reading *fines Caesaris n.* was discovered near its northeastern extremity at Baladız (Ramsay 1895: I, 336 no. 164; *CIL* III, 6882; Bean 1959: 84, 86). Some of the Roman property there may even have been used to establish the Roman colony of Baris, as was also the case with other Augustan colonies (Mitchell 1993: I, 157). Mitchell assumed that the northern Pisidian *ager publicus* had resulted from the campaigns of P. Servilius Isauricus and from the Augustan campaigns to pacify Pisidia.

In the village of Düger itself, Ramsay also found a second fragmentary inscription of the same type that had been hollowed out to form a drinking-trough (Ramsay 1886: 129). He later (1941: 236) restored it as if both stones had formed part of a group at the roadside, one facing north and the other one south, with a statue in-between. Thus, in his restoration of this second stone, he gave the right-hand side to Tymbrianassos and the left to Sagalassos. Bean however, restored the text to be word-for-word identical with Ramsay's first inscription (Bean 1959: 87 no. 30 Z).

A third (or fourth?) boundary stone of similar rectangular type with an identical, but much better preserved text mentioning the village of Tymbrianassos was discovered by Bean in the yard of house no. 44 at Düger. According to him it had been brought from a spot ca. 1 km to the north, where it had been used in a building (Bean 1959: 85 no. 30 Y; 87 nr. 44). Today, it can be found in the yard of the house of Osman Tekkin (Fig. 229).

As Bean rightly suggested, the occurrence of three (or four) identical copies of the inscription in the village of Düger, leaves no doubt that the boundary must have run at or very near Düger. Ramsay had taken a road as the dividing line, Bean however considered it equally possible that it was a river. Since the Boz Çayı runs a good hour (on foot) to the east of the village, he supposed that the three copies of Düger had been posted at intervals along the Düger Çayı (Bean 1959: 87-88). Mitchell considered this statement to be too precise although probably not far from the truth (Mitchell 1976: 118).

In 1989, French studied a newly recovered boundary-marker which one year before had been taken to the Burdur museum (French 1990: 11). It had been found in the fields of Farık Şengül, ca 300 m north of the Düger-Hacılar road and ca 1 km west of a bridge over the Bozçay (D. French, personal communication).

That same year, he also (personal communication) had found a similar marker to the northwest of the former, in the fields north of Düger. In 1999, he kindly provided us with a photograph of the stone and with a copy of his notes. Rapidly it became clear that this marker was identical with the one copied by us in 1996. In the view of French, because of the distribution of the six markers, there was a strong possibility that the via Sebaste had been used as the definitive boundary.

We believe that this was the case, at least for the northern part of the plain of Düger, but that, unless the bew boundary stone was not stainding *in situ*, in the southern half this role was perhaps taken over by a secondary road, corresponding with the Sultan Yolu (Fig. 231). As we have said, this road was located a bit to the north of the Roman republican road, built by M. Aquillius. Milestones belonging to the latter road have been discovered by French at Ördek Gediği near Harmanlı on the shores of Lake Çorak (milestone no. 221: French 1988: 106 no. 279), at Alanköy (milestone no. 224: French 1988: 101 no. 266) and at Yarışlı (milestones 223 and 227: French 1988: 111 nos 294-295). So the republican road came as near as Yarışlı, in the valley immediately to the southwest of the plain of Düger. The easiest course towards the Lysis valley, from where it descended towards Pamphylia, would have taken it through the southern part of the plain of Düger and then along the Lysis valley via Karaçal towards the south. In the Lysis valley, it was incorporated into the *via Sebaste*. French confirmed that he saw indeed well preserved parts of this road running along the southern edges of the plain of Düger, to the south of this last village.

Today a road, known as Sultan Yolu, comes from Yarışlı and joins the so-called Deve Yolu, which might be the descendant of the *via Sebaste,* a little to the northeast of Düger, near the above mentioned ancient necropolis (Kilise Mevkii; see Fig. 231).

Exactly along the Sultan Yolu, we discovered in 1996 a seventh boundary-marker, which later proved to have been copied already by D. French, but nog yet published (Figs 230, 231). Since it is located in the centre of a triangle formed by Aşağımüslimler, Yarıköy and Düger, it may still be possible that it corresponds with one of the unpublished boundary-markers copied by J. and L. Robert in 1948 "at Yarı", although the field in which it stands belongs to Düger. In 1989, D. French was told that it had been taken there from a nearby spot, apparently somewhere along the *via Sebaste*. Today, the border stone is still standing perfectly upright on the border of a piece of land belonging to Osman Ceylan. Since it has no connection whatsoever with any construction around it and since it was very deeply embedded into the soil, it seems to occupy its original location. It stands on the limit between two small fields and behind a small ditch (altitude 885 m a.s.l.; co-ordinates: 37°36,308' N; 30°02,352' E). Our 71 year old local guide, who forty years ago had taken also Bean around, claimed that the latter had refused to come and see this spot from of lack of time, but that the boundary-marker which he had copied at Düger (nr. 30 Y) also came from this area. The new marker is rectangular (total h.: 1.40 m; w.: 0.65 m above to 0.73 m below; th.: 0.30 m) and is rough on three sides. On its front, it carries a rather well preserved identical copy of the six other texts, that will soon be published elsewhere. The orientation of the field border with the boundary stone is nearly east–west

Fig. 228: Funerary column at Duğer.

Fig. 229: G. E. Bean's boundary-marker no. 30 Y at Düğer.

Fig. 230: The boundary-marker of Öztarlar *in situ (?)*

(N280°) and the inscription on the boundary stone is oriented towards the west, i.e. perpendicular to the orientation of the edge of the field. According to this inscription also, the fields on the left (i.e. to the north of the stone) were imperial property and located within the territory of Tymbrianassos, while those on the right (i.e. to the south of the stone) belonged to Sagalassos.

There is no trace of a stream in the immediate vicinity of the marker: it is located about 100 m to the east of the Düger Çayı and 2.5 km to the west of the Boz Çayı. Therefore, unless the river beds changed considerably, it is unlikely that the seven markers were posted along one of these streams.

Today, the landscape around the boundary stone rises ca. 30 m above the level of Lake Burdur, and bears several characteristics of humidity: it shows a humic clayey soil and is characteristic of an enclosured agricultural landscape. In this area, the Düger Çayı is not deeply cut, in sharp contrast to the river valley characteristics upstream. We therefore consider this lower lying area as a younger morphological unit, indicated on Fig. 231 as the 'swamps of Yarıköy'. Nowadays, the true marsh towards Lake Burdur is situated at altitudes below 875 m a.s.l. and begins at a distance of about 500 m to the north of the boundary stone. It is therefore not inconceivable that the boundary stone with the adjacent road were situated at the outer limit of a formerly more extensive marsh which could correspond with the Holocene lake bottom. According to Kis *et al.* (1989) and to Erol (1997), this area was still covered by a lake around 13,000-11,000 BP, the time during which coastal sandy sediments were deposited at an altitude of 905-910 m a.s.l. at Tozlutepe, 1 km to the northwest of Hacılar. According to data presented by the same authors, the area dried up around 9,000-7,400 BP, when at Suludere alluvial sediments were deposited at altitudes of about 870-880 m a.s.l.. This means that at that time the lake level was already lower. It should be clear, however, that our approach does not take into account eventual later tectonic movements, but it seems likely that the marches extended further south in Roman antiquity.

With the boundary stone at Öztarlar as anchor point, it is possible to suggest a reconstruction of the road pattern in the plain of Düger. If still *in situ*, as we believe, the apparently still original west-southwest east-northeast orientation of the stone allows us to assume that it must have been situated along a west-southwest east-northeast oriented road. Toward the west-southwest, exactly in the same line as the boundary stone, there exists a prominent earth road known as 'Sultan Yolu' (Fig. 232). The road cannot be traced in the Öztarlar area, but its prolongation towards the east-northeast still corresponds in some sections with a modern road that arrives at the Boz Çayı (Lysis r.) after a distance of 2.5 km, where the large necropolis (Kilise Mevkii) is situated, discussed above.

This site was thus not only situated near the crossing of the Sultan Yolu with the river, but also near a crossroad between the Sultan Yolu and the Deve Yolu. The latter, a north – south road that can still be followed without interruption over more than 10 kilometers, is situated parallel and at a distance of about 1 km to the west of the Boz Çayı. This Deve Yolu road could correspond with the course of the *via Sebaste*. Most probably, as already suggested by French (1990: 111), the Yarıköy boundary-markers seen by J. and L. Robert originally stood along this road.

Following the Sultan Yolu towards the northeast, and following a straight line, which corresponds with an existing road just east of the Boz Çayı, the Sultan Yolu reaches after 10 km the village of Suludere at the eastern border of the plain of Burdur. Suludere is located at the mouth of the Büğdüz Çayı, the river that has eroded the main valley through the badland area in an eastern direction. The entry to this valley is controlled by the site of the Çığırtkankaya Tepesi, rising 150 m above the plain of Düger. The Sultan Yolu thus may correspond with an old road system, perhaps going back to a prehistoric track. Its eastern prolongation along the southeastern shore of Lake Burdur may have existed already at the time of Cn. Manlius Vulso's expedition (see section 3).

All this evidence confirms that early in the reign of Nero, but at the request of his predecessor, the provincial governor, aided by an imperial procurator, fixed the boundary between Sagalassian territory and the village of Tymbrianassos which seems to have been the main settlement on an imperial estate located to the southwest of Lake Burdur. Most likely, this boundary was originally to some extent a natural one. It is very tempting to assume that it was formed by the Düger Çayı from the spot where it entered Lake Burdur in the north to its crossing with a secondary road corresponding with the modern Sultan Yolu in the south. It seems likely that the now almost completely dried up swamps of Yarıköy and Yazırköy reached as far south as this road (Fig. 233). Such a reconstruction would correspond very well with Polybios (XXI, 36) and Livy's description (XXXVIII, 15) of Cn. Manlius Vulso's expedition in 189 BC, where the author describes how the Roman consul after leaving Darsa (only mentioned by Livy and in our opinion the site of Ada Tepesi in Lake Yarışlı, see below section 8), continued "along the marshes" (respectively παρὰ τὴν λίμνην and *praeter paludes*), which correspond exactly with the location of the swamps near Öztarlar, where he met envoys sent by Lysinia. As we have already mentioned above and as suggested by Mitchell (1976: 58), the consul seems to have continued southeast of Lake Burdur, otherwise he would have crossed the territory of Lysinia, so that their embassy to meet him near the marshes would have been totally unnecessary. If he followed the line of the Sultan Yolu, he would have marched along the marshes to the south of Lake Burdur, which even today come as close as 500 m, but in antiquity may have reached as far as the road. According to our reconstruction of the city's boundaries, he would already have been skirting Sagalassian property on the south side of the road the moment he had entered the plain of Düğer, but it was only further east, perhaps where he crossed the Lysis or a road preceding the later *via Sebaste,* that he would actually have entered the city's territory. This topographical situation corresponds exactly with the writings of Polybios and Livy, who say that after marching past the marshes, where he was met by the Lysinian envoys, Cn. Manlius Vulso entered the fertile land of the Sagalassians (εἰς τὴν τῶν Σαγαλασσέων γῆν καὶ πολὺ πλῆθος ἐξελασάμενος κ.τ.λ. and *Inde in agrum Sagalassenum, uberem fertilemque omni genere frugum, ventum est*). It is likely that Quintus Petronius Umber and Lucius Pupius Praesens put a number of boundary-markers along this Sultan Yolu and that the whole Düğer plain located to the south of it belonged to Sagalassos, as far as the valley mouth giving access to the plain of Yarışlı. In the northern half of the valley, they most probably put their markers along the *via Sebaste,* since such inscriptions were meant to be seen by everybody. A position along a winding stream bed (of the Düğer Çayı), which even today is to a large extent surrounded by swampy land, seems therefore less likely. Yet, the rather strange addition in all the texts, that one fifth of the revenue of the imperial estate around Tymbrianassos had to be given to Sagalassos, might suggest that before the construction of the *via Sebaste,* which must have been a straight road, the real border had originally extended some hundred meters further west, as far as this stream. If this was the case, a boundary correction along the *via Sebaste* would have meant a small loss of territory, but the official attribution of one fifth of the revenues of the Tymbrianassos estate to the city would have been compensation. Bean was already puzzled by this strange financial arrangement and declared that the same purpose could have been achieved by fixing a slightly different boundary. In his eyes, the Imperial decision had been taken in order to have a clear and unmistakable dividing line, formed by the stream (Bean 1959: 88). Our own explanation takes the Roman road as a new boundary, which fulfilled the purpose of establishing a clear boundary even better than the winding river would have done, and the financial arrangement probably prevented a loss of income for the city. All this implies that in Imperial times Sagalassos must have controlled three quarters of the Düğer plain. The presence of at least seven boundary stones along these roads in the plain of Düğer, can be explained by the absence of a clear natural boundary – contrary to the other borders of Sagalassos' territory-, once this role was taken over by the *via Sebaste,* by the fact that the boundary stones also identified the boundaries of an Imperial estate, and by the publicity which they provided to the city among people travelling along the *via Sebaste.*

8. THE DISTRICT IMMEDIATELY SOUTH OF THE DÜĞER PLAIN

It is clear that the crest of the hill tops along the southern edge of the Düğer plain, comprising the Kara Tepe (1205 m a.s.l.), the Devedüsen Tepesi (1274 m a.s.l.), the Akalan Tepesi (1148 m a.s.l.), the Kireçocağı Tepesi (1332 m a.s.l.), and the Burgulutaş Tepesi (1196 m a.s.l.), must have formed the natural southern boundary of the city's possessions in this area. This line of hills was only interrupted by a large divide to the southwest of Düğer and by the Lysis river near Karaçal.

In 1996, during our efforts to identify Sagalassos' southwestern boundary, the survey team also ventured a little beyond this border, and studied the remains of two major sites, which are included in this report.

The first one is located on a peninsula, locally known as Yarımada (i.e. 'peninsula'), Ada Tepesi (i.e. 'the island hill') or Düğer Ada in the salt lake of Yarışlı. During the Bronze Age and Early Iron age it held one of the most important settlements in the area.

The site can be reached by a track along the northern shore of the salt lake, part of which was already cut in the rock in antiquity to accommodate the wheels of wagons or carts (Fig. 234). The site itself is located on a small elongated peninsula with an east–west orientation, projecting for 1 km into the lake (Fig. 235).

The estimated surface area of the lake is about 20 sq km (4 km east–west and 5 km north–south) and its water level is estimated at 900 m a.s.l. The lake is situated in a closed basin, at the mouth of the main drainage line coming from the west (Yeşilova). There are several indications that the lake level has dropped substantially this century. Our 71-year old local guide estimated the decline he had witnessed during his lifetime in the order of 5 m. As a result, the peninsula today is also linked to the surrounding plain by a previously submerged zone in the northwest (Fig. 236). We observed several very recent storm water-marks between the actual water level and + 8 m. The beach zone confirms these observations. In fact the soil surface of the lower beach zone and the former lake bottom is very efflorescent from salt crystallisation and bears no vegetation. The upper beach zone also contains salt, but is already covered with a salt-tolerant flora. It is suggested that the recent lowering of the lake level is related to a reduced influx of freshwater, mainly from the west, because of irrigation practices towards Yeşilova.

According to Erol (1997: 325): "Yarasly Lake was connected to Burdur Lake during the last (Würm?) pluvial period, but became an isolated water body during the

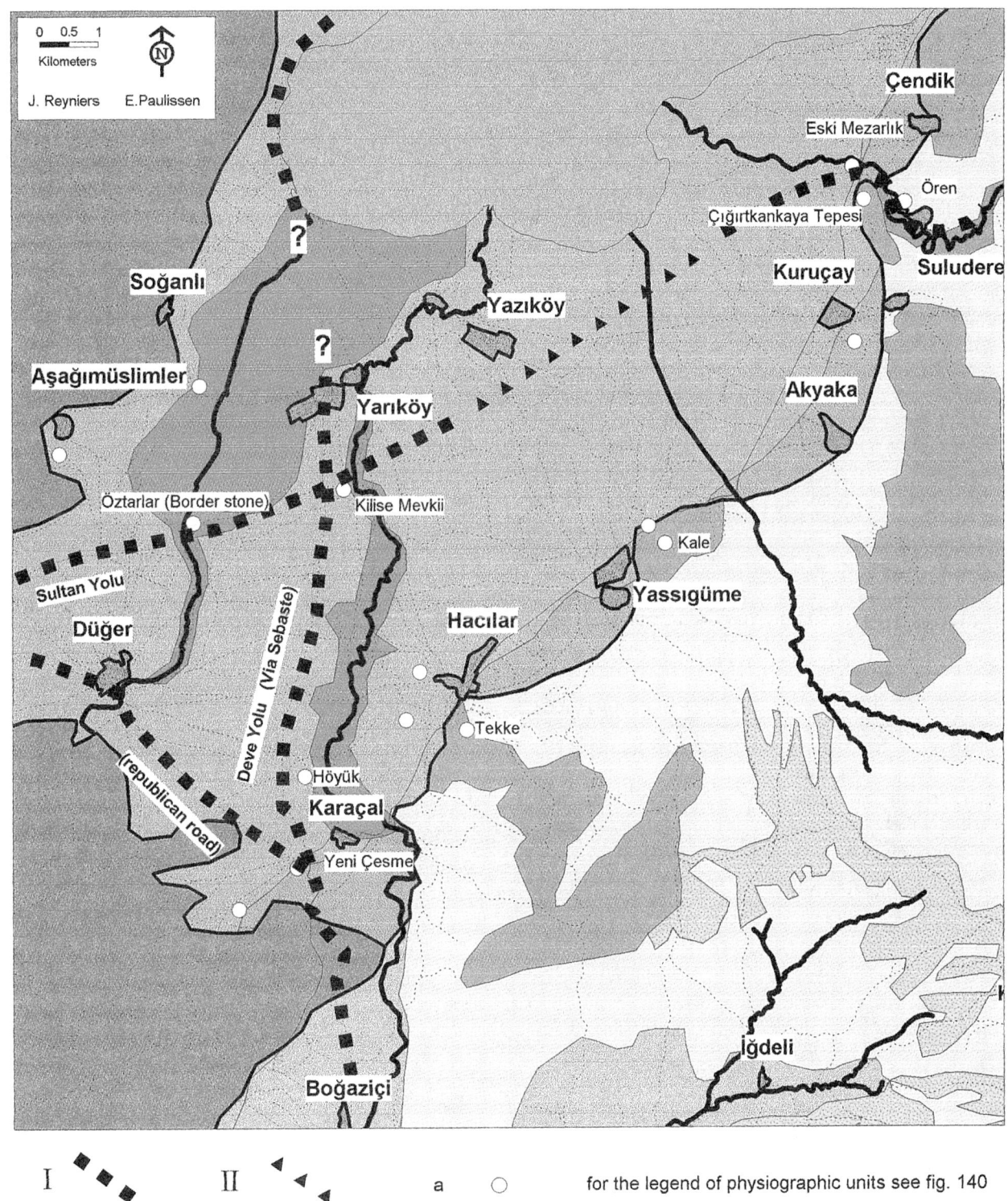

Fig. 231: Map of the plain of Düğer with the old and present-day road systems.
Road structure south of Lake Burdur

I Coinciding with present road system   II not coinciding with present road system

a Site

Fig. 232: View of the Sultan Yolu, immediately to the west of the border-marker.

Fig. 233: View of the Düğer plain from the site of Tymbrianassos. The green line in the middle represents the vegetation around the Öztarlar boundary stone and the stream bed of the Düğer Çayı. The white fields around it are dried-out marshes.

Fig. 234: Rock carved to accommodate the wheels of wagons or carts in the northern approach to Ada Tepesi.

Fig. 235: View of Lake Yarışlı with the peninsula of Ada Tepesi, seen from the north.

Fig. 236: The now exposed lake bottom to the northwest of the peninsula.

Fig. 237: The outlets of freshwater springs into the salty brine of Lake Yarışlı's northern shores.

Fig. 238: The hill site of Ada Tepesi inside Lake Yarışlı.

Fig. 239: View from the highest spot on the peninsula towards the west.

Fig. 240: The remains of the ruined Early Iron Age buildings at Ada Tepesi.

Fig. 241: The southwest cliff of Ada Tepesi with the 'Phrygian' tomb.

Holocene, and contains elevated early Holocene beaches, in the sands of which hundreds of pithos are found, a graveyard probably of the Bronze age"(sic; see below).

Within the closed lake basin, one can provisionally distinguish two levels based on the altitude of naturally eroded rock terraces. The youngest level of these terraces is situated at about +10 m (910 m a.s.l.) above the present lake level. A second level of naturally eroded rock terraces is located at about +20 m (920 m a.s.l.). These two former lake levels are undated, but appear to be both quite young (Holocene?) as the surfaces of the terraces are fresh, unweathered and not covered with slope deposits. It is clear that even with a +20/25 m lake level, the Yarışlı Lake would remain a closed lake, but that the peninsula could have been transformed into an island as its northern isthmus became submerged. With higher lake levels, the peninsula could even have been transformed into three small islands corresponding with the individual hilltops mentioned below. In any case, the present-day peninsula formed an ideal site, offering fresh water and a natural protection, only accessible from the north via the narrow isthmus.

In fact it is important to note that active freshwater springs still exist on the peninsula. These springs are situated close to the lake level and discharge fresh water directly into the lake. The springs can be found easily, since their outlets are marked with a freshwater flora and the fresh water itself creates an opening in the lake brine near the spring (Fig. 237).

The substrate of the peninsula consists entirely of limestone and forms an undulating topography of three hills separated by depressions (Fig. 238). The northernmost depression is at an estimated altitude of 920 m a.s.l., the others at 925 m a.s.l., or at +20/25 m above the actual lake level. These areas are covered with soil material and are cultivated. The altitudes of the hills are:
- the northern hill: its top is located at 950 m a.s.l. (+50 m) and is flat and elongated. No ceramics have been found there.
- the middle hill: top located at 930 m a.s.l. (+30 m). Some ceramics have been found there.
- the southern hill, the actual Ada Tepe, is the most important and also the highest one, with its top located at 965 m a.s.l. (co-ordinates: 37°34,416' N – 29°58,469' E). This hill dominates the lake and is a prominent observation point towards the west in the direction of Yeşilova and ancient Phrygia (Fig. 239). The summit of the Ada Tepesi dips gently towards the north, in accordance with the inclination of the layers, so that the highest point is situated at its western extremity. The hill is covered in huge amounts of ceramics and traces of buildings (Fig. 240). Most ceramics have been collected at the very top and near its northern border. Some of them are architectural terracotta fragments belonging to buildings that were looted in the 1960s and of which the scattered remains can still be seen at the surface (Fig. 240). The peninsula, an ideal location for a fortified site, may already have been inhabited by the people buried in the Bronze Age cemetery mentioned by Erol (1997: 325). Since this cemetery is located by Mellink at the northern end of Lake Yarışlı (1969: 212), it must have faced the Ada Tepesi peninsula. According to Mellink, it contained mostly Early Bronze Age pithos burials, but seems to have been used also in the second millennium BC. To this period belonged some squat Mycenaean alabastra of LH III type, purchased by the museum of Burdur in 1968 and said partly to come from this prehistoric cemetery. This cemetery may also have been the origin of the LBA pottery indicated on Mellaart's and Murray's map (1995: 101 map 1). The Mycenaean pieces collected by the museum in 1966 (Mellink 1967: 164) may have had the same provenance. The collection has been studied by E. French, who identified it as consisting of an imported pyxis and jug and of three local pyxides dated to the LH IIIA2-B period (Mee 1978: 126-127). Mee, who studied Middle and Late Bronze Age material from Anatolia, believed that the Mycenaean material from this necropolis had been imported along the Maeander valley (Mee 1978: 150). This fact, and the early Bronze Age date of most other evidence from the necropolis, is a strong indication that the site on the peninsula in Lake Yarışlı corresponds with an important Bronze Age stronghold. A study of the other ceramic evidence from the necropolis should reveal whether or not it belonged to Mellaart's EBA. 'southwestern group' of pottery, characteristic of the Upper Maeander valley from Dinar to Denizli and of the mountain country lying to the south of it (Mellaart 1954: 190). In this ceramic 'province', Mellaart distinguished two sub-groups, the first one of which included the plain of Yeşilova, whereas the second one occupied the plains of Elmalı and of Korkuteli. Yarışlı lies exactly in-between these two sub-groups, so that it would be interesting to see with what region it had most affinities (Mellaart 1954: 205). It would also be interesting to see the relationship with the EBA. Kusura culture, which is represented by several settlements in the plain of Isparta, but which seems also to have been present elsewhere in the Lake District and in the immediate (northern) vicinity of Lake Burdur (Goetze 1967[2]: 34).

Whether the site remained occupied during the Middle Bronze Age is uncertain. During the Late Bronze Age, however, it may have been one of the Arzawa settlements (see Waelkens 2000), linked by trade with the Mycenaean Aegean.

During the early Iron Age, the peninsula was clearly transformed into an important site, which seems to have been the seat of local rulers, either Phrygian princes, or Pisidian (?) dynasts who were strongly influenced by Phrygian culture.

It is known that the latter had even reached and strongly affected the district around Elmalı, as is shown by the tumuli at Bayındır excavated by the Antalya Museum, and by those around Elmalı, excavated by Mellink. By the seventh century BC at least, the kingdom of Phrygia's cultural sphere and artistic range, if not the kingdom itself, certainly extended south into the Burdur-Yeşilova region and into Lycia (Birmingham 1964: 33; Cummer 1970: 43).

During the Iron Age, the site must have contained various monumental structures of the Phrygian megaron type known from Gordion and from rock-cut shrines, decorated with exquisite terracottas. From 1964 onwards, terracotta revetments from the site turned up at Sotheby & Co. They were decorated with birds, spotted panthers, bovines, lotus flowers, egg-and-dart, astragal and guilloche patterns. Around the same time, similar fragments, probably with a similar provenance, also entered the Istanbul Museum (Mellink 1965: 143). A year later, more terracotta revetments from Yarımada were sold at Sotheby & Co, and the Birmingham City Museum acquired a large number of the previously auctioned lots (Mellink 1966: 153). A discussion of the revetments and their original position was published by Thomas (1965). In 1966, one plaque was acquired by the Berlin Museum (Greifenhagen 1966; Mellink 1967: 166). Fortunately several architectural terracottas from this plundered site could also be collected on the local market by the Burdur Museum, where some of them are now on display. A few fragments belong to the rider and griffin plaques that were sold in Europe, but most of the Burdur plaques show geometrical designs. Of the latter, only a few had been sold abroad.

The geometrical material was studied in detail by Cummer who could identify at least two major buildings with pitched roofs, but established that the total of the terracottas indicated at least three, and perhaps even six different buildings, or as many alterations to previous structures. Space was certainly not lacking since the citadel seems to cover an area that is almost as large as that of the Royal Enclosure at Gordion. The geometrically decorated tiles and revetments studied by Cummer could be compared with Phrygian parallels dated from the middle of the eight century BC onwards (Cummer 1970). The series with the figural reliefs were dated by some to the seventh–sixth centuries BC (Birmingham 1964: 33), by others to the third quarter of the sixth century BC or possibly somewhat later (Åkerstrøm 1964: 53; Greifenhagen 1966: 47). Prayon and Wittke attributed fibulae from the site, taken to the Burdur Museum, to the period 680-500 BC (Prayon and Wittke 1994). The surface material that we sampled on the peninsula (SA 96 S 26-27) belonged to the group of 'Phrygian' grey wares and painted 'Southwest Anatolian wares' attributed to the Early Iron Age (Mellaart 1954: 180). Birmingham dated the latter to the late eighth–sixth centuries BC and subdivided these wares into three fabrics. They show considerable external influence, especially from the East Greek settlements, reaching the district via the Maeander valley route. Later, Lydian fashion also seems to have become prominent. In the eastern part of the Burdur-Antalya-Denizli region, there is also a limited influence from the Cilician-Chypriot cultural zone that must have reached the plateau via Antalya. Finally, especially in the Burdur-Yeşilova region from the early seventh century BC onward, some sherds also show clear Phrygian influences (Birmingham 1964: 30-33). All this means that the area around Düğer in the early Iron Age must have had contacts with various outlying districts and been well aware of developments elsewhere.

Ada Tepesi is delimited by very steep to vertical limestone cliffs. In the upper part of a vertical cliff facing northeast, a monumental rock-cut tomb has been carved (Fig. 241). This had already been noted by Özsait (1980: 105). Originally, it could be approached by rock-cut steps, but the latter are interrupted now, so that we could not get inside. Its façade is decorated with a geometrical pattern (Fig. 242), partly carved, partly painted in red, reminiscent not of the tombs, but of the façades of some of the rock-cut sanctuaries from the Phrygian Highlands (Haspels 1971: figs 513-523). Despite its slightly different appearance, the monument is clearly of Phrygian inspiration, if not also carved by Phrygian craftsmen. The size of the monument and its richly decorated façade, together with the quality of the megaron-like buildings on the peninsula, identify the site as the seat of a family of regional rulers.

It is clear therefore that, during the Phrygian and Lydian period in Anatolia, the supposedly former Bronze Age site of Ada Tepesi remained or became a major settlement of regional importance. Yet, this settlement also continued to be inhabited to a much later date. The rather flat area on the north side of the hill carrying the Early Iron Age remains is littered with mostly coarse pottery. However, it also included early to late Imperial Sagalassos red slip wares. In the same area, the north-facing cliffs are decorated in at least two spots with rock-cut reliefs. One of them, located ca. 25 m above lake level, represents in a vaulted niche (h.: 0.99 m; w.: 0.62 m) a nude Herakles holding a club in his right hand (Fig. 243). This god must have been popular in the area, since he was also worshipped near Kozluca (see below). At a lower level, several other reliefs are completely weathered. Some 10 m further to the west, another rock surface has been smoothed. On this surface, a woman holding a small object in her right hand has been carved (Fig. 244). The identity of this female figure, goddess, priestess or worshipper could no longer be established, but it must be that this was a sacred area.

The peninsula thus must clearly have housed an Imperial settlement, which from its remains, was certainly no longer

Fig. 242: The rock-cut 'Phrygian' tomb in the southwest cliff of the Ada Tepesi.

Fig. 243: The Herakles relief at Ada Tepesi.

Fig. 244: The female relief at Ada Tepesi.

Fig. 245: The plain of Çallıca (ancient Lysis valley), seen from the pass to the south of Karaçal.

as important as the previous holder of the site. This could easily correspond with the small city of Palaiopolis mentioned by Hierokles in the sixth century AD between Olbasa (near Belenli in the Lysis valley) and Lysinia (on the north side of Lake Burdur) and issuing coins from Antoninus Pius to Alexander Severus (Ramsay 1888, pls II-III facing p. 20; Ramsay 1895: I: 326-327; Aulock 1977: 40; Hall 1986: 142). The name Palaiopolis ('the old city') would perfectly fit the site. But we believe that, even if our suggestion would be correct, the original name of the settlement was that of Darsa mentioned in Cn. Manlius Vulso's campaign by Livy (XXXVIII, 15). This author said that after a stop at Kormasa, probably located near Kozluca (see below) on the other side of the small ridge separating the Lysis valley from Lake Yarışlı, "*Darsa proxima urbs erat; eam, metu incolarum desertam, plenam omnium rerum copia invenit. Progredienti praeter paludes legati ab Lysinoe dedentes urbem venerunt. Inde in agrum Sagalassenum, uberem fertilemque omni genere frugum, ventum est.*" The description fits perfectly with the site at Ada Tepesi, located exactly between Kormasa and the marhses in the territory of Sagalassos. The Roman general may have crossed the low hills to the west of the Lysis valley, instead of entering the plain of Burdur by following the stream, in order to provide his troops with the necessary supplies from this old and important settlement which was apparently full of them, or in order to insure the loyalty of its inhabitants. A recent study of his journey clearly indicated how Cn. Manlius Vulso also systematically depleted potential Seleucid strongholds of their supplies (Grainger 1995). The early and middle Hellenistic history of the area could easily explain pro-Seleucid feelings in some of the older settlements. At the time of Vulso's journey, the site of Ada Tepesi may still have controlled most if not all of the Yarışlı basin. Later, an important settlement, Takina, developed near Yarışlı proper, much better situated geographically on the other side of the lake, on a hill called Asar (Bean 1959: 89-90), some 2 km from the lake and along the republican road built by M. Aquillius. In AD 212-213, Takina would file a complaint against soldiers leaving the road and helping themselves from the community's fields. From the rescript sent by Caracalla, one can also learn that, just like nearby Tymbrianassos, it was located within an imperial estate (Şahın and French 1987). Bean's description of a considerable building, "possibly a council house, with an apse at the north end" rather fits a church than a bouleuterion. Takina never issued coins. In a late antique itinerary, it is mentioned (as Tagina) as a *statio* on a road connecting Apamea (Dinar) with Kormasa (Belke and Mersich 1990: 397). Therefore, Darsa, perhaps renamed as Palaiopolis, may have remained the only independent settlement in the area.

In the past, Ramsay proposed to correct Livy's text from Darsa to Darsila and to see it as a Hellenised name of Ptolemy's Durzela, Zarzela, or Zorzila which he suggested might be identified with Burdur (Ramsay 1890: 408). A few years later however, since the version which we have of Polybios' narrative of the same journey (XXI, 36) did not mention a place called Darsa between Kormasa and Lake Burdur, he was inclined to doubt its existence and to suspect it as a duplication of Kormasa (Ramsay 1895: I, 327; also Mitchell 1976: 58; Syme 1995: 201). Finally, he changed his mind again and proposed to take Darsa for another name for Panemoteichos and to identify it with Düğer. In fact, he believed that Darsa might be a Hellenised version of an old Anatolian toponym Tursa ('walled town'), later 'translated' into Greek as Panemoteichos, and still later transformed again in Turkish Duvar-Düver, meaning 'wall'. The vernacular of the place would occur in the Tekmoreian lists as Tursènos and Darrènos (Ramsay 1941: 234-235; Bean 1959: 116). According to Bean however, the name of Düğer could have been derived from an influentual 'derebey' and therefore not be of ancient origin (Bean 1959: 117 nr. 89). Since Livy's manuscripts show no uncertainty with regard to the reading of Darsa (Bean 1959: 117 nr. 90), it is better not to consider it as a phantom city in the author's text. The rich site of Ada Tepesi fits exactly with his description. After the construction of the Roman roads in the area, which passed through the more fertile areas on the other side of Lake Yarışlı, the site may have lost its strategic importance, perhaps the main reason for its selection as a settlement originally, and dwindled into oblivion. The general prosperity of the Antonine and Severan period could have caused some renewed activity and the issuing of city coins, at least if our suggestion that it was perhaps called Palaiopolis then could be substantiated.

The 1996 survey took our team also to the east of Lake Yarışlı into the Lysis valley, locally known as the plain of Çallıca (former Eğneş). Karaçal must be the last village on Sagalassian territory. The road towards the south traverses a low pass 2 km south of Karaçal. This pass must have represented the Sagalassian border and offers a magnificent view of the plain of Çallıca (Fig. 245). Two km to the south of the pass the road splits into a branch to Acıpayam (southwest) and another to Antalya (southeast).

We believe that from the pass near Karaçal, as we have said above, the Sagalassian border must have continued eastward along the edge of the flat hills (part of the badlands) which dominate the plain to the northeast of Bogaziçi and Igdeli (watershed near Eskiköy Mevkii; Eskiköy Tepesi; Sariyer Tepesi: 1326 m a.s.l.; Çalça Tepesi; Kundurun Tepesi). This edge is covered with black pine and juniper (Fig. 246). The Çallıca plain itself, irrigated by the Lysis river (Fig. 247) is very fertile and contains several prehistoric mounds (Fig. 248). This was a district once inhabited by the Milyae (Hall 1986b: 152), who according to Strabon (XII.7.1 C 570;

XIII.4.17 C 631) were Sagalassos' southwestern neighbours. The southern part of this valley or Tefenni Ovası, where the Boz Çayı is called Eren Çayı, formerly Gebren Çay (Bean 1959: 96), was called the 'Makron Pedion' in antiquity, inhabited by the 'demos of the Makropedeitai', known from inscriptions at Akören, located to the northeast of Kemer (Duchesne 1879: 478; Ramsay 1895: I, 308 nos 120-121; Bean 1959: 96). In this area, at Kuştepealtı near Akçeören, there is a small ancient site (Bean 1959: 100). Ramsay, without any clear evidence, wanted to place the settlement of Alastos, known from inscriptions at Karamanlı (Collignon 1878: 173 and 262) and from a sculptor's signature at Gâvur Ören (see above), in this neighbourhood. He located a sanctuary for Zeus Sabazios there and considered the site to have been the centre of the area before the foundation of Olbasa. He even suggested the name of Palaiopolis for it (Ramsay 1895: I, 307 nos 114-115; 321-322).

On the opposite (west) side of the valley, around Bademli (ancient Polyetta, see Bean 1959: 97), to the north of Tefenni, lay the 'demos of the Ormeleis', known to have been part of the province of Asia (Duchesne and Collignon 1877: 363-375; Collignon 1878: 53-64).

Originally this very fertile plain remained almost empty of towns, since it was partially occupied by estates, some of which according to Ramsay (1895: I, 280) had already been Pergamenian royal property. In Roman imperial times, part of the area must have been the property of the colonists of the Augustan colony of Olbasa (near Belenli), but private (for example, Annia Faustina, wife of Marcus Aurelius) and Imperial estates continued to exist as well (Collignon 1878: 59; Ramsay 1895: I, 286-295; Levick 1967: 49). Levick suggested that Olbasa had possessed a long, narrow strip of land on the eastern edge of the Lysis valley. In her view, the Lysis river perhaps formed the city territory's southwestern and western boundary towards the Ormelian estates, and its northern boundary towards Kormasa (located by her at Eğneş), whereas the Elmacık Çayı, an eastern tributary of the Lysis, would have formed the border with the territory of Hadrianoi (located by her at Gâvur Ören; Levick 1967: 50). Even if Kormasa and Hadrianoi may have to be located elsewhere (see below), the proposed boundaries of Olbasa's territory may still be correct.

The Milyas, the region inhabited by the Milyae or Milyadeis, extended as far as here, but originally it must have occupied an even more extensive territory, stretching as far south as Isinda (near Korkuteli) and Termessos (Hall 1986b: 137). According to an inscription built into the bridge at Boğaziçi and dated to the year 5-4 BC, the middle part of the Lysis valley, immediately adjoining the plain of Düğer, had become in early Imperial times the district of the 'Milyadeis', but it also was inhabited by Thracian colonists, apparently introduced into this region as military settlers by the Seleucids in order to guard its vital roads. A third population group was that of Roman settlers with commercial interests in the district (Hall 1986b: 137, 153).

At Boğaziçi, the plain has an altitude of 960 m a.s.l. The village of Boğaziçi is located just downstream of the confluence of the Eren Çayı coming from the south and of the Harımruz Çayı coming from the east (direction of Kozluca and Iğdeli). Together they form the Boz Çayı, spanned by an old Ottoman bridge which is today disconnected from the modern road system. In fact, the bridge has suffered from severe river erosion. The gravel bed of the Boz Çayı is quite wide at this point, as it is swept by considerable flooding. When the water level is low, it shows several characteristics of a dissected river with gravel bars separating a number of channels. In June 1996, the river bed was nearly dry (Fig. 247).

An excellent study of the above mentioned Boğaziçi inscription by the late A.S. Hall traces its provenance and that of a number of Imperial dedications at Kozluca to a spot called Kınalı Taş, in the Kemer Çayı Mevkii of Kozluca village (Hall 1986b: 137-140). These other inscriptions, still to be found in the cemetery of the village, were erected for Caracalla and for Lucius Verus respectively, by the *boulè* and the *dèmos* of a city, in one case identified as that of Hadrianoi. Since Bean had wrongly assumed that all stones at Kozluca had been taken from the site at Gâvur Ören, this had induced him to identify the latter as Hadrianoi (see above).

In fact, the dedications came from the Kınalı Taş site (see Bean 1959: 108-110), located in the middle of the fields ca. 500 m to the east of the large Kozluca Hüyük, and clearly identified by the inscription in the Boğaziçi bridge as a Sebasteion, a sanctuary which in 5-4 BC was dedicated to the cult of Roma and Augustus by the Milyadeis, and by Thracian and Roman settlers. According to Hall, the sanctuary perhaps occupied the spot of an old meeting place of Cicero's *commune Milyadum*, but in middle Imperial times it seems to have developed into a regional centre for the Imperial cult, so that neighbouring communities, such as Hadrianoi, also erected monuments there (Hall 1986b: 142). It may even have served the cult of other deities as well, at least if the provenance of a large Herakles relief (h.: 1.30 m; w.: 0.74 m; th.: 0.43 m) standing near the school of Kozluca, which we were told in 1996 came from Kınalı Taş, was correct (Fig. 249). At the sanctuary itself (37°29,786' N; 30°04,279' E; altitude: 1012 m a.s.l.), there is still an uninscribed pedestal emerging from the soil (Fig. 250). The ground is covered with tile fragments, with coarse and Sagalassos red slip wares, but its surface material also contained a fragment of a late antique bracelet in blue glass.

The city of Hadrianoi appears as a bishopric in the *Notitiae* and in Council lists from the fifth to seventh centuries AD.

Fig. 246: View of the flat hills (background) to the north of the village of Iğdeli, which must have separated the Lysis valley from Sagalassian territory in the badlands. In the background, Mt. Beşparmak.

Fig. 247: The Lysis river near the bridge of Boğaziçi.

Fig. 248: One of the prehistoric mounds on the road to Çallıca (Eğneş).

Fig. 249: The Herakles relief at Kozluca.

Fig. 250: A pedestal at the Sebasteion site near Kozluca. The hüyük is visible in the background.

It is also mentioned on one of the statue bases from the cemetery at Kozluca. In 1985, Hall could read the city's name in a dedication to Diocletian and Maximian built into the bridge at Boğaziçi, probably taken again from the Sebasteion (Hall 1986b: 140 nr. 2). But he also found a text with the name of Hadrianoi at Çallıca (former Eğneş), near which there exists a large site, previously identified by Bean as that of Kormasa. Therefore, Hadrianoi must have been located there (Hall 1986b: 141 nr. 3). Most probably, the Lysis river formed its eastern boundary, while the hills southwest of Karaçal separated it from the Sagalassian estates in the Düğer plain. The name of the city undoubtedly goes back to the reign of Hadrian, but the type of monuments (tumuli with phallus stones, among others) seen there by Bean makes it unlikely that it was a completely new foundation (see also Levick 1967: 49). Whether this means that an existing city merely changed its name in honour of the emperor, or that a smaller community was raised to the rank of a 'city' has to remain uncertain.

The site near Eğneş had already been visited by Duchesne and Collignon, who considered it to be Sanaos (Duchesne and Collignon 1877: 371; Duchesne 1879: 478-479, 481). Ramsay took it successively for Tymbrianassos (1886: 128) and for Lysinia (1895: I, 322). Bean, however, who was told that many stones at Boğaziçi were taken from Eğneş, and who had found a tombstone in this village for a veteran *natus Cormasa*, suggested that it should be identified with Kormasa. He gave a good description of the site, located on the extreme western edge of the plain and covered over nearly a mile with great quantities of rough stones and of Roman sherds. He also noticed some 20 small tumuli (Bean 1959: 91-97; see also Mitchell 1976: 117) that had already been described by Sterrett in 1888 (Sterrett 1888: 115).

Whereas the 3 km wide plain to the west of the Lysis river can now be attributed to the territory of Hadrianoi, the part of the valley on the eastern side may originally have belonged to a large settlement formed by the Kozluca Hüyük, some 500 m to the west of the Sebasteion (Fig. 251). The mound (37°29,746' N; 30°03,981' E; altitude: ca. 1027 m a.s.l.) is located on the valley bottom ca. 200 m to the east of the river bed. In this area, the valley bottom is situated at about 975 m a.s.l. and has a width of ca. 1 km. The river itself is incised for nearly 20 m into a concave and very fertile plain ca. 5 km wide. The valley is cultivated with poppies and pomegranates, but also contains some wild olives, the remainder of an abandoned olive cultivation.

The mound covers an area of ca. 6000 m^2 (60 by 100 m) and rises 13 m above the plain. A very productive pit, probably a well, is located near the southwest corner of the mound, close to the river. Except for some collapsed rubble walls, there are no architectural structures visible on top of the mound which is entirely cultivated (Fig. 252). The surface, however, is absolutely littered with the same kind of archaic pottery as that found at Ada Tepesi, indicating a contemporary Early Iron Age occupation. Özsait (1996) identified 'Phrygian' pottery here. We also sampled lots of Hellenistic (Megarian bowls, among others) and Roman wares, beside worked pieces of lead (SA 96 S 30) and blue glass fragments (SA 96 S 29). The Roman pottery included early Imperial Sagalassos red slip ware (SA 96 S 28), while some of the Hellenistic sherds could be identified as a pre-sigillata production from Sagalassos. The mound thus represents at the latest an Early Iron Age site, which remained inhabited right into Roman times. Since the fields around the hüyük are also covered with mainly Roman pottery, the old mound may have become a kind of upper city, with a lower settlement and a cemetery located around it. The whole site is heavily affected by modern farming, which may have removed most surface material.

Since the site near Çallıca can now be identified as that of Hadrianoi, it is very tempting to follow Hall (1986 b: 141-142) and suggest that Kuzluca Hüyük corresponds with the old city of Kormasa mentioned by Livy during the journey of Cn. Manlius Vulso (see above), who thence continued towards Darsa and the territory of Sagalassos. The location near Lake Kestel suggested by Syme (1995: 201) cannot be possible. The tombstone of the veteran from Kormasa at Boğaziçi fits very well with Hall's suggestion. In Imperial times, the settlement may have been surpassed by its larger neighbour Hadrianoi, which eventually may even have incorporated Kormasa into its territory. There is however no reason to suggest, as Hall did, that the name of Kormasa was later transferred to Gâvur Ören, while the old mound received the name of Palaiopolis, which issued coins in the Antonine and Severan period (see Ada Tepesi). The fact that the site was not fortified does not exclude its identification as a small city site (so Bean 1959: 110; cf. Hall 1986 b: 140). If the city had dwindled into oblivion in Imperial times, its public structures may have been rather simple or almost non-existent and could easily have been obliterated by centuries of farming.

Kormasa is mentioned by Ptolemaios (V 5,4), which excludes its identification with Palaiopolis, still considered as a possibility by Bean. In subsequent ages, the city may have lost status (Syme 1995: 201). It occurs still as a 'statio' on a road connecting Themisonion with Perge in the *Tabula Peutingeriana* (Syme 1995: 201). This function corresponds very well with the fact that the famous edict of the emperor Tiberius' *legatus pro praetore*, Sextus Sotidius Strabo Libuscidianus, written ca. AD 13-15, concerning the organisation of requisitioned transport through the territory of Sagalassos (Mitchell 1976; French and Mitchell 1977: 216-218), ordered Sagalassos to take care of official transport as far as Kormasa. In fact, the *via Sebaste* must have passed very close to the site. A milestone from this road was discovered at Boğaziçi, located only 1.7 km to the north of Kozluca Hüyük (French 1988: 102 no. 267).

A loss of status and a 'shrinking' of the settlement in Imperial times could explain why no late Roman pottery was discovered on or around the mound. Nor is Kormasa ever mentioned as a bishopric in early Byzantine sources (von Aulock 1977: 40). The letter of Sotidius Libuscidianus suggests that Kormasa was a southern neighbour of Sagalassos. With Hadrianoi firmly established near Çallıca, the mound near Kozluca remains the most plausible candidate for Kormasa, which cannot be an older name of Hadrianoi since both toponyms co-existed into late antiquity. Yet, an incorporation of the old city into the territory of Hadrianoi in late Imperial times, similar to the early Imperial annexation of Keraitai and its territory by Kremna and Sagalassos (Waelkens *et al.* 1997a: 54-55), remains a possibility. In that case, Hadrianoi eventually controlled the complete middle Lysis valley.

9. NEW SITES IN THE CENTRAL PART OF THE CHORA OF SAGALASSOS

In 1996 and 1997, the detailed geological, geomorphological, pedological, palaeobotanical and archaeozoological surveys in the neighbourhood of Sagalassos, the results of which are presented as separate research articles in the *Sagalassos* volumes, also led to the discovery of a number of smaller 'special purpose' sites that went unnoticed during the 1994 and 1995 campaigns published in *Sagalassos IV* (Waelkens *et al.* 1997a). They are located in or around the valley of the Ağlasun Çayı, the valley of Çanaklı and that of Çeltikçi.

In the upper valley of the Ağlasun Çayı, near Başköy, three sites already studied in 1994 have been surveyed more intensively, so that new ceramic material could be sampled. A first site was the plateau of Tepe Düzen, where coarse and Imperial to early Byzantine Sagalassos red slip wares were found. A second was the limestone quarry of Sarıkaya, which produced early Imperial Sagalassos red slip ware, while the isolated rock of Adam Atacağı near it (a possible watchtower) contained on its top early Byzantine pottery. Finally, there was the village site of Körüstan, where additional early to late Imperial Sagalassos red slip ware and coarse wares were sampled. On the east slopes of Düzen Tepe a hitherto unnoticed small limestone quarry was discovered (Waelkens *et al.* 1997a: 44-52).

The valley of the Lower Ağlasun Çayı has already been discussed at length in the previous survey article (Waelkens *et al.*1997 a: 18-34). In 1996, a study was made of the division of potential zones for grazing and for farming. Today the whole area, up to an altitude of ca. 1250 m a.s.l., is used for agriculture, sometimes practiced on terraces. Drilling for soil analysis in the fields to the west of Yazırköy produced a Roman sherd at a depth of 0.45 m, providing evidence of colluviation. Up to an altitude of 1700 m, good grazing land is found. Higher up the slopes, grasses are no longer found and pines begin.

During these activities, two new sites were discovered near the western limit of the broad valley bottom of Köyünü, a southern affluent valley of the Ağlasunovası (Fig. 253).

The first is at the Erek Mevkii of Ağlasun. It is located on a gentle east-facing slope near the valley border, at an altitude of 1055 m a.s.l. (37°38,20' N; 30°34,111' E). Here, ceramics were found in a plough layer (5YR 3/4) on top of a red truncated chromic luvisol (5YR 3/6) in clay, containing charcoal fragments and sherds (SA 96 S 33). The survey team also sampled quite a few lumps of flint (SA 96 S 32), most of it unworked. All this material seems to have been removed by erosion from a spot higher up the slope. In fact, ca. 100 m to the north (37°38,231'N; 30°34,151 E; altitude: 1060 m a.s.l.), a second concentration of fine and coarse ceramics (SA 96 S 34) with many tiles, was found directly on the limestone substrate. They belonged to a ruined structure, made of rubble walls, situated on the lowest part of a limestone hill, very close to the contact zone with the fields. To the south of it, near a field road, the central part of an olive press (l.: 0.85 m; w.: 0.75 m; h.: 0.30 m), was seen (Fig. 254) providing evidence for the cultivation of olives in Roman antiquity. The pottery that was sampled included early Imperial Sagalassos red slip ware and probably middle to late Imperial coarse wares. The structure can be identified as an isolated farmstead, practicing olive cultivation and occupying a rocky hill that was itself unfit for farming, but surrounded by good arable land.

In the same valley, a second site, known as Kilocağı (37°37,563' N; 30°33,645 E; altitude: 1100 m a.s.l.), was discovered in the southern front, still worked, of a large clay quarry, exploited for the construction of a nearby irrigation dam. It contained a kiln which had been almost entirely destroyed during the quarrying activities (Fig. 255). Originally, the kiln had stood on an elevated spur, about 10 m above the plain, on top of ophiolithic formations, occupying a very limited area of the actual quarry. The *in situ* remains were located at a depth of ca. 0.70 m below the present surface. The width of the kiln was nearly 1.50 m. It was constructed of rubble walls, lined on the inside with clay, now baked red. The bottom of the kiln was covered with a 0.01 m thick layer of charcoal and ashes. Around the kiln, some tiles were found.

In the quarry walls, significant amounts of colluvial deposits containing Roman ceramics and charcoal frag-

Fig. 251: View of Kozluca Hüyük from the east.

Fig. 252: View from Kozluca Hüyük towards the northeast.

Fig. 253: View of the Köyünü valley, seen from the farm site at Erek Mevkii, Ağlasun.

Fig. 254: Central part of an olive press at Erek Mevkii.

Fig. 255: Remains of a kiln at Kilocağı near Ağlasun.

Fig. 256: One of the rock-cut tombs at Koca Boğaz in the plain of Çanaklı.

Fig. 257: View of the basin of Manastır Mevkii from the east.

Fig. 258: The cultivated valley leading to Manastır Mevkii.

Fig. 259: The cultivated fields at Manastır Mevkii.

Fig. 260: A well at Manastır Mevkii.

Fig. 261: Ruined tomb at Manastır Mevkii.

Fig. 262: The valley of the Peçenekboğaz Deresi, seen from the northeast.

ments are exposed. One of the quarry faces also contained the remains of a terracotta pipe. Ca. 10 m to the north of the kiln, there is an old well (diam.: 1.10 m) faced with rubble. All this indicates that in antiquity some ceramic production took place here. In the mean time, archaeometrical research has revealed that clay derived from flysh deposits around Köyünü sometimes was used as a temper in the coarse wares produced at Sagalassos (Degryse *et al.* 2000). Taken together with the tile kiln excavated at Taşkapı (Poblome *et al.* 2000) and with the remains of a production site near Bağsaray (Waelkens *et al.* 1997a: 60-61), this evidence clearly shows that the ceramic industry of Sagalassos was not limited to the city's potters' quarter alone, but that other sites of the territory contributed to the industry.

To the south of the Ağlasunovası, some of the valley bottoms and slopes around the plain of Çanaklı (Waelkens 1995) were further explored. In 1996, a small farm site (?) was discovered very close to the main road, on a small limestone hill ca. 6 m above the main level of the plain and very close to a modern well. The site, known as Kör Kuyu (37°36,011' N; 30°32,544' E), offers a splendid view over the plain. It contains the remains of a 10.20 by 16.10 m tall structure of well worked stone. Around it, flint (SA 96 S 43), coarse and (late) Imperial Sagalassos red slip wares (SA 96 S 45-46) were found. The same kinds of pottery and tile fragments also occur near the remains of a rubble structure, near the northwestern edge of the limestone hill. The size and location of the ruins suggest a Roman farm site.

On the other side of the plain, near the mouth of the small valley where the detritic clays were exploited that were the raw material for the production of the Sagalassos red slip ware, at the edge of the plain and below the Koca Boğaz pass leading to Çeltikçi, there is a small rock-cut necropolis. Two of the tombs are rather well preserved (Tomb 1: h. of niche: 0.60 m; w.: 0.55 m; Tomb 2: h. of niche: 0.90 m; w.: 0.83 m): they belong to the *arcosolium* type of tomb, known also from Sagalassos, where they seem to be dated to the middle Imperial period, and contain rock-cut coffins below vaulted niches (Fig. 256). This necropolis may be connected with Roman Imperial activity in the nearby clay quarry. Unfortunately, no pottery was found here.

The 1996 survey took us also to an intramontane bassin located immediately to the east of the Çanaklı plain. This basin, known as Manastır Mevkii, is located at a mean altitude of ca. 1350 m a.s.l. (Fig. 257). It can be reached both from Ağlasun and from Hisarköy. From the latter, a small valley to the west of the Büyük Tepe leads towards the hamlet of Manastır. In its lower part, this valley is cultivated on terraces that retain moisture. In its central area, the valley narrows down to ca. 30 m and the bottom is covered with gravel. Higher up, the river bed has eroded a 5 to 20 m deep gulley. Finally, in its highest part, the valley widens again and is once more cultivated on terraces (Fig. 258). There are indications that in the past this terrace agriculture continued to some extent further down. The valley slopes are covered with ceder and juniper trees on the east slopes, and with kermes oak on the opposite side. The intramontane basin of Manastır Mevkii is ca. 1.5 km (east–west) long and 800 m (north–south) wide. It is entirely cultivated with wheat, maize and chickpeas (Fig. 259). The hamlet contains eight inhabited houses and the same number of families. For their water supply they are dependent on three ancient wells (opening ca. 0.60 by 0.60 m) all located in the western part of the basin (Fig. 260). They are at least 15 m deep. One of the wells is additionally fed by a hollowed-out stone channel. Near this well, there are the remains of an old house. Higher up the slopes, on a limestone hill, are the ruins of a ca. 4 by 6 m ancient rectangular structure (Fig. 261). This structure, known as Kiz Kulesi ('the tower of the girl'; 37°36,295' N; 30°34,633' E) and built of medium-sized rough fieldstones, is accessible by a door from the east. Around it, lots of tiles and probably late coarse pottery are found. The structure, which dominates the whole basin, was probably a monumental tomb, a picture which corresponds with the situation in the farming communities in the limestone massif of the Beşparmak. There can be no doubt that at least in late antiquity, this intramontane basin was already under cultivation. Beside good farming land, it also offered its occupants excellent natural protection.

To the southwest of the Çanaklıovası, the small and steep valley of the Pecenekboğazı Deresi (Fig. 262) through which the road from Ağlasun to Çeltikçi and Bucak runs today, was already an important road connection in Roman times (Waelkens *et al.* 1997a: 14). It must have kept this function during the Ottoman and Turkish republican period. This is shown by a number of cisterns or wells at regular intervals in the valley bottom. The southernmost one (37°32,734' N; 30°30,995' E) is located near a recent well. It is pear-shaped with an interior diameter of max. 5.40 m, and has a rectangular opening of 0.80 by 0.90 m. Around it, some coarse, probably late Imperial sherds (SA 96 S 35) were found. Further north, there is a modern well. Finally, higher up the valley, there is a well-preserved cistern (Fig. 263) of the same type as the cisterns around Çanaklı (Waelkens 1995). It is built of plastered rubble walls (4 m by 14 m) and covered with a pitched roof.

In its lower reaches, to the west and parallel to the modern road Ağlasun-Bucak-Antalya, the valley bottom is concave and transformed by several alluvial fans originating from the affluent valleys. The road is situated in the lower reaches of the main valley and in an affluent valley in the prolongation of the main valley. This secondary valley contains considerable colluvial deposits at least 10 m thick.

Except near the southern cistern, no archaeological material was discovered here, so that the lower reaches of the main valley may have been largely uninhabited in antiquity.

This was certainly not the case with its higher areas. In fact, at about 2 km from the valley mouth, the main valley turns towards the west and follows an east–west orientation for nearly 1 km, before turning again to the north (Fig. 264). This section is known as the valley of Sulemiş. In 1996, only part of the east–west section of the main valley (Sulemiş), especially the valley bottom to the north of the *dere* and the lower reaches of the northern valley slope towards the Orta Tepe (altitude: 1081 m a.s.l.) were surveyed. These lower slopes are mainly on bare limestone, with sporadically a thin soil cover. They are overgrown with a scrub vegetation of Quercus calliprinos. In hollows on the slopes, there are some small cultivated terraces. The valley bottom itself is totally under cultivation watered by rainwater. There are also isolated stands of oak trees.

The Sulemiş part of the Peçenekboğazı Deresi valley, was certainly occupied in antiquity. A beautiful arrow-head or scraper was found near its mouth (SA 96 S 36). Higher up, there were two concentrations of ceramics. A terraced area at an altitude of 950 m a.s.l. (37°34,03' N; 30°30,511' E) thus contained a number of coarse ceramics of middle Imperial and mediaeval date, as well as tiny tile fragments (SA 96 S 37). This material may have been deposited here in loads of manure. A more important concentration of tiles and ceramics were found higher up the slopes (37°34,10' N; 30°30,511' E) on a limestone outcrop. The pottery here is similar to that found further down, but also contained some Imperial Sagalassos red slip ware fragments. There are also traces of at least three squarish or rectangular structures in rubble walls. The site, which offers a good view over the valley (Fig. 264), may have been a Roman Imperial farm site, placed in a non-arable part of the valley (limestone outcrop). Nearby, an old dried-up river bed, which may have provided the necessary water, was noticed.

The picture offered by the survey in the central part of the Sagalassian *chora* suggests that it must have included quite a number of dispersed farm sites. In the near future, this hypothesis will be checked by intensive surveys.

10. PRELIMINARY CONCLUSIONS CONCERNING THE OCCUPATION HISTORY

The archaeological survey was initiated in 1993 to improve our knowledge of the settlement history of the region and to define the most likely borders of the territory of Roman Sagalassos. During three previous campaigns, the eastern and southern areas have been explored (Waelkens 1995;
Waelkens *et al.* 1997a). The 1996 survey focused on the western part of the territory of the city (especially sheets M 24 c 1, M 24 c 4, M 24 d 2, M 24 d 3 and M 24 d 4 of the Isparta topographical map) and on some isolated spots in the immediate vicinity of Sagalassos, where activities continued also in 1997. The methodology of previous years, based on previous reports, on scrutinising topographical maps and on interviews with local villagers, was applied again in 1996. As a result, 86 sites could be recorded in 1996 (Fig. 1), some of which were already known from the scholarly literature.

Considering the PREHISTORIC period, 13 sites were recorded, 9 of which were known already from earlier discoveries. The surveys carried out by Özsait especially (1976-77, 1980, 1989, 1991) provided lots of data on the early occupation of the region. Combined with the distribution maps of protohistoric sites in the first volume of the Beyçesultan excavations publication (Lloyd *et al.* 1962), a satisfactory overview can be given of the pre- and protohistoric settlement pattern in the area. Moreover, the excavations at Hacılar and Kuruçay have also greatly increased our knowledge of the protohistoric occupation of the region (Fig. 265).

Among the best-documented prehistoric sites are the höyüks of Hacılar and Kuruçay. Both of them were excavated, respectively by Mellaart during the late 50s and early 60s and by Duru in the late 70s and early 80s. During the 1996 survey, both sites were revisited. They represent the earliest occupation in the area, going back to the Aceramic and the Early Neolithic period respectively, when larger settlements seem to have been limited to the edge of the fertile and perhaps still partly submerged plain of Düğer, where alluvial mud deposited by the receding lake had created favourable conditions for farming. Apart from the höyüks of Hacılar and Kuruçay that were still occupied in the Late Neolithic period, a settlement dating back to this era was also recorded and revisited at Yeşildağ (formerly Gölde). This last is located in an in tramontane basin immediately to the east of the plain of Lake Burdur.

During the Chalcolithic period, the number of known settlements increases. Early Chalcolithic traces were not only found at Hacılar and Kuruçay, but also at Kokar Pınar Hüyük near Yassıgüme, and at Çığırtkankaya. For the Late Chalcolithic period, settlements occur at Kuruçay, Hacılar II, Çığırtkankaya and Karaçal Hüyük. The nice distribution of sites along the eastern edge of the plain of Düğer, where lake levels may have dropped considerably, is characteristic of the Chalcolithic.

This quite dense occupation pattern continued into the Early Bronze Age. Settlements from this period are known at Hacılar II, Kuruçay, Karaçal and Yarıköy, this last now

Fig. 263: One of the Turkish cisterns in the lower valley reaches.

Fig. 264: View from the Sulemiş valley towards the southeast.

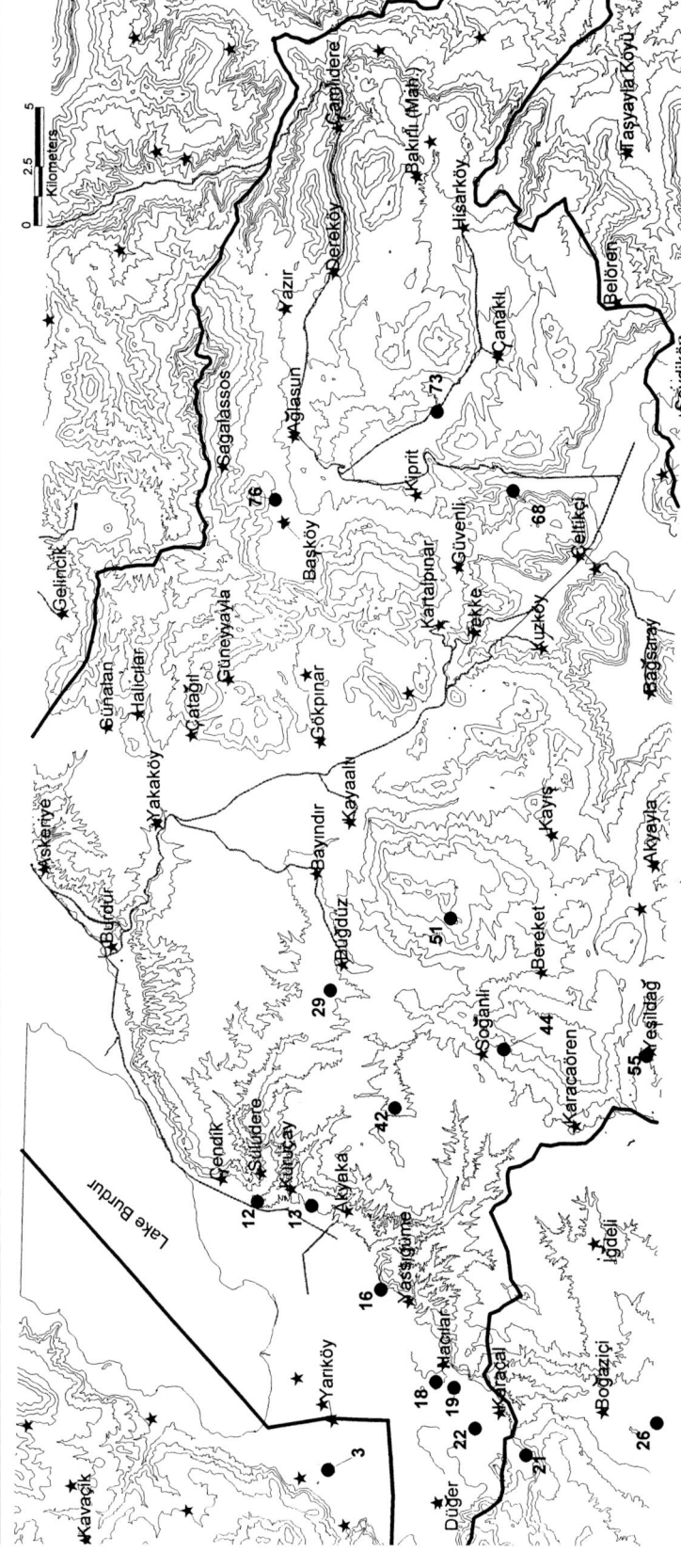

Fig. 265: The distribution of the prehistoric sites surveyed in 1996 and 1997.

Prehistoric sites (n = 17)

3. Gâvur Evi Tepesi (Yarıköy)
12. Çığırtkankaya
13. Kuruçay Höyük
16. Kokar Pinar (Yassıgüme)
18. Öz (Hacılar II)
19. Kerit (Hacılar I, Mellaart's Hacılar)
21. Kozaklı/Yeni Çeşme (Karaçal)
22. Höyük (Karaçal)
26. Höyük (Kozluca)
29. Göbecik Tepesi (Buğdüz)
42. İlyas Tepesi (Soğanlı)
44. Kale (Soğanlı)
51. Kale (Kökez)
55. Höyük (Yeşildağ)
68. Peçenek (Çeltikçi)
73. Kör Kuyu (Çanaklı)
76. Tepe Düzen (Başköy)

being located in the northwestern extremity of the plain of Düger. Apart from these sites whose existence was already known before, two new potential pre- (or protohistoric) sites that are still awaiting a more precise date, could be recorded (Oluk Beli at Yazırköy, Göbecik Tepe at Büğdüz).

When considering their settlement pattern, the density of the prehistoric sites is striking. Immediately to the east and the southeast of Lake Burdur, which means in the western part of the territory of Sagalassos, prehistoric settlements seem to be found at intervals of ca. 5 km. The great uniformity in topographical location of these settlements is also striking. They are all located in the plain bordering Lake Burdur (Figs. 1, 140) or in the valleys around it, on good arable land that is still intensively cultivated today, and always in close vicinity to water. Most of these settlements carry the toponym 'höyük'. However, not all 'höyüks' seem to have been occupied in pre- or protohistoric times and some of them were not necessarily built up by prolonged human occupation.

It is clear that the main function of these settlements was agricultural. Land that was easier to cultivate (the fertile grounds in the plain) was apparently occupied first. The dense occupation of the Burdur plain seems also to prove the success of early agriculture in the area. Only the site at Çığırtkankaya may have belonged to a different category being located on top of a steep hill, without easy access to water or good arable land. Yet, standing at Çığırtkankaya, all the main protohistoric centres in the area can be seen (Hacılar, Kuruçay, Yassıgüme). Moreover, the site guards the only eastern exit through the badlands, formed by the Büğdüz Çayı. It appears that this site already fulfilled a strategic function, which might indicate some degree of hierarchy among the settlements in the area and the creation of territorial units. The density of prehistoric settlements in the western part of the *chora* of Sagalassos stands in sharp contrast with the nearly total lack of permanent settlements in the valleys and the forested hills of the eastern half, where conditions for farming were less favourable. There, an economy based on gathering and hunting may have continued for a much longer period of time. This phenomenon has already been sufficiently discussed elsewhere (Vanhaverbeke *et al.* 1998,a-b; 2000; in press) and will not be treated further here.

For the PROTOHISTORIC period, however, which here corresponds with the Middle and Late Bronze Age, the situation requires more explanation. Except for the site of Darsa (Yarımada, Ada Tepesi or Düğer Ada) near Düger, that was located just beyond the southwestern border of Sagalassian territory, there is no material evidence for Middle and Late Bronze Age occupation in the territory. Near Darsa, a mostly Early Bronze Age cemetery, which seems to have been used also in the second millennium BC, was plundered in the 1960s. This necropolis also contained some Mycenaean imports, most likely imported via the Maeander valley, as well as some local imitations, showing that the local inhabitants had established contacts with the Aegean and with the Mycenaean civilisation. The site on the peninsula in Lake Yarışlı may thus correspond with an important Bronze Age site. Whether the site remained inhabited during the Middle Bronze Age is still uncertain. In the lake district, there is a hiatus in settlements towards the end of the Early Bronze Age (Goetze 1967[2]: 34), but during the Late Bronze Age, the settlement on the peninsula may have been one of the Arzawa settlements (see Waelkens 2000).

Despite the lack of material evidence, it is scarcely possible that the territory of Roman Sagalassos could have been totally devoid of Middle and Late Bronze Age settlements. Previous palynological research had already established that, near the beginning of the Late Bronze Age (3300 BP, uncalibrated date, or cal. ca. 1629 BC), human activity seems to have opened up the by then dominant coniferous forests in Northern Pisidia, while various types of orchards were introduced in the same area (Waelkens and the Sagalassos team 1997: 233-234). More recent drillings by our team in the Gravgaz marshes showed that in the territory of Sagalassos, a deforestation phase took place somewhat later, ca. 3170-2270 BP or cal. 1515/1420-310/240 BC. It is characterised by the disappearance of pine pollen, the dominance of pollen of the *Artemisia herba-alpa* type (up to 50%), and the spread of *Quercus cerris* (Vermoere *et al.* 2000). Although one cannot exclude climatic causes for such a change, it is likely that human activity was also involved in it. In fact, Hittite sources clearly indicate that during this period, Southwest-Anatolia, including Pisidia, already possessed some important settlements. The fact that, based on surface material, no such sites have been identified thus far, can only be explained by cultural superposition, whereby later, more important settlements have obliterated and completely covered older remains. For some settlements (Kolbasa and most probably Sagalassos, see Waelkens 2000), this can even be accepted as a certainty.

Darsa is a similar case: today the various surveys on the site have only produced surface material dated from the eight century BC to Roman Imperial times. Yet, the nearby Bronze Age necropolis could neither be linked with surface material from Darsa, which is the most obvious location for the corresponding settlement, nor with any other site in the vicinity.

A detailed discussion of the settlements and of the regional history during the Late Bronze Age is published by Waelkens (2000). The following remarks are only a summary of that article. Many of the Late Bronze Age military events mentioned in Hittite sources took place in Pisidia, although it is very difficult to identify the toponyms with any degree of certainty. Part of the problem may be the fact that the Hittite activities in the area took place over a longer span of time, during which the boundaries of states such as Arzawa or the Lukka lands probably changed several times, while the local toponomy may also have undergone changes. Sagalassos must have been located at one stage in or near Arzawa, and later also in or near the Lukka lands.

During the Bronze Age, Pisidia must have been settled by Luwians (Fig. 266). The latter, the predecessors of, *inter alia*, the Pisidians of classical times, occupied all of Southwest Anatolia, where they developed powerful states such as Arzawa, located in the periphery of the Hittite kingdom (Goetze 1967²: 49, 179). The state of Arzawa, which for long periods during the Middle Bronze Age seems to have dominated the western half of the peninsula, at least during the first half of the Late Bronze Age, when the Hittite kings had to organize various campaigns against it (Gurney 1975: 16), must have comprised parts of northern Pisidia (Waelkens 2000).

Towards the beginning of the Late Bronze Age, the site of Sagalassos seems to have been located in the region where some of Madduwatas military actions took place. The Madduwatas text tells how this ruler attacked king Kupanta-Kal-as of Arzawa, but was defeated by him. He managed to escape, but his complete household (wife, children and slaves), who fled into the mountains, was eventually taken captive. The Hittite king sent a military force to help Madduwatas. This auxiliary force rescued the latter's household in a place called Sallawassa (Sal-la-u-ua-as-si), where in turn the household and all possessions of Kupanta-Kal-as of Arzawa fell into Hittite hands and were given to Madduwatas (Goetze 1928: 15 §10 vs. 54-55; §11 vs. 58). The latter was reinstated in power, but he later stirred up a rebellion against the Hittites in the cities of Dalawa and Hinduwa.

Another country that turns up, in Hittite sources of the fourteenth – thirteenth century BC, is Luqqa (Lukka) or Lukki. To the Hittites, the Lukka lands must have been a rather vague term, for a group of Luwian-speaking countries in southwestern Anatolia, including Lycia and parts of Pisidia, and without clear political boundaries (Gurney 1997: 135-136, 139). However, towards the end of the Hittite Empire, Lukka seems to have corresponded specifically with eastern Lycia, perhaps including also western Pamphylia as far as the Kestros river, as well as central-southern Pisidia (Hawkins 1995: 55; see Gurney 1997: 135). During the first half or the middle of the thirteenth century BC, as mentioned in the so-called Tawagalawas letter, the Lukka lands were overrun by an enemy. Among the places that were invaded, were also Sallusa and Kuwalapassa.

Forlanini (1988: 156) suggested that Sallusa was perhaps identical with the mountain refuge of Sallawassa or Sallawassi from the Madduwattas episode (1988: 161). This was endorsed by Freu (1987: 131) and Gurney (1997: 137). The last Hittite kings seem also to have campaigned widely in the area (Waelkens 2000).

Bryce suggested that the toponyms mentioned in both the Madduwatas text and the Tawagalawas letter be subdivided into a number of 'clusters'. One of these clusters included Dalawa, Hinduwa and Iyalanda. Another cluster linked Dalawa to Kuwalapassa. since both places agreed to join forces with the Hittites in an attack on Iyalinda (Bryce 1974: 399). Most scholars now locate the cluster Dalawa-Hinduwa-Iyalinda and Kuwalapassa in western Lycia (Tlos-Kandyba-Oinoanda) and the adjoining part of northwestern Pisidia. In fact, Dalawa (as Talawa) is also mentioned together with Awarna (Xanthos), Pinali (Pinara) and Wiyanawanda (Oenoanda) on two hieroglyphic texts from the late thirteenth century BC (Hawkins 1995: 49, 52; Gurney 1997: 136). They show that the Dalawa-Hinduwa-Iyalinda cluster actually has to be placed in classical Lycia. Kuwalapassa is generally identified now with Kolbasa, located immediately to the south of Sagalassos (Forlanini 1988: 167; Hawkins 1995: 52 nr. 181, 56; Gurney 1997: 138). This means that, despite the general lack of Late Bronze Age surface finds in Southwest Anatolia, Lycia and even Pisidia already possessed several urban settlements, which continued to exist and prosper right into classical times.

Despite ongoing discussions among the Hittitologists about the identification of some of the toponyms, it is clear that Madduwatas' first military activities must have taken place somewhere to the north of Lycia with its cities of Dalawas, Hinduwa and Iyalanda and that this condottiere must have ruled over the Phrygo-Pisidian border district. All this makes it very tempting and even plausible, as Cornelius (1990⁴: 22, 265) suggested, to look for his base in the district around Lake Burdur, in which case, in our opinion Darsa would be a very valuable candidate. Whatever the location of Madduwatas's residence, the mountain site of Sallawassa (Sal-la-u-ua-as-si) where the families of Madduwatas and of Kupanta-Kal-as of Arzawa were taken captive, can most probably be identified with Sagalassos, as was already suggested by Freu (1987: 140-141, 147). The fact that the southern neighbour of Sagalassos, that is, Kuwalapassa-Kolbasa, at one stage joined forces with Dalawa to attack Iyalinda, whereas the last two cities are also mentioned shortly after the two Sallawassa episodes in the Madduwatas text, suggest that all these events took place within the same geographical region. Moreover, the clear similarity between the toponyms makes such an identification more plausible than Forlanini's suggestion of

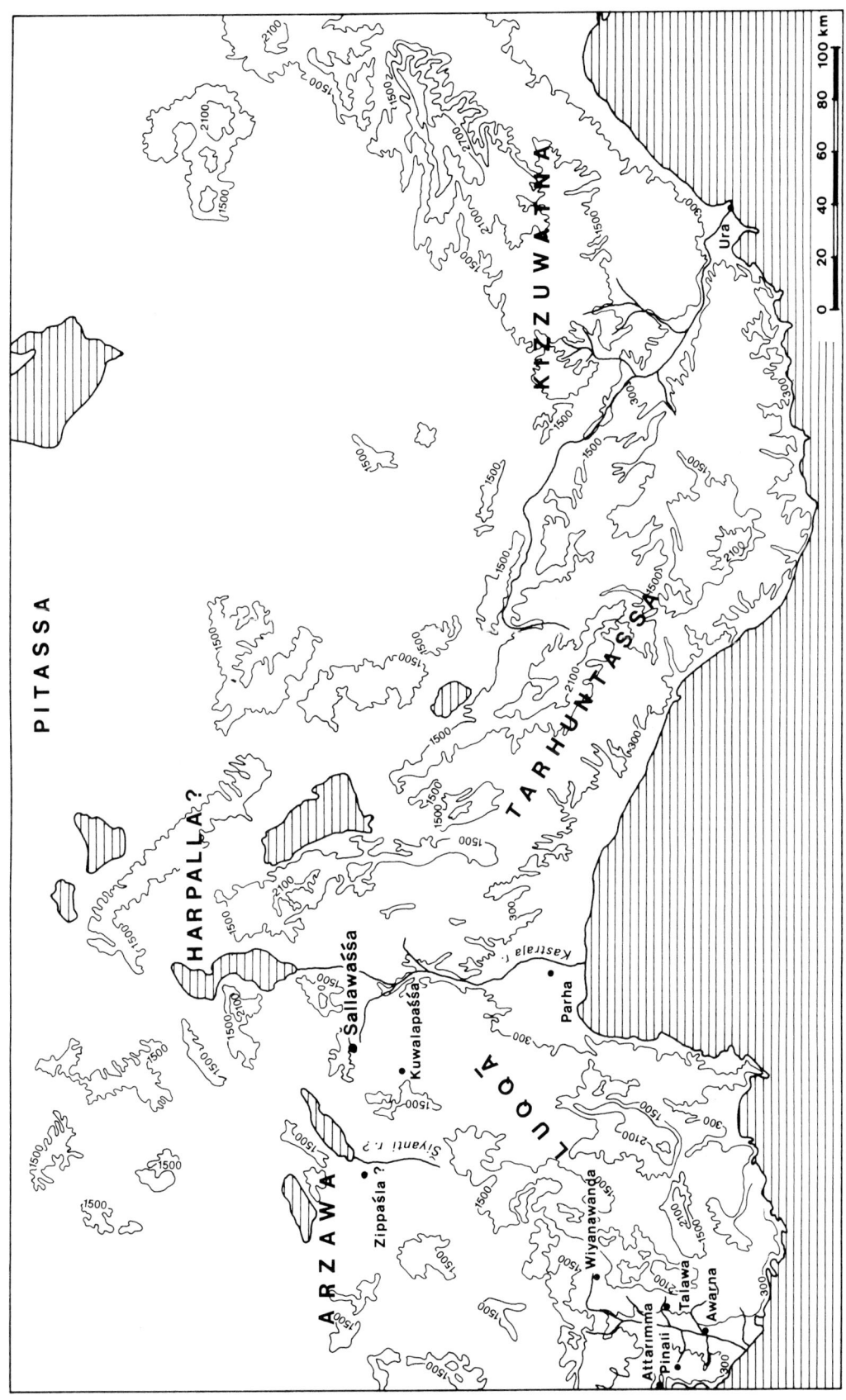

Fig. 266: Pisidia during the Late Bronze Age.

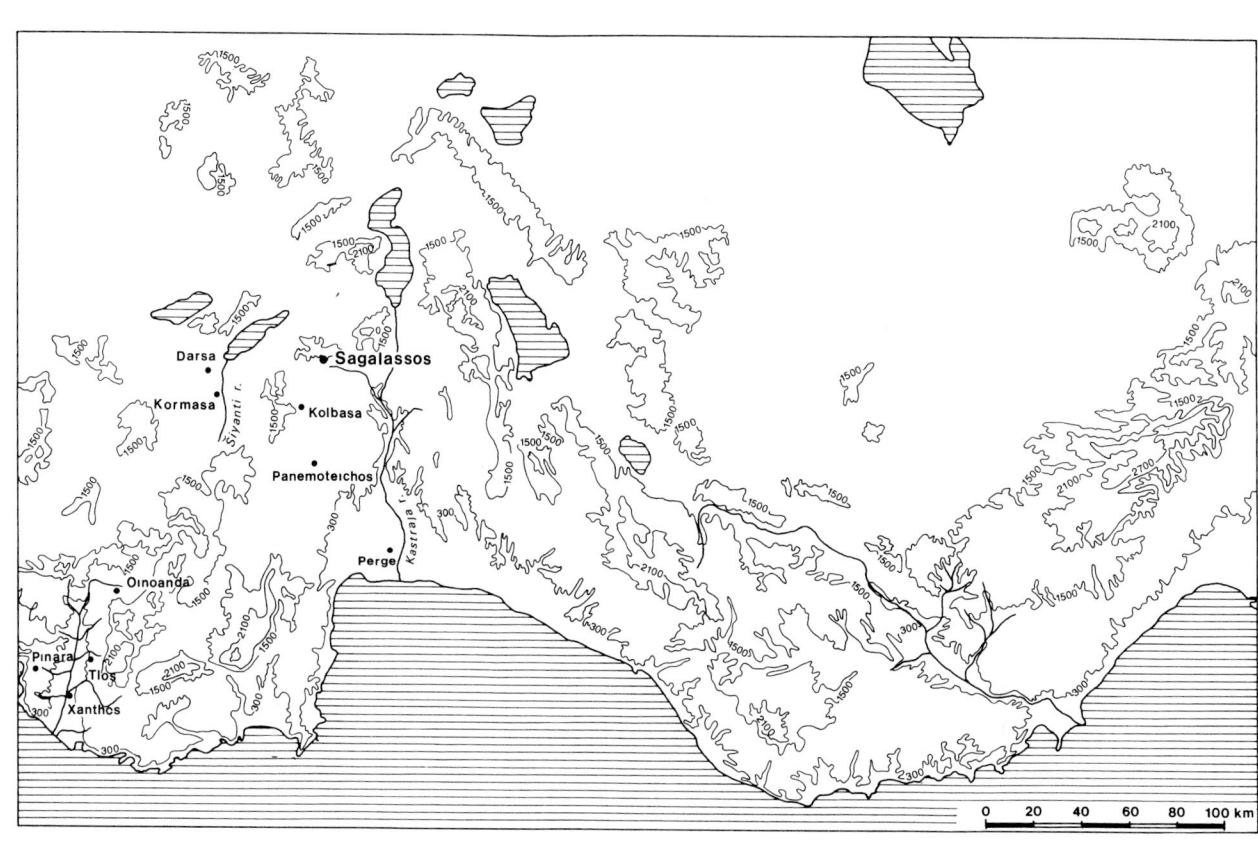

Fig. 267: West Pisidia during the Early Iron Age.

identifying Sallawassa with Pamphylian Sillyon (1988: 167). Sagalassos most probably therefore occurs already in fourteenth century BC Hittite texts as Sallawassa, and perhaps again in thirteenth century BC texts as Sallusa (Waelkens 2000). Originally, it must have been located in or near the princedom of Madduwattas. The description of the military events following his defeat by the king of Arzawa could suggest that Sallawassa was part of Arzawa, or at any rate located very close to it. After Mursilis II's campaigns, the place may have become part of the Hittite realm, but the upheaval following Hattusilis III's usurpation of the throne, may have placed it again beyond Hittite control. Depending on the much disputed northwestern boundary (near Akşehir?) of the vassal state of Tarhuntassa, which certainly further south, in Pamphylia, was formed by the Aksu, it may have been part of this kingdom, or perhaps already have been located in the Lukka lands, which seem to have been replaced Arzawa in this area. What the Hittite sources in any case reveal is the fact that many of the sites of classical Lycia (Xanthos, Tlos, Pinara, Oenoanda), Pisidia (Kolbasa, Sagalassos) and Pamphylia (Perge) existed already during the Late Bronze Age. This strongly corroborates the hypothesis of a cultural superposition in this district between protohistorical and classical sites and can explain the apparent lack of protohistorical settlements. The establishment of Luwians and the creation of chiefdoms and states from the Middle Bronze Age onward (Hittites, Arzawa, Kizzuwatna, Ahhiyawa, Lukka lands) may have introduced a new kind of society, no longer centred around höyüks in the middle of the rich agricultural plains or valleys, but around fortified or more easy defensible mountain sites. If this hypothesis is valid, in many places there may have been a continuum of settlement from the Middle/Late Bronze Age right into the historical period.

All this indicates that conditions were very unsettled in Southwest Anatolia towards the end of the Late Bronze Age, which must have also affected the area around Sagalassos (including Kolbasa). During the second half of the thirteenth century BC, the Lukka are mentioned in Egyptian sources among the Sea Peoples (Bryce 1974a: 395-397). Whatever remained of Arzawa most probably disappeared in the general turmoil around 1200 BC (Goetze 1967^2: 185).

In the EARLY HISTORICAL period (early Iron Age) the same phenomenon of cultural superposition may explain a similar lack of sites. In Central Anatolia most Hittite sites were burned around 1200 BC, and there may have been massive movements and migrations of people, but elsewhere on the peninsula life and settlements may have continued almost undisturbed. This may have been the case with some of the Luwian states in southern Anatolia, such as Tarhuntassa and the Lukka lands (Joukowsky 1996: 297-299). In the central and western part of the peninsula by the late ninth century BC, the power vacuum caused by the collapse of the Hittite state was filled gradually by the emergence of a Phrygian kingdom, at least partly ruled by immigrants from the Balkans. This short-lived political power, which lasted only one century, in the mid-eighth century BC extended as far as Lydia in the west. Yet, its cultural influence, which is even visible as far south as the Elmalı plain, was more long-lasting and continued up to the beginning of the Lydian domination of the peninsula. From the early seventh century BC until 546 BC, the Lydian kings, ruling from Sardis, extended their domination over most of western Anatolia, except for Cilicia which fell into Neo-Babylonian hands. They eventually reached the Halys river in the east (Joukowsky 1996: 368-372, 374, 402-407). During the years 546-338 BC, all of Anatolia became incorporated into the Persian Achaemenid empire. For the moment, however, it is far from clear how strongly Phrygian and Lydian rule was felt in the mountain sites of Pisidia, including Sagalassos. The Persians could hardly control the unruly Pisidians (Xenophon, *Hellenika* III.1.3).

The history of Southwest Anatolia during the Dark Ages is still a mystery. Mellaart (1954: 180) believed that numerous new settlements emerged, often on hitherto uninhabited and isolated rocks, which continued to be occupied until a later period (Xanthos, Pinara, Kaş, Aspendos). As we have seen, however, some of them were already important settlements during the Late Bronze Age. This may also have been the case with Sagalassos, which at the time of Alexander's conquest is described already as "not a small city" (Arrian, *Anabasis Alexandri* I, 28).

Unless some of the fortified mountain sites discovered during our surveys, are (partly) pre-Hellenistic in date, which is probable the case for at least some of them, the only major Early Iron Age sites are those of Ada Tepesi, Yarımada or Düğer Ada in Lake Yarışlı, and of Kozluca Hüyük, both located immediately to the southwest of Sagalassian territory. Recently, another site of similar date was discovered to the south of it, at Panemoteichos (Aydal et al. 1997). Together with Sagalassos, where so far no contemporary material evidence has been found, they may indicate the emergence of real city sites, probably controlling larger territorial units (Fig. 267)

The site of Ada Tepesi most probably should be identified with the small city of Darsa mentioned by Livy XXXVIII, 13-15, whereas that of Kozluca Hüyük may correspond with the city of Kormasa mentioned in the same episode. Both controlled a major road system linking Central and Western Anatolia with the Turkish south coast.

During the Early Iron Age, the peninsula in Lake Yarışlı, clearly became the seat of a local ruler, either of Phrygian origin, or a Pisidian (?) dynast strongly influenced by Phrygian culture. It is known that, if not the kingdom of Phrygia itself, its cultural sphere during the eighth to the sixth century BC extended south into the Burdur region and into Northern Lycia. During this period, Darsa contained various monumental structures of Phrygian type, including both real 'buildings' and a rock-cut tomb. Its ceramic surface material belonged both to the group of 'Phrygian' grey wares and to the painted 'Southwest Anatolian wares', attributed to the Early Iron Age (Mellaart 1954: 180). This means that the area around Düğer in the Early Iron Age must have had contacts with various outlying districts and have been well aware of developments elsewhere. It is hoped that the Sagalassos excavations will also some day produce similar sherds.

The transition from the Early Iron Age, with its Phrygian (?) remains at Ada Tepesi and Kozluca, to the historical period, is still hardly documented. As far as Sagalassos is concerned, the HISTORICAL period starts with the arrival of Alexander the Great in the spring of 333 BC and the beginning of the Hellenistic period. During the 1996 survey, fewer than ten Hellenistic sites (Fig. 268) could be recorded (Hellenistic pottery was collected at Ada Tepesi (Darsa) and on the höyük near Kozluca (Kormasa). Some of this pottery seems already to have been produced at Sagalassos. Hellenistic fortifications were recorded at the Kale's near Akyayla, Kökez and Soğanlı. Other Hellenistic fortlets or watchtowers were recorded at Tekke, close to Hacılar, and at Gâvur Evi Tepesi near Yarıköy, respectively on the eastern and the western edges of the plain of Düğer. Except for the latter, which could represent the site of a garrison of one of the Hellenistic kingdoms, the others probably played a role in the defences of the territorial boundaries of Hellenistic Sagalassos. They seem to belong to a ring of fortified lookouts, from which imminent danger could directly be signalled to the city. Even if in most cases, the 1996 surface material did not produce any conclusive evidence for such an early date, the highly strategic location of these fortifications, which would have become totally superfluous in Roman Imperial times, as well as the use of a good ashlar or emplekton technology might confirm a Hellenistic construction date. Traces of real (late) Hellenistic settlements may occur near Kayış, at Yeşildağ, at Bereket and at Yapımca Olak in the limestone district, and near Suludere and Karaçal along the eastern edge of the plain of Düğer.

Most of the mountain fortifications, except perhaps for the one above Soğanlı, cannot be considered to have been occupied by a permanent civilian population. They are much too small for that. Yet, it is very likely that some minor settlements may have developed near or around them, in order to provide the garrisons with food and other amenities, and the civilian population would in return find shelter or military protection at times of danger.

For the Imperial period, the number of sites recovered rises dramatically compared with the Hellenistic period. No less than 65 sites could be attributed to this period, some of which had already been (partly) described by earlier travellers. A certain number were already occupied before. Considering the sites dated to the Roman period (Fig. 269), we can make four points, two of which relate to the general characteristics of the settlement pattern of this period. It thus seems that settlements developed at this time in all sorts of topographical locations: plains and valleys, hillsides and mountain slopes. The explosion of sites must reflect a real expansion of occupation and settlement patterns. They are found in all the intramontane basins and valleys, usually representing a denser occupation pattern than the present one. The peace established by Augustus not only made it safer to occupy the whole territory of Sagalassos, but also provided a more favourable economic framework and material prosperity for a growing number of people with enough means to leave material evidence behind. Some of these people may also have played a prominent role in the economic development of their villages and may eventually have come to dominate them completely as the chief landholding families, constructing impressive family mausolea.

A second point related to the first is that there exists a clear hierarchy in these settlements, evidenced by the typology and number of buildings, by the occurrence of inscriptions and reliefs, and by the type and amount of ceramics. The smallest settlement unit, still recognisable as 'a site', consists of isolated find-spots. Most of these are characterised by coarse ceramics, found in relation to rubble walls and sometimes accompanied by cisterns or counter-weights for olive presses. These sites are found near or on arable land, mostly in the vicinity of water. It is striking that, wherever possible, they did not occupy good farming land, but had been built on top of nearby limestone spurs. Most probably, they represent 'isolated farmsteads', some of them ceramic production units. Another striking feature is the omnipresence of traces of olive cultivation. Whereas this cannot now be practised above an altitude of ca. 900 m a.s.l., remains of presses are found almost everywhere on the territory at much higher altitudes, ranging from ca. 990 m a.s.l. (Suludere) to 1445 m a.s.l. (Bereket). This can only indicate less harsh climatic conditions in Roman antiquity. Even if some of these presses may also have been used in viticulture, it is more likely that most of them served the processing of olives, of which the cultivation up to an altitude of 1200 m a.s.l. is also attested by pollen and by carbonized olive wood.

Next in rank are larger 'agricultural settlements' with similar characteristics, but containing more buildings with

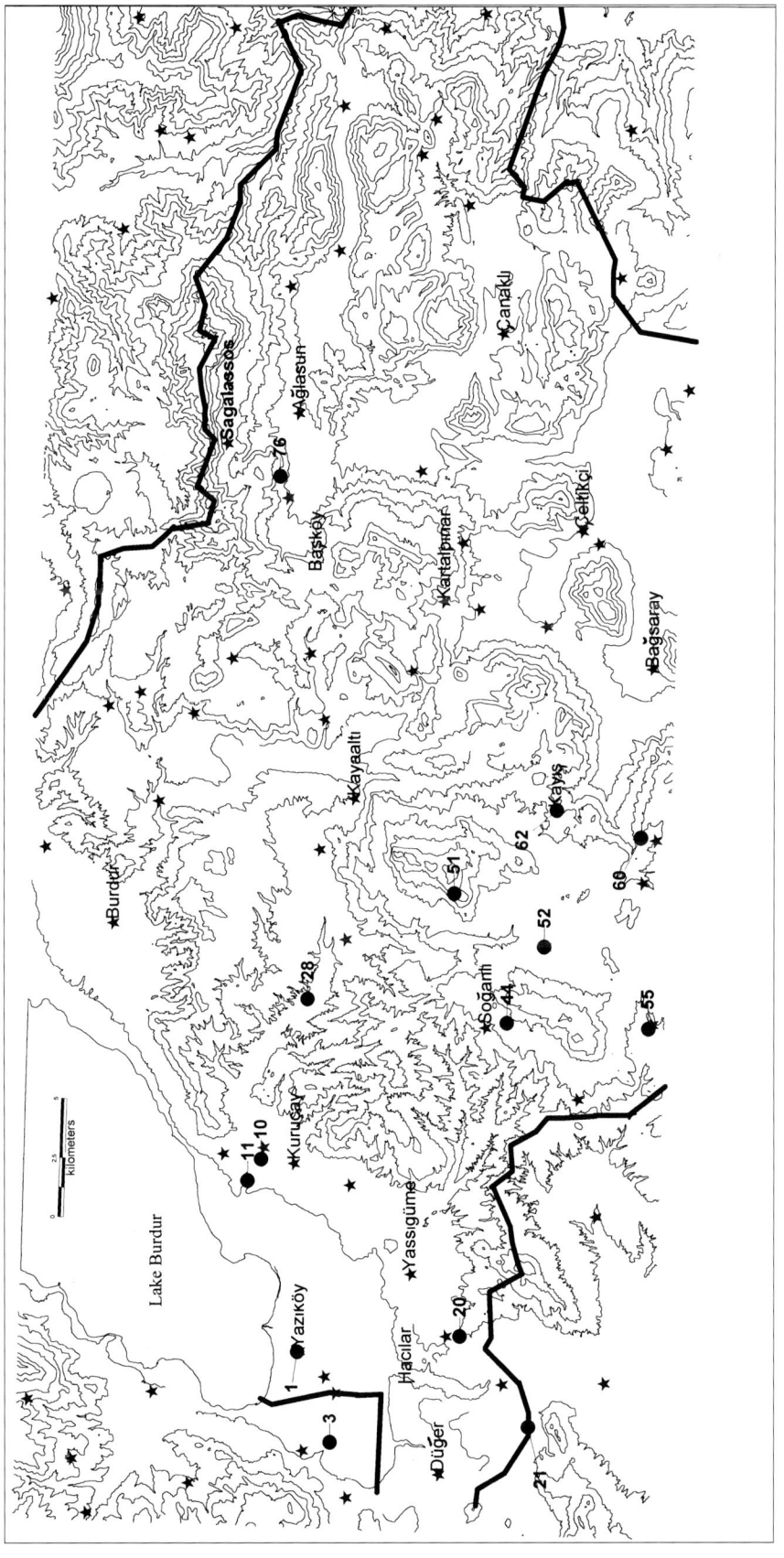

Fig. 268: Map with the Hellenistic sites discovered in 1996-1997.

Prehistoric sites (n = 14)

1. Yazıköy
3. Gâvur Evi Tepesi (Yarıköy)
10. Ören (Suludere)
11. Eski Mezarlık (Suludere)
20. Tekke (Hacılar)
21. Kozaklı/Yeni Çeşme (Karaçal)
28. Old Büğdüz
44. Kale (Soğanlı)
51. Kale (Kökez)
52. Bereket
55. Höyük (Yeşildağ)
60. Kale (Akyayla)
62. Kayış
76. Tepe Düzen (Başköy)

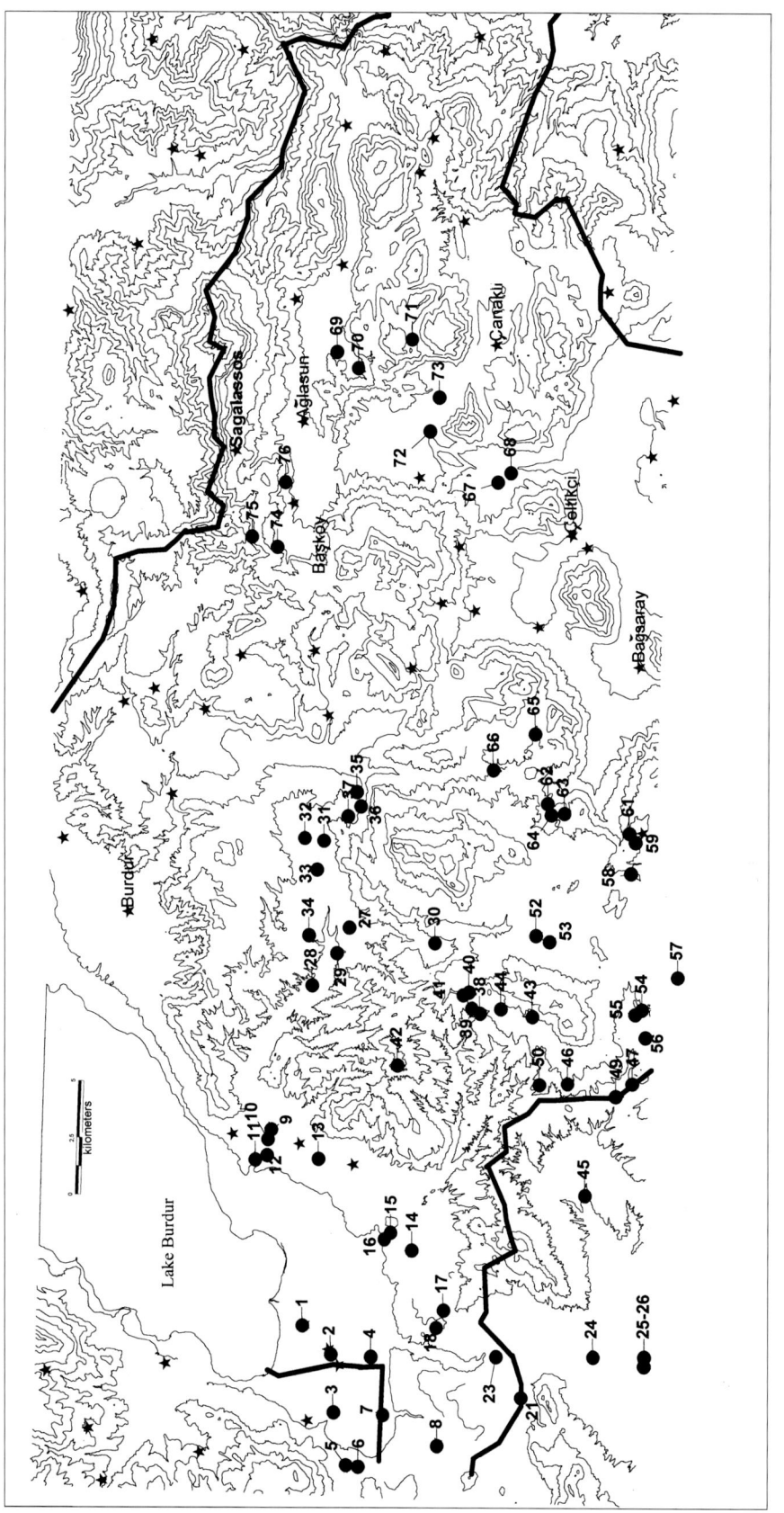

Fig. 269: The Roman sites studied during the 1996-1997 surveys.

sometimes a more elaborate character (e.g. with columns). Most of these represent monumental tombs of local landowning families who may have dominated these rural communities economically and politically.

Still higher in rank are 'minor centres', characterised by architectural remains of some standing (monumental buildings or tombs, a certain number of well-decorated building elements and inscriptions). One can imagine that Gâvur Ören near Karacaören and Kayış may have been such minor centres during the Imperial period.

A last type of settlement, apparently appearing from late Imperial times onwards and reflecting the changed conditions in the empire, are 'strategic sites', located near crossroads (Kilise Mevkii to the north of Düğer?) or in dominating locations without access to good farming land (Ilyas Tepesi, Çığırtkankaya Tepesi).

The third point we wish to make is the very pronounced role of the changing environment in the distribution of settlements. Chronologically speaking, the changing lake levels may have favoured or excluded specific areas for settlement, at least during the prehistoric period. The presence of water always remained a decisive factor, except for sites with a merely strategic function. But, even during the period of the greatest prosperity and economic expansion, large areas in the western part of the city's territory, that is, in the badlands, remained almost free of sites, because productive farming was not possible here. These zones however, may have had a use as pastures or as hunting grounds.

A fourth point is more specific and concerns the borders of the territory of Sagalassos in Imperial times. Some indications of the location of the western boundary of the territory were already known. Monuments erected by Sagalassos had thus been found at Yazıköy, at Yarıköy, and at Düğer. During the 1996 survey, an identical boundary stone, also dated to the reign of Nero, delimiting the territories of Sagalassos and Tymbrianassos, was found most probably *in situ* in a field along an ancient road near Düğer. This exceptional find permitted a more specific delimitation of the western and southwestern limits of Sagalassasian territory. Starting near the southernmost point of Lake Burdur, the boundary must have followed the *via Sebaste* southwards (perhaps replacing a previous boundary formed by the Düğer Çayı) as far as its crossing (a bit north of Düğer) with the Sultan Yolu (probably representing a secondary ancient road*)*. The area to the north of this road belonged to the village of Tymbrianassos, which was located on an imperial estate and gave one fifth of its revenues to Sagalassos. This means that the southern and eastern half of the valley to the south of Lake Burdur belonged to Sagalassos and that the hills immediately south and west of Düğer, at either side of the republican road coming from Yarışlı apparently formed a natural boundary to its territory. East of Düğer the hills at either side of the Lysis near Karaçal may have formed the border again, eventually turning eastwards along the southern edge of the badlands somewhere to the north of Igdeli and northeast of Kozluca. This southern boundary separated Sagalassos from the city of Darsa (Palaiopolis?), Hadrianoi and Kormasa. Gâvur Ören must have been a large settlement still located on Sagalassian territory. From there the boundary followed the hills towards the Kestel Dağı range, which separated Sagalassos from a number of small fortified cities further south (Kaynar Kalesi, Kolbasa, Kretopolis).

In the early Byzantine period, the number of sites with traces from this period is much less (Fig. 270). One of them, Asar near Akyayla, can be considered as a typical example of a Byzantine settlement: it is located near a rocky spur, with a good view over the surroundings, small in surface, and covered with mostly coarse wares. A similar location is at Yassıgüme. Another Byzantine settlement found at Manastır near Soganlı does not seem to have had a primarily strategic function. The latter was apparently a small, remote settlement without any fortifications although it was well protected by the dense forest surrounding it. The site of Manastır between Ağlasun and Hisarköy, located at a high altitude in an intramontane basin with good farming land, but with a difficult access, might also partly go back to this period. Byzantine remains have also been found at Bereket, Karacaören en Soğanlı, but on the whole the number of sites is drastically reduced, suggesting a serious abandonment of the area after the middle of the seventh century AD, probably caused by natural catastrophes and by the Arab raids.

For the later periods, we should mention the presence of most probably Ottoman cisterns, in the valley of Peçenek (Çeltikçi), along an old caravan road to Ağlasun. An exquisite Ottoman house (Fig. 53) was found at Yeşildağ (Gölde).

As a conclusion for the 1996 and 1997 surveys, we can say that the western part of the territory of Sagalassos had a very rich archaeological past. Its fertile arable land clearly attracted some of the earliest farmers of the Neolithic period. During the subsequent Chalcolithic and Early Bronze Age, the region became even more densely occupied, especially in the rich plain to the southeast of Lake Burdur. During the Middle and Late Bronze and during the Early Iron Age, traces of occupation are very rare. This could be due, however, to cultural superposition, meaning that those sites were continuously occupied until Hellenistic and Roman times, so that they basically present artefacts from those periods at their surface. This would imply that the arrival of the Pisidi-

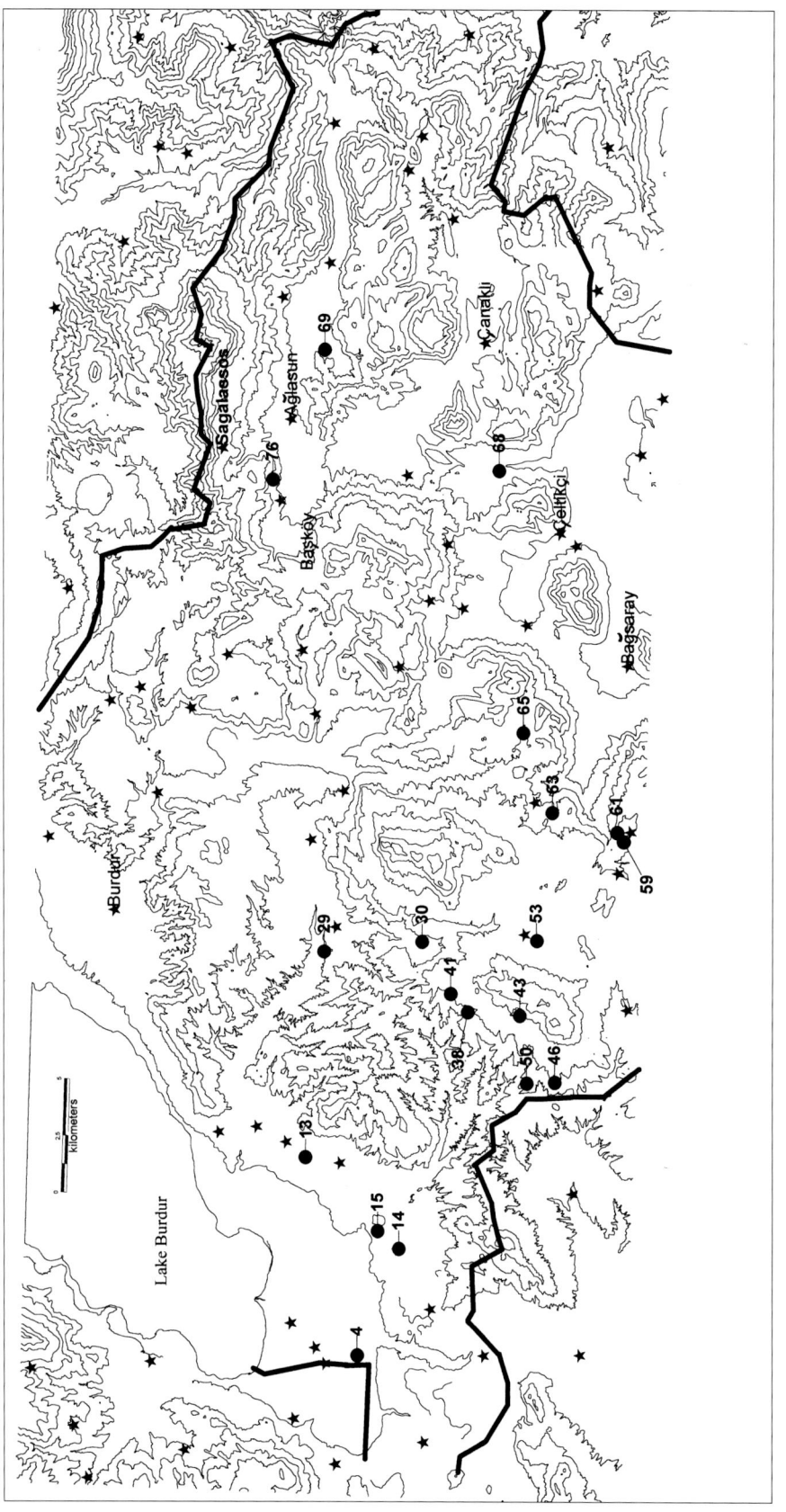

Fig. 270: The early Byzantine sites identified in 1996-1997.

Byzantine sites (n = 19)

4. Kilise (Yarıköy)
13. Kuruçay Höyük
14. Yassıgüme
15. Kale (Yassıgüme)
29. Göbecik Tepesi (Buğdüz)
30. Yayla (Buğdüz)
38. Soğanlı
41. Yapımca Olak (Soğanlı)
43. Monastır (Soğanlı)
46. Karacaören
50. Ören/Pazar
53. Kirselik (Bereket)
59. Kilise Yıkığı (Akyayla)
61. Asar (Akyayla)
63. Asar Tepesi (Kayış)
65. Eski Kayış (Kayış)
68. Peçenek (Çeltikçi)
69. Erek (Köyünü)
76. Tepe Düzen (Başköy)

ans, perhaps at some time during the seventeenth century BC, had involved a drastic change in settlement patterns. In fact, more unstable conditions may have caused the population to retreat to well-protected mountain sites, exactly the same as those of the Hellenistic period. That this was the case for at least some of them seems corroborated by Hittite sources. The close vicinity of good farming lands may have been no longer the priority for selecting a settlement site, but rather defence and military control. This pattern continued right into Hellenistic times.

During the Roman Imperial period the number of settlements leaving datable material evidence behind increased dramatically, with wide variations in their location and probable function. While some of the old mountain sites remained occupied, most people seem to have settled in farmsteads, hamlets, special purpose sites and minor centres spread all over the plains and valleys. In the Byzantine era, political instability and military threats (the Isaurian raids of the fifth-sixth century and the Arab invasions of the seventh century AD), as well as natural catastrophes (earthquakes in AD 518 and ca. AD 650, the plague of AD 541-542) may have triggered a new recession (Waelkens *et.al.* 2000), the fewer settlements being located again in remote places, protected by fortifications or by nature.

11. ACKNOWLEDGEMENTS

This text presents the results of the Belgian Programme on Internuniversitary Poles of Attraction initiated by the Belgian State, Prime Minister's Office, Science Policy Programming (IUAP 4/12). This research was also made possible thanks to an FWO-Vlaanderen research grant (FWO/G.0215.96) and to a GOA-programme (97/2). Scientific responsibility is assumed by its authors.

12. REFERENCES

A. Åkerstrøm (1966) *Die architektonischen Terrakotten Kleinasiens*, Lund.

N.II. Ἀνδριώτης (1931) art. Λιμνόρροια, in: Μεγάλη Ἑλληνικὴ Ἐγκυκλοπαιδεία, Athens: 143.

F.V.J. Arundell (1834) *Discoveries in Asia Minor Including a Description of the Ruins of Several Ancient Cities and Especially of Antioch of Pisidia* 2, London.

H. von Aulock (1977) *Münzen und Städte Pisidiens I* (Istanbuler Mitteilungen. Beiheft 25) Tübingen.

S. Aydal, S. Mitchell, Th. Robinson and L. Vandeput (1997) The Pisidian survey 1995, *Anatolian Studies* 47: 141-172.

G.E. Bean (1954) Sculptured and inscribed stones at Burdur, *Belleten* 18: 469-510.

G.E. Bean (1959) Notes and Inscriptions from Pisidia I, *Anatolian Studies* 9: 67-118.

G.E. Bean (1960) Notes and inscriptions from Pisidia II, *Anatolian Studies* 10: 34-92.

V. Bérard (1892) Inscriptions d'Asie Mineure, *Bulletin de Correspondance Hellénique* 16: 417- 438.

K. Belke and N. Mersich (1990) *Phrygien und Pisidien* (Tabula Imperii Byzantini 7) Wien.

J. Birmingham (1964) Surface finds from various sites, *Anatolian Studies* 14: 29-34.

J. Birmingham (1965) Recent acquisitions by Birmingham City Museum, in: *Archaeological Reports for 1964-65. Published by the Council of the Society for the Promotion of Hellenic Studies. British School of Archaeology at Athens*: 64-70, figs 4-14.

T.R. Bryce (1974) The Lukka problem and a possible solution, *Journal of Near Eastern Studies* 33: 395-404.

M. Christol and Th. Drew-Bear (1991) D. Fonteius Fronto, Proconsul de Lycie-Pamphylie, *Greek-Roman-and-Byzantine Studies* 32: 397-413.

M. Collignon (1878) Inscriptions d'Orméle en Phrygie, *Bulletin de Correspondance Hellénique* 2: 53-64, 170-174, 243-265.

M. Collignon (1879) Inscriptions de Pisidie et de Pamphylie, *Bulletin de Correspondance Hellénique* 3: 333-347.

F. Cornelius (1990^4) *Geschichte der Hethiter. Mit besonderer Berücksichtigung der geographischen Verhältnisse und der Rechtsgeschichte*, Darmstadt (unveränderte Auflage von durchgesehene Auflage 1976).

W.W. Cummer (1970) Phrygian rooftiles in the Burdur Museum, *Anadolu* 14: 29-71.

P. Degryse, R. Degeest, J. Poblome, W. Viaene, R. Ottenburgs, H. Kucha and M. Waelkens (2000) Mineralogy and geochemistry of Roman common wares produced at Sagalassos and their possible clay resources, in: M. Waelkens and L. Loots (eds) *Sagalassos V. Report on the Survey and Excavation Campaigns of 1996 and 1997* (Acta Archaeologica Lovaniensia Monographiae 11) Leuven University Press: 709-721

H. Devijver (†) and M. Waelkens (forthcoming) Roman inscriptions from the sixth and seventh campaigns at Sagalassos, *Sagalassos VI*.

L. Duchesne and M. Collignon (1877) Rapport sur un voyage archéologique en Asie Mineure, *Bulletin de Correspondance Hellénique* 1: 363-375.

L. Duchesne (1879) Sur deux villes de la Phrygie Pacatienne, *Bulletin de Correspondance Hellénique* 3: 478-482.

R. Duru (1980) Kuruçay Höyüğü kazıları, 1978-1979 çalışma raporu, *Anadolu Araştırma. Ek Yayın* 2.

R. Duru (1982) Kuruçay Höyüğü kazıları, 1980 çalışma raporu, *Anadolu Araştırma* 8: 1-33.

R. Duru (1983a) Kuruçay Höyüğü kazıları, 1981 çalışma raporu, *Anadolu Araştırma* 9: 13-38.

R. Duru (1983b) Kuruçay Höyüğü kazıları, 1982 çalışma raporu, *Anadolu Araştırma* 9: 81-89.

R. Duru (1985) Kuruçay Höyüğü kazıları, 1983 çalışma raporu, *Belleten* 194: 595-606.

R. Duru (1986) Kuruçay Höyüğü kazıları, 1984 çalışma raporu, *Belleten* 195: 247-259.

R. Duru (1987a) Kuruçay Höyüğü kazıları, 1985 çalışma raporu, *Belleten* 196: 305-313.

R. Duru (1987b) Kuruçay 1986, *Anatolian Studies* 37: 202-203.

R. Duru (1988a) Kuruçay Höyüğü 1986 çalışma raporu, *IX Kazı sonuçları toplantısı*, Ankara 1987: 65-70.

R. Duru (1988b) Kuruçay Höyüğü kazıları 1986-87 çalışma raporu, *Belleten* 203: 653-666.

R. Duru (1989) Kuruçay Höyüğü 1987 çalışma raporu, *X Kazı sonuçları toplantısı*, Ankara 1988: 57-60.

R. Duru (1990) Kuruçay Höyüğü kazıları 1988 çalışma raporu, *XI Kazı sonuçları toplantısı*, Ankara 1989: 81-90.

R. Duru (1994) *Kuruçay Höyük I. 1978-1988 Kazılarının sonuçları Neolitik ve Erken Kalkolitik çağı yerleşmeler / Results of the Excavations 1978-1988. The Neolithic and Early Chalcolithic*

Periods, Ankara.

R. Duru (1996) *Kuruçay Höyük II. 1978-1988 Kazılarının sonuçları Geç Kalkolitik ve Ilk Tunc çagı yerleşmeler / Results of the Excavations 1978-1988. The Late Chalcolithic and Early Bronze Settlements*, Ankara.

D. Eitam (1993) Selected oil and wine installations in ancient Israel, in: M.C. Amouretti, J.P. Brun and D. Eitam (eds), *Actes du symposium international organisé par le Centre Camille Jullian (Université de Provence-C.N.R.S.) et le Centre archéologique du Var (Aix-en-Provence et Toulon, 20-22 novembre 1991) (Bulletin de Correspondance Hellénique. Supplément XXVI)* Paris 1993: 91-106.

O. Erol (1997) Geomorphologic arguments for mid- to late Holocene environmental change in Central Anatolian (pluvial) lake basins, in: N. Dalfes, G. Kukla and H. Weiss (eds) *Third Millennium BC Climate Change and Old World Collapse (NATO SCI Series I, 49)* Berlin: 321- 350.

M. Forlanini (1988) La regione del Tauro nei testi Hittiti, *Vicino Oriente* 7: 129-169.

R. Frankel (1994) Ancient oil mills and presses in the land of Israel, in: R. Frankel, S. Avitsur and E. Ayalon (eds) *History and Technology of Olive Oil in the Holy Land*, Arlington-Tel Aviv: 19-89

D.H. French (1976) Roma devri mil taşları ve yolları üzerinde 1974 yılında yapılan araştırmalar, *Türk Arkeoloji Dergisi* 23,1: 51-54.

D.H. French and S. Mitchell (1977) Roma imparatorluğunun ilk devirlerinde Pisidia'da yollar ve ulaşım, *Türk Arkeoloji Dergisi* 24,1: 213-220.

D.H. French (1978) Roman roads in Central Anatolia, in: E. Akurgal (ed.) *Proceedings of the Tenth International Congress of Classical Archaeology*, Ankara: I, 293-294.

D.H. French (1979) RECAM: Burdur, *Anatolian Studies* 29: 6.

D.H. French (1980) The Roman road system of Asia Minor, in: H. Temporini and W. Haase (eds) *Aufstieg und Niedergang der römischen Welt* II.7.2, Berlin: 698-729.

D.H. French (1984) CIL CVII *Fasc.5*. Roads and milliaria of Asia Minor, *Anatolian Studies* 34: 10-11.

D.H. French (1988) *Roman Roads and Milestones of Asia Minor. Fasc. 2: An interim Catalogue of Milestones. Part 2 (British Institute of Archaeology at Ankara. Monograph n° 9; BAR Intern. Ser. 392 II)* Oxford.

D.H. French (1990) Roman roads and milestones of Asia Minor 1989, *Anatolian Studies* 40: 9- 11.

D.H. French (1991) Sites and inscriptions from Phrygia, Pisidia and Pamphylia, *Epigraphica Anatolica* 17: 51-62.

P. Freu (1987) Problèmes de chronologie et de géographie hittites. Madduwattas et les débuts de l'empire, *Hethitica VIII. Acta Anatolica E. Laroche oblata. Edidit R. Lebrun (Colloque anatolien, Paris, 1-5 juillet 1985)* Louvain-Paris: 123-175.

A. Goetze (1928) *Madduwattas (Hethithische Texte in Umschrift, mit Übersetzung und Erläuterungen herausgegeben von Ferdinand Sommer. Heft III. Mitteilungen der Vorderasiatischen Aegyptischen Gesellschaft. 32 Jahrgang)* Leipzig.

A. Goetze (1967^2) *Kleinasien (Kulturgeschichte des Alten Orients. Dritter Abschnitt. Erster Unterabschnitt. Handbuch der Altertumswissenschaft III.1)* München.

J. Grainger (1995) The campaign of Cn. Manlius Vulso in Asia Minor, *Anatolian Studies* 45: 23-42.

A. Greifenhagen (1966) Ein architektonisches Terrakottarelief aus Kleinasien, *Archäologischer Anzeiger*: 44-47.

O.R. Gurney (1975) The Hittites, London.

O.R. Gurney (1997) The annals of Hattusilis III, *Anatolian Studies* 47: 127-138.

A.S. Hall (1976) Notes and inscriptions from Eastern Pisidia, *Anatolian Studies* 66: 58-92.

A.S. Hall (1979) Burdur: RECAM, *Anatolian Studies* 28: 4.

A.S. Hall (1985) Kibyratis Survey, in: *Annual Report of the British Institute of Archaeology at Ankara*: 14-15.

A.S. Hall (1986a) Kibyratis Survey, *Anatolian Studies* 36: 10-11.

A.S. Hall (1986b) R.E.C.A.M. notes and studies N° 9: The Milyadeis and their territory, *Anatolian Studies* 36: 137-158.

C.H.E. Haspels (1971) *The Highlands of Phrygia. Sites and Monuments*, Princeton University Press.

J.D. Hawkins (1995) *The Hieroglyphic Inscription of the Sacred Pool Complex at Hattusa (SÜDBURG). With an Archaeological Introduction by Peter Neve (Studien zu den Boğazköy- Texten herausgegeben von der Kommission für den Alten Orient der Akademie der Wissenschaften und der Literatur. Beiheft* 3) Harassoswitz Wiesbaden.

E. Honigmann (1939) L'origine des noms de Balikesir, de Burdur et d'Eğirdir, *Byzantion* 14: 649- 656.

G.H.R. Horsley (1992) The mysteries of Artemis Ephesia in Pisidia: a new inscribed relief, *Anatolian Studies* 42: 120-150.

M. Jordan-Ruwe (1995) *Das Säulenmonument. Zur Geschichte der erhöhten Aufstellung antiker Porträtstatuen (Asia Minor Studien* 19) Habelt Verlag Bonn.

M. Sh. Joukowsky (1996) *Early Turkey. An Introduction to the Archaeology of Anatolia from Prehistory through the Lydian Period*, Dubuque Iowa.

J. Jüthner (1902) *Die Augusteia in Olbasa, Wiener Studien. Zeitschrift für klassische Philologie* 24: 285-291.

N. Kazancı and O. Erol (1987) Sedimentary characteristics of a Pleistocene fan-delta complex from Burdur Basin, Turkey. *Zeitschrift für Geomorphologie N.F.* 31: 261-275.

R.A. Kearsly (1994) The Milyas and the Attalids: a decree of the city of Olbasa and a new royal letter in the second century B.C., *Anatolian Studies* 44: 47-58.

H. Kiepert (1854) *Karte von Kleinasien*, Berlin-Leipzig.

H. Kiepert (1886) *Roads made in 1884 and 1885 by J.R.S. Sterrett in Ancient Lycaonia, Isauria and Pisidia*, Berlin.

M. Kis, O. Erol, S. Senel and M. Ergin (1989) Preliminary results of radiocarbon dating of coastal deposits of the Pleistocene pluvial lake of Burdur, Turkey, *Journal of the Islamic Academy of Sciences* 2: 37-40.

A. Kloner and N. Sagiv (1993) The olive presses of Hellenistic Maresha, Israel, in: M.C. Amouretti, J.P. Brun and D. Eitam (eds) *Actes du symposium international organisé par le Centre Camille Jullian (Université de Provence-C.N.R.S.) et le Centre archéologique du Var (Aix-en-Provence et Toulon, 20-22 novembre 1991) (Bulletin de Correspondance Hellénique. Supplément XXVI)* Paris 1993: 119-136.

B. Levick (1967) *Roman Colonies in Southern Asia Minor*, Oxford.

S. Lloyd and J. Mellaart (1962) *Beycesultan 1. The Chalcolithic and EBA Levels (Occasional Publications of the British Institute of Archaeology at Ankara* 6) London.

L. Loots, M. Waelkens and F. Depuydt (2000) The city fortifications of Sagalassos from the Hellenistic to the late Roman period, in: M. Waelkens and L. Loots (eds) *Sagalassos V. Report on the Survey and Excavation Campaigns of 1996 and 1997 (Acta Archaeologica Lovaniensia Monographiae* 11) Leuven University Press: 595-634.

Chr. Mee (1978) Aegean trade and settlement in Anatolia in the second millennium BC, *Anatolian Studies* 28: 121-155.

J. Mellaart (1954) Preliminary report on a survey of pre-classical Remains in Southern Turkey, *Anatolian Studies* 4, 175-240.

J. Mellaart (1970) *Excavations at Hacılar (Occasional Publications of the British Institute of Archaeology at Ankara* 9) 2 vol., Edinburgh.

J. Mellaart and A. Murray, Beycesultan III.2. The late Bronze Age

and Phrygian Pottery and the Middle and Late Bronze Age Small Objects London.

M.J. Mellink (1965) Archaeology in Asia Minor, *American Journal of Archaeology* 69: 143.

M.J. Mellink (1966) Archaeology in Asia Minor, *American Journal of Archaeology* 70: 153.

M.J. Mellink (1967) Archaeology in Asia Minor, *American Journal of Archaeology* 71: 164.

M.J. Mellink (1969) Archaeology in Asia Minor, *American Journal of Archaeology* 73: 212.

M.J. Mellink (1975) Archaeology in Asia Minor, *American Journal of Archaeology* 79: 24.

S. Mitchell (1976) Requisitioned transport in the Roman Empire: a new inscription from Pisidia, *Journal of Roman Studies* 76: 106-131.

S. Mitchell (1982) RECAM, *Anatolian Studies* 32: 6.

S. Mitchell (1991) The Hellenization of Pisidia, *Mediterranean Archaeology* 4: 119-145.

S. Mitchell (1993) *Anatolia. Land, Men, and Gods in Asia Minor. Volume I. The Celts and the Impact of Roman Rule*, Oxford Clarendon Press 1993.

S. Mitchell (1994) Three cities in Pisidia, *Anatolian Studies* 44: 129-148.

S. Mitchell and M. Waelkens (1998) *Pisidian Antioch. The Site and its Monuments*, Duckworth with the Classical Press of Wales, London-Swansea.

M. Özsait (1976-1977) Pisidya Bölgesinde Yeni Prehistorik İskân Yerleri I, *Anadolu Araştırmaları* IV-V: 71-95.

M. Özsait (1980) İlkçağ tarihinde Pisidiya, Istanbul.

M. Özsait (1983) 1982 yılı Burdur çevresi prehistori araştırmaları, *Araştırma sonuçları toplantısı* 1, Ankara: 7-12.

M. Özsait (1984) 1983 yılı Burdur-Isparta çevresinde prehistorik araştırmaları, *Araştırma sonuçları toplantısı* 2, Ankara: 205-220.

M. Özsait (1985) 1984 yılı Burdur-Isparta çevresi tarih öncesi araştırmaları, *Araştırma sonuçları toplantısı* 3, Ankara: 389-410.

M. Özsait (1989) Pisidya bölgesinde yeni prehistorik iskân yerlemeleri IV, *Anadolu Araştırmaları* XI: 22.

M. Özsait (1990) *Ilkça Tarihinde Pisidya*, Istanbul.

M. Özsait (1991) Nouveaux sites contemporains de Hacılar en Pisidie occidentale, *De Anatolia Antiqua I*: 59-118.

M. Özsait (1992) 1991 yılı Burdur-Çeltikçi ve Yeşilova yüzey araştırmaları, *Araştırma sonuçları toplantısı* 10, Ankara: 331-344.

M. Özsait (1996) 1995 yılı Antalya-Korkuteli ve Burdur yüzey araştırmaları, *Araştırma sonuçları toplantısı* 14,2, Ankara: 193-214.

J. Poblome, H.A. Ekinci, I. Öztürk, P. Degryse, W. Viaene and M. Waelkens. An early Byzantine tile and lime kiln in the territory of Sagalassos (2000), in: M. Waelkens and L. Loots (eds), *Sagalassos V. Report on the Survey and Excavation Campaigns of 1996 and 1997* (Acta Archaeologica Lovaniensia Monographiae 11) Leuven University Press: 669-683.

F. Prayon and A.M. Wittke (1994) *Kleinasien vom 12. bis 6. Jh.v.Chr.: Kartierung und Erläuterung archäologischer Befunde und Denkmäler* (TAVO Band 82) Wiesbaden.

W.M. Ramsay (1886) Notes and inscriptions from Asia Minor X. Fines Sagalassensium, *American Journal of Archaeology* 3: 128-131.

W.M. Ramsay (1887) Antiquities of Southern Phrygia and the border lands, *American Journal of Archaeology* 3: 345-363.

W.M. Ramsay (1888) Antiquities of Southern Phrygia and the border lands, *American Journal of Archaeology* 4: 5-21, 263-283.

W.M. Ramsay (1890) *The Historical Geography of Asia Minor*, Amsterdam 1967 (reprint of 1890 edition).

W.M. Ramsay (1895) *The Cities and Bishoprics of Phrygia I*, Oxford.

W.M. Ramsay (1941) *The Social Basis of Roman Power in Asia Minor. Prepared for the Press by J.G.C. Anderson*, Aberdeen.

J. and L. Robert (1948) Notes sur un voyage archéologique en Pisidie, en Carie et à Ankara, *Comptes-rendus de l'Académie des Inscriptions et Belles Lettres* 1948: 401-403, 430-432, 530-531.

L. Robert (1960) *Hellenica. Recueil d'épigraphie, de numismatique et d'antiquités grecques* XI-XII, Paris.

S. Şahin and D.H. French (1987) Ein Dokument aus Takina, *Epigraphica Anatolica* 10: 133-142.

W.H. Schoch (1995) Analyse van Holzkohlen in Schlacken von Sagalassos, in: M. Waelkens, J. Poblome (eds), Sagalasoos III. Report on the Fourth Excavation Campaign of 1993 (Acta Archaeologica Lvaniensia Monographiae 7), Leuven, 293-296.

N.V. Sekunda (1997) Nearchus the Cretan and the foundation of Cretopolis, *Anatolian Studies* 47: 217-223.

R.K. Sherk (1980) Roman Galatia. The governors from 25 BC to AD 114, in: H. Temporini and W. Haase (eds) *Aufstieg und Niedergang der römischen Welt* II.7.2, Berlin.

A.N. Sherwin-White (1977) Roman involvement in Anatolia, 167-88 BC, *Journal of Roman Studies* 67: 62-75.

A.H.M. Smith (1887) Notes on a tour in Asia Minor, *Journal of Hellenic Studies* 8: 222-267.

T.J. Smith, with an epigraphical appendix by N.P. Milner (1997) Votive reliefs from Balboura and its environs, *Anatolian Studies* 47: 3-50.

J.R.S. Sterrett (1888) *An Epigraphical Journey in Asia Minor* (Papers of the American School of Classical Studies at Athens II) Boston.

R. Syme (1995) *Anatolica. Studies in Strabo. Edited by A. Birley*, Clarendon Press Oxford.

N. Thomas (1965) Recent Acquisitions by Birmingham City Museum. *Archaeological Report 1964/1965 published by the council of the Society for the promotion of Hellenic studies and the British School of Archaelogy at Athens*.

L. Vandeput (1997) *The Architectural Decoration in Roman Asia Minor. Sagalassos: a Case Study* (Studies in Eastern Mediterranean Archaeology) I) Brepols Publishers Turnhout.

H. Vanhaverbeke, P.M. Vermeersch and M. Waelkens (in press, a) Living between the river and the lake. The Epipalaeolithic, Neolithic, Chalcolithic and EBA on the territory of Sagalassos, *Aegean Archaeology* 3:7-25.

H. Vanhaverbeke, P.M. Vermeersch, M. Waelkens (in press, b) What's in a name? The Epipalaeolithic, Aceramic and Early Neolithic on the territory of Sagalassos, *Near Eastern Archaeologist* 61,3:175-176.

H. Vanhaverbeke and M. Waelkens (1999) Lower, Middle and Upper Palaeolithic on the Territory of Sagalassos (SW Turkey). Problems and Prospects, *Anatolia Antiqua* VI: 1-19.

H. Vanhaverbeke (2000) How can there still be such a degree of uncertainty? Problems of chronology for the prehistoric periods on the territory of Sagalassos, in: M. Waelkens and L. Loots (eds) *Sagalassos V. Report on the Survey and Excavation Campaigns of 1996 and 1997* (Acta Archaeologica Lovaniensia Monographiae 11) Leuven University Press: 463-472.

H. Vanhaverbeke, M. Waelkens and P.M. Vermeersch (in press) People of the mountains versus people of the höyüks? The Neolithic, Chalcolithic and EBA in the territory of Sagalassos (SW Turkey), *International Symposium "The Aegean in the Neolithic, the Chalcolithic and the Early Bronze Age, Izmir-Urla, Turkey, 13-19 October 1997"*.

P.M. Vermeersch, I. Öztürk, H.A. Ekinci, P. Degryse, B. De Cupere, J. Poblome, M. Waelkens and W. Viaene (1999) Late Palaeolithic at the Dereköy Karain cave, in: M. Waelkens and L. Loots (eds), *Sagalassos V. Report on the Survey and Excavation Campaigns of 1996 and 1997* (Acta Archaeologica Lovaniensia Monographiae 11) Leuven University Press: 451-462.

M. Vermoere, M. Waelkens, H. Vanhaverbeke, I. Librecht, L. Vanhecke, E. Paulissen and E. Smets (2000) Late Holocone environmental change and the record of human impact at Gravgaz near Sagalassos, Southwest Turkey, *Journal of Archaeological Science.* 27,7:71-95.

G. Verstraeten, E. Paulissen, I. Librecht and M. Waelkens (2000) Limestone platforms around Sagalassos as the result of giant mass movements, in: M. Waelkens and L. Loots (eds), *Sagalassos V. Report on the Survey and Excavation Campaigns of 1996 and 1997* (*Acta Archaeologica Lovaniensia Monographiae* 11) Leuven University Press: 783-797.

M. Waelkens (1982) *Dokimeion. Die Werkstatt der rerpäsentativen kleinasiatischen Sarkophage. Chronologie und Typologie ihrer Produktion* (*Archäologische Forschungen* 11) Berlin.

M. Waelkens (1986) *Die kleinasiatischen Türsteine. Typologische und epigraphische Untersuchungen der kleinasiatischen Grabreliefs mit Scheintür*, Ph. von Zabern Mainz.

M. Waelkens (1995) The 1993 survey in the district south and east of Sagalassos, in: M. Waelkens and J. Poblome (eds) *Sagalassos III. Report on the Fourth Excavation Campaign of 1993* (*Acta Archaeologica Lovaniensia Monographiae* 7) Leuven University Press: 11-22.

M. Waelkens, E. Paulissen, H. Vanhaverbeke, I. Öztürk, B. De Cupere, H.A. Ekinci, P.M. Vermeersch, J. Poblome and R. Degeest (1997a) The 1994 and 1995 surveys on the territory of Sagalassos, in: M. Waelkens and J. Poblome (eds) *Sagalassos IV. Report on the Survey and Ecxavation Campaigns of 1994 and 1995* (*Acta Archaeologica Lovaniensia Monographiae* 9) Leuven University Press: 11-102.

M. Waelkens, P.M. Vermeersch, E. Paulissen, E. Owens, B. Arıkan, M. Martens, P. Talloen, L. Gijsen, L. Loots, C. Peleman, J. Poblome, R. Degeest, T. Patrício, S. Ercan and F. Depuydt (1997b) The 1994 and 1995 excavation seasons at Sagalassos, in: M. Waelkens and J. Poblome (eds) *Sagalassos IV. Report on the Survey and Excavation Campaigns of 1994 and 1995* (*Acta Archaeologica Lovaniensia Monographiae* 9) Leuven University Press: 103-216.

M.Waelkens and the Sagalassos Team (1997) Interdisciplinarity in classical archaeology. A case study: the Sagalassos Archaeological Research Project (Southwest Turkey), in: M. Waelkens and J. Poblome (eds) *Sagalassos IV. Report on the Survey and Excavation Campaigns of 1994 and 1995* (*Acta Archaeologica Lovaniensia Monographiae* 9) Leuven University Press: 225-252.

M. Waelkens, E. Paulissen, M. Vermoere, P. Degryse, D. Celis, K. Schroyen, B. De Cupere, I. Librecht, K. Nackaerts, H. Van Haverbeke, W. Viaene, Ph. Muchez, R. Ottenburgs, J. Deckers, W. Van Neer, E. Smets, G. Govers, G. Verstraeten, A. Steegen and K. Cauwenberghs (1999) Man and environment in the territory of Sagalassos, a classical city in SW Turkey, in: *Quaternary Science Reviews* 18: 697-709.

M. Waelkens (1999) Sagalassos. Religious life in a Pisidian town during the Hellenistic and Roman Imperial period, in: C. Bonnet and A. Motte (eds) *Colloque F. Cumont. Les syncrétismes religieux dans le monde méditerranéen antique. Rome, 25-27 septembre 1997,* Bruxelles - Brussel - Rome, 191-226

M. Waelkens (2000) Sagalassos and Pisidia during the Late Bronze Age, in: M. Waelkens and L. Loots (eds) *Sagalassos V. Report on the Survey and Excavation Campaigns of 1996 and 1997* (*Acta Archaeologica Lovaniensia Monographiae* 11) Leuven University Press: 473-488.

M. Waelkens, L; Vandeput, B. Arıkan, Ch. Berns, J. Poblome and E. Torun (2000). The Northwest Heroon at Sagalassos, in: M. Waelkens and L. Loots (eds) *Sagalassos V. Report on the Survey and Excavation Campaign of 1996 and 1997*) Acta Archaeologica Lovaniensa Monographiae 10) Leuven University Press 553-594.

M. Waelkens and L. Vandeput (in press) Regionalism in Hellenistic and Roman Pisidia, in: H. Elton and G. Reger (eds) *International Conference. Regionalism in Hellenistic and Roman Asia Minor. Tinity College, Hartford CT, 22-24 August 1997.*

H. Waldmann (1978) Ein Archimystes in Sagalassos, in M.B. De Boer and T.A. Edridge (eds) *Hommages à M.J.Vermaseren* (*Etudes préliminarires aux religions orientales dans l'Empire romain*) vol. III, Leiden: 1309-1315, Taf. CCLXIV.

A.M. Woodward and A.H. Ormerod (1909-1910) A journey in South-Western Asia Minor, *The Annual of the British School at Athens* 16: 76-136.

THE 1996 AND 1997 EXCAVATION SEASONS AT SAGALASSOS

M. Waelkens[1], J. Poblome[1], R. Degeest[1], L. Vandeput[1], L. Loots[1], E. Paulissen[2], F. Martens[1],
P. Talloen[1], J. Van den Bergh, V. Vanderginst, B. Arıkan, I. Van Damme, I. Akyel, M. Martens,
I. Uytterhoeven, T. Debruyne, D. Depraetere, K. Baran, B. Van Daele, Z. Parras, Ş. Yıldırım, S.
Bubel, H. Vanhaverbeke[1], C. Licoppe, F. Landuyt, T. Patrício[3], S. Ercan[3], K. Van Balen[3],
E. Smits[4], F. Depuydt[5], L. Moens[6] and P. De Paepe[7].

1 - Department of Archaeology, KULeuven, Blijde Inkomststraat 21, B-3000 Leuven, Belgium
2 - Geomorphology and Regional Geography, KULeuven, Redingenstraat 16, B-3000 Leuven, Belgium
3 - Center for Restoration R. Lemaire, KULeuven, Kard. Mercierlaan 94, B-3001 Heverlee, Belgium
4 - University of Amsterdam, Amsterdams Archeologisch Instituut (AAC),
Nieuwe Prinsengracht 130, 1018 VZ Amsterdam, The Netherlands
5 - Cartography, KULeuven, Redingenstraat 16, B-3000 Leuven, Belgium
6 - Laboratory of Analytical Chemistry, University of Ghent, Proeftuinstraat 86, B-9000 Gent, Belgium
7 - Geology and Earth Sciences, Geological Institute 98, Krijgslaan 281, B-9000 Gent, Belgium

The seventh excavation season at Sagalassos took place between the 6th of July and the 31st of August 1996. A total of 113 scientists and students and 63 Turkish workmen were involved. The Turkish Ministry of Culture was represented by Mrs Ümran Yüğrük (Efes Museum) and by Mr. Mustafa Akaslan (Isparta Museum). The eighth excavation campaign took place between the 6th of July and the 28th of August 1997 and a total of 122 scientists and students and 74 Turkish workmen took part. During the 1997 campaign, Mr. Recep Okçu (Çanakkale Museum) represented the Turkish Ministry of Culture. We are indebted to all three temsilci's for their much appreciated support and collaboration.

During the 1996 and 1997 campaigns, work was concentrated on the areas listed below. From 1997 the grid system was slightly altered and renumbered to make it correspond with the true North. This means that the grid numbers in the text do not correspond with those visible on the photographs from the 1996 season.

1. THE NORTHWEST HEROON (SITE)

During the 1996 and 1997 campaigns, excavations in this area continued and were more or less completed. Since the monument is discussed separately in this volume, we refer to that article (Waelkens *et al.* 2000)

2. THE DORIC TEMPLE (ZEUS SANCTUARY?)

2.1. The Augustan Propylon

From 1990 to 1992, the interior of a Doric temple, located to the southwest of the NW Heroon and its immediate surroundings to the west, to the north and to the south, were excavated (Waelkens 1993 b: 9-12). However, because the building had been radically converted long after it was built, these excavations did not produce any conclusive evidence to confirm stratigraphically its supposed first century BC date. In fact, around 400 AD, the building had been converted into a watchtower and incorporated into a fortification wall which henceforth linked it to the NW Heroon.

In 1996, these excavations resumed and two sectors (2250/2550, 2255/2550) as well as the western extremity of a third sector (2260/2550) were excavated to the east of the temple (Fig. 1). The year after, work continued in one sector immediately to the west of the late fortifications and to the north of the Doric temple (2250/2555). This excavation exposed a city gate in the late defences. During the same campaign, the southern part of two sectors located immediately to the east of this gate and to the north of the propylon (2255/2555 and 2260/2555) were also excavated.

In 1974, Fleischer had discovered the base of a half-column that was apparently part of a monumental entrance in this area but, at the end of his season, he had covered it over again (Fleischer 1979: Abb.1; Taf. 73,3). During our 1996 campaign, this half-column base was found immediately below the topsoil (layer 1, ca. 0.20 to 0.60 m th.) in sector 2260/2550. It proved to be the northeast corner of a propylon building that was squeezed in between the Doric temple to the west and the bouleuterion courtyard wall to the east. The plinth of a free-standing column was found 1.58 m to the north of this corner (Fig. 2). In sector 2255/2550, immediately to the west of the late Roman fortification wall, the northwest corner of the same propylon façade was discovered. This was another half-column still standing nearly 4 m above its base. Here again, a second free-standing column base stood 1.58 m in front of it (Fig. 3). At the time of its discovery, a small rubble wall ca 0.30 m wide was built over both bases. This wall formed the foundation of the late Roman fortification wall (see Fig. 26).

Today, only the propylon façade, framed by Corinthian half-columns at either side, has been partly preserved since it was incorporated into the late Roman city wall. The propylon was in the form of a Corinthian *distyle prostylos,* 6.48 m long and 4.66 m wide (Fig. 4). Its back wall had a door 1.64 m wide by 3.44 m high, framed by two windows (1.24 m wide by 1.60 m high). The door and the windows had nice frames and richly decorated lintels. The door lintel was supported by two consoles with a rich tendril decoration. The western half of the structure, including the corresponding window, is still standing to a level just below the capitals (h.: 3.66 m), but today is completely hidden from view by the late Roman fortification wall which is built perpendicularly against it. The eastern extremity of the back wall is broken obliquely just above the level of the eastern half-column base (Fig. 5).

On the south side (interior), the wall is heavily weathered and very much damaged, but largely plain. On this side, the whole area has been too much affected by later alterations to allow a reconstruction of its original appearance. In 1997, the 3.80 m wide space between the western courtyard wall of the bouleuterion and the early Byzantine construction against the temple (see 2.3) was excavated (sectors 2255/2550, 2260/2550, 2255/2545 and 2260/2545).

Here, below the topsoil, two destruction layers (layers 2 and 3) were found on top of an old floor. The latter consisted of two layers:
- a mortar layer (layer 4) with a thickness of about 0.10-0.15 m. This mortar layer had clearly been a bed for now removed pavement slabs. It varies considerably in thickness since its function was to level the cavities in the natural bedrock (a pink-grey breccia) the surface of which had been leveled. The deepest holes had been filled with stones. No diagnostic finds were discovered in it.
- layer 6: a fill of smaller stones, with scarcely any archaeological finds, approximately 0.80 m deep. This fill is mainly present along the eastern edge of this intermediate space, where the original bedrock slopes down towards the east and runs right up to the western courtyard wall of the bouleuterion.

The date of these layers can no longer be established, but they must represent the remains of one of several courtyard floors of the sanctuary.

In front of the propylon's north wall, an area of 7.60 m (E-W) by 2.64 m (N-S) had been paved with limestone slabs (Figs 6-7). Below them, the natural conglomerate bedrock shows traces of a stepped stone extraction sloping towards the east (see Fig. 8). Because of this, while at the western end the pavement slabs were laid directly on the bedrock, at the eastern end, one or two additional rows of smaller ashlars were laid underneath (Fig. 9). Below the late Roman fortification wall, however, this stone pavement had been removed and replaced by a rubble foundation (Fig. 26).

On top of the pavement, two column bases, at an interaxial distance of 2.32 m in front of the half-columns of the façade, had supported a pair of free-standing columns, more or less along the line of the bouleuterion's northern courtyard wall. Of the eastern column, only the square plinth was found *in situ* (Fig. 2), while the plinth still bore its column base (Fig. 6). Fragments of the Corinthian capitals have been recovered in later seasons. A limestone bench, with carved lion feet was placed along the eastern edge of the paved area, connecting the eastern column and half-column (Fig. 10). There would have been, most probably, an identical bench on the opposite side that was removed and replaced by the late Roman fortification wall. The free-standing columns supported a low gable of which most of the elements have been recovered (see Fig. 4).

On the east side the propylon abutted the west wall of the Bouleuterion courtyard (see Fig. 9) but the 2.20 m wide gap separating it from the Doric Temple to the west was closed by a wall of beautiful ashlar blocks in a pseudo-isodomic arrangement (Figs 5, 11 and 12). There can be no doubt that propylon and temenos wall were built during a single building operation which must have followed that of the construction of the Doric temple itself. Although the courses of the temenos wall correspond to a large extent with those of the krepis, the podium and the east wall of the temple, they all abut the latter rather than intersecting with them, although this would have made the wall structurally safer. The krepis steps and the upper and lower mouldings of the temple podium also continue through the temenos which seems to indicate that they were once completely visible. The adjoining stones of the temenos wall were cut to fit as well as possible to the mouldings (Fig. 11). This can also be seen where they touch the half-column base of the propylon (Fig. 12). The sequence of building in this area was thus clearly first the Doric temple, second the propylon, and

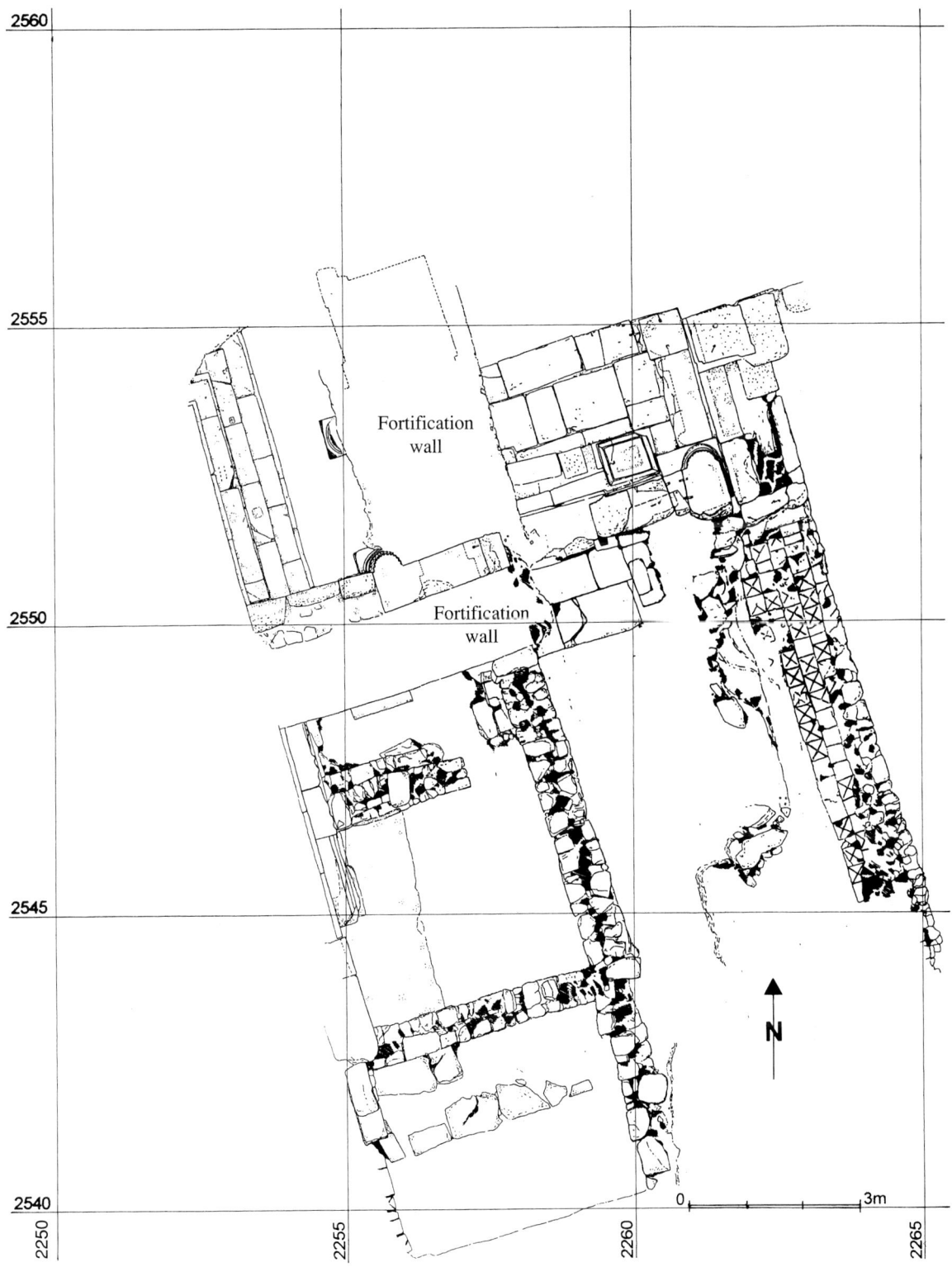

Fig. 1:. Plan of the area between the Doric temple and the NW Heroon with the propylon building.

Fig. 2: View of the northeast corner of the propylon façade, seen from the south.

Fig. 3: The northwestern half-column of the propylon façade, squeezed between the late Roman fortification wall to the left and the temenos wall to the right.

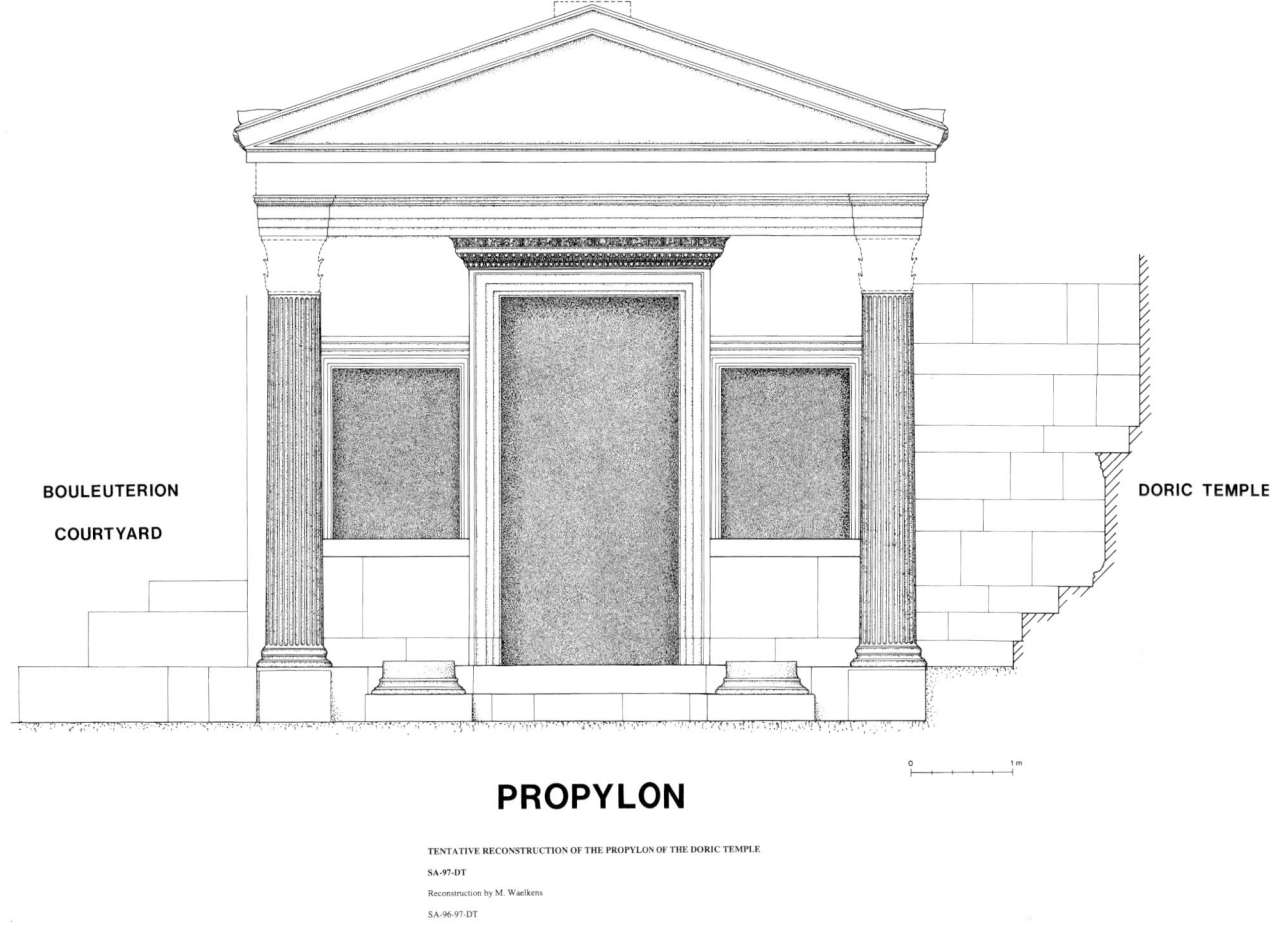

Fig.4. Preliminary reconstruction drawing of the Propylon.

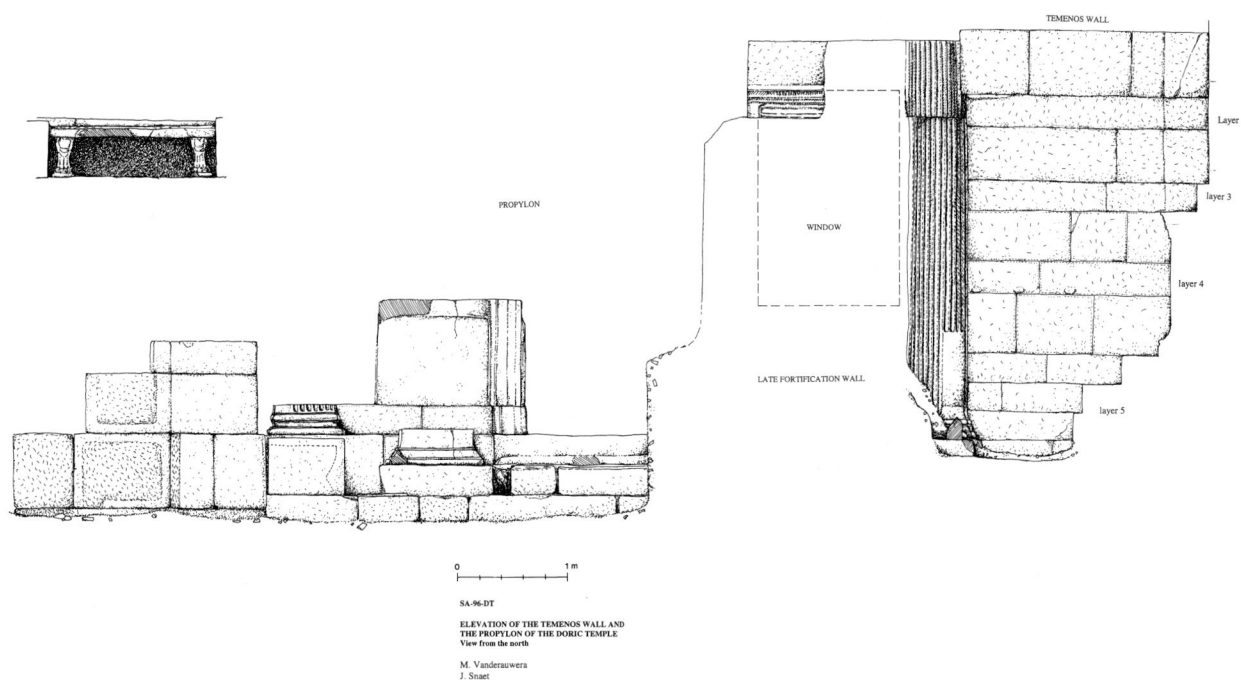

Fig. 5. Drawing of the *in situ* remains of the propylon, seen from the north.

Fig.6. Plan of the *in situ* remains of the Propylon.

Fig. 7: General view from the north of the propylon towards the end of the 1996 season. The late fortification wall can be seen in the middle, the Doric temple stands to the right.

Fig. 8. View of the stepped extraction of conglomerate blocks in front of the propylon.

Fig. 9: View of the foundations of the northeast corner of the propylon.
To the left: the corner with pilaster of the northern courtyard wall of the bouleuterion.

Fig. 10: The bench with lion feet along the eastern edge of the propylon.

Fig. 11: Blocks of the Doric temple's temenos wall carved to fit the mouldings of the temple podium.

Fig. 12: The temenos wall between Doric temple and propylon.

third the temenos wall connecting them.

The whole arrangement, with a temenos wall not surrounding the temple itself but built against it in such a way that the temple still projected 3.50 m beyond it, most probably indicates that the temenos was not planned here in this form from the beginning. Probably, its position 3.50 m behind the northeast corner of the temple was intended to bring into prominence the propylon 2.64 m to the front. On the east side, the propylon's columnar front was aligned with the bouleuterion's northern courtyard wall, which meant that, in effect, it was set back compared with the latter. So, its prostyle façade had to be emphasised on the opposite (western) side by recessing the temenos wall, explaining the wall's awkward position with regard to the Doric temple and creating a ' lost' corner of 2.64 m by 2.20 to the east of this latter. There is only one explanation for this apparent loss of space: the propylon could not project into the street, although the street was wide enough (10.80 m) to have allowed for this, because there was already another building there, whose aspect would have been blocked by the propylon. Or it may have been that the propylon itself would have been too much dwarfed by some building on the opposite side, if it had projected onto the street and, in fact, there is such a structure there, the NW Heroon.

Today, 11 layers of the temenos wall (pres.h.: 3.78 m; w.: 0.80 m) are still discernible. The lowest one was the *euthynteria* (vis.h.: 0.20 m), originally only visible in its upper part. Its upper level corresponds with that of the plinth of the propylon's western half-column. Part of it had to be cut down to fit below the lowest steps of the temple's krepis (Figs 5 and 11). It corresponds in level with a rubble foundation below the lowest row of steps of the temple podium. Perhaps in late antiquity, when the fortification wall was built and the original floor level raised, a pavement or a slightly projecting *euthynteria* was removed in front and below the outer edge of these steps (see Fig. 11). As a result, the stratigraphy corresponding with the construction of the temenos foundations was completely disturbed.

The three lowest visible rows of blocks of the temenos wall corresponded exactly in height with those of the krepis steps (from top to bottom: 0.24 m, 0.26 m and 0.26 m). The height of the temple's podium was equal to three ashlar layers of the temenos wall (from bottom to top: 0.52 m, 0.30 m and 0.45 m). From here onwards the courses are erected in a pseudo-isodomic arrangement (Figs 5 and 12) that is maintained throughout the four upper layers (from bottom to top: 0.24 m, 0.47 m, 0.27 m and 0.57 m).

Most stones of the temenos wall have been very carefully worked on the outside (with a fine point) with very fine drafted edges. The stones of the fifth visible row of blocks still possess three projecting bosses for moving them during construction, which had never been trimmed down. At Sagalassos, the extremely fine treatment of these temenos wall blocks is only seen again on some of the Augustan NW Heroon podium blocks on the other side of the same street. As we have already said, the original stratigraphy of the construction of the propylon and temenos had been completely disturbed when the early fifth century AD fortification wall was built. But enough decorative elements of the propylon remain to allow it to be dated by L. Vandeput exactly to the Augustan period (Vandeput, see below). Several parts of the highly decorated door lintel of the propylon were unearthed (Fig. 13) and its decorative motifs contain sufficient clues for dating the monument. The top moulding is enhanced with an anthemion in which the individual palmettes stand independently from one another, while their central leaves sprout from a small sheathing leaf. These elements occur especially from the early-Imperial period onwards (Vandeput 1997a: 44, 60). Equally important is the shape of the Lesbian cyma on the central moulding. Some of its intermediate flowers are completely developed and grow from their own stems, while others sprout from between adjacent stirrups. This development towards fully developed stirrup-framed leaf-and-darts essentially took place during the reign of Augustus (Ganzert 1983: 179; Vandeput 1997a: 151, with further literature). An intermediate phase occurs only on one other building at Sagalassos, the temple of Apollo Klarios, also dated on the basis of a stylistic analysis to the reign of Augustus (Vandeput 1997a: 51-52, 57, 151). The very low lower negative of the stirrup frames is also unusual, a feature which is echoed on the propylon of the portico on the agora of Magnesia near the Maeander. Based on stylistic analysis the latter building has been dated to the Augustan period (Rumscheid 1994: no. 142, pl. 90.1).

The anthemion on the top moulding is cut in a very shallow relief. The shallow carving and the general lay-out of the motif immediately recalls the anthemion on the pilaster capital of the early-Imperial NE Heroon further down the same road leading towards the theatre of Sagalassos (Vandeput in Kosmetatou *et al.* 1997: 355-356, figs 1-2). The same low relief is also found in most of the decoration of the Augustan sanctuary of Apollo Klarios (Vandeput 1997a: pl. 17.3, 18.2 and 20.3), although decorative patterns at Sagalassos are mostly characterised by high relief (Vandeput 1997: 183-18).

This Augustan date of the propylon provides both a *terminus ad quem* for the Doric temple and a *terminus post quem* for its preserved temenos section. Since a propylon without a temenos wall would have been useless, the wall must have been part of the same building works intended to close off the sanctuary from the street and to provide it with a monumental entrance. The temenos wall was clearly added as the last element of all, since its stones were adapted to those of the constructions on either side of it. The temple itself must have preceded the construction of the propylon, as the awkward position of temenos and propylon with regard to the temple, discussed above, seems to exclude their having been part of the original building project. The different order (Doric for the temple, Corinthian for its propylon) also implies this.

As we have noted, this awkward position was most probably dictated by the presence on the other side of the street of the NW Heroon, which also dates to the Augustan period (Waelkens *et al.* 2000a). Unfortunately, the architectural decoration of this building does not provide conclusive evidence, since the heroon and the propylon were clearly built by different *Bauhütten*. Whereas the decoration of the latter building fits perfectly with the local building tradition, that of the former shows strong Italic influences, perhaps transmitted via the Augustan colonies in Pisidia, and especially via Pisidian Antioch (see Waelkens *et al. a* 2000). Not enough is known of the still unexcavated NE Heroon, further east along the same street, to permit a good comparative study, but the few preserved elements suggest kinship with the NW Heroon (Kosmetatou *et al.* 1997).

The temenos wall must have had a counterpart to the west of the temple, but this wall may have been dismantled completely around 400 AD, when the temple was converted into a watchtower and incorporated into the late fortifications. However, it is unlikely that the time-span separating all these constructions was very long. The presence of a podium seems already to imply the influence of Roman religious architecture. At Pergamon, some third and second century BC temples needed a supplementary flight of steps only at the front since they led to the podium or terrace on which the temple stood. This arrangement, which was imposed by the fact that these buildings were set into a steep slope, gave rise in the second century BC to a local development of (low) podium temples that were built on more level ground (Waelkens 1989: 84). Theoretically, Pergamene influences cannot be excluded at Sagalassos since from 189 BC to 133 BC the city had been part of the Attalid kingdom. The survey article in this volume also shows that Attalid control of the area may have been much more pronounced than previously assumed. Because of the strong similarity of its podium mouldings to similar profiles from Pergamon, an early first century BC date was previously proposed for the Doric temple (Waelkens 1989: 85). We now believe that this early date needs to be adjusted towards the middle or even the second half of the century, thus slightly preceding the construction of the Augustan propylon. Even if the choice of a podium temple implies Roman influence, this does not necessarily mean that its construction date has to be early Imperial, when podium temples became popular in Anatolia especially in connection with the Imperial cult (Waelkens 1989: 85; Vandeput in press). One should not forget that the western half of the peninsula, including western Pisidia, had been subjected to nearly a century of Roman republican rule. The construction of a road by M. Aquillius, which as the survey article in this volume shows crossed the southwestern part of Sagalassos-held territory, originally served a military purpose – the protection of the vital connection between Asia's provincial capital at Pergamon and its former colony at Attaleia. The road must therefore have passed through territories under firm Roman control, indicating that Sagalassos must also have been incorporated into the province of Asia. During the first century BC, the city must have passed temporarily into the newly created province of Cilicia, before being reunited with Asia at the time of the Mithridatic wars. Sagalassos apparently remained part of Cilicia until 39 BC, when Marcus Antonius created a new kingdom composed of Phrygia Paroreios and Northern Pisidia, which he gave to Amyntas (see Devijver and Waelkens to be published in Sagalassos VI). The city must therefore have known almost a century of Roman republican rule and absorbed its first Roman influences. Such influences may have been facilitated by the city's easy access to *Aquillius' road,* which connected it directly with both the provincial capital and the Pamphylian ports (see survey article this volume). Recently, urban studies in Italy have shown the existence of networks of power and influence related to distance and the speed of travel, and of a hierarchy of information favouring towns situated on major roads and ports (Morley 1997: 48).

Between the Mithridatic wars and the creation of Amyntas' kingdom in 39 BC, Sagalassos must have known a period of relative prosperity and stability, which may have stimulated a resumption of public construction. This would be less likely during the reign of Amyntas (39-25 BC), since it was characterized by internal turmoil in the city and during the Sandaliote war by military campaigns on Sagalassian soil (Waelkens *et al.* 1997a: 29-31).

The plain Doric order of the temple would correspond very well with a date in late Hellenistic times. In fact, at Sagalassos the same Doric order was selected for the late Hellenistic fountain-house, which was probably almost contemporary in date (see below). However, from the early Imperial period onwards, all major monuments were built either in the Ionic order (Apollo Klarios) or in the even more elaborate Corinthian order (propylon of the Doric temple, NW Heroon, honorific columns and canopy monument on the upper agora, southwest gate of the lower agora: see Vandeput 1997, *passim*). It seems unlikely that a major religious monument of the early Imperial period, which dominated the whole city, would have been erected in a building order that was eclipsed by surrounding contemporary structures built in the more elaborate Corinthian order (propylon, NW Heroon, honorific columns on the upper agora).

Fig. 13: Fragment of the door lintel of the Doric temple's propylon.

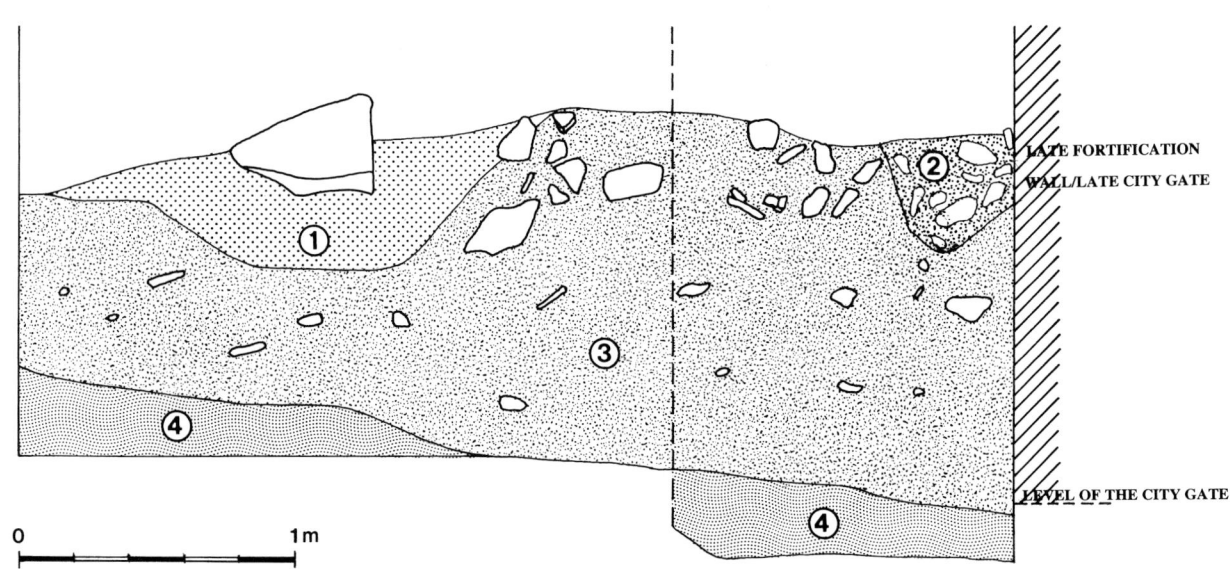

E-W SECTION (N PROFILE) THROUGH LAYERS 3 AND 4, WEST OF THE LATE ROMAN FORTIFICATION WALL AND NORTH OF THE CITY GATE 5

Fig. 14. Section through layers 3 and 4, immediately to the west of the late Roman fortifications and a bit to the north of the city gate.

But, the time-lapse between the temple and the propylon cannot be very wide. It is clear that the construction of the Doric temple, which may have replaced an older sanctuary, must also have included a plan to close it off from the structures around it, and especially from the street to the north of it, where its back wall was exposed. The unruly conditions under Amyntas' rule may however have interrupted the completion of this plan. When stability returned under Augustus, the city apparently launched an impressive building programme, which in the vicinity of the Doric Temple comprised the construction of the NW Heroon and the NE Heroon further east. This may have made it necessary to alter the original building plans. The original plan may be presumed to have comprised a simple, straight temenos wall connecting the more-or-less aligned back wall of the Doric temple to the north wall of the bouleuterion's Doric courtyard, and provided with a simple Doric entrance corresponding with the order of the buildings on either side. However, after the construction of the Corinthian NW Heroon, the plans may have been changed and a more elaborate propylon of the same order as the impressive memorial on the other side of the street may have been considered more appropriate. Letting this structure project onto the street may not have been acceptable, as it would have partly blocked the street (or small plaza) in front of it, while a vast space was necessary for exposing the heroon in its full glory. Moreover, a projecting propylon would have been completely dwarfed by the heroon. Therefore, in the new arrangement, the prostyle layout of the propylon columns was constructed flush with the originally planned position of the temenos wall, whereas a regressing position between the propylon and the Doric temple was chosen for the latter. This offered a perfect solution to make the propylon sufficiently impressive, especially to those entering the city from the north.

A recent study of the local cults suggests that the temple may have served the cult of Zeus, who is clearly identified as the city's protecting divinity by its municipal coinage (Waelkens 1999: 198-201).

2.2. The construction of the late Roman fortifications around AD 400 and the raising of the street level in front of the propylon after the AD 518 earthquake.

The stratigraphy of the excavations only documented the later history of the area. To the west of the late fortifications, in sector 2550/2250, the area immediately to the west of the late Roman city gate was excavated in 1997 (Fig. 14). Below the topsoil and a destruction layer (2) that had already been excavated in the early 1990s, layer 3 could be identified as a typical fill containing shards dated by Poblome to phase 8 of the local production of Sagalassos red slip wares (second half of the fifth–first half of the seventh century AD), bone (some of it worked), glass and metal. Underneath layer 3, a very compact layer of gravel was reached (layer 4). No diagnostic material was found here, but the layer was not completely excavated. It is a very compact anthropogenic layer, sloping down towards the east (from 1538.25 m a.s.l. to 1537.537 m), where it is level with the sill of the city gate (western extremity: 1538.915 m a.s.l.; eastern edge of gate's sill: 1537.537 m a.s.l.) after which it slopes further down again inside the fortifications (Figs 15-16). There were clearly no steps on either side of the city gate, but instead the whole approach had been arranged as a ramp. On the other side of the gateway, layer 4 contained pottery indicating a date after the 518 AD earthquake.

The floor slabs of the city gate (width: 3 m) were completely uncovered (Figs 15-17). There are three main rows of slabs, one of which forms the actual sill of the gate with post-holes in its corners. That on the south side (0.13 by 0.135 m) still has some remnants of lead in it. At 0.045 m north of it, there are clear marks left by a door hinge and probably also by the nails of the hinges. There are also orange iron stains on the stone. In the northern hole (0.17 by 0.14 m), no lead was found, but here again there are marks of hinges and of iron residues. A more detailed description of this gate, its closing system and the surrounding fortifications is given in the article by Loots et al. 2000.

On top of layer 4, immediately to the west of the city gate, a relief block representing Athena (facing left) was discovered (h.: 0.52 m). She wears a helmet and the *aegis* to which a Gorgoneion has been fixed (Figs 18-19). Inside the gate itself, a corresponding, but partly broken relief of Ares was found (Figs 20-21). Both frieze fragments clearly belonged to the late second - early first century BC bouleuterion façade and had been removed from there, together with other weaponry reliefs discovered round the gate and the Doric temple, when around 400 AD the walls were built with *spolia* and the temple converted into a tower. Most probably the busts of both gods of war had been built into the gate itself, whereas the other weaponry reliefs decorated wall sections (among others, in the converted temple) on either side of it.

To the south of the city gate, in the recess between the Doric temple and the late fortifications (sector 2250/2550 and the extremity of 2255/2550), where nothing had been touched in previous campaigns, the following layers were identified in 1996 (Fig. 22):
- layer 1: covered by a very deep heap of stones fallen from the Doric temple, the temenos wall and the propylon, layer 1 (th.: ca. 0.30 m) was an erosion layer which left only 0.15 m of the uppermost layer of the temenos wall uncovered and contained mixed ceramic material (SA 96-280/975-237) from the period AD 450-650.
- layer 2: another destruction or erosion layer (th.: ca. 0.80 m), reaching to nearly 0.10 m above the fourth course of the

temenos wall, it contained many small stones and ceramic material (SA 96-280/975-245) that was contemporary with that of layer 1. Light to middle brown in colour, layer 2 consisted of silty sand and was very loose.

- layer 3: could be identified as a middle to dark brown fill (th.: 0.45 m against the temenos, but sloping down towards the north). It started ca. 0.10 m below the upper moulding of the temple's podium on the north side, and in the middle of the third course (from above) of the temenos wall in the south (Fig. 23). It contained a fair amount of pottery (SA 96-280/975-253) from the same period as that of the two layers above it, as well as destruction material (stones, tiles, plaster, *tesserae*, glass fragments and metal).

- layer 4: this layer (th.: ca. 1.30 m) was another dark greyish to brown compacted fill reaching from ca. 0.10 m below the upper moulding of the temple's podium to ca. 0.10 m below the top of the upper step of the krepis. The ceramic material (SA 96-280/975-261) dated once more to the period AD 450-650. There was also a coin of Theodosius II, dated to the years 425-450 AD (Scheers 2000, cat. 156: SA 96 B 216). A second coin, a small *pentanummium* of Justinian I (543-565 AD; Scheers 2000, cat. 365: SA 96 B 289) was also found while excavating this layer, but since it was found in a joint between two of the temple's podium blocks it need not necessarily belong to the layer itself. This layer contained lots of smaller stones and mortar, *crustae* fragments, *tesserae* and plaster, bone, metal and glass. At his level, the northwest propylon half-column and the adjoining temenos wall section contained, still *in situ,* a lot of pink mortar, indicating that after the construction of the late fortifications, this recess may have been used as a shelter (to guard the nearby city gate?).

These two layers must represent successive stages of a filling operation in which destruction material and waste from the city were dumped in this corner. The whole operation may have been started at some point after the AD 518 earthquake, when the fortification walls apparently ceased to have any military function and a lot of debris was cleared from inside the city and piled up against these walls (Waelkens *et al.* 1997b: 192). However, if the coin of Justinian I entered its niche between the podium blocks during this operation, then it cannot have immediately followed the seismic catastrophe, or else dumping material in this corner continued over various generations.

- layer 5: another fill (th.: ca. 0.55 m), hard and gravelly with a dark brown colour, starting immediately above the *euthynteria* of the temenos wall. It contained less ceramic material (SA 96- 280/975-269) but of the same date as that from layers 3 and 4, as well as a coin of Constantinus II, dated to the years 351-355 AD (Scheers 2000, cat. 44: SA 96 B 314). There were also *crustae* fragments, *tesserae*, metal, glass and bones. The gravel in this layer corresponds with that in layer 4 to the north and must represent a levelling operation to create a new walking level on either side of the city gate (see below)

- layer 6: this fill just covered the top of the *euthynteria* of the temenos wall, as well as the column bases of the propylon. It also surrounded the rubble foundations of the late fortification system that were arranged on top of these column bases. Its ceramic material (SA 96-280/975-276) could be dated to the period AD 100-300, with some intrusive material from the final occupation phase of the town (AD 450-650). Some of this may have become part of the layer when, apparently after the 518 AD earthquake, some architectural elements from the propylon and the Doric temple collapsed on top of it (Fig. 24). This layer produced 27 boxes of tile fragments that were especially very concentrated against the temenos wall. The exposed lowest step of the Doric temple showed a graffito with the name of Klau(dios) Pios (Fig. 25).

- layer 7 below it (depth unknown) was discovered in a small sondage (0.52 by 0.83 m) against the east wall of the Doric temple's krepis and could be identified also as a fill, containing shards (SA 96-280/975-282) from the period AD 100-300 only (Fig. 26). This sandy layer, dark brown in colour, contained pebbles and produced lots of tile fragments and burnt wood.

Layers 6 and 7 have to be considered as the remains of the foundation trench of the later Roman fortification wall that was filled with second to early fourth century AD material. During this operation, part of the pavement in front of the propylon, as well as the soil level corresponding with the construction of the Doric temple must have been completely removed. The date of the material found inside layers 6 and 7 does not conflict with the supposed construction date around AD 400 of the fortification. The more recent shards in the upper layer of this fill must be considered as intrusive material.

To the east of the fortification wall (sectors 2255/2550, 2260/2550, and southern half of 2255/2555 and 2260/2555) in front of the propylon façade and covering its paved entrance, layers 1 and 2 (1 to 1.60 m thick) were identified in 1996 as a mixture of destruction material (from the surrounding buildings) and of slope deposits. Therefore, their ceramic material was not examined. These layers showed a pronounced downward slope to the east.

- layer 3 (th.: ca. 0.40 m) started ca. 0.45 m below the level of the propylon's east window and was of a middle to dark brown colour. This very hard soil was identified as a fill and contained many small to medium-sized stones and a few tiles. There was a rich harvest of archaeological material from it, especially ceramics and bone, but also fragments of *tesserae*, metal and glass. This material (SA 96-285/975-178) corresponded with that of layers 3 to 4 on the other

Fig. 15: View through the city gate from the east, at the level of layer 3.

Fig. 16. The city gate seen from the west.

Fig. 17: The sill of the city gate with the post holes and holes in the posts for closing the gate.

Fig. 18: The bust of Athena, at the time of its discovery.

Fig. 19: The bust of Athena after conservation.

Fig. 20: The bust of Ares inside the city gate, at the time of its discovery.

Fig. 21: The bust of Ares after conservation and repair.

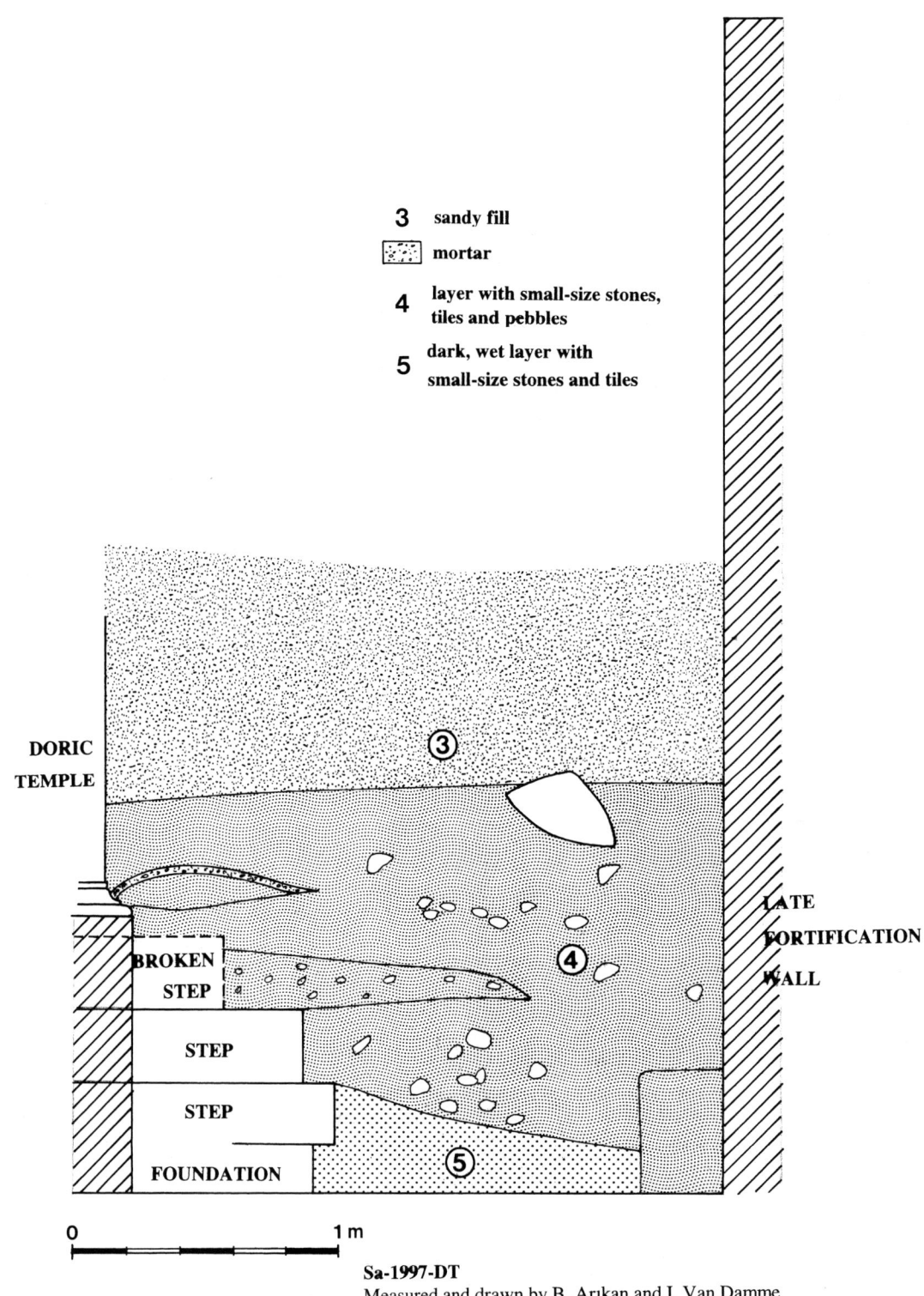

Fig. 22: Section of the stratigraphy in the 'recess' between Doric temple and late fortifications.

Fig. 23: Top of the fill (layer 3) piled up against the temenos wall in the 'recess' after the 518 AD earthquake.

Fig. 24. View of layer 6, which corresponds with the top of the construction trench for the later Roman fortifications. On top of it collapsed parts of the Doric temple and of the propylon.

Fig. 25: Graffito on the lowest step of the Doric temple.

Fig. 26: The area between propylon and Doric temple after the removal of layer 6. To the right, the foundation layer of the temple podium is visible below the lowest step.

Fig. 23: Top of the fill (layer 3) piled up against the temenos wall in the 'recess' after the 518 AD earthquake.

Fig. 24. View of layer 6, which corresponds with the top of the construction trench for the later Roman fortifications. On top of it collapsed parts of the Doric temple and of the propylon.

Fig. 25: Graffito on the lowest step of the Doric temple.

Fig. 26: The area between propylon and Doric temple after the removal of layer 6. To the right, the foundation layer of the temple podium is visible below the lowest step.

side of the fortification wall. Layer 3, therefore, has to be identified as a dump dated to the last occupation phase of the city. This must mean that, after the earthquake of AD 518, the propylon no longer functioned as a normal passageway. As we have said, parts of its upper structure must have collapsed during this catastrophe, but the excavations in the bouleuterion courtyard have revealed that the doorlintel only fell as the result of the seismic catastrophe of the mid-seventh century AD.
- layer 4: this layer, starting some 0.24 m above the level of the propylon's doorstep, must correspond with an old walking level (Fig. 27). This dark brown layer (th.: 0.20 to 0.50 m) was very hard and contained gravel, as well as small to medium-sized stones. Its ceramic material (SA 96-285/975-197) could be dated to the last occupation phase of the city (AD 450-650). There were also two coins, dated to the fourth-fifth century AD (Scheers 2000 cat. 224 and 156: SA 96 B 202: AE 3: fourth-fifth century AD; SA 96 B 216: Theodosius II, 425-430 AD). The layer contained two water-supply systems made of terracotta pipes that were connected to the reservoir built against the NW Heroon and to the systems discovered to the south of the heroon. These systems have been dated to the arrangements made after the 518 AD earthquake (Waelkens et al. 1997b: 192). One of the pipes was laid against the late Roman fortification wall and continued through the propylon door towards the south (fig. 27), the second one had a southeast orientation and ended in a large settling tank (diam.: 0.58 m) on top of the paved area in front of the propylon (Fig. 28). The rest of its course had been destroyed. Inside the settling tank (labelled as layer 5), a coin of Leo I and Verina dated to the years 457-474 AD was found (Scheers 2000, cat. 204: SA 96 B 210). At least some sections of layer 4 bore a pavement made of irregular, small slabs, of which two rows were found *in situ* in front of the propylon door (Fig. 27). Some of these slabs rested on tiles.

In some areas above the propylon's pavement, a layer 5 was found under layer 4. This should be considered as part of a same levelling operation but was less rich in archaeological material. Its ceramic finds (SA 96-285/975-217) were contemporary with those of layer 4. Immediately in front of the propylon, layer 4 directly covered the natural bedrock (conglomerate). Layer 4 corresponds with layer 5 in the recess on the other side of the fortification wall, and with layer 4 in sectors 2255/2555 and 2260/2555 to the north.

In 1997, the sixth century AD water-supply systems were removed from it in sectors 2255/2550 and 2255/2555. The southern part of the same layer was also excavated in sectors 2255/2555 and 2260/2555. Here again, layer 4 was a compact gravel layer with ceramic material (SA 97 H 266) dated to phase 8 of the local production of fine wares (second half of the fifth to first half of the seventh century AD). Layer 4 must thus represent a sloping, perhaps partly paved walking level which had been laid after the AD 518 earthquake. It is possible that it was originally completely paved, but that the small slabs had been removed at a later stage.

In sectors 2255/2555 and 2260/2555, two more layers could be identified during the 1997 excavations (Fig. 29):
- layer 5: this layer contains less gravel but larger rubble stones and more tiles than layer 4 above it and has to be distinguished from layer 5 in sector 2255/2550. The fine wares in it (SA 97 H 287) were dated to phase 2/3 of the local production, i.e. to a period between the middle of the first century AD to the first half of the third century AD (Poblome). This layer was not present everywhere.
- layer 6: this layer covered the top of the natural bedrock composed of a pinkish to brown conglomerate. The pottery in it (SA 97 H 292) was contemporary with that of layer 5 above it, but it also contained some intrusive material. The layer also contained medium-sized rubble stones, small tile fragments and quite a lot of non-residual pieces of plaster.

Layers 5 and 6 in sectors 2255/2555 and 2260/2555 must thus represent an older fill with material dated to the middle Imperial period. Since this material is roughly contemporary with that in fills 6 and 7 in the 'recess' between the Doric temple and the late fortifications, which was identified as the fill of the foundation trench of the fortifications, it is possible that layers 5 and 6 here represent the remains of a street level after the construction of these fortifications. However, in such a case one would certainly expect a lot of intrusive material dated to the period 400-518 AD. Therefore, it is much more likely that we have here a middle-Imperial fill under a street pavement that was completely removed after the AD 518 works. In any case, the stratigraphical relation of both layers to the early Imperial propylon floor seems to indicate a middle Imperial date at the earliest. In fact, layer 6 corresponds with the lower part of the *euthynteria* of the propylon and with the bottom of the plinth of the NW corner pilaster of the bouleuterion's late Hellenistic courtyard wall. Layer 5, on the other hand, covered the *euthynteria* and the lower part of the northern edge of the pavement of the propylon completely, which would have made an excellent walking level at the time of the propylon's construction. But it also covered the lower moulding of the courtyard's pilaster, which would hardly fit with the extreme care with which most of the early Imperial architecture in this area was treated.

A sondage further east, against the outer wall of the bouleuterion's courtyard, also suggested a raising of the original street level which covered the lower courses of the original courtyard wall in middle Imperial times (see 3.1).

Below these two layers, the conglomerate bedrock, shows a stepped extraction sloping in at least four steps towards the east (Fig. 8). The rather smooth surfaces on the edges suggest that they once supported steps. In early Imperial times, therefore, the street may have been (partially) laid out as a stairway between the propylon and the NW Heroon.

2.3. An early Byzantine construction behind the propylon (Fig.1)

During the 1996 campaign, excavation was also begun on sectors 2255/2545 and 2260/2545, as well as the adjoining parts of 2255/2550 and 2260/2550 located to the south of the facade of the propylon. Layers 1 and 2 corresponded with layers 1 and 2 on the north side of this wall.

However, to the south of the propylon façade, layer 2 was much thicker (ca. 1.50 m) as it contained more debris and architectural elements of those parts of the propylon, of the Doric temple and of the late fortification wall that had remained upright until the middle of the seventh century AD, when an earthquake destroyed them. In fact, layer 2 continued up to the first step of the temple krepis. It contained also a coin of Constantinus II, dated to the years 355-361 AD (Scheers 2000, cat. 46: SA 96 B 287). At the time of this disaster, the corner between the Doric temple and what remained standing of the propylon (basically its façade) was occupied by a construction made up of two or three rooms in a row, built against the Doric temple's east wall (Figs 6, 30).

The 1996 campaign only unearthed the northernmost room of this late construction (sector 2255/2545). The two other rooms (sectors 2255/2545 and 2255/2535) were exposed in 1997. The outer dimensions of the complex are 10.27 m (length) by 4.58 m (width). Its walls are made of mortared rubble (mean width: ca. 0.70 m) alternating with irregular layers of brick. This building had the same orientation as the Doric temple, of which the east wall, including the 1.30 m high podium, formed the room's western extremity.

- the northern room (Fig. 31): this room was the smallest of the three (interior dimensions: 1.30 m long by 3.36 m wide). Its east and south walls are mainly built with rubble stones and re-used blocks set in a mortar bed, but the south wall also has a course of bricks. The west wall is formed by the foundations of the temple podium, and the north wall by the late fortifications, which incorporated the temenos and the façade of the propylon. In the southeast corner, a small door gave access to the central room (sectors 2255/2545 and 2255/2540). Originally, the northern room could be entered from the outside through a small stepped door in its east wall (h.: 0.75 m). The sill of this door was formed by a re-used altar. Two additional steps (h.: 0.21 m upper one, 0.18 m lower one) below it descended into the room, whose floor level was thus considerably lower than the walking surface outside. However, during the final occupation phase of the room, this door seems to have been blocked off, at least in its lower level. As this was the only visible entrance to the northern and the central room from outside, it is unlikely that the door was completely walled up, since both rooms remained in use until the final disaster. Perhaps this alteration to the doorway only reflects a secondary raising of the door sill, corresponding with a gradual raising of the floor level outside, where at some time after the 518 AD disaster waste and debris had been dumped against the propylon and its entrance (see 2.2). The construction of the late building must even have entailed removing part of this dump. Another possibility may be that the entrance was only temporarily sealed off.

Within the room, the stratigraphy comprised five layers, all related to the construction of the late building. The bedrock (layer 8) and layer 6 were at first only exposed in a sondage of 0.50 m by 0.50 m, carried out 1.40 m to the east of the krepis of the temple and against the late fortification wall. Later on, however, the whole room was excavated until the bedrock was reached.

- the natural bedrock and the foundations of the podium and of the temenos: the natural bedrock in the western extremity of the room (here called layer 8) directly underlay the foundations of the podium krepis. Inside the room, its three steps had been completely removed below the lower moulding of the podium (Fig. 31). The three steps of the krepis had been supported by a foundation composed of three roughly finished steps (from bottom to top: 0.18 m, 0.21 m and 0.26 m), which were left *in situ*. Between the latter and the bedrock, there was an additional row of rougher, slightly projecting rubble stones (h.: ca. 0.30m).

On the other hand, along the northern extremity of the room, the foundations of the early Imperial temenos wall were also exposed. They consisted of a row of similar rubble stones, including a re-used small ashlar block (see Fig. 31).

- layers 7 and 9: whatever remained of the original layout of the courtyard surrounding the Doric temple had apparently been completely removed for the construction of the late building. The slope of the natural bedrock in this area was levelled using a dark, red brown clayish soil (layer 7) with a concentration of decayed cement in the middle (Fig. 31) and in the southeast corner of the room, a cone of dark, burnt soil (layer 9). Both layers contained pottery (respectively SA 97 DT 34 and SA 97 DT 52), belonging to the last phase of the local production (second half of the fifth- to first half of the seventh century AD). They included also some residual pieces.
- layer 6: a floor level composed of a dark soil with gravel. Its level corresponded with that of the lowest part of the Doric temple's podium. It contained lots of charcoal and pottery (SA 97 DT 12) contemporary with that of layers 7

Fig.27. The area in front of the propylon with the late pavement on top of layer 4.

Fig. 28: The settling tank (right) inside layer 4, in front of the propylon.

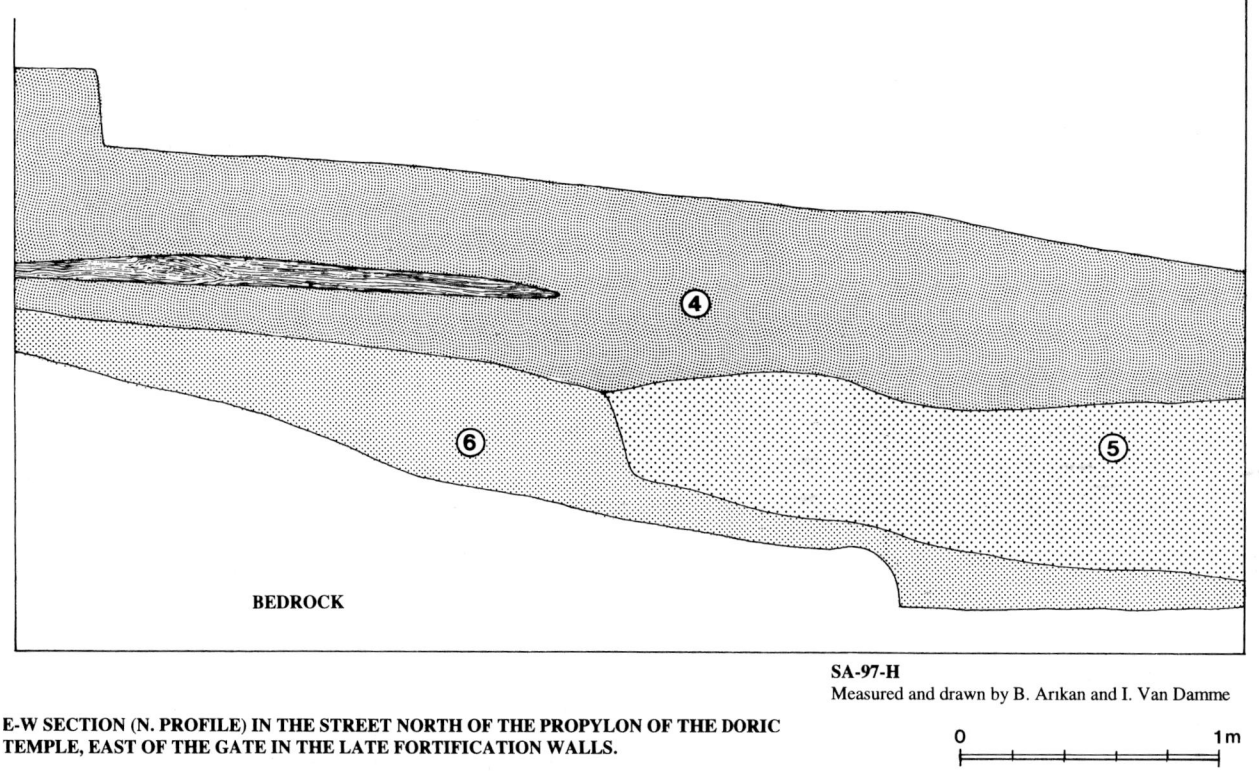

Fig. 29: North profile of the section through the street to the north of the propylon.

Fig. 30: View of the late structure built against the Doric temple, seen from the south.

Fig. 31: View of the kitchen at the level of layer 7. Left, the brick wall supporting the alcove (centre left); in the back, the foundations of the temple krepis; to the right the late fortification on top of the early Imperial temenos foundations.

Fig. 32: The west wall of the central room, with the remains of the temple's altered podium. The photograph is taken at the floor level of the room (layer 4).

Fig. 33. The southern room with the niche in its north wall and the older pavement slabs.

and 9, so that the three layers can be considered as one filling operation aimed at creating a floor level inside the northern room. This fill also contained three coins, dated to the second half of the fourth and the fifth century AD (Scheers 2000, cat. 293-295: SA 97 DT 18, 20-21). The fill of this floor level was sampled for research on mites, but this did not produce satisfactory results. However, most faunal remains were so fragmented that they could no longer be determined (674 in total), so that they might have been kitchen refuse. Among those that could be identified were ovicaprines (89), sheep (4), goats (3), pigs (52), cattle (11) and hare (1). Layer 6 also contained a slightly projecting brick wall below the southern rubble wall. It seems to have been built here as a support for a cooking alcove in the south wall.

- layer 5: the surface of the floor level was separated from the rest of layer 6, since it was clearly a hard packed walking surface, containing a lot of pottery (SA 97 DT 6) and other finds pressed into it. The pottery could all be dated to phase 8 (second half of the fifth-first half of the seventh century AD).

The floor still bore *in situ* a container (SA 97/ 5285-4975/6), standing in the middle of ashes, and dated to the mid-seventh century AD. During the winter of 1997, part of the nearly 1 m thick south wall of the room collapsed, thus exposing a small alcove oven, 0.33 m above the floor level, which had been left untouched during the summer. It still contained a locally produced cooking pot (SA 98 DT 103-1) of type 4G 101 (see Degeest 2000 a), dated by Degeest to the late sixth or first half of the seventh century AD.

It is clear that the northern room functioned as the kitchen of a dwelling occupied during the first half of the seventh century AD and still inhabited when an earthquake destroyed it around the middle of that century (see Waelkens *et al.* 2000 b).

This seventh century AD floor level was covered by the following destruction layers:
- layer 4: a 0.30 m to 0.50 m deep, greyish brown layer, composed of a loose, loamy silt, containing lots of rubble stones and small tiles (from the walls). It contained scarcely any diagnostic archaeological finds, except for a *nummus* of Anastasius, from AD 491-498 (Scheers 2000, cat. 357: SA 97 DT 148).
- layer 3: a brown layer consisting of compacted silty sand, full of rubble stones. This must have formed the upper part of the debris of the walls.
Layers 3 and 4 represent the destruction layers of the late dwelling and are mainly composed of material from the rubble walls.

- The central room: this room, which connected by a door in its north wall with the kitchen, has the same width as the latter (3.38 m) but is 3.80 m long and therefore much larger. Inside the room, the north wall still contains a niche with a width of 0.84 m, a depth of 0.20 m and a preserved height of 0.36 to 0.46 m. The bottom and lower west side of the niche are still covered with plain wall plaster. This niche must have functioned as a kind of cupboard. The west wall of the room was again formed by the remains of the podium of the Doric temple, but here part of the orthostats composing the podium's outer facing had been removed (and the gaps most probably plastered over). This made it possible to study the inner structure of the podium (Fig. 32), so that it became obvious that the front part of the temple had been completely rebuilt in a later period, most probably around 400 AD, when it was converted into a tower. As early as the 1986 survey, it had become clear that part of the façade was no longer original. At present, the inner part of the podium consists of 5 rows of well cut ashlars (lowest one 0.27 m high; four upper ones combined height of 0.87 m), a layer of bricks (h.: 0.025 to 0.04 m), and three layers of tufa blocks (combined height: 0.85 m). For conservation purposes a modern rubble wall was constructed in front of it. In this room, the natural bedrock had been cut away and smoothed on top, so that it forms a 1.55 m projecting natural terrace. Its upper level corresponded more or less with that of the floor level (layer 4) which for safety reasons (the front of the building is very unstable) could not be excavated (Fig. 32). In the southeast corner, the floor seems to have been originally covered by tiles, of which one was found *in situ*. On top of it, some crushed seventh century AD vessels and a number of heavily corroded metal objects, mostly hooks, were found.

Above the floor and below the topsoil, covered by a large amount of ashlars from the collapsed front of the temple, two destruction layers could be identified:
- layer 3: composed of medium to large stones embedded in a greyish brown silty soil, containing lots of tile fragments and tiny bits of mortar.
- layer 2: containing lots of smaller stones, tufa blocks, tile fragments and mortar.

- the southern room: to the south of the larger central room, a third space (visible length: 4.38 m by 3.30 width inside) was unearthed. For practical reasons (limitations in the movement of the crane), it was not possible to expose its south wall, so that the total length of the room remains unknown.

This room was apparently not connected to the central room, with which it shared a common wall. The south face of this wall contained a niche like that in the north wall of the central room. It has a width of 0.63 m, a depth of 0.30 m and a preserved height of 0.48 to 0.57 m. (Fig. 33). Within the-room, a lot of coloured wall-plaster fragments were recovered, unfortunately too fragmentary to reconstruct a particular scene or motif, although some flowers could be identified. The floor level of this room (layer 3) could not be excavated either. Its northern extremity, however, was formed by nicely laid limestone slabs, ending in a straight edge to the south, more or less aligned with the southern extremity of the Doric temple (Fig. 34). These slabs are at the same level as the smoothed bedrock in the central room. Both may therefore reflect the original layout of the temple square (or a later phase of it). In the northwest corner of this room, a seventh century AD dolium (SA 97/5285-4965/122) stood on the floor, while in the southeast corner there was a concentration of metal artefacts (SA 97/5285-4965/118), whose function has not yet been identified or studied (Fig. 35).

Below the top soil, the destruction layer (layer 2) above this floor contained quite a lot of tufa blocks.

2.4. Conclusion

The evidence from the 1996-1997 excavations combined with that of the area immediately to the east, excavated in previous years (Waelkens *et al.* 1997b: 192), suggests that the Doric temple may already have been planned before the reign of Augustus. But, under the rule of Rome's first emperor, this whole area underwent a drastic transformation, when first the NW Heroon was built and, shortly afterwards, a temenos surrounding the Doric temple and a monumental propylon. The latter's construction may not have followed the original plans but a slightly changed version inspired by the presence and the order of the NW Heroon on the other side of the street.

At some time during the third century AD, the originally perhaps partially stepped street may have been converted into a paved slope that would allow wheeled traffic to enter the street from the north. Yet, the sill has no traces of wheels.

A second, much more drastic change seems to have occurred around AD 400, when a construction trench was dug against the east side of the Doric temple in order to build a new city wall. This incorporated both the temenos wall and the western half of the propylon facade. The recess between the city wall and the Doric temple may then have been converted into a kind of shelter (for a guard?).

A third intervention seems to have taken place after the AD 518 earthquake, which seems to have destroyed the upper part of the propylon, as is suggested by some building material found between the propylon and the Doric temple, below the sixth century AD levels (Fig. 24). After this catastrophe, the street level was raised nearly 0.50 m by a layer of gravel and seems to have received a kind of new pavement, at least in front of the propylon entrance. During this operation, an effort was made to provide the city with new water-supply systems, connected to the reservoir in the corner between the NW Heroon and the late Roman city wall. During the same period, or during the final occupation phase, some areas adjoining the city gate, such as the abandoned shelter in the recess, but also the Propylon's entrance, were used as a dump, possibly continuing over various generations.

The area behind the propylon may also have been used at first for dumping material. However, during the (late sixth or) seventh century AD, part of this dump must have been removed for the construction of a structure made of rubble walls and brick layers, comprising at least three rooms. It was built against the east wall of the Doric temple, which by this time had become an already abandoned tower. This structure may have contained at least two separate units, the northern one composed of a room and a kitchen, inhabited until an earthquake destroyed the city around the middle of the seventh century AD. The second unit is only partly excavated, but seems to have been more lavishly decorated inside from the fact that its walls were covered with a plaster with floral motifs. The function of this structure is uncertain, but the northern unit at least seems to have been a simple kitchen.

3. THE BOULEUTERION

3.1. The courtyard of the bouleuterion (Figs 36-38)

The 1996 season saw an excavation begun in both the courtyard and in the bouleuterion proper. One of the aims of the 1996 campaign was to find the north wall of the open courtyard to the north of the Bouleuterion (see 3.2), from which the latter could be entered, and to determine its length. As a result, a surface of 225 m², spread over thirteen partially excavated sectors (2260/2550, 2265/2550, 2270/2550, 2260/2555, 2265/2555, 2270/2555, 2275/2555, 2280/2555, 2285/2555, 2275/2560, 2280/2560, 2285/2560, 2285/2565) located immediately north of the bouleuterion façade and the east of the Doric temple, was excavated in 1996. In these sectors, several layers of debris from the NW Heroon, the Doric temple, its propylon, and the bouleuterion filled the courtyard. In general, only one layer was removed in 1996.

The excavations also exposed the upper part of the northern courtyard wall, extending 22.21 m eastward and almost reaching the front of the terrace building on the north side of the upper agora. The northwest corner of the wall decorated with a pilaster (w.: 0.76 m on both sides) still stands upright, above a well-preserved socle moulding (Fig. 9). The northeast corner of the courtyard and its corner pilaster (w.: 0.77 m) has also remained *in situ* (Fig. 39). This pilaster is carved out of two joining ashlar blocks. Since its

Fig. 34: View from the southeast showing the alignment of the pavement slabs and the temple front.

Fig. 35:
One of the metal objects found inside the southern room.

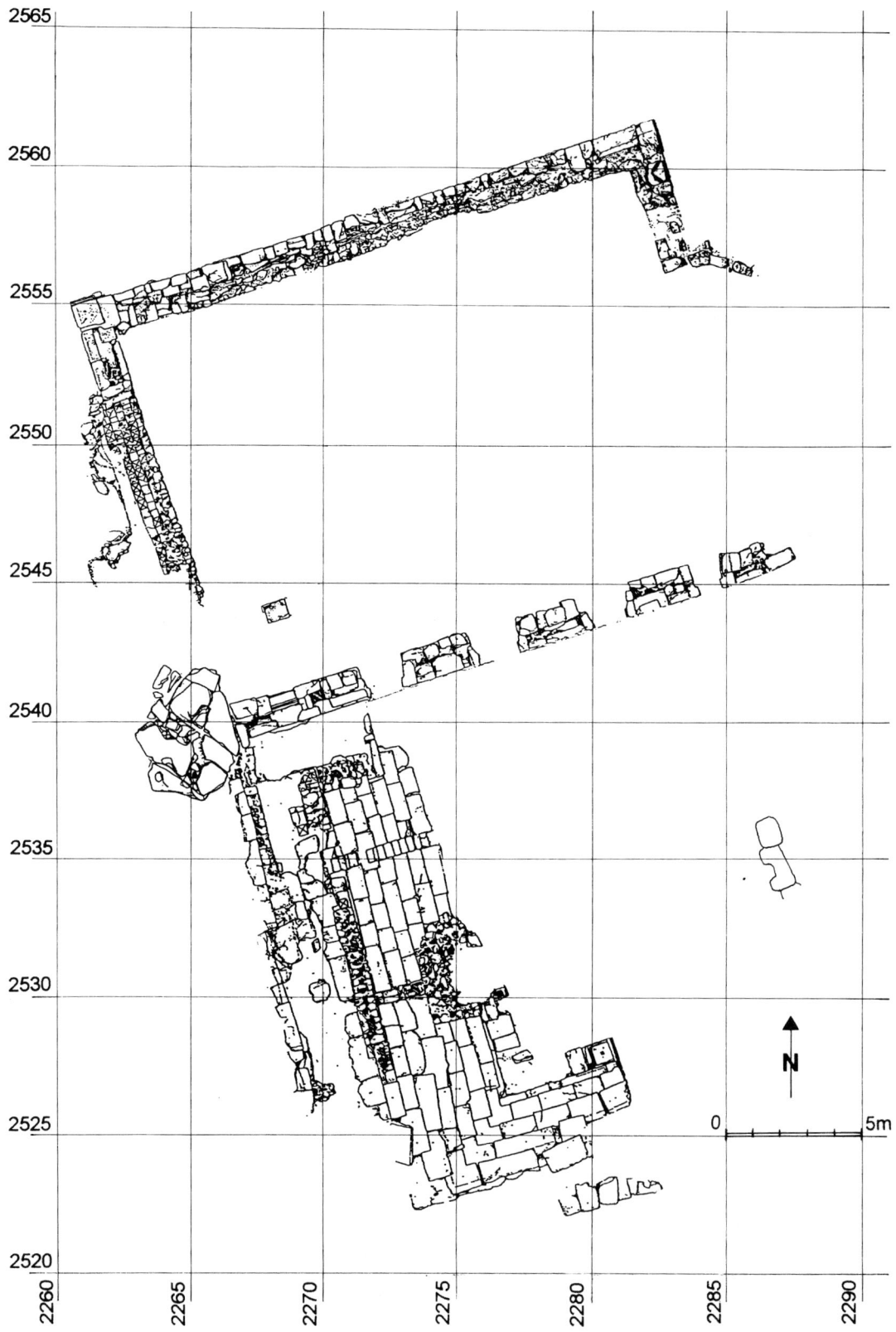

Fig. 36: Map of the bouleuterion and its courtyard (1987).

Fig. 37. View of the bouleuterion (left) and its courtyard (right), seen from the east, at the end of the 1997 season.

Fig. 38: The bouleuterion (background) and its courtyard (foreground), towards the end of the 1997 campaign. The view is taken from the north.

Fig. 39: The northeast corner of the bouleuterion courtyard wall, seen from the west.

Fig. 40: The northeast corner of the bouleuterion courtyard, seen from the northeast. A socle moulding is clearly visible.

Fig. 41: View of the north wall of the bouleuterion courtyard near its northwest corner.

Fig. 42: Part of the collapsed outer face of the northern courtyard wall, showing the original ashlar courses.

Fig. 43: Reused late Hellenistic/early Imperial ostothecae in the northern courtyard wall.

Fig. 44: View of the sondage exposing the lowest courses of the bouleuterion's northern courtyard wall.

Fig. 45: The upper part of the courtyard's west wall, with the remaining brick layers, seen from the north.

Fig. 46. General view of the bouleuterion's west wall, seen from the northeast.

Fig. 47. The southern half of the west wall with its irregular stone arrangement.

socle moulding is very high above the north side, it cannot have been at street level there, since the street level sloped down to the east. On the east side, it may have faced a stairway leading down in the level of the courtyard. A stairway was excavated here, but it is already of late Roman/early Byzantine date (see below).

Most of the northern courtyard wall (w.: ca. 1.20 m) consists of a kind of *emplekton* system with two outer ashlar faces filled with rubble. At regular intervals, however, stones of the outer layer intersect with those of the inner face. The northern face is made of rectangular courses of bossed ashlars with drafted edges and is in general quite well preserved (Fig. 41). Most of these ashlars must belong to the original layout of the wall (Fig. 42), but repairs show that it had been partly rebuilt at a later stage. In fact, near the northwest corner, even some late Hellenistic to early Imperial *ostothecae* had been re-used and adapted as stones for the outer facing (Fig. 43).

Except for the two corners, which still look completely original and are built with large ashlars, the inner face is almost completely a construction of later date and is less carefully built. It is predominantly made of mortared rubble and rows of brick. The rows of brick were inserted to level the courses of the wall's inner face, but sometimes also to fill up gaps in it. Therefore, even this wall seems to have undergone reconstructions or repairs in late antiquity. At present, the north wall also contains some re-used door- or window-sills and posts, which must have belonged to the original layout, although in a different position. The preserved parts indicate that there must have been at least one monumental gabled entrance, built in the Doric order.

Of the northern courtyard wall only the northwest extremity was further excavated in 1997. The fact that the structure in late antiquity had been rebuilt with brick sections and re-used blocks was confirmed. However, a sondage in the Upper Agora/North sector revealed that there may already have been an alteration in the second century AD.

In fact, in 1997, in an attempt to reach the foundations of the bouleuterion courtyard wall, a sondage was made in layer 7 of room XVIII (sector 2275/2560) of upper agora/North (see 4.4.2). Layer 7 proved to be a very thick fill (1.10 m) that contained fine wares from the second phase of the local production (SA 97 UA/N 110 and 116), i.e. the second half of the first and the first half of the second century AD. In room XVIII four ashlar courses of the courtyard wall were exposed (total height: 1.55 m). All the stones had a regular, rusticated surface to the north, but were completely rough at the back, confirming that the original wall was constructed by the *empklekton* method. The two upper courses were flush, but the two lower ones were each arranged as a slightly projecting step.

The outer surface of the third course is well finished so that it must have been completely visible. The lowest course has a much rougher surface treatment and therefore seems to have functioned as an *euthynteria*. It is supported by a projecting row of large rubble stones laid in a mortar bed. These are embedded in layer 8, which was not then excavated (Fig. 44). The fill of layer 7 covered the lowest three courses of the courtyard wall and therefore cannot have corresponded with the original layout. It must represent a later alteration, involving a considerable raising of the street level and perhaps a (partial) rebuilding of the courtyard wall. Originally, the street surface must have corresponded with the middle of the euthynteria. The pottery contained in layer 7 suggests that this alteration occurred during the first half or the middle of second century AD. This seems to correspond very well with the situation further west, in front of the propylon where, in sectors 2255/2555 and 2260/2555, layers 5 and 6 were identified as the remains of a middle Imperial street level, containing more or less contemporary material to that in layer 7 (see 2.2). If this alteration dates from the middle of the century (or even a bit later, which is still possible), these works may perhaps be connected with the rearrangement of the water-supply in this part of the upper city at the time of the construction of the Antonine nymphaeum on the upper agora. Another possibility is that it dates from repairs after a late first century AD earthquake, which also required considerable rebuilding in the area to the west of the late Hellenistic fountain house (Waelkens *et al.* 2000b).

Whereas the 1996 campaign focused on the north wall of the courtyard, the main aim of the 1997 season was to define the western and southern boundaries of the courtyard and to start clearing the inside, which was full of stones from the above-mentioned buildings high above it. Work was, therefore, carried out in the following sectors: 2260/2550, 2265/2550, 2260/2545, 2265/2545, 2270/2545, 2275/2545, 2265/2540, 2270/2540, 2275/2540 and 2280/2540.

The western courtyard wall is to a great extent carved from the natural bedrock, but it contains a mortared rubble fill inside the cracks and gaps. Its upper stretches, however, are made of rubble and small sized ashlars, topped by mortared bricks that are in some parts preserved up to a third row (Fig. 45) The wall has a thickness of 1.20 m and in 1997 it was exposed to a depth of nearly 2.50 m. Near the northwest corner of the courtyard, coloured wall plaster was found *in situ* against the bedrock. For the time being, it is difficult to get a picture of what the wall plaster represents: its edges are enclosed by a red and blue band, and within them there are green and yellow colours. This painted wall plaster indicates that, during the last occupation of Sagalassos, the original courtyard was converted into a covered space, whose function (a church) only became clear during the 1998 campaign.

Since the south wall of the courtyard is formed by the bouleuterion's façade, it will be described in the next section. At the end of the 1997 season, the internal dimensions of the courtyard were established as 19.70 m (east-west) by 11.80 (west side) to 12.70 m (east side).

From the interior of the courtyard several layers of collapsed building blocks were removed with the help of a mobile crane. Everything was covered by the following material:
- an erosion layer (topsoil) with a thickness of 0.40 to 1.20 m. It contained various coins spanning a time period from the first century BC to the late sixth century AD (Scheers 2000, cat. 13, 17, 19, 32, 81, 104, 135, 170, 226, 366 and 377: SA 97 DT 123, first century BC/early Imperial times; SA 97 B1 178, Sagalassos city coin from the reign of Hadrian; SA 97 DT 94, Sagalassos city coin from AD 193-211; SA 96 B 78, *antoninianus* of Valerian I, from AD 257; SA 97 DT 59, coin of Theodosius, dated to the years AD 383-395; SA 97 B1 125, coin of Arcadius from 395-401 AD; SA 97 B1 160, coin of Honorius from 393-395 AD; SA 96 B 94, *gloria Romanorum* coin from AD 408-423; SA 96 B 147, AE 4 from the fourth-fifth century AD; SA 96 B 77: *decanummium* of Justinian I from the year 562/3 AD; SA 96 B 89, *follis* of Phokas from the year 592/3 AD).
- a first destruction layer (2): this layer was removed all over the courtyard. Its depth varied from 0.20 to 1 m. It consisted of a loose, brown, slightly crumbly soil and contained several coins dated from the fourth to the sixth centuries AD (Scheers 2000, cat. 71, 102, 114, 123, 248 and 363: SA 96 B 102, *gloria Romanorum* coin of 364-375 AD; SA 97 B1 139, *salus rei publicae* coin from AD 383-395; SA 97 B1 172; coin of Arcadius from AD 395-401; SA 97 B 156; coin of Arcadius from AD 400-401 AD; AE 4 from the fourth-fifth centuries AD; SA 96 B 99: *follis* of Justinian I, from the year 541/2 AD).
- a second destruction layer (3) below it was nowhere fully excavated and contained a lot of mortar and tile fragments. During the 1996 and 1997 campaigns, two coins were recovered from it. They were dated to the fourth and fifth centuries AD (Scheers 2000, cat. 72 and 268: SA 97 DT 74, *gloria Romanorum* coin from 364-378 or 383-388 AD; SA 96 B 104, small bronze from the second half of the fourth or the fifth centuries AD).

3.2. The bouleuterion

3.2.1. The original council house

The bouleuterion is located on an intermediate terrace between the Doric temple to the west and the upper agora to the east (Figs. 36-38). The presence of a bouleuterion here with an open courtyard to its north had already been established since the 1986 survey (Mitchell and Waelkens 1987: 40-42; Mitchell and Waelkens 1988: 60-62). In fact, before the excavations were begun in 1996, some rows of seats near the southwest corner of the building, as well as the upper part of its north wall were already visible, suggesting a roofed building of roughly 21 by 22 m (Waelkens 1993a: 43-44).

The upper level of the east wall of the council-house apparently opened towards the agora via an open gallery with four half-column piers, Doric on the outside and Corinthian on the inside. Two of these supports, decorated with reliefs representing Athena and Ares, respectively with a male and a female prisoner at their feet, were visible at the surface. Loggias in upper wall sections had become popular since the early Hellenistic period in palace and house architecture (Lauter 1986: 141 Abb. 44a; Nielsen 1994: 83 fig. 42; 142-144 figs 75-75; Brands 1996). A similar, although completely Doric loggia, was found on the first floor of the so-called "*customs house*" at Selge, dated to the second half of the second century BC (Machatschek and Schwarz 1981: 85-88 Taf. 17). One of the corresponding capitals had already been stored, before the start of our activities, in the Belediye depot at Ağlasun. In the past (Waelkens 1993a: fig. 29), it had been dated to the late second or the beginning of the first century BC (Waelkens 1993a: 44). Since the 1986 season, three other capitals of half-column piers have been recovered. A fifth Corinthian capital, stored in the same Belediye depot and this time from a free-standing column, which in the past had been wrongly assumed to belong to the NW Heroon (Waelkens 1993a: 43 fig. 24), is clearly a product of the same *Bauhütte*, and most probably came from an internal support in the bouleuterion. Such supports would be necessary to span the width of the interior space. It is known that the bouleuterion at Priene, which had almost identical dimensions, was confronted with serious problems resulting from the width of the roof span. This had to be reduced, with the introduction of new supports, to 14.50 m, later even to 10.65 m (Rumscheid 1998: 56).

The date of the Corinthian capital from Sagalassos must therefore be brought forward and must be contemporary with that of the half-capitals from the bouleuterion. Recently, Rumscheid proposed a late Hellenistic-early Imperial date for this group of capitals (Rumscheid 1994: 150-152). However, compared to early Augustan capitals from Sagalassos studied by Vandeput (1997a), a date in the first century BC remains more likely. The whole arrangement may go back to the period of stability under Roman republican rule, before the outbreak of the Mithridatic wars which also affected Pisidia, or to the period immediately after these events. A detailed study and comparison with other late Hellenistic and all early Imperial remains from Sagalassos, should be undertaken in the near future in order to establish a more precise date.

Fig. 48: The bedrock separating the two different sections of the west wall.

Fig. 49: The northern section of the west wall in pseudo-isodomic ashlars.

Fig. 50: View of the interior (original) face of the north wall of the bouleuterion, seen from the west.

Fig. 51: The northwest corner of the bouleuterion, with the console (upper left corner) and the left door.

Fig. 52: The second door from the left in the north wall of the bouleuterion.

Fig. 48: The bedrock separating the two different sections of the west wall.

Fig. 49: The northern section of the west wall in pseudo-isodomic ashlars.

Fig. 50: View of the interior (original) face of the north wall of the bouleuterion, seen from the west.

Fig. 51: The northwest corner of the bouleuterion, with the console (upper left corner) and the left door.

Fig. 52: The second door from the left in the north wall of the bouleuterion.

The campaign of 1996 had not yet touched on the bouleuterion proper, but one of the aims of the 1997 season was to define the exact limits of the building which were still unclear along the south and east side. Therefore, excavations were initiated in sectors 2275/2540, 2265/2535, 2270/2535, 2275/2535 (western half), 2265/2530, 2270/2530, 2275/2530, 2280/2530 (western half), 2265/2525, 2270/2525, 2275/2525, and 2280/2525 which correspond more or less with the western half of the building.

- The bouleuterion walls:

The exterior dimensions of the building could be fixed at 20.75 m (E-W) by 20.20 m (N-S). With these dimensions the bouleuterion at Sagalassos almost has the same size as the bouleuterion of Priëne (south wall: 20.25 m; west wall: 21.06 m; east wall: 21.18 m), built around 200 BC (Rumscheid 1998: 51-57). The 1997 excavations only exposed the western half of the north wall (façade) and most of the west wall. The south wall had completely collapsed, at least above the level of the preserved seats.

- *west wall* (Fig. 46): this wall is mostly built against the natural bedrock, which also forms its northern extremity. The wall consists of two sections of a different building style and surface treatment. The southern section recedes some 0.40 m and is made of rather rough, mostly rectangular ashlars of greatly varying dimensions, thus forming four to five irregular courses (h.: ca. 1.60 m). Their surface has been shaped with a pick (Fig. 47). Towards the north, this wall rests upon a slightly projecting part of the natural bedrock that was left in place (Fig. 48). Most of this wall had collapsed but was put back in place, since the original location of the blocks was easy to identify. This wall section most probably represents an older building phase, when a smaller structure (an older council-house?) occupied this spot. In fact, unless this was merely a terrace wall, the surface treatment of the blocks suggests that they may have been plastered over.

On the other side of the projecting bedrock, and also partly supported by it, the northern wall section continued until it abutted another projecting section of more regularly worked bedrock in the northwest corner of the room (Fig. 49). Here as well, some of its courses were put back in place. The 5.10 m long northern wall section is made of beautifully carved ashlars placed in an almost pseudo-isodomic arrangement (5 courses). Its face, preserved over a height of ca. 2 m, has been worked with a fine pointed chisel. The edges are slightly bevelled.

- *north wall (façade)*: this wall (l.: 20.75 m; w.: 1.20 m) presents a completely different aspect and also shows two different construction phases on the outside and inside. Only the inner face is still original. The outside face, the façade itself, is a late Roman alteration built with re-used blocks.

Today, the wall still stands to a height of 4.95 m in the northwest corner, but gradually diminishes to a height of 2.02 m in the east (Fig. 50). The eastern extremity seems to have collapsed but, since this corner originally must have been linked to the eastern courtyard wall, only one block seems to be missing here (Fig. 36).

Inside the council-room, the wall is built of nicely carved ashlars, worked with a claw chisel and sometimes with drafted margins, arranged in a kind of pseudo-isodomic arrangement. However, around the doors, the regularity of the courses is interrupted, to better incorporate the posts and lintels. Only the western 7.20 m of the north wall was completely exposed to a level of 1.40 m above that of the door sills. Its western extremity is built against the smoothed bedrock in the room's northwest corner. The lowest row is made of orthostats (h.: 1.42 m). Above them, the height of the regular courses varies from bottom to top: 0.35 m, 0.56 m, 0.25 m, 0.52 m, 0.24 to 0.28 m, and 0.87 m.

At ground level this wall is interrupted by seven nicely built doors, slightly tapering towards the top. Only the two lefthand ones are sufficiently excavated for a more detailed description. The left (western) door is still buried below and has a very nice door lintel, with a cornice moulding, on top of its doorframe composed of three *fasciae* (Fig. 51). The upper width of the door opening is 0.83 m. Its height was most probably less than ca. 2 m. The next door, 2.14 m further east, which is completely exposed, is still standing up to the height of its collapsed lintel, i.e.: 2.70 m (Fig. 52). Its upper width is 1.20 m (lower width: 1.32 m), so that this door was considerably larger than the first one.

There must have been a row of windows at a higher level as the highest preserved stone between the two doors is clearly moulded along its southern edge as a window sill (Fig. 53). It shows that these windows were placed ca. 3.70 m above the foot of the north wall. In the northwest corner, the wall also contains a small *in situ* console (Fig. 51), which may have had some function in the roof structure (h.: 0.14 m; projection: 0.11 m).

Whereas the inner face of the bouleuterion façade is still original, its outer face was completely rebuilt in late antiquity, re-using at least part of the original structure. Its re-used material suggests that large sections of the façade was made of nicely carved ashlars with incised, but smooth 'false' drafted margins round an inner part worked with a point chisel. This arrangement is similar to that of the late Hellenistic bouleuterion at Termessos in Pisidia. This wall, however, had been completely dismantled. This most probably happened at the latest around AD 400, when the busts of Athena and Ares, together with a number of other parts of the weaponry frieze that originally crowned the bouleuterion's outer walls, were incorporated in and around the late Roman city gate (see 2.2).

During the 1997 season, various elements of this frieze, representing helmets, shields and cuirasses, which must have been re-used in the outer face of the north wall, were recovered from the mass of debris filling the courtyard (Figs 54-57).

But, the wall also contains several stones from other buildings, so that it presents a very irregular outlook (Fig. 58), suggesting that it had been plastered over during this final phase of the building's use. The outer wall sections above the doors seem to have had niches cut out, possibly to reduce the load on the door lintels (Fig. 59).

- The auditorium

The arrangement of the seats inside the bouleuterion reflects that of the old bouleuterion of Athens, but especially that of the Hellenistic bouleuteria from Priene, Assos, Notion and Heracleia on the Latmos, with three wings of seats running parallel to the W-, S-, and E-wall of the building. Between the northern extremity of the seats and the northern bouleuterion wall there was a corridor 1.95 m wide, which has not yet been excavated (Fig. 51).

On the west side all eight rows of seats (total length: 13.46 m below and 15.81 m above; total width below: 6.21 m) have been preserved (Fig. 60). The seats (0.40 m high, 0.62 m wide) show a rather heavy *cyma reversa* profile, with a band along the upper edge of the front only in the upper courses (Fig. 61). Over a width of 0.20 m the back part of each seat is hollowed out a few centimetres to keep the feet of each *bouleutès* away from the back of the council member sitting in front of him (Fig. 62). In theatres of Asia Minor, this type of seat, elaborately carved with curving lines, became widespread only during the first century BC – first century AD. But the beginning of this process can already been seen in the middle Hellenistic theatre of Erythrai (De Bernardi 1974: fig. 116; 109). However, similar shapes already occur in the bouleuterion of Priene, built around 200 BC (Rumscheid 1998: Abb. 37, 40-41), so that the seats themselves scarcely offer additional evidence concerning the exact date of the bouleuterion.

In the west wing, the seats are broken by two staircases of 16 steps (0.20 m high, 0.29 m wide, 0.50 m deep) each (Fig. 63). Between the uppermost seat and the back wall there was a walking area of nearly 2 m.

Of the south wing, only the western half has been excavated. This wing apparently comprised only five rows, of which only four are preserved now (length: 12.23 m below). Here as well there were apparently two small stairways, the western one of which is located at 4.45 m from the SW corner of the building. The excavations stopped in the middle of sector 2280/2525, where the row of seats seems to have been interrupted for a kind of straight passage to the south (Fig. 64).

Today, on the east side, only two rows of seats can be seen, but this area has not yet been excavated. This wing seems to have held two staircases located exactly opposite those on the west side.

At the end of the 1997 campaign only half of the auditorium had been exposed. If one accepts however a space of ca. 0.63 m width for each participant (Rumscheid 1998: 53-54), then the excavated seats must have accommodated in the west wing approximately sixteen to seventeen people on the lowest row, up to twenty-three or twenty-four on the highest one (one can assume an increase of one seat per row as one moves upwards). On the excavated part of the south side, these numbers are respectively thirteen and nine. This brings the total number of possible councillors seated in the excavated section up to 156/164 for the west wing and 55 in the southern wing.

A row of limestone slabs (1.20 m wide in front of the seats, 2.30 m wide in front of the north wall) ran parallel to the seats and surrounded a lower central space, which was not then excavated (Fig. 64).

3.2.2. The early Byzantine conversion of the bouleuterion

As we have noted above (3.2.1), when around 400 AD the weaponry friezes of its facade were re-used in and around the nearby city gate of the late Roman fortifications, the council-house must have undergone such a considerable transformation in its upper wall sections that the building can no longer have been roofed. The recycling of building material even seems to indicate that the council-house had already been abandoned. This is the more striking since in Asia Minor the fifth century AD was still a prosperous period (Grant 1998: X). There are, however, various possible explanations for the abandonment of the building. Possibly, as occurred at Priene, its wide span had caused such problems to the roof structure that it eventually collapsed. Or, the apparent neglect of, or lack of respect for the building could be that by that time it simply had lost its original function and was no longer used by the councillors. Both factors may have been in play at once.

Despite the fact that, during fourth century AD, society still remained urban, by the beginning of the century, the *ekklèsia* or popular assembly had already virtually ceased to exist, except for meetings in the theatres on the occasion of games or

Fig. 53: View of the upper part of the north wall, seen from the west. In the middle, the sill of a window is visible.

Fig. 54: Block of the weaponry frieze with a nicely carved helmet.

Fig. 55: Frieze block with the remains of a similar helmet.

Fig. 56: Weaponry frieze block with a cuirass.

Fig. 57: Cuirass on a frieze block from the bouleuterion.

Fig. 58: View of the north wall of the bouleuterion.

Fig. 59: Niche in the exterior face of the bouleuterion facade.

Fig. 60: View of the west wing of the bouleuterion seats.

Fig. 61: The seats of the bouleuterion. Only the upper section is completely finished.

Fig. 62: The bouleuterion seats of the west wing, seen from the north. Notice the space hollowed out for the feet.

Fig. 63: Stairway in the western wing of the bouleuterion.

agones (Foss 1979: 15; Jones 1994: 242). By the end of the same century, civic self-government had declined into the rule of small hereditary oligarchies, the *curiales*, whereby the *boulè* became the only institution through which self-government could still be practised (Liebeschuetz 1972: 101-102). However, the fact that the town councillors were held personally liable for any deficiency in collecting the Imperial taxes became such a heavy burden that they constantly tried to escape their duties (Foss 1979: 14). As a result, several laws, even laws including the enrolment of outsiders to fill up vacancies, had to be issued in order to keep their ranks filled (Jones 1994: 244- 247). Eventually, this led to a widening division between a minority of privileged leading citizens, the *prôteuontes*, who managed to manipulate the tax system to their advantage, and the rank and file of *bouleutai*. As a result, already by the late fourth century AD, most of the old notables in the Greek East were treated in the same violent way by the leading figures of their class who collaborated with the imperial authorities, as were members of the lower classes. They were increasingly held responsible for tax arrears and were even flogged in public. During the fifth century, this group pressure caused an unbridgeable split among the notables, when the *prôteuontes* began to form a province-wide nobility that no longer felt any loyalty to the smaller cities of their region, where the maintenance of law and order and of civic pride devolved increasingly on the bishop and his clergy (Brown 1992: 21, 26-28, 53, 150-151). As a result of this development, the numbers of town councillors constantly declined (Foss 1979: 13) and by the time of Justinian, the emperor could write in his *Novellae* that *"if one counts the city councils of our empire, one will find them very small, some well off neither in numbers, nor in wealth"*. In fact, after the reforms of Anastasius I (491-518 AD), when the central government took over the management of the cities' finances, the councils seem to have ceased to function in the East and shortly afterwards they disappeared from civic life (Foss 1979, 13; Jones 1994: 247). At Ephesos, the last datable dedication of the Council dates to the time of Theodosius II, while its activity is still attested in AD 431. But even here, in this provincial capital, the Council gradually became smaller and less influential and the governors thus increasingly usurped its former functions (Foss 1979: 14-15). At Aphrodisias, the Council still existed around AD 500 (Bowersock 1990: 3), but the great plague of 541-542 resulted there, as everywhere else, in the collapse of traditional city life before the end of the century (Roueché 1989: 140).

In late antiquity, the numbers of active councillors at Sagalassos must have dwindled rapidly, so that the building with its seating capacity of at least two hundred in the section excavated thus far may have outgrown the needs of what remained of the Council. Under such circumstances, one would understand why the by then centuries-old building was no longer well kept and its roof no longer maintained or repaired. In fact, a reduced Council could also meet in various other buildings (for instance, in the odeion).

However, after partially dismantling its façade, the auditorium was used for other purposes than the meetings of the Council. In fact, excavation revealed the existence of a late, two-room structure built on top of the western wing of the auditorium (Fig. 65). Its east wall (length: 11.60 m) stands on the edge of the uppermost row of seats of the auditorium. Its outer and inner walls are only preserved to a height of approximately 0.40 m and consist of mortared rubble. The structure consists of two rooms with access to one another, corresponding in length with the two different sections of the bouleuterion's western wall. In fact, the wall separating the rooms was built against that projecting part of bedrock that separated these two wall sections (Fig. 66). The building is in such a ruinous state that its north wall is completely missing, except for a wall section descending to the seats of the auditorium. The entrance can only have been from the south, but the 1.75 m wide opening in this wall seems far too wide to have been a door opening.

The southern room has a mortared floor, the northern one a floor made of terracotta tiles quite a few of which were still in place ("layer 5"). The floor of the southern room ("layer 3") consists of a compact soil with lots of small-sized rubble and pieces of mortar it. This floor level has not been excavated.

The rainwater from the roof of this structure was apparently collected and taken via terracotta pipes, laid inside the southern stairway of the auditorium, to a rough structure of mortared rubble (ca. 2.40 by 2.80 m) built on top of the three lowest rows of seats. The east wall of this structure, clearly a cistern, had collapsed (Fig. 67). Its corners were formed by seats from the auditorium, placed upright, while the wall was made of a re-used ostotheca.

The function of the structure on top of the west wing of the auditorium is not yet clear. The pottery that was found inside could be dated to the sixth and first half of the seventh century AD, which corresponds with the last phases of the occupation of Sagalassos. The building may therefore have had the same function as the similar three-room unit in the corner between the Doric temple and the propylon (see 2.3) and may represent an early Byzantine dwelling.

3.2.3. The final destruction of the bouleuterion complex

According to the last datable material from the simple dwelling (?), the latter must have been destroyed by the mid-seventh century AD earthquake that eventually wiped out the city. The destruction layers were slightly different in the various parts of the old auditorium. Inside the northern room of the early Byzantine structure on top of the west wing of the auditorium and inside the open space in the northwest corner of the auditorium, two destruction layers, specifically connected with the late dwelling (?), could be identified:

- layer 4: a layer composed of a dark brown, light silty earth and mortar fragments. It contained pottery (sixth to first half of the seventh century AD), bone, glass, *crustae*, stone, metal, stamped tiles, plaster and *tesserae*. The layer also filled the upper part of the small 'corridor' in the northwest corner of the auditorium. This layer contained a fourth century AD bronze coin (Scheers 2000, cat. 70: SA 97 B2 47, AE 3 from AD 364-378).

- layer 3: this layer, which reached as far as the north wall of the auditorium, consists of a fine, light brown earth containing very few tiles, ceramics, metal, bone, glass and crustae.

The other destruction layers covered the whole interior of the council-house. Some of their architectural remains must have fallen down from the early Byzantine structures along the east side of the Doric temple (see 2.3). Two such layers could be identified:

- layer 2: a 0.80 m deep layer characterised by a huge amount of tiles (ca. 60%) originating from the destruction of the late structure above the western section of the auditorium and from the contemporary dwelling on the temple terrace above it. The colour of its soil was rather dark brown and the earth was loose. It contained medium and small-sized stones, as well as ceramics, bone, glass, metal (including parts of a weighing-scales), stone, *tesserae*, plaster, fragments of small sculpture, coins and *crustae* fragments. In the lower part of the auditorium, layer 2 covered the original floor slabs along the edge of the bouleuterion's auditorium. Four fourth to early seventh centuries AD coins were recovered from it (Scheers 2000, cat. 131, 102, 181 and 379: SA 97 B2 119, coin of Honorius from AD 393-395; SA 97 B2 69, coin of Arcadius from AD 395-401; SA 97 B2 103, coin of Marcian from AD 450-457; SA 97 B2 127, *follis* of Heraclius from AD 613/4). In the vicinity of the late cistern, this layer also contained rather well preserved hooked chains belonging to no less than three weighing instruments (SA 97 B2 146, 149, 151; Figs 68-70), which could suggest some artisanal activity in the neighbourhood.

- layer 1 or topsoil (max. 0.70 m deep): in all sectors it consisted of dark brown, loose and silty earth, mixed with small and medium-sized rubble stones and some building blocks. There were also tile inclusions. The finds were ceramics, bone, metal, glass, *tesserae*, plaster, organic material *crustae* and two coins from the fourth-fifth centuries AD (Scheers 2000, cat. 124 and 179: SA 97 B2 28, *salus rei publicae* coin from AD 383-395; SA 97 B2 48, *victoria augg* coin from AD 408-ca 435).

- above this, there was a large pile of stones belonging to the Doric temple and its late alterations, to the bouleuterion's west wall and to the late structure described above.

In any case, neither the stratigraphy of the bouleuterion proper nor its courtyard produced any material evidence, coins or pottery, which could be dated after the middle of the seventh century AD. Apparently, after the earthquake (Waelkens *et al.* 2000b), this whole part of town was abandoned.

3.3. Conclusion

The 1996-1997 campaigns did not produce new evidence for dating the construction of the bouleuterion, but helped to establish the limits of both the council-hall and the courtyard in front of it. The building technique of the west wall could suggest that this building was already an enlargement of an older structure.

The whole complex certainly underwent various changes during its existence. In middle Imperial times, the street level to the north of the courtyard, if not the north wall itself, was raised considerably, either as a repair following earthquake damage, or as part of a reorganisation of the whole water-supply systems in this area when the Antonine nymphaeum was built on the upper agora.

A more drastic alteration must have occurred around AD 400. By that time, the council-hall had apparently lost its original function, either because of structural problems with its roof or following drastic changes in the role and size of the council. The outer face of the emplekton system of its façade was completely rebuilt and many of the original stones ended up in the late fortifications. Yet, when an earthquake disaster struck the remaining structure around AD 518, the courtyard apparently housed a roofed building, for which the façade of the bouleuterion had been rebuilt. Research in the following years revealed that this was a church.

What happened to the old council-hall itself still remains unclear. However, during the seventh century AD at the latest, a simple dwelling and a cistern had been established on top of the centuries-old seats of the old meeting hall's western wing.

4. THE 'TERRACE BUILDING' AND WORKSHOP AREA OF THE UPPER AGORA NORTH (Fig. 71)

From 1994 to 1995, a sixth to seventh century AD complex of workshops (and shops?) had been excavated on a terrace immediately north of the Antonine nymphaeum (AD 160-180) along the northern edge of the upper agora.
Originally, this area may have been partly occupied by a probably early Hellenistic 'market building' in rusticated

Fig. 64: The southwest corner of the auditorium, with on the left the seats of the south wing.

Fig. 65: View of the early Byzantine two room unit on top of the west wing of the auditorium.

Fig. 66: The division wall of the late structure, built against the projecting bedrock

Fig. 67: Cistern built on top of the lower part of the west wing of the auditorium.

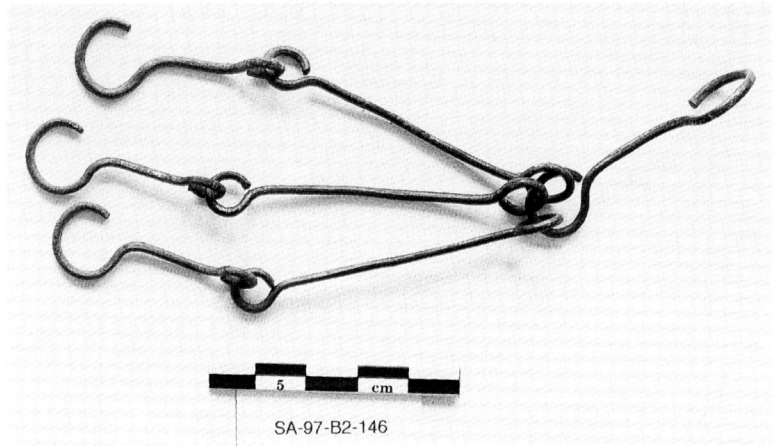

Fig. 68: Part of a weighing instrument from layer 2 inside the bouleuterion.

Fig. 69: Part of a weighing instrument from layer 2 inside the bouleuterion.

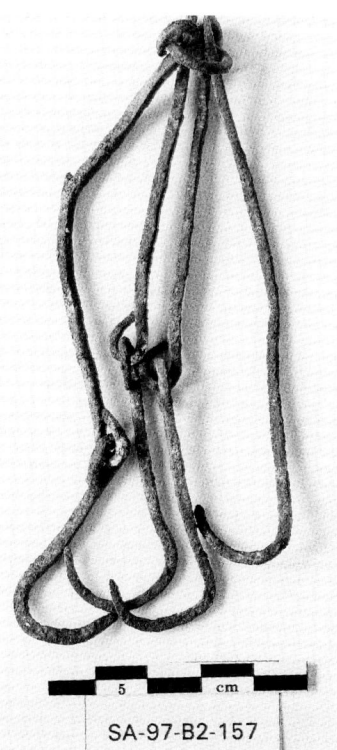

Fig. 70: Part of a weighing instrument from layer 2 inside the bouleuterion.

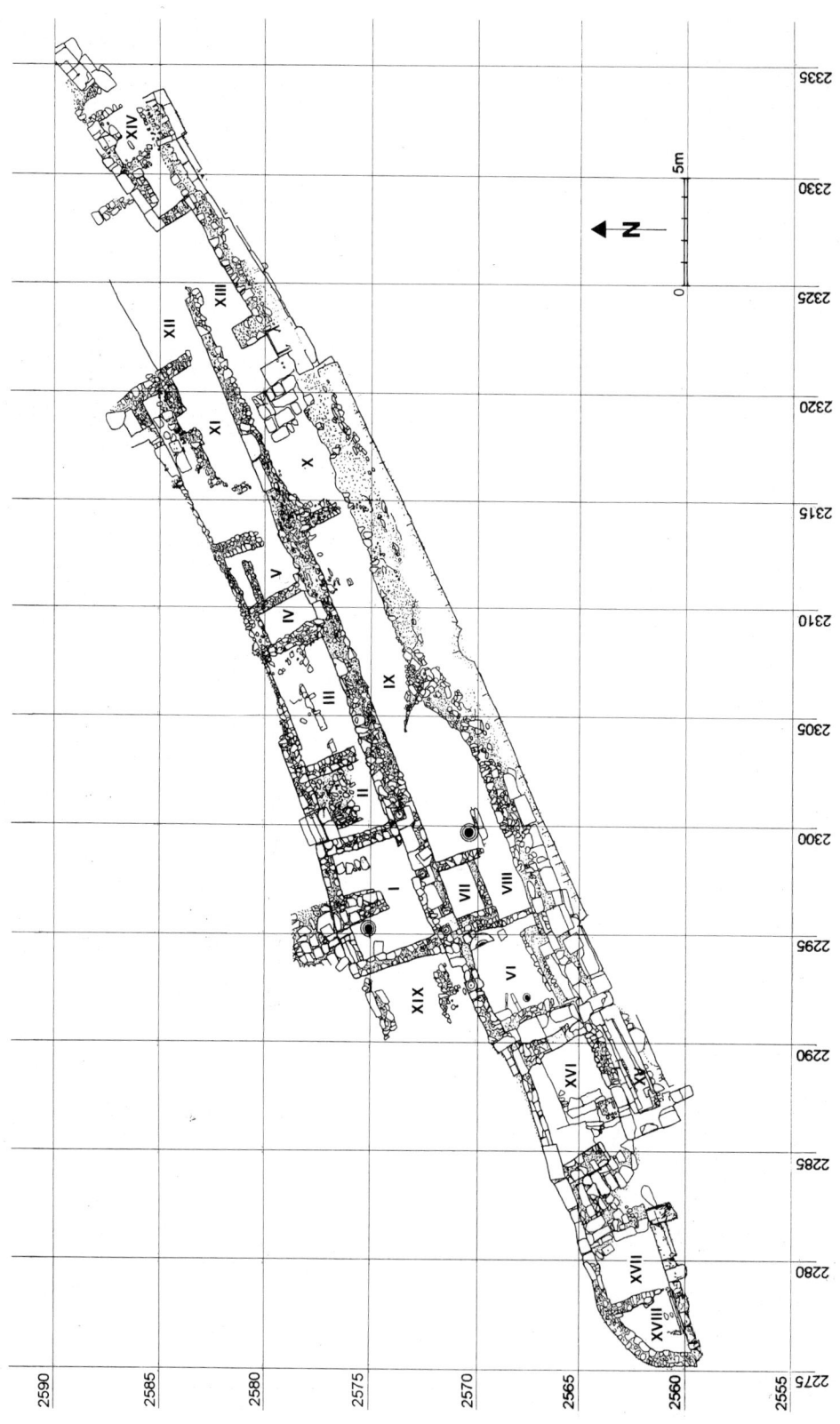

Fig. 71. Plan of the terrace building to the north of the upper agora.

blocks, which is still standing in the northeast corner of the square (Waelkens *et al.* 1997b: 127-130).

Probably during the early Imperial period, the western part of the building was replaced by a new 31.60 m long 'terrace building', henceforth occupying most of the northern edge of the upper agora and perhaps supporting a stoa of the Pergamene type. The lowest 4.10 m of the front wall (thickness: 2.70 to 2.90 m) of this 'terrace building' still stands upright, while its original fill seems to be preserved up to the same level (layer 13 S in southwest corner of room IX) (Waelkens *et al.* 1997b: 131-136).

At the time of the construction of the Antonine nymphaeum, around AD 160-180, this structure was partly dismantled in its central part to accommodate the curved central niche of the nymphaeum. Its front wall and walking level were also raised in order to accommodate the water-supply system of the fountain. At the same time, the front wall was apparently faced with mortared rubble inside, while a longitudinal wall divided the structure in two. The walking level of the northern part (layer 6 SD in room I) was at least 1.10 m higher than the highest floor level in the southern half. According to the excavations of 1995, the latter seemed to have comprised at least two 'rooms': a smaller room (VI: floor level 4 SB), which could have been the cellar of a room above it and which was used for storage, and a very long room (IX) to the east of it. The latter apparently had a much higher floor level (layer 8S) that lay over the water-supply system of the nymphaeum. The exact limits of the building to the north remained unknown (Waelkens *et al.* 1997b: 137-162).

During the late Roman period, most probably around 400 AD, this longitudinal wall, as well as the floor levels and perhaps even the front wall, were raised once more, retaining the different levels on either side of this wall. The lower sections of the north wall of the building go back to this period. In some parts of the 'terrace building', the floor level was raised by more than 1 m. This may also have been the case with the terrace wall itself. The longitudinal wall was also rebuilt and reinforced by a fill (layer 7S in room IX) containing fourth century AD material. The western extremity of room IX was divided into two small spaces (VII and VIII) and a new floor level created inside (3S in room IX, 2SC in room VII, completely eroded away in room VIII). It is assumed that the floor level of room VI (layer 4SB) was not altered, despite the fact that its side-walls were raised. At the same time, the northern part of the 'terrace building' was subdivided in various units (from west to east, rooms I, II, III, IV, V and XI) that were only accessible from a street running immediately to the north of the building.

In 1994-1995, only rooms I to III had been excavated. In the western part of room I, a sondage reached second century AD levels, whereas a fill with fourth century AD material was recovered only in its eastern half (layer 3SW). Two possibly contemporary strata were found in room II (layers 3S and 5S). Room III was only excavated as deep as the most recent occupation phase (seventh century AD). To the north of rooms I and II, the fills of a street level (5N), laid around 400 AD, were reached (Waelkens *et al.* 1997b: 162-170).

After the earthquake of AD 518, both the 'terrace building' and the street to the north of it were probably raised again. During this operation, some of the rooms were further subdivided into smaller spaces to create artisanal units of one to three rooms, many of them containing storage vessels. In the southern half of the 'terrace building', rooms VI and IX received new floors (respectively layer 3SB and 2SC). In room VI, a dolium was sunk into this layer, its base resting upon layer 4SB. Room X now had a paved floor.

In the northern part of the building, room I was subdivided into two smaller spaces, its floor raised another 0.10 m and covered with irregular limestone slabs (layer 2SW in the east, 3SD in the west). As the west wall of this room was completely (re)built on this occasion, the occupation level from 400 AD, still present in the eastern half of the room, was completely dug out and removed from the western half of the room. The street level to the north of it was also raised (layer 3 N). After these alterations, the smaller rooms (workshops?) were occupied until the final destruction of the city by the earthquake of the seventh century AD (Waelkens *et al.* 1997b: 170- 173).

In 1996, the Upper Agora North excavations were extended both towards the east and towards the west (Fig. 71). The eastern excavation was aimed at trying to find the connection between the UA/N structures and the northeast gate of the upper agora (see 5.2), while the western excavation was aimed at trying to establish a connection with the north wall of the bouleuterion courtyard and to define the western limit of the 'terrace building'.

During the 1996 campaign, eight sectors of 5 by 5 m were completely or partially excavated towards the east (2315/2580, 2320/2580, 2325/2580, 2325/2585, 2330/2585 and parts of 2310/2580, 2315/2585 and 2320/2585). Four 'rooms' (part of XI; rooms XII, XIII and XIV) were exposed here. But, in view of the planned anastylosis of the Antonine nymphaeum, for which an easy access to the back of the front wall of the 'terrace building' was required, it was not possible to expose the lower levels of this building on its east side. For this reason, the area was not touched in 1997.

On the west side, reaching the lower levels was not much of a problem but, since a road needed to be maintained here to make the area between the NW Heroon and the bouleuterion courtyard accessible for a mobile crane, only the southern part of the 'terrace building' could be fully explored. In 1996, the western part of sector 2290/2565, the southern part of 2285/2565, sectors 2285/2565, 2280/2560 and 2275/2560 were excavated. A total of four 'rooms' (rooms XV – XVIII) as well as the western part of VI were unearthed here. The 1997 season continued to expose the lower strata of rooms VI, XVI, XVII and XVIII, but also uncovered an additional room (XIX) in sector 2290/2570.

4.1. Early Imperial remains

In 1997, while excavating layer 2S in room VI, remains of a nearly 1 m thick ashlar wall (see Fig. 72) were discovered towards the west. Unfortunately, the wall could not be excavated over its total depth, but it may belong to the original west wall of the early Imperial terrace building, whose south front turns northwards exactly at this spot. To the west of room VI (room XVI, see 4.4.2), no remains from the 'terrace building' have thus far been identified.

4.2. The middle Imperial 'terrace building'

In room VI, the supposedly mid-Imperial level (4SB) already partly excavated in 1995 was further removed in 1997. Its absolute height varies around 1532.24 m a.s.l. This layer was directly covered by the early Byzantine layer 3SB. Its fine ware fragments were dated by Poblome to the second half of the first and the first half of the second century AD, thus confirming the middle Imperial date of this stratum. The lower part of a small dolium (h.: 0.50 m; diameter: 0.23 m) was sunk in it (Fig. 72). Since the storage vessel was completely covered by layer 3SB above it, it cannot have belonged to the early Byzantine phase, but must have been placed here at some time between the middle of the second and the early sixth century AD. In the northwestern part of room VI, layer 4SB also contained two water-supply systems made of terracotta pipes that could have been part of the original water supply system of the Antonine nymphaeum (Figs. 73, 83).

In the southern part of the room, layer 4SB covered another rubble wall and to the south of it a fill of *opus caementicium* (see Fig. 83). This must represent the concrete fill that, in the middle of the second century AD, was used to consolidate the back of the 'terrace building's' front wall.

Immediately to the west of room VI another room (XVI) was partially excavated in 1996 and its three upper layers removed. Four more layers were identified and researched in the following year. For safety reasons, the excavation of the room had to stop above layer 7SB, for which no chronological information is available. However, its level (ca. 1532.00 m a.s.l.) corresponds rather well with that of the middle Imperial levels in room VI (4SB: 1532.24 m a.s.l.), so that it may have been more or less contemporary with it. In the northwest corner of the room, this layer bore over most of its width (but still continuing in the north face of the trench) what was probably the foundation of two steps descending from the west (Fig. 74). These steps were composed of two ca. 1.50 m long but rather rough blocks (absolute height of lower one: 1532.336 m; of the upper one: 1533.075 m). It is possible that these are the remains of an abandoned stairway, giving access from the west to a middle Imperial phase of the 'terrace building' (in room VI). But it could also have led to whatever structure then occupied the space of room XV to the south of it. However, there is a fair chance that even this arrangement goes back to the period immediately before the sixth century AD earthquake (see 4.4.2).

In 1997, what may have been the eastern half of the northwest corner room of the 'terrace building' was excavated in sector 2290/2570. Immediately to the north of room VI and to the west of room I, another unit (XIX) was also discovered. However, because the mobile crane had to pass close by every day, it was not possible to descend to its deepest levels. Despite this limitation, a middle Imperial stratum could be reached:
- layer 5: this 0.30 to 0.35 m thick layer supported an east-west oriented wall of mortared rubble which was in a very ruinous state (Fig. 75). Only its northern half (5A) was fully excavated until the stratum below (6A) was reached. Layer 5A is a dark brown loose silty soil, containing medium- and small-sized rubble and small mortar fragments. Archaeologically, it was rather poor, but the pottery fragments could be attributed to phase 2 of the locally produced fine wares (second half of the first – first half of the second century AD). As a result, this stratum must correspond with the mid-century AD alterations of the early Imperial 'terrace building' at the time of the construction of the Antonine nymphaeum.

4.3. The late Imperial 'terrace building'

On the east side of the excavated zone, in order not to block the planned anastylosis of the Antonine nymphaeum built against the 'terrace building', the excavations could not expose the older levels. However, possibly late Imperial, if not older, levels were reached in rooms XII and XIII. There, below an early Byzantine floor level (3S), the upper surface of an earth beaten floor 5S (Fig. 76) and a mortared floor level (8 SA) were exposed. The latter (Fig. 77) may once have borne a pavement of the upper level of the 'market building'.

On the west side of the 'terrace building', in view of a consolidation of the longitudinal wall, it was necessary to remove a small part of layer 7S in room VII and IX. Sur-

Fig. 72: Room VI with the dolium embedded in layer 4SB. Behind the rubble wall, to the right, one can see the remains of what was perhaps the original west wall, made of ashlars of the 'terrace building'.

Fig. 73: Remains of the two water supply systems embedded in layer 4SB.

Fig. 74: View (from the northeast) of room XVI, layer 7SB, with to the right the foundations of a stairway (?) and in the upper right corner, the remains of a fire place. To the left, the rubble foundations of the reused ashlar wall as well as the rubble wall blocking the 'door' can be seen.

Fig. 75: View of room XIX from the west. Layers 5A and 5B are located on either side of the dividing wall.

Fig. 76: View of room XII from the east, with floor levels 5S (left) and 3S (right).

Fig. 77: View of the mortared floor (layer SA) of room XIII, seen from the east.

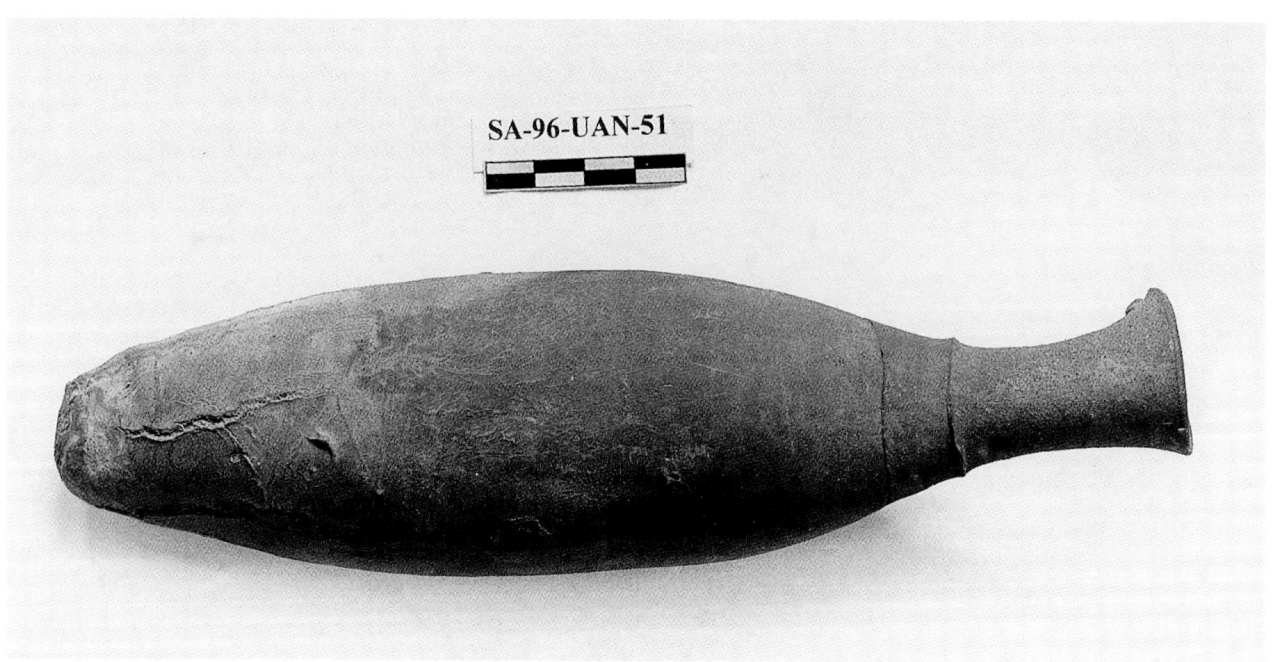

Fig. 78: Early Byzantine uguentarium from room XII.

Fig.79: One of the balance trays recovered from layer 2 in room XII.

prisingly, it only produced pottery (SA 97 UA/N 239 and 299) dated to the second phase of the locally produced fine wares (second half of the first and first half of the second century AD), whereas in the past, this layer had also produced fourth century AD sherds. For the moment, it is assumed that the small excavated area contained mainly residual material.

4.4. The early Byzantine workshop area.

4.4.1. The eastern extremity of the 'terrace building' and the 'market building'

In the eastern part of Upper Agora/North, the excavations confirmed that the subdivision of the northern part of the 'terrace building' into smaller units goes back to building work after the AD 518 earthquake. In fact, all the transversal walls dividing rooms IV, V, XI and XII are built on a floor level (3S) that contains pottery from the last phase (8) of the locally produced *red slip wares*, dated to the period 450-650 AD, but also comprising residual material (SA 96 UA/N 24, 51, 79). Among this pottery from layer 3S in room XII was a nice unguentarium (Fig. 78), a very popular item in the last occupation layers of Sagalassos (Degeest, 2000b). The pottery found in the destruction level 2S above it (SA 96 UA/N 20, 23, 39, 43, 70 and 72) and in the topsoil of these sectors (SA 96 UA/N 1, 3, 7, 29, 32, 59, 61) was contemporary with that of layer 3S, indicating that this area was no longer occupied after the mid-seventh century AD catastrophe. The coins recovered from the top soil in the area could all be dated between the (middle of the) fourth and the earlier sixth century AD and do not therefore contradict this statement (Scheers 2000, cat. 182, 230, 236 and 291: SA 96 UA/N 37, an AE 4 from AD 425-450; SA 96 UA/N 64, an AE 3 from the fourth-fifth century; SA 96 UA/N 36, a *follis* of Justin I from AD 518-527; SA 96 UA/N 49, a small bronze from the second half of the fourth-fifth centuries AD).

In room XII, destruction layer 2 also contained a small glass bottle and several parts belonging to a small weighing-scales made of a copper alloy (Figs 79-80), suggesting that valuable materials had once been processed, used or sold here.

Layer 3S was also found on top of the southern half of the early Hellenistic 'market building', where it bore the east wall of room XII. The construction of rooms XII and XIII above the terrace of the 'market building' must therefore also have happened in the sixth century AD.

In room XII, layer 3S covered some reinforcements of the northern extremity of the northeast gate of the agora (see 5.2). The latter contained a vertical drainpipe, most probably taking water from the roof of the early Byzantine workshop area to cisterns located inside the still unexcavated terrace of the 'market building'. Among the stones that were re-used for this reinforcement was an early Imperial frieze block with a garland suspended from a nicely carved horsehead (Fig. 81).

4.4.2. The western extremity of the 'terrace building' and the adjoining area

- Room VI: in the western part of the UA/N zone, the 1995 campaign had already partially removed an apparently early Byzantine layer 3SB inside room VI. A large dolium had been found in it, resting upon the middle Imperial layer 4SB.

In 1997, this layer, identified in 1995 as a raised floor level created after the AD 518 earthquake, was further excavated in the western half and along the northern edge of room VI. Along the western edge of the room, it bore a wall of mortared rubble built immediately against the older ashlar wall, as if to increase its load-bearing strength (see Fig. 72). In the northwest corner, layer 3SB also bore a re-used ashlar block placed upright. To the east, it bore another rubble wall, which formed an partition with room IX (and VII and VIII). The interior dimensions of room VI were thus diminished by the construction of additional side-walls (see Figs. 72 and 83).

The pottery from layer 3SB (SA 97 UA/N 130), except for some residual shards, belonged to phase 8 of the locally produced fine wares (450-650 AD). Among them, there was a complete lamp (SA 97 UA/N 135; Fig. 82). The layer also contained three coins, dated between the middle of the fourth century AD and the years 518-527 AD (Scheers 2000, cat. 62, 157 and 359: SA 97 UA/N 142, *spes rei publicae* coin from AD 355-361; SA 97 UA/N 143, coin of Theodosius II from AD 425-435; SA 97 UA/N 134, half *follis* of Justin I from AD 518-527). These finds thus seem to confirm that layer 3SB is the result of works undertaken after AD 518.

Along the southern edge of the room, a water-supply system, made of mortared rubble walls, at one point covered with a flat limestone lid (to allow cleaning), was found inside this layer (Fig. 83). It is built exactly above the concrete of the second century AD alterations of the 'terrace building's' original front wall. It could not be followed as far as the east wall of room VI, since this might have caused the latter to collapse. Most probably, this is the (or one of the) water supply system(s) feeding the nymphaeum during the sixth and seventh centuries AD.

- Room XVI: as we have noted above, the ashlar wall near the western edge of room VI was most probably part of the original west wall of the early Imperial 'terrace building' and perhaps contained an entrance to its southern half, reached by a stairway below the later room XVI. Despite the fact that around 400 AD the floor level inside the 'terrace building' had been considerably raised, the lower levels in room XVI seem not to have been altered at that time. In fact, all the strata excavated in 1997 could be attributed to the sixth-seventh century AD. This shows that, while the construction of 'workshops' inside the terrace building had already started around 400 AD, their encroachment upon public space beyond the latter, not only on its east side (above the 'market building'), but also on its west side, apparently happened only in early Byzantine times, i.e. from the sixth century AD onward.

In fact, the construction of 'room XVI' (ca. 5 m by 2.97 m) seems to have taken place completely during this period. Its walls, made of mortared rubble and of re-used ashlars, were supported by layer 7SB (see Fig. 74).

The south wall of this room is a rather nicely built ashlar wall, containing a partially blocked 'door' connecting the spaces of the later rooms XV and XVI. However, its building material includes at least one re-used block bearing part of an official inscription (to be published in our volume *Sagalassos* VI) mentioning the Sagalassians, carved in nice second century AD characters. Inside room XVI, the door-posts and the ashlars of the wall are supported by rubble masonry that continues below the door opening (see Fig. 74). This rubble wall functioned as a foundation and was completely embedded in layer 4S, which represents the floor level of the room. Inside room XVI, this rubble wall continued as deep as layer 7SB.

Layers 4SB to 6SB should thus be seen as a fill, intended to cover the foundations of the south wall of room XVI, which therefore was built during the sixth century AD. Above layer 4SB, the door was still blocked over another 0.30 m by rubble and a re-used ashlar block, so that it had a raised sill, possibly covered with mortar.

The north wall of the room is a double-faced ashlar wall with a rubble core, most probably also supported by 7SB and embedded in the three layers above it. This is certainly the case for the west walls of the room, which consist of large stone blocks combined with rubble. The east wall is formed by the ashlar wall belonging to room VI. Inside room XVI, the following layers could be identified:
- layer 6SB: a yellowish-brown silty layer (1532.158 m a.s.l.) with small- and medium-sized stones and small mortar fragments. It was quite loose but, in the east part of room XVI, there was a much harder area. Yet, this layer can hardly have been a real floor level. It covered the foundations of a middle Imperial (?) stairway descending from the west. The layer contained only a very small amount of finds. The fine ware fragments (SA 97 UA/N 227) could be attributed to the last phase of the local production (middle of the fifth to middle of the seventh century AD). Layer 6SB also produced one coin (Scheers 2000, cat. 175: SA 97 UA/N 238) dated to the years 408-423 AD (*gloria Romanorum* type).
- layer 5SB: a brown silty soil with lots of burnt spots coloring the soil completely black in places (1532.654 m a.s.l.). It also contained red-brown inclusions of a rather loamy soil, as well as small amounts of a greyish clay, mortar and many small charcoal fragments. There were also medium to larger rubble stones in it. The layer, clearly a fill, contained lots of archaeological material, both bone, tiles and pottery, many of them burnt. This may be partly because of the fireplace built in the northwest corner of the room and belonging to layer 4SB (see Fig. 74). Two big ashlars (l.: ca. 1.40 m), which delimited the fireplace in the layer above, were embedded in layer 5SB (Fig. 84). The pottery from this layer (SA 97 UA/N 182) could again be attributed to the last phase of the local production (mid-fifth to mid-seventh century AD), but the 78 bronze coins that were found in it perhaps suggest a more precise date (Scheers 2000, s.v. Upper Agora, room XVI, layer 5SB). In fact, except for a first century BC-early Imperial city coin of Sagalassos, all the other coins date from the fourth and fifth century AD, and mainly from the latter, the most recent coin being an AE of the emperor Zeno (AD 476-491). These dates could indicate that the construction of room XVI occurred shortly after the AD 518 earthquake. Part of the fill (including the traces of burning) may even represent debris from the city. Beside the coins, layer 5SB also contained a glass bead, a metal object and a terracotta figurine.
- layer 4SB: a dark brown silty soil containing only a small amount of small-sized rubble, and quite loose. It therefore cannot have been a real walking level, but may have had a tile floor on it that was removed later. In fact, the position of this layer towards the level of the fireplace in the southwest corner of the room, seems to suggest that it must correspond more or less with a floor level. The fireplace (0.90 by 0.70 m) was characterised by a corner of upright tiles embedded in reddish-brown hard-baked mud against the ashlars of layer 5SB (see Fig. 74), as well as by a clayish soil, with greyish ash on top of it and black burnt spots immediately below the surface. Archaeologically, layer 4SB was a very rich layer, with pottery (SA 97 UA/N 164) to be dated between the second half of the fifth and the first half of the seventh century AD. No coins were found in it, which might confirm that this layer had once been sealed off. On the other hand, it did contain metal objects (a key), a female figurine (SA 97 UA/N 171, Fig. 85), three complete oil lamps (SA 97 UA/N 174, 180 and 181; Figs 86-88), and two complete miniature vessels (SA 97 UA/N 172 and 178; Figs 89-90). The latter belong to a ware group that was probably imported because of its valuable content and can be attributed mainly to the first half of the sixth century AD, extending however into the

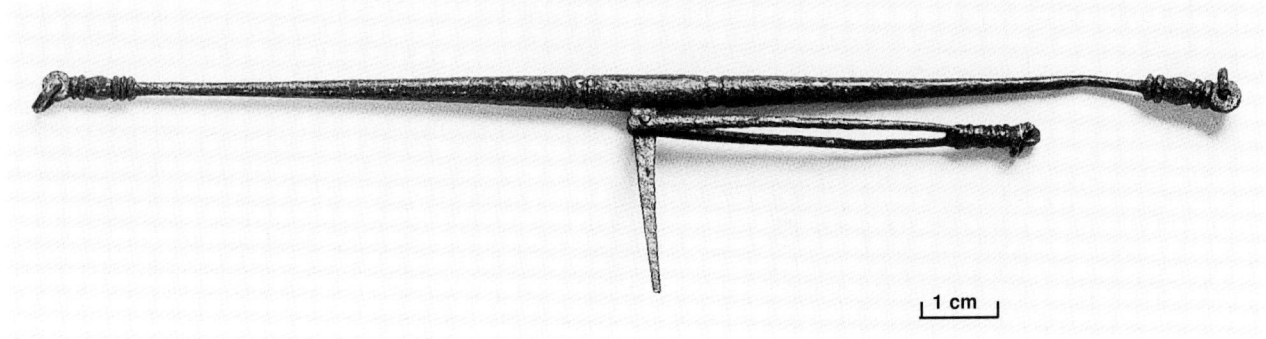

Fig. 80: Horizontal beam of a tray from layer 2 in room XII.

Fig. 81: Relief with garland and horse head reused in the reinforcements of the northeast gate of the upper agora.

Fig. 82: Lamp from layer 3SB in room VI.

Fig. 83: View of room VI from the east. On the left, the early Byzantine water supply system inside layer 3SB (notice the limestone lid in the upper left edge of the picture). Below it the concrete backfill of the 'terrace building's' front wall inside layer 5SB. In the upper right corner, the middle Imperial water supply system (terracotta pipes) in layer 4SB.

Fig. 84: View of room XVI from the northeast. The left half of the picture shows layer 5SB, the right half layer 4SB. The fire place is located to the right of the door.

Fig. 85: Female figurine from layer 4SB in room XVI.

Fig. 86: Lamp from layer 4SB in room XVI.

Fig. 87: Lamp from layer 4SB in room XVI

Fig. 88: Lamp from layer 4SB in room XVI.

Fig. 89: Miniature vessel from layer 4SB in room XVI. Fig. 90: Miniature vessel from layer 4SB in room XVI.

middle of the following century (Degeest et al. 2000c).

Layers 4SB to 6SB represent a fill that was thrown inside room XVI at the time of its construction to create a raised floor level and to cover the foundations of its walls. A similar raising of floor levels seems to have occurred everywhere in this area at some time after the AD 518 earthquake. This may have been done to dispose of the debris. The city seems also to have been drastically altered after this event, including the usurpation during the course of the century of a lot of formerly public space for private purposes.

Above these fills, two destruction levels were excavated:
- layer 3 SB: a clear destruction layer most of which was already excavated in 1996, and the remainder removed in 1997. The pottery from this layer (SA 96 UA/N 133; SA 97 UA/N 147) again dated to phase 8 of the local production (mid-fifth to mid-seventh century AD). It contained also a well-preserved miniature glass flask (SA 97 UA/N 150, an object which is frequently found in the most recent occupation levels at Sagalassos (Fig. 91).
- layer 2S: the upper part of the destruction layer containing pottery (SA 96 UA/N 108; SA 97 UA/N 122) that is contemporary with that in the previous layer. There was even a complete vessel among it (Fig. 92). This layer also contained four coins ranging in time from the middle of the fifth to the early seventh century AD (Scheers 2000, cat. 47, 150, 368, 381: SA 96 UA/N 150, Constantius II, AD 355-361; SA 96 UA/N 163, Arcadius, AD 395-408; SA 96 UA/N 170, *follis* of Justin II from AD 570/1; SA 96 UA/N 142, *follis* of Heraclius from AD 613/6). The other finds include a miniature glass bottle (SA 96 UA/N 172; Fig. 93) of the same type as that of layer 3SB.
These destruction layers were covered by topsoil.

- Room XV: in 1996 a small room was excavated immediately to the south of early Byzantine room XVI, in sectors 2285/2560 and 2290/2560, located in what then was still supposed to have been part of the bouleuterion courtyard. During that season, however, it became clear that this structure was located outside the courtyard and that it was linked to the workshop area that had developed on top and around the 'terrace building' of Upper Agora/North. The room measures 1.50 by 4.90 m. Its north wall, exposed over a length of 4.90 m, is identical with the south wall of room XVI and was exposed to a height of 2.70 m inside room XV. Whereas, today, the original front of this wall faces north, the many cramp holes on its inner side indicate that these ashlars were originally covered with wall veneering, and that this face represented the interior of the original structure. When it was exposed 1996, our first impression was that this wall represented an older building still *in situ*, of which the door had been blocked at a later date by the rubble wall filling its lower part. This impression was reinforced by the fact that, on this side, the wall stands on a very regular step or socle, supported by an euthynteria. However, the 1997 excavations in room XVI showed that neither the 'step' nor the euthynteria continued to the other side of the wall, as one would have expected for a real façade and that the latter even incorporated a re-used inscription. Finally, the fill dumped behind the rubble wall blocking the door left no doubt that the ashlar wall was only built as part of a drastic reorganisation of the whole area after the AD 518 earthquake. This was further confirmed by the lower stratigraphy in room XV.

The eunthynteria is thus supported by layer 11 (Fig. 94) and embedded in layer 10 (Fig. 95). The clear correspondence of this layer with the upper level of the euthynteria at first sight suggests that layer 10 was once a walking level and that the euthynteria and the 'step' above it belonged to an older structure (of which only the lowest courses were) left *in situ*. Two arguments could confirm this. If both courses had been built here merely as a support for the ashlar wall above it, one would expect the latter to have been placed closer to the front of the step, to ensure a better stability. Now, inside room XVI, the front of the ashlar wall rests up a rubble wall. Secondly, the level of the 'step' (1532.034 m a.s.l.) seems to correspond exactly with that of the surface of layer 7SB (ca. 1532 m a.s.l.) on the other side of the wall, thus assuring a perfect walking level for the step and the euthyntria on either side (respectively 7SB in room XVI and 11 in room XV). This 'step' is made of carefully carved blocks, with a height of 0.31 m, the usual height for a step (see Figs 94-95). Combined with the remains of a stairway in room XVI, the whole arrangement may have been a route along a stairway (with a north-south orientation) in room XVI leading to stepped terrace(s) (with an east-west orientation) in room XV, descending from the street located between the NW Heroon and the bouleuterion and continuing along the north side of the 'terrace building', towards the level of the courtyard or even towards the upper agora. If this hypothesis is correct, the construction of this arrangement must have happened already during the (early?) sixth century, as an intermediary phase before this public area was usurped by private structures in the course of the same century. In that case, layer 7SB in room XVI, and the stairway that it supported, must also belong to the early Byzantine period. The ceramic finds from layers 10 and 11 leave no doubt that even this arrangement dates from the sixth century AD. Since it is very difficult for the moment to come up with a fine chronology for the pottery of the last hundred and fifty years of the city's occupation, a plausible suggestion would be that the whole arrangement with the stairway and stepped terrace(s) belongs to the period immediately preceding the AD 518 catastrophe, whereas the wide-spread raising of floor levels belongs to the years after this event. Such a hypothesis is not contradicted by the material recovered from layers 10 and 11.

- layer 11 (Fig. 94): this layer (ca. 1531.31 m a.s.l., i.e. ca. 0.70 m below the 'step') is composed of a yellowish soil containing many mortar fragments and very fragmented tiles. The layer was only 0.15 to 0.25 m deep and covered the natural bedrock and a rubble bed. Therefore, it seemed to represent the lower part of a fill for levelling. It still bore one square stone in the southwest corner of the room (remains of a pavement?), but it also supported the euthynteria of the 'step'. The excavated section only produced three sherds (SA 96 B 84), dated to the early Byzantine period (sixth century AD).

- layer 10 (Fig. 95): a dark brown soil, contained small stones, roof-tiles and lots of pottery and bone. There was a concentration of charcoal in the eastern part of the room, close to the euthynteria, which is level with it. It looked as if this layer had represented the corresponding walking level to the south of the step. Layer 10 contained pottery from the sixth century AD (SA 96 B 64), including also a small proportion of residual material. In this layer, a coin of Constantinus II, dated to the years AD 351-355 was recovered (Scheers 2000, cat. 43: SA 96 B 68).

If our hypothesis of an early sixth century AD arrangement of stairs and stepped terraces in this area is correct, the latter were very rapidly usurped by private structures, most probably during the reconstruction of the city in the years following the AD 518 catastrophe. One of them was room XVI, built against the remains of the 'terrace building'. For the construction of this room, a nearby (?) ashlar structure was dismantled and partially rebuilt on top of the abovementioned 'step' of the terrace. The stairway descending from the west was stripped of its steps and the walking level was considerably raised.

Similar reconstructions also took place in room XV, where the stepped terrace (?) was covered with debris, which then supported the construction of a new room (XVI):

- layer 9 (Fig. 96): this layer with a depth of ca. 0.50 m covered the probably somewhat older walking level (layer 10) as well as the 'step'. It then bore the three other walls of the small and oblong room XV, made of mortared rubble. Since this room could only be entered from room XVI by means of the partially blocked 'door' and because of its small width, it should perhaps be interpreted as a storage facility for room XVI. The pottery from layer 9 (SA 96 B 57) was identified by Poblome as belonging to the sixth century AD, which fits well the successive stages of intervention discussed above.

After the construction of room XV, its floor level was further raised by the addition of layer 8 (Fig. 96), the surface of which was located some 0.30 m below that of the rubble wall which blocked the lower part of the entrance to room XVI. Its level therefore corresponded more or less with that of layer 4SB on the other side of the division wall. Layer 8 consists of a dark brown soil, containing a few rubble stones, tile and mortar fragments that are very fragmented. Unfortunately, the pottery in this (SA 96 B 33) had not yet been studied at the time of this report, but since that of layer 9 below was of sixth century AD date, layer 8 must have been deposited at the earliest during the same century. It contained a coin of Arcadius, dated to the years 392-395 AD (Scheers 2000, cat. 96: SA 96 B 55).

Room XV must have been destroyed or abandoned at the same time as room XVI to the north of it. Inside, a very thick destruction layer was found:

- layer 7: a loose whitish to light brown soil, full of large mortar fragments that had fallen from the walls and of larger parts of roof tiles. Unfortunately, the pottery from this layer (SA 96 B 46) has not been dated yet. Layer 7 filled the roof almost entirely. It was covered by an erosion layer (2).

- Room XIX: the 1997 excavation also exposed the alterations of the northern section of the 'terrace building' during the sixth and seventh centuries AD. First of all, the actual northwest corner of the present building was not erected around AD 400, as was the case further east, but only after the AD 518 catastrophe. The reason might be simply that the older corner had perhaps collapsed as the result of this event.

The same season confirmed once more that the wall separating rooms I and XIX was built at the same time. For the construction of this room, a deep trench seems to have been dug out during the sixth century AD, inside room I, thereby destroying and removing all the older strata up to the level of the new wall's foundations. On the other side of this trench, the floor level was raised with the addition of layer 3. This layer 3 was characterised in its northern part by a yellowish brown soil with lots of stones and in its southern part by a darker brown soil. When this distinction was underlined by the discovery of the east-west wall dividing the room during the middle Imperial period (see 4.2 and Fig. 75), but apparently abandoned in early Byzantine times, the northern part of the deeper sections of layer 3 was called 4A, while its southern part became layer 4B. Layer 4A has all the characteristics of a water-led fill, as was the case with several other strata of the 'terrace building' excavated in the past (Waelkens et al. 1997b). It also contained some small burnt spots. Layer 4B was the continuation of the southern part of layer 3. The pottery found within layers 3, 4A and 4B (SA 97 UA/N 309, 313 and 322) could all be dated to the final phase of the locally produced fine wares (middle of the fifth to middle of the seventh century AD).

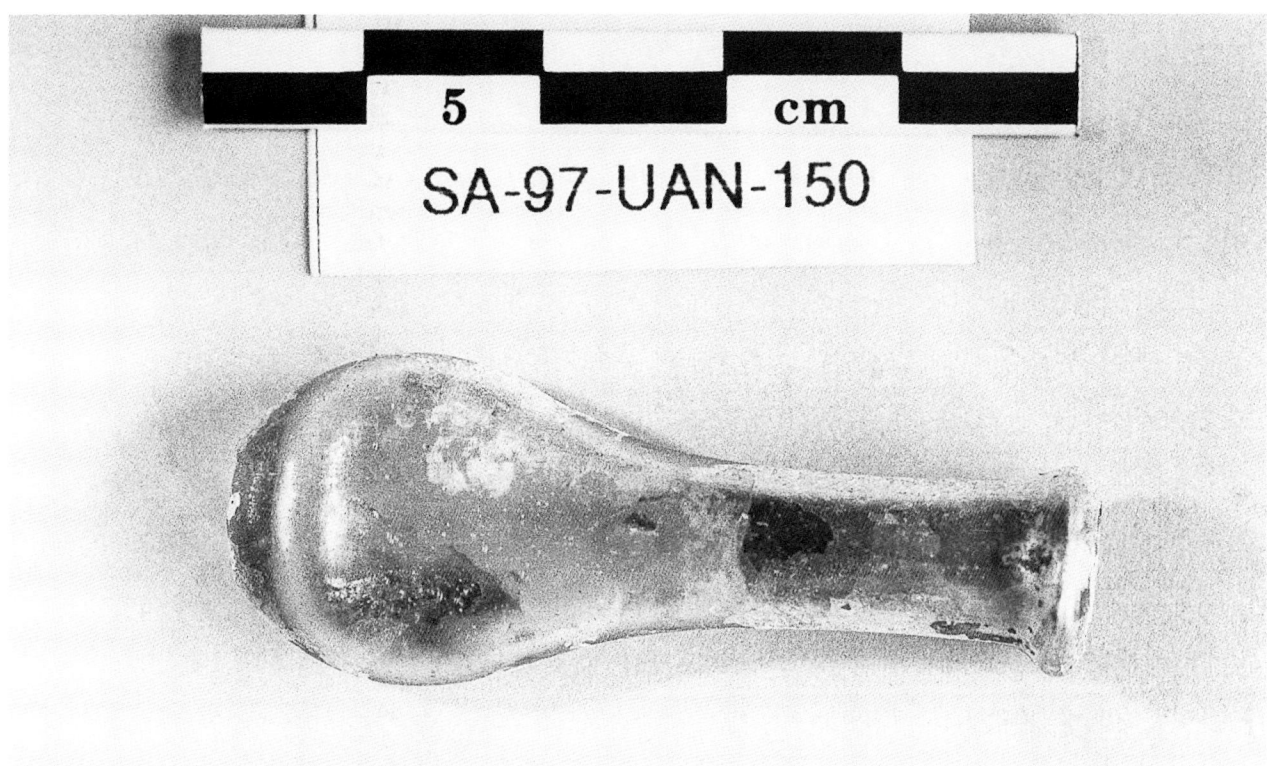

Fig. 91: Miniature flask from layer 3SB in room XVI.

Fig. 92: Complete coarse ware vessel from layer 2SB in room XVI.

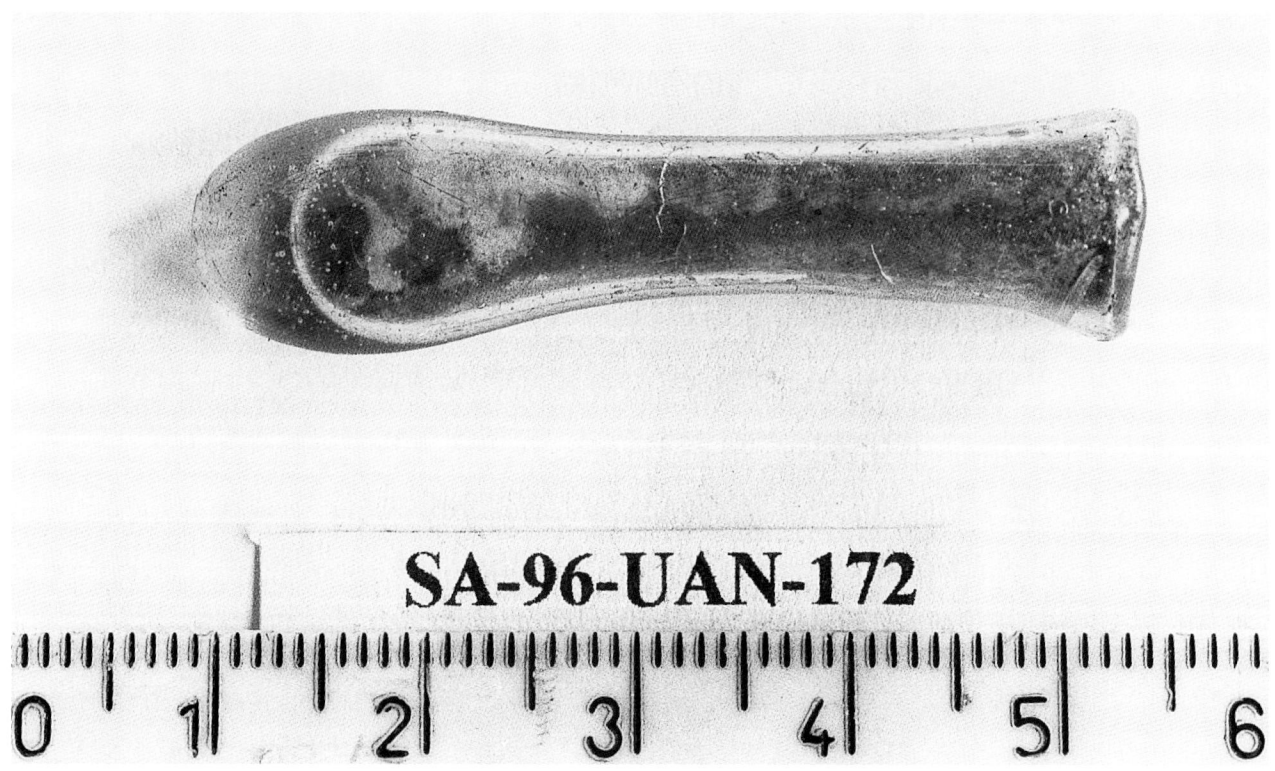

Fig. 93: Miniature flask from layer 2SB in room XVI.

Fig. 94: Layer 11 in room XV, seen from the west. In the lower part of the picture, the step, with the euthynteria below it. Above the step, the reused ashlar wall and the blocked door. In the upper part of the picture, the rubble wall supported by layer 9.

Fig. 95: View of layer 10 in room XV, seen from the west. The layer is clearly corresponding with the rougher stones of the projecting euthynteria. Above them the 'step'.

Fig. 96: View of layers 8 and 9 in room XV. The picture is taken from the east.

Fig.97: Head of a drunken Dionysos from the top soil of room XIX.

Fig. 98: View of the early Byzantine stairway from the south. Notice the reused rusticated ashlars from the northern courtyard wall of the bouleuterion.

The coins that were found in them were all attributed to the fourth and fifth centuries AD (layer 4B: 2000 this volume, cat. 116, 168 and 242: SA 97 UA/N 321, coin of Arcadius from AD 401-403; SA 97 UA/N 317, *gloria Romanorum* coin of AD 406-408; SA 97 UA/N 316, bronze coin of the fourth-fifth centuries AD; layer 3: Scheers 2000 cat. 109: SA UA/N 312, coin of Theodosius I or II from AD 401-403).

Layer 2 is a silty light brown soil, quite loose, containing small-sized rubble, a small amount of mortar pieces and only few pottery and tile fragments. The pottery (SA 97 UA/N 303) could be dated to the sixth and early seventh century AD. This layer supported both the door-sill of room XIX as well as its north wall. It contained three coins dated to the fourth-fifth centuries AD (Scheers 2000, cat. 59, 138 and 172: SA 97 UA/N 332, *Fel temp reparatio* from AD 346-361; SA 97 UA/N 306, coin of Honorius from AD 395-401; SA 97 UA/N 307, *gloria Romanorum* coin of AD 408-423).

Since this part of the slope was severely eroded, there was no real destruction layer left. But, the top soil produced a very nice terracotta head (SA 97 UA/N 298), according to the position of the hand on the head, apparently representing a drunken Dionysos (Fig. 97). It was possibly inspired by the two giant marble statues of Dionysos in both corner *aediculae* of the Antonine nymphaeum. They represent the drunken god in a similar position, supported by a satyr (Waelkens *et al.* 1997b: 152 fig. 71; 160 fig. 188).

- an early Byzantine stairway: during the 1996 and 1997 season, a 2.70 m wide stairway made of re-used ashlars was exposed immediately to the west of rooms XVI and XV, and to the east of rooms XVII and XVIII (see below). Since all those structures whose side-walls framed the steps could be dated to the sixth century AD, it is clear that this whole arrangement must have been planned simultaneously. Some of the steps were formed by rusticated blocks that may originally have belonged to the courtyard of the bouleuterion (Fig. 98). It is therefore very likely that this stairway was built some time after the AD 518 earthquake. It possibly replaced an older arrangement, partially visible in rooms XV and XVI, but abandoned after the seismic catastrophe. While excavating the steps, a nice altar (?) representing an *imago clipeata* of Helios was discovered (Fig. 99), together with a fragment of a military *diploma* in a copper alloy (Fig. 100).

- rooms XVII and XVIII: to the west of the early Byzantine stairway, a curved two-room unit, with a curvilinear wall (at least at its western extremity in room XVIII), was built against the north wall of the bouleuterion courtyard, in sectors 2275/2560 and 2280/2560. Whereas the four upper layers of room XVII and the three upper strata of room XVIII were excavated in 1996, the lower strata were only exposed in 1997. Despite the fact that these rooms were separated from the workshop area further east by the early Byzantine stairway, it is likely that they were part of a same sixth century AD building project. Both rooms were only accessible by means of a door located in the east wall of the eastern room (XVII), via which one could enter the western room (XVIII).

The curved north wall of the structure is made of rectangular limestone blocks with smaller irregular stones set in a mortar bed. The east wall is built with re-used blocks of limestone and irregular blocks of travertine joined with mortar. When this structure was already occupied, it was further subdivided into the present two units by means of a wall made of irregular limestone rubble and travertine blocks.

- Room XVII: the eastern room of the double unit contained the following stratigraphy:
- layer 7A: this was the lowest stratum of the room that was reached, but not excavated, in 1997. It bore the east wall that faced the early Byzantine stairway, from which it could be entered. The layer was covered with a lot of larger stones, some regular, some irregular, which seemed to represent earthquake debris that was used as a bed for supporting the floor level above it (Fig. 101). Almost certainly, this is the same layer as layer 7 in room XVIII, which represents a middle Imperial street level (see 3.1).
- layer 6A: a rather loamy brown layer with small-sized stones and a small amount of very fine plaster pieces, which was also the case in the adjoining section of layer 5S in room XVIII. In fact, it appeared to be a floor level corresponding exactly with layer 5S of room XVIII. Both were also very rich in contemporary finds. The north-south dividing wall was clearly built on them, so that this wall may represent a later subdivision of the original unit into two rooms. The north wall of the whole structure was embedded into these layers. A lot of destruction material was found on the floor. The pottery (SA 97 UA/N 53) found in layer 6A was contemporary with that of layer 5S in the next room (mid-fifth to mid-seventh century AD). It also contained 11 bronze coins, belonging to the second half of the fourth and the fifth century AD (Scheers 2000, cat. Upper Agora/North, Room XVII, layer 6A). As in the corresponding layer 5S in the next room, layer 6A contained a large amount of faunal remains. Sieving the soil produced 355 undetermined mammal, 9 bird and 3 fish remains. It also produced 2 bones from Cyprinidae, 1 bone of a stone partridge, 11 cattle bones, 32 ovicaprine remains, 1 sheep and 3 goat bones, 37 pig fragments and 16 chicken bones. The quantity and fragmentation of these bones seem to suggest that they represent refuse from consumption, so that the surface of layer 6A must have been a real floor level and not merely a fill. In that case, the original structure may have been a dwelling or eating house-rather than a simple workshop or shop, unless one accepts that the owner ate at his work, which is certainly possible.

Above the floor level, the following destruction layers could be identified:
- layer 5S: a layer mainly composed of rubble, small ashlars and tiles from the collapsed upper part of the room
- layer 4S: a light brown layer full of white mortar and small- to medium-sized rubble stones. This layer also contains the remains of collapsed walls.
- layer 3S: a layer full of mortar fragments and rubble.
The material of floor levels 3S and 4S could be dated to the sixth-seventh centuries AD.

These destruction levels were covered by an erosion layer (2S) and by topsoil.

- Room XVIII: the room immediately to the west of room XVII and only accessible from the layer produced the following stratigraphy:
- layer 8: this is the lowest stratum that was reached in 1997 by a sondage to check the date of the northern courtyard wall of the bouleuterion. It was not excavated (see 3.1).
- layer 7: this 1.10 m deep fill of middle Imperial date (see 3.1) was, like the corresponding layer 7A in room XVII, covered with earthquake debris (Fig. 102). Especially in the southern part of the room it included a remarkable concentration of big irregular stones from a collapsed wall, without any doubt the upper part of the bouleuterion's northern courtyard wall. This spot also contained a concentration of red stucco fragments, suggesting that the collapsed wall had been plastered. In that case, the bouleuterion courtyard must have been roofed. This earthquake debris, most probably the result of the AD 518 earthquake, was left *in situ* where it fell and later used as a base for layer 6. The pottery inside layer 7 however (SA 97 UA/N 110 and 116) could be dated to the mid-first to mid-second century AD.
– layer 6: a nearly 0.50 m deep fill containing only a small amount of finds. Among them was some pottery dated to phase 8 of the local production (mid-fifth to mid-seventh century AD).
- layer 5S: a brownish, silty layer that contained a lot of gravel and in its eastern part also small plaster fragments. It had an average depth of only 0.10 m and was clearly an occupation layer, corresponding with layer 6A in room XVII. In the southeast corner of the room, there was a rather large burnt surface. Layer 5S contained so many fragmented animal bones (SA 97 UA/N 29), that it was decided to sieve the soil. It produced a total of 235 undetermined mammal bones, 16 undetermined bird remains and 5 undetermined fish bones. Of those which could be determined, De Cupere counted 19 cattle bones, 35 ovicaprine remains, 5 sheep and 3 goat bones, 34 pig remains, 25 chicken bones and 2 bones of a hare. The layer also contained a number of fish (2 of Cyprinidae, 2 of carp, 3 of a Bagrus from the Nile) and bird bones (4 of stone partridge, 1 of duck, 1 of pigeon). This variety of small, fragmented faunal remains seems to identify this layer as a floor level, and the room perhaps as a kitchen. Its identification as a floor level (beaten earth floor) may also explain the high number of sherds (SA 97 UA/N 28 and 48) that could be dated to phase 8 (middle of the fifth to middle of the seventh century AD) and of bronze coins (33 in total), ranging in time from AD 335 to the year 607/8 AD. Most of them belong to the fourth and fifth centuries AD (Scheers 2000, Upper Agora North, Room XVIII, layer 5S). There was also a weight of 6 *nomisma* (Scheers 2000, cat.; 387: SA UA/N 46) which can be dated between the third and fifth centuries AD (Fig. 103).

This floor surface was covered by two destruction layers:
- layer 4S a very silty light-brown layer, with lots of tiles, white mortar and rubble stones.
- layer 3C: a dark grey layer with lots of mortar and rubble stones. Its pottery (SA 96 B117; SA 96 UA/N 188) was not specifically studied, but it contained seven coins ranging from the fourth to the fifth centuries AD (Scheers 2000, cat. Upper Agora/North, room XVII, layer 3C).

The two upper layers corresponded with those in room XVII.

It is clear that after an earthquake, doubtless the catastrophe of AD 518, some wall debris from a roofed structure in the former bouleuterion courtyard, had collapsed towards the north, where it fell on a middle Imperial street level and was left *in situ*. It was covered with a fill that later bore an oblong curvilinear structure, perhaps a dwelling or eating place, built against the remainder of the courtyard wall. At some time during its occupation, this structure seems to have been subdivided into two units of which the western one may have functioned as a kitchen.

4.5. Conclusion

The 1996 and 1997 seasons, which extended the ongoing excavations around the early Imperial 'terrace building' both to the east and to the west, did not produce any new evidence concerning the first phase of the building.

They did however establish that in middle Imperial times, its western limit was probably formed by rooms VI and XIX. The first room also produced evidence of what may have been part of the water-supply of the Antonine nymphaeum. At that time, the southwest corner of the building was most probably free-standing. But, unless this had been brought about by a first century AD earthquake that caused considerable damage in the city, the mid-second century AD building works undertaken in and around the building to accommodate the water-supply system of the Antonine nymphaeum did necessitate a considerable raising of the street level to the north of the bouleuterion courtyard and of the 'terrace building'.

Fig. 99: Altar with the *imago clipeata* found on top of the early Byzantine steps.

Fig. 100: Fragment of a military *diploma* found on top of the stairway.

Fig. 101: View of layer 7A with the earthquake debris in room XVII.

Fig. 102: Layer 7 in room XVIII before its removal. Notice the curved north wall of the structure. The ashlars belong to the northern courtyard wall of the bouleuterion.

Fig. 99: Altar with the *imago clipeata* found on top of the early Byzantine steps.

Fig. 100: Fragment of a military *diploma* found on top of the stairway.

Fig. 101: View of layer 7A with the earthquake debris in room XVII.

Fig. 102: Layer 7 in room XVIII before its removal. Notice the curved north wall of the structure. The ashlars belong to the northern courtyard wall of the bouleuterion.

Fig. 103: Weight of six *nomisma* from floor level 5S in room XVIII.

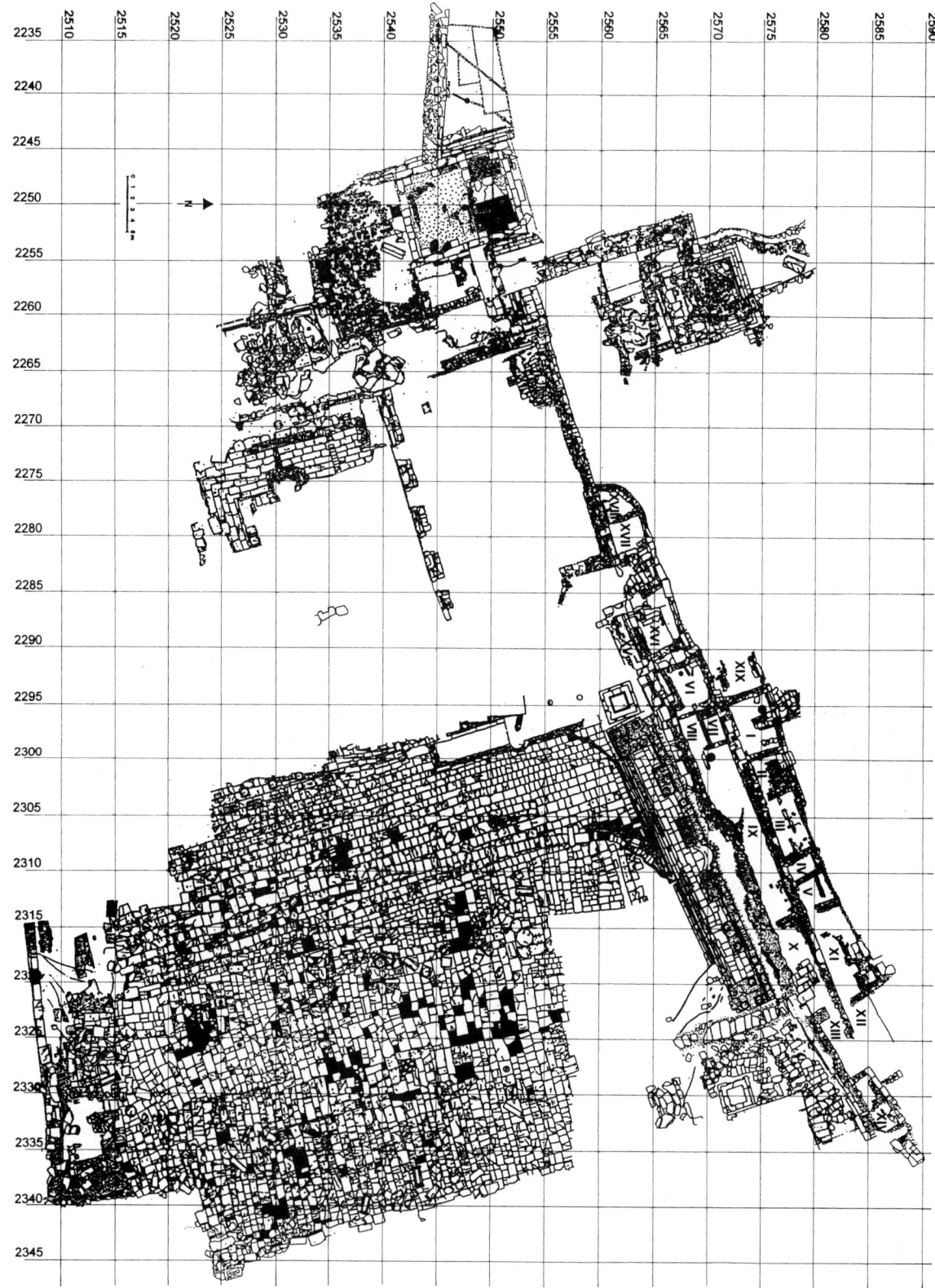

Fig. 104: Map of the upper agora.

No remains of the early fifth century AD alterations of the 'terrace building' have been discovered to the west of it. This suggests that these works were mainly limited to the 'terrace building' itself which was subdivided into smaller units. Its currently visible north wall was actually built then, together with the section of the street immediately to the north of it. The fact that no contemporary levels were found to the north of the bouleuterion courtyard and in the propylon area suggests that in general the middle Imperial street level was maintained into late Roman times. The construction of the north wall of the workshop area, then established in the 'terrace building' may have necessitated the change in the street level only in the immediate vicinity of this building.

There is a strong possibility that, during the early sixth century AD, a new connection between the upper city and the upper agora was created immediately to the west of the terrace building. It may have consisted of a stairway and a (number of) stepped terrace(s). But, within a short time after the creation of this new layout, the city may have been struck by the AD 518 earthquake. A roofed structure inside the bouleuterion's courtyard partly collapsed on the middle Imperial levels to the north of it. Since the city had to dispose of considerable amounts of debris, as we have noted in the propylon area, not all the collapsed remains were removed. Some were just covered, and served as a base for a considerable fill that raised the old walking levels. These activities may have continued for a considerable period. The AD 541-2 plague, which seems to have had a negative effect on civic life and responsibilities (see 3.2), may have inspired a different attitude among the survivors: instead of repairing former public spaces, at least in the area to the west of the 'terrace building', these spaces were henceforth usurped for the construction of workshops and/or simple dwellings. A rather rude stairway, partially built with ashlars from the bouleuterion courtyard wall, replaced the older arrangement now buried below a new workshop. There are traces of continuing alterations, sometimes leading to additional partitioning in the course of the century. Yet, when a massive earthquake levelled this area around the middle of the seventh century AD, it seems to have been abandoned forever.

5. THE UPPER AGORA: THE MARKET BUILDING AND NORTHEAST GATE

The objective of the 1996 campaign was to uncover the northeast corner of the agora, where the remains of a partly collapsed arched gateway were visible at the surface. We also expected to find the postament of an honorific column over 10 m tall that would have been a counterpart to similar columns in the three other corners of the square. At the same time, we intended to investigate the interior of a tunnel that seemed to cross the market building along the northeast corner of the square.

5.1. The upper agora (Fig. 104):

5.1.1. The northeast corner of the upper agora (Fig. 105)

In 1996, two complete sectors (2325/2570 and 2325/2575) and parts of seven others (2320/2570, 2320/2575, 2325/2580, 2330/2580 and 2330/2570, 2325/2565 and 2330/2565) were excavated in the northeast corner of the upper agora. In view of the planned anastylosis of the Antonine nymphaeum, the excavations could not proceed any further than the early Byzantine, mostly paved levels of the square. Therefore, the exact date of some structures and water management systems that were exposed has not yet been established.

In sectors 2325/2570 and 2330/2570, a postament that originally supported a tall honorific column was found (Fig. 106). Its shape and dimensions are completely identical with those of a corresponding honorific column and postament exposed in the northwest corner of the upper agora (Waelkens et al. 1997b: 130-131, figs 37-38). As was the case with the latter, the new postament (again 1.52 m by 1.52 m) stood on a square socle, shaped as a bench to sit on and measuring 2.42 m by 2.42 m. This is carried by a plain socle of which only the north-south dimension (3.04 m) could be determined (Fig. 107). The postament itself is less well-preserved than its counterpart in the northwest corner. In fact, half of it and the plate forming the upper moulding, were not found in situ. The column drums did not bear a legible inscription either, so that the identity of the statue on top of the monument could no longer be established. However, the completely identical shape and dimensions of the postament and the corresponding treatment of the Corinthian capital of the column (Fig. 108) are sufficient proof that the northwest and northeast honorific columns were contemporary monuments and part of a single building project. These two columns belonged to a group of four more or less identical columns bearing bronze portrait statues erected in the four corners of the upper agora (Vandeput 1993; Waelkens et al. 1997b: 130-136; see Waelkens in press). The identity of two of the statues, in the southwest and in the northwest corner of the square respectively, is known: an inscription on the columns states that the 'dèmos' honoured Krateros and Ilagoas, both sons of Kallikles son of Kallikles (Devijver 1996:107). The type of monument itself is completely Greek. The practice of placing votive gifts in sanctuaries on top of columns or pillars can be traced back to the seventh century BC but, during the fourth century BC, the original anathemata were sometimes replaced by portrait statues representing the dedicators themselves, transforming the votive column into a memorial. At the same time, the cities began to produce portraits to thank their benefactors for political or economic assistance. Such memorials became rather popular in Hellenistic times but normally they remained confined to the sacred atmosphere of a sanctuary (Vandeput 1993; Jordan-Ruwe 1995: 8-21, 43-45; 49; Rose 1997: 109-110). However, this kind of monument was first divorced from its sacred milieu in a series of Attalid pillar monuments placed in carefully selected spots along the Panathenaic road in Athens, and aimed at a public display of Attalid power. The honorific columns on the upper agora of Sagalassos may have served a similar purpose. The reason for their dedication is not specified in the two preserved inscriptions but it may have been made sufficiently clear by the fact that the columns marked the corners of the square. Because the latter had been enlarged and repaved during that period (Waelkens et al. 1997b: 130-136), it is possible that the sons of Kallikles had played a role in this renovation and that the erection of the columns marked its completion. These columns not only emphasized the four corners of the new, enlarged square, but they actually formed a rectangle, thus giving the trapezoidal agora a more 'regular' appearance. The date of the whole arrangement, based on the treatment of the Corinthian capitals, seems to be late Augustan (Vandeput 1997a: 46-49). Since the honoured persons on the northwest and the southwest columns were brothers, the northeast column may have honoured another member of the same family.

The honorific columns in the northern corners of the square were placed on tall pedestals (Waelkens et al. 1997b: 131-132, figs 38, 40), while those in the southern corners stood on simpler bases (Vandeput 1997a: 46-49). This may have been to increase the visibility of the statues in the northern part of the upper agora so that they could also be seen from the lower city. Decrees continually specified that images should be erected in the most visible spots, so most of them were set up in locations that guaranteed the greatest public exposure (Rose 1997: 110, 113). The size of the columns, their elaborate capitals and their richly decorated statue supports (Vandeput 1997b: 46-47) must have made them very expensive and attractive monuments.

Some 4.30 m to the south, in sectors 2325/2565 and 2330/2565, the remains of a semicircular exedra were exposed (see Fig. 106). Its stone benches were found more or less in situ, but the back support pieces were dispersed around it. The exedra measured 2.70 by 3.75 m. Because of its location on that part of the upper agora which was enlarged in early Imperial times, the monument was most probably built during the Imperial period, but for the moment a more precise chronology cannot be established. It is even possible that the monument originally occupied a different position.

The excavated zone also comprised a certain number of water-supply and drainage systems. Immediately behind the exedra, a water-supply system of terracotta pipes was visible in an unpaved section of the agora. It could be traced over a distance of 3.70 m in a northwest-southeast direction and may have transported water from the Antonine nymphaeum, although it may not necessarily date from the latter's construction.

A second water-supply system made of terracotta pipes was found along the wall of the 'market building' (Fig. 109) embedded in a layer 6. This stratum, found in sectors 2320/2575, 2325/2575, 2325/2580 and 2330/2580, is a thin layer of up to 0.10 m depth located immediately above and between the pavement slabs of the agora. It consisted of a light-colored compacted sandy soil with gravel and small fragments of tiles, ceramic and bones. This layer may be detritus that accumulated before the final earthquake on the pavement slabs of the agora, in the corner between the Antonine nymphaeum and the 'market building'. At the base of the 'market building', it covered a terracotta water-pipe and in sector 2330/2580 it became quite humid. The terracotta pipes found in this layer perhaps reflect a newly arranged or repaired water-supply system of early Byzantine times. In fact, layer 6 contained eight coins, most of which could be attributed to the fourth and fifth centuries AD (Scheers 2000, cat. Upper Agora, layer 6).

The excavated area also contained an impressive sewage channel extending from the entrance of the tunnel in the 'market building' (see below) towards the south (Fig. 110). It was connected with another sewage channel coming from the east through the northeast gate (see Fig. 109). Both channels had been built with re-used ashlars and column drums, with smaller stones filling the gaps in between. These systems must be a late Roman or early Byzantine repair of an older arrangement. The main sewer, which could be followed over a distance of 18.80 m along the eastern edge of the square, has a width of 1.10 m.

5.1.2. Stratigraphy of the destruction and erosion layers covering the upper agora

In general, the stratigraphy of the removed soil was quite simple, as the deposit represented mainly a destruction layer of remains of the Antonine nymphaeum, the 'terrace building' behind it, and the workshops that were built above the latter in late antiquity. However, some distinctions could be made in the various sectors:
- layer 5, removed in sectors 2320/2575, 2320/2570, 2325/2575 and 2325/2570, consisted of a very dark brown-black soil with many charcoal remains and burnt material. The soil had left black (burnt) traces on the walls of the 'market' and the 'terrace building'. This seems to suggest that the seventh century AD earthquake was accompanied by fires. The layer had a thickness of 0.50 m and contained lots of sherds, bone, window glass, small stones, but almost no tiles.

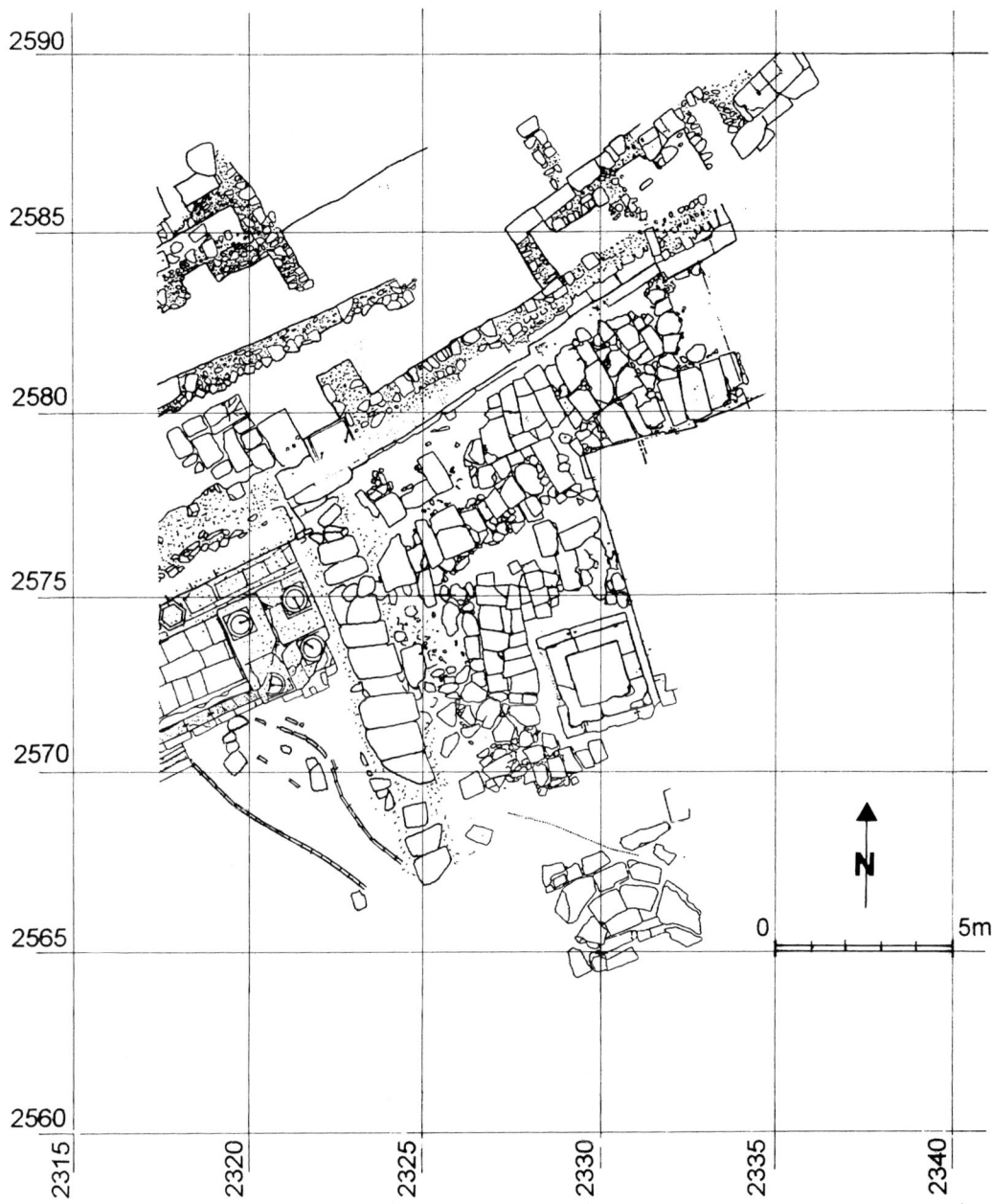

Fig. 105: The northeast corner of the upper agora.

Fig. 106: View of the exedra (front) and the honorific column's postament (centre) in the northeast corner of the upper agora.

Fig. 107: The southern extremity of the postament of the northeast honorific column and its support.

Fig. 108: The capital of the northeast honorific column.

Fig. 109: View of the northeast corner of the upper agora, seen from the northeast gate. To the left, along the wall and in the background, the two sewage systems with their raised covers. To the right, at the bottom of the 'market building', the terracotta water supply system

Fig. 110: The sewage system crossing the east side of the upper agora, seen from the south.

Fig. 111: View of the front wall of the market building seen from the southwest.

In sector 2325/2570, layer 5 surrounded the postament of the northeast honorific column and there it had a depth of 0.70 m. It contained eight coins, ranging in date from the reign of Honorius (AD 395-408) to that of Justinian I (AD 543-565; Scheers 2000, cat. Upper Agora, layer 5).

- layer 4: was not present in this part of the agora.
- layer 3, excavated in sectors 2320/2575, 2325/2575, 2325/2580 and 2330/2580, was the main destruction layer, with a depth of 1 m. Its soil was greyish-green in color, probably due to the many mortar fragments from collapsed structures above the 'market building'. It contained large, medium and small stones and tiles. The few archaeological finds were found in patches throughout the layer. In sector 2325/2580 along the terrace wall, large tiles and bricks with mortar still attached to them were found. As is illustrated by their north-south orientation, they must have fallen from the workshop area located at a higher level. In sector 2330/2580, closer to the gate, layer 3 contained fewer mortar fragments and was finer in texture. The eleven coins that were found in this layer could mainly be dated between the late fourth and the final years of the sixth century AD (Scheers 2000, cat. Upper Agora, layer 3).
- layer 2: an erosion layer with a loose fine soil containing roots, and of a much lighter colour. The layer contained ceramic, bone, glass and metal finds as well as small and larger stones and tiles. Nine coins were found in it. They could be dated between the (second half of the) fourth century and the reign of Heraclius (AD 616/7 or 617/8). The coin finds from layers 2, 3 and 5 confirm once more a mid-seventh century AD date for the destruction of the city, followed by total abandonment.
- the topsoil (layer 1) covered the whole excavated area. It consisted of a loose and fine, dark soil full of plant roots, with a depth of ca. 0.20 m. At the surface, many small and larger stones were found along with weathered sherds, glass and a few metal objects. One coin (Scheers 2000, cat. 95: SA 96 UA 15) belonged to the reign of Arcadius (AD 392-395).

5.2. The Hellenistic market building

During the 1995 campaign, a tall structure of rusticated ashlar, with a partially vaulted tunnel inside, was discovered immediately to the east of the second century AD nymphaeum. It was identified as a probable 'market building', with storage facilities in its lower levels and perhaps a stoa-like structure above (Waelkens et al. 1997b: 127-130). In 1996, the excavation of the building was extended towards the east. In the upper area of the terraced structure, the excavations had to stop at the level of the late Imperial to early Byzantine workshops (?) that had been built on top of it (see 4.3 and 4.4.1). A hole in the floor of room XIII made it possible to see that the 'market building' below it contained a number of rooms, partially filled with debris, that may originally have functioned as storage rooms or cisterns. Since no external access has been discovered thus far, these facilities were apparently only accessible from above. In 1996, the front wall of the building was exposed over its total length of 12.30 m, between the second century AD nymphaeum and the northeast gate of the upper agora. Originally, the building had continued further west and may have occupied a location along a street giving access from the east to the Hellenistic agora, which was at that time less wide. However, when in Augustan times the agora was enlarged towards the east and a 'terrace building' erected along its northern edge, the western extremity of the 'market building' was removed as far as could be done without endangering the tunnel. Parts of its left archivolt, however, had to be sacrificed (Waelkens et al. 1997b: 127-130).

Since the street level in front of the building slopes towards the west, its eastern extremity has only five courses of irregular rusticated ashlar (instead of six near the western extremity) with a medium total height of 3.10 m (Fig. 111). Above them, there are two layers of re-used stones, added in antiquity to raise the floor level. The interior of the tunnel was already partially explored in 1995 and it was excavated in 1996 (Fig. 112). The tunnel is 1 m wide and in the vaulted sections it is 1.60 m high. The first 3.40 m are horizontal and paved with nice slabs, after which is a 4.50 m long and 1.35 m high stairway (Fig. 113) comprising seven steps (h. of the steps, ca.: 0.20 m). This very gentle slope (30%) is covered by a ceiling of identical slope, made of flat slabs placed next to one another (Fig. 114). After this first stairway, there is a second horizontal stretch of 2 m of which 1.55 m is horizontally vaulted. Then there is a second stepped section that rises only 0.70 m over a distance of 4 m. It comprises five broad steps (h. ca: 0.10 m) that together make a slope of 17.5% (Fig. 115). It is followed by a third horizontal, vaulted section of 1.75 m, and by another 1 m long section with the same floor level, but covered by a horizontal slab. After this, the tunnel becomes a sharply rising stairway (slope of 108%) of seven steps that over a distance of a mere 2.25 m rise 2.45 m. The stairway is covered by five flat slabs, placed stepwise next to one another. At a distance of 18.5 m from the entrance, a brick arch occurs in this stepped ceiling through which a room above the tunnel can be detected from the north (Fig. 116). In this room, two massive rough columns still bear a stone ceiling. The room, however, is filled with rubble and at the moment cannot be entered. The brick arch may have served to aerate either the tunnel or the room above it. This very steep stairway is followed by a fourth horizontally vaulted section of 1.75 m (Fig. 117), after which the tunnel rises again 2.45 m over a distance of 2.05 m by six steps (slope of 119%). This section is covered by flat slabs placed next to one another and at the same slope as the stair. After this fourth stairway follows a 1.90 m long horizontal section, which is blocked however by a wall.

The alternation of horizontal vaults and ceilings made of slabs laid obliquely or in steps that was used to create the slope of the tunnel seems to indicate a date before the technique of sloping barrel-vaults was mastered, and might suggest an early Hellenistic date (early third century BC at the latest) or even before. The treatment of the wall blocks of the 'market building's' façade fits very well with such a date (Waelkens *et al.* 1997b: 127). The interior dimensions of the tunnel preclude its ever having been used for normal traffic. Originally, it may have had a military purpose: to surprise an enemy who may have come too close to the city walls. In fact, it seems to continue beyond the late Roman fortifications, which in this particular area seem to occupy the position of an older Hellenistic wall (Loots *et al.* 2000). The last sections of the system could not be explored because of the danger of collapse and the fact that the tunnel had been blocked by a wall. This wall, 24.60 m from the entrance, is made of rubble, tiles and mortar. Through a hole in the rubble wall (thickness: 0.90 m), the continuation of the tunnel can be seen for another 2 m. It is partially filled with earth, but this fill nowhere reaches the ceiling.

The tunnel is likely to have been blocked in late Roman/early Byzantine times, either because its last section had become too dangerous to enter (problems with the roof) or to prevent an enemy using it in the opposite direction. In the former case, even today the tunnel is very damp and the soil on the floor gets moister towards the north. Some of the stones of the walls and ceiling have even been damaged and cracked by water that enters the tunnel from outside.

In 1995, some pottery and the scattered remains of a human being, a cow and a sheep were found inside the tunnel. They may be victims of the mid-seventh century AD earthquake who had sought refuge inside this solid structure but were trapped when its entrance was closed off by debris (layers 5 and 3) from the structures above. Recent research in the Roman baths has revealed that by that time, Sagalassos had become a very rural society, so that the presence of a shepherd or a farmer with two animals on the upper agora need not surprise us. None of the other finds were later than the seismic catastrophe either. The pottery that was found inside (SA 96 UA 131) all belonged to phase 8 of the local production (mid-fifth to mid-seventh century AD), while the four coins ranged in date from the late fourth to the late sixth centuries AD (Scheers 2000, cat. 93, 100, 362 and 371: SA 96 UA 213, *virtus exerciti* coin from AD 393-408; SA 96 UA 139, coin of Arcadius from AD 392-395; SA 96 UA 137, *follis* of Justinian I from AD 538/9; SA 96 UA 140, follis of Justin II from AD 570/1).

5.3. The 'northeast building'

In the northeast corner of the upper agora, in sectors 2330/2575 and 2330/2570, the 1996 campaign exposed the (west) wall of a rectangular building immediately to the east of the northeast honorific column. The interior of this structure has not yet been exposed. Today, its northern extremity is hidden from view by a late Roman wall aligned with the south wall of the northeast gate (see 5.4). Most of the south wall of the building has collapsed and is still buried. The eastern limit of the structure has not yet been established, so that at present only its west wall could be studied.

This west façade is carefully built of nice ashlar blocks and is 6.25 m long (Fig. 118). The ashlars are very well worked with a claw chisel and form regular courses up to a preserved height of 2.90 m. Today seven courses are visible: from bottom to top, their height varies from a visible height of 0.30 m for the lower course, to 0.565 m, 0.53 m, 0.29 m, 0.49 m, 0.53 m and 0.495 m for the successive layers above it. The ashlars from the northwest corner are carved in such a way that in the upper three rows they form a slightly projecting pilaster 0.47 m wide. The stones below them project stepwise towards the south (Fig. 119).

The function and the date of this structure have not yet been established. However, its position along the upper agora, of which it forms the eastern edge, and its alignment with the Augustan expansion of this square and with the late Augustan northeast honorific column placed against it indicates that the construction of this building was following this layout. As we have said above, the Hellenistic square may have had a slightly different orientation, which was also confirmed by a sondage in 1998. As a result the 'northeast building' must either have been part of the (late) Augustan rearrangement of the upper agora, or have been built shortly afterwards. In fact, the extreme care with which the ashlars were treated and joined can only be compared at Sagalassos with the building technology of early Imperial structures (NW Heroon, propylon of the Doric temple, southeast agora gate of the lower agora).

This carefully constructed west façade of the building contrasts very sharply with its current north wall (Figs 120-121). The latter, which is 4.30 m long, 1.04 m wide and now 2.98 m high, is made of six to seven courses of re-used material, in the lower levels especially including numerous inscriptions of Imperial date that may have been removed from the nearby agora (Devijver and Waelkens to be published in Sagalassos VI). These inscriptions even continue inside the gutter. This wall must therefore have been built in late Roman/early Byzantine times in front of the early Imperial 'northeast structure' to connect the latter's northwest corner with the south wall of the northeast gate. Since the northwest corner of the 'northeast building' is still pre-

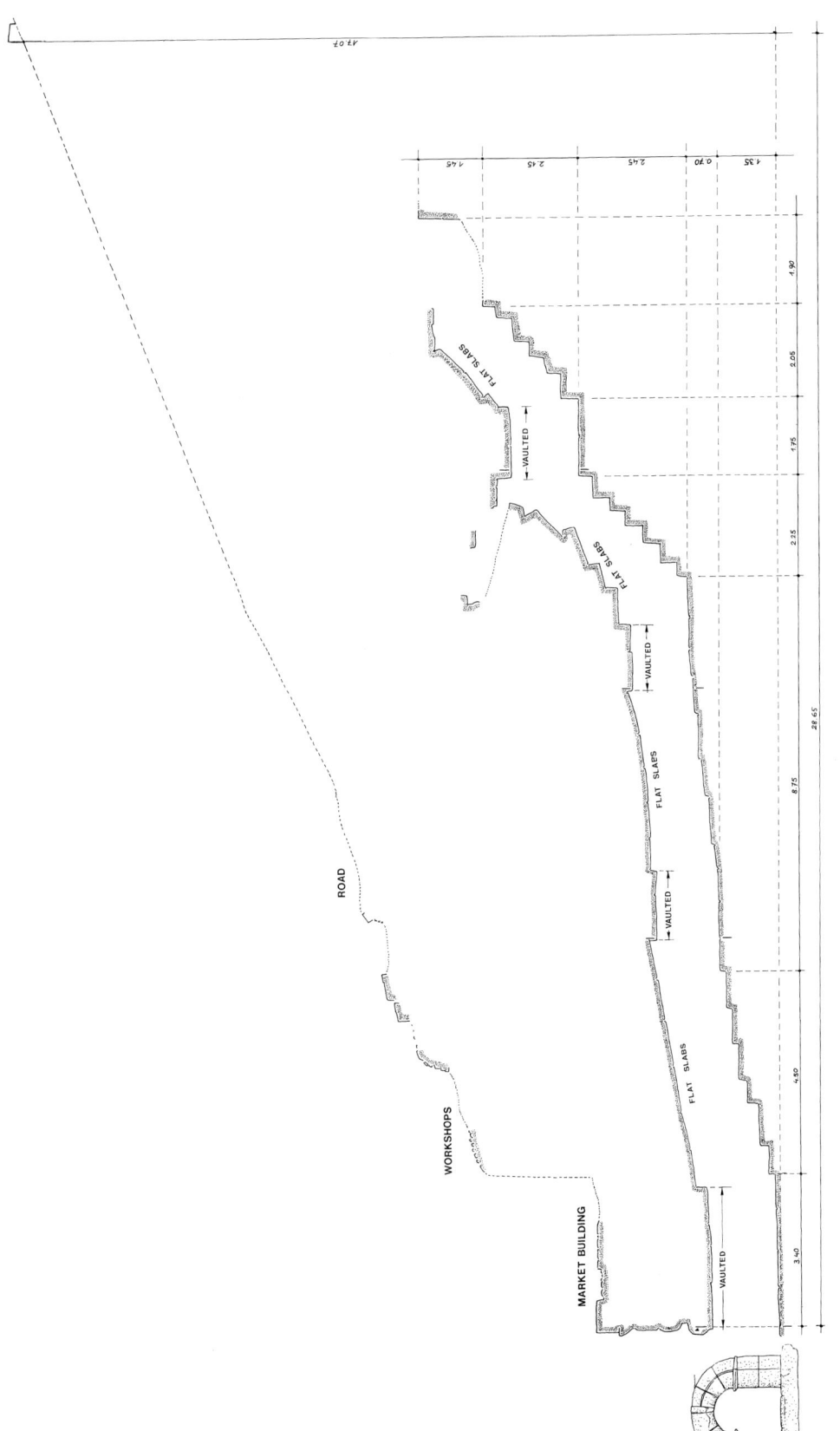

Fig. 112: Section of the tunnel.

Fig. 113: View of the first horizontal and stepped section of the tunnel, seen from the south.

Fig. 114: The ceiling above the first stairway inside the tunnel, seen from the south.

Fig. 115: The second stairway with its very broad and low steps, seen from the south.

Fig. 116: The brick arch in the ceiling immediately in front of the fourth horizontal vault.

Fig. 117: View of the very steep third stairway,
with the fourth horizontally vaulted section behind it, seen from the south.

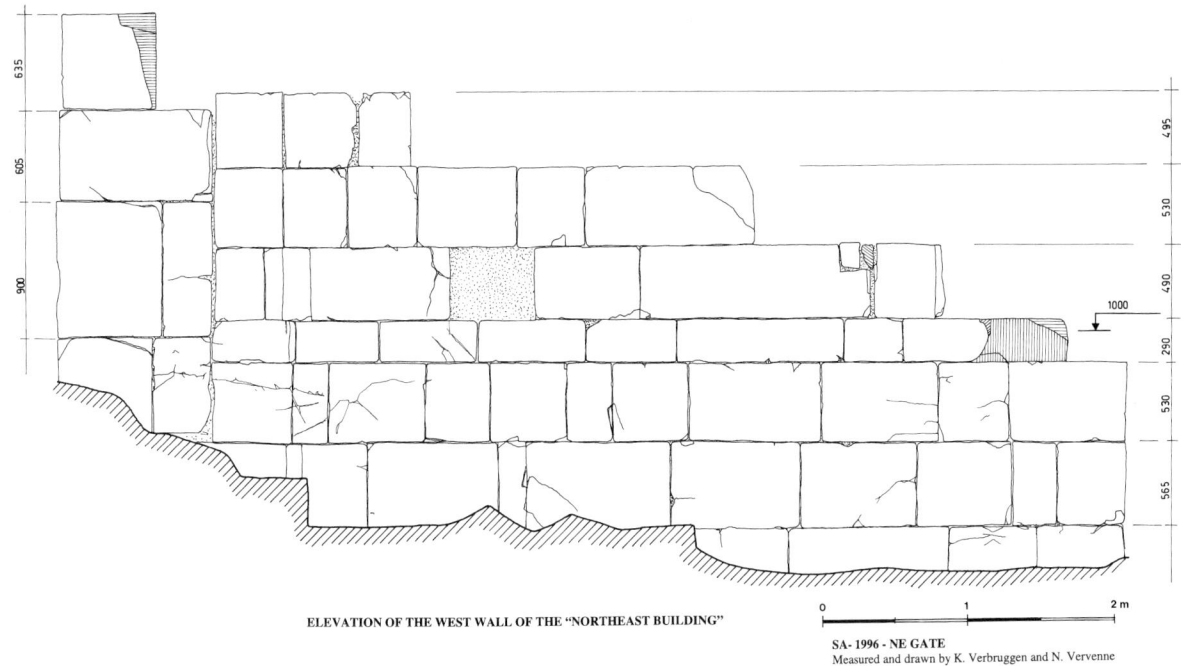

Fig. 118: The west façade of the 'northeast building'. To the left, the late Roman/early Byzantine extension.

Fig. 119: The northwest corner of the 'northeast building'.

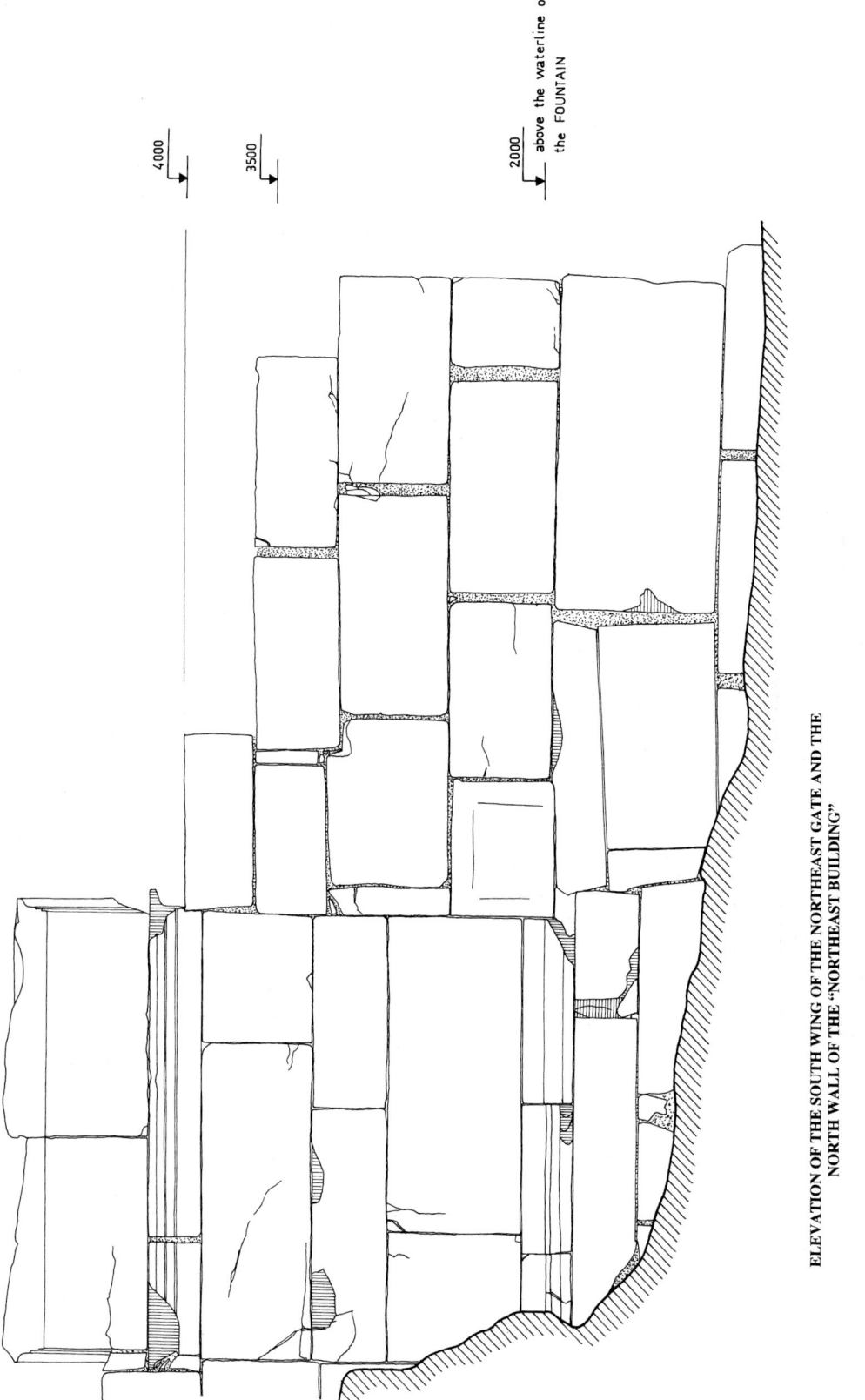

Fig. 120: The north wall of the 'northeast building'.

served and visible, its north wall cannot have been replaced by the new wall, unless it was intended to block possible entrances to this building from that side. One result of this operation was that the width of the street entering the upper agora from the northeast was reduced by 1 m.

5.4. The northeast gate of the upper agora

To the east of the market building, an arched gateway of Roman Imperial date was exposed in sector 2230/2580. It lay over the street that entered the upper agora near its northeast corner, some 10 m before the square was reached (Figs 122-125). To the north, this street was flanked by the early Hellenistic (?) 'market building', while to its south stood the early Imperial 'northeast building'. Since these two structures were of different orientation, aligning themselves respectively with the Hellenistic and the Augustan lay-out of the upper agora, the resulting street was wedge-shaped. Its width of 4.80 m near the eastern extremity of the market building was reduced to 3.90 m in early Imperial times (by the northwest corner of the 'northeast building') and even 2.90 m in late Imperial times (by the corner of the late wall) at the spot where it entered the square. When the arch was built, the then visible extremity of the 'market building' was partially destroyed. In fact, some of the ashlars from the lower courses had to be reduced in size (Fig. 122). The aim of the arch was most probably to give the funnel-like entrance to the upper agora a more regular appearance and to hide some irregularity behind it, possibly a change in direction of the street further east or the beginning of other, less imposing buildings.

The architect who was responsible for this construction had therefore to reconcile the arch with a section of street that was not parallel-sided. This was achieved by giving the arch two side walls that clearly followed the alignment of the sides of the street, while the arch above them followed a different orientation and had almost parallel sides. Therefore, the springing of the arch receded a mere 0.05 m behind the edge of the upper moulding of the side walls near their eastern extremity, but some 0.18 m near their western edge (see Fig. 125). The resulting span of the arch was 4.75 m. Its depth was exactly 2.40 m.

The two side walls were built in an identical way (Figs 124, 126-127). Below, there were two steps, of which the lower one (visible height: 0.30 m) projected some 0.13 m towards the centre of the arch. The second was 0.34 m high with its upper edge was shaped like an Egyptian throat. Above it, there was a 0.28 m high cyma reversa socle moulding that was not completely finished over its whole length. This bore a 1.80 m high straight wall section of three courses (from bottom to top 0.76 m, 0.42 m and 0.62 m). They were crowned by an upper moulding (height: 0.30 m) made up of a band, a cyma recta and an astragal above a recessed straight section.

Apparently as the result of an earthquake, this upper moulding, together with the arch above it, had shifted some 0.05 m to the south on both sides of the street (see Fig. 123). It was this moulding which carried the archivolt, composed of three fasciae crowned by an oblique moulding. While on the south side only one row of voussoirs survived in situ (Fig. 126), on the north side the two lowest rows survived, since three rows of blocks above them, which held them with interlocking joints, were left in situ (Figs 123-124). At the beginning of the excavation, most of the other voussoirs were discovered near the surface. Although they had not collapsed during the final earthquake, they were no longer connected to one another, despite being partially supported by other debris (Fig. 128) and had to be removed for safety reasons.

In the upper levels of this debris some pieces of entablature were found, comprising a nicely carved tendril frieze, the decoration of which at first sight appears a bit older than that of the Antonine nymphaeum (Fig. 129). It most probably belonged to the upper part of the archway, which in that must have been built around or shortly before the middle of the second century AD.

Below it, the road slopes towards the west and is covered with large slabs, many of them re-used. There is no evidence of cartwheels, as this kind of traffic would have been impossible here because of a small step in front of the gate. Further down, several large slabs forming a stepped surface, which may represent the remains of an earlier stairway, can also be seen (Fig. 109).

5.5. Conclusion

The 1996 season confirmed the drastic changes that the upper agora must have undergone in Augustan times. Not only was the square considerably enlarged towards the east and repaved, its edges were also neatly marked by the construction of the 'northeast building' and the erection of four honorific columns in its four corners. These gave the trapezoidal square a more rectangular appearance. Most probably around the middle of the second century AD, the wedge-shaped northeastern entrance to the square was also given a more regular look by the construction of an arched gateway, some 10 m behind the corner of the square. Its location in this recess was most probably chosen to hide some irregularity (change in direction of the street, change in buildings) behind it. However, at the same time it may have been intended to create a kind of esplanade that integrated the old 'market building' better into the square.

Earthquakes in late antiquity also affected this corner of the agora. The first one (AD 518) perhaps made it necessary to build a wall of re-used material, in front of the 'northeast building's' north face, thus reducing the width of the street by one metre. The second, even more catastrophic, earthquake, which levelled the city around the middle of the seventh century AD, made the upper parts of the northeast gate collapse and may have buried a human being together with two animals inside the tunnel crossing the 'market building'. Neither the tunnel, nor the northeast gate were ever cleared. This means that the northeast entrance of the square was given up forever.

6. THE LATE HELLENISTIC FOUNTAIN HOUSE

During the 1996 and 1997 campaigns, some small-scale excavations were carried out around the late Hellenistic fountain house excavated in 1990-1993, in relation to the ongoing anastylosis there (Waelkens *et al.* 1997b: 110-114; Ercan *et al.* 1997; Patrício *et al.* 2000). In 1996, a first sondage was undertaken immediately to the north of the fountain house, below the ancient street level, with the aim of finding the water-supply system that still fed the building. A number of steps belonging to the western portico and of some of the steps giving access to the courtyard were also removed. The last stairway was also further dismantled in 1997. However, this season mainly focused on the excavation of the water-basins of the three porticoes with the view of rendering them waterproof again. At the end of the campaign, the building was inaugurated and was restored to its original function (Figs. 130-132). A detailed report on the completion of the anastylosis will be published in the next volume. After these two seasons it was possible to confirm the supposed late first century BC date of the building and to document some of the later changes.

6.1. The construction of the fountain house.

In 1995, the early sixth century AD water-supply system, including a settling tank and three terracotta pipes, had been excavated behind the service window in the back wall of the north portico of the fountain house, which formed an opening for access to the water supply. At that time, the 'service room' for the fountain, formed by two walls built behind the fountain house, was dry and was therefore closed off again. In fact, the water at that time entered through the back wall of the northern portico, a metre to the east of the 'service room' (Waelkens *et al.* 1997b: 110-114). To channel this source, after removing some of the street slabs, a new sondage (4 m E-W; ca. 2.90 m N-S) was carried out in 1996, behind the northeast corner of the building. It showed that over the winter the water-course had altered direction again and now infiltrated into the 'service room' through its northern profile. After cleaning out the original terracotta water-supply system in the northeast corner of the room, the water eventually emerged from the pipe, but it still disappeared through a hole in the southeast corner of the trench.

Therefore, a cistern in stone masonry plastered with a hydraulic lime mortar was built inside the 'service room' and connected to the original water-supply. As a result, the water today enters the fountain again through the original slit-like opening in the northern portico's back wall and fills the original water-basins. From there, it disappears into the original sewage system, which is still functioning. Neither the provenance of the water, nor its final destination have been identified thus far, but in the meantime the whole system is working again as it did before the mid-seventh century AD earthquake. After this work, a roof was constructed over the 'service room' and this space was covered with the original earth fill and paving slabs.

Despite the fact that the 1996 sondage eventually proved to have been unnecessary as far as controlling the water-supply was concerned, it did provide us for the first time with stratigraphical evidence about the construction date of the original building. The sondage continued to a depth of ca 4.50 m below the level of the pavement slabs, where the water-table was reached half way down layer 8. The following layers could be identified as the original back fill of the fountain house:

- layer 8: a compact soil (depth in some spots at least 1.80 m) composed of an almost black clay containing a lot of large stones. Below it were some large stones that covered almost the entire surface of the trench. This stone layer marked the end of the excavation (Fig. 133). The black clay was not horizontally distributed all over the trench, but seemed to slope from east to west. For safety reasons, it could only be examined in a 1 m wide section in the middle of the trench. The few sherds (SA 96 N 54) that it contained belonged to the first phase of the locally produced fine red slip wares (25 BC/25 AD – 50 AD).

- layer 7: a 1.70 m deep layer (1538.43 to 1538.49 m a.s.l. and ca. 2 m below the street level), which is rather compact and very wet (Fig. 134). It contained a lot of small rubble stones and gravel. The amount of finds (bone, pottery) was low, but the sherds (SA 96 N 50) were contemporary with those of layer 8.

- layer 6: a 0.80 m deep layer (1539.22 to 1539.31 m a.s.l. and ca. 1.40 m below the street level).

This layer is characterised by the great amount of large rubble, of which the largest pieces were clearly piled up against the back wall of the fountain house (see Fig. 134). The soil between was rather loose and contained few finds (bone, metal). The sherds (SA 96 N 44) were again contemporary with those of layers 7 and 8.

- layer 5 was a 0.30 m deep (1539.46 to 1539.61 m a.s.l. and ca. 0.90 m below the street level), gravel-rich layer containing lots of smaller stones ceramics, bone, tesserae, and metal. The pottery in it (SA 96 N 39) once more belonged to phase 1 of the locally produced fine wares.

Layers 5-8 represent a single filling operation and contained

Fig. 121: View of the northeast gate and the adjoining north wall of the 'northeast building'.

Fig. 122: View of the northeast gate of the upper agora, seen from the west. To the right, the late Roman wall, built in front of the northwest corner of the 'northeast building' can be seen.

Fig. 123: North-south cross-section through the standing remains of the northeast gate, seen from the west.

Fig. 124: The north wing of the northeast gate (left), with the adjoining 'market building.

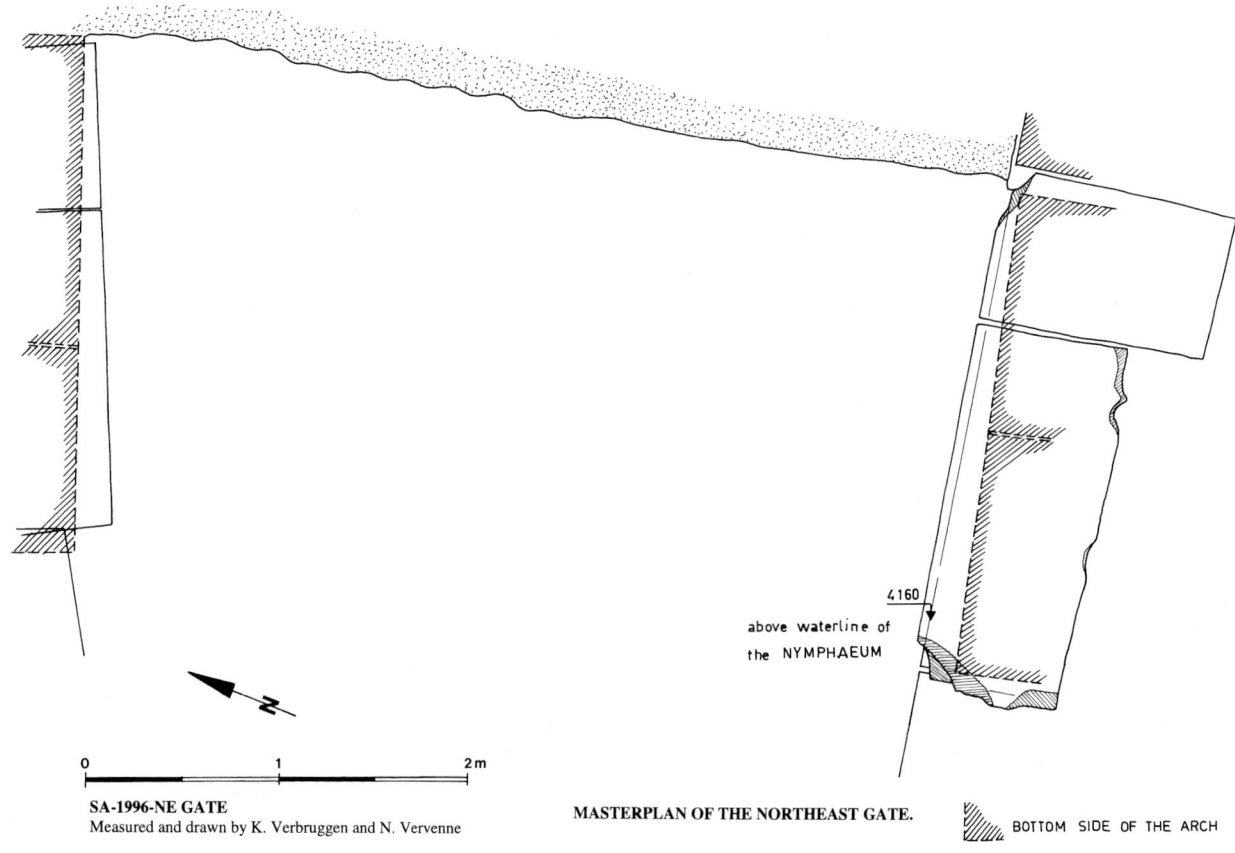

Fig. 125: Plan of the northeast gate.

Fig. 126: The south wing of the northeast gate, with the adjoining late wall.

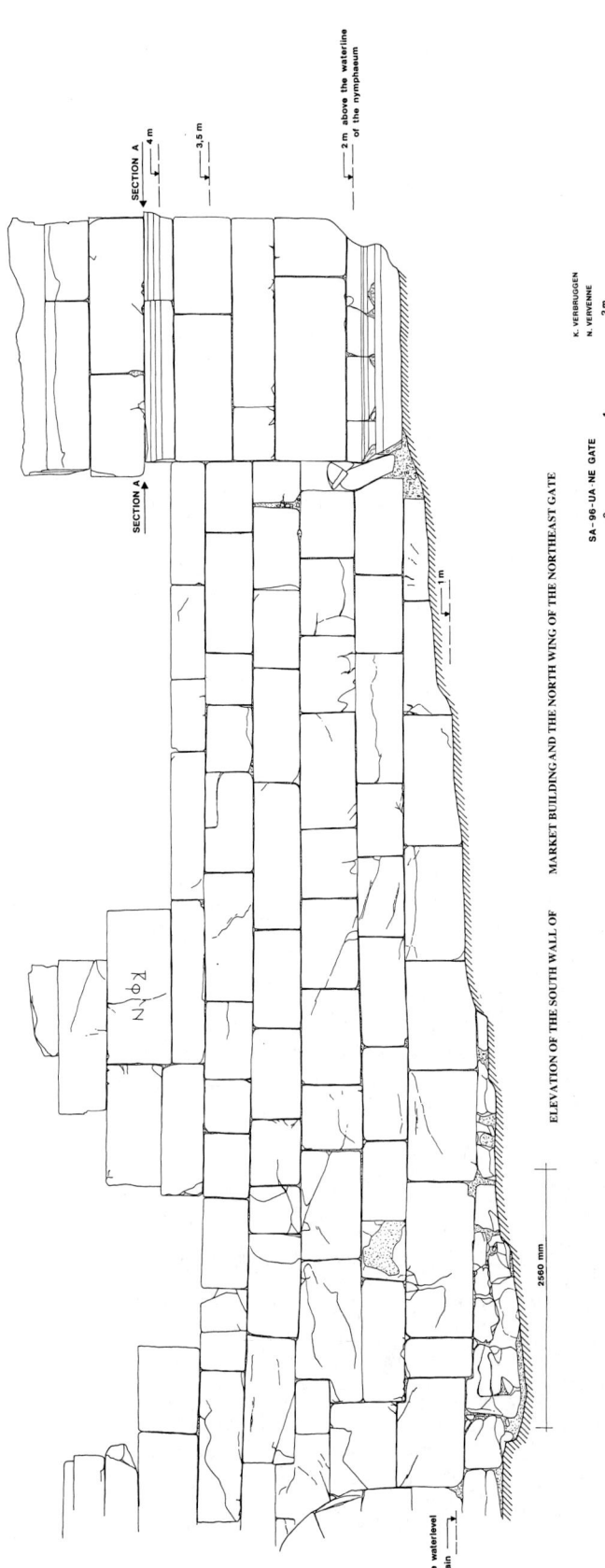

Fig. 127. Drawing of the north wing of the Northeast Gate.

Fig. 128: View of the collapsed upper part of the northeast arch at the beginning of the 1996 season.

Fig. 129: View of entablature blocks that may have belonged to an upper section of the northeast arch.

Fig. 130: View of the late Hellenistic fountain house at the end of the 1997 campaign.

Fig. 131: The western part of the courtyard after the 1997 anastylosis.

Fig. 132: The eastern half of the courtyard after the 1997 inauguration.

Fig. 133: View of the sondage behind the northeast corner of the late Hellenistic fountain house, at the level of layer 8.

Fig. 134: View of layer 7 behind the fountain house. To the left, the rubble from layer 6 is still visible.

Fig. 135: The original floor level inside the east basin.

Fig. 136: View inside the west basin. In front, the original mortar floor bearing the steps of the east portico. At the back, the early Imperial fill no. 4 (no. 9 in the picture) with the second mortar floor above it.

Sagalassos red slip wares of the first production phase (at present, 25 BC/25 AD to 50 AD). This fill may therefore be connected with the building of the fountain house during the (late) first century BC, but it may also represent an early first century AD repair. For the moment, it is unfortunately not possible to tell the difference between material from the late first century BC and that from the early first century AD, nor to date the beginning of the mass production of the locally produced wares precisely. However, the 1997 excavations inside the west basin of the fountain house revealed that an original date of construction during the later first century BC is likely.

In fact, in view of the anastylosis of the fountain building, excavations were undertaken inside the water-basins of its three porticoes. The ultimate aim was to plaster them again with a waterproof coating. Therefore, the last floor level inside the basins had to be removed so that the original level could be reached. The latter (floor 1) consists of a reddish coating composed of a hydraulic mortar containing lots of fragments of brick near the edges of the basins. Especially in the east basin, some small volcanic particles that made the mortar more waterproof could be distinguished (Fig. 135). While the back walls of the porticoes continued below this floor, the steps supporting the parapets of the porticoes had been placed on it. They must have been covered with a now lost hydraulic mortar. In the western portico, it became clear that only the two lowest courses of stones in its back wall were still original (Fig. 136) and indeed we had previously discovered that the rest of the wall had been rebuilt during the second century AD (Waelkens *et al.* 1997b: 110-114).

As was to be expected, the level of the original floor was somewhat higher inside the north basin (Fig. 137), which is separated from the basins on either side by a single ashlar block creating a kind of settling tank in between (floor level: 1534.815 m a.s.l. near its western end and 1534.865 m a.s.l. near its eastern end). The floor level of the west basin (1534.755 m a.s.l. near its northern end and 1534.625 near its southern end) and the east basin (1534.72 m a.s.l. near its northern end and 1534.69 m a.s.l. near its southern end) sloped gently towards the south.

At some point, this floor level has been raised by the addition of two layers:
- layer 4: a ca. 0.30 m deep fill, containing almost exclusively rubble, and almost no soil at all. But, it did include some bone, metal, marble fragments and sherds (SA 97 N 31 and 33). The latter could be dated to the first phase of the local production. This layer clearly served as a base for the mortar layer above it (see Fig. 136). In the east basin, this layer was excavated as a layer 2 and contained a city coin from Selge, dated to the second-first century BC (Scheers 2000, cat. 25: SA 97 NEB 28). The rubble from this layer was not mixed with mortar.

- a 0.05 to 0.25 m deep mortar layer (floor 2).

The total thickness of both layers varied from 0.49 m in the east basin to 0.56 m in the west basin.

In the southeast corner of the west basin, an outlet consisting of a terracotta pipe was still *in situ* (Fig. 138). Since it went straight through layer 4, it must belong to this raised floor level. The 1997 excavations thus revealed that the original floors of the fountain house's water-basins had already been altered during the late first century BC or early first century AD. Since pottery belonging to the same phase was also discovered in the fill (layers 5-8) around the 'service room', two possible explanations can be given. It may be that both fills (layer 4 inside the basins and layers 5-8 behind the back wall of the north portico) represent one single building operation wherein the original floor level of the water-basins was raised, perhaps because of a change in the water-table or a seismic event that necessitated an alteration to the original water-supply system. In that case, this intervention must have occurred between the end of the first century BC and the middle of the second century AD and neither fill therefore represents the original situation.

A more plausible explanation however, seems to be that the original arrangement to the north of the fountain house had been altered in order to accomodate the water supply tunnel carrying surplus water towards the upper agora (Waelkens *et al.* 1997b: 112-113 Figs 13-14). The fact that part of the water supply thus was carried away before reaching the fountain house's water spout, must have reduced the fountains output and could explain alterations in its basins.

A second possibility would be that layers 5-8 behind the back wall of the north portico do still represent the original arrangement, while the raising of the floor level inside the basins was done in a second stage, following the first one so closely that the pottery from both fills cannot be distinguished chronologically.

The first explanation seems to be more logical, not only because of the great similarity between the sherds of both fills, but also because raising the original floor level of the basins most probably reflected changes in the water supply. In the first case, a (late) first century BC date for the original construction is more than probable. But even with this second explanation, the necessary time-lapse between both filling operations would rather suggest a first century BC date for the original construction. In the first case, the construction date of the building would most probably be pre-Imperial; in the latter, the fountain house would appear to have been an early Imperial construction.

6.2. The second century AD repairs.

We had previously established that the fountain house and

its surroundings, both to the east and to the west, had been considerably altered during the first half of the second century AD, perhaps when around the year 120-130 AD the Neon Library was built immediately behind the fountain house (Waelkens *et al.* 1997b: 110-114). The 1996 campaign showed that these changes also extended along the north side of the building behind and next to the 'service room'.

Above the late first century BC-early first century AD fills 5-8 of the 1996 sondage (see 6.1) the following layers could be identified:

- layer 4: a thin layer (depth: 0.13 m to 0.26 m; 1539.69 m to 1539.76 m a.s.l., ca. 0.70 m below the street level) that was only present in the northern part of the trench. The soil of this dark brown, rather wet layer was rather fine-grained and compact. It contained little rubble, except for the area immediately behind the back wall of the northern portico, where a large amount of rubble had been piled dry. This layer contained a water-supply system (1539.73 m a.s.l. in the east to 1539.71 m in the west) running from the northwest to the southeast (Fig. 139). In 1992, its continuation in this direction had been exposed as the 'lower drain' inside layer 10E, then dated to the second century AD (Waelkens 1993c: 50; 78 fig. 43; 79 fig. 45). In the meantime, a more precise date was established: all the pottery from layer 4 (SA 96 N 24) could be attributed to the first half of the second century AD. It also contained a Sagalassos city coin dated to the first century BC-early Imperial times (Scheers 2000, cat. 8: SA 96 N 28).

- layer 3: a 0.20 m deep dark brown layer (1539.82 m to 1539.97 m a.s.l.; ca. 0.50 m below the street level) that was full of rubble. This rather loose soil covered a second water-supply system made of terracotta pipes (1539.76 m a.s.l.), with a slightly different orientation from that in layer 4, which it crossed (Figs 140-141). These pipes again had already been exposed in 1992 as the 'upper drain' inside layer 10E to the east of the fountain house (Waelkens 1993c: 50; 78 fig. 43; 79 fig. 45). Layer 3 contained ceramics, bone, and tesserae. Its pottery (SA 96 N 13) is contemporary with that of layer 2. Layer 3 also contained two coins, one of which was a Sagalassos city coin from the first century BC-first century AD, while the other was a coin of Augustus (respectively, Scheers 2000, cat. 9 and 31: SA 96 N 21 and SA 9 N 15).

- layer 2: the layer immediately below the current street pavement (level 1) was called layer 2 (1540.10 m a.s.l.). It was clearly a fill with a depth of approximately 0.20 m. Near the northeast corner of the fountain house, it contained a terracotta water supply system (1540.13 m a.s.l.), running at first parallel to the back wall of the fountain, but eventually turning to the south (Figs 141-142). This southward run of pipe was not discovered during the 1992 season east of the fountain (Waelkens 1993c) and may have been destroyed during the early third century AD transformation of the area. Layer 2 contained bone, tesserae, crustae, metal, and glass as well as pottery dated to the period 100-150 AD. This water channel located immediately below the pavement slabs was protected by rubble, which flanked it on either side (see Fig. 142). The pottery inside this layer (SA 96 N 6) was contemporary with that of the two layers below it. Therefore, the three water-supply systems seem to belong to one building operation at some time during the first half of the second century AD. It was most probably related to the construction of the Neon Library behind the fountain in the years 120-130 AD (Waelkens 1993b: 13-15). In fact, the construction of the Neon Library may have destroyed or at least affected the old water-supply systems, so that new gutters and supply systems needed to be built. The three terracotta supply systems discovered in layers 2-4, as well as the sewers and tunnels at either side of the fountain, excavated in previous years (Waelkens 1993c; Waelkens *et al.* 1995a), may all belong to this building operation. In fact layers 2 to 4 only represent successive phases of a single filling operation. The uppermost terracotta pipe system (layer 2) was apparently partially removed to the east of the fountain when, shortly after 200 AD, an esplanade was built around the fountain house in front of the Neon Library (Waelkens 1993c).

6.3. An early sixth century AD (?) operation in the courtyard

After the construction during the second century AD of a wall closing the fountain courtyard to the south and the laying of an esplanade around it ca. 200 AD, the fountain courtyard was only accessible by a stairway that was repaired once more during the sixth century AD (Waelkens 1993c). During its reconstruction, some steps had to be removed in 1996, and cleaned and restored. This was done in successive stages so that small fills between the steps could be studied. The fill between the fourth and the fifth step from below was called layer 1 and contained a few sherds (SA 96 N 60). That between the lowest steps was identified as layer 2, which also produced some pottery (SA 96 N 66). Since the sherds from both 'layers' could be attributed to the last phase of the local production (AD 450-650), the present-day steps must have been rearranged shortly before the fountain courtyard was filled with debris at some time after the earthquake of AD 518 (see Waelkens 1993c). It is very unlikely that this rearrangement of the stairs would have been done after this catastrophe, since they had no longer any function.

6.4. The post-earthquake alterations of the sixth century AD

During the 1997 season, the fill inside the basins of the fountain house and that covering the second floor level was also completely removed, except for the stone supports

Fig. 137: View of the north basin. In the left part of the picture, the original mortar floor; in the centre, the sixth century AD wall used as a support for terracotta pipes.

Fig. 138: The terracotta pipe used as a drain for the second mortared floor level in the southeast corner of the west basin.

Fig. 139: View of layer 4 with its water-supply system (left), seen from the east. To the right, remains of the terracotta pipes inside layer 3.

Fig. 140: View of layer 3 with its water-supply system (left), seen from the northwest. To its right, the terracotta pipes in layer 4.

Fig. 141: View of the sondage from the northwest with, to the left, the water-supply system in layer 3, and behind it the terracotta pipes in layer 2.

Fig. 142: The water-supply system in layer 2, seen from the east.

Fig. 143: View of the mosaic floor of the pedestrian way to the northeast of the library with the late structure above it.

Fig. 144: The building protecting the library, seen from the southeast.

inside the north basin. After the AD 518 earthquake, the fountain house was no longer used as a public fountain: three holes were cut through the back wall of the north portico, so that the water within could be directly transported by three terracotta pipes to well-chosen spots within the city. These water-supply systems were partially supported by a wall made of re-used stones inside the north basin and inside the courtyard, while a deep earth fill thrown inside the basins and inside the courtyard formed at the same time a support and a protective cover (Waelkens 1993c).

Inside the northern and western basin, remains of two terracotta pipes, one of them still embedded in mortared rubble, were removed. The mortared rubble was called layer 2, the fill around it was separated into a western (layer 2) and an eastern half (layer 1). The pottery in these layers (SA 96 N 1 and 6) all belonged to phase 8 of the local production (AD 450-650). Layer 3 of the west basin contained a Sagalassos city coin dated to the reign of Caracalla, AD 197-217 (Scheers 2000, cat. 21: SA 97 NEB 13), while layer 1 in the north basin produced a coin of the *spes rei publicae* type, dated to the years 355-361 AD (Scheers 2000, cat. 61: SA 97 NEB 18). These finds only confirm the already accepted date for this final intervention at some time after the AD 518 earthquake.

7. THE NEON LIBRARY

7.1. The street to the east of the library

In 1996, in view of the construction of the east wall of the building to cover the remains of the Neon Library and its restored mosaics, a small sondage of 1.5 m by 5 m was carried out near the library's southeast corner. The 1990 excavations had exposed in front of the library a 13.50 m long and 4 m wide 'pavement' laid with black and white mosaics. Towards the east, a 1.25 m high stairway led to a continuation of this pavement at a higher level (Waelkens *et al.* 1991: 202-203, fig. 5; pl. xxviii b; Waelkens 1993a: 48, fig. 63). Later, this was identified as the remains of a pedestrian way of a colonnade running along the north side of the street connecting the upper agora with the theatre. Its *tesserae* of black and white limestone formed a geometric pattern of octagons, separated from one another by elongated hexagons. Every other side of the octagons and four sides of the hexagons formed the bases of black triangles. This pattern was framed at the edges by a black band and by a row of elongated black diamonds, which in the four corners were replaced by black triangles. A detailed study revealed that the library mosaics were contemporary with the floor of the pedestrian way for which a date during the second half of the fourth century AD, and most probably during the reign of Julian (AD 361-363), is suggested (Waelkens *et al.* 2000c, figs 4-5).

The 1996 sondage revealed that the higher section of the pedestrian way to the northeast of the section in front of the Neon Library had also been paved with mosaics (1543.07 to 1543.11 m a.s.l.). They form a simple geometric pattern of squares and triangles outlined in black *tesserae* against a white background and must be contemporary with the floor in front of the library (Fig. 143).

At some point the new mosaic floor had been partially destroyed for the construction of a simple rubble structure of roughly 1.50 m (E/W) by 1.75 m (N/S), of which only one course of stones was found *in situ* (see Fig. 143). The structure had collapsed towards the north and was filled inside with a large amount of rubble and tiles. To the east of it, the mosaic floor was covered with a lot of burnt material. All this was covered by a destruction or erosion layer (2), with a max. depth of 0.40 m, mainly made up of rubble. This layer also contained some third to fifth century AD coins (Scheers 2000, cat. 35, 196 and 233: SA 96 LE 14, *antoninianus* of Aurelian from AD 270-275; SA 96 LE 15, AE from AD 425-450; SA 96 LE 13, AE from the fourth-fifth centuries AD).

The function of the structure could no longer be established. Its dimensions suggest that it might have been an oven but the burnt material was found outside, not inside its remains. It should most probably be linked to the late fourth/early fifth century AD dwelling immediately to the east of the Library (Waelkens 1993b: 15).

7.2. The shelter for the Library.

The construction of a building to shelter the remains of the Neon Library, designed by Patrício and Ercan and financed by the **ABB Insurance Company** (Belgium), was started in 1995 and completed during the 1996 season. Its steel roof consists of five main trusses supported by removable steel columns. Galvanised steel panels with perfect insulation properties were used to roof over an area of roughly 17 m by 15 m. Curtain walls made of mortared rubble alternating with rows of brick fill the gaps between the steel columns.

The whole building was built in such a way that it is completely reversible and well integrated into the surrounding landscape. The roof, which follows what was the original slope before excavations started here in 1990, was covered by light volcanic material and earth. Plants from the immediate surroundings were inserted in it, so that the roof will eventually not look too obtrusive (Fig. 144).

The insurance company also financed the restoration of the mosaic floor. In 1996 and 1997, a team from the Başkent Meslek Yüksek Okulu (Ankara University) directed by Kökten and Şener completed the restoration of the fourth century AD mosaics inside and in front of the library building

(Waelkens *et al.* 2000c). Inside the building, wooden walkways were arranged for visitors (Fig. 145). The building was inaugurated and officially opened to the public on September 3, 1997.

8. THE DOMESTIC AREA 1

During the 1995 season, some 125 m² of a domestic unit in the central part of the city were excavated. They cover the southeast corner of sector 2450/2480, the southern half of 2455/2480, the western half of 2460/2480, the eastern half of 2450/2475, the western half of 2460/2475 and of 2460/2470, as well as the complete sectors 2450/2470, 2455/2475 and 2455/2470 of the new grid system (Fig. 146). In these sectors were discovered the remains of what most probably had been originally two terrace houses, located along the east side of one of the streets leading from the central part of the city to its upper quarters. Originally, these houses had been located on two successive terraces and were separated from one another by a narrow paved alley ('room V'). The 1995 campaign exposed only the southwest corner of the house on the upper terrace, where three rooms were identified (I-III), apparently destroyed by a fire during the first half of the sixth century AD.

Of the southern house, only one room (VI) was partially unearthed. It seemed to have been destroyed on the same occasion. It was assumed then that this catastrophe had been the AD 518 earthquake and that after this event the two houses, together with part of the street to the west of it ('rooms VII and VIII'), had been incorporated into a single housing unit, and the floor levels of the original structure raised with earthquake debris. Since no paved or covered floor levels were identified, it was assumed that they may have been removed before the final destruction of the building. In fact, stratigraphical evidence appeared to suggest that the 'new' house had been occupied for a rather short period during the sixth century AD, but that it had been soon abandoned and gradually filled in with destruction and erosion material before the remaining structure collapsed during the mid-seventh century AD earthquake (Waelkens *et al.* 1997b: 193-199).

In 1996, the 1995 excavation trench of Domestic Area 1 was enlarged to the west and north by opening another 25 m² corresponding with the eastern half of sector 2450/2480, the northern half of sector 2455/2480, the western half of sector 2460/2485 and the complete sector 2455/2485 (Fig. 146).

This campaign confirmed that the house contained two groups of rooms of a slightly different orientation in the north (rooms II-IV, IX and X) and south (rooms VI, VIII). A small paved inner courtyard (V), previously assumed to be an alley, and part of the street running west of the houses, which had been walled off to form another small outer courtyard (room VII), formed a gradual transition between the two former units.

The 1996 excavations focused on rooms III and IV, and on the northern part of room VII. In the northern part of the trench, after removing the topsoil (ca. 0. 30 m deep), the excavations stopped in layer 2. This layer, at least 1.80 m deep here, is clearly a debris layer that also includes material from buildings higher up the slope. The amount of archaeological material in it was very limited (pottery, almost no bone or metal). In these sectors, a new room (IX) of the house was discovered.

- Room IX:
Only the upper wall sections of this room were exposed. Its internal width is 3.755 m, its visible length is 6 m, but the northern extremity has not yet been reached. The west wall of the room was exposed over a length of 6 m. It is ca 1.30 m thick and made of two leaves with an internal cavity of ca.0.40 m. The outer face (vis. length: 5 m) is made of rubble, the inner one (vis. length: 6.10 m) of rubble alternating with courses of brick. The cavity may have served to collect rain water, since its southern extremity is located exactly above a deep gutter made of large tiles which is visible below the floor in the northwest corner of room III (Fig. 147). Against this inner face, a third rubble wall (length: 3.05 m; thickness: 0.55 m) was discovered at a lower level inside room IX. This brings the total thickness of the west wall in its final phase to 1.88 m, suggesting that room IX may have been vaulted or had to be well insulated from the exterior to keep the warmth inside. Recently, the 'gutter' in the northwest corner of room III (Fig. 149), has been identified as a toilet (Martens in press).

However, is likely that the cavity wall and the one built against its inner face were not constructed as part of the same building operation. The former was most probably built after room IX. In fact, the wall technique of the lower, inner section of the west wall is of a much better quality than that of the higher outer part (with the cavity) and identical with that of the room's south wall, built at a slightly oblique angle against it. This south wall, already excavated in 1995, consists of two mortared rubble segments at either side of a door opening (Waelkens *et al.* 1997b:197, fig. 48). It is possible that the mortared rubble alternated with brick courses in the higher levels of the wall.

The visible part of the room's east wall is again formed by a massive wall consisting of rows of brick and mortared rubble sections, still partly rendered with mortar. The southern half of the wall (vis. length: ca. 2.08 m; width: 1.25 m) survives to a higher level than the northern segment (length: 1.20 m; width: ca. 0.40 to 0.30 m), which is much thinner

Fig. 145: View inside the building protecting the Library after the 1997 inauguration.

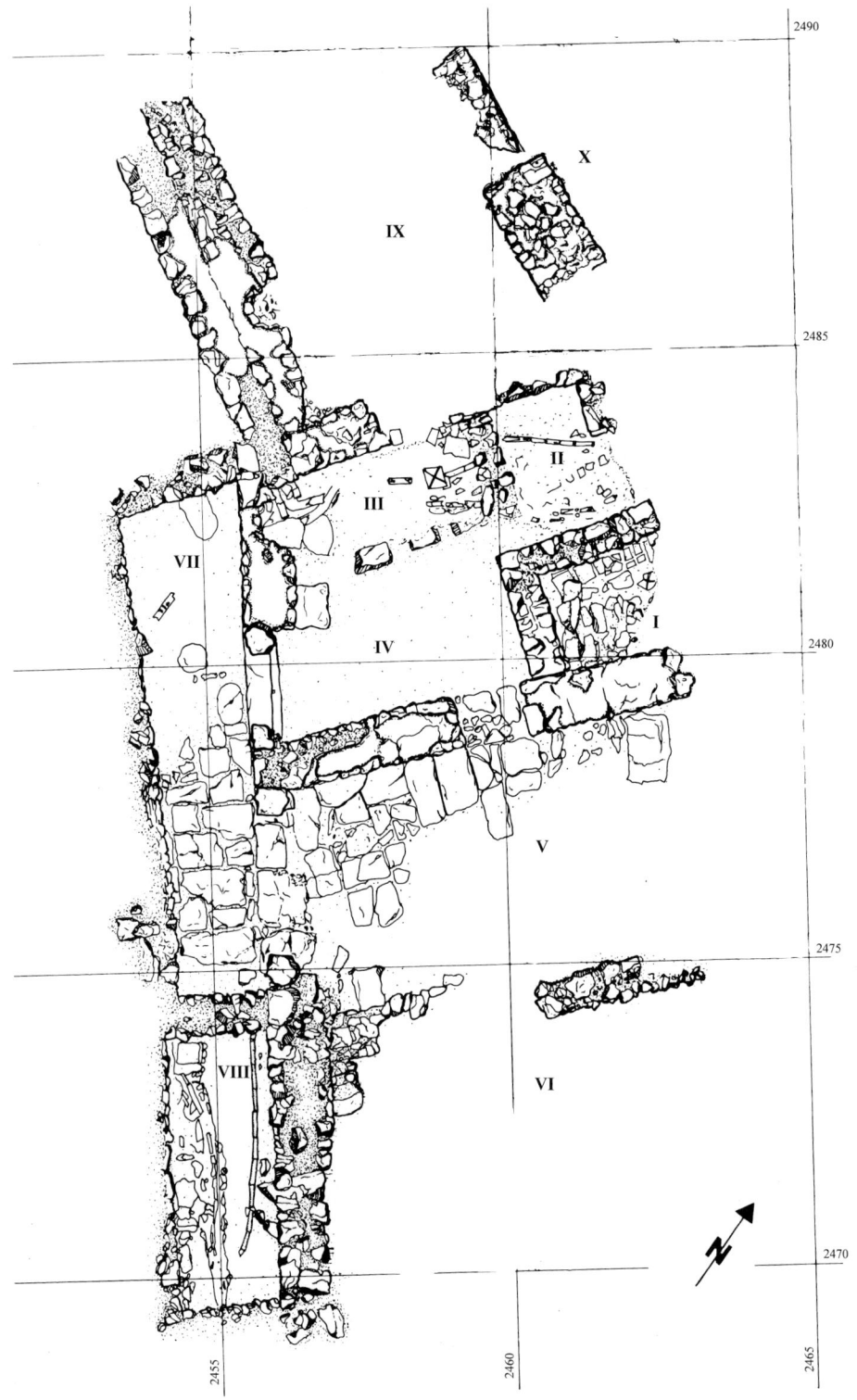

Fig. 146: Plan of Domestic Area I after the 1996 season.

Fig. 147: The inner courtyard III/IV at the level of layer 5E, with the cavity in the west wall of room IX above the water collecting arrangement in the northwest corner of the courtyard.

Fig. 148: The inner courtyard III/IV at the level of layer 5E, seen from the west.

Fig. 149: The water collecting arrangement (toilet) in the northwest corner of the inner courtyard III/IV.

Fig. 150: The outer courtyard VII with layer 5W covering the older street pavement. In the middle, the limestone block ('elbow') in which the terracotta pipes changed directions.

as if it might have contained a niche. It is not clear yet how this wall continues to the south. Since no floor level has been reached, the exact chronology of the successive building phases of room IX has not yet been established.

- The inner courtyard (III/ IV):

To the southwest of room IX, the excavations reached deeper levels inside the western part of rooms III and IV. These two rooms proved to have been in fact one single inner courtyard. Room II may have been another part of it, but was separated from the rest of the courtyard by a short low rubble wall, which either belonged to an older building phase or had been the base of a light structure (Waelkens *et al.* 1997b: fig. 148). The excavations went as deep as a layer 5E and produced the following stratigraphy:

- layer 5E (Figs 147-148): a ca. 0.20 m deep, rather compact layer (1498.324 m to 1498.97 m a.s.l.), full of bone and pottery. A lot of this material was burnt and clearly results from some sort of destructive activity. It corresponds with the layer 5 that was excavated in 1995 in rooms II and III and that contained pottery from the first half of the sixth century AD (Waelkens *et al.* 1997b: 194). The sherds recovered in 1996 (SA 96 DA1 67) could be dated to the last phase of the locally produced fine wares (mid-fifth to mid-seventh century AD). The layer also produced three coins, ranging in date from the first century BC to the fifth century AD (Scheers 2000, cat. 7, 161 and 272: SA 96 DA1 74, Sagalassos city coin from the first century BC; SA 96 DA1 68, a coin of the *gloria romanorum* type from the years 402-408 AD; SA 96 DA1 72 a bronze from the second half of the fourth/fifth centuries AD). Their date more or less corresponds with that of the 45 coins recovered from layer 5 in 1995. This layer also contained a well preserved part of weighing-scales, some rubble and bits of terracotta water pipe, spread over the whole area although in greater numbers along the north wall. Beside these traces of older (?) water-supply systems, layer 5E also contained two rather well preserved systems. The first ran in a northeast-southwest direction, while the second more or less followed the north wall to a water-collecting arrangement (a toilet) in the northwest corner of the courtyard, below the void in the outer west wall of room IX. This arrangement consists of a kind of funnel made of brick walls and floored with tiles (Fig. 149). The fact that this compact layer contained some nearly complete water systems and a water outlet (NW corner) shows that it was not just a destruction level, but rather a beaten earth floor made with debris from some fire catastrophe that must have occurred between the middle of fifth and the middle of the seventh century AD. If this fire was caused by an earthquake, which need not necessarily have been the case, the AD 518 catastrophe is the most likely candidate. If we are correct in believing that layer 5E was a beaten earth courtyard floor, we need no longer assume that the original floor level had been removed at a later date and that the house had been abandoned before it eventually collapsed.

- layer 4E: clearly a genuine destruction layer (1497.984 m a.s.l. to 1498.539 m a.s.l.) that covered the step of the door towards room VII. It is ca. 0.35 m deep, full of rubble, tiles and other archaeological material that is found in greater quantities and is more varied than that of layer 3 above it. It represents the collapse of the upper wall sections of the house. Its pottery (SA 96 DA1 51) can be dated to 450-650 AD, which probably means that the building was destroyed in the mid-seventh century AD earthquake.

- layer 3: another ca 0.60 m. deep destruction layer, containing fewer wall blocks. In this layer, a small statue base was found which may belong to some of the statue fragments found in 1995 (now in the Burdur museum). This layer also contained in the middle of the courtyard a concentration of roof tiles and, along the walls, large amounts of painted plaster. The layer most probably represents a gradual collapse of the parts of the house that had survived the earthquake. Its pottery (SA 96 DA1 35) is contemporary with that of layer 4E.

- layer 2: a ca. 0.70 m deep layer that corresponds with the debris and erosion material of layer 2 in room IX. It contained a huge amount of *tesserae*, some of them still embedded in mortar, as well as painted plaster fragments. These had most probably fallen down from an upper floor of the house or washed in from the northern slopes.

- The outer courtyard (VII):

The 1996 excavation exposed the remaining northern part of a small trapezoidal courtyard (west wall: 7.85 m; north wall: 2.07 m; east wall: 8.35 m; south wall: 1.50 m). This courtyard was formed by enclosing part of the street immediately to the west of courtyard III/IV with mortared rubble walls. While the part of it that was uncovered in 1995 still possessed its original paving slabs (Waelkens *et al.* 1997b: figs 153-154), the newly uncovered section had a beaten earth floor (Fig. 150). The following stratigraphy was established:

- layer 5W: a compact layer full of burnt material, identical with layer 5E inside courtyard III/IV. It covered the remains of the street and contained a largely destroyed water-supply system coming through the north wall. Originally, it had been connected to a hollow limestone block which formed an 'elbow' from which water had been distributed in two different directions (Fig. 150). Its pottery (SA 96 DA1 63) was contemporary with that of layer 5E. The layer contained one coin, dated to the reign of Honorius (AD 392-395; Scheers this volume, cat. 58: SA 96 DA1 58).

In the northern unpaved section of this small courtyard, layer 5W covered a vaulted tunnel running below the street level from north to south. This must clearly have been one of the

major sewage systems of Sagalassos and layer 5W must have represented the final walking level of this courtyard.
- layer 4W: a destruction layer (1498.816 m a.s.l. to 1499.018 m a.s.l.) containing contemporary pottery (SA 96 DA1 44) as that of layer 4E inside courtyard III/IV. It also contained a lot of burnt brick, and even parts of burnt mud-brick walls (from an upper floor?).
- layers 2-3: these two destruction and erosion layers had the same characteristics as the corresponding layers in the rest of the excavated zone.

- Conclusion: the 1996 season only confirmed that the mid-seventh century AD earthquake destroyed the early Byzantine occupation of housing unit DA 1, which had been rebuilt after a fire, possibly but not necessarily resulting from the AD 518 seismic catastrophe, had destroyed an older dwelling some time after the mid-fifth century AD. There was no new evidence for establishing the construction date of the house. The interior spaces excavated so far seem to have been mainly courtyards and small shelters with beaten earth floors. Room IX, however, of which only the upper wall sections were exposed, seems to represent a more elaborate, possibly vaulted room. There are also indications that the house comprised a rather elaborate upper floor level with painted wall plaster and mosaics, which may however have been partly made of mudbrick.

9. THE ROMAN BATHS (Fig. 151)

During the campaigns of 1994 and 1995, the southwestern part of a huge bath complex located to the east of the lower agora was excavated thanks to a generous grant from the family **L. Lamberts-Van Assche**. The complex comprises three superposed levels: a vaulted ground level, an intermediary *hypocaustum* floor, and the actual bathing complex on the first floor. The excavations of 1995 had revealed the remains of a first *caldarium* (1) of which the enormous brick vaulted ceiling had collapsed, thus destroying the room's marble paved floor and exposing the 1.25 m high *hypocaustum* system made of round terracotta pillars below.

The 1994-1995 campaigns also showed that, below this *hypocaustum*, there still existed a well-preserved brick-vaulted ground floor, accessible through a rectangular door in the west facade of the complex. The southwest corner of this floor was illuminated by a large rectangular window in the west and a by large vaulted opening (entrance?) in its south wall (Waelkens *et al.* 1997b: 199-205).

During the 1996 campaign, the excavations of the baths focused on the southern part of *caldarium* 1 and the adjoining parts of the same floor, both to the south and to the west of this room. The work was carried out in fourteen sectors of 25 m^2 each (2360/2390, 2360/2395, 2360/2400, 2365/2390, 2365/2395, 2365/2400, 2370/2385, 2370/2390, 2370/2395, 2370/2400, 2375/2380, 2375/2385, 2375/2390 and 2375/2395). They corresponded roughly with *caldarium* 1 located along the western edge of the baths, with the northern half of its *praefurnium* 1 immediately to the south of it, with the western edge of a second *caldarium* 2 on a slightly higher level to the southeast of the latter, and with the corresponding *praefurnium* 2 located to the south (Fig. 151). The western edge of *caldarium* 2 was composed of a pool (*alveus*) that contained an almost intact *hypocaustum* system with square pillars and arched wall sections.

The aim of the 1997 season was to excavate the remaining part of *caldarium* 1 and to obtain a clear picture of the situation in front of the southwest corner of the bath complex. Work was therefore focused on the northern part of *caldarium* 1, located in grids 2360/2405, 2365/2405, 2370/2405 and 2375/2405. The excavations exposed the complete room as far as the preserved marble floor along its eastern edge, and as far as the floor of the *hypocaustum* system in the rest of it. In grids 2370/2380, 2370/2385 and 2370/2390, *praefurnium* 1 was completely unearthed.

On the ground level, nine grids (2355/2380, 2355/2385, 2355/2390, 2360/2380, 2360/2385, 2360/2390, 2365/2380, 2365/2385 and 2365/2390) were excavated in front of the bath complex. During the same campaign, it also became possible to enter for the first time a series of well-preserved vaulted rooms on the ground level of the baths. In two rooms (1 and 4) the upper strata were excavated, while the other rooms were only entered for a quick examination.

9.1. Upper floor

9.1.1. *Caldarium* 1

This *caldarium,* located along the most northern of the 'angles' that form the western edge of the bath complex, was 13.50 m wide (E-W) and 16.50 m long (N-S). While its marble floor was still *in situ* along the eastern edge of the room, most of it had been crushed under the weight of the thick brick vaults that had fallen on it (Figs 152-153).
- the *hypocaustum*: its floor consisted of square floor tiles in the southern part and rectangular tiles in the northern part of the room (Fig. 154). A square tile supported each of the brick pillars. Close to the east wall the latter were square, but the others were round. Each pillar (total h.: 1.44 m) was covered by two square bricks of different sizes: 0.30 m by 0.30 m by 0.06 m and 0.40 m by 0.40 m by 0.06 m. They supported heavy terracotta slabs of 0.80 m by 0.80 m by 0.10 m. The interaxial distance of the brick pillars varied from 0.90 m to 1 m.

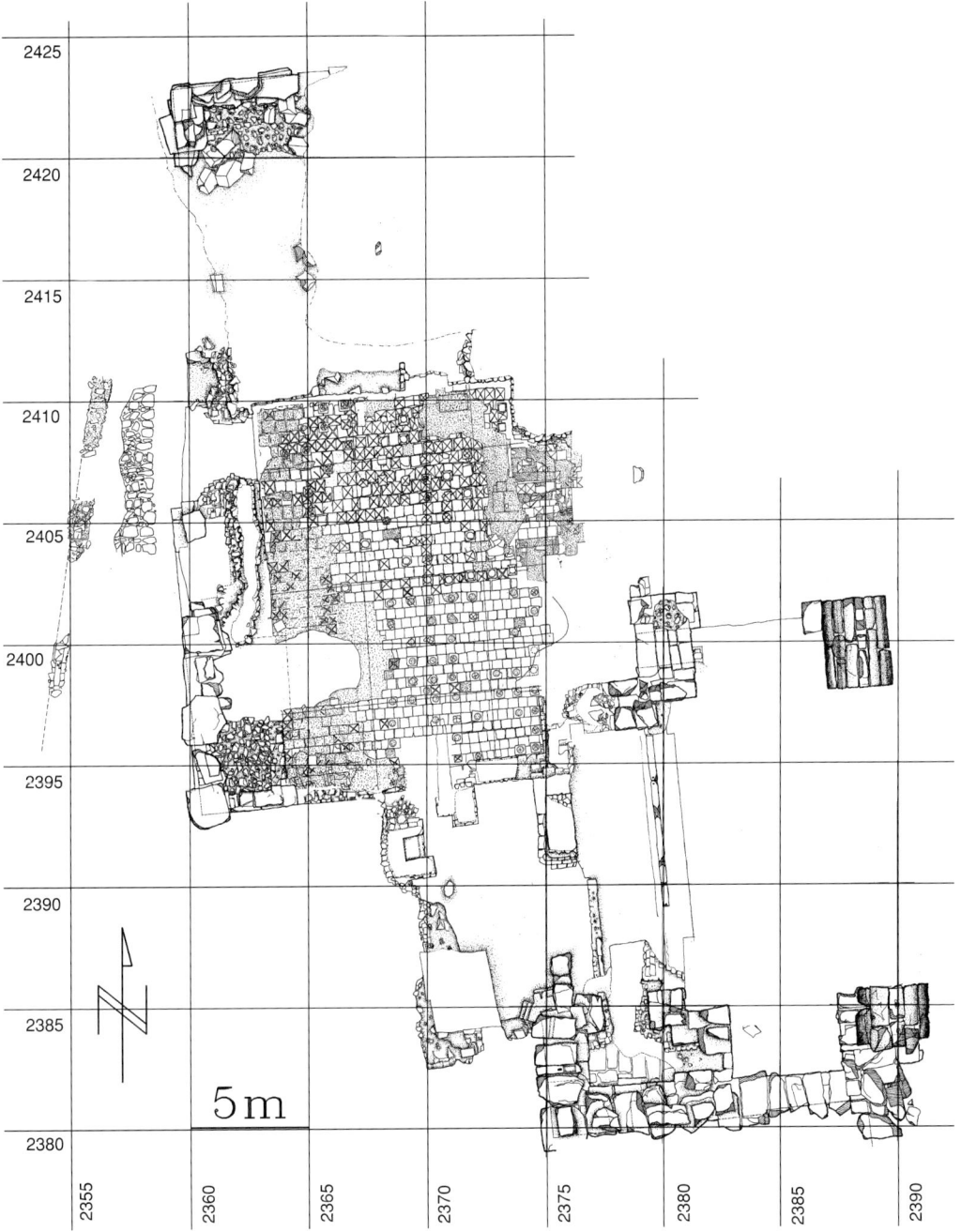

Fig. 151: Ground plan of the excavated section of the Roman Baths after the 1997 campaign.

Fig. 152: View of *caldarium* 1 from the north.

Fig. 153: *Caldarium* 1, seen from the southeast.

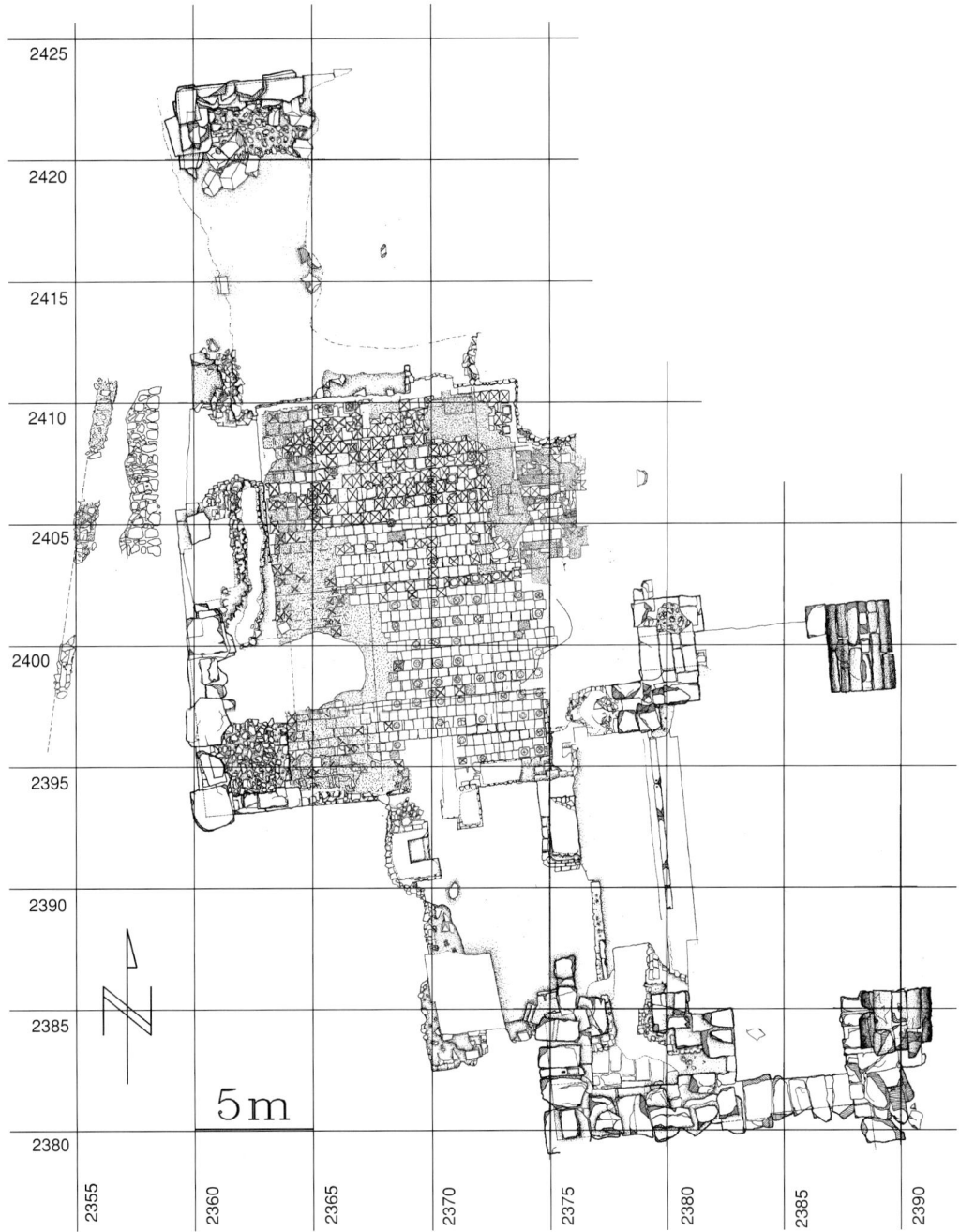

Fig. 151: Ground plan of the excavated section of the Roman Baths after the 1997 campaign.

Fig. 152: View of *caldarium* 1 from the north.

Fig. 153: *Caldarium* 1, seen from the southeast.

- the *caldarium* floor: the large terracotta slabs were covered by two mortar layers (Fig. 155): the lower one was 0.12 m thick and contained coarse fragments of broken ceramics, small pieces of wood and *tesserae*, and was of a greyish-pinkish color. The second, greyish layer above it, was only 0.055 m thick. It bore large marble slabs, some of them clearly re-used wall veneering slabs of different sizes. In grids 2370/2405 and 2375/2405 some of these slabs were still found *in situ*, while others had left a clear imprint in the mortar layer (Fig. 156). They were of rather large dimensions: 0.635 m by 0.34 m, 0.68 m by 0.50 m and 0.68 m by 0.68 m. These *in situ slabs* were located immediately to the west of the eastern passageway described below.

-the *caldarium* walls: the west wall was 3.20 m thick of which the exterior 1.25 m was composed of the ashlars of the building's west façade. The inner face consisted of mortared rubble alternating with brick courses. The south wall is almost completely gone today (Fig. 152), but seems to have been formed by a 1.90 m thick mortared rubble wall. This certainly no longer represented the original façade, which must have been made of ashlars and had perhaps been destroyed during the AD 518 earthquake, which seems to be the most logical explanation for its disappearance. The north wall, which was a partition wall, is 1.95 m thick and built of alternating layers of square bricks and mortared rubble (Fig. 153). In sector 2370/2405 it still contained some of the metal clamps for keeping the marble wall veneering *(crustae)* in place. In the corner of this sector, the wall showed traces of burning, especially on the bricks and mortar layers. The east wall of the room seems to have been built in the same technique as the north wall, but also included ashlar sections and has not yet been excavated. In sectors 2375/2395 and 2375/2400, it comprised an ashlar passageway, which is aligned, albeit at much a higher level (in fact on the first floor), with the window in the ground floor façade to the west (Room IV). This seems to indicate that at least some wall systems continue throughout the various floors. Some gray-pinkish mortar, but no *crustae*, was still attached to the lower courses of the passageway. Several metal clamps used to attach the various types of *crustae* to the wall were found around it. The above-mentioned sectors also produced bricks with small circular holes, most probably the remains of clamp holes. Near the northeast corner of the passageway, a short brick wall (0.62 m thick) continued eastward. It seems to represent the north wall of *caldarium* 2. The enormous thickness of the walls was necessary to support a large brick and mortared rubble vault of which the largest thrust came down on the west and east walls of the *caldarium*.

Inside *caldarium* 1, nearly 40 tons of wall-veneer in Docimian marble were recovered (Waelkens *et al.* in press). Some panels of the latter were inscribed in an exquisitely fine lettering, apparently dating from the second century AD, or carried graffiti.

The walls of *caldarium 1* had been completely covered with marble slabs. The long walls seem to have been divided into panels by half-pilasters in marble, supporting Corinthian pilaster capitals (Fig. 157). The latter bore a false entablature consisting of a fasciated architrave and a cornice with dentils. Along the upper edge of the short sides ran similar marble archivolts. In between the pilasters, the wall sections were divided into rectangular moulded panels. The marble veneering of the room consisted of various varieties of Docimian marble (*pavonazetto,* Afyon *bal,* Afyon *şeker*). At least some of the slabs and architectural elements may have been re-used. For the moment it is very difficult to see how many building phases are represented among the dozens of capitals and other decorative elements. At this stage of the excavation, only the Corinthian capitals provided clues for the following dating effort by L.Vandeput, but even this information is not uniform.

The pilaster capitals are built up of one or two rows of acanthus leaves, topped by volutes and helices. Caules and bracts are completely absent. However, the actual shape of the acanthus of the individual capitals varies strongly. A similar variation occurs among the capitals from the late Antonine period at Sagalassos, especially in the nymphaeum on the upper agora, which was attributed to the reign of Marcus Aurelius (Vandeput 1997a: 104-105, pls 4; 3-4; Vandeput 1997b: 402-403, figs 1-2, 9-10). Both acanthus of the 'normal' type and several simplified shapes are represented on the capitals and the consoles of this monument. At first glance, the different types of acanthus on the pilaster capitals of the baths compare very well with those of the nymphaeum. The acanthus leaves of the 'normal' type from the Antonine nymphaeum (Vandeput 1997a: pl. 43.4) and from *caldarium* 1 (Fig. 158) are especially closely related to one another, so that an Antonine date for the marble decoration of *caldarium* 1 seemed to be a reasonable possibility. However, some of the capitals have 'twisted' acanthus leaves (Fig. 159), as became popular in late Roman times. Moreover, whereas some capitals have nicely carved leaves (see Fig. 158), others are heavily drilled (Fig. 160). Since it is known that the designs and acanthus shapes of the second century AD stood as a model for those of later periods (Kramer 1994: 8), several if not all presently known capitals from *caldarium* 1 may well date from the later third or fourth century AD. Parallels from this period can be found, both in the general lay-out and in specific details, such as the shape of the helices and the volutes. In fact, some of the *caldarium* capitals (Fig. 160) have the typical 'snail-like' volutes that are characteristic of late Roman times (Kramer 1994: 8-9), whereas others compare very well with late third-fourth century AD examples from Kramer's catalogue (1994: 132-135, pls 5 and 6: catalogue numbers 28-35). In view of their monumental size, it is very unlikely that the baths were built towards the end of the third or during the fourth century AD. More recent campaigns in the meantime confirmed that the construction of the vaulted ground levels goes back as far as the early second century AD. However, the dimensions of the complex suggest that its completion may have taken several generations. One also has to bear in mind that the huge building may have undergone several repairs or restorations, some of them due to earthquake damage. During these interventions the function of some rooms may have been altered, and some of the original veneering may have been moved and re-used together with later material. As far as *caldarium* 1 is concerned, no apparent alteration of the room's function was noticed, so it may have functioned as a hot water room since the beginning.

For the moment, the most plausible, although complex, explanation seems to be that some of the wall veneer of *caldarium* 1 (certainly the re-used inscribed panels, perhaps some capitals) goes back to the second century AD, most likely to the Antonine period, whereas most of it should be linked to an extensive intervention during the later third-fourth centuries AD, which re-used the older material. Theoretically, it is still possible that, during these interventions, at least the northern section of the *caldarium*'s west façade was rebuilt. In fact, in order to repair the broken door lintel of a doorway at the ground level of this wall, part of the courses above it, which now form the outer facing of the *caldarium*'s west wall, had to be removed. They proved to have belonged to the Doric architrave of an older structure, of which the original front with the *regula* and *guttae* is still preserved on the inward face of the wall, although totally obscured by the mortared rubble inner lining of the facade (Waelkens *et al.* 1997b: 203 fig.163). However, the date of this recycling can no longer be established, so that it is possible that these building elements were actually re-used at the time of the original construction of the complex. In fact, when the Antonine nymphaeum was built on the upper agora, the terrace wall behind it was also raised by means of re-used architectural elements (Waelkens *et al.* 1997b: 137). A study of all building parts will hopefully permit a more precise chronology.

It is also difficult to date the construction of the present *hypocaustum* floor. However, the renewal of the wall veneering during the later third-fourth century AD seems to have been quite drastic, so that it may have been part of a larger building programme. It is possible therefore that the floor was also altered at the same occasion. Some of the marble slabs are clearly re-used wall veneering slabs. Traces of interventions along the east wall, in which another type of *hypocaustum* pillars (square ones instead of round ones) were introduced, seem to be connected with the creation of a *tepidarium* (see 9.1.2) and a second *caldarium* (9.1.4) on the other side of the wall, where similar square *hypocaus-*

tum pillars were found. Theoretically, the rounded pillars could go back to the original second century AD layout, and the square ones to a drastic intervention during the later third-fourth centuries AD. This would have involved the creation of a new *caldarium* (9.1.4) and a new *tepidarium* (9.1.2) in the central part of the building, the construction of a new extension of the complex between the first and the second angle of the west facade (9.2.2 and 9.2.3) in order to support a new *praefurnium* (9.1.3), and the complete renewal of the wall veneering inside *caldarium* 1. Yet, for the moment we are more inclined to believe that, except for the last intervention, the rest of the above mentioned building programme was carried out at a later date. In fact, there is evidence for later interventions. The debris inside the *caldarium* contained not only several stamped tiles (Loots *et al.* 2000b), but also a brick fragment with a Christian graffito ("*Lord help us*"), showing that the building was still repaired in Christian times. The excavations of the destruction layers, especially those inside *caldarium* 1, also produced a substantial number of fourth and fifth century AD coins (Scheers 2000, s.v. C. Roman Baths, layers 2 and 3). While some of them may have been lost inside the building, others had most probably been mixed accidentally with the mortared rubble and concrete of walls and vaults. This evidence could suggest that, even after its renewal in late antiquity (later third-fourth centuries AD), the bath complex still underwent repairs, most probably because of the AD 518 earthquake. This catastrophe also seems to be the best explanation of why the south facade of *caldarium* 1, in the final stages of the building was no longer made of ashlar, but rebuilt in mortared rubble and bricks. The construction of an extension in the same material, housing two new heating places immediately to the south of it, was most probably done as part of the same repair. As a result, for the time being, it seems more reasonable to attribute the final transformation of the building to a period after the fourth century AD, most probably after AD 518.

Inside *caldarium* 1, the following stratigraphy was observed:
- layer 4: a 0.07 m deep ash layer covering the *hypocaustum* floor.
- layers 3: a dark brownish 0.50 m deep layer, containing a lot of building ceramics (roof tiles, brick vault fragments, square and round tiles of the *hypocaustum* pillars) and disintegrated mortar. This layer mainly contained elements from the collapsed *caldarium* floor and from the *hypocaustum* below it, together with parts of the collapsed ceiling and walls (two chunks of bricks and mortared rubble had a weight of 1150 and 1980 kg, respectively). Large chunks of the collapsed ceiling of *caldarium 1* were still lying in a slanted position when discovered. They had destroyed most of the *hypocaustum* system in sectors 2370/2395 and 2370/2400. The hypocaustum floor to the west of it had

Fig. 154: The *hypocaustum* pillars in the southeast corner of *caldarium* 1.

Fig. 155: View of the double mortar layer between the *caldarium* floor and the supporting pillars.

Fig. 156: The preserved *caldarium* floor section against the east wall of the room.

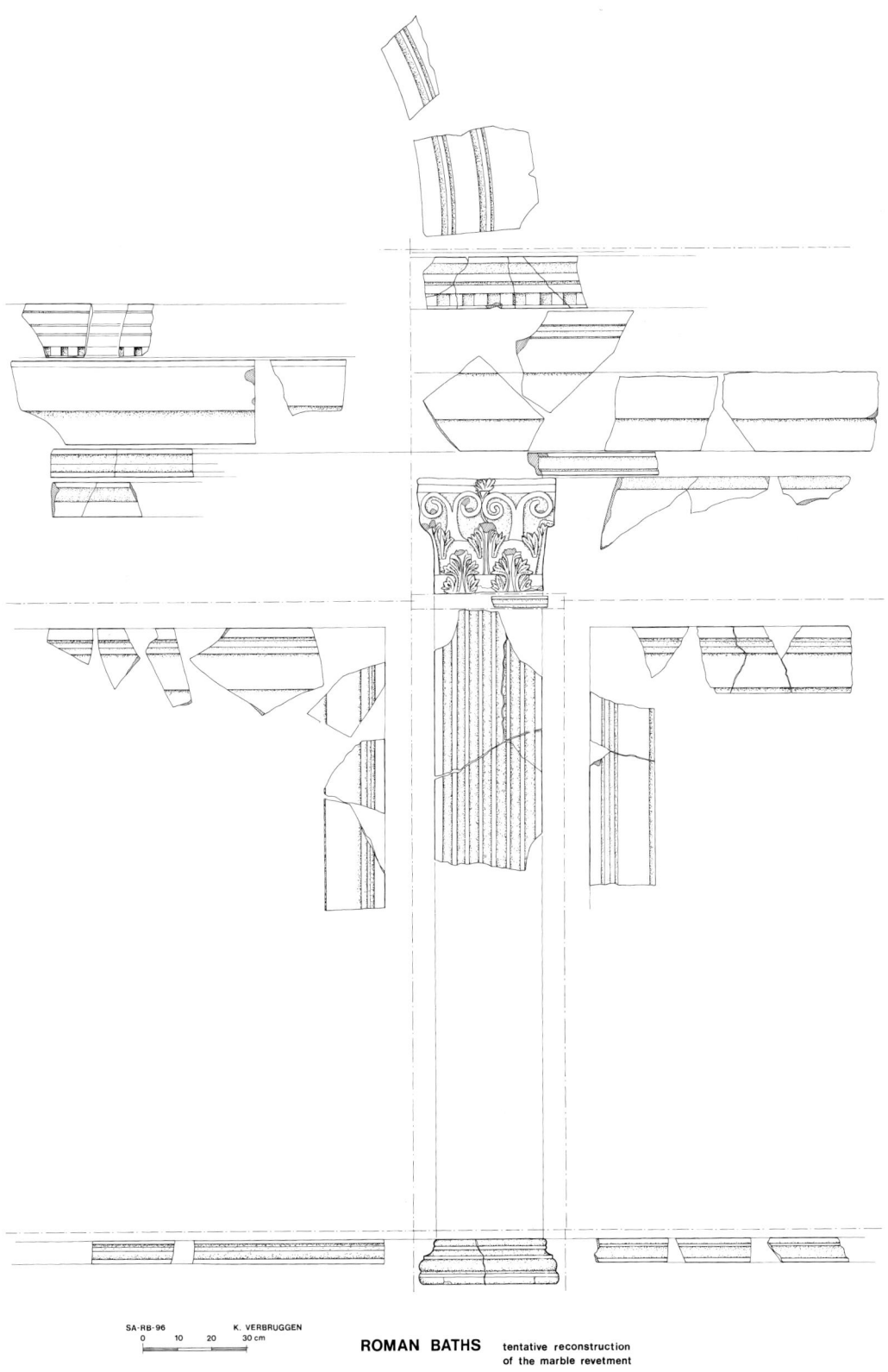

Fig. 157. Composition of the false architecture in the wall veneering of *caldarium* 1.

Fig. 158: Pilaster capital of the 'normal' type from *caldarium* 1.

Fig. 159: Pilaster capital with twisted leaves from *caldarium* 1.

Fig. 160: Pilaster capital with 'snail-like' volutes and drilled leaves from *caldarium* 1.

Fig. 161: View of the heating channels between *caldarium* 1 and the *tepidarium* to the east of it.

Fig. 162: The southwest angle of the Roman baths seen from the west. The three arched openings in the ground level belong to room 1, which was added later and supports *praefurnium* 1.

Fig. 163: *Praefurnium* 1 seen from the south. The actual firing place is seen in the left half of the picture; to the right of it, the northeast corner that was filled with ashes.

completely collapsed, but in the zones towards the north and the south, most of the round pillars were still standing. The lower levels of layer 3 also contained a large number of beautiful Corinthian capitals that were dated to between the Antonine period and the fourth century AD (Figs 158-160).
- layer 2: a very deep brownish-grey destruction layer of nearly 2 m depth. It contained a lot of disintegrated mortar, rubble, building ceramics from vaults and inner walls (e.g. roof tiles, wall and vault bricks), parts of rounded columns, some tufa blocks and big limestone ashlars from the outside walls and from the supporting structures inside the building, bone, *tesserae* and metal. This material clearly comes from the collapsed upper part of the whole structure. Inside *caldarium* 1, the layer contained various concentrations (among others, at the edge of sector 2370/2405 and in sector 2380/2400) of mostly moulded marble *crustae*, as well as some burnt spots. More *crustae* were found deeper inside layer 2. Two large limestone consoles were also discovered, while in sector 2375/2400 part of a collapsed brick vault from the ceiling of *caldarium* 1 was exposed. Several huge cornice blocks had to be removed near the southwest corner of the room. There were plenty of inscribed tiles (with single letters) as well as different stamped tiles (Loots *et al.* 2000b).
- topsoil: was full of rubble and brick fragments.

9.1.2. A *tepidarium* (?)

In sectors 2370/2405 and 2370/2450, near the northeast corner of *caldarium* 1, its *hypocaustum* system was connected with a corresponding system from a space in the angle between *caldarium* 1 to the west and *caldarium* 2 to the south. Since this room was situated at a considerable distance from both *praefurnia*, it may have served as a tepid room or *tepidarium*. The height of its *hypocaustum* floor was the same as that of the corresponding floor of the southern *caldarium*, so that it may stem from the same building phase as the latter. It also seems to be provided with the same square *hypocaustum* pillars. A vaulted passage at the *hypocaustum* level gave access to three heating channels (width: 0.60 m) connected to one another by corbelled triangular vaults in the brick walls between the channels (Fig. 161). Several details indicate alterations to the system. The floor tiles here also were of different dimensions (0.73 m by 0.73 m by 0.05 m).

9.1.3. The *praefurnium* 1

The heating room of *caldarium* 1 was located to the south of it and seems to have been added later, since its outer walls were not made of ashlar, but of bricks throughout, and since it is supported below by a room (1: see 9.2.2) with mortared rubble and brick walls, which clearly represents a later addition to the bath complex (Fig. 162). The interior dimensions of the heating room were 10.20 m by 5 m (Fig. 163). The fireplace itself was in the northwest corner and projected 0.80 m inside the room. The hot air was conducted to the *hypocaustum* system of *caldarium 1* (Fig. 164) via a small brick vaulted corridor (width: 0.50 m; length: 2.40 m). To the east of this vent, but only in this area, the earth covering the tile floor (layer 4) was dark grey to black and eventually became a pure ash layer.

The two uppermost layers inside the room were identical in character with those inside *caldarium* 1 and represent debris from the collapsed side walls and vault. Below them, the following strata could be identified:
- layer 4: this lowest stratum contained an enormous amount of bone from cows, birds, and especially ovicaprines (goat and sheep), as well as glass, lots of pottery (SA 96 RB 1 194, mostly kitchen-wares, but also some finer table wares, from the last phase of the local production, AD 450-650), and eight coins. The latter all belong to the fourth-fifth centuries AD (Scheers 2000, cat. Roman Baths, *praefurnium* 1, layer 4). However, none of the objects, except for the rim and base sherds of the cooking pots, showed any trace of burning. This implies that these remains belong to a spoil heap that may have been dumped here after the *praefurnium* had become disused.
- layer 3: this layer produced lots of ceramics, two coins dated to the second half of the fourth and the fifth century AD (Scheers 2000, cat. 279-280: SA 96 RB 221 and 225), small metal pins, large clamps, nails, some metal instruments, lots of window glass, small rim fragments of glass vessels, and large quantities of animal bones. This layer must also represent the upper part of the same dump. It contained two coins dated to the second half of the fourth/fifth century AD (Scheers 2000: cat. 279 and 280).

Since this dumped material was covered by the actual destruction layer of the Roman Baths, *caldarium* 1 and its corresponding *praefurnium* must have been abandoned before an earthquake destroyed both spaces around the mid-seventh century AD.

9.1.4. The *caldarium* 2

To the south of the ashlar passageway inside the bath building (Fig. 165), inside sectors 2375/2385, 2375/2390 and 2375/2395), the western edge of a second *caldarium (2)* was exposed together with its *praefurnium* (heating system) located to the south of it. Significant concentrations of bricks around the passageway probably derived from the collapsed ceiling of this second *caldarium*, of which only some 2 m along the western edge have been unearthed thus far. This part of the space is occupied by the remains of a large plunge pool (*alveus*) of ca. 10 m by 2 m. The excavated part contained a piece of broken parapet with an early

Byzantine graffito, which had fallen inside the pool (Fig. 166), as well as lots of window glass.

- the *hypocaustum*: the *caldarium* floor is supported by a *hypocaustum* system (h.: 1.47 m) made of mostly square (Figs 167-168) pillars and rows of vaults, which is 0.03 m higher than the pillar *hypocaustum* system below *caldarium* 1. There are also traces of heart-shaped pillars, made up of three round pillars built against one another (Fig. 169). The vaults (Fig. 170) most probably supported the parapet of the pool, which has not yet been found inside *caldarium* 2. Both pillars and vaults are covered with soot. Inside this *hypocaustum* system a plastic comb and a rusted metal bottle cap were found, indicating that people must have ventured inside previously during the twentieth century.
- the *caldarium* floor: the floor of the pool seems to be almost intact. Even parts of the marble slabs were still found *in situ* (Fig. 171). Some of them were re-used *crustae*. They covered a deep mortar layer above several layers of floor tiles
- the walls: so far none of the side walls has really been excavated, but clamp holes on the northwestern ashlar corner of the pool, which in the final building phase were hidden by *tubuli* of the heating system of the walls, indicate that this room originally must have had a function other than as a *caldarium*. This is also confirmed by the fact that, at a later date, a passage in the southwest ashlar pier of the room had also been blocked by the construction of a fireplace inside *praefurnium* 2.

Below layers 1 and 2, identical in composition and finds with the corresponding strata elsewhere in the complex, the floor of the pool was covered by a thin, dark-coloured, sandy layer (layer 3), which could represent the decantation material from the pool's last water content.

9.1.5. The *praefurnium* 2

This second *caldarium* was heated by means of a *praefurnium* of 6 m by 2.50 m, located in the second (calculated from the north) southwest 'angle' of the bath complex, in sectors 2375/2380 and 2380/2380). There was a large window in its western facade (Fig. 172). In front of it, a lot of coloured window glass (blue, green) was found. Along the room's eastern edge, a brick vault contained two terracotta pipes set at different heights, which probably led to chimneys in the roof and may have been used for regulating the heat inside (Fig. 173). This vaulted fireplace had blocked a former entrance to the room, which had originally connected it to the space then occupied by *caldarium* 2.

A small 3.60 m long and 0.80 m wide vaulted passage made of bricks, which functioned as a vent for the hot air, was connected via four arched openings (two on its northern and two on its western extremity) with the *hypocaustum* system of *caldarium* 2 (Fig. 174).

The pavement of the room consists of large ashlar slabs some of which bore lines showing the original placement of now gone walls. It was clear from this that the room must originally have served another purpose than that of being a heating room. In the eastern extremity of the room, below the vaulted structure with the ventilation pipes (Fig. 173), these original pavement slabs were partly covered by a 0.15 m thick floor (layer 4) composed of a rubble layer with tiles on top. Since the tiles were completely burnt, this floor may represent the actual fireplace, while the already mentioned terracotta pipes immediately above and behind it may have functioned as *tuyères* to increase the temperature. The purpose of this arrangement may have been to protect the limestone ashlars and slabs from the excessive heat of the fireplace.

In fact, along the western extremity of the room and inside the heating channel, no tile floor has been found. The heating channel linking the *praefurnium* with the southern *caldarium's hypocaustum* shows two consecutive building phases, in which at a later date a new brick wall was built against an older brick structure, thus narrowing the width of the vent. This shows that *praefurnium* 2 had been altered at least once after its original layout.

Below the two uppermost layers, which correspond with the destruction layers elsewhere in the bath complex, *praefurnium* 2 contained a layer 3 (0.25 to 0.30 m deep), blackish in color and containing pieces of charcoal. This layer, which covered the pavement of the room, was rather loosely packed. The lowest 0.02 m, probably representing the remains of heating activities, were very black and contained a greater concentration of charcoal. The upper part of the layer contained smaller chunks of charcoal, lots of *crustae*, glass, and some ceramics. A column was also discovered, about 0.90 m high and 0.25 m thick, broken in 7 pieces, which probably fell down from the room above, together with a number of tufa building blocks.

Near the southwest corner of the room, layer 3 also contained a root, which ran from an opening in the southern wall and crossed the room. A piece of this root, which was most probably intrusive, has been preserved for further study. Further excavations should reveal the original function of *praefurnium* 2.

9.2. The ground floor

9.2.1. The area in front of the bath complex

In the area immediately to the west of the bath complex, nine grids (2355/2380, 2355/2385, 2355/2390, 2360/2380, 2360/2385, 2360/2390, 2365/2380, 2365/2385 and 2365/2390) were excavated in 1997. Here the terrain sloped

Fig. 164: The heating channel between *praefurnium* 1 and *caldarium* 1.

Fig. 165: The ashlar passageway connecting *caldarium* 1 to *caldarium* 2.

Fig. 166: Parapet block from the plunge pool with an early Byzantine graffito.

Fig. 167: View of the square pillars belonging to the *hypocaustum* system below *caldarium* 2.

Fig. 168: View inside the *hypocaustum* system below *caldarium* 2.

Fig. 169: Remains of a heart-shaped pillar made up of three round pillars.

Fig. 170: The vaulted structure inside *hypocaustum* 2, below the supposed parapet of the pool above it.

Fig. 171: The floor of the plunge pool along the western edge of *caldarium* 2, seen from the north.

Fig. 172: View of the window in *praefurnium* 2, seen from the west.

Fig. 173: View of the vaulted brick containing a ventilation system against the east wall of *praefurnium* 2.

Fig. 174: View of the heating channel connecting *praefurnium* 2 with the *hypocaustum* system of *caldarium* 2.

rather steeply. This slope originally started from the northern *caldarium* (1) on the first floor and gradually sloped down towards the south-southwest. The following stratigraphy was observed:
- layer 1: a topsoil of ca. 0.30 m depth, which covered the original slope. It contained *tesserae*, glass, ceramics, tiles (some of them stamped) and metal.
- layer 2: a 1 to nearly 2 m deep destruction layer containing ceramics, glass, *crustae, tesserae* bone and metal. This layer also contained segments of collapsed rubble walls. This layer became very deep towards the east.

During the 1996 and 1997 campaigns it became clear that there is a clear correspondence between the inner walls at ground level and those in the upper floor, as all the supporting structures seem to continue right through the *hypocaustum* level in between them. Some of the ground-level rooms, which are either partly or largely filled with earth, mortar and rubble were entered during the 1996 season. Some of them were excavated the year after (Fig. 175). For the time being, the following rooms can be described or were (partially) excavated:

9.2.2. Room 1

This room is between the first and the second southwest angle of the ashlar section of the baths (measured from the north). Its different building materials, mortared rubble and brick, used for the exterior walls clearly indicate that this room must be interpreted as a later addition to the original bath complex (Figs 176-177). The building technology of the room also distinguishes it from the much more carefully constructed brick vaults in rooms 2, 3 and 4. Moreover, its east wall is clearly built against the already existing corridors 1, 2 and 3 (see below and Fig. 179). The purpose of this room was to bear *praefurnium* 1. Originally, it was connected to a now collapsed room located immediately to the south of it (see 9.2.3), and must have been part of the final transformation of the bath complex, when *caldarium* 1, which in its current shape mostly dates back to the fourth century AD, received a new *praefurnium*. Also, a large hall located to the southeast of it, was converted into a second *caldarium*, heated by a *praefurnium* inside a small corner room in the second southwest angle of the baths (9.1.5). The date of this conversion cannot yet be established, but at the earliest it would be during the fourth century AD, when *caldarium* 1 had most of its walls veneered; however, most probably, it was somewhat later. In fact, the construction of room 1 and of a collapsed room to the south of it (see 9.2.3) seems to have been part of a single building phase during which a large hall to the east was converted into a second caldarium and during which both *praefurnia* were established in this corner. As we have already mentioned above, it seems most likely to have been after the damage caused to the city by the AD 518 earthquake. Only the upper fill of room 1 was removed during the 1997 campaign.

The space (8 m by 3.50 m) occupied by room 1 is also much smaller than that of most of the other rooms located on the ground level of the baths. Room 1 has a vaulted ceiling (h. in the middle today: 2.60 m), made of alternating rows of tufa blocks and bricks, and is oriented north-south. The north wall is built of rubble combined with ashlar blocks. An older doorway or window opening towards room 4 here had been blocked up at a later date. The south wall is entirely made of bricks and contains a 1.50 m wide doorway, with a staircase leading into the collapsed room to its south (Fig. 178). The east and west walls are brick walls, intersected by three vaulted openings. Of those in the west wall the two outer ones must have functioned as windows, while the central one was a doorway (Fig. 177). The north window is 1.40 m wide, the south window, originally 1.25 m wide was later narrowed to 0.60 m. The central door is 1.65 m wide.

The three vaulted openings in the east wall gave access to three corridors, numbered one to three from north to south. It is clear however that these corridors correspond with an older arrangement and that the 1 m thick east wall of room 1 had been built against them (Fig. 179). Corridor 1 is 6.05 m long and 1.50 m wide and consists of a single brick vault supported by rubble walls. It ends in a *cul de sac* against a rubble wall and is not visible in the corresponding west wall of room 2. Corridor 3 (the southern one) is completely identical with the first one except for the fact that its east wall contains horizontal rows of bricks. A pile of small stones showing evidence of a small fire together with remnants of plastic found inside corridor 3 shows that the corridor had been entered during the twentieth century. Corridor 3 also contained eggshells and small animal bones. Between these two corridors, there is another corridor, which gives access to room 2. The first meter of this corridor, corresponding with the thickness of the east wall of room 1 is wider (1.90 m) than the original part of the corridor (1.45 m). The latter is 7.25 m long and has a double brick vault supported by mortared rubble walls. It nicely intersects with the brick ceiling of room 2.

9.2.3. A collapsed room to the south of room 1

In 1997, the remains of another mortared rubble and brick structure were unearthed and left *in situ* immediately to the south of room 1 and to the west of *praefurnium* 2 (see 9.1.5, in sector 2370-2380 (Fig. 180). They belonged to a collapsed vaulted room, which could be reached from room 1 through a door with a small stairway (Fig. 178). This room must have been built simultaneously with room 1, at the time when a new *praefurnium* (no. 2) was established inside the corner room of the second southwest angle (seen from the north) of the receding bath complex.

After this conversion, the now collapsed room must have provided the only possible access to *praefurnium* 2 located at a higher level immediately to its east, which henceforth was only accessible through the former window in its west wall. At the same time, the collapsed room must have provided the only possible entrance to *praefurnium* 1, located immediately to the north of it, although on a higher level. In fact, during the final phase of use of the bath complex, both *praefurnia* could only be entered from the space located directly above the collapsed room. The stepped entrance in its north wall (Fig. 178) therefore may have continued as a stairway leading to a room directly above it.

The fact that room 1 and its collapsed neighbour to the south are built with a different material (rubble and brick walls) from the usual ashlar of the complex's outer walls, together with the fact that the room housing *praefurnium* 2 originally had a different function, show that in late antiquity the bath complex must have undergone yet further (a) considerable change(s). For the time being, it looks as if *caldarium* 2 may only have become a heated room during the final stage of the building's use. However, as we have said above, the datable parts of the northern *caldarium*'s wall veneer seem to indicate a (re)construction date of that room during the fourth century AD, with possible later alterations. The fact that their *hypocaustum* systems were built using a different technique (shape of the pillars) and to a different height, suggest that the construction of the *caldaria* was not carried out at the same time. The use of square pillars along the eastern edge of the northern *caldarium*'s *hypocaustum*, instead of rounded pillars as found in the rest of the room, but corresponding in layout with the pillars in *caldarium* 2, might reflect a repair at the time when *caldarium* 2 was laid out as a hot-water bath. The fact, however, that their *praefurnia* do seem to have be laid out as part of a single building phase and that, contrary to *caldarium* 2 (see *praefurnium* 2), no obvious change could be discerned in the function of *caldarium* 1, might suggest that the latter had already functioned as a *caldarium* before the final transformation of the complex. In that case, its original *praefurnium* must have been located elsewhere.

Some remains of the mortared rubble and brick wall sections belonging to the collapsed rooms (on ground and first floor), which eventually gave access to both *praefurnia*, measure up to 1.5 m in length and ca. 1 m in width. These remains also included several vaulted features. One wall fragment still contained two terracotta pipes. Below one of the smaller wall sections, a very brittle powder-like 'mortar' with green inclusions was found. Some of the wall remains were completely black (called layer 3) as the result of a fire. A completely burnt root was also found below the 'window' in the west wall of the southern *praefurnium*. Most probably, it is connected with the burnt layer 3. The find location of the wood, together with the fact that at this point the ashlar wall of the baths as well as the southern part of sector 2370-2380 are of a definite black colour, could suggest a connection with the black layers found inside both *praefurnia*, or indicate that the collapsed room was destroyed by fire.

Above its remains, the following stratigraphy was unearthed in sector 2370-2380:
- Layer 2: this deep layer (up to 2 m) was light brown in color and loosely compacted. The depth is difficult to estimate as the area slopes. Moreover, the end of this layer was not reached everywhere. The inclusions found in it were rubble, building ceramics and disintegrated mortar. This extensive layer should be interpreted as a destruction layer containing the debris from the collapsed southwest corner of the baths (destroyed by an earthquake?).
- Layer 1: this ca. 0.25 m deep layer was of a dark brown color and a very loosely compacted. Fieldstones, building ceramics and plant remains were found as inclusions. The common finds from this layer were *crustae*, glass, ceramic, metal and *tesserae*. This layer should be interpreted as topsoil, a humus layer following the natural slope overlying the destruction layer (layer 2).

9.2.4. Room 2

This large room (12 m by 6.70 m) is located to the east of room 1 with which it is connected by a 7.25 m long corridor. Its vaulted ceiling (h. in the center today: 2.50 m) is completely made of large tiles and continues downward to form the long walls. It is not clear whether this ceiling has a double or a single layer of tiles. It is important to note that there is no visible trace of corridors 1 and 3 in room 2. The quality of the brick vaulting is excellent.

The north wall is made of rubble and medium-sized ashlars in its lower part. It is punctuated by two vaulted corridors composed of a double row of bricks, which form the upper part of the wall (Fig. 181). The left (west) corridor is 1.13 to 1.20 m wide and at present 1.70 m high. Today, its lower half has been blocked by a mortared rubble wall. After 1.90 m, this corridor narrows down to ca. 1 m width and continues as a (triple?) vaulted brick-lined corridor towards the north (see Fig. 181).

To the left of this smaller corridor, at a somewhat lower level, a 1.20 m wide, 0.40 m high and 7.72 m long corridor with a double brick vault supported by rubble walls leads towards room 4. Today, this corridor is filled with stones and is only accessible by lying flat. Entering it from room 2, the double brick vault of this corridor is horizontal over its first 2.62 m, while the rest of the corridor slopes downwards towards room 4. Inside the corridor, at a distance of 4.62 m

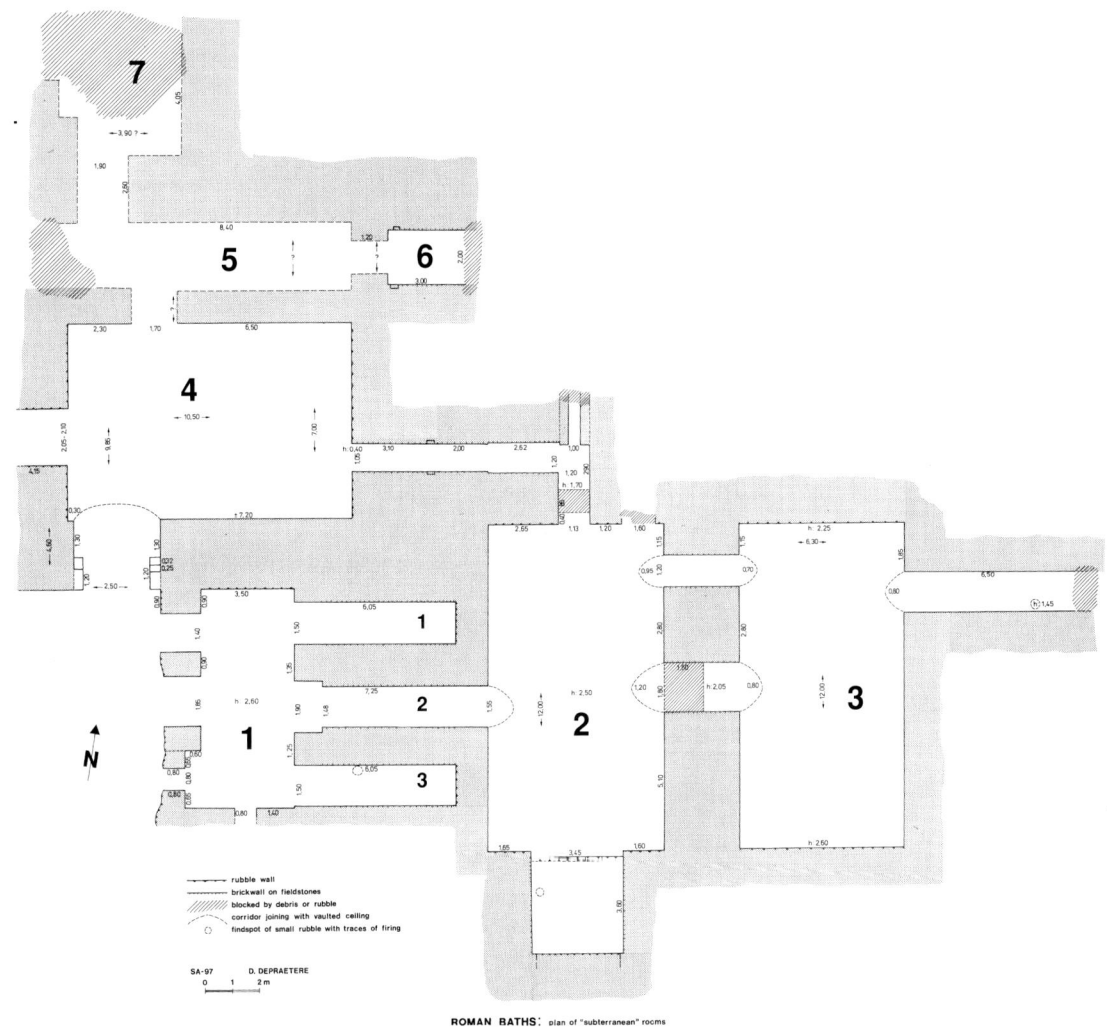

Fig. 175: Plan of the rooms located at ground level.

Fig. 176: View of the Roman baths from the west, towards the end of the 1997 campaign.

Fig. 177: View of room 1 at the ground level of the Roman baths. The picture is taken from the southwest.

Fig. 178: View of the stairway inside room 1 leading to the collapsed room to the east of it.

Fig. 179: View of corridor 2. The picture clearly shows that the east wall of room 1 was built against it at a later date.

Fig. 180: View of the collapsed remains in front of *praefurnium* 2, seen from *praefurnium* 2.

Fig. 181: View of room 2 from the south.

from its east entrance, both side-walls have a small niche which probably functioned as a lamp holder. The brick ceiling of the corridor is supported by rubble walls. The dimensions of both the northern and the western branch of the left corridor in room 2's north wall suggest that these must have functioned as service corridors, either for ventilation, or for the transport of water, as future seasons should confirm.

At 1.20 m to the right of this first corridor in the north wall, there is another brick-vaulted entrance with a lesser width of 1.50 m (Fig. 181). Most of it, however, is covered by the vaulted ceiling of room 2 and blocked with debris. As this corridor is partly obscured and hidden by the east wall of room 2, one is forced to conclude that the vault of room 2 was built at a later date against an already existing structure, which henceforth formed its north wall.

The south wall of room 2 is built as a rubble wall, but contains a 3.45 m wide brick vault which spans most the width of the wall. This suggests that in a later phase a large, vaulted opening had been blocked off. Originally, this opening gave access to an almost square room (3.45 m by 3.60 m) located to the south of it, but later the latter was completely separated from room 2.

The south wall of this south room, which can be entered by means of a hole that seems to have been cut recently, is today partially blocked by a rubble wall. Most of the room is filled with deposits that came down from the outside. The original south wall was formed by a large ashlar vault similar to that in the south wall of room 4 (see below) and spanned almost the total width of the room. This vault is located exactly below the south façade of the baths in this location, so that it may have been a vaulted entrance to a kind of vestibule leading into room 2.

The brick-vaulted ceiling of this southern vestibule is lower than the vault of room 2. In fact, the brick vault visible in the south wall of room 2 is nothing other than the beginning of the brick ceiling in this vestibule. Inside the latter, fragments of a large early Byzantine vessel were found (inv. no. 143) near evidence of a more recent fire (a concentration of small animal bones and plastic on a pile of small stones as in corridor 3 from room 1 and the eastern corridor of room 3).

In the east wall of room 2, two single brick-vaulted, 3 m long corridors lead towards room 3. The southern one is wider (1.60 m) than the northern one (1.20 m), but partially blocked by loose rubble blocks. Both vaulted corridors perfectly intersect with the vaults of rooms 2 and 3, so that they must be contemporary with them.

The floor of room 2 is filled with black muddy deposits that flowed into it from room 3, via both corridors.

9.2.5. Room 3

This room is nearly as large (12 m by 6.20 m) as room 2, but filled with a deeper black muddy layer sloping up towards the eastern half of the room, which had arrived in the room via the only east corridor of the room. Both the north and the south wall (Fig. 182) are made of rubble and medium-sized ashlars in the lower parts. In the east wall of the room there is one corridor, which continues 6.50 m towards the east before being blocked by debris. Most probably, it provided an entrance to another room further east which is almost completely filled with debris. Ca. 5 m inside this east corridor was found a similar concentration of small stones, bones, remains of a fire and plastic as in corridor 3 in room 1 and in the southern vestibule of room 2. The surface of room 3 and of its eastern corridor also contained small concentrations of pottery.

9.2.6. Room 4

This room occupying the first southwest angle of the bath's ground floor (calculated from the north) is oriented west-east instead of the north-south orientation of rooms 1, 2 and 3. Its internal dimensions (10.50 m by 7 m) are also smaller than those of rooms 2 and 3. Yet, near its southwest corner, room 4 has a square (2.50 m by 2.50 m) wide side-room opening to the south via a 1.20 m deep ashlar vault (Figs 183-184). Behind it, a double brick vault sloped downwards before intersecting with the barrel-vaulted ceiling of room 4 itself. At this intersection, part of the room's ceiling had collapsed.

At first it was thought that the sloping vault suggested that a staircase went down into the room, but later excavations have proved that this was not the case and that the large vaulted opening was a window rather than a door.

Originally, room 4 had a double brick barrel-vaulted ceiling. Most of the outer row of bricks is gone, but there are still some remains *in situ*, especially along the east side. The east wall is a mortared rubble wall with a double vaulted opening towards the already mentioned 'service' corridor that connects it with room 2 (Fig. 185). The west wall of the room, composed of a mortared rubble facing behind an ashlar wall, contains a 2.05 to 2.10 m wide niche with a large rectangular window apparently partially blocked by a rubble wall below. In the north wall of the room, a largely destroyed vaulted doorway leading towards room 5 is visible.

At the time of its discovery, room 4 was almost filled to its ceiling with mortar and small brick fragments. Although the upper part of this fill was removed, it did not contain any larger brick fragments, suggesting that these had already been removed in the past. There was also only one ashlar block in it, which had fallen through the hole at the intersection of the south window's sloping vault and room 4's barrel vault.

9.2.7. Room 5

This room, located to the north of room 4 from which it could be entered by means of a now partially destroyed doorway, is also oriented west-east. This brick-vaulted space is almost completely filled with debris, which is mostly mortar. As a result, no correct measurements could be taken, but the room looked rather like a long corridor or vestibule. In fact, its west wall, now completely obscured by debris, must contain a large door opening that is visible in the west facade of the baths' ground floor. Its east wall, made of mortared rubble, seems to contain an opening to another space (room 6) further east. Another vaulted passage in the north wall gave access to room 7.

9.2.8. Rooms 6 and 7

Room 6 has not yet been explored because of the level of debris filling it. But a brick vaulted ceiling located at a higher level than that of room 5 is visible. It is rather well preserved and is supported by mortared rubble walls. Its orientation is also east-west. The west wall is a nicely built rubble wall with, in its centre, a double brick vault. At either side of the room, there is a niche similar to the ones present in the corridor connecting room 4 with room 2.

Room 7 again is almost completely blocked by debris. To the left, there seems to be a connection towards the west façade of the baths. This room also seems to continue towards the north. According to the plan, it must almost have reached the northern edge of the bath building.

9.2.9. Conclusion

The bath complex at Sagalassos seems to be one of the larger and best preserved buildings of this type in Asia Minor. Reused wall veneering slabs suggest that the original bath section on the first floor had been completed during the second century AD, most probably under the Antonines. Later seasons have shown that the vaults of the ground floor were built during the first half of the second century AD, which would fit rather well with a date of completion of the upper part in the middle of the century. Most probably, *caldarium* 1 already fulfilled this purpose in the original construction, but the room seems to have been almost completely renovated as far as its wall veneering (and possibly its heated floor) is concerned during the later third-fourth century AD.

There is however plenty of evidence suggesting later interventions and repairs. For the time being, it is assumed that the AD 518 earthquake can be held responsible for drastic changes involving a rebuilding of the first *caldarium*'s south wall and the addition of a new heating system to its south. This served both *caldarium* 1 and a second *caldarium* inside a hall that had formerly had a different function, located to the southeast of the old *caldarium*.

The vaulted rooms of the ground floor show also various alterations that for the time being cannot be dated. Christian graffiti indicate that the bath complex remained in use until the early Byzantine period. Yet, evidence of a dump inside *praefurnium* 1 suggests that, at the time of the building's collapse, most probably as a result of the mid-seventh century AD earthquake, at least that part of the complex was no longer in use.

10. THE LOWER AGORA

The objectives of the 1996 and 1997 campaigns were to clear as much as possible the west side of the lower agora and the stairway around the Tiberian gateway. Whereas the 1996 season had mainly uncovered the rest of the agora gate, the 1997 season focused on the exposure of the central section of the west portico (Fig. 186).

In 1996, eight sectors of 25 m^2 each were partially excavated: old grid numbers 5325-4770 (cleaning only), 5325-4775, 5325-4780, 5325-4785, 5330-4775, 5330-4780; 5330-4785 and 5335-4785, corresponding more or less with the new grids 2320-2350, 2320-2355, 2320-2360, 2320-2365, 2320-2370, 2325-2360 and 2325-2365. In 1997, the following sectors were partially excavated: old grid numbers 5325-4785, 5325-4790, 5325-4795, 5330-4785, 5330-4790, 5330-4795, 5335-4785, 5335-4790 and 5335-4795 corresponding more or less with the new grids 2320-2370, 2320-2375, 2320-2380, 2325-2370, 2325-2375 and 2325-2380.

10.1. The agora gate

During the campaign of 1995, the remains of a monumental gateway had been discovered near the southwest corner of the lower agora. Since then, this monument has been studied and prepared for a partial anastylosis by C. Licoppe. It consisted of two parallel podia (2.64 m by 0.75 m; 1.44 m high), the so-called 'side wings', set at 9.70 m from one another in the upper part of a stairway giving access to the square. Each podium supported two Corinthian columns, while a row of probably four hexagonal pedestals supported similar columns in between. They bore an elaborately decorated entablature composed of an architrave, a frieze with theatre masks supporting fruit garlands, a cornice and a kind of *attica* with a palmette decoration (Fig. 187). A detailed study by C. Licoppe to be published in the next Sagalassos

Fig. 182: View of room 3 from the north.

Fig. 183: The recess with the vaulted window in the south wall of room 4.

Fig. 184: The vaulted window in the south wall of room 4, blocked off towards the end of the 1997 season.

Fig. 185: View of room 4 seen from the west. The top of the eastern 'service' corridor is visible in the back wall of the picture.

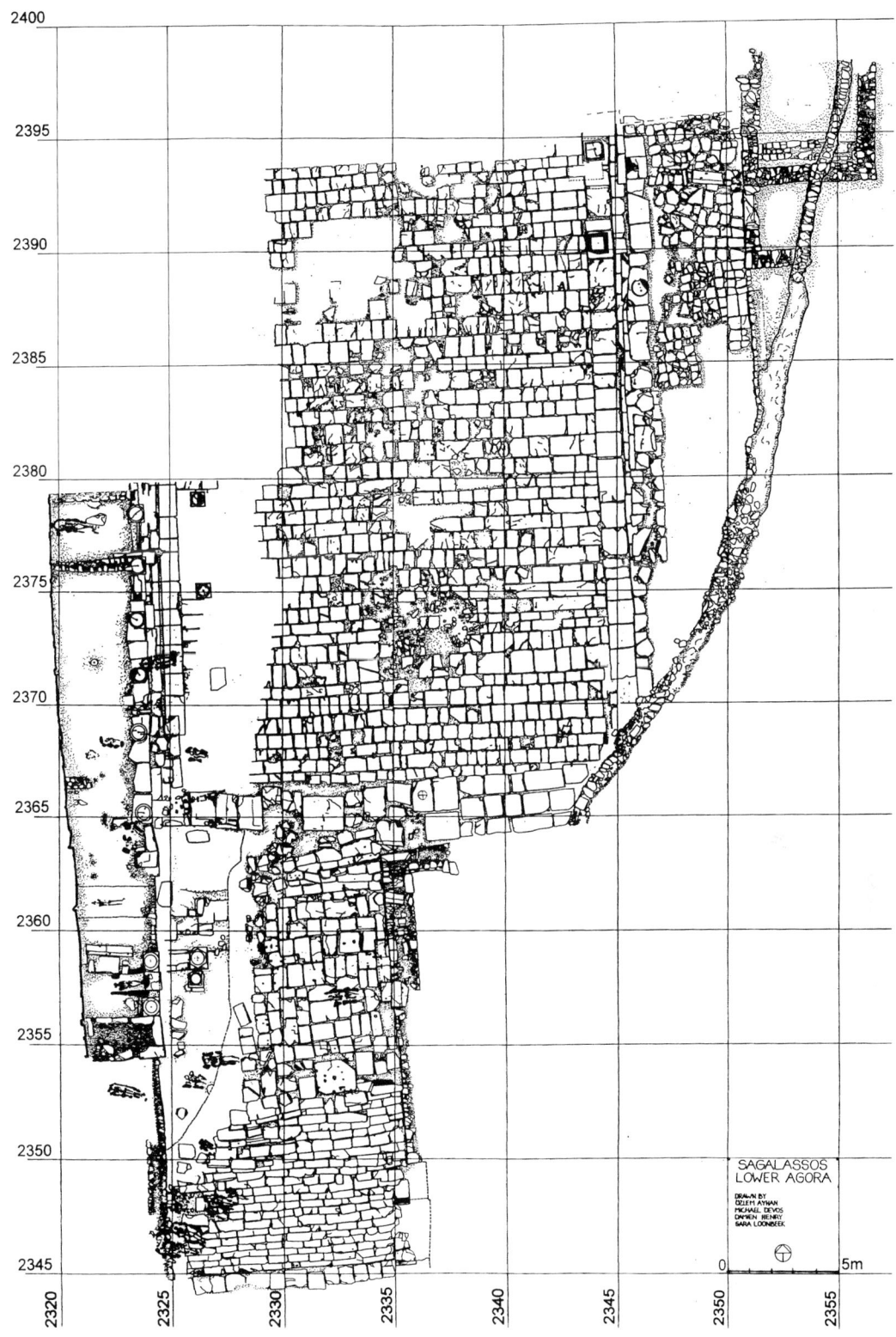

Fig 186: Plan of the lower agora as excavated in 1996-1997.

Fig. 187. Reconstruction drawing of the second phase of the Agora Gate on the Lower Agora (C. Licoppe).

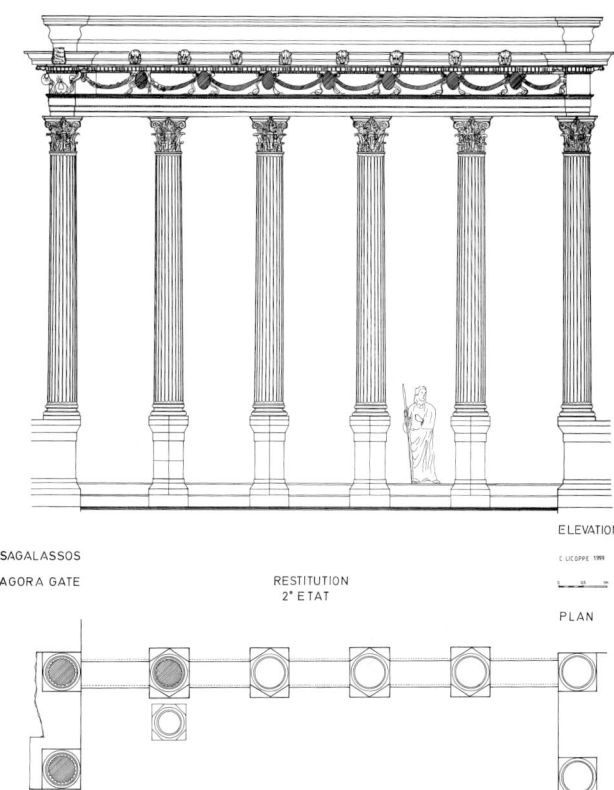

Fig. 188: Reconstruction drawing of the final phase of the Agora Gate on the Lower Agora (C. Licoppe).

volume, has revealed that this monument represented what was already the second stage of the gateway. In fact, the lateral wings seem to have been shortened in order to make the side wings fit to the two podia mentioned above. As a result, the Tiberian date (14-37 AD) that was established for the monument refers to an older and somewhat larger version of the gateway of which the exact location has not yet be established. Most probably, however, the structure occupied a similar position. For the time being, the occasion and the reason for the rebuilding of the original structure in a somewhat reduced version on top of the podia and the intermediary pedestals remains unknown, but this must have happened between the first and the sixth century AD. Ceramic evidence from the fill behind the west podium may suggest that this second building phase occurred during the third century AD (see 10.3).

During the earthquake of 518 AD, most of the second stage of this gateway seems to have collapsed, except for its west wing. Together with the first adjoining column of the central wing, the west wing was maintained as part of an angular monument that corresponded with the northwest corner of the former gateway (Fig. 188). During this transformation, the remaining entablature of the central part of the monument was adapted to its new position. At the same time, most probably because the original was lost, the capital of the only remaining column of the central wing was replaced by a mid-second century AD capital from another monument (Waelkens *et al.* 1997b, 208 fig. 172).

During the same intervention, a new monumental stairway of 32 steps, even incorporating parts of the old gate (with the cornices now transformed into steps), was established above the remains of its predecessor. Four steps of the latter were found immediately east of the west podium, in sectors 2325-2355 and 2325-2360 (Fig. 189). Since these steps still bore the west pedestal of the agora gate's central wing and a hexagonal statue base placed in front of it, they must be either contemporary to the second phase of the agora gate or older. The statue base was placed on top of the inverted upper moulding of an older honorific monument (Fig. 190).

The new sixth century AD stairway consisted of a stairway with twenty-one steps leading south. The total height of this stairway was 4.81 m (west) to 5.01 m (east). To the north of it, there was an 8.75 m wide landing, also sloping to the south (0.26 m in the east to 0.35 m in the west). From here, an additional stairway composed of only six steps (with the top, however, destroyed) led to the agora. Its height was more or less 1.42 m. The stairway, just like the pavement of the upper agora itself, sloped both to the south and to the west.

Apparently, when after the AD 518 earthquake the new stairway was built, an area of ca. 2.50 to 3 m in front of the west podium of the agora gate, comprising the still standing remains of this monument, remained unpaved. This area was filled with earth covering a terracotta water supply system installed against the west podium (Fig. 189). This fill (layer 6) contained pottery dated to the last phase of the local production (AD 450-650: SA 96-5330/4770-85 and SA 96-5330/4775-52) and a number of bronze coins dated to the fourth and fifth centuries AD (Scheers 2000 s.v. Agora Gate, layer 6). This evidence corresponds well with a rearrangement of the area during the early sixth century AD.

During the 1996 campaign, the lower parts of the three columns belonging to the final phase of the agora gate were placed back into their original position (Fig. 191). During the 1997 season, the heavily fragmented original Corinthian capitals were restored by C. Licoppe (Figs 192-193).

10.2. The west portico of the lower agora

During the campaigns of 1996 and 1997, the remains of a portico, nearly 3.10 m deep, which flanked the western extremity of the lower agora, was unearthed over a length of nearly 20 metres (Figs 194-195). The portico has a three-stepped *krepis* (total height ca. 0.915 to 0.94 m) of which the *euthynteria* below the lowest step becomes more visible to the south in order to overcome a slight inclination of the agora pavement in that direction (0.25 m in the area exposed in 1996). There was also an inclination to the west. All of this made sense, since a gutter made of hollowed out border stones had been built at the bottom of the *krepis*. Four column bases of the Ionic-Attic order were found, of which only the three northern ones were standing more or less *in situ* (Fig. 195). They are placed at an interaxial distance of ca. 2.50 m. Several smooth column drums were also found in the position where they fell during the mid-seventh century AD earthquake (Fig. 196). Some of them still contained their dowels (Fig. 197). A number of broken Ionic capitals, not all of them of similar type (which indicates a re-use of material) were also recovered (Fig. 198), together with large parts of the entablature, consisting of an architrave with three *fasciae* and a plain pulvinated frieze (Fig. 199). The columns (including capitals and bases) had an original height of ca. 4.30 m, while the combined height of the entablature was ca. 0.57 m (Fig. 200). Most of the capitals and the plain entablature bear a striking similarity to the corresponding elements of the Apollo Klarios temple, higher up the slope, as it was when rebuilt during the year AD 103-104 (Vandeput 1997a: 55-59, Pls 19-21). This plain architecture seems to have been characteristic at Sagalassos during the second half of the first and the beginning of the second century AD. In fact, it is also seen in the later first–early second century AD odeion (Waelkens 1993 a: 46 note 99) and in the still unpublished monument that was dedicated by Claudia Severa to the emperor Trajan near

Basilica E1. The original date of the construction of the West Portico should therefore be attributed to the same period.

In front of the excavated section of the west portico, two pedestals were replaced into their original position (Fig. 195). Their date and function could no longer be established.

However, the portico that collapsed in the middle of the seventh century AD was no longer the original construction, but a portico that had been rebuilt after an earthquake, undoubtedly the catastrophe of AD 518. On this occasion, the back wall of the original portico, composed of rusticated ashlar blocks, was almost completely rebuilt, whereby, especially in the southern part and central part of the portico, the original position of the stones was no longer observed (Figs 194-195). This irregularity was certainly obscured by plaster rendering. Today, this back wall continues as far south as the southern extremity of the agora gate, but originally it may have been shorter.

In sector 2320-2365, the top of the reconstructed back wall also contained an early third century AD inscription (Fig. 201) dedicated to a L. Gellius Maximus from Sagalassos, who became the private doctor of the emperor Caracalla and eventually the director of the famous library at Alexandria (Devijver 1997: 119-150 n°.3). In 1997, in the above mentioned grid, a small sondage was carried out behind this back wall. Here, a layer 3 was partially exposed, which appeared to be a very disturbed and eroded layer with small mortar lenses and reddish-brown-to-blackish inclusions directly covering the natural bedrock. In the excavated sector, this layer seemed to have been cut vertically to accommodate the back wall of the west portico. Unfortunately, the small section of it that could be examined did not produce any diagnostic features.

10.3. The early Byzantine conversion of the West Portico.

After the AD 518 earthquake, the whole area underwent a drastic transformation. Initially, the west portico may have resumed its original function, but within a few generations mortared rubble walls were built in between the columns, and in between these and the back wall, dividing the long walkway into a number of separate units, only accessible from the east. Remains of such a mortared wall were found against the back wall of the west portico in the middle of the first intercolumnium (from the south) of the west portico as it stands today (Fig. 202).

The west podium of the agora gate, now transformed into a two-sided corner monument with only three of the original columns standing, became incorporated into a structure built on top of the west podium (Fig. 203). This building must have reached a considerable height since the heads and garlands on the west side of the old agora gate were knocked off, apparently to make the entablature fit better against the new walls.

The south wall of the new (tower like?) structure was built on a stone base made of ashlars (ca. 3.70 m by 1.90 m), built at a right angle against the south column of the agora gate and against the (extended?) back wall of the sixth century AD west portico. A second wall further north, connected the northwest column of the agora gate to the same back wall, thus delimiting an internal space of ca. 2.90 by 2.70 m. This north wall apparently contained the entrance to this room, since it contained a large doorstep. To its south, the remains of a mortared floor (layer 5) were exposed. However, to the north of the doorstep, no clear floor level could be identified.

Layer 5 was made up of a very compact mortar floor. Below it, a fill (layer 9) was partially excavated. This fill can only have arrived here after the AD 518 earthquake, since it occupied the space behind the agora gate's west podium and the (extended?) back wall of the west portico, and the latter had been completely rebuilt (and extended?) after this seismic catastrophe. Layer 9 is very loose and dark brown, and composed of a sandy clay mixed with stones. It contained bone, metal, *tesserae*, plaster fragments, glass and ceramics. The latter (SA 96-5325/4775-38) mainly comprised sherds belonging to phases 3 (AD 100-150) to 5 (third century AD) of the local production, mixed with sherds from phase 8 (AD 450-650). This content may possibly indicate that the original backfill of the podium, and therefore the construction of the second phase of the agora gate itself, date from the third century AD, and the original fill got mixed with later material during the reconstruction of the sixth century AD.

10.4. The mid seventh century AD destruction and the early Byzantine graveyard

Within a few generations after its transformation into a shop or workshop area, the west portico of the lower agora was completely destroyed by a massive earthquake, which we could attribute to the mid-seventh century AD (Waelkens *et al.* 1997b: 212; Waelkens *et al.* 2000b). The debris that covered the stairway leading to the lower agora as well as the western edges of this square and rendered them unusable was never removed (Figs 204-205). This shows that most of the city must have been abandoned after the catastrophe. Nothing of the front of the building remained standing, and the upper half of the restored back wall collapsed again, especially in the southern and central parts of the former portico.

Fig. 189: View of the older stairway (left), below the level of the sixth century AD stairway (right). To the left, against the west podium of the agora gate, a sixth century AD water supply system made of terracotta pipes is visible.

Fig. 190: The hexagonal statue base in front of the west pedestal of the agora gate's central wing.

Fig. 191: The partially restored northwest corner of the final phase of the agora gate.

Fig. 192: One of the original capitals from the west wing of the Tiberian agora gate on the lower agora, after its 1997 restoration.

Fig. 193: Second capital from the west wing of the Tiberian agora gate.

Fig. 194: Southern section of the west portico on the lower agora as excavated in 1997.

Fig. 195: Northern section of the west portico on the lower agora as excavated in 1997.

Fig. 196: Columns in the position where they fell during the mid-seventh century AD earthquake.

Fig. 197: One of the column drums with its dowel, next to the corresponding base.

Fig. 198: Fragments of the Ionic capitals of the west portico.

Fig. 199: Parts of the entablature of the west portico.

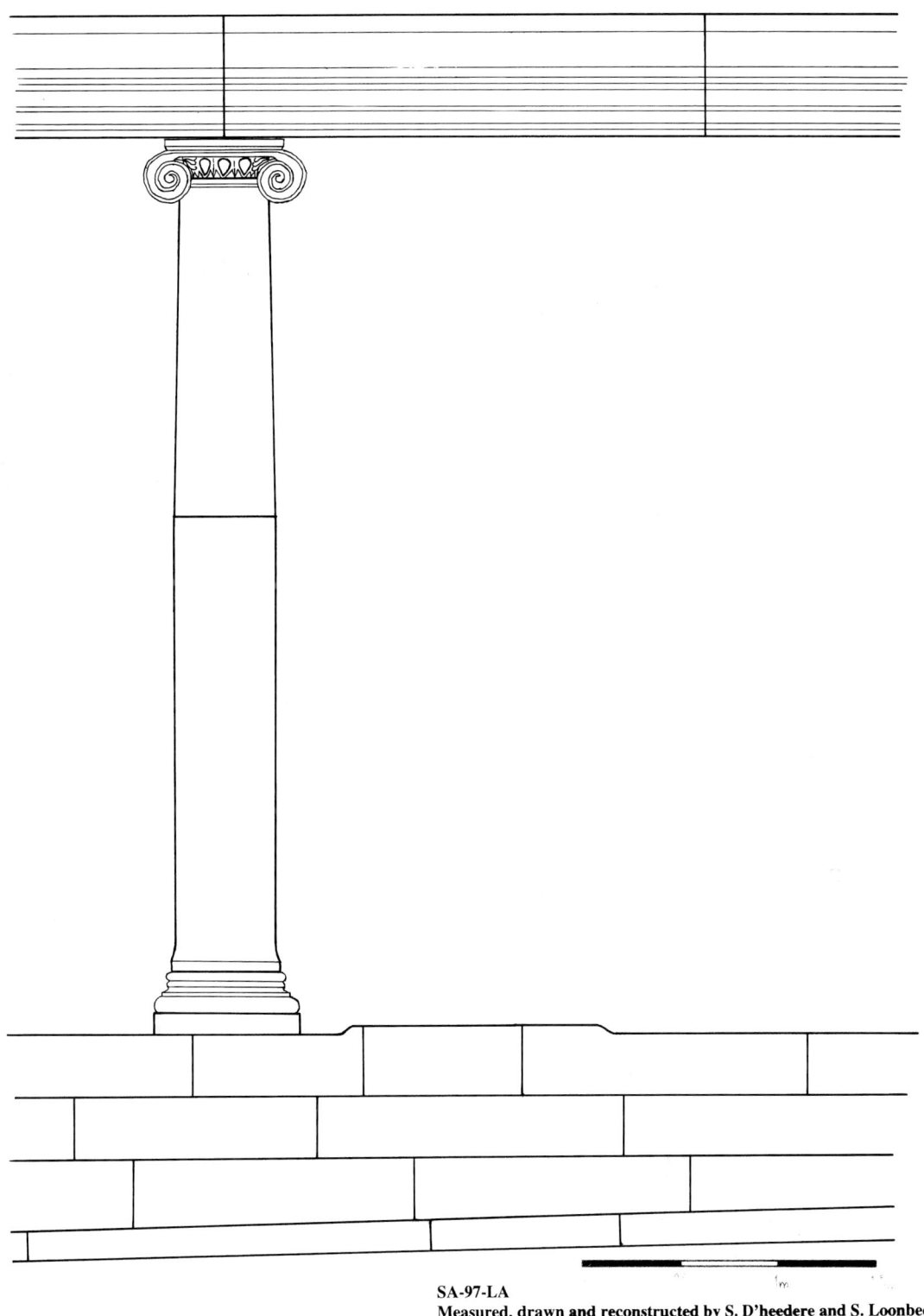

SA-97-LA
Measured, drawn and reconstructed by S. D'heedere and S. Loonbeek

ELEVATION OF THE WEST PORTICO OF THE LOWER AGORA

Fig. 200: Reconstruction of the elevation of the west portico.

Fig. 201: Inscribed base dedicated to L. Gellius Maximus re-used in the back wall of the west portico.

Fig. 202: The (at present) first intercolumnium of the west portico with the remains of a partition wall against the back wall.

On top of these ruins however, an early Byzantine graveyard was established. In 1993-1994, a total of 17 tombs were discovered in the Agora Gate area. Since several of these tombs, either simple holes dug out in the debris or stone-lined pits, had been multiple burials, a total of 20 skeletons were recovered. A study of the skeletons by E. Smits revealed that these bodies were not earthquake victims, but that according to stratigraphical evidence they were people who had died fairly soon after this event i.e. during the second half of the seventh century AD. The occurrence of adults, children and infants in one tomb may suggest that they may have been victims of an epidemic disease (Waelkens *et al*. 1997b: 212). This hypothesis was confirmed by the fact that preliminary DNA analysis of some of the skeletons from these multiple burials did not produce any evidence of a maternal relationship (Jehaes *et al*. 2000).

In the debris caused by the mid-seventh century AD earthquake, the following layers were distinguished:

- Inside the late structure built on top of the west podium of the former agora gate, the same destruction layers as those inside the west portico were discovered. Layers 2 and 3 had already been removed in previous years, but layer 4 was excavated in 1996. It contained tiles, metal, bone, glass, *crustae* fragments and pottery from the final phase of the local production (AD 450-650: SA 96-5325/4775-6). The discovery of two coins was significant, respectively dated to the reigns of Arcadius (Scheers 2000, cat. 99: SA 96 AG 10 from the years 392-395 AD) and Heraclius (Scheers 2000, cat. 382: SA 96 AG 19: a *follis*, class 3 from AD 615/6).

Inside the 'units' created inside the west portico, the following destruction layers were distinguished:
- layer 4: in 1996, this layer covering the floor of the west portico was only partially exposed in sector 2320-2365. It must correspond with the first destruction level of the 'units' established inside the former west portico. The layer contained lots of tile fragments (33 crates in this sector alone), bone, glass, metal, ceramics, *tesserae, crustae* and an early fifth century AD coin (Scheers 2000, cat. 166: a *gloria Romanorum* coin dated to the years 406-408 AD).

During the 1997 campaign, most of this layer was removed from sectors 2320-2365 and 2320-2375. It produced *in situ* a large dolium (SA 97-5325/4785-118) that had been knocked over and destroyed during the earthquake (Fig. 205).
- layer 3: the central part of the destruction layer, found on top of the portico's steps and inside the building. This light brown layer was of a rather loose structure and was very sandy. It contained lots of rubble, but also medium-sized tufa blocks and bricks (from the partition walls inside the west portico) and tiles (92 crates). The coins from this layer all belonged to the late fourth to late fifth century AD (Scheers 2000 s.v. B. Lower Agora, layer 3).
- layer 2: this was the upper part of the destruction levels, immediately below the topsoil. It contained larger stones from the back wall of the west portico and from the church (the former Apollo Klarios sanctuary) above it.

Five more tombs were discovered in the 1996 campaign and a sixth in 1997, in layer 2 (see Fig. 186). The mid-seventh century AD date of the earthquake that levelled the city was once more confirmed by the pottery (SA 96-5330/4785-30, 37 and 52; SA 97 LA 147) from layer 2 (phase 8: 450-650 AD) and by its coins, which range in date from the late third to the fifth century AD (Scheers 2000, s.v. B. Lower Agora, Layer 2). Layer contained many roof tiles (156 crates) and plaster fragments from the final occupation of the west portico, glass, bone (including worked bone: hairpins), metal, *tesserae* and crustae.

Four of the 1996 tombs were found in the southern half of grids 2320-2365 (tombs 18 and 19) and 2325-2365 (tomb 20), and overlapping grids 2320-2370 and 2325-2370 (tomb 21). A fifth one (tomb 22) was exposed above the remains of the west podium of the collapsed agora gate in grid 2320-2355. The 1997 tomb (tomb 23) was discovered in grid 2320-2375 (the head of the skeleton slightly crossing into grid 2315-2375). All tombs were dug ca. 0.50 m down in layer 2. In sectors 2320-2365 and 2325-2365, layer 2 directly covered the stairs of the west portico of the lower agora, as well as the pavement slabs of the square. A detailed study of the skeletal remains by E. Smits will be published in the next Sagalassos volume.

- Tomb 18 (tomb 1 of old grid 5325-4785): a tomb of ca. 0.60 m by 0.50 m, oriented west-east, placed against the back wall of the west portico. The tomb was not lined with stones, but simply dug into layer 2 (Fig. 206), so that the skeleton had been less protected and its bones were no longer articulated but in a very poor condition (50% of it is missing). The remains belonged to a child buried on its back, facing east. Based on the dentition, E. Smits could establish its age as ca. 1.5 years (+/- 6 months). The tomb contained some non-datable intrusive material (ceramics, glass, *tesserae*).
- Tomb 19 (tomb 2 of old grid 5325-4785): this tomb is located ca. 0.50 m to the southeast of tomb 18. Its edge was outlined with stones on the south side only, but the rest of the outline may have eroded away (Fig. 207). This burial was less disturbed than the one in tomb 18. Its skeletal remains, though recently fragmented, were almost complete, except for some missing hand and foot bones. They belonged to a child, buried on its back and facing east, whose the age was established by E. Smits as ca. 1.5-2 years (based on the length of the *humerus* and on the dentition).

Across the chest two small bronze crosses were found (Figs 208-209). A small metal ring discovered below the skull may have been part of a necklace holding both crosses.

- Tomb 20 (tomb 1 of old grid 5330-4785): a tomb of nearly 1 m by 0.60 m, oriented west-east. The south, west and north sides of the tomb were edged by five medium-sized rubble stones (Fig. 210). As with many other tombs, the east edge of the tomb and of the skeleton inside had suffered from erosion on the rather steep slope. Inside, the remains of a child, identified by E. Smits as a child of ca. 1.5 years (+/- 6 months) were found. The child was buried on its back, facing east. The legs were stretched and the arms flexed. The bone remains that were found were still well articulated and in a very good state of preservation. Some of the hand and foot bones were missing. Near the missing edge of the tomb, but just outside it, a glass bead and a coin (SA 96 LA 76: Scheers 2000, cat. 169: *gloria Romanorum* coin from AD 408-423) were found inside layer 2. Apparently, there was no direct connection with the tomb content. The tomb contained also some intrusive ceramic material composed of unidentifiable Sagalassos red slip ware sherds (SA 96-5330/4785-79).

- tomb 21 (tomb 2 of old grid 5330-4785): a tomb of ca. 1.75 m by 0.60 m, lined with small and medium-sized stones and some tiles (Fig. 211). A large stone, the only remains of a possible cover was placed across the *tibia*. The tomb contained the remains of an adult individual, buried on its back and facing east, with the legs stretched and the arms crossed over the chest. The skeleton was almost complete, except for some bones of hands and feet. The latter were sticking outside the stone edging of the tomb, but this was probably because the stone casing had eroded away towards the east. E. Smits could identify the skeleton as belonging to a female of ca. 1.66 m height and ca. 16-18 years old (based on the epiphyseal closure).

- tomb 22 (tomb 2 of old grid 5325/5330-4775): this tomb was arranged on top of the west podium of the agora gate, so that the eastern end of the tomb was exactly between the two column bases of the gateway's west wing (Fig. 212). The eastern end had eroded away, together with part of the feet of the skeleton. The tomb was ca. 1.70 m by 0.70 m and placed against a late wall to the south. The north side was lined with large stones. The tomb was partly dug through the mortared floor of the late structure on top of the west podium and the body was covered with rubble. The skeleton belonged to an adult individual, buried on its back, facing east, with stretched legs and arms folded over the chest. Except for some hand and foot bones, the skeleton was almost complete. E. Smits identified it as the remains of a male, of ca. 40-50 years, with a stature of ca. 1.77 m.

- tomb 23 (tomb 1 of the old grid 5325-4795): this tomb was inside the remains of a workshop (?) built inside the fifth intercolumnium (from the south) in the west portico. The tomb, oriented west-east, was almost completely edged with small- to large-sized stones (Fig. 213) and was apsidal in shape (ca. 2.40 m by 0.70 m). Except for a few hand- and foot-bones, the skeleton was almost complete. It was buried on its back, facing east, the legs crossed and both arms folded over the chest. E. Smits identified these remains as belonging to a female of ca. 21-23 years old, with a stature of ca. 1.61 m.

After the abandonment of the city, the graveyard became covered with topsoil. Near the surface this produced in 1996 an anonymous *follis* class A 2, dated to the reign of Basil II (976-1025 AD) or Romanus III (1028-1034 AD) (Scheers 2000, cat.385, SA 97 LA 36), showing that the population, which had moved down to Ağlasun by that time, still frequented the area occasionally.

10.5. Conclusion

The 1996 and 1997 campaigns showed that the southwest gate of the lower agora originally occupied a different position. Possibly during the third century AD, it was placed in its present location, but the side wings at least had to be reduced in length to fit the podia that bore them. During the second half of the first or the early second century AD, a long portico was constructed along the western edge of the agora. Together with most of the agora gate, it collapsed as a result of the AD 518 seismic catastrophe. Both buildings were rebuilt, however: the west portico using the original building parts, but also incorporating some other elements, while the Agora Gate was henceforth reduced to a two-sided monument composed of three columns with corresponding entablature. The rest of the monument disappeared in a newly built monumental stairway leading to the agora.

Within a few generations, however, the west portico was partitioned into smaller units, accessible from the front only, and the original colonnade had been completely blocked by walls linking the columns to one another. This structure collapsed during the earthquake that struck the city around the middle of the seventh century AD. For a short time, the survivors seemed to have used the debris covering the west side of the lower agora for a graveyard, most probably because there was a church higher up the slope (inside the former sanctuary of Apollo Klarios). The fact, however, that the earthquake debris covering this important public square and blocking its access was never removed, indicates that the city must have been almost completely abandoned after this catastrophe.

11. THE POTTERS' QUARTER

In 1987, the urban survey identified a potters' quarter on a plateau to the east of the theatre (Mitchell and Waelkens 1988: 60). An area of about six hectares is still littered with ceramic waste. Between 1989 and 1991, a first series

Fig. 203: The remains of the late structure built on top of the west wing of the agora gate.

Fig. 204: View of the collapsed west portico.

Fig. 205: Dolium found inside the west portico.

Fig. 206: View of the scattered remains of tomb 18.

Fig. 207: View of tomb 19.

Fig. 208: One of the small crosses from the child burial in tomb 19.

Fig. 209: The second cross from the child burial in tomb 19.

Fig. 210: View of tomb 20 seen from the east.

Fig. 211: Tomb 21 seen from the east.

Fig. 212: Tomb 22 on top of the west podium of the agora gate, seen from the north.

Fig. 213: Tomb 23 seen from the south.

of excavations was undertaken there (sites D and F) in collaboration with the Museum of Burdur. At both sites, a middle Imperial family tomb was discovered that had been looted already in antiquity. The tomb of site F was vaulted and still contained some of its original contents in human remains and grave goods. The tomb of site D, however, was no longer roofed and already in antiquity it had been used as a dump (Waelkens *et al.* 1990; 1991: 206-213; 1992: 91-98). At the surface of the potters' quarter the remains of more collapsed tombs can be seen. At least some of them seem to have been part of larger complexes laid out on terraces and surrounded by enclosure walls. The size of some of these compounds suggests that they had gardens, as was usual in Roman antiquity. Sagalassos thus seems to be another example of how an ancient city buried part of its dead in the same area where its industrial activities were established. This was also the case, for example, at Athens (Morris 1992: 128-155) and at Pergamon (Erdemgil and Özenir 1982).

By exposing large quantities of waste material, the early excavations in the potters' quarter confirmed the existence of a local pottery industry. However, after the 1991 season, it was decided to interrupt the excavations to permit the classification, identification and dating of this entirely new line of products. The typo-chronological studies of both the fine and common wares were largely based on the excavations in the urban centre of Sagalassos (Poblome 1999; Degeest 2000). On the other hand, by 1990, a complementary full-scale archaeometrical programme was initiated with the aim of fingerprinting the local fabrics and reconstructing the production technology (for Sagalassos red slip ware: Poblome *et al.* 1997; for the Sagalassos common wares: Degeest *et al.* 1997; Degeest 2000a; Degryse *et al.* 2000).

As a result, the typology and chronology of the locally produced wares were first established, with their technological features. The local pottery production includes tablewares, jugs and jars, oil lamps, figurines, *oinophoroi*, storage vessels, bricks, tiles, water-pipes, cooking vessels, amphorae and pithoi from a mass production covering a fairly long and continuous timespan from the reign of Augustus to early Byzantine times. In a next stage, the economic importance of Sagalassos red slip ware, which was distributed throughout the eastern Mediterranean and even beyond, was established (Poblome 1996). The fact that comparable pottery manufactures have not been located, let alone excavated, resulted in a decision to launch another research programme in the potters' quarter with the aim of studying in detail all the possible aspects of mass producing ancient pottery.

The dominant topographical feature of the potters' quarter is its central depression, which opens towards the southeast and measures about 50 m across. A platform to the west of it contains a second smaller depression. An *arcosolium* datable to the Imperial period, carved in a limestone outcrop, provides a landmark at about the highest point of the slope to the east of the depression. To the north, the potters' quarter is bounded by the mountain range overlooking the site of Sagalassos. The scree material originating from this limestone front reaches as far as the northern edge of the quarter. To the south, a low, long ridge with limestone outcrops forms the border of the central depression (Fig. 214).

Apart from some minor, localised concentrations, production waste is still visible at the surface in four areas of the potters' quarter: the area of Site D, the area of site F, the eastern slope of the quarter and the southeast opening to the central depression. The area of Site D contains a mixture of material, but predominantly late Roman wares, while the area of Site F comprises mainly middle Imperial waste material. Two different concentrations were noted on the eastern slope, one located in front of the *arcosolium* containing predominantly early Imperial material, while the other with mainly late Roman sherds was found higher on the slope and more towards the north. The concentration near the southeast opening of the depression is less dense and contains mainly tile fragments and kiln debris.

In order to explore the main features of this extensive area and to locate potential elements of workshop infrastructure, the eastern slope of the quarter, where the concentrations of production waste are most dense, was surveyed in 1996 by R. Degeest and R. Ottenburgs, using an active scan EM31 geo-conductivity meter. A primary area of 70 m by 100 m and a secondary zone of 50 m by 60 m were gridded with lines at 1 m intervals, so that readings were taken at 1 m intervals. The total number of readings exceeded 14,000. An area with consistently higher conductivity readings was located in the first sector, near the ridge of the eastern slope. Except for a distinctive line of very low readings, which may be the course of a buried aqueduct, the second sector did not produce any anomalies.

Between the 22nd and 29th of July 1997, a series of sondage excavations was carried out in the potters' quarter (Fig. 215). Trench 1 (5 m by 5 m) was located on the spot where the anomaly with higher conductivity readings had been located in sector 1 in 1996. The high readings could have been caused by, for example, the presence of fired clay or a kiln, which are both more conductive than natural deposits. However, the excavation immediately exposed bedrock in this area, consisting of, as elsewhere in Sagalassos, an undulating tectonised ophiolitic platform. This parent material was reached at a depth between 0.60 m and 0.80 m below walking level. The ferro-magnetic nature of the ophiolitic sequence easily explained the anomaly. Thus, the results of the electro-magnetic survey could no longer be considered a potential source of information. The deposits on top of the bedrock were erosional in nature and consisted of a dark brown clayey matrix with small limestone fragments. They contained a chronological mixture of ceramic material and one coin, a Sagalassos city coin dated to the reign of Augustus (Scheers 2000, cat. 16: Sa-97-PQ-3). A thin top-soil layer of 0.10 m to 0.20 m had formed in the upper face of these deposits.

Taking into account the limited value of the geo-conductivity measurements, it was decided to carry out sondages in different units in the quarter to understand its stratigraphical and geomorphological components and build up a picture of the internal organization in terms of function and chronology

Three more trenches (trench 2, 3 and 4: each 5 m by 2 m) were dug on the eastern slope, following the direction of trench 1. In each of these trenches a ceramic dump was exposed, containing mainly but not exclusively waste material of Sagalassos red slip ware. Based on the results of the quantification process, these layers of waste products could be attributed to the second century AD (Fig. 216). This dump layer can therefore be seen as the continuation of the material found at the surface in front of the *arcosolium*. In Trench 2 a very dense concentration of this waste material was found in a dark brownish clayey layer, 1.20 m to 1.30 m thick, on top of which a thin top-soil had formed. A city coin from Eukarpeia, dated to the second-third century AD (Scheers 2000, cat. 1: SA 97 PQ 8), was found inside the dump layer. The pottery had been directly dumped on the ophiolitic bedrock. This was also the case in trench 4, where the less compacted second century AD dump material formed part of the same dark brown clayey layer, measuring 1.30 m to 1.60 m in thickness and containing a coin of the emperor Julian, dated to the years AD 355–361 (Scheers 2000, cat. 54: SA 97 PQ 11). In this trench, however, another layer was found on top of the second century AD stratum. It is 0.40 m to 0.70 m thick and consists of a dark greyish clayey matrix with small to medium-sized stones, mainly in the lower part of the layer. The layer contains mainly early Byzantine waste products. This upper layer resulted from a process of erosion that replaced material from the northeast, where concentrations of early Byzantine material can still be found at the surface. Only in trench 3 was an older phase found below the second century AD dump. The lower deposits stretched horizontally and contained in their upper face a 0.20 m thick dark grey ashy matrix, over a 0.60 to 0.70 m thick orange to red stratum comprising mainly kiln debris and ash lenses, on top of a 0.60 m thick brownish clayey matrix with medium-pebbles and a concentration of misfired tableware dating to the early first century AD (Fig. 217). These lower deposits had been dumped on the ophiolitic bedrock. The upper deposits containing a dense concentration of the second century AD waste products measured 1.60 m to 1.70 m in thickness.

Trench 5 (5 m by 2 m) was 30 m to the south of Trenches 1 to 4, at the bottom of the eastern slope. The intention was to check at this point the stratigraphy of the slope and to follow a terracotta water pipe, which was first discovered in the upper deposits of trench 3. The pipe continued in trench 5 but was broken in its southern part and did not appear in the southern profile of the trench. It must have carried fresh water from a collection point connected to one of the eastern aqueducts of Sagalassos (Owens 1995: 91-95) to an unknown destination. Once more, ophiolitic bedrock was encountered at a depth of about 1 m. The stratigraphy of the trench consisted of a dark brown clayey matrix with small pebbles. It was erosional in nature and contained a chronological mix of ceramics.

When building a theoretical profile of the eastern slope based on trenches 1 to 4 (Fig. 218), the differences in depth of the ophiolitic bedrock between the trenches is striking. Where the bedrock was found in trench 3 there is a marked dip in the slope compared to the gradient of the actual walking level. Together with the fact that in each level that could be checked the bedrock did not slope but was horizontal and appeared to be a freshly cut face, without an overlying clayey weathered horizon, we were led to the conclusion that this weathering horizon may have been quarried in antiquity in a stepped open mining system. Recent interdisciplinary research has confirmed the existence of quarrying activities in the potters' quarter and has shown that the local potters did indeed use the local clay deposit (Degryse *et al.* 2000). The presence of this good quality clay source may of course have influenced the choice of the location of this industrial activity.

A second set of sondages was dug in the southern part of the potters' quarter. The quarter ends here in a low and long ridge, overlooking the central depression. Trench 6 (4 m by 4 m) was dug in a small depression immediately to the west of the ridge. trenches 7 (10 m by 1.50 m) and 8 (2 m by 2 m) were dug on the approximately 10 m wide platform along the foot of the ridge, facing the central depression. Excavations were stopped in trench 6 at a depth of about 1.50 m without reaching bedrock. The stratigraphy consisted of a package of eroded material, mainly containing medium-sized stones in a greyish clayey matrix. Only a couple of late Roman sherds were recovered, which had clearly been transported. No indication of any past activity was recorded.

Neither trench 7 nor 8 were continued to the level of the bedrock and excavations were stopped at about 1 m depth. In both cases, the stratigraphy consisted of material that had eroded from the northern face of the ridge, containing mainly medium-sized stones in a greyish clayey matrix and a few scraps of pottery from different periods. In trench 7, a fragment of a late Hellenistic to early Imperial ostotheca

Fig. 214: General view of the potters' quarter from the northwest.

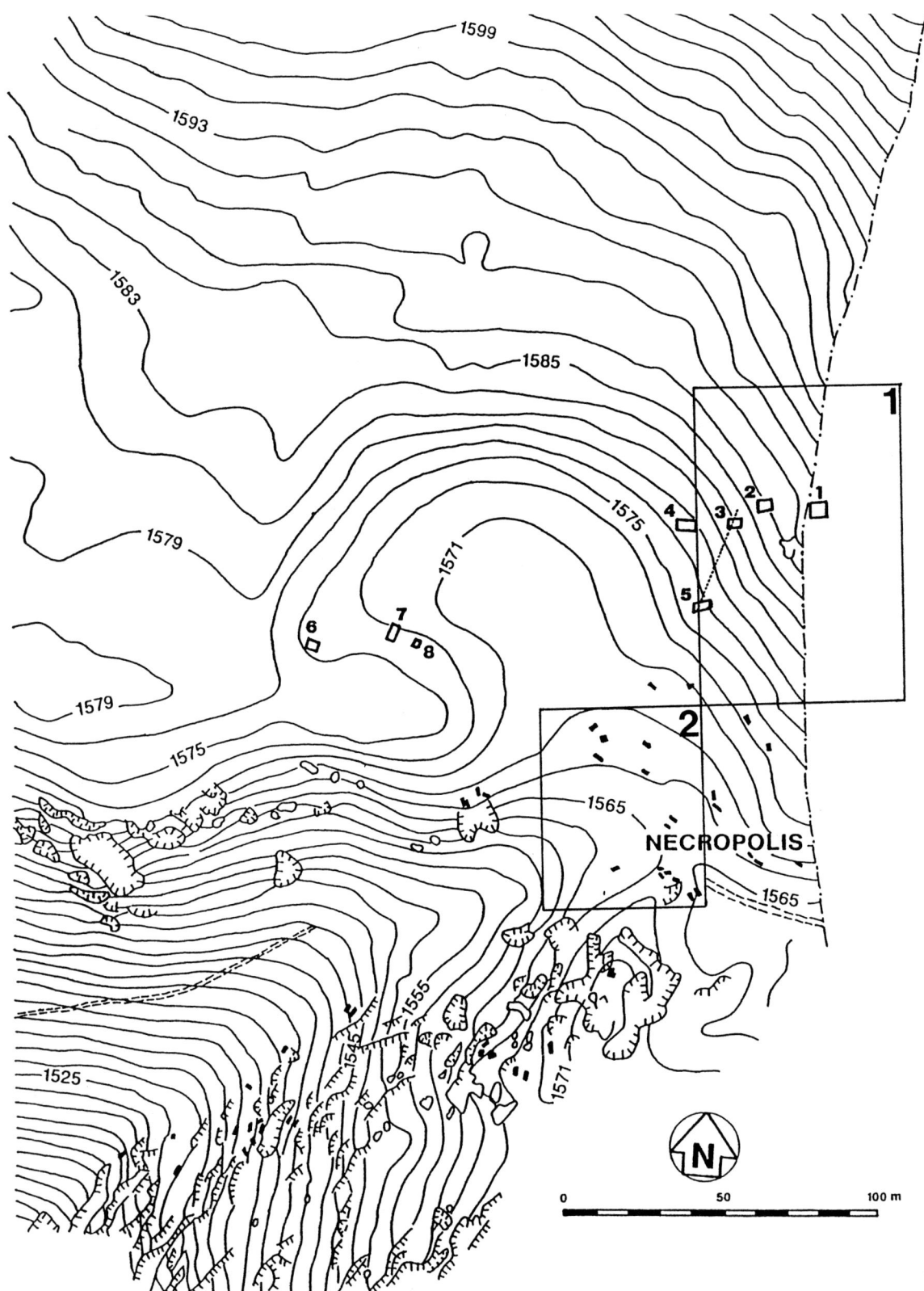

Fig. 215. Topographical map of the potters' quarter, indicating the surveyed sectors of 1996 and the sondages of 1997.

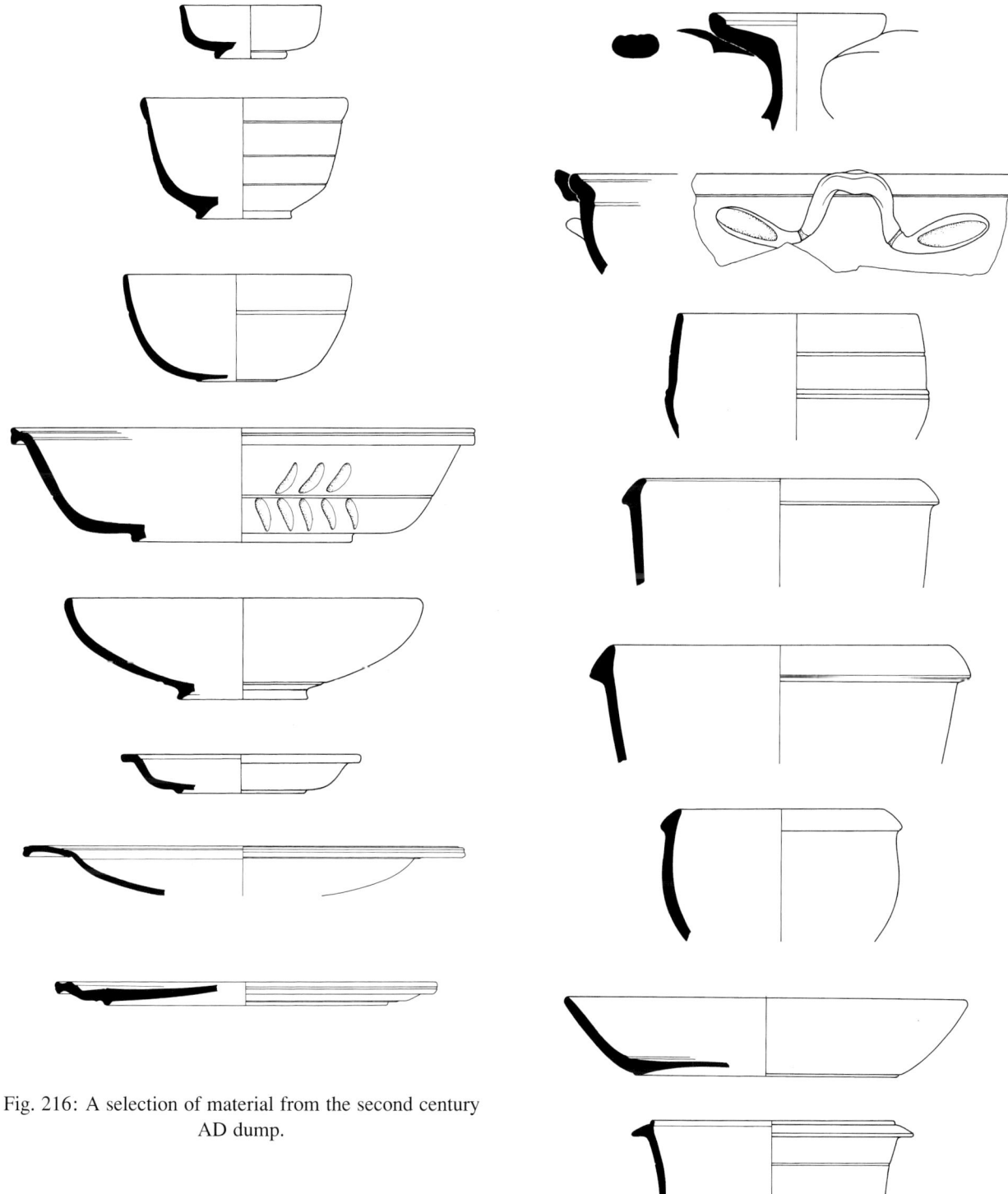

Fig. 216: A selection of material from the second century AD dump.

Fig. 217: A selection of material from the early Imperial dump in trench 3.

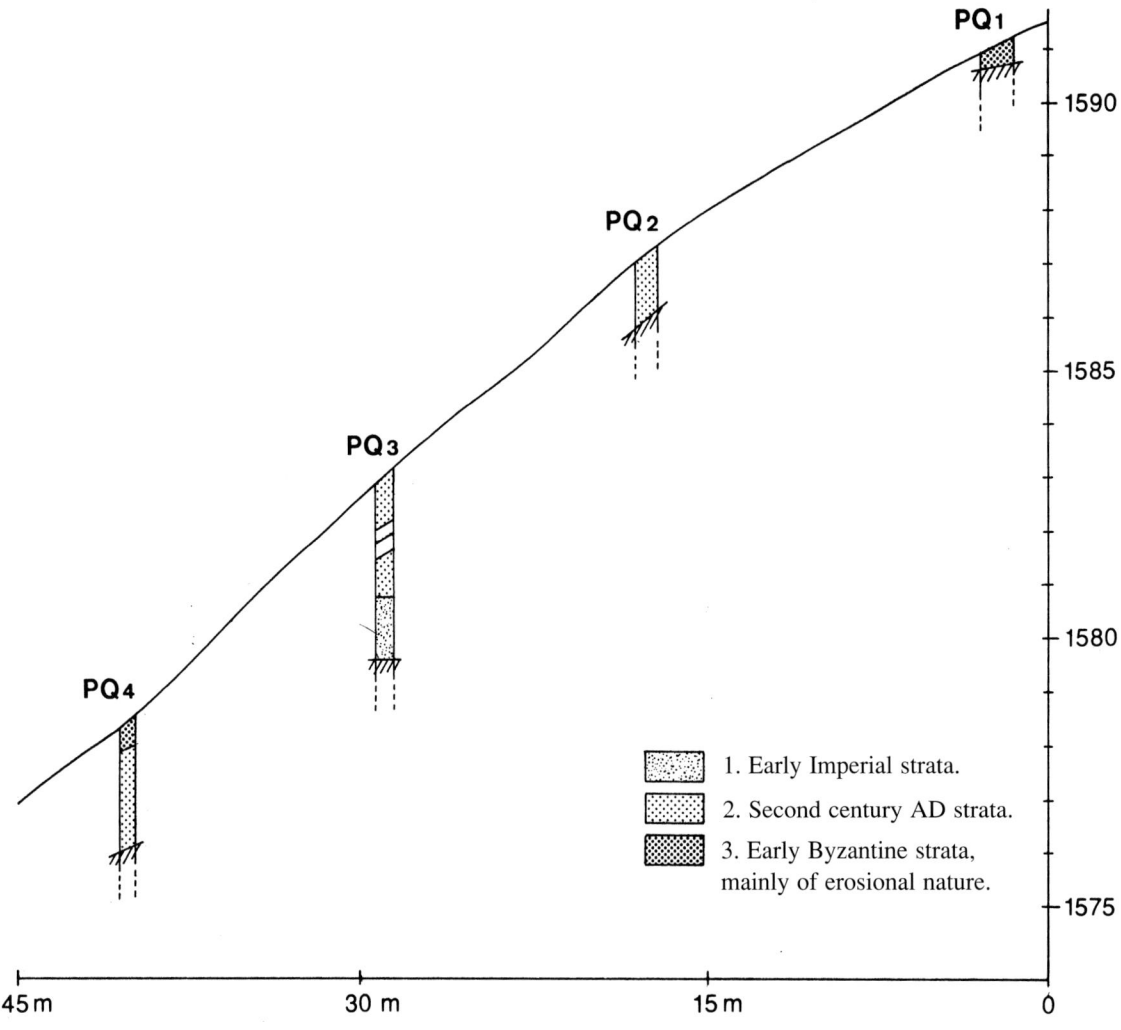

Fig. 218: Theoretical section through the eastern slope of the potters' quarter.

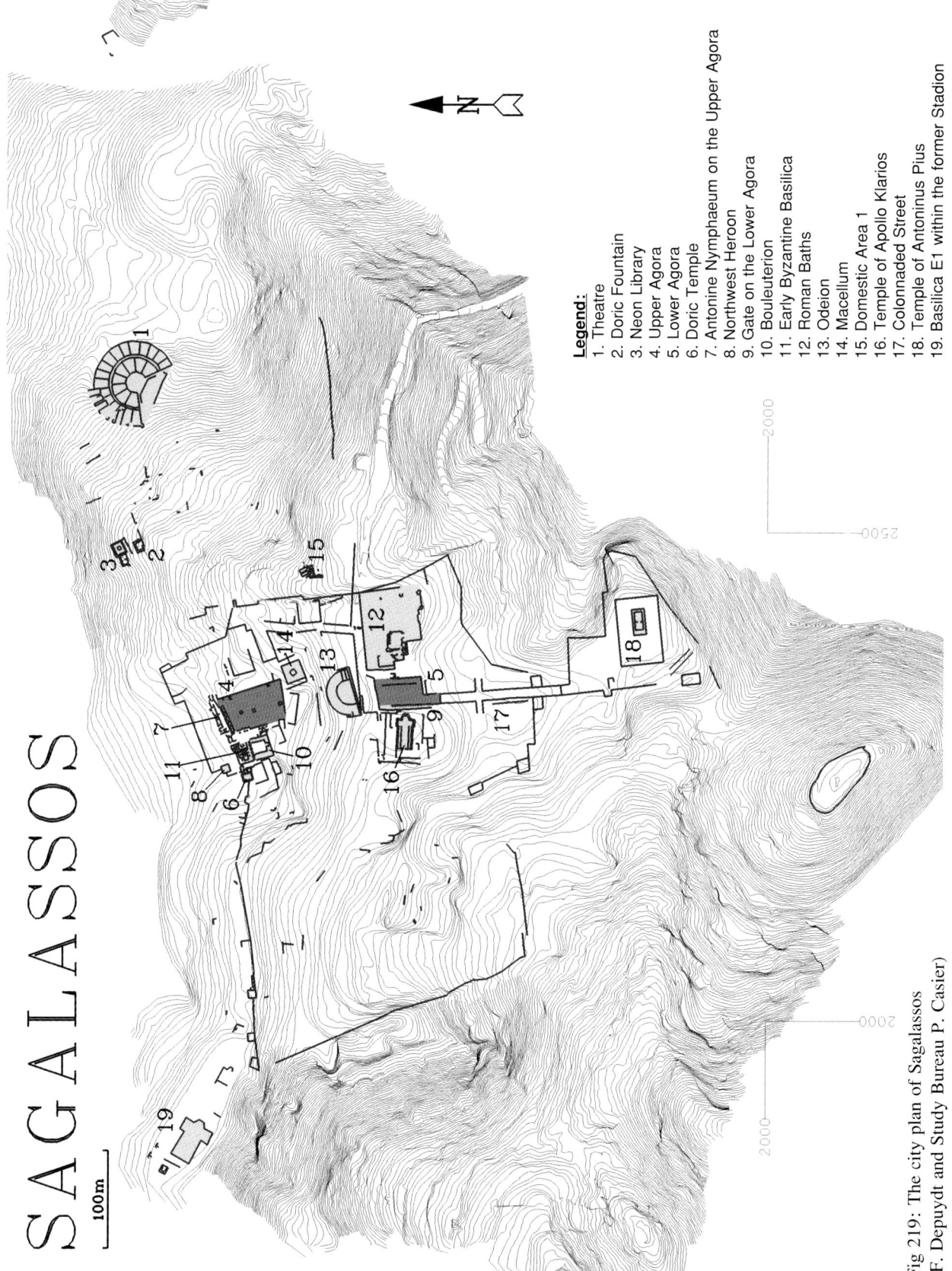

Fig 219: The city plan of Sagalassos
(F. Depuydt and Study Bureau P. Casier)

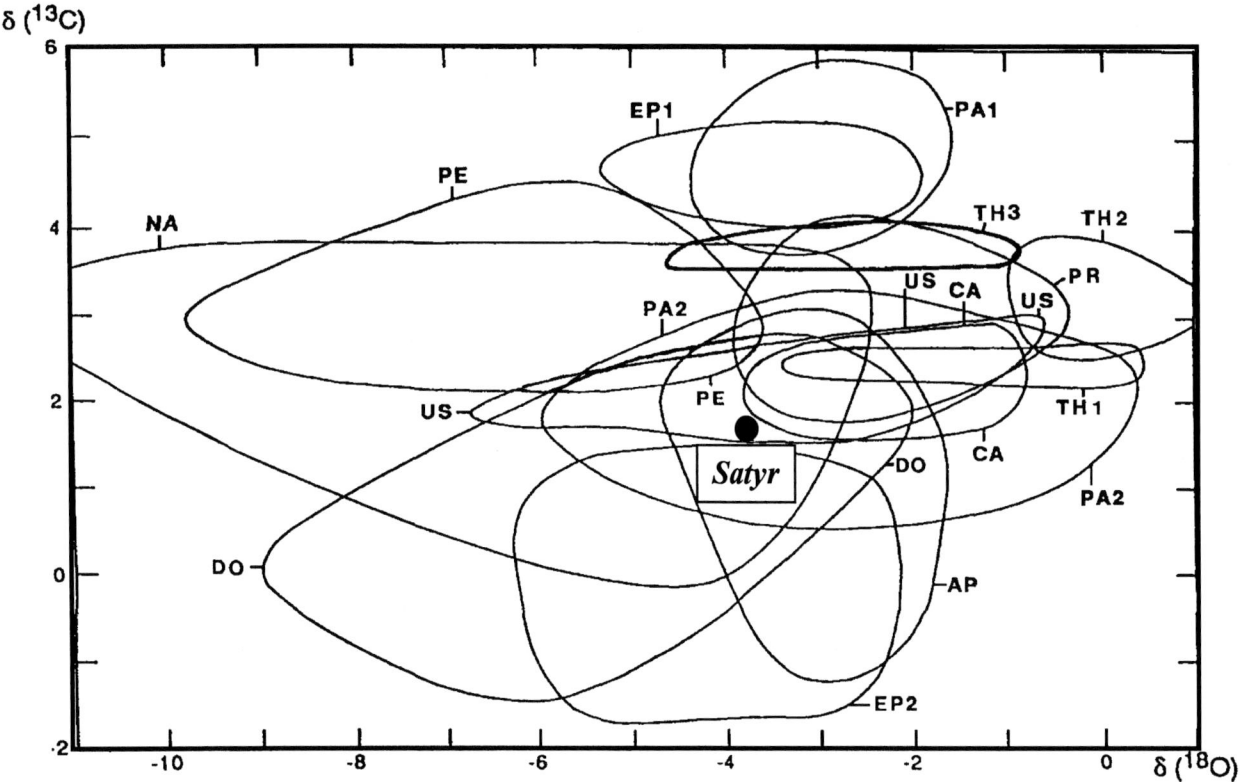

Fig 220: Isotopic fields of the major antique quarry districts (NA = Naxos, DO = Dokimeion, PE=Pentelikon, US=Uşak, EP=Ephesos, PA=Paros, AP=Aphrodisias, CA=Carrara, PR=Proconnesos, TH=Thasos).

SAGALASSOS

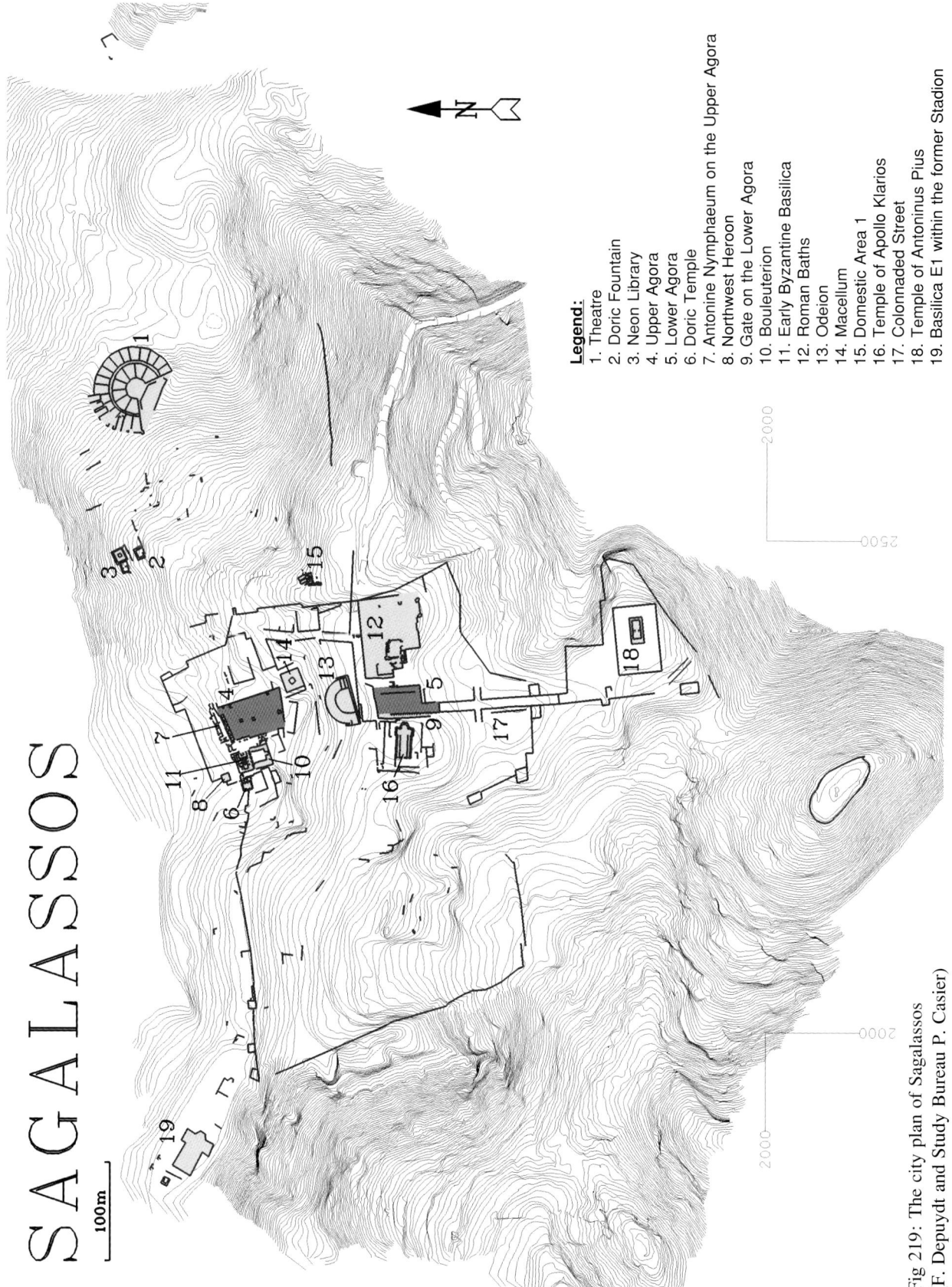

Fig 219: The city plan of Sagalassos
(F. Depuydt and Study Bureau P. Casier)

Legend:
1. Theatre
2. Doric Fountain
3. Neon Library
4. Upper Agora
5. Lower Agora
6. Doric Temple
7. Antonine Nymphaeum on the Upper Agora
8. Northwest Heroon
9. Gate on the Lower Agora
10. Bouleuterion
11. Early Byzantine Basilica
12. Roman Baths
13. Odeion
14. Macellum
15. Domestic Area 1
16. Temple of Apollo Klarios
17. Colonnaded Street
18. Temple of Antoninus Pius
19. Basilica E1 within the former Stadion

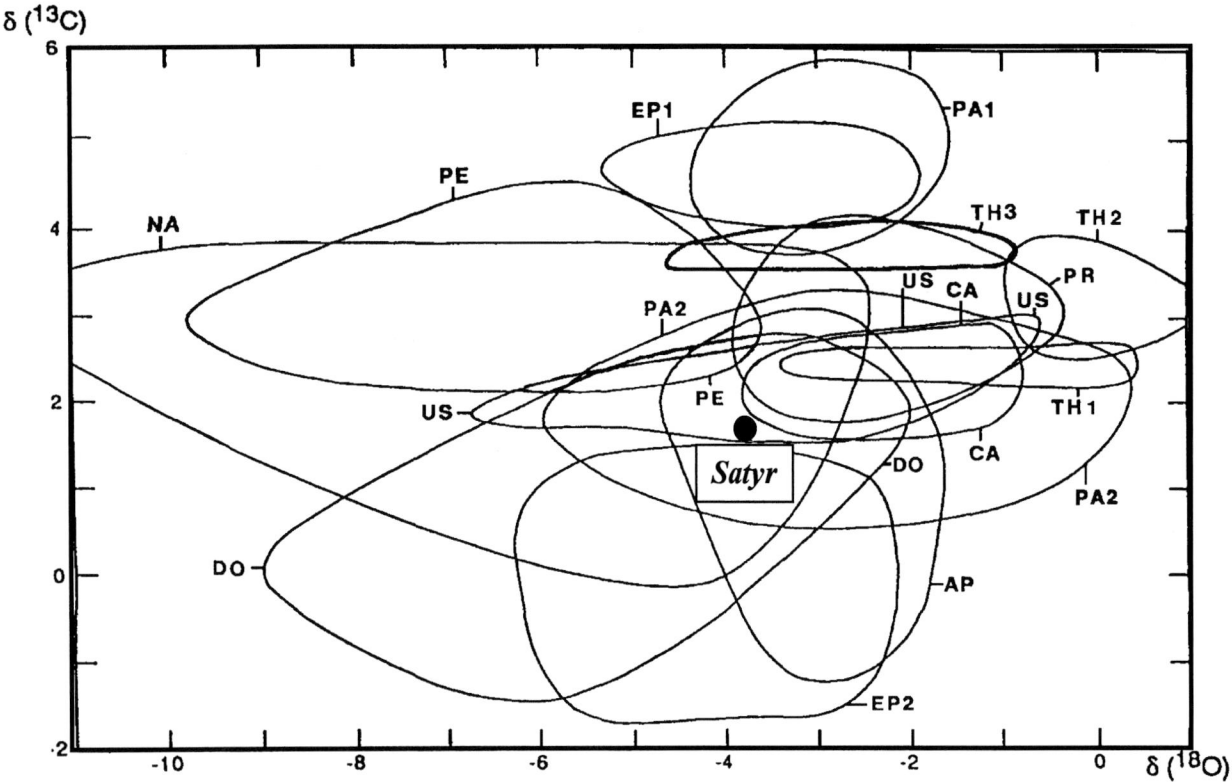

Fig 220: Isotopic fields of the major antique quarry districts (NA = Naxos, DO = Dokimeion, PE=Pentelikon, US=Uşak, EP=Ephesos, PA=Paros, AP=Aphrodisias, CA=Carrara, PR=Proconnesos, TH=Thasos).

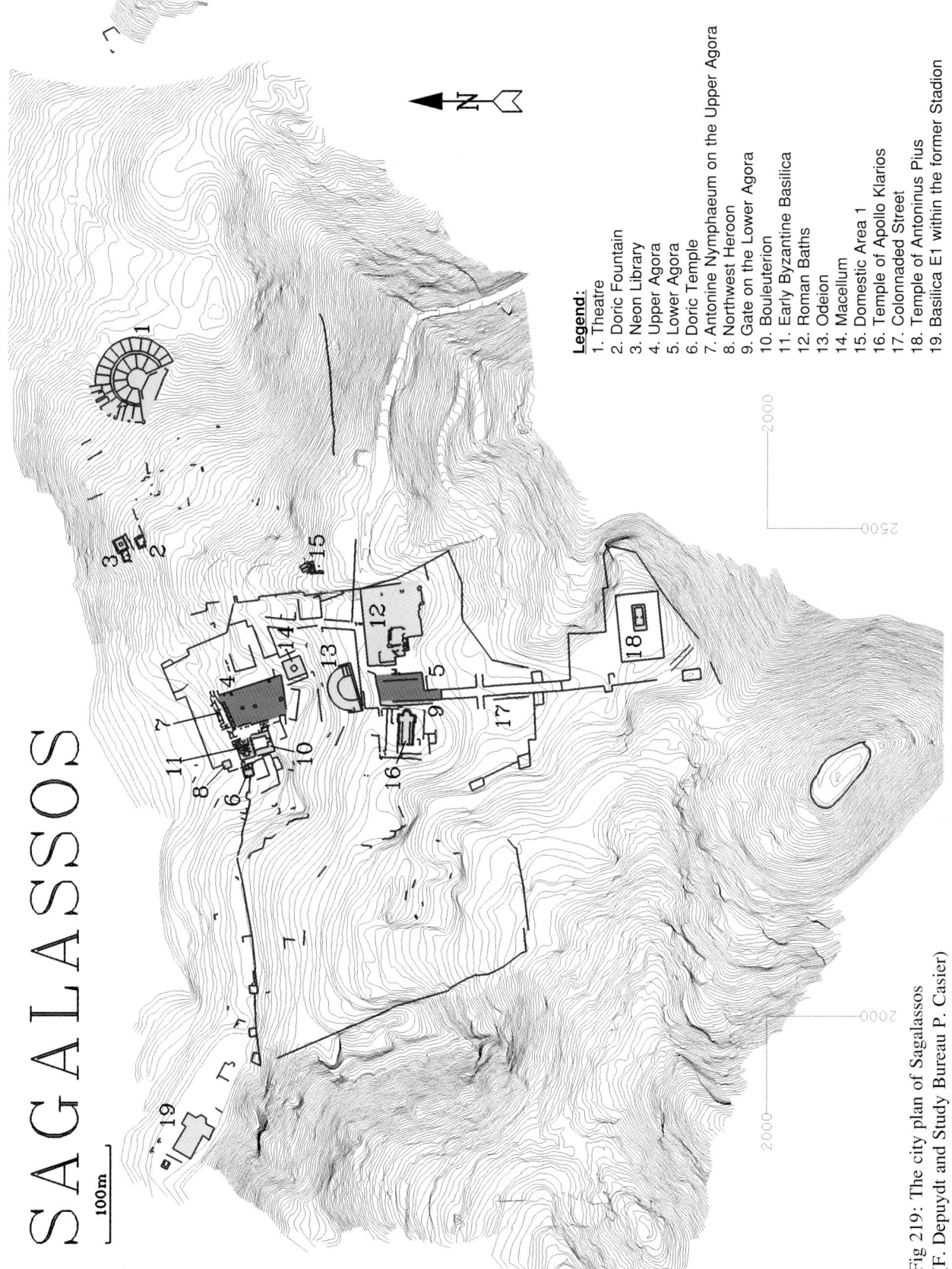

Fig 219: The city plan of Sagalassos
(F. Depuydt and Study Bureau P. Casier)

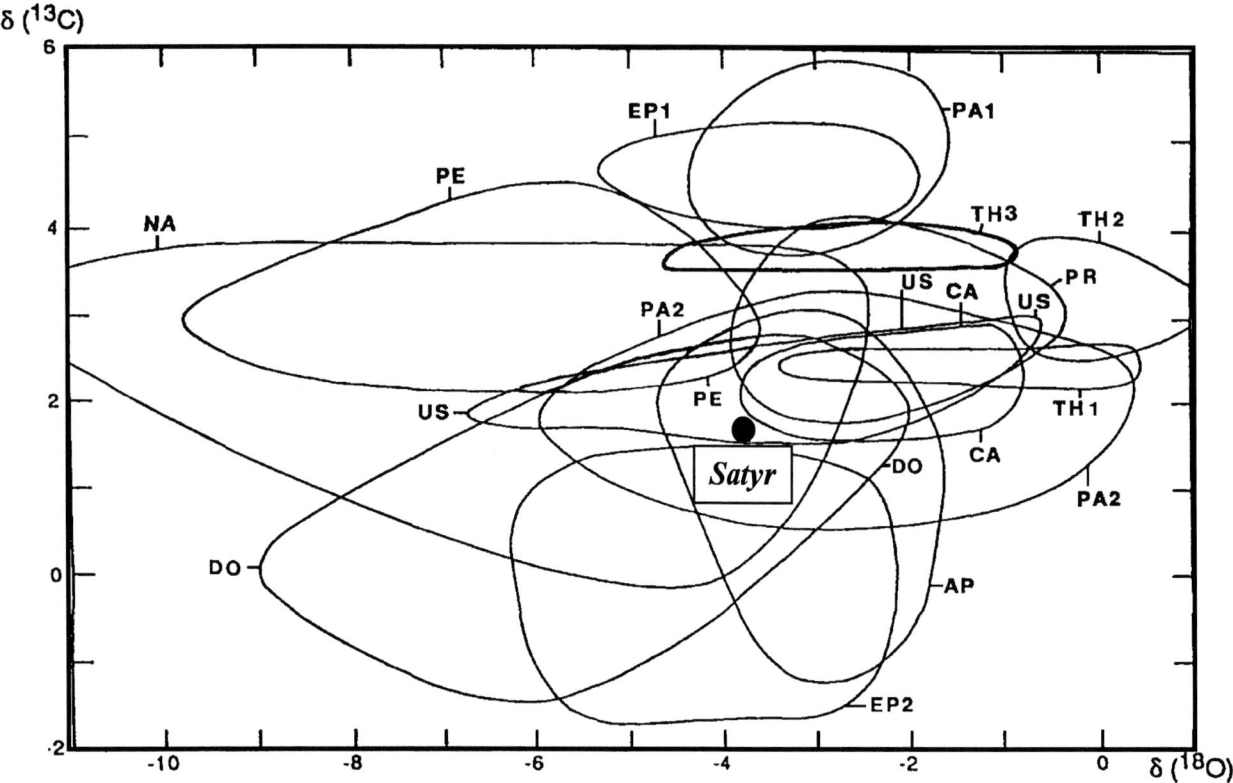

Fig 220: Isotopic fields of the major antique quarry districts (NA = Naxos, DO = Dokimeion, PE=Pentelikon, US=Uşak, EP=Ephesos, PA=Paros, AP=Aphrodisias, CA=Carrara, PR=Proconnesos, TH=Thasos).

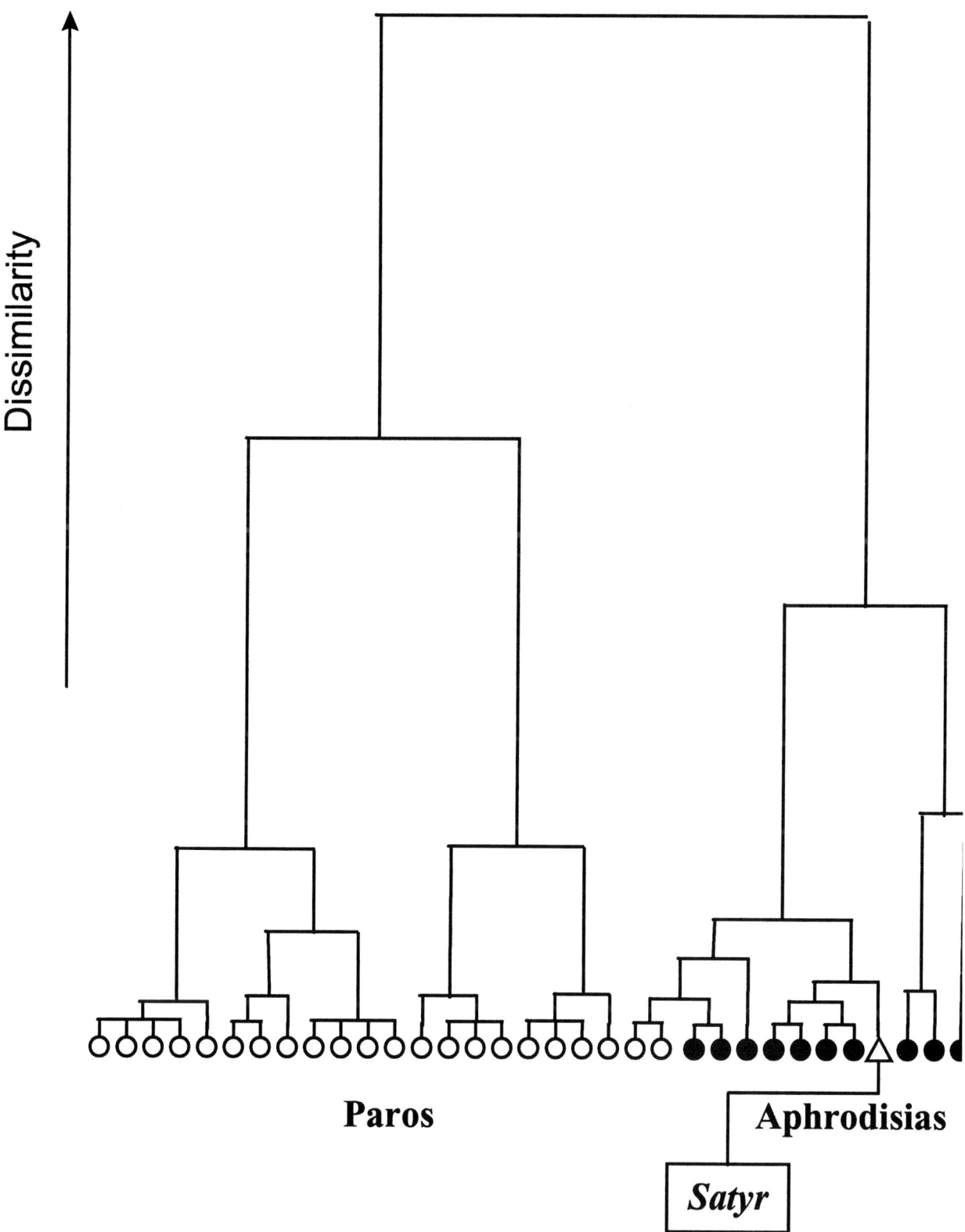

Fig. 221: Cluster analysis on the chemical and pertrographical data for quarry samples from Paros and Aphrodisias and for the statue of a satyr.

(SA 97 PQ 19) was found in this eroded layer. In a small section of trench 7, the excavation was continued to a depth of an additional 1.10 m and a distinctive yellow-brownish loamy matrix was discovered containing a lot of small limestone fragments but no artefacts. This loam represents a weathered fraction of the limestone platform that forms the bedrock in this southern part of the potters' quarter.

12. CARTOGRAPHY

During the 1996 season, the topographical map of the site, at a scale of 1:500, was nearly completed in the southwestern part of the city. In 1997, a team of cartographers (H. Roose, M. Schreurs, J. Theelen, V. Vanacker) completed the map at 1:500 in the western and southern part of the site. In the meantime, a complete city map has been produced and digitised (Fig. 219), also thanks to the help of **SPC (Studiebureau P.Casier, Leuven)**.

13. APPENDIX. AN ARCHAEOMETRIC STUDY OF THE PROVENANCE OF THE DIONYSOS AND SATYR GROUP FROM THE EAST TABERNACLE OF THE MIDDLE ANTONINE NYMPHAEUM (L. Moens and P. De Paepe)

In 1995, a 2.65 m high, 1.12 m wide and 0.60 m deep marble statue representing a drunken Dionysos supported by a satyr was found in and near the sixth *aedicula* of the above-mentioned nymphaeum. It has already been described in the fourth Sagalassos volume, where it was thought to have been made of Docimian marble (Waelkens *et al.* 1997b: 157-161 fig. 88). The statue formed a somewhat taller counterpart for the Aphrodisian Dionysos and satyr group in the first *aedicula* of the same building (see Moens *et al.* 1997: 373, fig.7). While restoring the statue some holes had to be drilled for fibreglass dowels. The extracted core could thus be analysed, and the following results identified this statue group as also originating from Aphrodisias.

- Sample preparation
During the restoration of the sculpture, a sample was taken from one of the fragments with a cylindrical core drill. Integrating the sampling with the restoration process in general permits the hole made in the fragment either to be used to insert a dowel, in which case the scientific analysis implies no additional damage to the artifact, or to be filled immediately by the conservation team and covered with spare marble grains from the same statues. In any case, the sample is taken from a broken surface and in most cases this surface will no longer be visible after restoration. The sampling and subsequent decontamination procedures have been described in more detail elsewhere (Moens *et al.* 1986: 399-406; Moens *et al.* 1997: 367-383).

- Analytical Methods
In previous papers, the multi-method analytical approach has been thoroughly discussed (Waelkens *et al.* 1988: 11-28; Moens *et al.* 1988: 243-250; Moens *et al.* 1997: 367-383). In summary, the material taken from the artifact was subjected to petrography, isotopic (stable C and O isotopes) analysis and analysis of minor and trace elements. Microscopic investigation of thin sections yields a complete petrographic description of the marble. The most important information derived from petrographic analysis concerned the texture of the material and the size of the calcite grains, for which the maximum grain size was used. Isotopic analysis after acid hydrolysis produces the isotopic signature of the marble expressed by the $*^{18}O$ (‰) and $*^{13}C$ (‰) values. Finally, chemical analysis via neutron activation analysis (NAA) and atomic absorption spectrometry (AAS) yields accurate concentration values for many minor and trace elements. The concentration pattern also was found to be a valuable criterion to distinguish between different marble quarries.

- Information extraction
The combined analytical information can be used as a fingerprint and comparison of the data from the artifact with those from quarry samples permits the provenance of the marble to be determined with high probability in most cases. The quarry information, obtained by the analysis of numerous samples collected at the major antique quarries, was stored in a data-base, described in previous work (Waelkens *et al.* 1988: 11-28; Moens *et al.* 1997: 367-383). Comparison is made by first plotting the isotopic signature of the artifact on a two-dimensional diagram (see Fig. 220) showing the isotopic fields characterizing the major antique quarry regions. The result of this comparison is rarely conclusive since the isotopic fields overlap to a large extent. However, the comparison often allows the elimination of several of the quarry. If, in addition, the maximum grain size of the marble from the artifact is compared to the values in the data-base, further elimination is possible, occasionally leading to a clear conclusion. In general, it will be necessary, however, to complement the isotopic information with the combined information of the petrographic and minor- and trace-element analysis. The latter information is extracted from the data set by cluster analysis, permitting a comparison of the data for the artifact with those for the quarries in a stepwise elimination process (Moens *et al.* 1988: 243-250).

The procedure has already been successfully applied to more than hundred artifacts and proved to be highly reliable (Chamay *et al.* 1990: 138-148; De Paepe *et al.* 1992: 255-262; Ramseyer *et al.* 1992: 287-292; Moens *et al.* 1992: 269-276; Moens *et al.* 1997: 367-383). It also allows marble specimens, originating from quarry regions that are not represented in the reference material data-base, to be recognized as such and is therefore proof against any erroneous positive identification of such artifacts. It is of course inevitable that occasionally artifacts will be offered for analysis that are not made of marble from any of the major quarry districts but of marble from one of the numerous quarries of local or regional importance only.

- Results and discussion

Table 1 summarizes the relevant analytical data for the marble of the Dionysos group. In figure 220 its isotopic signature is plotted in the isotope fields diagram showing the major antique quarries. Obviously, isotopic analysis is inconclusive since the isotopic signature of the marble is situated in a zone of overlap between the fields of Dokimeion, Naxos, Paros (2), Aphrodisias and Uşak and even Ephesos, Carrara and Proconnesos cannot be ruled out completely.

The marble from these quarries, except Dokimeion and Carrara, is characterized by a maximum grain size range compatible with the value measured for the statue. Therefore, the chemical information was essential in determining the actual provenance. Stepwise elimination revealed that the marble originates from Aphrodisias. One dendrogram is shown in Figure 221. This dendrogram clearly rules out Paros as a possible provenance since Paros and Aphrodisias form separate clusters and the statue sample is shown as a typical Aphrodisias sample. Similar dendrograms were obtained after cluster analysis applied to the data for the artifact plus the data from any pair of quarry regions from the data-base. All other quarries were thus ruled out when compared to the Aphrodisian quarry region.

The analysis therefore allows us to state with a high degree of probability that the marble of the Dionysos group originates from Aphrodisias.

14. ACKNOWLEDGEMENTS

Parameter	Value	Parameter	Value
Na (ppm)	7,9 (0.2)	Zn (ppm)	4.50 (0.09)
Mg (ppm)	1900 (10)	Sr (ppm)	139 (3)
Al (ppm)	29.0 (0.1)	La (ppb)	152 (2)
Si (ppm)	166 (1)	Ce (ppb)	190 (20)
Ca (%)	39.6 (0.1)	Th (ppb)	5.0 (0.5)
Sc (ppb)	12.2 (0.2)	U (ppb)	590 (90)
V (ppb)	900 (100)		
CR (ppm)	16.5 (0.3)	Maximum grain size (mm)	2.3 (0.1)
Mn (ppm)	65.5 (0.9)		
Fe (ppm)	76.7 (0.8)	$*^{13}C$ ()	1.62 (0.02)
Co (ppb)	25.7 (0.4)	$*^{18}O$ (‰)	-3.44 (0.04)

Table 1: Parameters characterizing the sample of the Satyr (analytical uncertainty between parentheses).

This text presents the results of the Belgian Programme on Interuniversity Poles of Attraction initiated by the Belgian State, Prime Minister's Office, Science Policy Programming (IUAP 4/12). This research was also made possible thanks to an FWO-Vlaanderen research grant (FWO/G.0215.96) and to a GOA-programme (97/2). Scientific responsibility is assumed by its authors.

15. REFERENCES

G. Bowersock (1990) *Hellenism in Late Antiquity*, Cambridge University Press.

G. Brands (1996) Halle, Propylon und Peristyl. Elemente hellenistischer Palastfassaden in Makedonien, in: W. Hoepfner and G. Brands (eds) *Basileia. Die Paläste der hellenistischen Könige. I*, Mainz: 62-72.

P. Brown (1992) *Power and Persuasion in Late Antiquity. Towards a Christian Empire*, The University of Wisconsin Press.

J. Chamay, J.-L. Maier, L. Moens, P. De Paepe, V. Barbin, K. Ramseyer, D. Decrouez, P. Roos and M. Waelkens (1990) l'Origine des marbres blancs de quelques statues du Musée d'Art et d'Histoire de Genève. Etude scientifique plurodisciplinaire, *Antike Kunst* 33: 138-148.

D. De Bernardi Ferrero (1974) *Teatri classici in Asia Minore. 4. Deduzioni e proposte*, Roma.

R. Degeest, R. Ottenburgs, W. Viaene, H. Kucha, D. Laduron, A. Bocquet and M. Waelkens (1997) Characterization of the common wares manufactured in Roman Sagalassos. An overview, in: M. Waelkens and J. Poblome (eds) *Sagalassos IV. Report on the Survey and Excavation Campaigns of 1994 and 1995* (*Acta Archaeologica Lovaniensia Monographiae* 9) Leuven University Press: 519-531.

R. Degeest (2000a) *The Common Wares of Roman Sagalassos* (*Studies in eastern Mediterranean Archaeology* 3) Brepols Publishers.

R. Degeest, P. Degryse, R. Ottenburgs, W. Viaene and M. Waelkens (2000b) The late Roman unguentaria of Sagalassos, *Bulletin Antieke Beschaving* 74, 1999[2000]: 247-272

R. Degeest, P. Degryse, R. Ottenburgs, W. Viaene and M. Waelkens (2000c) Miniature jars of Sagalassos. An analytical, quantitative and typological overview of a series of very small pottery vessels from late antiquity, in: M. Waelkens and L. Loots (eds) *Sagalassos V. Report on the survey and Excavation Campaigns of 1996 and 1997 (Acta Archaelogica Lovaniensia Monograephiae 10)* Leuven: 697-738

P. De Paepe, L. Moens, P. Roos, V. Barbin, D. Decrouez, K. Ramseyer, L. Thommen, E. Berger and K. Faltermeier (1992) An analytical investigation of white marble sculptures from the Basel Museum of Ancient Art and Ludwig Collection, Switzerland, in: M. Waelkens, N. Herz and L. Moens (eds) *Ancient Stones: Quarrying, Trade and Provenance (Acta Archaeologica Lovaniensia Monographiae 4)* Leuven University Press: 255-262.

P. Degryse, R. Degeest, J. Poblome, W. Viaene, R. Ottenburgs, A. Kucha and M. Waelkens (2000) Minerology and geochemistry of Roman common wares produced at Sagalassos and their possible clay resources, in: M. Waelkens and L. Loots (eds) *Sagalassos V. Report on the Survey and Excavation Campaigns of 1996 and 1997 (Acta Archaelogica Lovaniensa Mongographae 10), Leuven University Press:* 709-721.

H. Devijver (1997) Local elite, equestrians and senators: a social history of Roman Sagalassos, *Ancient Society* 27, 1996 [1997] 105-162.

H. Devijver and M. Waelkens (forthcoming) Roman inscriptions from the sixth and seventh campaigns at Sagalassos, *Sagalassos VI.*

S. Ercan, T.C. Patrício and K. Van Balen (1997) The structural restoration of the late Hellenistic nymphaeum: principles, laboratory tests and field applications, in: M. Waelkens and J. Poblome (eds) *Sagalassos IV. Report on the Survey and Excavation Campaigns of 1994 and 1995 (Acta Archaeologica Lovaniensia Monographiae 9)* Leuven University Press: 423-440.

Hierapolis di Frigia 1957-1987 (1987), Fabri editori.

S. Erdemgil and S. Özenir (1982) Preliminary report on the kilns excavated in the Ketios Valley, *Rivista di Archeologia* 6: 109.

K.T. Erim (1987) *Aphrodisias. City of Venus Aphrodite.* Introduction by J.J. Norwich, London.

R. Fleischer (1979) Forschungen in Sagalassos 1972 und 1974, *Istanbuler Mitteilungen* 29: 273- 307.

Cl. Foss (1979) *Ephesos after Antiquity. A Late Antique, Byzantine and Turkish City*, Cambridge University Press.

J. Ganzert (1983) Zur Entwicklung Lesbischer Kymationformen, *Jahrbuch des Deutschen archäologischen Instituts* 98: 123-202.

M. Grant (1998) *From Rome to Byzantium. The Fifth Century AD*, Routledge.

F. Hueber (1997) *Ephesos. Gebaute Geschichte. Mit zwei Beiträgen von S. Erdemgil und M. Büyükkolancı (Sonderhefte der Antiken Welt)* Mainz.

E. Jehaes, M. Waelkens, A. Muyldermans, J.J. Cassiman, J. Poblome, P. Lambrechts and M. Decorte (2000) DNA analysis of archaelogicael human remains from Sagalassos in: M. Waelkens and L. Loots (eds) *Sagalassos V, Report on the Survey and Excavation Campaigns of 1996 and 1997 (Acta Archaelogica Lovansiensa Monographae 10), Leuven University Press:* 821-832.

A.H.M. Jones (1994[12]) *The Decline of the Ancient World*, Longman.

M. Jordan-Ruwe (1995) *Das Säulenmonument. Zur Geschichte der erhöhten Aufstellung antiker Porträtstatuen (Asia Minor Studien* 19) Bonn.

E. Kosmetatou, L. Vandeput and M. Waelkens (1997) The NE Heroon at Sagalassos, in: M. Waelkens and J. Poblome (eds) *Sagalassos IV. Report on the Survey and Excavation Campaigns of 1994 and 1995 (Acta Archaeologica Lovaniensia 9)* Leuven University Press: 353-366.

J. Kramer (1994) *Korinthische Pilasterkapitelle in Kleinasien und Konstantinopel. Antike und Spätantike Werkstattgruppen (Istanbuler Mitteilungen Beiheft 39)* Tübingen.

H. Lauter (1986) *Die Architektur des Hellenismus*, Darmstadt.

L. Loots, M. Waelkens and F. Depuydt (2000a) The city fortifications of Sagalassos from the Hellenistic to the late Roman period, in M; Waelkens and L. Loots (eds) *Sagalassos V. Report on the survey and Excavation campaigns of 1996 and 1997 (Acta Archaeologica Lovaniensia Mongraphiae 10)* Leuven, University Press: 595-634.

L. Loots, M. Waelkens, W. Clarysse, J. Poblome and G. Hibner (2000b) A Catalogue on the tile stamps found at Sagalassos, in: M. Waelkens and L. Loots (eds) *Sagalassos V. Report on the Survey and Excavation Campaigns of 1996 and 1997 (Acta Archaelogica Lovaniensia Monographiae 10), Leuven, University Press:* 685-696.

J.H.W.G. Liebeschuetz (1972) *Antioch: City and Imperial Administration in the Later Roman Empire*, Oxford.

A. Machatschek and M. Schwarz (1981) *Bauforschungen in Selge (TAM, Erg.-B. 9)* Vienna.

F. Martens (in press) Urban water management at Sagalassos. Studying urban development from an hydrological perspective, in: K. Demoen (ed.) *The Greek City from Antiquity to the Present. Historical Reality, Philosophical Concept, Literary Representation*, Leuven.

S. Mitchell and M. Waelkens (1987) Sagalassos and Cremna, *Anatolian Studies* 37: 40-42

S. Mitchell and M. Waelkens (1988) Cremna and Sagalassos, *Anatolian Studies* 38: 60-65

L. Moens, J. De Rudder, P. De Paepe and M. Waelkens (1986) Preparation of white marble samples for instrumental neutron activation analysis, *Bulletin des Societes Chimiques Belges* 95: 399-406.

L. Moens, P. Roos, J. De Rudder, P. De Paepe, J. Ven Hende and M. Waelkens (1988) A multi-method approach to the identification of white marbles used in antique artifacts, in: N. Herz and M. Waelkens (eds) *Classical Marble: Geochemistry, Technology, Trade (NATO ASI Series, Series E: Applied Sciences, 153)* Dordrecht: 243-250.

L. Moens, P. Roos, J. De Rudder, P. De Paepe, J. Van Hende and M. Waelkens (1990) Scientific provenance determination of ancient white marble sculptures, using petrographic, chemical and isotopic data, in: *Art Historical and Scientific Perspectives on Ancient Sculpture*, Malibu: 111- 125.

L. Moens, P. Roos, P. De Paepe and R. Lunsingh Scheurleer (1992) Provenance determination of white marble sculptures from the Allard Pierson Museum in Amsterdam, based on chemical, microscopic and isotopic criteria, in: M. Waelkens, N. Herz and L. Moens (eds) *Ancient Stones: Quarrying, Trade and Provenance (Acta Archaeologica Lovaniensia Monographiae 4)* Leuven University Press: 269-276.

L. Moens, P. De Paepe and M. Waelkens (1997) An archaeometric provenance study of white marble sculptures from Sagalassos (Turkey), in: M. Waelkens and J. Poblome (eds) *Sagalassos IV. Report on the Survey and Excavation Campaigns of 1994 and 1995 (Acta Archaeologica Lovaniensia Monographiae 9)* Leuven University Press: 367-383.

N. Morley (1997) Cities in context: urban systems in Roman Italy, in: H.M. Parkins (ed.) *Roman Urbanism. Beyond the Consumer City*, Routledge London-New York: 42-58.

I. Morris (1992) *Death-Ritual and Social Structure in Classical Antiquity*, Cambridge.

I. Nielsen (1994) *Hellenistic Palaces. Tradition and Renewal (Studies in Hellenistic Civilization* V) Aarhus University Press.

T. Patricio, S. Ercan and K. Van Balen (2000) The restoration of the Late Hellenistic Fountain Houser field works in: M. Waelkens and L. Loots (eds) *Sagalassos V. Report on the Sur-*

vey and Excavation Campaigns of 1996 and 1997 (Acta archaelogica Lovaniensia Mongrophiae (10), Leuven University Press: 319-418

E.J. Owens (1995) The aqueducts of Sagalassos, in: M. Waelkens and J. Poblome (eds) *Sagalassos III. Report on the Fourth Excavation Campaign of 1993 (Acta Archaeologica Lovaniensia Monographiae 7)* Leuven University Press: 91-113.

J. Poblome (1996) Production and distribution of Sagalassos red slip ware. A dialogue with the Roman economy, in: M. Hertfort-kock, U. Mondel and U. Schädler (eds) *Hellenistische und kaiser zeitliche keramik das östlichen Mittelmeergebiets. Kolloquium Frankfurt 24-25. April 1995*, Frankfurt am Main; 75-103

J. Poblome, W. Viaene, H. Kucha, M. Waelkens, D. Laduron and F. Depuydt (1997) Clay raw materials of Sagalassos red slip ware. A chronological evaluation, in: M. Waelkens and J. Poblome (eds) *Sagalassos IV. Report on the Survey and Excavation Campaigns of 1994 and 1995 (Acta Archaeologica Lovaniensia Monographiae 9)* Leuven University Press: 507-518.

J. Poblome (1999) *Sagalassos Red Slip Ware. Typology and Chronology (Studies in Eastern Mediterranean Archaeology* 2) Brepols Publishers.

K. Ramseyer, D. Decrouez, V. Barbin, S. Burns, L. Moens, P. De Paepe, P. Roos, J. Chamay and J.-L. Maier (1992) Provenance investigation of marble artefacts now in the collection of the Museum of Art and History in Geneva, in: M. Waelkens, N. Herz and L. Moens (eds) *Ancient Stones: Quarrying, Trade and Provenance (Acta Archaeologica Lovaniensia Monographiae 4)* Leuven University Press: 287-292.

Ch. Roueché (1989) *Aphrodisias in Late Antiquity. With Contributions by J.M. Reynolds (Society for the Promotion of Roman Studies. Journal of Roman Studies Monographs N° 5)* London.

B. Rose (1997) The imperial image in the Eastern Mediterranean, in: S. Alcock (ed.), *The Early Roman Empire in the East (Oxbow Monograph* 95) Oxford: 108-120.

F. Rumscheid (1994) *Untersuchungen zur kleinasiatischen Bauornamentik des Hellenismus*, 2. Vol. (*Beiträge zur Erschliessung hellenistischer und kaiserzeitlicher Skulptur und Architektur* 14) Mainz.

F.Rumscheid (1998) *Priene. Führer durch das "Pompeji Kleinasiens". Mit Beiträgen von W. Königs*, Istanbul.

S. Scheers (2000) Coins found in 1996 and 1997, in: M. Waelkens and L. Loots (eds) *Sagalassos V. Report on the Survey and Excavation Campaigns of 1996 and 1997 (Acta Archaelogica Lovaniensia Monographiae 10)* Leuven University Press:509-551.

L.Vandeput (1993) Honour where honour is due: regional features on honorific monuments of Pisidia?, *Anatolian Studies* 48: 193-202.

L.Vandeput (1997a) *The Architectural Decoration in Roman Asia Minor. Sagalassos: a Case Study (Studies in Eastern Mediterranean Archaeology* 2) Brepols Publishers Turnhout.

L.Vandeput (1997b) An Antonine nymphaeum to the north of the Upper Agora at Sagalassos, in: M. Waelkens and J. Poblome (eds) *Sagalassos IV. Report on the Survey and Excavation Campaigns of 1994 and 1995 (Acta Archaeologica Lovaniensia Monographiae 9)* Leuven University Press: 385-403.

L. Vandeput (in press) Frühkaiserzeitliche Tempel in Pisidien, in: H. von Hesberg, L. Vandeput, Ch. Berns and M. Waelkens (eds) *Kontinuität und Diskontinuität in den frühkaiserzeitlichen Städten Kleinasiens (Bulletin Antieke Beschaving Supplements)*.

M. Waelkens, P. De Paepe and L. Moens (1988) Quarries and the marble trade in Antiquity, in: N. Herz and M. Waelkens (eds) *Classical Marble: Geochemistry, Technology, Trade (NATO ASI Series, Series E: Applied Sciences, 153)* Dordrecht: 11-28.

M. Waelkens (1989) Hellenistic and Roman influence in the imperial architecture of Asia Minor, in: S. Walker and A. Cameron (eds) *The Greek Renaissance in the Roman Empire (Papers from the Tenth British Museum Classical Colloquium. Bulletin Supplement* 55) University of London: 77-88.

M. Waelkens, S. Başer, M. Lodewijckx, W. Viaene and R. Degeest (1990) Sagalassos 1989. The rescue excavation in the Potters' Quarter and the "Sagalassos ware", *Acta Archaeologica Lovaniensia* 28-29: 75-98.

M. Waelkens, A. Harmankaya and W. Viaene (1991) The excavations at Sagalassos 1990, *Anatolian Studies* 41: 197-213.

M. Waelkens, E. Owens, A. Hasendonckx and B. Arıkan (1992) The excavations at Sagalassos 1991, *Anatolian Studies* 42: 79-98.

M. Waelkens (1993a) Sagalassos. History and archaeology, in: M. Waelkens (ed.) *Sagalassos I. First General Report on the Survey (1986-1989) and Excavations (1990-1991) (Acta Archaeologica Lovaniensia Monographiae 5)* Leuven University Press: 37-82.

M. Waelkens (1993b) The 1992 season at Sagalassos. A preliminary report, in: M. Waelkens and J. Poblome (eds) *Sagalassos II. Report on the Third Excavation Campaign of 1992 (Acta Archaeologica Lovaniensia Monographiae 6)* Leuven University Press: 9-42.

M. Waelkens (1993c) The excavations of a late Hellenistic fountain house and its surroundings (site N), in: M. Waelkens and J. Poblome (eds) *Sagalassos II. Report on the Third Excavation Campaign of 1992 (Acta Archaeologica Lovaniensia Monographiae 6)* Leuven University Press: 43-87.

M. Waelkens, E. Paulissen, B. Arıkan, L. Gijsen, M. Martens, V. Mataouchek and K. Van Daele (1995a) The 1993 excavations in the fountain house-library area, in: M. Waelkens and J. Poblome (eds) *Sagalassos III. Report on the Fourth Excavation Campaign of 1993 (Acta Archaeologica Lovaniensia Monographiae 7)* Leuven University Press: 47-90.

M. Waelkens, D. Pauwels and J. Van den Bergh (1995b) The 1993 excavations on the upper and lower agora, in: M. Waelkens and J. Poblome (eds) *Sagalassos III. Report on the Fourth Excavation Campaign of 1993 (Acta Archaeologica Lovaniensia Monographiae 7)* Leuven University Press: 23-46.

M. Waelkens, E. Paulissen, H. Vanhaverbeke, I. Öztürk, B. De Cupere, H.A. Ekinci, P.M. Vermeersch, J. Poblome and R. Degeest (1997a) The 1994 and 1995 surveys on the territory of Sagalassos, in: M. Waelkens and J. Poblome (eds) *Sagalassos IV. Report on the survey and excavation campaigns of 1994 and 1995 (Acta Archaeologica Lovaniensia Monographiae 9)* Leuven University Press: 11-102.

M. Waelkens, P.M. Vermeersch, E. Paulissen, E.J. Owens, B. Arıkan, M. Martens, P. Talloen, L. Gijsen, L. Loots, Ch. Peleman, J. Poblome, R. Degeest,T.C. Patricio, S. Ercan and F. Depuydt (1997b) The 1994 and 1995 excavation seasons at Sagalassos, in: M. Waelkens and J. Poblome (eds) *Sagalassos IV. Report on the Survey and Excavation Campaigns of 1994 and 1995 (Acta Archaeologica Lovaniensia Monographiae 9)* Leuven University Press: 103-217.

M. Waelkens (1999) Sagalassos. Religious life in a Pisidian town during the Hellenistic and Roman Imperial period, in: C. Bonnet and A. Motte (eds) *Les syncrétismes religieux dans le monde méditerranéen antique. Actes du Colloque International en l'honneur de Franz Cumont à l'occasion de sa mort. Rome, Academia Belgica, 25-27 septembre 1997*, Bruxelles-Brussel-Rome: 191-226.

M. Waelkens, L. Vandeput, Ch. Berns, B. Arıkan and E. Toruss, (2000a) The northwest heroon at Sagalassos, in: M. Waelkens and L. Loots (eds) *Sagalassos V. Report on the survey and Excavation campaigns of 1996 and 1997 (Acta Archaeologica Lovaniensia Mongraphiae 10)* Leuven University Press 553-594.

M. Waelkens, M. Sintubin, Ph. Muchez and E. Paulissen (2000b) Archaeological, geomophological and geological evidence for a major earthquake at Sagalassos (SW Turkey) around the middle of the seventh century AD, in: W.J. McGuire, D.R. Griffiths, P.L. Hancock and I.S. Stewart (eds) *The Archaeology of Geological Catastrophes (Geological Society of London. Special Publications* 171) London: 373-383.

M. Waelkens, H. Kökten Ersoy, K;. Severson, F. Martens and S. Senen (2000c) The Sagalassos Neon Library mosaic and its conservation, in: M. Waelkens and L. Loots (eds) *Sagalassos V. Report on the Survey and Excavation Campaigns of 1996 and 1997 (Acta Archaelogica lovaniensia Monographiae 10)*, Leuven, Unversity Press 419-450.

M. Waelkens (in press) The transformation of the public and sacred landscapes in early Imperial Sagalassos, in: H. von Hesberg, L. Vandeput, Ch. Berns and M. Waelkens (eds) *Kontinuität und Diskontinuität in den frühkaiserzeitlichen Städten Kleinasiens (Bulletin Antieke Beschaving Supplements)*.

M. Waelkens, Ph. Muchez, L. Loots, P. Degryse, L. Moens and P. Depaepe (in press) Marble and the marble trade at Sagalassos (Turkey), in: *Fifth International ASMOSIA Conference, 11-15 June 1998, Boston Museum of Fine Arts.*

M. Waelkens and L. Vandeput (in press) Regionalism in Hellenistic and Roman Pisidia, in: H. Elton and G. Reger (eds) *Regionalism in Hellenistic and Roman Asia Minor. Trinity College, Hartford CT, 22-24 August 1997.*

RESTORATION OF THE LATE HELLENISTIC FOUNTAIN HOUSE: FIELD WORKS

Teresa C. PATRÍCIO[1], Semih ERCAN[2] and Koenraad VAN BALEN[1]

1 - R. Lemaire Centre for Conservation, KULeuven, Kardinaal Mercierlaan 94, B-3001 Heverlee, Belgium
2 - Department of Archaelogy, KULeuven, Blijde Inkomststraat 21, B-3000 Leuven, Belgium

1. INTRODUCTION

A restoration project applying anastylosis techniques has been proposed for the stone structure of the late Hellenistic fountain house. The aim of this project was to preserve the monument by rebuilding it, re-using all the original elements in their original places while preserving their original structural behaviour. The physical reconstitution also aimed to reinstate the building's original function as a fountain, as its natural spring is still in existence.

The first phase of the work, which took place in 1991 and 1992, included the full documentation of the discovered material with a view to its restoration (Patrício and Van Balen 1993: 87-105). The second phase began in 1993 and led to a partial anastylosis of some parts of the building from fragments and blocks. At the same time, the first reconstitution models were drawn (Patrício and Van Balen 1995: 143-163). A preliminary study of the architectural elements in 1992 led to the first laboratory experiments and tests (Van Balen and Patrício 1995: 165-174) as well as a detailed study of the architectural elements by direct observation (Patrício 1995:143-163). The materials and techniques to be used in the structural restoration were examined during the laboratory research. The third phase started in 1994 with the restoration of the damaged building blocks and is still proceeding (Ercan *et al.* 1997: 423-437). The architectural research also focussed on the position in which the stones were found at the time of the excavations and on their relative positions within the structure (Patrício and Van Balen 1996: 101-109). The last phase of the work began in 1996 when the restored blocks started to be replaced into position. The reconstitution model was updated every year with new information obtained during the progress of the work. This research continued until all the blocks, were re-assembled in the building (Patrício and Van Balen 1993: 87-105).

More specifically, the works during the 1996 campaign included the following activities:

- continuation of the architectural investigation; restoration of the stone blocks;
- consolidation and levelling of the foundations;
- correction of the west wall's distortion;
- controlling and canalising the natural spring water with testing of mortars for the water basins;
- final anastylosis of parts of the building.

2. ARCHITECTURAL INVESTIGATION

The scientific study of ancient Greek architecture by architects and archaeologists has developed considerably during the last two centuries. The main purpose of the scientific study and architectural investigation of the late Hellenistic fountain house was to provide the necessary documentation for the restoration project. The aim of the project was to restore the building using the existing original stone blocks, which have collapsed over the years. However *Bauforschung,* or architectural investigation of the late Hellenistic fountain house, is not limited only to providing a tool for restoration or the documentation that is strictly necessary for that particular restoration. On the one hand, research on the monument and its parts before its reinstatement by anastylosis provides a unique opportunity to analyse and develop scientific knowledge on architectural history, architectural details and construction techniques. On the other hand, *Bauforschung* itself is the first step in the preservation of historical information. Since 1992, *Bauforschung* has been carried out on the fountain house and its elements, either *in situ* or removed. In 1993, the first results of this investigation already emerged (Patrício and Van Balen 1995:143-163).

Investigation on the structural study, building construction methods and techniques continued through the last campaigns. The study of the construction elements afforded some important conclusions for the final reconstitution of the original building.

Before describing these final results, we wish to emphasise that the description of the *in situ* and the removed material of a historic building should not be dissociated from its theoretical reconstitution and that every single element in the building must be included.

2.1. Construction techniques

The structure of the fountain house consists of three walls making a U-shape with three porticoes, supported by three parapets, running parallel to them. The parapets and walls form three water basins. Cornices supported by the walls and porticoes connect those elements, making a roof over the basins. The entablature consists of an architrave and frieze together with their cornices (Patrício and Van Balen 1995: 143-164). At both extremities of the north portico, there are two connecting beams (corner architraves with a plain moulding leading from east to west) between the corner columns of the porticoes and the west and east walls (Van Balen and Patrício 1995: 165-174).

Normally, the last block would be put in place with a lewis (Adam 1994: 48-49). But no lewis holes were found either on the upper surface of the architraves or on the cornices. Three cornice blocks are missing: one from the central part of the north portico, and two from the south part of the east and west porticoes.

A study of the connection points of the entablature with the walls showed that the construction is very simple and that no lewis was necessary for the placement of the blocks because the last architraves and cornices were simply placed on top of the walls. From the study of the architraves it became clear that the construction might not have proceeded from the corners toward the centre. The structure was probably assembled as follows:

1 – Columns and capitals were placed in their final position.
2 – For the architraves, the construction started from the north portico with the east connection beam block N808 and continued from east to west. The architrave N808 was built in the east wall. The last architrave to be placed was N292, the west connection beam. This architrave was not built in the west wall but only positioned on it (Fig. 1).
3 – The east and west portico architraves were put in place from north to south. Only afterwards was the south wall built against the porticoes.
4 – The planning of the work of placing the cornices was exactly the same as for the architraves, starting from the north portico with the first cornice from the east side, block N826 (Fig.1). The cornice was built in the east wall and built into the street pavement. The construction continued from east to west. The last cornice was the final and highest stone N 290 of the west wall (Fig.1).

The blocks were apparently lifted with thin ropes and placed into their final positions. The architraves have a projecting boss on their rear surfaces (Fig. 2). Initially this was interpreted as a lifting boss, but a closer study indicates that these projecting bosses were probably so that a pry-bar could be used for the precise and final positioning of the block (Fig. 3).

3. RESTORATION OF THE STONE BLOCKS

Because seismic activities and deterioration processes over the centuries had caused the collapse of the structure, most of the building blocks were found fragmented in many pieces and with serious cracks. Moreover, some fragments of the broken blocks were still missing. The first problem to solve for the re-erection of the dismembered building was to make up sound blocks, as strong as they had been originally. Broken fragments had to be joined together and where parts of the blocks were missing they needed to be completed for structural integrity. The interventions conducted for the restoration of the stone blocks were based on the principle of minimal intervention and protection of the original material. The materials and techniques, after being studied and improved through laboratory tests between 1994 and 1996 in the Reyntjens Laboratory of the Civil Engineering Department of the KULeuven, were then applied for the restoration of the fountain house (Ercan *et al*. 1997: 573-584).

The restoration of the stone blocks, which started in 1994, can be divided into four main activities: joining the broken parts, completing the missing parts, consolidation and cleaning of the blocks.

3.1. Joining of the broken blocks
An epoxy-based adhesive mixed with a limestone powder filler was used to glue small fragments. By mixing the epoxy adhesive with an inert filler of powdered limestone the strength of the adhesion and cohesion has been reduced to almost the strength of the stone itself.

For joining the structurally important broken blocks, such as column drums, architraves and cornices, fibreglass rods were used together with the epoxy adhesive. Two conditions were imposed on this work. First, the broken blocks should be joined in such a way that the strength of the joined block would not exceed the limit state strength of the monolithic block. Second, if the joined block were to break, it should break again in the original place. To fulfil these requirements, the application area of the epoxy glue was limited to only half of the broken surface and the fibreglass reinforcing rods were designed appropriately according to these considerations. The brittle nature of the fibreglass is

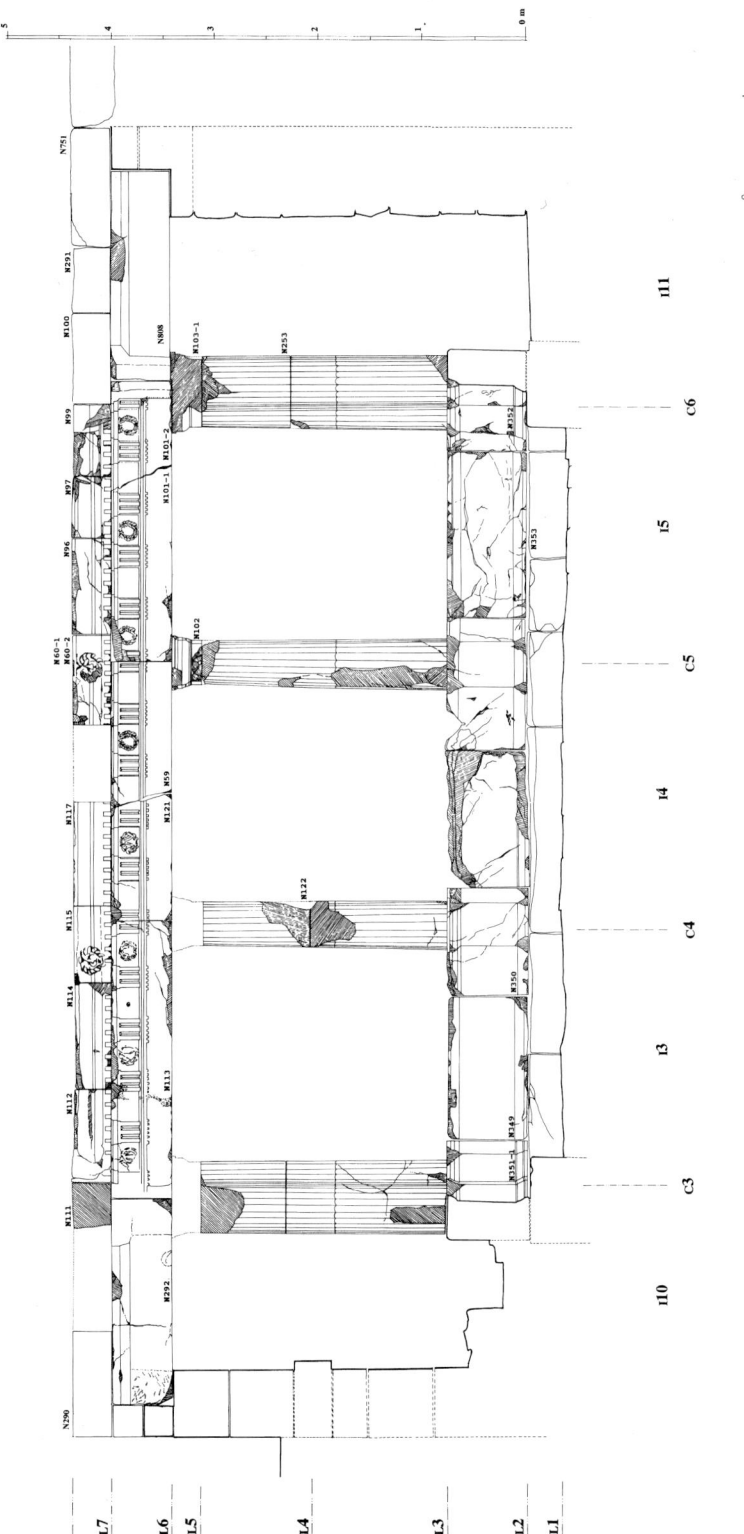

Fig. 1 – Graphic synthesis of the north portico.

Fig. 2: View of the rear surface of the architrave N196. Two projecting bosses are visible in the lower part.

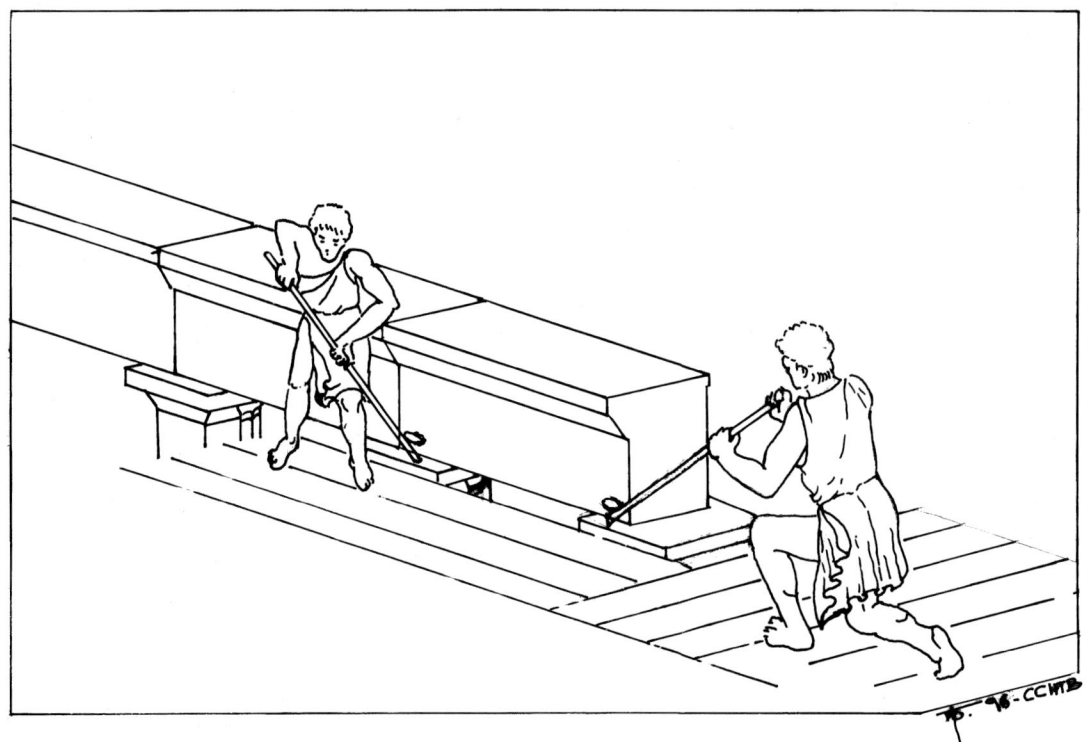

Fig. 3: Reconstruction drawing of the use of the pry-bar for the positioning of the fountain house architraves.

Fig. 4: View of an architrave after the existing fragments were joined. The fibreglass reinforcing rod is visible. The missing parts of the block still need to be completed for structural integrity.

Fig. 5: View of a column drum after the existing fragments were joined. The missing parts of the block still need to be completed.

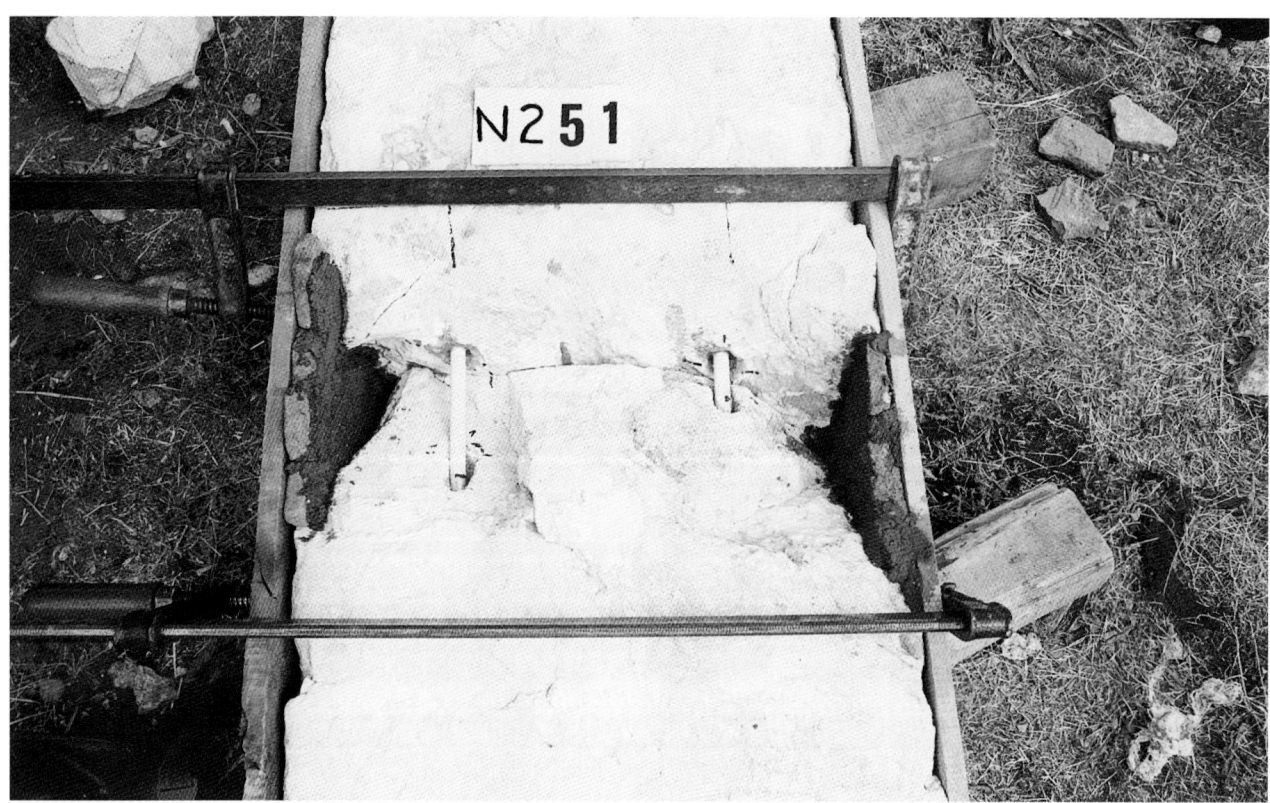

Fig. 6: View of a joined cornice block, before the missing parts were completed.

Fig. 7: The cornice block after its missing parts were completed by an epoxy mortar.
The epoxy mortar will then be covered by the covering mortar.

Fig. 8: A completed column drum. The surface of the epoxy mortar was prepared prior to the application of the mineral covering mortar.

Fig. 9: Restored column drum after the mineral covering mortar was applied.

Fig. 10: Structural consolidation of a cracked block by pinning with a fibreglass rod, embedded in epoxy grout.

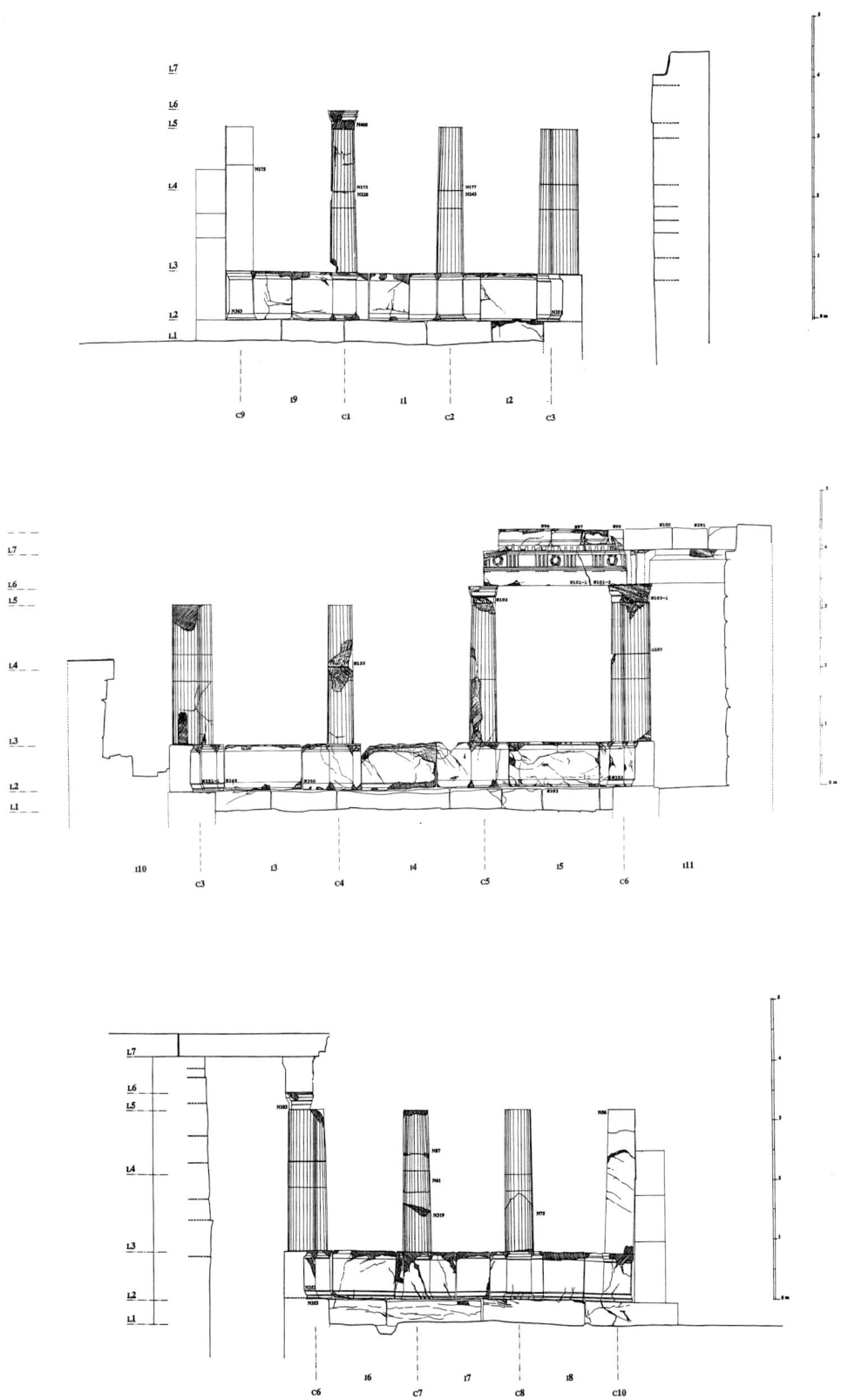

Fig. 11: Reconstruction drawing of the first anastylosis stage, west, north and -east porticoes.

an advantage here, as it means that the reconstruction can be altered at any time in the future, as the broken reinforcement can be removed and replaced by a similar system. The number, size and length of the reinforcing rods varied according to the broken parts of the block and its structural function. For the blocks under flexural stress, like architraves and cornices, the rods should have a certain anchorage length, so that they would not be pulled out. Generally 4 fibreglass rods of 34 cm length and 16 mm diameter were used for joining these blocks (Fig. 4). Shorter rods are sufficient for joining the column drums, as the main structural stress on them would be in shear. Generally 4 fibreglass rods of 20 cm length and 12 mm diameter were used to join the column drums (Fig. 5).

3.2. Completing the missing parts of the blocks

After joining the fragments composing a block, missing parts had to be completed to fulfil the structural integrity. An epoxy mortar obtained by mixing epoxy adhesive with a well-graded crushed limestone filler was used for this purpose. The maximum particle size of the filler was 2 mm and the binder to filler ratio of the mortar varied between 1:5 to 1:8 by volume, according to the application. The epoxy mortar, which was tested earlier in the laboratory, has similar physical properties to the original stone. Its mechanical properties are slightly weaker than the original stone and it also has a more elastic behaviour than the stone. The epoxy mortar was applied in a few layers, where each layer was compacted firmly. According to the volume to fill and the structural function of the block to be completed, fibreglass bars were sometimes used for a stronger bond between the epoxy mortar and the stone blocks (Fig. 6, 7, 8). As epoxy mortars discolour under ultraviolet radiation and in order to create a proper surface texture, a 1 to 2 cm thick covering mortar was applied over the dried epoxy mortar fillings (Fig. 9). The covering mortar used was a zinc chloride-based mineral mortar, which was also tested in the laboratory before being used. This quick setting and non-shrinking covering mortar has a very similar colour to the stone and its shape and texture can be finished easily by carving.

3.3. Structural consolidation of the stone blocks

Structural consolidation was necessary for stone blocks of structural importance that had severe cracks. First the cracks in the stones were detected by inspection and sound testing, then structural consolidation was undertaken where necessary by pinning fibreglass rods, anchored by an epoxy grout, through the cracks (Fig. 10). Fibreglass rods of 7 and 8 mm diameter and at least 20 cm length were used. Some of the *in situ* blocks, like the window lintel and some wall blocks, were also consolidated *in situ* using the pinning method.

3.4. Non-structural consolidation

The fissured and flaking stone blocks of no structural importance were consolidated *in situ* by injection of a water-porous glue. Different materials were tested and evaluated for this purpose. The most important criterion was that the sealed crack should allow water vapour through, so that the wet and very fine sand present in the crack could dry. In this way, frost damage due to the expansion of the water trapped in the crack is avoided. After these consolidations, all the fissures and cracks were sealed with a zinc chloride-based covering mortar, to avoid water seeping in, which could cause further frost damage.

3.5. Cleaning of the blocks

All the restored blocks were cleaned by cold water under pressure (100 to 200 bars of pressure). A chemical cleaning method was applied to the biological dirt deposits that did not come off with water. A cleaning product 'complexion paste' was used for this. The paste was applied on the stone surface with a brush and was covered with a plastic cling-film to prevent drying out. After two days the paste was washed away with water under pressure. The cleaning product, which does not leave or generate harmful salts on the stone, was tested earlier in the laboratory. The final cleaning was done after putting the blocks in place.

4. REPLACING MISSING PARTS OF THE BUILDING

4.1. The need for anastylosis

The architectural investigation of the fountain house revealed that some complete stone blocks from the original structure were missing, viz.: wall blocks from the south and west wall, steps blocks from the entrance stair and three cornices and capitals. Since the start of the fountain house restoration project, the principle of minimum intervention has been a fundamental aspect in our philosophy. Following this principle, it is clear that the missing blocks are only replaced by new elements when it is strictly necessary for the positioning of an existing one. Bearing this in mind, three stages have been defined for the anastylosis project:
- the first stage was the positioning of the existing architectural elements without the insertion of new elements. This was possible until the top level of the columns C2, C3, C4, C6, C7, C8, C9 and C10; and the top level of the capitals C1, C5 and C6. Capitals C5 and C6 made it possible to place two architraves and four cornices (Fig. 11);
- the second stage was the positioning of the architraves of the three porticoes and the cornices of the north and east portico. It was necessary therefore to integrate into the structure some completely new elements, viz., the capitals (Fig. 12);
- the third and last stage of the anastylosis was the positioning of the cornices of the west portico. For this final work it

was necessary to complete the west wall with new stone blocks to serve as support for the back of the cornices (Fig.12).

4.2. Carving new stone blocks to replace the missing ones

The discussion above clarifies the question of the insertion of new blocks. For the replacement of the missing blocks by new elements, two other problems arose: the determination of the shape and dimensions of the missing stone blocks and the choice of the material to produce them. As sufficient information was available on the missing elements from the study of the existing architectural material, the definition of the shape, dimensions and proportions was not a difficult task to accomplish. However the choice of the material was more complicated.

Nowadays, different materials are being used in various restoration projects, such as artificial stone, concrete (Yorulmaz *et al.* 1989: 447-456; 407-414) and stone (Papanikolaou 1994: 137-150; Korres 1994: 111-136), etc. The missing parts in a building that need to be replaced for structural reasons should use a material with physical and mechanical properties similar to the original parts of the structure. In our opinion, the use of pre-cast concrete was out of the question. The cements sold in Turkey have a very high salt content, which could cause future problems to the structure. It was decided to prepare new blocks by carving natural stone. This material is not expensive in Turkey and being a similar material to the original allowed us to remain faithful to the materials, construction techniques and structural behaviour of the ancient building. Furthermore, the use of natural stone cannot harm the building, its long-term durability is known and it is highly compatible with the original material from an aesthetic and structural point of view (Patrício *et al.* 1997:371-334).

Nowadays, concern for the preservation of the authenticity of a historic building also tends to take into account craftsmanship as an authentic value. Apart from the earlier mentioned argument, this opinion reinforced our decision to carve new stones to replace missing stone blocks.

After making an investigation to find a similar stone to the limestone used in the original elements and after evaluating its geological properties, it was decided to use limestone from a quarry at the village of Yarışlı, near the city of Burdur. For the carving of the new capitals we took the profiles and proportions of the existing capital C5 (Fig.13), the only one that is complete. The craftmanship for carving the stones was provided through collaboration with City and Guilds of London Art School. The stones were purchased with approximate dimensions and carved on site using traditional tools (Fig. 14).

During the study of the removed fragments found during the excavations, we found some small fragments belonging to the missing capitals and, after some investigation, were able to determine the exact position of these small fragments. As the main goal of the project was to preserve the original material it was decided to integrate all the capital fragments found into the new carved ones. For a correct architectural integration, the new capital was first carved. Afterwards, by direct measurement the fragment was shaped on the new capital and the negative form of it was carved (Fig. 15). The original fragments were integrated into the new one using epoxy mortar and fibreglass rods (see section 3.1) (Fig. 16). To improve the aesthetic integration, the final shades and decorations of the new carved stones, as well as matching the integrated original fragments, were further finished when the new stone blocks were in their final position on the structure (1997 campaign). The final surface carving was integrated into the ancient one to guarantee a more satisfactory aesthetic result without constituting a violation of the principle that the modern parts should remain distinguishable from the older ones (Venice Charter: 1964).

5. CONTROLLING AND CANALISING THE NATURAL WATER SPRING

As the natural water spring of the fountain house still exists, we planned to recover the original function of the building as a fountain by canalising the water flow once more into the basins of the fountain house. Just to the north of the building, therefore, the stone slabs of the street were removed and the back of the north wall was examined (Waelkens *et al.* 2000). The water source was reached and the settling tank that had collected and distributed the water was found (Fig. 17). The water distribution system of the settling tank was repaired and it was connected to the water source again. In this way a control room for the water source, accessible through the window on the north wall of the fountain house, as it was in antiquity, was recreated. Then a roof was constructed over the collector to close the control room. Finally, the top of the roof was filled with earth and the stone slabs were put back in place.

An *in situ* test was carried out to test the behaviour of the natural hydraulic lime mortar which we planned to use to seal the basins and contain the water. A small partition wall of rubble was constructed in the east basin of the fountain house. All the walls were plastered to seal the pool. Those walls consisted of the parapet stones, the big stones of the east and the south wall and, to the north, a small rubble wall built after AD 518 to carry one of the terracotta pipes taking the water directly to the city. The bottom of the small test pool was made of different layers of well-graded sand and hydraulic lime mortar.

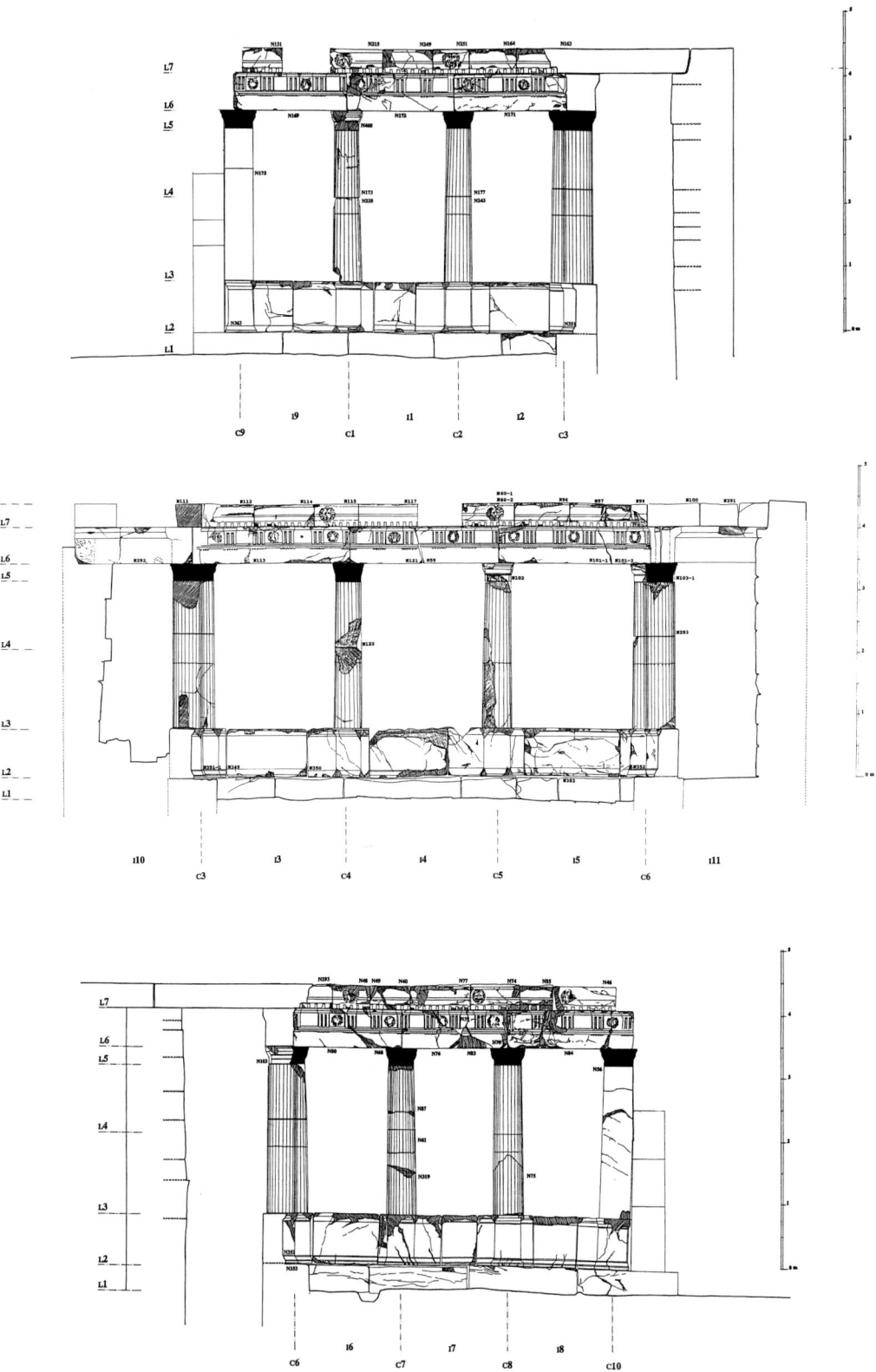

Fig. 12: Reconstruction drawing of the second anastylosis stage, north and east porticoes. Reconstruction drawing of the second and third anastylosis stage, west portico.

Fig. 13: Front view of the existing capital C5. This capital was used as a model for the new carved capitals. August 1996.

Fig. 14: Front view of the new carved capital C4. August 1996.

Fig. 15: Preparing a new carved capital for the insertion of the existing fragment from the original capital.

Fig. 16: Insertion of original fragments in a new carved capital.

Fig. 17: General view of the original water system found in the excavations behind the north wall.

Fig. 18: General view of the small water basin built for testing the mortar that was applied inside the water basins.

Fig. 19: Excavations during the 1991 campaign. The collapsed west wall and west portico are visible.

Fig. 20: Model of the column C2 built during field work, at a scale of 1:1. The model is made out of the original and restored stone blocks.

Fig. 21: Placing the columns of the west and north porticoes for trial and verification of the levels. Situation at the end of the 1996 campaign.

Fig. 22: Detail of the connection between the west and south walls. The inclination of the west wall to the east is very clear.

The natural hydraulic lime mortar used for the finishing of the surfaces and the sealing has two different grades of filler. The mortar of the P1 layer had a filler with maximum sized particles of 1 mm, while the P2 layer was composed of mortar with a filler of up to 2 mm particles. Plastering was done afterwards with a hydraulic lime mortar. The surfaces were well prepared and then two layers of P2 mortar were applied first and afterwards two layers of P1. The finer filler of the last layers allowed a very smooth finish. For the final touch, the surface of the last layer was redone several times by wetting and trowelling it. In this way, small cracks appearing at the surface from drying could be worked out, even after a few days. This demonstrated clearly the particular behaviour of natural hydraulic lime of curing only after a certain time, although giving some mechanical strength after the initial setting. As the climate at the site is rather hot during the day, the surfaces had to be wetted regularly and protected against fast drying.

After the mortar was completely hardened, the pool was filled with water to see if seeping would occur through the mortar after a severe winter. (Fig.18) This proved to be successful.

6. ANASTYLOSIS WORKS

The architectural research on the existing in situ remains during the 1992 and 1993 campaigns (Patrício and Van Balen 1993: 87-105) demonstrated and quantified the movement suffered by the structure during earthquakes (Patrício and Van Balen 1993: 88). The earthquake forces induced a movement of the structure in the southwest/northeast directions. This resulted in the total collapse of the west and east porticoes (Fig. 19), in a partial destruction of the west wall and in inducing a strong tilt in the wall to the east and the consequent slipping of the foundations of the east and west porticoes. Since the beginning of the excavations of the fountain house and its consequent restoration, we wanted to avoid dismantling the still *in situ* remains of the structure so as to preserve, as far as possible, the structure's original integrity. Therefore the observed distortions, that is, the deformation of the west and east porticoes foundations and the inclination of the west wall were incorporated into had to be allowed for in the final anastylosis of the structure.

6.1. Trial of parts of the building for the final anastylosis

A theoretical reconstitution of the original building was drawn up from the study of the stone blocks and *in situ* remains. This reconstitution was the basis for the final anastylosis of the building. We were aware that the proposed reconstitution could present some errors in the measurements. Conscious that the earthquake destruction had deformed the *in situ* ruin and that the stone blocks were broken into many pieces, it became clear that it was impossible to check and correct the measurements for the final anastylosis by only taking into account the graphic survey. It was therefore decided to work also with three-dimensional (test) models on a 1:1 scale built with the original and restored material itself. When blocks were restored parts of the building were reconstituted in the field (Fig. 20). The partial reconstitution of the building, three-dimensional models made with the original architectural material, allowed it to be surveyed in various aspects and consequently corrected on the drawing-board. This method of working was also carried out extensively on the building itself. Models on a scale of 1:1 made it possible to correct measurements, verify levels and study connections, to understand more clearly the relation between stone blocks found during the excavations and the *in situ* remains (Fig. 21).

6.2. Correction of the foundation deformation

Soundings all around the basin foundations were carried out first to verify the conditions and stability of the existing foundations. We could observe voids in between the top surface of the stone foundations and the step of the basin parapet. The architectural survey revealed that the level of the north portico foundations was still the correct one and that it should be taken as a reference to correct the west and east foundations. For planning the intervention there were three possibilities:

1 – The complete dismantling of the west and east parapet and steps of the basins. This could cause a large loss of information and uncontrollable errors.

2 – Dismantling portico by portico, starting from the first blocks at the north part of the portico, taking the corner columns of the north portico as reference level. Proceeding with this method stone by stone from north to south. Once again, however, this way of working could create incremental errors.

3 – Dismantling portico by portico, starting from the first blocks at the south part of the portico, correcting the top level of the foundation in relation with the corner columns of the north portico. Proceeding with this method stone by stone from south to north. Starting from the biggest correction to the smallest appeared to be the most appropriate way of working. The errors were controllable and reduced to a minimum.

The basins, parapets and steps from the west and east side porticoes were entirely dismantled stone by stone and the foundation level corrected following this third procedure. The material used for the levelling was natural hydraulic lime mortar mixed with small rubble, which provided a correctly levelled bed for the stone of the step. The steps were then replaced, and finally all the foundations were strengthened by the injection of a plastic hydraulic mortar to increase the contact area between the stones of the foundations and the stones of the bed rock on which they were placed.

6.3. West wall anastylosis

The observed and measured distortions of the west wall were a problem in its final anastylosis as well as the final anastylosis of the west portico entablature. As a consequence of seismic effects the wall had an inclination of 35 cm (Fig. 22) to the east and about 10 cm to the south. The dismantling of the still *in situ* wall was inevitable to allow for the correct repositioning of the stone blocks, particularly the cornices. Moreover, since the 1993 campaign, research had been carried out on excavated original material with the view of finding the stone blocks belonging to that wall. Hypotheses were made but to reach conclusions it was first necessary to correct the distortions.

For the correction of the distortions the work was planned in four phases:
1 – Registration and inventory. The wall was photographed and, after completing all the already existing graphic survey, we started to work with the first upper layer of stone blocks. Each stone block was given a number and registered on the drawings. A *topography* of the stones was done, the site of each stone was defined with three reference points and the points defined by the three axes X, Y and Z. Detailed photographs were taken of the layers and a detailed graphic survey drawn on a scale 1:20.
2 – The stones of the first layer were removed. The first and second step of the planning was applied and repeated layer by layer, stone by stone. It was necessary to dismantle 4 layers of stones to reach the correct position of the wall.
3 – When necessary the removed stones were restored. Mainly small fragments were glued.
4 – The stones were placed back into their original positions. The reference points measured during the first phase of the works were verified to correct the distortions as much as possible.

After correcting the distortions of the wall it was possible to begin the anastylosis of the wall with the material found out of position during the excavations. Some of the original stone blocks of the wall were missing. In order to reach the level of the cornices from the west entablature it was necessary to carve new stone blocks. This work was executed during the 1997 campaign.

7. CONSIDERATIONS ON ONGOING WORKS

The anastylosis of the fountain house showed the importance of approaching anastylosis as a process of consecutive and inter-related steps. The original concept of the building and its structural behaviour was understood and allowed to establish the criteria for choosing restoration techniques. Based on those criteria and the general principles of monument conservation, new techniques were developed in the laboratory and applied at the site. The restored stone blocks allowed the reconstitution of the monument structure and enable the anastylosis to progress smoothly. The restoration was completed by the end of the 1997 campaign.

8. ACKNOWLEDGEMENTS

Thanks are due to the personnel of the Reyntjes Laboratory for their technical advice and permission to use the laboratory infrastructure, and also to the JNICT – Junta Nacional de Investigação Ciêntifica e Tecnológica, Lisbon, for a grant for the planning of architectural conservation research. This research is supported by the Belgian Programme on Interuniversity Poles of Attraction (IUAP 4/12) initiated by the Belgian State, Prime Minister's Office, Science Policy Programming. The text also presents the results of the Concerted Action of the Flemish Government (GOA 97/2) and the Fund for Scientific Research-Flanders (Belgium) (FWO) (G.2145.94). Scientific responsibility is assumed by its authors.

9. REFERENCES

J.P. Adam (1994) *Roman Building. Materials and Techniques*, London.

S. Ercan, K. Van Balen and T. Patrício (1997) The structural restoration of the late Hellenistic nymphaeum: principles, laboratory tests and field applications, in: M. Waelkens and J. Poblome (eds) *Sagalassos IV. Report on the Survey and Excavations Campaigns of 1994 and 1995* (Acta Archaeologica Lovaniensia Monographiae 9) Leuven University Press: 423-437.

S. Ercan, K. Van Balen and T. Patrício (1997) Structural restoration of the late Hellenistic nymphaeum at Sagalassos in Turkey, in: G. Özen (ed.) *Studies in Ancient Structures. Proceedings of the International Conferenc, Istanbul 14-18 July 1997*, Istanbul: 573-584.

M. Korres (1994) The restoration of the Parthenon, in: R. Economakis (ed.) *Acropolis Restoration. The CCAM Interventions*, London: 111-136.

R. Martin (1965) *Manuel d'architecture grecque. Matériaux et techniques*, Paris.

A. Papanikolaou (1994) The restoration of the Erechtheion, in: R. Economakis (ed.) *Acropolis Restoration. The CCAM Interventions*, London: 137-150.

T. Patrício and K. Van Balen (1996) The Nymphaeum at Sagalassos, Turkey. The Anastylosis and the applicability, in: *Archae-*

ological Remains-In situ Preservation, ICOMOS-ICAHM-The International Committee for Archaeological Heritage Management, 11-15 October 1994, Montreal: 101-109.

T. Patrício and K. Van Balen (1993) The nymphaeum at Sagalassos and the anastylosis, in: M.Waelkens and J. Poblome (ed.) *Sagalassos II. Report on the Third Excavation Campaign of 1992 (Acta Archaeologica Lovaniensia Monographiae* 6) Leuven University Press: 87-105.

T. Patrício and K. Van Balen (1995) Architectural analysis of the nymphaeum at Sagalassos. First results, in: M.Waelkens and J. Poblome (eds) *Sagalassos III. Report on the Fourth Excavation Campaign of 1993 (Acta Archaeologica Lovaniensia Monographiae* 7) Leuven University Press: 143-163.

T. Patrício, S. Ercan, K. Van Balen and M. Waelkens (1997) The restoration project of the nymphaeum at Sagalassos in Turkey, in: A. Moropoulou *et al.* (eds) *Proceedings of the 4th International Symposium on the Conservation of Monuments in the Mediterranean. Rhodes 6-11 May 1997* Vol. 4, Athens: 371-384.

K. Van Balen and T. Patrício (1995) Preparative tests for the structural consolidation of the Hellenistic nymphaeum at Sagalassos, in: M. Waelkens and J. Poblome (eds) *Sagalassos III. Report on the Fourth Excavation Campaign of 1993 (Acta Archaeologica Lovaniensia Monographiae* 7) Leuven University Press: 165-174.

Venice Charter – International Charter for the Conservation and Restoration of Monuments and Sites. Approved at the 2nd International Congress of Architects and Technicians of Historic Monuments, which met in Venice from 25th to 31st May 1964. Adopted by ICOMOS in 1965

M. Waelkens, J. Poblome, R. Degeest, L. Vandeput, L. Loots, P. Talloen, F. Martens, E. Paulissen, J. Van Den Bergh, V. Vanderginst, B. Arıkan, I. Van Damme, I. Akyel, M. Martens, I. Uytterhoeven, T. Debruyne, D. Depraetere, K. Baran, B. Van Daele, Z. Parras, Ş. Yıldırım, S. Bubel, H. Vanhaverbeke, C. Licoppe, F. Landuyt, T. Patrício, S. Ercan, K. Van Balen, E. Smits, F. Depuydt, L. Moens and P. De Paepe (2000) The 1996 and 1997 excavation season at Sagalassos, in: M. Waelkens and L. Loots (eds) *Sagalassos V. Report on the Survey and Excavation Campaigns of 1996 and 1997 (Acta Archaelogica Lovaniensia Monographiae* 10) Leuven University Press: 217-398.

M. Yorulmaz, F. Cili and Z. Ahunbay (1989) Anastylosis of the Apollo Temple in Side/Antalya, Turkey, in: Brebbia (ed.) *Structural Repair and Maintenance of Historic Buildings,* Southampton: 447-456.

M. Yorulmaz, G. Tanyeli and U. Izmirliğil (1989) Anastylosis of the arch of Demetrius-Apollonius in Perge, in: C.A. Brebbia (ed.) *Structural Repair and Maintenance of Historical Buildings,* Southampton: 407-414.

THE SAGALASSOS NEON LIBRARY MOSAIC AND ITS CONSERVATION[1]

Marc WAELKENS[1], Hande KÖKTEN ERSOY[2], Kent SEVERSON[3], Femke MARTENS[1] and Selçuk SENER[2]

1 - Department of Archaelogy, KULeuven, Blijde Inkomststraat 21, B-3000 Leuven, Belgium
2 - A.Ü. Başkent Meslek Yüksekokulu, D.T.C.F. Ek Binası, Sıhhiye, 06100 Ankara, Turkey
3 - 35 Queensberry Street 9, Boston, Massachusetts 02215, USA

1. THE BUILDING AND ITS MOSAIC FLOOR
(M. Waelkens and F. Martens)

1.1. The excavations

From 1990 to 1994, a tall structure, later identified as a library, was excavated on a terrace immediately above and to the north of the late Hellenistic fountain house at Sagalassos. The building was located in a commanding position in front of a kind of esplanade, which offered a wide and undisturbed view towards the south, almost halfway along the street connecting the upper agora with the theatre of the city (Fig. 1). Since the southern extremity of the esplanade was formed by the late Hellenistic fountain house, of which the flat roof was located at the esplanade level, the façade of the 'library' must have been visible from most spots within the city and even from many places in the valley below it (Waelkens *et al.* 1992: 85-88; Waelkens 1993: 13-15, Waelkens *et al.* 1995: 53-89; Waelkens *et al.* 1997: 114-126).

At first, it was thought that the remains were those of a basilica, but it soon appeared that the building had been a library, showing at least three building phases. These phases have been described and illustrated in the report on the 1992 season (Waelkens 1993: 13-15). The final study of this structure and of its mosaics will be published elsewhere, but some preliminary remarks are presented here, as an introduction to the description of the conservation of the mosaic floor.

The building consists of a single room, from the time of its construction onwards flanked by single-room *tabernae* which at a later date were converted into housing units (Waelkens *et al.* 1997: 114-126). At present, the room consists of a 11.80 by 9.90 m internal space which, thanks to generous assistance from the **ABB-Insurance Company** (Belgium), was covered by a protective building and conserved. The restoration of the mosaic floor was part of this conservation and restoration project which eventually resulted in the re-opening of the whole building on September 3, 1997.

- The first building phase

As already mentioned, at least three building phases can be distinguished (for a detailed description, see Waelkens 1993: 14-15). Epigraphical evidence has firmly dated the original building phase to the beginning of Hadrian's rule, around the year 120 AD, or shortly after. The building was erected by a local aristocrat T. Flavius Severianus Neon in memory of his deceased father P. Flavius Dareius (Devijver 1993: 114). At that time, Sagalassos was most probably still part of the Roman province of Asia (Devijver and Waelkens to be published in Sagalassos VI). The construction, between 112/14 and 117 AD, of a magnificent library in the provincial capital of Ephesos, by T. Julius Aquila in memory of his father C. Julius Celsus Polemaeanus, may thus have inspired a member of one of the leading families of Sagalassos to do the same in his home town.

Only the back wall of the building still belongs to this original building phase. Inside, it consists of a 2.35 m high limestone podium with ornate upper and lower mouldings, the former also carrying an inscribed kind of *attica* moulding

---

[1] This article is dedicated to the mosaicist Dioskoros, who designed and made the emblema of the mosaic, and to the workmen from Ağlasun who helped the conservation team during the 1996 and 1997 campaigns.

with seven inscriptions with the names of members of Neon's family, and their careers. This limestone podium contains eight curved and vaulted niches (Fig. 2), possibly meant for the smaller sculpture of which some fragments were recovered during the excavations. The upper wall sections above the podium were made of mortared rubble outside, but of solid brick inside (Waelkens *et al.* 1997: 114-126). Here again, the Ephesian prototype may have served as a model, since it was the first building in Asia Minor with – also in its upper section- walls of solid brick throughout. This choice of materials there was clearly made to advertise the *romanitas* of Aquila and Celsus, who both, respectively in 92 and 110 AD, had been consuls at Rome, where walls in *opus latericium* or *testaceum* had by then become common practice (Waelkens 1987: 86).

At Sagalassos this upper wall section contained a large semicircular niche for a tall bronze statue in the middle, between two rectangular niches (0.90 m deep) on either side, the outer ones being slightly smaller than the inner ones (1.20 m versus 1.50 m). Theoretically, they could have contained statuary as well, although there is no correspondence between the arrangement of the niches and the seven inscriptions on the moulding below them. Most probably there was a second row of four rectangular niches in a now last upper section of the back wall.

The strongly projecting upper profiles of the limestone podium, which change direction in both corners (Fig. 3), show without any doubt that originally a similar arrangement continued along both side walls, where two more superposed rows of four niches each could have been present.

At first sight, the whole lay-out closely resembles that of the *Kaiser-* or *Marmorsaal* in many bath-gymnasia complexes of Asia Minor. Because of this resemblance, Russell recently went as far as to suggest that the hall might have been devoted by Neon to the imperial cult. In that case, the large bronze statue in the central niche would have been occupied by the image of an emperor (Hadrian, or perhaps Trajan?), while statues of other members of the Imperial family would have filled the flanking niches to right and left (Russell 1997: 542).

There are, however, a number of problems in such an interpretation. Firstly, Neon's structure was not a part of a larger complex and we know of no other isolated halls of similar shape in the East that were dedicated to the Imperial cult. At the time of our excavations, it appeared that the 'Sebasteion' of Boubon in Southwest Pisidia (the Kabalis) might have been such an example. Between 1960 and 1967, robber trenches cut in a successful search for statues had exposed the remains of a 'Sebasteion'. A first rescue excavation uncovered a 6.20 by 5.80 m space, walled on three sides, which the excavator even thought might have been open to the sky (Inan 1977-78). The short back wall had over its total length a 0.60 m projecting socle with inscriptions including the emperors Nero (partly erased), Domitian? (erased), Nerva and Caracalla (?), as well as the empress Poppaea Sabina. A second projecting socle in front of the greater part of the east wall carried inscriptions honouring Julia Domna, Salonina, Gallienus, Caracalla and Septimius Severus. Finally, a number of isolated statue bases were also placed against the west wall. The first one was a re-used base with an inscription to a prominent local citizen, the others had once carried the statues of Caracalla, Gordian III and either Commodus or a later emperor (Jones 1977-78). A second rescue excavation in 1990 produced evidence for statues of Lucius Verus, Philippus Arabs, Decius or Trebonianus Gallus, and Valerianus, while a third campaign in 1993 showed that this 'Sebasteion' had been covered with a roof and had at least one more room in front of it (Ekinci 1994). The overall schema of both rooms remains unknown, but it is clear by now that they were part of a larger complex which now bears no resemblance to the structure excavated at Sagalassos.

A second objection to explaining the Sagalassos structure as an Imperial hall is the fact that the seven inscriptions on the north socle all identify members of Neon's family, who were honoured by the *Boulè* and the *Dèmos* of the city. The fact that these inscriptions occupied the most prominent and visible part of the whole building is hard to reconcile with the possibility that the statues in the niches above them could have represented members of the Imperial family. The inscriptions clearly identify the building as a monument to the glory of Neon's family. At Bubon, except for a statue base which had been re-used later, the inscriptions mentioned only the names of emperors, whose statues were still present in the building until their removal by robbers in the 1960s.

At Sagalassos, the only statues recovered by the excavations were fragments of the large bronze statue from the central niche, and several fragments of smaller statuary, either from the podium niches, or from the rounded niches in the side wall (?). Nothing was found that could be connected with either Imperial statues, their socles or their dedicatory inscriptions.

An isolated hall dedicated to the Imperial cult would also have been a very odd feature at Sagalassos at the beginning of Hadrian's reign. In fact, under the rule of his predecessor Trajan, either in 103-104 or in 115-116 AD, the local Temple of Apollo Klarios had been greatly rebuilt and (re)dedicated to the cult of Apollo and of the Imperial House (Devijver and Waelkens 1997: 295) and it is most probable that

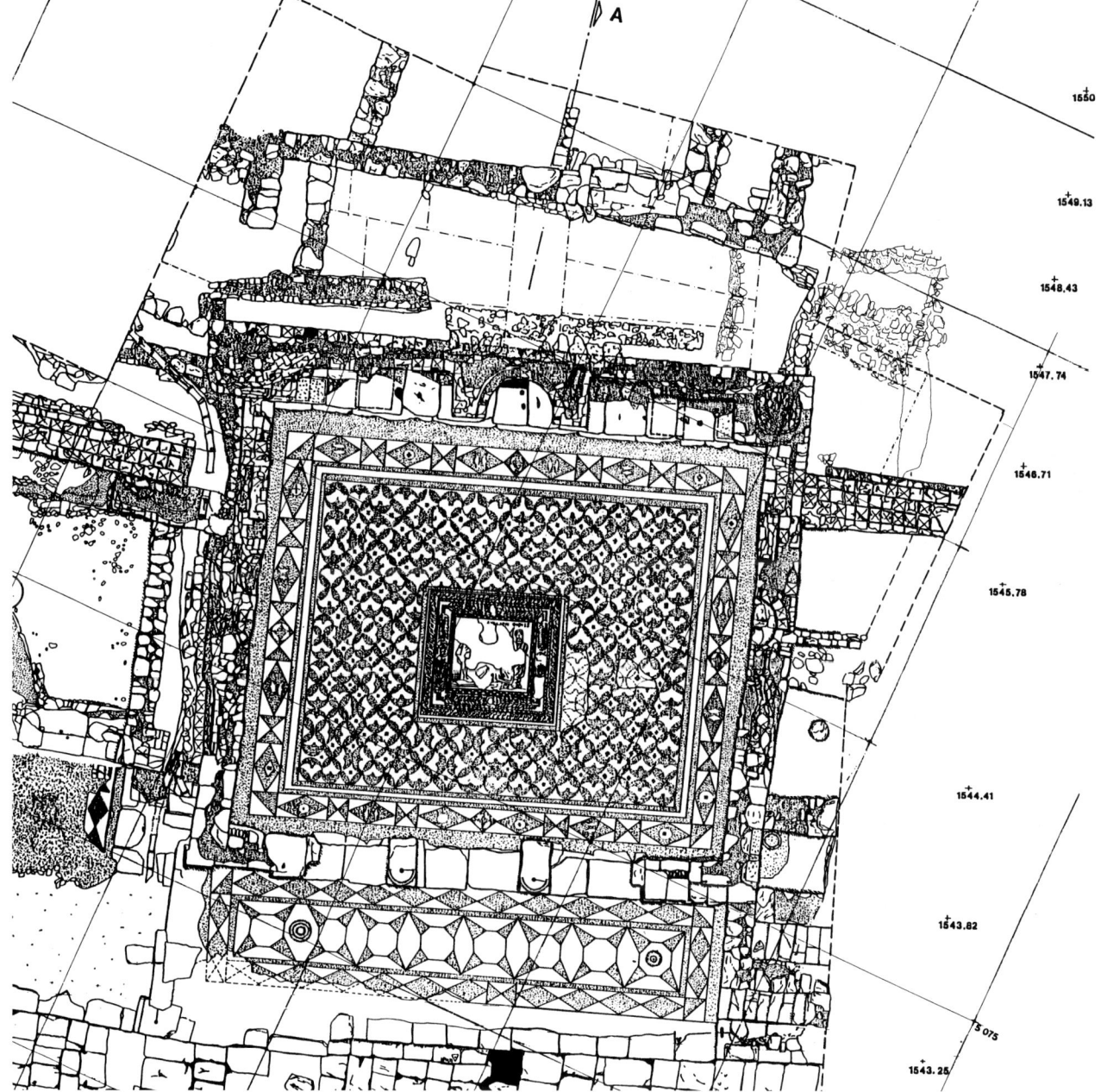

Fig.1: Plan of the Neon Library after the 1993 seasons.

Fig. 2: View of the Neon Library after the 1992 season.

Fig. 3: Detail of the northwest corner of the library's podium, showing the turn of the upper moulding towards the original west wall.

422

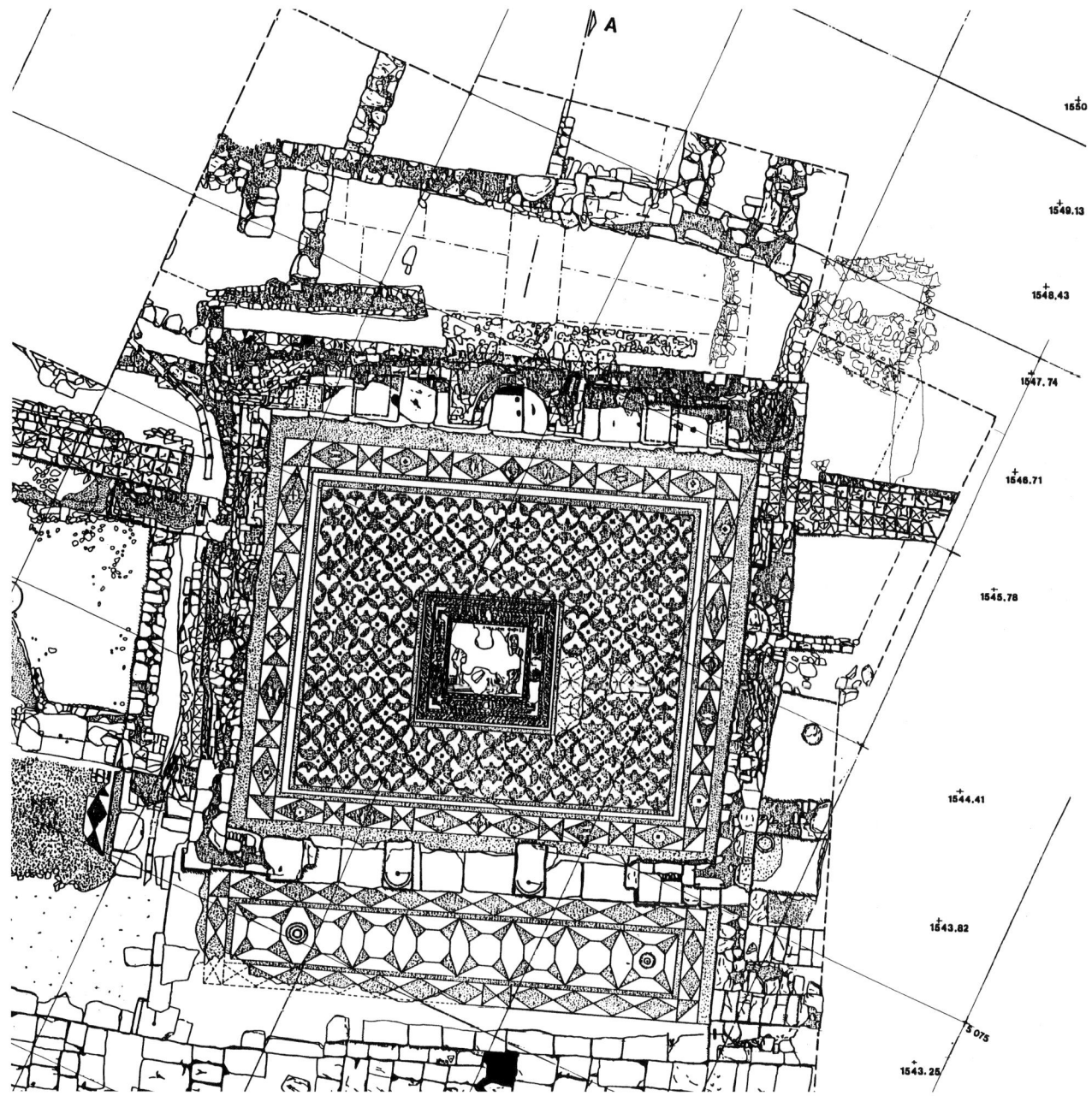

Fig.1: Plan of the Neon Library after the 1993 seasons.

Fig. 2: View of the Neon Library after the 1992 season.

Fig. 3: Detail of the northwest corner of the library's podium, showing the turn of the upper moulding towards the original west wall.

this sanctuary had housed the imperial cult from the Flavian period onwards (Waelkens in press). During the second half of Hadrian's reign, a second, more magnificent, sanctuary for the Imperial cult would be erected on a promontory in the southern part of the city, but be completed only under Antoninus Pius (Vandeput 1997: 64-77; Devijver and Waelkens 1997: 312). Therefore, a hall for the Imperial cult built by a private family would have seemed superfluous during Neon's lifetime.

If the lateral niches on either side of the central niche were meant for statuary, it would be more likely that they represented members of Neon's family. In that case, the building could have been a kind of heroon or 'dynastic' monument for Sagalassos' most prominent family of the time. In any case, the building did not contain an actual grave. During the excavation, it was thought that P. Flavius Dareius was perhaps buried below the central niche of the back wall, just as Celsus had been buried in a similar situation below his library at Ephesos. In 1996, the covering stones of the podium were lifted but no cavity was found underneath. If the building had been a kind of heroon for Neon's family, of which half of the members mentioned in the inscriptions were still alive at the time of its construction, one could perhaps look to the first century BC heroon of Diodoros Pasparos at Pergamon for a parallel. The most monumental feature of this heroon was also an 8 by 8 m square cult room with a large rectangular niche for a statue of Pasparos in the back wall. After the 17 AD earthquake this niche was converted into an apsidal exedra and during the second century AD it was flanked by two smaller statue niches. In 17 AD, the room was also transformed into a kind of *Marmorsaal* with a 2.50 m high marble podium decorated with reliefs referring to Pasparos' virtues along the walls (Radt 1998: 279-285). Pasparos' cult room certainly offers a better architectural parallel for Neon's building at Sagalassos than does Bubon's 'Sebasteion'. However, if it was a heroon, the 'statue niches' did not correspond with the inscriptions on the upper podium moulding below them. These inscriptions are not placed exactly below the niches and honour three members of the family on either side of the central niche, whereas there were only two niches above them.

It would appear to be more likely therefore that, if they were intended to be statue niches, the niches would have contained the images of mythological or allegorical figures. One of the second century AD niches flanking the apsis of Pasparos' cult room at Pergamon also contained the small statue of a youth (Radt 1998: 284). At Sagalassos, the size of the niches is such, however, that they must have contained larger statuary.

But here again, there are strong objections to the identification of Neon's building as a family heroon. Firstly, the total lack of any remains of statues from the lateral niches in the back wall remains an enigma. It does not seem likely that they would have been removed before the destruction of the building, since this apparently was not the case with the smaller statuary elsewhere in this building, nor with the bronze statue of the central niche of which a massive thumb and other fragments were recovered. Even more problematic, however, is the fact that this cult room stands in splendid isolation and was not a part of a larger complex of public buildings. Such a bold expression of a family's power and such a monumental instrument of self-representation would perhaps have been acceptable during the late Hellenistic and even during the early Imperial period (Waelkens in press) but, under the Empire, local self-advertisement adopted more subtle ways and generally took the form of constructing buildings for common use, such as fountains, gateways, libraries, gymnasia or baths, and theatres. Even the cult room for Diodoros Pasparos at Pergamon was only the central part of a much larger gymnasium complex which under the Empire was actually enlarged to incorporate a small bath. There is no doubt that the room at Sagalassos was completely isolated from all the structures around it (viz. a housing complex to the north, and *tabernae* to the west and to the east). It is our opinion, therefore, that to interpret this building as a family heroon is also wrong.

This brings us back to the explanation of the building as a monument for public use through which Neon wanted to express his family's prominence at the local level. In that respect the best parallel is offered by the almost contemporary Celsus Library at Ephesos. The latter consisted of a single, isolated hall of 16.70 by 10.90 m, with a central small apse for a statue, no doubt representing Celsus himself. Tiers of rectangular niches round three sides of the room housed the cupboards for the books. They were preceded by balustraded galleries supported by columns that were carried by a 1.20 m projecting and 1 m high podium (Ward-Perkins 1981: 289-290).

The general resemblance of this building, both in general shape and size, and in its internal arrangements, with that of Neon at Sagalassos induced us to identify this latter also as a library. However, some objections against our identification have been voiced by Russell (1997). Firstly, there is the height of the podium (2.35 m) which in Russell's view would mean that access to the shelves could have been achieved only by means of a movable ladder with at least 7 rungs. In the Celsus Library, the podium below the lower row of book niches was only 1 m in height and therefore could be reached by means of a simple two- or three-stepped box (Russell 1997: 541). This is certainly correct, as far as the back wall of Neon's building is concerned. However, the present sidewalls of Neon's building are not the original ones, so that we have no idea about their appearance or about the width of the podium in front of them. We cannot exclude for the moment that this podium might have originally provided a similar arrangement to that at Ephesos. During the second building phase the transformation of the side walls and of the adjacent *tabernae* was such that no clues about their original appearance were left. It is possible that, at least during the final period of use of the structure, a wooden gallery ran in front of both side walls. If this were the case, it could also have given access to the corner niches of the back wall (see below). Such a wooden construction might have replaced an older one placed on top of the podium that was removed during the second building phase. Although made of perishable material, its appearance might have been very similar to that of the columnar screen inside the Celsus Library although such a presumption in our opinion is not necessary.

In fact, one has to remark that the access to the book niches in the Celsus Library was not so easy as Russell seems to imply. The columns of the interior columnar screen in front of the niches, as shown by the dowel holes in the top of the projecting podium (see Hueber 1997: 79 Abb. 99), were placed so close to the back wall that they must have excluded any movement from one niche to the other. The width of the podium, less the thickness of the wall veneering and the balustrade, makes it clear that the function of the whole screen must have been purely aesthetic. An imitation of a construction of the *Marmorsaal* type was probably intended. How one could get to the niches in the upper level is not clear either. The 1.10 m voids between the library and the surrounding buildings, in the past explained as a stairway to the upper floor and at the same time a measure against damp, seem actually to have been a rainwater collector (Hueber 1997: 79). In any case, the upper part of the walls was not sufficiently preserved to confirm the idea that it might have been connected with this void by the putative stairway. So if there was a second row of niches, as seems very plausible, they also may only have been accessible by means of removable ladders. The same equipment may even have been necessary to reach the books on the highest shelves in the lower row of niches. Today, removable ladders can be found in many bookstores and public libraries. Above all, one should not forget that both the Celsus and the Neon Libraries were essentially monuments to glorify the builder's family and his own *paideia*, and that most probably the 'books' which they contained were not so much in demand as to require constant and direct access to them. Most probably, an attendant would have been able to get the volumes whenever someone asked for them and this could easily be achieved by means of a removable ladder.

Russell (1997: 542 note 12) also remarked that, especially in Asia Minor, Roman libraries had double walls which formed narrow passages around the building. Previously these were thought to have been cavities to prevent damp from building up in the vicinity of the shelves. But, as Russell rightly said and as we have mentioned above, in the case of the Celsus Library, these spaces were designed to collect rainwater from adjacent buildings, so the absence of such a structure at Sagalassos cannot be cited against the interpretation of Neon's building as a library. But, at least during its last building phase, the west wall of the library did have a 0.10 to 0.12 m wide void behind the niches, which contained terracotta pipes for collecting rain water. The north wall, on the other hand, showed in its different layers of mortar adapted to the degree of exposure of each zone, a great care to protect the interior of the building against moisture or water damage (Waelkens *et al.* 1995: 60; Waelkens *et al.* 1997: 116-117).

All these remarks, together with the general resemblance of the structure to the Library of Celsus at Ephesos, which offers the best, almost contemporary, parallel, in our view makes the interpretation of Neon's monumental building as a library still the most plausible explanation.

- The second building phase

At some time, both side walls of the library were rebuilt. The new walls were made of layers of mortared rubble alternating with brick (Fig. 4), covered with marble *crustae* and wall plaster. The arrangement in both north corners shows that at the time the internal width of the building was reduced. In the first building phase, the angle of the upper moulding above the podia on the side walls had been carved in the corner stones of the back wall's podium and these latter still present a right angle with a smooth surface for joining. During this first alteration, the podia along the side walls were removed and new walls were built in front of the position of the original walls. After this, only the extremity of the smooth joint which had formed the turn of the moulding remained visible. The original span of the roof had perhaps caused stability problems, so that the side walls needed to be moved closer and the problem may have continued later, since the preserved mosaic floor of the last building phase showed near three corners of the central *emblema* impressions caused by wooden supports which had made the floor sink under their weight and in one case had even cracked it completely.

After this first intervention, each side wall had two rows of four niches with a width of 1.10 to 1.20 m. Rectangular niches (depth: 0.45 m) alternated with semicircular ones (depth: 0.58 m). All the niches had plaster frames, the ornaments of which indicate a (late) second or early third century AD date. Although at the moment precise dating is very difficult, it is possible that the construction of the new side walls of the library was part of a thorough rearrangement of the whole area in front of the building that took place during the Severan period (Waelkens *et al.* 1995; Waelkens *et al.* 1997).

During the third building phase, except for their southern extremities that were completely rebuilt, the alterations of the side walls seem to have been limited to a new plaster coating, in which, as many joining fragments reveal, the new layer was simply applied above the older one. For the rest, the appearance of the side walls hardly changed. It is very likely therefore that the function of the niches in the side walls did not change either. Their dimensions correspond very well with those of the Celsus Library (1.06 to 1.07 m wide in the back wall, 1.15 to 1.20 m wide in the side walls; depth: 0.57 m) and it is most likely that they served the same purpose.

Russell (1997) remarks that book niches are generally rectangular in shape, which is the case for only half of those in Neon's building. On the other hand the semicircular niches were certainly deep enough to contain wooden shelves too, unless they were meant as an aesthetic relief and filled with smaller statuary.

- The third building phase

At a certain date, the front wall and the southern extremities of both side walls were completely rebuilt (Figs 2 and 4). The new sections of the side walls and the façade of the building were constructed by re-using ashlar *spolia* from older structures, some of which could be dated to the later second century AD (Waelkens 1993: 15 figs 16-17). The wall covering, including the frames around the niches in the side wall were completely redone. A firm date for this alteration could not be established, but it is likely to have been contemporary with the laying of the mosaic floor which both inside and in front of the building does not show any traces of repair and seems to have been laid after the completion of the present walls. In 1992, a drilling operation by the geomorphologists inside one of the gaps in the mosaic pavement provided evidence for the presence of an older mosaic floor (with white *tesserae*) at a depth of ca. 1.20 m. However, it could not be established whether it had belonged to a structure preceding the library, or to an older building phase of the latter. In this last case, however, it would mean that this floor had sunk considerably since the difference in level cannot correspond with mere successive building phases.

In the end, the whole building was destroyed by a massive fire and filled in with dumped material, mostly industrial waste, that was thrown in while the fire was still raging, either to bury the structure, or to extinguish the fire. It is clear that the interior had been looted before the structure was torched: the two left figures of the *emblema* in the mosaic floor had apparently been deliberately smashed (Figs 10-11), whereas the rest of the floor remained largely intact. A number of cracks in this floor (Figs 4-5), seem to have been caused by earthquakes or by massive slope movements at a later date. The fire had baked the *tesserae* very solidly to their mortar substrate and thus prevented them from disintegrating completely during later seismic or slope movements (Waelkens *et al.* 2000). A few fragments of the large bronze statue from the central niche in the back wall, including a massive thumb, and several fragments of small marble statues from the niches in the limestone podium (or the curved niches in the side walls?) were found spread over the building's floor. The latter was covered with thick calcinated beam sections from the roof structure (Fig. 4) and some of them were still clad in smaller transverse timbers. But, in front of the side walls, especially along the east side, there was also a concentration of smaller timber lying below the roof beams and fallen in a different direction. Unless they belonged to a lower part of the roof construction, it is possible that they were part of a wooden gallery running along the side walls. A re-used column base, placed on the mosaic floor against the east wall, may have supported one of these beams. At first sight, such a construction must have hindered the view of the side walls, but in fact it may have resembled the columnar screen of the Celsus Library On the other hand, aesthetic considerations apparently did not prevent the last users of the building from placing internal supports around the *emblema* of the mosaic floor, right in the centre of the room, as we mentioned above. Three round depressions near the corners of the *emblema,* one of which had even completely come adrift from the rest of the floor (Fig. 6), suggest that in the end wooden supports helped to support the central part of the roof system.

During the excavations, seven layers could be identified inside the building. A 0.06 to 0.64 m thick burnt layer (7) covered the floor. It contained many elements of the internal decoration of the building (wall plaster, *crustae*) and of roof fragments, as well as the lowest part of the fill which had been dumped inside. This was also the case with the 0.08 to 0.98 m thick layer 6 above it. The metal slag, bone waste and pottery from this dumped material were sometimes completely coagulated as the result of the fire and heavily burned. The 1 to 1.06 m thick layer 5 above the two lowest strata contained the same type of material but with less trace of burning, since it represented a higher level of the fill which had been thrown inside, apparently after the extinction of the fire. This layer just covered the inscriptions of the back wall. The excavators were convinced that for a short time it had acted as a top layer as it was covered with a layer of thin ash which appeared to be washed in or eroded soot from the burnt out building whose upper wall sections must have remained standing for a while. Eventually, however, everything collapsed and layer 5 was covered with four layers of debris and dumped material (respectively max. 1.02, 0.86, 0.92 and 0.30 m thick; see Waelkens 1993: 13-14).

A study of the fine material from layers 1-7 later suggested that the fill had been thrown inside in one single operation, immediately following the fire. This was deduced from the fact that the ceramic assemblage was very homogeneous and could be dated to the first half of the fourth century AD, tending to the middle of the century. Moreover, this picture was apparently also matched by the very homogeneous numismatic evidence, with 23 coins ranging in date from Augustan times to the reign of Arcadius (one coin in layer 5). Fourteen coins belonged to the fourth century (Poblome 1999: 277-278). However, the study of the common wares from the fill, and especially the clear shift in the proportion between fabric 1 and fabric 4, confirmed that layers 5-7 represented the original man-made fill, whereas the material from the upper layers was thrown in or eroded in at a somewhat later date, albeit probably still within a fairly short timespan (Degeest 2000: 204-206).

The material from this fill only provides a *terminus post quem* for this event, and suggests a date for the catastrophe starting at the third quarter of the fourth century AD. If layer 5 was only one stratum of a single filling operation, the *terminus post quem* could be as late as the reign of Arcadius (383-423 AD). If however, it was an upper layer, even for a very short time, this could suggest that the surface had been formed at some time during or after this reign and in that case the original catastrophe could be somewhat earlier.

There is also, however, other evidence which provides a *terminus ante quem* for the fire which destroyed the library. In fact, the *tabernae* at either side of the building in late antiquity were converted into simple dwellings. Their destruction levels, also caused by fire, indicate a second catastrophic event in the early fifth century AD (Waelkens 1995; Poblome 1999; Degeest 2000). Since these levels did not contain any material which could be identified as coming from the library proper, the destruction of the houses must have occurred at a later date. The construction of both dwellings therefore must have followed the destruction of the library. At some point, the latter's front wall was dismantled and its building elements re-used elsewhere, most likely in the construction of the late Roman fortifications built during the reign of Arcadius, in the first years of the fifth century AD. As a result, part of the fill collapsed on the street in front of the library's ruin.

One thus can conclude that the library had apparently been looted before it was torched. This event must have occurred during the third or the last quarter of the fourth century AD. Its possible cause will be discussed below. The construction date of the third building phase can be placed between the Severan period and the end of the fourth century AD. A study of the mosaic floor may help to suggest a more precise date.

1.2. The mosaic floor

In 1990-1992 the excavations exposed a rather well-preserved mosaic pavement covering the floor of the library and a 4 m wide pedestrian way in front of it. This last must have belonged to a colonnade running along the north side of the street connecting the Upper Agora with the theatre (Fig. 7).

The floor of this pedestrian way was composed of larger *tesserae* in black and white limestone. They formed a geometric pattern of octagons outlined in black on a white background and separated from one another by elongated hexagons. Two of the latter were filled with black circles. Every other side of the octagons and four sides of the hexagons formed the bases of black triangles. The points of adjoining pairs of triangles touched one another. From a distance the whole pattern looked like a series of four-pointed stars (Fig. 8). This pattern was enclosed on four sides by a black band and by a row of elongated black diamonds. In the four corners, the diamonds were replaced by black triangles. On both small sides and along its front, a second black band formed the external border of the mosaic pavement. Along the façade, part of it is only visible in the northeast corner of the pedestrian way. At first sight, this could suggest that the original pavement had been reduced during one of the transformations which the library underwent. But, the edges do not show any trace of such an alteration, so that it rather looks as if the mosaic pavement was laid like that from the start. The pedestrian way is not completely rectangular, so that the geometric pattern had to be adapted. In the western part, some of the border's black diamonds were cut by the façade of the building, but at the slightly receding northwest corner they had to be made larger. Here, the mosaic covered the lower moulding of the re-used (?) corner pilaster, so that it must have been posterior to the construction of the façade. The *tesserae* along the edge are sometimes placed in a more irregular pattern, but this may have been caused by the fact that the mosaicists had to adapt their geometric design to the available space and need not necessarily indicate a later repair. Similar, less carefully executed spots occur in some of the four-pointed stars in the centre of the pavement, and these also need not necessarily be explained as repairs. Such spots are sometimes hard to interpret and later interventions are sometimes also difficult to spot. Even in figured mosaics of high quality, later repairs sometimes escape an experienced eye (Balty 1995: 16). Only when figural panels were raised and reassembled did they sometimes show visible mistakes (Ling 1998: 27).

Inside the library, the greater part of the floor was covered by a black and white mosaic pavement, executed in much finer *tesserae*. Here, on four sides, the border is composed of a wide black band, followed inside by a white background covered with a row of black elongated diamonds alternating with black triangles ranged point to point like an hourglass. In the centre of each side, the hourglass is replaced by a pitched square enclosing a white circle surrounding a black curvilinear diamond with a smaller white diamond in its cen-

Fig. 4: Overall view of the mosaic before cleaning; note the sintered burial accretions along the north wall and some of the calcinated roof timbers.

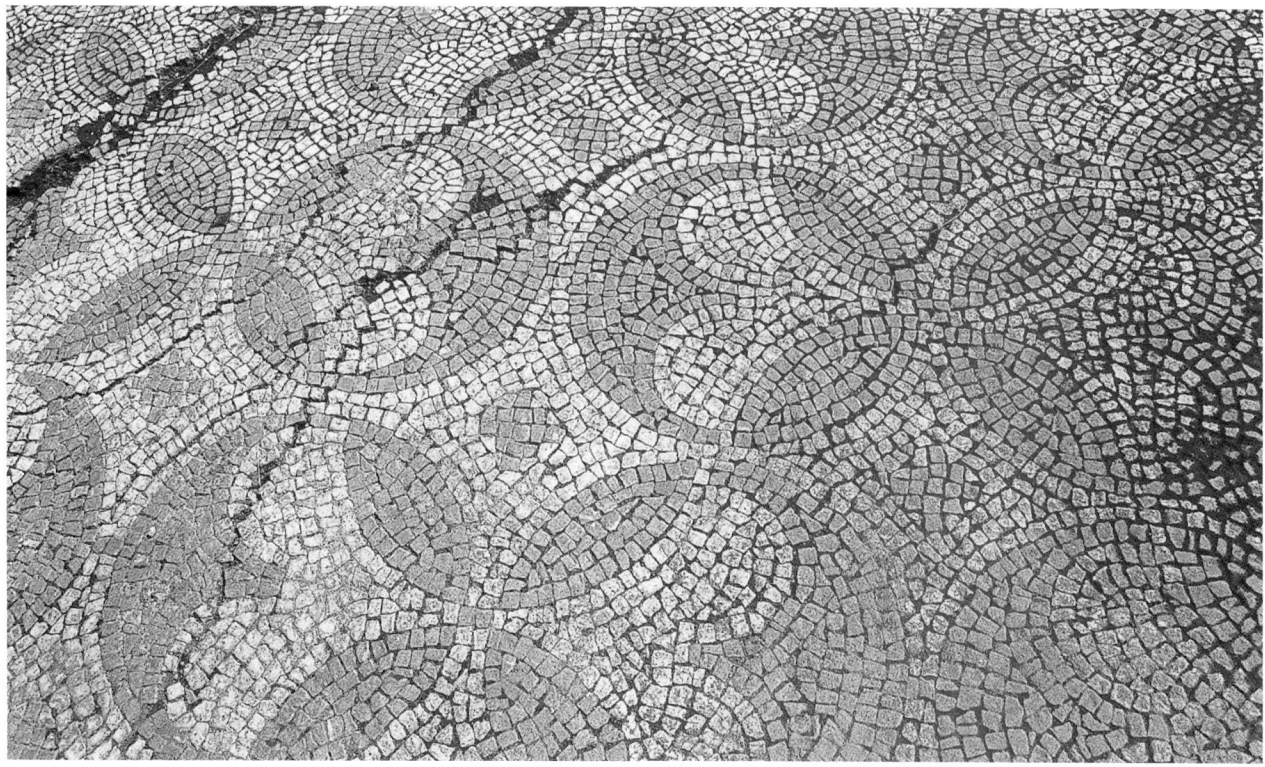

Fig. 5: Detail of the of the *peltae* and quatrefoil decoration of the black and white mosaic floor.

Fig. 6: Deep vertical cracks and losses partially filled with foundation mortar, scored to receive compensation mortar. (photograph: Hande Kökten Ersoy).

Fig. 7: The mosaic floor of the pedestrian way in front of the Neon Library after its 1990 provisional treatment.

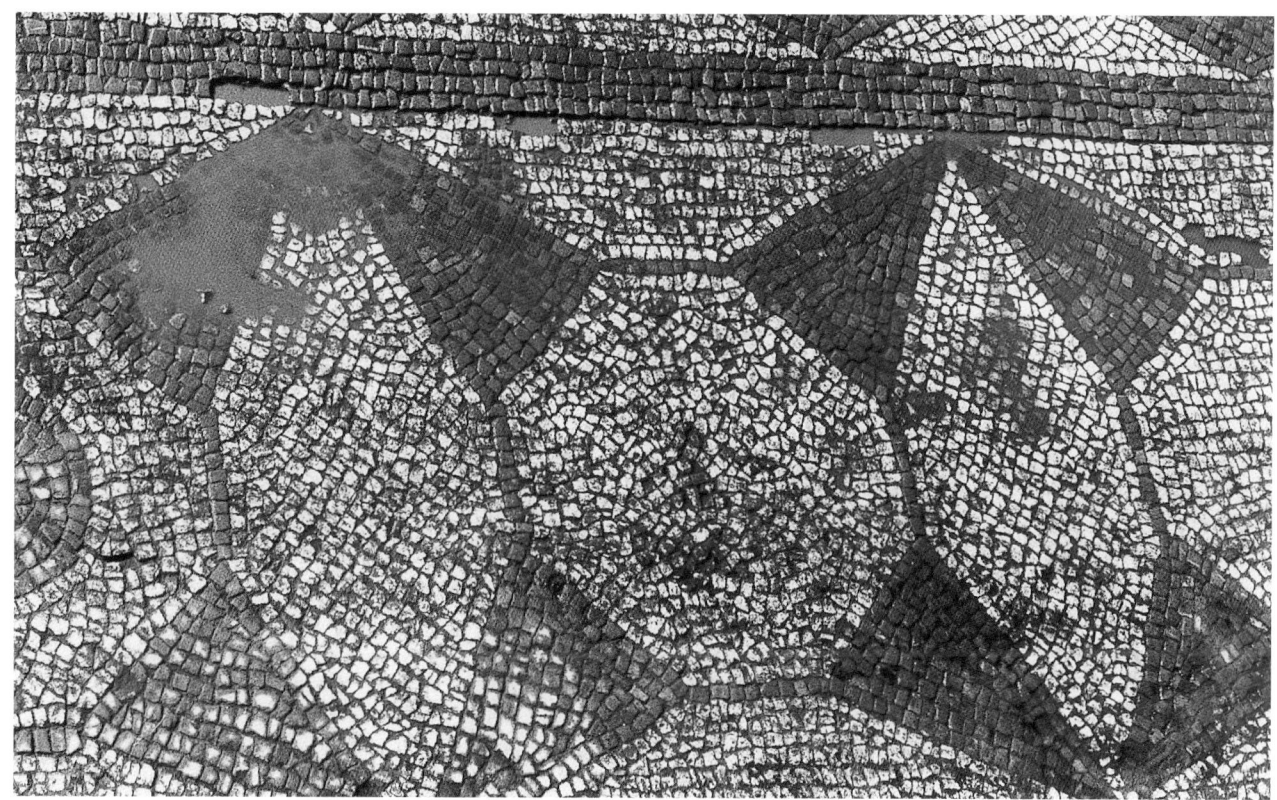

Fig. 8: Detail of the four-pointed stars on the pedestrian way.

Fig. 9: View of the southern half of the Neon Library's black and white mosaic floor, after the 1991 excavation season.

Fig. 10: The *emblema* after the 1992 provisional treatment.

Fig. 11: General view of the *emblema*, after the 1997 treatment.

tre. The centres of the elongated black diamonds are filled alternately with pairs of white *peltae* and white circles. The alternation of both motifs is not always continued or arranged symmetrically towards the central square of each border. Towards the centre of the room are three narrower bands in black, white and black. The width of the central bands is constant throughout, but that of the outer one is somewhat thinner along the shorter sides than on the back or the front wall. It is unlikely however that this could be because the room was reduced in size at the time of its first alteration (Fig. 1). If the mosaic floor already belonged to the original structure, the complete replacement of its side walls and later the front wall would have caused considerable damage to the pavement, which however does not show clear traces of repair corresponding with such a major event. The mosaics even follow closely the irregular internal contours of the front wall (Fig. 9).

Within the border, the pavement is covered with a geometric pattern in black and white *tesserae*. It is formed by intersecting circles forming black quatrefoils alternating with pairs of black *peltae*. The latter are placed either vertically or horizontally (Figs 5,9). Seen from the entrance, all the *peltae* in the outer row of intersecting circles around the room are aligned horizontally (Fig. 1). This could suggest that the mosaicist drawing the design before the *tesserae* were placed had worked from the borders towards the centre. In its alternation of horizontal and of vertical *peltae*, the rest of the floor does not show any consequent pattern anymore. In fact the random use of either horizontal or vertical peltae in the rest of the floor means that the coherence of the pattern was lost. Most of the vertically-aligned *peltae* occur in the west part of the pavement, where quite frequently they alternate with horizontal ones, whereas vertical *peltae* are much less abundant in the eastern half. This could suggest that the different parts were laid by different teams. The white curvilinear diamonds formed by the black motifs contain a small black diamond.

The centre of the floor, at 2.60 m behind the entrance, is formed by a *pseudo-emblema* in bright colours, approximately 2.40 m wide and 3.45 m long (Figs 10-11). It is clear that this is not a real *emblema* produced in a workshop and later brought to the library, but that it was made *in situ*, as became common practice for Eastern *pseudo-emblemata* during the Imperial period (Balty 1995: 68). It may even have been placed in position first. In fact, when the mosaicists who laid the much simpler black and white pavement reached this central panel, their geometric pattern did not match exactly the borders of the *pseudo-emblema* so the transition was formed by a row of white *tesserae*. Along the smaller sides of the panel, they fitted quite well, but on the south side there was not enough space left to close the upper edge of the intersecting circles along the *emblema*, so that they had to be trimmed. On the north side, however, a second row of white *tesserae* had to be introduced to meet the circles (Fig. 10). All this suggests again that the mosaicists worked from the border towards the *pseudo-emblema*. There is no evidence at all to suggest that the central panel was laid or added later. If this had been the case, traces of repairs along the edges of the pavement would have been visible.

From the outer edge, the *pseudo-emblema* is contained in a black and a white band. Then follows a row of two-strand guilloche outlined in black and forming white eyelets. Although there are three sets of colours, they form a simple two-strand twist rather than a three-strand guilloche. The colour sets are composed of black and red with white, black and yellow with white, and black and brown with white. Inside he guilloche are stepped pyramids in black on white and then a rather wide, yellow band filled with two opposed garlands on each side of the *pseudo-emblema*. Their leaves are coloured from white to grey, to bluish grey and dark blue and surround white to yellow flowers below and red pomegranates above. A stem links each pair of garlands round the corners of the central panel. In the middle of each side the opposed garlands are separated from one another by female busts, perhaps representing the Four Seasons. Unfortunately, only one of them was completely preserved (Figs 12 and 13). On the inside, the garland band is framed by a ribbon twist in three shades. The white ribbon is backed by whitish yellow, yellow and reddish brown inside, and by whitish yellow, yellow and dark red outside. Finally, a black linear square frames the figural part of the *pseudo-emblema* (Fig. 11).

The latter depicts a mythological scene with three standing figures which overlapped in the lower part of the white background of the panel. The faces and upper part of the bodies of two of them were deliberately damaged in late antiquity when the building was torched. The left figure was a woman, perhaps Thetis, Achilleus' mother. She is clad in a wide floating yellow and blue cloak. Both other figures were male and are identified by an inscription in black characters around their head respectively as Achilleus and his mentor and protector Phoinix. The head of Phoinix was well preserved, with the upper part of a bird sitting on his right shoulder. The lower left corner of the scene (Fig. 11) contained the signature of the mosaicist Dioskoros, again written in black characters (Διόσκορος ἐψηφοθέτει). The verb of the signature (ψηφόω) is common for such signatures (Balty 1995: 16). Dioskoros is not known from other places.

If mosaics are not dated by an inscription, a practice which only became widespread in the Near East from the end of the fourth century AD onwards, the most reliable chronological evidence has to be provided by the political history or by the stratigraphy of the site (Balty 1995: 17). In our case, however, the building history and the stratigraphy provide us only with a very wide chronological frame, between 120 AD and the transition from the fourth to the fifth century AD. Since the mosaic does not show any trace of extensive repairs, as one would expect if it had been older than the later alterations of the building which eventually replaced three of its four walls, all the evidence indicates its being laid at the time of the building's final repair. This narrowing of the chronological frame still leaves us with a period of nearly two centuries, extending from the Severan period, when the first alteration was undertaken, to the end of the fourth or the beginning of the fifth century AD, when the façade was dismantled and the houses on either side of the already destroyed library burned down. The result is that only a stylistic comparison can produce a more specific time frame. Such a dating technique however, is only reliable if one has at one's disposal abundant material from the same site or from the same region, and if one takes into account the general concept of the floor, the spatial rendering of the figures, the composition of the pavement and its ornamental parts (Balty 1995: 20). And even then, additional problems may be caused by the fact that a stylistic evolution is not always consistent through a certain time span, so that 'old fashioned' and 'revolutionary' tendencies might occur next to one another (Balty 1995: 22).

Even in a city like Antioch (Antakya), where nearly 300 mosaics are known, spanning a period of four centuries (Levi 1947, Campbell 1988, Ling 1998: 49), only relative chronologies are possible (Balty 1995: 15). At Sagalassos, other mosaic pavement fragments in black and white were found along the same footpath, further south and north of the library (Waelkens *et al.* 1997: 121). The rather badly preserved fragments contain black and white *tesserae* forming intersecting circles and triangles. These mosaic pavements must be contemporary with those in front of the library and be part of the same colonnade. During the 1998 season, a well-preserved mosaic floor, which is still being excavated, was discovered in an early Christian cathedral built inside the courtyard of the former bouleuterion. It represents a rich, partly vegetal, mostly geometric polychrome row of borders surrounding a central multicoloured labyrinth and seems to date to the fifth century AD. Finally, during the same excavation season, a simple but coloured geometric mosaic pavement was also unearthed inside the *apodyterium* (?) of a private bath belonging to a sixth century AD urban villa. This means that no other contemporary or older mosaics from Sagalassos proper are available in order to make local comparisons.

If we turn to other places, the problem is that, except for Cilicia and the Hatay, our knowledge of mosaics in Asia Minor is still very limited and very dispersed, both chronologically and geographically (Bingöl 1997). Even here, it is likely that there may have existed several cultural 'provinces' and that mosaics from outlying regions in present-day Turkey may not always offer better parallels than those from adjacent countries (Greece, Cyprus, even Italy). An additional problem is that most examples come from houses, or from bath complexes, whereas the internal space of the library presented a completely different challenge. Even in the case of Antioch, most evidence came from the periphery of the city, whereas the mosaic floors of the more prestigious buildings in the city centre remain largely unknown (Balty 1995: 15).

As far as the general concept with its rather small *pseudo-emblema* facing the entrance of the building is concerned, the mosaic pavement of the Neon Library still respects Hellenistic prototypes. Thus far, these are best known from Delos, where polychrome figured or abstract *emblemata*, generally oriented for viewers entering the room and isolated within patterned borders, or within areas of plain surfacing (white *tesserae*, chip pavements) were apparently the rule (Bruneau 1972; Ling 1998: 27). Similar mosaics also occurred in Asia Minor (Bingöl 1997: 81-85, 98-100, figs 57-58, 63). At least in luxurious contexts, for instance in the richer dwellings or palaces of Pergamon, Arsameia and Samosata, the evolution during the late Hellenistic period seems to have been towards the borders becoming more illusionistic, richer, more colourful and wider, so that eventually they occupied most of the floor (Bingöl 1997: 100-110, Figs 65-76).

But, even during the first century AD, mosaics with very simple compositions and a more limited pattern of colours, closely resembling the older Delian examples, were still produced in the Near East (Balty 1995: 30, pl. I,1). The Sagalassos pavement maintains the general composition and the small proportions of the *emblema* of its Hellenistic prototypes, but the neutral background has been replaced already by a black and white geometric pattern.

The latter originated in late Republican Italy, where from the Second Pompeian Style onwards, the elaborate wall paintings necessitated more simple and abstract floor decorations instead of Greek style pictorial mosaics. In fact, the 'trompe l'oeil effects' and rich colouring of these illusionist wall paintings made floors with elaborate figural motifs and richly coloured borders totally inappropriate if one wanted to avoid a distracting and 'overwhelming' effect (Ling 1998: 35). Therefore, the Italian mosaicists gradually seemed to have turned towards the bichrome pavements of their own tradition (*opus signinum*) as a source of inspiration (Joyce 1979: 262). As a result, by the time of Augustus and well into the first half of the first century AD, two-dimensional systems in black and white became predominant in Italy. They introduced abstract styles born of the western *opus signinum* tradition and made use of meanders, grids of diamonds, and scale ornaments in black and white. Squares surrounding roundels replaced the colourful *emblemata* of the past. During the rest of the first century AD, various design dominated Italian mosaic art including simple black and white geometric pavements with bands or meanders as borders surrounding grids of octagons and hexagons, eight-lozenge stars enclosing large square panels, all-over meanders, systems of large and small squares or oblongs with inset geometric figures (roundels, squares, diamonds and triangles, ranged above one another or point to point like an hourglass). Within and alongside these schemes, silhouette figures (plant scrolls, objects, animals or even people) gradually made their appearance (Ling 1998: 36-38). During the second and early third century AD, figures of the black on white silhouette style, enriched sometimes with floral motifs (the so-called 'floral style'), became the trademark of Italian mosaics. They transformed the whole concept of mosaic pavement: whereas the Hellenistic picture-*emblema* as Ling put it "had treated the floor as a wall with a picture hung on it, …" the lack of landscape and the even distribution of the figures over the whole floor eventually transformed the latter into a continuous field (Ling 1998: 40-41, 47). This black and white style was certainly the major Italian contribution to the history of ancient mosaics. Yet, even in such floors with geometric black and white patterns, a limited use of polychrome *emblemata* can be traced occasionally as late as the second century AD, for instance in Hadrian's Villa at Tivoli dated around 118-121 AD (Ling 1998: 35, 47 fig. 31). In that respect, except perhaps for the dominance of *peltae* in the geometric floor, which in the West became popular before it did in the East (see below), the whole concept of the Neon Library's mosaic pavement could theoretically fit with the pavements of the time of the building's construction. For a while, except for the *emblema* itself, we had to accept that it was possible that this floor was the original pavement of the library. But we believe now that, if the *emblema* which certainly belongs to the fourth century AD (see below), had been introduced later, traces of such an alteration would have been more obvious along its edges with the geometric black and white pattern. Again, the replacement of three out of the building's four walls would also have left much clearer traces in the exterior border zones.

During the third century AD, Italy witnessed a revival of coloured mosaics and of perspectival patterns originating in the Hellenistic period. By the next century, coloured mosaics had won the day (Ling 1998: 48).

In the Near East (from Cilicia to Egypt), however, from the beginning of the second century AD onwards, the development of mosaic pavements followed a completely different path. Here, the Hellenistic tradition of the polychrome mosaic with pictorial *emblema* continued for at least three more centuries. Polychromy remained a distinguishing feature of the region throughout the Imperial and Byzantine period. Instead of the unified concept of the Italian black and white mosaic pavements, the attention of the viewer continued to be dominated by a usually mythological *pseudo-emblema* in bright colours, surrounded by borders of geometric patterns or of leaf-scrolls. The figures of the central scene were also set within a realistic spatial setting by which they continued to impose a specific viewpoint. Another characteristic of these *pseudo-emblemata* was that they were monumentalised, as the framing area (Hellenistic wave crest, Imperial two-dimensional meanders, stepped pyramids, two-strand guilloches) was reduced in importance. A new decorative border motif which would enjoy a lasting popularity in the East was the undulating ribbon with its careful exploitation of different colour gradations which suggest a sinuous and three-dimensional curvature. Often however, the old Hellenistic, concentric borders were abandoned in favour of a network of geometric, usually coloured ornaments (intersecting circles, diagonal grid systems, etcetera). In smaller spaces the figured parts occupied almost the whole floor surface, except for its small frame. In larger rooms they were multiplied and the floor was divided into several figured panels, placed either directly next to one another, or separated by geometrical pavements. The Severan period introduced a more baroque style as well as new motifs (e.g. the star with eight diamonds). Personifications, old (the Four Seasons) and new (abstract concepts like *Ananeosis*, etcetera), became also increasingly popular. From the third century AD onwards, these abstract images became labelled. Gradually, this practice spread to mythological scenes too. As in third century AD Italy, perspectival patterns became popular again from the middle of the century onwards. Other, new ornamental patterns were developed, octagons and *peltae* which sometimes in rather fashion occupied the whole floor. Fourth century AD mosaics became more balanced again, with a repetition of geometric motifs covering almost the entire floor. The reigns of Constantine and of Constantius II saw a revival of the figural *pseudo-emblemata* which would flourish a last time-in classicized forms- during the reign of the emperor Julian. During the fourth century AD, labels had become ubiquitous in figured panels. Another novelty of the period, which had already become common practice at a much earlier date in the West, was the fact that the spatial setting of the scenes was sometimes reduced in importance, or even completely replaced by a neutral white background. After Julian's death, however, the principle of the *emblema* was quickly abandoned completely and mosaic pavements became a continuous field covered with colourful geometric figures. The style continued right into the earlier part of the fifth century AD until the middle of the century, when due to

Sassanid influences the human figure was reintroduced, especially in increasingly popular hunting scenes (Balty 1995: 30-31, 69-71, Ling 1998: 49-59).

The cathedral mosaic from Sagalassos fits rather well within this development, the mosaic from Neon's Library does not. All one can say is that its *pseudo-emblema* cannot be much later than the reign of Julian. The labelling of its figural scene and its neutral white background would perfectly fit within the Near Eastern mosaic tradition of the fourth century AD. But the black and white pavement which surrounds it would seem totally out of place there in Imperial times. This can only suggest that the Sagalassos mosaicists did not turn to the Near East for their inspiration.

In Cyprus, there seems to have been a mixture of Italian and of oriental traditions, so that some motifs (for instance *peltae*) made an earlier appearance there than they did in the Near East (Balty 1995: 31). Similar mixed traditions may also have characterised the development of mosaics in Greece. Some of its mosaic floors continued the Hellenistic *emblemata* tradition. But, as in the Near East, the *emblema* was monumentalised and occupied most of the floor, or the floor was divided into several decorative polychrome panels. Yet, during the second century AD, simple black and white mosaics, presenting linear or geometric patterns also made an appearance beside more colourful floors. Unlike Italian practice however, the black and white mosaic floors of Roman Greece usually did not cover the whole surface (Bruneau 1981: 327-328,339, 340, 345 355; Hellenkemper Salies 1986: 280; Ling 1998: 59).

As far as Asia Minor is concerned, except for Cilicia which stylistically seems to have formed a single cultural province with Antioch, it has been suggested that the old Hellenistic mosaic tradition was interrupted as the result of the general economic stagnation and the political upheaval of the unruly first century BC. When prosperity resumed and increased the demand for luxury floors during the later first and second centuries AD, mosaicists would have turned to the West for inspiration and thus would have become influenced strongly by the mosaic tradition of Italy and that of other western provinces. This would explain the adoption of black and white geometric and silhouette figure mosaics strongly resembling those of Italy. The polychromy and illusionistic styles which can also be found here from the third century AD onwards, would also not necessarily indicate Near Eastern influence, since by then they had become part of the mosaic tradition in Italy too (Ling 1998: 59). A detailed overview of the Anatolian mosaic development during the Imperial period has not been written, but there are several published examples of simple black and white geometric mosaic floors dating from the middle Imperial period onwards (Bingöl 1997: 129-130 fig. 92). The mosaic floors of the *Hanghäuser* at Ephesos, especially units 1 and 2 of *Hanghaus* 2, include also various geometric floors with intersecting circles in black and white, or in three colours (black, white, and yellow or red-brown) some of which belong to the later first or second century AD (Jobst and Vetters 1977: 42-43), while most were laid as late as the second half of the fourth century AD, especially the last quarter of it, and even later (Jobst and Vetters 1977: 45-48 figs 78-81; 52-54 fig. 90; 56-58 fig. 95; 59-64 figs 98, 103; 84-86 figs 152-155; 97-101 figs 176-180). Generally, the geometric pattern is surrounded by a broad, white band with a dispersed, simple rosette decoration and in some cases it contains a coloured figured *pseudo-emblema* in its centre (Jobst and Vetters 1977: 47 figs 78-81). All this shows that, as far as its general composition is concerned, the mosaic floor of the Neon Library at Sagalassos does fit rather well within the middle to late Roman Imperial mosaic tradition of Western Anatolia.

A closer look at some of the motifs may provide evidence for a more precise dating. Intersecting circles formed one of the most popular geometric patterns in the Roman East. At Antioch (Antakya), they usually form quatrefoils and curvilinear squares decorated with crosslets or smaller squares or diamonds. They occur from Hadrian's reign onwards until the reign of the Severi, but they never cover the whole floor. Instead, they form smaller geometric panels set between figured or other geometric floor sections. All of them seem to have been multi-coloured (Levi 1947: 54 pl. IXa; 57 pl. XCVa; 105 pl. XCVIIa: 106, 109 pl. XCIX a,c; Campbell 1988: 25 pl. 77). During the second half of the fourth century AD, similar floors turned up again in the Antioch area (Campbell 1988: 41 pl. 101; 46 pl. 136). During the same period, almost identical mosaic pavements can be found in Turkey, at Carian Aphrodisias, where they extend into the fifth century. Here as well, most of them were multicoloured and they filled just a few panels of a more complex geometric pattern (Campbell 1991: 2 pl. 8; 12 pl. 41; 14-15 pls 47-54, 16-17 pls 55-68). However, some multicoloured, late fourth to late fifth century AD examples belong to central panels which covered a greater floor surface (Campbell 1991: 23. pl. 81; 25 pls 91-92; 28-29 fig. 17 and pl. 105). At Ephesos, but also at Miletus and Side, bi- and tri-coloured pavements of intersecting circles, forming quatrefoils and curvilinear squares with internal diamonds or other small ornaments, created geometric patterns which, except for a white border, extended over most of the floors of the corridors and rooms in some of the *Hanghäuser*. They range in date from the second to the fourth century AD and were especially popular during the last quarter of the fourth century AD (Jobst and Vetters 1977: 45-48 figs 78, 81; 52-55 fig. 90; 59-65 figs 98, 103; 84-86 figs 152-155; 97-102 figs. 176-180). Some dated to a repair after an earthquake in 356-368 AD, even surrounded a figural *pseudo-emblema* (Jobst and Vetters 1977: 47 figs 78-81).

In the Near East, *peltae* patterns were introduced only during the second half of the third century AD (Levi 1947: 180 pl. XLIIa: here alternating vertical and horizontal pairs), but in the West and on Cyprus they made an earlier appearance, possibly as early as the beginning of the century, if not before (Balty 1995: 18-20). In Roman Britain, bi- or tri-coloured patterns of interlaced circles forming quatrefoils or patterns of horizontally and/or vertically placed running *peltae*, sometimes covering complete floors (except for the borders), were very popular during the fourth century AD (Neal 1981: 41 nr. 5, 42 nr. 6, 79, nr. 46, 97 nr. 70, 99 nr. 72, 112 nr. 84). The authors know of no other parallel where intersecting circles and *peltae* are combined in a single motif as is the case at Sagalassos.

Lozenges, some of them filled with circular motifs, as in the border of the library, were also popular as a border pattern in Roman Britain during the fourth century AD (Neal 1981: 48 nr. 12, 109 nr. 83). As far as the mosaic floor of the path is concerned, borders of tangent pitched squares, as well as four-pointed stars enclosing lozenges in different colours, occur at Antioch from the Severan period onwards (Levi 1947: 106 pl. XCVIIIa; Campbell 1998: 25 pl. 77). They are also known at Ephesos during the last quarter of the fourth century AD (Jobst and Vetters 1977: 47-48 figs 79-80).

A closer look at the geometric pattern of the black and white mosaic floor of Neon's Library at Sagalassos thus shows that the local mosaic tradition appears to have been a combination of older Hellenistic features (the rather small *pseudo-emblema*) and of strong western influences (the black and white style). However, unlike the paving tradition in Italy, in western Asia Minor, but also in Roman Britain, black and white or tri-coloured geometric pavements of larger size remained popular throughout the later fourth century AD. The motifs that were used in the Neon Library appear to have been in vogue during the third, but especially during the fourth century AD.

A date during this last century is suggested also by the *pseudo-emblema*. Its border certainly does not contradict such a date. In fact, there are good fourth century AD examples of similar three-shade twisted ribbons at Carian Aprodisias (Campbell 1991: pls 7, 64-65). The tri-coloured two-strand twist is also found in that city in mosaics dated to the second half of the fourth and the early fifth century AD (Campbell 1991: 2-4 pls 4-7, 9-11). On the other hand, the garland of the border is already far removed from second and third century AD realistic vegetal borders and seems to prefigure the more stylised garlands of the Ananeosis Mosaic of Antioch, dated to the third quarter of the fifth century AD (Levi 1947: 626 pl. LXXIII; Campbell 1988: 27-28 pls 81-82). The small size of the *pseudo-emblema* could fit very well with a later fourth century AD date when in the Near East the classicizing tendencies during Julian's reign reintroduced such *emblemata*, set into large geometric patterns (Balty 1977: 8). A fourth century AD date would also answer very well, at least in the same geographic area, with the white background and lack of spatial setting in the figured panel. It has to be stressed however that these features appeared much sooner in the West.

The actual theme apparently represents a woman (Thetis?) next to Achilleus in the company of his tutor, Phoinix. The depiction of Phoinix as tutor of Achilleus comes from the *Iliad* (IX B; XVI, 96; XIX, 326). According to Homer, Peleus had entrusted Phoinix with Achilleus' education and sent them off together to Troy. This choice of subject fits very well with the function of the building. Homer still played an enormous role in the *paideia* of the Greeks during the fourth century AD, when explaining Homer by means of a symbolic *exegesis* to youngsters was one of the major tasks of the *grammatikos* (Festugière 1959: 226-227; Schouler 1984: 470 ff.). Homer is one of the authors most commonly discussed in the works of the famous rhetor Libanios, who rose to prominence during the rule of Julian. Libanios also wrote several biographies of Achilleus (Schouler 1984: 442, 457). So the choice of an episode of this Greek hero's life for representation in the *emblema* of the Neon Library's mosaic floor would perfectly fit the spirit of the age of Libanios and the rule of Julian.

A summary of all these factors thus appears to suggest a date for the mosaic during the second half of the fourth century AD, and most likely during the reign of Julian (AD 361-363). Historical events could corroborate this date. In fact, such a splendid repair of the building would be perfectly in line with this emperor's policy, supported by many members of the urban elite, to give a new boost to the old Hellenic culture. But, if the building was constructed as a monument devoted to the Imperial cult or as a heroon for the founder's family, its repair in the later fourth century AD would have been totally incomprehensible.

During the third quarter of the fourth century, Libanios saw the maintenance of Greek civilization, the preservation of by then discarded books and the restoration of the schools, as one of the major tasks of the city councillors of Antioch, where he was teaching (Liebeschuetz 1972: 102). This is not so surprising, since in the East many of the prominent families remained pagan until the fifth and sometimes even as late as the sixth century AD (Brown 1992: 129-130; Jones 1994: 325; Grant 1998: 67-68). Between the reigns of Marcian and Justin I (AD 450-527) society in Aphrodisias had both Christians and pagans occupying prominent positions (Rouaché 1989: 86). The same was true at Ephesos and in many other major cities (Foss 1979: 32). But even the Christian elite remained faithful to the ideals of the classical Greek *paideia*. One should not forget that certainly before Constantine's 'conversion' in 312 AD, Christianity had not become a really 'popular' movement. Its followers came mainly from the urban lower classes and only occasionally from the notables too (Brown 1992: 76; Jones 1994: 322). Throughout the fourth century, *paideia* remained a distinguishing feature of the elite of both the Greek and the Latin world. Both the governing class of the empire (e.g. the governors) and the notables of each region, Christians and pagans alike, constantly emphasised their devotion to the Muses and proclaimed the existence of a common culture. At a time when general literacy began to diminish, the leaders of society still possessed a high degree of literary culture and maintained the services of professional teachers, which might guarantee a future career to their sons. So, *paideia* became a sign of good birth and wealth and made its possessors the natural leaders of society (Brown 1992: 33-37). As Brown rightly says, "The ideal of the cultivated governor, the carefully groomed product of a Greek paideia, was a commonplace of the political life of the eastern empire ... Paideia united potentially conflicting segments of the governing class. It joined imperial administrators and provincial notables in a shared sense of common excellence" (Brown 1992: 38-39).

This picture must have been true of Pisidia too. During his stay at Syrian Antioch, in the years 361-62 and 362-63 respectively, the rhetor Libanios, the dominant figure of fourth century AD Greek culture, had two prominent Pisidians (both *curiales*) among his students at Antioch. The first one (Faustinus) later became a Christian bishop, while the second one (Julianos XV) was a pagan who upon his return played a prominent role in his home town (Petit 1957: 27-28, 54, 55, 63-64, 112, 114,138, 149, 151, 157-158, 161, 167-168). The restoration of the Neon Library would thus fit perfectly with the spirit of the age of Libanios and the emperor Julian. Julian even restored the civic taxes, which in the early fourth century AD had been taken over by the Imperial government, in order to allow the cities to maintain and restore their public buildings (Roueché 1989: 78).

During most of the fourth century, pagan teachers and philosophers were allowed to practice (Foss 1979: 32). Many Christians, including St. Basil, recognised the values of Greek education and managed to dissociate ancient authors from pagan cults (Festugière 1959: 217-225). Others, like John Chrysostom however, were more reluctant and began to warn against Greek culture (Festugière 1959: 225-240). Attacks on pagan temples had started already during the reign of Constantius II, but Julian's pagan reaction put a temporary end to them. Between his death and the mid-380s the pagan cults even enjoyed a last period of *de facto* toleration (Fowden 1978: 59- 62). The accession in 384 AD of Maternus Cynegius as Praetorian Prefect of the East eventually turned the machinery of persecution, which Theodosius I had mobilised already against Christian heretics, against pagans too. Quickly, the destruction of pagan temples started again and reached a peak in the 390s (Fowden 1978: 63-65; Brown 1992: 107, 114). A new equilibrium would only be achieved in the course of the reign of Theodosius II, from 408 to 450 AD (Brown 1992: 119).

Before this happened however, during the last decades of the fourth century, bishops and monks joined forces and showed that they could sway the will of the powerful (Brown 1992: 4). As Brown recently wrote, during the last decades of that century, "Christian spokesmen, representing the needs of Christian congregations in the cities, began to intervene in the politics of the empire ..... they frequently did so by taking on roles, in their confrontation with those in power, that had originally been elaborated by men of paideia ..." (Brown 1992: 34).

Therefore, the apparently deliberate destruction of the Neon Library should not necessarily indicate a Christian reaction following the news of the emperor Julian's death. The impressions in the mosaic floor that were caused by the central supports suggest a certain period of use of the building before its destruction. If layer 5 was not a temporary upper surface, but part of the filling operation, the coin dated to the reign of Arcadius that was found in it could confirm this too. In any case, the fire catastrophe occurred before the end of the century.

It is known that in the East, the fourth century, and especially the generations preceding the reign of Theodosius I, was a period of civil turmoil and of urban upheaval, during which the urban elite repeatedly faced real danger from rioting lower classes. The latter attempted on many occasions to put to the torch the residences of the powerful, or attacked and destroyed ancient buildings (Brown 1992: 86-88, 90, 119). At Ephesos and in the rest of the province of Asia, considerable disturbances had already begun as the result of the persecution of magicians under Valens (372-378 AD), but they would continue later in the century too, and spread into the fifth and sixth centuries AD. By then, they had become associated with the factions of the Blues and the Greens (Foss 1979: 17). Often these riots were provoked by individual congregations of believers mobilised by (Christian) controversies, or they were led by less educated members of Christian society. Monks especially were blamed for this. Although they belonged to various social backgrounds, Christian writers constantly described the monks as uneducated peasants and as the enemies of Greek culture or the educated upper classes (Foss 1979: 17; Brown 1992: 71). Libanios described them as *apoliades*, i.e. opposed to urban culture, and despised them as the most fierce opponents of the *Hellenikos bios*. They were held responsible for the destruction of many temples and other 'pagan' buildings, and for the growing polarisation between Christianity and Greek culture that was henceforth linked with paganism (Festugière 1959: 237-239; Fowden 1978: 67-69). The reason for this animosity seems to have been the fact that, instead of the highly formalised rhetoric which had been used by the upper classes to maintain their authority, monks became the spokesmen of a certain Christian populism and used the simple words of the masses (Brown 1992: 72-74). Especially towards the end of the fourth century, the populist component of Christianity reached its most aggressive peak. Its 'universal' appeal and the fact that it addressed all classes made it a 'social' challenger of the old ideal of the 'paideia' adopted by the urban elites. The fact that only the bishop, who during this period proclaimed himself a 'lover of the poor', could control these unruly believers, would turn him into a new type of urban leader (Brown 1992: 76-78, 89). But even during the next century, many bishops would still need *paidea* in order to live in peace with their pagan neighbours (Brown 1992: 122).

In view of the historical developments of the later fourth century AD, it is likely that Neon's Library eventually fell victim to a city riot during this period. The fact that in AD 363 the mother of one of Libanios' Pisidian pupils, a certain Julianos who was originally from some unidentified Pisidian town, was murdered, illustrates that Pisidia did not escape the unruly conditions of that period. But, this event should not necessarily be linked with the destruction of the Neon Library as we previously suggested (Waelkens *et al.* 1993: 15). In fact, upon his return, Julianos was received with great honours by his fellow citizens (Petit 1957: 55, 157-158). But a riot by less educated people might very well explain why this prestigious building was looted and torched, and why the *emblema* of its mosaic floor which apparently reflected the old *paideia* system, was deliberately destroyed. Shortly afterwards, a splendid mosaic pavement would be placed inside the courtyard of the old Council House of the city, transformed into a Christian cathedral.

2. THE CONSERVATION OF THE MOSAIC
(H. Kökten Ersoy, K. Severson with S. Şener)

2.1. Provisional stabilisation

In August of 1992, the condition of the mosaic was documented and provisional stabilisation measures undertaken by conservator John Stewart[2]. In addition to the general archaeological documentation, surviving areas in the central *emblema* were drawn at a scale of 1:1 on polythene sheets and photographed in an approximately 0.60 by 0.60 m grid[3]. Losses in the *emblema* and the length and depth of the large northeast-southwest fissures across the width of the mosaic were documented and it was noted that some of the fissures extended into the side walls of the library building. Areas of settling were also recorded, particularly in the centre of the mosaic at the *emblema*.

The large black and white tesserae, used in the geometric pattern forming most of the mosaic, were found to be relatively secure, except around the edges of fissures and gaps. In spite of the survival of a good deal of jointing mortar between *tesserae* in many areas, preliminary sounding by tapping revealed 'extensive loss of adhesion' between the *tesserae* and the mortar substrate. Loss of adhesion was estimated to occur in 60 to 80 percent of the black and white geometric pattern[4]. In the *emblema*, the general loss of jointing mortar and the small size of the *tesserae* made that area more unstable than the rest and put the *emblema* "… at risk of dismemberment, particularly around existing lacunae."[5] Detachment of the *tesserae* from the bedding mortar in the *emblema* was estimated to be approximately 90 percent[6].

In order to secure loose *tesserae* in the *emblema*, the edges of lacunae and fissures were quickly edged at the end of the 1992 season. Time constraints and problems in obtaining certain materials forced the team to use an edging mortar consisting of lime putty and river sand, with small amounts of white cement and polyvinyl acetate emulsion[7]. In areas of loose and jumbled *tesserae*, the loose stones were removed and stored. In the *emblema*, where *tesserae* were loose but still remained in the correct location within the design, they were faced with cotton muslin, adhered in place with dilute polyvinyl acetate emulsion (Fig. 10). Large-scale facing of the *emblema* was avoided due to uncertainties about the behaviour of the resin in that environment[8]. Because of lack of time and concern for the stability of the mosaics during the winter, the remaining large cracks in the black and white geometric areas were hastily filled with cement-based mortar at the end of the season.

---

[2] The account of the 1992 work is taken from the report submitted by J. D. Stewart after his visit to the site: *Sagalassos Library Mosaic, Condition and Conservation Report*, unpublished report (London1993). The authors wish to thank the Sagalassos Expedition for free use of this material.
[3] Assistance was provided by K. Norman, L. Hibler-Vandenbulcke, B.Daniëls, L.Bijnens and H.Smolders, *ibid.* p.1.
[4] *Ibid.* p. 6 and Appendix 7.
[5] *Ibid.* p.4, ff.
[6] *Ibid.* p. 6.
[7] *Ibid.* p. 8; these materials were used in the following proportions: lime putty: white cement: river sand: polyvinyl acetate emulsio (3:1:12:.75).
[8] *Ibid.* p. 9. "Polysan Tutkal," a locally produced polyvinyl acetate emulsion, was used in these operations (as reported in Appendix 1). It is fortunate that facing was limited to the edges of the lacunae as this product is notorious for rapidly becoming insoluble. Removal of the small amount of facing that was applied was extremely laborious (see below).

2.2. Planning the 1996-97 project

The report on the 1992 stabilisation measures included recommendations for temporary protection of the mosaic as well as suggestions for more permanent solutions for their preservation. Recommendations for long-term protection of the mosaic offered three main options: reburial, consolidation *in situ* with partial lifting and relaying on a new mortar bed, or complete lifting and relaying on a new foundation[9].

In the spring of 1996, the staff of Ankara University's Başkent Meslek Yüksek Okulu were invited to prepare a plan for the conservation of the library mosaics[10]. Between 1992 and 1996, the Sagalassos Archaeological Research Project had designed and initiated the construction of a permanent shelter for the protection and display of the mosaics, in conjunction with the reconstruction of the first century AD fountain house located on the hillside directly below the library. The construction of this substantial building eliminated any need to consider reburial as an option for long-term preservation of the mosaic. It therefore remained to determine whether to consolidate the mosaic *in situ*, to lift and relay the *emblema* only, or to lift the entire mosaic and relay it on a new foundation.

Lifting and relaying a large mosaic is always a major undertaking, requiring specialised expertise and considerable monetary expenditure for equipment, supplies and labour[11]. While sometimes necessary, the removal of mosaics from the bedding on which they were constructed is also full of serious risks, such as equipment failure and catastrophic damage from fire or flood while work is in progress[12]. Above all, ancient mosaics are an integral part of the buildings in which they were originally installed and every effort should be made to preserve them within that context[13]. In recent years, *in situ* treatment has been increasingly accepted as the most appropriate method for conservation of excavated mosaics. With a protective roof in place, it was hoped that the Library mosaics could be successfully treated without lifting[14].

2.3. Initial cleaning and documentation

During the years between the excavation and the construction of the new protective structure, the mosaic was covered with a layer of loose synthetic polymer netting and approximately 0.15-0.20 m of soil (Fig. 14). Although there was no noticeable growth of large plants on the surface of the soil during this period, the area was quickly covered with native grasses and other low growth. At the beginning of the 1996 excavation season, the mosaic remained covered with the thick layer of soil to provide continuing protection from the elements as well as from the traffic and hazards of construction. As soon as the roof was in place, shielding the area from rain and excessive sun (and the conservators from falling debris), re-excavation could proceed. The main hall was cleared at the beginning of the 1996 season, while the pedestrian way in front of the building was not cleared until the beginning of the 1997 season.

Removal of the bulk of the soil revealed that roots from low plants and grasses had penetrated the soil and synthetic mesh to the level of the mosaic (fig. 15). In the areas of black and white patterns, where the *tesserae* were larger and the grouting mortar was relatively sound, the roots ran along the surface of the mosaic until they located a crack. The considerable width of many of the cracks allowed the roots to penetrate the mosaic without causing additional damage. Where there were small losses in the grout mortar, or other discontinuities in the surface, the roots had penetrated the mosaic, disrupting previously sound *tesserae*. In the *emblema*, where there was greater loosening and displacement of the *tesserae* prior to excavation, the roots formed a dense layer which penetrated the muslin facing as well as the exposed bedding mortar.

Removal of the roots by pulling would clearly have resulted in additional disruption of the *tesserae*. So they were painstakingly cut at the surface of the mosaic, or slightly below the level of the *tesserae* wherever possible, before further cleaning could proceed. With the roots cut and most

---

[9] *Ibid.* pp. 11-12. Also included in this part of the report were rough work plans, material requirements and cost estimates for each of these options and notes on locally available materials.

[10] The project was planned by Dr. Hande Kökten and Selçuk Sener, of Ankara Üniversitesi Başkent Meslek Yüksekokulu, in consultation with Kent Severson (private conservator, Boston, Massachusetts, U.S.A.). Conservation was carried out by students Derya Elmalı (1996), Serap Çelik (1997), and Onur Çelebi (1997), from Ankara Üniversitesi Başkent Meslek Yüksekokulu, and Zeynep Pehlivanoğlu (1996-97) from Istanbul Üniversitesi, Klasik Arkeoloji Bülümü, under the supervision of conservators Hande Kökten Ersoy, Kent Severson and Selçuk Sener, and assistant conservator Nil Baydar.

[11] As, for example: *The Conservation of the Orpheus Mosaic at Paphos, Cyprus* (1991) Getty Conservation Institute, Malibu.

[12] At the Bath/Gymnasium complex at Sardis, Turkey, in 1997, a fire seriously damaged a series of mosaics in storage. Those mosaics had been lifted from the excavation to explore the strata beneath; they were faced and awaiting backing when the unfortunate incident occurred. The fire burned the facings and there were considerable losses. A plan for recovery is currently being formulated.

[13] The desirability of this approach was clearly stated in the 1964 *International Charter for the Conservation and Restoration of Monuments*, the so-called -"*Charter of Venice,*"- Article 8.

[14] International consensus concerning the desirability of *in situ* preservation was well formed by 1980 as demonstrated in Mora (1980: 11). A recent and very successful treatment *in situ* was undertaken by R. Nardi in Zippori, Israel (Nardi 1996: 120-132).

Fig. 12: Portrait of one of the female heads in the border of the *emblema*, after treatment.

Fig. 13: Detail of the border of the *emblema* with its undulating ribbon, the garland, the stepped pyramids and the guilloche

Fig. 14: Massive amounts of roots, along with some soil and the netting, removed for the 1996 treatment (photograph: Hande Kökten Ersoy).

Fig. 15: Penetration of the netting and the mosaic by roots during temporary burial (photograph: Hande Kökten Ersoy).

of the covering soil removed, the mosaic was dusted with soft bristle brushes to remove the remaining soil.

Using the temporary mortar fills and facings applied to the mosaic in the 1992 stabilisation as indicators, along with the archaeologists' photographic documentation, it could be demonstrated that very little additional subsidence, freeze-thaw cracking or other damage had occurred during the temporary reburial[15]. The documentation was updated in advance of the further treatment by marking the location of all fractures, both treated and untreated, on a photocopy of the architects' documentary drawing of the room. Additional 35 mm colour slides and black and white prints were taken before continuing the treatment and at all subsequent stages of the treatment.

Intensive soil removal, not undertaken in 1992, revealed a thin layer of burial over large areas of the mosaic. In some areas, such as the northwest corner and the north side near the centre, the accretions appeared to have been slightly sintered by the heat of the fire which destroyed the roof of the building in antiquity. The accretions in these areas were redder and considerably harder than elsewhere. All burial accretions were removed mechanically by scraping with steel scrapers and/or knives, or with small chisels and hammers.

During cleaning, the voids beneath the *tesserae* were mapped by tapping on the surface in a regular pattern while listening for changes in tonality. The locations of voids were marked on the surface of the mosaic with chalk and indicated on the drawing of the mosaic floor for conservation records. Loose, scattered *tesserae* no longer in recognisable position were removed during cleaning and stored.

2.4. Removal of temporary fills

With the mosaic surface fully exposed in the main hall, the technical and aesthetic effectiveness of the cement-based fill material, applied to the long fractures in the 1992 stabilisation project, was reassessed. It was decided to remove the fills for the following reasons:

1 – The mortar was quite hard and appeared to form a non-permeable barrier which could lead to moisture accumulation beneath the surface of the mosaic. In the cold environment of a Sagalassos winter, it was feared that this moisture accumulation could lead to damage in the freeze-thaw cycle.
2 – The cement mortar was tightly bound to the *tesserae* surrounding the fractures. It is well known that Sagalassos is located in a zone of high risk from seismic activity. In the event of an earthquake, the hard, inflexible mortar would pull *tesserae* away from previously undamaged areas.
3 – Removal of the fill material in several test areas revealed that the cement only partially filled the deep fractures over which it was applied. The shallow fills did nothing to fill the horizontal voids separating the *tesserae* from the bedding mortar and were blocking access to these voids for subsequent stabilisation treatment.
4 – Finally, the texture and colour of the cement fills did not harmonise with the visible bedding mortar or the colours of the mosaic.

Removal of the cement fills was accomplished mechanically with small chisels. The strong adhesion of the cement to the *tesserae* made this a time-consuming operation and inevitably some *tesserae* were loosened in the process; control over loose *tesserae* was maintained by tacking them in their original locations with masking tape until they could be permanently re-adhered. Beneath the fills, the fractures proved to be quite deep and filled with a variety of debris, including small stones, soil, sand, roots and a few displaced *tesserae*. All this material was removed in advance of further treatment. To avoid additional losses in the *emblema* during cleaning, the temporary edgings around lacunae were not removed until just before the consolidation process (see below). A last cleaning of the entire mosaic surface and the fractures before consolidation was accomplished by dusting with a jet of compressed air.

2.5. Treatment

With the surface of the mosaic freed of soil, burial accretions and most of the temporary fills, it was immediately apparent that there was no need to lift and re-bed the mosaic and that even the most damaged areas of the *emblema* could be treated *in situ*.

2.5.1. Conservation materials

The bedding mortars and *tesserae* were consolidated by injection of grout, followed by application of lime-based edging and compensation mortars to lacunae and fractures. In current conservation practice, lime-based mortars and grouts are the materials of choice for consolidation and edging because of their similarity in physical properties to the original bedding mortar used in the construction of most Roman mosaics. These properties include similar porosity,

---

[15] This was suggested by Stewart (1993) *Sagalassos Library Mosaic*: 10. Appendix 6 of this report contains the text of a letter from E. Paulissen, geomorphologist at the Catholic University of Leuven, describing a core sample taken from the floor of the mosaic at the location of a previous loss. The sample was apparently taken to assess the potential for ongoing subsidence. In addition to finding evidence of a previous mosaic floor beneath the current one, the letter points to the need for a permanent shelter over the mosaic to reduce the potential for ongoing subsidence due to water infiltration and frost.

hardness and coefficient of thermal expansion (Torraca 1988: 28-29, 70, 80-81). Matching coefficients of thermal expansion prevents stress-cracking at the interface between the old and new material during normal thermal cycles while matching porosity prevents the introduction of a moisture barrier in the mosaic matrix. Should further seismic activity or subsidence occur, the relatively soft lime mortar will fracture before loosening sound *tesserae*. If it becomes necessary to reverse this treatment, the lime-based mortars can easily be broken away mechanically with small tools.

The injection grouts and mortars used in this treatment were based on those developed elsewhere for consolidation of ancient mosaics and wall paintings[16]. Lime-based mortars were used exclusively in this treatment. A small amount of Primal AC-33® acrylic emulsion was added to most mixtures to help prevent cracking during initial drying and to provide extra adhesion and mechanical strength until the application was fully cured[17]. The addition of a small amount of crushed ancient brick provided the mortars with some slight hydraulic properties.

All mortars were prepared from locally acquired slaked lime (lime putty) and mixed by hand. The lime was screened before mixing and the sand lime mixture prepared in large batches. Mixing included repeated chopping and pounding and all the mortar mixes were stored under a damp cloth until used. Crushed brick and acrylic resin were added to a limited quantity of sand/lime mix at the beginning of the day of use only. Mortar formulations are presented in Table I.

2.5.2. Work space

During the treatment of the mosaic, all equipment and conservation materials were kept in the main hall of the Library on a wooden platform covered with plastic sheeting. Mortars, consolidation solutions, and grouts were prepared outside the building. The presence of a nearby well-organised restoration project, that is, the restoration of the late Hellenistic fountain house just below the Library, aided the mosaic conservation team by providing electrical supply and an air-compressor, as well as the lime, sand and ancient brick needed to prepare lime mortars. Continuously flowing, clean, potable water from the ancient fountain was collected in a tank nearby for use in the conservation projects. During work, access to the Library was restricted to conservation team members. Dividing the mosaic into convenient sections for work, the conservation team worked in three groups, using the documentation drawings to record specific treatments applied to each area. All containers, buckets and hand tools were kept on plastic sheets near the work to prevent staining from spills and drips.

2.5.3. Consolidation

Voids beneath the surface had previously been located during cleaning. Where there were nearby fractures and lacunae, these were used for access points for deep consolidation. Where no access points were available, two or three *tesserae* were removed mechanically above the voids. *Tesserae* removed for consolidation were temporarily kept in place by taping to the floor with masking tape.

The area to be consolidated was first thoroughly wetted with 3% ethyl alcohol in water. Wetting was followed by injection of a slurry of lime water in 5% Primal-AC 33 acrylic emulsion, generally in a ratio of 1:1. An initial injection grout consisting of slaked lime, marble dust, sand, brick dust, and 5% acrylic emulsion was applied through large-bore syringes or from squeeze bottles fitted with synthetic plastic extension tubes. (See Table I, A. Injection Grout). Depending on the size and depth of the fracture and the extent of the void, the viscosity of the grout was adjusted for each area. Grout was injected until the area sounded solid when tapped.

In the event of future earth movement, no injection treatment could provide protection against further splitting of the mortar beds or mosaic. However, filling the voids left by previous subsidence allowed the low-viscosity injection grouts to flow into the horizontal gaps between the mortar beds. Partial filling of the vertical fissures with loose gravel reduced the amount of injection grout necessary and helped to reduce cracking during curing (Fig. 16). As the voids were filled and injection neared completion, a lime-based foundation mortar was applied to bring the fill uniformly up to the level of the top of the original bedding mortar in preparation for the application of the final final visible layer. (Table I, B. Foundation Mortar). *Tesserae* removed for injection were reset in the same mortar.

Because of the advanced state of deterioration of the *emblema*, the presence of the polyvinyl acetate and cotton muslin facing, and the cementitious mortar edging applied in the 1992 stabilisation, a slightly different approach was used during consolidation. The edging was removed mechanically, one small section at a time. The exposed *tesserae* were injected with the alcohol/water mixture, the acrylic emulsion solutions, and the injection grout as described above. The mosaic was then reinforced with lime-based edging mortar. (Table I, C. Edging Mortar). When the

---

[16] Grout and mortar formulations are similar to those presented in Ferragni *et al.* (1984: 110-116). See also: Nardi (1996: 128-130).

[17] Primal™ acrylic emulsions are manufactured by Rhom and Haas, Philadelphia, Pennsylvania, U.S.A., and are readily available from a variety of sources in Turkey.

Fig. 16: Deep vertical void, partially filled with gravel during injection grouting (photograph: Hande Kökten Ersoy).

Fig. 17: Compensation with *tesserae* in geometric patterns (photograph: Hande Kšökten Ersoy).

Fig. 18: Interior of the library with walkways for tourist traffic after completion of the project.

Fig. 19: General view of the interior of the library after the 1997 inauguration.

mortar had set, the cotton facing, softened by the water from the injection materials, was removed with scalpels. With one section secured in this way, work progressed around the perimeter of each lacuna until all areas of the *emblema* was stable. In many places, individual loose *tesserae* were lifted, a small amount of thick grout injected in the void, and immediately reset. The large cracks running through the centre of the *emblema* were consolidated in the same way as the other fissures, finishing with foundation mortar, scored to receive the final finish mortar during the compensation phase of the treatment[18].

2.5.4. Compensation

Although there are no universally accepted rules regarding the making up of losses in the conservation of ancient material, it is a generally accepted principle that compensation should be kept to a minimum and that all compensation should be readily distinguishable from the original material. With mosaics, it is common practice to fill small losses in geometric patterns with loose *tesserae* collected from badly damaged areas, setting the replacements in lime-based bedding mortar of a slightly different colour than the original mortar. Compensation using *tesserae* is usually restricted to small areas where there is no problem about the nature of the loss, as in geometric patterns and areas of solid colour. Larger losses, and those losses which include complicated figural decoration or inscriptions, are usually filled with a solid coloured mortar, tinted to harmonise with the surviving mosaic[19].

Small losses in the Library mosaic were filled with *tesserae* recovered from the debris of badly damaged areas, set in the same, untinted mortar used as the basis for the injection grout and the temporary edging in the *emblema*. Compensation was limited to filling areas of fracture where the losses were no more than one or two tesserae wide and which consisted solely of geometric patterns (Fig. 16).

All losses not filled by *tesserae* were filled with a flat, uniform hydraulic lime-based mortar. A light brown colour, similar to the soil from the surrounding area, was created by using local sand and a small amount of mineral pigment, added to lime and crushed brick to yield a very dry mortar mix. (Table I, D. Compensation Mortar) The mixture was prepared in large batches in advance of application to assure uniformity of colour in the bigger gaps at the centre of the *emblema* and in the narthex. Although somewhat stiff, the mortar was prepared with as little additional water as possible to help prevent micro cracking during curing. It was applied with spatulas and trowels, and smoothed to a uniform level approximately 3 mm below the surface of the *tesserae*. The surface was then tamped down with stiff bristle brushes to compact the mortar and provide a slightly rough texture. When the mortar was partially set, it was dabbed with a slightly wet sponge to expose the aggregate. Following finishing treatment, areas filled with compensation mortar were covered with plastic sheeting. The mortar was kept moist by occasional misting with a hand-held spray bottle for a minimum of five days. After initial setting, the plastic sheeting was removed and the mortar allowed to air dry. The final effect was a soft, uniformly textured surface which contrasted with the texture of the mosaic but harmonised with the lightest tonalities of the *tesserae*, the colour of the original mortar, and the colour of the soil visible between the *tesserae*.

In areas where the original jointing mortar between the *tesserae* was lost or where *tesserae* had been removed and reset during consolidation, the jointing mortar was replaced with the same mortar used in filling the large lacunae. The mortar was thinned slightly with water and spread over the surface of the mosaic, pushing it into the interstices with a damp sponge. When partially dry, excess mortar was removed with a clean sponge damped with clean water.

2.5.5. Final cleaning and consolidation

Although most of the soil and burial accretions had been removed prior to consolidation, a fine layer of dark, burned soil dulled the surface of the mosaic and remained in the spaces between the *tesserae*. At the end of the 1997 work season, with all the consolidation complete, four teams were formed from the available conservators and archaeologists to undertake a final cleaning. The mosaic was divided into zones and each team was equipped with three buckets, brushes and sponges. A good supply of tap water was made available from a storage tank outside the library. The entire floor was brushed with stiff dry brushes. Following dry brushing, the floor was wet with clean water containing a small amount of non-ionic detergent. The detergent solution was agitated with stiff brushes and the residues removed with clear water on clean sponges. While the entire main hall and portico could be vigorously scrubbed during this process, the *emblema* required particular attention from the conservators to prevent loss of small *tessera*. During the entire cleaning process, not a single *tessera* was dislodged, in spite of the numerous workers involved and the traffic of workmen carrying buckets of water across the room for the cleaning teams.

---

[18] Approximately two thirds of the main hall, including the *emblema*, were consolidated during the 1996 season. The remaining portion of the main hall and the portico were treated in the 1997 season.

[19] As per Mora (1980: 12-14) and Nardi (1996: 130). The publication of the Paphos project (note 11, above) does not discuss the rationale, but follows this policy. For a slightly more restrictive approach, see Baron (1983: 179 note 9).

Finally, to improve the visibility of the polychrome border frame, the fragmentary figures of Thetis and Achilles, and the signature of the mosaicists in the *emblema*, a solution of 5% Primal AC-33 in water was applied by brushing. This last consolidate was introduced, in a single soaking application, to the *emblema* only. Upon drying, the slightly saturated surface was considerably more legible with only a very slight gloss.

2.6. Preparations for public display

Prior to presentation of the library to the public, the remaining walls around the mosaic were cleaned by intensive brushing. Also, a separate conservation team cleaned the inscriptions and niches on the back wall of the library mechanically. During these operations the mosaic was carefully covered with plastic sheeting. Similar protection was used during the installation of ventilation windows high on the side walls and in the façade of the protective structure.

In order to prevent ongoing foot traffic from damaging the mosaic, wooden walkways were erected to control tourist access inside the building (Figs 18-19). Where the platforms bridged the portico, the short supporting columns were padded with heavy neoprene rubber at the surface of the mosaic. At the stylobate which separates the pedestrian way from the main hall, the walkway forms a viewing platform, running from one side of the building to the other. Tourists can also walk part-way up the outside of the west side wall of the library building to view the mosaics.

3. ACKNOWLEDGEMENTS

This research is supported by the Belgian Programme on Interuniversity Poles of Attraction (IUAP 4/12) initiated by the Belgian State, Prime Minister's Office, Science Policy Programming. The text also presents the results of the Concerted Action of the Flemish Government (GOA 97/2) and the Fund for Scientific Research-Flanders (Belgium) (FWO) (G.2145.94). Scientific responsibility is assumed by its authors. Femke Martens is research assistant of the Fund for Scientific Research Flanders – Belgium (F.W.O.).

4. REFERENCES

J. Balty (1977) *Mosaïques de la Syrie,* Brussels.
J. Balty (1995) *Mosaïques antiques du Proche-Orient. Chronologie, iconographie, interprétation* (Centre d'Histoire Ancienne. Volume 140; Annales Littéraires de l'Université de Besançon 551) Paris.
Z. Barov (1983) Recent developments in mosaic lifting techniques and new supports for removed floor mosaics, in: *Mosaics No. 3: Conservation in situ,* ICCROM, Aquileia: 163-183.
O. Bingöl (1997) *Malerei und Mosaik der Antike in der Türkei (Kulturgeschichte der Antiken Welt Band 67)* Ph. von Zabern Mainz.
P. Brown (1992) *Power and Persuasion in Late Antiquity. Towards a Christian Empire,* The University of Wisconsin Press.
Ph. Bruneau (1972) *Les mosaïques (Exploration archéologique de Délos* 29) Paris.
Ph. Bruneau (1981) Tendances de la mosaïque en Grèce à l'époque impériale, in: *Aufstieg und Niedergang der römischen Welt II.12.2.,* Berlin: 320-346.
S. Campbell (1988) *The Mosaics of Antioch (Subsidia Mediaevalia* 15) Toronto.
S. Campbell (1991) *The Mosaics of Aphrodisias in Caria (Subsidia Mediaevalia* 18) Toronto.
R. Degeest (2000) *The Common Wares of Roman Sagalassos (Studies in Eastern Mediterranean Archaeology* 3) Brepols Publishers.
H. Devijver (1993) The inscriptions of the Neon-Library of Roman Sagalassos, in: M. Waelkens and J. Poblome (eds) *Sagalassos II. Report on the Third Excavation Campaign of 1992 (Acta Archaeologica Lovaniensia Monographiae* 6) Leuven University Press: 107-123.
H. Devijver and M. Waelkens (1997) Roman inscriptions from the fifth campaign at Sagalassos, in: M. Waelkens and J. Poblome (eds) *Sagalassos IV. Report on the Survey and Excavation Campaigns of 1994 and 1995 (Acta Archaeologica Lovaniensia Monographiae* 9) Leuven University Press: 293-314.
H. Devijver and M. Waelkens (forthcoming) Roman inscriptions of the sixth and seventh campaigns at Sagalassos, *Sagalassos VI.*
H.A. Ekinci (1994) Boubon kurtarma kazısı 1993, in: *V. Müze kurtarma kazıları semineri,* Ankara: 333-343.
D. Ferragni *et al.* (1984) Injection grouting of mural paintings and mosaics, *Adhesives and Consolidants,* IIC, London: 110-116.
A.J. Festugière (1959) *Antioche païenne et chrétienne. Libanius, Chrysostome et les moines de Syrie (Bibliothèque des Ecoles Françaises d'Athènes et de Rome* 194) Paris.
C. Foss (1979) *Ephesus after Antiquity: A Late Antique, Byzantine and Turkish City,* Cambridge University Press.
G. Fowden (1978) Bishops and temples in the eastern Roman Empire AD 320-435, *The Journal of Theological Studies.* New Series 29: 53-78.
M. Grant (1998) *From Rome to Byzantium. The Fifth Century AD,* Routledge, London-New York.
G. Hellenkemper Salies (1986) Römische Mosaiken in Griechenland, *Bonner Jahrbücher* 186: 241-284.
F. Hueber (1997) *Ephesos. Gebaute Geschichte (Sonderhefte der Antiken Welt)* Mainz am Rhein.
J. Inan (1977-78) Der Bronzetorso im Burdur-Museum aus Bubon und der Bronzekopf im J. Paul-Getty Museum, *Istanbuler Mitteilungen* 27-28: 267-287.
International Charter for the Conservation and Restoration of Monuments and Sites (1964).
ICOMOS and the Second International Congress of Architects and Technicians of Historic Monuments, Venice.
W. Jobst and H. Vetters (1977) *Römische Mosaiken aus Ephesos I: Die Hanghäuser des Embolos (Forschungen in Ephesos. Veröffentlicht vom Österreichischen Archäologischen Institut. Band VIII.2)* Wien.
A.H.M. Jones (1994) *The Decline of the Ancient World* (12th edition) Longman Publishers.
C.P. Jones (1977-78) Some new inscriptions from Bubon, *Istanbuler Mitteilungen* 27-28: 288-296.
H. Joyce (1979) Form, function and technique in the pavements of Delos and Pompei, *American Journal of Archaeology* 83: 253-263.

D. Levi (1947) *Antioch Mosaic Pavements*, Princeton-London-The Hague.

J.H.W.G. Liebeschuetz (1972) *Antioch. City and Imperial Administration in the Later Roman Empire*, Oxford.

R. Ling (1998) *Ancient Mosaics*, British Museum Press.

P. Mora *et al.* (1980) *Mosaics No. 2: Safeguard*, ICCROM, Rome.

R. Nardi (1996) Zippori, Israel: the conservation of the mosaics of the Building of the Nile, *Archaeological Conservation and its Consequences*, IIC, Copenhagen: 127-132.

D.S. Neal (1981) *Roman Mosaics in Britain*, London.

P. Petit (1957) *Les étudiants de Libanius. Un professeur de faculté et ses élèves au Bas Empire*, Paris.

J. Poblome (1999) *Sagalassos Red Slip Ware. Typology and Chronology* (Studies in Eastern Mediterranean Archaeology 2) Brepols Publishers.

N.S. Price (ed.) (1991) *The Conservation of the Orpheus Mosaic at Paphos, Cyprus*, Getty Conservation Institute, Malibu.

W. Radt (1998) *Pergamon. Geschichte und Bauten, Funde und Erforschung einer antike Metropole*, DuMont Buch Verlag Köln.

Ch. Roueché (1989) *Aphrodisias in Late Antiquity* (Society for the Promotion of Roman Studies. Journal of Roman Studies Monographs 5) London.

J. Russell (1997) Sagalassos in Pisidia, *Journal of Roman Archaeology* 10: 537-544.

B. Schouler (1984) *La tradition hellénique chez Libanios II*, Lille-Paris.

G. Torraca (1988) *Porous Building Materials* (3rd ed.) ICCROM, Rome.

L. Vandeput (1997) *The Architectural Decoration in Roman Asia Minor. Sagalassos: a Case Study* (Studies in Eastern Mediterranean Archaeology 1) Brepols Publishers.

M. Waelkens (1987) The adoption of Roman building techniques in the architecture of Asia Minor, in: S. Macready and F.H. Thompson (eds) *Roman Architecture in the Greek World* (The Society of Antiquaries of London. Occasional Papers X) Thames and Hudson: 94-105.

M. Waelkens, E. Owens, A. Hasendonckx and B. Arıkan (1992) The excavations at Sagalassos 1991, *Anatolian Studies* 42:79-98.

M. Waelkens (1993) The 1992 season at Sagalassos. A preliminary report, in: M. Waelkens and J. Poblome (eds) *Sagalassos II. Report on the Third Excavation Campaign of 1992* (Acta Archaeologica Lovaniensia Monographiae 6) Leuven University Press: 9-42.

M. Waelkens, E. Paulissen, E. Owens, B. Arıkan, L. Gijsen, M. Martens, V. Matauochek and K. Vandaele (1995) The 1993 excavations in the fountain house-library area, in: M. Waelkens and J. Poblome (eds) *Sagalassos III. Report on the Fourth Excavation Campaign of 1993* (Acta Archaeologica Lovaniensia Monographiae 7) Leuven University Press: 47-89.

M. Waelkens, P.M. Vermeersch, E. Paulissen, E.J. Owens, B. Arıkan, M. Martens, P. Talloen, L. Gijsen, L. Loots, Ch. Peleman, J. Poblome, R. Degeest, T.C. Patrício, S. Ercan and F. Depuydt (1997) The 1994 and 1995 excavation seaons at Sagalassos, in: M. Waelkens and J. Poblome (eds), *Sagalassos IV. Report on the Survey and Excavation Campaigns of 1994 and 1995* (Acta Archaeologica Lovaniensia Monographiae 9) Leuven University Press: 103-216.

M. Waelkens, M. Sintubin, Ph. Muchez and E. Paulissen (2000) Archaeological and geological evidences for a major earthquake at Sagalassos (SW Turkey) around the middle of the seventh century AD, in: W.J. McGuire, D.R. Griffiths, and I.S. Stewart (eds) *The Archaelogy of Geological Catastrophes (Geological Society of London. Special Publications 171)* Londen; 373-383.

M. Waelkens (in press) The transformation of the public and the sacred landscape in Early Imperial Sagalassos, in: Ch. Berns, H. von Hesberg, L. Vandeput and M. Waelkens (eds), *Kontinuität und Diskontinuität in den Städten des frühkaiserzeitlichen Kleinasien. Kolloquium in Köln, 19-21. November 1998*.

J.B. Ward-Perkins (1988) *Roman Imperial Architecture* (The Pelican History of Art) Pelican Books.

PRINTED ON PERMANENT PAPER • IMPRIME SUR PAPIER PERMANENT • GEDRUKT OP DUURZAAM PAPIER - ISO 9706

ORIENTALISTE, KLEIN DALENSTRAAT 42, B-3020 HERENT

SAGALASSOS V

Dedicated to the memory of Hubert DEVIJVER (1936-1997),
who made the Sagalassos families speak again

and to the memory of Richard VAN STEEN (1933-1997)
member of the L. Baert-Hofman family; one of our major sponsors.

ACTA ARCHAEOLOGICA LOVANIENSIA
MONOGRAPHIAE
11/B

VOLUME II

KATHOLIEKE UNIVERSITEIT LEUVEN
AFDELING ARCHEOLOGIE
LEUVEN (BELGIUM)

SAGALASSOS V

REPORT ON THE SURVEY AND EXCAVATION CAMPAIGNS
OF 1996 AND 1997

Edited by
M. Waelkens and L. Loots

Leuven University Press
2000

Published with the financial support of the K.U. Leuven Commissie voor Publicaties.

© 2000 Universitaire Pers Leuven / Leuven University Press /
Presses Universitaires de Louvain
Blijde-Inkomststraat 5, B-3000 Leuven (Belgium)

All rights reserved. Except in those cases expressly determined
by law, no part of this publication may be multiplied, saved in
an automated data file or made public in any way whatsoever
without the express prior written consent of the publishers.

ISBN 90 5867 079 1

D/2000/1869/77

CONTENTS

VOLUME I

Marc Waelkens
Introduction 7
Summary of research 10

PART I. THE SURVEY AND EXCAVATIONS IN 1996 AND 1997
PRELIMINARY REPORTS

Marc Waelkens, Etienne Paulissen, Hannelore Vanhaverbeke, Jeroen Reyniers, Jeroen Poblome, Roland Degeest, Willy Viaene (†), Jozef Deckers, Bea De Cupere, Wim Van Neer, Haci Ali Ekinci and Mustafa Oral Erbay
The 1996 and 1997 Surveys in the Territory of Sagalassos 17

Marc Waelkens, Jeroen Poblome, Etiene Paulissen, Peter Talloen, Julie Van Den Bergh, Vanessa Vanderginst, Burcu Arikan, Inge Van Damme, Ipek Akyel, Femke Martens, Marleen Martens, Inge Uytterhoeven, Tom Debruyne, David Depraetere, K. Baran, Bernard Vandaele, Zissis Parras, Şahin Yildirim, Shawn Bubel, Hannelore Vanhaverbeke, Corinne Licoppe, Frédérique Landuyt, Roland Degeest, Lutgarde Vandeput, Lieven Loots, Teresa Patrício, Semih Ercan, Koenraad Van Balen, Elisabeth Smits, Frans Depuydt, Luc Moens and Paul De Paepe
The 1996 and 1997 Excavation Seasons at Sagalassos 217

Teresa Patrício, Semth Ercan and Koenraad Van Balen
Restoration of the Late Hellenistic Fountain House: Field Works 399

Marc Waelkens, Hande Kökten Ersoy, Kent Severson, Femke Martens and Selçuk Sener
The Sagalassos Neon Library Mosaic and its Conservation 419

VOLUME II

PART II. PRE- AND PROTO HISTORICAL RESEARCH

Pierre M. Vermeersch, Ilhame Öztürk, Haci Ali Ekinci, Patrick Degryse, Bea De Cupere, Jeroen Poblome, Marc Waelkens and Willy Viaene (†)
Late Palaeolithic at the Dereköy Karain Cave 451

Hannelore Vanhaverbeke
How Can There Still Be Such a Degree of Uncertainty? Problems of Chronology for the Prehistoric Periods in the Territory of Sagalassos. 463

Marc Waelkens
Sagalassos and Pisidia during the Late Bronze Age 473

PART III. HISTORICAL STUDIES

Katlijn Vandorpe
Negotiators' Laws from Rebellious Sagalassos in an Early Hellenistic Inscription 489

Simone Scheers
Coins Found in 1996 and 1997 509

PART IV. URBANISM AND ARCHITECTURAL STUDIES

Marc Waelkens, Lutgarde Vandeput, Christof Berns, Burcu Arikan, Jeroen Poblome and Ebru Torun
The Northwest Heroon at Sagalassos 553

Lieven Loots, Marc Waelkens and Frans Depuydt
The City Fortifications of Sagalasoss from the Hellenistic to the Late Roman Period 595

An Steegen, Kris Cauwenberghs, Gerard Govers, Edwin Owens, Marc Waelkens and Philip Desmet
The Water Supply to Sagalassos 635

Kristof Callebaut, Willy Viaene (†), Marc Waelkens, Raoul Ottenburgs and Jean Naud
Provenance and Characterization of Raw Materials for Lime Mortars used at Sagalassos with Special Reference to the Volcanic Rocks 651

PART V. CERAMIC STUDIES

Jeroen Poblome, Hacı Ali Ekinci, Ilhame Öztürk,
Patrick Degryse, Willy Viaene (†) and Marc Waelkens
An Early Byzantine Tile and Lime Kiln in the Territory of
Sagalassos   669

Lieven Loots, Marc Waelkens, Willy Clarysse,
Jeroen Poblome and Gerhild Hübner
A Catalogue of the Tile Stamps Found at Sagalassos   685

Roland Degeest, Patrick Degryse, Raoul Ottenburgs,
Willy Viaene (†) and Marc Waelkens
Miniature Jars of Sagalassos. An Analytical, Quantitative
and Typological Overview of a Series of Very Small
Pottery Vessels from Late Antiquity   697

Patrick Degryse, Roland Degeest, Jeroen Poblome,
Willy Viaene (†), Raoul Ottenburgs, Harry Kucha
and Marc Waelkens
Mineralogy and Geochemistry of Roman Common Wares
Produced at Sagalassos and their Possible Clay Sources 709

PART VI. ENVIRONMENTAL STUDIES

Kristien Donners, Marc Waelkens, David Celis,
Kris Nackaerts, Jozef Deckers, Marleen Vermoere
and Hannelore Vanhaverbeke
Towards a Land Evaluation of the Territory of Ancient
Sagalassos   723

Kristof Schroyen, Marleen Vermoere, Ireen Librecht,
Patrick Degryse, Philippe Muchez, Willy Viaene (†),
Eric Smets, Etienne Paulissen, Eric Keppens and
Marc Waelkens
Preliminary Study of Travertine Deposits in the Vicinity of
Sagalassos. Petrography, Geochemistry, Geomorphology
and Palynology   757

Gert Verstraeten, Etienne Paulissen, Ireen Librecht,
and Marc Waelkens
Limestone Platforms around Sagalassos Resulting from
Giant Mass Movements   783

Ireen Librecht, Etienne Paulissen, Gert Verstraeten
and Marc Waelkens
Implications of Environmental Changes on Slope
Evolution near Sagalassos   799

PART VII. ANTHROPOLOGICAL AND ARCHAEOZOOLOGICAL STUDIES

Els Jehaes, Marc Waelkens, Ann Muyldermans,
Jean-Jacques Cassiman, Elisabeth Smits, Jeroen
Poblome, Paul Lambrechts and Ronny Decorte
DNA Analysis of Archaeological Human Remains from
Sagalassos   821

Wim Van Neer, Ruud Wildekamp, Fahrettin Küçük,
Mustafa Ünlüsayın, Marc Waelkens and
Etienne Paulissen
Results of the 1996 Survey of the Fish Fauna of the Aksu
River (Kestros) and Some Lakes in Southwestern Anatolia,
and the Implications for Trade at Sagalassos   833

Ingrid Beuls, Bea De Cupere, Marleen Vermoere,
Leo Vanhecke, Hugues Doutrelepont, Luc Vrydaghs,
Ireen Librecht and Marc Waelkens
Modern Sheep and Goat Herding near Sagalassos and
its Revelance to the Reconstruction of Pastoral Practices in
Roman Times   847

Zissis Parras
An Experimental Approach to Understanding the Bone
Working Industry at Roman Sagalassos   863

PART II

PRE- AND PROTO-HISTORICAL RESEARCH

LATE PALAEOLITHIC AT THE DEREKÖY KARAIN CAVE

Pierre M. VERMEERSCH[1], Ilhame ÖZTÜRK[2], Haci Ali EKINCI[2], Patrick DEGRYSE[3], Bea DE CUPERE[4], Jeroen POBLOME[5], Marc WAELKENS[5] and Willy VIAENE (†)[3]

1 - Laboratory of Prehistory, KULeuven, Redingenstraat 16, B-3000 Leuven, Belgium
2 - Archaeological Museum Burdur, Burdur Turkey
3 - Laboratory of Mineralogy, Physico-Chemical Geology, KULeuven, Celestijnenlaan 300C, B-3001 Heverlee, Belgium
4 - Royal Museum of Central Africa, B-3080 Tervuren, Belgium
5 - Department of Archaeology, KULeuven, Blijde Inkomststraat 21, B-3000 Leuven, Belgium

1. SITE SITUATION

The cave of Karain near the village of Dereköy is located approximately 13 km from Ağlasun, alongside and to the north of the road from Ağlasun to Isparta, halfway between the villages of Yazır and Çamlıdere (Fig. 1). It has the following geographical co-ordinates: 37°38.171 North and 30°39.409 East. The road follows the incised valley, which is drained by the Ağlasun Çayı, a small intermittent river. The slopes of the valley are very steep (average of 75 %), leading from the valley floor at 1000 m above sea level to an altitude of 1635 m. The northern valley slope, where the cave is located, is covered with a forest of red pine, juniper and evergreen kermes oak (*Quercus coccifera*)[1].

The cave lies on the valley slope at approximately 40 m above the Ağlasun Çayı. It is formed by karst processes in a breccia of consolidated limestone scree of unknown age. Some pipes within the cave are still active intermittently. The cave is 13 m wide and is, at its largest extent, 5 m deep and 3 m high. Its floor consists of a breccia (Fig. 2) which is probably the same as that in which the cave is formed. The cave apparently lacks any kind of more recent fill. The ceiling and sides of the cave are covered with a calcite crust and blackened by smoke. The cave still receives visits of shepherds and their herds.

The cave terrace is composed of a fine unconsolidated limestone scree, which, in its western part, has been quarried, apparently for road mending. The quarry face therefore truncates the western part of the terrace slope. The base of the terrace was cut into by recent road works. The terrace has a slope of approximately 25% and is covered with limestone blocks that outcrop from the fine terrace deposits.

Some flint and obsidian artefacts were found on the surface of the cave terrace during the 1995 survey (Waelkens *et al.* 1997: 18-19). It was unclear if the artefacts had emerged from the terrace deposits by erosion. Hence, it was decided to organise an excavation to check the stratigraphical position of the artefacts. A joint excavation consisting of the Archaeological Museum of Burdur, which officially directed the research, and the Sagalassos group was planned.

2. EXCAVATION

The excavations were conducted by the authors[2] and took place from 14.07.1997 until 20.07.1997. The aim of the excavation, in such a short time span, was not to excavate the whole site, but rather to understand its potential. Should the site produce important data, it would then be excavated further during a later campaign. Our approach to the site was to survey the terrace in front of the cave, since the cave itself did not contain any deposit. A topographical plan (Fig. 2) was drawn, and a field reference system was set up. A baseline, 20 m long, was laid down. It is orientated in an east-west direction on the highest terrace level in front of the cave. The base points were called 40N0E and 40N20E. We gave the last point a conventional elevation of 20 m.

Several test trenches were surveyed (Fig. 2): 39N0E (T1), 39N9E (T2), 40N17E (T3), 36N6E (T4), 31N11E (T5), 27N15E (T10), 25-27N8E (T7), 22-24N9E (T8), 19-21N10-

---

[1] Identified by M. Vermoere
[2] Özlem Buyuran, student, and some workers, to whom the authors express their gratitude, assisted the authors.

11E (T9) and an incomplete trench along the quarry face at approximately 29-30N5E (T6). The deposits from the test trenches were sieved in a 6 mm sieve.

2.1. Stratigraphy of the terrace deposits

Our first priority was to investigate the lower part of the slope, since most finds were discovered there. At first, some quadrants (T7 and T8) along the quarry border were excavated. Our excavation found that the prehistoric artefacts were scattered from the surface to well below it. The stratigraphy was very difficult to comprehend here because all sediments were very unconsolidated, probably due to the quarrying works. We then decided to start excavations in T9.

The northern east-west profile (Fig. 3) at T9 provided a succession of deposits in which numerous roots were observed down to about 0.6 m below the surface, whereas rootlets occur down to about 1.4 m below the surface, producing a significant bioturbation of the deposits. Deposits from layers 1-3 are moreover very heterogeneous in their composition. From top to base the following layers were found.

1 – black clayey deposit in a sandy matrix containing angular to rounded limestone or breccia fragments, many organic remains, flint artefacts and early Byzantine and also more recent ceramics throughout the entire area. There were no concentrations of artefacts. The base is formed by a concentration of large limestone blocks.
2 – black clayey deposit, similar to the previous deposit, but richer in its stony content, and less rich in organic remains; some flint artefacts, Sagalassos red slip ware, and protohistoric body sherds throughout the whole layer. The base is formed by a concentration of large limestone blocks.
3 – Similar deposit but with fewer limestone fragments than in the upper deposits; scattered flint artefacts and protohistoric body sherds. Deposits have a slight dip towards the east. The base is formed by a concentration of large limestone blocks.
4 – Progressive browning of the sediments that remain stony and clayey. There are still flint artefacts and protohistoric body sherds.
5 – Fine, brown to whitish, angular limestone debris. We still found flint artefacts in the upper part, but there were no longer any sherds.
6 – Horizontally layered fine angular limestone debris. Neither flint artefacts nor ceramics have been recovered.

A profile along the quarry front at 28-33N5E was cleaned (Fig. 4) and we searched for the location of artefacts in that profile. From this profile it was clear that a gully, starting at 33.5N, dissects the underlying deposits. The gully floor consists of one or two layers of large to small slightly rolled limestone fragments. The gully fill is composed of limestone fragments in a matrix of loose black clayey humic deposits. Below the gully floor, the deposits are similar to those above but they are less humic and are somewhat brownish. In between the two large blocks the deposits are composed of fine limestone fragments in a matrix of brown clayey sand. No ceramics have been found, but flint artefacts do occur (T6), scattered throughout the whole thickness of the profile.

In T8 numerous flint artefacts were encountered scattered throughout the whole depth of the deposits in our trench (± 1 m). The deposits consist, as in the other trenches, of a heterogeneous deposit of a very humic matrix with limestone fragments on the top, becoming more brownish farther below the surface. In addition to flint artefacts, some bone remains and ceramics were encountered. There was clearly no archaeological horizon in which artefacts occurred in concentration.

The deposits in T10 are very loose and heterogeneous. Down to a depth of 0.9 m flint artefacts occur together with glass fragments and apparently Roman ceramics. The deposits in 36N6E consist of an upper 0.3 m of black clayey deposits, containing recent to sub-recent ceramics and glass fragments. They are resting upon a deposit of fine brown limestone fragments, which, in its upper part, is rich in mostly unbroken artefacts. No ceramics have been collected here. However, no vertical concentration of artefacts was present. Below 0.6 m limestone outcrops appear. In T1 little archaeological material was found. In quadrant 39N9E, limestone blocks occur at a depth of 0.5 m. Above, there is an accumulation of brownish limestone fragments in a humic clayey matrix with some flint artefacts and some protohistoric body sherds.

To understand the sedimentology in front of the cave it is important to note the profile that was created for the widening of the road by truncating the cave terrace base. We did not clean up the profile but we made a sketch of the terrace truncation (Fig. 5). A deep gully is filled with the black deposits that are well represented on the terrace. Its floor is paved with small and large limestone blocks, similar to those which are described in Figs 3 and 4, where they represent the base of a single or of multiple erosion phases of the underlying deposits. An inspection of the surface of the slope in the vicinity of the cave suggests that the gully originated from an erosion and sediment flow from northeast to southwest with its centre just south of the large outcropping rock.

An important observation was made on a profile (Fig. 6) bordering the quarry in 36N3W. The upper 30 cm of this profile consists of typical black deposits which we also found in the upper deposits of the other quadrants. In between the brown and the black deposits lie large breccia blocks, which had probably fallen from the roof of the cave. The lower deposit consists of mostly angular limestone

Fig.1 :

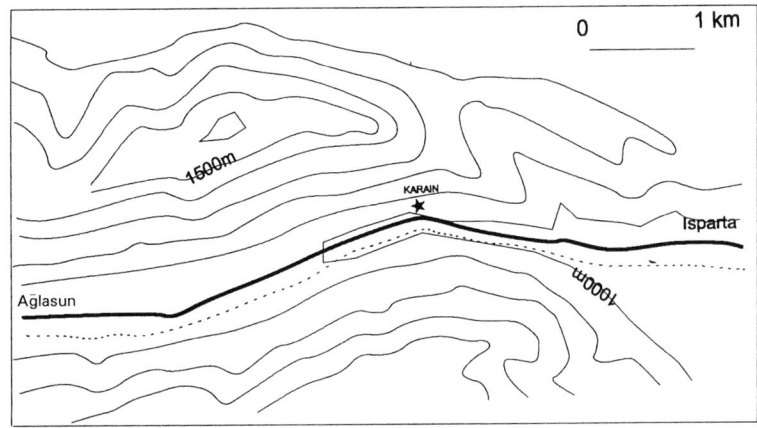

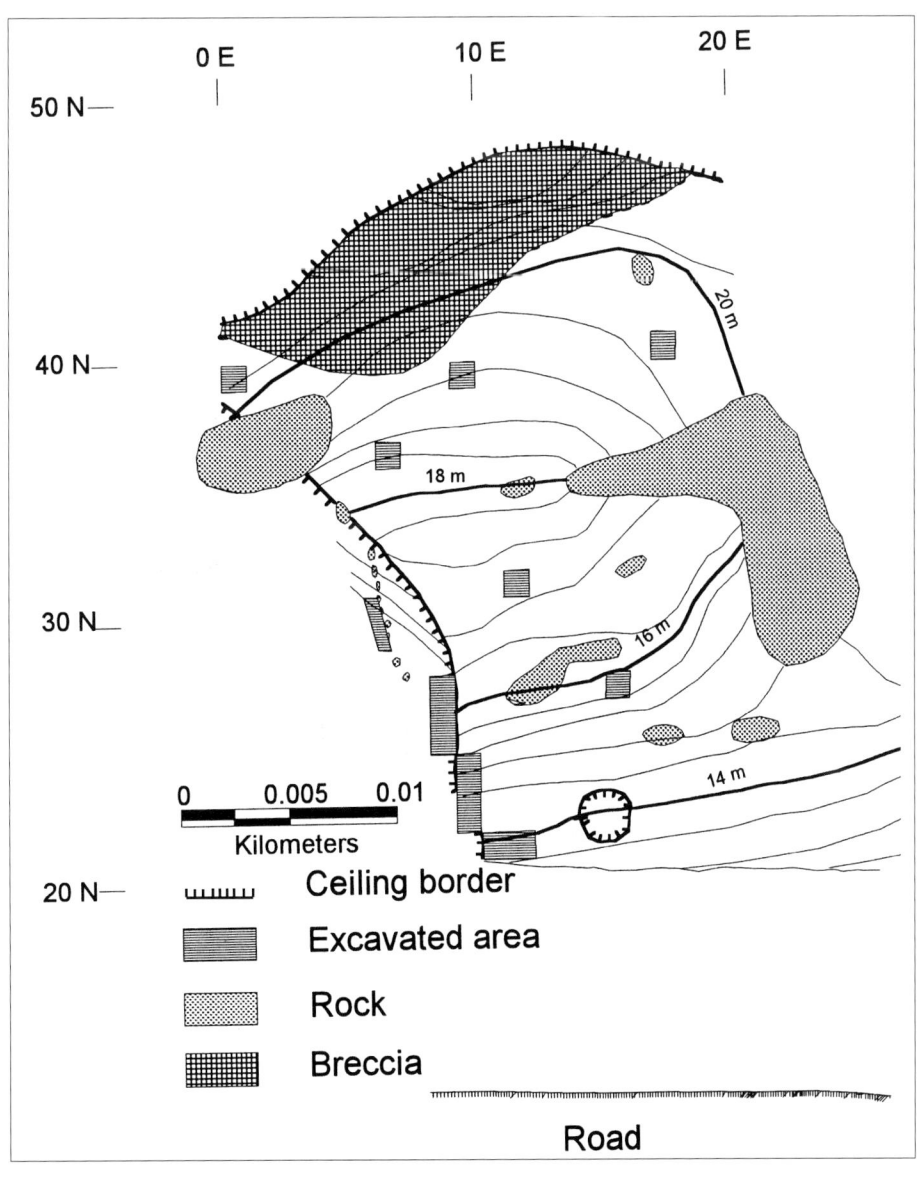

Fig. 2: Plan of the cave and its terrace.

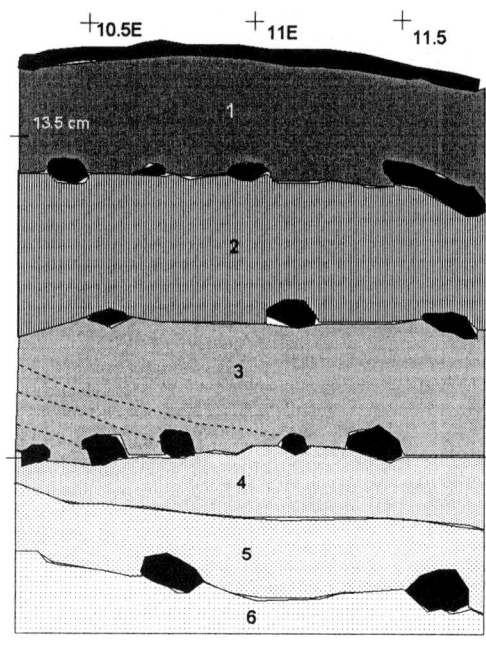

Fig. 3: Profile at 20N10-11E.

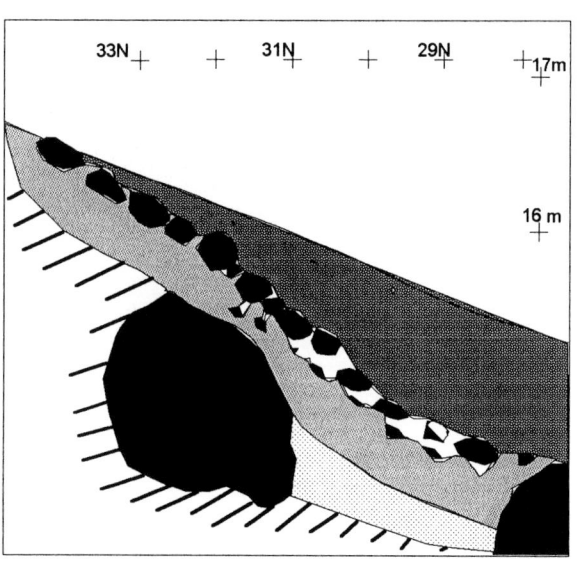

Fig. 4: Profile along the quarry front at 28-33N5E.

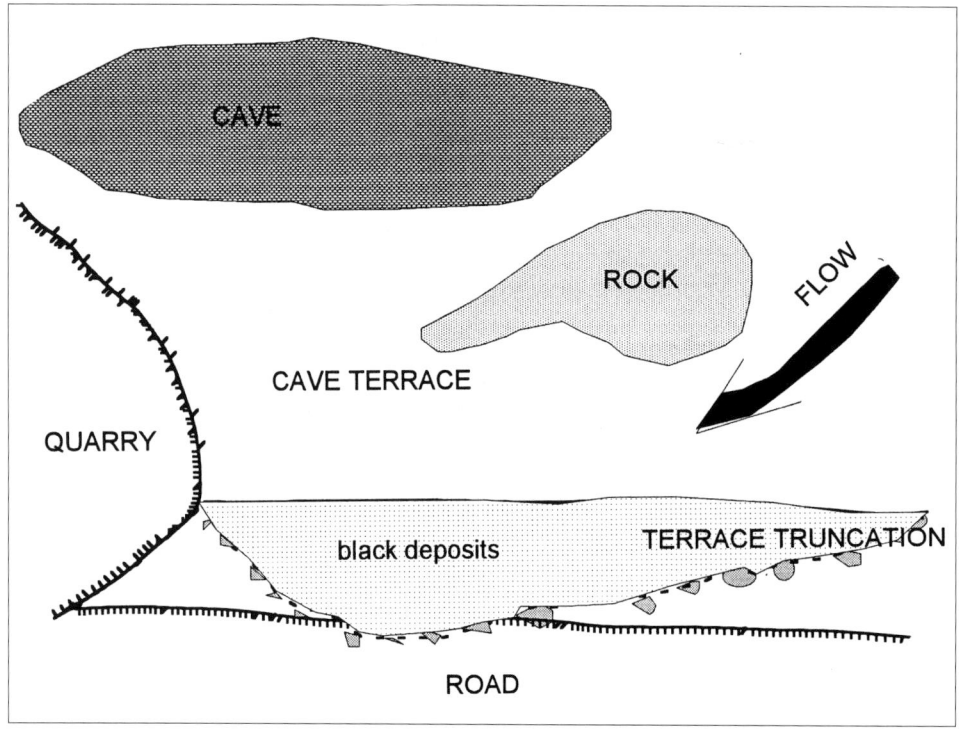

Fig. 5: Sketch of the terrace truncation profile.

Fig. 6: Profile along the northern quarry face at 36N3W.

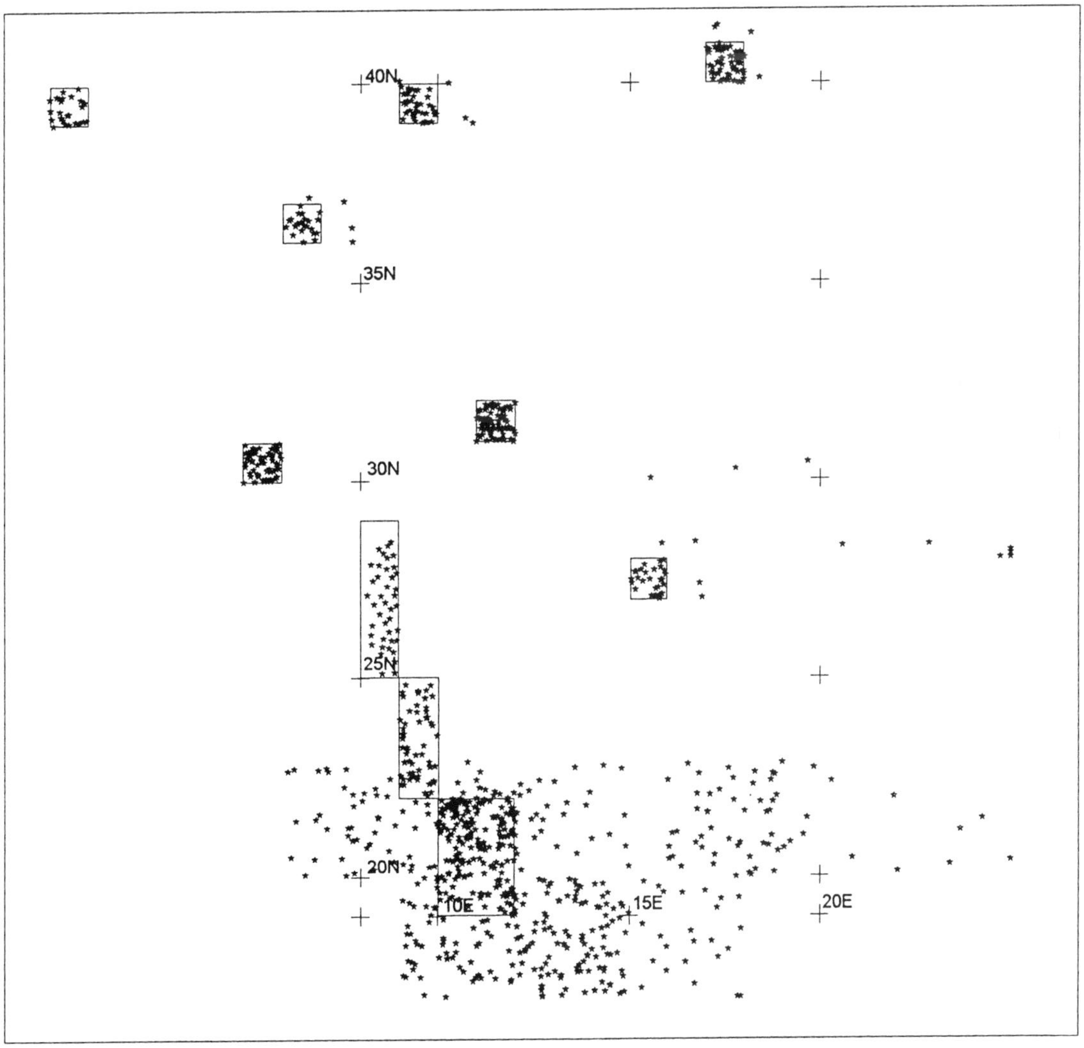

Fig. 7: Distribution of all recovered artefacts from the surface and below the surface.

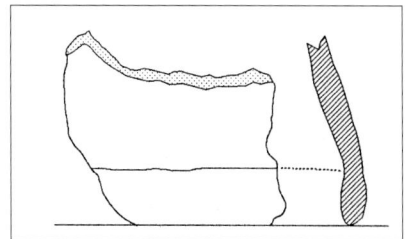

Fig. 8: Rim sherd (type 1B210) from a late Roman/early Byzantine vessel.

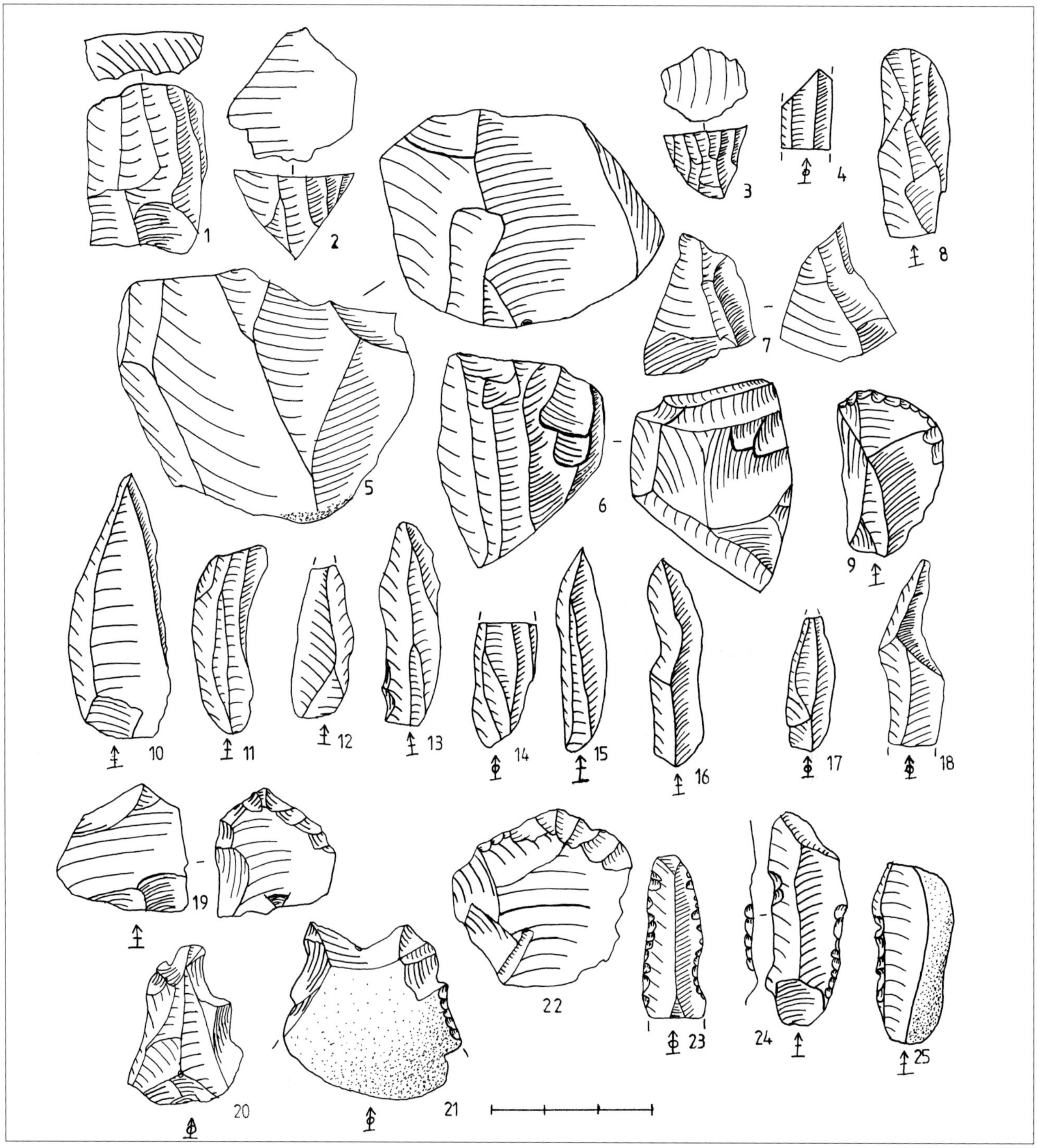

Fig. 9: Flint artefacts. (P.-M. Vermeersch)

fragments, with a maximum length of about 5 cm, brownish at the top and becoming progressively whiter below. The top of the lower deposit does not indicate a clear stratification, whereas the lower whitish part of the layer is horizontally stratified. The contact-zone between the two layers is rich in brown to black humic material. The sequence below the breccia blocks represents a mollisol developed on a scree slope. Two flint artefacts, of a similar technique as the artefacts from other parts of the site, were found situated in the brownish limestone debris, at 40 and 55 cm below the surface. This profile shows us that the artefacts are integrated in a scree slope deposit of limestone cryoclasts. The cryoclasts can be attributed to climatic conditions during the Last Ice Age, when the scree slope deposits accumulated. From the Holocene on they have been submitted to a process of soil formation which resulted here in a mollisol. This means that the artefacts had been deposited in cryoclastic deposits and therefore belong to the (late?) Glacial period. We also refer to the observations in T9 layer 5, where the lowest artefacts in the profile present an identical pedo-stratigraphical position.

2.2. Interpretation of the stratigraphy

The best hypothesis to explain all the field observations would be that there was a prehistoric settlement in the cave, or on the terrace in front of the cave, during the end of the Last Ice Age, or possibly during the Tardiglacial. According to Paulissen *et al.* (1993) Sagalassos is situated in a cold to very cold and subhumid to humid environment when measured by Mediterranean standards. We may expect that such conditions were able to generate during the Last Ice Age and during the Tardiglacial a significant frost wedging of the limestone and breccia. Cryoclastic and slope processes were very active and produced a mass of fine limestone grit. When the occupants abandoned the settlement, many artefacts remained on the surface. These artefacts have been moved by slope evolution and covered by other cryoclasts after the end of the cold conditions. Holocene pedogenesis resulted in the formation of a mollisol, creating a superficial humus-rich A-horizon and a brownish B-horizon. The surface, which was created by those deposits incorporating the prehistoric artefacts, was covered by limestone blocks from the collapse of a ceiling, probably somewhere in the first part of the Holocene. During protohistoric times a new occupation took place, leaving some ceramics on the surface. After that occupation, large-scale erosion created a deep gully through the glacial deposits. This gully descends from the hillside on the eastern side of the cave. It is filled with black A-horizon soil sediments, containing both prehistoric flint artefacts and pre- or protohistoric sherds. A later (early Byzantine and also more recent) occupation resulted in even more erosion and re-deposition of the earlier deposits.

Clearly, due to the intensive erosion of the cave terrace, we cannot expect to find any prehistoric artefacts *in situ*. The site was already destroyed by slope evolution before the end of the Last Ice Age and renewed occupational erosion by gullying resulted in a re-deposition of earlier sediments and their archaeological content.

2. SPATIAL DISTRIBUTION OF THE ARCHAEOLOGICAL MATERIAL

Due to the reworking of the deposits containing the archaeological material, analysis of their spatial distribution is of restricted value. Fig. 7, which for evident reasons does not differentiate between material from the surface and that from below, gives an idea of the distribution. Apparently the artefacts are evenly scattered. There is a denser scatter in the southern part of the cave terrace because the road cutting uncovered a greater surface inside the deposits. In the trenches, artefacts are well represented but, as we have said above, mainly in old or recently disturbed positions. No conclusions relating to the prehistoric occupation can be drawn from such a distribution.

3. THE ARCHAEOLOGICAL MATERIAL

3.1. Ceramics

In addition to recent ceramics, late Roman to early Byzantine, Sagalassos red slip ware and protohistoric ceramics were recovered. A sherd of type 1B210 (Fig. 8) from a vessel with a rim diameter of about 12 cm is attributed to the late Roman to early Byzantine period. The Sagalassos red slip ware dates from 25 BC up to AD 600/650. This Roman to early Byzantine or even later ceramic evidence probably represents the passage of shepherds. At present, it is very hard to give a precise chronological or cultural definition of the restricted and undistinctive assemblage of pre- or protohistoric material. In general, it may range from the later Neolithic period into the Bronze age.

3.2. Lithic material

3.2.1. Raw material

Several raw materials have been used by the knappers on the site. The best-represented flint quality is a fine burgundy flint, which was introduced on the site in small (3-5 cm) nodules. The green flint is very similar in texture to the burgundy flint, but is less frequent. Black and grey flint is well represented but of heterogeneous quality within a single nodule. Nodules seem to be larger than those of the burgundy flint. Beige flint is generally translucent. The multicoloured flint is of bad quality, allowing only occasionally the production of regular flakes. The other flint qualities are

rare. About 20, mostly small, artefacts have been subjected to heat.

Cherts and flints are abundantly present in the allochthonous and autochthonous limestones in the region. In the Tertiary allochthonous nappes, mostly consisting of Mesozoic limestones, beige-brown and red cherts are abundant, but they are too brittle to be exploited and cannot be used for flaking. The autochthonous limestones, with extensive outcrops in the area of Dereköy and Köyünü a few kilometers to the southwest, contain a wide variety of cherts suitable for exploitation. In these outcrops at Köyünü, sections and alluvial fans were sampled for cherts. These were compared with the lithic artefacts found at Dereköy on the basis of their colour, texture and brittleness or strength.

The fine green flint and fine burgundy flint, together with the multicoloured flint were not observed in the area of Köyünü. Their texture and variation in colours indicate a sedimentary-diagenetic origin, which is possible in limestones as well as in clay-rich rocks. Black obsidian is represented almost solely by bladelet fragments. Its origin is unknown but is unlikely to be of local provenance. The nearest volcanic deposits can be found at Gölcuk (about 15 km from the excavation site), but the volcanic glasses found there are unlike the black obsidian found at Dereköy. Only small amounts of volcanic glass can be found in the matrix of volcanic tuffs, and the glass shows signs of incipient crystallisation of lath-shaped feldspars (Callebaut et al. 2000). Hence the black obsidian is probably transported from further away to the excavation site because of its superior quality.

The beige, light-coloured and black to grey heterogeneous flints can be found in large quantities at the nearby locality of Köyünü. They occur as nodules of up to 10 cm in diameter in the local autochthonous limestones of Cretaceous to Eocene age. The nodules are formed by silica-rich fluids flowing through the limestone and replacing the $CaCO_3$ on their way. The silica originates from radiolaria and sponge spicula fossils which are abundant in these limestones (Degryse et al. in preparation). These flints are thus of a local origin.

Nodules of other colours can also be found in the autochthonous limestones at Köyünü, such as brittle yellow flint and coarse reddish-brown flint. These materials however are of a too poor quality to be used for flaking. Similar material is not found in the artefacts at Dereköy.

	N	%
black obsidian	13	1.0
fine green flint	193	14.8
fine burgundy flint	354	27.1
red flint	10	0.8
beige flint	100	7.7
light coloured flint	74	5.7
dark spotted flint	9	0.7
multicoloured flint	35	2.7
black heterogeneous flint	171	13.1
grey heterogeneous flint	342	26.2
banded flint	5	0.4
Total	1306	100.2

Table 1: Flint raw material qualities.

	N	%
cores	21	16.1
flakes	330	25.3
bladelets	31	2.4
chips	678	51.9
chunks and nodules	246	18.8
Total	1306	100

Table 2: General composition of the flint artefact assemblage.

fragments, with a maximum length of about 5 cm, brownish at the top and becoming progressively whiter below. The top of the lower deposit does not indicate a clear stratification, whereas the lower whitish part of the layer is horizontally stratified. The contact-zone between the two layers is rich in brown to black humic material. The sequence below the breccia blocks represents a mollisol developed on a scree slope. Two flint artefacts, of a similar technique as the artefacts from other parts of the site, were found situated in the brownish limestone debris, at 40 and 55 cm below the surface. This profile shows us that the artefacts are integrated in a scree slope deposit of limestone cryoclasts. The cryoclasts can be attributed to climatic conditions during the Last Ice Age, when the scree slope deposits accumulated. From the Holocene on they have been submitted to a process of soil formation which resulted here in a mollisol. This means that the artefacts had been deposited in cryoclastic deposits and therefore belong to the (late?) Glacial period. We also refer to the observations in T9 layer 5, where the lowest artefacts in the profile present an identical pedo-stratigraphical position.

2.2. Interpretation of the stratigraphy

The best hypothesis to explain all the field observations would be that there was a prehistoric settlement in the cave, or on the terrace in front of the cave, during the end of the Last Ice Age, or possibly during the Tardiglacial. According to Paulissen *et al.* (1993) Sagalassos is situated in a cold to very cold and subhumid to humid environment when measured by Mediterranean standards. We may expect that such conditions were able to generate during the Last Ice Age and during the Tardiglacial a significant frost wedging of the limestone and breccia. Cryoclastic and slope processes were very active and produced a mass of fine limestone grit. When the occupants abandoned the settlement, many artefacts remained on the surface. These artefacts have been moved by slope evolution and covered by other cryoclasts after the end of the cold conditions. Holocene pedogenesis resulted in the formation of a mollisol, creating a superficial humus-rich A-horizon and a brownish B-horizon. The surface, which was created by those deposits incorporating the prehistoric artefacts, was covered by limestone blocks from the collapse of a ceiling, probably somewhere in the first part of the Holocene. During protohistoric times a new occupation took place, leaving some ceramics on the surface. After that occupation, large-scale erosion created a deep gully through the glacial deposits. This gully descends from the hillside on the eastern side of the cave. It is filled with black A-horizon soil sediments, containing both prehistoric flint artefacts and pre- or protohistoric sherds. A later (early Byzantine and also more recent) occupation resulted in even more erosion and re-deposition of the earlier deposits.

Clearly, due to the intensive erosion of the cave terrace, we cannot expect to find any prehistoric artefacts *in situ*. The site was already destroyed by slope evolution before the end of the Last Ice Age and renewed occupational erosion by gullying resulted in a re-deposition of earlier sediments and their archaeological content.

2. SPATIAL DISTRIBUTION OF THE ARCHAEOLOGICAL MATERIAL

Due to the reworking of the deposits containing the archaeological material, analysis of their spatial distribution is of restricted value. Fig. 7, which for evident reasons does not differentiate between material from the surface and that from below, gives an idea of the distribution. Apparently the artefacts are evenly scattered. There is a denser scatter in the southern part of the cave terrace because the road cutting uncovered a greater surface inside the deposits. In the trenches, artefacts are well represented but, as we have said above, mainly in old or recently disturbed positions. No conclusions relating to the prehistoric occupation can be drawn from such a distribution.

3. THE ARCHAEOLOGICAL MATERIAL

3.1. Ceramics

In addition to recent ceramics, late Roman to early Byzantine, Sagalassos red slip ware and protohistoric ceramics were recovered. A sherd of type 1B210 (Fig. 8) from a vessel with a rim diameter of about 12 cm is attributed to the late Roman to early Byzantine period. The Sagalassos red slip ware dates from 25 BC up to AD 600/650. This Roman to early Byzantine or even later ceramic evidence probably represents the passage of shepherds. At present, it is very hard to give a precise chronological or cultural definition of the restricted and undistinctive assemblage of pre- or protohistoric material. In general, it may range from the later Neolithic period into the Bronze age.

3.2. Lithic material

3.2.1. Raw material

Several raw materials have been used by the knappers on the site. The best-represented flint quality is a fine burgundy flint, which was introduced on the site in small (3-5 cm) nodules. The green flint is very similar in texture to the burgundy flint, but is less frequent. Black and grey flint is well represented but of heterogeneous quality within a single nodule. Nodules seem to be larger than those of the burgundy flint. Beige flint is generally translucent. The multi-coloured flint is of bad quality, allowing only occasionally the production of regular flakes. The other flint qualities are

rare. About 20, mostly small, artefacts have been subjected to heat.

Cherts and flints are abundantly present in the allochthonous and autochthonous limestones in the region. In the Tertiary allochthonous nappes, mostly consisting of Mesozoic limestones, beige-brown and red cherts are abundant, but they are too brittle to be exploited and cannot be used for flaking. The autochthonous limestones, with extensive outcrops in the area of Dereköy and Köyünü a few kilometers to the southwest, contain a wide variety of cherts suitable for exploitation. In these outcrops at Köyünü, sections and alluvial fans were sampled for cherts. These were compared with the lithic artefacts found at Dereköy on the basis of their colour, texture and brittleness or strength.

The fine green flint and fine burgundy flint, together with the multicoloured flint were not observed in the area of Köyünü. Their texture and variation in colours indicate a sedimentary-diagenetic origin, which is possible in limestones as well as in clay-rich rocks. Black obsidian is represented almost solely by bladelet fragments. Its origin is unknown but is unlikely to be of local provenance. The nearest volcanic deposits can be found at Gölcuk (about 15 km from the excavation site), but the volcanic glasses found there are unlike the black obsidian found at Dereköy. Only small amounts of volcanic glass can be found in the matrix of volcanic tuffs, and the glass shows signs of incipient crystallisation of lath-shaped feldspars (Callebaut *et al.* 2000). Hence the black obsidian is probably transported from further away to the excavation site because of its superior quality.

The beige, light-coloured and black to grey heterogeneous flints can be found in large quantities at the nearby locality of Köyünü. They occur as nodules of up to 10 cm in diameter in the local autochthonous limestones of Cretaceous to Eocene age. The nodules are formed by silica-rich fluids flowing through the limestone and replacing the $CaCO_3$ on their way. The silica originates from radiolaria and sponge spicula fossils which are abundant in these limestones (Degryse *et al.* in preparation). These flints are thus of a local origin.

Nodules of other colours can also be found in the autochthonous limestones at Köyünü, such as brittle yellow flint and coarse reddish-brown flint. These materials however are of a too poor quality to be used for flaking. Similar material is not found in the artefacts at Dereköy.

	N	%
black obsidian	13	1.0
fine green flint	193	14.8
fine burgundy flint	354	27.1
red flint	10	0.8
beige flint	100	7.7
light coloured flint	74	5.7
dark spotted flint	9	0.7
multicoloured flint	35	2.7
black heterogeneous flint	171	13.1
grey heterogeneous flint	342	26.2
banded flint	5	0.4
Total	1306	100.2

Table 1: Flint raw material qualities.

	N	%
cores	21	16.1
flakes	330	25.3
bladelets	31	2.4
chips	678	51.9
chunks and nodules	246	18.8
Total	1306	100

Table 2: General composition of the flint artefact assemblage.

fragments, with a maximum length of about 5 cm, brownish at the top and becoming progressively whiter below. The top of the lower deposit does not indicate a clear stratification, whereas the lower whitish part of the layer is horizontally stratified. The contact-zone between the two layers is rich in brown to black humic material. The sequence below the breccia blocks represents a mollisol developed on a scree slope. Two flint artefacts, of a similar technique as the artefacts from other parts of the site, were found situated in the brownish limestone debris, at 40 and 55 cm below the surface. This profile shows us that the artefacts are integrated in a scree slope deposit of limestone cryoclasts. The cryoclasts can be attributed to climatic conditions during the Last Ice Age, when the scree slope deposits accumulated. From the Holocene on they have been submitted to a process of soil formation which resulted here in a mollisol. This means that the artefacts had been deposited in cryoclastic deposits and therefore belong to the (late?) Glacial period. We also refer to the observations in T9 layer 5, where the lowest artefacts in the profile present an identical pedo-stratigraphical position.

2.2. Interpretation of the stratigraphy

The best hypothesis to explain all the field observations would be that there was a prehistoric settlement in the cave, or on the terrace in front of the cave, during the end of the Last Ice Age, or possibly during the Tardiglacial. According to Paulissen et al. (1993) Sagalassos is situated in a cold to very cold and subhumid to humid environment when measured by Mediterranean standards. We may expect that such conditions were able to generate during the Last Ice Age and during the Tardiglacial a significant frost wedging of the limestone and breccia. Cryoclastic and slope processes were very active and produced a mass of fine limestone grit. When the occupants abandoned the settlement, many artefacts remained on the surface. These artefacts have been moved by slope evolution and covered by other cryoclasts after the end of the cold conditions. Holocene pedogenesis resulted in the formation of a mollisol, creating a superficial humus-rich A-horizon and a brownish B-horizon. The surface, which was created by those deposits incorporating the prehistoric artefacts, was covered by limestone blocks from the collapse of a ceiling, probably somewhere in the first part of the Holocene. During protohistoric times a new occupation took place, leaving some ceramics on the surface. After that occupation, large-scale erosion created a deep gully through the glacial deposits. This gully descends from the hillside on the eastern side of the cave. It is filled with black A-horizon soil sediments, containing both prehistoric flint artefacts and pre- or protohistoric sherds. A later (early Byzantine and also more recent) occupation resulted in even more erosion and re-deposition of the earlier deposits.

Clearly, due to the intensive erosion of the cave terrace, we cannot expect to find any prehistoric artefacts *in situ*. The site was already destroyed by slope evolution before the end of the Last Ice Age and renewed occupational erosion by gullying resulted in a re-deposition of earlier sediments and their archaeological content.

2. SPATIAL DISTRIBUTION OF THE ARCHAEOLOGICAL MATERIAL

Due to the reworking of the deposits containing the archaeological material, analysis of their spatial distribution is of restricted value. Fig. 7, which for evident reasons does not differentiate between material from the surface and that from below, gives an idea of the distribution. Apparently the artefacts are evenly scattered. There is a denser scatter in the southern part of the cave terrace because the road cutting uncovered a greater surface inside the deposits. In the trenches, artefacts are well represented but, as we have said above, mainly in old or recently disturbed positions. No conclusions relating to the prehistoric occupation can be drawn from such a distribution.

3. THE ARCHAEOLOGICAL MATERIAL

3.1. Ceramics

In addition to recent ceramics, late Roman to early Byzantine, Sagalassos red slip ware and protohistoric ceramics were recovered. A sherd of type 1B210 (Fig. 8) from a vessel with a rim diameter of about 12 cm is attributed to the late Roman to early Byzantine period. The Sagalassos red slip ware dates from 25 BC up to AD 600/650. This Roman to early Byzantine or even later ceramic evidence probably represents the passage of shepherds. At present, it is very hard to give a precise chronological or cultural definition of the restricted and undistinctive assemblage of pre- or protohistoric material. In general, it may range from the later Neolithic period into the Bronze age.

3.2. Lithic material

3.2.1. Raw material

Several raw materials have been used by the knappers on the site. The best-represented flint quality is a fine burgundy flint, which was introduced on the site in small (3-5 cm) nodules. The green flint is very similar in texture to the burgundy flint, but is less frequent. Black and grey flint is well represented but of heterogeneous quality within a single nodule. Nodules seem to be larger than those of the burgundy flint. Beige flint is generally translucent. The multicoloured flint is of bad quality, allowing only occasionally the production of regular flakes. The other flint qualities are

rare. About 20, mostly small, artefacts have been subjected to heat.

Cherts and flints are abundantly present in the allochthonous and autochthonous limestones in the region. In the Tertiary allochthonous nappes, mostly consisting of Mesozoic limestones, beige-brown and red cherts are abundant, but they are too brittle to be exploited and cannot be used for flaking. The autochthonous limestones, with extensive outcrops in the area of Dereköy and Köyünü a few kilometers to the southwest, contain a wide variety of cherts suitable for exploitation. In these outcrops at Köyünü, sections and alluvial fans were sampled for cherts. These were compared with the lithic artefacts found at Dereköy on the basis of their colour, texture and brittleness or strength.

The fine green flint and fine burgundy flint, together with the multicoloured flint were not observed in the area of Köyünü. Their texture and variation in colours indicate a sedimentary-diagenetic origin, which is possible in limestones as well as in clay-rich rocks. Black obsidian is represented almost solely by bladelet fragments. Its origin is unknown but is unlikely to be of local provenance. The nearest volcanic deposits can be found at Gölcuk (about 15 km from the excavation site), but the volcanic glasses found there are unlike the black obsidian found at Dereköy. Only small amounts of volcanic glass can be found in the matrix of volcanic tuffs, and the glass shows signs of incipient crystallisation of lath-shaped feldspars (Callebaut *et al.* 2000). Hence the black obsidian is probably transported from further away to the excavation site because of its superior quality.

The beige, light-coloured and black to grey heterogeneous flints can be found in large quantities at the nearby locality of Köyünü. They occur as nodules of up to 10 cm in diameter in the local autochthonous limestones of Cretaceous to Eocene age. The nodules are formed by silica-rich fluids flowing through the limestone and replacing the $CaCO_3$ on their way. The silica originates from radiolaria and sponge spicula fossils which are abundant in these limestones (Degryse *et al.* in preparation). These flints are thus of a local origin.

Nodules of other colours can also be found in the autochthonous limestones at Köyünü, such as brittle yellow flint and coarse reddish-brown flint. These materials however are of a too poor quality to be used for flaking. Similar material is not found in the artefacts at Dereköy.

	N	%
black obsidian	13	1.0
fine green flint	193	14.8
fine burgundy flint	354	27.1
red flint	10	0.8
beige flint	100	7.7
light coloured flint	74	5.7
dark spotted flint	9	0.7
multicoloured flint	35	2.7
black heterogeneous flint	171	13.1
grey heterogeneous flint	342	26.2
banded flint	5	0.4
Total	1306	100.2

Table 1: Flint raw material qualities.

	N	%
cores	21	16.1
flakes	330	25.3
bladelets	31	2.4
chips	678	51.9
chunks and nodules	246	18.8
Total	1306	100

Table 2: General composition of the flint artefact assemblage.

3.2.2. Debitage

The flint artefacts are very fragmented, especially in the lower parts of the terrace slope, apparently a result of postdepositional processes. The technological composition bears witness to some flaking having been done on the site. The representation of the chips is certainly somewhat biased because sieving was performed only during the excavations of the quadrants. In surface material, which was only hand-picked and not sieved, chips are certainly under-represented. Chunks are numerous and some of them seem to be very small nodule fragments that show restricted traces of flaking.

No cores have been registered from the following raw materials: grey flint, multicoloured flint, light coloured flint, beige flint and obsidian, representing together 36 % of all raw materials. We may conclude that no nodules or cores from these raw material types have been introduced on the site. Most of those artefacts were introduced as such on the site. We may infer that those raw materials have been introduced from some distance, whereas the raw materials from which cores could be found on the site represent a nearby source of origin. Most often, the cores are small – sometimes not longer than 1.5 cm – and entirely exhausted, suggesting a parsimonious utilisation of raw material. They have been used for bladelet production but in their final stage of production they only produced small flakes and chips.

single platform cores	5
pyramidal single platform cores	4
opposed platform core	5
double adjacent platform core	1
multi-platform core	1
irregular cores	5
Total	21

Table 3: Cores

Three tiny pyramidal single platform cores (Figs 9.2 and 3) produced very regular bladelets, apparently with a punch technique. Their platform is unfaceted. A multi-platform core (Fig. 9.5) was flaked using a hard hammer technique, with the core table as a platform. Production aimed mainly at producing elongated bladelets. One of the single platform cores is irregular. A large opposed platform core had become thin because of the core table exhaustion (Fig. 9.1), whilst another is very reduced (Fig. 9.7). A double adjacent platform core has traces of a careful maintenance of the core table (Fig. 9.6). Irregular cores are, in such parsimonious flint economy, reduced to very small artefacts. The cores clearly suggest a bladelet-oriented flaking technology, which is, however, not reflected in the bladelet/flake ratio (Table 2). This is probably because the nodules needed a lot of flaking before the desired bladelets could be produced. Except for obsidian bladelets that are very thin and have parallel edges (Fig. 9.4), bladelets are thin with irregular edges (Figs 9.10-12, 14-18). Flakes are irregular and mostly small, apparently because of the reduced dimensions of the nodules. Bladelets and flakes are often broken.

end-scrapers on a flake	3
denticulated bladelets	3
retouched bladelet	2
retouched flakes	2
inverse retouched flake	1
notched pieces	2
denticulates	3
splintered piece	1
Total	17

Table 4: Tools

3.2.3 Tools

Tools are rare and none of them is very specialised. They consist mainly of end-scrapers on a flake, retouched bladelets and flakes, some denticulates and notches and an uncharacteristic splintered piece. The scraper-edge from one of the end-scrapers (Fig. 9.9) is thin but obtained by regular retouches. Another end-scraper (Fig. 9.22) has a large flake blank. One of the retouched bladelets (Fig. 9.23) has an obsidian blank. Retouches are numerous and occur also on the ventral face. Another retouched bladelet (Fig. 9.24) has inverse and normal retouches. The other retouched bladelets have a tendency to be denticulated bladelets (Fig. 9.13 and 25). The inverse retouched flake (Fig. 9.19) presents regular retouches. The notched pieces have a chunk blank rather than a flake blank. Denticulates are made on rather thick flakes (Figs 9.20-21).

3.3. Bone remains

The site also contained bone remains, but it is impossible to link these with a specific settlement period. A total of 239 bone fragments were collected. Due to the high degree of fragmentation only a few finds could be identified. A small fragment of a horncore was from a goat. The distal end of a metacarpal was probably from a sheep. In both cases it was not possible to establish the domestic or wild status of the animal. Thirteen finds, namely 7 tooth fragments, 1 humerus shaft, 1 radius shaft, 1 metacarpal shaft, 1 metatarsal shaft, 1 proximal end of a first phalanx and 1 proximal end of second phalanx, could not be narrowed down to a species, but were classified as ovicaprine. The distal end of a first phalanx was identified as from a pig. Again, it was not possible to establish the wild or the domestic status of the animal. One mandible and one femur came from a mole rat (*Spalax* sp.). The other finds (n = 221) remained unidentified, although the majority probably represent small ruminants such as sheep and goats; only three bone fragments belonged to a large animal. Many of the bone fragments were burnt and black coloured.

4. DISCUSSION AND INTERPRETATION

The assemblage from Dereköy Karain will be considered as an homogeneous assemblage. We must, however, be aware that this is only a guess, not substantiated by field evidence. It is not impossible that several different occupations occurred on the site. Post-depositional processes have obliterated the eventual existence of a multi-layered settlement. We presume, as there is some technological homogeneity in the material, that we have the remains of a single occupation.

From the stratigraphy it was deduced that the occupation can be dated to the end of the Late Glacial or in the Tardiglacial. For that period very few sites from the area are known. We can refer to the Karain B Cave, the Öküzini Cave and the Beldibi site, all located near Antalya ca. 100 km to the south, where microlithic assemblages have been identified. As far as one can judge from the available drawings, the production technique for bladelets seems similar to those from Dereköy Karain. As no microliths have been found at Dereköy Karain, it is impossible to associate that assemblage definitely with a specific one from Öküzini where several different assemblages have been recognised.

The Öküzini sequence (Léotard *et al.* 1996; Yalçınkaya *et al.* 1995) comprises four assemblages. The lower one comprises layers XII-VII and is dated around 15,740-13,620 BP. On top of it there is a transitional or mixed zone (layers VI-V). A new homogeneous assemblage is found in layers IV-II, dating from 12,420-11,565 BP. Some mixed layers overlay this stratigraphic sequence. Double platform cores for bladelets occur in layers XI and X, whereas pyramidal cores are found in layers IV-II.

At Karain B cave (Albrecht 1988; Albrecht *et al.* 1992), pyramidal cores occur in the archaeological horizon AH29, whereas double platform cores are more characteristic in the archaeological horizon AH18. In the AH29, a single obsidian flake was recovered. Even though there are some difficulties involved with the absolute dating of Karain, an AMS-date of 17,630 ± 140 BP (ETH-8036) for a charcoal sample from AH29 can be accepted. Another charcoal sample from AH18 is 14C-dated at 12,550 ± 400 BP (Hv-14374), but a 14C-date on bone from the same level is much later: 11,250 ± 200 (HD 10028-10227).

As we lack characteristic tools and microliths it is not easy to correlate the Dereköy material with that of the dated cave sequences. We presume that the material from Dereköy Karain, because of the presence of some pyramidal cores, may correspond with the assemblage from layers IV-II at Öküzini. It should however be observed that the sequence of the most important core type at Öküzini is different from the sequence at Karain B. Pyramidal cores are more numerous in the older layers at Karain B and in the later layers at Öküzini. Taking into account the data from the well-dated sequence from the site of Öküzini and the less well-dated sequence from Karain B cave, we provisionally prefer to correlate the Dereköy Karain assemblage with that of Öküzini. When we accept this correlation, the Dereköy Karain assemblage could be dated somewhere around 12,000 BP. We were able to observe that artefacts were included in cryoclastic slope deposits in front of the cave. This implies that, after the Late Palaeolithic occupation, probably during a cold spell of the Tardiglacial, cryoclasts could be produced and/or moved along the slopes of the Ağlasun Çayı at an elevation of 1000 m above sea level. This cryoclastic activity and concomitant slope evolution may be responsible for a first (important?) postdepositional reworking of the Late Palaeolithic remains. Our test pits evidence an intense destruction of the Late Palaeolithic occupation at the site during successive occupations that could be attributed to the pre- or protohistoric, the Roman, the Byzantine and more recent periods.

We therefore preferred not to continue the excavations, even when there is no doubt that more extensive excavation could produce significant prehistoric material. We cannot unfortunately hope to recover any assemblage in its original position.

5. ACKNOWLEDGEMENTS

This research is supported by the Belgian Programme on Interuniversity Poles of Attraction initiated by the Belgian State, Prime Minister's Office, Science Policy Programming (IUAP 4/12). This research was also made possible thanks to a FWO-Vlaanderen research grant (FWO/G.0251.96) and to the GOA-programme (97/1). Scientific responsibility is assumed by the authors. Jeroen Poblome is Post Doctoral Fellow of the Fund for Scientific Research - Flanders (FWO).

6. REFERENCES

G. Albrecht (1988) Preliminary results of the excavation in the Karain B cave near Antalya/Turkey: the Upper Palaeolithic assemblages and the Upper Pleistocene climatic development, *Paléorient* 14/12: 211-222.

G. Albrecht, B. Albrecht, H. Berke, D. Burger, J. Moser, W. Rähle, W. Schoch, G. Storch, H.P. Uerpmann and B. Urban (1992)

Late Pleistocene and Early Holocene finds from Oküzini: a contribution to the settlement history of the bay of Antalya, Turkey, *Paléorient* 18/2: 123-141.

K. Callebaut, W. Viaene (†), M. Waelkens, R. Ottenburgs and J. Naud (2000) Provenance and characterization of raw materials for lime mortars used at Sagalassos with special reference to the volcanic rocks, in: M. Waelkens and L. Loots (eds) *Sagalassos V. Report on the Survey and Excavation Campaigns of 1996 and 1997* (Acta Archaeologica Lovaniensia Monographiae 11) Leuven University Press: 651-665.

J.-M. Léotard, M. Otte, I. Lopez-Bayon, 1. Yalcınkaya and M. Kartal (1996) Le Tardiglaciaire de la grotte d'Okuzini (sud-ouest de l'Anatolie), *Anthropologie et Préhistoire* 107: 157-170.

E. Paulissen, J. Poesen, G. Govers and J. De Ploey (1993) The physical environment at Sagalassos (Western Taurus, Turkey). A reconnaissance survey, in: M. Waelkens and J. Poblome (eds), *Sagalassos II. Report on the Third Excavation Campaign of 1992* (Acta Archaeologica Lovaniensia Monographiae 6) Leuven University Press: 229-247.

M. Waelkens, E. Paulissen, H. Van Haverbeke, I. Öztürk, B. De Cupere, H.A. Ekinci, P.M. Vermeersch, J. Poblome and R. Degeest (1997) The 1994 and 1995 surveys on the territory of Sagalassos, in: M. Waelkens and J. Poblome (eds), *Sagalassos IV. Report on the Survey and Excavation Campaigns of 1994 and 1995* (Acta Archaeologica Lovaniensia Monographiae 9) Leuven University Press: 11-102.

1. Yalçınkaya, J.-M. Leotard, M. Kartal, M. Otte, O. Bar-Yosef, I. Carmi, A. Gautier, E. Gilot, P. Goldberg, J. Kozlowski, D. Lieberman, I. Lopez-Bayon, M. Pawlikowski, S. Thiebault, V. Ancion, M. Patou, A. Emery-Barbier and D. Bonffian (1995) Les occupations tardiglaciaires du site d'Öküzini (sud-ouest de la Turquie). Résultats preliminaires, *L'Anthropologie* 99: 562-583.

HOW CAN THERE STILL BE SUCH A DEGREE OF UNCERTAINTY? PROBLEMS OF CHRONOLOGY FOR THE PREHISTORIC PERIODS IN THE TERRITORY OF SAGALASSOS

Hannelore VANHAVERBEKE

Department of Archaeology, KULeuven, Blijde Inkomststraat 21, B-3000 Leuven, Belgium

1. INTRODUCTION

"Chronology is the backbone of archaeology as well as of history. For, without a time framework, there can be no established sequence of events, no clear picture of what happened in the past, no knowledge of which significant development came first" (Renfrew 1991: xiii).

The title of this contribution summarizes its subject. The problems of chronology will be considered for the prehistoric periods attested on the territory of Sagalassos. Two restrictions are implied in this title:
1 – We will only take into consideration the chronological problems for the prehistoric periods.
Anatolia is said to enter (proto-)historical times at the beginning of the second millennium BC, during the Middle Bronze Age, with the appearance of written documents at the site of Kültepe in Central Anatolia. Here, traders from Assyria were permanently settled. They introduced their (cuneiform) writing system into Anatolia. It is through the inscribed clay tablets, which were found during excavation, that we have the first historical evidence for Anatolia (Joukowsky 1996: 214).
2 – Only those prehistoric periods will be dealt with for which we have archaeological evidence in the city's territory, i.e. the Epipalaeolithic, the Neolithic, the Chalcolithic and the Early Bronze Age. The Lower, Middle and Upper Palaeolithic are therefore omitted[1]

2. A HISTORY OF CHRONOLOGY

Archaeology – and chronology- has come a long way from the cumbersome calculations of James Ussher, a seventeenth-century Irish archbishop who managed to date the Creation of the World precisely to the year 4004 BC and the Flood to 2348 BC, based on chronological indications in the Bible. At that time, Ussher's verdict was widely received as final and early chronologists had to operate within the chronological constraints defined by him. Since no archaeological monuments could possibly have survived the Flood, the extinct creatures known from fossil finds could be explained only by relegating them to an antediluvian era before Noah. This was the insoluble problem faced by Joseph Scaliger (1540-1609), the leading Protestant scholar of his time. He was the first to make a systematic and critical study of the chronological material in the Bible, together with that from the pagan classical world. His conclusions seemed impossible to reconcile with the Christian view of world history. He had recovered new evidence: a Byzantine summary of the writings of Manetho, a Graeco-Egyptian priest of the second century BC who had recorded a history of Egypt back to its first kings. Scaliger set the start of the First Egyptian Dynasty in 5285 BC, long before the Creation of the World as dated by Ussher (James et al. 1991: 6-7).

By post-Renaissance times the intellectual straight jacket of the biblical chronology was gradually becoming very uncomfortable. By the eighteenth century, a provisional

---

[1] An overview of the causes of this lack of early traces and a proposal for remedying this blank in our knowledge can be found in Vanhaverbeke and Waelkens 1998.

Manethonian chronology had been generally accepted. With the decipherment of Egyptian hieroglyphs in 1822 by the French scholar Jean-François Champollion, the writings of the ancient Egyptians themselves were now accessible and nothing in them appeared to contradict the dates already derived from Manetho.

The vital breakthrough in understanding the prehistoric record was made by Christian Thomsen (1788-1865), a Danish businessman and collector, who developed the 'Three-Age System', a technological succession from Stone to Bronze to Iron. This new framework permitted a sensible way of ordering prehistoric finds. His broad chronology had found general favour across Europe by the 1860s, as a continual stream of new finds confirmed his results. Thomsen's sequence enabled the finds to be arranged in a relative order. However, fixed points in time still remained elusive. The absolute dating of finds was still dependent on historical chronologies, such as those developed for Egypt (James *et al.* 1991: 8).

As first conceived by Thomsen and his followers, the Three Ages system was not truly 'evolutionary'. Instead of a gradual development from one age to another, the changes in technology were viewed as abrupt and attributed to waves of invaders. By the last third of the nineteenth century, however, after the revelations of Charles Darwin on evolution and natural selection had taken hold, the succession of the 'ages' was viewed as reflecting the natural law of 'progress' (Waldbaum 1978: 10).

It was only in the 1950s that a breakthrough occurred in dating methods. An entirely new dating technique was discovered and developed by Willard Libby. The radiocarbon method provided the first independent check on the age of prehistoric cultures. Archaeologists now had at their disposal a new means of obtaining dates independent of the interpretations of cultural historical processes. They were freed from the obvious circular reasoning of first arranging the finds into temporal order according to typological criteria and then detecting typological variation from the same temporal order (Siiriäinen 1992: 204).

In the meantime, a range of dating techniques was developed and became available for archaeologists. These techniques can be subdivided into two categories: relative and absolute (for a good overview, see Renfrew and Bahn 1991: 101-147).

Dates based on stratigraphical, typological, linguistic and climatic arguments are of a *relative* nature. They place one object in relation to another and work with a geo-archaeologically, culturally or environmentally defined concept of time. *Absolute* dates, such as those furnished by ancient calendars and historical chronologies, varves, tree-rings, the radiocarbon method, thermoluminescence, electro-spin-resonance, the Potassium/Kalium-Argon method, Uranium-series, fission-tracks, obsidian hydration, amino-acid racemization, cation-ratio and archaeomagnetism, all tie an object to an absolute place in time and work with the notion of 'physical' time.

In spite of this array of possible dating methods, there still seems to be a lot of uncertainty concerning the dates of several cultures or phases. This led James *et al.* (1991: xix) to wonder in their controversial book, *Centuries of Darkness*, "How can there still be such a degree of uncertainty? After all, scientific methods of dating, such as the radiocarbon technique, have now been available for a generation".

It is true that despite -or rather due to- the different methods available, one is confronted with huge problems when trying to sketch the changes which took place in the settlement pattern throughout time. The main causes for this are problems inherent in the methods used and in the hidden corollaries of each method which influence all statements concerning change and evolution in an implicit, but profound way.

In the following sections, these factors will be rendered explicit for each dating method to enhance a greater awareness and critical attitude. However, we will only concentrate on those dating methods which have been used for sites on the territory of Sagalassos: stratigraphical and typological evidence and radiocarbon dates[2].

3. THE DATING METHODS USED: THE STRATIGRAPHICAL, TYPOLOGICAL AND RADIOCARBON DATING METHODS

The *stratigraphical* method is obviously only applicable in excavations. Its central paradigm is that a succession of layers provides a relative chronological sequence – usually from earliest at the bottom to latest at the top- for the objects that are associated with these layers (Renfrew and Bahn 1991: 102-3). It is clear that geo-archaeology and geomorphology have an important role in assessing whether this paradigm is actually correct in a specific case.

On the territory of Imperial Sagalassos only two excavated sites, Hacılar (Mellaart 1970) and Kuruçay (Duru 1994, 1996), have yielded a well documented multi-period sequence. Other excavated sites, such as Baradız (Kansu

---

[2] Other objects have been dated as well, which are not strictly archaeological in nature, such as pollen diagrams and travertine deposits (by radiocarbon and Uranium-Thorium method).

1943, 1945), Dereköy (Vermeersch *et al.* 2000) and the caves at Sagalassos (Waelkens *et al.* 1997b: 103-110) are either disturbed or one-period in nature.

Underlying the *typological* method are two assumptions. The first is that the products of a given period and place have a recognizable style (and technology). The second idea is that the change in style (or technology) of artefacts is evolutionary, a view which is influenced by the Darwinian theory concerning the evolution of species (Renfrew and Bahn 1991: 104). Studies of style thus should allow the establishment of chronologies, and should in turn reflect the history and relationships of the culture(s) concerned through changes, similarities, differences and exchanges.

Once a sequence of changes in artefacts has been determined for one site, artefacts characteristic of that site which are found in undated contexts can be used to furnish a *terminus post quem* for the undated context. This method, derived from typological dating, is referred to as cross-dating. Cross-dating actually assumes that changes in artefacts at several sites follow the same sequence at the same time as the sequence at the exemplary key site. Thus, the method depends on an assessment of the comparability of artefacts at two or more sites. When they are judged to be the same (identical or closely similar), then the deposits in which they occur are assumed to be contemporary (Hole 1987: 559; Manning 1995: 40-41).

The stratigraphical and typological dating methods can actually be considered as one. The sequences (e.g. of pottery) that are established on the basis of their association with certain layers in a well-known stratigraphy, are generally used to date the evidence found at other sites which have not been excavated. In doing so, both principles, the stratigraphical and typological, are applied at the same time since the change in the styles and types which are observed throughout the stratigraphical layers is applied as a dating criterion.

All prehistoric sites recorded on the territory of Sagalassos have been dated by using this combined stratigraphical-typological method. Reference is either made to the exemplary sequence at Hacılar, or to sequences established for other regions in Turkey.

The *radiocarbon* dating method developed by Willard Libby, "the single most useful method of dating for the archaeologist" in the words of Renfrew and Bahn (1991: 121-122), is presumed to be generally known and will not be explored in detail (for a good introduction see Bowman 1990). On the territory of Sagalassos, radiocarbon dates are only available for Hacılar and Kuruçay.

4. THE PROBLEMS

4.1. The stratigraphical-typological dating method

Several problems are inherent in the stratigraphical-typological dating method. First, the basis of archaeological classification throughout the world is still Thomsen's simple Three-Age System. However, since Thomsen's day, this terminology has strayed far from its original – technological – meaning. With the further growth and development of archaeology, connotations of a different nature became attached to these technological terms, e.g. cultural, functional, diffusionist, economic and chronological (Bruins and Mook 1989: 1019). In the Eastern Mediterranean for instance, these terms are now in use to describe cultural phases which are generally defined by their pottery (James *et al.* 1991: 10). As a result, confusion has ensued since many archaeologists confuse time units – as originally implied in Thomsen's system-, and archaeological units -as understood now under Stone, Bronze and Iron Age (Bruins and Mook 1989: 1019; Mellink 1965: 105; Joukowsky 1996: 34). Thus, to assume that a site is dated by labelling it 'Late Bronze Age' is incorrect, since this term does not have a primarily chronological but a cultural meaning: it does not date the site, but places it in a relative cultural sequence.

Secondly, the general terms as introduced by Thomsen have, in the course of generations of archaeologists, been subdivided into smaller units. One example is Evans' tripartite division for the Aegean Bronze Age (Early, Middle and Late), a system that has become so popular that one might imagine that it was the natural and obvious way to classify material. However, the suggestion that a tripartite system necessarily conveys images of growth and decay -as Evans did- is surely wrong; it can simply imply a beginning, middle and end (Manning 1995: 9). Attempts to force archaeological evidence, mostly pottery, into this terminological straight jacket have delimited the research of an entire generation of archaeologists: pottery seriation has in many cases become an end in itself and promoted to be a focus of research (Knapp 1994: 276). Moreover, Early, Middle and Late divisions, while providing a device for pursuing generalised comparisons, can also serve to distort and homogenise temporal and spatial variability, thus overlooking rapid and discontinuous changes (Mathers and Stoddart 1994: 13).

Thirdly, developments which are particular to a given geographic area or chronological span, are often held to be characteristic of large regions or of a time period as a whole. Thus, regional differences in the rate of technological progress, as well as the existence of contemporaneous cultural differences within even small areas, seriously discredit the use of terms such as 'Late Bronze Age' as chronological denominators (Bruins and Mook 1989: 1019). The result has been the creation of highly artificial zones of cultural uniformity and the obscuring of localised changes within one and the same period (Mathers and Stoddart 1994: 13).

Cross-dating obviously creates the same problem. Underlying this method is the same assumption that cultural phases in separate sites and regions are of equivalent length and chronological significance. However, once the network of correlation synchronisms of archaeological artefacts is extended beyond the immediate region, the links become progressively more questionable with geographic as well as with cultural distance (Manning 1995: 74). Moreover, the method poses problems for those who wish to segment their sequences on an absolute timescale since it does not provide either a theoretical or an empirical basis for assessing chronological equivalence between sites with artefacts that are merely 'similar' rather than 'identical' and between sites that are widely separated in space. Only when synchronous patterns in two or more areas have been worked out in detail and tied to an independent method of dating (such as radiocarbon) can one be certain that the sequential segmentation has chronological significance.

Finally, there remains the necessity and difficulty of determining if and when there is a complete sequence in any site or region. Gaps are usually difficult to recognize and there is a tendency to assume that they do not exist. When virgin soil is not reached, the possibility of unrecognized earlier phases or antecedent cultures is real (Hole 1987: 559-560).

Considering all the problematic consequences of the use of this dating method, we can wonder why the Three-Age System and its later subdivisions are still in use. At a time when this system is increasingly being replaced by radiocarbon chronologies it might seem anachronistic to employ terms such as 'Bronze Age'. However, while it may be preferable to reform the tripartite subdivisions of the Bronze Age with their implicit notions of development-florescence-decadence, or abandon the concept of this and other cultural phases altogether, any major alteration of the traditional nomenclature and cultural-chronological boundaries would inevitably lead to widespread confusion (Manning 1995: 14, 21).

4.2. The radiocarbon dating method

The problems relating to the application of radiocarbon dates are two-fold: a number of them are inherent in its methodology, while others are due to external factors.

1 – Inherent problems[3]

A first and basic problem caused by radiocarbon dating is that radiocarbon determinations are not dates as such, but Gaussian probability distributions with standard deviations around a central value ("date") (Bruins and Mook 1989: 1023). The scepticism amongst many archaeologists referred to below, has mainly been caused by this aspect of radiocarbon dating. One erroneous solution to this problem has been the calculation of averages for several radiocarbon dates from a similar context (e.g. as advocated by Yakar 1979: 53). This method is in total contradiction to the definition of radiocarbon dating itself (Gasco 1987: 154). The non-monotonic relationship between radiocarbon ages and calendar ages (see below) renders the averaging of various radiocarbon dates inappropriate for different samples (Manning 1995: 130 note 15). The continuing use of averages in the literature undoubtedly reflects their ease of creation, not their correctness (Manning 1995: 136,138).

A partial solution to the problem is the use of more suitable samples (see below) and the application of the AMS-method (Accelerator Mass Spectrometry). This method needs smaller samples, is quicker, and has a wider time range. More important, AMS does not measure the decay rate of carbon-14, with all its biases, but determines the number of carbon-14 atoms present (Bruins and Mook 1989: 1023; Bowman 1990: 34-37; Nelson 1990: 271 table 1, 273; Thomsen 1995: 38; Manning 1995: 126-127). A second factor inherent to radiocarbon dating has been alluded to above, i.e. the fact that radiocarbon years do not correspond to calendar years (Evin 1995: 13) due to the interference of isotope fractionation, i.e. a differential intake of carbon-14 by different organisms, and the de Vries effect, i.e. fluctuations in atmospheric carbon-14 levels (Bowman 1990: 16-18, 20-23; Manning 1995: 127). Therefore, radiocarbon dates need to be calibrated. In order to do so, the most recent calibration curve should be used (Stuiver et al. 1998) or the calibration computer program freely available on the internet (http://www.rlaha.ox.ac.uk/oxcal/oxcal.html). Even then, due to wiggles in the calibration curve, a radiocarbon date can still result in wide or multiple possible calibrated date ranges. In time areas where the calibration curve has a steep slope, the standard deviation of the calibrated date may become smaller than the precalibrated date in conventional radiocarbon years. In time areas with a more horizontal or irregular calibration curve the opposite occurs, widening the probability range of the radiocarbon date (Bruins and Mook 1969: 1023).

---

[3] A good overview of the chemical and physical principles, problems and solutions of radiocarbon dating is presented by Mook and Streurman 1983, Waterbolk 1983 and Bowman 1990.

Archaeological wiggle-matching is the technique which recently has been applied to counteract this to some degree. The technique uses the archaeological, or the approximate historical sequence as observed stratigraphically and typologically, to provide the framework for the curve fitting, and the radiocarbon dates are best-fitted on a probabilistic basis. In other words, archaeological wiggle-matching takes the prior archaeological observation that a given series of radiocarbon dates are known to derive from several phases of relative time, and best-fits this known relative calendar sequence to the radiocarbon year BP curve. The conceptual idea is that the stratigraphic sequence is seen as the proxy calendar timescale: the radiocarbon dates from the stratigraphy thus approximate the relevant part of the calibration curve, except that the precise calendar intervals are not known. Archaeological wiggle-matching is the method of estimating those unknown intervals (given prior knowledge of seriation, and a relative sequence from stratigraphy, and/or ceramic seriation, and/or other 'knowledge'). A substantial series of dates, and dates which have relatively small standard errors, is required to do so. However, one should beware of self-fulfilling prophecies: the best fit may not be the real one; analyses of significant numbers of dates from a significant number of phases should be carried out to prevent this bias (Manning 1995: 141).

A third problem facing the use of radiocarbon dates is the precautions and recommendations which have to be kept in mind when sampling. A considerable variation in radiocarbon determinations can be caused by different materials. Some materials should preferably not be used for dating, such as bone (Henry and Servello 1974: 19; Mook and Streurman 1983: 51; Evin 1987: 111), although dates from the collagen part of bone are more reliable (Mook and Streurman 1983: 51; Evin 1987: 111). Dates derived from other sources, such as shell, soil and burned matrix have also proved to be inconsistent (Henry and Servello 1974: 19; Evin 1987: 111-113). Given the procedures currently employed in the radiocarbon dating technique, the most reliable sources for dating are carbonised wood, peat, or other plant-related materials, especially the short lived varieties (Henry and Servello 1974: 19; for a good overview, see Evin *et al.* 1990).

In addition to the limitations of the radiocarbon technique, there exist numerous inherent biasing factors attributed to natural contaminants, improper collection, inadequate pretreatment, insufficient sample size, and errors in the processing and counting of samples (Henry and Servello 1974: 19). Due to these potential dating errors, caution must be used in evaluating single determinations. A series of determinations should be used when evaluating the temporal placement of archaeological occurrences. Ancillary chronological evidence (i.e. stratigraphy, palaeo-environmental data, typologic seriation) can also be useful as a check on relationships within and between series of determinations (Henry and Servello 1974: 19-20).

Finally, it appears that differences in dating occur which are related to the lab which dates the samples. Firstly, the dates produced in the early years of radiocarbon dating show differences in quality due to the lack of internationally uniform standards, the inability of the counters to produce precise measurements, the imperfect pretreatment of the samples (e.g. removal of humic acid with NaOH), the fact that no corrections were made for isotopic fractionation, and the fact that the measuring process was not kept under continuous computerized control. Secondly, in 1983, the laboratory of Glasgow compared series of dates of 20 laboratories on 8 samples of homogenized tree ring materials spread over an interval of 200 years with an age of ca. 5000 years BP. There was evidence both for systematic bias up of to 200 years and for variability which was not accounted for by the standard deviation given to each measurement. Although all samples should date between 5000 and 5200 BP, the determination ranged from 4650-5460 BP (Waterbolk 1987: 41-42; Waterbolk 1990).

2 – External problems
A first problem that still occurs, albeit to a diminishing extent, is the lack of understanding of the method on the part of archaeologists which has led to the submission of large numbers of samples of little or no value in dating the contexts from which they come (James *et al.* 1991: xix). In addition, the literature contains a number of examples of considerable naivety on the topics of what a radiocarbon date represents, and how it should be seen in calendar terms (Manning 1995: 36).

Secondly, the problems inherent in the radiocarbon method, as enumerated above, have often led to an unnecessary delay in its application since it still meets with scepticism amongst archaeologists, especially amongst those scholars who have been working with historical chronologies. The Egyptian- and Mesopotamian-based chronologies are generally believed to be fixed and, of the relatively few radiocarbon results available, many conflict with the present understanding. Moreover, the standard deviation is often too large to provide a check on or to improve historical dates. Because of this, most archaeologists working in the area are not fully convinced by the method (James *et al.* 1991: 23), a view which is clearly expressed in the following statements:

"C14 dates are not useful for exact dating. Even if the carbon samples come form indisputably stratified contexts and are correctly pretreated, we still have margins of error of about 50 to 250 years. C14 dates thus have little or nothing to contribute to the absolute chronology of the Aegean Middle Bronze Age." (Astrøm *et al.* 1984: 4-5).

"Radiocarbon dates are as yet too inconsistent and, after calibration, have too wide a range to permit replacement of the historically derived chronology." (Warren 1987: 210).

"... recent recalibrations of radiocarbon... have highlighted the large margins of error connected with radiocarbon-based chronologies. As a consequence, it is arguable whether the absolute time frames currently available in much of the Mediterranean provide any greater precision than traditional classification schemes." (Mathers and Stoddart 1994: 14)

"Nevertheless, some system of historical phasing and material classification seems required. It is still not possible to use absolute dates. Rather, the basis for discussing development of any kind must be a relative chronology, based upon regional classification systems. The results can be correlated within broad phases that ideally should reflect stages in historical development, and if possible these phases can then be given absolute dates" (Manning 1995: 11).

This scepticism has entailed two consequences. Sometimes a dozen or so radiocarbon dates are included in an archaeological site report merely as scientific window-dressing. This attitude is clearly reflected in a regrettably common practice: when a radiocarbon date agrees with the expectations of the excavator it appears in the main text of the site report; if it is slightly discrepant it is relegated to a footnote; if it seriously conflicts it is left out altogether (James et al. 1991: xviii-xix).

The second consequence is more widespread: scepticism has prevented more systematic sampling and this has led to a lack of sufficient dates. This lack of systematic sampling, in turn, means that radiocarbon dating is still too blunt a tool to date cultural phases accurately (James et al. 1991: xix; 26) and thus the prevailing scepticism is reinforced.

After having enumerated the corollaries of radiocarbon dating and its many limitations, it may seem strange to stress the fact that there is reason for optimism. The "eventual development of an independent calibrated radiocarbon chronology of Near Eastern archaeology will be the natural outcome of current progress in radiocarbon dating" (Bruins and Mook 1989: 1022). In order to reach this goal, i.e. the establishment of a calibrated radiocarbon chronology of Near Eastern archaeology, the basic requirements may be summarized as follows:

1 – formation of a database of all available radiocarbon dates for the region, with continuous updating. This might be accomplished in the framework of the pilot project *Paleoenvironment and Human History in the Southeastern Mediterranean* of the IRDB (Intern Radiocarbon Data Base) as proposed by Kra (1988a, 1988b).
2 – production of internally consistent series of precise radiocarbon dates from carefully selected archaeological sites, strata and artefacts
3 – evaluation of each radiocarbon date: sample material, time range of sample, archaeological association, standard deviation
4 – calibration according to internationally agreed guidelines, with graphic and numerical expression of the result
5 – chronological ordering of the radiocarbon according to area, age and association with archaeological and historical periods (Bruins and Mook 1989:1025).

5. PROBLEMS OF CHRONOLOGY FOR THE PREHISTORIC PERIODS ON THE TERRITORY OF SAGALASSOS

Within the territory of the city, 199 sites dating from the Epipalaeolithic to Ottoman times have been recorded by various scholars especially M. Özsait and S. Mitchell, and by the Sagalassos survey team from 1993 to 1996[4]. Of these sites, three have been dated to the Epipalaeolithic period, 5 were Neolithic in age, 13 yielded Chalcolithic material and 22 belonged to the Early Bronze Age[5].

However, these 'dates' are all cultural attributions. The only exception is Hacılar where Mellaart in the 1950s had to start from a virtual blank in the knowledge of the prehistoric periods in Pisidia. Basing his observations on the stratigraphy and the (ceramic and faunal) assemblages included within these stratigraphical units, he called the several cultural assemblages (from bottom to top): Aceramic Neolithic, Late Neolithic and Chalcolithic. Subsequently, radiocarbon dates were attached to these cultural units (Mellaart 1970: 93):

P-315	Early Chalco	level IA	6990+/-121	BP
P-326A	Early Chalco	level II	7170+/-134	BP
P-313A	Late Neo	level VI	7350+/-85	BP
BM-48	Late Neo	level VI	7550+/-180	BP
BM-125	Late Neo	level VII	7770+/-180	BP
P-314A	Late Neo	level IX	7340+/-94	BP
BM-127	Aceramic Neo	level V	8700+/-180	BP

At the time of drafting this and the subsequent tables, an older version of the Oxcal program was used (M. Stuiver, A. Long & R.S. Kra, OxCal v2.18, *Radiocarbon 35(1)*). The data based on that version have been included here since no major changes in the general chronological framework deducted from these tables could be noted.

---

[4] These sites are discussed in the survey articles: Waelkens 1995; Waelkens et al. 1997a; Waelkens et al. 2000

[5] A discussion of these sites and of the changes which can be observed in the settlement pattern has been published (Vanhaverbeke et al. 1998a).

The excavations at Kuruçay in 1978-88 (Duru 1994, 1996) actually worked along the same lines: cultural units were defined in the stratigraphy, mainly on the basis of comparison with the finds at Hacılar, and with other Anatolian sites for the one period which was not attested at Hacılar (the Early Bronze Age), and radiocarbon dates were determined for these (Duru 1983: 43; 1994: 89; 1996: 143):

HD 9988-10341	Late Chalco	levels 6A-6b	4620+/-60BP
HD 9989-10360	Late Chalco	levels 6A-6b	4740+/-50BP
HD 9990-10361	Late Chalco	levels 6A-6b	4690+/-60BP
HD 9991-10362	Late Chalco	levels 6A-6b	4720+/-60BP
HD 9992-10363	Late Chalco	levels 6A-6b	4650/+-55BP
Hacettepe	Late Chalco	level 6b	4795+/-82BP.
Hacettepe	Late Chalco	level 6c	5450+/-52BP
Hacettepe	Early Chalco	level 7	5170+/-70BP
Hacettepe	Early Chalco	level 7	7214/+-68BP
HD 12917-12830	Late Neo	level 11	7045+/-95BP
HD12916-1267	Early Neo	level 12	7140+/-35BP
HD 12915-1267	Early Neo	level 13	7310+/-70BP

Subsequently, surface finds at other sites were dated using the cultural sequence established at Hacılar and Kuruçay as a basis.

Several of the problems relating to both dating methods, the typological-stratigraphical and the radiocarbon dating, which have been mentioned above, recur here, especially when one wants to make inter-site comparisons or study the changes in settlement pattern which have occurred through the ages. Central to a study of the first is the concept of contemporaneity. However, because the majority of the sites are only known through surface finds, contemporaneity is very difficult to establish (Vanhaverbeke 1997: 257). What is more important in this narrative, however, is the fact that sites which have been given labels such as 'Late Neolithic' are not really dated. Such labels actually merely summarize the characteristics of the cultural assemblage (mostly pottery) found at a specific site by referring to rather/very similar or identical assemblages found elsewhere, close by or further afield, which were called 'Late Neolithic'. Several of the risks referred to above come to mind. It is clear that, if one considers these sites as being 'dated', one is confusing time units with cultural units. 'Late Neolithic' refers to a cultural stage, not to an absolute timespan. Moreover, including in a comparison remote sites, such as Troy which is very often referred to even in a Pisidian context, obviously assumes that cultural phases in separate sites and regions are of the same duration and date. It should be clear that most of the time this will not have been the case. Moreover, subjectivity almost unavoidably comes into play when one has to assess to what degree several assemblages are similar or identical and, thus, whether they can really be considered as being contemporaneous.

Tracing and trying to explain long-term changes in settlement patterns meets essentially with the same problems. The most recurrent problem here is the confusion arising from the use of cultural dates. If one wants to sketch changes in settlement pattern, one first has to arrange all the sites according to their age which should mean arranging sites from Epipalaeolithic, through Neolithic and Chalcolithic to the Early Bronze Age. In theory, then, one should be able to synthesize the changes which occur and the similarities and seek an explanation for them. However, these 'ages' are merely cultural and do not have a real chronological value. Strictly speaking, Epipalaeolithic, Neolithic, Chalcolithic and Early Bronze Age all may have been present as cultural traditions within one and the same time span[6]. Clarifying long-term changes thus becomes extremely awkward.

It would seem that radiocarbon dates are the preferred solution to all these problems, especially seeing the justified optimism expressed above. However, for the prehistoric periods on the territory of Sagalassos, the list of available radiocarbon dates is extremely short, which is mainly due to the lack of prehistoric excavations in the area[7]. Moreover, one must stress the fact that in the case of Hacılar we are dealing with an excavation carried out during the late 1950s. Bearing in mind the strictures listed above concerning older radiocarbon dates, these should be applied with caution and the latest calibration curves (Stuiver et al. 1998) should be used. However, the wide standard deviations occurring for the Hacılar dates cannot be counteracted.

For the time being, therefore, a strictly chronological framework into which the cultural sequence for the prehistoric evidence on the territory of Sagalassos can be fitted, must still be built up not only by using local radiocarbon dates from Hacılar and Kuruçay, but also incorporating regional dates obtained from excavations such as at the caves of Karain and Öküzini in the Bay of Antalya for the Epipalaeolithic (Albrecht et al. 1990: 131 table 1; Yalçınkaya et al. 1995: 572-574), and supra-regional published dates for Anatolia as a whole for the Neolithic and subsequent periods (Aurenche and Evin 1987; Breunig 1987; Cauvin 1987; Ehrich 1992: 173, 178; Manning 1995: 168-173; Mellaart 1957; Treuil 1983).

In Appendix 1 the radiocarbon dates which are easily available, i.e. published in compendia, for the periods which are attested on the territory of Sagalassos are listed according to the cultural

---

[6] That this was possibly the case in the sense that the Epipalaeolitihic tradition continued up through the Neolithic and in a modified way until the Early Bronze Age on the territory of Sagalassos, is argued in Vanhaverbeke et al. (1998a and 1998b).

[7] Several excavations have been undertaken bij P.M. Vermeersch in collaboration with the Burdur Museum (Waelkens et al. 1997b: 103-110; Vermeersch et al. 1997, 2000).

phase to which they belong. It must be stressed here that the cultural phases as distinguished by each excavator have been maintained and copied. It is not within the scope of this study to evaluate the excavation data. However, it should be mentioned that the preferred way of working would be to list all radiocarbon dates and then divide the resulting time span into regionally differentiated cultural sequences, and not *vice versa* -as is necessarily done here- starting from defined sequences and subsequently dating them absolutely. This list is not meant to be exhaustive. Troy, for example, has been omitted because of the lack of general publications on its dates.

On the basis of these radiocarbon dates, a chronological framework for the cultural periods attested on the territory of Sagalassos can be proposed: the Epipalaeolithic in Southern Turkey can be said to go back to ca. 16,000. The Neolithic way of life began to appear around 10,000/9000 BP, lasting to ca. 7500 BP (ca. 9500/8000-6500/6000 BC). The Chalcolithic cultural period covers the time span from ca. 7500 BP to ca. 4400 BP (ca. 6500/6000- 3000 BC). The Early Bronze Age began after ca. 4400 BP and lasted until ca. 3500 BP (ca. 3000-1800 BC)[8].

6. CONCLUSIONS

To conclude this discussion, two remarks may be made. First, both relative (stratigraphical- typological) and absolute (radiocarbon) dating have their own unique assets and limitations. A 'scholarly' attitude towards radiocarbon dating as a mere indication of probability not to be taken seriously, is as unhelpful in the search of the past reality as 'scientific' derision of archaeo-historical dating as merely subjective interpretation of layers and antiquities with no semblance of probability. Together, and in tune with each other, they constitute a comprehensive approach to the archaeo-historical past, by which some of the outstanding chronological controversies might be resolved (Bruins and Mook 1989:1026).

Secondly, however, an absolute timeframe, independent of material culture must be the preferred solution (Mathers and Stoddart 1994: 14). In the area of absolute chronology, priority should be accorded to the independent radiocarbon and, where culturally related, tree-ring data, as this direct evidence for the ages of samples offers – in principle- the only means to avoid the cumbersome step-wise transfers that are inherent to historical or cultural dating (Waterbolk 1987: 40). Moreover, new scientific work in progress holds out interesting prospects for absolute chronology. Apart from the IRDB project, more definite results may come from the ongoing development of a tree-ring sequence for ancient Anatolia and Greece (James *et al.* 1991: xix-xx;

Dickinson 1994: 18; Mathers and Stoddart 1994: 14).

Dendrochronology seems to be very promising as demonstrated by the tedious but successful work of P.I. Kuniholm in Anatolia and the Aegean where a floating chronology is now available which stretches over 1503 years (Kuniholm *et al.* 1983; Kuniholm *et al.* 1987; Kuniholm 1992; Kuniholm *et al.* 1996). Kuniholm and his colleagues have tried to fix this floating chronology. To this end they have first compared high-precision radiocarbon determinations on a sequence of decadal samples, and matched the results with the precisely dated decadal variations in radiocarbon ages known for European wood. The entire 1503-year dendrochronology accordingly begins in 2223 BC and runs to 731 BC (+76/-22 years). Moreover, Kuniholm *et al.* proposed to equate a major tree ring growth anomaly lasting 36 annual rings from Porsuk (South-Central Anatolia) with the one seen in 1628/1627 BC in Europe and the United States (Kuniholm *et al.* 1996). This anomaly is believed to represent the effects of a major volcanic eruption which Kuniholm *et al.* (1996) wish to relate to the eruption of Thera, thus providing a second anchor for their floating chronology. However, this equation is not obvious and has been discussed immediately after its publication by Renfrew (Renfrew 1996).

As for the prehistoric sites on the territory of Sagalassos, the present state of prehistoric research in the area does not allow a firmly established local absolute chronological framework for the different cultural periods present. Regional and supra-regional radiocarbon dates must be invoked to do so. This deficit can only be remedied by more (multi-period) local excavations with controlled sampling for radiocarbon dating.

In the meantime, we can use the cultural attributions furnished by different scholars for the prehistoric sites on the city's territory. Bearing in mind the remarks and recommendations mentioned above, these attributions can be used only as indicators of a certain cultural phase, and *not* as chronological denominators.

7. ACKNOWLEDGEMENTS

This research is supported by the Belgian Programme on Interuniversity Poles of Attraction (IUAP IV/12) initiated by the Belgian State, Prime Minister's Office, Science Policy Programming, by a Concerted Action of the Flemish Government (GOA 97/2) and by the Fund for Scientific Research-Flanders (Belgium) (FWO) (G. 2145.94). The author is postdoctoral fellow of the Fund for Scientific Research Flanders – Belgium (F.W.O.). Scientific responsibility is assumed by the author.

---

[8] These calibrated dates have been obtained by using the computerized calibration programma developed by Stuiver *et al.* 1998.

8. REFERENCES

G. Albrecht, B. Albrecht, H. Berke, D. Burger, J. Moser, W. Rähle, W. Schoch, G. Storch, H.P. Uerpmann and B. Urban (1992) Late pleistocene and early holocene finds from Öküzini: a contribution to the settlement history of the bay of Antalya, Turkey, *Paléorient* 18/2: 123-141.

P. Astrøm, L.R. Palmer and L. Pomerance (1984) *Studies in Aegean Chronology*, Gothenburg.

O. Aurenche and J. Evin (eds) (1987) *Chronologies du Proche Orient/Chronologies in the Near East. C.N.R.S. International symposium, Lyon (France), 24-28 November 1986* (BAR International Series 379) Oxford.

S. Bowman (1990) *Radiocarbon Dating. Interpreting the Past*, London.

P. Breunig (1987) *14C-Chronologie des vorderasiatischen, südost- und mitteleuropäischen Neolithikums*, Köln.

H.J. Bruins and W.G. Mook (1989) The need for a calibrated radiocarbon chronology of NE archaeology, *Radiocarbon* 31/3: 1019-1029.

J. Cauvin (1987) Chronologie relative et chronologie absolue dans le néolithique du Levant nord et d'Anatolie entre 10.000 et 8.000 BP, in: O. Aurenche and J. Evin (eds) *Chronologies du Proche Orient/Chronologies in the Near East. C.N.R.S. International symposium, Lyon (France), 24-28 November 1986* (BAR International Series 379) Oxford: 325-341.

O.T.P.K. Dickinson (1994) *The Aegean Bronze Age*, Cambridge.

R. Duru (1983) Kuruçay Höyüğü kazıları. 1981 Çalışma raporu/Excavations at Kuruçay Höyük 1981, *Anadolu Araştırmaları* 9: 13-40/41-50.

R. Duru (1994) *Kuruçay Höyük, I: 1978-1988 Kazılarının sonuçları Neolitik ve erken Kalkolitik çağı yerleşmeleri/Results of the Excavations 1978-1988. The Neolithic and Early Chalcolithic Periods*, Ankara.

R. Duru (1996) *Kuruçay Höyük, II: 1978-1988 Kazılarının sonuçları geç Kalkolitik ve ilk Tunç çağı yerleşmeleri/Results of the Excavations 1978-1988. The Late Chalcolithic and Early Bronze Settlements*, Ankara.

R.W. Ehrich (ed.) (1992) *Chronologies in Old World Archaeology*, Chicago.

J. Evin (1987) Problèmes posés par certains matériaux de datation en provenance du Proche Orient, in: O. Aurenche and J. Evin (eds) *Chronologies du Proche Orient/Chronologies in the Near East. C.N.R.S. International symposium, Lyon (France), 24-28 November 1986* (BAR International Series 379) Oxford: 105-120.

J. Evin, O. Aurenche and J. Gasco (1990) Techniques for the classification, selection and interpretation of a series of 14C dates from the Near East, in: W.G. Mook and H.T. Waterbolk (eds) *Proceedings of the Second International Symposium. 14C and Archaeology. Groningen 1987* (PACT 29) Strasbourg: 105-124.

J. Evin (1995) Possibilité et nécessité de la calibration des datations C-14 de l'archéologie du Proche-Orient, *Paléorient* 21/1: 5-16.

J. Gasco (1987) Traitements graphiques des dates radiocarbone: application au Proche Orient, in: O. Aurenche and J. Evin (eds) *Chronologies du Proche Orient/Chronologies in the Near East. C.N.R.S. International symposium, Lyon (France), 24-28 November 1986* (BAR International Series 379) Oxford: 151-176.

D.O. Henry and A.F. Servello (1974) Compendium of carbon-14 determinations derived from Near Eastern prehistoric deposits, *Paléorient* 2/1: 19-44.

F. Hole (1987) Issues in Near-Eastern archaeology, in: O. Aurenche and J. Evin (eds) Chronologies du Proche Orient/Chronologies in the Near East. C.N.R.S. International symposium, Lyon (France), 24-28 November 1986 (BAR International Series 379) Oxford: 559-566.

P. James, I. Thorpe, N. Kokkinos, R. Morkot and J. Frankish (1991) *Centuries of Darkness. A Challenge to the Conventional Chronology of Old World Archaeology*, London.

M.S. Joukowsky (1996) *Early Turkey. Anatolian Archaeology from Prehistory through the Lydian Period*, Dubuque.

Ş.A. Kansu (1943) Anadoluda Mezolitik kültür buluntaları, *Dil ve Tarih Cografya Fakültesi Dergisi* 2/5: 673-682.

Ş.A. Kansu (1945) Isparta, Burdur illeri çevresinde T.T.K. adına 1994 haziranında yapılan prehistorya araştırmalarına dair ilk rapor, *Belleten* 34/9: 277-287.

A.B. Knapp (1994) Emergence, development and decline in Bronze Age Cyprus, in: C. Mathers and S. Stoddart (eds) *Development and Decline in the Mediterranean Bronze Age*, Sheffield: 271-304.

R.S. Kra (1988a) Updating the past: The establishment of the international radiocarbon data base, *American Antiquity* 53: 118-125.

R.S. Kra (1988b) The first American workshop on the international radiocarbon data base, *Radiocarbon* 30/2: 259-260.

P.I. Kuniholm and C.L. Striker (1983) Dendrochronological investigations in the Aegean and neighbouring regions, 1977-1982, *Journal of Field Archaeology* 10: 411-420.

P.I. Kuniholm and C.L. Striker (1987) Dendrochronological investigations in the Aegean neigbouring regions, 1983-1986, *Journal of Field Archaeology* 14: 385-398.

P.I. Kuniholm (1992) A 1503-year chronology for the Bronze and Iron Ages; 1990-1991 progress report of the Aegean dendrochronology project, *VII Arkeometri Sonuçlar Toplantısı, Çanakkale 27-31 Mayıs 1991*, Ankara: 121-130.

P.I. Kuniholm (1996) The prehistoric Aegean: dendrochronological progress as of 1995, *Acta Archaeologica* 67: 327-335.

P.I. Kuniholm, B. Kromer, S.W. Manning, M. Newton, C.E. Latini and M.J. Bruce (1996) Anatolian tree rings and the absolute chronology of the eastern Mediterranean, 2220-718 BC, *Nature* 381: 780-783.

S.W. Manning (1995) *The Absolute Chronology of the Aegean Early Bronze Age: Archaeology, Radiocarbon and History*, Sheffield.

C. Mathers and S. Stoddart (1994) Introduction, in: C. Mathers and S. Stoddart (eds) *Development and Decline in the Mediterranean Bronze Age*, Sheffield: 13-20.

J. Mellaart (1957) Anatolian chronology in the Early Bronze Age and Middle Bronze Age, *Anatolian Studies* 7: 55-88.

J. Mellaart (1970) *Excavations at Hacılar*, Edinburgh.

M. Mellink (1965) Anatolian chronology, in: R.W. Ehrich (eds) *Chronologies in Old World Archaeology*, Chicago: 101-131

W.G. Mook and H.J. Streurman (1983) Physical and chemical aspects of radiocarbon dating, in: W.G. Mook and H.T. Waterbolk (eds) *Proceedings of the First International Symposium. 14C and Archaeology* (PACT 8) Strasbourg: 31-55.

D.E. Nelson (1990) Radiocarbon dating in archaeology: comparing the AMS and radiometric methods, in: W.G. Mook and H.T. Waterbolk (eds) *Proceedings of the Second International Symposium. 14C and Archaeology. Groningen 1987* (PACT 29) Strasbourg: 269-280.

C. Renfrew (1991) Foreword, in: P. James, I. Thorpe, N. Kokkinos, R. Morkot and J. Frankish (eds) *Centuries of Darkness. A Challenge to the Conventional Chronology of Old World Archaeology*, London: xiii-xv.

C. Renfrew and P. Bahn (1991) *Archaeology. Theories, Methods and Practice*, London.

C. Renfrew (1996) Kings, tree rings and the Old World, *Nature* 381: 733-734.

A. Siiriäinen (1992) Time in archaeology, in: T. Hackens, H. Jungner and C. Carpelan (eds) *Time and Environment. A Pact Seminar, September 25-28, 1990 – Helsinki, Finland* (PACT 36) Rixensart: 203-208.

M. Stuiver and J. Van der Plicht (eds) (1998) Calibration issue, *Radiocarbon* 40 (3) (http://www.rlaha.ox.ac.uk/oraw.html).

M.S. Thomsen (1995) 14C dating by the accelerator technique, in: T. Hackens, L.-K. Königsson and G. Possnert (eds) *14C Methods and Applications. A Symposium Dedicated to I. Olsson on the Occasion of a Birthday (PACT* 49) Rixensart: 29-38.

R. Treuil (1983) *Le néolithique et le bronze ancien égéens*, Paris.

H. Vanhaverbeke (1997) Interpreting junk. The reliability of surface finds for archaeological research in the Mediterranean, in: M. Waelkens and J. Poblome (eds) *Sagalassos IV. Report on the Survey and Excavation Campaigns of 1994 and 1995 (Acta Archaeologica Lovaniensia Monographiae* 9) Leuven University Press: 253-261.

H. Vanhaverbeke and M. Waelkens (1998) Lower, Middle and Upper Palaeolithic in the territory of Sagalassos (SW Turkey)? Problems and prospects, *Anatolia Antiqua* 6: 1-19.

H. Vanhaverbeke, P.M. Vermeersch and M. Waelkens (1998a) Living between the river and the lake: the evolution of the prehistoric settlement pattern on the territory of Sagalassos (Pisidia, southwestern Turkey), *Aegean Archaeology* 3, 7-25.

H. Vanhaverbeke, P.M. Vermeersch and M. Waelkens (1998b) What's in a Name? The Epipalaeolithic, the Aceramic and the Early Neolithic on the Territory of Sagalassos (Pisidia, Turkey), *Near Eastern Archaeology/Arti-Facts* 61:3, 175-176.

P.M. Vermeersch, H.A. Ekinci, I. Öztürk, J. Poblome, B. De Cupere, R. Degeest and M. Waelkens (1997) A sondage excavation at Düldül Izi (Osman Pinari), in M. Waelkens and J. Poblome (eds) *Sagalassos IV. Report on the Survey and Excavation Campaigns of 1994 and 1995 (Acta Archaeologica Lovaniensia Monographiae* 9) Leuven University Press: 217-224.

P.M. Vermeersch, I. Öztürk, H.A. Ekinci, P. Degryse, B. De Cupere, J. Poblome, M. Waelkens and W.Viaene (2000), Late Palaeolithic at the Dereköy Karain cave, in: M. Waelkens and L. Loots (eds) *Sagalassos V. Report on the Survey and Excavation Campaigns of 1996 and 1997 (Acta Archaeologica Lovaniensia Monographiae* 11) Leuven University Press: 451-462.

M. Waelkens (1995) The 1993 survey in the district south and east of Sagalassos, in: M. Waelkens and J. Poblome (ed.) *Sagalassos III. Report on the Fourth Excavation Campaign of 1993 (Acta Archaeologica Lovaniensia Monographiae* 7) Leuven University Press: 11-22.

M. Waelkens, E. Paulissen, H. Vanhaverbeke, I. Öztürk, B. De Cupere, H.A. Ekinci, P.M. Vermeersch, J. Poblome and R. Degeest (1997a) The 1994 and 1995 surveys on the territory of Sagalassos, in: M. Waelkens and J. Poblome (eds) *Sagalassos IV. Report on the Survey and Excavation Campaigns of 1994 and 1995 (Acta Archaeologica Lovaniensia Monographiae* 9) Leuven University Press: 11-102.

M. Waelkens, P.M. Vermeersch, E. Paulissen, E.J. Owens, B. Arıkan, M. Martens, P. Talloen, L. Gijsen, L. Loots, C. Peleman, J. Poblome, R. Degeest, T.C. Patricio, S. Ercan and F. Depuydt (1997b) The 1994 and 1995 excavation seasons at Sagalassos, in: M. Waelkens and J. Poblome (eds) *Sagalassos IV. Report on the Survey and Excavation Campaigns of 1994 and 1995 (Acta Archaeologica Lovaniensia Monographiae* 9) Leuven University Press: 103-216.

M. Waelkens, E. Paulissen, H. Van Haverbeke, J. Reyniers, J. Poblome, R. Degeest, W.Viaene, J. Deckers, B. De Cupere, W. Van Neer, H.A. Ekinci, M.O. Erbay (2000) The 1996 and 1997 surveys, in: M. Waelkens and L. Loots (eds) *Sagalassos V. Report on the Survey and Excavation Campaigns of 1996 and 1997 (Acta Archaeologica Lovaniensia Monographiae* 11) Leuven University Press: 17-216.

J.C. Waldbaum (1978) *From Bronze to Iron. The Transition from the Bronze Age to the Iron Age in the Eastern Mediterranean*, Gothenborg.

P.M. Warren (1987) Absolute dating of the Aegean Late Bronze Age, *Archaeometry* 29/2: 205- 211.

H.T. Waterbolk (1983) Ten guidelines for the archaeological interpretation of radiocarbon dates, in: W.G. Mook and H.T. Waterbolk (eds) *Proceedings of the First International Symposium. 14C and Archaeology (PACT* 8) Strasbourg: 57-70.

H.T. Waterbolk (1987) Working with radiocarbon dates in southwestern Asia, in: O. Aurenche and J. Evin (eds) *Chronologies du Proche Orient/Chronologies in the Near East. C.N.R.S. International symposium, Lyon (France), 24-28 November 1986 (BAR International Series* 379) Oxford: 39-60.

H.T. Waterbolk (1990) Quality differences between radiocarbon laboratories illustrated on material from SW Asia and Egypt, in: W.G. Mook and H.T. Waterbolk (eds) *Proceedings of the Second International Symposium. 14C and Archaeology. Groningen 1987 (PACT* 29) Strasbourg: 141-157.

J. Yakar (1979) Troy and Anatolian Early Bronze Age chronology, *Anatolian Studies* 29: 51-67.

I. Yalçınkaya, J.M. Léotard, M. Kartal, M. Otte, O. Bar-Yosef, I. Carmi, A. Gautier, E. Gilot, P. Goldberg, J. Kozlowski, D. Lieberman, I. Lopez-Bayon, M. Pawlikowski, S. Thiebault, V. Ancion, M. Patou, A. Emery-Barbier and D. Bonjean (1995) Les occupations tardiglaciaires du site d'Öküzini (Sud-Ouest de la Turquie). Résultats préliminaires, *l'Anthropologie* 99/4: 562-583.

SAGALASSOS AND PISIDIA DURING THE LATE BRONZE AGE

Marc WAELKENS

Department of Archaelogy, KULeuven, Blijde Inkomststraat 21, B-3000 Leuven, Belgium

One of the most striking features of our surveys in the territory of Roman Sagalassos is the near total lack of surface remains that can be attributed to the Middle and the Later Bronze Age. A recent intensive survey in the territory of not too far distant Balboura to the southwest of Sagalassos produced similar negative results for the same period (Coulton 1988). Except for the site of Darsa (Yarımada, Ada Tepesi or Düğer Ada) near Düğer, that was just beyond the southwestern border of Sagalassian territory, there is no material evidence for Middle and Late Bronze Age occupation in the territory (Waelkens et al. 2000). Near Darsa, a mostly Early Bronze Age cemetery, which seems to have been also in use in the second millennium BC, was plundered in the 1960s. This necropolis also contained some Mycenaean imports, most probably imported via the Meander valley, as well as some local imitations, showing that the local inhabitants had established contacts with the Aegean and with the Mycenaean civilization. The site on the peninsula in Lake Yarışlı must thus have been an important Bronze Age site (Waelkens et al. 2000). Whether the site remained inhabited during the Middle Bronze Age is still uncertain. In the lake district, there is a hiatus in settlements towards the end of the Early Bronze Age (Goetze 1967²: 34), but at the latest during the Late Bronze Age, the settlement on the peninsula may have become one of the Arzawa settlements (see below).

Despite the lack of material evidence, it is scarcely possible that the territory of Roman Sagalassos could have been totally devoid of Middle and Late Bronze Age settlements. Previous palynological research has established that, near the beginning of the Late Bronze Age (3300 BP, uncalibrated date, or Cal. ca. ~1629 BC), the then dominant coniferous forest in Northern Pisidia was to some extent affected by human intervention, while various types of orchards were introduced in the same area (Waelkens and the Sagalassos team 1997: 233-234). More recent research has added to this picture (Eastwood et al. 1998). This period of increased anthropogenic activity, which has been called the 'Beyşehir occupation phase', characterized by forest clearance, crop cultivation (cereals and weeds) and arboriculture (walnut, olives, manna and vines, depending on the area), is documented from Lake Beyşehir in Pisidia to Lake Gölçük near Sardis (Lydia). This landscape clearance may have been started first near Lake Beyşehir, where it is already in evidence at ~3500 ^{14}C BP or Cal. ~1800 BC (Eastwood et al. 1998: 77). Drilling by our team in the Gravgaz marshes, ca. 25 km to the southwest of Sagalassos, showed that in the territory of this city, a deforestation phase took place somewhat later, at ca. 3200-2300 ^{14}C BP or Cal. ~1520/1430-410/240 BC and is characterized by the disappearance of pine pollen, the dominance of pollen of the *Artemisia herba-alpa* type (up to 50%), and the spread of *Quercus cerris* (Vermoere et al. 2000). Recent drilling at Lake Gölhisar near Kibyra produced a date for the beginning of the 'Beyşehir occupation phase' that was even more recent and almost synchronous with its appearance at nearby Pınarbaşı (to the west of Lake Burdur) and Lake Söğüt at ~3000 BP or Cal. 1240 BC (Eastwood et al. 1998: 77). Although climatic causes may have contributed, it is likely that human activity was also involved. It might suggest a gradual increase of farming and arboriculture starting in the Lake District and spreading towards the mountain zones of inner Pisidia, during the Late Bronze Age. Hittite sources clearly confirm that during this period, there were already some important settlements in Southwest-Anatolia, including Pisidia. The fact that, based on surface material, no such sites have so far been identified, may be explained by inefficient surveying techniques or undiagnostic pottery, but also by cultural superposition, whereby later, more considerable settlements have obliterated and completely covered older remains. For some settlements (Kolbasa and most probably Sagalassos, see below), this can be accepted as certain.

Darsa is a similar case: today the various surveys on the site have only produced surface material dated from the eight century BC to Roman Imperial times. Yet, the nearby

Bronze Age necropolis could neither be linked with surface material from Darsa, which is the most obvious location for the corresponding settlement, nor with any other site in the vicinity.

During the Bronze Age, Pisidia must have been settled by Indo-European Luwians (Bryce 1999: 54-55). These people, the predecessors of, *inter alia*, the Pisidians of classical times, occupied all of Southwest Anatolia, where they developed powerful states such as Arzawa, and in the oldest phase Kizzuwatna (eastern Cilicia), both located in the periphery of the Hittite kingdom (Goetze 1967[2]: 49, 179). The state of Arzawa, which was the largest and most populous region of Luwian settlement in Anatolia, seems to have dominated the western half the peninsula for long periods during the Middle Bronze Age (Gurney 1975: 16). According to Bryce (1999: 55) the whole Arzawa region during the fifteenth and fourteenth centuries, would only occasionally have formed confederacies for specific military purposes, without ever creating a united and politically coherent kingdom under the rule of a single king. Only during military episodes would the king of the heartland (Arzawa Minor) have become a kind of *primus inter pares* among the other chiefs and rulers of the Arzawa lands. Towards the end of the fourteenth century BC the once mighty Arzawa had been dissolved into at least four separate districts: Mira-Kuwaliya, Wilusa, Hapalla, and the lands of the river Seha (Goetze 1967[2]: 102; Wainwright 1954: 47). A recent study by Hawkins (1998) has produced a more varied picture of the development of Great Arzawa and of its various districts.

The first Hittite king, Labarna, may already have been involved in a military conflict with Arzawa, but after the death of Mursili I, the Hittite kingdom weakened and Arzawa was no longer threatened by Hittite expansion (Goetze 1967[2]: 84; Gurney 1975: 22; Cornelius 1990[4]: 101).

In the meantime, another new powerful 'state' had emerged in the west -Ahhiyawa- which sometimes joined forces with Arzawa against the Hittites (Goetze 1967[2]: 185). Until recently it was commonly accepted that Ahhiyawa could be conflated with the Mycenaean Greeks, either those of the mainland or those installed on the Anatolian coast and the offshore islands from where they sometimes ventured further inland, or both (Gurney 1975: 53; Freu 1987: 146; Bryce 1999: 59-61). The Anatolian west coast and the Aegean were already in close contact during the Late Bronze Age I-II, when Minoan influences reached the East Greek islands, from Patmos to Rhodes, and on the opposite coast, from Miletos to Knidos (Mountjoy 1998: 33). Miletos and Trianda (Rhodes) may even have been Minoan colonies (Niemeier 1998) or were at least part of a Minoan trading network. During the LM II / LH II B period, this Minoan presence gradually disappeared and the Mycenaean culture slowly took over. From the reign of Tudhaliya I/II onward the Anatolian coast was subject to the strongest Mycenaean influence so far known, in its so-called Upper Interface between the Aegean and Anatolian worlds, from Troy in the north down to Chios in the south, but especially in the Lower Interface, from Miletos down to Rhodes. According to Mountjoy (1998) however, this was not the result of a Mycenaean colonization, but of the fact that the local inhabitants of the East Aegean became absorbed into the Mycenaean culture, adopting its burial customs and pottery styles to produce a hybrid culture of their own. Based on a careful analysis of literary and archaeological evidence, she suggests that at some point this Lower Interface, that is coastal Anatolia and the offshore islands, presumably populated by Luwians who had undergone a strong Mycenaean acculturation, must have been formed into a maritime kingdom with two pivotal centres, Miletos, now firmly identified as Millawanda (see recently Hawkins 1998: 2), in the north and Rhodes, where Trianda may have been the capital, in the south. Mountjoy suggests that this was the kingdom known in Hittite sources as Ahhiyawa.

This kingdom is mentioned for the first time when, towards the beginning of the New Kingdom, an adventurer from Ahhiyawa, Attarissiyas, began to interfere in western Anatolia, most probably in the southwest of the area (Mountjoy 1998: 47, 51). From this time onwards the relations between the Hittites and Arzawa is fairly well documented. The whole event is described in detail in the so-called Indictment of Madduwata (Goetze 1928; Hawkins 1998: 25-26; Bryce 1999: 140-148). Previously, this episode was dated to the reign of Tudhaliya IV (last quarter of the thirteenth century BC) and his successor Arnuwanda III (end of the thirteenth century BC), shortly before the collapse of the Hittite state (Goetze 1928: 158; *idem* 1967[2]: 85; Gurney 1975: 38, 51; Waelkens and the Sagalassos team 1997: 234-235). Later, however, it was attributed firmly to the fifteenth-fourteenth centuries BC. Hoffmann suggested a date under Suppiluliuma I (1984), but it was finally shown by Otten that the episode took place during the reigns of Tudhaliya I/II and his son Arnuwanda I, i.e. during the first half of the fourteenth century BC (Otten 1967: 62; Otten 1969: 36; Gurney 1982: 561-563; Freu 1987: 124-125, 136; Forlanini 1988: 162; Bryce 1999: 140).

According to the so-called Indictment, a local Arzawan ruler, Madduwata, driven out of his chiefdom by Attarissiyas, fled to the Hittites and received from them a small vassal state made up of the mountain land Zippasla and later also the land of the Siyanta river, both presumably strategic in nature and apparently located close to Arzawa. His Arzawan neighbour, Kupanta-Kurunta, got mixed up in the tortuous affairs of Madduwata, first as his enemy, later as his ally. In fact, still during the reign of Tudhaliya I/II and in direct violation of his status as a vassal of the Hittite king, Madduwata invaded the territory of Kupanta-Kurunta, but his expedition ended in disaster and the invader had to flee for his life, whereupon his territory was occupied by the Arzawan ruler. However, Tudhaliya I/II came to his rescue, driving Kupanta-Kurunta back to his own land and restoring Madduwata, to his vassal throne. The fact that Madduwata was not punished may have been because Arzawa at that time posed a continuing threat to the security of Hittite-controlled territory and that Madduwata's actions provided Tudhaliya with an excuse for inflicting a resounding defeat on the Arzawan king (Bryce 1999: 143). He may even have conquered some territory in the borderland between classical Lycia and Caria to the west of Fethiye (Hawkins 1998: 28), although most of Arzawa remained independent. Tudhaliya rescued Madduwata a second time, when Attarissiyas invaded Hittite territory with the aim of capturing and killing Madduwata. The latter, instead of opposing Attarissiyas, fled once more but, despite his failure to defend his own territory, was restored a second time to his vassal throne. Later, Madduwata ambushed a Hittite army to which he had promised his help and that was moving against the rebel cities of Talawa and Hinduwa, that were at least nominally subject to Tudhaliya, possibly in revenge for Hittite troops remaining in the area to keep an eye on him. His treason ended by killing its two commanders. Amazingly, the Hittite king did not intervene to punish the treacherous vassal, who even concluded a peace with the Arzawan king Kupanta-Kurunta and sealed it by a marriage alliance with his daughter. Perhaps through a combination of force and diplomacy he eventually took over Arzawa and added it to his own kingdom. However, he still acknowledged Hittite overlordship.

During the reign of Tudhaliya's successor, Arnuwanda I, another kingdom of the Arzawan complex, Hapalla, which lay close to Madduwata's own state, became hostile to the Hittites. At Arnuwanda's request, Madduwata conquered Hapalla but added it to his own realm, as he did with a group of lands in the border area of classical Caria and Lycia that were also claimed by the Hittites who may have seized them during Tudhaliya's Arzawa campaign (Hawkins 1998: 25, 28). He even won the elders of the Land of Pitassa, part of the Hittite realm, away from their Hittite allegiance. In the end, he was forced to return Hapalla, but then, in collaboration with his former enemy, Attarissiyas from Ahhiyawa, he raided Cyprus (Alasiya), which however, he may have returned to Hittite control (Bryce 1999: 146-147).

Shortly before the middle of the fourteenth century BC, Arzawa appears not to have been a unified state. Power seems to have been shared by competing princes, while some parts of it (Hapalla, Madduwata's kingdom) still recognized Hittite suzerainty. However, the fact that the Hittite kings did not really intervene, when their control over the area had clearly slipped out of their hands, shows that Arzawa was emerging as a formidable force, slowly eating away at the peripheral subject territories of the Hittites.

In the reign of Aruwanda's son and successor, Tudhaliya III, around the middle of the fourteenth century BC, the Hittite New Kingdom faced a first major crisis in its history and was confronted with disaster and invasions. When the Kaskans attacked from the north and sacked Hattusa, the forces of Arzawa, built up since the reign of Arnuwanda, overran the Lower Land and the southern territories of the Hittite kingdom, establishing their power as far as Tuwanuwa (classical Tyana) near the Cilician gates. This meant that most of southern Anatolia was taken over by Arzawa. This state emerged as a dominant force in the region, which is clearly shown by the diplomatic overtures made by the Egyptian pharaoh Amenophis III towards the king of Arzawa, Tarhundaradu, even seeking one of his daughters in marriage to cement an alliance between Egypt and Arzawa (Hawkins 1998: 10; Bryce 1999: 160-161). Since the two rulers corresponded on equal terms (Wainwright 1954: 47; Gurney 1975: 5, 28), this might suggest that Tarhundaradu had become the sole ruler of a unified Arzawan state. For a short time, he may have ruled over most of the Luwian-speaking territories in Anatolia.

But, before Tarhundaradu could capitalize on his military successes, Tudhaliya III embarked on a military campaign to recover his lost territories and, together with his son and successor Suppiluliuma, laid the foundations for a completely changed political landscape in the Near East. It was Suppiluliuma who eventually stopped the Arzawa army and recovered the south. After securing the Hittite homeland and its northern boundaries, he conquered the city of Sallapa (according to some, Gözören in Lycaonia: Bryce 1999: 163 n. 90; according to others, Sivrihisar in Galatia: Hawkins 1998: 22) at the border with Arzawan held territories and gradually re-established Hittite control over the Lower Land. However, Arzawan military resources were so substantial that it may have taken Suppiluliuma twenty years to recover all lost territories (Bryce 1999: 164-165). In fact, his Arzawa campaigns continued into his own reign and were partly carried out by his general Hannutti. During these hostilities, a number of Arzawan princedoms are mentioned. One of them was Hapalla, which was conquered by Hannuti. Based on its location in the military campaign, Hawkins recently suggested its identification with the Lake District in Pisidia (between the Sultan Dağları and Lakes Eğirdir and Beyşehir). Another princedom that appeared for the first time during this period, was Mira, whose prince Mashuiluwa fled to Suppiluliuma. At this time, Arzawa Minor, the nucleus of Arzawa, was apparently ruled by a king called Uhhaziti, who may not have directly controlled the other Arzawa lands (Hawkins 1998: 14). The second Mursili's later claim on Attarimma (probably Telmessos, see Hawkins 1998: 26) might suggest that Suppiluliuma had even campaigned in the Carian-Lycian borderland (Hawkins 1998: 28).

In any case, it was Suppiluliuma, who during the second half of the fourteenth century BC transformed the Hittite state into a superpower again (Cornelius 1990[4]: 132-135, 140-143; Freu 1987: 127; Bryce 1999: 168-205). He also refined the system of vassal states and according to Cornelius would even have imposed this status on Arzawa. This might be reflected in the fact that Suppiluliuma's son, Mursili II, during a dispute between two princes for the succession in one of the northern Arzawa states, the Seha River Land, was able to place one of them, Manapa-Tarhunda, on the throne. If Arzawa had still been a unified state at this time, this intervention would have been highly improbable. Suppiluliuma also managed to make a treaty with Kizzuwatna and recreated it as an autonomous state, which he recognized as an equal partner. It formed thenceforth a buffer against the Mitanni and against Arzawa. It was only during the second half of his reign that he eventually also annexed Kizzuwatna itself (Cornelius 1990[4] : 145-147).

Another district of southwest Anatolia that is mentioned in Hittite sources during the fourteenth-thirteenth century BC, sometimes as an ally, but often as an enemy, is Luqqã (Lukka) or Lukki. Lukka was never an organized political entity, nor a state with a clearly defined political organization with which the Hittites could make treaties. It was rather a conglomerate of Luwian communities with close ethnic affinities living in the same area. They later formed the main ethnic component of the classical Lycians. Some of these Lukka people may have been subjected to certain of the Hittite kings following their Arzawa campaigns (Tudhaliya I/II, Suppiluliuma, Mursilis?), but most of the time they may have been under little more than nominal control (Bryce 1999: 56-57). They were apparently a difficult people, experienced in seafaring and often resorting to piracy. At some time during the reign of Suppiluliuma, the king of Alasiya (Cyprus) complained to Akhenaton of Egypt about Lukka attacks on Cyprus. They may even have played a role in Madduwatta's raids on the island. Later, Lukka men participated as allies of Muwatalli at the battle of Qadesh.

Suppiluliuma's second successor Mursili II (later fourteenth-beginning of the thirteenth century BC) restricted the diplomatic and military freedom of Arzawa considerably, but the country remained autonomous as far as its internal policy went (Goetze 1967[2]: 98-99, 102; Cornelius 1990[4]: 177-179, 198-199, 208, 215). This was after the king had crushed Arzawa in a campaign which lasted two years (Hawkins 1998: 14-15; Bryce 1999:209-214). The *casus belli* was the Arzawan king Uhhaziti's refusal to surrender Hittite rebels from three cities, one of which was the city of Attarimma (Telmessos?). According to Bryce, Uhhaziti, apparently in collaboration with the king of Ahhiyawa, attempted to win Hittite subject states in southwest Anatolia away from their allegiance to Mursili. Mursili's itinerary took him to Sallapa (see above) from where he reached Walma on the river Astarpa, where he defeated Uhhaziti's son Piyama-Kurunta. This river henceforth would form one of the boundaries of the state of Mira-Kuwaliya (Hawkins 1998: 22, 24; Bryce 1999: 210 n. 12) and according to Hawkins and others, should be identified with the Akar Çayı in southern Phrygia (Hawkins 1998: 22). At the end of this first year, Mursili also conquered Arzawa's capital Apasa (Ephesos according to Güterbock 1983; Cornelius 1990[4]: 177; rejected by Freu 1987: 127; Habesos near Kaş on the Lycian coast according to Freu 1987: 147; Forlanini 1988: 167; Gurney 1997: 135; now convincingly identified with Ephesos by Hawkins 1998: 1, 22-23). Uhhaziti fled from Apasa to one of the Aegean islands of the Ahhiyawa, where he died. After the winter, Mursili completed his campaign: he mopped up the last resistance in Uhhaziti's former kingdom of Arzawa Minor which according to Bryce (1999:214) may have been completely depopulated and possibly even disappeared forever. During these hostilities Millawanda (Miletos), which may already have belonged to Ahhiyawa during Mursili's reign (Mountjoy 1998: 50-51), seems also to have been raided by Hittite generals and destroyed (Hawkins 1998: 28). Mursili II may even have conquered part of Ahhiyawa itself (Gurney 1975: 47).

The hieroglyphic inscriptions and reliefs from the pass of Karabel in the Tmolos range between Ephesos and Sardis, have been recently attributed to kings of Mira, one of the Arzawa states emerging after Mursili's intervention. This state therefore may be considered as the successor of Arzawa Minor surviving, at least in part, under a different name and dynasty (Hawkins 1998: 1). At the end of his campaign, Mursili reorganized Arzawa and installed Hittite nominees in its various chiefdoms. Despite the fact that he had allied himself with Uhhaziti, Manapa-Tarhunda was reconfirmed as ruler of the Seha River land. According to the recently deciphered Karabel inscription this land cannot have been the Meander valley, as had been assumed, but was apparently the Hermos valley and may have been a predecessor of the Early Iron Age Lydian kingdom. The Seha River land may also have included the Kaikos and even the Makestos valleys (Hawkins 1998: 2, 23-24, 28). The land of Hapalla (in the Lake District?) was given to Targasnali, and prince Mashuiluwa, who had sought help from Suppiluliuma whose daughter he eventually married (Gurney 1975: 32-33), was placed on the throne of the new state of Mira-Kuwaliya (Hawkins 1998: 14-15; Bryce 1999: 212-213).

Hawkins believes that this new kingdom incorporated the rump of the former Arzawa Minor (also Heinhold-Krahmer 1977: 136-147, 211-219) and would have reached from the neighbourhood of Afyon in Phrygia to the coast. The Meander valley would thus have been the spine of the state and the backbone of its communications, making it possible to control such a vast area (Hawkins 1998: 1, 24). However, some of the Arzawa leaders proved to be unreliable again, since ten years later Mashuiluwa instigated anti-Hittite intrigues in Pitassa, as Madduwata had previously. Eventually he was replaced by his nephew and adopted son Kupanta-Kurunta whom Muwatalli united under oath with the two other Arzawan rulers (Hawkins 1998:15; Bryce 1999: 230-234).

According to Heinhold-Krahmer and Hawkins (1998: 15-16), the three vassal states created by Mursili II in the former Arzawa area may not have been 'kingdoms', but only 'dukedoms', while their rulers, established on the throne by Mursili II, were at first only 'lords' subject to the Hittite king.

It comes as no surprise therefore that at the battle of Qadesh (1274 BC), Arzawa is mentioned as having provided auxiliary troops against Ramesses II to Mursili's son, Muwatalli II (early thirteenth century BC) (Goetze 1967[2]:12). But, in the early years of Muwatalli's reign, a certain Piyamaradu, according to Bryce (1999: 244) a renegade Hittite of high birth, but according to others an Arzawan prince, possibly even of the royal line of Uhhaziti (Hawkins 1998: 17), stirred up trouble again in the west. He had managed to take Wilusa, apparently located in the Troad (Bryce 1999: 245), which seems to have remained loyal to the Hittites from the time of Labarna onward (Gurney 1975: 34; Cornelius 1990[4]: 228). But the rulers of the Seha River land and of Mira-Kupaliya opposed Piyamaradu and helped to drive him out of the region (Hawkins 1998: 16; Bryce 1999: 244-248).

Muwatalli confirmed the Arzawa princes in their positions and drew up a new treaty with the legitimate heir to the throne of Wilusa, Alaksandu. The stability created by Mursili's Arzawa settlement and the reliability of its alliances may in fact have enabled Muwatalli II to establish control over this more remote western country. This treaty is significant in that it now addresses the four rulers in western Anatolia (Alaksandu of Wilusa, Kupanta-Kurunta of Mira-Kuwaliya, the new ruler Urahatusa of Hapalla, and Manapa-Tarhunda of the Seha River land, who later in Muwatalli's reign was deposed by the Hittite king in favour of his son, Masturi) as the four kings in the Arzawa lands (Hawkins 1998: 16). As far as can be judged, Mursili's political settlement may even have lasted into the reign of his grandson Tudhaliya IV, in the later thirteenth century BC (Hawkins 1998: 10, 15). In the middle of his reign, Muwatalli moved his capital from Hattusa to the city of Tarhuntassa (or Dattassa) in Cilicia, closer to the North Syrian provinces and further away from the constant threat of the Kaskans in the north, and appointed his brother Hattusili as ruler of the northern regions in the face of the Kaskan threat (Bryce 1999: 251-255).

Hattusili dominated the short reign of his nephew Urhi-Tesub, the son of Muwatalli and a concubine, who adopted the name Mursili (III) and moved the capital back to Hattusa (Bryce 1999: 277-280). After seven years of submission however, he usurped the throne for another thirty years reigning as Hattusili III. The king installed Muwatalli's second son Kurunta (or Ulmi-Teshup) as king of the newly created kingdom of Tarhuntassa (named after its capital, for a short time also the capital of Hatti), which was made into a vassal state, and thus inherited the role of buffer state previously attributed to Kizzuwatna. It controlled the south Anatolian coast from Perge in the west to Kizzuwatna in the east and may have extended inland almost as far as Konya (Hawkins 1995: 52). In the Arzawa lands Hattusili's usurpation of the throne did not go unnoticed. Masturi, who had been forced by Urhi-Tesub to accept his deposed father's return to River Seha land (Bryce 1999: 278), understandably supported Hattusili III, but Kupanta-Kurunta of Mira remained loyal to Urhi-tesub (Hawkins 1998: 17).

The surviving fragments of the king's annals also mention a major uprising in the Lukka lands, which rebellion extended all over classical Lycaonia, Pisidia and Lycia. These annals mention that the Lukka lands were overrun by an enemy (according to Forlanini 1988: 157: Piyamaradu; see also Bryce 1999: 320 n. 82), who eventually even moved into Hittite territory as far as Watarwa, Nahita and Sallusa. Kuwalapassa was also invaded (Freu 1987: 130-131, 139; Hawkins 1995: 56; Gurney 1997: 132). Hattusilis III lost many formerly Hittite territories and had to undertake military operations against Lukka and/or Arzawa which had apparently regained its independence (Gurney 1975: 37; Freu 1987: 131). During this campaign, the Hittite king went as far as Kuwalapassa, which he left because of lack of water (Forlanini 1988: 158; Hawkins 1995: 56; Gurney 1997: 131-133). This must have been located immediately to the south of Sagalassos (see below).

Whether or not this enemy was in fact Piyamaradu, the latter was involved in contemporary problems involving the Lukka people, as is shown by the so-called Tawagalawa letter, now generally recognized as having been written by Hattusili III to a king of Ahhiyawa (Forlanini 1988: 157; Gurney 1997; Hawkins 1998: 17; Bryce 1999: 321-324). By the time of the reign of Hattusili III, Ahhiyawa did control Millawanda (Miletos) as part of its kingdom and Ahhiyawa's king was then recognized as a Great King, in contrast to the kings of

Mira-Kuwaliya and the Seha River land who, despite their royal titles, still had vassal status (Mountjoy 1998: 51). At the time of the Lukka uprising, the Ahhiyawa king's brother Tawagalawa resided in the coastal part of Ahhiyawa (according to Cornelius 1990[4]: 218, somewhere in Pamphylia), while Millawanda then was governed by a certain Atpa. Atpa had married the daughter of the former usurper of Wilusa's throne, Piyamaradu. The events in the Tawagalawa letter suggest that Piyamaradu was involved in the Lukka uprising. As Hattusili III prepared to retaliate against the rebellion, Piyamaradu seems to have taken some of their fugitives to Tawagalawa for asylum, but at the same time forcibly removed some loyal Hittite subjects from their homeland (he destroyed Attarima/Telmessos?). These then appealed to Tawagalawa and to Hattusili III to rescue them, and both of them came (Hawkins 1998: 26). The Hittite king moved to Sallapa and only when Piyamaradu refused to submit to him and even asked to receive a kingdom (perhaps Mira-Kuwaliya, whose ruler had remained faithful to Urhi-Tesub or may have died in the mean time as Hawkins 1998: 17 n. 17 suggested), did Hattusili continue westwards. From Waliwanda he sent an unsuccessful ultimatum to Piyamaradu who had occupied Iyalanda (probably classical Alinda in Caria, see Hawkins 1998: 21, 26). Hattusili thus proceeded to conquer Iyalanda and went to Millawanda to ask Atpa to hand over Piyamaradu, his father-in-law. Piyamaradu, who was clearly supported by the king of Ahhiyawa, could escape to one of its islands, from where he apparently continued to raid Hittite held territory after Hattusili's unsuccessful campaign. The fact that Piyamaradu's actions remained unpunished shows how shaky the Hittites' hold of their western territories had become (Bryce 1999: 331).

Shortly after his accession to the throne, Hattusili's son, Tudhaliya IV (last quarter of the thirteenth century BC) renewed the treaty with Kurunta of Tarhuntassa. Among the witnesses of the treaty were two of the Arzawa kings: Masturi, king of the Seha River land, and Alantalli, king of Mira, who may have been a son of Kupanta-Kurunta (Hawkins 1998: 17). This treaty, preserved on the famous bronze tablet discovered at Hattusa in 1986 (Otten 1988), gives a detailed description of the state of Tarhuntassa and of its boundaries. The western boundary (according to Otten, bordering Arzawa, but according to Cornelius bordering the Lukka lands (Cornelius 1990[4]: 241)), was formed by the Ka-as-ta-ra-ia-as or Kastraja river, which corresponds with the Kestros (Aksu) of classical times. Cornelius' hypothesis seems to be confirmed by a recently discovered hieroglyphic text at Yalburt (Hawkins 1995: 55-56). On the other side of the Kestros river lay the city of Parha, which is Pamphylian Perge (see Hawkins 1995: 51 n. 178). The Hittite king guaranteed that whatever land Kurunta could conquer on that side of the river (i.e. Pisidia and western Pamphylia), would remain in his power (Otten 1988: 37). This western boundary of Tarhuntassa must have come very close to Sagalassos, whose eastern territorial boundary in classical times was formed by the Kestros, one of the main tributaries of which originated near the city. According to Hawkins (1995: 52) the boundary went inland, up the Aksu valley as far as the neighbourhood of Akşehir.

The recently discovered Luwian hieroglyphic inscription from Yalburt (Poetto 1993) shows that Tudhaliya IV himself campaigned in Lycia and went as far as Awarna/Xanthos, Pinali/Pinara and Talawa/Tlos in the Lukka lands, and Wiyanawanda/Oenoanda, located according to Bryce (1999: 337 n. 43) in the border zone of the kingdom of Mira-Kuwaliya, where he forced submission on women and children. This submission, together with the attack on Awarna and Pinali, is also mentioned in a contemporary hieroglyphic text from Emirgazı (Hawkins 1995: 49-50, 66; Gurney 1997: 136; Bryce 1999: 336). References to "the hostages of Awarna and Pinali" in the so-called Milawata (Milawanda) letter sent to the ruler of this place, now securely date this letter to Tudhaliya's reign (Hawkins 1998: 19; Bryce 1999: 340).

From this letter it becomes clear that the father of its recipient had been at war with Tudhaliya: in fact he exchanged hostages from Awarna and Pinali held by the Hittite king for hostages which he had taken himself in Hittite controlled territory, at U(tima) and At(riya) (Hawkins 1998: 27: Idyma and Idrias/Stratonikeia in Caria). He also seems to have intervened against Hittite interests in the kingdom of Wilusa. In the past, the recipient of this Milawata letter, whom the Hittite king apparently had put on the throne, has been identified as a ruler of the Seha River land (Singer 1983: 214-216) or as a putative son of Atpa of Millawanda (Bryce 1985: 39-44; 1999: 341-342). Bryce even suggests, from the way in which Tudhaliya addresses the recipient, that the king had been reduced to an unprecedented power-sharing in the west (against Ahhiyawa), whereby a local ruler was being granted direct authority over at least one other vassal kingdom (Wilusa) in the region. The fact that Millawanda would have been under the control of a king appointed by the Hittite Great King would have seriously curtailed, if not terminated Ahhiyawa's power (Bryce 1999: 342-343). Yet, recent studies might suggest that Ahhiyawa continued to flourish even after the Hittite collapse (Mountjoy 1998; see below). Moreover, Hawkins has recently suggested the identification of the recipient of the Milawata letter as the king of Mira, whose name he had read in the Karabel hieroglyphic inscription as Tarkasnawa and whom he supposes to have been the son of king Alantalli, one of the witnesses in Tudhaliya's treaty with Kurunta (Hawkins 1998: 18-19). In his view, the royal line of Mira thus would have defected again from Tudhaliya IV. It is known that Tudhaliya IV also had to intervene in another of the Arzawan kingdoms, the Seha River land, where with the support of Ahhiyawa, an usurper Tarhunaradu had seized the throne and rebelled against the Hittites. His attempt failed and Tudhaliya claims to have restored a member of the old royal family to this vassal throne (Bryce 1999: 338-339).

All this indicates a new political situation in western Anatolia towards the end of the thirteenth century BC, in which Hittite power started to wane again. Tudhaliya's son and the last Hittite king, Suppiluliuma II (late thirteenth-early twelfth century BC), in his turn also undertook a wide-ranging military campaign from the Lukka lands in the southwest to Tarhuntassa in the south and claimed to have annexed both (Hawkins 1995: 61; Gurney 1997: 136). It has been shown recently that Kurunta of Tarhuntassa eventually took the title of Great King, while it has also been suggested that the Great King Hartapu of Karadağ-Kızıldağ was another ruler of Tarhuntassa before rather than after the fall of Hattusa and the end of the Hittite Empire (Hawkins 1998: 20). Some evidence suggests that in the last years of Hittite power, Tarhuntassa might have become a hostile force (Bryce 1999: 354-355, 364). Hawkins even suggests the possibility that during the reign of Suppiluliuma II a third superpower, after that of the Hittites and Tarhuntassa, may have emerged in the West. In his opinion, king Parhuitta, an Arzawan who according to a letter sent to him by a Hittite king, had almost acquired the status of a Great King, was not a ruler of Millawanda or the Seha River land, as assumed by others, but may have been a successor to Tarkasnawa of Mira, and a contemporary of Suppiluliuma II, who had managed to create another Great Arzawa. Hawkins thus regards it as possible that towards the end of the Late Bronze Age Mira-Arzawa revived as a major power, a clear match for Tarhuntassa and even Hattusa (Hawkins 1998: 20-21). If his identification of the recipient of the Milawata letter is correct, this process would already have been prepared under Tudhaliya IV.

All this indicates that conditions were very unsettled in Southwest Anatolia towards the end of the Late Bronze Age, which must have also affected the area around Sagalassos (including Kolbasa). During the late thirteenth century BC, the Lukka are mentioned in Egyptian sources among the Sea Peoples (Bryce 1974a: 395-397). It has been assumed that whatever remained of Arzawa most probably disappeared in the general turmoil around 1200 BC (Goetze 1967[2]: 185). In fact, Arzawa is one of the countries recorded as being destroyed by the Sea Peoples in the eighth year of Ramesses III (Hawkins 1998: 21).

However, the Dark Ages may have been less dark than is generally assumed, and it is possible that some of the old states continued to exist, although perhaps on a reduced scale, right into the Early Iron Age. The lack of material remains should not be considered as an indication to the contrary since, except for the Karabel reliefs, hardly any material remains have thus far come to light from any of the Arzawan states mentioned above. The kingdom of the River Seha land might eventually have been succeeded by the Heraclid kingdom of the Lydians. A recent study by Mountjoy also showed that in the post-Hittite phase, during the Early to Middle LH III C period (ca. 1190-1070 BC), the activities of the Sea Peoples had hardly affected the Lower Interface, identified by her as the kingdom of Ahhiyawa. With the exception of Rhodes, which started to produce a completely different pottery style, the rest of the former territories of Mountjoy's Ahhiyawa reveal a flourishing pottery style which is very homogeneous and has been called by her "the East Aegean Koine". The typology and decoration of this suggests a continuity of inhabitants and only Rhodes may have been populated by newcomers with Minoan interests. Unless the kingdom of Ahhiyawa had been fragmented, perhaps as the result of the activities of the Sea Peoples, with Rhodes henceforth acting as a separate unit, Mountjoy suggests that it is possible that the kingdom was still a unit in early post-Hittite times.

The Lukka people as well, together perhaps with some immigrants from the Aegean, may also have continued to live in their homeland. The same was probably the case with the Luwian population of what was to become Pisidia. But further east also the Luwian element was not extinguished as a political force: the kingdom of Tarhuntassa may even have survived for centuries after the Hittite collapse (Bryce 1999: 382-383). Further research in Anatolia should reveal whether some of the former Arzawan states continued to exist to some extent as well.

Many of the above-mentioned events clearly took place in Pisidia, although it is very difficult to identify the toponyms with any degree of certainty. Part of the problem may be the fact that the Hittite activities in the area took place over a longer span of time, during which the boundaries of states such as Arzawa or the Lukka lands probably changed several times, while the local toponymy may also have undergone changes.

As far as the larger geographical or political units are concerned, there has been much discussion concerning the exact location of (Great) Arzawa. Goetze located it between the mountains to the southwest of Konya and the Mediterranean (Goetze 1928: 148-149, 153). In his opinion, the eastern districts of Arzawa thus included Pisidia, Pamphylia and Isauria, while its western boundary would be formed by the Mediterranean. Wainwright (following Garstang) even considered Pisidia to have been the centre of Arzawa, which in his opinion extended from the inland plains to the north of the Taurus as far as the coast (Wainwright 1954: 46).

Freu identified Arzawa Minor with eastern Lycia and Pamphylia, so that it must have adjoined Pisidia (Freu 1987: 148). Forlanini considered it to have corresponded with the district between Afyon, Lycia, the middle Hermos and the middle Meander, thus including Pisidia (Forlanini 1988: 166). Only Cornelius, who had equated Pitassa with Pisidia (1958: 393, 396; 1990[4]: 198), located the country further west, that is, in the valley of the Gediz Çayı (Hermos) and in the valleys around Miletos and Ephesos (Cornelius 1976: 20). Macqueen considered two alternatives: Arzawa Minor was either located to the southwest of the Salt Lake reaching as far as the Pamphylian and Lycian coast, which he considered doubtful however, because of the lack of physical evidence of its settlements, or it lay in the area of classical Lydia along the Aegean coast around classical Ephesos and Smyrna (Macqueen 1996: 38-39, figs. 21-22).

Hawkins' recent reading of the Karabel hieroglyphs (1998) had led him to suppose that Arzawa Minor formed the backbone of Mira-Kuwaliya. If this is so, then it must have corresponded roughly with the Kaystros and Meander valleys between Ephesos and Dinar. Greater Arzawa then must have extended beyond the Meander valley and roughly have covered the district proposed by Goetze.

Today, most scholars agree that Pitassa or Pedassa, a Hittite dependency which formed a kind of buffer between the Hittite homelands and Arzawa, was located to the west or northwest of the Tuz Gölü -according to Hawkins (1998: 22) even more precisely between Polatlı and Kadınhanı- perhaps overlapping with parts of Pisidia (so Bryce 1974a: 397; Forlanini 1988: 150, 153, 160). Only Forlanini located it in the mountain and lake area to the southeast of Konya (Forlanini 1988: 150). In either case, Greater Arzawa, which adjoined Pitassa, must have comprised parts of northern or northwest Pisidia, including the territory of classical Sagalassos.

The Lukka lands, which played a major role during the thirteenth century BC, are difficult to locate since they never formed an organized state. To the Hittites, the Lukka lands were a rather vague term, for a group of Luwian-speaking countries in southwestern Anatolia, including Lycia and parts of Pisidia and even Pamphylia, and without clear political boundaries (Gurney 1997: 135-136, 139). They were located by some in Caria and perhaps also in western Lycia (Freu 1987: 148), but by others further east, in a wider area including southwest Lycaonia, Pisidia, Pamphylia and Lycia (see Bryce 1974a: 397; 1999: 56), or including parts of Pisidia (between the lakes and Pamphylia), Rough Cilicia (also Cornelius 1958: 381) and Isauria (Forlanini 1988: 163, 166). Others believe that they corresponded with Lycaonia only (Cornelius 1958: 381). That the Lukka territory in a wider sense possibly reached as far as Konya is suggested by a late Imperial (Suppiluliuma II) hieroglyphic inscription from Hattusa (Hawkins 1995: 29). Forlanini wrongly believed that Millawanda, from where Piyamaradu invaded the Lukka lands, was not Miletos, as is generally accepted now, but the Milyas (1988: 164). Gurney considered this suggestion to be rather improbable mainly since the Milyas (except for Darsa?) left no material remains from this period (Gurney 1997: 136). Still others believe that the geographical distribution of the Lukka people may have varied chronologically and that, since they never formed a unified and organized 'state', the Lukka people may have established themselves at various stages in both Lycia and Lycaonia (Bryce 1974a: 404; Freu 1987: 131; Cornelius 1990[4]: 262-263; Gurney 1997; Bryce 1999: 56, 320-321). Gurney was at first reluctant to accept the equation of Lycia with the Lukka lands (Gurney 1975: 47, 56). Yet, the recently published Luwian hieroglyphic text from Yalburt (Poetto 1993) recording a military campaign of Tudhaliya IV as far as Lycian Awarna/Xanthos, Pinali/Pinara, Talawa/Tlos and Wiyanawanda/Oenoanda in the Pisido-Lycian border land (Kabalis), implies clearly that the latter are to be located generally in classical Lycia. In this text, Wiyanawanda is mentioned in juxtaposition with the Lukka lands, which is also the case in the second Suppiluliuma's hieroglyphic text from Hattusa (Hawkins 1995: 49, 54; Gurney 1997: 139). Finally, Gurney also realized that, during the reign of Hattusili III, the Lukka lands were closely involved in the military events around Kuwalapassa (Kolbasa), either as attackers or as victims (Gurney 1997: 132, 138). Towards the end of the Hittite Empire, Lukka thus may have corresponded specifically with Lycia, perhaps including also western Pamphylia as far as the Kestros river, as well as central-southern Pisidia (Hawkins 1995: 55; see Gurney 1997: 135). In the reign of Hattusili III they had certainly invaded the country of Kolbasa, immediately south of Sagalassos.

Gurney believes that the Lukka lands were originally part of Arzawa but that, after the Hittites' conquest of this state (Mursili II), they had been occupied by the Lycians who, during the dark ages following the collapse of the Hittites, would have pushed even into Lycaonia.

Whatever the changes, Sagalassos must have been located in Great Arzawa, and at one stage even in or near Arzawa Minor. Later it must have temporarily adjoined (or even have been located in) the Lukka lands.

Towards the beginning of the Late Bronze Age however, the site must have been located in the region where some of Madduwata's military actions took place. Zippasla, the power base of Madduwata, is located by Goetze in Southern Phrygia (Goetze 1928: 148-149, 153) and by Freu (1987: 126) "near Pisidia", while Cornelius even located another of his fiefs, i.e. the land of the Siyanta river, in the plain of Burdur, so that this river would have corresponded with the

Lysis of classical times (Cornelius 1990[4]: 22, 265). Freu also postulated its location in the vicinity of the Pisidian lakes (1987: 149).

According to the Annals of Mursili II, the Siyanta river apparently formed the boundary of Great Arzawa and later of Mira, while the Astarpa river, which the Hittite armies usually reached coming from Sallapa, would have formed the boundary of Kuwaliya, joined by Mursili II to Mira to form a single vassal state (Bryce 1974b; Freu 1987: 128; Hawkins 1998: 22). As we have mentioned above, some scholars locate Sallapa in Lycaonia, but Hawkins, who assumes that Mira-Kuwaliya extended far in a northeast direction, rather followed Garstang and identified Sallapa with Sivrihisar (Spalia) and Astarpa with the Akar Çayı to the south of Afyon. In his opinion however, the Siyanta river was probably not the Banaz Çayı, as Garstang had proposed, but one of the upper tributaries of the Sakarya, either the Porsuk (Tembris), or the Seydi Çayı (Parthenios). The latter alternative would have included in Mira the site of Malatça Höyük, a Bronze Age mound, which eventually became the Byzantine city of Meiros and is viewed by some as a late survival of Mira. But, as Hawkins stressed, it is hard to believe that such a remote eastern site could have given its name to the state of Mira. Despite these doubts, Hawkins locates Mira and the Siyanta river in this general area, which would mean that Madduwata's fief was located somewhere in the Phrygian Highlands. Macqueen also located Mira in the Afyon-Kütahya area (1996: 55). Kuwaliya is located by Hawkins along the upper branches of the Meander, between Dinar and the Akar Çayı. In his opinion, Beycesultan could have been a city, if not the principal city, of Kuwaliya, although he also considers it possible that it was a part of Mira (Hawkins 1998: 22, 24 fig. 11).

Whatever the exact locations of the Siyanta river and of Kuwaliya, a closer look at the geographical descriptions in the Madduwatta text indicates that the core of his power base in the territory of Mount Zippasla and the Siyanta River land must have adjoined Hapalla which was seized by Madduwata (see Hawkins 1998: 25 n. 153). Hapalla has been located rather convincingly by Hawkins in the Lake District to the northeast of Sagalassos (so also Macqueen 1996: 55), and rather close to Pitassa (still further northeast), where Madduwata instigated a rebellion against the Hittites. On the other hand, his original vassal state also adjoined Arzawa Minor (the Meander valley) and the Lycian-Carian border district of classical times (with Attarimma/Telmessos?, Dalawa/Tlos, Hinduwa) which he both invaded. Finally, this original fief was located in a region where he could easily be attacked from Ahhiyawa (Attarissiyas). The only region which seems to fulfil all these topographical requirements seems to me to have been the border area comprising South Phrygia (Dinar) and Northwest Pisidia (the district around Lake Burdur). This might even be confirmed by the toponyms of the text. A location in the Phrygian Highlands does not seem to be a possibility.

The Madduwata text tells how this ruler attacked king Kupanta-Kurunta of Arzawa, but was defeated by him. He managed to escape, but his complete household (wife, children and slaves), who fled into the mountains, was eventually taken captive. The Hittite king sent a military force to help Madduwata. This auxiliary force rescued the latter's household in a place called Sallawassa (Sal-la-u-ua-as-si), where in turn the household and all the possessions of Kupanta-Kurunta of Arzawa fell into Hittite hands and were given to Madduwata (Goetze 1928: 15 '10 vs. 54-55; '11 vs. 58). As we have mentioned above, Madduwata was reinstated in power, but shortly afterwards initiated a military conflict with the ruler of Ahhiyawa, named Attaris(s)ijas, who had previously chased Madduwata out of his first chiefdom. Once more, he was saved by a Hittite intervention, but despite this he stirred up a rebellion against the Hittites in the cities of Dalawa and Hinduwa, which ambushed and defeated a Hittite force and eventually paid tribute to the traitor. The latter teamed up again, through a dynastic marriage, with Kupanta-Kurunta of Arzawa. In the end, he subdued Arzawa and managed to set Kupanta-Kurunta, the land of Pitassa and Ahhiyawa, against the Hittites. (Goetze 1928: 17-37,' 13-16, 21-22, 24, 26-27, 35-36).

After studying the topography in both the Tawagalawa letter and the Madduwata text, Bryce suggested that their toponyms be subdivided into a number of 'clusters'. One of these clusters included Dalawa, Hinduwa and Iyalanda. Another cluster (mentioned in KUB XXIII, 83) linked Dalawa to Kuwalapassiya, undoubtedly the same as the Kuwalapassa of Hattusili's annals (Forlanini 1988: 158), since both places agreed to join forces with the Hittites in an attack on Iyalanda. Hittite Dalawa is usually considered to correspond with Tlava, which was the Luwian/Lycian name for the Greek 'Tlos'. In Bryce's opinion, this last place corresponded either with the Lycian city of Tlos or with an unidentified Pisidian settlement with the same name (Steph. Byz. s.v. Tlos), while Hinduwa would have been the predecessor of Kandyba, located to the west of Kaş (Bryce 1974a: 399). Freu however, identified Dalawa with a Carian Tlos and Hinduwa with Carian Kindiya (Freu 1987: 149-150). Iyalanda was also identified by him, by Bryce and by Hawkins with Carian Alinda (Bryce 1974a: 402; Freu 1987: 148; Hawkins 1998: 26). Forlanini had placed it wrongly to the south of Lake Burdur (Forlanini 1988: fig.1). Most scholars now locate the cluster Dalawa-Hinduwa-Iyalinda and Kuwalapassa in western Lycia (Tlos-Kandyba) and the adjoining parts of Caria

(Iyalanda/Alinda) and northwestern Pisidia. In fact, Dalawa (as Talawa) is also mentioned together with Awarna (Xanthos), Pinali (Pinara) and Wiyanawanda (Oenoanda) in two hieroglyphic texts from the reign of Tudhaliya IV, from Yalburt and Emirgazı respectively (Hawkins 1995: 49, 52; Gurney 1997: 136). They show that the Dalawa-Hinduwa-Iyalinda cluster actually has to be placed in classical Lycia and adjoining Caria. A recently discovered hieroglyphic text from the 'Südburg' at Hattusa, dated to the reign of Suppiluliuma II, records what was probably a single year's campaign of the king to Wiyanawanda and four other countries, including Luka and Ikuna, which seem to represent a coherent group (Hawkins 1995: 54; Gurney 1997: 136). Kuwalapassa is generally identified now with Kolbasa, located immediately to the south of Sagalassos (Forlanini 1988: 167; Hawkins 1995: 52 n. 181, 56; Gurney 1997: 138; Hawkins 1998: 26 n. 163). This means that, despite the general lack of Late Bronze Age surface finds in Southwest Anatolia, Lycia, Caria and even Pisidia already possessed several urban settlements, which continued to exist and prosper right into classical times.

As we have said above, under Hattusili III, an enemy invaded the Hittite realm as far as Nahita, Sallusa and Kuwalapassa (Freu 1987: 130-131, 139; Hawkins 1995: 52 n. 181). Nahita was identified by Freu (1987: 131) with Niğde, but by Cornelius, Forlanini (1988: 159) and Hawkins (1995: 56 n. 199) with Nagidos east of Anamur. Hawkins proposed to identify Sallusa with Selinous in Rough Cilicia (Hawkins 1995: 52 n. 181). It is also mentioned in the famous bronze tablet of Tudhaliya IV as one of the border places of the kingdom of Tarhuntassa, together with Tatta and Dasa. These places were considered by Otten to have been located inland on a line running parallel to the coast. He thought it possible that Tatta corresponded with the Daddassi of other Hittite sources (Otten 1988: 13 '8, 56-64; 37 n. 35; 38). Forlanini located it near Lake Suğla (1988: 156) and suggested that Sallusa was perhaps identical with the mountain refuge of Sallawassa or Sallawassi from the Madduwatta episode (1988: 161). This was endorsed by Freu (1987: 131), de Martino (1996: 44-496869) who placed it in (Southern Pisidia or) Pamphylia, and Gurney (1997: 137). Gurney believed moreover that the list of places in Hattusili's annals was merely a list of places and not an itinerary, so that nothing could be gathered from juxtapositions (Gurney 1997: 137). In that case, the identification of Sallusa with Sallawassa becomes more plausible. The site of Sallawassa (Sal-la-u-ua-as-si), mentioned in the Madduwata text, perhaps recurs as Za-al-la-ua-as-si-in in a fragmentary fifteenth-fourteenth century BC Hittite treaty between the Hittites and a certain Huhhazalma, who had conquered the port of Ura (near Silifke in Cilicia) and a place called Mutamutasi. The latter also occurs in the Madduwata text as Mutamutassa. The similarity of the toponyms in both texts thus suggests that the Huhhazalma treaty concerned the same geographical area. (Otten 1967: 61-62). In Bryce's view, Mutamutassa was part of the Lukka lands (Bryce 1974a: 398) while, according to Forlanini, it was located along the border of it (Forlanini 1988: 163). Recently an identification has been proposed with Mylasa in Caria (see Hawkins 1998: 27). Huhhazalma was considered by Forlanini to be a later king of Arzawa or even a successor of Madduwata (1988: 162).

Despite the discussions among the Hittitologists, it is clear that Madduwata's first military activities must have taken place somewhere to the north of the Lycian-Carian border land with its cities of Dalawas, Hinduwa and Iyalanda and to the southwest of the Pisidian Lake District (Hapalla) so that this condottiere must have ruled over the Phrygo-Pisidian border district. All this makes it very tempting, as Cornelius suggested, to look for his base in the district around Lake Burdur, in which case, in our opinion Darsa could perhaps be a valuable candidate. This site could easily control the plain of the Lysis which for some corresponds with the Siyanti river (Cornelius 1990[4] : 22, 265; see also Freu 1987: 149). This district would also be a good location for Mt. Zippasla: it abounds in mountains with peaks above 2000 m a.s.l. (Akdağ, Beşparmak, Kestel, Davras) with enough peculiar shapes (especially the Beşparmak and Kestel) to name a region after them. Moreover, our surveys revealed a large number of fortified mountain sites and fortresses, which by lack of distinctive features or pottery have been attributed to the Hellenistic period or before. Some of them could easily be of much older date and even go back to the late second millennium BC (Waelkens et al. 1997; Waelkens et al. 2000).

Whatever the location of Madduwata's residence, the mountain site of Sallawassa (Sal-la-u-ua-as-si) where the families of Madduwata and of Kupanta-Kurunta of Arzawa were taken captive, can probably be identified with Sagalassos, as was already suggested by Freu (1987: 140-141, 147). The fact that the southern neighbour of Sagalassos, that is, Kuwalapassa-Kolbasa (which would be an excellent location for a fortified Bronze Age settlement) at one stage joined forces with Dalawa-Tlos to attack Iyalinda-Alinda, and that these last two cities are also mentioned shortly after the two Sallawassa episodes in the Madduwata text, suggest that all these events took place within the same geographical region. Moreover, the clear similarity between the toponyms makes such an identification more plausible than Forlanini's suggestion of identifying Sallawassa with Pamphylian Sillyon (1988: 167).

Sagalassos most probably therefore occurs already in fourteenth century BC Hittite texts as Sallawassa, and possibly again in thirteenth century BC texts as Sallusa. Originally, it must have been located in or near the princedom of Madduwatta, who may have ruled over the Phrygo-Pisidian borderlands. It must certainly have been included in the Greater Arzawan kingdom which Maduwatta eventually controlled at the time of Arnuwanda I. The beginning of the landscape clearance in the area, revealed by palynological research, could possibly reflect the expansion of Maduwatta's kingdom. The region of Sagalassos certainly was included again in Tarhundaradu's Greater Arzawan kingdom under Tudhaliya III, in the middle of the fourteenth century BC. After Suppiluliuma's conquests, it may have remained either in Great Arzawa or perhaps have become part of the vassal state of Hapalla. After Mursili's settlement and continuing into the reign of Muwatalli II, it may have witnessed a relative peace and stability within the vassal kingdom of Mira-Kuwaliya or Hapalla. However, the upheaval following Hattusili's usurpation of the throne may have placed it again beyond Hittite control in the earlier thirteenth century BC. Hattusili III had to campaign as far as the classical city's southern neighbour, Kolbasa. Depending on the much disputed northwestern boundary (near Akşehir?) of the new state of Tarhuntassa, which further south, in Pamphylia, was certainly formed by the Aksu, Sagalassos may have been part of this kingdom, have been temporarily controlled by the Lukka, or more probably still have belonged to the vassal kingdom of Mira. Under the last two Hittite kings, however, when new forces emerged in the west, the region may have been located in the border district between Tarhuntassa and a new Greater Arzawa, most probably as part of the latter. How much the area was affected by the collapse of the Hittite empire remains uncertain, but some continuity is certainly not improbable.

What the Hittite sources in any case reveal is the fact that many of the sites of classical Caria (Alinda), Lycia (Xanthos, Tlos, Pinara, Oenoanda), Pisidia (Kolbasa, Sagalassos) and Pamphylia (Perge) existed already during the Late Bronze Age. Since so far no Bronze Age remains have come to light, this strongly suggests a cultural superposition in this district of classical sites on protohistorical sites and can explain the apparent lack of protohistorical settlements. The establishment of Luwians and the creation of chiefdoms and states from the Middle Bronze Age onward (Hittites, Arzawa, Kizzuwatna, Ahhiyawa, Lukka lands) may have introduced a new kind of society, no longer centred around höyüks in the middle of the rich agricultural plains or valleys, but around fortified or more easy defensible mountain sites. If this hypothesis is valid, in many places there may have been a continuum of settlement from the Middle/Late Bronze Age right into the historical period.

ACKNOWLEDGEMENTS

This text presents the results of the Belgian Programme on Internuniversitary Poles of Attraction initiated by the Belgian State, Prime Minister's Office, Science Policy Programming (IUAP4/12). This research was also made possible thanks to an FWO-Vlaanderen research grant (FWO/G.0215.96) and to a GOA-programme (97/2). Scientific responsibility is assumed by the author.

REFERENCES

T.R. Bryce (1974a) The Lukka problem and a possible solution, *Journal of Near Eastern Studies* 33: 395-404.

T.R. Bryce (1974b) Some geographical and political aspects of Mursilis Arzawa campaign, *Anatolian Studies* 24: 103-116.

T.R. Bryce (1985) A reinterpretation of the Milawata letter in the light of the new join piece, *Anatolian Studies* 35: 13-23.

T.R. Bryce (1999) *The Kingdom of the Hittites*, Oxford Clarendon Press (paperback version of the 1998 hardback edition).

F. Cornelius (1958) Geographie des Hethiterreiches (*Orientalia New Series* 27).

F. Cornelius (1990^4) *Geschichte der Hethiter. Mit besonderer Berücksichtigung der geographischen Verhältnisse und der Rechtsgeschichte*, Darmstadt (unveränderte Auflage von durchgesehener Auflage 1976).

J. J. Coulton (1988) 'Balboura Survey', *Annual Report of the British Institute of Archaeology at Ankara* 40: 13 -15.

S. de Martino (1996) *L'Anatolia occidentale nel medio regno ittita*, Firenze.

W.J. Eastwood, N. Roberts and H.F. Lamb (1998) Palaeoecological and archaeological evidence for human occupance in southwest Turkey: the Beyşehir occupation phase, *Anatolian Studies* 48: 69-86.

M. Forlanini (1988) La regione del Tauro nei testi Hittiti, *Vicino Oriente* 7: 129-169.

P. Freu (1987) Problèmes de chronologie et de géographie hittites. Madduwattas et les débuts de l'empire, *Hethitica VIII. Acta Anatolica E. Laroche oblata. Edidit R. Lebrun (Colloque anatolien, Paris, 1-5 juillet 1985)* Louvain-Paris: 123-175.

A. Goetze (1928) *Madduwattas (Hethithische Texte in Umschrift, mit Übersetzung und Erläuterungen herausgegeben von Ferdinand Sommer. Heft III. Mitteilungen der Vorderasiatischen Aegyptischen Gesellschaft. 32 Jahrgang)* Leipzig.

A. Goetze (1967^2) *Kleinasien (Kulturgeschichte des Alten Orients. Dritter Abschnitt. Erster Unterabschnitt. Handbuch der Altertumswissenschaft* III.1) München.

O.R. Gurney (1975) *The Hittites*, London.

O.R. Gurney (1982), Review of S. Heinhold-Krahmer, I. Hoffmann, A. Kammenhuber and G. Mauer, *Probleme des Textdatierung in der Hethithologie (Beiträge zu umstrittenen Datierungskriterien für Texte des 15. Bis 13. Jahrhunderts v.Chr.)* Heidelberg 1979, in *Orientalistische Literaturzeitung* 77: 560-563

O.R. Gurney (1997) The annals of Hattusilis III, *Anatolian Studies* 47: 127-138.

H.G. Güterbock (1983) The Hittites and the Aegean world, *American Journal of Archaeology* 87: 133-138.

J.D. Hawkins (1995) *The Hieroglyphic Inscription of the Sacred Pool Complex at Hattusa (SÜDBURG). With an Archaeological Introduction by Peter Neve (Studien zu den Boğazköy- Texten herausgegeben von der Kommission für den Alten Orient der Akademie der Wissenschaften und der Literatur. Beiheft* 3) Harassoswitz Wiesbaden.

J.D. Hawkins (1998) Tarkasnawa king of Mira "Tarkondimos", Boğazköy sealings and Karabel, *Anatolian Studies* 48: 1-31.

S. Heinhold-Krahmer (1977) Arzawa, *Theth* 8: 136-219.

I. Hoffmann (1984) Einige Überlegungen zum Verfasser des Madduwatta-Textes, *Orientalia New Series* 53: 34-51.

J.G. Macqueen (1996) *The Hittites and their Contemporaries in Asia Minor. Revised and enlarged edition*, Thames and Hudson.

P.A. Mountjoy (1998) The East Aegean-West Anatolian interface in the Late Bronze Age: Mycenaeans and the Kingdom of Ahhiyawa, *Anatolian Studies* 48: 33-67.

W-D. Niemeier (1998) The Mycenaeans in Western Anatolia, in: S. Gitin, A. Mazar and E. Stern (eds) *Mediterranean Peoples in Transition, in Honor of Trude Dothan*, Jerusalem: 27-28.

H. Otten (1967) Ein hethitischer Vertrag aus dem 15./14. Jahrhundert v.Chr. (Kbo XVI 47), *Istanbuler Mitteilungen* 17: 55-62.

H. Otten (1969) Sprachliche Stellung und Datierung des Madduwatta-Textes, *Studien zu den Boğazköy Texten* 11: 36.

H. Otten (1988) *Die Bronzetafel aus Boğazköy. Ein Staatsvertrag Tuthaliyas IV (Studien zu den Boğazköy-Texten. Herausgegeben von der Kommission für den Alten Orient der Akademie der Wissenschaften und der Literatur. Beiheft* 1) Wiesbaden.

M. Poetto (1993) *L'iscrizione luvia-geroglifica di Yalburt. Nuove acquisizioni relative alla geografia dell' Anatolia sud-occidentale* (*Studia Mediterranea*) Pavia.

I. Singer (1983) Western Anatolia in the thirteenth century B.C. according to Hittite sources, *Anatolian Studies* 33: 205-219.

M.Vermoere, M. Waelkens, H. Vanhaverbeke, I. Librecht, L. Vanhecke, E. Paulissen and E. Smets (in press), Late Holocene environmental change and the record of human impact at Gravgaz near Sagalassos, southwest Turkey, *Journal of Archaeological Science*. 27:571-591.

G.A. Wainwright (1954) Keftiu and Karamania (Asia Minor), *Anatolian Studies* 4: 33-47.

M. Waelkens and the Sagalassos Team (1997) Interdisciplinarity in classical archaeology. A case study: the Sagalassos Archaeological Research Project (Southwest Turkey), in: M. Waelkens and J. Poblome (ed.) *Sagalassos IV. Report on the Survey and Excavation Campaigns of 1994 and 1995* (*Acta Archaeologica Lovaniensia Monographiae* 9) Leuven University Press: 225-252.

M. Waelkens, E. Paulissen, H. Vanhaverbeke, J. Reyniers, J. Poblome, R. Degeest, W. Viaene, J. Deckers, B. De Cupere, W. Van Neer, H.A. Ekinci and M.O. Erbay (2000) The 1996 and 1997 survey seasons at Sagalassos, in: M. Waelkens and L. Loots (eds) *Sagalassos V. Report on the Survey and Excavation Campaigns of 1996 and 1997* (*Acta Archaeologica Lovaniensia Monographiae* 11) Leuven University Press: 17-216.

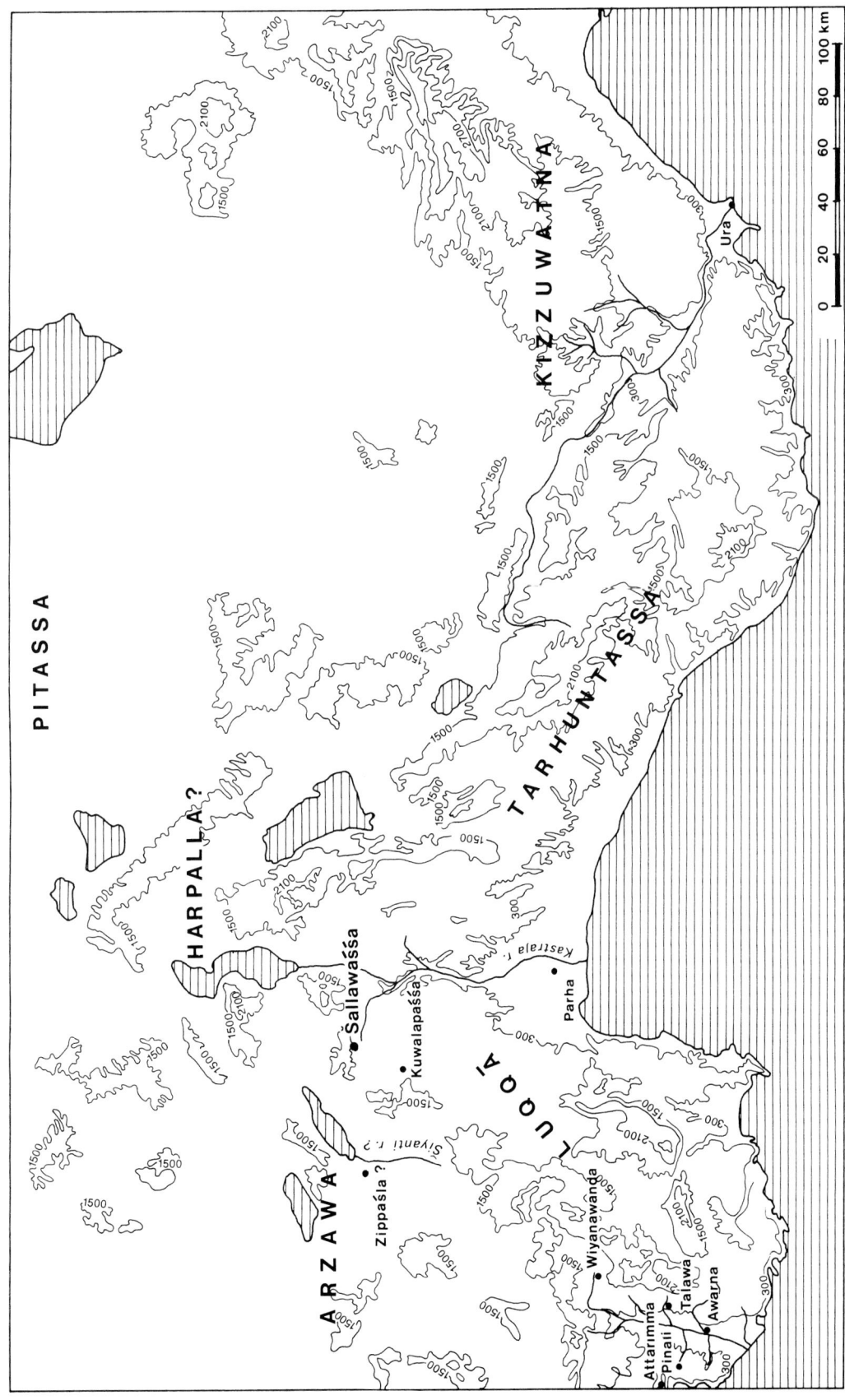

Fig. 1: Map of Pisidia during the Late Bronze Age

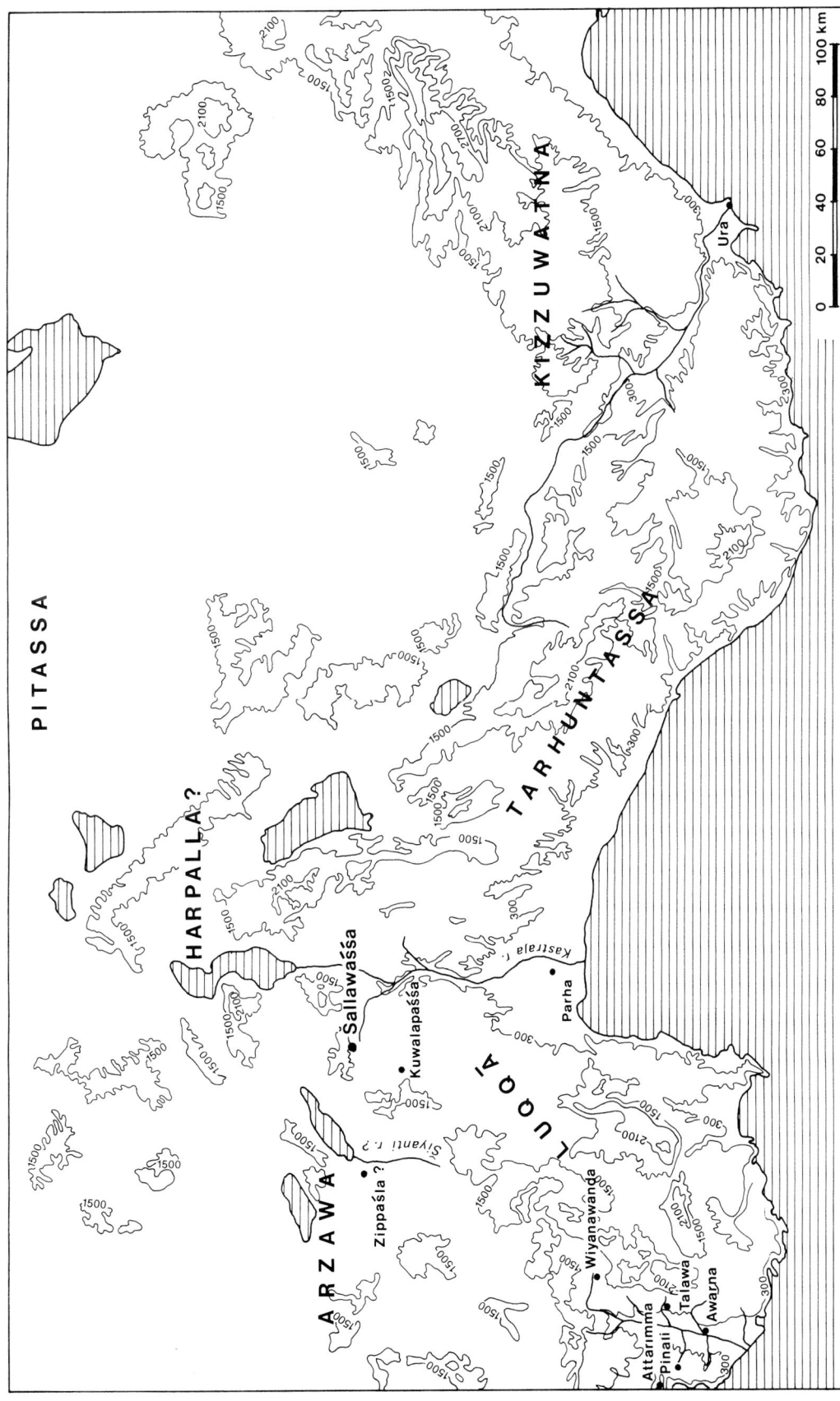

Fig. 1: Map of Pisidia during the Late Bronze Age

PART III

HISTORICAL STUDIES

NEGOTIATORS' LAWS FROM REBELLIOUS SAGALASSOS IN AN EARLY HELLENISTIC INSCRIPTION

Katelijn VANDORPE

Department of Ancient History, KULeuven, Blijde Inkomststraat 21, B-3000 Leuven, Belgium

1. INTRODUCTION

Arrian wrote that the inhabitants of Sagalassos "were thought to be the most warlike of these warlike people Pisidians" (*Anabasis Alexandri* I.28.2). In general, the people of Pisidia "with a sprinkling of superficially Hellenised cities" are portrayed as undisciplined barbarians always ready to go to war (Levick 1967: 17). S. Mitchell has warned not to confuse "a propensity for war with un-Hellenised barbarian behaviour" and points to the Hellenization process of the Pisidian communities (Mitchell 1991: 122). The new, early Hellenistic Sagalassos inscription perfectly illustrates this double panel of the painting, putting an end to a rebellion by Greek negotiators' laws.

An early Hellenistic inscription from Teos (Ionia) reveals the fear that the guard of the *akra* of Kyrbissos would seize this highest, fortified part of the city: several measures are taken in order to avoid a revolt (see below, 4. Content). The inscription published here suggests that such a rebellion has actually taken place, this time on the *akra* of Sagalassos: radical measures are taken to put an end to this situation.

2. DESCRIPTION

The stele (Figs 1 and 2) was discovered during the 1996 campaign in front of the northeast gate on the upper agora (see Waelkens *et al.* 2000). In late Roman times the structures around this gate, the Hellenistic market building and a so far unidentified structure in the northeast corner of the square, had been partly rebuilt, especially in their upper courses. The stele had apparently been re-used in one of them. A dowel hole in the centre of its front shows that this side was not visible during this or some former re-use. In fact, the stone seems to have been re-used at least twice. A clamp hole in the lower part of the right side indicates that at one stage the stele had been re-used resting on its left side. The anathyrosis along the front edge of the right side probably represents a reworking of the original surface (completely smooth on the left). The rather careful treatment of the reworked right side during this phase might suggest that the stele had already been re-used once during the Imperial period. The dowel hole in its front, implying that this was either a bedding or a resting surface, most probably belongs to a second phase of recycling.

At present, the stele is broken at the top. Both upper corners were broken off and have been re-attached. This fragmentation explains why some letters are damaged along the crack in the left corner and why the end of lines 4-15 is missing on the right side.

- *Inventory number*: G 96/98
(now in the depot of the excavation house)
- *Dimensions*: 0.594 (total w.) by 0.962 (h.) by 0.232 (th.) m.
- *Letter height*:
0.8 cm. (for O and Θ) – 1.6 cm. (average h.) – 2.2 cm. (especially lines 1-3)
- *Letter shapes*: see below (date).

x+1 Ἐὰν δὲ δια[κρ]ατήσωσιν οἱ καταλ[αβόμε]νοι τὴ-
2 ν ἄκραν κἀγβαλῶσίν τινας ἐκ τῆς πόλε[ω]ς ζη-
3 τείτω ἥ τε πόλις κἀναγέτω καὶ οἱ θεοὶ ἀνάστατα
4 πάντα ποιο[ῦ]ντες ἕως ἂν ἀγάγωσιν αὐτοὺς καὶ ὅσα ἂν [ἔχω-]
5 σιν τῶν ἐγβληθέντων οἱ ἐγβαλόντες καὶ ὅσα ἂν ἀπ[ῆι.]
6 Ἀναβάντων δὲ αὐτῶν τινετώσαν ἅπαντα ἐκ τ[ῶν]
7 ἰδίων καὶ τοῖς θεοῖς ὑπόχοι ἔστωσαν καὶ ἀποκτειν[έτω-]
8 σαν αὐτῶν τρεῖς τοὺς ἄρξαντας, οἱ δὲ λοιποὶ τέως δ[?ώ-]
9 δεκα τινέτωσαν ἀνὰ μνᾶς δέκα ἀργυρίου καὶ ἔστω ἱε[ρὸν]
10 ἅπαν [[......]]
11 Περὶ κλοπῆς. Ὅς ἂν κλέψηι τι οὗ πρότερον ἦσαν μναῖ τρε[ῖς]
12 νῦν δ' ἔστω θάνατος ἡ ζημία ἐλεγχθέντι vac.
13 Αἱ δὲ ὁμολογίαι καὶ αἱ συνθῆκαι ἐγένοντο ἐπὶ
14 ἀρχόντων Μο.οιτου Μοασιος Ιδααδιος vac.

15 Τοναωλλιος Μαλλου Νου Εννεις Κουας Νανει[ς]
16 Σοας Μαγισιλβις Οαδεις Οας Αλουπαις *vac.*
    or ¹⁵Νανει-¹⁶ς Οας
17 Οις Αρμοας Ιβδαμοας Κιλασαρβης Σανεις Πονα-
    or Οισαρμοας or   Κιλας Αρβης
18 σαμις- Κιλασαρβης Σιλλαβος Μοακλωιας *vac.*
    or   Κιλας Αρβης
19 Κοτβασις

(x+1) If those who have seized the *akra*, continue to hold it and if they exile some people from the city, the city should look for them and bring them back, and the gods (will be) destroying everything until they have brought them back as well as everything which those who exiled (citizens) have taken from those who have been exiled and everything which is missing. When (the exiles) return, (the rebels) should pay back everything out of their own pockets and they should be subject to the gods and they should put to death three of them who were the leaders. The rest of them,?up to now?twelve (in number), should pay at the rate of ten silver minas each and everything should be consecrated.

(11) (Law) concerning theft. He who steals something for which (the punishment) used to be three minas, let the punishment now be death if he is convicted.

(13) The agreements and accords have been made under the *archontes* Mo oites, Moasis, Idaadis, Tonaollis, Mallos, Nous, Enneis, Kouas, Naneis, Soas, Magisilbis, Oadeis, Oas, Aloupais, Ois, Armoas, Ibdamoas, Kilasarbes, Saneis, Ponasamis, Kilasarbes, Sillabos, Moakloias, Kotbasis.

3. DATE

(End fourth – third century BC, probably first half third century BC)

Only an approximate dating is possible. A possible *terminus post quem* is 333 BC: I assume that the text does not predate Alexander the Great. A possible *terminus ante quem* is the end of the third century BC, when Hellenization in Pisidia (Sagalassos, Termessos) was accelerated and Greek colonists were probably settled in several cities (see below 5.3). The Greek inscription listing at the end 24 leaders all bearing Pisidian names (with Greek endings), suggests that Hellenistic civilisation had permeated sufficiently to enable the inhabitants to use the Greek language and script and yet not to such an extent that they assumed Greek names or that Greek people settled in their city.

On palaeographical grounds, the inscription belongs to the late fourth or early third century BC; since the Greek script in inland Sagalassos may have developed less rapidly than in seaside cities, the second half of the third century BC may also be a possibility[1].

Typical of the period of the late fourth – first half third century BC[2] are the curved strokes sometimes found for A, Λ, M, Y; the Θ, O and Ω are still small; the diagonal strokes of the K do not yet reach the upper and lower limits of the line; the M still has 'branching' hastae; the second hasta of the N has not yet descended to the lower line; the second hasta of the Π is in only very few cases equal to the first in length, but is normally short; the Σ does not yet have parallel forms, only 'branching' ones. On the other hand, typical characteristics of the second century BC, such as a broken cross-bar for the A or apices decorating the ends of some letter-strokes, are totally lacking. If the inscription dated from the second century BC, one would expect these or other second century BC characteristics even in inland Sagalassos, since they are found in other inscriptions from Pisidian cities such as Termessos[3], Amblada[4], Olbasa[5] and possibly Pogla[6].

Some inscriptions from Asia Minor show the same letter forms and a similar careless arrangement of the text as the Sagalassos inscription: two building inscriptions from Alexandreia Troas, which are dated on palaeographical and internal grounds to the late fourth – early third century BC[7]. More interesting is a dated inscription from the closer Laodikeia on the Lykos[8], an inland city like Sagalassos. The letter forms are very similar and even somewhat more evolved (the second hasta of the N has often descended to the lower line). The Laodikeia text dates from year 45 of the reign of Antiochos and Seleukos, that is 267 BC. Good parallel inscriptions from Pisidia are found in nearby Termessos (written in the fifth year of Ptolemy II or 281 BC[9]) and in Pednelissos (early Hellenistic)[10]. The letter forms of both these inscriptions are even more evolved in comparison to the Sagalassos inscription. The latter text was most probably redacted in the first half of the third century BC, as were

---

[1] For the script of the second half of the third century, see, for instance, Rey-Coquais 1978: 315-320.
[2] Compare, for instance, Welles 1934: l-liii.
[3] *TAM* III.1.2 (reign of Eumenes II or Attalos II, see Magie 1950: 1136, no. 12.
[4] Swoboda-Keil, *Denkmäler* no. 74-75
[5] Kearsley 1994, plates VI-VII (159 BC).
[6] Bean 1960.
[7] *IK* 53.1 (squeeze p. 25); *IK* 53.2 (photograph p. 35); the only different letter form is the Ξ: in the Sagalassos inscription the Ξ consists only of three horizontals, in the building inscriptions from Alexandra Troas the three horizontals are connected by a vertical, a phenomenon which is found in all periods.
[8] *IK* 49.1 (photograph p. 9) = Wörrle 1975 (photograph Taf. 17).
[9] Robert 1966: 53-58 (photograph pl. III). For year 5=281/80 rather than 279/8, see R.A. Hazzard, in *Phoenix* 41 (1987): 156; id. 2000: 21.

the above-mentioned parallels from Laodikeia on the Lykos, Termessos and Pednelissos.

4. CONTENT

An agreement made by two Sagalassian parties. – The inscription records 'agreements and accords' (Αἱ δὲ ὁμολογίαι καὶ αἱ συνθῆκαι, l.13). Since the stone is broken at the top and since the text starts *in medias res*, it is obvious that only part of these agreements have come down to us. Moreover, the use of the connective particle δέ at the very beginning of the preserved part (Ἐὰν δὲ δια[κρ]ατήσωσιν) strongly suggests that (an)other article(s) preceded it[11]. What article(s) may be lost, is discussed below.

Agreements presuppose at least two parties. Those two groups are not defined as such in the inscription. We have only twenty-four names at the end of the text. Those twenty-four people made the agreement. The twenty-four names are all Pisidian, none is Greek (see below 6); since no city or town is mentioned, all twenty-four Pisidians must be inhabitants of Sagalassos, where the inscription was found.

The reason for the agreement: rebels have seized the ἄκρα. – As only the last part of the inscription has come down to us, the circumstances in which the agreements came off are not clear. There are two possibilities: either the inscription records general provisions in connection with, for instance, the establishment of a fortress on the *akra* and wants to avoid that the *akra* and the city would be seized by rebels, or the inscription wants to put an end to a rebellion. I prefer the second possibility. First of all, the new law on theft ("He who steals something for which the punishment used to be three minas, let the punishment now be death if he is convicted") is stringent and shows that there were serious problems at the time. Secondly, l. 1 suggests that the *akra* (with the fortress) has already been seized ("If those who have seized the *akra*, continue to hold it"). If I am right, why then are these negotiators' laws engraved on a stele? In my view, the stipulations are also valid in the future and contain at least one new sction of the city's law code: the above-mentioned article on theft (l. 11-12).

The first lines make the situation clear and explain why the agreements were made by the two rival groups of Sagalassians. The 'highest part' (ἄκρα) has been seized (καταλ[αβόμε]νοι)[12] by a group of rebels. The verb καταλαμβάνεθαι points to a non-legal action and the medium is often found in agreements between cities in the Hellenistic period. The citizens of Kos and Kalymna, for instance, swear in an oath not "to seize (καταλαψεῦμαι) under any pretext any of the forts or the *akra*, whether for my own possession or in collaboration with someone else"[13].

What exactly is meant by the ἄκρα or 'highest part'? ἄκρα is here to be interpreted "im militärischem Sinn"[14]. The highest part must be a part of the city or at least control it, since it is possible that the rebels could expel the citizens. Other Anatolian cities and some Greek islands are known to have had such an ἄκρα; the evidence even dates to the same period as the Sagalassos inscription. The ἄκρα is usually explicitly distinguished from the city (πόλις) itself[15] and is, contrary to the polis, often controlled by a military officer such as the phrourarch (in Priene and in Kition on Cyprus). Where the city is already situated on a hill or mountain, the ἄκρα rises above the city near or at the top of the hill[16]. It is girded by fortification walls, is usually difficult to reach and rarely encloses public buildings or sanctuaries, if at all.

The topographical situation is most clear in third century BC Priene[17]. The city is built on a terrace of the hill, above which rises the fortified ἄκρα called Teloneia. The ἄκρα does not contain public buildings or temples and is quite difficult to reach. It is controlled by a phrourarch, as is the ἄκρα of third century BC Kition (Cyprus)[18]. The Carian cities of Iasos and Theangela apparently had several ἄκραι. According to Robert, the ἄκραι of Theangela mentioned in a decree of 310 BC, refer to the two highest parts of the mountain, separated by a depression and enclosed by fortifications which, according to Robert, must have been built before the second century BC and probably already existed

---

[10] Comparetti 1916-1920: 143-148 = *SEG* 2 710. The letter forms and the mention of the Persian siglos suggest an early Hellenistic date contrary to the suggestion of Comparetti: "dei tempi imperiali non molto inoltrati" (I owe the reference to the kindness of S. Mitchell). A last inscription from Pisidia which may date to the early Hellenistic period is TAM III 1 (on palaeographical grounds).

[11] The particle δέ is always a connective (pure connection 'and' or contrast 'but', with all that lies between); exceptions (δέ with the value of δή) are not applicable here, see Denniston 1954²: 162.

[12] The verb καταλαμβάνω has also been used by Arrian (*An.* I.28.2) when he describes how the Sagalassians had occupied (κατειληφότες) the hill (λόφος) in front of their city (the later Alexander Hill) and there awaited Alexander who came to attack the city. The medium is often attested, for instance in Polybius 1.19.5: καταλαβόμενοι τὸν λόφον.

[13] *Staatsverträge* III 545, l. 123-125; see also Chaniotis 1996 no. 31, 37, 38 and 61.

[14] See Robert 1970: 595-596.

[15] Thus in Priene, Iasos and Theangela, see below; for examples outside Asia Minor, see Piejko 1981: 108-109.

[16] Compare Piejko 1981: 108: "Naturally a command over the citadel implies ultimate control (or protection) over the city".

[17] See *Inschriften von Priene*, index p. 261 s.v. ἄκρα.

[18] *SEG* 31.1348 (246-221 BC) and see Piejko 1981.

at the time the decree was promulgated[19]. The ἄκραι of Iasos, recorded during the reign of Ptolemy I, could refer to a similar situation of several "befestigte Höhen oder auch vorspringende Landzungen, von denen aus man die Einfahrt in den Hafen kontrollieren konnte, oder auch beides"[20].

There can be little doubt as to the meaning of ἄκρα at Sagalassos. It is clear that it has to be identified with the early to middle Hellenistic fortress located on the Tekne Tepe (1885 m) which dominates the city to the northwest (see Loots *et al.* 2000). Its location is very similar to that of the ἄκρα at Priene. Whoever was master of this fortress had complete control of the upper parts of Sagalassos and in fact could force people to flee by using artillery.

Who were the rebels? – The information on the rebels is scarce. They have seized and are in control of the *akra* of Sagalassos. Three of them are desribed as τοὺς ἄρξαντας, "the former leaders" and the rest of them are apparently twelve in number (τέως δ[ώ-δεκα], l. 8-9). In total only 15 rebels are recorded, at first sight an unacceptably low number: the fortress on the *akra* measures 41 by 58 m and can harbour more people. An inscription from Teos (Ionia, third cent. BC)[21] informs us on the guard of the *akra* of Kyrbissos: the phrourarch or military officer of the *akra* may take at least 20 citizens as watchmen. L. Robert comments "c'est peut-être la seule inscription que nous ayons sur le nombre des gardes dans un phrourion"[22]. The 15 rebels recorded in the inscription from Sagalassos may have been the guard of the *akra* and may have been supported by some other citizens or by an enemy. The above-mentioned inscription from Teos very well illustrates the fear of the city that the guard of 20 men would revolt and seize the *akra*; therefore, several measures are taken to avoid such a rebellion: the watchmen are citizens, not mercenaries; the guard is appointed for only four months and has to take an oath before they watch the *akra*; several chastisements are listed in case the phrourarch revolts. The fear that the guard of the *akra* would revolt is revealed throughout the inscription; L. Robert concluded: "On est frappé à la lecture de ces prévisions de rébellion du phrourarque, de combat et de sanction. Apparemment les Teiens avaient eu quelque expérience malheureuse dans une de leurs fortresses."[23]

The terms of the agreement. – The rebels got into a tight spot, since some of them negotiated a peace with the non-rebellious Sagalassians and accepted the hard terms. There are no parallel inscriptions for the terms of agreement. The fear that a small group of people would seize the *akra* of the city is expressed by the above-mentioned stele from Teos, but the clauses of this agreement are quite different.

The preserved part of the agreements consists of two items: an elaborate one on the rebellion (l. 1-10) and one on the punishment for theft. The stonecutter probably first began to write the first two words of the second part on theft (Περὶ κλοπῆς) immediately after the first (l. 10), but then erased the two words and started again on the next line (l. 11). Both items were then separated by a paragraphus, as were probably the other parts which are now lost.

I.
The article on the rebellion starts with a dubious conditional clause: "if (Ἐὰν δέ) those who have seized the highest point, continue to hold it (δια[κρ]ατήσωσιν) and if they exile people from the city, ..."; then follows the punishment of the rebels and their leaders. The rebels are apparently to be punished not for having seized the highest point of the city, but for holding it in their possession and for driving people out. It also seems that this condition has not yet been fulfilled.
But if the latter condition is fulfilled, a series of measures is listed:
(1) measures to be carried out by the city,
(2) punishment of the rebels and rebel leaders.

    (1) The city must look for the exiles and bring them back, because the gods will ruin everything (οἱ θεοὶ ἀνάστατα πάντα ποιο[ῦ]ντες[24]) until they have brought them back (ἕως ἂν ἀγάγωσιν αὐτοὺς)[25] as well as everything which the rebels have taken and everything which is missing (ἀπ[ῆι])[26].

    (2) When the exiles have returned, the rebels have to pay everything back out of their own pockets (that is everything which they have taken from the exiles and everything which is missing). Furthermore, they have to be subjected to the gods (τοῖς θεοῖς ὕποχοι[27]). This statement is probably inspired by the fact that rebels or enemies are in general considered to be ungodly, sacrilegious (ἀσεβής)[28].

    "They" also have to put to death (ἀποκτειν[έτω]σαν) three of the rebels who have been

---

[19] Robert 1936: 81-86.
[20] *IK* 28/1.2 (passim) and comment on l. 11.
[21] Robert 1976 = *SEG* 26 1306 and see *SEG* 30 1376.
[22] Robert 1976: 206-214.
[23] Robert 1976: 213.
[24] The expression ἀνάστατα ποιέω is also found in an Athenian inscription of 446-445 BC, in which the Athenians swear not to drive the Chalkidians out of Chalkis οὐδὲ τὴν πόλιν ἀνάστα-τον ποήσω; thus the Athenians will preserve the city of Chalkis (Tod 1985 no. 42).
[25] Undoubtedly ἄγειν for ἀνάγειν.
[26] Given the length of the lacuna, the supplements ἀπ[ολώλη] or ἀπ[όληται] are too long.
[27] For the expression, see the speech of Klearchos in Xenophon *An.* 2.5.7, where he states that everything is everywhere subject (ὕποχα) to the gods.
[28] See, for instance, *Inschriften von Priene* 17 on the Gauls.

(the) leaders²⁹; it is not clear whether the rebels are still the subject of the verb or the non-rebellious Sagalassians are meant. The following clause is problematic: "The rest of them, τέως? twelve (in number), should pay at the rate of ten silver minas each…".

The remaining twelve rebels each have to pay a penalty of ten minas. The fine the latter have to pay for their misbehaviour is to be dedicated to the gods³⁰.

What is the meaning of τέως in the phrase οἱ δὲ λοιποὶ τέως δ[?ώ]δεκα τινέτωσαν? This adverb is rarely found in inscriptions. Only³¹ the meaning of 'hitherto, up to the present' can be possible, a meaning used in decrees in Attica at the end of the fifth century BC³². The use of τέως, 'for the present', only makes sense if it accompanies δ[ώ]δεκα and not the verb τινέτωσαν: the remaining leaders are thus "for the present twelve (in number)". Is that as long as none of them has surrendered or is killed in the battle which may put an end to the uprising?

The total of the fine adds up to a rounded number: 2 talents (10 minas x 12). If the rebels are the guard of the *akra*, then this fine of 10 minas or 1000 drachmas may be compared to their wages: the above-mentioned inscription from Teos (third cent. BC) informs us on the wages of the guard; each man receives 1 drachma a day³³: a fine of 1000 drachmas represents three years work.

II.
The item on theft is less problematic. It is a legal section introduced by the title Περὶ κλοπῆς: *(Law) concerning theft. He who steals something for which (the punishment) used to be three minas, the punishment will now be death if he is convicted.*

The punishment for (a) theft used to be (πρότερον) three minas; this clause shows there was already a (most probably Greek) law code at Sagalassos before the rebellion at the end of the fourth- (early) third century BC, that is, in a very early stage of the Hellenization process. Several Greek cities of Asia Minor drew up a code of law or decrees with legal items at the end of the fourth beginning of the third century BC.

It is not clear what kind of theft is in question. This must have been obvious when the earlier section of the law was consulted. In Athens, for instance, there were four types of theft: three categories of aggravated theft and one of simple theft. The three aggravated thefts were theft by night, theft of more than 50 drachmas by day and theft from public places; they were punishable by death (θάνατον τὴν ζημίαν). Simple theft (theft of less than 50 drachmas by day) was punishable by a double penalty plus five days in the stocks³⁵.

The punishment for (a) theft for which (the punishment) used to be three minas, is changed to death if the accused is convicted. The measure was undoubtedly taken to discourage looting. The addition of ἐλεγχθέντι ('if convicted, if proven guilty') is significant: there must be proof that the suspect is guilty³⁶.

Archontes in Sagalassos: commanders or magistrates? – The interpretation of the term 'archontes' is somewhat problematic, especially since little is known about the third-century BC institutions in Pisidia and neighbouring regions. Except for the southern Pisidian cities under Ptolemaic rule such as Termessos³⁷, the first Pisidian polis structures turn up (at the end of the third³⁸ or) in the second century BC with a varying picture of magistrates (strategoi, archontes, geraioi). A decree of 159 BC is promulgated by the *boulè* and the *demos* of Olbasa (western Pisidia: the Milyas) on the motion of their three *strategoi*³⁹. In Pogla (the Milyas) a decree of the second or first century BC mentions the polis and its *archontes*⁴⁰. Finally, two Attalid letters are addressed to the 'polis and the γεραιοί of Amblada (eastern Pisidia)⁴¹.

---

²⁹ For a parallel construction and a similar measure, see the measure taken by an *aisymnetes* from Miletos: τῶν δὲ κοινωνῶν τῶν φόνου τρεῖς ἀπέκτεινε, τοῖς δὲ ἄλλοις φυγὴν προ<σ>εῖπεν ("of the accomplices in murder he had killed three, for the others he proclaimed banishment"), see Nicolas from Damascus, *FGrHist* 90 F 53.

³⁰ Compare, for instance, a law from Elis (before 450 BC): disobedient people or people who provoke a rebellion, have to pay a fine which in most cases has to be dedicated to Zeus of Olympia (Van Effenterre *et al.* 1994 no. 56).

³¹ Τέως does neither stand for ἕως, as ἕως is used in l.4, nor is it used as correlative to ἕως nor followed by an answering phrase ('for a time…, then…).

³² *IG* I² 57, l. 21 and 108, l. 48.

³³ Robert 1976: 216.

³⁵ Cohen 1983, esp. p. 40.

³⁶ Compare *IK* 24.1. 736, an inscription from Smyrna (?121/122 AD): τὸν δ'εὑρεθέντα καὶ ἐλεγχθέντα τι το[ιούτων πεποιηκέναι?] δηναρίων ἑκατὸν εἰς τὸν θεὸν ζημ[ι, "Wer aber ertrappt und überführt wird, daß er etwas [derartiges getan hat, soll] eine Strafe von hundert Denaren [zahlen?] für den Gott". See also *IG* XII. Suppl. 644, l. 32 (ca. 200 BC, Chalkis): ἐλεγχθέντες παθέτωσαν, "If proven guilty, they have to undergo the punishment which…"; *Fouilles de Delphes* III 479, l. 8 (ca. 281 BC): ἐκόλασα[ν δ'εἴ τις ἐλεγχθείη?] τῶν ἐ[πα]ναχθέντων πρὸς αὐτοὺς κ[ακουργήσας?] κρίναντες κατὰ] τὸν νόμον, "If anyone of those who have been referred to them, has done evil and is proven guilty, then they judged according to law and punished them".

³⁷ In the southern Anatolian cities under Ptolemaic rule such as Termessos (see below, Historical context), an *ekklesia* and/or δικασταί are found already in the third century BC (compare Bagnall 1976: 232); for the 'elders' of Termessos attested in 319 BC, see the note on *gerousia* (below).

³⁸ Polybius (5.75.7) mentions a meeting of the *ekklesia* of Selge in 218 BC.

³⁹ Kearsley 1994.

⁴⁰ Bean 1960: 59-60.

The mention of a *gerousia*⁴² made Jones (1971²: 130) concluded that under the Attalids "republican institutions were still rudimentary in the more backward Pisidian communities"; Van Rossum (1988: 46), however, showed that 'polis' can stand for 'boule and demos'; Amblada most probably had a democratic regime.

Archontes are twice mentioned in the Sagalassos inscription:

(1) The twenty-four names of the persons who made the agreement, are introduced by ἐπὶ ἀρχόντων:

the first six names are in the genitive, corresponding to ἀρχόντων;

the remaining eighteen names are in the nominative for an unclear reason.

(2) In l.8 at least three (of the) rebels are called τοὺς ἄρξαντας.

(a) Are the 'archontes' the chief magistrates (usually three in number) of the polis (l. 2-3) Sagalassos? In this case, the three archontes are listed in l. 14-15 where ἐπὶ ἀρχόντων is followed by six names in the genitive, that are the three names of the archontes with their father's names (without the article τοῦ): Mo.oites?son of Moasis, Idaadis?son of Tonaollis, Mallos?son of Nous. The remaining eighteen names in the nominative may have been the names of the negotiators.

(b) The term 'archontes' can also be a general term for all the magistrates of a city, as, for instance, an early Hellenistic inscription from Kaunos⁴³ (probably under Ptolemaic rule at the time) lists the names of at least eleven of the ex-magistrates of the city who were active in the year when Apollonios was eponymous priest ([οἱ ἄρ]ξαντες ἐν τῶι ἐπὶ ἱερέως [Ἀπολ]λωνίου ἐνιαυτῶι). In this case, the 24 names preceded by ἐπὶ ἀρχόντων may refer to 24 magistrates of Sagalassos.

(c) The word ἄρχοντες may simply to be interpreted as 'leaders, commanders' and not as the title for the (chief) magistrates of a polis. The expression τοὺς ἄρξαντας in l. 8 undoubtedly refers to 'leaders', that is, the former leaders of the rebels who are supposed to surrender.

An agreement enforced by a Hellenistic king? – The rebellion is in my view not (only) the result of internal problems in an independent city. It is an uprising by some of the Sagalassians against a Hellenistic monarch (see below 5). I also believe that the agreement between the rebels and the other Sagalassians was enforced by this Hellenistic king⁴⁴. All this would explain the Greek character of the agreement in a city which was scarcely Hellenised at that time (end fourth -(early) third century BC) as well as the imperative mood and the threat of the gods which the city itself imposes ("the city should look (ἥ τε πόλις ζητείτω) for the exiles and bring them back (κἀναγέτω)", l.3; "and the gods (are) destroying everything until they have brought them back", l. 3-4).

Other agreements from Greek and Hellenistic cities in dispute – Most Greek inscriptions recording agreements are treaties between cities, some between a Hellenistic monarch and a city⁴⁵. Other agreements are aimed at settling disputes between rival groups within one city and are to be seen in the context of the democratization process of the Greek poleis. They put an end to the situation of στάσις or discord, a subject studied by Gehrke (1985) for the Greek cities of the fifth and fourth centuries BC. The agreement of the inhabitants of Sagalassos, a city without a Greek past, does not really fit the picture: it is an agreement between rival groups, but they are not political groups supporting for example the democratic or oligarchic cause.

The way in which the Sagalassians settle their dispute, though, is typically Greek: by ὁμολογίαι καὶ συνθῆκαι⁴⁶. According to Gehrke (1985: 261) a στάσις can be ended by appealing to an arbitrator from another city⁴⁷ or by drawing up a decree (ψήφισμα) or an agreement (ὁμολογία, etc). Such decrees or agreements dealing with a στάσις generally

---

⁴¹ Swoboda-Keil, *Denkmäler* no. 74-75.

⁴² *Gerousiai* found in Hellenistic Asia Minor are either pure political institutions or associations. The *gerousia* becomes a normal feature of the Greek cities in the Eastern part of the Roman Empire, having a somewhat hybrid character with characteristics of a political institution and of an association, see especially Van Rossum 1988.

The members are usually called γέροντες or γερουσιασταί; in a large region of southern Anatolia they always bear the name γεραιοί; that region is formed by cities of Lycaonia, Phrygia, Pisidia (Amblada in the Hellenistic period and Sagalassos in the Roman period), Pamphylia, Caria and Lycia; in Roman Ephesos the term is used alongside γέροντες and γερουσιασταί; there are no *geraioi* attested in Hellenistic Telmessos (Lycia) nor in Hellenistic Termessos (Pisidia; in 319 BC, there was a group of elders in Termessos, called πρεσβύτεροι (versus the νέοι, see Diodorus 18.46.4), but they are probably not to be identified with the institution of the γεραιοί). According to Welles (1934: 239) the members are called γεραιοί instead of γέροντες, because the institution may be a pre-Hellenic inheritance; this assertion is refuted by Van Rossum, but the latter does not give an alternative reason for the use of the term γεραιοί, see Van Rossum 1988: 3 and 45-46, notes 31 and 32 and *SEG* 28.1225.

⁴³ Bean 1953: 21 no. 5 = *SEG* 12.463 and see L. Robert in *Bull. ép.* 1954 no. 229.

⁴⁴ Compare the two letters from Antigonos Monophthalmos to the people of Teos, in which the king forces his subjects to an agreement with neighbouring Lebedos (ποεῖν ἀμφοτέρους συνθήκην) and to settle their disputes, see Welles 1934 no. 3 and Ager 1996 no. 13. Compare also the edict of Alexander in 324 BC, commanding the immediate restoration of all exiles (φυγάδες), resulting in agreements or decrees settling possible disputes between those who stayed in the city and the exiles who returned (Tod 1985.II: 297).

⁴⁵ For these two groups, see especially Ager 1996.

⁴⁶ The combination ὁμολογίαι καὶ συνθῆκαι as such is not attested in inscriptions; συνθήκα ὁμόλογος is found once in a

include some typical elements. These are described by Gehrke (1985: 266-267) and are often more complex and more elaborate than in the Sagalassos inscription, when they reflect a more complicated situation[48]: "Sehr haüfig finden wir die Amnestie (…). Dem korrespondiert, daβ von einer Bestrafung oft ausdrücklich nur die Rädelsführer, also die jeweiligen Exponenten, betroffen waren. Angesichts der Tatsache, daβ Verbannung und Verfassungsänderung das wichtigste Stasis-Element sind, nehmen die Regelungen gerade auf sie besondere Rücksicht (…). Meistens wird den Emigranten jedoch die Rückkehr selbst gestattet (…). Am wichtigsten dabei war selbstredend, daβ ihnen ihr ehemaliger, im Zuge der Stasis enteigneter Besitz restituiert wurde." Sometimes a special commission is given the job of drawing up a (new) law code. This is apparently not the case at Sagalassos, as in the agreement itself a section of the existing law code which concerns theft is changed (Περὶ κλοπῆς, l. 11-12).

5. HISTORICAL CONTEXT

(End fourth – (early) third century BC)

The rebellion recorded in the inscription marvellously fits the picture of Pisidia as a region harbouring rebellious, warlike tribes and cities. *It remains difficult, however, to link the new data to a particular event of the late fourth -(first half of the) third century BC*, mainly because very little is known about the history of early Hellenistic Sagalassos. The new inscription is the only epigraphical evidence for this period. The literary sources only record the conquest of Alexander in 333 BC and coins are lacking until ca. 200 BC. As far as archaeological remains are concerned, there are some parts of the fortifications (Loots *et al.* 2000), a market building[49] and perhaps some ostothekai[50] that might be dated to this period. Near the limits of the city's territory one can cite the early Hellenistic fortress of Insuyu in the Çineovası, which may have served as a lookout guarding the approach to the city from the west[51].

However, to supply some answers, we have to turn to the history of Pisidia[52] and neighbouring regions, especially Pamphylia. The events in the regions of Southern Anatolia are as confused as the history of the Diadochs and Descendants. The situation becomes even more complicated by the rivalry between some Pisidian cities: Selge comes into collision with Sagalassos, Termessos, Pednelissos and Pamphylian Aspendos[53]. I have not systematically included the data on the Pisidian mercenaries found in the Ptolemaic, Seleucid or Attalid armies[54], since this kind of evidence does not give any exact information on the powers in control of Pisidia at that time[55].

5.1. Antigonos Monophthalmos and the Alketas episode

After Alexander's conquest of Pisidia in 333 BC, the region became part of the new satrapy of Greater Phrygia controlled by Antigonos Monophthalmos. In order to get a better control of the region, a new city was founded near the territory of Sagalassos: Kretopolis, inhabited by Cretan mercenaries of the Macedonian army[56]. After the settlement of Babylon, a conflict arose between Perdikkas and Antigonos which eventually brought Pisidia under the control of Perdikkas' younger brother Alketas. The latter was supported by an army amounting in 319 BC to circa 20,000 soldiers, at least 6,000 of them being Pisidian mercenaries devoted to their charismatic leader. When in 319 BC Alketas had to face Antigonos in the territory of Kretopolis, he withdrew and went into hiding in Termessos, where he was supported by his Termessian mercenaries. The elders of the city, however, betrayed Alketas and surrendered him to Antigonos. Alketas' followers "initially decided to retaliate for their leader's betrayal. They threatened their city with civil war, but eventually chose to organize guerilla bands who raided the territory"[57]. The remaining years of Antigonos' reign (319-301 BC) were apparently peaceful. If the Sagalassos inscription is to be linked to the Alketas' episode, then some of the Sagalassians who were probably mercenaries in Alketas' army and supported his cause, may

---

treaty and alliance between the Aitolian and Akarnanian leagues (263-262 BC?, Ager 1996 no. 33). Inscriptions usually have either ὁμολογίαι or συνθῆκαι to denote agreements, often in the plural to emphasize the several articles of the agreement, compare, for instance, Chaniotis 1996: 63. Both terms are sometimes combined with ὅρκοι, when both parties have to swear to keep their commitments, see, for instance, Ager 1996, index *s.v.*

The combination is only found in a dialogue of Plato (*Cra* 384d) where Hermogenes, Kratylos and Sokrates have a discussion on the correctness of names and Hermogenes says that there is no "correctness of names other than convention and agreement (συνθήκη καὶ ὁμολογία)".

[47] See on this subject in general Piccirilli 1973; Ager 1996: 515-517.
[48] For instance, the return of exiles whose possessions have been acquired by people in legal purchases.
[49] Waelkens *et al.* 1997a: 127-136.

[50] Kosmetatou *et al.* 1997; Mitchell 1991: 142; Bracke 1993: 25.
[51] Bean 1960: 43; Waelkens *et al.* 1997b: 78-82, figs 85-88.
[52] The exact boundaries of Pisidia are difficult to define, see Kosmetatou 1997.
[53] Bracke 1993: 19.
[54] For Pisidian mercenaries, see Launey 1949: 471-476 (Neoptolemos listed on p. 473 is not a Pisidian, see Robert 1990); Rey-Coquais 1978: 321-323 [= *SEG* 27.973bis]; Bracke 1993: 19-20; Kosmetatou *et al.* 1997; Kosmetatou 1997; for addenda on Launey 1949, see especially Brandt 1992: 88-89.
[55] Compare Brandt 1992: 90: "zwar unabhängig von den politischen Machtverhältnissen im südwestlichen Anatolien".
[56] Cohen 1995: 345-346; for a convincing location of Kretopolis, see Mitchell 1994: 129-136; on the foundation of Kretopolis, see now Sekunda 1997.
[57] Kosmetatou 1997.

have seized the city's acropolis, when Antigonos had eliminated Alketas and tried to get control over Pisidia. The other citizens did not then want to oppose Antigonos, like the elders of Termessos, and negotiated a peace with the rebellious inhabitants. The attribution of the Sagalassos inscription to this early period is, however, unlikely, since Sagalassos, at the time of the rebellion referred to in the inscription, already had a (Greek?) legal code (see line 11).

5.2. The threat to independence by Ptolemies and Seleucids

Selge[58]. – According to Strabo 12.7.3, the Pisidian city of Selge enjoyed independence since it was founded. It was also the only city in the region of Pamphylia and Pisidia that managed to keep an autonomous mint (based on the Persian standard) throughout the third century BC[59].

Pamphylia and southern Pisidia. – There is no evidence to suggest that Lysimachos took control of Pisidia or Pamphylia after Antigonos' defeat at Ipsos in 301 BC[60]. Part of Pamphylia and Pisidia may have become temporarily or permanently under Ptolemaic control: an inscription from Aspendos shows that the city was defended by two Ptolemaic commanders and by mercenary troops, listing among others Pamphylians, Lycians and Pisidians. The text may be dated to the reign of Ptolemy I, less probably to the early years of Ptolemy II[61]. The presence of Pisidians in the army of Ptolemy I could indicate a Ptolemaic influence or dominance in Pisidia, probably only in the southern part (as was the case under Ptolemy II). This situation is continued and was consolidated under Ptolemy II: Lycia, Pamphylia (where the king founded the cities of Ptolemais and Arsinoe)[62] and the southern Pisidian cities Termessos and Etenna are part of the Ptolemaic possessions. According to an honorary inscription dating to the fifth year of Ptolemy II (281-280 BC) Termessos was governed by the Pamphyliarch[63]; Etenna presumably was subjected to the Ptolemies as it stopped minting its independent coinage (see below)[64]; in addition, several Pisidian mercenaries serving in the Ptolemaic army appear to be from Etenna (Ἐτεννεύς)[65].

After Alexander's conquest and until ca. 301 BC the Pamphylian cities of Side and Aspendos, as well as the southern Pisidian cities of Etenna and Selge, had been allowed to (continue to) strike their own coins based on the Persian standard[66]. The Ptolemies, however, introduced a royal coinage of their own and this was the only coinage allowed within their kingdom[67]. As a consequence, the cities of southern Anatolia which came under Ptolemaic control in the third century BC, ceased minting their own coins[68]. It had only recently become clear that Ptolemaic coins were used in the region[69], but there were no mints established in it which issued Ptolemaic coins[70].

Ptolemaic rule in Pamphylia (and apparently not in Lycia[71]) was interrupted by the second Syrian war (260-253 BC). The Pamphylian cities of Perge and Aspendos began to mint their own coins again during this brief period of independence[72]. Ptolemy III Euergetes re-established power in Pamphylia during the third Syrian war (246-241 BC) and called it, in the Adoulis inscription, a separate conquest, whereas Lycia is said to be an inherited possession[73]. Evidence for Pisidia is lacking: possibly only the southern part of Pisidia remained under Ptolemaic control (administered by a Pam-

---

[58] See in general, J. Nollé and F. Schindler in *IK* 37: 13-19.
[59] For bibliography, see Von Aulock 1979.
[60] Kosmetatou 1997.
[61] *SEG* 17.639; Bagnall 1976: 111-113; Hauben 1988.
[62] Bagnall 1976: 110-114; Kosmetatou 1997.
[63] Robert 1966.
[64] See Kosmetatou 1997.
[65] Launey 1949: 471-476.
[66] Head 1977²: 699; Von Aulock 1979; *Coin Hoards* VIII 1994 no. 210 (silver coin from Selge found in a hoard from Cilicia; burial ca. 310 BC). For the other cities of Pamphylia and Pisidia no mints are attested for this period.
[67] Le Rider 1986: 39-51; Howgego 1995: 52-54.
[68] Aspendos and Side still issued their own bronze coins through the third century BC.
[69] Bagnall (1976: 198-200) lists some reports recording very few (bronze) Ptolemaic coins in southern Asia Minor and concludes that "it does not appear that there was an active monetary policy in effect". Recent new evidence, however, changes this picture: a hoard found in Antalya, the heart of Pamphylia, contains Ptolemaic gold coins of Berenike, Arsinoe II, the Theoi Adelphoi and Polemy IV, buried during the late third century BC (*Coin Hoards* I 1975 no. 69); another hoard discovered in the Fethiye region (Lycia) was buried ca. 300-200 BC and contains silver tetradrachmas of Ptolemy I and II (*Coin Hoards* VIII 1994 no. 246); a large hoard buried in 240-235 BC originates from Meydancıkkale (near Gülnar in Cilicia Tracheia), where a Ptolemaic garrison was settled: of the 5215 silver coins, 2158 are Ptolemaic (type Ptolemy I and Arsinoe II) (*Coin Hoards* VIII 1994 no. 308). Thus Ptolemaic coins apparently circulated in the region of southern Anatolia conquered by the Ptolemies. (It is noticeable that in general almost no Ptolemaic coins are found in hoards of Asia Minor. According to Le Rider (1986: 43-44) "La quasi-absence des Ptolémées dans les trésors d'Asie s'explique par le fait que cette monnaie, à cause de son poids particulière, n'avait pas sa place dans les transactions commerciales de la zone d'étalon attique et que son éventuel possesseur était tenu de la convertir au préalable en alexandres, en numéraire séleucide ou attalide").
[70] Bagnall 1976: 194-198.
[71] Bagnall 1976: 108.
[72] Perge issued for a period of 13 years their own series of silver coins and Aspendos once more struck their own silver staters based on the Persian standard, see H. Seyrig in *Revue Numismatique* 1963: 40; Bagnall 1976: 197; Price 1991: 358.
[73] *OGIS* 54, l. 15.

phyliarch as in the reign of Ptolemy II), otherwise the region would doubtless have been mentioned among the Ptolemaic possessions in Euergetes' Adoulis-inscription. Anyway, the Ptolemies were mainly interested in the cities and harbours along the coast of southern Asia Minor, or to quote Polybius (5.34.7): the Ptolemaic kings reigning before Ptolemy IV "had the chief cities, strong places and harbours in their hands all along the coast from Pamphylia to the Hellespont"[74].

Northern Pisidia. – But what happened to northern Pisidia? Did it come under Seleucid control after 281 BC, or was it independent like Selge? Or did it become a base for operations by the Galatians as some Phrygian towns did? I will here tentatively suggest ascribing the Sagalassos inscription to the same period as its paleographic parallels from Laodikeia (267 BC) and Termessos (281/280 BC) (see above, date) and link the rebellion to the Galatian invasion in Asia Minor, which has been thoroughly studied by Mitchell (1993). This suggestion is, however, purely hypothetical.

After 301 BC the northern part of the region probably regained its independence for some time, as already suggested by Bevan (1902: 100), but there is no evidence for this. At some point, Antiochos I (280-261 BC) had to cope with the terrifying Galatians, who arrived in Asia Minor in 278/277 BC[75]. As Bevan (1902: 140) says, the Galatians "hampered the authority [of the Seleucids] by being always there to furnish material to any antagonist of the paramount power. All the opponents with whom the house of Seleucus had hitherto to deal, all future rebels, had now an unfailing source of strength on which to draw. (...) To the Greek cities the result was twofold. (...) According as they looked at the matter from this side or that, they saw in the barbarians a danger and in the kings the saviours of Hellenism, or in the kings a danger and in the barbarians a safeguard." Bevan's statement is partly based on the Greek Historian Memnon of Heraklea Pontika who describes how the Galatian arrival in Asia Minor was at first considered as a threat, but how in the end the poleis saw the kings as the enemies of their "demokratia", and the Galatians rather as its protectors[76].

Sagalassos, if defying external control during the period 301-281 BC, was undoubtedly one of those cities that saw in the Galatian incursions a safeguard of its independence against the Seleucids. The Galatians must have been very near Sagalassos as Galatian arm rings (dated to the third century BC) have been found near Isparta[77]. We know furthermore that the Galatians threatened the region where later Laodikeia on the Lykos was founded, which was at the time private property that Achaios had received from Antiochos I (see below). Pausanias relates how the Galatians made a raid on Themisonion, to the south-east of Laodikeia on the Lykos (10.32.4) as well as on Kelainai (near Dinar), to the north-west of Sagalassos (10.30.9)[78]. The Galatians probably went even further south reaching the south coast of Lycia which was under Ptolemaic control: they apparently threatened Limyra, where an imposing monument was dedicated to Ptolemy II and Arsinoe in the 270s BC, including a relief that clearly refers to a victory over the Galatians[79]. At Finike a Celtic belt-buckle (first half third century BC) has been found[80] and the following text may show that the Galatians threatened the Lycian city of Tlos. An epigram[81] in honour of Neoptolemos son of Kraisis, describes how this Ptolemaic general saved the inhabitants of Tlos. According to the interpretation of Robert (1990), the second part of the epigram runs as follows:

οὕνεκεν ὧν Πισίδας καὶ ...ᾶνες ἠδ' Ἀγριᾶνας
καὶ Γαλάτας τόσσους ἀντιάσας στόρεσα

"c'est pour eux (les citoyens de Tlos) que Pisidiens, (Péoniens?) et Agrianes
et Gaulois en si grand nombre je les ai affrontés pour les abattre."

The epigram suggests that the warlike Pisidians joined the Galatians and Agrianes (a Thracian tribe)[82] during their raids in Lycia (at Tlos and maybe also at Limyra and Finike, see above)[83]. When exactly Neoptolemos son of Kraisis,

---

[74] Translation by W.R. Paton.
[75] Wörrle 1975: 63; Strobel 1991: 116; Mitchell 1993: 15.
[76] *FGrH* III.3 no. 434 (11): τῶν γὰρ βασιλέων τὴν τῶν πόλεων δημοκρατίαν ἀφελεῖν σπουδαζόντων, αὐτοὶ (the Galatians) μᾶλλον ταύτην ἐβεβαίουν, ἀντικαθιστάμενοι τοῖς ἐπιτιθεμένοις.
[77] Müller-Karpe 1988: 195-196.
[78] These Galatian raids on Kelainai and Themisonion may also date to a later period, see Stähelin 1907²: 9. For the dating in the reign of Eumenes II, see Magie 1950: 731, note 11. For the possible dating of these raids in the 270s or 260s BC, see Wörrle 1975: 65; Mitchell 1993: 17; Cohen 1995: 326 on Themisonion ("Gallic invasion of 278 BC or later raids of the 230s BC, when the Gauls were allied with Antiochos Hierax").
[79] Borchhardt-Stanzl 1990: 79-84; Mitchell 1993: 18.
[80] Mitchell 1993: 18, note 58; see, however, the reservations by Strobel 1991: 125, note 166.
[81] Stephanus Byz., *s.v.* Ἀγρίαι.
[82] For Thracians joining the Galatians in their raids in Asia Minor as far south as Lycia in the first half of the third century BC, see Robert 1990: 242.
[83] See Robert 1990: 258: "Les Pisidiens s'étaient joints aux envahisseurs gaulois"; see also Mitchell 1993: 17-18. This hostility of the Pisidians towards the Lycians continues in the second century BC as revealed by the Araxa-decree, see Bean 1948; *Bull. ép.* 1950 no. 183; Robert 1990: 254-255.

who was an eponymous priest in Alexandria in 252-251 BC[84], defeated them, is under discussion[85], but a date before the defeat of the Gauls by Antiochos I ca. 269/268 BC (see below) is certainly possible[86] and would place the events in the same period as the withdrawal of the Galatians from the region of Limyra in the 270s (see above).

After the First Syrian War (274-271 BC), Antiochos I could again concentrate on the Galatians and won an important victory in a battle now dated to ca. 269/268 BC[87], in which the enemy was frightened by the sight of the King's elephants. The Gauls were most probably driven away from southern and western Anatolia and were active later in Bithynia and Pontus[88]. As Mitchell points out (1993: 18), the victory over the Gauls was "as decisive for the security of Asia as the battle of Lysimacheia was for Thrace and Macedonia". From then on, Antiochos assumed the title of *Soter*.

The attitude of the Anatolian cities towards Antiochos was varied and reflects the support which he got from them during the war. (1) Cities like those of the Ionian League (see below) may have remained more or less neutral, probably hoping to become independent if Antiochos lost his cause, but after the war submitted subserviently to the Seleucid regime. (2) Other cities, like the later city of Laodikeia on the Lykos (see below), were honoured for having supported the king. (3) Still other cities, probably including Sagalassos (see below), would not give up their independence and revolted against Antiochos.

(1) The decree of the Ionian League in honour of Antiochos I (ca. 267-262 BC) was promulgated after an important victory[89], undoubtedly that over the Gauls. They offer their congratulations and express their hope that they will continue to be free and autonomous and live according to their own traditional laws. A similar, unfortunately fragmentary, decree was issued by the city of Erythrae for 'a' king Antiochos. The answer of the king is in this case preserved: he promises that the city will be autonomous and will be free of paying 'for Galatian matters' (a war fund?)[90]. It is, however, still under discussion which Antiochos is referred to here[91].

(2) Shortly after Antiochos' victory in 267 BC, a decree was set up in the territory of the later city of Laodikeia on the Lykos; two agents of Achaios (see above) are honoured for their services in the Galatian war (τὸν πόλεμον τὸν Γαλατικὸν)[92]. (3) There was also "an active policy of defence by which the Seleucids [especially Antiochos I] founded a string of military colonies at strategic points in the headwaters of the valleys that led from central Anatolia to the west coast, and marked the possible routes of invasion"[93]. Thus Seleukeia Sidera was founded (probably by Antiochos I) on the western side of Lake Eğirdir, to the north-east of Sagalassos, and as Bevan (1902: 166) notes "this may also have been intended to keep a watch on Sagalassos and the Pisidian towns to the south".

All this suggests that Antiochos I had now got a firmer grip on the region and, *if* the Sagalassos inscription is to be linked to this series of events, Antiochos apparently forced rebellious Sagalassos to negotiate a peace between the supporters and opponents of Seleucid power. That some of the Sagalassians withstood the Seleucids, but in Roman times adopted the Indian elephant as state official seal – a symbol of Seleucid power and maybe even a reference to their victory over the Galatians[94] - does not tell against our hypothesis. The Sagalassians also resisted Alexander, but afterwards honoured him as a hero in, for example, representing the Macedonian conqueror on their coins of the Imperial period[95].

5.3. The Hellenization of Pisidia under Antiochos III

We are better informed on the history of Pisidia and neighbouring regions from the 220s BC onward[96]. Except perhaps for cities in the south, such as Termessos, Pisidia did not apparently submit to Antiochos III until after the defeat of the usurper Achaios in 216 BC. Seleucid control allowed a certain degree of autonomy. It is for palaeographical reasons less likely that the revolt described in the Sagalassos inscription is to be ascribed to this point of history, when the Sagalassians again lost their independence.

During the reign of Antiochos III the Hellenization of Sagalassos was accelerated as is indicated by indirect but

---

[84] Clarysse-Van der Veken 1983: 8.
[85] Robert 1990 (between 278-252 BC). Recently, Strobel 1991: 125-126, places the victory during the Second Syrian War (260-253 BC) and puts forward the thesis that the group of Thracians, Pisidians and Galatians is a "Formation seleukidischer Kräfte mit antigonidischer Unterstützung".
[86] For similar cases where a military officer becomes an eponymous priest after ca. 20 years of duty, see Ijsewijn 1961: 62-118, passim.
[87] Wörrle 1975: 63-72; Strobel 1991: 123 and note 152; Mitchell 1993: 18.
[88] Mitchell 1993: 19.

[89] *OGIS* 222 and Piejko 1991.
[90] *IK* 1.30 and 31.
[91] Antiochos I: Habicht 1970²: 93-99; Antiochos I or II: see *IK* 1. 30-31; Antiochos III: Piejko 1991: 131, n. 7.
[92] Wörrle 1975; *IK* 49.1.
[93] Mitchell 1993: 20; see also Orth 1977: 141, n. 13; Cohen 1978: 15; Cohen 1995: 418.
[94] Vandorpe 1995.
[95] Kosmetatou 1997.
[96] See especially, Schmitt 1964: 158-175; Bracke 1993; Beyer-Rotthoff 1993: 72-80; Syme 1995: 198-199; Kosmetatou 1997. For the history of Pisidia after 200 BC, I refer to the stud-

nevertheless persuasive evidence (see next paragraph). The Sagalassos inscription cannot be dated to this period of Hellenization, since it lists at the end twenty-four names, all Pisidian, none Greek.

Several ostothekai decorated with a Macedonian shield[97] were found at Sagalassos. They can be dated from their reliefs to the third – first centuries BC and may thus bear witness to the settlement of Greek colonists in the area already in the third century BC[98]. Furthermore, traces of Seleucid dominion are found in later architectural features[99]. Sagalassos also issued Alexander coins under Antiochos III, of which one specimen has been found (see below).

Recently, similar conclusions were reached for the region of the Milyas (to the south-west of Sagalassos). A decree from Olbasa published by Kearsley (1994) shows that "Olbasa was a city with a Greek democratic constitution and strong Greek influence in nomenclature before the middle of the second century (...) a thorough Hellenization had occurred already by that time". Kearsley is searching out Greek influence and Greek settlers from the third century, when Asia Minor was under Seleucid control.

Finally, I want to discuss in more detail the oldest preserved autonomous coin from Sagalassos, a posthumous Alexander dating from the reign of Antiochos III. This silver tetradrachma, listed by Hill in the *Numismatic Chronicle* of 1917 (p. 16-17) and by Price in his catalogue of 1991 (no. 2985), has been largely ignored. Usually Sagalassos is said not to have minted coins before it started its own coinage about the time of Amyntas in the first century BC.

Alexander and the Hellenistic kings after him (who thus wanted to indicate their right to the succession) tried to introduce a unified monetary system based on the Attic standard. The coins referred to as 'Alexanders' and 'posthumous Alexanders' were struck during his lifetime and in his name (or in the name of Philip III) after his death, until 294 BC, and again during the third and second centuries BC, by cities with a certain degree of autonomy.

Alexander's monetary system mainly consisted of silver tetradrachmas of the Attic standard. In Asia Minor smaller coins have also been minted, such as drachmas; smaller silver coins were a more familiar medium of exchange for the people of Asia Minor who were used to the smaller coins of the Persian standard; at the end of third – beginning of the second century, the tetradrachmas became the staple coinage[100].

The unified monetary system that Alexander and Antigonos wanted to introduce in the East was at first not very successful in Southern Anatolia[101]. What happened in northern Pisidia in the period 301-ca. 221 BC is not clear, but the situation was very unstable and not suited to the minting of coins. Which coins circulated in the region also remains unclear. They were undoubtedly Alexanders, the dominant currency of the Seleucid empire, as in other parts of Asia Minor[102].

The rule of Antiochos III allowed a certain degree of autonomy: several cities of Pamphylia and Pisidia, among them Termessos and Sagalassos, began to mint their own posthumous Alexander tetradrachmas and instituted new dating eras. Thus, many of the coins are dated with sequence numbers referring to the new city era[103] (thus Perge, Sillyum, Termessos[104]). The minting in Pisidia and Pamphylia was interrupted by the revolt in 218-216 BC of the above-mentioned Achaios. After the rebellion, the minting continued and a new era began at Magydos and at Aspendos (Price 1991: 346-368). Side began to issue Alexanders, but changed to silver coins of a civic type (with Athena and

---

ies of Mitchell 1991, Brandt 1992, Bracke 1993, Waelkens 1993 and Kosmetatou 1997. An important new inscription from the city of Olbasa in the Milyas (to the west of Pisidia) has to be added to the evidence of the second century BC, recording a Pisidian war (ὁ Πισιδικὸς πόλεμος) between the Pisidians and the city's citizens. Kearsley (1994) relates the events to the Pergamene campaigns in Pisidia ca. mid-second century BC.

[97] If not of Pisidian origin, see J. Nollé and F. Schindler in *IK* 37: 13-14, n. 11.
[98] Mitchell-Owens-Waelkens 1989; Kosmetatou and Waelkens 1997.
[99] Waelkens 1993: 42.
[100] Thompson-Bellinger 1955 (on Alexander drachmas); Göbl 1978: 65-69, 155-156; Thompson 1981 (on a small group of drachmas issued at Side); Price 1991: 73-79; Howgego 1995: 48-51; see especially Le Rider 1986.
[101] Only the Pamphylian port and city of Side (which also struck its own coins) minted Alexander silver tetradrachmas and drachmas between 323 and 317 BC (Price 1991 no. 2966-2974; ? 2948-2965). It is doubtful whether the Alexanders from Pisidian Termessos were issued in the period 319-301 BC (*Pace* Kosmetatou 1997); they were probably minted at the end of the third century BC (see below). Silver Alexanders were circulating inland, for instance, in the region of Denizli (to the west of Pisidia) (*Coin Hoards* VII 1985 no. 61 (ca. 300 BC)).
[102] Le Rider 1986: 32-39; esp. p. 27: "au IIIe siècle, en Asie Mineure et dans l'Orient séleucide, lorsque des transactions comportaient un paiement en drachmes, celles-ci étaient dans leur très grande majorité des monnaies aux types d'Alexandre". Hoards of Asia Minor buried in the period 272-225 BC consist mainly of Alexanders (Le Rider 1986: 32-39; see also *Coin Hoards* VIII 1994 no. 267 (:silver tetradrachmas and drachmas mainly issued in the name of Alexander and Philip III; burial ca. 280 BC)). Most of these Alexanders were issued in the name of Alexander before 301 BC; the money thus circulated for rather a long time (Le Rider 1986: esp. p. 2).
[103] There is much discussion on the exact starting point of the eras, see especially Price 1991: 346-348.
[104] The only date found on the five specimens from Termessos has the sequence number 13 and probably coincides with the Perge-era; see Cox 1966: 35-36; Price 1991 no. 2986-2987 [the attribution of the two coins of no. 2987 to Termessos is very probable, though not certain]; for a fifth posthumous Alexander from Termessos preserved in the collection of the American Numismatic Society, see Kosmetatou 1997, n. 43.

Nike; Price 1991: 363).
The one silver tetradrachma from Sagalassos from this period is said 'to stand alone. The attribution is, however, certain from the letters in the field [ΣΑΓΑ], but the style is rather individual' (Price 1991 no. 2985). In addition, the bucranium-symbol beneath Zeus' throne clearly refers to Sagalassos, as this symbol is also found on the city's autonomous coins of the first century BC. The coin is not dated by a sequence number and was probably issued in 200-189 BC. In addition, a silver drachma of the civic type struck at Side in the period 205-190 BC (see above), was found at Sagalassos[105]. These are the only two references to coins in or from Sagalassos during the earlier Hellenistic period.

6. A LIST OF PISIDIAN PERSONAL NAMES

The early Hellenistic inscription contains at the end a long list of indigenous, Anatolian personal names. They are an important enrichment of our knowledge of Pisidian anthroponymy. Pisidian as well as Lycian, Sidetan (Pamphylia), Isaurian and Cilician belong to the Luwian language group, whereas Carian and Lydian are part of Hittite-Luwian[106]. Consequently, in the Hellenistic period, Luwian names are found mainly in the region of the Taurus mountains (Lycia, transitional regions between South-Phrygia and Pisidia/Lycia and between East-Phrygia and Pisidia, Pamphylia, Lycaonia, Isauria, Cilicia)[107]. Most of the Anatolian names listed in the Sagalassos inscription are indeed Luwian and some elements of the names are often found in the other regions where Luwian names have been found[108]. According to Houwink ten Cate, Pisidia has produced "a relatively larger number of names with no Luwian connections", originating from newcomers from the north[109]. There are, however, no names of foreign origin found in the early Hellenistic Sagalassos inscription.

Indigenous Anatolian names which are rendered in *scriptio continua* without Greek endings, are often difficult to split. This is the case in the 'epichoric' inscriptions of Pisidia, which were found in the region between the Eğirdir and the Beyşehir lakes and date to the Roman imperial age[110]. Fortunately, the names of the Sagalassos-inscription can in most cases be split since most have a Greek ending:
- Greek endings (or indigenous endings coinciding with the Greek endings): -ος gen. -ου, -ις gen. -ιος (i-stem declined like πόλις), -ας, -ης gen. -ου, -ους gen. -ου
- Indigenous ending(s) are: -εις (an ending frequently found in Anatolia) and -αις (if not for -ιας, see below: Αλουπαις).[111]

Laminger-Pascher (1973: 66-67) has already indicated that: "ein und derselbe Name nach verschiedenen (griechischen) Deklinationsarten flektiert wird (…). Auffällig ist, daβ solche Varianten gerade bei häufig gebrauchten Namen am zahlreichsten sind". For instance, the frequently occurring name Ναννεις is written as Ναν(ν)ας, Ναν(ν)ος, Νανιος, Νανης, Νανων, Ναννεις (see below, s.v. Νανεις).

There are other problems of interpretation: (1) Are there (grand)father's names listed? The first six names are in the genitive corresponding with ἀρχόντων. Then the scribe apparently changed to the nominative for the following ca. 18 names. It is less likely that there are father's names among the first six names in the genitive, since they are missing for the last 18 names in the nominative. (2) Are there names of tribes listed? The names ending in -εις (Εννεις, Οαδεις and Σανεις) could theoretically be names of tribes. Οαδεις could refer to the inhabitants of the Phrygian town Οαζα (ethnic: Ουαζηνος), Σανεις to the Phrygian town Σαναος or Σανις[112]. However, tribes or inhabitants with such names have not appeared in Pisidia. Therefore, I prefer to interpret them as personal names: anthroponyms with the ending -εις are typical of Anatolia (see above); Εννεις and Οαδεις are well-known personal names; Σανεις may be a variant of Σανυς.

Only a few anthroponyms are attested elsewhere, though sometimes in a variant form or with variant endings (see above). Most of them are new names, compounded with known elements. The names or elements ιβδα-, -κλωιας, Μαλλου (gen.), Οις or Οισ-, -παις, Σιλλαβος and τονα- are problematic (for our interpretation, see below).

6.1. Survey of the compounding elements

-αδι in Ιδααδιος (gen.)
αλου- in Αλουπαις
αρβη- in Αρβης or do we have to read Κιλασαρβης?
-αρμοα in Αρμοας

---

[105] Scheers 1993 no. 4 and 1995: 315.
[106] Zgusta 1963; see also Laroche 1966, Table between 367-368; Neumann 1980: 172; for Lydian anthroponymy, see also Gusmani 1988.
[107] Houwink ten Cate 1961: 192.
[108] Compare Houwink ten Cate 1961, appendix.
[109] "In Lycia and Cilicia Apsera, the two regions most isolated from the interior [by the Taurus mountains, which approach the shore in both these regions], the Luwians were best able to maintain themselves as a separate group. Foreign population groups evidently penetrated the other sections of the southern coast [which have a coastal plain, for instance Pamphylia]." (Houwink ten Cate 1961: 192 and 1).
[110] Published by Ramsay 1895; Borchardt-Neumann-Schulz 1979; Brixhe-Gibson 1982; Brixhe-Drew Bear-Kaya 1987; see Zgusta 1957 and 1963; Neumann 1980: 176. The inscriptions (except for Brixhe-Drew Bear-Kaya 1987) have been gathered by Brixhe 1988.
[111] For the Greek and indigenous endings in Anatolian names, see Laminger-Pascher 1973: 52-86.
[112] Zgusta 1984 §959-2 and §1156.

-βασις in Κοτβασις
εννει- in Εννεις
ιβδα- in Ιβδαμοας
ιδα- in Ιδααδιος (gen.)
κιλα- in Κιλας (or? Κιλασαρβης)
-κλωια in Μοακλωιας
κοτ- in Κοτβασις
κουα- in Κουας
(-)μοα(-) in Ιβδαμοας, Μοακλωιας, Μοασιος (gen.)
νανει- in Νανεις
οα- in Οας, Οαδεις
? οισ- in Οις or Οισαρμοας
-παι in Αλουπαις
πονα- in Πονασαμις
-σαμι in Πονασαμις
? σιλλα- in Σιλλαβος
τονα- in Τοναωλλιος (gen.)
-ωλλι in Τοναωλλιος (gen.)

6.2. Commentary on the names

Αλουπαις (new name)
αλου- is probably the same element as in the names Αλλους (Pisidia[113]; the alteration λ /λλ is common and insignificant) and Αλοητος (Pisidia[114]). Zgusta links the element also with the names Αλιους (Lycaonia), Αλλακοας (Pisidia, Termessos), Αλλεας (Caria) and the woman's name Αλλαγα found in western Pisidia[115]. Is this compound element to be connected with the element *alu-*, Greek αλυ-, found in Hittite (*Aluluwa* etc.) and Lydian names (*Alus*, Αλυς, Αλυάττης etc.)[116]?
-παις: There are no clear parallels for this compound element. There exists, however, a name ending in -β(ε)αις found only in Pisidia (the alteration of voiced and voiceless consonants is common and not significant): Ουρουβαις (on the condition that the nominative is correctly reconstructed[117]) and Βεκκωβεαις (Termessos[118]). For the ending -αις in the latter name Neumann refers to the ancient Phrygian names on -ais: according to Lejeune[119], the ending -αις in those Phrygian names could be a syncope of -αιος. The same element is perhaps found in a variant form in Ιγδαμπαιης (Olbia, North Shore Black Sea[120]) or at the beginning of the name in ΠαιαϜας, Lycian *Pajawa* (*Pam*phylia and Lycia[121]).
The endings -παις and -βαις (in Ουρουβαις) are probably not variants of the frequently found endings -πιας, -βιας, -πις, -πεας, etc[122]. The well-known ending on -πιας originates from Luwian *-piya* ('gift by') and is found in the names Αρμαπιας, Ερμαπιας, Ερπιας, Κουλαπιας, etc[123].

? Αρμοας (name attested) or Οισαρμοας, see *s.v.*
Personal names compounded with *Arma-*, the name of the Hittite-Luwian moon-god, are well attested among the Anatolian anthroponyms of the Greco-Roman period: Αρμοας, Αρμοασις, Αρμαστα, etc[124]. In Pisidia the names Αρμαστα, Αρμαστις and Ερμαστα are found.

Εννεις (variant of the name attested)
This name is found in various forms: Ενας, Εννης, Εννις (South-Phrygia-Pisidia, South- Phrygia-Lycia, Isauria, Cilicia, Lydia[125]). The name Ενεις (Pisidian genitive) is probably also found in an epichoric Pisidian inscription[126]. The variant Εννεις found in the Sagalassos-inscription is new.

Ιβδαμοας (new name compounded with the known element -μοας)
-μοας: For the Luwian compound element -μοας, see the name Μοασις.
ιβδα-: There are no clear parallels for the element ιβδα-. It is probably found in the anthroponym Βδευασις (or Βαευασις?; Pisidia[127]) and in the Carian place name Σιβδα[128]. According to Sundwall (1913: 176) -βδα- is a transcription of Lycian *pdda, compare the name *pdda-knta*[129].
There is another possible etymology. The groups βδ, κβ, κδ, τβ, γδ, etc. in Anatolian names are found exclusively in Pisidia, Isauria, Cilicia and Lycia and are apparently the result of a syncope. Thus Γδα-ομοασις is undoubtedly a syncope of Κιδα-μουασις[130]. In the case of Ιβδαμοας a prothetic *i* has to facilitate the pronunciation[131]. Thus ιβδα- could be a syncope of Παδα-, attested in the names Παδαμουρις and Παδαμουριανος (Pisidia[132]) or of Πιδα-, attested in the names Πιδασις and Πιδενηνις (Lycia[133]) and ?Πιδος(Pisidia[134]).

Πιατηραβις (Pisidia; Zgusta 1964 §1251-2), compare the Hittite names with **Piyatar-* (Laroche 1966 no. 986-988).

---

[113] Zgusta 1964 §52-2.
[114] Zgusta 1964 §54.
[115] Zgusta 1964. PNsippen: 37-38; Zgusta 1964 *s.v.*
[116] See for the names with *alu-* Laroche 1966 no. 38-41; Zgusta 1964 §56 and the article on 'Il tipo onomastico ALUS' by Innocente 1990; for the alteration in Greek o / ου / υ (from Hittite-Luwian /u/) see Brixhe 1988: 139-140; Blümel 1992: 31.
[117] Zgusta 1964 §1173 and note 177.
[118] Neumann 1992: 27.
[119] Lejeune 1969: 292.
[120] *SEG* 40.631.
[121] Zgusta 1964 §1190-1/2.
[122] For the alteration παι / πια I may refer to the name Παιταροβης, a hapax attested in Pisidia, Termessos (Zgusta 1964 §1192) and a variant of the well-known anthroponym
[123] Houwink ten Cate 1961: 175-177; Masson 1990: 168-170.
[124] Houwink ten Cate 1961: index; Zgusta 1964.PNsippen §19.
[125] Zgusta 1964 §334.
[126] Brixhe 1988: 133; otherwise Zgusta 1964 §334-6 note 38.
[127] Zgusta 1964 §157.
[128] Zgusta 1984 §1207.
[129] Zgusta 1964 §1228.
[130] Zgusta 1964; Brixhe 1988: 140.
[131] Compare the prothetic *e* in Εστλεγιιυς cited by Brixhe 1988: 140.
[132] Zgusta 1964 §1187.
[133] Zgusta 1964 §1256.
[134] Zgusta 1964 §1256, note 175. Compare also the Hittite names using *Pidda/Pitta*, Laroche 1966 no. 1025-1033: is no. 1033 *Pitta-zzi* = Πιδασις?

*Ιδααδις, gen. Ιδααδιος (new name compounded with the known element ιδα-)

ιδα-: The element is well known from names such as Lycian *Ida*, Pisidian Ιδαλωβασις, Carian Ιδαγυγος, Lycian Ιδαγρης = *Idakre*, Lycian Ιδακλοα, etc[135].

-αδις, gen. -αδιος: The element -αδις has parallels in names such as Καρταδις (*Lycia*[136]) and ?Μισσαυαδιος (genitive[137]; Pisidian name[138]).

? Κιλασαρβης (new name compounded with the known element κιλα-) or ? Κιλας Αρβης

It is not clear whether we have to read Κιλασαρβης or split the name into Κιλας Αρβης: the name Κιλας is well-known, the name Αρβης is not attested, but the compound Αρβησις[139] is. As ΚΙΛΑΣΑΡΒΗΣ is encountered twice in the inscription and as it would be strange that the same two names Κιλας and Αρβης follow each other twice, I prefer not to split the name.

κιλα-: The element κιλα- is well attested. It coincides with the Greek names Κίλλης and variants, but the names with κιλα- found in, for instance, Pisidia are undoubtedly indigenous, as Zgusta has already proposed[140]. The element is used to form the simplex Κιλας and Κιλης (Caria, Pisidia, Lycaonia/Lycia) and several compounds such as κιλαριος (Pisidia-Lycaonia[141]), κιλαλοας (Caria[142]), κιλαμουεις (Lycaonia[143]), etc.

-σαρβης: The element -σαρβης is unclear.

Κοτβασις (new name compounded with the known elements κοτ- and -βασις)

κοτ-: This compound element is well-known[144]. The simplex Κοτ(τ)ης is frequently attested in Pisidia, for instance, at Termessos and in the region of Burdur (also in Pamphylia and Lycia)[145]. The element κοτ- is furthermore found in the front position in the compounds Κοττονεις and variants (Pisidia, Isauria[146]), Κοτοβης (Lydia[147]), Κοτοραλημις (Cilicia, Lycia[148]), Κοτυσις/ Κοτασις (Pisidia, Lycia[149]), Κοτβελημος (= Κυτβελημος; Caria[150]).

-βασις: The element -βασ(σ)ις is always found in last position[151]: Αρυνβασις (Lycia[152]), Λογβασις (Pisidia[153]), Λουβασις or βουλουβασις or Τουλουβασις (South-Phrygia-Lycia[154]), Ουαββασις (Isauria, Cilicia[155]), Ουανγδιβασσιν (Lycaonia[156]), Σωσοβασις (Cilicia[157]).

Κουας (name attested)

An element *kuwa* is encountered in a few Hittite names as a simplex and in compound names[158]. The simplex *kuwa* is rendered in Greek as Κουας (Cilicia[159]), Κοας (Pisidia, Lycia[160]), Κυας (Pisidia[161]) and ΚουϜαυ (gen.; Pamphylia[162]). The variant with κουα- is also found in Pisidia in the compound Κουαδαπεμις. The alteration ο / ου / υ in the Greek rendering of Hittite-Luwian names is often attested, since there is no *o*-sound, only an *u*-sound in the latter language group[163]. There are compounds with-κο(υ)α- in front and end positions attested in Pisidia, Pamphylia and Cilicia[164].

The names compounded with the element *kuwa* are attested in Lycia, Pamphylia, and especially in Pisidia and Cilicia. In Western Pisidia the name Κουαδαπεμις is found (see above), in Termessos the names Κυας, Κοας, Πιλλακοας, Παλακοας, Αλλακοας and Μιλικουας[165].

Μαγισιλβις (variant of the name attested)

The variant Μαγασιλβις is found in a text discovered near Burdur, in the vicinity of Sagalassos[166]. The first element is also found in the name ΜαγασιψϜας (Pamphylia[167]), the second in Σιλβος (South-Phrygia-Pisidia, Caria[168]).

---

[135] Sundwall 1913: 86; Zgusta 1964 §451; Blümel 1992: 14; Masson 1990: 21;? Laroche 1966 no. 477: *Idahakab*.
[136] Zgusta 1964 §543-1.
[137] Zgusta 1964 §931 and p. 694.
[138] See Robert 1963: 103-104 and 1970: 366 and n.3; Blümel 1992: 19.
[139] Αρβησις is made up of the elements *arpa* ('Ungunst, Misserfolg') and the suffix -*zi*, see Houwink ten Cate 1961; Zgusta 1964 §85; Zgusta 1964.PNsippen §11.
[140] Sundwall 1913: 105-106; Robert 1963: 400, n. 4; Zgusta 1964 §607; Zgusta 1970 §607-9a; Laminger-Pascher 1973: 104; Blümel 1992: 16.
[141] Zgusta 1964 §607-9.
[142] Zgusta 1964 §607-8.
[143] *SEG* 42.1269.
[144] Sundwall 1913: 127.
[145] Zgusta 1964 §707-3 and 4; *SEG* 40.1268; Robert 1948: 12; Robert 1963: 283.
[146] Zgusta 1964 §708; *SEG* 42. 1276; *IK* 37.1.
[147] Zgusta 1964 §707-1.
[148] Zgusta 1964 §707-2.
[149] Zgusta 1964 §706.
[150] Blümel 1992: 17 and *SEG* 40.992.

[151] Sundwall 1913: 236-237.
[152] Zgusta 1964 §113.
[153] Zgusta 1964 §821.
[154] Zgusta 1964 §948 and 1590-2.
[155] Zgusta 1964 §1130-2.
[156] Zgusta 1964 §1139-2.
[157] Zgusta 1970 §1491a.
[158] Houwink ten Cate 1961: 152-153; Zgusta 1964.PNsippen §4; Laroche 1966 no. 659-662.
[159] Zgusta 1964 §713-1.
[160] Zgusta 1964 §638; *EA* 24 (1995): 95-126 no. 41.
[161] Zgusta 1964 §762-1.
[162] Brixhe 1976 no. 96.
[163] Brixhe 1988: 139-140; Blümel 1992: 31; see also Laminger-Pascher 1973: 99-101.
[164] Sundwall 1913: 127-128; Houwink ten Cate 1961: 152-153; Zgusta 1964 §713-3; 714; Robert 1963: 427; Brixhe-Drew Bear-Kaya 1987: 158-159; Neumann 1992: 32.
[165] Zgusta 1964.PNsippen: 39-41; Zgusta 1964 *s.v.*
[166] Zgusta 1964 §840-1; Robert 1954: 78.
[167] Zgusta 1964 §840-2; not in Μαγα", see Zgusta 1964 §840-3.
[168] Zgusta 1964 §1426.

*Μαλλος, gen. Μαλλου (new name)

The personal name Μαλλος is not yet attested, except for the legendary founder of the city of Μαλλος in Cilicia. There are four cities in Anatolia bearing the name Μαλλος (Cilicia, Phrygia, Galatia and Pisidia). They have all been located. The most famous one is Marlos, Hellenized as Mallos, in Cilicia[169]. The town of Μαλλος or Μαλος (ethnic Μαληνός) in Pisidia, located near Sarridiris to the north-east of Lake Eğirdir, has produced coins from the period first century BC- first century AD[170]. Finally, I would like to add *mala*, the Anatolian name for the Euphrates, attested as a personal name in Hittite texts[171]. There could also be a link with the element μαλο- in the name Μαλοσωος (Caria[172]).

*Μοασις, gen. Μοασιος (new name compounded with the known elements μοα-)
The Hittite-Luwian element *muwa* is widespread in the onomastics of earlier periods and is especially attested in the Greco-Roman period in the regions of Caria and Lydia (producing names with Hittite connections) as well as in Lycia, Pisidia, Pamphylia, Lycaonia, Isauria and Cilicia (producing names with Luwian connections)[173]. The element *muwa* appears as a simplex, rendered in Greek as Μοας, Μουας, Μως. In compounds *muwa* is found in front as well as in second position:
- In front position: μο-, μοα-, μου-, μυα-, μω-[174]. The Sagalassos-inscription has the new compounds Μοακλωιας (see *s.v.*) and Μοασις. For the rendering μοα- in Pisidia, see for instance the name Μοαβις (Termessos[175]). Μοασις is doubtless the rendering of *muwa* + the well-known suffix -*zi*[176]. The suffix was already attested in connection with μοα-, but only in compounds such as Οπραμουασις (versus Οπραμοας; Cilicia, Pamphylia, Lycaonia-Isauria[177]), Κιδαμουασις (Cilicia[178]) and Τουαμουσι[179].
- In last position: -μοας, -μυας, -μ(ο)υης, -μως. The Sagalassos inscription has the new compounds Ιβδαμοας and ?Οισαρμοας (see *s.v.*). Known compounds are listed in Houwink ten Cate (1961: 167-169) and Zgusta 1964 (reverse index); to these should be added Εκαμυης (Caria[180]), Οξαμοας (Pisidia-Lycaonia[181]), Στaναμοας (Pisidia[182]).

Μοακλωιας (new name compounded with the known element μοα-)
μοα-: For the element μοα-, see Μοασις.
-κλωιας: There is no exact parallel for the element -κλωια. It is most probably to be connected with -κλοα, -γλοα in Ιδακλοα (Lycia[183]) and Ναλαγλοας (Pisidia-Lycaonia[184]).
Μο.οιτου (gen.), probably Μοκοιτου (variant of the name attested)
The third sign is damaged and fits the letters κ, τ, ρ or ι. I prefer to read Μοκοιτου (gen.) as the traces fit this reading well and because the name Μοκωτης (gen. Μοκωτου) is attested in the Pisidian region (third century AD, South-Phrygia-Pisidia[185]).

Νανε[ις] or Νανε[ι]ς (variants of the name attested)
The Luwian noun *nani* probably means 'brother' and is already attested in Hittite texts. The simplex Ναν(ν)ας, Ναν(ν)ος, Νανιος, Νανης, Νανων, Ναννεις etc. is widespread all over Asia Minor. The form Νανεις with one -ν- is new[186]. There also exist compounds[187].

*Νους, gen. Νου (name attested)
The name Νους, gen. Νου is attested in Cilicia; Zgusta remarks that the name has a Greek form, but that "man ihn im Grunde als einheimisches Sprachgut auffassen dürfen wird[188]". This is confirmed by the Sagalassos text where the name is listed among exclusively Anatolian names.

Οαδεις (variants of the name attested)
Variants of the name are: Οαδας (Isauria), Ουαδις (East-Phrygia) and Ουαδους (Lycaonia)[189]. οαδ- is also part of the name Καροαδις (Lycia[190]).
οα-: For the element οα-, see the name Οας.
-δεις: Variants of this ending are apparently -δας, -δις, -δους. The same kind of variants -εις, -ας, -ις are found in a common name of the south coast Τροκονδας (Lycia, Pisidia, Pamphylia, Lycaonia, Isauria), Τροκονδεις (Lycaonia-Isauria), Τροκονδις (Cilicia-Isauria)[191]. -δεις probably corresponds to the element -*da* found in, for instance, *Kuwa-da* or Lycian *Kuwata* = Κοατα or Pisidian Κουαδα-πεμις or perhaps Isaurian-Cilician Κουδεις[192].

---

[169] Imhoof-Blumer 1883; Zgusta 1984 §773.
[170] Zgusta 1984 §756-6. The Pisidian town Mallos is cited in the *Notitiae* and by Hierokles; for the location of Pisidian Mal(l)os, see Mersich 1985.
[171] Laroche 1966: 277.
[172] Blümel 1992: 18.
[173] Friedrich 1927-1930; Houwink ten Cate 1961: 166-169; Zgusta 1964.PNsippen §23; Laroche 1966: 322-324; Robert 1954 II: 77; W. Blümel, in *IK* 34: 9.
[174] Brixhe-Drew Bear-Kaya 1987: 136, 154, 156; Sundwall 1913: 160-163; Zgusta 1964 §940, §978, §1003; Zgusta 1970: 117.
[175] Zgusta 1964 §940-3.
[176] Houwink ten Cate 1961: 185-186; Laroche 1966: 333.
[177] Zgusta 1964 §602-6.
[178] Zgusta 1964 §602-6.
[179] Brixhe-Drew Bear-Kaya 1987: 152.
[180] Blümel 1992: 12.
[181] Zgusta 1970 §1094-9.
[182] Zgusta 1970 §1472a.
[183] Zgusta 1964 §451-6.
[184] Zgusta 1964 §1010-1, see also Sundwall 1913: 109.
[185] Zgusta 1964 §945.
[186] See Zgusta §1013-18, note 52.
[187] Sundwall 1913: 166; Houwink ten Cate 1961: 142-144; Zgusta 1964 §1013; Zgusta 1964.PNsippen §8; Laroche 1966: 326; Robert 1954: 77; Blümel 1992: 19; Neumann 1992: 30.
[188] Sundwall 1913: 170; Zgusta 1964 §1052; Zgusta 1970 §1052.
[189] Zgusta 1964 §1132-1/3.
[190] Zgusta 1964 §541.
[191] Houwink ten Cate 1961: 126.
[192] Houwink ten Cate 1961: 153; Zgusta §640; 713-3; 718-1.

Οας (name attested)
This name probably corresponds to *uwa* (? 'Family', 'Rind')[193], compare the name *Uwa* in Hittite texts[194]. In Greek the name is rendered as Οα (frequently attested in Pisidia, also found in Isauria[195]) and Οας (East-Phrygia-Galatia, ?Cilicia[196]), in compounds as οα- and ουα- (compare Οαδεις, *supra*). In Pisidia one usually finds οα and not ουα[197].

?Οις or ?Οισαρμοας
I prefer to split this into Οις Αρμοας, as the name Αρμοας is attested (see *s.v.*). If one reads Οισαρμοας (compound with the element -μοας, see Μοασις), there are no parallels for the element οισαρ- or σαρ- except perhaps for Οσαρτηνμος of which the reading is very uncertain[198].
For the element οι- in Οις I refer to names compounded with the element οι-/ ουι-. According to Sundwall (1913: 236-238) this element derives from *uwa (see Οας), variant *uwi, see for instance the Lycian name *Uwa-tise* or *Uwa-ta* probably rendered in a Pisidian text as Ουιτασις. The element οι-/ ουι- is apparently found in the names Ουιω (Pisidia[199]) and Οιω (East-Phrygia[200]), as well as in several compounds of which I only give those attested in Pisidia: Οιμοτης[201], Οιταλοιος[202], Ουιτασις[203], ?Ουιαρος = Lycian *Uwihairi*[204], ?Οιδα[205].

Πονασαμις (new name compounded with the known elements πονα- and -σαμις)
πονα-: The Luwian element *puna-* is already found in names in Hittite texts; the meaning is unknown. It is a well-known part of Luwian names in the Greco-Roman period and *puna-* is rendered by πονα- or πυνα-. In Pisidia, for instance, one finds Πονασατης. The element always appears in compounds and always in the front position[206]. Thus our interpretation Πονασαμις (and not Πονα[18] Σαμις) is safe[207].
-σαμις: The element is found as a simplex in the Pisidian name Σαμης (Termessos) and in the name Σαμος, being an indigenous name of Pisidia, Pamphylia and Caria[208]. σαμ- is met in the compound Σαμασσις (Caria)[209]. The element has not yet been found in the end position[210].

Σανεις (new name or variant of Σανυς)
For the ending, compare the names Κανεις, Μανεις, Νανεις. It is difficult to explain the name as a variant of the Pisidian names Σανβεις[211] or Σανδα (= Σανδας, Σανδης[212]). Is Σανεις a variant of Σανυς (Caria[213])? It has been doubted whether Σανυς is an equivalent of the Greek name Σαννης or not. If Σανυς and Σανεις of the Sagalassos inscription are to be equated, then the names must be indigenous, like all the other names of the inscription.

Σιλλαβος (new name)
Is this new name to be connected with Σιλβος (South-Phrygia-Pisidia, Caria[214])? Or is the element σιλλα- also found in the names Σιλαις (or Σιλλις: reading uncertain; Isauria-Cilicia) and Σιλλεας (Kibyra). Zgusta (1964 §1425, n. 73) considers these rare names as variants of the Greek anthroponyms Σίλλας etc. The ending -βος is well-attested in Anatolian names, see Zgusta, reverse index p. 671.

? Σοας or Οας (see line 15-16)
For Οας, see *s.v.*
The name Σοας is attested in Isauria[215] and originates most probably from the element *zuwa*: the names *Zuwa* and compounds with *Zuwa-* are found in Hittite texts[216].

Τοναωλλις (new name compounded with the known element ωλλι-)
Τονα-: The element is otherwise unknown. The reading τονα- (and not πονα-, a well-known compound element) is clear. Is the same element found in the Pisidian name Τοινα[217] or in the Pisidian place name Τυναδα[218]?
-ωλλις: The element -ωλλι (variant probably -ωλδι[219] and

---

[193] Sundwall 1913: 236 ('Family'); Neumann 1992: 30 ('Rind').
[194] Laroche 1966 no. 1461.
[195] Zgusta 1964 §1129-2; *SEG* 41. index.
[196] Zgusta 1964 §1129-4 and p. 685.
[197] Zgusta 1963: 476.
[198] See *EA* 16 (1990): 40, n. 32; O. Masson, in *Bull. ép.* 1990: 360; Blümel 1992: 20 and n. 70.
[199] Zgusta 1964 §1160-1.
[200] Zgusta 1964 §1160-2.
[201] Zgusta 1964 §1078.
[202] Zgusta 1964 §1079-1.
[203] Zgusta 1964 §1161.
[204] Zgusta 1964 §1158 and note 158.
[205] Zgusta 1964 §1076-1.
[206] Except maybe for Πανις, see Zgusta §1197-1. For the element *puna-*, see Houwink ten Cate 1961: 158; Zgusta §1288; Laroche 1966: 322 and no. 1050-1051.
[207] In addition, the name Πονα would be the only name in the inscription that does not have a Greek ending, as there is no space left at the end of line 17 to add an ending as, for instance, -ς.
[208] Σαμος is a well-known Greek name, but according to Zgusta (1964 §1365-2), the name must be indigenous in regions where other names compounded with the element σαμ- are found; see also Robert 1954: 78.
[209] Zgusta 1964 §1361; Blümel 1992: 24. For the splitting Σαμασσις, see Robert 1954: 78, n. 11. The Carian names Σαμβακτυς, Σαμπακτυης probably consist of the elements σαν- and -πακτυης, see Blümel 1992: 24.
[210] The name Σαδασαμις (Zgusta §1353-2) does not exist, see Zgusta 1970 §1353-2.
[211] Zgusta 1964 §1368.
[212] Zgusta 1964 §1370.
[213] Zgusta 1964 §1372; Zgusta 1970 §1372; Blümel 1992: 24.
[214] Zgusta 1964 §1426; Blümel 1992: 25.
[215] Zgusta 1964 §1449.
[216] Sundwall 1913: 253 and Laroche 1966 no. 1577-1585.
[217] Brixhe-Drew Bear-Kaya 1987: 152.
[218] Zgusta 1984 §1385-1.
[219] Blümel 1992: 31 n. 111.

-αλλι) is well attested among the Anatolian names and is most likely to be connected with the suffix *alla/i* found in Hittite texts[220]. It is found in the end position in especially Carian names: Θυσσωλλος (Caria[221]), Ιβανωλλις (Caria[222]), Κασβωλλις, Κασβαλλις (Caria[223]), Κοστωλλις (Caria[224]), Ογωλλις (South-Phrygia-Lycia[225]), Οδωλλος (Pisidia[226]), Πακτυωλλις (Caria[227]), Υσσωλλος (Caria[228]). Compare also the Carian epiklesis of Zeus: Οσογωλλις[229].

7. ACKNOWLEDGEMENTS

This research is supported by the Belgian Programme on Interuniversity Poles of Attraction (IUAP 4/12) initiated by the Belgian State, Prime Minister's Office, Science Policy Programming. The text also presents the results of the Conserted Action of the Flemish Government (GOA 97/2) and the Fund for Scientific Research-Flanders (Belgium) (FWO) (G.2145.94). The scientific responsibility is assumed by its author. The contents of this paper was improved by discussions with W. Clarysse, S. Mitchell, D.J. Thompson, M. Waelkens and L. Zgusta, for which we are grateful. Furthermore, I would like to thank several members of the British Epigraphy Society (especially M. Crawford, Ch. Crowther and J. Roy) and of the Classical Department of Cambridge. The author is a Postdoctoral Fellow of the Fund for Scientific Research – Flanders (Belgium) (Γ.W.O)

8. REFERENCES

8.1. General bibliography

For the abbreviations of epigraphical editions and periodicals, see F. Bérard et al. (1989²) *Guide de l'épigrafiste. Bibliographie choisie des épigraphies antiques et médiévales*, Paris.

S.L. Ager (1996) *Interstate Arbitrations in the Greek World, 337-90 B.C.*, Berkeley-Los Angeles-London.

R.S. Bagnall (1976) *The Administration of the Ptolemaic Possessions Outside Egypt* (Columbia Studies in the Classical Tradition 4) Leiden.

G.E. Bean (1948) Notes and inscriptions from Lycia, *Journal of Hellenistic Studies* 68: 40-58.

G.E. Bean (1953) Notes and inscriptions from Caunus, *Journal of Hellenistic Studies* 73: 10-35.

G.E. Bean (1960) Notes and inscriptions from Pisidia. II, *Anatolian Studies* 10: 43-82.

E.R. Bevan (1902) *The House of Seleucus. A History of the Hellenistic Near East under the Seleucid Dynasty*, London.

B. Beyer-Rotthoff (1993) *Untersuchungen zur Aussenpolitik Ptolemaios' III*. (Habelts Dissertationsdrucke. Reihe alte Geschichte 37) Bonn.

H. Bracke (1993) Pisidia in Hellenistic times (334-25 B.C.), in: M. Waelkens (ed.) *Sagalassos I. First General Report on the Survey (1986-1989) and Excavations (1990-1991)* (Acta Archaeologica Lovaniensia Monographiae 5) Leuven University Press: 15-36.

H. Brandt (1992) *Gesellschaft und Wirtschaft Pamphyliens und Pisidiens im Altertum* (Asia Minor Studien 7) Bonn.

J. Borchhardt and G. Stanzl (1990) Ein hellenistischer Bau des Herrscherkultes: Das Ptolemaion in Limyra, in: *Götter, Heroen, Herrscher in Lykien*, Wien: 79-84.

BMC Pisidia = G.F. HILL, *A Catalogue of the Greek Coins in the British Museum. Catalogue of the Greek Coins of Lycia, Pamphylia and Pisidia*, London 1897.

A. Chaniotis (1996) *Die Verträge zwischen kretischen Poleis in der hellenistischen Zeit* (Heidelberger Althistorische Beiträge und Epigraphische Studien 24) Stuttgart.

W. Clarysse and G. Van der Veken (1983) *The Eponymous Priests of Ptolemaic Egypt* (Papyrologica Lugduno-Batava 24) Leiden.

D. Cohen (1983) *Theft in Athenian Law* (Münchener Beiträge zur Papyrusforschung und antiken Rechtsgeschichte 74) München.

G.M. Cohen (1978) *The Seleucid Colonies. Studies in Founding, Administration and Organization* (Historia. Einzelschriften 30) Wiesbaden.

G.M. Cohen (1995) *Hellenistic Settlements in Europe, the Islands, and Asia Minor* (Hellenistic Culture and Society 17) Berkeley-Los Angeles-Oxford.

D. Comparetti (1916-20) Iscrizione di Pednelissos (Pisidia), *Annuario della R. Scuola Archeologica di Atene e delle Missioni Italiane in Oriente* 3: 143-148.

D.H. Cox (1966) Gordion hoards III, IV, V, and VII, *American Numismatic Society Museum Notes* 12: 19-55.

J.A. Cramer (1971) *A Geographical and Historical Description of Asia Minor*, 2 vol., Amsterdam.

J.D. Denniston (1954²) *The Greek Particles*, Oxford.

H.J. Gehrke (1985) *Stasis: Untersuchungen zu den inneren Kriegen in den griechischen Staaten des 5. und 4. Jahrhunderts v. Chr.* (Vestigia: Beiträge zur alten Geschichte 35) München.

R. Göbl (1978) *Antike Numismatik*.I, München.

Ch. Habicht (1970²) *Gottmenschentum und griechische Städte* (Zetemata 14) München.

H. Hauben (1988) Philocles, king of the Sidonians and general of the Ptolemies, in: E. Lipinski (ed.) *Studia Phoenicia V. Phoenicia and the East Mediterranean in the First Millennium B.C.* (Orientalia Lovaniensia Analecta 22) Leuven University Press: 413-427.

R.A. Hazzard (2000) *Imagination of a monarchy: Studies in ptolemaic propaganda* (Phoenix Suppl. 37) Toronto.

B.V. Head (1977²) *Historia Numorum. A Manual of Greek Numismatics*, London.

G.F. Hill (1917) Greek coins acquired by the British Museum 1914-1916, *Numismatic Chronicle* 1917: 1-10.

C. Howgego (1995) *Ancient History from Coins*, London-New York.

J. Ijsewijn (1961) *De sacerdotibus sacerdotiisque Alexandri Magni et Lagidarum eponymis* (Verhandelingen van de Koninklijke Vlaamse Academie voor Wetenschappen, Letteren en Schone Kunsten van België. Klasse der Letteren 42) Brussel.

---

[220] Laroche 1966: 329.
[221] Zgusta 1964 §445-2; Blümel 1992: 14.
[222] Zgusta 1964 §450; Blümel 1992: 14.
[223] Zgusta 1964 §545; Blümel 1992: 15.
[224] Zgusta 1964 §705; Blümel 1992: 17.
[225] Zgusta 1964 §1070.
[226] Zgusta 1964 §1072.
[227] Blümel 1992: 21.
[228] Zgusta 1964 §1629-6/8; Blümel 1992: 27.
[229] EA 16 (1990): 34-35.

A.H.M. Jones (1971²) *The Cities of the Eastern Roman Provinces*, Oxford.

R.A. Kearsley (1994) The Milyas and the Attalids: a decree of the city of Olbasa and a new royal letter of the second century BC, *Anatolian Studies* 44: 47-57.

E. Kosmetatou and M. Waelkens (1997) The "Macedonian" shields of Sagalassos, in: M. Waelkens and J. Poblome (eds) *Sagalassos IV. Report on the Survey and Excavation Campaigns of 1994 and 1995* (Acta Archaeologica Lovaniensia Monographiae 9) Leuven University Press: 277-291.

E. Kosmetatou (1997) Pisidia and the Hellenistic kings from 323 to 133 B.C., *Ancient Society* 28:5-37.

M. Launey (1949-50) *Recherches sur les armées hellénistiques* (Bibliothèque des Ecoles Françaises d'Athènes et de Rome 169) 2 vol., Paris.

G. Le Rider (1986) Les Alexandres d'argent en Asie Mineure et dans l'Orient séleucide au IIIe siècle av. J.-C. Remarques sur le système monétaire des Séleucides et des Ptolémées, *Journal des Savants* 1986: 3-51.

B. Levick (1967) *Roman Colonies in Southern Asia Minor*, Oxford.

L. Loots, M. Waelkens and F. Depuydt (2000) The city fortifications of Sagalassos from the Hellenistic to the late Roman period, in: M. Waelkens and L. Loots (eds) *Sagalassos V. Report on the Survey and Excavations Campaigns of 1996 and 1997* (Acta Archaeologica Lovaniensia Monographiae 11) Leuven University press: 595-634.

D. Magie (1950) *Roman Rule in Asia Minor to the End of the Third Century after Christ*, Princeton (N.J.).

S. Mitchell, E. Owens and M. Waelkens (1989) Ariassos and Sagalassos, *Anatolian Studies* 39: 53-65.

S. Mitchell (1991) The hellenization of Pisidia, *Mediterranean Archaeology* 4: 119-145.

S. Mitchell (1993) *Anatolia. Land, Men, and Gods in Asia Minor. I. The Celts and the Impact of Roman Rule*, Oxford.

S. Mitchell (1994) Three cities in Pisidia, *Anatolian Studies* 44: 136-144.

A. Müller-Karpe (1988) Neue galatische Funde aus Anatolien, *Istanbuler Mitteilungen* 38: 195- 197.

W. Orth (1977) *Königlicher Machtanspruch und städtische Freiheit: Untersuchungen zu den politischen Beziehungen zwischen den ersten Seleukidenherrschern und den Städten des westlichen Kleinasien* (Münchener Beiträge zur Papyrusforschung und antiken Rechtsgeschichte 71) München.

L. Piccirilli (1973) *Gli arbitrati interstatali greci. 1. Dalle origini al 338 a.C.* (Relazioni interstatali nel mondo antico. Fonti e studi 1) Pisa.

F. Piejko (1981) A Cyrenaican dedication and some congeners, in *Zeitschrift für Papyrologie und Epigraphik* 44: 105-109.

F. Piejko (1991) Decree of the Ionian League in honor of Antiochus I, ca. 267-262 BC, *Phoenix* 45: 126-147.

M.J. Price (1991) *The Coinage in the Name of Alexander the Great and Philip Arrhidaeus. A British Museum Catalogue.* I. *Introduction and Catalogue*, London.

J.P. Rey-Coquais (1978) Inscription grecque découverte à Ras Ibn Hani: stèle de mercenaires lagides sur la côte syrienne, *Syria* 55: 313-325.

L. Robert (1936) *Collection Froehner.I. Inscriptions grecques*, Paris.

L. Robert (1966) Décret hellénistique de Termessos, in: id., *Documents de l'Asie Mineure méridionale* (Centre de recherches d'histoire et de philologie III. Hautes études du monde gréco-romain 2) Genève-Paris.

L. Robert (1970) review of: F.G. Maier (1961) Griechische Mauerbauinschriften, *Gnomon* 42: 579-603.

L. Robert and J. Robert (1976) Une inscription grecque de Téos en Ionie. L'union de Téos et de Kyrbissos, *Journal des Savants*: 154-235.

L. Robert (1990) Une épigramme hellénistique de Lycie, in *Opera Minora Selecta* 7, Amsterdam: 241-258.

S. Scheers (1993) Catalogue of the coins found in 1992, in: M. Waelkens and J. Poblome (eds) *Sagalassos II. Report on the Third Excavation Campaign of 1992* (Acta Archaeologica Lovaniensia Monographiae 6) Leuven University Press: 249-260.

S. Scheers (1995) Catalogue of the coins found in 1993, in: M. Waelkens and J. Poblome (eds) *Sagalassos III. Report on the Fourth Excavation Campaign of 1993* (Acta Archaeologica Lovaniensia Monographiae 7) Leuven University Press: 307-323.

H.H. Schmitt (1964) *Untersuchungen zur Geschichte Antiochos' des Großen und seiner Zeit* (Historia. Einzelschriften 6) Wiesbaden.

N. V. Sekunda (1997) Nearchus the Cretan and the foundation of Cretopolis, *Anatolian Studies* 47: 217-223.

F. Stähelin (1907²=1973) *Geschichte der kleinasiatischen Galater*, Osnabrück.

K. Strobel (1991) Die Galater im hellenistischen Kleinasien: historische Aspekte einer keltischen Staatenbildung, in: J. Seibert (ed.) *Hellenistische Studien. Gedenkschrift für H. Bengtson* (Münchener Arbeiten zur Alten Geschichte 5) München: 101-134.

R. Syme (1995) *Anatolica. Studies in Strabo*, Oxford (chapter 17. Pisidia and the Milyas; 18. Campaigns in the Milyas; 19. The Pacification of Pisidia and Lycaonia).

M. Thompson and A.R. Bellinger (1955) Greek coins in the Yale collection.IV. A hoard of Alexander drachms, *Yale Classical Studies* 14: 3-45.

M. Thompson (1981) The Cavalla hoard (IGCH 450), *American Numismatic Society Museum Notes* 26: 44-48.

M.N. Tod (1985) *Greek Historical Inscriptions*, Chicago.

K. Vandorpe (1995) A Sagalassos city seal, in: M. Waelkens and J. Poblome (eds) *Sagalassos III. Report on the Fourth Excavation Campaign of 1993* (Acta Archaeologica Lovaniensia Monographiae 7) Leuven University Press: 299-305.

H. Van Effenterre and F. Ruzé (1994-95) *Nomima. Recueil d'inscriptions politiques et juridiques de l'archaïsme grec* (Collection de l'École Française de Rome 188) 2 vol., Rome.

J.A. Van Rossum (1988) *De Gerousia in de Griekse steden van het Romeinse rijk*, Leiden- Haarlem (PhD).

H. Von Aulock (1977 and 1979) *Münzen und Städte Pisidiens* (Deutsches Archäologisches Institut. Abt. Istanbul. Istanbuler Mitteilungen. Beihefte 19 and 22) 2 vol., Tübingen.

M. Waelkens (1993) Sagalassos, history and archaeology, in: M. Waelkens (ed.) *Sagalassos I. First General Report on the Survey (1986-1989) and Excavations (1990-1991)* (Acta Archaeologica Lovaniensia Monographiae 5) Leuven University Press: 37-81.

M. Waelkens, P.M. Vermeersch, E. Paulissen, E.J. Owens, B. Arıkan, M. Martens, P. Talloen, L. Gijsen, L. Loots, C. Peleman, J. Poblome, R. Degeest, T.C. Patricio, S. Ercan and F. Depuydt (1997a) The 1994 and 1995 excavation seasons at Sagalassos, in: M. Waelkens and J. Poblome (eds) *Sagalassos IV. Report on the Survey and Excavation Campaigns of 1994 and 1995* (Acta Archaeologica Lovaniensia Monographiae 9) Leuven University Press: 103-216.

M. Waelkens, E. Paulissen, H. Vanhaverbeke, İ. Öztürk, B. De Cupere, H.A. Ekinci, P.M. Vermeersch, J. Poblome and R. Degeest (1997b) The 1994 and 1995 surveys on the territory of Sagalassos, in: M. Waelkens and J. Poblome (eds) *Sagalassos IV. Report on the Survey and Excavation Campaigns of 1994 and 1995* (Acta Archaeologica Lovaniensia Monographiae 9) Leuven University Press: 11-102.

M. Waelkens, J. Poblome, R. Degeest, L. Vandeput, L. Loots, E.

Paulissen, P. Talloen, J; Van Den Bergh, V. Vanderginst, B. Arıkan, I. Van Damme, I. Akyel, F. Martens, M. Martens, I. Uytterhoeven, T. Debruyne, D. Depraetere, K. Baran, B. Vandaele, Z. Parras, Ş. Yıldırım, S. B. Bubel, H. Vanhaverbeke, C. Licoppe, F. Landuyt, T. Patrício, S. Ercan, K. Van Balen, E. Smits, F. Depuydt, L. Moens and P. De Paepe (2000) The 1996 and 1997 Excavation seasons at Sagalassos, in: M. Waelkens and L. Loots (eds) *Sagalassos V. Report on the Survey and Excavation Campaigns of 1996 and 1997* (Acta Archaeologica Lovaniensia Monographiae 11) Leuven University Press: 217-398.

P. Weiß (1992) Pisidien: eine historische Landschaft im Licht ihrer Münzprägung, in: E. Schwertheim (ed.) *Forschungen in Pisidien* (Asia Minor Studien 6) Bonn: 143-165.

C.B. Welles (1934) *Royal Correspondence in the Hellenistic Period. A Study in Greek Epigraphy*, New Haven.

M. Wörrle (1975) Antiochos I., Achaios der Ältere und die Galater, *Chiron* 5: 59-87.

8.2. Anatolian languages and onomastics (especially Pisidia)

W. Blümel (1992) Einheimische Personennamen in griechischen Inschriften aus Karien, *Epigraphica Anatolica* 20: 7-33 (contains addenda on Zgusta 1964 for the region of Caria).

J. Borchhardt, G. Neumann and K. Schulz (1979) Vier pisidische Grabstelen aus Sofular, *Kadmos* 14: 68-79.

Cl. Brixhe (1976) *Le dialecte grec de Pamphylie* (Bibl. de l'Institut Français d' Etudes Anatoliennes 26) Paris.

Cl. Brixhe and E. Gibson (1982) Monuments from Pisidia in the Rahmi Koç collection, *Kadmos* 21: 130-169.

Cl. Brixhe, T. Drew-Bear and D. Kaya (1987) Nouveaux monuments de Pisidie, *Kadmos* 26: 122- 170.

Cl. Brixhe (1988) La langue des inscriptions épichoriques de Pisidie, in: Y.L. Arbeitman (ed.) *A Linguistic Happening in Memory of B. Schwartz. Studies in Anatolian, Italic and other Indo-European Languages*, Louvain-la-Neuve: 131-155.

J. Friedrich (1927-1930) Zu den kleinasiatischen Personennamen mit dem Element *muwa*, in: F. Sommer and H. Ehelolf, *Kleinasiatische Forschungen. I*, Weimar: 359-378.

R. Gusmani (1988) Anthroponymie in den lydischen Inschriften, in: Y.L. Arbeitman (ed.) *A Linguistic Happening in Memory of B. Schwartz. Studies in Anatolian, Italic and other Indo-European Languages*, Louvain-la-Neuve: 179-195.

H.J. Houwink ten Cate (1961) *The Luwian Population Groups of Lycia and Cilicia Aspera during the Hellenistic Period* (Documenta et Monumenta Orientis Antiqui 10) Leiden.

M.F. Imhoof-Blumer (1883 [= 1979]) *Mallos, Megarsos, Antioche du Pyramos. Étude géographique, historique et numismatique*, Paris.

L. Innocente (1990) Una nuova attestazione del tipo onomastico ALUS, *Kadmos* 29: 38-46.

G. Laminger-Pascher (1973) *Index grammaticus zu den Inschriften Kilikiens und Isauriens.I* (Österreichische Akademie der Wissenschaften. Philosophisch-historische Klasse 284.3) Wien (II.B: Einheimische Deklination; III. Wortbildung einheimischer Namen).

E. Laroche (1966) *Les noms des Hittites* (Études Linguistiques 4) Paris.

M. Lejeune (1969) Notes paléo-phrygiennes, *Revue des Etudes Anciennes* 71: 292.

O. Masson et al. (1990) *Onomastica Graeca Selecta*. I, Nanterre.

M. Mersich (1985) Malos in Pisidien, *Jahrbuch der Österreichischen Byzantinistik* 35: 51-54.

G. Neumann (1961) *Untersuchungen zum Weiterleben hethitischen und luwischen Sprachgutes im hellenistischer und römischer Zeit*, Wiesbaden.

G. Neumann (1980) Kleinasien, in: *Die Sprachen im römischen Reich der Kaiserzeit. Kolloquium 8. bis 10. April 1974* (Beihefte der Bonner Jahrbücher 40) Köln: 167-185.

G. Neumann (1992) Sprachwissenschaftliche Erläuterungen zu den epichorischen Namen, die in "Epigraphische Forschungen in Termessos und seinem Territorium I-II" vorkommen, in: B. S.I.B. Iplikçioğlu, G. Celgin and G. Neumann (1991-1994) *Epigraphische Forschungen in Termessos und seinem Territorium I-II* (Österreichische Akademie der Wissenschaften. Philosophisch- historische Klasse 575, 583, 610) Wien.

W.M. Ramsay (1895) Inscriptions en langue pisidienne, *Revue des Universités de Midi* 1.17: 353- 362.

L. Robert (1948) *Hellenica. Recueil d'épigraphie, de numismatique et d'antiquités grecques. VI. Inscriptions grecques de Lydie*, Paris.

L. Robert (1954) *La Carie. Histoire et géographie historique. II. Le plateau de Tabai et ses environs*, Paris.

L. Robert (1963) *Noms indigènes dans l'Asie-Mineure gréco-romaine* (Bibliothèque archéologique et historique de l'Institut Français d'Archéologie d'Istanbul 13) Paris.

L. Robert (1970) *Études anatoliennes. Recherches sur les inscriptions grecques de l'Asie Mineure* (Études orientales publiées par l'Institut Français d'Archéologie de Stamboul 5) Amsterdam.

J. Sundwall (1913) *Die einheimischen Namen der Lykier nebst einem Verzeichnisse kleinasiatischer Namenstämme* (Klio. Beiträge zur Alten Geschichte 11) Leipzig.

L. Zgusta (1957) Die pisidischen Inschriften, *Archiv Orientalni* 25: 570-610.

L. Zgusta (1963) Die epichorische pisidische Anthroponymie und Sprache, *Archiv Orientalni* 31: 470-482.

ZGUSTA 1964 = L. Zgusta, *Kleinasiatische Personennamen*, Prag 1964.

ZGUSTA 1964.PNsippen = L. Zgusta, *Anatolische Personennamensippen*, Prag 1964.

L. Zgusta (1970) *Neue Beiträge zur kleinasiatischen Anthroponymie*, Prag.

L. Zgusta (1984) *Kleinasiatische Ortsnamen* (Beiträge zur Namenforschung N.F. Beihefte 21) Heidelberg.

Fig. 1: The negotiator's law inscription from Sagalassos.

Fig. 2: Detail of the inscription.

COINS FOUND DURING 1996 AND 1997

Simone SCHEERS
(Table of stratigraphically related coins by Lieven Loots and Marc Waelkens)

Department of Archaeology, KULeuven, Blijde Inkomststraat 21, B-3000 Leuven, Belgium

1. GREEK AUTONOMOUS AND IMPERIAL COINS

1.1. Phrygia

1.1.1. Eucarpeia

2nd – 3rd cent. AD
[ ] Head of young Demos r., bareheaded
Rv. [ευκα-ρπ-εων] Artemis standing to front, drawing with r. hand arrow from quiver at her shoulder, and with l. holding bow; to l., stag; to r., female cult image.
BMC Phrygia 11; Lindgren A 948A
1. AE, 9.58g
   inv. SA-97-PQ-8

1.2. Pamphylia

1.2.1. Attaleia

early imperial period
Dolphin
Rv. ΑΤΤΑ-ΛΕΩΝ Rudder
SNG PfPs 150; Baydur 79-90.
2. AE, 1.57g
   inv. SA-96-Y-8

1.2.2. Perge

Hadrian (117-138 AD)
ΑΔΡΙΑ – [καις] Bust of emperor r., laureate, draped
Rv. ΑΡΤΕΜΙΔΟΣ – ΠΕΡΓΑΙΑΣ Quiver
SNG PfPs 282; *SNG Paris* 404
3. AE, 1.57g
   inv. SA-97-S-8

Septimius Severus (193-211 AD)
AVT KAC[ ]IN Bust of emperor r.
Rv. ΠΕΡ[γα]ΙΩΝ Artemis standing r., bow in r. hand, arrow in l.

cf. *SNG PfPs* 312-314.
4. AE, 2.44g
   inv. SA-96-LA-99

[ ]VH[ ] Head of Septimius Severus (?) r., laureate
Rv. ΠΕΡΓ[ ] Distyle temple in which cult image of Artemis Pergaia
SNG Copenhague -; *SNG PfPs* -; *SNG Paris* -; *SNG von Aulock* -
5. AE, 1.99g
   inv. SA-97-H-307

Tranquillina (Gordian III, 241-244 AD)
[cαβει] TPANKVΛΛEINA[ν cεβ] Bust r., draped, with stephane, crescent behind shoulder
Rv. ΠΕΡΓΑΙ-ΩΝ CIΔHTΩN OMONOIA To l., Artemis standing; to r., Athena standing; between them, stag
SNG von Aulock 4700.
6. AE, 12.21g, homonoia-coin with Side
   inv. SA-96-Y-2

1.3. Pisidia

1.3.1. Sagalassos

1st cent. BC – early imperial times
Head of Athena r., in crested Corinthian helmet
Rv. ΣΑΓΑ-ΛΑΣΣ [ ] Nike advancing r., holding in extended r. hand wreath, in l. palm-branch
BMC 3-4; *SNG Paris* 1733-1734; *SNG von Aulock* 5155.
7. AE, 2.28g
   inv. SA-96-DA 1-74

1st cent. BC – imperial times
Head of Zeus r., bearded, laureate
Rv. Two goats confronted, standing on hind legs; between them, caduceus, below CAΓA
BMC 195; *SNG Paris* 1736.
8. AE, 2.56g
   inv. SA-96-N-28

As above. Rv. Two goats confronted. between them, bucranium; [below, cαγα]
9. AE, 2.18g
inv. SA-96-N-21

As above. Rv. Two goats confronted; between them, cornucopiae; below CAΓA
BMC 194; *SNG Copenhague* 194; *SNG von Aulock* 5157; *SNG Paris* 1735
10. AE, 2.27g
inv. SA-96-UA-218
11 AE, 2.32g
inv. SA-97-UAN-255

As above. Rv. Two goats confronted standing on hind legs, symbol uncertain
cf. *SNG Copenhague* 191-195; *SNG Paris* 1735-1741
12. AE, 2.54g, legend below uncertain
inv. SA-96-UA-167
13. AE, 4.05g, below [cα]Γ[α]
inv. SA-97-DT-123

As above. Rv. Illegible
cf. *SNG Copenhague* 191-195
14. AE, 3.27g
inv. SA-97-H-213

1st. cent. BC – imperial period
Head of Heracles r.
Rv. CAΓ within laurel-wreath
BMC 198; *SNG Copenhague* 198; *SNG von Aulock* 5159; *SNG Paris* 1744
15. AE, 2.4g
inv. SA-96-UA-175

Augustus (27 BC – 14 AD)
[καις cεβα] Bust of Augustus r.
Rv. [cαγαλαccεων] Head of Zeus r., laureate
RPC 3523.2; *SNG Paris* 1749
16. AE, 4.16g
inv. SA-97-PQ-3

Hadrian (117-138 AD)
ADRIANOC K[αιcαρ] OΛYNΠIOC Bust of Hadrian r., laureate, wearing paludamentum
Rv. [cαγαλαc]-CEΩN Cybele, turreted, seated l. on throne flanked by two lions, holding in r. patera, l. resting on throne
BMC Pisidia-; *SNG Copenhague* -; *SNG Paris* -; *SNG von Aulock* -
17. AE, 21.2g
inv. SA-97-B1-178

Marcus Aurelius (161-180 AD)
[αυτ] KAI [αντ]ΩNI Head r., laureate

Rv. The Dioscuri standing confronted, each holding spear
SNG Paris 1781
18. AE, 4.12g
inv. SA-97-S-9

Septimius Severus (193-211 AD)
AVT KAI Λ CEΠ OVCEOVHPOC ΠE Bust of emperor r., laureate, draped
Rv. [cαγ]AΛ[αccε]-ΩN Tyche, turreted, seated l. on rock; in extended r. hand, branch (?); at her feet, river-god (Kestros) swimming l.
BMC Pisidia -; *SNG von Aulock* -; *SNG Paris* -
19. AE, 26.93g
inv. SA-97-DT-94

AV KAI Λ C CEOV-HPOC ΠEPT Head of emperor r., laureate
Rv. CAΓAΛA-CCEΩN Heracles running l., carrying infant Dionysius on l. arm
BMC Pisidia -; *SNG Paris* -; *SNG von Aulock* -
20. AE, 3.9g
inv. SA-97-H-286

Caracalla (197-217 AD)
AV K M AV [αντω]NEINOC CEB Head of Caracalla r., laureate
Rv. CAΓAΛACCEΩN Tyche standing l., wearing modius, holding rudder and cornucopiae
SNG Paris 1794-1795
21. AE, 4.3g
inv. SA-97-NEB-13

Gordian III (238-244 AD)
AVT K [μ αν γορδιανοc αν] Bust r., radiate, draped
Rv. CAΓAΛAC-CEΩN Mên standing to l., crescent behind shoulders; wears Phrygian cap, chlamys, short chiton; in r. hand, patera, l. resting on sceptre
SNG von Aulock 5184 (obv.) – 5187 (rev.), but described as Lakedaimon, helmeted, cuirassed, patera in r. hand, spear in l.
22. AE, 15.18g
inv. SA-96-Y-1

Philip II (244-249 AD)
AVT KA MA IOV ΦIΛIΠ[ποχ] Bust r., laureate, cuirassed, with mantle
Rv. CAGALACCEΩN Two arched shrines, each containing circular altar, adorned with a crescent and surmounted by a star; between them, tall column; under, snake
Imhoof-Blümer, *Klein-Asiatische Münzen*, II, 1902, p. 394, n° 17; *SNG von Aulock* 5191 (obv.) – 5194 (rev.)
23. AE, 11.81g
inv. SA-96-UAN-68

Claudius II (268-270 AD)
AV K M AVP – KΛAVΔION Bust of Claudius r.
Rv. CAΓAΛ-A-CCE-Ω-N Demeter, holding torch, standing in car drawn by winged serpents; below I
SNG Paris 1860-62; *SNG Copenhague* 225; *SNG von Aulock* 5204
24. AE, 19.76g, 10 assaria
 inv. SA-97-H-151

1.3.2. Selge

2nd-1st cent. BC
Bearded Heracles facing, wreathed with styrax; lion's skin round neck; behind, club appearing over l. shoulder
Rv. Forepart of stag r., head l.; above, ΣE-Λ
SNG Copenhague 261-262; *SNG von Aulock* 5286; *SNG Paris* 1969-1976
25. AE, 2.15g
 inv. SA-97-NEB-28

2nd-1st cent. BC
Head of Heracles r., laureate; at shoulder, club
Rv. Winged thunderbolt; on r., bow; in field, Σ – E
SNG Copenhague 263; *SNG von Aulock* 5288-5289: *SNG Paris* 1981-1982
26. AE, 3.71g
 inv. SA-97-H-228

1.4. Uncertain city coins

Lion's head to r.
Rv. Owl facing or cantharos?
27. AE, 0.76g
 inv. SA-96-B-25

Obv. uncertain
Rv. Animal (stag?) r.
28. AE, 2.45g
 inv. SA-97-N-70
The coin may be from Selge, cf. *SNG Paris* 1963-1968, but its bad conservation allows no certain identification.

Bust of emperor to r.
Rv. Figure to l.
29. AE, 3.21g, Empire, 1st-3rd cent.AD
 inv. SA-96-UA-149

Bust of emperor to r., laureate
Rv. Seated figure (Zeus?) to l.
30. AE, 5.02g, Empire, 1st-3rd cent. AD
 inv. SA-96-AG-90
 Sagalassos (?)

2. ROMAN EMPIRE

2.1. Augustus (27BC-14 AD)

CAES [ ] Head of Augustus, bare, r.
Rv. [AVGVSTVS in one line in] laurel-wreath
RIC 485; Giard 963-971
31. AE, 4.58g, as (halved), Ephesus or Pergamum, c. 25 BC or 27-23 BC
 inv. SA-96-N-15

2.2. Valerian I (253-268 AD)

IMP C P LIC VALERIANVS PF AVG Bust r., radiate, draped
Rv. ORIE-N-S AV-GG Sol, radiate, naked, except for cloak flying out behind him, advancing l., raising r. hand and holding whip in l.
RIC 106
32. BI, antoninianus, 3.07g, Rome, 257 AD
 inv. SA-96-B-78

2.3. Claudius II (268-270 AD)

[imp c]LAVDI[us aug] Bust r., radiate, draped
Rv. [mars ultor] Mars, helmeted, naked except for cloak flying out behind him, advancing r., holding spear in r. hand and trophy over l. shoulder
RIC 66
33. BI, antoninianus (fragment), Rome, 268-270 AD
 inv. SA-96-N-234

2.4. Aurelian (270-275 AD)

[ ]S AVG Bust r., radiate, draped
Rv. IOV[i conser] The emperor, bare-headed, in military dress, standing r., receiving globe from Jupiter, naked except for cloak, standing l., sceptre in l. hand; $\overline{A}$
RIC 48
34. BI, antoninianus, 3.28g, Rome, 270-275 AD
 inv. SA-96-UA-196

[ ]AVRE[ ] Bust r., radiate
Rv. Apparently two standing figures (only the r. one is discernible)
35. BI, antoninianus, 2.79g, uncertain mint
 inv. SA-96-LE-14

2.5. Diocletian (284-305 AD)

IMP C C VAL DIOCLETIANVS PF AVG Bust r., radiate, draped, cuirassed, seen from front
Rv. CONCORDIA MIL-ITVM Prince standing r. in military dress receiving small Victory on globe from Jupiter standing l.; <u>HA</u>

RIC 13 and 21
36. AE, 2.36g, light radiate fraction, Heraclea, c. 295-298 A D
inv. SA-97-LA-62

2.6. Constantinus I (306-337 AD)

IMP CONSTA-NTINVS AVG Bust r., laureate, helmeted, cuirassed
Rv. VICTORIAE LAETAE PRINC PERP Two Victories facing one another, holding on column shield inscribed VOT/PR; $\overline{\text{PARL}}$
RIC 191, 194
37. AE, follis, 3.05g, Arles, 319 AD
inv. SA-97-RB1-92

[ ]NVS MA[x] AVG Bust r., laureate
Rv. [glo]R-IA EXE[rc-itus] Two soldiers standing, each holding spear and leaning on shield; between them, one standard
38. AE, follis, 0.7g, uncertain mint, 335-337 AD
inv. SA-97-UAN-45

2.7. Constantinus II (317-340 AD)

[const]ANTINVS IVN NOB C Bust r., laureate, cuirassed
Rv. GLOR-IA EXER-CITVS Two soldiers standing, each holding spear and leaning on shield; between them, one standard; $\overline{\text{CONS}\Theta}$
LRBC 1026; *RIC* 138.
39. follis, 0.95g, Constantinople, 336-337 AD
inv. SA-96-UA-160

2.8. Constantius II (337-361 AD)

DN CONSTAN-TIVS PF AVG Bust r., draped, diademed
Rv. GLOR-[ia exerc]-ITVS Two soldiers standing, each holding spear and leaning on shield; between them, one standard; $\overline{\text{CONSA}}$
LRBC 1051; *RIC* 42
40. AE, follis, 1.14g, Constantinople, 335-341 AD
inv. SA-97-UAN-41

DN CONS[tan]-TIVS PF AVG Bust r., diademed
Rv. VOT/XX/MVLT/[x]XX within a wreath; $\overline{\text{[con]SA}}$
LRBC 1064; *RIC* 69
41. AE, follis, 1.3g, Constantinople, 347-348 AD
inv. SA-97-UAN-276

DN CONSTAN-TIVS PF AVG Head r., diademed
Rv. VOT/XX/MVLT/XXX within a wreath; $\overline{\text{[consa]}}$*
LRBC 1071; *RIC* 76
42. AE, follis, 1.12g, Constantinople?, 347-348 AD
inv. SA-97-RB2-129

DN CONSTAN-TIVS PF AVG Bust r., diademed, draped
Rv. FEL TEMP REPARATIO Helmeted soldier to l., shield on l. arm, spearing falling horseman, shield on ground at r., $\dfrac{\Gamma\ |}{\overline{\text{SMN}\Gamma}}$
LRBC 2300 *RIC* 84
43. AE 2, 5.55g, Nicomedia, 351-355 AD
inv. SA-96-B-68

DN CONSTAN-TIVS PF AVG Bust r., draped, diademed
Rv. [fel temp re]-PARATIO Helmeted soldier to l., spearing fallen horseman; $\dfrac{\text{E}\ |}{[\quad]}$
LRBC 2036 or 2629; *RIC* 115 or 144
44. AE 2, 3.38g, Constantinopel or Antioch, 351-355 AD
inv. SA-96-B-314

DN CONSTAN-TIVS PF AVG Bust r., draped, diademed
Rv. [fel temp reparatio] Helmeted soldier to l., spearing fallen horseman
45. AE 3, 2.32g, uncertain mint, 355-361 AD
inv. SA-96-LA-53

[ ]STAN-[ ]AVG Bust r., draped, diademed
Rv. FEL TEMP RE-PARATIO Helmeted soldier spearing fallen horseman; $\dfrac{\text{M}\ |}{[\quad]}$
46. AE 3, 1.42g, uncertain mint, 355-361 AD
inv. SA 96-B-287

DN CONSTAN-[tius pf] AVG Bust r., draped, diademed
Rv. SPES REI-PVBLICE Emperor in military dress standing r., holding globe and spear, $\overline{\text{SMKA}}$
LRBC 2504; *RIC* 117
47. AE 4, 2g, Cyzicus, 355-361 AD
inv. SA-96-UAN-150

DN CON[stan]-TIVS PF AVG Bust r., draped, diademed
Rv. SPES REI-PVBLICE Emperor in military dress standing r., holding globe and spear
48. AE 4, 1.67g, uncertain mint, 355-361 AD
inv. SA-96-Y-4

DN [cons]TANT-IVS PF AVG Bust r., draped, diademed
Rv. SPES REI-PVBLICE Emperor in military dress standing r., holding globe and spear
49. AE 4, 1.99g, uncertain mint, 355-361 AD
inv. SA-97-H-79

[dn con]STAN-[tius pf aug] Bust r., draped, diademed
Rv. SPES [reipublice] Emperor in military dress standing r., holding globe and spear
50. AE 4, 0.95g, uncertain mint, 355-361 AD
inv. SA-97-UAN-72

2.9. *Gloria exercitus*, one standard (337-341 AD)

DN CONSTA[ ] Head r., laureate
Rv. GLOR-IA EX(er-citus) Two soldiers standing, each holding spear and leaning on shield; between them, one standard; SM(N?)
RIC 8
51. follis, 1.66g, Nicomedia (?), 337-340 AD
inv. SA-96-AG-59

2.10. Julian (354-361 AD)

[ ]IVS NOB [caes] Bust r., bareheaded
Rv. [fel temp re]-PARATIO Helmeted soldier to l., spearing fallen horseman; [•]M• | [con]SA
LRBC 2051; *RIC* 140
52. AE 3, 1.51g, Constantinople, 355-361 AD
inv. SA-96-RB-191

DN IVLIAN-VS [nob caes] Bust r., draped, bareheaded
Rv. [fel temp reparatio] Helmeted soldier to l., shield on l. arm, spearing falling horseman raising l. arm
53. AE 3, 1.7g, uncertain mint, 355-361 AD
inv. SA-97-RB2-120

DN CL FL IVLI-ANVS PF AVG Bust r., draped, diademed
Rv. SPES REI-[publice] Emperor in military dress standing r., holding globe and spear; * | [ ]
54. AE 4, 1.29g, uncertain mint, 355-361 AD
inv. SA-97-PQ-11

2.11. *Fel temp reparatio* (346-361 AD)

[ ] Bust. r., draped, diademed
Rv. [ ] Helmeted soldier to l., spearing fallen horseman
55. AE 3, 1.17g, uncertain mint
inv. SA-96-AG-76
56. AE 3, 1.2g, uncertain mint
inv. SA-97-UAN-277

DN [ ] Bust r., draped, diademed
Rv. FEL TEMP [reparatio] Helmeted soldier to l., shield on l. arm, spearing falling horseman raising l. arm
57. AE 2, 1.24g, uncertain mint
inv. SA-97-UAN-296

[ ] Bust r.
Rv. [ ] Helmeted soldier to l., spearing falling horseman raising l. arm
58. AE 3, 2g, uncertain mint
inv. SA-97-UAN-214

[ ]CONSTAN-[ ] Bust r., draped, diademed
Rv. [ ] Helmeted soldier to l., spearing fallen horseman
59. AE 3, 1.06g, uncertain mint
inv. SA-97-UAN-332

2.12. *Spes reipublice* (355-361 AD)

[ ] Bust r., draped, diademed
Rv. SPES [reipublice] Emperor in military dress standing r., holding globe and spear
60. AE 4, 1.66g, uncertain mint
inv. SA-96-B-113

[ ] Bust r., draped
Rv. [ ] Emperor in military dress standing r., holding globe and spear
61. AE 4, 0.91g, uncertain mint
inv. SA-97-NEB-18

DN [ ] Bust r., draped
Rv. [spes rei] PVBLICE Emperor in military dress standing r., holding globe and spear;]N[
62. AE 4, 1.81g, uncertain mint
inv. SA-97-UAN-142

DN[ ] Bust r., draped
Rv. [spes] REI-[p]VBLICE Emperor in military dress standing r., holding globe and spear
63. AE 4, 1.78g, uncertain mint
inv. SA-97-UAN-219

DN[ ] Bust r., draped, diademed
Rv. [spes] REI [publice] Emperor in military dress standing r., holding globe and spear;]M or N[
64. AE 4, 1.23g, uncertain mint
inv. SA-97-UAN-270

[ ] Bust r., draped, diademed
Rv. [spes] REI-PVBLI[ce] Emperor in military dress standing r., holding globe and spear
65. AE 4, 1.31g, uncertain mint
inv. SA-97-UAN-275

2.13. Valentinian I (364-375 AD)

DN VALENTIN[ ] Bust r., draped, diademed
Rv. [restitutor reipub]LICAE Emperor standing facing, head r., holding standard and Victory on globe

66. AE 1, 0.61g (fragment), uncertain mint, 364-365 AD
inv. SA-96-RB-81

2.14. Valens (364-378 AD)

DN VALEN-S PF AVG Bust r., draped, cuirassed, diademed
Rv. RESTITVTOR-[reipublicae] Emperor standing facing, head r., holding standard and Victory on globe; SMNA
LRBC 2322; *RIC* 7b

67. AE 1, 7.13g, Nicomedia, 364-367 AD
inv. SA-97-UAN-260

2.15. Valentinian I (364-375 AD) or Valens (364-378 AD)

DN VALEN[ ] Bust r., draped, diademed
Rv. [gloria ro]-MANORVM Emperor advancing r., with r. hand dragging captive and holding labarum in l.

68. AE 3, 1.62g, uncertain mint, 364-378 AD
inv. SA-96-B-10

DN VALEN[ ] Bust r., draped, diademed
Rv. [g]LORIA RO-[manorum] Emperor advancing r., with r. hand dragging captive and holding labarum in l.

69. AE 3, 2.4g, uncertain mint, 364-378 AD
inv. SA-97-UAN-38

2.16. Gratian (367-383 AD)

DN GRATI[a-nus pf aug] Bust r., draped, diademed
Rv. [gloria ro]-MANORVM Emperor advancing r., with r. hand dragging captive and holding labarum in l.

70. AE 3, 1.88g, uncertain mint, 364-378 AD
inv. SA-97-B2-47

2.17. *Gloria romanorum* (364-378, 383-388 AD)

[ ] Bust r., draped, diademed
Rv. [gloria ro]-MANORVM Emperor advancing r., with r. hand dragging captive and holding labarum in l.

71. AE 3, 1.88g, uncertain mint
inv. SA-96-B-102
72. AE 3, 1.68g, uncertain mint
inv. SA-97-DT-74

DN[ ] Bust r., draped, diademed
Rv. GLORIA RO-[manorum] Emperor advancing r., with r. hand dragging captive and holding labarum in l.

73. AE 3, uncertain mint
inv. SA-97-S-36

2.18. Valentinian II (375-392 AD)

DN VALENTINIA-NVS IVN PF AVG Bust r., draped, diademed
Rv. VRBS ROMA Roma seated l., holding Victory on globe and spear; below, cuirass; $\frac{|*}{SMNB}$
LRBC 2345; *RIC* 34

74. AE 3, 2.82g, Nicomedia, 378-383 AD
inv SA-97-S-15

[dn valen]TINIANVS P[f aug] Bust r., draped, diademed
Rv. [salus rei]- PVBLI[ce] Victory advancing l., trophy on shoulder, dragging captive; $\frac{\text{⚒} \,|}{CO[NSA]}$
RIC 86 and 90

75. AE 4, 0.61g, Constantinople, 388-395 AD
inv. SA-96-B-107

2.19. Theodosius I (379-395 AD)

DN THEODO-SIVS PF AVG Bust r., draped, diademed
Rv. VOT/X/MVLT/XX within wreath; SMNA
LRBC 2382; *RIC* 38b

76. AE 4, 0.9g, Nicomedia, 383 AD
inv. SA-97-LA-114

DN THEODO-SIVS PF AVG Bust r., draped, diademed
Rv. VICTORIA AVGGG Two Victories facing one another, each holding wreath; $\frac{:}{[RP]}$
LRBC 790; *RIC* 57c

77. AE 4, 1.24g, Rome, 383-387 AD
inv. SA-96-UAN-97

[dn t]HEODO-SIVS PF AVG Bust r., draped, diademed
Rv. SALVS REI-PVBLICAE Victory advancing l., trophy on shoulder, dragging captive; to l.✝; SMNΓ
LRBC 2407; *RIC* 45b

78. AE 4, 1.4g, Nicomedia, 388-392 AD
inv. SA-97-S-25

DN THEODO-SIVS PF AVG Bust r., draped, diademed
Rv. SALVS [rei publicae] Victory advancing l., trophy on shoulder, dragging captive

79. AE 4, 0.82g, uncertain mint, 388-395 AD
inv. SA-97-UAN-78

[dn] THEODO-SIV[s pf aug] Bust r., draped, diademed
Rv. [salus rei publicae] Victory advancing l., trophy on shoulder, dragging captive

80. AE 4, 1.2g, uncertain mint, 388-395 AD
    inv. SA-97-UAN-264

[dn theod]O-SIVS PF AVG Bust r., draped, diademed
Rv. [salus rei] PVBLICE Victory advancing l., trophy on shoulder, dragging captive
81. AE 4, 0.93g, uncertain mint, 388-395 AD
    inv. SA-97-DT-59

DN THEODO-SIVS PF AVG Bust r., draped, diademed
Rv. GLORIA ROMANORVM Emperor standing facing, head r., holding labarum and globe; SMNA
LRBC 2422; *RIC* 46a
82. AE 2, 3.95g, Nicomedia, 392-395 AD
    inv. SA-96-LA-43
83. AE 2, 5.54g, Nicomedia, 392-395 AD
    inv. SA-97-UAN-99
84. AE 2, 5.04g, Nicomedia, 392-395 AD
    inv. SA-97-UAN-247

DN THEODO – SIVS PF AVG Bust r., draped, diademed
Rv. GLORIA – ROMANORVM Emperor standing, facing, head r., holding labarum and globe; ANTA
LRBC 2779; *RIC* 68a
85. AE 2, 4.49g, Antioch, 392-395 AD
    inv. SA-97-H-199

for Aelia Flacilla
AEL FLAC -[cilla aug] Bust r., mantled, with headdress; above head, hand holding wreath or diadem
Rv. SALVS REI – PVBLICAE Victory seated r., writing, ☧ on shield resting on small column; SMKA
LRBC 2567; *RIC* -
86. AE 2, 2.50g, Cyzicus, 383-388 AD
    inv. SA-96-Y-7

2.20. Theodosius I (379-392 AD) or Theodosius II (402-450 AD)

DN T[ ] Bust r., draped
Rv. illegible
87. AE 3 or 4, 1.16g, uncertain mint
    inv. SA-97-UAN-209

2.21. Arcadius (383-408 AD)

DN ARCADIVS PF AVG Bust r., draped, diademed
Rv. VOT/X/MVLT/XX within wreath; ANT[ ]
LRBC 2735; *RIC* 56d
88. AE 4, 1.17g, Antioch, 383 AD
    inv. SA-96-UA-88

DN AR[ ] Bust r., draped, diademed
Rv. [victor]-IA AV[gg] Two Victories facing one another, each holding wreath and palm; • RP
LRBC 788; *RIC* 57e
89. AE 4, 0.84g, Rome, 383-387 AD
    inv. SA-97-UAN-71

DN ARCADIVS PF AVG Bust r., diademed, draped
Rv. SALVS REI-PVBLICAE Victory advancing l., trophy on shoulder, dragging captive; ☧ | CONSA
LRBC 2185 and 2194; *RIC* 86c, 90c
90. AE 4, 0.82g, Constantinople, 388-395 AD
    inv. SA-96-UA-197

[dn a]RCADIVS [pf aug] Bust r., draped, diademed
Rv. SALVS [rei] PVBLICAE Victory advancing l., trophy on shoulder, dragging captive; SMNΓ
LRBC 2404, 2429; *RIC* 45c, 48b
91. AE 4, 0.61g, Nicomedia, 388-395 AD
    inv. SA-97-UAN-251

DN ARCADIVS PF AVG Bust r., draped, diademed
Rv. SALVS REI-PVBLICAE Victory advancing l., trophy on shoulder, dragging captive
92. AE 4, 1.46g, uncertain mint, 388-395 AD
    inv. SA-97-LA-77

DN ARCADIVS PF AVG Bust r., draped, diademed
Rv. SALVS [rei]-PVBLICAE Victory advancing l., trophy on shoulder, dragging captive; to l., ☧
93. AE 4, 1.11g, uncertain mint, 388-395 AD
    inv. SA-97-UAN-213

DN ARCADIVS PF AVG Bust r., draped, diademed
Rv. SALVS REI-PVBLICAE Victory advancing l., trophy on shoulder, dragging captive; to l.☧; S[ ]
94. AE 4, 0.55g, uncertain mint, 388-395 AD
    inv. SA-97-UAN-39

DN ARCADI-VS PF AVG Bust r., draped, diademed
Rv. GLORIA [romanorum] Emperor, in military dress, standing facing, head r., holding labarum and globe; CONSΔ
RIC 88b
95. AE 2, 5.68g, Constantinople, 392-395 AD
    inv. SA-96-UA-15

DN ARCADI-VS PF AVG Bust r., draped, diademed
Rv. GLORIA ROMANORVM Emperor, in military dress, standing facing, head r., holding labarum and globe; CONSΓ
RIC 88b2

96. AE 2, 5.24g, Constantinople, 392-395 AD
    inv. SA-96-B-55
97. AE 2, 3.95g, Constantinople, 392-395 AD
    inv. SA-96-UA-76

   DN ARCADI-VS PF AVG Bust r., draped, diademed
   Rv. GLORIA – ROMANORVM Emperor, in military dress, standing facing, head r., holding labarum and globe; $\overline{\text{SMNB}}$
   RIC 46b
98. AE 2, 3.58g, Nicomedia, 392-395 AD
    inv. SA-96-UAN-69

   DN ARCADI-VS PF AVG Bust r., draped, cuirassed, diademed
   Rv. GLORIA – ROMANORVM Emperor, in military dress, standing facing, head r., holding labarum and globe
   RIC 27b
99. AE 2, 4.3g, Cyzicus, $\overline{\text{SMKB}}$, 392-395 AD
    inv. SA-96-AG-10
100. AE 2, 4.96g, Cyzicus, $\overline{\text{SMK}\Gamma}$, 392-395 AD
    inv. SA-96-UA-139

   DN ARCADI-VS PF AVG Bust r., draped, diademed
   Rv. GLORIA – RO[manorum] Emperor, in military dress, standing facing, head r., holding labarum and globe, $\overline{\text{SM[ ]}}$
101. AE 2, 3.89g, uncertain mint, 392-395 AD
    inv. SA-96-UAN-84

   DN ARCADI-VS PF AVG Bust r., draped, diademed
   Rv. VIRTVS – EXERCITI Emperor standing l., head r., holding spear and resting l. hand on shield. Victory to l. holds palm-branch in l. hand and crowns him
   LRBC 2205; *RIC* 60
102. AE 3, 1.74g, Constantinople, $\overline{\text{CONSA}}$, 395-401 AD
    inv. SA-97-B2-69
103. AE 3, 1.45g, Constantinople, $\overline{\text{CONSB}}$, 395-401 AD
    inv. SA-97-B1-172
104. AE 3, 2.2g, Constantinople, $\overline{\text{CO[ ]}}$, 395-401 AD
    inv. SA-97-B1-125
105. AE 3, 1.82g, Constantinople, [c]O[ ], 395-401 AD
    inv. SA-96-UAN-163

   DN ARCADI-VS PF AVG Bust r., draped, diademed
   Rv. VIRTVS – EXERCITI Emperor standing l. crowned by Victory; [s]$\overline{\text{MNB}}$
   LRBC 2436; *RIC* 62
106. AE 3, 2.24g, Nicomedia, 395-401 AD
    inv. SA-97-H-28

   DN ARCADI-[us pf aug] Bust r., draped, diademed
   Rv. VIRTVS – EXERCITI Emperor standing l. crowned by Victory; [a]$\overline{\text{NTA}}$
   LRBC 2791; *RIC* 70
107. AE 3, 2.08g, Antioch, 395-401 AD
    inv. SA-97-UAN-205

   [dn arc]A[dius pf aug] Bust r.
   Rv. [virtus exerciti] Victory to l. crowns [emperor to r.] and holds palm-branch in l. hand
108. AE 3, 0.48g (fragment), eastern mint, 395-401 AD
    inv. SA-97-UAN-63

   DN ARCADI[us pf aug] Bust cuirassed, facing, helmeted, holding spear and shield
   Rv. CONCOR[dia augg] Constantinopolis enthroned facing, head l., holding sceptre and Victory on globe; prow under r.foot
109. AE 3, 2.03g, eastern mint, 401-403 AD
    inv. SA-97-UAN-312

   DN ARCADI-VS PF AVG Bust r., draped, diademed
   Rv. CONCOR – [dia aug/auggg] Cross; $\overline{\text{CONS[ ]}}$
   LRBC 2202 or 2221; *RIC* 107 or 127
110. AE 4, 0.85g, Constantinople, 404-406 AD
    inv. SA-96-B-115

   DN ARCADI-VS PF AVG Bust r., draped, diademed; behind, *
   Rv. GLORI-A ROMA-NORVM Three emperors standing facing; smaller centre figure holds spear in r. hand; emperors on l. en r. hold shield and spear; $\overline{\text{SMNA}}$
   LRBC 2446; *RIC* 145
111. AE 3, 1.43g, Nicomedia, 406-408 AD
    inv. SA-97-UAN-223

   [dn arc]ADI-VS PF AVG Bust r., draped, diademed; behind, *
   Rv. GLORI-A ROMA-NORVM Three emperors standing facing, holding spear and shield, the smaller centre figure only spear
112. AE 3, 1.89g, eastern mint, 406-408 AD
    inv. SA-97-UAN-265

   DN ARCADI-VS [pf aug] Bust r., draped, diademed
   Rv. illegible
113. AE 4, 1.01g, uncertain mint
    inv. SA-97-H-31

for Eudoxia

   AEL EVDO-XIA AVG Bust of empress r., diademed, draped, crowned by the Hand of God
   Rv. GLORIA RO-MANORVM Empress enthroned facing, hands folded over breast, crowned by the Hand

of God; |+ / SMNA
LRBC 2450; *RIC* 80
114. AE 3, 1.46g, Nicomedia, 400-401 AD
inv. SA-97-B1-156

[ae]L EVDO-XIA AVG Bust of empress r., diademed, draped, crowned by the Hand of God
Rv. SALVS REI-PVBLICAE Victory seated r. on cuirass, writing ☧ on shield resting on small column
115. AE 3, 1.68g, eastern mint, 401-403 AD
inv. SA-97-UAN-210

[ael eudo]XIA AVG Bust of empress r., diademed, draped, crowned by the Hand of God
Rv. [salus rei] PVBLICAE Victory seated r. on cuirass, writing ☧ on shield resting on small column
116. AE 3, 1.72g, eastern mint, 401-403 AD
inv. SA-97-UAN-321

[ael eudoxia aug] Bust of the empress r., diademed, draped, crowned by the Hand of God
Rv. [salus reipublicae] Victory seated r., writing ☧ on shield resting on small colum
117. AE 3, 1.52g, eastern mint, 401-403 AD
inv. SA-97-S-30

2.22. *Vot x mult xx* (383 AD)

[ ] Worn
Rv. VOT/X/MVLT/XX within wreath; CON[ ]
LRBC 2158-2159
118. AE 4, 1.08g, Constantinople
inv. SA-96-UA-145

[ ] Bust r., draped, diademed
Rv. VOT/X/MVLT/XX within wreath
119. AE 4, 0.91g, uncertain mint
inv. SA-97-UAN-256

[ ] Bust r.
Rv. [vot/x *or* xx]/MV[lt]/X[x *or* xx] within wreath; AN[ ]
120. AE 4, 0.58g (fragment), Antioch
inv. SA-97-UAN-189
The coin is probably from Arcadius, as the legend, which can not be read, shows no break.

2.23. *Salus reipublicae* (383-395 AD)

[ ] Bust r., draped, diademed
Rv. [salus rei]-PVLICAE Victory advancing l., trophy on shoulder, dragging captive

121. AE 4, 1.01g, uncertain mint
inv. SA-96-LA-93

[ ] Bust r., draped, diademed
Rv. [ ] Victory advancing l., trophy on shoulder, dragging captive
122. AE 4, 1.54g, uncertain mint
inv. SA-96-UA-43

[ ] Bust r., draped, diademed
Rv. [ ] Victory advancing l., trophy on shoulder, dragging captive; to l., ⚹
123. AE 4, 1.31g, uncertain mint
inv. SA-97-B1-139

[ ]IVS PF AVG Bust r., draped, diademed
Rv. [salus rei] PVBLICAE Victory advancing l., trophy on shoulder, dragging captive
124. AE 4, 1.22g, uncertain mint
inv. SA-97-B2-28

[ ]AVG Bust r., draped, diademed
Rv. [sa]LVS RE[ipublicae] Victory advancing l., trophy on shoulder, dragging captive; [c]ONS
125. AE 4, 0.81g, Constantinople
inv. SA-97-H-175

[ ]PF AVG Bust r., draped, diademed
Rv. [salus] REI PVBLI[cae] Victory advancing l., trophy on shoulder, dragging captive
126. AE 4, 1.22g, uncertain mint
inv. SA-97-N-101

[ ]IVS PF AVG Bust r., draped, diademed
Rv. [sal]VS REI[publicae] Victory advancing l., trophy on shoulder, dragging captive
127. AE 4, 1.1g, uncertain mint
inv. SA-97-UAN-81

[ ] Bust r.
Rv. [salu]S REI-PVB[licae] Victory advancing l., trophy on shoulder, dragging captive; to l.,
128. AE 4, 0.76g, uncertain mint
inv. SA-97-UAN-112

[ ] Bust r., draped, diademed
Rv. [ ] Victory advancing l., dragging captive
129. AE 4, 1.24g, uncertain mint
inv. SA-97-UAN-221

2.24. Honorius (393-423 AD)

DN HONORIVS PF AVG Bust r., draped, diademed
Rv. GLORIA ROMANORVM Emperor standing fac-

ing, head r., holding labarum and globe; $\overline{\text{CONSA}}$
LRBC 2188; *RIC* 88c1
130. AE 2, 3.81g, Constantinople, 392-395 AD
inv. SA-96-UAN-95

DN HONORIVS PF AVG Bust r., draped, diademed
Rv. GLORIA – ROMANORVM Emperor standing facing, head r., holding labarum and globe;
LRBC 2424; *RIC* 46c
131. AE 2, 4.5g, Nicomedia, $\overline{\text{SMN}\Gamma}$, 392-395 AD
inv. SA-97-B2-119
132. AE 2, 4.57g, Nicomedia, $\overline{\text{SMN[ ]}}$, 392-395 AD
inv. SA-97-UAN-74
133. AE 2, 4.41g, Nicomedia, $\overline{\text{SMN[ ]}}$, 392-395 AD
inv. SA-92-DA 1-58

DN HONORIVS PF AVG Bust r., draped, diademed
Rv. GLORIA ROMANORVM Emperor standing facing, head r., holding labarum and globe; $\overline{\text{ANT}\Delta}$
RIC 68e
134. AE 2, 6.89g, Antioch, 392-395 AD
inv. SA-96-UAN-204

DN HO[norius pf au]G Bust r., draped, diademed
Rv. GLORIA ROM[anorum] Emperor standing facing, head r., holding labarum and globe
135. AE 2, 2.94g (fragment), eastern mint, 392-395 AD
inv. SA-97-B1-160

DN HONORI-VS PF AVG Bust cuirassed, facing, helmeted, holding spear and shield
Rv. CONCORDI-A AVGG Constantinopolis seated facing, head helmeted r., holding spear and Victory on globe, prow by r.foot; $\overline{\text{CONSA}}$
LRBC 2211; *RIC* 88
136. AE 3, 3.39g, Constantinople, 401-403 AD
inv. SA-96-UA-126

DN HONORI-VS PF AVG Bust r., draped, diademed
Rv. [virtus exer]CITI Emperor standing l., head r., holding spear and resting l. hand on shield, crowned by Victory holding palm-branch in l. hand
137. AE 3, 1.92g, eastern mint, 395-401 AD
inv. SA-97-UAN-266
138. AE 3, 2.3g, eastern mint, 395-401 AD
inv. SA-97-UAN-306

DN HONORI-[us pf aug] Bust r., draped, diademed; behind, *
Rv. [gloria romanorum] Two emperors standing facing, each holding shield and spear
cf. *RIC* 395-406
139. AE 3, 2.15g, eastern mint, 408-423 AD
inv. SA-97-LA-165

DN HONORI-[us pf aug] Bust r., draped, diademed; behind, *
Rv. GLORI-[a roma]-NORVM Two emperors standing facing, each holding shield and spear
140. AE 3, 1.4g, eastern mint, 408-423 AD
inv. SA-97-UAN-190

[dn] HON[ ] Bust r.
Rv. illegible
141. AE 3, 1.19g, uncertain mint
inv. SA-97-UAN-285

2.25. *Virtvs exerciti* **(395-401 AD)**

DN[ ]I-VS PF AVG Bust r., draped, diademed
Rv. VIRTVS EXERCITI Emperor facing, head r., holding spear in r. hand, l. resting on shield, is crowned by Victory to l., holding palm-branch; $\overline{\text{CONSA}}$
cf. *LRBC* 2205-2206; cf. *RIC* 60-61
142. AE 3, 2.46g, Constantinople
inv. SA-96-UA-213

[ ] PF AVG Bust r., draped, diademed
Rv. [virtus] EXERCITI Emperor standing l., head r., holding spear in r. hand, l resting on shield, is crowned by Victory, holding palm-branch
143. AE 3, 1.74g, eastern mint
inv. SA-97-RB1-52

[ ]S PF AVG Bust r., draped, diademed
Rv. [virtus] EXE[rciti] Emperor standing l., holding spear and resting l. hand on shield, is crowned by Victory, holding palm-branch
144. AE 3, 1.18g (fragment), eastern mint
inv. SA-97-LA-134

[ ] VS PF A[ug] Bust r.
Rv. [virtus exer]C[iti] Emperor standing l., holding spear and resting l. hand on shield, is crowned by Victory, holding palm-branch; $\overline{\text{SMNA}}$
cf. *RIC* 62-63
145. AE 3, 1.55g, Nicomedia
inv. SA-97-UAN-222

DN [ ] Bust r., draped, diademed
Rv. [virtus] EXERCITI Emperor standing l., head r., holding spear and resting l. hand on shield, is crowned by Victory, holding palm-branch; $\overline{\text{SMN (or H)A}}$
cf. *RIC* 62-63
146. AE 3, 2.62g, eastern mint (Nicomedia or Heraclea)
inv. SA-97-UAN-263

[ ] Bust r., draped, diademed
Rv.[ ] Emperor facing, head r., holding spear in r. hand, l. resting on shield, is crowned by Victory to l., holding palm-branch
147. AE 3, 2.5g, eastern mint
inv. SA-96-LA-41

2.26. *Concordia augg* (401-403 AD)

[ ]VS PF AVG Bust cuirassed, facing, helmeted, holding spear and shield
Rv. [concordi]-A AVGG Constantinopolis enthroned facing, head l., holding sceptre and Victory on globe; prow under r. foot; [a]NTΓ
cf. *LRBC* 2797-2999; cf. *RIC* 97-100
148. AE 3, 2.27g, Antioch
inv. SA-97-UAN-40

[ ] Bust cuirassed, facing, helmeted, holding spear and shield
Rv. [Concordia augg] Constantinopolis enthroned facing, head l., holding sceptre and Victory on globe
149. AE 3, 1.04g, uncertain mint
inv. SA-97-UAN-287

2.27. Theodosius II (402-450 AD)

DN THEODO-SIVS PF [aug] Bust cuirassed, facing, helmeted, holding spear and shield
Rv. [concordia augg] Constantinopolis enthroned facing, head l., holding sceptre and Victory on globe; prow under r. foot
150. AE 3, 1.93g, eastern mint, 401-403 AD
inv. SA-97-UAN-76

DN THEODO[sius pf aug] Bust r., draped, diademed
Rv; [concordia augg] Constantinopolis enthroned facing, head l., holding sceptre and Victory on globe; prow under r. foot
151. AE 3, 1.64g, eastern mint, 401-403 AD
inv. SA-96-RB-205

DN THEODO-SIVS PF AVG Bust r., draped, diademed; behind, *
Rv. GLORI-A ROMA-NORVM Three emperors standing facing; smaller centre figure holds spear in r. hand; emperors on l. and r. hold shield and spear
152. AE 3, 2.13g, eastern mint, 402-408 AD
inv. SA-96-H-85

[dn theodo]SIVS PF AVG Bust r., draped, diademed; behind, *
Rv. GLORI-A ROMA-NORVM Two emperors standing facing, each holding shield and spear; SMNA
LRBC 2455; *RIC* 402
153. AE 3, 1.57g, Nicomedia, 408-423 AD
inv. SA-97-UAN-84

DN THEO[dosius pf aug] Bust r., draped, diademed
Rv. [gloria romanorum] Two emperors standing facing, each holding spear and supporting between them a globe
154. AE 3, 1.56g, eastern mint, 408-423 AD
inv. SA-97-UAN-126 A

[ ] Bust r.
Rv. Monogram ⌘
155. AE 4, 1.1g, uncertain mint, 425-450 AD
inv. SA-96-UA-189

DN THEODO-SIVS [pf avg] Bust r., draped, diademed
Rv. Cross within wreath; C[on]
LRBC 2234 or 2238; *RIC* 443 or 445
156. AE 4, 1.08g, Constantinople, 425-435 AD
inv. SA-96-B-216

[dn theodo]SIVS PF A[ug] Bust r., draped, diademed
Rv. Cross within wreath; CO[n]
LRBC 2238; *RIC* 445
157. AE 4, 0.84g, Constantinople, 425-435 AD
inv. SA-97-UAN-143

[dn theodos]IVS PF AVG Bust r., draped, diademed
Rv. Wreath (with cross within?)
158. AE 4, 0.92g, uncertain mint, 425-435 AD
inv. SA-97-UAN-211

DN T[heodosius] PF AVG Bust r., draped, diademed
Rv. Cross within wreath
159. AE 4, 0.99g, uncertain mint, 425-435 AD
inv. SA-97-UAN-226

Obv. illegible
Rv. [vt]/XXX/V/ within wreath; CON
RIC 457
160. AE 4, 0.75g, Constantinople, 435 AD
inv. SA-97-UAN-34

2.28. *Gloria romanorum*, 3 emperors (402-408 AD)

[ ] Bust r., draped, diademed
Rv. [gloria roman]ORV[m] Three emperors facing, holding spear and shield, the smaller centre figure only spear
161. AE 3, 1.28g, eastern mint
inv. SA-96-DA 1-68

[ ] Bust r., draped, diademed
Rv. GLORI-[a romanorum] Three emperors facing, holding spear
162. AE 3, 1.48g, eastern mint
inv. SA-96-Y-5

[ ] Worn
Rv. [gloria roma]NORVM Three emperors facing, holding spear, but only the centre and the r. figure are visible.
163. AE 3, 0.53g, eastern mint
inv. SA-96-UA-78

[ ] Bust r.
Rv. [gloria]ROM[anorum] Three(?) emperors standing facing
164. AE 3, 1g, eastern mint
inv. SA-96-UAN-96

DN[ ] Bust r., draped, diademed; behind, *
Rv. GLORI-[ia romanorum] Three emperors standing facing
165. AE 3, 1.43g, eastern mint
inv. SA-97-LA-153

[ ] Bust r., draped, diademed
Rv. [gloria roma]NORVM Three emperors standing facing
166. AE 3, 1.83g, eastern mint
inv. SA-97-LA-193

DN [ ] Bust r., draped, diademed; behind, *
Rv. [gloria romanorum] Three emperors standing facing
167. AE 3, 0.86g, eastern mint
inv. SA-97-RB2-137

[ ]-VS [pf] AVG Bust r., draped, diademed; behind, *
Rv. [ ] Three emperors standing facing; [ ]NΔ
cf. *LRBC* 2446-2448; *RIC* 145-147
168. AE 3, 1.94g, Nicomedia (?)
inv. SA-97-UAN-317

2.29. *Gloria romanorum*, **2 emperors (408-423 AD)**

DN[ ]PF AVG Bust r., draped, diademed; behind, *
Rv.[gloria]ROMA-NORVM Two emperors, standing facing, heads turned r. and l., holding spear and supporting globe between them
cf. *RIC* 407-418
169. AE 3, 2.03g, eastern mint
inv. SA-96-LA-76

[ ] Bust r., draped, diademed, behind, *
Rv. [gloria roman]ORV[m] Two emperors, standing facing, holding spear and supporting globe between them
170. AE 3, 1.32g, eastern mint
inv. SA-96-B-94

[ ] Worn
Rv. [glo]RI[a romanorum] Two emperors, standing facing, holding spear and supporting globe between them
171. AE 3, 0.35g, eastern mint
inv. SA-96-UA-202

[ ]VS PF AVG Bust r., draped, diademed
Rv. GLORIA RO-[manorum] Two emperors standing facing, heads turned r. and l., supporting globe between them
172. AE 3, 1.88g, eastern mint
inv. SA-97-UAN-307

Obv. illegible
Rv. [gloria romanorum] Two emperors standing facing supporting globe between them
173. AE 3, 0.58g, eastern mint
inv. SA-97-UAN-335

[ ] Bust r., draped, diademed
Rv. [gloria roma]-NORVM Two emperors standing facing, each holding shield and spear
cf. *RIC* 395-406
174. AE 3, 1.27g, eastern mint
inv. SA-97-S-39

[ ]-VS PF AVG Bust r., draped, diademed
Rv. GLORI-[a romanorum] Two emperors standing facing, each holding spear and shield
175. AE 3, 1.64g, eastern mint
inv. SA-97-UAN-238

[ ] Bust r.
Rv. [ ] Two emperors standing facing
176. AE 3, 1.11g, eastern mint
inv. SA-97-UAN-62
177. AE 3, 0.97g (fragment), eastern mint
inv. SA-97-UAN-257

2.30. *Victoria augg* **(408-c. 435 AD)**

[ ] AVG Bust r., draped
Rv. [ ] Victory advancing l., holding wreath and palm-branch, P |
              [ ]
178. AE 4, 1.57g, Rome
inv. SA-97-UAN-252

[ ] Bust r., draped, cuirassed, diademed
Rv. VICTOR-[ia augg] Victory advancing l., holding wreath and palm-branch; S|‾RM

179. AE 4, 0.8g, Rome
    inv. SA-97-B2-48

2.31. *Concordia aug (425-450 AD)*

[ ] Bust r., draped, diademed
Rv. CONCOR – [dia aug] Victory facing, wreath in each hand

180. AE 4, 0.69g, eastern mint
    inv. SA-96-UA-56

2.32. Marcian (450-457 AD)

DN M[arcianus p]F AVG Bust r., draped, diademed
Rv. Within wreath, monogram ☧; CO[n]
LRBC 2248; *RIC* 543

181. AE 4, 0.57g, Constantinople, 450-457 AD
    inv. SA-97-B2-103

[ ] Bust r.
Rv. Within wreath, monogram ☧

182. AE 4, 1.06g, eastern mint, 450-457 AD
    inv. SA-97-N-73

[ ] Bust r., draped, diademed
Rv. Within wreath, monogram ☧

183. AE 4, 0.77g, eastern mint, 450-457 AD
    inv. SA-97-UAN-232

2.33. Cross within wreath (425-457 AD)

[ ]VS PF AVG Bust r., draped, diademed
Rv. Cross within wreath

184. AE 4, 1.05g, uncertain mint
    inv. SA-96-UAN 37

[ ]S PF AV[g] Bust r.
Rv. Cross within wreath

185. AE 4, 0.5g, uncertain mint
    inv. SA-97-UAN-280

[ ] Bust r., draped, diademed
Rv. Cross within wreath

186. AE 4, 0.5g, uncertain mint
    inv. SA-96-AG-83
187. AE 4, 0.86g, uncertain mint
    inv. SA-96-UA-195
188. AE 4, 0.82g, uncertain mint
    inv. SA-97-S-12
189. AE 4, 0.61g, uncertain mint
    inv. SA-97-UAN-44
190. AE 4, 0.78g, uncertain mint
    inv. SA-97-UAN-89
191. AE 4, 0.62g, uncertain mint
    inv. SA-97-UAN-191
192. AE 4, uncertain mint
    inv. SA-97-UAN-208
193. AE 4, 0.96g, uncertain mint
    inv. SA-97-UAN-224

Obv. illegible
Rv. Cross within wreath

194. AE 4, 0.65g, Constantinople, [ ]O[ ]
    inv. SA-97-UAN-102
195. AE 4, 0.88g, uncertain mint
    inv. SA-96-UA-174
196. AE 4, 0.58g, uncertain mint
    inv. SA-96-LE-15
197. AE 4, 0.6g, uncertain mint
    inv. SA-96-UA-136
198. AE 4, 0.74g, uncertain mint
    inv. SA-97-UAN-82
199. AE 4, 0.96g, uncertain mint
    inv. SA-97-UAN-106
200. AE 4, 0.62g, uncertain mint
    inv. SA-97-UAN-253

Obv. illegible
Rv. Cross

201. AE 4, 0,62g, uncertain mint
    inv. SA-97-UAN-111
202. AE 4, uncertain mint
    inv. SA-97-UAN-126 B

Small bust r. (?)
Rv. Wreath (with cross?)

203. AE 4, 0.52g, uncertain mint
    Inv. SA-96-RB-235

2.34. Leo I and Verina (457-474 AD)

[dn le]O Small bust r., draped, diademed
Rv. Empress standing facing, holding cross on globe and transverse sceptre
LRBC 2272; *RIC* 714

204. AE 4, 0.98g, Constantinople?, 457-474 AD
    inv. SA-96-B-210

[p]F [aug] Bust r., draped, diademed
Rv. Empress standing facing, holding cross on globe and transverse sceptre; in field, [b]-E
LRBC 2272-2275; *RIC* 715

205. AE 4, 1.02g, eastern mint, 457-474 AD
    inv. SA-97-UAN-70

[dn l]EO Small bust r., draped, diademed
Rv. Emperor standing facing, in r. hand long cross, l. hand on head of captive
206. AE 4, 1.17g, eastern mint, 457-474 AD
inv. SA-96-UA-194

[ ] Bust r., draped, diademed
Rv. Within wreath, monogram ℟
207. AE 4, 0.86g, eastern mint, 457-474 AD
inv. SA-97-S-34

DN L[eo p]F AVG Bust r., draped, diademed
Rv. Lion crouching l., in wreath
RIC 680
208. AE 4, 0.84g, uncertain mint, 457-474 AD
inv. SA-97-UAN-83

[ ]VS PF [aug] Bust r., diademed
Rv. Two emperors nimbate enthroned;
V(?)KO[?] (or V?NO)
RIC 724 var.
209. AE 4, 1.55g, eastern mint, 473-474 AD
inv. SA-97-UAN-225
As Leo I is the only emperor with this reverse, this coin has been attrubuted to him, although the obv. legend seems different.

[ ] LEO Bust r.
Rv. Illegible
210. AE 4, 0.64g, eastern mint, 457-474 AD
inv. SA-97-UAN-220

2.35. Zeno (474-475, 476-491 AD)

[ ] Bust r.
Rv. Within wreath, only left part of monogram ℟
LRBC 2281; cf. *RIC* 958-976
211. AE 4, 0.96g, eastern mint, 476-491 AD
inv. SA-97-S-32

[ ] Bust r.
Rv. Within wreath, monogram ℟
LRBC 2281; cf. *RIC* 958-976
212. AE 4, 0.74g, eastern mint, 476-491 AD
inv. SA-97-S-38

Obv. illisible
Rv. Within wreath, monogram ⨆
213. AE 4, 0.72g, eastern mint, 476-491 AD
inv. SA-97-S-10

[ ] Bust r.
Within wreath monogram ℟
214. AE 4, 0.48g, eastern mint, 476-491 AD
inv. SA-97-LA-113

[ ] Bust r.
Rv. [ze] – NO Emperor standing facing, head l., holding long cross and globe
cf. *RIC* 953-957
215. AE 4, 1.22g, eastern mint, 476-491 AD
inv. SA-97-UAN-259

2.36. Imitations

]Λ[Barbaric bust r., draped, diademed
Rv. [vic]TORIA[ ] Victory to l.
216. AE 4, 1.36g, imitation of *Victoria augg* (408-c. 435 AD)
inv. SA-97-UAN-33

Blundered legend. Bust r., draped, diademed
Rv. Victory advancing l., holding wreath and dragging captive with l. hand; in l. field ⚔; all within wreath made up of I's
217. AE 3, 0.9g, imitation of SE-CN-coin of Zeno (476-491 AD), cf. *RIC* 949 (prototype)
inv. SA-97-UAN-60

Blundered legend. Bust r., diademed
Rv. illegible
218. AE 4, 1.02g, 4th-5th cent. AD
inv. SA-97-RB2-121

2.37. AE 3 and AE 4 (4th and 5th cent.AD)

[ ]-IVS PF AVG Bust r., draped, diademed
Rv. [ ]CAE Figure standing l.
219. AE 4, 1.34g
inv. SA-96-UA-178

DNVALEN[ ] Bust r., draped
Rv. illegible
220. AE 4, 1.36g
inv. SA-96-B-116
Maybe Valentinian III (?)

[dn] HO(?)[ ] Bust r., draped, diademed
Rv. illegible
221. AE 3, 1.17g
inv. SA-96-UA-65

Bust r., draped, diademed
Rv. Victory to l.
222. AE 3, 1.24g
inv. SA-96-AG-45
223. AE 3, 1.54g
inv. SA-96-UA-127

224. AE 3, 1.41g
    inv. SA-96-B-202
225. AE 3, 1.54g
    inv. SA-96-RB-131

[ ]PF AVG Bust r., draped, diademed
Rv. Two Victories? (only the r. one visible)
226. AE 4, 0.61g
    inv. SA-96-B-147

Bust r., draped, diademed
Rv.]IAR[Standing figure facing with spear(?)
227. AE 4, 1.06g
    inv. SA-96-Y-3

Bust r.
Rv. Standing figure facing
228. AE 4, 0.94g
    inv. SA-96-AG-77

Bust r., draped, diademed
Rv. Standing figure (?)
229. AE 3, 1.01g
    inv. SA-96-UAN-131

Bust r.
Rv. Traces of legend. Type illegible
230. AE 3, 1.35g
    inv. SA-96-UAN-64

Bust r., draped, diademed
Rv. illegible
231. AE 4, 0.8g
    inv. SA-96-UA-214
232. AE 4, 0.8g
    inv. SA-96-RB-192
233. AE 4, 0.45g
    inv. SA-96-LE-13

Small bust r.
Rv. illegible
234. AE 4, 0.8g
    inv. SA-96-UA-105
235. AE 4, 0.19g
    inv. SA-96-RB-228
236. AE 4, 1.04g
    inv. SA-97-UAN-36

[ ] PF AV[g] Bust r., draped, diademed
Rv. illegible
237. AE 4, 1.22g
    inv. SA-96-RB-171

DN [ ] Small bust r.
Rv. illegible
238. AE 4, 0.7g
    inv. SA-96-LA-64
    Obv. shows confused image. The only recognisable letter is V
    Rv.]TO[Building with two colums (?). Confused image, maybe overstrike?
239. AE 3 or 4, 0.92g
    inv. SA-97-UAN-199

[ ]VG Bust r., draped
Rv. Monogram (of Marcian?)
240. AE 4, 1.1g
    inv. SA-97-LA-160

Bust r.
Rv. Figure to l.
241. AE 4, 1.01g
    inv. SA-97-H-299

Bust r., draped
Rv. Standing figure
242. AE 4, 1.5g
    inv. SA-97-UAN-316
243. AE 4, 0.69g
    inv. SA-97-UAN-85

Bust r., draped
Rv. Wreath?
244. AE 4, 0.99g
    inv. SA-97-UAN-188

DN [ ] Bust r.
Rv. illegible
245. AE 3, 0.62g (fragment)
    inv. SA-97-UAN-279

Bust r., draped; behind, *
Rv. illegible
246. AE 4
    inv. SA-97-S-40 B

Bust r., draped
Rv. illegible
247. AE 4, 1.38g
    inv. SA-96-AG-84
248. AE 4, 1.5g
    inv. SA-97-B1-126
249. AE 4, 0.32g,
    inv. SA-97-S-43
250. AE 4, 1.24g
    inv. SA-97-UAN-37
251. AE 3, 0.91g
    inv. SA-97-UAN-61
252. AE 4, 1.04g

inv. SA-97-UAN-65
253. AE 4, 1.0g
inv. SA-97-UAN-69
254. AE 4, 0.37g
inv. SA-97-UAN-87
255. AE 4, 0.91g
inv. SA-97-UAN-88
256. AE 4, 0.26g
inv. SA-97-UAN-193
257. AE 4, 0.41g
inv. SA-97-UAN-194
258. AE 4, 0.9g
inv. SA-97-UAN-254
259. AE 3, 1.13g
inv. SA-97-UAN-261

2.38. Uncertain bronze coins, mostly 2nd half 4th-5th cent. AD

260. inv. SA-96-AG-26-0.63g
261. inv. SA-96-AG-64-1.02g
262. inv. SA-96-AG-72-0.36g
263. inv. SA-96-AG-73-0.68g
264. inv. SA-96-AG-74-0.14g
265. inv. SA-96-AG-75-0.68g
266. inv. SA-96-AG-80-0.5g
267. inv. SA-96-AG-81-0.62g
268. inv. SA-96-B-104-0.27g
269. inv. SA-96-B-111-0.25g
270. inv. SA-96-B-112-0.48g
271. inv. SA-96-B-114-0.47g
272. inv. SA-96-DA 1-72-0.7g
273. inv. SA-96-H-137-0.51g
274. inv. SA-96-LA-42-0.35g
275. inv. SA-96-LA-65-0.89g
276. inv. SA-96-N-92-0.37g
277. inv. SA-96-RB-189-0.54g
278. inv. SA-96-RB-206-0.24g
279. inv. SA-96-RB-221-0.82g
280. inv. SA-96-RB-225-0.43g
281. inv. SA-96-RB-226-0.78g
282. inv. SA-96-RB-227-0.51g
283. inv. SA-96-RB-239-0.53g
284. inv. SA-96-UA-91-0.37g
285. inv. SA-96-UA-147-0.76g
286. inv. SA-96-UA-148-1.18g
287. inv. SA-96-UA-162-0.75g
288. inv. SA-96-UA-170-1.33g
289. inv. SA-96-UA-181-0.23g
290. inv. SA-96-UA-220-0.33g
291. inv. SA-96-UAN-49-4.12g – Greek city-coin?
292. inv. SA-96-UAN-105-0.46g
293. inv. SA-97-DT-18-0.87g
294. inv. SA-97-DT-20-0.42g
295. inv. SA-97-DT-21-0.53g
296. inv. SA-97-H-320-7.08g (Greek imperial or Byzantine?)
297. inv. SA-97-LA-146-0.36g
298. inv. SA-97-LA-159-0.33g
299. inv. SA-97-RB2-107-0.24g
300. inv. SA-97-RB2-151-0.73g
301. inv. SA-97-S-14-0.24g
302. inv. SA-97-S-31-0.88g
303. inv. SA-97-S-33-0.34g
304. inv. SA-97-S-35-0.72g
305. inv. SA-97-S-37 A
306. inv. SA-97-S-37 B
307. inv. SA-97-S-37 C
308. inv. SA-97-S-37 D
309. inv. SA-97-S-37 E
310. inv. SA-97-S-40 A – 0.57g
311. inv. SA-97-S-40 C – 0.29g
312. inv. SA-97-S-41 B – 0.80g
313. inv. SA-97-S-42-0.6g
314. inv. SA-97-UAN-35-0.62g
315. inv. SA-97-UAN-42-0.48g
316. inv. SA-97-UAN-66-0.6g
317. inv. SA-97-UAN-68-1.31g
318. inv. SA-97-UAN-75-0.35g
319. inv. SA-97-UAN-77-0.43g
320. inv. SA-97-UAN-79-0.61g
321. inv. SA-97-UAN-80-0.56g
322. inv. SA-97-UAN-86-0.73g
323. inv. SA-97-UAN-187-0.38g
324. inv. SA-97-UAN-192-0.6g
325. inv. SA-97-UAN-196-0.35g
326. inv. SA-97-UAN-197-0.52g
327. inv. SA-97-UAN-198-0.66g
328. inv. SA-97-UAN-203-0.93g
329. inv. SA-97-UAN-204-0.8g
330. inv. SA-97-UAN-206-0.6g
331. inv. SA-97-UAN-207-0.77g
332. inv. SA-97-UAN-215-0.47g
333. inv. SA-97-UAN-216-0.58g
334. inv. SA-97-UAN-217-0.44g
335. inv. SA-97-UAN-218-0.95g
336. inv. SA-97-UAN-235-0.64g
337. inv. SA-97-UAN-248-0.78g
338. inv. SA-97-UAN-249-0.76g
339. inv. SA-97-UAN-258-0.71g
340. inv. SA-97-UAN-262-0.75g
341. inv. SA-97-UAN-267-0.34g
342. inv. SA-97-UAN-268-0.24g
343. inv. SA-97-UAN-269-0.32g
344. inv. SA-97-UAN-271-2.00g
345. inv. SA-97-UAN-272-1.36g
346. inv. SA-97-UAN-273-0.41g
347. inv. SA-97-UAN-274-0.61g
348. inv. SA-97-UAN-278-0.22g

349. inv. SA-97-UAN-281-0.83g
350. inv. SA-97-UAN-282-0.82g
351. inv. SA-97-UAN-283-1.39g
352. inv. SA-97-UAN-284-0.48g
353. inv. SA-97-UAN-286-1.07g
354. inv. SA-97-UAN-334-0.22g
355. inv. SA-97-UAN-336-0.68g

3. BYZANTINE EMPIRE

3.1. Anastasius (491-518 AD)

[ ] Bust r., draped, diademed
Rv. Within wreath monogram ⋈
DOC I, 15
356. AE, nummus, 0.49g, Constantinople, 491-498 AD
inv. SA-97-UAN-73

[ ] Bust r., draped, diademed
Rv. Within wreath monogram ⋈
357. AE, nummus, 0.69g, Constantinople, 491-498 AD
inv. SA-97-DT-148

3.2. Justin I (518-527 AD)

DN IVSTI-[nus pp]AVC Bust r. with diadem, cuirass and paludamentum
Rv. Large M; above, cross; to l. and r., stars (*); beneath, ϵ in exergue, CON
DOC I, 8e7
358. AE, follis, 16.84g, Constantinople
inv. SA-96-UAN-36

DN IVSTIN-[us pp auc] Bust r.
Rv. Large K; to l., long cross; above and below, star; to r., Ⱥ
DOC I, 15a
359. AE, half follis, 10.43g, Constantinople
inv. SA-97-UAN-134

3.3. Justin I or Justinian I

[ ] Bust r.
Rv. Large ⋇ No letters discernible on both sides
360. AE, pentanummium, 0.31g
inv. SA-96-H-125
The very small size of this coin and the absence of letters on the reverse make this coin difficult to place. The pentanummia struck by Justin I and Justinian I at Constantinople and Nicomedia are larger and heavier and have always letters on both sides of the cross on the reverse. This is maybe an imitation?

3.4. Justinian I (527-565 AD)

[ ] Bust r.
Rv. Large A̅
DOC I, 36.2
361. AE, nummus, 0.4g, Constantinople, 527-538 AD
inv. SA-97-S-41 A

[dn iu]STINI-ANVS PP AVC Bust facing, in helmet, with diadem and cuirass; in r. hand, globe crucigerus, on l. shoulder, shield; in field r., cross
Rv. Large M; above, cross; to l., A/N/N/O; to r., XII; beneath B; in exergue, CON
DOC I, 37b
362. AE, follis, 23.14g, Constantinople, 538/9 AD
inv. SA-96-UA-137

DN[ ]-ANVS PP AVC As above
Rv. As above; but to r., X/Ч; beneath, Δ, in exergue, CON
DOC I, 40d
363. AE, follis, 22.56g, Constantinople, 541/2
inv. SA-96-B-99

[ ] Small bust r.
Rv. Large ϵ in a circle; to r., B
cf. *DOC* I, 97b
364. AE, small pentanummium, 1.35g, Constantinople, 543-565 AD
inv. SA-96-UA-66

Obv. illegible
Rv. Large ϵ
DOC I 97
365. AE, small pentanummium, 0.88g, Constantinople, 543-565 AD
inv. SA-96-B-289
The very small size of this coin seems to point to Justinian I

Bust r. with diadem, cuirass and paludamentum
Rv. Large I surmonted by a cross; to l., A/N/N/O; to r., X/XXϚ; in exergue, NIK
DOC I, 159
366. AE, decanummium, 3.46g, Nicomedia, 562/3 AD
inv. SA-96-B-77

DN IVSTINI-[anu]S PP AVC Bust r.
Rv. Large M; above, cross; beneath, Γ; to l. and r., star; in exergue, +THE Ч [ ]
DOC I, 210c
367. AE, follis, 15.69g, Antioch, 533-537 AD
inv. SA-97-LA-63

3.5. Justin II (565-578 AD)

DN IVSTI-NVS PP AVC Justin, on l., and Sophia, on r., seated, nimbate, on double throne. He holds in r. hand globe crucigerus, she holds cruciform scepter
Rv. Large M; above ☧; beneath A; to l., A/N/N/O; to r., Ϛ ; in exergue, CON
DOC I, 28 a

368. AE, follis, 14.82g, Constantinople, 570/1 AD
inv. SA-96-UAN-170

DN IVS[tin]VS PP A[uc) As above
Rv. Large M; above, cross; beneath, A; to l., A/N/N/O; to r., X/II; in exergue, CON
DOC I, 42a

369. AE, follis, 13.63g, Constantinople, 576/7 AD
inv. SA-96-B-43

[dn iusti]- NVS PP AVC As above
Rv. Large K, above, Φ+C; to l., A/N/N/O; to r., XI/II; beneath, TES
DOC I, 85

370. AE, half follis, 5.75g, Thessalonica, 577/8 AD
inv. SA-96-UA-190

[dn iustinus] PP AVC As above
Rv. Large M; above, cross; to l., A/N/N/O; to r., Ϛ beneath A; in exergue, NIKO
DOC I, 96a

371. AE, follis, 15.16g, Nicomedia, 570/1 AD
inv. SA-96-UA-140

3.6. Maurice (582-602 AD)

δNmΛV-RITIbE Bust facing, wearing cuirass and helmet with plume; in r. hand, globe crucigerus
Rv. Large K; above, cross; to l., A/N/N/O; to r., Ϛ; beneath, A
DOC I, 22

372. AE, half-follis, 5.9g, Constantinople, 588/9 AD
inv. SA-96-N-89

OmAVRIC – TIbER PPA Bust facing, wearing cuirass and crown; in r. hand, globe crucigerus; on l. shoulder, shield
Rv. Large M; above, cross; to l., A/N/N/O; to r., Ϛ; beneath, B; in exergue, KYZ
DOC I, 122

373. AE, follis, 11.15g, Cyzicus, 587/8 AD
inv. SA-97-H-254

[ ]mARI-TIbERIP Bust facing, wearing cuirass and helmet with plume; in r. hand, globe crucigerus; on l. shoulder, shield
Rv. Large K; above, cross; to l., A/N/N/O; to r., Ϛ, X/I; beneath, A
DOC I, 143a

374. AE, half-follis, 5.46g, Cyzicus, 592/3 AD
inv. SA-96-UA-151

δNmAVΓI – CNPA 'Γ Bust facing, in consular robes and crown with trefoil ornament; in r. hand, mappa; in l., eagle-topped sceptre
Rv. Large M; above, cross; to l., A/N/N/O; to r., X/I; beneath, Γ; in exergue, THEЧP'
DOC I, 163b

375. AE, follis, 11.21 g, Antioch, 592/3 AD
inv. SA-96-LA-58

δNmAЧ R – [ ]P AV Bust facing, in consular robes and crown; in r. hand, mappa; in l., eagle-topped sceptre
Rv. Large K; above, cross; to l., A/N/N/O; to r., XI; in exergue, R (for Ҏ)
DOC I, 186 (but XI instead of IX)

376. AE, half follis, 5.23g, Antioch, 592/3 AD
inv. SA-97-H-232

3.7. Phocas (602-610 AD)

δN FOCAS [perp auc] Bust facing, wearing consular robes and crown with cross; in r. hand, mappa; in l., cross.
Rv. XXXX; above, ANNO; to r., Ч; in exergue, CON[ ]
DOC II.1, 29

377. AE, follis, 10.64g, Constantinople, 606/7 AD
inv. SA-96-B-89

δN FOCAS – PERP AV Bust facing, wearing consular robes and crown with cross; in r. hand, mappa; in l., cross.
Rv. Large XXXX; above, ANNO; to r., Ϛ; in exergue, KYZB
DOC II.1, 73b

378. AE, follis, 10.01g, Cyzicus, 607/8 AD
inv. SA-97-UAN-67

3.8. Heraclius (610-640 AD)

ddNN hE[ ] To l., Herclaius, and [to r., Heraclius Constantine, both standing]; each wears chlamys and crown with cross and holds globe crucigerus in r. hand. – Underlying type: Large M; to r., Ϛ I/II; in exergue, [co]N
Rv. Large M; above ☧; to l., A/N/N/O; to r., date uncertain [II]/II (?); beneath, B; in exergue, CON – Underlying type:]-NVS PP AV[ ] Sophia nimbate facing

Overstruck on follis of Justin II of year 573/4 AD (*DOC* I, 36)
DOC II.1, 79b

379. AE, follis, 13.24g, Constantinople, 613/14 AD
inv. SA-97-B2-127

[dNheracli]-PERP AVC Bust bearded, facing, wearing cuirass with shield and plumed helmet; in r. hand, globe crucigerus
Rv. Large K; above, cross; to l., A/N/N/O; to r., I; beneath, Γ
DOC II.1, 72

380. AE, half-follis, 5.53 g, Constantinople, 610/11 AD
inv. SA-96-H-116

[ ] To l., Heraclius, and to r., Heraclius Constantine, both standing; each wears chlamys and crown with cross and holds globe crucigerus in r. hand.; between heads, cross. Underlying type: [XXXX]; above, ANNO; to l., Ч; in exergue, NIKOB
Rv. Large M; above ☩; to l. A/N/N/O; beneath, Γ; in exergue, CON. Underlying type: dɱ FOCA [ ]PER AV Consular bust of Phocas
DOC II.1, 82. Overstruck on a follis of Phocas struck at Nicomedia in 606/7 (*DOC* II, 1, 66)

381. AE, follis class 2, 12.03g, Constantinople, 613-616 AD
inv. SA-96-UAN-142

Heraclius (center), Heraclius Constantine (to r.) and Martina (to l.), standing facing, each wears chlamys and crown with cross and holds globe crucigerus; crosses in upper field to l. and r.
Rv. Large M; above, cross; to l., A/N/N/O; to r., Ϛ; beneath, E; in exergue, CON
Overstrike
DOC II,1, 89d

382. AE, follis class 3, 9.58g, Constantinople, 615/6 AD
inv. SA-96-AG-19

[dn]hR – ACLIPP Bust facing, wearing cuirass, paludamentum and helmet; in r. hand, globe crucigerus
Rv. Large K turned to l.; above, cross; to r., Ϛ, A/N/N/O; to l., I[?]; beneath, A (?)
The type on the reverse die was mistakenly engraved in the wrong direction.
DOC II.1, 156a

383. AE, half follis, 5.32g, Nicomedia, 611/12 AD
inv. SA-97-H-235

dM hERACCC NK (blundered inscription) To l., bust of Heraclius; to r., smaller bust of Heraclius Constantine; each wears chlamys and crown with cross; between heads, cross
Rv. Large M; to l., A/N/N/O; to r., Ч I ; beneath, A; in exergue, ISAYR
The coin has been restruck and overturned (ISAYR is upside down above the large M)
DOC II, 1, 183.

384. AE, follis, 11.27g, Isaura, 616/7 or 617/8 AD
inv. SA-96-UA-184

3.9. Basil II (976-1025 AD) – Romanus III (1028-1034 AD)

+[emma – novH]Λ Bust of Christ facing, bearded, with nimbus, wearing tunic and himation; r. hand raised in blessing, l. holds book with ornate cover. In field, [IC] – XC
Rv. –∴– / +IhSЧS / XRISTЧS / BASILEЧ/ BASILE/– ∴ -
DOC III, p. 673, n° A 2.48

385. AE, anonymous follis class A 2, 15.11g, c. 976 (?) – c. 1030/35 AD
inv. SA-97-LA-36

4. LATE ROMAN BRONZE WEIGHTS FROM THE EAST (ca. third – fifth cent. AD)

Within double incuse circle, N̊ Γ (3 nomisma), letters decorated with small points
Rv. Double incuse circle, small hole in centre
Dürr, n° 125.

386. Bronze square, 18 mm, weight unknown.
Weight of three nomisma
inv. SA-97-H-3
Obv. Within double relief circle, N S (6 nomisma), decorated with small points, on each side of central hole. Rv. Blank

387. Bronze circular disk, 23 mm, weight unknown.
Weight of 6 nomisma
inv. SA-97-UAN-46

5. COMMENTARY

The excavations of 1996-97 confirm the statements already discussed in previous publications.

5.1. The civic coins

As may be expected there is a preponderance of the local coinage of Sagalassos (59 coins or 51.75 % of all the civic coins). Coins of the other Pisidian cities are scarce, Selge being the best represented (6 coins or 5.26 %). Perge, apparently the most frequented harbour, accounts for two-thirds of the Pamphylian coins (23 out of 32 coins, or 20.17 % of all the civic coins), followed by Attaleia (6 coins or 5.26 %). The coinage of Sagalassos started apparently during the reign of the Galatian king Amyntas (36-25 BC). Of the 27 early coins of Sagalassos, dating from 36-25 BC and the early Imperial times, the majority, i.e. 17 bronzes, bear on the obverse the head of Zeus and on the reverse two goats confronted. All the other types are less well represented. The Zeus/goats type may have been struck in large quantities and over a significant period of time. It was the only Sagalassian bronze in the Ariassos-hoard, buried after 24

type	total	references to Scheers, Catalogues I to V
Head of Zeus / two goats confronted	17	symbol *bucranium*: Scheers I, 8; III, 13, 15; V,9 symbol *caduceus*: Scheers III, 16;IV, 12; V, 8 symbol *cornucopiae*: Scheers V, 10, 11 symbol uncertain: Scheers II, 7, 8; III, 14, 17; IV, 13; V, 12, 13, 14
Head of Zeus / CAΓ within wreath	3	Scheers II, 5-6; V, 15
Head of Athena / Nike standing r.	2	Scheers III, n° 19; V, n° 7
Head of Hermes / boar	1	Scheers IV, n° 14
Bucranium / *caduceus* CΛ-GΛ	1	Scheers III, n° 18
Humped bull r. / horseman	2	Scheers IV, n° 15;II, n° 17 (classified as uncertain) There is no legend, but the type is close to SNG Paris 1746, which has ΣΑΓΑΛ under the horseman
Butting bull r. /CΛ within wreath	1	Scheers III, n° 20 (listed as uncertain, but a second coin in the 1998 excavations permits to identify the revers with certainty)

Table 1: The early bronze coins of Sagalassos found in the excavations from 1990 to 1997 (with some corrections to the earlier publications in the case of previously unknown or unpublished coins).

BC (see further).

The coins with Imperial heads range from Augustus to Claudius II, but the series is less abundant than might be expected. Further excavations will no doubt reach the earlier layers of the city and provide more information about this period.

The series from Perge consists mainly of imperial issues, ranging from Hadrian to Gallienus. We have listed under Perge the two small coins bearing a bust of Artemis and on the reverse a standing figure (Dionysos?), although their attribution is uncertain (Scheers I, 1; III, 25). We attributed the first coin tentatively to Grymenothyrae (Scheers I, 1), but the legend, which remains uncertain, is too short. Also, the presence of the two coins at Sagalassos means that the mint cannot be far away. A Pisidian or Pamphylian origin seems likely, and Perge is the likeliest candidate (Scheers III, 25), as the cult of Artemis is well attested at Perge and her coins are frequent at Sagalassos. But we may be wrong in our attribution. A better preserved coin will no doubt settle the matter.

Bronze coins represent the movements of individuals. Although the total of civic coins is still small, some observations can be made. Sagalassian citizens apparently travelled to the north (Phrygia), the south (Pamphylia) and the west (Pisidian cities, Lydia, Caria). No such contacts can be traced with the eastern countries. It is strange that there are no coins from the Roman colony Antiochia Pisidiae, although its series are very abundant. Nor have Cilician and Syrian coins been recorded yet at Sagalassos. But it is still too soon to make historical generalisations from this, as further finds may alter this image considerably.

There is only one Pisidian hoard with which some comparison can be made. The so-called Ariassos hoard, as it is thought to come from the neighbourhood of that city, has been discussed by von Aulock (1977: 27-29). Of the 207 bronze coins, 166 or 80.2% are from Pisidia, 31 or 14.98% from Pamphylia, a few coins originate from Mysia (6), Lycia (1), Phrygia (2), while a bronze of king Amyntas (36-25 BC) is of uncertain mint. The last coin of Termessos major dates from year 32 (39 BC). Von Aulock proposes 25 BC (year 1) for the Isinda bronze, and 24 BC (year 2) for the Ariassos bronze, both coins using an era starting with the creation of the province of Galatia by Augustus in 25 BC (although Isinda may also use an era ending with the death of Augustus in 14 AD, which brings year 2 down to 9 BC). The hoard was certainly buried during the reign of Augustus, probably after 24 BC. It is interesting to note that it shows a circulation pattern similar to that of Sagalassos. The majority consists of Pisidian coins (166 coins or 80.2%; the best represented cities being Ariassos with 133 coins or 64.25% of the total amount and Termessos major with 20 coins or 9.66%). Of the 31 Pamphylian coins, 24 were issued at Perge (i.e. 11.6% of the total amount). Because of the southern origin of the hoard, Phrygian coins are few (2 coins), but the western regions are represented by one Lycian and 6 Mysian coins. As at Sagalassos, there are no coins from eastern countries, such as Cilicia and Syria.

The coin circulation in Pisidia seems to be essentially local and regional, showing strong ties with the port of Perge and in a more general way with western Asia. Contacts with eastern regions, such as Cilicia, Syria, Cappadocia, seem to have been scarce or non-existent.

5.2. The halved coins

The halved coin found in 1996 (catalogue no. 16) is an as of Augustus struck at Ephesus or Pergamum between 29 and 19/18 BC, although the authors of *RPC* situate the series more firmly about 25 BC. The legend CAES[ ] behind the long neck on the obverse is sufficiently clear to classify the coin. The very broad flan (27 mm) supports this identification and distinguishes it from the smaller Syrian variant. These coins are rather common and circulated throughout Asia (*RPC*: 380; Howgego 1982: 2-7 pl. 2/3 (Asian as) and 4 (Syrian as). It is the third cut coin from the excavations at Sagalassos. Two halved bronzes were found in 1992 (Scheers 1993b: nos 70-71). One of them (no. 70) still shows traces of a head r., but both coins are completely worn and the types illegible. These halved coins are somewhat smaller (26 mm) and weigh less (3.47g and 3.16g) than the 1996 coin (27 mm, 4.58g).

Halved coins are not unknown in the Roman East, although they are less abundant than in the West. A preliminary study is published by Leonard (1993). Halving of coins began in the East as early as the reign of Augustus as is shown by the presence of two cut asses of the CAESAR/AVG in wreath type at Tell Abou Danne, which was abandoned ca. 15-20 AD. Halved coins of this type occur in Syria, at Sardes (22), Aphrodisias (1), Seleucia Pieria (3), Antioch (68) and Tell Abou Danne (2). The finds from Sagalassos prove that halved coins also circulated in central Asia Minor. In the West, the phenomenon is linked to the monetary reform of Augustus in 18 BC. The halving of the old bronzes tended to assimilate them to Augustus' new lighter copper asses.

At Sagalassos, the practice cannot be dated with certainty, but an Augustan date cannot be ruled out. The two 1992 halves were found in the fill of a gutter, east of the fountain, which also yielded four coins of Sagalassos, three from the first century BC – early Imperial period and one of Septimius Severus, as well as an unidentified coin. The 1996 halved as was also found in a fill behind the fountain, in the same layer as an early Sagalassian Zeus/two goats bronze (cat. no. 10).

It is not impossible that the halved coins are linked in some way with the countermarked coins of Sagalassos. Two worn coins bear on the obverse a circular countermark with the letters CΛ (Scheers 1993b, no. 16 and 1997, no. 16) which is not in Howgego's catalogue. To our knowledge, it is only found on the coins excavated at Sagalassos. It seems logical to interpret it as the first two letters of the city's name. The half-round sigma (C) as well as the A without a bar are frequently used on the early bronzes of Sagalassos.

There is no doubt that the countermark was meant to prolong the circulation of the nearly totally worn and illegible coins. The underlying types cannot been identified, although both coins bear on the obverse a head to the right. They seem to represent different denominations as shown by their dimensions and weights, the largest one measuring 22/24 mm and weighing 13.15g, the smaller one 20/21 mm and 7.41g. As both coins are single finds, the archaeological context cannot be used for chronological purposes.

We must await further finds to reach a better understanding of both practices and the eventual link between them.

5.3. The Roman and Byzantine coins

Roman coins are very scarce before the third century AD. A few, mostly plated, denarii are of the second century and belong to the reigns of Trajan, Hadrian and Commodus. The presence of a bronze quadrans of Hadrian is rather unexpected.

The antoninianus appears about the middle of the third century AD, from the reign of Trebonianus Gallus onward, but the numbers are never important, not even after Claudius II, when the striking of civic coins ceased.

The majority of the coins date from the fourth to the seventh century AD and cover the later occupation of the city. In this period, the coin circulation at Sagalassos was implemented by the eastern mints, especially Constantinople, Nicomedia, Cyzicus and Antioch. Coins from western mints, mainly Rome, are present only in small quantities in the fourth and fifth century AD.

From the fifth century AD onward, the mint of Constantinople predominates and this remained so under the Byzantine emperors until it became the sole mint under Heraclius, about 610 AD. It is interesting to note the presence of a follis struck in 617/18 at the mint of Isaura (catalogue no. 384), the modern Zengibar Kalesi in the Cilician Mountains not far from Seleucia (Silifke). Seleucia and Isaura were both temporary mints striking folles in 616/17 and 617/8 AD. They probably came into existence as a result of the Persian war and replaced the mints of Alexandria and Cyzicus, both then in Persian hands. The folles of Isaura are not very common and are struck from 3 obverse and 5 reverse dies (Morrisson: 258: Grierson: 120-121).

5.4. The late Roman bronze weights
(catalogue nos 386-387)

The 1997 excavation yielded the first small bronze weights, one for 3 nomisma, another for 6 nomisma. It is a great pity that no chronological data are available as both weights are surface finds.

6. AKNOWLEDGEMENTS

This research is supported by the Belgian Programme on Interuniversity Poles of Attraction (IUAP 4/12) initiated by the Belgian State, Prime Minister's Office, Science Policy Programming. The text also presents the results of the Conserted Action of the Flemish Government (GOA 97/2) and the Fund for Scientific Research-Flanders (Belgium) (FWO) (G.2145.94). Scientific responsibility is assumed by the author. Lieven Loots is research assistant of the Fund for Scientific Research Flanders – Belgium (FWO).

7. ABBREVIATIONS

BMC = H. Mattingly and R.A.G. Carson (1923-1976-77) *Coins of the Roman Empire in the British Museum*, 6 vol., London 1923-1976-77.
BMC Phrygia = B.V. Head (1906), *Catalogue of the Greek Coins of Phrygia*, London.
BMC Pisidia = G.F. Hill (1897), *Catalogue of the Greek Coins in the British Museum. Lycia, Pamphylia and Pisidia*, London.
Baydur = N. Baydur (1875-76), Die Münzen von Attaleia in Pamphylien, *Jahrbuch für Numismatik und Geldgeschichte* 25: 33-72 and 26: 37-78.
DOC = A.R. Bellinger and P. Grierson (1992) *Catalogue of the Byzantine Coins in the Dumbarton Oaks Collection and in the Whittemore Collection*, 4 vol., Washington (2 ed).
Dürr = N. Dürr (1964) Catalogue des poids byzantins, Musée d'Art et d'histoire de Genève, *Geneva*, 12.
Giard = J.-B. Giard (1988) *Bibliothèque nationale. Catalogue des monnaies de l'empire romain. I. Augste*, Paris.
Grierson = Ph. Grierson (1982) *Byzantine Coins*, London, Berkeley - Los Angeles.
Howgego = C.J. Howgego (1985) *Greek Imperial Countermarks*, London

Imhoof-Blümer = F. Imhoof-Blümer (1901-1902) *Kleinasiatische Münzen*, 2 vol., Wien.
LRBC = P.V. Hill and J.P.C. Kent (1965) *Late Roman Bronze Coinage, A.D. 324-498*, London.
Lindgren = H.C. Lindgren and F.L. Kovacs (1985) *Ancient Bronze Coins of Asia Minor and the Levant from the Lindgren collection*, San Francisco.
Morrisson = C. Morrisson (1970), *Catalogue des monnaies byzantines de la Bibliothèque nationale (491-1204)*, 2 vol., Paris.
RPC = A. Burnett, M. Amandry and P. Pau Ripollès (1992), *Roman Provincial Coinage*, I. *From the Death of Caesar to the Death of Vitellius (44 BC – AD 69)*, London-Paris.
RIC = H. Mattingly *et al.* (1923-1994) *The Roman Imperial Coinage*, 10 vol., London.
SNG Copenhague = *Sylloge Nummorum Graecorum. The Royal Collection of Coins and Medals. Danish National Museum. VI. Phrygia to Cilicia*, Copenhague 1948-1956.
SNG Paris = *Sylloge Nummorum Graecorum. France. 3. Cabinet des médailles. Pamphylie, Pisidie, Lycaonie, Galatie*, Zürich, 1994.
SNG PfPs = *Sylloge Nummorum Graecorum Deutschland. Pfälzer Privatsammlungen. 4. Pamphylien Nr. 1-960*, München 1993.
SNG von Aulock = *Sylloge Nummorum Graecorum. Collection of Greek Coins from Asia Minor from H. von Aulock*, 4 vol., Berlin 1987 (2nd ed.).

8. REFERENCES

H. von Aulock (1977) *Münzen und Städte Pisidia I*, Tübingen.
C.J. Howgego (1982) Coinage and military finance: the Imperial bronze coinage of the Augustan East, *NC* 142.
R.D. Leonard (1993) Cut bronze coins in the Ancient Near East, *Proceedings of the XIth International Numismatic Congress, Brussels 1991*, Louvain-la-Neuve: 363-370.
S. Scheers (1993a) Catalogue of the coins found during the years 1990 and 1991, in: M. Waelkens (ed.) *Sagalassos I. First General Report on the Survey (1986-1989) and Excavations (1990-1991) (Acta Archaeologica Lovaniensia Monographiae* 5) Leuven University Press: 197-205.
S. Scheers (1993b) Catalogue of the coins found during the year 1992, in: M. Waelkens and J. Poblome (eds) *Sagalassos II. Report on the Third Excavation Campaign of 1992 (Acta Archaeologica Lovaniensia Monographiae* 6) Leuven University Press: 259-260.
S. Scheers (1995) Catalogue of the coins found in 1993, in: M. Waelkens and J. Poblome (eds) *Sagalassos III. Report on the Fourth Excavation Campaign of 1993 (Acta Archaeologica Lovaniensia Monographiae* 7) Leuven University Press: 307-323.
S. Scheers (1997) Coins found during 1994 and 1995, in: M. Waelkens and J. Poblome (eds) *Sagalassos IV.Report on the Survey and Excavation Campaigns of 1994 and 1995 (Acta Archaeologica Lovaniensia Monographiae* 9) Leuven University Press: 315-350.

	total	uncertain	2nd cent. BC	1st cent. BC	1st cent. AD	2nd cent. AD	3rd cent. AD
Pisidia:							
- Baris	2						2
-Cremna	1						1
-Sagalassos	59	4		27	8	4	4, 12
-Selge	6		6				
-Termessos	1			1			
Phrygia:							
-Eukarpia	1						1
-Hierapolis/Sebaste	1					1	
-Laodikeia	1				1		
-Prymnessos	1					1	
Pamphylia:							
-Aspendos	2			1			1
-Attaleia	6			1	4	1	
-Perge	23	2		3		5	3, 12
-Side	1		1				
Lydia:							
-Apollonis	1				1		
Caria:							
-Mylasa	1		1				
Uncertain cities	7						

Table 1: Greek autonomous and Imperial coins at Sagalassos

	Civic coins (Sagalassos between brackets)	Romain coins
Augustus, 27 BC - 14 AD	4 (4) 3 halved AE 2 counter-marked AE	
Tiberius, 14-37		
Caligula, 37-41		
Claudius, 41-54		
Nero, 54-68	2 (2)	
Vespasian, 69-79		
Titus, 79-81		
Domitian, 81-96	1	
Nerva, 96-98	1 (1)	
Trajan, 97-117		1 (AR pl.)
Hadrian, 117-138	7 (2)	2 (AR, AE)
Antoninus Pius, 138-161	1	
Marcus Aurelius, 161-180	3 (2)	1 (pl.)
Lucius Verus, 161-169	2	
Commodus, 180-192		
Septimius Severus, 193-211	8 (4)	
Caracalla, 211-217	2 (1)	
Diadumenian, 217-218	1 (1)	
Elagabal, 218-222	5 (1)	
Severus Alexander, 222-235	2	
Maximinus, 235-238		
Gordian III, 238-244	2 (1)	
Philip I and II, 244-249	2 (1)	
Trajan Decius, 249-251		
Trebonianus Gallus, 251-253	1 (1)	1
Volusian, 251-253	1	
Valerian I, 253-260		1
Gallienus, 253-268	4 (1)	1
Claudius II, 268-270	4 (4)	2
Aurelian, 270-275		5
Tacitus, 275-276		
Probus, 276-282		2
Carus, 282-283		1
Diocletian, 284 to 294		1
Maximian, 284 to 294		1

Table 2: Provincial and Romain coins until the reform of Diocletian.

	Arles	Rome	Aquileia	Siscia	Thessalonica	Constantinople	Nicomedia	Heraclea	Cyzicus	Antioch	Tripolis	Alexandria	eastern mint	western mint
2nd cent.									3	6			1	
3rd cent.		4						1	24	5	1	1	36	1
4th cent.	1	5	1	2	1	30	45	3	1	2			60	
5th cent.		6				21	6		3	5				
6th cent.		4			3	31	6		1	1	Isaura 1			
7th cent.						27	4							

Table 3: Roman and Byzantine coins according to their mint (all mints represented).

TABLE OF THE STRATIGRAPHICALLY RELATED COINS
(Lieven Loots and Marc Waelkens)

A. AGORA GATE

- Layer 1

Gloria exercitus (one standard)	follis, 337-341 AD	cat.51, SA96-AG-59

- Layer 4

Arcadius	AE 2, 392-395 AD	cat.99, SA96-AG-10
Heraclius	AE, follis class 3, 615/6 AD	cat.382, SA96-AG-19

- Layer 6

Fel temp reparatio	AE 3, 346-354 AD	cat.55, SA96-AG-76
AE 3 and AE 4	AE 4, 4th-5th cent. AD	cat.228, SA96-AG-77
AE 3 and AE 4	AE 4, 4th-5th cent. AD	cat.247, SA96-AG-84
cross within wreath	AE 4, 425-450 AD	cat.186, SA96-AG-83
uncertain	AE 5, 1st-3rd cent. AD	cat.30, SA96-AG-90
uncertain	2nd half 4th-5th cent. AD	cat.261, SA96-AG-64
uncertain	2nd half 4th-5th cent. AD	cat.262, SA96-AG-72
uncertain	2nd half 4th-5th cent. AD	cat.263, SA96-AG-73
uncertain	2nd half 4th-5th cent. AD	cat.264, SA96-AG-74
uncertain	2nd half 4th-5th cent. AD	cat.265, SA96-AG-75
uncertain	2nd half 4th-5th cent. AD	cat.266, SA96-AG-80
uncertain	2nd half 4th-5th cent. AD	cat.267, SA96-AG-81

B. LOWER AGORA

- Layer 1

Perge (Septimius Severus)	AE 2, 193-211 AD	cat.4, SA96-LA-99
Virtvs exerciti	AE 3, 395-401 AD	cat.144, SA97-LA-134
Basil II – Romanus III	AE, anonymous follis class A 2 ca. 976 AD(?)	cat.385, SA97-LA-36

- Layer 2

Diocletian	AE, 295-298 AD	cat.36, SA97-LA-62
Constantius II	AE 3, 351-361 AD	cat.45, SA96-LA-53
Arcadius	AE 4, 383-395 AD	cat.92, SA97-LA-77
Theodosius I	AE 2, 392-395 AD	cat.82, SA96-LA-43
Virtus exerciti	AE 3, 393-408 AD	cat.147, SA96-LA-41
AE 3 and AE 4	AE 4, 4th-5th cent. AD	cat.238, SA96-LA-64
Gloria romanorum (3 emperors)	AE 3, 406-408 AD	cat.165, SA97-LA-153
Gloria romanorum (2 emperors)	AE 3, 408-423 AD	cat.169, SA96-LA-76
Justinian I	AE, follis, 533-537 AD	cat.367, SA97-LA-63

Maurice	AE, follis, 592/3 AD	cat.375, SA96-LA-58
uncertain	AE 4, 4th-5th cent. AD	cat.240, SA97-LA-160
uncertain	2nd half 4th-5th cent. AD	cat.274, SA96-LA-42
uncertain	2nd half 4th-5th cent. AD	cat.275, SA96-LA-65
uncertain	2nd half 4th-5th cent. AD	cat.298, SA97-LA-159
uncertain	2nd half 4th-5th cent. AD	cat.297, SA97-LA-146

- Layer 3

Theodosius I	AE 4, 383 AD	cat.76, SA97-LA-114
Salus rei publicae	AE 4, 383-395 AD	cat.121, SA96-LA-93
Honorius	AE 3, 408-423 AD	cat.139, SA97-LA-165
Zeno	AE 4, 476-491 AD	cat.214, SA97-LA-113

- Layer 4

Gloria romanorum (3 emperors)	AE 3, 406-408 AD	cat.166, SA97-LA-193

C. ROMAN BATHS
- Layer 1

AE 3 and AE 4	AE 4, 4th-5th cent. AD	cat.237, SA96-RB-171

- Layer 2

Julian Caesar	AE 3, 355-361 AD	cat.52, SA96-RB-191
Virtvs exerciti	AE 3, 395-401 AD	cat.143, SA97-RB1-52
AE 3 and AE 4	AE 3, 4th-5th cent. AD	cat.225, SA96-RB-131
Gloria romanorum (3 emperors)	AE 3, 406-408 AD	cat.167, SA97-RB2-137
uncertain	2nd half 4th-5th cent. AD	cat.277, SA96-RB-189
uncertain	2nd half 4th-5th cent. AD	cat.299, SA97-RB2-107

- Layer 3

Spes rei publicae	AE 4, 355-361 AD	cat.66, SA96-RB-81
Julian	AE 3, 355-361 AD	cat.53, SA97-RB2-120
Constantius II	AE, follis, 347-348 AD	cat.42, SA97-RB2-129
AE 3 and AE 4	AE 4, 4th-5th cent. AD	cat.232, SA96-RB-192
uncertain	2nd half 4th-5th cent. AD	cat.279, SA96-RB-221
uncertain	2nd half 4th-5th cent. AD	cat.280, SA96-RB-225
uncertain	2nd half 4th-5th cent. AD	cat.300, SA97-RB2-151
uncertain	AE 4, 4th-5th cent. AD	cat.218, SA97-RB2-121

- Layer 4

Constantinus I	AE, follis, 319 AD	cat. 37, SA97-RB1-92
AE 3 and AE 4	AE 4, 4th-5th cent. AD	cat. 235, SA96-RB-228
Theodosius II	AE 3, 402-408 AD	cat. 151, SA96-RB-205
cross within wreath	AE 4, 425-450 AD	cat.203, SA96-RB-235
uncertain	2nd half 4th-5th cent. AD	cat.278, SA96-RB-206
uncertain	2nd half 4th-5th cent. AD	cat.281, SA96-RB-226
uncertain	2nd half 4th-5th cent. AD	cat.282, SA96-RB-227
uncertain	2nd half 4th-5th cent. AD	cat.283, SA96-RB-239

D. SITE DA1
- Layer 5 east

Sagalassos	AE 2, 1st cent. BC	cat.7, SA96-DA1-74
Gloria romanorum (3 emperors)	AE 3, 402-408 AD	cat.161, SA96-DA1-68
uncertain	2nd half 4th-5th cent. AD	cat.272, SA96-DA1-72

- Layer 5 west

Honorius	AE 2, 392-395 AD	cat.133, SA96-DA1-58

E. UPPER AGORA
- Layer 1

Arcadius	AE 2, 392-395 AD	cat.95, SA96-UA-15

- Layer 2

Sagalassos	AE	cat.15, SA96-UA-175
Arcadius	AE 4, 383 AD	cat.88, SA96-UA-88
Arcadius	AE 2, 392-395 AD	cat.97, SA96-UA-76
Gloria romanorum (3 emperors)	AE 3, 402-408 AD	cat.163, SA96-UA-78
cross within wreath	AE 4, 425-450 AD	cat.195, SA96-UA-174
Concordia augg	AE 4, 425-450 AD	cat.180, SA96-UA-56
Heraclius	AE, follis, 616/7 AD or 617/8 AD	cat.384, SA96-UA-184
AE 3 and AE 4	AE 4, 4th-5th cent. AD	cat.219, SA96-UA-178
uncertain	2nd half 4th-5th cent. AD	cat.284, SA96-UA-91

- Layer 3

Aurelian	BI, antoninianus, 270-275 AD	cat.34, SA96-UA-196
Vot xx mult xx	AE 4, 383 AD	cat.118, SA96-UA-145
Arcadius	AE 2, 383-395 AD	cat.90, SA96-UA-197
Salus rei publicae	AE 4, 383-395 AD	cat.122, SA96-UA-43
Gloria romanorum (2 emperors)	AE 3, 408-423 AD	cat.171, SA96-UA-202
Theodosius II	AE 4, 425-450 AD	cat.155, SA96-UA-189
cross within wreath	AE 4, 425-450 AD	cat.187, SA96-UA-195
Leo I and Verina	AE 4, 457-474 AD	cat.206, SA96-UA-194
Justin II	AE, half follis, 577/8 AD	cat.370, SA96-UA-190
Maurice	AE, half follis, 592/3 AD	cat.374, SA96-UA-151
uncertain	AE 3, 1st-3rd cent. AD	cat.29, SA96-UA-149

- Layer 5

Honorius	AE 3, 395-408 AD	cat.136, SA96-UA-126
cross within wreath	AE 4, 425-450 AD	cat.197, SA96-UA-136
Justinian I	AE, small pentanummium, (543-565 AD)	cat.364, SA96-UA-66
AE 3 and AE 4	AE 4, 4th-5th cent. AD	cat.234, SA96-UA-105
AE 3 and AE 4	AE 3, 4th-5th cent. AD	cat.223, SA96-UA-127
AE 3 and AE 4	AE 3, 4th-5th cent. AD	cat.221, SA96-UA-65
uncertain	2nd half 4th-5th cent. AD	cat.285, SA96-UA-147
uncertain	2nd half 4th-5th cent. AD	cat.286, SA96-UA-148

- Layer 6

Constantinus II	follis, 335-337 AD	cat.39, SA96-UA-160
Sagalassos	AE 2	cat.12, SA96-UA-167
Sagalassos	AE	cat.10, SA96-UA-218
AE 3 and AE 4	AE 4, 4th-5th cent. AD	cat.58, SA96-UA-214
uncertain	2nd half 4th-5th cent. AD	cat.287, SA96-UA-162
uncertain	2nd half 4th-5th cent. AD	cat.288, SA96-UA-170
uncertain	2nd half 4th-5th cent. AD	cat.289, SA96-UA-181
uncertain	2nd half 4th-5th cent. AD	cat.290, SA96-UA-220

- Inside tunnel

Arcadius	AE 2, 392-395 AD	cat.100, SA96-UA-139
Virtus exerciti	AE 3, 393-408 AD	cat.93, SA96-UA-213
Justin II	AE, follis, 570/1 AD	cat.371, SA96-UA-140
Justinian I	AE, follis, 538/9 AD	cat.362, SA96-UA-137

F. SITE UAN

a. Room VI

- Layer 1S

Theodosius I	AE 4, 383-387 AD	cat.77, SA96-UAN-97
Honorius	AE 2, 393-395 AD	cat.130, SA96-UAN-95
Gloria romanorum (3 emperors)	AE 3, 402-408 AD	cat.164, SA96-UAN-96
uncertain	2nd half 4th-5th cent. AD	cat.292, SA96-UAN-105

- Layer 3 SB

Spes rei publicae	AE 4, 355-361 AD	cat.62, SA97-UAN-142
Theodosius II	AE 4, 425-435 AD	cat.157, SA97-UAN-143
Justin I	AE, half follis, 518-527 AD	cat.359, SA97-UAN-134

b. Room XII-XIII

- Layer 1S

cross within wreath	AE 4, 425-450 AD	cat.182, SA96-UAN-37
Justin I	AE, follis, 518-527 AD	cat.236, SA96-UAN-36

c. Room XIV

- Layer 1S

Arcadius	AE 2, 392-395 AD	cat.98, SA96-UAN-69
AE 3 and AE 4	AE 3, 4th-5th cent. AD	cat.230, SA96-UAN-64

- Layer 2S

Arcadius	AE 2, 392-395 AD	cat.101, SA96-UAN-84

d. Room XV

- Layer 1

uncertain	AE	cat.27, SA96-B-25

- Layer 1S

AE 3 and AE 4	AE 3, 4th-5th cent. AD	cat.229, SA96-UAN-131

- Layer 2

Gloria Romanorum	AE 3, 364-375 AD	cat.68, SA96-B-10

Justin II	AE, follis, 576/7 AD	cat.369, SA96-B-43

- Layer 8

Arcadius	AE 2, 392-395 AD	cat.96, SA96-B-55

- Layer 10

Constantinus II	AE 2, 351-355 AD	cat.43, SA96-B-68

e. Room XVI
- Layer 2S

Constantius II	AE 4, 355-361 AD	cat.47, SA96-UAN-150
Arcadius	AE 3, 395-408 AD	cat.105, SA96-UAN-163
Justin II	AE, follis, 570/1 AD	cat.368, SA96-UAN-170
Heraclius	AE, follis class 2, 613/6 AD	cat.381, SA96-UAN-142

- Layer 5SB

Sagalassos	AE, 1st cent. BC – imperial times	cat.11, SA97-UAN-255
Fel temp reparatio	AE 3, 346-361 AD	cat.58, SA97-UAN-214
Fel temp reparatio	AE 3, 346-361 AD	cat.56, SA97-UAN-277
Constantius II	AE, follis, 347-348 AD	cat.41, SA97-UAN-276
Spes rei publicae	AE 4, 355-361 AD	cat.63, SA97-UAN-219
Spes rei publicae	AE 4, 355-361 AD	cat.64, SA97-UAN-270
Spes rei publicae	AE 4, 355-361 AD	cat.65, SA97-UAN-275
Salus rei publicae	AE 4, 383-395 AD	cat.129, SA97-UAN-221
Valens	AE 1, 364-367 AD	cat.67, SA97-UAN-260
Vota	AE 4, 383 AD	cat.120, SA97-UAN-189
Vota	AE 4, 383 AD	cat.119, SA97-UAN-256
Theodosius I	AE 4, 383-395 AD	cat.80, SA97-UAN-264
Theodosius I or Theodosius II	AE 3 or 4	cat.87, SA97-UAN-209
Theodosius I or Theodosius II	AE 2, 392-395 AD	cat.84, SA97-UAN-247
Arcadius	AE 4, 383-395 AD	cat.93, SA97-UAN-213
Arcadius	AE 4, 383-395 AD	cat.91, SA97-UAN-251
Arcadius	AE 3, 395-401 AD	cat.107, SA97-UAN-205
Arcadius	AE 3, 401-403 AD	cat.115, SA97-UAN-210
Arcadius	AE 3, 406-408 AD	cat.111, SA97-UAN-223
Arcadius	AE 3, 406-408 AD	cat.112, SA97-UAN-265
Concordia augg	AE 3, 401-403 AD	cat.149, SA97-UAN-287
Virtvs exerciti	AE 3, 395-401 AD	cat.145, SA97-UAN-222
Virtvs exerciti	AE 3, 395-401 AD	cat.146, SA97-UAN-263
Honorius	AE 3, 395-401 AD	cat.137, SA97-UAN-266
Honorius	AE 3, 408-423 AD	cat.140, SA97-UAN-190
Honorius	AE 3	cat.141, SA97-UAN-285
Gloria romanorum (2 emperors)	AE 3, 408-423 AD	cat.177, SA97-UAN-257
Victoria augg	AE 4, 408-ca.435 AD	cat.178, SA97-UAN-252
Theodosius II	AE 4, 425-435 AD	cat.158, SA97-UAN-211
Theodosius II	AE 4, 425-435 AD	cat.159, SA97-UAN-226
cross within wreath	AE 4, 425-457 AD	cat.191, SA97-UAN-191
cross within wreath	AE 4, 425-457 AD	cat.192, SA97-UAN-208
cross within wreath	AE 4, 425-457 AD	cat.193, SA97-UAN-224
cross within wreath	AE 4, 425-457 AD	cat.200, SA97-UAN-253

cross within wreath	AE 4, 425-457 AD	cat.185, SA97-UAN-280
Marcian	AE 4, 450-457 AD	cat.184, SA97-UAN-232
Leo I and Verina	AE 4, 457-474 AD	cat.209, SA97-UAN-225
Leo I and Verina	AE 4, 457-474 AD	cat.210, SA97-UAN-220
Zeno	AE 4, 476-491 AD	cat.215, SA97-UAN-259
uncertain	AE 3 or AE 4, 4th-5th cent. AD	cat.239, SA97-UAN-199
uncertain	AE 4, 4th-5th cent. AD	cat.244, SA97-UAN-188
uncertain	AE 4, 4th-5th cent. AD	cat.256, SA97-UAN-193
uncertain	AE 4, 4th-5th cent. AD	cat.257, SA97-UAN-194
uncertain	AE 4, 4th-5th cent. AD	cat.258, SA97-UAN-254
uncertain	AE 3, 4th-5th cent. AD	cat.259, SA97-UAN-261
uncertain	AE 4, 4th-5th cent. AD	cat.245, SA97-UAN-279
uncertain	2nd half 4th-5th cent. AD	cat.323, SA97-UAN-187
uncertain	2nd half 4th-5th cent. AD	cat.324, SA97-UAN-192
uncertain	2nd half 4th-5th cent. AD	cat.325, SA97-UAN-196
uncertain	2nd half 4th-5th cent. AD	cat.326, SA97-UAN-197
uncertain	2nd half 4th-5th cent. AD	cat.327, SA97-UAN-198
uncertain	2nd half 4th-5th cent. AD	cat.328, SA97-UAN-203
uncertain	2nd half 4th-5th cent. AD	cat.134, SA97-UAN-204
uncertain	2nd half 4th-5th cent. AD	cat.330, SA97-UAN-206
uncertain	2nd half 4th-5th cent. AD	cat.331, SA97-UAN-207
uncertain	2nd half 4th-5th cent. AD	cat.332, SA97-UAN-215
uncertain	2nd half 4th-5th cent. AD	cat.333, SA97-UAN-216
uncertain	2nd half 4th-5th cent. AD	cat.334, SA97-UAN-217
uncertain	2nd half 4th-5th cent. AD	cat.335, SA97-UAN-218
uncertain	2nd half 4th-5th cent. AD	cat.336, SA97-UAN-235
uncertain	2nd half 4th-5th cent. AD	cat.337, SA97-UAN-248
uncertain	2nd half 4th-5th cent. AD	cat.338, SA97-UAN-249
uncertain	2nd half 4th-5th cent. AD	cat.339, SA97-UAN-258
uncertain	2nd half 4th-5th cent. AD	cat.340, SA97-UAN-262
uncertain	2nd half 4th-5th cent. AD	cat.341, SA97-UAN-267
uncertain	2nd half 4th-5th cent. AD	cat.342, SA97-UAN-268
uncertain	2nd half 4th-5th cent. AD	cat.343, SA97-UAN-269
uncertain	2nd half 4th-5th cent. AD	cat.344, SA97-UAN-271
uncertain	2nd half 4th-5th cent. AD	cat.345, SA97-UAN-272
uncertain	2nd half 4th-5th cent. AD	cat.346, SA97-UAN-273
uncertain	2nd half 4th-5th cent. AD	cat.347, SA97-UAN-274
uncertain	2nd half 4th-5th cent. AD	cat.348, SA97-UAN-278
uncertain	2nd half 4th-5th cent. AD	cat.349, SA97-UAN-281
uncertain	2nd half 4th-5th cent. AD	cat.350, SA97-UAN-282
uncertain	2nd half 4th-5th cent. AD	cat.351, SA97-UAN-283
uncertain	2nd half 4th-5th cent. AD	cat.352, SA97-UAN-284
uncertain	2nd half 4th-5th cent. AD	cat.353, SA97-UAN-286
uncertain	2nd half 4th-5th cent. AD	cat.355, SA97-UAN-336

- Layer 6SB

Gloria romanorum (2 emperors)	AE 3, 408-423 AD	cat.175, SA97-UAN-238

f. Room XVII
- Layer 3C

Spes rei publicae	AE 4, 355-361 AD	cat.60, SA96-B-113
Valentinian II	AE 4, 383-395 AD	cat.75, SA96-B-107

Arcadius	AE 4, 395-408 AD	cat.110, SA96-B-115
AE 3 and AE 4	AE 4, 4th-5th cent. AD	cat.220, SA96-B-116
uncertain	2nd half 4th-5th cent. AD	cat.269, SA96-B-111
uncertain	2nd half 4th-5th cent. AD	cat.270, SA96-B-112
uncertain	2nd half 4th-5th cent. AD	cat.271, SA96-B-114

- Layer 6A

Salus rei publicae	AE 4, 383-395 AD	cat.127, SA97-UAN-81
Theodosius II	AE 3, 408-423 AD	cat.153, SA97-UAN-84
Gloria romanorum (2 emperors)	AE 3, 408-423 AD	cat.173, SA97-UAN-335
cross within wreath	AE 4, 425-457 AD	cat.198, SA97-UAN-82
cross within wreath	AE 4, 425-457 AD	cat.190, SA97-UAN-89
Leo I and Verina	AE 4, 457-474 AD	cat.208, SA97-UAN-83
uncertain	2nd half 4th-5th cent. AD	cat.321, SA97-UAN-80
uncertain	AE 4, 4th-5th cent. AD	cat.243, SA97-UAN-85
uncertain	2nd half 4th-5th cent. AD	cat.322, SA97-UAN-86
uncertain	AE 4, 4th-5th cent. AD	cat.254, SA97-UAN-87
uncertain	AE 4, 4th-5th cent. AD	cat.255, SA97-UAN-88

g. Room XVIII
- Layer 4S

Honorius	AE 2, 392-395 AD	cat.134, SA97-UAN-204

- Layer 5S

Constantinus I	AE, follis, 335-337 AD	cat.38, SA97-UAN-45
Constantius II	AE, follis, 347-348 AD	cat.40, SA97-UAN-41
Constantius II	AE 4, 355-361 AD	cat.50, SA97-UAN-72
Valentinian I or Valens	AE 3, 364-379 AD	cat.69, SA97-UAN-38
Theodosius I	AE 4, 383-395 AD	cat.79, SA97-UAN-78
Arcadius	AE 4, 383-395 AD	cat.94, SA97-UAN-39
Arcadius	AE 4, 383-387 AD	cat.89, SA97-UAN-71
Arcadius	AE 3, 395-401 AD	cat.108, SA97-UAN-63
Honorius	AE 2, 393-395 AD	cat.132, SA97-UAN-74
Concordia augg	AE 3, 401-403 AD	cat.148, SA97-UAN-40
Theodosius II	AE 3, 401-403 AD	cat.150, SA97-UAN-76
Theodosius II	AE 3, 408-423 AD	cat.154, SA97-UAN-126 A
Gloria romanorum (2 emperors)	AE 3, 408-423 AD	cat.176, SA97-UAN-62
cross within wreath	AE 4, 425-457 AD	cat.202, SA97-UAN-126 B
cross within wreath	AE 4, 425-457 AD	cat.189, SA97-UAN-44
Theodosius II	AE 4, 435 AD	cat.160, SA97-UAN-34
Anastasius	AE, nummus, 491-498 AD	cat.356, SA97-UAN-73
Phocas	AE, follis, 607/8 AD	cat.378, SA97-UAN-67
Leo I and Verina	AE 4, 457-474 AD	cat.205, SA97-UAN-70
immitation (*Victoria augg*)	AE 4	cat.216, SA97-UAN-33
immitation (SE-CN-coin of Zeno)	AE 3	cat.217, SA97-UAN-60
uncertain	AE 4, 4th-5th cent. AD	cat.253, SA97-UAN-69
uncertain	AE 4, 4th-5th cent. AD	cat.358, SA97-UAN-36
uncertain	AE 4, 4th-5th cent. AD	cat.184, SA97-UAN-37
uncertain	AE 3, 4th-5th cent. AD	cat.251, SA97-UAN-64

uncertain	AE 4, 4th-5th cent. AD	cat.252, SA97-UAN-65
uncertain	2nd half 4th-5th cent. AD	cat.320, SA97-UAN-79
uncertain	2nd half 4th-5th cent. AD	cat.314, SA97-UAN-35
uncertain	2nd half 4th-5th cent. AD	cat.315, SA97-UAN-42
uncertain	2nd half 4th-5th cent. AD	cat.319, SA97-UAN-77
uncertain	2nd half 4th-5th cent. AD	cat.316, SA97-UAN-66
uncertain	2nd half 4th-5th cent. AD	cat.23, SA97-UAN-68
uncertain	2nd half 4th-5th cent. AD	cat.318, SA97-UAN-75
weight(6 nomisma)	3rd-5th cent. AD	cat.387, SA97-UAN-46

- Layer 6

Salus rei publicae	AE 4, 383-395 AD	cat.128, SA97-UAN-112
Theodosius I or Theodosius II	AE 2, 392-395 AD	cat.83, SA97-UAN-99
cross within wreath	AE 4, 425-457 AD	cat.194, SA97-UAN-102
cross within wreath	AE 4, 425-457 AD	cat.199, SA97-UAN-106
cross within wreath	AE 4, 425-457 AD	cat.201, SA97-UAN-111

h. Room XIX
- Layer 1

Fel temp reparatio	AE 2, 346-361 AD	cat.57, SA97-UAN-296
uncertain	2nd half 4th-5th cent. AD	cat.354, SA97-UAN-334

- Layer 2

Fel temp reparatio	AE 3, 346-361 AD	cat.59, SA97-UAN-332
Honorius	AE 3, 395-401 AD	cat.138, SA97-UAN-306
Gloria romanorum (2 emperors)	AE 3, 408-423 AD	cat.172, SA97-UAN-307

- Layer 3

Theodosius I or Theodosius II	AE3, 401-403 AD	cat.109, SA97-UAN-312

- Layer 4B

Arcadius	AE 3, 401-403 AD	cat.116, SA97-UAN-321
Gloria romanorum (3 emperors)	AE 3, 406-408 AD	cat.168, SA97-UAN-317
uncertain	AE 4, 4th-5th cent. AD	cat.242, SA97-UAN-316

i. Northeast Gate
- Layer 1S

Sagalassos (Philip II)	AE, 244-249 AD	cat.23, SA96-UAN-68
uncertain	2nd half 4th-5th cent. AD	cat.291, SA96-UAN-49

G. SITE BOULEUTERION COURTYARD (B1)
- Layer 1

Sagalassos	AE, 1st cent. BC – imperial times	cat.13, SA97-DT-123
Sagalassos (Septimius Severus)	AE, 193-211 AD	cat.19, SA97-DT-94
Sagalassos (Septimius Severus)	AE, 193-211 AD	cat.19, SA97-DT-94
Theodosius I	AE 4, 383-395 AD	cat.81, SA97-DT-59

Sagalassos (Hadrian)	AE, 117-138 AD	cat.17, SA97-B1-178
Valerian I	BI, antoninianus, 257 AD	cat.32, SA96-B-78
Theodosius I	AE 4, 383-395 AD	cat.81, SA97-DT-59
Honorius	AE 2, 393-395 AD	cat.135, SA97-B1-160
Arcadius	AE 3, 395-401 AD	cat.104, SA97-B1-125
Justinian I	AE, decanummium, 562/3 AD	cat.366, SA96-B-77
Phocas	AE, follis, 592/3 AD	cat.377, SA96-B-89
Gloria romanorum (2 emperors)	AE 3, 408-423 AD	cat.170, SA96-B-94
AE 3 and AE 4	AE 4, 4th-5th cent. AD	cat.226, SA96-B-147

- Layer 2

Gloria Romanorum	AE 3, 364-375 AD	cat.71, SA96-B-102
Salus rei publicae	AE 4, 383-395 AD	cat.123, SA97-B1-139
Arcadius	AE 3, 395-401 AD	cat.103, SA97-B1-172
Arcadius	AE 3, 400-401 AD	cat.114, SA97-B1-156
Justinian I	AE, follis, 541/2 AD	cat.363, SA96-B-99
uncertain	AE 4, 4th-5th cent. AD	cat.248, SA97-B1-126

- Layer 3

Gloria romanorum	AE 3, 364-378 AD or 383-388 AD	cat.72, SA97-DT-74
uncertain	2nd half 4th-5th cent. AD	cat.268, SA96-B-104

H. SITE BOULEUTERION (B2)
- Layer 1

Salus rei publicae	AE 4, 383-395 AD	cat.124, SA97-B2-28
Victoria augg	AE 4, 408-ca.435 AD	cat.179, SA97-B2-48

- Layer 2

Honorius	AE 2, 393-395 AD	cat.131, SA97-B2-119
Arcadius	AE 3, 395-401 AD	cat.102, SA97-B2-69
Marcian	AE 4, 450-457 AD	cat.181, SA97-B2-103
Heraclius	AE, follis, 613/4 AD	cat.379, SA97-B2-127

- Layer 4

Gratian	AE 3, 364-378 AD	cat.70, SA97-B2-47

I. SITE H
- Layer 1

Sagalassos	AE, 1st cent. BC – imperial times	cat.14, SA97-H-213
Salus rei publicae	AE 4, 383-395 AD	cat.125, SA97-H-175
Theodosius I	AE 2, 393-395 AD	cat.85, SA97-H-199

- Layer 2

Selge	AE, 2nd-1st cent. BC	cat.26, SA97-H-228
Constantius II	AE 4, 355-361 AD	cat.49, SA97-H-79
Maurice	AE, half follis, 592/3 AD	cat.376, SA97-H-232
Heraclius	AE, half follis, 611/2 AD	cat.383, SA97-H-235
uncertain	2nd half 4th-5th cent. AD	cat.273, SA96-H-137
uncertain	2nd half 4th-5th cent. AD	cat.296, SA97-H-320

- Layer 3

Perge (Septimius Severus)	AE, 193-211 AD	cat.5, SA97-H-307
Theodosius II	AE 3, 402-408 AD	cat.152, SA96-H-85
Arcadius	AE 4, 383-408 AD	cat.113, SA97-H-31
Arcadius	AE 3, 395-401 AD	cat.106, SA97-H-28
Justin I or Justinian I	AE, pentanummium	cat.360, SA96-H-125
Maurice	AE, follis, 587/8 AD	cat.373, SA97-H-254
Heraclius	AE, half follis, 610/11 AD	cat.380, SA96-H-116

- Layer 4

Sagalassos (Septimius Severus)	AE, 193-211 AD	cat.20, SA97-H-286

- Layer 6

Sagalassos (Claudius II)	AE, 268-270 AD	cat.24, SA97-H-151

J. SITE DT

a. Propylon, early Byzantine structure
- Layer 2

Constantinus II	AE 3, 355-361 AD	cat.46, SA96-B-287

- Layer 4

Anastasius	AE, nummus, 491-498 AD	cat.357, SA97-DT-148

- Layer 6

uncertain	2nd half 4th-5th cent. AD	cat.293, SA97-DT-18
uncertain	2nd half 4th-5th cent. AD	cat.294, SA97-DT-20
uncertain	2nd half 4th-5th cent. AD	cat.295, SA97-DT-21

b. Propylon, street
- Layer 4

Theodosius II	AE 4, 425-450 AD	cat.156, SA96-B-216
AE 3 and AE 4	AE 3, 4th-5th cent. AD	cat.224, SA96-B-202

- Layer 5

Leo I and Verina	AE 4, 457-474 AD	cat.204, SA96-B-210

c. Propylon, recess

Constantinus II	AE 2, 351-355 AD	cat.44, SA96-B-314
Justinian I	AE, small pentanummium	cat.365, SA96-B-289 (543-565 AD)

K. SITE LE
- Layer 2

Aurelian	BI, antoninianus, 270-275 AD	cat.35, SA96-LE-14
cross within wreath	AE 4, 425-450 AD	cat.196, SA96-LE-15
AE 3 and AE 4	AE 4, 4th-5th cent. AD	cat.233, SA96-LE-13

L. SITE LW (fill behind terrace wall)
- Layer 1
Selge (?)	AE 2, 2nd-1st cent. BC	cat.28, SA97-N-70
Salus rei publicae	AE 4, 383-395 AD	cat.126, SA97-N-101
Marcian	AE 4, 450-457 AD	cat.182, SA97-N-73

M. SITE N
Sondage to the northeast of the fountain
- Layer 3
Sagalassos	AE 2	cat.9, SA96-N-21
Augustus	AE 4, 27 BC-14 AD	cat.31, SA96-N-15

- Layer 4
Sagalassos	AE 2, 1st cent. BC – imperial times	cat.8, SA96-N-28

Water basins of the fountain
a. North basin
- Layer 1
Spes rei publicae	AE 4, 355-361 AD	cat.61, SA97-NEB-18

b. East basin
- Layer 2
Selge	AE, 2nd-1st cent. BC	cat.25, SA97-NEB-28

c. West basin
- Layer 3
Sagalassos (Caracalla)	AE, 197-217 AD	cat.21, SA97-NEB-13

N. SITE PQ
Julian	AE 4, 355-361 AD	cat.54, SA97-PQ-11
Sagalassos / Augustus	AE, 27 BC-14 AD	cat.16, SA97-PQ-3
Eucarpeia	AE, 2nd-3rd century AD	cat.1, SA97-PQ-8

O. SURFACE FINDS
Sagalassos (Gordian III)	AE, 238-244 AD	cat.22, SA96-Y-1
Perge (Gordian III)	AE, 241-244 AD	cat.6, SA96-Y2
Constantius II	AE 4, 351-361 AD	cat.48, SA96-Y-4
Theododius I	AE 2, 383-392 AD	cat.86, SA96-Y-7
Gloria romanorum (3 emperors)	AE 3, 402-408 AD	cat.162, SA96-Y-5
AE 3 and AE 4	AE 3, 4th-5th cent. AD	cat.222, SA96-AG-45
AE 3 and AE 4	AE 4, 4th-5th cent. AD	cat.227, SA96-Y-3
AE 3 and AE 4	AE 4, 4th-5th cent. AD	cat.241, SA97-H-299
uncertain	2nd half 4th-5th cent. AD	cat.260, SA96-AG-26
weight (3 nomisma)	3rd-5th cent. AD	cat.386, SA97-H-3
Maurice	AE, half follis, 588/9 AD	cat.372, SA96-N-89

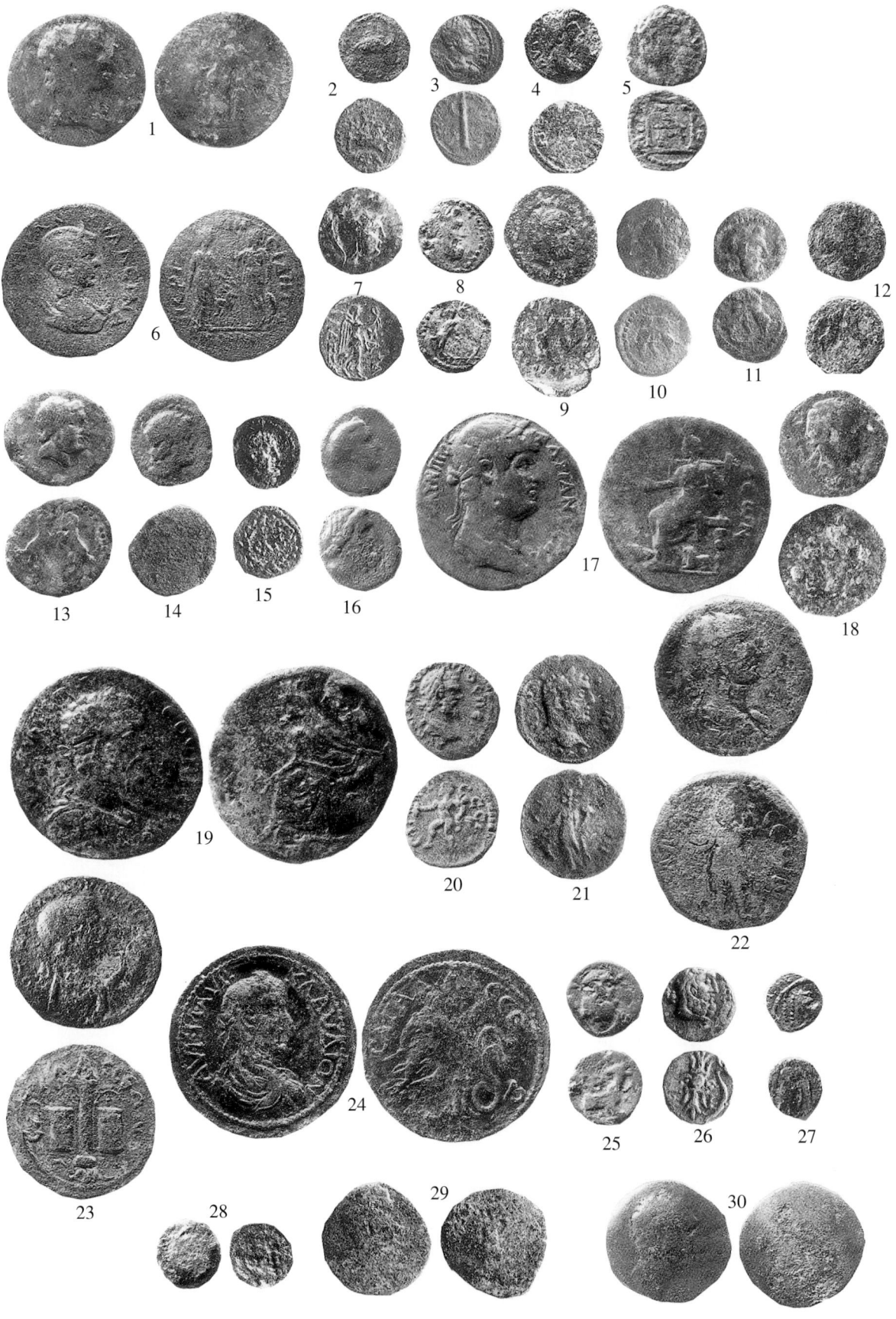

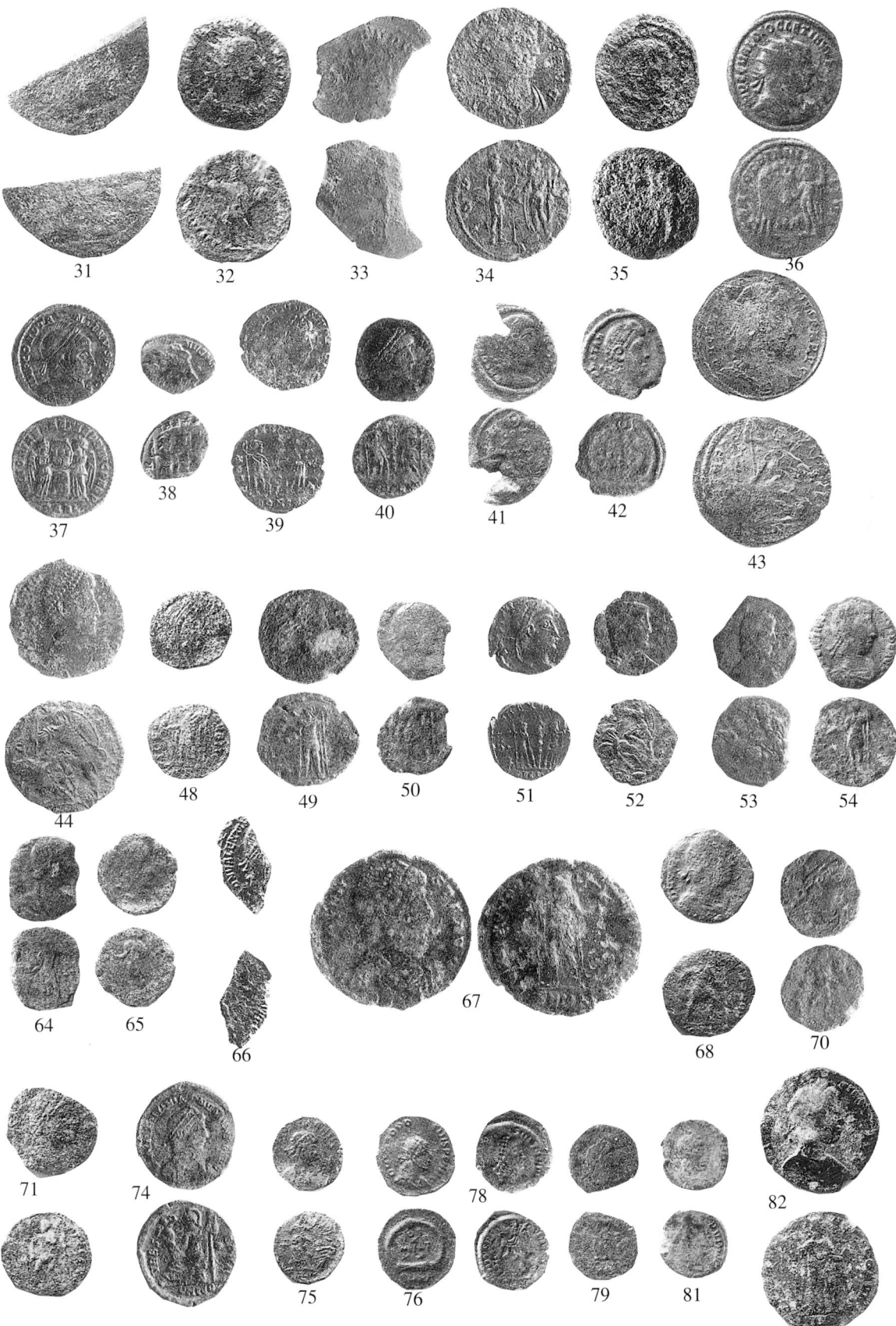

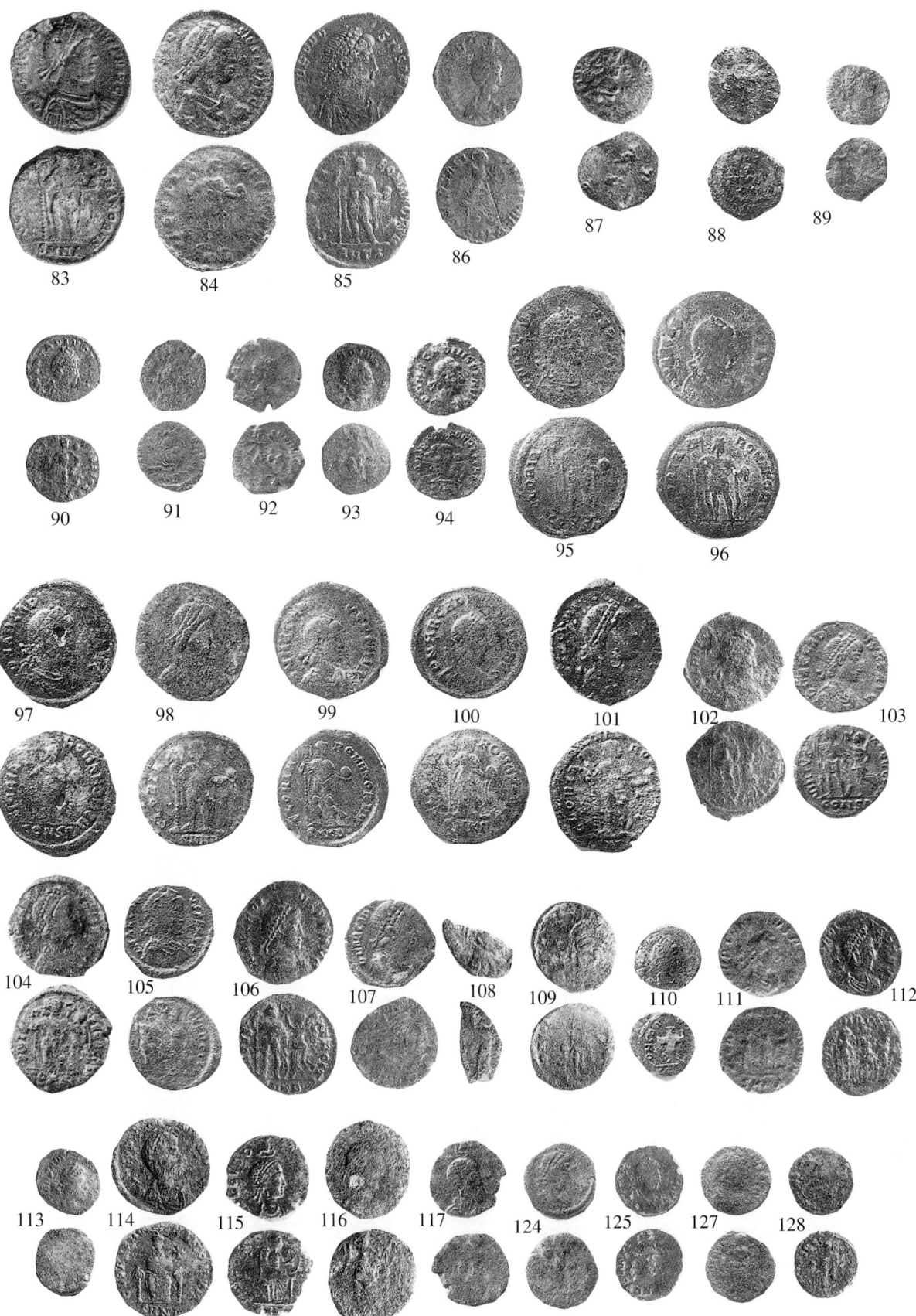

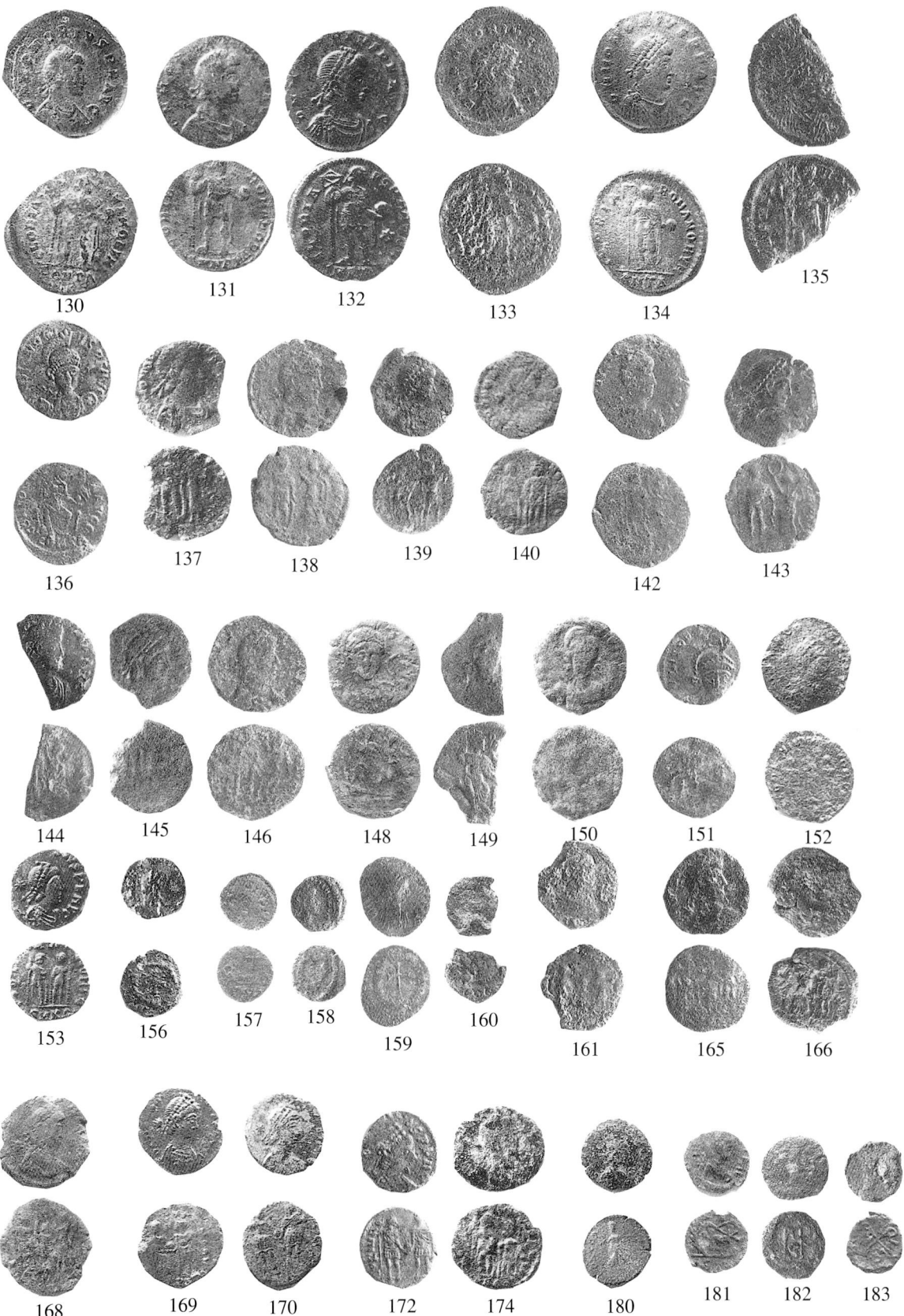

PART IV

URBANISM AND ARCHITECTURAL STUDIES

THE NORTHWEST HEROON AT SAGALASSOS

Marc WAELKENS[1], L. VANDEPUT[1], Ch. BERNS[2], B. ARIKAN[3], J. POBLOME[1] and E. TORUN[1]

1 - Department of Archaelogy, KULeuven, Blijde Inkomststraat 21, B-3000 Leuven, Belgium
2 - Junior fellow of the KULeuven Research Council, Department of Archaeology,
KULeuven, Blijde Inkomststraat 21, B-3000 Leuven, Belgium
3 - Department of Classics, University of Cincinnati 410, Blegen Library, P.O.Box 210226, Cincinnati, OHIO 45221 USA

1. INTRODUCTION: THE MONUMENT
(M. Waelkens and E. Torun)

The Northwest Heroon at Sagalassos is located in the upper part of the monumental city centre, to the northwest of the upper agora and to the northeast of the Doric temple (Fig. 1). It borders a street running to the north of the upper agora, although at a higher level. The excavations of the monument began in 1994 and continued for four excavation seasons during which 25 squares of 25 m² were excavated. The main objective of the excavations in this area was to uncover, investigate and date the monument and to better define the fortification system in the northwest part of Sagalassos, into which it had been incorporated in late antiquity.

Before the excavations were begun, the socle frieze of the NW Heroon, composed of a row of dancing girls holding the tips of each others' cloaks, was well known. In fact, some of these slabs, apparently already lying on the surface then, were praised by G. Hirschfeld during his visit to the city in 1875, as the best sculptures of the area (Hirschfeld 1880: 310 note 1). Two of the three slabs, representing four dancers, were drawn by K. Lanckoronski's team and published in his report (Lanckoronski 1982: 139-140, figs 109-110).

A century later, the friezes caught the attention of R. Fleischer, who in 1972 and 1974 studied the monument in detail and exposed five more dancers (Fleischer 1979 with further literature). In 1994, M. Waelkens resumed research on the monument, with the excavation being supervised by B. Arıkan. An extensive report of the 1994 and 1995 seasons has already been published by Waelkens (Waelkens et al. 1997: 173-195), with some important preliminary conclusions on the date and the original appearance of the monument. The first two excavation seasons (1994-95) thus increased our understanding of the elevation of the monument, and this was recently further improved thanks to the study of the architecture by E. Torun, L. Vandeput and M. Waelkens. E. Torun, who is responsible for the anastylosis of the monument with the support of **BACOB (Artesia Banking Corporation)**, managed to produce very accurate measurements of the whole structure (Figs 2-5).

The actual heroon was supported by an ashlar socle (7.62 m east-west; 8.23 m north-south) that was built directly on top of natural bedrock which slopes towards the south (Fig. 6). As a result, the height of this socle is different on all four sides, being at its lowest at the back, where the socle proper only consists of two courses of ashlar (total height: ca. 1.26 m; upper course: 0.60 m high). The ashlar surface has been worked with a point, instead of being smooth, clearly aiming at creating an impression that the socle was growing out of the bedrock (Fig. 7). On the eastern side, the total height has not yet been established, since in late antiquity a water-collecting system had been built against it (Waelkens et al. 1997: 175 fig. 112). Here, the visible height varies from 0.60 m (one course) at the northeastern corner to 2.22 m (four courses) at the southeastern corner. The four courses of ashlar blocks (h. of the courses from top to bottom: 0.60 m, 0.665 m and 0.58 m; the fourth course not completely visible) again have a rough surface worked with a pointed chisel, presumably again to imitate natural rock (Fig. 8). This is again the case on the west side, where the socle is visible over a total height of 0.10 m (northwestern corner) to 2.475 m (southwestern corner). Here a total of four courses (h. from top to bottom: 0.59 m, 0.67 m, 0.62 m and 0.595 m) have been exposed (Fig. 9). The socle reached its maximum height on the south side, the actual façade, where the bedrock slopes very steeply. Here the socle reaches a height between 2.655 m at the southwestern and 2.815 m at the southeastern corner. On this side, the socle comprises six ashlar courses (h. from top to bottom: 0.595 m, 0.665 m, 0.62 m, 0.595 m, 0.715 m, ca. 0.43 m), of which only the two lower ones, immediately above the bedrock, show the rougher treatment with the pointed chisel (Waelkens *et al.* 1997: 175 fig. 111) The four upper courses are completely smooth, and have been worked with a very fine claw chisel (Fig. 10). On all four sides, the upper course of the socle is crowned by a slightly projecting upper moulding (h.: 0.39 m; 7.79 m east-west; 8.58 m north-south) composed of a ledge chamfered above and below, a widely projecting *cyma reversa*, an astragal and a *scotia* (Waelkens *et al.* 1997: 175 fig. 113).

Behind the very well-dressed ashlar facings, the core of the podium, at least on the south side, is of rubble faced with small stones in a mortar bed.

Its blocks supported a *krepis* (7.01 m east-west; 7.85 m north-south) of three steps, of which the height decreases from bottom to top (respectively 0.39 m, 0.32 m and 0.31 m), thus creating an illusion of height. An elegant socle moulding (h.: 0.365) crowned these three steps (Fig. 11). It is composed of an *apophyge*, a *cyma reversa*, a *trochilus* and a plinth (Waelkens *et al.* 1997: 175 fig. 114). At this level, the centre of the whole monument was filled with larger stones and medium-sized rubble.

This socle moulding once carried a row of 1.18. m high orthostats, of which those at the back (north side) remained smooth (Waelkens *et al.* 1997: 175 fig. 117), while those on the three other sides were decorated with the famous frieze of the dancing girls, five on each side (Waelkens *et al.* 1997: figs 118-128 m). The north dancer on the eastern side is unfortunately still missing. A row of smaller ashlars (h.: 0.32 m) separated the frieze from an upper moulding (h.: 0.465 m). From top to bottom, this is composed of a *cyma recta*, a fillet, a cavetto, an astragal, a quarter-round and an astragal and created a second podium of 5.57 m (east-west) by 6.35 m (north-south). The steps and the mouldings clearly distinguished this part of the building from the volumes above and below.

Above this podium rose a *distyle in antis* naiskos (dimensions at the level of the step below: 5.29 m east-west by 6.03 m north-south) of which the columns and *antae* had already been removed in late antiquity. The naiskos is supported by a 0.28 m high step, which bore a 0.32 m high Ionic-Attic plinth. This carried a row of plain orthostats (h.: 0.89 m) with bevelled edges on the sides and below, above which six courses of wall blocks with bevelled edges (except for the lowest course) had been placed in a pseudo-isodomic arrangement (from top to bottom: 0.415 m, 0.37 m, 0.59 m, 0.445 m, 0.59 m and 0.30 m). The four corners of the naiskos were worked as slightly projecting pilasters with elaborately worked Corinthian capitals (Waelkens *et al.* 1997: 186 fig. 131). The latter corresponded with a scroll frieze (h.: 0.53 m) on the visible north, east and west sides of the naiskos. Friezes at this level seem to have been a North Pisidian feature (Waelkens *et al.* 1997: 182; Waelkens and Vandeput in press). On the front, inside the *pronaos*, this course remained smooth, since it could not be seen from the outside. Outside, immediately below this course, attention was focused on the elaborately decorated door lintel of the structure (Waelkens *et al.* 1997: 182 fig. 130).

The wall frieze and Corinthian capitals bore on all four sides an entablature composed of an architrave with three *fasciae* (h.: 0.315 m), a "Pfeiffenfries" or fluted frieze (h.: 0.285 m) and a *geison* (h.: 0.30 m) with false lion spouts. It supported a 1.13 m high gable (the one at the back decorated with a round shield) and a roof, like the rest of the building, completely made of semi-crystallized white to pinkish limestone. The corners of the gable carried supports for akroteria. The roof slabs imitated *tegulae* and *imbrices* ending in antefixes decorated with very elegant palmettes (Fig. 12). The total height of the naiskos was 10.785 m, that of the heroon 14.795 m.

The workmanship and finish of all the building elements is of superb quality. Its decoration had already permitted us to date the monument to the early Imperial period, more specifically to the reign of Augustus (Vandeput 1997: 21; Waelkens *et al.* 1997: 182-184 and Vandeput this article). The construction seems to have been part of a building programme during which this area was transformed into a kind of *area sacra*, including also the NE Heroon a few dozen metres further east (Kosmetatou *et al.* 1997). A small stepped socle, immediately left of the NW Heroon and covered by the late fortifications may have belonged to another, albeit much smaller religious or honorific monument (Fig. 13).

The naiskos itself once housed a marble statue more than 3.50 m high, representing an almost completely naked young men with a cloak on his left shoulder. The statue, which shows pronounced Polycleitan features in the treatment of the hair and of the face, was tentatively identified by Waelkens as perhaps representing a young Alexander (Moens *et al.* 1997: 371-372 figs 3-6). However, for the moment, and without any dedicatory inscription, it is safer to leave the question of the statue's identity open. Its marble was identified as coming from the quarries at Dokimeion (Moens *et al.* 1997: 375-382).

2. THE EXCAVATIONS OF THE HEROON AND THE LATER TRANSFORMATIONS OF THE AREA (M.Waelkens, B.Arıkan and J. Poblome)

During the first years of the present excavations of the heroon, 1994 and 1995, work was concentrated on sectors to the southwest, south and southeast of the heroon. During the 1996 season, activities focused on the eastern side, which proved to be very different from the west and south sectors.

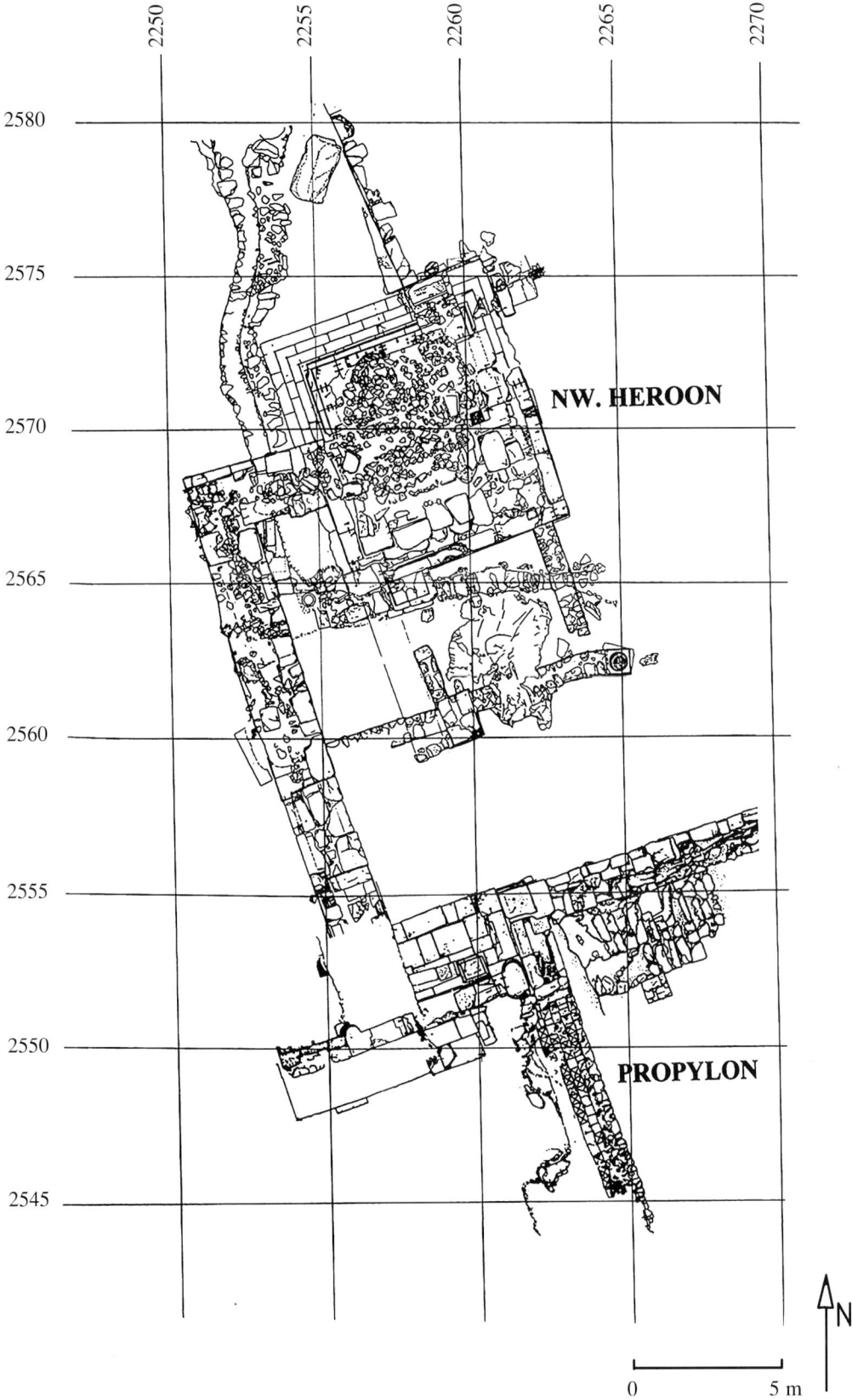

Fig. 1: Plan of the NW Heroon area.

Fig. 2. Preliminary draft of the reconstruction of the north side of the Heroon (restitution and drawing by E. Torun and L. Vandeput 1999).

Fig. 3. Preliminary draft of the reconstruction of the west side of the Heroon (restitution and drawing by E. Torun and L. Vandeput 1999).

Fig. 4. Preliminary draft of the reconstruction of the south side of the Heroon (restitution and drawing by E. Torun and L. Vandeput 1999).

Fig. 5. Preliminary draft of the reconstruction of the east side of the Heroon (restitution and drawing by E. Torun and L. Vandeput 1999).

Fig. 6: View of the ashlar socle of the NW Heroon, seen from the southeast.

Fig. 7. The ashlar socle of the NW Heroon, seen from the north.

Fig. 8: View of the east side of the heroon's ashlar socle.

Fig. 9: View of the southwest corner of the Heroon's ashlar socle. The stones of the west side are visible in the right side of the picture.

Fig. 10: The south side of the ashlar socle of the heroon showing the different treatment of the lower and upper parts of the structure.

Fig. 11: The socle moulding crowning the steps of the heroon on the north side of the building.

Fig. 12: Palmette antefix from the NW Heroon.

The 1997 excavation season finalised the research on the north side of the heroon, in the sectors adjacent to the building itself (sectors 2250-2570, 2255-2570, 2250-2575 and 2255-2575).

These excavations allowed M. Waelkens to trace the post-construction history of the excavated monument and its immediate vicinity. It thus became clear that the area around the heroon changed considerably through the centuries that followed the original Augustan lay-out. The fact that the heroon was directly built on bedrock and that the area around it was considerably altered in late antiquity, explains why no stratigraphical evidence could be recorded to confirm the original construction date of the monument.

2.1. The area to the west and to the south of the NW Heroon

To the west and south of it, the whole area seems to have been remodelled in consecutive phases.

- A first intervention may be represented by a rock-cut channel (width: ca. 0.50 m; depth: ca 0.90 m), which coming from the north first runs parallel with the west side of the monument before turning round its southwest corner and continuing in an east-southeast direction (Fig. 14). This channel, covered by rough limestone slabs set in a hard pink mortar, clearly follows a course defined by the position of the heroon itself, so that it must be either contemporary with it or be a later addition. However, since the construction of the NW Heroon must have affected the water management in the area, it is likely that the channel may have been part of the Augustan building phase.

- Most probably during the second century AD, the two right slabs of the dancers' frieze on the south façade were replaced. In fact, the three right-hand dancers on this front, could be identified as copies of respectively the first, third and fourth (not the fourth and the third, as previously thought) dancers on the east side. These three pairs of figures are identical, except for the completely different treatment of their drapery and eyes. While the folding of the drapery of all the original figures was carved by very fine chiselling, the drapery of the three right front dancers was largely shaped by drilling. Also, the surviving heads of the original figures had blank eyes, whereas the only surviving head of the three right dancers on the front has eyes with carved pupils and irises (Waelkens *et al.* 1997: 176 figs 120-128). This means that, for a so far unknown reason, the east corner on the front must have been so damaged that not enough was left of the original dancers and the repair had to rely on copying three figures of the adjoining east side.

- At some point two ashlar piers were built to the south of the heroon (Fig. 15). The northern one (0.76 m by 1.10 m; preserved h.: 1.65 m; 5 ashlar courses) rested on a socle (1 by 1.50 m) built against the south wall of the socle of the heroon, 1.30 m from its west corner and over the above mentioned rock-cut water channel. The second or southern pier (1.08 by 1.44 m; preserved h.: 1.515 m; 3 ashlar courses) also stood on a socle (1.16 m by 1.52 m) directly resting on the bedrock, 3.34 m to the south of the first one. The slightly different orientation of the piers implies that they must be independent structures (Waelkens *et al.* 1997: 184-185). Since these two piers, which may have carried statuary or other decorative elements, masked the view of the heroon, they probably belonged to the late Imperial period.

- Around AD 400, when the late fortifications were built, a fortification wall made of spolia was erected 2.20 m to the west of the NW Heroon, eventually turning ninety degrees to join the heroon 3.14 m behind its southwest corner (Fig. 16). This fortification wall also continued to the east of the monument. The latter was now transformed into a tower, guarding, together with the Doric temple on the south side of the same entrance, the northwestern entrance to the city (Waelkens *et al.* 1997: 134; Loots *et al.* 2000). During this operation, the prostyle front of the naiskos seems to have been removed completely, since thus far, except for a fragmented Corinthian capital, no remains of the prostyle arrangement have been recovered. Along the west wall, all projecting mouldings were cut off, so that they could not be used for climbing the monument, now turned into a defensive structure.

At the time of these transformations, new arrangements were also laid out to reorganise the distribution of water in the upper city.

A small water reservoir (2.40 by 1.60 m) was thus built in the corner of the western side of the NW Heroon and the fortification wall (Fig. 17). Its west and south walls are made of re-used smaller ashlars and of mortared rubble. It had a vaulted roof made of flat stones bedded in mortar, sloping towards the west, covering an internal space 1 to 1.20 m wide, with a maximum height of 1.20 m (Waelkens *et al.* 1997: 187 fig. 137). A 0.34 m wide opening in the south wall gave access to the reservoir via five tile steps. The floor inside the reservoir was made of large terracotta slabs. The reservoir was drained by the old rock-cut channel and received its water supply by means of a small opening (0.34 m wide; 0.60 m high) built into its north wall. This opening was connected with a well-built water-channel discovered on the other side of the fortification wall (see below 2.3). Recently, a study by F. Martens identified the reservoir as a kind of *lacus*, collecting an intermittent flow of water. Chemical analysis of the calcite deposits covering the walls of the channel suggests that the water conducted by this channel was most probably from melted snow. It may therefore have brought melt-water from the mountains to the city

(Martens in press). The channel or another water-supply system most probably originally continued towards the north, below the levels excavated in 1997 on the other side of the late Roman fortifications. After the construction of the latter it was fed by the early fifth century AD supply system mentioned below (2.3).

Inside this collector, a layer 4, composed of a very light and silted soil was found. It contained many stones obviously rounded by water, thus suggesting a rather long period of use. At one point, however, the entrance had been completely blocked by larger stones.

Perhaps at the time of the arrangement of this reservoir, a simple mortared rubble wall was built between the northern extremity of the late Roman city gate and the south pier in front of the NW Heroon (Fig. 18). This wall, 1.30 m wide and 3.80 m long, and directly resting upon the bedrock, is now reduced to a couple of rubble courses. It may have belonged to a construction protecting the water-collecting system, or it may have offered some shelter to soldiers guarding the entrance gate. If there ever was such a shelter, it must have remained open towards the east, while its roof may have been supported by the two ashlar piers (Waelkens et al. 1997: 187 fig. 140). The date of this construction is uncertain, but it was most probably contemporary with the transformation of the area around AD 400.

When the NW Heroon became incorporated into the late fortifications, a second water collector was constructed along its northeast corner (Fig. 19). Here, a small area level with the third step of its krepidoma, between the northeast corner of the monument and the late fortification wall built against it, was paved with a large terracotta slab (0.735 by 0.735 m) in order to collect rainwater from the upper part of the fortifications or of the heroon (Waelkens et al. 1997: 187 fig. 138).

This slab rested upon a 0.60-0.65 m thick gray earth layer full of ash, but without any finds. It was covered by a thin layer of reddish earth.

The water of this rainwater collector was run off through a 0.50 m wide drain, made of two rows of mortared rubble lined with tiles and covered with small stone slabs (Fig. 20). It is built directly on the natural bedrock and consequently has an exceptionally steep gradient, taking the water to an unknown destination (Waelkens et al. 1997: 187 fig. 139). The soil that was removed from the inside contained a lot of bird bones.

- At some point, the whole area in front of the heroon was transformed again and the wall linking the south pier to the city walls removed, except for its two lowest courses. The whole area was levelled with a very hard layer full of pebbles, called layer 4 in its western half and layer 5 further east. Since it also covers the foundations of the late fortifications, these must have been completely exposed at this time. This layer, which in its eastern extremity is very hard and reddish, sits directly on top of the natural bedrock. In the western part of the area, it is at least 0.20 m deep and there it covers the remains of the demolished rubble wall linking the south pier to the fortifications. It clearly served as a floor level of the simple construction (4.40 by 4.30 m) which henceforth occupied the space immediately to the south of the NW Heroon and to the east of the ashlar piers, both incorporated into the new structure. The walls of this last were built directly on this floor level and did not have any foundations sunk into it (Fig. 21).

The west wall of this structure is 0.60 m wide and 1.80 m long, leaving a 1.50 m wide doorway next to the north pillar. The south wall has a width of 0.70 m and a length of 4.30 m. In its central part, it sits directly on the bedrock, elsewhere layer 5 continues underneath it. After 4.30 m, the south wall made a right angle and joined the podium of the heroon. This wall now projects 1.55 m from the southeast corner of the heroon towards the south and had been partly demolished to make room for water pipes that later emerged from the west reservoir against the heroon (see below).

This structure, which could only be entered from the west and incorporated both the ashlar piers and the podium of the heroon into its wall system, perhaps had a military function. However, in its southwest corner, a lime dump was found. The floor level (layers 4-5) contained a nice gem with a representation of a Nike (Fig. 22: SA 95 H 127), a bronze oil lamp (Fig. 23: SA 95 H 129) and several coins ranging in date from the second to the fourth/fifth century AD. The pottery, however, was dated to the first half of the sixth century AD. Since this material was clearly contemporary with that of the layers covering the building after its destruction, the structure was most probably rather short-lived, suggesting that it had been built shortly before the AD 518 earthquake (Waelkens et al. 1997: 191 fig. 143).

- After the AD 518 seismic catastrophe, only the water collectors built against the west and east sides of the podium of the NW Heroon remained in place, whereas the square building built against the south façade was levelled and removed. Its debris was covered by a 0.40 m thick layer (layer 3 in the western part, layer 4 in the eastern one) which was full of pottery dated to the first half of the sixth century and which contained lots of fourth and fifth century AD coins. The fill itself was composed of a light brown moist earth with many small stones and tile fragments. It covered the lowest course of the heroon's podium, as well as the lowest course of the ashlar piers. The archaeological material from this fill is clearly contemporary with that of the dumps excavated to the northwest and to the east of the

Fig. 13: Remains of the smaller socle monument to the west of the NW Heroon, covered by the late Roman fortifications. The steps are visible in the left part of the picture.

Fig. 14: Rock-cut water channel along the south side of the ashlar socle of the NW Heroon.

Fig. 15: View of the two ashlar piers to the south of the NW Heroon.

Fig. 16: The fortification wall linking the NW Heroon to the Doric temple seen from the west. The NW Heroon is in the centre of the picture.

Fig. 17: The water collector built against the west side of the heroon's podium.

Fig. 18: View of the simple rubble wall linking the southern ashlar pier to the late Roman fortifications.

Fig. 19: The water collecting system against the northeast corner of the heroon.

Fig. 20: The water drainage system from the collector to the east of the NW Heroon.

Fig. 21. The square rubble structure built against the façade of the NW Heroon shortly before AD 518.

Fig. 22: Gem with the representation of a Nike from the floor level of the square rubble structure.

Fig. 23: Bronze oil lamp from the floor level of the rubble structure.

Fig. 24: View of the sixth century AD terracotta pipe system with the settling tank to the southwest of the NW Heroon.

Doric temple, in which earthquake debris was apparently piled up against the now abandoned fortifications. Inside the fill were various water-supply systems made of terracotta pipes and draining water from the collector against the west side of the heroon. One of them, following a north-south course and continuing through the door of the propylon of the Doric temple, included in its course a terracotta basin used as a settling tank (Fig. 24). A second one ran to the southeast towards the tufa basin mentioned below (Fig. 25). Sections of the west and east walls of the square building had been destroyed to make way for it (Waelkens *et al.* 1997: 193-194 figs 142-143).

Near the southeast corner of the abandoned square building in front of the NW Heroon, layer 4 also supported a pedestal (h.: 0.55 m; 0.77 by 0.77 m) 4.40 m to the south of the monument's southeast corner (Fig. 26). It bore a reused monolithic limestone column (h.: 2.20 m; lower diameter: 0.44 m) carrying a first century AD limestone sundial, set up by a certain Tiberius Claudius Polypeithes (Waelkens *et al.* 1997: 193 fig. 145). The foot (h.: 0.43 m; 0.37-0.40 m wide) of the sundial was in the shape of a lion's paw, of which the hair on the back grew into a floral pattern surrounding the ring of the dial. The piece of lead that once held the *gnomon* was still visible. The ring itself, the inside of which was marked with the hours, was considerably bent downwards so that spectators below it could see the time indication. As a result, the sundial must have originally stood high above the ground (Fig. 27).

- When a fatal earthquake levelled the city around the middle of the seventh century AD, the column collapsed and broke in two and the sundial was smashed in seven pieces. Lots of building and statuary fragments were found scattered over layer 4. This was covered by a debris layer (layers 2 and 3, respectively in the western and in the eastern part of the area in front of the heroon). This debris layer varied in thickness and composition. To the southwest of the NW Heroon, in sector 2255-2560, it was mainly composed of collapsed ashlars from the late fortifications and also contained mortar, rubble stones, bricks and tiles, but very little archaeological material. Further south, in sector 2255-2555, layer 2 contained many blocks from the late Roman city gate, some of them decorated (Waelkens *et al.* 1997: 187 fig. 136). On the other side of the gateway, in sector 2250-2555, layer 2 also produced several fragments of marble statues, which may have been built into the late fortifications. Among them were the head of a calf, two fragments of a leg and part of a fluted marble stand.

Immediately west of the heroon, in sector 2255-2565, layer 2 was 1.50-2 m deep and reached as deep as the vaulted cover of the water reservoir. Here, the debris layer contained real concentrations of rubble and tiles and was full of archaeological material, including sherds, bones, glass, nails, lead fragments from the dowelling and cramping systems of the heroon, architectural fragments and a finger of a marble statue. To the south of the monument, layer 2 was slightly different. In fact, concentrations of mortar were only present in the western parts of the area, in sector 2255-2560, which still contained a lot of debris of the late fortifications. Further south in sectors 2255-2555 and 2260-2555, more fragments of marble statuary, among other things a hand resting on a club, most probably from a Herakles statue, were exposed within this layer.

2.2. The area to the east of the NW Heroon

Some interventions, such as the construction of the late fortifications and the arrangement of a water collector between them and the monument's northeast corner, have already been discussed above. Other interventions in the area, however, were not actually linked to the heroon itself.

- At some time in late antiquity, the area a few metres east of the NW Heroon also underwent a considerable transformation. The bedrock, which most probably contained a partially natural crevice or cavity, seems to have been transformed into a kind of cistern, surrounded by re-used ashlars. Adjoining it to the east, a small fountain house was built (Fig. 28). Since the whole area is still covered under huge amounts of debris from the late fortifications to the north, this has not yet been fully excavated and a precise date still needs to be established. The debris on top and in front of the fountain reached over three metres in some places. It contained bricks and tiles, mortar, lots of mosaics, medium-sized rubble and architectural elements from all the surrounding structures. There also were mortared bricks from a brick arch.

The fountain house was a vaulted structure with an arched entrance leading to a small room with a dome (1.42 by 1.45 m). Inside, its east and west walls both had an arched doorway (w.: 0.60 m and h.: 1.267 m in the east wall; w.: 1.63 m and h.: 1.75 m in the west wall) leading respectively into a second room and into the cistern. The interior walls of the fountain house were originally veneered in Docimian *pavonazetto* marble attached to the brick and tufa walls with iron clamps (18 in total). These wall plates were only *in situ* on the north wall up to a height of 1.40 m where they were crowned by a moulding (h.: 0.10 m), and at either side of the arched doorway in the east wall (Fig. 29). At the top of the marble revetment on the north wall, beneath its moulded crown, there is a square recess holding a piece of glass. The same moulded crown could be seen on the east wall. The walls on the south side (0.91 to 0.87 m wide, 1.95 m high; with an addition of 0.40 m into the basin) were plastered. The entrance to the fountain house consisted of a semicircular basin, lined with onyx revetments, apparently the variety known in antiquity as *marmor Hierapolitanus* (quarries located by M. Waelkens at Gölemez near Pamukkale).

Inside the structure, five vertical terracotta pipes were built into the dome, four at the corners and one at the centre. The collapsed material that blocked the doorways to the east and the west showed traces of intense heat, indicating that at some point there must have been a fire. Because of the danger involved in excavating the fountain with all the weight of a metre-high mass of material above, the fountain was closed after a preliminary consolidation of its wall plaster.

In front of the fountain house, there seems to have been a *piazetta* bordered by a 4.85 m long wall along its western edge (Fig. 30). It extends from the above-mentioned cistern (Fig. 31) towards the south and runs parallel to the drainage system built laid the east side of the heroon's podium. This wall was built of two thick stone paraments with a rubble fill in between. No mortar was used in the construction of this wall, of which the function is not yet certain.

A similar, but much less well-preserved wall bordered the southern extremity of the *piazzetta*. A simple water system was discovered attached to this south wall. Its sides are made of brick supported by rubble on the north side and it is covered by tiles. Near the southwest corner of the *piazzetta*, built against the outer stone parament of its south wall, an apsidal tufa basin (h.: 0.56 m; 1.30 by 1.18 m) was exposed. It was fed by the sixth century AD terracotta pipes draining water from the collector near the heroon's west podium. This means that the tufa basin and perhaps the whole water-works to the east of the heroon must belong to the transformation of the area after the AD 518 earthquake. A layer 3 was also found in the *piazzetta*, which was very similar in material and composition to that of the post AD 518 earthquake fill in front of the heroon (layers 3 and 4) and contained coins of the sixth and early seventh century BC (Scheers 2000: SA 96 H 125: a *pentanummium* of Justin I or Justinianus I; SA 96 H 116: a half *follis* of Heraclius dated to the year AD 610/611). They seem to confirm that this small square had been in use during this period.

- To the east of the NW Heroon, in sector 2260-2570, destruction layer 2 also contained material from the collapse of the structure on top of the fountain house adjoining the heroon. This may have been a simple dwelling and was partially excavated in 1998. This could explain why layer 2, from bottom to top, consisted of a thick layer of mortar, full of bricks and tiles, and medium-sized rubble. Large architectural elements from the heroon and from the dwelling (?) above the small fountain house regularly appeared in the upper part of the layer. It also contained a considerable amount of *tesserae*.

In the area of the *piazzetta* in front of the sixth century AD (?) fountain house, layer 2 contained many pieces of marble sculpture. Among these were a piece of an arm and the torso of a male statue, naked except for a cloak covering the left shoulder (Fig. 32), a leg fragment belonging to the body, four other leg fragments of which one was attached to a tree trunk, a statue base with one complete and one broken foot, an arm, an almost complete back of a head, pieces of hair and drapery. A sixth leg fragment in white marble (h.: 1.25 m) attached to a huge piece of drapery (h.: 1.00 m; w.: 0.50 m) was also excavated (Fig. 33). From its size, it must have belonged to the giant statue originally set up inside the NW Heroon. This must mean that it was standing there until the mid-seventh century BC earthquake. In fact, its head was also found on top of the sixth century AD fill in front of the building (Fig. 34).

All the statue fragments were found among blocks from the heroon. Among these also was a slab with a dancing girl, from the east frieze.

- All the remains were covered by a topsoil layer, 0.10 to 0.50 m deep, composed of dark, dry earth, full of plant roots and containing only very little archaeological material. This covered the south face of the heroon's podium. Since part of the edge of the latter had collapsed, it was possible to study its internal structure. Layer 1 still contained many elements from the dancers' frieze, showing that some of the slabs had only fallen and been damaged in a sub-recent period. Four slabs, representing five of the dancers from the southeast corner and east side of the monument were found in it.

This means that only one dancer from the east side remains missing. Layer 1 contained also many small to medium-sized pieces of statuary. Among them, a shoulder and cloak fragment from the huge marble statue that originally stood inside the heroon, as well the face of one of the girls and the complete head of another. At least some of the statue fragments were most probably incorporated into the late fortifications.

2.3. The area to the north of the NW Heroon

Both the stratigraphy and the structures behind the heroon presented a more complicated picture than on the other sides. Since the area to the north of the heroon was outside the late Roman city walls, most of the finds there had no connection whatsoever with the areas described above. The only link with the latter was a water channel coming from the north and protected along its western edge by a retaining wall built against the west side of the podium of the heroon (Fig. 35). Although the channel, made of mortared rubble, was not opened, its sharp dive to the south made it clear that it passed through the late fortification and that it connected with the

Fig. 25: The sixth century water supply system immediately south of the heroon, for which the rubble walls of the square structure were partially destroyed.

Fig. 26: Location of the column (right) that formerly bore a sundial to the southeast of the NW Heroon.

Fig. 27: The sundial paid for by Polypeithes.

Fig. 28: View of the sixth century AD fountain house to the east of the NW Heroon.

Fig. 29: View of the interior of the fountain house with some of the marble veneer still attached to the walls.

Fig. 30: View of the piazetta with its west enclosure wall, seen from the east.

Fig. 31: View of the cistern between the NW Heroon and the sixth century AD fountain house.

Fig. 32: Male marble torso found to the east of the NW Heroon.

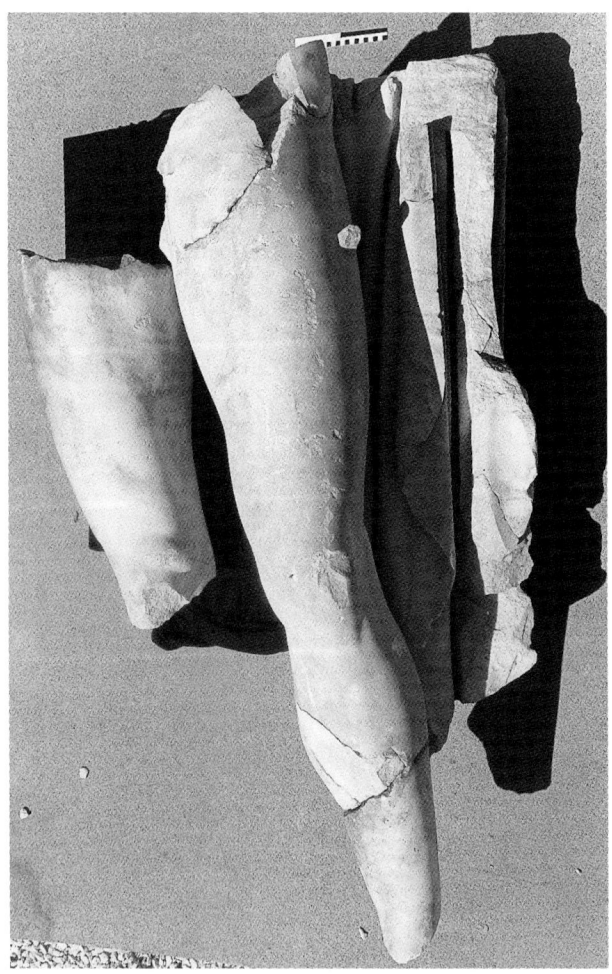

Fig. 33: Legs and cloak fragment of the huge statue that was at one time inside the NW Heroon.

Fig. 34: Head of the colossal statue from the NW Heroon in the position where it fell.

Fig. 35: View from the north of the water channel (5) taking mountain water through the late Roman fortifications. The retaining wall that protected it is visible in the right part of the picture.

Fig. 36: View of the stratigraphy and the foundation of the ashlar podium on the north side of the NW Heroon.

Fig. 37: View of the fourth century AD construction with the blocked entrance, to the northeast of the heroon.

narrow opening in the north wall of the reservoir uncovered during the 1994 excavations. Since this channel was clearly built at the same time as the fortifications, it confirms the early fifth century AD date of the whole water-supply system constructed at that time on either side of the fortifications. As we have said above, the late Roman collector that it supplied on the south side of the city walls was drained by an early Imperial rock-cut channel and this latter bore traces of the transport of melt-water. Whether or not the late Roman water channel to the north of the heroon also carried melt-water is not certain, but it is at least possible since it seems to have carried water from a source in the mountain face, less than 100 m to the north of the NW Heroon.

The stratigraphy of the excavated areas could only be completely studied to the east of the water channel. It produced evidence for the following building phases:

- The original arrangement: in the northwest corner, the north face of the podium of the NW Heroon sat directly on the limestone bedrock, whereas in the east a deep layer of three large blocks with rough facing had been inserted to level the limestone foundation (Fig. 36). The three blocks were placed over ophiolite. Below the upper line of these blocks, the area had been levelled with clay, green ophiolite fragments, chips resulting from the levelling of the natural bedrock or from the shaping of the blocks themselves, and some charcoal pieces. Geological research suggests that the heroon had been built on one of the limestone islands or *klippen*, which are very common in the northern side of the site and at Sagalassos in general.

Whether or not the area to the north of the structure had remained rough bedrock or had been levelled in one way or another could no longer be established.

- A mid-Imperial levelling operation to the north of the heroon that was represented by a fill of two layers:
1 – layer 9: this was the deepest layer that could be reached in this sector, as it sat directly on the natural bedrock. It represented the lowest part of a fill which also included layer 8. Six large tufa blocks made it difficult to dig through it. It consisted of reddish, very hard and silted clay. There was still archaeological material in this layer, especially pottery (SA 97 H 202) dated to the second half of the first century AD–first half of the second century AD, but containing some intrusions as well.
2 – layer 8: this layer represented the upper part of the same fill. Its pottery (SA 97 H 195) was dated to the second half of the first and the first half of the second century AD and did not contain any intrusions. It also contained many naturally rounded stones, dark earth, lots of broken glass, metal pieces, slag, crustae and bones. A broken dolium was found next to the heroon wall. This fill (layers 8 and 9), which is later than the construction of the NW Heroon, must represent some construction work that took place after the middle of the first century AD to level the area to the north of the NW Heroon (see Fig. 36).

- The construction of an unidentified building to the northeast of the NW Heroon:
To the northeast of the heroon, the late fortifications also seem to have incorporated another structure made of ashlar (Fig. 37). In fact, while exposing that face of the fortifications, it became clear that a wall built perpendicularly to the northeast corner of the heroon had originally been the west wall of another building of which the plan and function could not yet be established. It contained a large door that had been blocked up when it was incorporated into the late fortification wall. At that point, the wall was also connected to the heroon via a very crude mortared rubble wall.

This façade was exposed over a length of 2.48 m. The doorsill could be reached by a step of 0.80 m length. The step and the door-sill made up the difference in level of 0.85 m between the inside of the structure and the walking level in front of it. This last was made up of the following layers, all containing pieces of charcoal, numerous bones and archaeological material:
- layer 7 (in 2255-2575): a loose lens of dumped material, excavated as layer 6 in sectors 2250-2570 and 2255-2570. Beside some residual pieces, its pottery (SA 97 H 146 and SA 97 H 133) could be attributed to phase 6 of the production of Sagalassos red slip wares, dated to the first half of the fourth century AD. The layer also contained a coin from the reign of Claudius II, AD 268-270 (Scheers 2000: cat. 24).
- layer 6 (in 2255-2575): this layer was excavated as layer 5 in 2255-2570 and as layer 4 in 2250-2570. The ceramic material (SA 97 H 128,138 and 154) ranged in date from the second half of the first to the first half of the fourth century AD.

This seems to suggest that the unidentified structure to the northeast of the NW Heroon had been built around the middle of the fourth century AD or shortly after, but in any case before the beginning of the fifth century, when it had already been incorporated into the new fortifications.

- A levelling operation between the NW Heroon and the unidentified structure. After the latter had become part of the city's late Roman defences and its entrance had been blocked, there was no longer any need to maintain the doorstep.

Layer 4, level with the top of the sill and with the top of the heroon's ashlar podium, has probably to be seen as a fill connected with the construction of the retaining wall protecting the west side of the water channel (see Fig. 35). It covered the water channel completely, but its top was level with that of the retaining wall. The pottery from this fill (SA 97 H 40) could be dated to a period between the middle of the fifth and the middle of the seventh centuries AD, but contained several residual pieces. This is most probably an intervention after the AD 518 earthquake, when the water channel, which must already have existed since the time of the construction of the late fortifications, was dug up again and protected by a retaining wall built against its west face. Layer 4 then represents the fill spread out in the area after this operation.

- After this intervention, this area also seems to have been used as a dump for earthquake debris, represented by layer 3. This was a light brown soil, containing a significant number of mosaics, tile and brick fragments. The pottery from this layer (SA 97 H 25, 34, 65 and 90), was identical in date (with the same kind of residual pieces) as that from fill no. 4, thus confirming that the creation of both the fill and the dump must have occurred within a very short space of time.

Layers 1 and 2 represented the collapse of the upper parts of the late Roman city walls after the mid-seventh century AD earthquake.

On the west side of the water channel and its retaining wall, the situation was a little different. Here, the top of the channel was protected by another fill: earth had been laid over the channel and stones piled on top. This fill covered all the area between the retaining wall and the west side of the heroon. On the west of the retaining wall, beneath destruction layer 2, a fill was reached with lots of archaeological material, corresponding with that of layer 3 in sector 2255-2570. Even if the layers were different on either side of the retaining wall, they were deposited there as part of a single building operation.

3. THE DATE OF THE NORTHWEST HEROON: AN AUGUSTAN MONUMENT AT SAGALASSOS (L. Vandeput).

In the past few decades, the construction date of the Northwest Heroon at Sagalassos has been the subject of discussion on different occasions. After his survey of the monument in the seventies, Fleischer dated it to the second half of the second century BC (Fleischer 1979: 292-303). This, however, was not accepted by Froning (1981: 129-130) who decided in favour of a construction date around the middle of the first century BC at the earliest. Both authors based their dating of the monument on stylistic analysis of the socle frieze with the dancing girls.

Unexpectedly for a heroon located in such an imposing position in the city, no dedicatory inscription has been recovered so far. This must be, however, because the complete pronaos was apparently removed when the heroon was incorporated into the early fifth century AD city walls as a tower (see 1, this article). Most probably, the inscription is somewhere built into the buried or collapsed parts of these fortifications. As mentioned above (see 2), the fact that the monument was directly built upon natural bedrock, without any levelling around it, also resulted in a total absence of any stratigraphical evidence related to its construction. Therefore, only a study of the architectural decoration of the monument offers any possibility of defining its date of construction. Before the excavations, the visible architectural decoration had also given rise to different proposals for the construction date of the monument.

In the late eighties, Sagalassos was studied by the team of the Pisidia Survey Project under direction of S. Mitchell. The heroon was one of the first monuments to receive attention. The linking of a beautifully carved Hellenistic Corinthian capital in the depot in the present village of Ağlasun with the heroon seemed to favour its Hellenistic date (Waelkens et al. 1997: 176; Mitchell et al. 1988: 62, n. 26; Waelkens 1993: 45). At that time, a single block of a tendril frieze was visible in the neighbourhood of the heroon. Originally, it was thought to belong to the heroon (Mitchell et al. 1987: 38; Waelkens et al. 1987: 234, fig. 6), but later Waelkens dated the tendril to the beginning of the first century BC (Waelkens 1993: 44). Rumscheid (I 1994: 155, 292-294), however, disagreed with the attribution of the tendril frieze to the beginning of the first century BC. Because of the frieze, he dated the heroon with the Corinthian capital to the Augustan period[1].

Between 1994 and 1997, the heroon has been excavated and many new building elements were unearthed. As it turned out, the capital upon which the date for the heroon was based did not belong to the building. Before the excavations, the above mentioned frieze block was the only visible part of a splendid wall frieze most of which was recovered during the excavations. Rumscheid's early-Imperial date for the frieze block proved to be correct. Several other richly decorated building elements were found during the excavations, revealing that the entablature was composed of a large wall frieze, crowned by an architrave with plain mouldings, a frieze decorated with flutes and plain cornices with lion spouts. All the

---

[1] See also Vandeput 1995: 533-535, where the heroon is still wrongly dated to the second century BC on the basis of the Corinthian Capital.

Fig. 38: Sagalassos, NW Heroon. Wall frieze block.

Fig. 39: Sagalassos, NW Heroon. Wall frieze block with central acanthus bush.

the west side of the water channel (see Fig. 35). It covered the water channel completely, but its top was level with that of the retaining wall. The pottery from this fill (SA 97 H 40) could be dated to a period between the middle of the fifth and the middle of the seventh centuries AD, but contained several residual pieces. This is most probably an intervention after the AD 518 earthquake, when the water channel, which must already have existed since the time of the construction of the late fortifications, was dug up again and protected by a retaining wall built against its west face. Layer 4 then represents the fill spread out in the area after this operation.

- After this intervention, this area also seems to have been used as a dump for earthquake debris, represented by layer 3. This was a light brown soil, containing a significant number of mosaics, tile and brick fragments. The pottery from this layer (SA 97 H 25, 34, 65 and 90), was identical in date (with the same kind of residual pieces) as that from fill no. 4, thus confirming that the creation of both the fill and the dump must have occurred within a very short space of time.

Layers 1 and 2 represented the collapse of the upper parts of the late Roman city walls after the mid-seventh century AD earthquake.

On the west side of the water channel and its retaining wall, the situation was a little different. Here, the top of the channel was protected by another fill: earth had been laid over the channel and stones piled on top. This fill covered all the area between the retaining wall and the west side of the heroon. On the west of the retaining wall, beneath destruction layer 2, a fill was reached with lots of archaeological material, corresponding with that of layer 3 in sector 2255-2570. Even if the layers were different on either side of the retaining wall, they were deposited there as part of a single building operation.

3. THE DATE OF THE NORTHWEST HEROON: AN AUGUSTAN MONUMENT AT SAGALASSOS (L. Vandeput).

In the past few decades, the construction date of the Northwest Heroon at Sagalassos has been the subject of discussion on different occasions. After his survey of the monument in the seventies, Fleischer dated it to the second half of the second century BC (Fleischer 1979: 292-303). This, however, was not accepted by Froning (1981: 129-130) who decided in favour of a construction date around the middle of the first century BC at the earliest. Both authors based their dating of the monument on stylistic analysis of the socle frieze with the dancing girls.

Unexpectedly for a heroon located in such an imposing position in the city, no dedicatory inscription has been recovered so far. This must be, however, because the complete pronaos was apparently removed when the heroon was incorporated into the early fifth century AD city walls as a tower (see 1, this article). Most probably, the inscription is somewhere built into the buried or collapsed parts of these fortifications. As mentioned above (see 2), the fact that the monument was directly built upon natural bedrock, without any levelling around it, also resulted in a total absence of any stratigraphical evidence related to its construction. Therefore, only a study of the architectural decoration of the monument offers any possibility of defining its date of construction. Before the excavations, the visible architectural decoration had also given rise to different proposals for the construction date of the monument.

In the late eighties, Sagalassos was studied by the team of the Pisidia Survey Project under direction of S. Mitchell. The heroon was one of the first monuments to receive attention. The linking of a beautifully carved Hellenistic Corinthian capital in the depot in the present village of Ağlasun with the heroon seemed to favour its Hellenistic date (Waelkens *et al.* 1997: 176; Mitchell *et al.* 1988: 62, n. 26; Waelkens 1993: 45). At that time, a single block of a tendril frieze was visible in the neighbourhood of the heroon. Originally, it was thought to belong to the heroon (Mitchell *et al.* 1987: 38; Waelkens *et al.* 1987: 234, fig. 6), but later Waelkens dated the tendril to the beginning of the first century BC (Waelkens 1993: 44). Rumscheid (I 1994: 155, 292-294), however, disagreed with the attribution of the tendril frieze to the beginning of the first century BC. Because of the frieze, he dated the heroon with the Corinthian capital to the Augustan period[1].

Between 1994 and 1997, the heroon has been excavated and many new building elements were unearthed. As it turned out, the capital upon which the date for the heroon was based did not belong to the building. Before the excavations, the above mentioned frieze block was the only visible part of a splendid wall frieze most of which was recovered during the excavations. Rumscheid's early-Imperial date for the frieze block proved to be correct. Several other richly decorated building elements were found during the excavations, revealing that the entablature was composed of a large wall frieze, crowned by an architrave with plain mouldings, a frieze decorated with flutes and plain cornices with lion spouts. All the

---

[1] See also Vandeput 1995: 533-535, where the heroon is still wrongly dated to the second century BC on the basis of the Corinthian Capital.

Fig. 38: Sagalassos, NW Heroon. Wall frieze block.

Fig. 39: Sagalassos, NW Heroon. Wall frieze block with central acanthus bush.

Fig. 40: Sagalassos, NW Heroon. Pilaster capital with part of the wall frieze.

Fig. 41: Sagalassos, NW Heroon. Pilaster capital with part of the wall frieze.

decorated architectural elements, the wall frieze with the capitals and the doorframe, imply a construction date under the reign of Augustus (Vandeput 1997: 21; Waelkens *et al.* 1997: 182-184).

Among the decorative motifs, the fine tendril frieze forming the wall frieze (Figs 38-39) offers important leads for dating the NW Heroon (Waelkens *et al.* 1997: 185 fig. 129). In the centre of the north, east and west walls of the naiskos, the main stems of the tendrils sprout from acanthus bushes and run off in opposite directions towards the corners where they end just next to the pilaster capitals. They are executed in a very high and delicate relief.

The tendril is composed of a well-articulated main stem, progressing in a wave-like movement and occupying the complete height of the frieze moulding (see Figs 2-5). At regular intervals, secondary stems bend backwards from this main stem and end in a flower or fruit after a short turn inward. Both the main and the secondary stems are composed of successive fluted caules that grow from elegantly shaped bracts. Those on the main stem are worked in an acanthus-like way, the ones on the secondary stem are composed of two small, plain leaves. The flowers and fruits that grow from the secondary stem are very large and richly varied. The tendril is enriched with small, fancifully shaped off-shoots, growing from the bracts and ending in all sorts of small flowers. In spite of this very rich design, the structure of the tendril always remains very clear and its background is clearly demarcated.

Parallels for this elegant and evenly structured frieze appear in tendrils on early-Imperial monuments elsewhere in Asia Minor. Our first comparable decoration can be seen in the tendrils on the inside of the cornices of Honorific Monument I on the upper agora at Sagalassos, dated to the reign of Augustus (Vandeput 1997: 43-45, pl. 12). Here, however, the tendrils are composed differently. Unlike those on the heroon, they are very fancifully and irregularly shaped. The main and secondary stems are hard to distinguish from one another, which is partly due to the limited length of the tendrils and partly to the fact that they are of the same shape. Although all the stems end in large flowers, the tendril itself is less florally worked than the one of the heroon, where the bracts of the stem are worked in an acanthus-like way. In general, the tendril of the heroon is much more balanced and better worked.

The best known example of an early-Imperial tendril frieze in Asia Minor is the frieze on the Gate of Mazaeus and Mithridates at Ephesos, dedicated in 4/3 BC (Alzinger 1974: 109-110, figs 4, 5, 161-163; Rumscheid 1994 II: pl. 37). However, there are significant differences between this frieze and the one on the NW Heroon at Sagalassos. The secondary stems on the gate at Ephesos are more often formed by backward-curving volutes than by flowers. Unlike at Sagalassos, these elements occupy a secondary position and are clearly of lesser importance than the main stem. This is also seen in the fact that the secondary stems received a different treatment from the main one and are not composed of fluted caules. The small off-shoots that enliven the tendrils at Sagalassos appear less frequently at Ephesos. On the other hand, the pilaster capitals of the gate at Ephesos have a rich spectrum of different types of flowers recalling the arrangement at Sagalassos.

Friezes that have the same general structure with large central elements figuring in circles, formed by the progressing main stem and the backward-curving secondary stem appear also at Pergamon (Kraus 1953: Pls 19-21; Rumscheid 1994 II: nos 188, 24; 261; 262; 279). These tendrils were often dated to the Hellenistic period, but were later attributed to the late-Hellenistic or the early-Augustan period by Rumscheid (1994 I: 292-293 with further literature). Although the general lay-out of these friezes is identical to that on the NW Heroon at Sagalassos, their actual appearance differs markedly. While the structure at Sagalassos always remains clear, the floral features at Pergamon are so lush that the overall structure of a single progressing main stem is unclear.

The same goes for the wall frieze of the Temple of Augustus at Pisidian Antioch[1] where the general lay-out recalls that at Sagalassos, but the actual execution of the tendrils is quite different. As in the tendril frieze at Pergamon, the floral elements overgrow much more of the background than at Sagalassos, because they are richer and thicker (Robinson 1926: figs 4-12; Vandeput 1997: pl. 70, 1-2; Mitchell and Waelkens 1998: pls 80-84).

At the Temple for Augustus at Ankyra, constructed during his lifetime (Waelkens 1986: 57-58; Rumscheid 1994 II: no. 11), a tendril frieze forms the wall frieze of the monument, as was the case in the temple at Pisidian Antioch and in the NW Heroon at Sagalassos. Unfortunately it is in a rather bad state of preservation. However, the circles formed by the main and secondary stems are still clearly discernible as are the large motifs that decorate their cen-

---

[1] New research has revealed that the propylon of the Temple at Antioch does not date from ÀD 50 or 62, but from 2/1 BC (Mitchell and Waelkens 1998: 146-147). Altough this does not necessarily imply that the temple was completely ready by then, we believe with Mitchell that its construction must have begun significantly earlier and that it was most probably completed by the end of Augustus' reign (Mitchell and Waelkens 1998: 166-167).

tres. Remains of numerous off-shoots (Krencker and Schede 1936: Taf. 22, 30-32; Waelkens 1986: 54; Rumscheid 1994 II: pl. 4) seem to indicate that the frieze at Ankyra was originally enlivened like those at Pisidian Antioch, Ephesos, Pergamon and Sagalassos.

In spite of these differences, significant details recur on all early-Imperial friezes. The caules from all the examples are fluted and large flowers of very varying shapes play an important role in the decoration. All the friezes have flowers with leaves worked in an acanthus-like way. The flowers are of different types and often have hybrid shapes, indicating that reproduction of a realistic tendril was not the aim. This impression is reinforced by the fact that bunches of grapes figure among the central elements of the tendril at Sagalassos (Waelkens *et al.* 1997: 185, fig. 129). On several of the other friezes there are even living figures. So the frieze of the Gate at Ephesos is enlivened by small cupids flanking the central figure from which the tendril sprouts (Alzinger 1974: fig. 5, 161). Elsewhere on the same frieze small birds appear. The central element from which the tendrils sprout at Ankyra and at Antioch equally incorporates a human figure. Small female figures appear as the central element of frieze sections of the frieze at Ankyra (Rumscheid 1994 II: pl. 4, 1 and 5, 7.1). Another detail that recurs on several of the friezes is twisted elements, perhaps as an off-shoot, ending in a spiral or a twisted pistil of a flower (Figs 39, 41) (Pergamon: Rumscheid 1994 II: pl. 114, 6; Pisidian Antioch: Rumscheid 1994 II: pl. 6, 5; Ephesos: Rumscheid 1994 II: 36.7, 37; 2).

It is often indicated that the early-Imperial tendril friezes in Ankyra and especially Pisidian Antioch were strongly influenced by contemporary decoration in Italy (Waelkens 1986: 55; Rumscheid 1994 I: 155, 293), where early Augustan tendril friezes were evenly structured and carried large flowers, a type of tendril which was developed in the first years of the second half of the first century BC (Schörner 1995: 38-39). Certain features of the frieze of the NW Heroon at Sagalassos also indicate the influence of western examples. In Italy, specific details of the vegetal worked stems permit us to date monuments more precisely (Schörner 1995: 29). In the case of the frieze of the NW Heroon, details such as the shape of the bracts where a secondary stem grows from the main stem, composed of an acanthus leaf and a small plain leaf, or the fact that the main and secondary stems are treated in the same way, would be important indicators for an attribution of the tendril to the early Augustan period in Italy (Schörner 1995: 29, 41). The fact that the small plain leaves forming the bracts on the secondary stems are not worked in an acanthus-like way seems to point to even older examples, since on most early-Augustan tendrils from Italy they are worked more elaborately. The floral execution of the tendrils reached its climax during the remainder of the Augustan period, when it was influenced by the decoration of the Ara Pacis and of the Forum of Augustus in Rome (Schörner 1995: 72-73, pl. 31). These tendrils show bracts and sheathing leaves that are all worked in an acanthus-like, lushly shaped way. The stems themselves are now enriched with additional details and the shape of the flowers varies markedly. All these details recur on the friezes of Ankyra and Antioch. The tendril of the NW Heroon at Sagalassos seems rather to belong to an earlier phase in the development of the ornament, but also seems to draw heavily on the developments in the West.

A second element that provides clues for the dating of the heroon and also refers to architectural decoration in the West, is the acanthus of the bushes from which the tendrils of the wall frieze sprout and the acanthus of the Corinthian pilaster capitals. The motif is worked in very varied ways (Fig. 39). The acanthus bushes of the wall frieze are composed of three acanthus leaves of which only the central one is depicted in front view and the flanking ones in profile. The seven leaflets of the central leaf, composed of five well-articulated lobes, sprout from both sides of the pronounced mid-rib at a rather sharp angle and are clearly demarcated. The central lobe of each leaflet is very pronounced and projects strongly. The central rib seems to be separated from the rest of the leaf by two sharply cut flanking veins. The pendulous top leaflet of this central leaf is broken, but one of the side leaves is completely preserved. A considerable part of its top is folded back and appears in front view. Although these side leaves are elegantly curved and the folded part clearly represents an attempt to imitate the folds of real leaves, sharp lines and deep, dry cutting reduce their natural qualities. The unnatural way in which the top leaf of the acanthus bush is bent backwards reinforces this impression and shows that, despite much labour, a certain provincialism in the decoration cannot be denied.

The arrangement of the leaves of the central acanthus bushes of the wall frieze differs from the leaves of the pilaster capitals (Figs 40-41). An important distinction is in the organisation of the leaflets. Unlike those of the acanthus bushes, the leaflets of the capitals are composed of four lobes only and are arranged in a fan-like way. The points of the individual lobes are much sharper than those of the frieze. The acanthus of the pilaster capitals represents the normal type of acanthus in Asia Minor (Vandeput 1997: 132) and is therefore fairly similar to that of the large Augustan capitals of the honorific columns on the upper agora at Sagalassos (Vandeput 1997: 46-47, pls 13.2, 15.2, 16.1-2), even if its lobes are thinner and more sharply pointed. The wide base of the leaves of the lower row of the pilaster capitals is especially reminiscent of those of the SW column.

It is more difficult to compare the acanthus of the frieze (Fig. 39) to that of other monuments at Sagalassos.

Although of lesser quality, the acanthus of the central bush on the interior frieze of the cornices of Honorific Monument I on the upper agora, which has been dated to the reign of Augustus, offers the best parallel (Vandeput 1997: 43, 45, pl. 12.2). A better one is offered by a sheathing leaf on the wall frieze of the Temple of Augustus in Pisidian Antioch, which is moulded in a very similar way (Rumscheid 1994 I: 155-156; II: pl. 7, 3 top block). Both are strongly influenced by examples from the West. In fact, the leaflets are grouped like those on certain monuments in the West, such as the capitals of the Temple of Mars Ultor at Rome or the Maison Carrée at Nîmes (Heilmeyer 1970: pl. 2, 1; 40). However, they are slightly more pointed and deeper, which can probably be explained as an adaptation to the commonly used type of acanthus in Asia Minor.

An element that also seems to refer back to the West is the fact that the acanthus bushes of the wall frieze on the NW Heroon grow from basal leaves (Fig. 2). Basal leaves, mostly of an acanthus-like shape are practically omnipresent on friezes from the second half of the first century BC (Schörner 1995: 39, 42) and from the Augustan period in Italy (Schörner 1995: 73). In Asia Minor, however, they occur only randomly. One example is found on a relief from Pergamon, now in the museum at Istanbul (Börker 1973: fig. 12b), which has often been dated to the Hellenistic period, but was recently considered to be of early-Imperial date by Rumscheid (1994 I: 292-293). Another example occurs in the frieze of the monopteros at Termessos, convincingly attributed to the early-Imperial period by Rumscheid (1994 I: 169-170), who assumed a western influence for the Termessian frieze. Western influence can be deduced not only from the basal leaves on the wall frieze, but also from their shape. The motif can best be seen as a strongly simplified (and partly misunderstood?) imitation of a so-called "Herzblattkymation", a type of Lesbian cyma that regularly appears on monuments in the West (Leon 1971: 262), but which was mainly restricted to that part of the Roman empire.

The two pilaster capitals (Figs 40-41) that were recovered during the excavations of the heroon belong to the pilasters from the back of the small monument[1]. They fit well with other early Imperial Corinthian capitals at Sagalassos. The oldest preserved early Imperial examples in the city are the nicely carved capitals of the honorific columns on the upper agora, which can be dated to the second half of the reign of Augustus (Vandeput 1997: 46-47, 49, pls 13.2, 15.2, 16.1-2). Although strong similarities between the capitals are obvious, significant differences should be noted as well. In general, the rows of acanthus leaves on the pilaster capitals seem to reach slightly higher than those of the capitals of the honorific columns. As a consequence, helices and volutes rise less steeply to the abacus, but really seem to bear its weight. Also, the helices and volutes of the capitals of the NW heroon are clearly supported by the bracts from which they grow. These elements seem to indicate a further developed apparatus in carving the pilaster capitals of the heroon than those of the honorific columns. The drilling, however, is less pronounced than on the capitals of the SW Gate of the lower agora at Sagalassos, a monument that was dated to the reign of Tiberius (Vandeput 1997: 58-59, 63, pl. 22.1-2). The modelling of the few fully finished leaves is also more delicate than the carving of the leaves of the SW Gate of the lower agora.

In spite of the fact that the capitals of the NW Heroon were clearly executed at some point in the later Augustan period, certain elements of the carving differ from those of the other monuments at Sagalassos. One example is the treatment of the individual lobes. Those of the pilaster capitals are significantly smaller, more strongly pointed and carved less deeply, which gives a very dry appearance to the ornament of the pilaster capitals of the NW Heroon.

Not only were pilaster capitals unearthed during the excavations of the NW Heroon, but also a badly damaged Corinthian capital (Fig. 42), which turned up in the excavations immediately north of the heroon. It was found lying on layer 7 and partially covered by layer 6. Although the position of the capital could suggest at first sight that it belonged to the heroon, its acanthus is worked in a completely different way from elsewhere on this monument.

Nothing is preserved of the decoration that must originally have covered the upper half of the capital, as opposed to the leaves of the rows of acanthus, a larger part of which has survived. These leaves are more slender than those of the pilaster capitals and unlike the latter, the leaves of the lower row are partly placed in front of the upper row, thus creating a very high relief and a very delicate play of light and shadow. Unlike a strict arrangement with a central mid-rib and a small number of clearly cut flanking veins, several slightly opening veins accompany the mid-rib of the leaves of the column capital, providing a more dynamic and coherent idea of the leaf. The leaflets of the individual leaves are also of a different appearance. Unlike the leaves on the pilaster capitals, those of the column capital are not really grouped in a fan-like arrangement, but the lobes of the larger leaflets are placed two by two. The outline of the leaf as a whole is thus much more respected than in the leaves of

---

[1] The capitals were never finished, as the different treatment of the individual leaves clearly shows. On very few only was the carving articulating the mid-rib indicated. On one of the pilaster capitals, the caules are hardly worked, while those of the other capital are carefully finished.

the pilaster capitals. All this indicates a different date for the capital and the pilaster capitals, and consequently the capital cannot originally have belonged to the NW Heroon. A close examination revealed, however, that it strongly resembles the half-column capital that was found in the courtyard of the bouleuterion and dated to the beginning of the first century BC by Waelkens (in Mitchell *et al.* 1987: 42; Vandeput 1997: pl. 4.1). The capital probably therefore originated from there, but it is not clear when it was removed from its original position. It was found in the upper part of a fourth century AD fill, but because of its weight, it may have sunk into this position and have been part of the sixth century AD earthquake debris that was dumped here.

A further motif that offers clues for the construction date of the monument is the Lesbian cyma. A nicely worked example decorates the door lintel of the heroon (Fig. 43). As Waelkens has said earlier (Waelkens *et al.* 1997: 182), it is a fully developed stirrup-framed cyma, but compared to the examples of the Temple of Augustus at Antioch, the stem of the intermediate flower is less marked and much thinner (Rumscheid 1994 II: pl. 7, 5-6). A better parallel is offered by a Lesbian cyma from the Temple at Ankyra, where the examples from the top mouldings of the architraves of the pronaos especially (Rumscheid 1994 II: pl. 4,4) compare well with those of the door-lintel at Sagalassos. In both cases, the intermediate flowers are composed of two petals and an extra central element that distinguishes them from the commonly depicted two-petalled intermediate flowers in Asia Minor and seems to be an attempt to give them a more floral appearance. A florally worked Lesbian cyma also decorates the top moulding of the wall frieze of the Temple at Ankyra and clearly recalls western examples, where this type of cyma was very popular in the early-Imperial period. Rather simply worked intermediate flowers, not unlike the examples at Sagalassos, appear for instance on the architraves of the Forum of Augustus in Rome (Leon 1971: pl. 68, 1) and seem to indicate that the shape of this motif, too, goes back to western influences.

The rather roughly worked kymation on the cornice of the cella door is more difficult to place (Fig. 44). It is executed in a shallow relief only and the intermediate flowers consist of two small petals represented by a drill hole and a very small stem. Unlike the example from the door lintel, the stem of these intermediate flowers does not reach down between successive stirrups. This kyma therefore provides a less developed example than that of the hyperthyrion. Its shallow and unclear execution is most probably because it must have hardly been visible on the lowest moulding of the cornice above the door.

The larger crowning anthemion (Fig. 44), on the contrary, was probably well visible and was therefore given a more elaborate treatment. The anthemion is composed of closed palmettes, alternating with lotus flowers. Anthemia of such composition frequently occur in the Hellenistic period, but in this example the adjacent elements do not touch, a feature which became especially fashionable from the early Imperial period onwards and which already appears on Honorific Monument I on the upper agora at Sagalassos (Vandeput 1997: 44, pl. 12.1). Another significant detail is the small sheating leaf in front of the central leaf of the palmettes, a small addition which occurs especially on early Imperial monuments and is found for example on the SW Gate of the lower agora at Sagalassos (Vandeput 1997: 60, pl. 22.3). Altogether, the decorated patterns discussed above indicate that the NW Heroon was built during the early Imperial period, more specifically during the reign of Augustus. Several decorative elements, such as the anthemion and the pilaster capitals, compare very well with other early Imperial monuments at Sagalassos and permit us to fit the decoration of the heroon into already known early Imperial decorative patterns.

Other parts, however, are carved differently from comparable elements at Sagalassos. One example of this is the tendril that decorates the wall frieze of the heroon. It can be assumed that the early Imperial tendril friezes in Asia Minor heavily depend on western examples. The best parallels for the frieze at Sagalassos are seen on the Temples of Augustus at Pisidian Antioch and at Ankyra, two monuments that frequently attracted attention because of the western influences in their decoration. But, while these examples show a marked relationship to the Italian decoration from the second half of the reign of Augustus, influenced by the Ara Pacis Augustae, that at Sagalassos rather seems to reflect features of tendrils from the early Augustan period in Italy. Apart from the tendril, the acanthus of the acanthus bushes and their basal leaves as well as the Lesbian kymation on the door lintel reveal strong similarities with examples from the West.

The existence of this clear influence from the West in the early Imperial decoration from the heroon at Sagalassos, can probably be related to the fact that the area was incorporated into the Roman empire after the death of king Amyntas in 25 BC. Consequently, several Roman colonies were founded in Pisidia and thousands of veterans of Augustus's army were settled in the area around Sagalassos (Mitchell 1993: 70-79). It can therefore be assumed that the inhabitants of Sagalassos became familiar with decorative techniques, influenced by Italian fashion via the large building programmes in these colonies, of which nearby Pisidian Antioch was the most important. It is also possible that the veterans of Italian origin who were settled through the whole region had themselves a direct knowledge of Italian design.

4. TYPOLOGY AND FUNCTION OF THE NORTH WEST HEROON (Ch. Berns)

Perhaps the most striking feature of the monument's appearance was its hybrid form, which combined elements not

Fig. 42: Sagalassos, near NW Heroon. Capital found during the excavations.

Fig. 43: Sagalassos, NW Heroon. Detail of the door lintel.

Fig. 44: Sagalassos, NW Heroon. Cornice above the door.

Fig. 45: Sagalassos, NW Heroon, dancers frieze from the west side.

Fig. 46: Sagalassos, NW Heroon, first and second dancer from the south side.

Fig. 47: Sagalassos, NW Heroon, central dancer on the south side.

Fig. 48: Sagalassos, NW Heroon, fourth dancer on the east side.

Fig. 49: Sagalassos, NW Heroon, third and fourth dancer on the west side.

belonging together traditionally (Figs 2-3). The upper part of the building, for example, had the shape of a small temple. Its corners were articulated by pilasters bearing an entablature and a gabled roof. The front may be imagined as having two columns in antis, even if the Corinthian capital that had been previously assumed to belong to the monument did not in fact do so (Vandeput this article, s.v. 3). Unlike a normal temple, however, a monumental frieze had been fitted between its stylobate and the lower layers of the krepis (Figs 2-3). This frieze shows motifs well known from luxurious marble objects such as candelabras or vases (Cain 1985; Grassinger 1991 – see below). Moreover, the temple and the frieze have been placed on a high podium, which must have made the temple a prominent feature of the skyline of Sagalassos, at the same time preventing the building from being used as place of ritual as nobody was able to enter it.

As the 'heroon' appears to have been a highly individual monument, there is no point in looking for exact typological parallels or even antecedents. In general, however, the shape of the 'heroon' is reminiscent of monumental tombs of the second and first century BC such as the Lion Monument at Knidos (Newton 1863: 480 pl. 51-66) or the so-called Oktogon at Ephesos (Fig. 52) (Thür 1990). These and similar monuments were nearly of the same size and also show a close structural parallel in the use of various architectural units presented on a high podium.

4.1. The temple

The most characteristic architectural unit of the 'heroon' at Sagalassos was the small temple, which formed a considerable part of the whole monument and was elaborately worked in its decorative details (Vandeput this article, s.v. 3). Small temples like this were to be found in numerous places within the cities of the Hellenistic world (see Lauter 1986: 189-194). They served not only for the worship of gods, but also the honour of private individuals, for example, the small Doric prostylos on the Agora of Assos. This was the tomb of two brothers who had been benefactors of their city and are called "Heroes" in the inscription on the architrave (Clarke *et al.* 1902: 109-117 with figures; Merkelbach 1976: 59 no. 27). In contrast to this and other examples, however, the temple at Sagalassos is decorated in the Corinthian order. This gives the building a more sumptuous appearance, which is also stressed by the wall frieze showing carefully carved tendrils with a great variety of flowers (Figs 38-39).

4.2. The dancers' frieze

As we have said above, a monumental frieze had complemented the architecture of the temple, between the stylobate and the rest of the krepis. This frieze shows several girls performing a round dance, joined by holding the ends of each other's garments. Every dancer is presented as an isolated figure in an individual pose. This kind of composition is well known from the so-called Neo-Attic reliefs, a type of marble furniture very popular in the late Hellenistic and early Imperial periods. The respective pieces are decorated with figural scenes, mostly taken from a certain repertoire of often, although not only, classical models (cp. e.g. Fuchs 1959; Cain and Dräger 1994).

In the frieze at Sagalassos the basic pattern is a group of three girls linked to each other by holding the ends of their garments. The oldest examples of this pattern are known from Hellenistic votive reliefs of the nymphs, which originate from Attica. The lost original is assumed to date from around 340/30 BC on the grounds of style (Svoronos 1908: 443 no. 144 pl. 73; 451 no. 148 pl. 74; Fuchs 1959: 21-27 [Type A]). In the decoration of 'Neo-Attic' products this three-figure group of girls was widely used in various contexts. For the frieze of the 'heroon', however, it was extended to a total of 15 dancers, each based on the 'Neo-Attic' repertoire. The first dancer on the east side, for example, which was later copied as the middle dancer on the south side (Fig. 47) is a girl wearing a thick garment. Moving to the right, the upper part of her body is turned to the observer and her head is looking back. It is one of the figures from the early Hellenistic votive reliefs mentioned above (see Svoronos 1908: 451 no. 148 pl. 74 – the right one), which was also used for later marble furniture. On a puteal of about the middle of the second century BC, in the Villa Albani, the figure is shown the other way round bringing up the rear of a round dance (Fig. 51) (Cain in: Bol 1990: 236-248 no. 219 fig. 2 pl. 172; Golda 1997: 100-101 no. 49 pl. 18,4 Beil. 15,2). The central figure of the same group (Cain in: Bol 1990 pl. 171; Golda *loc. cit.*) corresponds to the fourth dancer from the east side of the Sagalassos frieze (Fig. 48). The fourth figure on the west side of that frieze is a Maenad moving to the right (Fig. 49). Standing on the tip of her toes, the upper part of her body turned to the front, she carries a thyrsus on her shoulder. The same type can be found in the decoration of some candelabras (cp. Cain 1985: 129 "Mänade 5" with Beil. 12). The "dancer with cithara" from the south side (Fig. 46) is also a figure familiar on decorative products. Probably going back to a Hellenistic statue type of Apollo Kitharoidos, it was already used for the decoration of so-called "Applikenkeramik", where its precise meaning remains unclear (see Bruneau 1991: 624 no. 33 with fig.; Hübner 1993: 146-147; 203 no. 256 fig. 32 pl. 54). At about the same time, the figure occurs as a female dancer on late Hellenistic marble puteals (Golda 1997: 58 "Tänzerin 1" with Beil. 13). To the right of the "dancer with cithara" eventually appears a girl in front view (Fig. 46). Her beautifully draped garment creates the effect of a *parapetasma* . While the long *chiton* fans out at the bottom, the *himation*, wrapped round both arms, is blown into a half circle behind the head of the dancer. The same type is used on a puteal that used to be in the Antiquario Municipale in Rome (Golda 1997: 59 "Tänzerin 7" Beil. 13).

The use of these patterns, well known from marble furniture, for the embellishment of a monumental building is at first surprising. It is reminiscent of a number of round friezes that have been found in different places of the Mediterranean world. Examples include several copies of a frieze of Maenads (see Caputo 1948: 6-10, 14-16 with references to earlier publications) as well as friezes with dancers from the Via Praenestina in Rome (von Steuben in: Helbig 1969: 49-50 no. 2148; Froning 1981: 125-131), from Pergamon (Fig. 50) (Winter 1908: 272-277 no. 344 pl. 38; Mendel 1913: 198-301 no. 575) and from Ancona (Pellegrini 1910: 358-359 fig. 26)[1]. While most of these monuments seem to date from the Imperial period, the frieze from the Via Praenestina is dated to the middle of the first century BC and the one from Pergamon to the middle of the second century BC (Fuchs 1959: 153-154; Froning 1981: 125-131). Thus, both are older than the monument at Sagalassos. Being between ca. 1.50 and 2 m high with diameters between ca. 1.50 and 2.30 m, these friezes will have formed part of some small construction in each case, although their precise function is difficult to determine. However, two of them, the one in Ancona and the one from Via Praenestina, were found in the area of a necropolis[2] and therefore most probably belonged to a funerary monument. In view of their round shape they may well have decorated the podium of a small monopteros bearing the portrait statue of the deceased. The frieze from Pergamon may have had a similar function. Reused into a late wall near the Upper Agora it is sometimes interpreted as part of a choregic monument. It need not necessarily be connected with the Dionysic sphere, however, but may actually have belonged to any kind of votive monument in the public space or may have been part of a small round base for a statue.

The round dance shown on the friezes may then be intended to refer to some aspect of the person commemorated by the monument, as has already been suggested by Fleischer (1979: 304-306) with respect to the example from Sagalassos. Without having a precise meaning, the iconography generally alludes to rituals depicted on Dionysic altars (cp. e.g. Fraser 1977: 31 no. 165 fig. 85f) and thereby implies that the person honoured is deserving of a cultic worship. Despite the iconographic parallels between the round monuments and the 'heroon' frieze, the latter remains unique, however. This is not so much for its quality or dimension (it is of course much longer, but at 1.80 m scarcely higher than that from Pergamon, for example, with a preserved height of 1.45 m) but for its integration into a comparatively large building[3].

4.3. The podium

The third element of the architecture of the 'heroon' was the approximately 2.80 metres high podium. Panelled with plain ashlar and crowned with a simple upper moulding it was of a very restrained shape. It seems likely, therefore, that its only purpose was to raise the small temple placed on it. At the same time, it detached the monument from the observer, who was not able to enter or even approach the temple, but could only look at it from a certain distance.

Such podia were familiar among monumental tombs and memorial architecture of the late Hellenistic period, and they always have the described effect. A good example is the already mentioned 'Oktogon' at Ephesos, an octagonal temple with a pyramidal roof placed on a podium more than three metres high (Fig. 52) (Thür 1990: 47 fig. 3). Here, as with the 'heroon' at Sagalassos, it was not possible to enter the podium, so that the seats arranged within the peristasis appeared as a mere architectural formula. The same goes for the cella that is ostensibly placed in the centre of the peristasis, which in fact is a massive construction with a false door. In contrast to the later monuments, examples from the early Hellenistic period give out different message, for example, in the so-called Charmyleion at Kos (Fig. 53) (see Schazmann 1934). Here two doors dominate the front of the podium. The monument could be entered through these, so that people could not only examine it from distance, but could also to interact with the architecture – a message also stressed by the size and the beautiful carving of the doors.

4.4. The function of the monument

It is instructive to consider the function of the 'heroon' by starting from two striking features connected with one another – its hybrid shape and its isolation from the onlooker. Both clearly show that the purpose of the monument was not to define ritual space, as one would expect from a heroon in its original sense. Admittedly, the term 'heroon' is generally used in a wide range of meanings, often just to describe a monumental tomb (e.g. Kader 1995). Similarly, the term 'Heros' is not applied consistently in the sources of the Hellenistic and Roman period (see Fraser 1977: 76-81). It is, however, useful to restrict the use of the term to a precise meaning and to understand it as describing the place of an institutionalised cult of a Heros (e.g. Deneken 1886-90: 2491-2496). This Heros, then, can be an old city founder, as for example Battos at Kyrene, but he can also be a rich man announcing himself as a person who deserves a cult, like the

---

[1] I am indebted to H. von Hesberg for helpful hints on these friezes.
[2] This fact is explicitly mentioned for the frieze from Ancona (cp. Pellegrini 1910: 358-359). On the Via Praenestina, as on all major roads to Rome, several tomb monuments have been found (cp. e.g. Quilici 1977).
[3] A similar, but much smaller frieze from Sagalassos is kept in the Museum of Burdur, but has not yet been published in detail. For preliminary pictures, see Waelkens (1993) Figs 20-22.

Fig.50: Istanbul, Arkeoloji Müzesi, Round frieze from Pergamon (photo: Staatliche Museen zu Berlin; plan: after Winter 1908: nr 344, abb. 342 A).

Fig. 51: Rome, Villa Albani Marble puteal (after Golda 1997: Pl. 18,4).

Fig. 52: Ephesos, Oktogon (after Thür 1990: 46 Fig. 3).

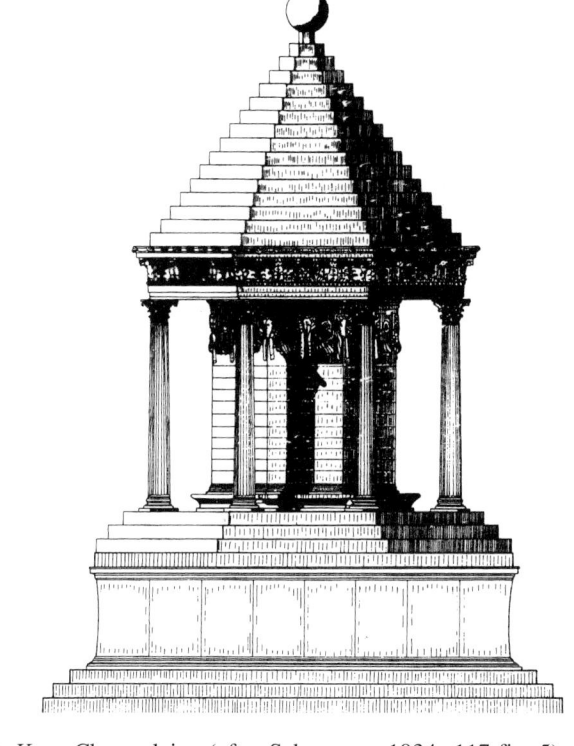

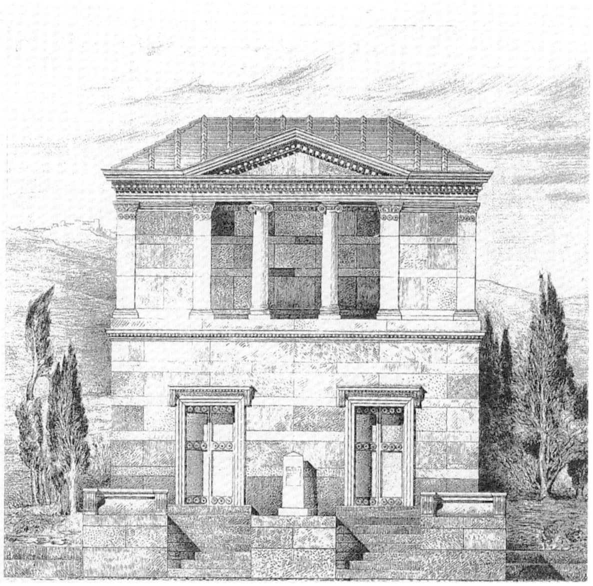

Fig. 53: Kos: Charmyleion (after Schazmann 1934: 117 fig. 5).

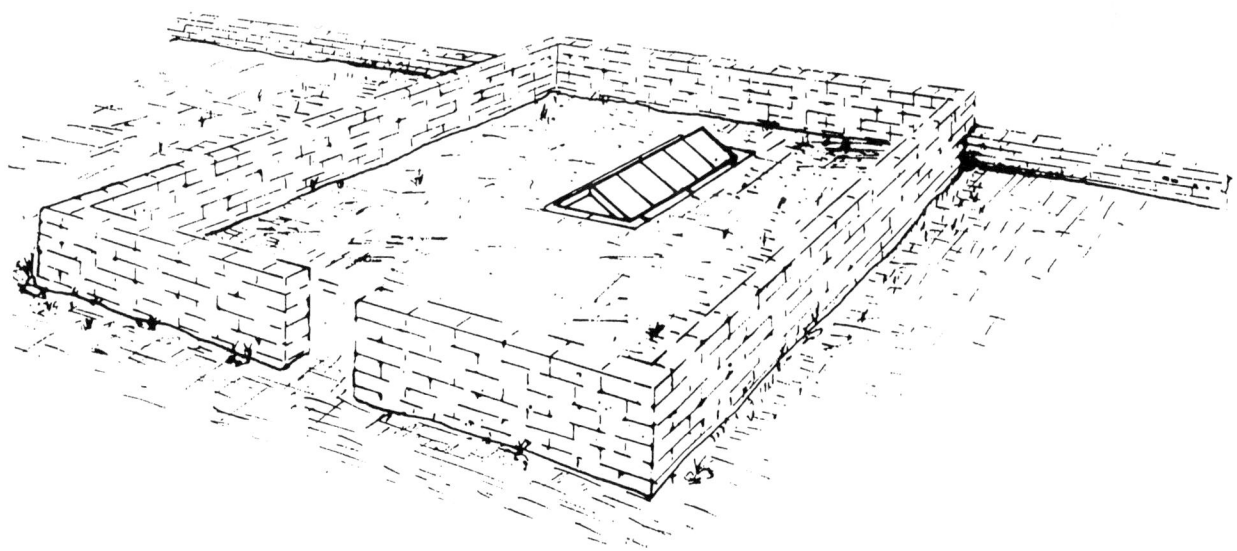

Fig. 54: Kyrene, Heroon of Battos (after Stucchi 1965: 143 Fig. 76).

well-known Leon at Kalydon in the second century BC. While the Heroon of Battos, after a renovation in the fourth century BC during the Hellenistic and Imperial period, consisted of a simple tomb monument within a walled temenos (Fig. 54) (Stucchi 1965: 139-142), the one of Leon was more sumptuous. There, several chambers embellished with architectural decoration and sculptures were arranged round a spacious courtyard (Dyggve *et al.* 1934). From the outside, however, the building appeared extremely reserved and it seems as if, like the Heroon of Battos, the main purpose of the Leonideion was to define ritual space.

The message of the 'Northwest Heroon' at Sagalassos was perhaps opposite to that. Of course, the temple architecture and the frieze seem to have been suggesting that the honorand deserved cult, too. But, as the cult could not have been practised at the monument itself, these elements rather announced a certain quality of the honoured person than actually requiring ritual actions. Moreover, they were part of a more complex statement about the honorand. This included the general richness of the decoration and the frieze pattern familiar on luxurious marble furniture, both speaking of this person's presumed wealth, as well as the exposed place of the 'heroon' within the monumental city centre, showing his or her importance for Sagalassos. Furthermore, there was also apparently a colossal marble statue of a young men in heroic pose in the small temple, thereby complementing the message of the monument (Waelkens *et al.* 1997: 184).

The 'Northwest Heroon' thus speaks a language typical of monumental tombs or memorials of private individuals[1] in the late Hellenistic period and on into the Augustan period. Numerous examples of this kind of architecture have been erected along the so-called Kuretenstraße in Ephesos, where they functioned as a medium of competition in the local society (Kader 1995: 212-220; Berns in press). Their different designs show attempts to outdo existing monuments by the innovative forms of the new ones. Moreover, the varying elements might stress different qualities of the honoured person, as we have already said in connection with the 'heroon' at Sagalassos. It is often difficult to decide whether these monuments were actually tombs or honorific monuments, because the burials may have been very simple. But in view of the structural parallels between, for example, the mentioned 'Oktogon' (Fig. 52), which has a burial chamber, and the so-called Memmiusbau in Ephesos, which has not, the question is perhaps less important. In any case, both monuments were elements in the local competitiveness. In a similar way, the 'Northwest Heroon' at Sagalassos may have been an answer to the 'Northeast Heroon', erected perhaps a few years earlier about hundred metres to the east (Waelkens in: Kosmetatou *et al.* 1997: 356-357).

5. ACKNOWLEDGEMENTS

This text presents the results of the Belgian Programme on Interuniversity Poles of Attraction initiated by the Belgian State, Prime Minister's Office, Science Policy Programming (IUAP G/12). This research was also made possible thanks to an FWO-Vlaanderen research grant (FWO/G.0215.96) and to a GOA-programme (97/2). Scientific responsibility is assumed by its authors.

6. REFERENCES

W. Alzinger (1974) *Augusteïsche Architektur in Ephesos* (*Sonderschriften herausgegeben vom österreichischen archäologischen Institut in Wien* 16) Vienna.

Ch. Berns (in press) *Kleinasiatische Grab- und Memorialbauten des späten Hellenismus und der frühen Kaiserzeit*.

P. Bol (1990) (ed.) *Forschungen zur Villa Albani. Katalog der antiken Bildwerke II*, Berlin.

Chr. Börker (1973) Neuattisches und pergamenisches an den Ara Pacis-Ranken, *Jahrbuch des deutschen archäologischen Instituts* 88: 283-317.

Ph. Bruneau (1991) La céramique pergaménienne à reliefs appliqués de Délos, *Bulletin de Correspondance Hellénique* 115: 597-666.

H.U. Cain (1985) *Römische Marmorkandelaber*, Mainz.

H.U. Cain and O. Dräger (1994) Die sogenannten neuattischen Werkstätten, in: G. Hellenkemper-Salies (ed.) *Das Wrack. Der antike Schiffsfund von Mahdia Vol. 2*, Bonn, 809-829.

G. Caputo (1948) *Lo scultore del grande bassorelievo con la danza delle Menadi in Tolemaide di Cirenaica*, Rome

J.T. Clarke, F.H. Bacon and R. Koldewey (1902) *Investigations at Assos*, Cambridge, Mass.

F. Deneken (1886-90) Heros, in: W.H. Roscher, *Ausführliches Lexikon der griechischen und römischen Mythologie I 2*, Leipzig: 2441-2589.

E. Dyggve, F. Poulsen and K. Rhomaios (1934) *Das Heroon von Kalydon*, Copenhague.

R. Fleischer (1979) Forschungen in Sagalassos 1972 und 1974, *Istanbuler Mitteilungen* 29: 273- 307.

R. Fleischer (1981) Der hellenistische Fries von Sagalassos in Pisidien, *Antike Welt* 12.1: 3-16.

R. Fleischer (1984) Zur Datierung des Frieses von Sagalassos, *Archäologischer Anzeiger*: 141- 144.

P.M. Fraser (1977) *Rhodian Funerary Monuments*, Oxford.

H. Froning (1981) *Marmor-Schmuckreliefs mit griechischen Mythen im 1.Jh. v. Chr.* (*Schriften zur antiken Mythologie* 5) Mainz.

W. Fuchs (1959) *Die Vorbilder der neuattischen Reliefs* (*20. Jahrbuch des deutschen archäologischen Instituts. Ergänzungsheft*) Berlin.

Th. Golda (1997) *Puteale und verwandte Monumente*, Mainz.

D. Grassinger (1991) *Römische Marmorkratere*, Mainz.

W.D. Heilmeyer (1970) *Korinthische Normalkapitelle. Studien zur Geschichte der römischen Architekturdekoration* (*Mitteilungen des deutschen Archaeologischen Instituts. 26. Ergänzungsheft*) Heidelberg.

---

[1] The presumed identification of the colossal statue just mentioned with Alexander the Great (cp. Waelkens *et al.* 1997: 184) is in my opinion less probable. Its head shows only general similarities to the known Alexander portraits, which may easily be explained by the influence of the Alexander portrait on the image of the Hellenistic hero in general (cp. Hölscher 1971: 43-51).

W. Helbig (1969) *Führer durch die öffentlichen Sammlungen klassischer Altertümer in Rom*, 4th ed. Vol. III, Tübingen.

G. Hirschfeld (1880) Vorläufiger Bericht über eine Reise im südwestlichen Kleinasien, *Monatsberichte der Königlichen Preussischen Akademie der Wissenschaften Berlin* 1879 : 299-312.

Th. Hölscher (1971) *Ideal und Wirklichkeit in den Bildnissen Alexanders des Großen* (Abhandlungen der Heidelberger Akademie der Wissenschaften, Phil.-Hist. Klasse) Heidelberg.

G. Hübner (1993) *Die Applikenkeramik von Pergamon* (Pergamenische Forschungen 7) Berlin.

I. Kader (1995) Heroa und Memorialbauten in: M. Wörrle and P. Zanker (eds) *Stadtbild und Bürgerbild im Hellenismus* (Vestigia 47) München: 199-229.

E. Kosmetatou, L. Vandeput and M. Waelkens (1997) The NE "Heroon" at Sagalassos in: M. Waelkens and J. Poblome (eds) *Sagalassos IV. Report on the Survey and Excavation Campaigns of 1994 and 1995* (Acta Archaeologica Lovaniensia Monographiae 9) Leuven University Press: 353-366.

Th. Kraus (1953) *Die Ranken der Ara Pacis. Ein Beitrag zur Entwicklungsgeschichte der augusteïschen Ornamentik*, Berlin.

D. Krencker and M. Schede (1936) *Der Tempel in Ankara* (Denkmäler antiker Architektur 3) Berlin-Leipzig.

K. Lanckoronski (1892) *Städte Pamphyliens und Pisidiens. I. Pisidien*, Wien-Prag-Leipzig.

H. Lauter (1986) *Die Architektur des Hellenismus*, Darmstadt.

Ch. Leon (1971) *Die Bauornamentik des Trajansforums und ihre Stellung in der früh-und mittelkaiserzeitlichen Architekturdekoration Roms* (Publikationen des österreichischen Kulturinstituts in Rom. 1. Abteilung. Abhandlungen 4) Vienna.

L. Loots, M. Waelkens and F. Depuydt (2000) The City Fortifications of Sagalassos from the Hellenistic to the late-Roman period, in: M. Waelkens and L. Loots (eds) *Sagalassos V. Report on the Survey and Excavation Campaigns of 1996 and 1997* (Acta Archaelogica Lovaniensia Monographiae 10) Leuven, University Press: 595-634.

F. Martens (in press) Urban water management at Sagalassos. Studying urban development from an hydrological perspective, in: K. Demoen (ed.) *The Greek City from Antiquity to the Present. Historical Reality, Philosophical Concept, Literary Representation*, Leuven.

G. Mendel (1913) *Catalogue des Sculptures Grecques, Romains et Byzantines aux Musées Impériaux Ottomans* Vol. 2, Istanbul.

R. Merkelbach (1976) *Die Inschriften von Assos* (Inschriften griechischer Städte aus Kleinasien 4) Bonn.

S. Mitchell and M. Waelkens (1987) Sagalassus and Cremna 1986, *Anatolian Studies* 37: 37-48.

S. Mitchell and M. Waelkens (1988) Cremna and Sagalassus 1987, *Anatolian Studies* 38: 53-65.

S. Mitchell (1993) *Anatolia, Land, Men and Gods in Asia Minor I. The Celts in Anatolia and Impact of Roman Rule*, Claredon Press-Oxford.

S. Mitchell and M. Waelkens (1998) *Pisidian Antioch. The Site and its Monuments*, London.

L. Moens, P. De Paepe and M. Waelkens (1997) An archaeometric provenance study of white marble sculptures from Sagalassos (Turkey), in: M. Waelkens and J. Poblome (eds) *Sagalassos IV. Report on the Survey and Excavation Campaigns of 1994 and 1995* (Acta Archaeologica Lovaniensia Monographiae 9) Leuven University Press: 367-383.

C.T. Newton (1863) *A History of Discoveries in Halicarnassus, Cnidus and Branchidae*, London.

G. Pellegrini (1910) Ancona, *Notizie degli Scavi* 1910: 333-366.

J. Poblome (1995) Sherds and Coins. A Question of Chronology, in M. Waelkens and J. Poblome (eds) *Sagalassos III. Report on the Fourth Excavation Campaign of 1993* (Acta Archaeologica Lovaniensia Monographiae 7) Leuven University Press: 177-205.

L. Quilici (1977) *La Via Prenestina. I suoi monumenti, i suoi paesaggi*, Rome.

D.M. Robinson (1926) Roman Sculptures from Colonia Caesarea (Pisidian Antioch), *The Art Bulletin* 9: 5-69.

F. Rumscheid (1994) *Untersuchungen zur kleinasiatischen Bauornamentik des Hellenismus*, 2. Vol. (Beiträge zur Erschliessung hellenistischer und kaiserzeitlicher Skulptur und Architektur 14) Mainz.

P. Schazman (1934) Das Charmyleion, *Jahrbuch des deutschen archäologischen Instituts* 49: 110-127.

S. Scheers (2000) Coins found in 1996 and 1997, in: M.Waelkens and L. Loots (eds) *Sagalassos V. Report on the Survey and Excavation Campaigns of 1996 and 1997* (Acta Archaelogica Lovaniensia Monographiae 10) Leuven University Press: 509-552.

G. Schörner (1995) *Römische Rankenfriese* (Beiträge zur Erschließung hellenistischer und kaiserzeitlicher Skulptur und Architektur 15) Mainz.

S. Stucchi (1965) *L' agora di Cirene I* (Monografie di archeologia Libica 7) Rome.

J.N. Svoronos (1908) *Das Athener Nationalmuseum*, Athens.

H. Thür (1990) Arsinoe IV, eine Schwester Kleopatras VII, Grabinhaberin des Oktogons von Ephesos? Ein Vorschlag, *Jahreshefte des österreichischen Instituts* 60, 43-56.

L. Vandeput (1995) review of F. Rumscheid, *Untersuchungen zur kleinasiatischen Bauornamentik des Hellenismus*, 2. Vol, (Beiträge zur Erschließung hellenistischer und kaiserzeitlicher Skulptur und Architektur 14) Mainz 1994, *L'Antiquité Classique*: 533-535.

L. Vandeput (1997) *The Architectural Decoration in Roman Asia Minor. Sagalassos: a Case Study* (Studies in Eastern Mediterranean Archaeology 1) Turnhout.

M. Waelkens (1986) The Imperial Sanctuary at Pessinus: Archaeological, epigraphical and numismatic evidence for its date and identification, *Epigraphica Anatolica* 7: 37-73.

M. Waelkens (1993) Sagalassos. History and archaeology, in: M. Waelkens (ed.) *Sagalassos I First General Report on the Survey (1986-1989) and Excavations (1990-1991)* (Acta Archaeologica Lovaniensia Monographiae 5) Leuven University Press: 37-81.

M. Waelkens and S. Mitchell (1987) Sagalassus 1986, in: *V. Araştırma sonuçları Toplantısı*, Ankara: 231-246.

M. Waelkens, P.M. Vermeersch, E. Paulissen, E.J. Owens, B. Arıkan, M. Martens, P. Talloen, L. Gijsen, L. Loots, Ch. Peleman, J. Poblome, R. Degeest,T.C. Patrício, S. Ercan and F. Depuydt (1997) The 1994 and 1995 Excavation seasons at Sagalassos, in: M. Waelkens and J. Poblome (eds) *Sagalassos IV (Acta Archaeologica Lovaniensia Monographiae* 9) Leuven University Press: 103-216.

M. Waelkens and L. Vandeput (in press) Regionalism in Hellenistic and Roman Pisidia, in: H. Elton and G. Reger (eds) *Regionalism in Hellenistic and Roman Asia Minor. Trinity College, Hartford CT, 22-24 August 1997*.

F. Winter (1908) *Die Skulpturen, Altertümer von Pergamon* VII.2, Berlin.

THE CITY FORTIFICATIONS OF SAGALASSOS FROM THE HELLENISTIC TO THE LATE ROMAN PERIOD

Lieven LOOTS[1], Marc WAELKENS[1] and Frans DEPUYDT[2]

1 - Department of Archaelogy, KULeuven, Blijde Inkomststraat 21, B-3000 Leuven, Belgium
2 - Cartography, Department of Geography, KULeuven, Redingenstraat 16, B-3000 Leuven, Belgium

1. INTRODUCTION

The ancient city of Sagalassos is located at an elevation between 1450 and 1600 m on the lower south-facing slopes of the Ağlasun Dağları in the western Taurus mountain range. Above the city, the Ağlasun Dağları form a steep cuesta front, ca. 250 m high (Paulissen et al. 1993: 230). Despite its elevation, the city is relatively vulnerable to enemy attacks. Compared with the strategic position of other Pisidian cities such as Termessos (Winter 1966: 128) or Cremna (Mitchell 1989a: 311), Sagalassos is more easily accessible from the south, east, north and west. Thus, the existence of city fortifications from Hellenistic times onward, and probably even before, was not only probable, but a necessity. The remains of these fortifications are still partly visible at the site and in its immediate surroundings.

2. HISTORY

During its history, Sagalassos has been exposed to many military threats and has been involved in several military conflicts. In response, the inhabitants built an extensive defence system in and around the city and thus the military history of the city and of Pisidia should not be neglected. Xenophon (*Anabasis* I, 1.11) was the first author to mention the rebellious Pisidians and their defiant attitude to the Persian king. But the involvement of Sagalassos itself in an armed conflict is mentioned for the first time by Arrian (*Anabasis Alexandri* I, 28) describing how Alexander the Great attacked and conquered the city in 333 BC. His *Anabasis Alexandri* is the only source dealing with the pre-Hellenistic city fortifications at Sagalassos, of which no datable remains have been identified.

After Alexander's death the continuous feuding between the Hellenistic monarchs and the cities posed a regular threat to Pisidia. The Pisidians were a warlike people who not only fanatically defended themselves against foreign intruders, but who also fought one another. During inter-city conflicts, they often appealed to Hellenistic rulers for help, as for example Pednelissos did with Achaois in its conflict with Selge (see below). In conflicts with Helllenistic rulers, for example Eumenes II's campaign against Selge in 164 BC, they even invoked the help of the Roman senate (Bracke 1993: 17). As mercenaries, the Pisidians were popular in the armies of the Hellenistic monarchs. Alketas thus ruled over southern Asia Minor during the first years following Alexander's death (322-320 BC) with the help of an army mainly composed of Pisidians (Bracke 1993: 17). In 319 BC, however, he was defeated at Kretopolis by Antigonos Monophthalmos, who must have passed through Sagalassian territory on his way from Cappadocia to the battle field. Kretopolis has been positively identified by Mitchell as a site near Bucak, some 30 km south of Sagalassos (1994a: 129). Alketas managed to escape to Termessos, where he was supported by the younger citizens. Since close ties existed between Termessos and Sagalassos, as is illustrated by Alexander's military campaign, when Sagalassos received support from Termessian soldiers, it is possible that the young people of Sagalassos also supported Alketas. Even so, Alketas was betrayed by the elders of Termessos, and Antigonos eventually conquered the whole region. Thus, the greatest threat to Sagalassos during this period may have come from Antigonos rather than Alketas.

Antigonos himself was defeated by Lysimachos almost 20 years later, in the battle of Ipsos (301 BC) after which Lysimachos assumed control over southern Asia Minor. The troop movements of both parties in this war undoubtedly caused much disturbance throughout Anatolia. A similar upheaval may have occurred in the year 281 BC, when Lysimachos was defeated at Kouropedion by Seleukos I, who henceforth controlled Pisidia. But Pisidia remained a much disputed area. It may have been temporarily conquered by Attalos I, between 228 and 223 BC (Mitchell 1995a: 22). Afterwards, it was subject to the Seleucid usurper Achaios (218-216 BC), who in 218 BC, at the request of the Pednelissians, intervened in a conflict with Selge (Bracke 1993: 17; Mitchell 1994a: 129). Following Achaios' expulsion and death, Antiochos III seized power over the area, but in 193 BC had to deal with a revolt of Pisidians living to the north of Side, approximately 100 km south of Sagalassos (Bracke 1993: 17; Waelkens 1993a: 42). All this means that most conflicts between the Hellenistic monarchs were fought in or near Pisidia. During this period Pisidia had to face many other threats as well.

In the years 275-268 BC, at the time of the Seleucid domination over Pisidia, the Galatians ravaged the inland regions of Asia Minor (Mitchell 1993: 18). There are indications that these Celtic tribes, who succeeded in pushing through as far as Lymira on the south coast of Asia Minor, also either crossed, or passed near the territory of Sagalassos (Müller-Karpe 1989: 195; Vandorpe 1995: 299-305). They were ultimately defeated by Antiochos I, in a battle which earned him the cognomen 'Soter'.

Another eventual important player in the history of Asia Minor was Rome. In fact, the Romans were increasingly inclined to intervene directly into conflicts in Asia Minor. Thus, in 189 BC, Antiochos III was defeated by a coalition led by Rome in the battle of Magnesia. Following this victory the Roman general Cnaius Manlius Vulso undertook a campaign to punish the Galatians and other partners of the Seleucids (Grainger 1995). This journey brought him also to Sagalassos, which city had to pay a huge ransom as a punishment for not sending envoys to welcome him in its territory (Livy 38.15).

After the defeat of Antiochos III in Magnesia and the treaty of Apamea (188 BC), most of Pisidia had become part of the Attalid kingdom. In 165 BC Eumenes marched against Selge, as did his successor Attalos II some years later (Bracke 1993: 17). A possible friction between Pergamon and the Termessians who did not accept Attalid domination and even tried to expand their territory at the expense of the Attalid foundation Attaleia, may be illustrated by the Kapıkaya wall to the east of Termessos, built by the Attalids against possible Termessian attacks (Winter 1966: 127-132; Bracke 1993: 18).

Following the death of Attalos III in 133 BC, Rome inherited the Attalid kingdom. Its first task was to suppress a rebellion by Aristonikos. A few years later the Romans created the new province of Asia to which most of Pisidia may have belonged. In reality, however, Pisidia remained largely autonomous. Brigands and pirates operated undisturbed in the region right into the first century BC. With the exception of a campaign against the pirates in 102 BC, there were no Roman troops stationed in Asia Minor until the outbreak of the Mithridatic wars in the years 88-72 BC (Mitchell 1993: 29-30; Mitchell 1995a: 29). During these wars, Mithridates' troops conquered Lycia and Pamphylia. Termessos was even occupied by his general Eumachos. Not long after, however, Mithridates was defeated by the Roman general Lucullus and the autonomy of Termessos was re-established and henceforth guaranteed by the Romans. During the late Hellenistic period, the Romans once again were obliged to intervene against robbery and piracy in Pisidia and Pamphylia. In 77 BC the Roman general Publius Servilius Isauricus eventually defeated the pirate king Zeniketes. He also undertook a campaign against the Isaurians and further inland suppressed the Pisidian Orondeis (Ormerod 1992: 35-52; Bracke 1993: 19).

In 39 BC Mark Antony gave Pisidia and Phrygia Paroreios to the Galatian aristocrat Amyntas who, three years later, also acquired parts of Lycaonia and Pamphylia, and eventually became king of Galatia (Mitchell 1993: 38; Bracke 1993: 19). Amyntas tried to strengthen his position through a series of wars against the local tribes of the Taurus, from Cilicia through Pisidia as far as Phrygia Paroreios. One of the major conflicts in which the Pisidian cities were involved was the war to conquer Sandalion, a stronghold located at Sandal Asar to the east of Sagalassos (Waelkens et al. 1997a: 21-31). An inscription by the inhabitants of Typallion honoured the Termessian Trokondas as their "saviour and benefactor" in the Sandaliote war. Typallion has been tentatively identified by Mitchell and Waelkens with the Hellenistic site of Kapıkaya to the east of Sagalassos (Waelkens et al. 1997a: 22-29). Recently, however, the discovery of a *milliarium* at Patara describing the Lycian roads and their distances (to be published by S. Şahın) has cast some doubt upon this identification, since a hitherto unknown Typallion is located there to the southwest of Termessos. Unless there were two places with this toponym, the Kapıkaya site remains unidentified. Whatever the exact location of Typallion was, the Sandaliote war must certainly have directly affected Sagalassos (Waelkens et al. 1997a: 31). A probably military lookout (Ispır Deresi), discovered during the 1998 survey in the Ağlasunovası on the road to Sandalion might be related to this war (to be published in Sagalassos VI). Cremna, the southern neighbour of Sagalassos, was also besieged and eventually conquered by Amyntas (Mitchell 1994b: 96). It seems probable that Sagalassos and Selge signed a treaty with Amyntas to secure themselves, just as Termessos had done previously with the Romans (Mitchell 1994b: 104; Levick 1967: 27). Sagalassos in any case formed part of Amyntas' kingdom (Waelkens 1997a: 31). The Pisidian cities thus reacted differently to Amyntas' rule. Sagalassos may have lived through it, remaining largely unharmed. However, a Sagalassian decree for a Termessian citizen may reveal that during this period, Sagalassos had to face civilian unrest and internal strife (Mitchell 1994b: 97; Waelkens *et al.* 1997a: 31). In 25 BC Amyntas was killed in battle against the Homonadeis. The Romans now annexed his kingdom and created the province of Galatia, thus establishing Roman rule over Pisidia. To control the unruly district the Romans established five colonies in or near Pisidia, i.e. Antioch ad Pisidiam, Cremna, Parlais, Olbasa and Comama (Levick 1967: 33).

During the first three centuries of Roman rule the *Pax Romana* brought peace to Pisidia. Only during the second half of the third century AD did the Gothic invasions (AD 255-277) and the war with Zenobia of Palmyra (AD 270) directly threaten Anatolia. However, it is very unlikely that the Pisidian cities were much influenced by these events (Waelkens 1993a: 47). The first time that Sagalassos may have been confronted with a military campaign, although it was not directly involved in it, was the rebellion of the Isaurian chief Lydios, who established himself at Cremna, resulting in the siege and conquest of that city in AD 278 by the emperor Probus (Mitchell 1995a: 210). Towards the end of the fourth and the beginning of the fifth centuries AD, Sagalassos may have been threatened more directly by the revolt of the Ostrogothic mercenaries under Tribigild, in AD 399, and the following raids of the Isaurians during the years 404-406 AD (Waelkens 1993a: 48; Belke and Mersich 1990: 66). During the next centuries the city maintained, however, a relatively peaceful existence until it was finally abandoned at the time of the first Arab invasions, most likely mainly due to a massive earthquake which seems to have hit the city around the middle of the seventh century AD (Waelkens 1993a: 49; Waelkens *et al.* 2000a).

3. THE PRE-HELLENISTIC AND HELLENISTIC PERIOD

3.1. The pre-Hellenistic period

In his *Anabasis Alexandri* (I.28), Arrian, relying on second century BC sources, mentioned the siege of Sagalassos by Alexander the Great and the importance during this battle of a conical hill located "in front" of the city. The inhabitants of Sagalassos and a contingent of Termessians waited for Alexander on top of this hill, but were defeated after Alexander's heavily armed troops stormed it. Based upon Arrian's description this hill can only be identified with an impressive, conical hill located immediately to the south of the city. Arrian wrote that the hill "was as strong for defensive operations as the wall itself" (καὶ τότε τὸν λόφον τὸν πρὸ τῆς πόλεως ὅτι καὶ οὗτος οὐ μεῖον τοῦ τείχους ὀχυρὸς ἐς τὸ ἀπομάχεσθαι ἦν κατειληφότες προσέμενον). There is room for doubt whether this passage should be translated: "as strong [...] as **the wall itself**", or as "the hill in front of the city which was as strong for defensive operations as **a wall**". The small difference can have far reaching consequences. The first translation, which is to be preferred from an archaeological as well as from a philological point of view, indicates that Sagalassos was defended by a city wall during the pre-Hellenistic period. Indeed, Alexander's Hill alone, as it is called now, was not sufficient to defend the city. Whether or not the hill was fortified at that time and if so how this was organised is not clear for the moment. Arrian did not use the term φρούριον ("fortified stronghold"), meaning that it may not have been considered necessary to fortify the hill, given its steep and hardly accessible slopes. However, the use of ὀχυρὸς in a military context may indicate the existence of fortifications. It is possible that an earthen rampart or a wooden palisade once surrounded the hill top, perhaps only built in an attempt to withstand Alexander's troops. Thus, the hill would have played only a limited, albeit important role in controlling and protecting the southern approach to the city. If, however, the hill was the most important part of the city's defence system, it is most likely that it would have been permanently fortified and have become a φρούριον. Arrian also wrote that many of the defenders after their defeat "unencumbered (i.e. by armour) and knowing the country (i.e. the paths) got away easily", rather than hiding in the city. This should not be interpreted as meaning that the city was undefended. Rather, the escape routes to the city may have been blocked by Alexander's troops, or the defenders may have realised the hopeless situation. Moreover, the fact that Alexander, according to Arrian, "took the city by force" and lost some of his soldiers during this capture, may rather suggest that it was well protected. Anyhow, one can conclude that Alexander's Hill formed part of the defence system of the city and that the hill was located outside the city wall. Because of its strategical position dominating the ancient approach towards the city from the south, the hill may have resumed this function in later times, as is clear from the remains of a rubble wall surrounding its top (11 on Fig. 1). Inside this wall no remains of buildings are visible today.

The urbanistic expansion of Sagalassos from the first to the fifth century AD obliterated most if not all pre-Hellenistic fortifications. Some undatable stretches of wall may go back to this period, but they could also be Hellenistic or even Roman in date since they contain no obvious datable elements. One of these walls is located to the northeast of the promontory with the sanctuary of Antoninus Pius (12 on Fig. 1; Fig. 2).

3.2. The Hellenistic city wall

As is clear from the short summary of Pisidia's military history, the many threats and conflicts during the Hellenistic period must have necessitated the construction and constant adaptation of city walls. At Sagalassos only a small portion of these fortifications has been preserved. Most were probably dismantled as the result of the extensive building programmes during the Roman period. Only three sections of a late Hellenistic city wall may have survived. These sections have been identified mainly by their appearance and by their relation to the later Roman city wall (fourth to fifth century AD). No excavations in these areas of the site have been started yet. The first part of the late Hellenistic wall (wall section 1) lies to the west of the city centre. The second part (tower *f* in wall section 7) is located on the main north-south oriented street of the city, to the south of the lower agora. The third part of the wall (wall section 9) is situated to the west of the former.

Wall section 1, still visible on the site today, was part of the city's northern defences and is situated to the west of the monumental Roman city centre. It has been incorporated into the late Roman defences (Fig. 1). This re-used late Hellenistic part of the city wall can be distinguished from its late Roman counterpart by its appearance, by its ashlar structure and by its monumentality. Wall section 1, made of a pseudo-isodomic ashlar wall, is approximately 1.80 to 2.20 m wide and consists of two ashlar casings with a mortar and rubble fill. Within the 130 m long stretch of the wall the remains of four monumental towers can be identified. In one place the preserved height of the wall is 3.40 m (*e* on Fig.1; Fig. 3). The overall quality of the ashlar masonry, in which no *spolia* are incorporated, is much better than that of the late Roman city wall. However, traces of later Roman repairs such as the incorporation of re-used cornice blocks in the wall between tower *a* and *b* are apparent. The four monumental towers testify that the wall was originally very carefully planned, unlike the late Roman city wall. Both the pseudo-isodomic ashlar masonry and the use of mortar as a fill between the inner and outer casing indicate a late Hellenistic date (Winter 1971: 325; Lawrence 1979: 209-210). Towards the south, the wall is connected to wall section 10, running through the valley. Towards the east, it connects with wall section 2, running up the slope towards the Doric temple (see 4.3.2).

The remains of four towers in wall section 1 can be reconstructed as more or less rectangular towers measuring 8 m by 8 m to 10 m by 10 m and consisting of 2 m thick walls with an inner and an outer casing filled with mortar and rubble (Fig. 4). The lower floors of the towers seem to have a fill of stones and earth. Due to the positioning of the wall, which is not the best strategically, the towers stand close to one another (see below). All the towers project to the north, that is, to the outside of the wall. The towers are built at an oblique angle to the wall, eliminating blind spots in the firing field of the defenders (Winter 1971: 197-198). The shape of the towers alone does not permit a precise dating. During the Hellenistic period the shape of a tower was mainly based on the preference of the architects and no chronological implications can be extracted from its plan, in contrast to the towers of the archaic and classical period (Winter 1971: 200). But Mitchell believes that small square towers, with neat masonry and incorporating a vault are typical of the late Hellenistic military architecture of Pamphylia and Pisidia. Examples can be found at Side, Perge, Sia, Adada and Pednelissos (Mitchell 1995a: 47). One corner of tower *d* is still standing, with a height of approximately 7 m (Fig. 5) and with a cornice moulding 3.50 m above the ground. Similar cornice mouldings are also found in a tower at Herakleia on the Latmos, dating to the end of the fourth and the beginning of the third century BC (Krischen 1922: 41-42). At Herakleia this moulding carried off rain water from an open platform on top of the tower. The cornice moulding in tower *d* at Sagalassos may have had a similar function, but this is by no means sure. Above the moulding, the tower rises another 3.50 m, implying that above this level, there was at least one room, most likely roofed. Fragments of roof tiles found among the remains of the tower also support such a reconstruction. Thus, the cornice moulding would mark an upper floor level inside the tower. The possible function of carrying off rain water should not be excluded completely. A pierced cornice has been re-used in the wall between tower *a* and *b*, showing that at least this cornice fragment functioned as a gutter at some time. It is by no means certain, however, whether this cornice belonged to one of the towers or to another building. It may simply have been re-used while repairing the wall during the late Roman period. Fragments of roof tiles clarify that towers *a* and *b* were also roofed and may have had similar cornice mouldings. The re-use of the cornices clearly indicates that, when the Sagalassians incorporated wall section 1 into their late Roman city wall, they also partially rebuilt it. During the early and middle Imperial period, however, the wall had probably remained untouched since it was located away from the monumental city centre.

The position of wall section 1 on top of a cliff, which slopes down steeply inside the wall, and at the foot of a steep mountain slope, does not at first seem very reasonable from a defensive point of view. In fact, the slope immediately to the north of the wall is broken by a vertical cliff rising ca. 25 m, above which a Roman road runs towards the northwest. An enemy positioned on top of this cliff would seem to have been able to harass the city undisturbed. However, it was almost impossible to take heavy siege machinery up the steep slopes from the south, while the barrier walls on the other side of the mountain

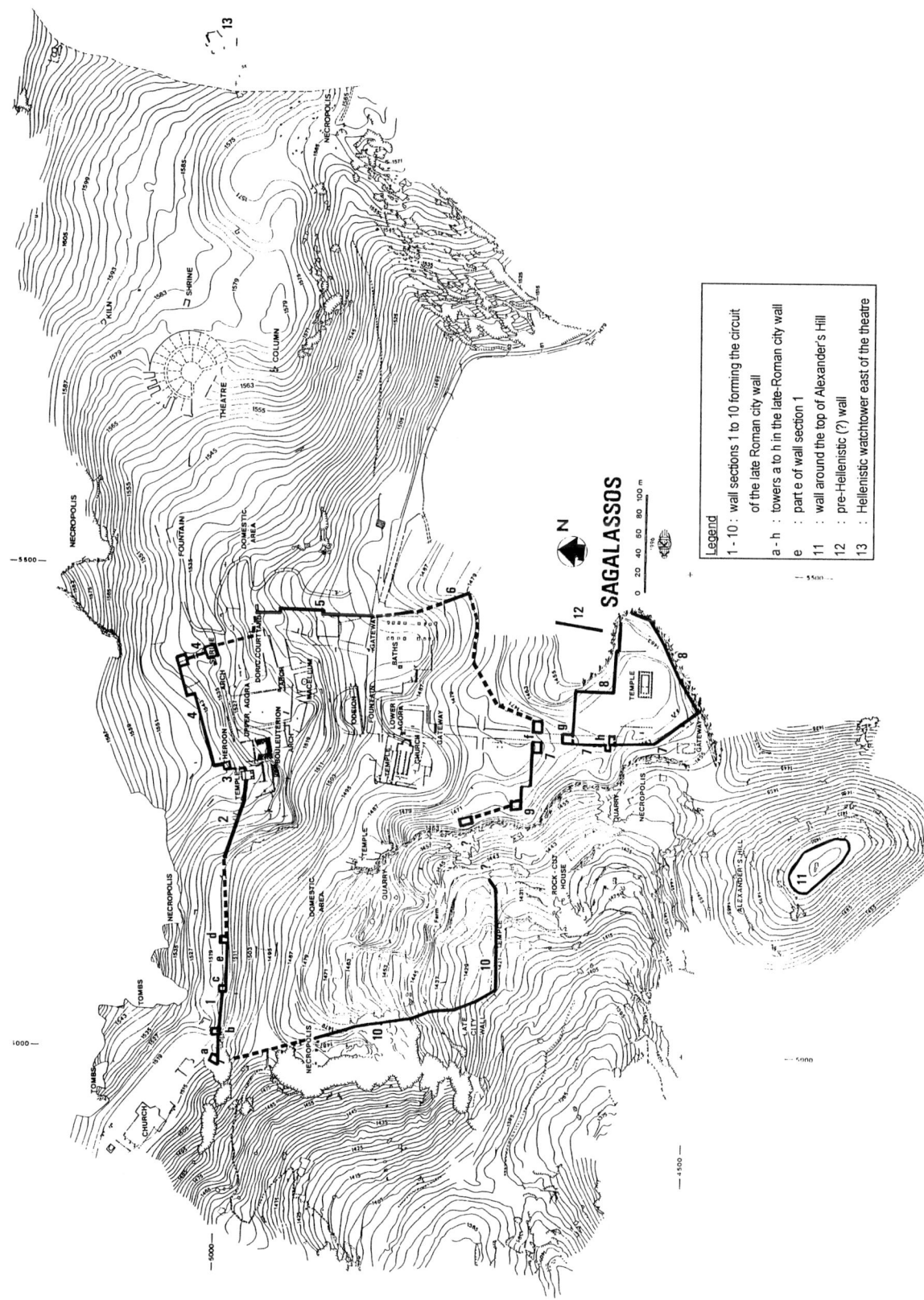

Fig. 1: The late Hellenistic and late Roman city wall.

Fig. 2: Wall blocking the valley to the northeast of the Antoninus Pius Temple.

Fig. 3: Standing part of wall section 1.

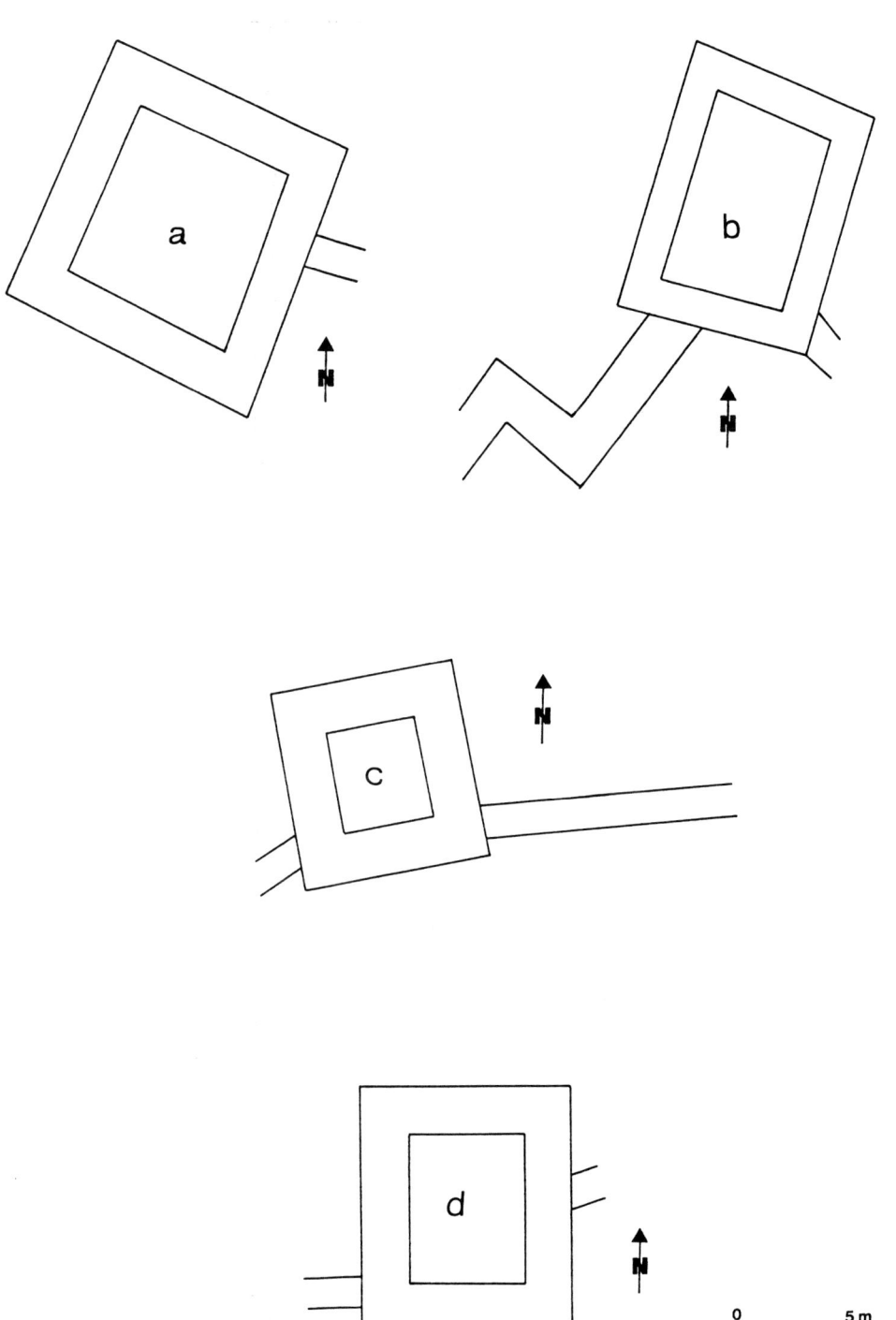

Fig. 4: Plans of the towers in wall section 1.

Fig. 5: Standing corner of tower *d* in wall section 1.

Fig. 6: Wall section 9.

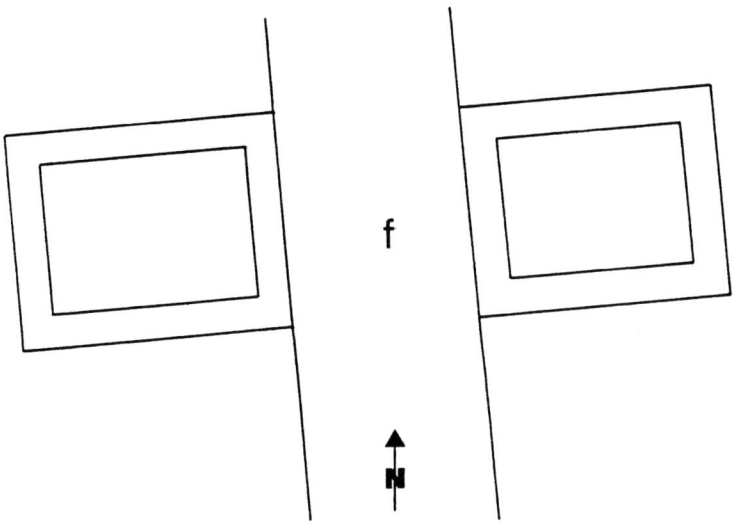
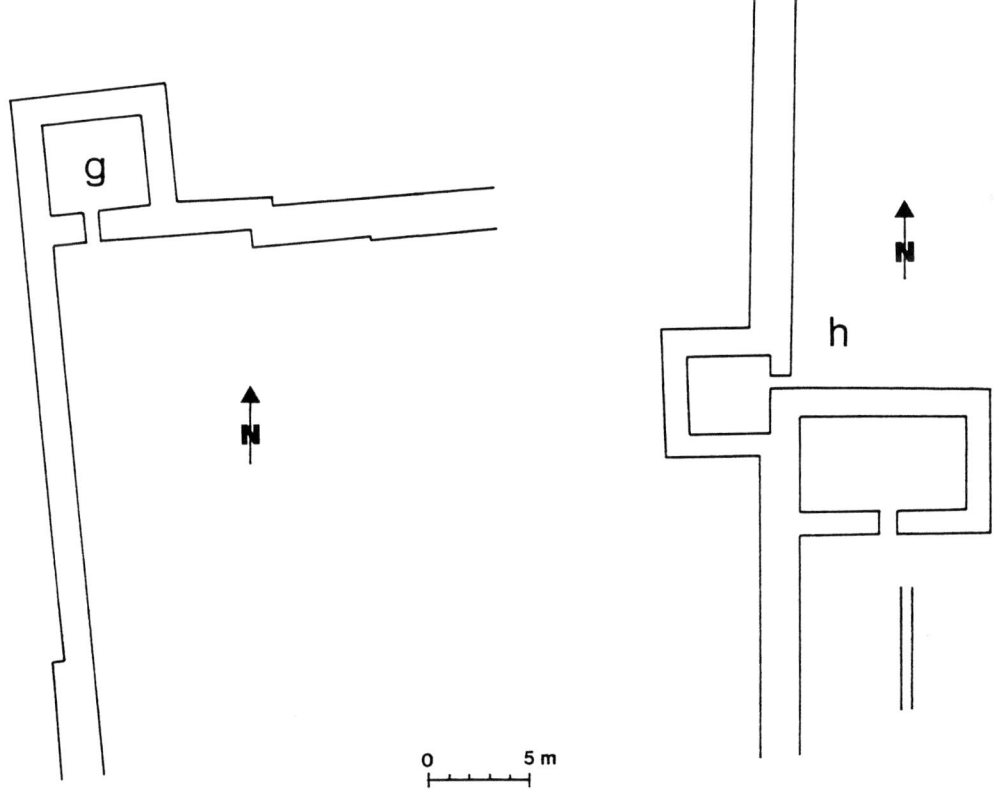

Fig. 7: Plans of the towers in wall section 7.

Fig. 8: Hellenistic weaponry frieze, found inside the ruins of tower *f*, in wall section 7.

Fig. 9: The Ağlasun Dağları from the south. From left to right: Koyaklının Tepe, Tekne Tepe, Çinçinkirik Tepe. The location of Sagalassos is indicated by an arrow.

(see 3.3.2) prevented an enemy from crossing the mountain crest and descending towards the vertical cliff. The only advantage left for an enemy upon reaching the top of the cliff would have been its position overlooking the city and its wall. However, in that position they would have been an easy target for the defenders occupying the fortress above them (see 3.3.1). The 50 m wide, rather flat, area between the wall and the foot of the cliff would also have neutralised an enemy's advantage. This distance could easily be covered by a bow or a sling, the only long-distance weapons which could be transported to the top of the cliff, but these weapons were not capable of damaging the wall itself. Moreover, the flat area between the wall and the cliff could easily accommodate one or more trenches or earthen ramparts to interrupt rocks rolling down from the mountain side. If the Sagalassians had built their wall on top of the cliff, it would have been more difficult to stop falling blocks before they reached it. The difficult and slow descent of an enemy down the slope would also give the defenders enough time to position and use their artillery against him. In order to really threaten the city wall, an enemy would first have to descend towards the flat area in front of it, where he would be trapped between the wall and the cliff rising above it. Consequently, the position of the wall was the only reasonable one, unless one had to built a 'great circuit wall'. The fortress and the barrier walls on top of the mountain rim, coupled with the inaccessibility of the south slope therefore guaranteed the safety of the city and hence no 'great circuit wall', incorporating the higher slopes around the city, from where an enemy could easily threaten it, was needed. The construction of such a 'great circuit wall' at Sagalassos would have posed an almost impossible financial burden. Most of these walls, in fact, were financed by Hellenistic rulers (e.g. Krischen 1922: 49; von Gerkan 1935: 125; Lessing and Oberleitner 1978: 41)

Two other parts of the late Hellenistic city wall at Sagalassos can be identified. Wall section 9, to the west of the great north-south colonnaded street, consists of a partly preserved tower which overlooks the valley to the west where wall section 10 is located. The tower measures approximately 7 m by 12 m and seems to have been built of an inner and an outer casing, filled with mortared rubble. The west wall of the tower is supported by two buttresses, presumably to overcome stability problems, since the tower was built on top of a steep slope (Fig. 6). Also in the west wall the remains of a 1.35 m wide window, that could be closed off by means of shutters and was probably reinforced by bars, are preserved. Wall section 9 was also incorporated into the late Roman city wall. Late Roman repairs resulted in a rather slapdash stonework.

A third remnant from the circuit of the late Hellenistic city wall is tower f, located along the north-south colonnaded street (wall section 7). This wall section comprised two towers, probably interconnected, at either side of the street (f on Fig. 7). The eastern tower measures 10.50 m by 13.50 m, the western tower 10.50 m by 12.50 m. Both have an inner and an outer ashlar casing filled with mortared rubble. The lower floors of the towers have a fill of stones and earth comparable to the fill of the towers in wall section 1. This fill indicates that the actual rooms were on the first floor. A block with a relief depicting a piece of Hellenistic armour, similar to those of the second century BC East Gate at Side (Mansel 1968: 262-279) and some of the Hellenistic city gates at Selge (Machatschek and Schwartz 1981: 40), now lies between the two towers (Fig. 8). This relief suggests a Hellenistic date for the tower or for another building which may have stood in its neighbourhood. Together with another Hellenistic weaponry frieze approximately 20 m to the south of the tower and which also may have come from it, the armour relief indicates that this part of the city had at least been partially developed during the Hellenistic period. The presence of the reliefs, although not *in situ*, leads one to believe that tower f was the Hellenistic south gate of Sagalassos. Tower f lies on a narrow tongue of land leading towards the city. This tongue could easily be blocked, making it an excellent location to build a gate that could be effectively defended. Three other indications support this hypothesis. The fill of the ground floor of the towers is not apparent in any of the other late Roman towers along the colonnaded street (see 4.3.7), but also occurs in the towers of the late Hellenistic wall section 1. Another indication of an early date might be that tower f does contain hardly any *spolia*, while this frequently occurs in the other towers along the colonnaded street. Tower f is also connected with wall section 9, also likely to be of Hellenistic date. Although the present day connection clearly dates to the late Roman period, one can presume that those two constructions were already connected during the Hellenistic period. The original connection was probably dismantled during the Imperial period, when the city was spreading further south. Wall section 9 and tower f were incorporated into the late Roman fortifications.

3.3. The Hellenistic outer defences

3.3.1. The fortress and the watchtowers

In mountainous areas such as at Sagalassos (Fig. 9), no city defence system could function properly without a belt of watchtowers situated outside the city. They provided a view of those areas surrounding the city that were not visible from the city itself. Such towers frequently occur in the defence of the Hellenistic cities in ancient Asia Minor. Examples can be found around Ephesos (Jobst 1978: 447-456) and around Herakleia on the Latmos (Krischen 1922: 44).

The northern and southern approaches to Sagalassos thus were controlled by a fortress on the Tekne Tepe and by three watchtowers (Fig. 10). One of these watchtowers is situated to the north of the city, on the Çinçinkirik Tepe, another to the southwest of the city, on the Zencirükin Tepe and a third one to the east of the potter's quarter of Sagalassos. The last probably controlled a road which led to the city. The fortress and the three watchtowers probably date to the Hellenistic period, as is suggested by their general appearance, by their masonry, by the study of archaeological parallels and by the regional history. An extensive belt of watchtowers surrounding a city is characteristic of the Hellenistic period. It is possible, however, that at Sagalassos one or more of the elements of this system date back to the pre-Hellenistic period. Yet, their definitive development is almost certainly Hellenistic, a time when it was of the utmost importance for the city to be able to spot enemy movements as soon as possible. The watchtowers surrounding the city were probably in sight of the watch and guard towers located in the territory, thus enabling the exchange of signals (Waelkens *et al.* 1997a: 31, 100, Waelkens *et al.* 2000b).

The fortress on the Tekne Tepe (1885 m), located immediately to the northwest of the city and dominating it, measures approximately 41 m by 58 m and has a slightly oval form which is determined by the topography of the mountain top (Fig. 11). It is composed of a double wall made up of roughly cut polygonal rocks and of a rubble fill. In some places the remaining walls stand 1.20 m high, incorporating bedrock in the south and in the northwest corner. There are two 1.25 m wide entrances; one in the east, built into the wall (Fig. 12) and one in the west, cut into the bedrock. Within this wall other structures are visible, five of which consist of rooms, each measuring 4.5 m by 5 m to 6 m by 10 m. Their function is not clear. A rock-cut cistern, 1.25 m by 4 m, lies next to rock-cut stairs which probably led towards the parapet of the fortress wall (Fig. 13). On the north side of the fortress the remains of a watchtower (7.5 m by 9 m) with a 0.75 m wide southern entrance can be seen. This tower's double walls also consist of roughly cut polygonal stones with a rubble fill. The location of this tower indicates its function, i.e. the control of the northern approaches to the city (Loots *et al.* 1999). Indeed, Sagalassos itself was not visible from the watchtower, although one could easily see the city from the south wall of the fortress. Remains of sixth century AD ceramics were found inside the fortress. This fortress on the Tekne Tepe was most probably continuously manned during the Hellenistic (and late Roman) period to defend the barrier wall on the north slope of the mountain rim (see below) in times of danger (Loots *et al.* 1999). The presence of a fortress, together with the immediate availability of soldiers, was very important for the defence of the city which could easily be attacked if an enemy reached the mountain crest. Parallels for the general appearance of the fortress can be found at Ephesos (Lawrence 1979: 178-179, 180; Jobst 1978: 449) and at Ören Tepe, near Boğazıçı (Panemouteichos) in Pisidia (Mitchell 1995b: 17). At Ephesos the fortress controlled part of the shore and a road that was not visible from within the city itself. The fortress of Ören Tepe was built on an isolated rocky outcrop located in a plain and measures 200 m by 300 m. Although this fortress is much larger, its irregular form, the two entrances, the rooms built against the inside of the wall and the rock-cut cisterns can also be seen in the fortress on the Tekne Tepe. The function of the fortress on the Ören Tepe was to control two roads leading through the plain, and in this it clearly differed from that of the fortress at Sagalassos. A possible date for the Ören Tepe fortress is the second century BC, at the time of the founding of Attaleia in Pamphylia by the Attalids (Mitchell 1995b: 17). The fortress on the Tekne Tepe almost certainly corresponds with the ἄκρα mentioned in a probably third century BC inscription from Sagalassos, another confirmation of its early date (Vandorpe 2000).

Of the watchtower on the top of the Çinçinkirik Tepe (2045 m), located ca. 750 m further east, immediately to the northeast of Sagalassos, only a few stretches of wall and a 1.20 m wide entrance in the west remain (Fig. 14). The polygonal watchtower measures approximately 6 m by 18.5 m by 10.5 m by 20 m. Its walls consist of a double ashlar casing filled with rubble. The watchtower is located on a rocky outcrop in the northern section of a small plateau which covers the mountain top and, as such, does not offer any view over Sagalassos itself. The main function of this watchtower would have been to control the northern approaches towards the city (Loots *et al.* 1999). A small northern extension of the watchtower was built using roughly cut polygonal stones, indicating two different building phases. As in the fortress on the Tekne Tepe sixth century AD ceramics were found.

The watchtower on top of the Zencirükin Tepe (1666 m), located immediately to the southwest of Sagalassos (Fig. 15), is only poorly preserved, and cannot be dated from its sparse remains. A few roughly cut polygonal stones are still visible, making it possible to reconstruct the polygonal plan of the watchtower (9.20 m by 10.30 m by 10.20 m). Observations in the field revealed that this watchtower offers a very good view of the mountain pass west of the Zencirükin Tepe and of the valleys just south and southeast of Sagalassos (Loots *et al.* 1999). Because it seems to form part of the Hellenistic system of watchtowers around Sagalassos it probably dates from the Hellenistic period as well.

To the east of the theatre stands a third watchtower, built against the southern edge of a rocky outcrop, and overlooking two small valleys towards the east and the southeast (13 on Fig. 1; Fig. 16). The function of this watchtower, unlike those mentioned above, was not to guard a large area, but to control a road approaching the city from the east, that was not visible from the city (Waelkens 1993a: 37). This rectangular watchtower measures 15 m by 25 m. The 1.50 m wide east wall and a large part of the south wall still stand

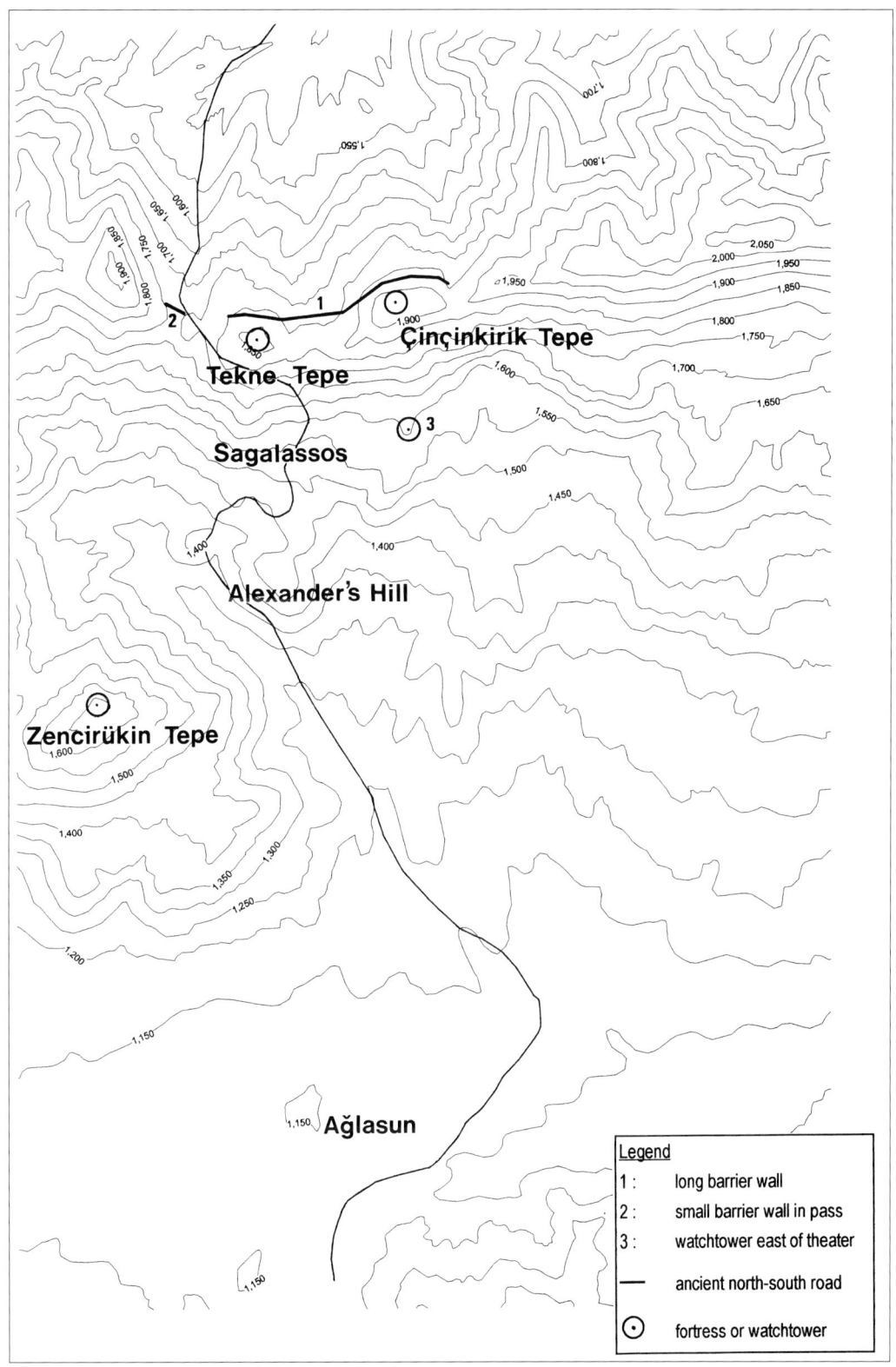

Fig. 10: Plan of the outer defences around Sagalassos.

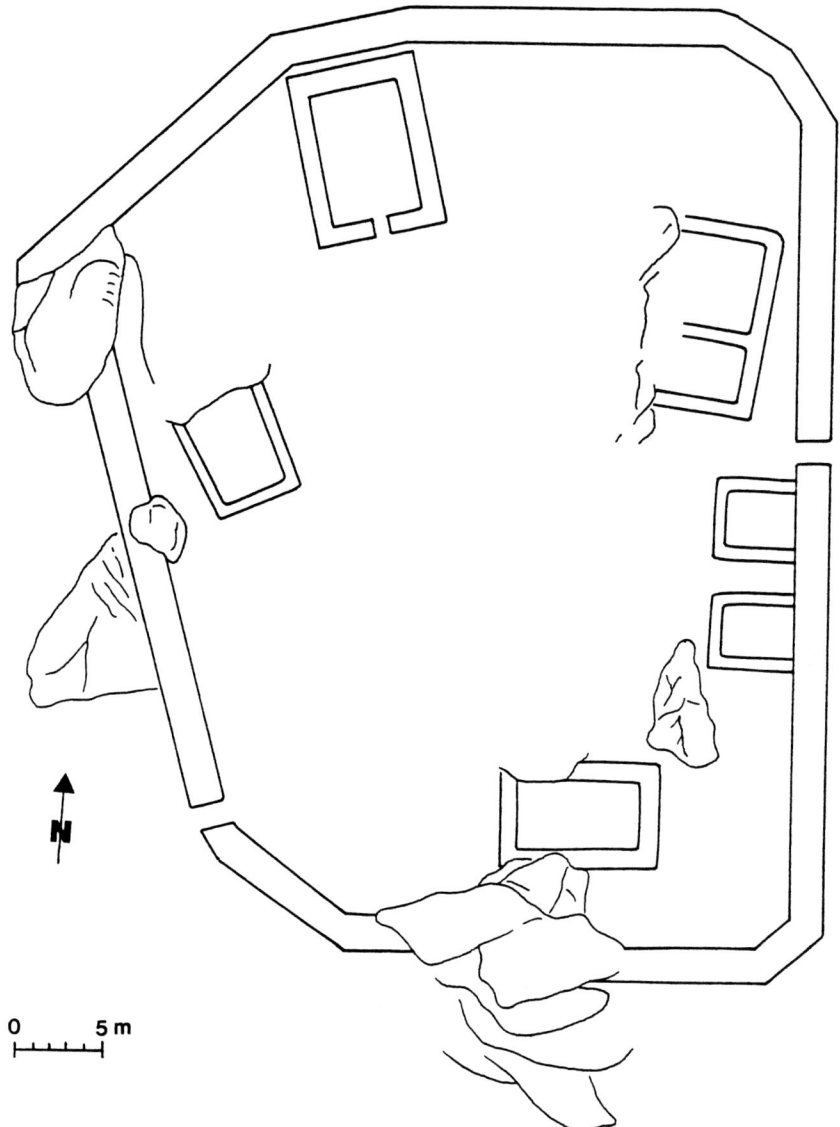

Fig. 11: Plan of the fortress on the Tekne Tepe (E. Owens).

Fig. 12: The eastern entrance to the fortress on the Tekne Tepe. In the background, the Çinçinkirik Tepe.

Fig. 13: Rock-cut steps leading to the parapet of the fortress wall on the Tekne Tepe.

Fig.14: The southeastern corner of the watchtower on the Çinçinkirik Tepe.

Fig. 15: View of the Zencirükin Tepe from Sagalassos.

Fig.16: Tower east of Sagalassos seen from the west.

Fig.17: Southeast corner of the tower east of Sagalassos.

Fig.18: Preserved part of the long barrier wall seen from the north.

Fig.19: Preserved part of the small barrier wall seen from the north.

Fig.20: Re-used gable from a monumental tomb in wall section 2.

approximately 3 m high. They were built using large roughly cut polygonal stones. The lower floor of the watchtower is filled with earth and stones, levelling the slope on which the watchtower is located. Based on ceramics found in and near it, the watchtower has been dated to the Hellenistic period (Waelkens and Mitchell 1988: 60). This early date may be confirmed by its masonry which is similar to the masonry of part of the Hellenistic city wall at Kaunos (Schmaltz 1994: 190-192). Parallels for such a watchtower controlling a single road, can be found at Ephesos (Jobst 1978: 448) and at Arpas in Caria (Marchese 1992: 47-52). At Ephesos the fairly large watchtower in ashlar masonry dates to the time of Lysimachos. The watchtower at Arpas most probably dates to the early Hellenistic period.

3.3.2. The barrier walls

Together with the fortress on the Tekne Tepe and the watchtower on the Çinçinkirik Tepe, two barrier walls guarded the northern approaches to Sagalassos (Fig. 10). The slopes to the north of the mountain crest are deeply dissected by major valley systems running northwards. The main valley heads often almost reach the southern cuesta front, limiting the flat level of the mountain top to merely a few 100 m on the level of the valley heads. One of the western valleys contains a well-defined pass at about 1730 m, but even the other slopes further east were easier to climb from the southern mountain face. This situation certainly caused defence problems and explains the presence of a fortification system along the northern edge of the mountain ridge above the city (Paulissen *et al.* 1993: 231). The long barrier wall on the north slope of the mountain rim was clearly meant to solve these problems. It is almost 1500 m long and runs in an east-west direction from the foot of the Çinçinkirik Tepe towards the foot of the Tekne Tepe. In 1979 Fleischer mentioned "mehrere Spermauern, die jeweils in engen Stellen der verschiedenen Felsrinnen gesetzt sind" (Fleischer 1979: 306-307). This description leads one to believe that Fleischer refers to both the small barrier wall in the pass (see below) and to the long barrier wall. This is only partially confirmed by the position he gives for the wall, i.e. west and northwest of the fortress on the Tekne Tepe. Several parts of the long barrier wall to the northeast of the Tekne Tepe are also preserved, but are not mentioned by Fleischer. He must have known these sections, however, since he gives a short description of the fortress on the Tekne Tepe and of the watchtower on the Çinçinkirik Tepe. This makes one wonder if he did not identify the long barrier wall as a sequence of different barrier walls to the north and northwest of the Tekne Tepe instead of one continuous wall.

Both the eastern and western ends of the long barrier wall are set against a steep rock cliff. The wall has mainly collapsed, but a few parts, standing on bedrock, still reach a height of approximately 3 m. All the preserved parts of the 2 to 2.5 m wide wall indicate the same building technique, consisting of an inner and outer casing of very roughly cut polygonal stones filled with rubble in between (Fig. 18). The stones making up the outer, northern casing are larger than those of the inner, southern casing. Although it does not form part of a 'great circuit wall', the long barrier wall at Sagalassos can be compared to the upper stretch of the 'great circuit wall' at Priene, which encloses the acropolis, dominating the city from above (Schede 1964: 21). Another example of this layout can be found at Ephesos (Forschungen in Ephesos 1906: 40, fig. 10). The long barrier wall at Sagalassos, however, does not form part of a real circuit wall and must be considered as a mixture of a 'great circuit wall' and a barrier wall. The long barrier wall had to incorporate the mountain crest within the fortified area around the city in order to prevent an enemy from seizing this strategically important position. In case of danger, this wall was an absolute necessity in the defence of the city and could not be abandoned. The fortress on the Tekne Tepe would most probably have been continuously manned and, because of its excellent view over the long barrier wall, defence of the latter could have been organized from there. This does not exclude the possibility that both structures were not exactly contemporary and that the long barrier wall was only added later. Yet the similarity in their masonry indicates that their construction was certainly not spread over a longer period.

Arrian describes Sagalassos as "not a small city" (*Anabasis Alexandri* I, 28), making it not unlikely that the first phase of the long barrier wall predates Alexander the Great's siege of the city in 333 BC. This would also mean that the fortress on the Tekne Tepe already existed in the pre-Hellenistic period. The fact that the long barrier wall seems to have formed an essential element of the city's defence systems might suggest that it was not necessarily built as a response to an immediate enemy threat. However, some historical events may have played a part. If not older and part of the same defence system as the fortress on the Tekne Tepe which most probably existed already in the first decennia of the third century BC, the construction of the long barrier wall could have taken place during the years 275 to 268 BC, when raids by the Galatians disturbed life in the interior of Asia Minor (Mitchell 1993: 18). A Celtic bracelet from the Archaeological Museum of Isparta (10 km north of Sagalassos) probably originating from the neighbourhood of this city, indicates the presence of Celtic tribes such as the Galatians immediately north of Sagalassos (Müller-Karpe 1989: 299-305). By using Indian elephants, much later adopted as the city's symbol on a seal from Sagalassos (Vandorpe 1995), Antiochos I was eventually able to defeat the Galatians ca. 270 BC. A Celtic shield on a relief of the honorific monument for Ptolemy II and Arsinoe at Lymira, dating to

280-270 BC, indicates that the Galatians may even have operated a few 100 km south of Sagalassos (Borchhardt 1986: 205-206; Borchhardt 1989: 178-179; Mitchell 1989b: 118; Mitchell 1993: 18). However, it is by no means certain whether or not the building of the long barrier wall was caused by this Galatian threat. A newly discovered inscription from Sagalassos, plausibly dated to exactly that period, even suggests that part of the city's population may have welcomed the Galatians against a Seleucid domination and occupied the fortress (Vandorpe 2000). It is possible therefore that the barrier wall also existed then and that it was not necessarily a defence against the Galatians. On the other hand, it is also possible that it had been built precisely after this rebellion of part of the city against the Seleucid power, at the instigation of or even with the help of Antiochos I, which might explain its enormous size reminiscent of that of the 'great circuit walls'. In that case it could have been constructed as a protection against future Galatian raids. The establishment of Macedonian colonists in the city (Kosmetatou and Waelkens 1997) could have been intended for a support of the pro-Seleucid part of the population and an additional safeguard against the Galatians who had helped their opponents. Repairs and rebuilding of parts of the wall during the Hellenistic period are more than likely, but cannot be concluded from the present ruinous state of the long barrier wall.

The small barrier wall blocking the northern approach through the pass northwest of Sagalassos is situated some 100 m to the north of this pass (1730 m) and ca. 250 m to the west of the long barrier wall (Fig. 10). This northeast to southwest orientated wall is 84 m long. Its eastern section was built against a steep rock cliff, while its western section disappears under the talud of a medieval caravan road running through the pass. The 1.10 to 1.20 m wide wall still stands approximately 3 m high and consists of two casings of small polygonal stones with a fill of rubble (Fig. 19). Because the pass in which the small barrier wall stands was not visible from the fortress on the Tekne Tepe, it would be more difficult to control this easy approach from the fortress (Loots *et al.* 1999). But an enemy approaching along the mountain pass could be seen from the fortress before he reached the small barrier wall. If necessary, the latter could also be manned from the fortress. The aim of the small barrier wall would in any case have been to stop or at least slow down an enemy approaching the city from the north.

3.4. Conclusion

It is clear from this description that Sagalassos possessed a well-developed defence system in the pre-Imperial times. Part of it may even have dated back to the pre-Hellenistic period. During the earlier third century BC, if not before, the northern approaches to the site were guarded by a fortress and probably also by two barrier walls. A Seleucid intervention in the construction of the latter cannot be excluded. The series of watchtowers surrounding the city could date back to the same period. Wealthy cities, such as Rhodes, could finance their own city walls, but generally long fortifications such as the 'great circuit walls' were financed by the Hellenistic monarchs. Examples are Herakleia on the Latmos and Ephesos, where the early Hellenistic 'great circuit walls' were built by respectively Pleistarchos and Lysimachos (Krischen 1922: 49; Lessing and Oberleitner 1978: 41; Peschlow-Bindokat 1996: 30) and Miletos, where new city walls were built by Mithridates VI around 85 BC (von Gerkan 1935: 125). Eventually, the city wall and the fortress, the watchtowers and the barrier walls, were indispensable for the defence of the city. Comparable Hellenistic defence systems have also been found at other Hellenistic cities in Asia Minor. The continuous feuding of the Hellenistic monarchs and the Hellenistic cities often escalated into fierce wars, forcing the cities to extend and continuously adapt their fortifications. This may also have been the case at Sagalassos, where the actual city walls, of which one still can see some traces, clearly belong to the late Hellenistic period, i.e. the second century BC or even later. Since Sagalassos was a rich city at that moment as is clear from Livy (38.15) it probably built its own city walls, as so many Hellenistic cities in Asia Minor did at that time.

4. THE LATE ROMAN CITY WALL

4.1. Circuit

Most of the wall sections at present visible at Sagalassos belong to the late Roman period. This city wall can be divided into 10 sections which form a highly irregular circuit (Fig. 1). Most of these wall sections date to the late Roman period, but a few stretches of the late Hellenistic city wall were incorporated into the circuit (wall section 1, tower *f* of wall section 7 and wall section 9). The circuit of the late Roman city wall can be almost completely reconstructed. To the west of the city, east of basilica E, the wall ascends along a slope eastwards, towards the Doric temple. This temple and the nearby Northwest Heroon were incorporated into the city wall as towers protecting a newly built city gate in between them. Northeast of the Northwest Heroon the wall runs eastwards over a distance of 110 m to the north of the upper agora and then diverts southwards. Immediately south of this turn lay two towers which protected another city gate. This gate faces the gate near the Doric temple and closed one of the main streets of the city leading eastwards towards the theatre. South of this second gate the wall descends along the slope east of the monumental city centre, towards the northeast corner of the Roman bath building. The wall follows the eastern edge of this building and approximately 15 m southeast of it, it turns to the west, leading to the colonnaded street. Here, the main late Roman city wall connected with the probably late Hellenistic tower *f*. South of tower *f* another tower (*g*) had been built over the colonnaded street. From tower *g* the wall follows the colonnaded street further south, towards a third tower (*h*) and then turns to run over the promontory on which the temple of Antoninus Pius is located towards the southeast. The wall runs over the southeast flank of the promontory, encircles it, and connects with wall section 8 on the northern slope of the promontory, to the east of the colonnaded street. This part of the city wall runs towards the west and connects again with tower *g* on the colonnaded street. The late Roman wall around the promontory was most probably not connected with the main late Roman wall around the city centre (see 4.3.7). From tower *f* the main city wall runs towards the west flank of the promontory and connects with wall section 9, probably a late Hellenistic tower which overlooked the generally domestic quarters of the city in the valley to the west of it. On this west flank, approximately 20 m north of wall section 9, traces of another construction connected with wall section 9 are visible. From here the wall probably descended into the valley and connected with wall section 10. However, today, this connection is no longer visible. Wall section 10 crosses the valley and after 120 m, turns towards the north. There, the wall runs over a small hill that forms the western border of this valley. The wall finally connected with the steep rock cliff on which wall section 1 stands (see 3.2). It is apparent that the late Roman city wall did not even include half of the Roman Imperial city. A large portion of the domestic quarters to the southeast and the southwest of the colonnaded street, the whole area between the monumental city centre and the theatre, and the potters' quarter to the east of the theatre were not included within the walled area, although they were definitely part of the city during the late Roman period.

The inhabitants of Sagalassos in the late Roman period thus made the logical choice of decreasing the defensible area of the city, fortifying only the monumental city centre (Waelkens 1993b: 16). This is a common phenomenon in the late Roman period when city populations diminished throughout the Roman empire. Examples of this process are numerous and are attested by the construction of various late Roman city walls, for example, during the fifth century AD at Sagalassos (for the date see 4.2), or as protection against the Gothic incursions of the second half of the third century AD at Sardis (Hanfmann and Waldbaum 1975: 4, 36), Pergamon (Wulf 1994: 172-173, figs a-d), at Ephesos (Lessing and Oberleitner 1978: 59; Foss 1979: 106) and at Side (Mansel 1963: 11, 40). At Sagalassos the late Hellenistic city wall had largely been dismantled as the result of the city's expansion during the first three centuries AD and could no longer be re-used. Only a few stretches of wall or towers had survived. A similar state of affairs can be seen at Side where most of the Hellenistic Sea Wall had been taken down during the Roman occupation (Mansel 1963: 27). By fortifying the monumental centre of their city, the Sagalassians secured the political as well as the commercial heart of their city. The fortified area of the city most probably served as a refuge in case of danger, which meant that only a small part of the domestic quarters of the city needed to be included. The potters' quarter, still active well into the sixth or even the seventh century AD, did not need any protection since its activities would have been useless during a siege.

As we have mentioned above, the possibility of re-using existing walls was another factor that must have played a part in planning the circuit of the late Roman city wall. Several wall sections consist of completely or partly re-used walls or buildings. These include former city wall sections (wall section 1), monumental buildings (the Doric temple and the Northwest Heroon in wall section 3) and even the colonnaded street in wall section 7. Parallels to such a recycling can be seen in the above mentioned cities and elsewhere in Asia Minor. At Side the rear wall of the theatre was incorporated into the third century AD city wall (Mansel 1963: 27). At Miletos parts of the Hellenistic south cross wall were incorporated into the third century AD Gothic Wall (Kleiner 1968: 32). Large buildings and other constructions generally stood in the monumental centre of the cities, making their defence easier.

The local topography also played a part in planning the late Roman city wall at Sagalassos. Wherever possible and where it was not restricted by the re-use of earlier walls, the late Roman city wall was built on places that were easy to defend. The crest of the hill used in wall section 10 is a good example. The promontory on which the temple of Antoninus Pius is located was clearly incorporated within the circuit of the wall for strategic reasons. The emperors' cult had ceased to exist long before, and there are no traces of other buildings on the promontory that could justify its incorporation within the late Roman wall. However, if the promontory had not been walled, the Sagalassians would not have been able to control the southern approach to their city and a base for a possible attack would have been left undefended.

4.2. Date

A *terminus post quem* for the construction of the late Roman city wall can be established by studying the *spolia* used in this wall. In wall section 2 parts of a funerary monument (Fig. 20) dating to the middle of the second century AD, have been re-used (Waelkens 1993a: 47; Vandeput 1993: 141-148). In wall section 7 and 8 more or less contemporary architectural elements from the temple of Antoninus Pius were re-used (Waelkens *et al.* 1990: 193). The podium of a temple dating to the second half of the third century AD was incorporated into wall section 10 (Vandeput 1997: 117-118).

However, a more precise date for the late Roman city wall can be established using the results from the excavations in and around the Doric temple and the Northwest Heroon, in the years between 1990 and 1996 (Waelkens *et al.* 1991: 204-206; Waelkens *et al.* 1992b: 90-91; Waelkens 1993b: 9-12; Waelkens *et al.* 1997b; some remarks on the excavation and its results can be found in Poblome 1995: 185-186). The Doric temple was incorporated into the late Roman fortifications of Sagalassos following its abandonment in favour of Christianity. To the northwest of this temple, piled up against the city wall, a fill was identified on top of the original floor of the temple terrace. In its lowest stratum, this fill contained a water supply system of terracotta pipes. The earth of this layer contained two coins of the late fourth or early fifth century AD (Scheers 1993a: 202). On top of this, several layers containing late Roman lamps, ceramics from the second half of the fourth century AD to the third quarter of the sixth century AD, and coins from the late third to the early fifth century AD were found. J. Poblome considers these layers to be a fill originating inside the city and dumped there after the earthquakes of AD 518 or AD 528 (Poblome 1995: 192-193). The fill of earth, stones and disintegrated mortar to the south of the wall west of the Doric temple, cannot be considered as a parallel, but as the remains of an artificial slope, built to enable the defenders to reach the top of the wall (see 4.3.2).

Excavations inside the Doric temple and to the south and the east of the Northwest Heroon yielded more information. In the late Roman period the Doric temple and the Northwest Heroon were incorporated into the wall as towers. The surroundings of the temple and the temple itself had therefore to be rebuilt (Waelkens *et al.* 1991: 206). The fill inside the temple consisted mainly of rubble from the collapse of the tower itself, containing few archaeological specimens. In the fill a coin from the reign of Theodosius II (AD 423-425) was found (Scheers 1993a: cat. 35). On the floor of the tower 18 bronze coins were discovered, dating from AD 346 to AD 408, most of them from AD 383 to AD 408 (Scheers 1993b: 249-255). In the southwest corner of the tower, immediately on top of the mortar floor that was laid out when the temple was converted into a tower, nine coins from the reign of Theodosius I (AD 383-392) were found (Scheers 1993b: 249-255). These coins give a clear and fixed chronological date for the transformation of the temple into a tower. In the late Roman terraces built to the south of the temple, a coin of Theodosius I was found as well (Waelkens *et al.* 1992b: 88). A coin of Anastasius I (AD 491- 518), found inside the temple, gives an indication of the time span during which the tower was in use (Poblome 1995: 190).

The excavations in 1994 and 1995 revealed the remains of a small construction (4.40 m by 4.30 m) to the south of the Northwest Heroon which was built with mortared rubble walls and had a floor of beaten earth that covered an earlier wall to the south of it (for the preliminary report on the excavations of the Northwest Heroon and its immediate surroundings, see Waelkens *et al.* 1997b: 173-193; Waelkens *et. al.* 2000c). Both constructions may have had a military function connected with the city gate. Following the destruction of the small building, probably due to the earthquake of AD 518, its debris was removed and the area was filled. This fill can be related to the fill to the northwest of the Doric temple. The floor level of the small building and the fill on top of it contained several coins from the late fourth to the early fifth century AD (Waelkens *et al.* 1997b: 191). The pottery could all be dated to the first half of the sixth century AD. No discrepancy exists between the ceramic evidence from the floor level and from the fill above, implying a short occupation phase for this construction. The ceramics from the first half of the sixth century AD give a rough date for the end of the use of the small construction to the south of the heroon and probably of the late Roman wall itself. This evidence from the excavations around the Northwest Heroon thus confirms the probable time span during which the Doric temple and the heroon were used as towers.

All these data suggest that the transformation of the Doric temple and the Northwest Heroon into towers guarding the late Roman northwest city gate did not happen before AD 392. A precise *terminus ante quem* for the building and the use of the towers and the late Roman city wall cannot be given. Most of the coins date from no later than AD 408 and indicate that the towers were mainly in use during the first decades of the fifth century AD. The coin from the reign of Anastasius I indicates how long the towers were occupied. The date of the transformation of the Doric temple and the Northwest Heroon is confirmed by our knowledge of the historical events in Pisidia in the late fourth to early fifth centuries AD. In AD 399 the Ostrogothic mercenary chief Tribigild, not having been paid for his services, started a revolt against the Romans. This revolt grew dangerous when several Gothic soldiers of the Roman army joined Tribigild. It resulted in the pillaging of a large part of Asia Minor, including Pisidia. Tribigild was only stopped at the border of Pisidia and Pamphylia when locals ambushed him near Selge (Wolfram 1979: 176; Waelkens 1993a: 48). After three centuries of relative peace, only interrupted by Lydios' short-lived seizure of Cremna, the revolt of Tribigild brought unrest to Pisidia, and encouraged the Isaurians to emerge once more from their hideouts in the Taurus mountains and

Fig. 21: North-face of hte excavated part of wall section 2, to the west of the Doric temple.

Fig. 22: South face of the excavated part of wall section 2, to the west of the Doric temple.

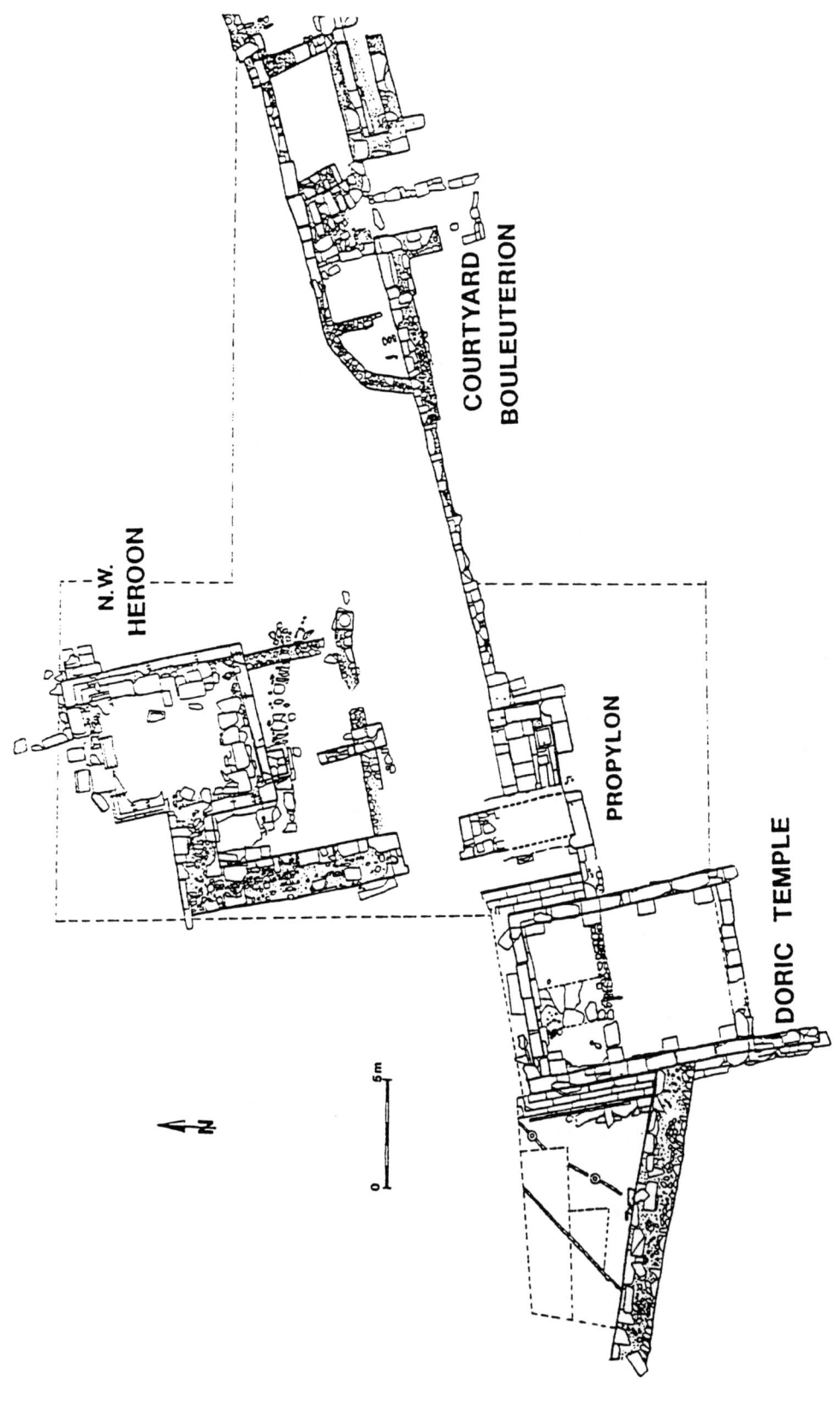

Fig. 23: Plan of the Doric temple and the Northwest Heroon area.

to start pillaging again (for the history of the Isaurians in the fourth century AD and before, see Rougé 1966). Between AD 404 and AD 406 Pisidia was continuously ravaged by Isaurian tribes. These events at the end of the fourth and the beginning of the fifth centuries AD were most probably the cause of the building of the late Roman city wall at Sagalassos. The revolt of Tribigild must have put the Pisidians on the alert, but did not necessarily lead to the building of Sagalassos' city wall. Tribigild's raid through Pisidia was a sudden and single event and therefore would rather have resulted in the construction of a primitive and hastily built wall. The late Roman city wall at Sagalassos, however, is of a better quality and was certainly not built in panic. It can more probably be linked to the general climate of insecurity caused by Tribigild's passage, and/or to the later raids of the Isaurians during the years AD 404-406.

Thus, at the latest during the period of the Isaurian pillaging, Sagalassos must have possessed a city wall. Excavations, to the east of the monumental city centre and outside the late Roman city wall (site LW and LE) revealed many traces of burning, perhaps related to the events of the late fourth to early fifth centuries AD (Waelkens 1993a: 48; Waelkens 1995: 61). It seems likely that the Isaurians effectively threatened Sagalassos and may have partially destroyed the city. Following the Isaurian raids, the Doric temple remained in use as a tower until the first half of the sixth century AD. The towers and the late Roman city wall were probably given up due to the earthquake of AD 518 and were not rebuilt. Earthquake debris piled up on either side of the wall, at least near the Doric temple and the Northwest Heroon, had abrogated its defensive value (Waelkens *et. al.* 2000).

4.3. The wall

4.3.1. Wall section 1

The remains of the late Hellenistic city wall were re-used and partly rebuilt in the late Roman period. A description of this late Hellenistic city wall has been given above (3.2).

4.3.2. Wall section 2

To the east, the late Hellenistic city wall (wall section 1) is connected with wall section 2, ascending the slope towards the Doric temple (Fig. 1). A small part of this wall section was excavated in 1990 and 1991, together with the Doric temple (see Waelkens *et al.* 1991; Waelkens *et al.* 1992b; Waelkens 1993b). Re-used blocks feature heavily in this wall. Among these are two cornices and the gable from a funerary monument (Fig. 20) dated to the middle of the second century AD (Waelkens 1993a: 47; Vandeput 1993: 141-148). The eastern end of wall section 2, built against the west wall of the Doric temple, still stands 3.60 m high. The 2.00 m thick wall consists of a mortared rubble fill between a northern, outer casing and a southern, inner casing. The northern casing consists of an assembly of re-used and reworked ashlars and of other architectural elements (Fig. 21); the southern casing is built of smaller, roughly cut and re-used blocks (Fig. 22). South of the wall a fill of sand, small stones and disintegrated mortar was excavated, which was most probably the remains of a rampart (Waelkens 1993b: 11). The presence of a parapet on top of the wall, as identified by the excavators (Waelkens *et al.* 1992b: 90), is very unlikely. The wall is only partly preserved, nowhere reaching its original height, so no parapet would have been apparent during the excavations and indeed such a parapet may have never existed. The wall itself probably functioned as a parapet, protecting the defenders who stood on the earthen rampart behind the wall. North of the wall a fill of destruction material from inside the city was found. Seven layers could be identified, dumped on top of a late Roman earthen surface. However, they all contain contemporary dumped material (Poblome 1995: 185-186). The latter contained part of a water supply system made of terracotta pipes (Waelkens 1993b: 19, fig. 1). These pipes were connected to a drainage system within the late Roman city wall, south of the Northwest Heroon. The earthen surface contained two coins of the late fourth or early fifth century AD (Scheers 1993a: cat. 27, cat. 33).

4.3.3. Wall section 3

This wall section consists of the Doric temple, the Northwest Heroon and the late Roman northwest city gate located between them (Fig. 23). The temple and the heroon date respectively to the late Hellenistic and to the early Imperial period and were incorporated into the wall and converted into towers around AD 400. The rise of Christianity at Sagalassos must have put an end to the religious connotations of both structures. As a result, their character must have already changed before the building of the city wall. Yet, this area remained an important *area sacra*: the 1998 campaign revealed the presence of a fifth century AD church, built inside the courtyard of the bouleuterion immediately east of the Doric temple. It is easy to see why they chose to re-use both the Doric temple and the Northwest Heroon. The temple stands on the highest point of the city centre, dominating the slope towards the west on which wall section 2 lies, thus offering an almost complete control over this stretch of the late Roman city wall. The passage between the temple and the heroon could easily be closed. During this conversion the Doric temple was partially rebuilt (for the preliminary reports on the excavations of this building see Waelkens *et al.* 1991: 204-206; Waelkens *et al.* 1992b: 90-91; Waelkens 1993b: 9-12). A new door was erected in its south wall. Eight pilasters, equally divided over the east and the west wall, were built inside the temple. They consist of alternating tuff blocks, tiles and rubble in a mortar bed (Fig. 24). The second row of pilasters from the north was linked by a small rubble wall. A doorway in this wall connected two rooms, a northern one with an earthen floor, and a southern room with a mortar floor. The pilasters originally must have reached to the top of the temple and may have supported a wooden platform or a gallery running along the inner walls. A massive destruction layer found inside the temple not only supports the hypothesis that its walls had been raised using mortared brick, but seems also to be the result of the collapse of a roof which covered the whole building and not just the section with the mortar floor that certainly needed some sort of weather protection, as previously suggested by Waelkens (1993b: 12). The smaller room with the beaten earth floor only opened towards the southern room, probably indicating that it was a storage room that could have easily been included within the roofing system of the tower. Indeed, in this room a large number of vessels for storage, including dolia, and cooking vessels were found (Degeest 2000). The span of 3.50 m between the pilasters would have provided no problem to covering the complete building. As we have mentioned above, nine coins dating from the years AD 383-392 were found on the mortar floor of the southern room. Together with several other coins (AD 346-408) they offer clear chronological evidence for the conversion of the temple into a tower. A separate coin of Anastasius I (AD 491-518) found inside the temple gives an idea of the time span that the tower remained in use (see 4.2).

The stretch of the late Roman city wall in which the northwest city gate is built leans against the outside of the Doric temple, approximately 8 m behind its eastern anta. This wall still stands 3.50 m high and measures 1.85 m wide to the north and 1.95 m wide to the south of the gate. The wall is built with re-used blocks and incorporates the western half of the propylon built against the east wall of the Doric temple. In the corner between the fortification wall and the west side of the heroon a reservoir collected water supplied by a channel coming from the north (Fig. 25). This channel leads through an opening measuring 0.60 m by 0.34 m, built into the wall. The vaulted reservoir, with a floor of large tiles, was made of mortared rubble and measures 2.40 m by 1.60 m. On the east side of the heroon's podium a second drain collected rainwater either from the upper part of the fortifications or from the heroon itself (Waelkens *et al.* 1997b: 187; Waelkens *et.al.* 2000c).

The late Roman northwest gate measures 2.90 m wide on the east and 2.50 m wide on the west side. It is 1.90 m deep. These rather large dimensions for a city gate indicate its importance as one of the main entrances into the city (Fig. 26). The upper part of the gate was composed of an arch of which the central keystone, depicting in an unfinished relief an eagle holding a snake, was found in 1995. During the excavations in 1997, several weaponry reliefs as well as busts of Ares and Athena, the old pagan war gods, all originating from the façade of the nearby bouleuterion, were found. These were probably re-used in the city wall. Similar weaponry frieze blocks discovered in or around the Doric temple or to the west of the Northwest Heroon suggest that not only the gate itself, but also the wall sections on either side of it, had been decorated with these re-used frieze blocks from the bouleuterion. Several andesite archivolts that were found during the excavations may belong to the arch of the gate. Only the lower part of the gate is preserved *in situ*. The threshold of the gate, excavated in 1997, offers evidence for a possible reconstruction (Fig. 27). There were two doors, probably suspended in a wooden frame. The square holes in which the doorposts were located can be seen on either side of the gate. The northern hole measures 17.5 cm by 15 cm; the southern 13 cm by 13.5 cm. Some lead still remains in the southern hole, probably used to secure an iron pin on which this door was hinged (Fig. 28). On the threshold of the gate next to the holes one can see circular, parallel grooves and iron stains, 10 cm to 11 cm wide, resulting from the way the doors were suspended. In the middle of the gate, 1.03 m from its north side, a small square hole measuring 5 cm by 5 cm, is visible in the threshold. This hole most probably served to lock the larger southern door (1.80 m wide). Since the gate incorporates one step of approximately 5 cm, it seems unlikely that chariots could have passed through it. Indeed, no traces of cart wheels have been found on the threshold of the gate. The smaller northern door would have measured approximately 0.90 m wide. The holes for the closing mechanism of the gate are still visible 1.20 m above the foundations of the city wall. From these dimensions one can reconstruct the total height of the gate. It would have been some 2 m high up to the spring of the arch. The maximum height of the passage would have been between 2.50 m and 3.00 m. The closing mechanism of the gate consisted of a 3.50 m long wooden bar with an overall diameter of 0.20 m, which slid into the holes present in both inner sides of the gate. It was then secured by means of a wedge-and-bolt system (Winter 1971: 253-268). It seems likely that, when the gate was open, this wooden bar was stored in the south wall of the gate. The hole in this wall measures 0.21 m by 0.29 m and is, unlike the northern one which only measures 0.13 m by 0.13 m, not cut into the stone, but spared out in the wall (Fig. 29). Unfortunately there is a lot of earth inside this hole, making it impossible to verify whether it extends further inside the wall. A parallel for this mechanism can be found at Termessos where the bar was stored in one of the rooms next to the gate, by sliding it through a hole in the wall between the gate and this room (Winter 1966: 134-137).

Only the podium of the Northwest Heroon (7.52 m by 8.37 m)

Fig. 24: Pilasters inside the Doric temple.

Fig. 25: Reservoir west of the Northwest Heroon.

Fig. 26: Threshold of the late Roman city gate.

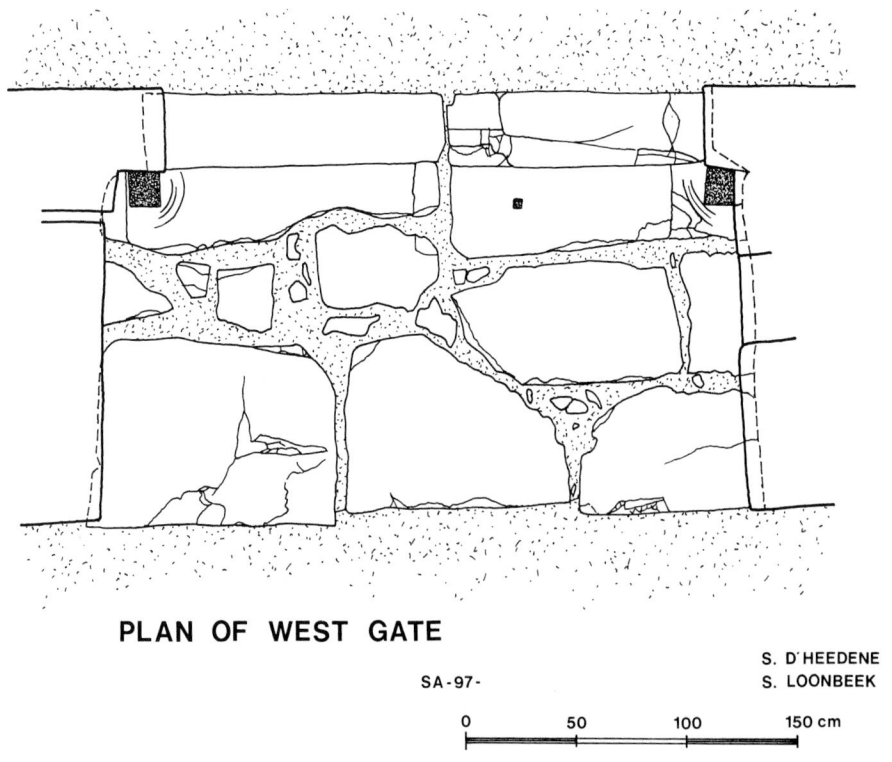

PLAN OF WEST GATE

SA-97-

S. D'HEEDENE
S. LOONBEEK

0 50 100 150 cm

Fig. 27: Late Roman city gate between the Doric temple and the Northwest Heroon.

622

Fig. 28: Hole for the southern doorpost in the threshold of the gate.

Fig. 29: Hole for the wooden bar in the southern post of the gate.

Fig. 30: Late Roman structures in front of the Northwest Heroon.

Fig. 31: Terrace wall in wall section 4.

has been preserved *in situ*. Both its west and north sides are incorporated into the city wall, which is partly supported by it (Fig. 23). To the north, this wall connects with wall section 4. In the late Roman period, the area between the heroon and the city gate was occupied by several structures (for a description and the dating of the different layers and structures south of the Northwest Heroon, see Waelkens *et al.* 1997b: 184-193; Waelkens *et. al.* 2000c). These include a mortared rubble wall, of which only the two lowest courses are preserved. They run from the northern extremity of the city gate towards the southern of two pillars in front of the heroon. A second and later structure covering the previous wall, consists of mortared rubble and contained a beaten earth floor (4.40 m by 4.30 m) (Fig. 30). These rubble walls still stand 0.20 m to 0.50 m high. Both constructions probably had some function in connection with the gate, serving as a guardroom or as a shelter for city officials collecting tolls. After the guardroom was deserted and probably destroyed by the earthquake of AD 518, the surface was raised and several terracotta water pipes were connected with the reservoir built against the west side of the heroon. They distributed water to the south, east and west and were arranged inside a thick fill of destruction material, probably resulting from cleaning the city after the earthquake.

4.3.4. Wall section 4

From the Northwest Heroon the late Roman city wall runs eastwards over a distance of approximately 110 m to the north of the upper agora (Fig. 1). Above the upper agora the wall consists of a large re-used terrace wall built with large, carefully worked stones, and supported by buttresses along its south side (Fig. 31). This part of wall section 4 probably dates to an early phase in the urban development of Sagalassos. The wall forms the first of several terrace walls descending from the north towards the upper agora. It is even possible that it was contemporary with the laying out of the upper agora during the second century BC (Waelkens 1993a: 43).

Towards the east the terrace wall has been extended by a late Roman wall. Within the north-south oriented part of wall section 4, a late Roman city gate, flanked by two towers measuring ca. 8.5 m by 10 m, can be identified (Fig. 32). Because of the ruinous state of the towers and of the gate, it is not possible to reconstruct them. One can only presume that this city gate resembled the northwest city gate in wall section 3. The presence of voussoirs indeed indicates that the northeast city gate was arched. The entrance was probably not much wider than 3 m. The gate is part of the road which entered the city through the northwest gate, then continued to the north of the upper agora and left the walled city centre again through the northeast gate, continuing eastwards towards the theatre. The street itself formed an important east-west axis, leading towards the industrial activities of the potters' quarter.

4.3.5. Wall section 5

Between wall section 4 and 5, the late Roman city wall is no longer visible, but can be reconstructed as a simple stretch of wall connecting both sections (Fig. 1). In wall section 5 several well-built walls of earlier monumental structures belonging to the eastern edge of the monumental city centre were incorporated (Fig. 33). The open spaces between these structures had been blocked by means of late Roman constructions consisting of a double casing with a fill of mortared rubble. In wall section 5 no traces of towers can be identified. However, since this wall section is 160 m long, it is very unlikely that no towers at all would have been planned here. Towards the south, wall section 5 disappears underneath the medieval caravan road to the north of the Roman bath building.

4.3.6. Wall section 6

The connection between wall section 5 and wall section 6 is no longer visible today and it is not clear how it should be reconstructed. It seems likely that part of the east wall of the Roman bath building had been incorporated into the late Roman city wall. However, wall section 6 itself lies to the southeast of the bath complex and is not connected with it (Fig. 1). The north-south oriented wall section 6 is 25 m long and can be divided into two different sections (Fig. 34). The pseudo-isodomic masonry of the northern section contained re-used ashlars of different dimensions, placed in a double casing with a fill of mortared rubble. The western casing of this wall is obscured by the slope behind it. This part of wall section 6 still stands to a height of 2.60 m. Against its southern extremity, a second wall has been built, still standing 2.50 m high and consisting of small and rough polygonal stones alternating with a few ashlars. This southern part of wall section 6 also has a fill of mortared rubble.

The northern part of wall section 6 seems to represent an earlier wall, re-used inside the city wall. While building the late Roman city wall, this part of wall section 6 was probably extended to the southwest by erecting the southern, polygonal wall against it. Near its southern end the polygonal wall turns sharply to the west and follows the slope to the south of the bath building towards the colonnaded street. There, wall section 6 was probably connected to tower *f* of wall section 7. This connection was discovered in 1995 when a small part of it was unearthed during the construction of an earth road to evacuate excavated material from the lower agora.

4.3.7. Wall section 7

Wall section 7 incorporates the southern half of the large colonnaded street leading from the lower agora towards the south (Fig. 1). This street follows the western slope of the promontory carrying the temple of Antoninus Pius. Wall section 7 follows the west side of the street and is 210 m long. Towards the south it diverts across the promontory towards the east. This last section is connected with wall section 8 located on the east slope of the promontory. The drop in level between the northern and the southern extremity of the colonnaded street is almost 25 m. This drop in level was overcome by monumental stairways, two of which were covered by late Roman towers (towers *g* and *h*). Wall section 7 consists of two faces with re-used architectural blocks and a fill of mortared rubble in between. The use of *spolia* from the temenos wall of the Antoninus Pius sanctuary offers a *terminus post quem* for the construction of wall section 7 (Waelkens *et al.* 1990: 193) (Fig. 35). The wall is approximately 2 m wide and in some places still stands 1.50 m high. Today, no connection between towers *f* and *g* is visible, but such a connection cannot be completely dismissed. It is possible that both sides of the colonnaded street were fortified between these towers, thus creating a passage between the main part of the fortified late Roman city and the walled off promontory to the south of it. However, the gap between towers *f* and *g* is only 28 m wide and could easily be controlled and defended from the towers. Thus, the probably late Hellenistic tower *f* (see 3.2) may have formed an important element in the connection between the two walled off sections of late Roman Sagalassos.

Tower *g* was built over the colonnaded street, 25 m south of tower *f*, and 160 m south of the lower agora. This tower forms both the beginning and the end of the late Roman wall around the southern promontory. Towards the south this wall leads to tower *h*; towards the east tower *g* is connected with the southwestern part of wall section 8. The tower forms the second important element in the connection between the main city wall and the wall around the promontory. In fact tower *g* forms the northwest corner of the latter. This rectangular tower measures 7 m by 8 m and has 1.50 m thick walls consisting of two casings filled with mortared rubble (Fig. 7). Like the rest of wall section 7, the walls of the tower were built using *spolia* from the temenos wall of the temple of Antoninus Pius. The existence of a 0.50 m wide entrance in the south side of the tower, instead of in the north where it would have faced tower *f*, is a further indication that the towers were not linked. Thus, the promontory, devoid of important buildings during the late Roman period since the emperor's cult ceased to exist, had a circuit wall of its own. Indeed, the promontory was strategically too important not to be incorporated within the circuit of the late Roman defences. Without fortifying it the southern approach to the city could never be controlled adequately. On the other hand, by fortifying the promontory, the inhabitants of Sagalassos also took a serious risk. An enemy who conquered the promontory would also obtain an ideal base from which to besiege the lower city.

Tower *h* is located 35 m to the south of tower *g*, and 195 m to the south of the lower agora. The north, east and south walls of this rectangular tower are 1.20 m thick. The 2.00 m thick west wall forms part of the late Roman circuit wall around the promontory. All these walls consist of two casings of re-used blocks with a fill of mortared rubble. The tower contains two rooms (Fig. 7). The main, eastern room measures 7 m by 11.5 m. The entrance to the tower is situated in its south wall and is 0.80 m wide. The second room, measuring 5.5 m by 6 m, projects from the late Roman circuit wall towards the west. Both rooms may have been connected by means of a doorway in the northeast corner of the main room. One of its doorposts still seems to stand *in situ*. The similarities in building techniques and building materials between the rooms make it very unlikely that they would represent two different building phases.

Approximately 20 m further south, wall section 7 turns to the east and crosses the promontory, approximately 40 m to the north of a monumental city gate dated to the first century AD (Fig. 1). Similar to the rest of wall section 7, this section consists of a wall with a double casing of re-used building blocks from the temenos wall of the temple of Antoninus Pius. A second, smaller wall runs parallel to the double wall, 2 m to the south of it. Between these walls several cross walls have been built. It is not clear whether these walls represent one or more building phases. It seems likely that somewhere within this 60 m long section, an entrance to the promontory existed of which today no traces can be seen. If there was no such entrance, there would have been only a few small sally ports, necessary for entering and leaving the promontory. The complexity of the section in the south of the promontory may be connected with the presence of the strategically important Alexander's Hill located to the southwest of the promontory.

4.3.8. Wall section 8

Southeast and east of the temple of Antoninus Pius, only a few remains of the circuit wall surrounding the promontory are preserved (Fig. 1). These walls consist either of re-used terrace walls built with large ashlars (Fig. 36) or of late Roman walls made of *spolia*. A smaller wall of rough polygonal stones, with a fill of rubble can also be seen. All these walls can be linked and form a slightly curved line of defence along the southeast slope of the promontory. The northern extremity of this eastern part of wall section 8 was built against a rocky outcrop, incorporated into wall section 8. To the northwest of this outcrop lies the northeastern section of wall section 8. Of the series of walls on the southeast slope of the promontory, the re-used terrace walls were most probably built first. The walls made of *spolia* probably date to around 400 AD, when the late Roman city wall was built. The date of the small polygonal wall is not clear. Wall

Fig. 32: The ruins of the late Roman northeast city gate.

Fig. 33: Wall of a building re-used in wall section 5.

Fig. 34: Wall section 6.

Fig. 35: *Spolia* of the temple of Antoninus Pius in wall section 7.

Fig. 36: Re-used terrace walls in wall section 8.

Fig. 37: *Spolia* of the temple of Antoninus Pius in the northeast part of wall section 8.

Fig. 38: Eastern part of wall section 10.

section 8 on the southeastern slope of the promontory seems not to have been built according to the technology used in the rest of the late Roman city wall, probably because this very steep slope already offered a good protection against attack.

On the northern slope of the promontory, wall section 8 can be divided in two parts. Against the rocky outcrop forming the northeast corner of the promontory, there is a wall completely made of *spolia* from the temenos of the temple of Antoninus Pius (Fig. 37). These include column drums, bases and a Corinthian capital. The 1.60 m thick wall consists of two facings and a fill of mortared rubble. Towards the west it has partly collapsed. This wall was probably linked to the bedrock which supports part of a huge terrace wall carrying the temenos of Antoninus Pius. This terrace wall has probably been incorporated into the late Roman wall, and was probably linked to the second part of wall section 8 on the northern slope of the promontory. A few blocks lying *in situ*, immediately west of the terrace wall offer an indication of such a connection. Here, wall section 8 mainly re-used the walls of an earlier building, made of nice ashlar. Towards the west, this building is connected with tower *g* on the colonnaded street. The late Roman connection consists of two casings of re-used building blocks and a fill of mortared rubble.

4.3.9. Wall section 9

The remains of a probably late Hellenistic tower were re-used in wall section 9. For a description of this wall section see 3.2.

4.3.10. Wall section 10

Wall section 10 runs through the valley to the west of the promontory with the Antoninus Pius temple, turning to the north after 120 m. It continues across a small hill that borders the valley in the west (Fig. 1). Towards the east, the connection between wall sections 9 and 10 is not clear. The wall may have run slightly towards the north along the western slope of the promontory and be linked to a tower (?), from where it would then have descended towards the valley. Towards the northwest, wall section 10 was built against the steep rock cliff which carries wall section 1. The eastern part of wall section 10 consists of a double wall built of large re-used ashlars with a rubble fill (Fig. 38). The rest of this wall section is in a very ruinous state. Towards the west as well as towards the north, on top of the small hill, only a heap of rubble can be seen. Towards the northwest, wall section 10 cuts through a necropolis. It is not clear whether any of the sarcophagi have been re-used in the wall.

Wall section 10 encloses part of the domestic quarters of Sagalassos. The reasons for this are threefold. At the time of the construction of the late Roman city wall Sagalassos was still a fairly densely populated settlement, so it may have been necessary to include at least a part of the domestic quarters within the wall. However, other domestic and industrial areas of the city were not protected. This indicates that the fortified city centre mainly functioned as a refuge at times of danger. Thus, there may have been another argument for including the northern half of the domestic area in this valley. The possibility of re-using part of the late Hellenistic city wall (wall section 1) may have been decisive. However, a third argument can be suggested. A small well, which nowadays flows a few meters to the south of wall section 10 but which in Roman times may have surfaced to the north of the wall, may have been important enough to be included within the walled city. A combination of these arguments can explain the inclusion of the northern half of the valley to the west of the promontory within the walled circuit of the city.

5. CONCLUSIONS

The city fortifications of Sagalassos form an important chapter in the urban development of the city. The city walls not only provided a defence for the city, but also expressed its power and emphasized its identity. One could say that, when the city became part of the Roman empire in 25 BC and most of its late Hellenistic walls were dismantled during the next two or three centuries, part of this identity was lost. Yet, the *Pax Romana* which established peace in Pisidia, made city fortifications superfluous. Only towards the end of the fourth or the beginning of the fifth centuries AD did the Ostrogoth uprising and the swiftly following raids of the Isaurians force the inhabitants of Sagalassos to fortify part of their city again. This evolution is parallelled by a growing instability in the rest of the empire. Two phases of city fortifications, a pre-Roman and a late Roman one, can be distinguished at Sagalassos.

The existence of pre-Hellenistic city fortifications at Sagalassos can be inferred from Arrian's *Anabasis Alexandri*. It seems probable that the pre-Hellenistic city was walled and that the defensive function of the Alexander's Hill was limited. However, no traces of these pre-Hellenistic defences can be identified with certainty on the site, unless part of the fortifications on the mountain ridge above it might date back to this period.

In fact, the Hellenistic fortifications of the city are twofold. There was a system of outer defences with a belt of watchtowers and a fortress on the mountain peaks overlooking the city and barrier walls that may or may not be contemporary with them. In any case, the fortress, watchtowers and barrier walls are certainly older than the preserved parts of the late Hellenistic city wall. The principles of this system can be found throughout Asia Minor. Its function was to control those approaches to the city that were not visible from it. The heart of this system at Sagalassos is the fortress on the Tekne Tepe. From here the defence of the barrier wall to the north of the mountain crest could be organised. The long barrier wall near the mountain crest and the small barrier wall in the pass to the west of the Tekne Tepe, did not form a mere addition, but were necessary elements of the Hellenistic city defence system at Sagalassos because of the less steep northern slopes of the mountain. The fortress most probably existed already during the first decades of the third century BC. If the barrier walls were not contemporary, their construction perhaps took place during the reign of Antiochos I.

The late Hellenistic city wall of Sagalassos is only partly preserved, making it impossible to reconstruct its full circuit. The probably late Hellenistic city gate in the south of the city shows that the Hellenistic city had already expanded to that point before the arrival of the Romans. During the first three centuries AD, most of the late Hellenistic city wall was dismantled. Even if the remaining parts were re-used in the late Roman city wall, it is unlikely that the complete late Hellenistic wall was followed, so that the exact size of the Hellenistic defences and the extent of the city can no longer be established.

During the *Pax Romana* of the first centuries AD city fortifications were no longer needed at Sagalassos. However, towards the end of the fourth and the beginning of the fifth centuries AD, military threats posed by the Ostrogoth uprising under Tribigild and the raids of the Isaurians, forced the inhabitants of Sagalassos to fortify their city once more. This late Roman wall fits very well into the pattern of contemporary fortifications elsewhere in Asia Minor. Only the centre of the city was fortified and many existing buildings and *spolia* were incorporated within the new circuit. The parts of the late Hellenistic city wall that were still standing were also re-used. Sixth century AD ceramics found inside the fortress on the Tekne Tepe and inside the watchtower on the Çinçinkirik Tepe, indicate that at least part of the outer defences remained or returned to use during the late Roman to early Byzantine period. The late Roman fortifications at Sagalassos were not maintained and well kept for very long. A century after their construction, some sections at least were already abandoned, since debris from an earthquake was piled up against them. This could suggest that the defence system had been damaged beyond repair during the 518 AD seismic catastrophe.

It is clear that the fortifications at Sagalassos can be compared with the general pattern of fortifications found in the rest of Asia Minor. Only elements that are determined by the local topography are specific. The function of the long barrier wall, for example, can be compared with that of a 'great circuit wall', but unlike this kind of wall, it was not part of a closed wall circuit. The construction of the long barrier wall was imposed by the topography on the north side of the mountain ridge which dominates Sagalassos. Enormous building costs and practical problems may have excluded the construction of a 'great circuit wall' to incorporate the mountain crest within the city's defences. The system of watchtowers on the mountain peaks overlooking Sagalassos has similarities at Ephesos and at Herakleia on the Latmos. The pseudo-isodomic masonry and the square plan of the towers of the late Hellenistic city wall also reflects building practices at other Pisidian sites, such as Termessos and Cremna. The use of *spolia*, the reduction of the walled off city area and the incorporation of earlier monumental buildings in the late Roman city wall finally resemble a large number of contemporary defences in other cities of Asia Minor.

This article is by no means a complete study of the city fortifications of Sagalassos, but only a starting point. Most of the observations are based on survey data and not on excavations. Thus, no conclusions can be drawn with absolute certainty, and most of the proposed reconstructions and hypotheses are open to further refinement and discussion.

6. ACKNOWLEDGEMENTS

This text presents research results of the Belgian Programme on Interuniversity Poles of Attraction (IUAP 4/12) initiated by the Belgian State, Prime Minister's Office, Science Policy Programming. This research was also made possible thanks to an FWO-Vlaanderen research grant (FWO/G.0215.96) and to the GOA-programme (97/1). Lieven Loots is research assistant of the Fund for Scientific Research Flanders – Belgium (F.W.O.). Scientific responsibilty is assumed by its authors.

7. REFERENCES

Forschungen in Ephesos (1906) I, Wien.
K. Belke and N. Mersich (1990) *Phrygien und Pisidien (Tabula Imperii Byzantini* 7) Wien.
J. Borchhardt (1986) Limyra, *Anatolian Studies* 36: 205-206.
J. Borchhardt (1989) Limyra, *Anatolian Studies* 39: 178-179.
H. Bracke (1993) Pisidia in Hellenistic times (334-25B.C.), in: M. Waelkens (ed.) *Sagalassos I. First General Report on the Survey (1986-1989) and Excavations (1990-1991) (Acta Archaeologica Lovaniensia Monographiae* 5) Leuven University Press: 15-30.
R. Degeest (2000) *The Common Wares at Roman Sagalassos (Studies in Eastern Mediterranean Archaelogy* 3) Brepols Publishers.

R. Fleischer (1979) Forschungen in Sagalassos 1972 und 1974, *Istanbuler Mitteilungen* 29: 273-307.

C. Foss (1979) *Ephesos after Antiquity: a Late Antique, Byzantine and Turkish City*, Cambridge.

A. von Gerkan (1935) *Die Stadtmauern (Milet. Ergebnisse der Ausgrabungen und Untersuchungen seit dem Jahre 1899* II.3) Berlin.

J. Grainger (1995) The campaign of Cn. Manlius Vulso in Asia Minor, *Anatolian Studies* 45: 23- 42.

G.M.A. Hanfmann and J.C. Waldbaum (eds) (1975) *A Survey of Sardis and the Major Monuments Outside the City Walls (Archaeological Exploration of Sardis* 1) Cambridge.

W. Jobst (1978) Hellenistische Außenfortifikationen um Ephesos, *Studien zur Religion und Kultur Kleinasiens. Festschrift für F.K. Dörner*, Leiden: 447-456.

G. Kleiner (1968) *Die Ruinen von Milet*, Berlin.

E. Kosmetatou and M. Waelkens (1997) The "Macedonian" shields of Sagalassos, in: M. Waelkens and J. Poblome (eds) *Sagalassos IV. Report on the Survey and Excavation Campaigns of 1994 and 1995 (Acta Archaeologica Lovaniensia Monographiae* 9) Leuven University Press: 277-292.

F. Krischen (1922) *Die Befestigungen von Herakleia am Latmos (Milet. Ergebnisse der Ausgrabungen und Untersuchungen* III.2) Berlin.

A.W. Lawrence (1979) *Greek Aims in Fortification*, Oxford.

E. Lessing and W. Oberleitner (1978) *Ephesos. Weltstadt der Antike*, Wien.

B. Levick (1967) *Roman Colonies in Southern Asia Minor*, Oxford.

L. Loots, K. Nackaerts and M. Waelkens (1999) Fuzzy viewshed analysis of the Hellenistic city defense system at Sagalassos, Turkey, in: *Archaeology in the Age of the Internet – CAA97. Computer Applications and Quantitative Methods in Archaeology. 25th Anniversary Conference. University of Birmingham. April 1997 (BAR S750)* Oxford.

A. Machatschek and M. Schwarz (1981) *Bauforschungen in Selge*, Wien.

A.M. Mansel (1963) *Die Ruinen von Side*, Berlin.

A.M. Mansel (1968) Osttor und Waffenreliefs von Side (Pamphylien), *Archäologische Anzeiger*: 239-279.

R. Marchese (1992) Ancient remains in Caria: the watchtower at Arpas, *Anatolian Studies* 42: 47-52.

A. McNicoll (1982) Developments in techniques of siegecraft and fortification in the Greek world ca. 400-100 B.C., in: *La fortification dans l'histoire du monde grec (CNRS Colloque International* 614): 305-313.

S. Mitchell (1989a) The siege of Cremna, in: *The Eastern Frontier of the Roman Empire (BAR International Series* 553) Oxford: 311-328.

S. Mitchell (1989b) Archaeology in Asia Minor, *Journal of Hellenistic Studies. Archaeological Reports* 1989/90: 118.

S. Mitchell (1993) *Anatolia. Land, Men and Gods in Asia Minor I: The Celts in Anatolia and the Impact of Roman Rule*, Oxford.

S. Mitchell (1994a) Three cities in Pisidia, *Anatolian Studies* 44: 129-148.

S. Mitchell (1994b) Termessos, king Amyntas, and the war with the Sandaliôtai. A new inscription from Pisidia, in: D. French (ed.) *Studies in the History and Topography of Lycia and Pisidia. In Memoriam A.S. Hall (British Institute of Archaeology at Ankara. Monograph* 19): 95-105.

S. Mitchell (1995a) *Cremna in Pisidia. An Ancient City in Peace and War*, London.

S. Mitchell (1995b) Pisidian survey, *Anatolian Archaeology. Reports on Research Conducted in Turkey* 1: 15-18.

A. Müller-Karpe (1989) Neue galatische Funde aus Anatolien, *Istanbuler Mitteilungen* 38: 189-199.

H.A. Ormerod (1992) The campaigns of Servilius Isauricus against the pirates, *Journal of Roman Studies* 12: 35-52.

E. Paulissen, J. Poesen, G. Govers and J. De Ploey (1993) The physical environment at Sagalassos (western Taurus, Turkey). A reconnaissance survey, in: M. Waelkens and J. Poblome (eds) *Sagalassos II. Report on the Third Excavation Campaign of 1992 (Acta Archaeologica Lovaniensia Monographiae* 6) Leuven University Press: 229-248.

A. Peschlow-Bindokat (1996) *Der Latmos, Eine unbekannte Gebirgslandschaft an der türkischen Westküste (Zaberns Bildbände zur Archäologie)* Mainz.

J. Poblome (1995) Sherds and coins. A question of chronology, in: M. Waelkens and J. Poblome (eds) *Sagalassos III. Report on the Fourth Excavation Campaign of 1993 (Acta Archaeologica Lovaniensia Monographiae* 7) Leuven University Press: 185-205.

J. Rougé (1966) L'histoire Auguste et L'Isaurie au IVe siècle, *Revue des études anciennes* 68: 282-315.

M. Schede (1964) *Die Ruinen von Priene*, Berlin.

S. Scheers (1993a) Catalogue of the coins found during the years 1990 and 1991, in: M. Waelkens (ed.) *Sagalassos I. First General Report on the Survey (1986-1989) and Excavations (1990-1991) (Acta Archaeologica Lovaniensia Monographiae* 5) Leuven University Press: 197- 205.

S. Scheers (1993b) Catalogue of the coins found in 1992, in: M. Waelkens and J. Poblome (eds) *Sagalassos II. Report on the Fourth Excavation Campaign of 1992 (Acta Archaeologica Lovaniensia Monographiae* 6) Leuven University Press: 249-260.

B. Schmaltz (1994) Kaunos 1988-1991, *Archäologisch Anzeiger*: 185-237.

L. Vandeput (1993) Remains of an Antonine monument at Sagalassos, in: M. Waelkens (ed.) *Sagalassos I. First General Report on the Survey (1986-1989) and Excavations (1990-1991) (Acta Archaeologica Lovaniensia Monographiae* 5) Leuven University Press: 141-148.

L. Vandeput (1997) *The Architectural Decoration in Roman Asia Minor. Sagalassos: a Case Study (Studies in eastern Mediterranean Archaeology* 1) Brepols Publishers.

K. Vandorpe (1995) A Sagalassos city seal, in: M. Waelkens and J. Poblome (eds) *Sagalassos III. Report on the Fourth Excavation Campaign of 1993 (Acta Archaeologica Lovaniensia Monographiae* 7) Leuven University Press: 299-305.

K. Vandorpe (2000) Negotiator's laws from rebellious Sagalassos in an early Hellenistic inscription, in: M. Waelkens and L. Loots (eds) *Sagalassos V. Report on the Survey and Excavation Campaigns of 1996 and 1997 (Acta Archaeologica Lovaniensia Monographiae* 11) Leuven University Press: 489-508.

M. Waelkens and S. Mitchell (1988) Cremna and Sagalassos 1987, *Anatolian Studies* 38: 53-66.

M. Waelkens, S. Mitchell and E. Owens (1990) Sagalassos 1989, *Anatolian Studies* 40: 185-198.

M. Waelkens, A. Harmankaya and W. Viaene (1991) The excavations at Sagalassos 1990, *Anatolian Studies* 41: 197-214.

M. Waelkens (1992a) Die neue Forschungen (1985-1989) und die belgischen Ausgrabungen (1990-1991) in Sagalassos, in: *Forschungen in Pisidien (Asia Minor Studien* 6): 43-60.

M. Waelkens, E. Owens, A. Hasendonckx and B. Arıkan (1992b) The excavations at Sagalassos 1991, *Anatolian Studies* 42: 79-98.

M. Waelkens (1993a) Sagalassos. History and archaeology, in: M. Waelkens (ed.) *Sagalassos I. First General Report on the Survey (1986-1989) and Excavations (1990-1991) (Acta Archaeologica Lovaniensia Monographiae* 5) Leuven University Press: 37-81.

M. Waelkens (1993b) The 1992 excavation season. A preliminary report, in: M. Waelkens and J. Poblome (eds) *Sagalassos II. Report on the Third Excavation Campaign of 1992 (Acta*

Archaeologica Lovaniensia Monographiae 6) Leuven University Press: 9-41.

M. Waelkens (1995) The 1993 excavation in the fountain house-library area, in: M. Waelkens and J. Poblome (eds) *Sagalassos III. Report on the Fourth Excavation Campaign of 1993 (Acta Archaeologica Lovaniensia Monographiae* 7) Leuven University Press: 47-89.

M. Waelkens, E. Paulissen, H. Vanhaverbeke, I. Öztürk, B. De Cupere, H.A. Ekinci, P.M. Vermeersch, J. Poblome and R. Degeest (1997a) The 1994 and 1995 surveys on the territory of Sagalassos, in: M. Waelkens and J. Poblome (eds) *Sagalassos IV. Report on the Survey and Ecxavation Campaigns of 1994 and 1995 (Acta Archaeologica Lovaniensia Monographiae* 9) Leuven University Press: 11-102.

M. Waelkens, P.M. Vermeersch, E. Paulissen, E. Owens, B. Arıkan, M. Martens, P. Talloen, L. Gijsen, L. Loots, C. Peleman, J. Poblome, R. Degeest, T. Patrício, S. Ercan and F. Depuydt (1997b) The 1994 and 1995 excavation seasons at Sagalassos, in: M. Waelkens and J. Poblome (ed.) *Sagalassos IV. Report on the Survey and Excavation Campaigns of 1994 and 1995 (Acta Archaeologica Lovaniensia Monographiae* 9) Leuven University Press: 103-216.

M. Waelkens, M. Sintubin, Ph. Muchez and E. Paulissen (2000a) Archaeological and geological evidence for a major earthquake at Sagalassos (SW Turkey) around te middle of the seventh century AD, in: B. McGuire, D. Griffiths and I. Stewart (eds) *The Archaelogy of Geological Catastrophes (Geological Society, Special Publications 171)* London: 373-383

M. Waelkens, E. Paulissen, H. Vanhaverbeke, J.Reyniers, J. Poblome, R. Degeest, W. Viaene (†), J. Deckers, B. De Cupere, W. Van Neer, M.A. Ekıncı and M.O. Erbay (2000b) The 1996 and 1997 surveys in the territory of Sagalassos, in: M. Waelkens and L. Loots (eds) *Sagalassos V. Report on the Survey and Excavation Campaigns of 1996 and 1997 (Acta Archaeologica Lovaniensia Monographiae 11)* Leuven University Press: 17-216.

M. Waelkens, L. Vandeput, Ch. Berns, B. Arıkan, J. Poblome and E. Torun (2000c) The Northwest Heroon at Sagalassos, in M. Waelkens and L. Loots (eds) *Sagalassos V. Report on the Survey and Excavation Campaigns of 1996 and 1997 (Acta Archaelogica Lovaniensia Monographiae* 10) Leuven University Press: 553-594.

F.E. Winter (1966) Notes on military architecture in the Termessos region, *American Journal of Archaeology* 70: 127-137.

F.E. Winter (1971) *Greek Fortifications*, London.

H. Wolfram (1979) *Geschichte der Goten. Von der Anfangen bis zur Mitte des sechsten Jahrhunderts. Entwurf einer historischen Ethnographie*, Munchen.

U. Wulf (1994) Der Stadtplan von Pergamon, *Istanbuler Mitteilungen* 44: 135-175.

THE WATER SUPPLY TO SAGALASSOS

An STEEGEN[1], Kris CAUWENBERGHS[1], Gerard GOVERS[1], Marc WAELKENS[2], Edwin J. OWENS[3] and Philip DESMET[1]

1 - Laboratory for Experimental Geomorphology, KULeuven, Redingenstraat 16, B-3000 Leuven, Belgium
2 - Department of Archaeology, KULeuven, Blijde Inkomststraat 21, B-3000 Leuven, Belgium
3 - Department of Classics and Ancient History, University College of Swansea, Swansea SA28PP, United Kingdom

1. INTRODUCTION

Water, as an essential of life, certainly played a major role in the selection of the location of an ancient city. In Roman times many cities were fed by aqueducts. These can be found both in the western part of the Roman empire and in the east. Several cities of Asia Minor have well-preserved aqueducts, e.g. Pergamon, Side and Cremna (Owens 1991).

The six aqueducts of Sagalassos have already been described by Owens (1995) but, at the time, the detailed topographical and morphological information necessary to estimate the possible flow was not available. It was also then unclear which springs may have contributed to the supply of the aqueducts and how the total present-day flow of these springs compared to the carrying capacity of the aqueducts. This last point may be an important indicator of environmental change in the area: if present-day flow is much lower than the flow the aqueduct was designed for, then it is probable that in historic times the flow from the springs was greater. In order to obtain more information on this topic a detailed map was made of three of the six aqueducts and a field survey was carried out to map all the springs in the area and to measure their present-day flow and water quality.

The survey of the aqueducts and springs was also carried out with another purpose in mind. When an aqueduct was built, it formed a reference line in the landscape. Apart from deliberate human action, any disturbance of this line may be ascribed to geomorphological and/or tectonic activity. The fills of the old aqueduct channel were therefore surveyed in detail, so that the average mechanical erosion rates of the upslope areas could be determined and sequences of cut-and-fill could be identified. It was also possible, by determining the hardness of the spring water, to estimate the present-day chemical erosion rates. Comparison of both figures allows a preliminary evaluation to be made of the contribution of both types of processes to the geomorphological evolution of the area.

2. MATERIALS AND METHODS

2.1. Spring survey

A study area of about 13 km^2 was delimited for the spring survey. Based on the earlier work by Owens, this area is considered the potential source area for the aqueducts which brought water to the site from the west and east (Fig. 1). The area is bounded by the watershed north of the site, including the summit of the Akdağ (2271 m), and the contour line of 1250 m to the south. This area was systematically surveyed by field walking. When a spring was found, its position was pinpointed by means of a handheld GPS receiver with an accuracy of +/- 70 m (one standard deviation). The flow of each spring was measured. Depending on the situation, a large or small triangular weir was used and the springwater was collected in a bottle or bucket for a certain length of time (Fig. 2). In an existing concrete channel near a modern trout farm (Kırazlı) a propeller current meter was used and the surface velocity in the channel was measured. One spring near to the city site was monitored several times to examine temporal variations.

Furthermore, three variables describing water quality were measured. Temperature was measured by means of a conventional alcohol thermometer. pH was measured with the help of a portable pH meter with a precision of 0.01, while carbonate hardness was measured by means of acidimetric titration with a precision of 1°d (1°d = 17.8 mg $CaCO_3$/litre).

2.2. Aqueducts

Three aqueducts are located to the east of the city and three to the west (Owens 1995). None of these is entirely preserved. The aqueducts may have suffered severe damage in the major earthquake of 518 AD (Waelkens 1993 and again in another around the middle of the seventh century

(Waelkens *et.al.* 2000). Also, significant erosion occurred on the slopes where the aqueducts were built, and at several places the aqueducts have completely disappeared. The remains of the upper (probably Hellenistic) and the middle rock-cut aqueducts on the eastern side of the city, as well as the Roman Imperial middle aqueduct to the west of the city are relatively well preserved. These aqueducts can be followed over significant distances and only these aqueducts were mapped in detail.

An automatic theodolite was used for mapping the aqueducts. This instrument is able to measure the height as well as the planimetric position of points with an accuracy of a few millimeters, so that the trajectory could be determined very accurately.

A major problem during mapping was that the aqueducts are nowadays often filled with hillslope debris. To determine the height of the channelbed (which is necessary to determine the hydraulic gradient), some holes were dug in the channel until its bottom was reached. Another method was to hammer an iron pin into the sediment layer. When this pin could no longer be driven into the fill, it was assumed that the bottom was reached.

First, the visible parts of the aqueducts were mapped. Because the channels are interrupted in several places, a method had to be developed to establish the most likely line of the aqueducts on the slope segments where no remains could be found. The place where the aqueducts crossed the slopes was estimated using a level. Then, small cross-profiles of 5 points were measured on the hillslope. Two of these points were located directly above and two below the estimated level of the aqueduct, whilst the fifth was taken at the level itself. By a linear interpolation of the height of the aqueduct between two known points, the most likely position of the aqueduct on the hillslope could then be determined. This method ensured that the topography of the slopes was taken into account when determining the trajectory of the aqueduct and that the length of the missing part of the channel between two known parts was not underestimated.

We have mentioned that the aqueducts around the city are to some extent filled with sediment that was eroded from the slopes above the channel after the aqueduct was abandoned. Because the city was abandoned in the seventh century AD (Waelkens *et al.* 2000), it may be assumed that sediment accumulation in the aqueducts continued for at least 1300 years. This can also then be considered as a long-term experiment to measure the mechanical erosion on these hillsides.

Four sections were chosen on the upper aqueduct east of Sagalassos, each with a length between 50 and 100 m. The volume of the sediment in each section was calculated. Dividing these values by the surface area of the slope above the channel that was the source of the sediment, and taking into account the fact that the mass density of the sediment is different from that of the limestone rock, we obtained an erosion rate for the slope.

3. THE SPRINGS AROUND SAGALASSOS

3.1. The location of the springs

In the study area, 45 natural and 4 other springs were found. Furthermore, it became clear that a large amount of surface water from the Akdağ mountain drained towards a trout farm located at Kırazlı in the southeast of the study area (Fig. 1). Paulissen *et al.* (1993) suggested that most of the springs were situated at the base of an escarpment, which is the contact plane between an upper limestone formation and a lower ophiolite formation which is relatively less permeable. A comparison of the position of the springs with a geological map of the area shows that the situation is more complicated. More than half of the springs are situated below the contact plane and nearly forty percent of them are located in the ophiolite formation. Thus, there is no clear 'line of springs'. Springs are most frequently found within the ophiolite zone as a whole, with a vertical range between 300 and 1000 m. However, significant water sources can also be found in the limestone above the ophiolites.

3.2. The flow of the springs

The total outflow of all 48 springs was 39.6 litre per second (l/s) and at the trout farm an outflow of 49 ($\pm$ 8) l/s was recorded. More than 90% of the springs had a flow of less than 1 l/s. The flow of the spring C1 was measured several times during the field campaign. Over a period of one month, its flow decreased from 2.3 to 1.9 l/s.

Measurements were taken at the end of the summer period, when they can be expected to be relatively low. In order to be able to recalculate the discharges for yearly average values, hydrographs of springs from Southeastern Turkey (Korkmaz 1989; Dinçer and Payne 1971) were examined. The trend at Sagalassos appeared to accord well with the levels recorded on the hydrographs. Assuming that their studies are representative for the Sagalassos area and taking into account seasonal variations, the yearly average flow of a spring in the study area (including the outlet at the trout farm) could be estimated as ca. 115 l/s or about 10 million litres per day. Expressed as an equivalent precipitation measurement for the study area, the spring discharge then equals ca. 0.28 m per year.

This estimate is based on the assumption that the situation in 1995 is representative for a longer time period. Databases

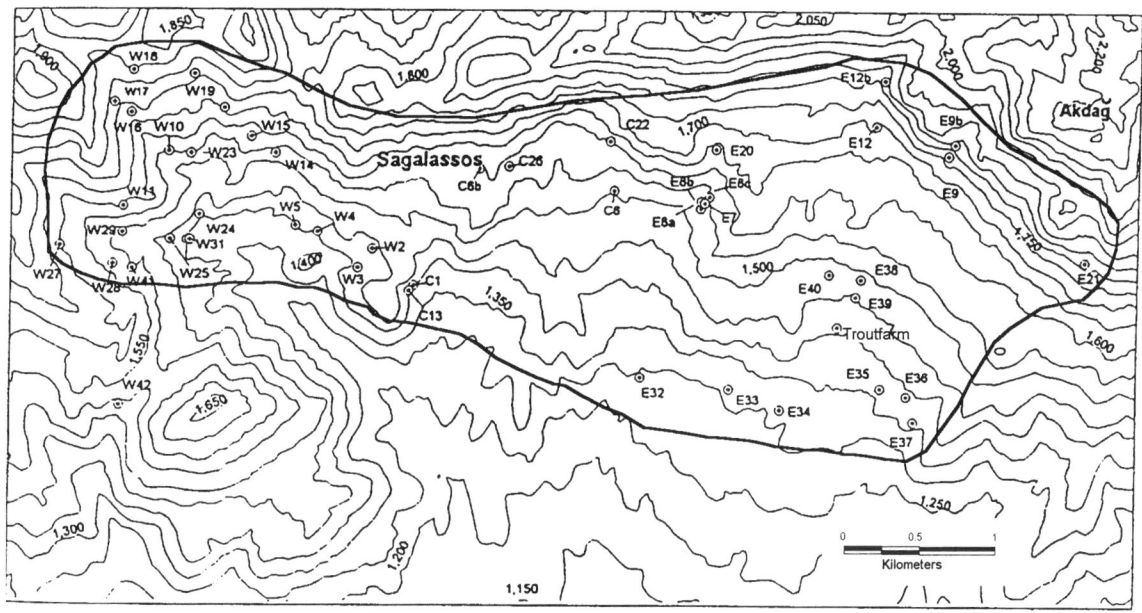

Fig. 1: Limitation of the surveyed area with indication of all springs.

Fig. 2: Weir used to measure the discharge of the springs.

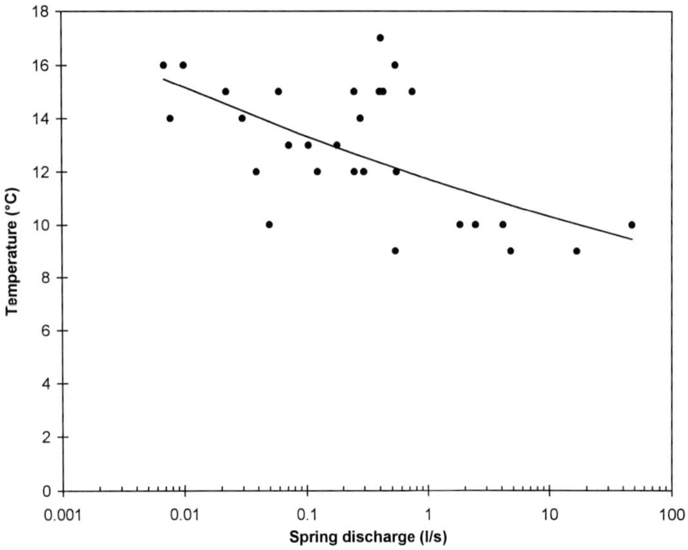

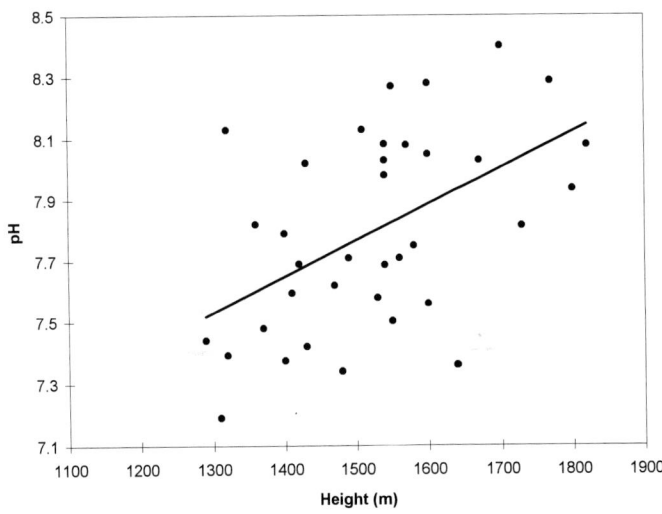

Fig. 3: Correlation between the temperature and the discharge of the springs in the study area.

Fig. 4: Positive correlation between pH and height of the springs.

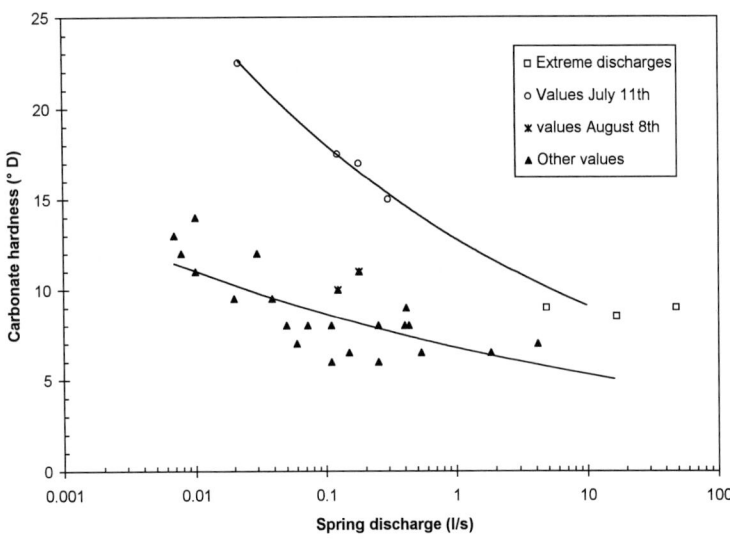

Fig. 5: Negative correlation between discharge and carbonate hardness.

638

Fig. 6: Section of the upper eastern aqueduct with a depth of more than 10 metres.

Fig. 7: Rock-cut section of the middle western aqueduct.

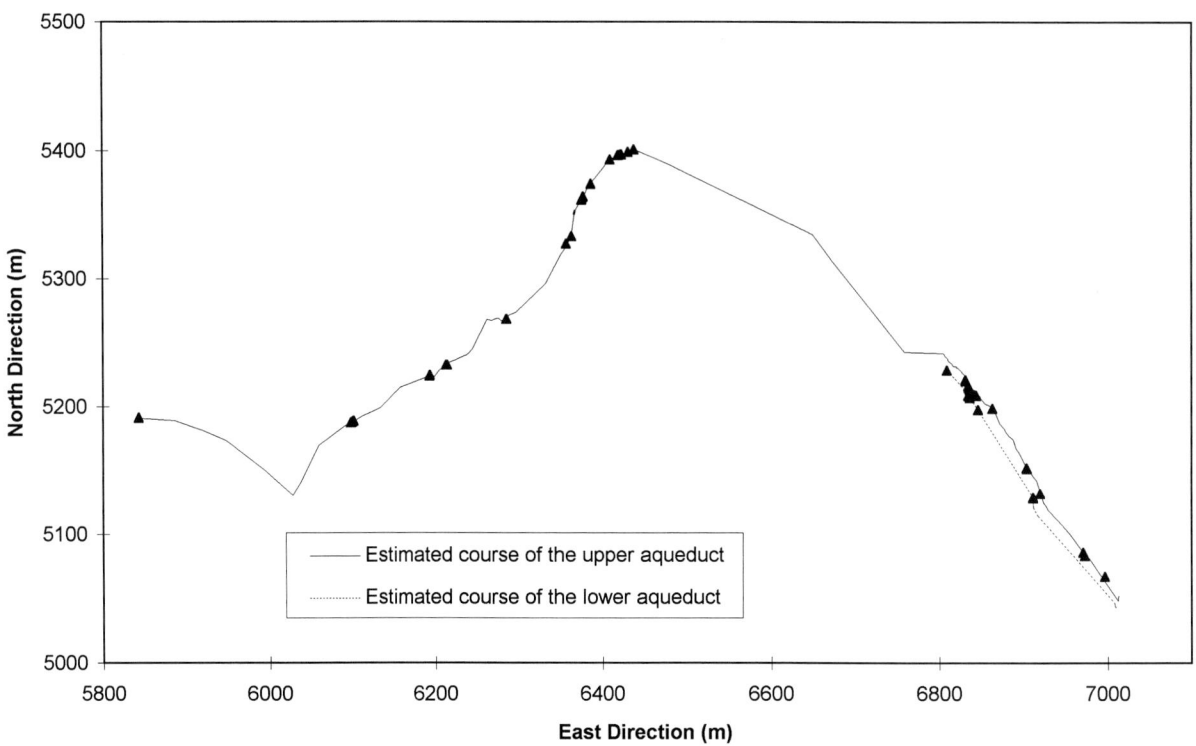

Fig. 8: Planimetric form of the eastern aqueducts.

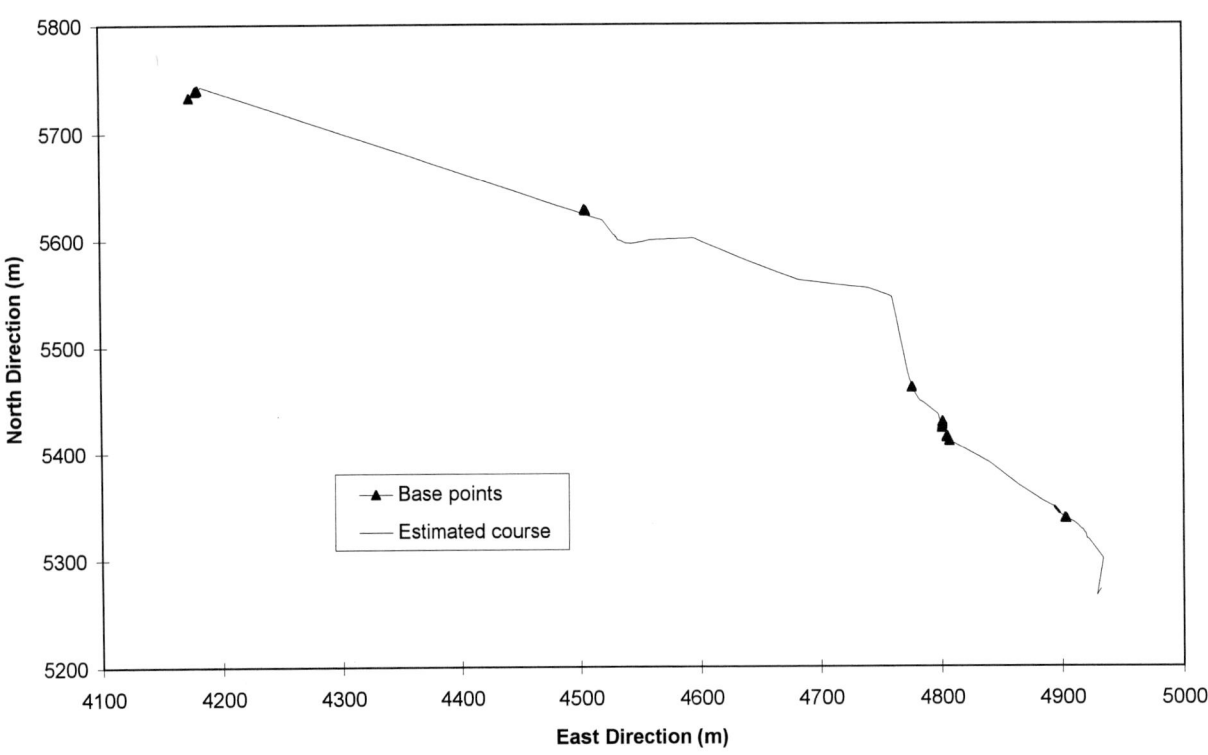

Fig. 9: Planimetric form of the middle western aqueduct.

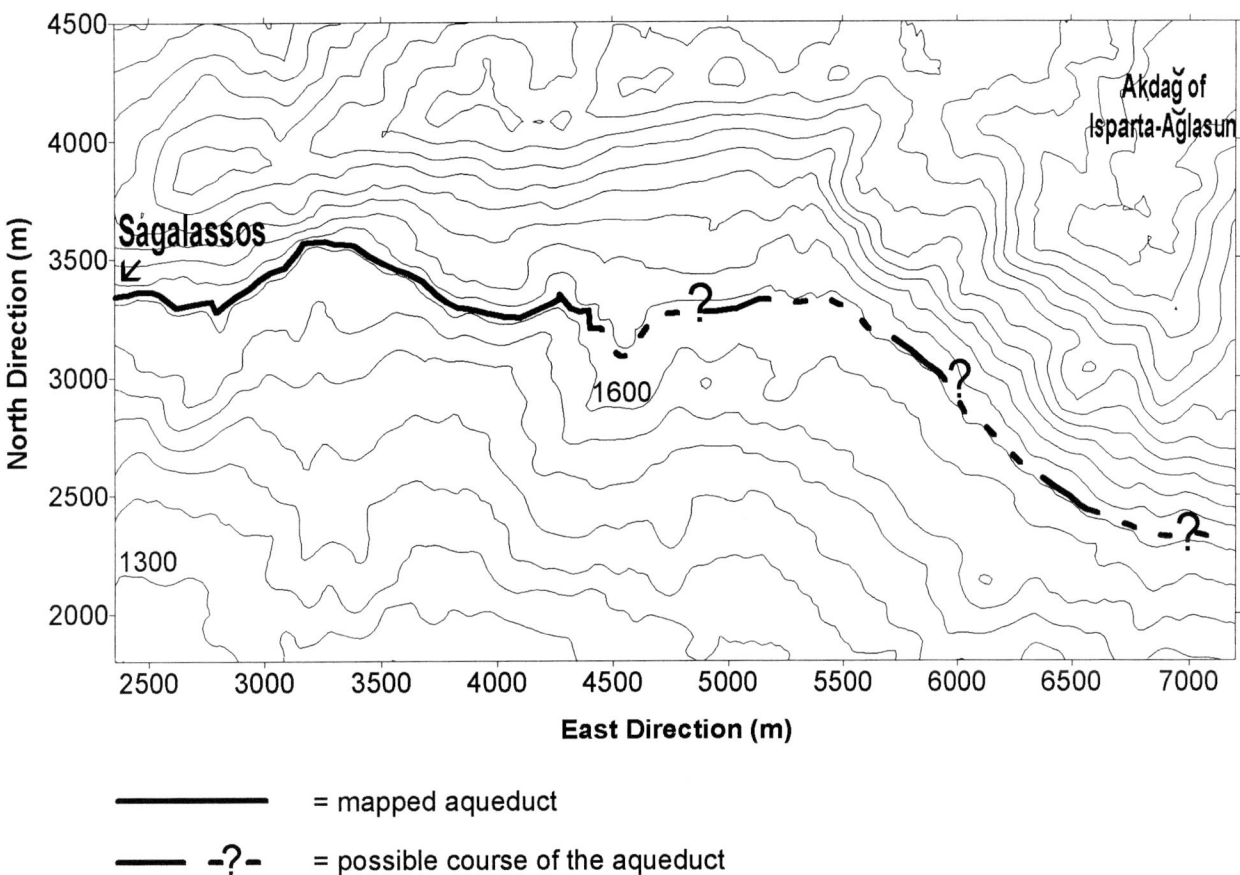

Fig. 10: Upper eastern aqueduct on the topographical map of Sagalassos.

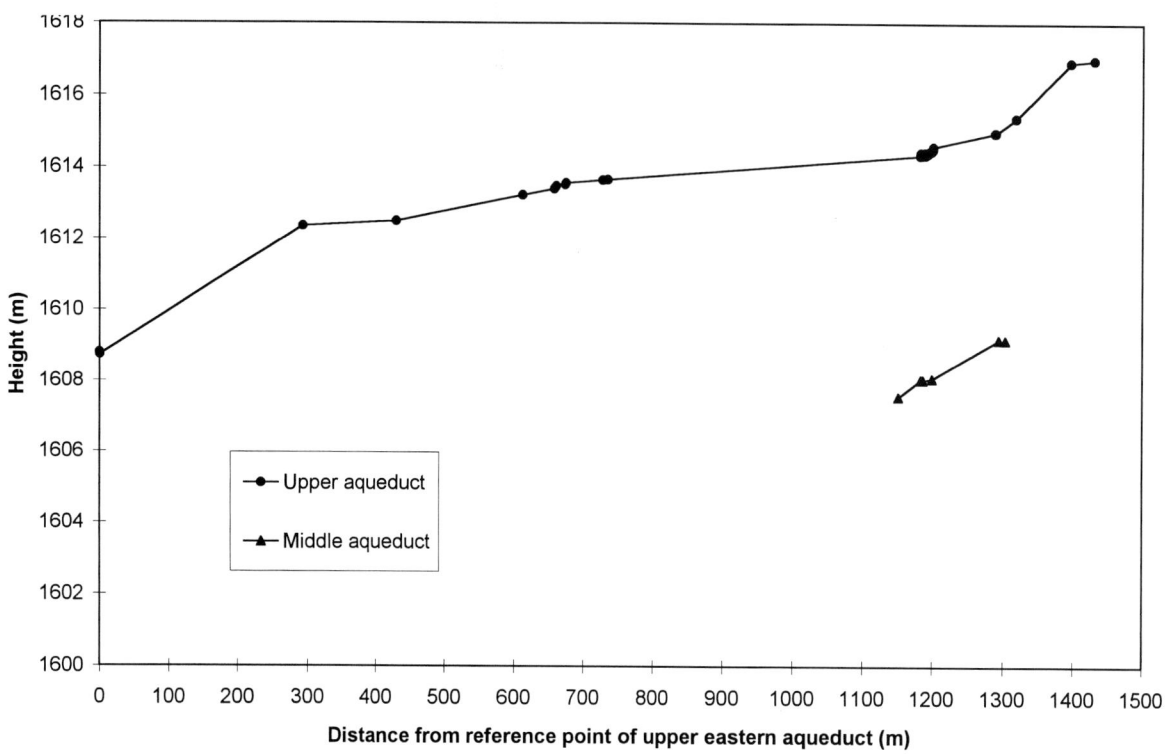

Fig. 11: Length profile of the eastern aqueducts.

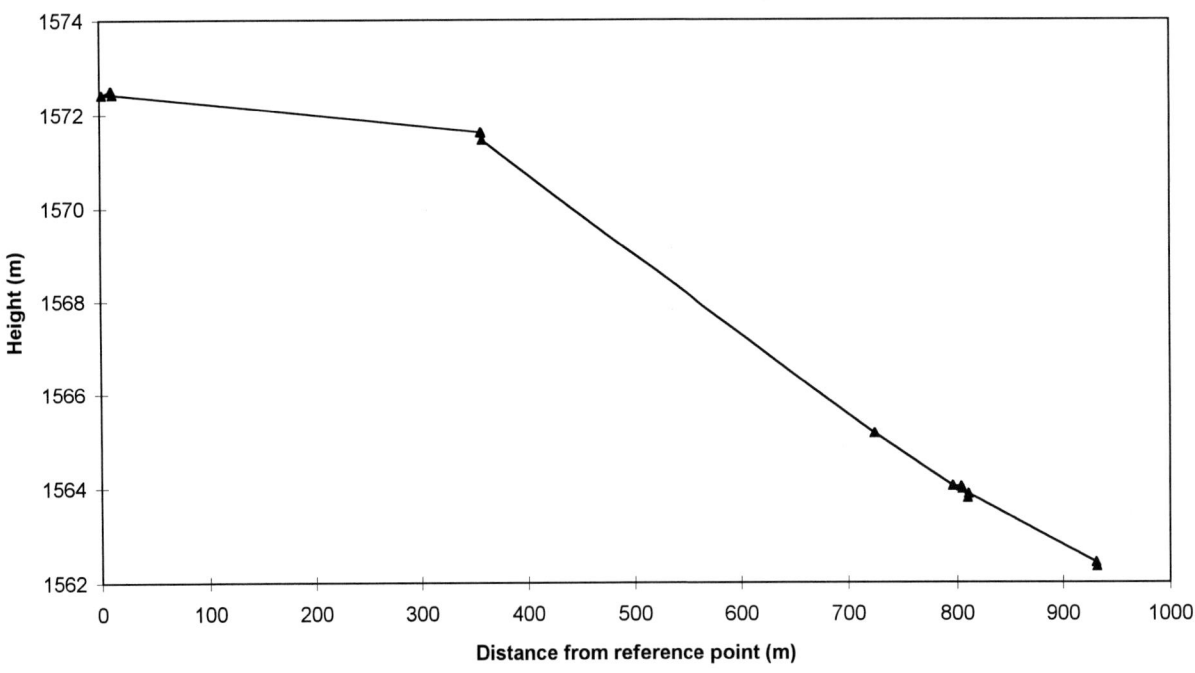

Fig. 12: Length profile of the middle western aqueduct.

available on the internet (http://rainbow.ldeo.columbia.edu/) show a decline in rainfall from the end of the 1970s until 1993 for the stations Antalya and Isparta. During 1995 the rainfall at the stations of Antalya and Isparta was between respectively 98 and 90% of their averages for this century. This trend, which was still continuing, was also confirmed in 1998 by I. Kancı of the Forestry Ministry for the whole of the province of Burdur. This implies that the estimated spring flow may be somewhat too low.

3.3. Physico-chemical characteristics

The spring water averaged 13 °C and had a range between 9 and 17 °C. Thus at present no indications for the occurrence of thermal water were found.

Although it was expected that the temperature would be positively correlated with the altitude of the springs, no such correlation was found. On the other hand, the temperature was inversely related to the flow (Fig. 3). This means that large springs must originate from deep aquifers and that the water was transported quickly towards the surface by dissolution tunnels. Smaller springs having a less deep origin would flow out slower.

The pH of the springwater averaged 7.8 with minimum and maximum values of 7.2 and 8.26. A significantly positive correlation was found between pH and altitude of the spring (Fig. 4). The negative correlation between acidity and altitude may be explained by the greater density of the vegetation cover and the production of humic acids at low elevations.

The carbonate hardness has a positively skewed distribution with an average of 178 mg/l. A negative correlation between the flow and the hardness was found, which may be attributed to the longer time travelled by the water emerging from the smaller springs (Fig. 5). Also, the water from springs located at low altitudes with a lesser flow of warm, acid water will tend to be harder.

4. THE AQUEDUCTS OF SAGALASSOS

4.1. The eastern aqueducts

The shape of the rock-cut sections of the aqueducts is rectangular, with a mean width of 0.40 m. The depth of the aqueducts varied according to the location. Some sections are over 10 m deep (Fig. 6). The walls of the channels were covered with a hydraulic mortar, most of which has disappeared with time. In areas covered with a thick layer of regolith, the water was conducted through terracotta pipes. These pipes have a typical diameter of 0.25 m.

The aqueducts have not yet been dated exactly. The general appearance of the two rock-cut aqueducts to the east of the city and the fact that they must have served the upper part of the city as far back as the Hellenistic period, where it includes a late Hellenistic fountain house, rather suggest a (late) Hellenistic date. But rock-cut water channels, albeit of much greater dimensions, such as parts of the aqueduct of Pamphylian Side, were still being built in Imperial times (Fahlbusch 1987). A (probably early) Imperial date cannot therefore be excluded.

Observations on the ground suggest that the upper eastern aqueduct is later than the middle aqueduct. Firstly, the upper aqueduct is not so eroded as the middle one: it is therefore possible that the upper one was constructed because the middle one had been damaged, e.g. by an earthquake and/or landslides (Verstraeten et al. 2000). This is also suggested by the fact that the aqueducts ran parallel to each other. Moreover, as we will show later, a single channel was generally sufficient to transport the outflow of all the springs to the east of the city.

4.2. The western aqueducts

The slopes to the west of Sagalassos are greatly eroded by debris flows and other processes so that only small sections of the western aqueducts could be recognised. Most remains which were found belong to the middle western aqueduct, which is situated above the old road to Isparta (Fig. 7). This aqueduct is mostly rock-cut, but includes some boulder sections carrying terracotta pipes (Owens 1995). On the whole, it was much more visible and more accessible to an enemy than the eastern aqueducts and so may have been constructed in a peaceful period, i.e. the Roman Imperial period. The rock-cut sections of this aqueduct have an average width of 0.35 m. The western aqueducts are much shorter than the eastern ones.

4.3. The trajectory of the aqueducts

The topographic points obtained with the theodolite were connected by a curve (Figs. 8 and 9). Transferring this line to a map shows that the eastern aqueducts followed the contour lines well (Fig. 10). The gradient of these aqueducts determines how well they function. A disturbance of the gradient of an aqueduct may stem from either of two causes: (1) the aqueducts may have been constructed wrongly or (2) tectonic activity occurred in the region of Sagalassos.

When calculating the gradients, only the topographic points for which the bottom of the channel was accurately located were used. The resulting profiles are shown in Fig. 11 and 12. The overall gradients of the known parts of the eastern aqueducts are between 5.75 ‰ and 11.26 ‰, the local gradients between 2.62 ‰ and 17.16 ‰. This means that the aqueducts had a slope of only a few meters per kilometer. These values are well above the 2.5‰ to 5‰ recommended by Vitruvius (*De Architectura* VIII.6) and the mean values of 1.3‰ for most of the aqueducts of Rome itself. Some of the longer stretches of the Roman Imperial Madradağ aqueducts of Pergamon, however, had gradients of more than 30‰ (Garbrecht 1987: 37).

The upper eastern aqueduct began with a steep gradient (12.21 ‰), followed by a section with a very shallow gradient (2.62 ‰). At the end, the aqueduct descends to the city with a gradient of 14.39 ‰. The total difference in height between the end and the beginning of the known parts of the aqueduct is 8.22 m. The explanation for the shallow gradient of the middle part of this aqueduct is probably the geomorphological activity on the slope at that area. The aqueduct crosses the 'Three Ladies', the debris cones east of the city (for its location see Steegen 1996). To avoid damage to the aqueduct, it was carried above these debris cones, which meant that a shallow gradient had to be maintained. Then, to reach the city, it needed a steeper gradient at the end.

At a distance of ca. 1200 m from the lower end point of the surveyed section, the aqueduct floor shows a relatively sudden drop of ca. 0.20 m. This is also the point at which the aqueduct takes a sharp bend from northwest to north. This discontinuity is not due to tectonic activity as this section in entirely cut out of bedrock: it is probably the point where two separate sections of the channel, constructed by different groups of workers, were connected.

Only a small part of the lower aqueduct east of Sagalassos could be reconstructed. The distance between the beginning and the end of the aqueduct is only 152 m which is too short to make meaningful calculations of the gradient.

It is also possible to divide the western aqueduct into two sections. The western part is very extensively eroded making it possible that the real length of the aqueduct was underestimated and consequently that the gradient was overestimated. It is clear that this part has only a small gradient. The second slope of the aqueduct is rather steep, namely 17.16 ‰. This is the highest measured gradient of the aqueducts of Sagalassos. Table 1 gives an overview of the gradients in Sagalassos.

	Aqueduct	Length (m)	Height difference (m)	Slope (‰)
1	Upper Eastern			
	A. Overall	1429.89	8.22	5.75
	B. Divided into 3 parts			
	1.	292.73	3.58	12.21
	2.	995.98	2.61	2.62
	3.	141.18	2.03	14.39
2	Lower Eastern	151.85	1.62	10.65
3	Western			
	A. Overall	895.91	10.01	11.26
	B. Divided into 2 parts			
	1.	353.60	0.81	2.29
	2.	540.43	9.27	17.16

Table 1: Gradients of the three aqueducts in Sagalassos.

By way of comparison, Table 2 summarises some of the aqueduct gradients found in the literature. By comparing these values with those of Table 1, it is clear that the gradients in Sagalassos are rather high, but not exceptional. Besides, it must be taken into account that only small sections of the aqueducts of Sagalassos are known.

Place	Length (km)	Slope (‰)	Discharge (m³/day)
Arles (France)	48	6.25	8,000
Bologna (Italy)	17.8	1	35,000
Carthage (Tunisia)	132	1.5	25,000
Caesarea Maritima (Israel):			
- *Upper aqueduct*	8.5/17	0.15	22,000/39,000
Lyon (France)	26/28	1.5/3.27	10,000
Nîmes (France)	50	0.34	20,000
Pergamon (Turkey):			
- *Hellenistic Madradağ*	42	Lowest value 0.04	2,700
- *Kaikos aqueduct*	53	0.031	20,000
Segovia (Spain)	15	16.4	1,700
Side (Turkey)	35	1	max. 173,000

Table 2: Some gradients of aqueducts in other cities (Adam 1984; Bailhache 1983; Colas 1983; Hauck *et. al.* 1987; Hodge 1992; Rakob 1983; Garbrecht 1987; Peleg 1987; Giorgetti 1988; Burdy 1988; Fisches and Paillet 1988).

Fig. 13: Fragment of a terracotta pipe with a typical diameter of 25 centimetres.

All the aqueducts slope towards the city of Sagalassos. No sections sloping in the opposite direction and/or major discontinuities were found. Thus, there is no indication of any 'differential' tectonic or other major geomorphological movements in the region of the aqueducts. Of course, it remains possible that the region in its entirety has undergone tectonic movement.

5. ARCHAEOLOGICAL IMPLICATIONS

Owens (1995) reported that the aqueducts originated a 100 m away from the last known point of the upper east aqueduct. He recognised a dry spring and a rectangular limestone block, which was the remains of a small basin, as the head of the aqueduct. Around this point, the vegetation is typical of a damp environment, but no running water was observed. Furthermore, there is only a very small spring with a negligible flow between the city and the starting point proposed by Owens.

But it is unlikely that a fairly significant aqueduct was built only to capture the flow from two minor springs. They may have been only part of the catchment system. Other springs situated high enough to feed the aqueducts were therefore searched for. Field observations indicated that there were some significant springs further to the east on the slopes of the Akdağ of Isparta-Ağlasun (Paulissen et al. 1993). Near these springs, several fragments of terracotta pipes were found (Fig. 13). These pipes were probably used to lead the water from the springs to the main aqueduct channel. Furthermore, another rock-cut section of an aqueduct was discovered. These observations suggest that most of the water for the aqueducts was captured on the slopes of the Akdağ mountain and that the aqueduct extended much further to the east than previously supposed. However, the exact eastern end of the aqueduct remains unknown.

Of most interest is the quantity of (spring)water that could be conducted by gravity towards Sagalassos during ancient times. From the present location of the 45 natural springs, only four springs in the eastern study area could definitely reach Sagalassos via the upper aqueduct. They have an estimated yearly average flow of ca. 2.6 litre per second or almost 225,000 litres per day. Another four springs east of Sagalassos (9.9 l/s), located at an altitude of 1540 m, could only have reached the lower parts of the city. Owens (1995) found near this location the traces of the lower aqueduct dated to the Imperial period (which was not surveyed in detail).

A question which remains in this context is whether the water which now emerges at the Kırazlı trout farm at a height of ca. 1350 m (estimated yearly average flow: 58 l/s) could have been diverted towards the city in ancient times.

From personal contacts with the owner of the farm and from the topographical map and photos of the Akdağ of Isparta-Ağlasun, we know that the trout farm tapped an aquifer in the debris slopes of the Akdağ for its water. In the neighbourhood of the tapping point, which is at a height of ca. 1800 m, the noise of flowing groundwater can be heard. It is therefore probable that the flow which now supplies the trout farm was also used to supply Sagalassos in ancient times.

Owens (1995) reported the presence of a watermark at a height of 0.50 m above the bottom of the upper eastern aqueduct. Using the local gradient, the channel geometry and the Manning equation, the flow passing through the aqueduct can then be estimated as 530 l/s or nearly 45,000 m^3/day (Table 3).

It is obvious that this value is much higher than the present average flow of the springs to the east of the city (115 l/s). However, it should be taken into account that the spring flows show a considerable seasonal variation. At the end of the winter period, the total spring flow is estimated to be ca. 150 l/s, which is still far lower than the calculated ancient flow. On the other hand, the water mark is an indication of maximum rather than average flow. Maximum flow may only be reached during extremely wet years. It is of course possible that other springs, located even further to the east, contributed to the aqueduct. It is also possible that the springs may have been much more active during the Roman period.

	Upper Eastern aqueduct
Cross section (m^2)	0.2
Hydraulic radius (m)	0.1429
Slope (‰)	14.39
Manning roughness coefficient (n)*	0.0125
Velocity (m s^{-1})	2.66
Discharge (m^3 s^{-1})	0.53

Table 3: Calculation of the discharge running through the aqueduct using Manning equation. (Hauck et al. 1987).

The total average spring flow now corresponds to a daily average of ca. 10,000 m^3/day. Table 2 shows that in many cities much longer aqueducts were built to obtain such a flow. During the second – third centuries AD ten aqueducts provided Pergamon with a total average of ca. 40,000 m^3/day for a population of ca. 160,000, implying a potential daily consumption of 250 l/day (Garbrecht 1987: 43). Taken into account that Sagalassos was at most a fifth as big as Pergamon, and that there were also three western aqueducts, the city's inhabitants certainly had more than enough water at their disposal. The above consumption figures for Pergamon are rather high since they also include water devoted to non-domestic purposes (public buildings and ornamental fountains). This also explains why Rome seems to have lavished up to 1,135 l/day on each of its inhabitants. According to Sextus Julius Frontinus (*De Aquaeductibus Urbis Romae* 78) Rome used slightly more than 3% of its water supply in ornamental fountains, and slightly more than 16% in public structures (for example, baths). However, since the flow rates of water were difficult to measure, those figures are only approximate (White 1984: 167). For a much smaller city, such as Roman Corinth, it has been assumed that the maximum figure of water devoted to non domestic purposes would be 20%. There, the *per capita* rate of water consumption has been established as between 4.1 litres per person per day, which represents an absolute minimum for any settled population, and 12.3 litres a day (Engels 1990: 180). Applied to Sagalassos, these figures once more confirm the generous water supply which the inhabitants had at their disposal, a fact which is also supported by archaeological evidence. In fact, water supply systems turn up in any small trench which is opened in the city.

At present, no significant flow from the western study area can reach Sagalassos by gravity. Two large springs with a total flow of 29 l/s were found, but they are situated ca. 150 m below the level of the middle aqueduct. It is possible that the outlet point of these springs was previously located higher up the slope and/or that some of the higher springs had significantly greater flows in Roman times. This requires further investigation.

A final archaeological implication can be drawn on the quality of the water delivered to Sagalassos. The temperature of the water is rather cold (10 °C). Due to the southern exposure, heating of the water in the aqueducts may have been quite significant during summer. The weighted average pH of the contributing springs equals 7.68, being nearly the same as the pH for the whole study area. The water contains on average 155 mg/l calcium carbonate so this water can be classified as soft to moderately hard.

6. AQUEDUCTS AS INDICATORS OF THE GEOMORPHOLOGICAL EVOLUTION ON THE SLOPES AROUND SAGALASSOS

The calculated erosion rates of the slopes above the selected four channel sections vary between 1 and 265 mm per 1000 year, depending on local geomorphological conditions (Table 4). Section 4, which is located between two deep rock-cut sections of the aqueduct, yields an erosion rate of ca. 30 mm per 1000 years, based on the accumulation of material in the aqueduct. However, the evolution is more complex: at present, the level of the slope between the rock-cut sections is several meters below the top level of the aqueduct fill. This indicates that a period of major deposition on the slope was followed by a period of significant denudation.

The high value of 265 mm per 1000 year was reached at a section that was divided in two by a debris cone. The volume of this cone was incorporated in the total sediment and we assumed that the debris cone built up once the aqueduct was abandoned. Because it is not clear whether the debris cone already existed before the aqueducts were abandoned, no further conclusions can be made.

Section	Length (m)	Volume (m³)	Erosion rate (mm/1000 year)
1	50	31	1
2	60	161	265
3	100	98	6
4	97	549	31

Table 4: Estimated erosion rates for the four sections on the upper eastern aqueduct.

Certain characteristics of the slopes, such as the hardness of the rock, vegetation cover, debris, the joints and gradients, were used to examine the erosion rates of the slopes but no correlation was obtained. Conacher (1988) concluded that a correlation between present-day measurements and processes of the past was problematic. The same can be said for Sagalassos.

7. KARST

During the field campaign in Sagalassos the water flows and hardness were measured. The calcium carbonate content of the water is the result of the dissolving of limestone underground. A chemical denudation rate from spring erosion can be obtained by multiplying the flow of each spring by its carbonate hardness. In total, the study area loses 19 gram calcium carbonate per second or 600 tons per year. By taking into account the total area contributing to the springs, we obtain a denudation rate between 43 mm and 101 mm per 1000 year depending on the assumptions made about the contributing area and the role of surface karst in the area. This value relates to subsurface dissolution and does not necessarily represent a reduction of the topographical height.

Comparing this value with the one on mechanical erosion, it can be concluded that the mechanical and chemical denudation rates are of a similar order of magnitude. However, the limestone rock eroded on the slopes by mechanical processes remains on the slopes and does not move out of the area, while the limestone dissolved in the water is conducted away from the area. Thus, there is no genuine mechanical export, but there is a significant chemical export of limestone.

8. CONCLUSIONS

Six aqueducts supplied the city and several springs were found in the region. The combination of several data types (a detailed survey of the aqueduct, a detailed survey of the springs in the area and indications of possible flows) led to the conclusion that the upper eastern aqueduct extended much further to the east than previously thought: the major springs contributing to the aqueduct are found on the southern side of the Akdağ of Isparta-Ağlasun.

The present-day flow of the springs above the aqueducts east of Sagalassos is 2.6 l/s. The water which is nowadays used at a trout farm was probably in earlier times also directed to the upper east aqueduct. The total flow of all the springs in the region of Sagalassos is 60.6 litre per second or more than 5 million litres water per day. This was certainly sufficient to supply the city and its citizens with water.

It is unclear whether major changes in the springs have occurred since Roman times. The total present-day flow of the springs above the eastern aqueducts is certainly sufficient to warrant the construction and maintenance of an aqueduct. It needs to be further investigated whether the western aqueducts were fed by springs which are still active nowadays, or whether some significant springs have disappeared from the area.

Only local gradients were measured because the complete trajectories of the aqueducts were not known. This may explain why they are rather high in comparison with other cities. There is no indication of disturbance of the aqueducts by tectonic movements or other large-scale geomorphological processes (see however, Verstraeten *et al.* 2000).

The present-day chemical erosion of limestone in the region of Sagalassos corresponds to a value of 43-101 mm per 1000 years. The rates obtained for mechanical hillslope erosion show a large variation, but they are of the same order of magnitude.

9. ACKNOWLEDGEMENTS

This research is supported by the Belgian Programme on Interuniversity Poles of Attraction (IUAP 4/12) initiated by the Belgian State, Prime Minister's Office, Science Policy Programming. The text also presents the results of the Concerted Action of the Flemish Government (GOA 97/2) and the Fund for Scientific Research-Flanders (Belgium) (FWO) (G.2145.94). Scientific responsibility is assumed by its authors. We would like to thank Eng. J. Meersmans for the construction of the two V-shaped weirs which were used at Sagalassos to measure the flow of the springs.

10. REFERENCES

J.P. Adam (1984) *La construction romaine: matériaux et techniques*, Paris.
M. Bailhache (1983) Etude de l'évolution du débit des aqueducs Gallo-Romains, in: *Journées d'études sur les aqueducs romains, Lyon 26-28 mai 1977*, Paris: 19-49.
J. Burdy (1988) Lugdunum/Lyon, in: *Die Wasserversorgung antiker Städte (Geschichte des Wasserversorgung* 3) Mainz: 190-198.
K. Cauwenberghs (1996), *Een hydrologische en geomorfologische studie van de bronnen rond Sagalassos (Z.W. Turkije)*, unpublished M.Sc. thesis, KULeuven.
J.L. Colas (1983) Présentation des aqueducs de Lyon: Problèmes anciens – Observations nouvelles, in: *Journées d'études sur les aqueducs romains, Lyon 26-28 mai 1977 Paris*: 179-205.
A.J. Conacher (1988) The geomorphic significance of process measurements in an ancient landscape, *Catena Supplement* 1: 147-164.
T. Dinçer and B.R. Payne (1971) An environmental isotope study of the southwestern karst region of Turkey, *Journal of Hydrology* 14: 233-258.
H. Elkhatib and G. Günay (1993) Potential of remote sensing techniques in karst areas: southern Turkey, in: *Hydrogeological Processes in Karst Terrains* (*Proceedings of the Antalya Symposium and Field Seminar, October 1990*) (*IAHS Publ.* 207): 47-51.
D. Engels (1990) *Roman Corinth. An Alternative Model for the Classical City*, Chicago.
H. Fahlbusch (1987) Side, in: *Die Wasserversorgung antiker Städte (Geschichte der Wasserversorgung* 2) Mainz: 218-221.
J.L. Fisches and J.L. Paillet (1988) Nîmes, in: *Die Wasserversorgung antiker Städte (Geschichte der Wasserversorgung* 3) Mainz: 207-214.
G. Garbrecht (1987) *Die Wasserversorgung des antiken Pergamon*, in: *Die Wasserversorgung antiker Städte (Geschichte der Wasserversorgung* 2) Mainz: 11-48.
G. Garbrecht (1988) Mensch und Wasser im Altertum, in: *Die Wasserversorgung antiker Städte (Geschichte der Wasserversorgung* 3) Mainz: 13-44.
D. Giorgetti (1988) Bologna, in: *Die Wasserversorgung antiker Städte (Geschichte der Wasserversorgung* 3) Mainz: 180-185.
G.F.W. Hauck, F. Asce, R.A. Novak and M. Asce (1987) Interactions of flow and incrustation in the Roman aqueduct of Nîmes, *Journal of Hydraulic Engineering* 113/2: 141-157.
T.A. Hodge (1992) *Roman Aqueducts and Water Supply*, London.
N. Korkmaz (1989) Estimation of groundwater recharge from spring hydrographs, *Hydrological Sciences* 35/2: 209-217.
E.J. Owens (1991) The Kremna aqueduct and water supply in Roman cities, *Greece and Rome* 38: 41-58.
E.J. Owens (1995) The aqueducts of Sagalassos, in: M. Waelkens and J. Poblome (eds) *Sagalassos III. Report on the Fourth Excavation Campaign of 1993* (*Acta Archaeologica Lovaniensia Monographiae* 7) Leuven University Press: 91-114.
E. Paulissen, J. Poesen, G. Govers and J. De Ploey (1993) The

physical environment at Sagalassos (Western Taurus, Turkey). A reconnaissance survey, in: M. Waelkens and J. Poblome (eds) *Sagalassos II. Report on the Third Excavation Campaign of 1992* (*Acta Archaeologica Lovaniensia Monographiae* 6) Leuven University Press: 229-248.

J. Peleg (1987) Caesarea Maritima, in: *Die Wasserversorgung antiker Städte (Geschichte der Wasserversorgung* 2) Mainz: 176-179.

J. Poesen, G. Govers, E. Paulissen and K. Vandaele (1995) A geomorphological evaluation of erosion risk at Sagalassos, in: M. Waelkens and J. Poblome (eds) *Sagalassos III. Report on the Fourth Excavation Campaign of 1993* (*Acta Archaeologica Lovaniensia Monographiae* 7) Leuven University Press: 341-356.

F. Rakob (1983) Die Römische Wasserleitung von Karthago, in: *Journées d'études sur les aqueducs romains, Lyon 26-28 mai 1977*, Paris: 309-332.

A. Steegen (1996) *De aquaducten van Sagalassos (Turkije): een hydraulische en geomorfologische studie*, unpublished M.Sc. thesis, KULeuven.

G. Verstraeten, J. Paulissen, I. Librecht and M. Waelkens (2000) Limestone platforms around Sagalassos, resulting from giant mass movements, in: M. Waelkens and L. Loots (eds) *Sagalassos V. Report on the Survey and Excavation campaigns of 1996 and 1997* (*Acta Archaeologica Lovaniensia Monographiae* 11) Leuven, University Press 783-798.

M. Waelkens (1993) Sagalassos. History and archeology, in: M. Waelkens (ed.) *Sagalassos I. Report on the Second Excavation Campaign of 1991* (*Acta Archaeologica Lovaniensia Monographiae* 5) Leuven University Press: 37-82.

M. Waelkens, M. Sintubin, Ph. Muchez and E. Paulissen (2000) Archaeological, geomorphological and geological evidence for a major earthquake at Sagalassos (SW Turkey) around the middle of the seventh century AD, in: B. McGuire, D. Griffiths and I. Stewart (eds) *The Archaeology of Geological Catastrophes (Geological Society. Special Publications* 171) London: 373-383

K.D. White (1984) *Greek and Roman Technology*, Ithaka N.Y.

PROVENANCE AND CHARACTERIZATION OF THE RAW MATERIALS OF LIME MORTARS USED AT SAGALASSOS WITH SPECIAL REFERENCE TO THE VOLCANIC ROCKS

Kristof CALLEBAUT[1], Willy VIAENE (†)[1], Marc WAELKENS[2], Raoul OTTENBURGS[1] and Jean NAUD[3]

1 - Laboratory of Mineralogy, Physico-Chemical Geology, KULeuven, Celestijnenlaan 200C, B-3001 Heverlee, Belgium
2 - Department of Archaeology, KULeuven, Blijde Inkomststraat 21, B-3000 Leuven, Belgium
3 - Laboratory of Geology and Mineralogy, UCLouvain, Bâtiment Mercator, Place Louis Pasteur 3, B-1348 Louvain-la-Neuve, Belgium

1. INTRODUCTION

The mortars used at Sagalassos have been discussed in a previous publication (Viaene et al. 1997). These mortars consist of a lime matrix and of various aggregates and admixtures. It was suggested that the lime originated from the burning (calcining at 800-1000 °C) and slaking (hydration of the burnt lime) of local Triassic limestones which are abundant in the area around Sagalassos. Three types of aggregates have been found so far in the mortars: limestone, crushed ceramics (chamotte) and volcanic fragments. The latter two are pozzolanic materials. The volcanic fragments consist of tuff and lava fragments, the first being a porous volcanic rock, the latter a dense volcanic rock.

Two main groups of lime mortars have been distinguished. Firstly, there are building mortars which consist of a lime matrix with aggregates mainly of volcanic origin. Secondly, there are mortars used in constructions that were related to water and these mortars consist of a lime matrix with (mainly) chamotte as an admixture. These admixtures (chamotte, volcanic rock fragments and volcanic powder) can be defined as pozzolanas, that is, siliceous and aluminous mineral substances which, though not having cementitious qualities themselves, will, at atmospheric temperatures in the presence of water, react with lime to form cementitious compounds (Blanks and Kennedy 1955) and give the mortar hydraulic properties. Such mortars can harden under water and obtain a higher strength than air-hardening lime mortars. The use of hydraulic lime mortars, first using volcanic powder and later also ceramic fragments, was already known to the Greeks in the sixth and fifth centuries BC and became more widespread during the fourth century BC (Viaene et al. 1997: 405). The Romans increased this knowledge of the hydraulic properties of mortars made of lime mixed with volcanic sands, which could harden under water and were an important element in the building of harbours and aqueducts. They also produced high quality hydraulic mortars made of a mixture of lime and chamotte. Their experiments with admixtures (*caementa*) eventually led to the introduction of 'Roman concrete' (Viaene et al. 1997: 406).

The previous study of the lime mortars from Sagalassos distinguished various raw materials: limestone, used both in the production of lime and as aggregates, and crushed ceramics and volcanic rock fragments (lava and tuff), that were used as admixtures. Thus far, the provenance of the different raw materials has been discussed in the framework of a broader study on the origin of the building materials themselves (stone, architectural ceramics, mortars, ...). The main aim of this paper is to identify the provenance of the various raw materials present in the lime mortars, based on petrographical, mineralogical and geochemical analysis. Special emphasis is given to the use of volcanic rocks as pozzolanic admixtures, because much work has already been done on limestones (Viaene et al. 1993) and on ceramics (Kucha 1995; Degeest 1997). The previous studies confirmed also that economic considerations at Sagalassos, particularly the problems of bulk transport over long distances, had forced builders to use local materials (Lamprecht 1987: 142), certainly in the case of chamotte and limestone (Viaene et al. 1997: 142). The lack of good sand may also have forced them to turn to volcanic materials as an alternative for use in building mortars, where strength in compression rather than hydraulic qualities, was needed (Viaene et al. 1997: 420, table 1). So far, the local provenance of these volcanic materials had not yet been established through comparative analysis. Therefore, a volcanic region of about 30 km² located immediately to the northwest of Sagalassos over the ancient mountain pass (Loots et al. 2000) was investigated to determine the characteristics of these rocks and to compare them with the admixtures used in the lime mortars. Only the southern part of this volcanic region, about 1 km to the north of the site, was examined during this study (Fig. 2).

2. GEOLOGICAL SETTING

On geological maps and in the field, five important stratigraphic units can be distinguished in the area around Sagalassos (Fig. 1). These are:

a – Mesozoic limestones (Trias-Jura): these form autochthonous and allochthonous series in the vicinity of Sagalassos. The limestone mountain range to the north of the site is part of an allochthonous nappe (Akdağ formation) and consists of white, mostly coarse crystalline limestone sometimes with chert layers and radiolarite.

b – An ophiolite sequence (Cretaceous): these occur as nappes obducted in the Tertiary (Eocene). This sequence consists of strongly serpentinised volcanic rocks and sediments. In the field, they are seen as considerably altered and weathered, mostly red-brown, rocks. The site of Sagalassos is located on an ophiolite sequence (not shown on the map).

c – A flysch sequence (Miocene): shales, marls, sandstones and conglomerates. Outcrops are present in the hills to the south of Sagalassos.

d – Volcanic rocks (Pliocene): tuffs and lava layers in a volcanic region to the northwest of Sagalassos and situated around Lake Gölçük (prov. Isparta). These volcanic rocks are deposited on a palaeo-relief of limestones.

e – Alluvial deposits (Quaternary): clays, sandstones, travertines and gravel present in the valleys around Sagalassos.

The volcanic region to the northwest of Sagalassos developed during the Tertiary-Quaternary volcanic activity in the western Taurides. According to Lefèvre et al. (1983) the volcanic region is of the Pliocene age (4.07 ± 0.20 to 4.70 ± 0.50 Ma using the K-Ar method). Lake Gölçük is supposed to be the eruption centre of this volcanic activity. The deposits consist mainly of lava layers and of volcanic tuffs.

3. MATERIALS AND METHODS

Samples were collected in the southern part of the volcanic region over an area about 5 km² (Fig. 1). Tuff samples were taken from various layers according to differences in colour, size and type of inclusions, compaction and resistance against weathering. Samples of a lava layer were also taken.

In fact, only one lava layer could be distinguished in this part of the volcanic region, but lava layers occur more abundantly around lake Gölçük. That region, however, was not sampled systematically. Different sections (n=17) were made, with the intention of composing a lithological column for the southern part of the volcanic area.

Samples were examined by standard petrographical methods using polarized light. The porous samples were impregnated in a vacuum with a resin that was coloured with a blue dye. Characterization of the various mineral phases was carried out using a scanning electron microscope (SEM) and X-ray diffraction analysis (XRD). Chemical analyses were carried out by dissolving the samples in Li-metaborate and by estimating the concentrations of SiO_2, Al_2O_3, Fe_2O_3, MnO, MgO, CaO, TiO_2 and P_2O_5 by atomic emission spectrometry (AES), using a Spectrojet III spectrometer. Na_2O and K_2O were analysed by atomic absorption spectrometry (AAS), using a Varian Techtron AA6 flame atomic absorption spectrometer. The loss on ignition (LOI) was determined by heating the sample from 105 °C to 1050 °C and determining the weight difference. On individual crystals (augites, plagioclases) a semi-quantitative chemical analysis was carried out using a scanning electron microscope (type JSM-6400) with an energy dispersive detector (SEM-EDX). Trace elements (Ba, Ce, Co, Cr, Cu, La, Nb, Ni, Pb, Rb, S, Sr, W, Y, Zn and Zr) were determined using X-ray fluorescence analyses (analyses carried out by Prof. J. Naud, Louvain-la-Neuve).

4. RAW MATERIALS OF THE LIME MORTARS: PROVENANCE AND CHARACTERIZATION

The various raw materials used in the production of lime mortars at Sagalassos will now be discussed. Since the limestones and the ceramics have already been intensively studied (Viaene et al. 1997), only a brief summary of the results will be given.

4.1. Limestones

Limestone is the raw material for lime production. Crushed limestone ($CaCO_3$) is first burnt at 800-1000 °C, which produces CaO and CO_2. This burnt lime (quicklime, CaO) is then hydrated by sprinkling water on it in 'lime pits' or by immersing a basket filled with quicklime in water until no further gas escapes ("dry-slaking", see: Kraus et al. 1989; for archaeological evidence see Viaene et al. 1997: 407). This slaked lime ($Ca(OH)_2$) is mixed with aggregates and admixtures and left to harden. If no pozzolanas are added and the lime contains no clayey impurities, the hardening will proceed by carbonation with CO_2 from the air ($Ca(OH)_2 + CO_2 \rightarrow CaCO_3 + H_2O$). If on the other hand, pozzolanas are added or if the lime contains clayey impurities, then hardening is the result of hydration (with the forma-

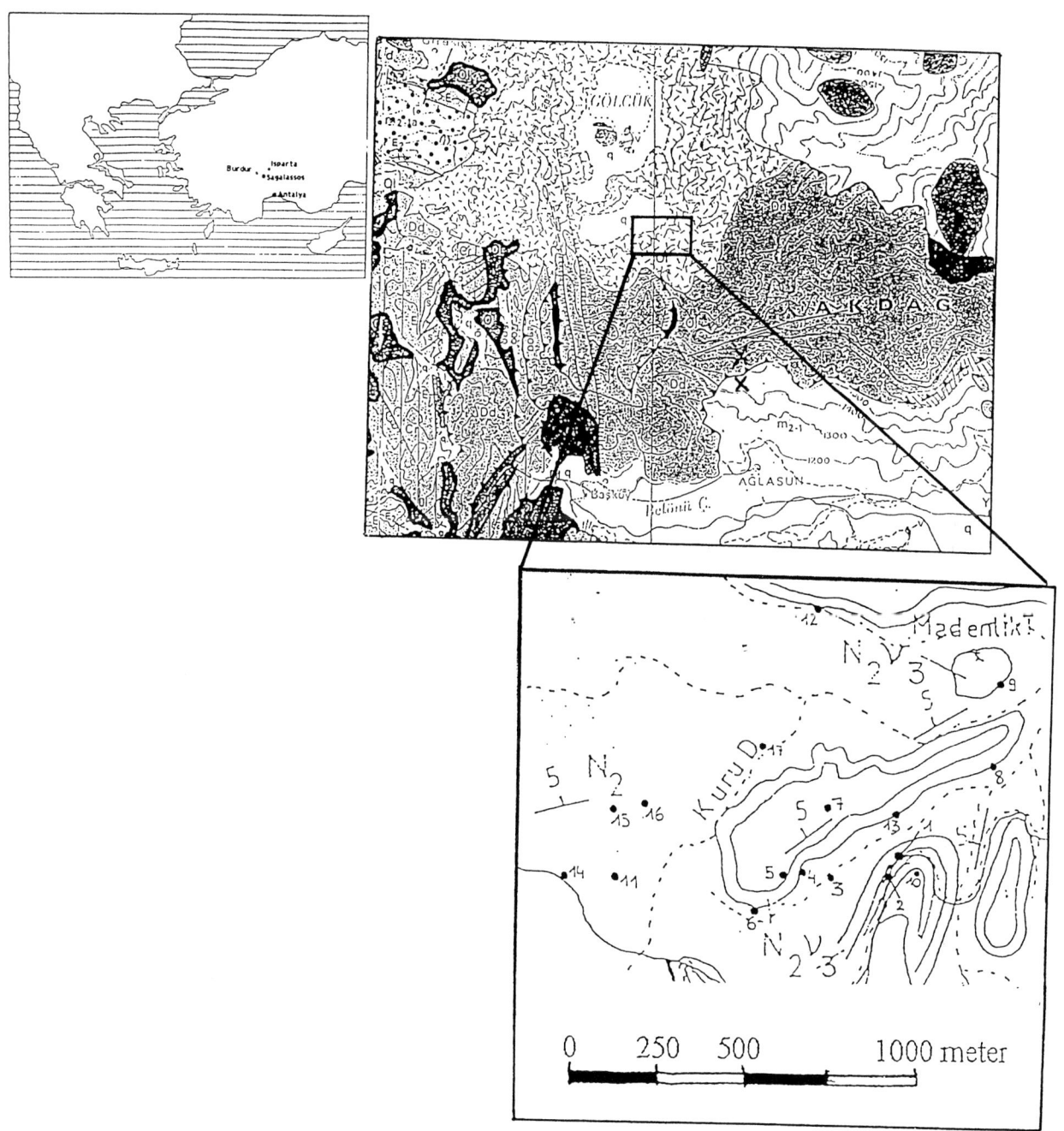

Fig. 1: Geological map showing the different tectonostratigraphic units around Sagalassos (**X**) (after Poisson *et al.* 1983). Scale: 1/100000. **Dd**: Trias limestone; **Ol**: Cretaceous ophiolite sequence, obducted in the Tertiary; **m$_{2-1}$**: Miocene flysch; **v**: Pliocene volcanics; **q**: Quaternary alluvial deposits. The studied area of the volcanic region (indicated by the rectangle) is enlarged (Yalçınkaya, 1983) and the numbers refer to the different sections made. **N$_2$**: Pliocene volcanics; **N$_2$v$_3$**: Pliocene volcanic tuffs.

Fig. 2: View of the southern part of the volcanic region (studied area). Hills of loose, 'sandy' tuff can be observed on the slopes and the hard tuff layers form cliffs.

tion of hydraulic compounds) and only partly of carbonation (Adam 1984: 76; Lamprecht 1987: 135-140).

The limestone found around Sagalassos is fairly pure. White limestone or marble were preferred by the Romans as raw materials for their lime (Vitruvius, *De Architectura* II.5). Because lumps of lime were found in the mortars, one can conclude that this lime was dry slaked (Kraus *et al.* 1989).

The limestone fragments used as aggregates show the same characteristics as those identified in the building stone of Sagalassos (Viaene *et al.* 1993): veinlets of calcite, which are a general feature in the limestones around Sagalassos, recrystallized calcite (transformation from micrite into sparite), radiolaria and twinned calcite crystals. Both micritic (fine) and sparitic (coarse) limestones have been used. The same petrographic features are found in the limestones around the site, so the lime and the crushed limestones both originate from the local Triassic limestones, which are abundant in the locality (Fig. 1, unit Dd).

4.2. Chamotte

Crushed ceramics are used as pozzolanic admixtures in lime mortars. The practice of mixing crushed ceramics with a lime-based mortar to obtain mortars with hydraulic properties was well-known to both Greek and Roman builders (Viaene *et al.* 1997: 405-406). Architects of the Roman period used this type of mortar throughout the empire whenever volcanic sands (as pozzolanas) were not available and a hydraulic mortar was needed (Baronio *et al.* 1997). A limited reaction rim indicates the pozzolanic properties of the chamotte (Viaene *et al.* 1997).

The fabric of the crushed ceramics is similar to that of the locally produced common ware or coarse ceramics. The presence of hematite dust in the fragments makes them reddish to almost opaque. A wide variety of mineral inclusions is present in the chamotte: feldspars, quartz, partly or wholly decomposed micas, pyroxenes and amphiboles and, more rarely, rock fragments of limestone, sandstone and volcanics. The same petrographical features are found in the coarse ceramics produced at Sagalassos (Degeest *et al.* 1997). Whether crushed ceramics of a specific type were selected or whether the chamotte was simply randomly crushed common wares (rejected pottery, tiles or bricks), is not yet clear.

4.3. Volcanic materials

Volcanic sand and crushed volcanic fragments were also used as pozzolanic admixtures in lime mortars. Both Greek and Roman builders were familiar with the practice of adding volcanic sand to lime mixtures. In Greece, volcanic dust from Santorini was even exported as far as Athens for the production of a mortar which was resistant to water (Martin 1965: 424; Orlandos 1966: 150). With the addition of volcanic sand, at first that from the area around Mt. Vesuvius and particularly Pozzuoli, the Romans also obtained a high quality hydraulic mortar (Plinius, *Naturalis Historia* 35.16; Adam 1984: 37-78). The rocks from the volcanic region located to the northwest of Sagalassos (Fig. 1) will therefore be discussed as a potential possible raw material for the lime mortars used there.

4.3.1. Field observations

The volcanic region consists mainly of volcanic tuffs. These tuffs can be seen as hills of loose, 'sandy' material and of hard tuff layers (Fig. 2). They originate from the weathering and erosion processes of the tuff layers. The hard layers are easily distinguished in the field because they form cliffs. These layers dip gently towards the north (ca. 5 °N) and are deposited on a palaeo-relief of limestone.

The tuffs have a light-coloured matrix with many inclusions, such as pumice, lava and sandstone fragments, and mineral grains. Two types of tuff can be distinguished: a fine-grained tuff with very small inclusions (mm size) and a coarse-grained tuff that is very porous and contains large inclusions (up to 0.01 m size). The tuff layers are poorly sorted and have varying thicknesses. One lava layer was found in the studied area. It consists of a grey, fine-grained matrix with phenocrysts of pyroxenes, biotite, etc.

A composed lithological column, showing 13 different layers, was constructed based on differences in colour, type and size of inclusions, compaction and wether or not it followed the hard layers in the topography (Fig. 3). These correspond to 13 different eruptions. One andesite layer was also found in the study area. This lithological column forms a sequence which is representative of the southern part of the area under study.

According to the mode of transport of the fragments Philpotts (1990) distinguishes three groups of pyroclastic deposits: pyroclastic fallout, pyroclastic surges and pyroclastic flow. The tuff deposits around Sagalassos are pyroclastic flow deposits: they are poorly sorted, the deposits are thickest in depressions, inclusions are up to 0.1 m and the deposits show no internal structure.

According to Özgür *et al.* (1990) the volcanic activity in the Gölçük region can be divided into three stages (Fig. 4): (I) As a result of the development of a 'graben' system, a basic tephriphonolite was extruded near Lake Gölçük and was accompanied by local eruptions. The lavas of the tephriphonolite have since been intensively eroded. The second stage (II) is characterized by powerful volcanic explosions round the centre of the recent Gölçük caldera, resulting in great masses of friable tuffs, ignimbrites and pumice tuffs which dominate the recent landscape. Trachyandesite and trachyte are not found. After the explosive expulsion of a great part of the material from the magma chamber, the surface collapsed, thus forming the Gölçük caldera. Finally, isolated extrusions of trachyandesites and trachytes occurred (III) at various localities in the centre and in the surrounding area of the caldera (dikes, volcanic domes).

The first stage described by Özgür *et al.* (1990) is not clearly recognizable in the study area. Only one sample plots chemically in the field of tephriphonolite (see Fig. 11). However, most of the lava layers are situated around the lake Gölçük and that part of the volcanic area has not yet been systematically sampled. The tuffs of the area under study belong to the second stage. Because fragments of (trachy)andesite were found alongside intrusive fragments (syenite) in the tuff layers, a stage of lava extrusion must have occurred before the explosive eruption of the tuffs. Most of the lava fragments found in this study were trachyandesites and trachytes. The last stage corresponds with field observations and is visible on the geological map (Fig. 1) as isolated lava domes around lake Gölçük. A more detailed study of the volcanic region could better define the different stages of the volcanic activity.

4.3.2. Mineralogy and petrography of the volcanic rocks

Samples were analysed with X-ray powder diffraction on bulk samples. Anorthite and sanidine are the main phases and augite is abundant in all samples. Diopside and hornblende are present in small quantities in most samples while magnetite and quartz are accessory minerals.

With the scanning electron microscope titano-magnetite and pyrite are observed and the zoning of the plagioclases and the augites has been studied (see below).

Petrographically, the volcanic rocks consist of:
1 – a cumulate of mostly submicroscopic crystals and a glass phase. This cumulate is defined as the *matrix*.
2 – inclusions of varying size. These inclusions include polycrystalline particles, which we define as rock fragments and monocrystalline, mono-mineral inclusions.

- Matrix
The matrix consists of submicroscopic crystals, which are distinguished as anorthite and sanidine by XRD, and a glass phase. In thin sections individual needle-shaped crystals (ca. 0.01 mm – 0.03 mm) with Carlsbad twins or plagioclase twins are observed. The glass phase is visible as an isotropic substance. In thin sections, because of variations in the brown colours, this matrix has a cloudy appearance. In the matrix, inclusions such as rock fragments and crystals are dispersed. The size of these inclusions differs from sample to sample and varies from some 0.01 mm to some 0.01 m. The matrix is more important in the fine-grained tuff type.

- Inclusions
Pumice, lava fragments and sporadic sandstone fragments are observed as rock fragments in the volcanic tuffs. They do not appear in lava layers: only a matrix and monocrystalline inclusions (phenocrysts) can be distinguished. Pumice fragments (Fig. 5, compare also with Fig. 5 in Viaene *et al.* 1997) are very porous fragments with only a thin glass wall between the pores. This vesicular volcanic glass with spheric pores originates from high vapour pressure during explosive eruptions. Sometimes, crystals (biotite, augite) can be observed in these pumice fragments. The fragments are mostly rounded by the cooling in the air and as the result of friction with other fragments during eruption.

Lava fragments (andesite and trachyandesite) are observed as irregular dark coloured inclusions of different sizes (smaller than 1 mm to some 0.01 m) which are not porous. These fragments have also a fine-grained, submicroscopic matrix with different phenocrysts (Fig. 6, see also fig. 6 in Viaene *et al.* 1997). The crystals in the matrix (mostly needle-shaped) often show a lineation which indicates the direction of flow. The matrix consists of plagioclases and alkali-feldspars. The phenocrysts are identified as feldspars (plagioclases and alkali-feldspars), augite, biotite, magnetite and sporadically hornblende. The plagioclases and the augites are mostly zoned parallel to the rims. The crystals are very similar to the crystals in the tuff, except that the augite is more zoned in the lava fragments. The lava fragments have the same petrographic characteristics as the lava layers, which implies that these were mixed in with the tuffs during eruption.

Sandstone fragments only occur sporadically. A typical red-brown colour originates from the presence of iron oxides. In this red-brown matrix, quartz grains can be distinguished. These sandstone fragments may originate from the Tertiary flysch found in the vicinity and be included in the tuffs during an explosive eruption.

Plagioclases, alkali-feldspars, augites, diopsides, biotites and hornblendes are seen as individual crystals. Plagioclases (Fig. 7) and augites (Fig. 8, compare also with fig. 8 in Viaene *et al.* 1997) are strongly zoned parallel to the rim. The zoning of these minerals is caused by variation in their composition (more details in the next section).

4.3.3. Geochemistry of the volcanic rocks around Sagalassos

- Semi-quantitative chemical analysis of crystals

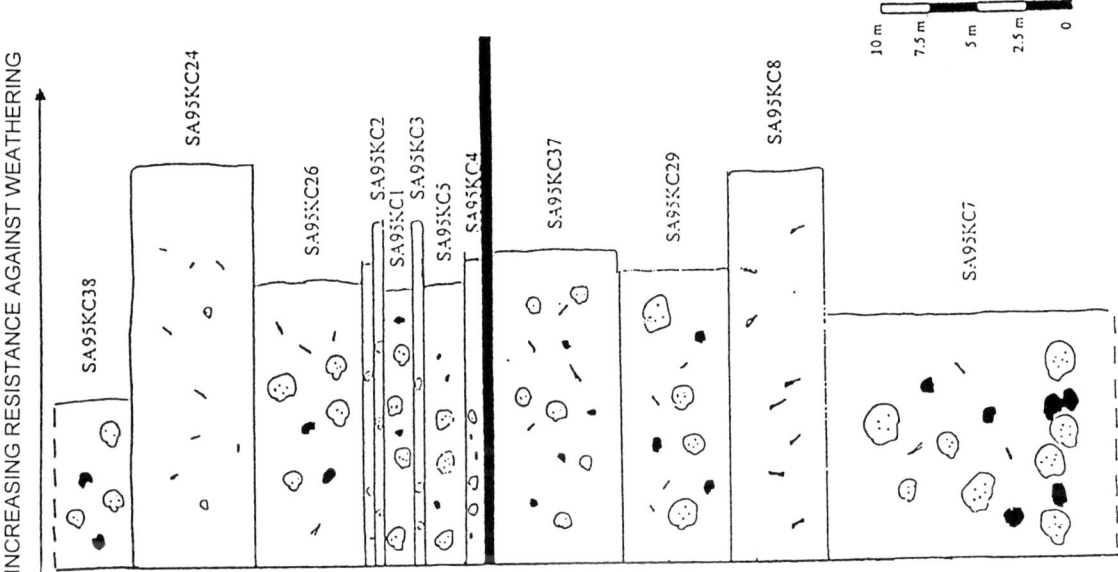

Fig. 3: Lithological column of tuff layers in the studied area. The lava layer (black) is the most resistant and the coarse-grained tuff (for example SA95KC27) is the least resistant against weathering. ⊙ = pumice inclusion; ● = andesite inclusion; ＼／ = pyroxene or biotite inclusion; ▬ = lava layer.

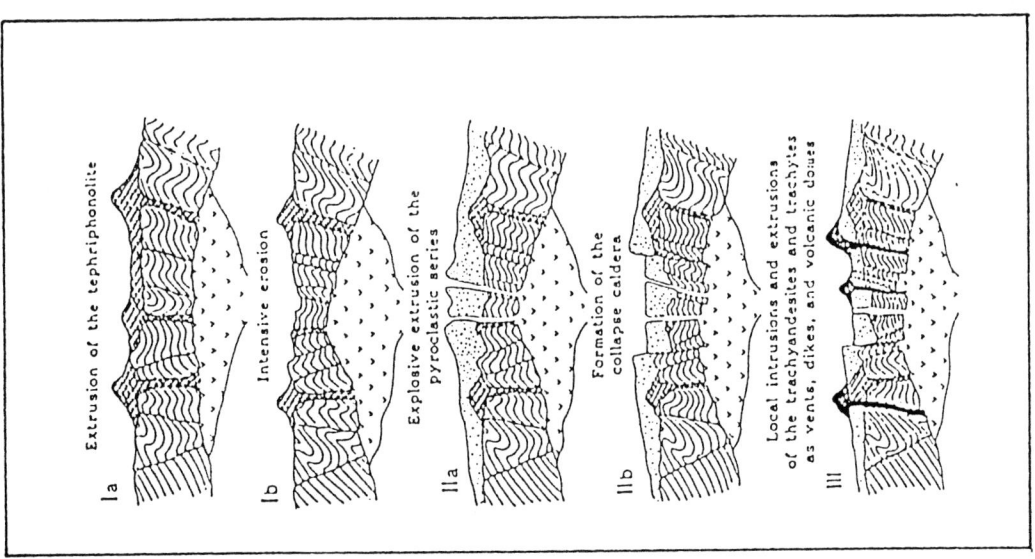

Fig. 4: Schematic evolution of the volcanic activity in the Gölcük area (Özgür et al. 1990). Not to scale.

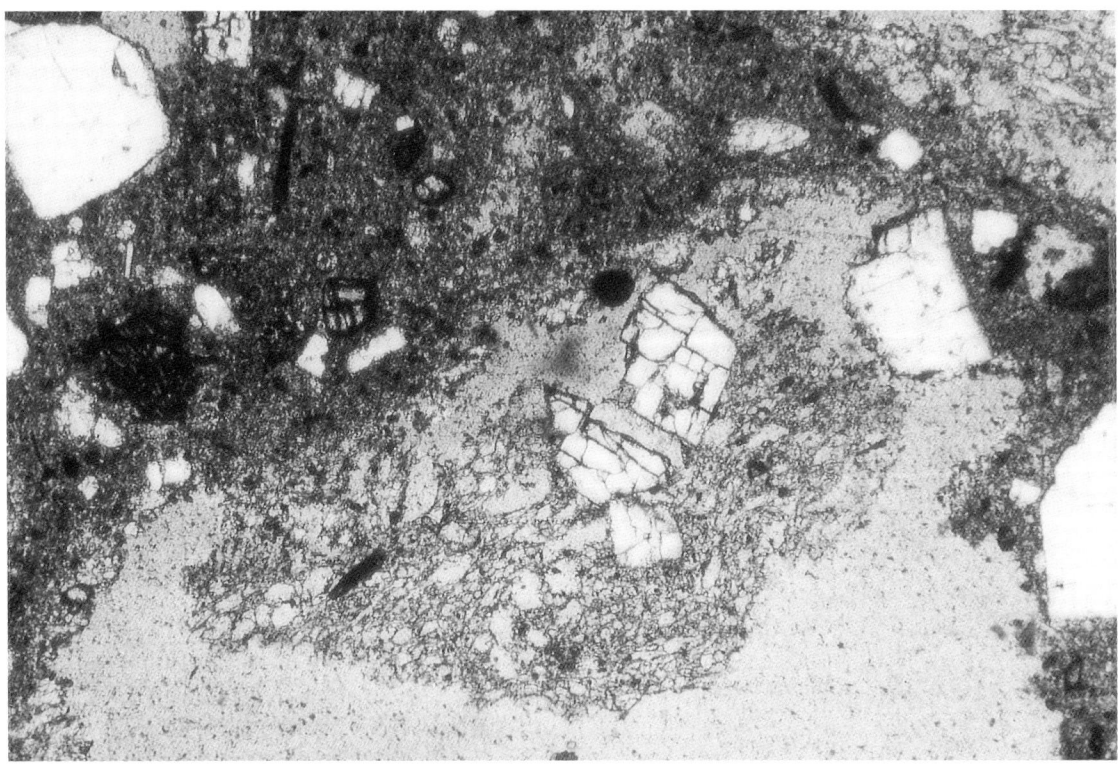

Fig. 5: Pumice inclusion in a tuff sample. The pumice is very porous and contains feldspar crystals (white). The pumice is partly gone due to preparation of the thin section. Sample SA95KC4. Scale: 1 cm = 625 μm.

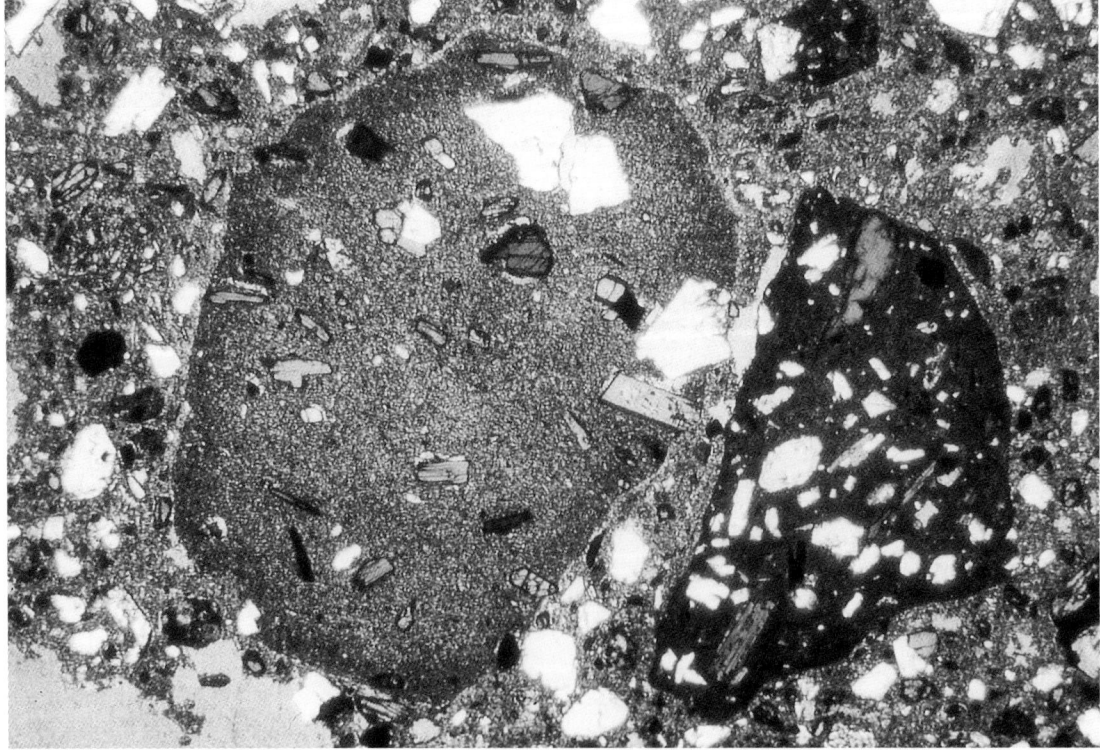

Fig. 6: Lava (andesite) inclusion in a tuff sample. The matrix of the lava inclusion is very fine and crystals of feldspar (white), biotite (brown) and augite (green) can be observed. Sample SA95KC4. Scale: 1 cm = 625 μm.

Fig. 7: Zoned plagioclase crystal in a fine-grained andesite matrix. The same crystals are also observed in tuff layers. Sample SA95KC42. Scale: 1 cm = 0.1 mm.

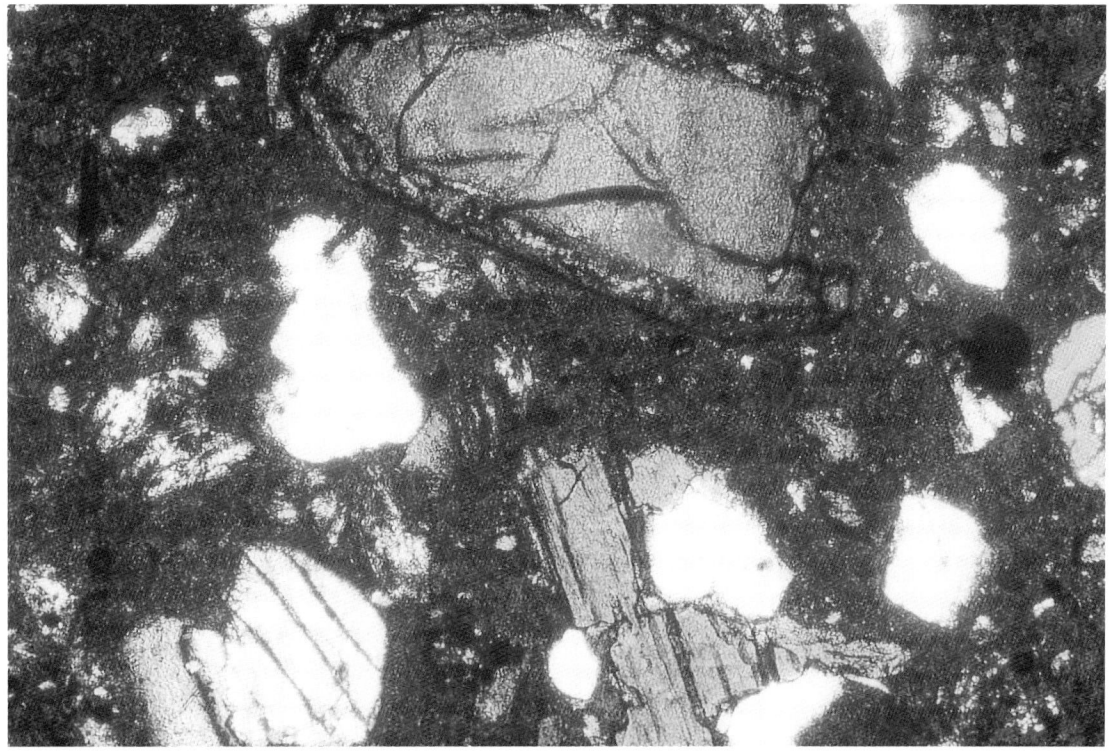

Fig. 8: Zoned augite crystal in a coarse-grained tuff layer. Sample SA95KC3. Scale: 1 cm = 0.1 mm.

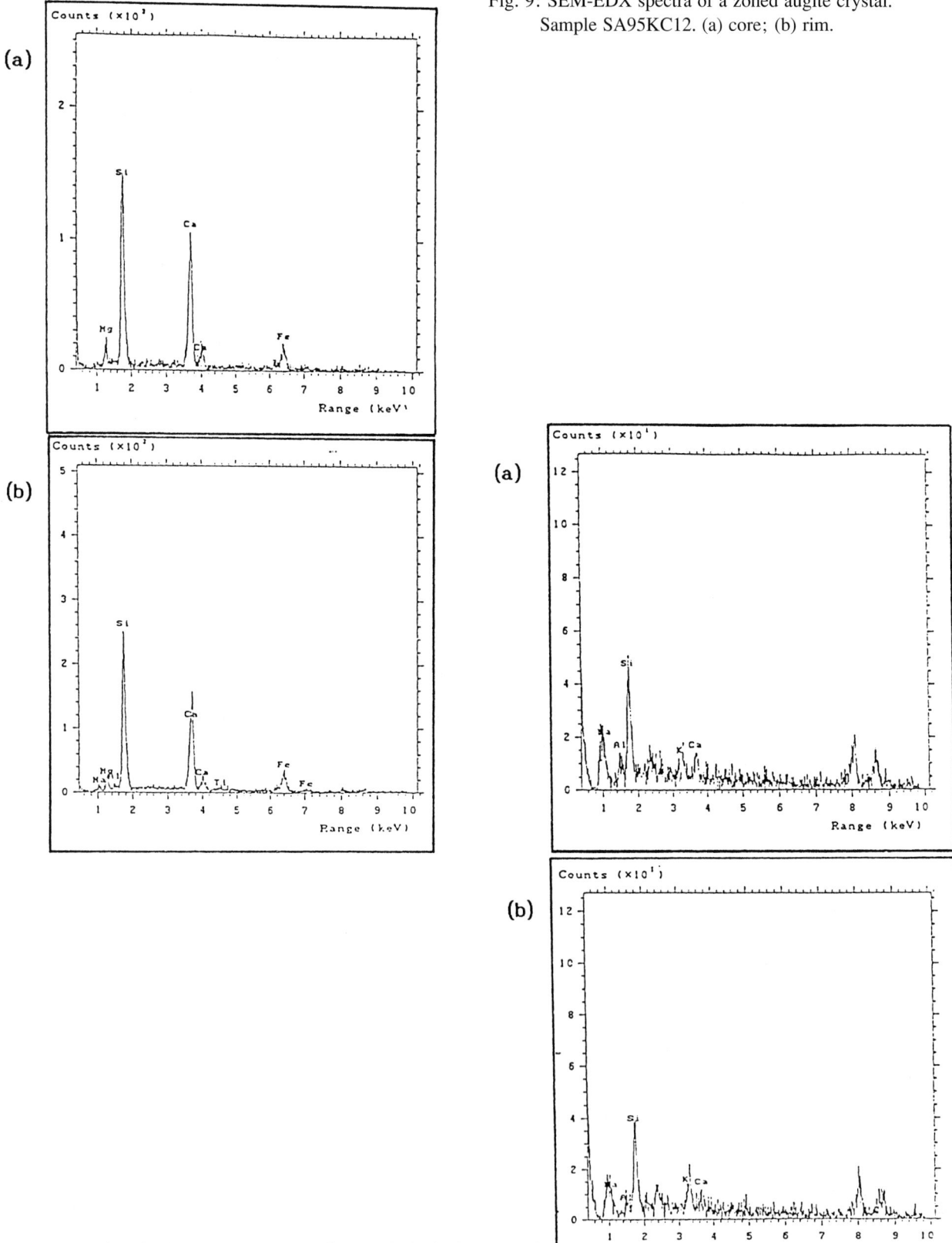

Fig. 9: SEM-EDX spectra of a zoned augite crystal. Sample SA95KC12. (a) core; (b) rim.

Fig. 10: SEM-EDX spectra of a zoned plagioclase crystal. Sample SA95KC11. (a) core; (b) rim.

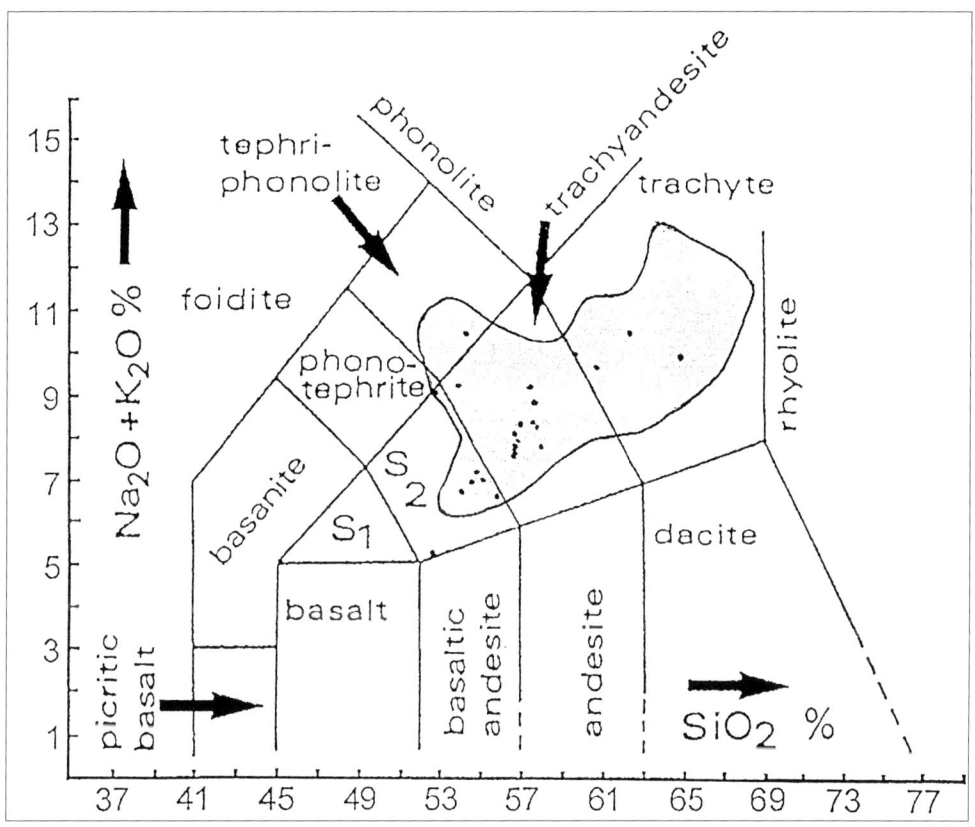

Fig. 11: Discrimination of the sampled tuff and lava layers (•) according to the classification scheme of Le Maitre (1984). The coloured area consists of samples analysed by Özgür et al. (1990). S_1: trachybasalt; S_2: benmoreite (Na) or shoshonite (K).

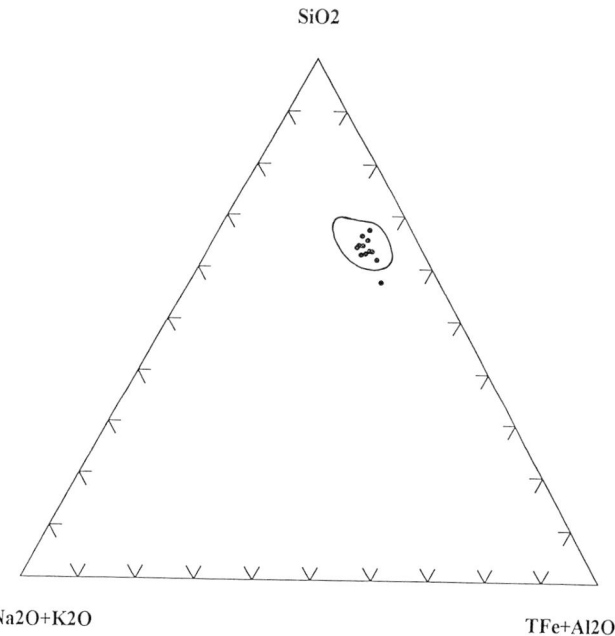

Fig. 12: Comparison of chemical analyses from lime mortars with only volcanic additives and rocks from the volcanic area. Mortar samples are identified by •. The encircled area contains the chemical analyses of volcanic rocks from the studied area.

With the SEM-EDX system, semi-quantitative chemical analyses on small volumes of plagioclases and augites were performed to characterize the zoning of these crystals. The zoning of augites (Fig. 9) is caused by a decrease of the Mg- and Ca-content and by an increase of the Fe- and Na-content from core to rim. The ratio of intensity of Si to Ca and Mg increases from core to rim (Si/Ca in the core is 1.3 and increases to 1.7 at the rim, Fig. 9). According to Deer *et al.* (1980) the first pyroxenes that crystallise have a diopside composition with a decreasing Ca-content and an increasing Fe- and Na-content during further growth. The zoning of the plagioclases is also caused by a variation in composition. The Ca- and Al-content decreases towards the rim while the K-content increases (Fig. 10). According to Deer *et al.* (1980) the zonation of plagioclases is often related to a Ca-rich core (bytownite) and a Na-rich rim. Here however, the ratio Si/Na is rather constant (Si/Na ca. 2 in core and rim). Quantitative analysis (e.g. with a microprobe) could characterize the zonation of the plagioclases.

- Chemical analyses of bulk samples from volcanic rocks

The results of the chemical analyses with AES and AAS are given in Table 1. The samples are classified by increasing SiO_2-content. The differences between the samples are not great, except for the SiO_2-content. The LOI-content is rather high and a distinction between lava and tuff can be made based upon this LOI-content. The LOI-content of the tuffs is higher than that of the lava samples. This high LOI-content can be explained by the loss of gases from the glass matrix and by dehydration of biotite and hornblende.

The higher Al_2O_3-content in sample SA95KC29 can be explained by the greater amount of feldspars which can be observed petrographically. The difference between the two types of tuff (fine-grained and coarse-grained) is not made clear through chemical analysis. The fine-grained tuff has a slightly higher K_2O-content and a slightly lower CaO-, MgO- and TFe-content. No evolution in composition relating to the lithological column (Fig. 3) can be seen.

In Fig. 11, the samples are plotted in a binary diagram, together with the field of data obtained by Özgür *et al.* (1990). All samples, except one (SA95KC29) plot within this field. Most of the samples are trachyandesites and trachytes, with some benmoreites or shoshonites. One sample (SA95KC16g) plots within the area of tephriphonolite, which could correspond with a relic of the first volcanic stage recognized by Özgür *et al.* (1990, see Fig. 4).

- Trace element analysis from volcanic rocks to the northwest of Sagalassos

Trace elements can be used to classify volcanic rocks and to determine the origin of the magma. The results of the analyses with XRF are given in Table 2. Very high amounts of Sr and Ba are observed. These amounts are higher than expected in volcanic rocks. Fisher and Schmincke (1984) mention an average value for Sr of ca. 300 ppm and for Ba of ca. 500 ppm. These high figures can be explained by substitution of Ba and Sr in feldspars. Rather high amounts of Ba can substitute in K-feldspars and Sr can substitute in feldspars in a range from about 100 to 5000 ppm (Yung *et al.* 1975). SA95KC8 especially shows an extremely high value of Ba and indeed more K-feldspars can be observed in this sample. Francalanci *et al.* (1990) mention Ba- and Sr-values of two ultra-potassic rocks around Isparta with values for Ba of 2384 ppm and 2354 ppm and for Sr of 2326 ppm and 2219 ppm. The values analysed here are clearly higher. Generally, we can conclude that the amount of most trace elements varies widely. Only elements in small quantities (Co, Cr, ...) show an almost constant value. Sulphur has a fairly constant value with the exception of two samples with high values. These samples contain more opaque minerals, including sulfides. More research on this subject is necessary for an explanation of the trace element content and for a better determination of the origin of the magma.

Trace elements can also be used to identify the provenance of the volcanic additives that were used in the mortars of Sagalassos. This will be dealt with in a following paper.

5. RELATIONSHIP BETWEEN THE VOLCANIC ROCKS AND THE VOLCANIC ADMIXTURES IN THE LIME MORTARS

The main aim of this study was to identify the provenance of the raw materials used in the lime mortars. The provenance of the lime and the chamotte is already clear. For the volcanic admixtures, the following observations could be made:

1 – petrographically, the volcanic rocks used as admixtures in the mortars and those from the volcanic region located immediately northeast of the city are similar. Both lava and pumice fragments are found in the mortars and in the tuff layers. The zoned augites and plagioclases, a characteristic feature in the rocks from the volcanic area, can also be observed in the mortars (compare Fig. 8 with fig. 8 in Viaene *et al.* 1997). The fragments in the mortars often have broken rims, so the inhabitants of Sagalassos must also have used the hard tuff and the lava layers, after crushing, instead of sandy tuff.

2 – chemically, the analyses of the mortars with volcanic admixtures only and the volcanic rocks from the volcanic region are also similar. This can be seen in Fig. 12, where the chemical analyses of mortars are plotted in a ternary dia-

Sample	SiO$_2$	Al$_2$O$_3$	TFe	MnO	MgO	CaO	Na$_2$O	K$_2$O	TiO$_2$	P$_2$O$_5$	LOI	Sum	description
SA95KC16w	52.46	17.20	6.62	0.14	3.60	7.53	3.52	5.60	0.70	0.57	1.59	99.53	lava
SA95KC29	52.52	21.39	4.34	0.13	1.40	4.52	2.32	2.78	0.60	0.31	9.10	99.41	tuff (p)
SA95KC11	53.77	16.93	6.67	0.12	2.95	7.11	3.95	5.16	0.79	0.48	1.57	99.50	lava
SA95KC25	53.91	18.54	4.26	0.12	2.14	5.66	2.18	4.68	0.51	0.28	6.99	99.27	tuff (p)
SA95KC16g	53.99	16.45	5.42	0.13	3.41	7.81	4.30	5.77	0.70	0.56	0.83	99.37	lava
SA95KC44	54.37	15.69	5.89	0.12	2.85	6.44	2.98	4.07	0.62	0.38	6.08	99.49	tuff (p)
SA95KC33	54.68	17.09	5.31	0.10	2.96	6.16	2.61	4.57	0.64	0.36	4.94	99.42	tuff (p)
SA95KC48	55.61	15.20	5.41	0.11	2.79	6.61	2.44	4.38	0.61	0.36	5.99	99.51	tuff (p)
SA95KC32	56.42	17.36	4.65	0.11	2.66	4.93	2.82	4.99	0.60	0.32	4.46	99.32	tuff (p)
SA95KC26	56.44	16.78	4.08	0.11	2.05	5.33	2.66	5.11	0.55	0.35	5.68	99.44	tuff (p)
SA95KC5	56.52	16.29	4.65	0.12	2.20	5.76	2.72	4.98	0.59	0.30	5.18	99.31	tuff (p)
SA95KC4	56.53	16.41	4.56	0.13	2.07	5.57	2.79	5.02	0.58	0.28	5.41	99.35	tuff (p)
SA95KC1	56.54	16.23	4.57	0.13	2.42	5.46	3.15	4.91	0.59	0.27	5.09	99.36	tuff (p)
SA95KC7	56.66	16.42	4.72	0.14	2.29	5.65	3.01	4.90	0.58	0.31	4.65	99.33	tuff (p)
SA95KC2	56.85	16.15	4.37	0.12	2.33	5.78	3.09	5.08	0.57	0.27	4.78	99.39	tuff (p)
SA95KC43	57.15	18.05	4.82	0.16	1.94	4.44	3.84	5.34	0.53	0.28	2.77	99.32	tuff (p)
SA95KC30	57.19	17.40	4.78	0.12	2.67	4.77	3.45	5.04	0.57	0.27	2.95	99.21	tuff (p)
SA95KC31	57.31	17.49	4.71	0.11	2.63	4.64	3.48	4.98	0.59	0.29	3.02	99.25	tuff (p)
SA95KC3	57.42	16.31	4.51	0.11	2.14	5.08	3.97	4.94	0.58	0.26	3.97	99.29	tuff (p)
SA95KC8	57.86	16.59	3.44	0.18	1.86	4.26	2.65	5.27	0.44	0.22	6.54	99.31	tuff (p)
SA95KC39	59.32	18.03	4.67	0.13	1.81	4.30	4.78	5.27	0.57	0.35	0.17	99.40	lava
SA95KC24	60.53	17.46	2.49	0.08	1.09	3.09	4.24	5.40	0.34	0.16	4.27	99.15	tuff (p)
SA95KC12	62.18	17.01	3.85	0.08	1.42	3.54	5.49	4.94	0.47	0.19	0.19	99.36	lava
SA95KC42	64.66	16.85	3.60	0.05	0.79	2.39	4.83	5.18	0.48	0.24	0.43	99.50	lava

Table 1: chemical analysis results (weight%) of the volcanic rocks from the area to the northwest of Sagalassos. Tuff (p): porous coarse tuff type; tuff (f): fine compact tuff type; TFe: total Fe-content, expressed as Fe$_2$O$_3$.

Sample	Ba	Ce	Co	Cr	Cu	La	Nb	Ni	RB	Sr	W	Y	Zn	Zr	Pb	S
SA95KC1	3396	458	20	18	255	281	46	52	322	7498	41	17	71	363	116	119
SA95KC2	3787	475	19	25	326	282	41	45	229	8208	51	16	75	317	142	120
SA95KC3	3646	413	17	15	244	294	47	73	481	6525	50	19	77	380	107	112
SA95KC4	5248	481	20	19	377	302	45	50	229	8279	55	16	70	338	118	139
SA95KC5	3895	463	19	20	262	320	41	43	238	6990	64	14	68	320	103	183
SA95KC7	3346	488	19	18	228	298	44	35	142	7105	40	18	70	338	104	119
SA95KC8	13867	424	14	12	613	355	52	49	184	6084	40	14	83	406	98	175
SA95KC11	3311	563	17	19	195	498	56	56	102	5464	59	22	60	455	92	732
SA95KC12	2255	163	14	14	126	157	34	48	155	3679	59	13	44	383	69	100
SA95KC16	3658	431	19	27	218	312	36	38	97	5580	44	16	56	373	78	1493
SA95KC24	2292	330	13	19	146	233	35	33	176	3859	61	11	78	362	125	81
SA95KC29	4573	785	18	10	218	389	78	44	69	4852	36	32	80	596	115	133
SA95LC30	4649	568	20	29	227	363	37	48	172	4109	34	17	95	355	123	236
SA95KC42	1795	259	13	17	85	162	35	46	147	2008	88	16	43	376	78	96
SA95KC48	3074	499	20	27	189	304	34	41	168	4466	48	17	94	333	102	103

Table 2: trace element analysis results (ppm) of the volcanic rocks from the area to the northwest of Sagalassos.

gram which also includes the field of analyses of rocks from the volcanic region. Only elements which are characteristic for the volcanic rocks (SiO_2, Na_2O, K_2O, TFe and Al_2O_3) are plotted, so that there is no danger of misinterpretation from the lime matrix. All the mortar samples but one (SA94RO34) plot in the field of the volcanic rocks. From this it is suggested that the volcanic rocks of the study area were used as admixtures in the mortars. Further analyses of trace elements of mortars containing only volcanic rock admixtures could confirm the provenance of the volcanic rocks.

An experimental study on the mortars was begun in order to observe the influence of the different admixtures on lime mortars. Different mixtures of lime and volcanic rocks from the volcanic region or chamotte were made and the change in strength through time was observed. Preliminary conclusions were that mortars made with lime and volcanic admixtures reached a strength comparable to that of the Roman mortars from Sagalassos (Callebaut 1996). Further study of different mixtures is in progress.

6. CONCLUSIONS

As was to be expected for economic reasons, the raw materials used in the mortars of Sagalassos all have a local origin. The lime probably originates from Triassic limestones in the vicinity of Sagalassos. In fact, the limestone fragments that were used as aggregates show the same features as those of the Triassic limestone (veinlets of calcite, recrystallised calcite, radiolaria and twinned calcite crystals). The fabric of the crushed ceramics used as admixture is also similar to that of the locally produced coarse ceramics from Sagalassos. The same petrographical features are found. This paper focuses on the study of the volcanic rocks that were used as admixtures in the mortars of the ancient city.

There was a strong possibility that the volcanic rocks to the northwest of Sagalassos were a source of raw materials. These can be observed almost immediately north of the mountain pass as tuff layers with varying thickness and resistance against weathering. These hills consist of material which eroded from these tuff layers. Lava layers are only abundant around Lake Gölçük. According to differences in inclusions, i.e. size and type (lava fragments, crystals, sandstone fragments, ...), colour, compaction and whether or not the layer followed the hard layers in the topography, thirteen different eruptions could be distinguished in the southern part of the volcanic region. Petrographically, a matrix and different inclusions can be observed. These inclusions are divided into rock fragments (pumice, lava and sandstone fragments) and crystals (plagioclases, alkali-feldspars, augites, diopsides, biotites and hornblendes). Chemically, these volcanic rocks can be classified mainly as trachyandesite and trachyte.

Petrographically, the tuffs show features identical to those of the volcanic inclusions in the lime mortars. These inclusions consist of pumice and lava fragments which also occur in the tuffs. In the lava fragments from the mortar and from the tuffs strongly zoned augites as well as zoned plagioclases can be observed. Chemically, the tuffs and the volcanic admixtures also show the same range of content of SiO_2, Na_2O, K_2O, Fe_2O_3 and Al_2O_3, elements which are characteristic for volcanics. Thus, it is clear that the volcanic deposits located immediately to the north of the mountain pass (Loots *et al.* 2000) were exploited by the inhabitants of Sagalassos as mortar admixtures for their building projects. The area also contains an important limestone quarry of Roman imperial date (Waelkens *et al.* 1997: 46-47, fig. 40).

7. ACKNOWLEDGEMENTS

This research is supported by the Belgian Programme on Interuniversity Poles of Attraction (IUAP 4/12) initiated by the Belgian State, Prime Minister's Office, Science Policy Programming. The text also presents the results of the Concerted Action of the Flemish Government (GOA 97/2), the Fund for Scientific Research-Flanders (Belgium) (FWO) (G.2145.94) and the National Fund for Collective Fundamental Research of Belgium. Scientific responsibility is assumed by its authors. The Turkish authorities are thanked for granting permission to export and study mortar and volcanic rock samples. Finally, the technical assistance of S. Lens, D. Coetermans, H. Nijs and D. Steeno is also gratefully acknowledged.

8. REFERENCES

J.P. Adam (1984) *La construction romaine*, Paris.
G. Baronio, L. Binda and N. Lombardini (1997) The role of brick pebbles and dust in conglomerates based on hydrated lime and crushed bricks, *Construction and Building Materials* 11: 33-40.
R.F. Blanks and H.L. Kennedy (1955) Pozzolanic cements, in: R.F. Blanks and H.L. Kennedy (eds) *The Technology of Cement and Concrete*, New York: 164-198.
K. Callebaut (1996) *Mineralogie van vulkanische tuffen rond Sagalassos (Turkije) en hun gebruik in mortels*, unpublished M.Sc. dissertation, KULeuven.
W.A. Deer, R.A. Howie and J. Zussman (1980) *An Introduction to the Rock Forming Minerals*, London.
R. Degeest, R. Ottenburgs, W. Viaene, H. Kucha, D. Laduron and M. Waelkens (1997) Characterization of the common wares manufactured in Roman Sagalassos. An overview, in: M. Waelkens and J. Poblome (eds) *Sagalassos IV. Report on the Survey and Excavation Campaigns of 1994 and 1995 (Acta Archaeologica Lovaniensia Monographiae* 9) Leuven University Press: 519-533.

R.V. Fisher and H.U. Schmincke (1984) *Pyroclastic Rocks*, Berlin.

L. Francalanci, L. Civetta, F. Innocenti and P. Manetti (1990) Tertiary-quaternary alkaline magmatism of the Aegean-Western Anatolian area: a petrographical study in the light of new geochemical and isotopic data, in: M.Y. Savasçın and A.H. Eronat (eds) *IESCA 1990 volume* II: 385-396.

K. Kraus, S. Wisser and D. Knöfel (1989) Uber das Löschen von Kalk vor der Mitte des 18. Jahrhunderts – Literaturauswertung und Laborversuche, *Arbeitsblätter für Restauratoren* (*Gruppe* 6) 1: 206-221.

H. Kucha (1995) *Ceramics of Sagalassos. Their Mineralogy and Trace Element Chemistry*, internal report.

H.O. Lamprecht (1987) *Opus Caementitium: Bautechnik der Römer*, Dusseldorf.

M. Lefèvre, H. Bellon and A. Poisson (1983) Présence de leucitites dans le volcanisme pliocène de la région d'Isparta (Taurides occidentales, Turquie), *Comptes Rendus de l'Academie de Sciences* 267 (*série* II): 367-372.

R.W. Le Maitre (1984) A proposal by the IUGS subcommission on the systematics of igneous rocks for a chemical classification of volcanic rocks based on the total alkali silica (TAS) diagram, *Australian Journal of Earth Sciences* 31: 243-255.

L. Loots, M. Waelkens and F. Depuydt (2000) The city fortifications of Sagalassos from the Hellenistic to the late Roman period: in M. Waelkens and L. Loots (ed.) *Sagalassos V. Report on the Survey and Excavation Campaigns of 1996 and 1997 (Acta Archaeologica Lovaniensia Monographiae* 11), Leuven University Press: 595-634.

R. Martin (1965) *Manuel d'architecture grecque 1. Matériaux et techniques*, Paris.

A. Orlandos (1966) *Les matériaux de construction et la technique architecturale des anciens grecs* 1, Paris.

N. Özgür, A. Pekdeger, H.J. Schneider and A. Bilgin (1990) Pliocene volcanism in the Gölcük area, Isparta/Western Taurides, in: M.Y. Savasçın and A.H. Eronat (eds) *IESCA 1990 volume* II: 411-419.

A.R. Philpotts (1990) *Principles of Igneous and Metamorphic Petrology*, New Jersey.

A. Poisson (1977) *Recherches géologiques dans les Taurides occidentales (Turquie)* (Thèse de doctorat d'état Université de Paris-Orsay).

W. Viaene, R. Ottenburgs, P. Muchez and M. Waelkens (1993) The building stones of Sagalassos, in: M. Waelkens (ed.) *Sagalassos I. First General Report on the Survey (1980-1986-1989) and Excavations (1990-1991) (Acta Archaeologica Lovaniensia Monographiae* 5) Leuven University Press: 85-92.

W. Viaene, M. Waelkens, R. Ottenburgs and K. Callebaut (1997) An archaeometric study of mortars used at Sagalassos, in: M. Waelkens and J. Poblome (eds) *Sagalassos IV. Report on the Survey and Excavation Campaigns of 1994 and 1995 (Acta Archaeologica Lovaniensia Monographiae* 9) Leuven University Press: 404-422.

S. Yalçınkaya (1983) *Geological map of Isparta – M25 – d.1, 1:25000*.

R.A. Yung, D.B. Steward, J.V. Smith and P.H. Ribbe (1975) Feldspar mineralogy, in: P.H. Ribbe (ed.) *Mineralogical Society of America Short Course Notes* 2: sm18-sm29.

PART V

CERAMIC STUDIES

AN EARLY BYZANTINE TILE AND LIME KILN IN THE TERRITORY OF SAGALASSOS

Jeroen POBLOME[1], Haci Ali EKİNCİ[2], Ilhame ÖZTÜRK[2], Patrick DEGRYSE[3], Willy VIAENE (†)[3] and Marc WAELKENS[1]

1 - Department of Archaeology, KULeuven, Blijde Inkomststraat 21, 3000 Leuven, Belgium
2 - Burdur Müzesi, Burdur, Turkey
3 - Physical and Chemical Geology, Laboratory of Mineralogy, KULeuven, Celestijnenlaan 200C, 3001 Heverlee, Belgium

INTRODUCTION

From the eleventh until the fourteenth of June 1996 a small-scale rescue excavation was undertaken at the village of Taşkapı, southern Turkey in the province of Burdur. This excavation was directed by the Archaeological Museum of Burdur, represented by its director Haci Ali Ekinci and his assistant Ilhame Öztürk, in collaboration with the Sagalassos Archaeological Research Project.

During the 1993 survey of the western part of the territory of the ancient town of Sagalassos (Waelkens 1995; Waelkens *et al.* 1997), locals from the village of Taşkapı pointed out a concentration of misfired tile fragments and kiln wall fragments on the surface. Most of these fragments were probably brought to the surface when the kiln structure itself had been damaged by the construction of a road leading to newly built houses to the east of the site (Figs. 3 and 4). Further illegal digging by locals had caused additional harm to the kiln structure (opening in the back wall, see Fig. 5). The goal of the small-scale rescue excavation was, therefore, to salvage and record the remains of the kiln structure, and identify and date its production.

2. TOPOGRAPHICAL SITUATION

The site is situated in the territory of the modern village of Taşkapı, at a distance of ca. 10 km to the west of the ilçe of Ağlasun and some 20 km to the southeast of the town of Burdur. In antiquity, this area was part of the extensive territory of the ancient town of Sagalassos. Farming communities within this rural territory formed the traditional backbone of the economy of the town of Sagalassos.

The kiln itself was dug and built into a south-facing slope, overlooking a small circular valley, which is enclosed by mountains (Figs. 1-4). The heavy back or southern wall of the kiln protected it from erosion by retaining the slope of the hill (Fig. 5). The entrance of the kiln faced towards the small valley (Fig. 6).

In the immediate surroundings of the kiln the locals pointed out more wall fragments, the remains of a farmstead (?), a water well (?), and a necropolis.

3. THE STRUCTURE

The excavated kiln is of the up-draught kiln type. The plan of the kiln is not circular but square, with one side measuring ca. 4 m (Fig. 7). The kiln was constructed within a pit dug into the slope. The back wall and the back part of the two side walls were constructed with limestone rubble set in mud. The back wall was preserved to a height of ca. 1 m above the raised floor of the kiln, while only the lowest row of stones of the side walls remained *in situ*. A thick layer of mud plaster lined the front part of the kiln. The raised floor was supported by a central short wall (tongue support), and a set of arches covering the two combustion chambers. The walls of the kiln were covered with two layers of mud plaster, totalling some 0.05 m thick. The greenish clay soil into which the kiln had been dug was coloured red around the kiln because of the heat produced by repeated firings. The front part of the raised kiln floor had been destroyed, probably due to the construction of the new road.

The flue or fire tunnel is in the lower part of the slope, in the middle of the front wall. This part of the kiln could only be partially excavated so the length of the flue could not be determined. It is ca. 1 m wide and lined irregularly with limestone blocks. The floor of the flue consists of clay, coloured red from the heat of the kiln, and containing a large amount of charcoal. This part of the kiln was most probably not covered. The 0.95 m wide entrance of the kiln was flanked by two limestone blocks. Nothing else remained of the door, but it was probably made of clay, in the same way as the rest of the kiln, and was presumably vaulted (Fig. 6).

Inside, two furnace or combustion chambers were arranged, separated by a short central wall, constructed of rubble and covered with a thick layer of mud plaster (Fig. 8). This wall was completely preserved, ca. 1.70 m high, 1.70 m long and 0.5 m wide. It was built against the rubble back wall of the kiln, ending 1 m short of the door. The off-set of an arch was found, constructed at the front end of this wall, spanning the distance to the door. The arch itself was not preserved (Fig. 5).

Of the two combustion chambers, the western one is ca. 2.70 m long, 1 m wide and 1.40 m high, while the eastern one is ca. 2.50 m long, 1.10 m wide and 1.40 m high (Figs 8-9). A mud floor, hardened from the firing, was completely preserved in both rooms. This floor stopped at the entrance. The mud lining was also applied to the side walls of the kiln and over the arches spanning the rooms. Each room was roofed by four arches, constructed of 0.08 to 0.10 m thick moulded lumps of clay with triangular pieces of tile inserted in between. Three of the arches over both rooms were supported by the central wall. The fourth arch of each combustion chamber was supported by the arch between the central wall and the door of the kiln. This fourth arch was no longer preserved, but the off-set on the side walls of the kiln was found. In the eastern room, the inner three arches were completely preserved. In the western room, the arch at the front of the central wall was badly preserved and was taken away during excavation for safety reasons. From the back wall to the front side of the kiln the four arches of the western room were respectively ca. 0.36, 0.28, 0.20 and 0.26 m thick, and the four arches of the eastern room ca. 0.24, 0.26, 0.22 and 0.22 m thick. The arches were placed at irregular distances from each other, which were different in both rooms so that they did not form a continuous line through the two chambers (Figs. 10 and 11).

Between the arches, pieces of tile were placed to make squarish vent holes to take the heat of the combustion chambers into the kiln. These vent holes are 0.05 to 0.10 m in diameter. The raised floor of the kiln was made of two to three layers of tile fragments, laid on the arches and leaving the vent holes open. These layers of tile fragments were covered by a 0.05 to 0.08 m thick layer of mud, into which small pebbles and tile fragments were mixed. The raised floor was preserved to the second arch from the back above the western room, and up to the third arch from the back above the eastern room. The floor measured 3.40 m between the two side walls (Fig. 12).

Patches of mud plaster were found *in situ* on the inner side of the back wall. Most probably the complete superstructure would have been made of clay, but no evidence was found to determine how the superstructure of the kiln would have appeared. Ethnographical research provides evidence for both open and closed superstructures for kilns of this type.

The square plan, the nature of the kiln spacers, the quantity of misfired tile fragments, the lack of ceramics or misfired pottery found in and around the kiln, and comparable structures excavated at other sites within the Roman and early Byzantine empire, all indicate that this kiln was used to fire tiles and not pottery.

Two handle fragments and a rim sherd were found in the ashes preserved on the floor of the combustion chambers (Fig. 13). These indicate a date in the early Byzantine period for this tile kiln. These sherds are not products of the town of Sagalassos, where pottery was mass-produced from around the start of our era into the first half of the seventh century AD (Poblome 1999), but from the production centre which was found during the 1995 and 1996 surveys of the territory of Sagalassos in the modern village of Bağsaray (Waelkens *et al.* 1997). In the fields in the immediate neighbourhood of what is considered by locals to be a kiln, a lot of misfired pottery and kiln spacers can be collected. Two types of wares were made at this production centre of regional importance. A coarse ware, with a reddish, sandy fabric with easily recognisable lime fragments, and a tableware with a pale yellowish, sandy fabric. Typological analysis and the analysis of the stratigraphical contexts in which those sherds occur at Sagalassos, indicate that the centre was active during the sixth and seventh centuries AD. The production centre of Bağsaray at first imitated Sagalassos red slip ware, but clearly continued its production even after the town of Sagalassos was abandoned around the middle of the seventh century AD.

4. ARCHAEOMETRICAL RESEARCH

In order to study the organisation of the small-scale production unit of Taşkapı in more detail, the chemical and mineralogical composition of samples of the kiln structure, tile fragments and a kiln spacer, together with the local clays, were analysed using atomic absorption and emission spectrography, X-ray diffractometry and thin section analysis. Samples of the thick ash layer on the floor of the combustion chambers were also examined.

Fig. 1: View of the hillside into which the kiln was built.

Fig. 2: View from the kiln towards the north.

Fig. 3: View from the kiln towards the west.

Fig. 4: View from the kiln towards the east.

Fig. 5: General view of the kiln, from the northwest.

Fig. 6: Detail of the entrance of the kiln, flanked by limestone blocks, and the flue or fire tunnel.

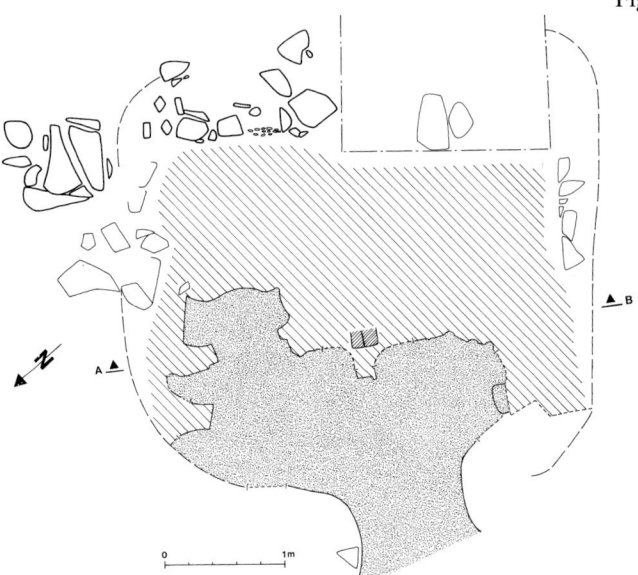

Fig. 7: General plan of the kiln at Taşkapı.

Fig. 8: Floor-plan of the combustion chambers.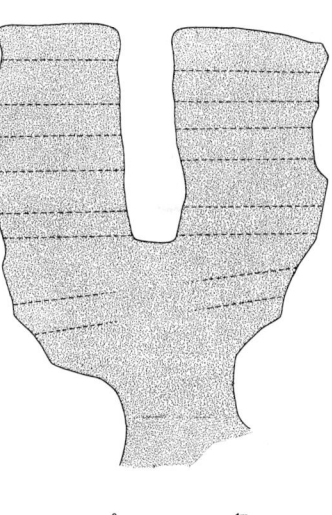

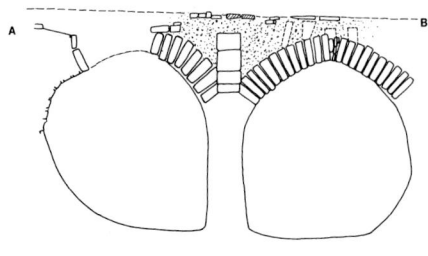

Fig. 9: Cross-section of the kiln at Taşkapı.

Fig. 10: View inside the western combustion chamber.

Fig. 11: View inside the eastern combustion chamber.

Fig.12: General view of the raised floor of the kiln.

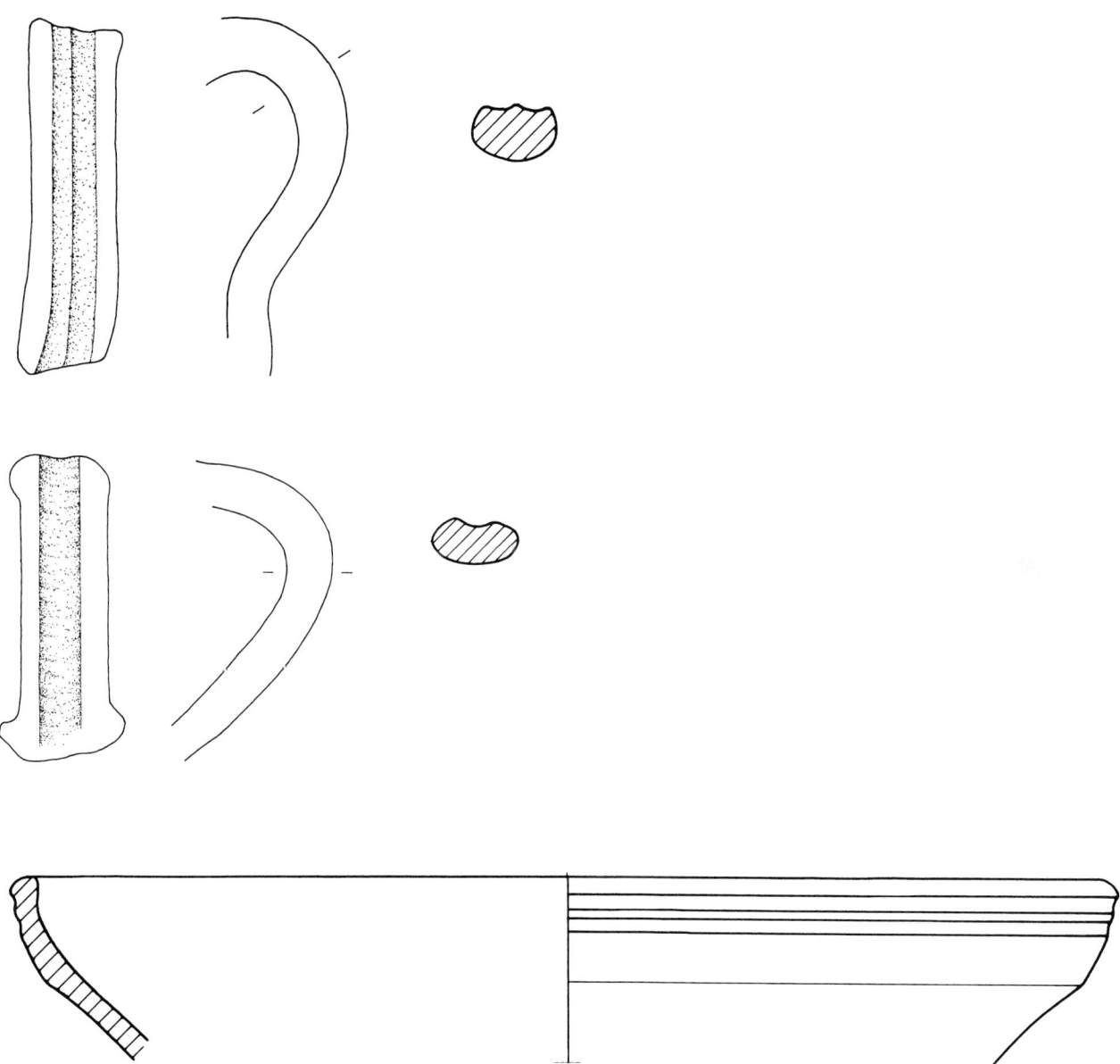

Fig. 13: Sherds found on the floor of the combustion chamber.

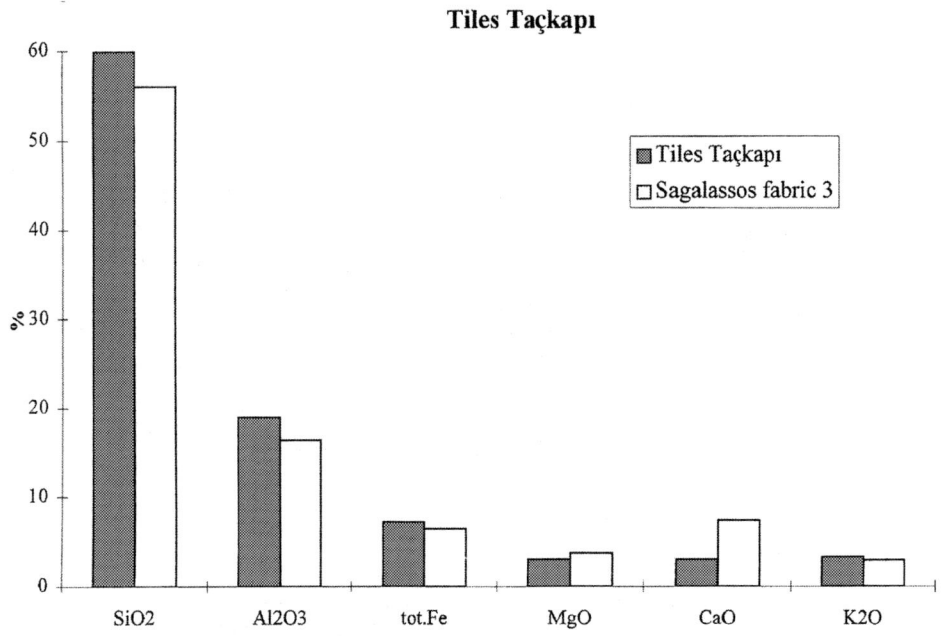

Fig. 14: The main chemical composition of the tiles produced at Taşkapı compared with the tiles made at Sagalassos.

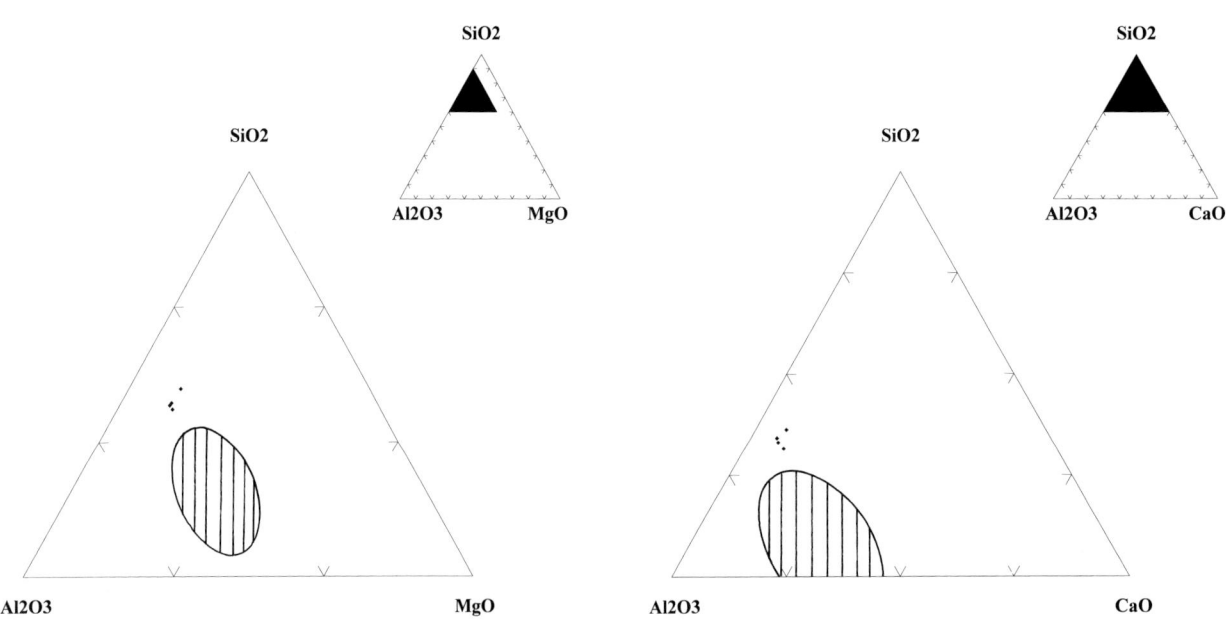

Fig. 15: Comparison of the chemical composition of tiles produced at Taşkapı (dots) and local clay resources (hatched area).

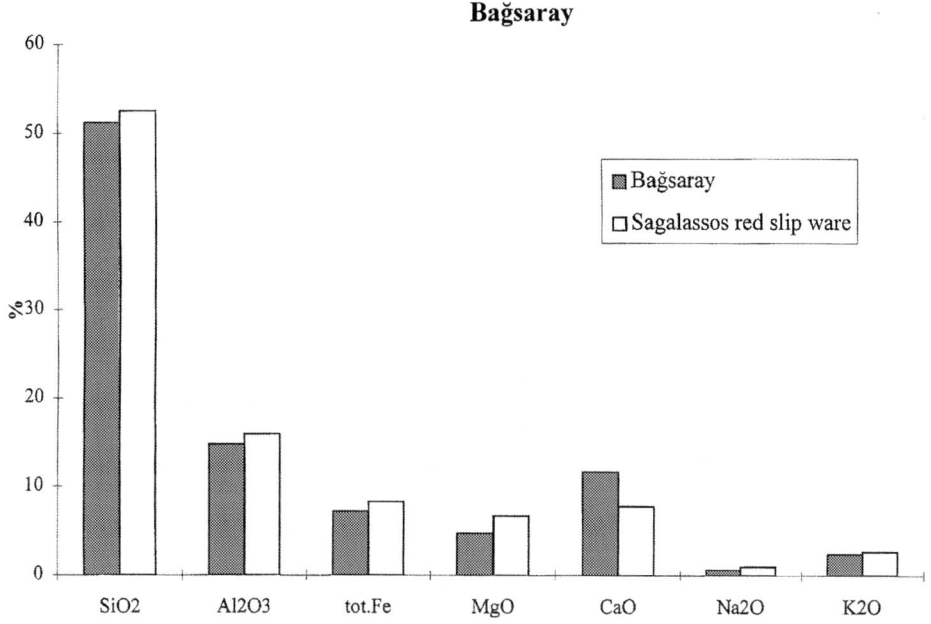

Fig. 16: The main chemical composition of the Bağsaray wares compared to Sagalassos red slip ware.

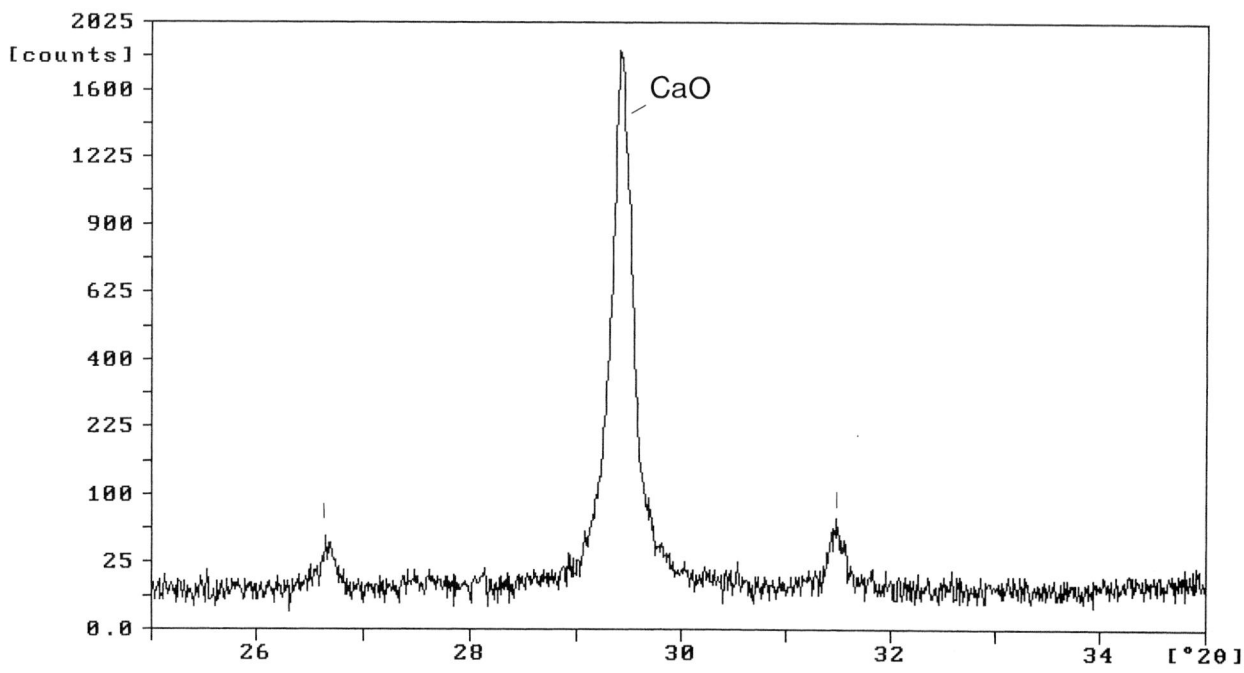

Fig. 17: X-ray diffractogram of CaO in the ashy deposits.

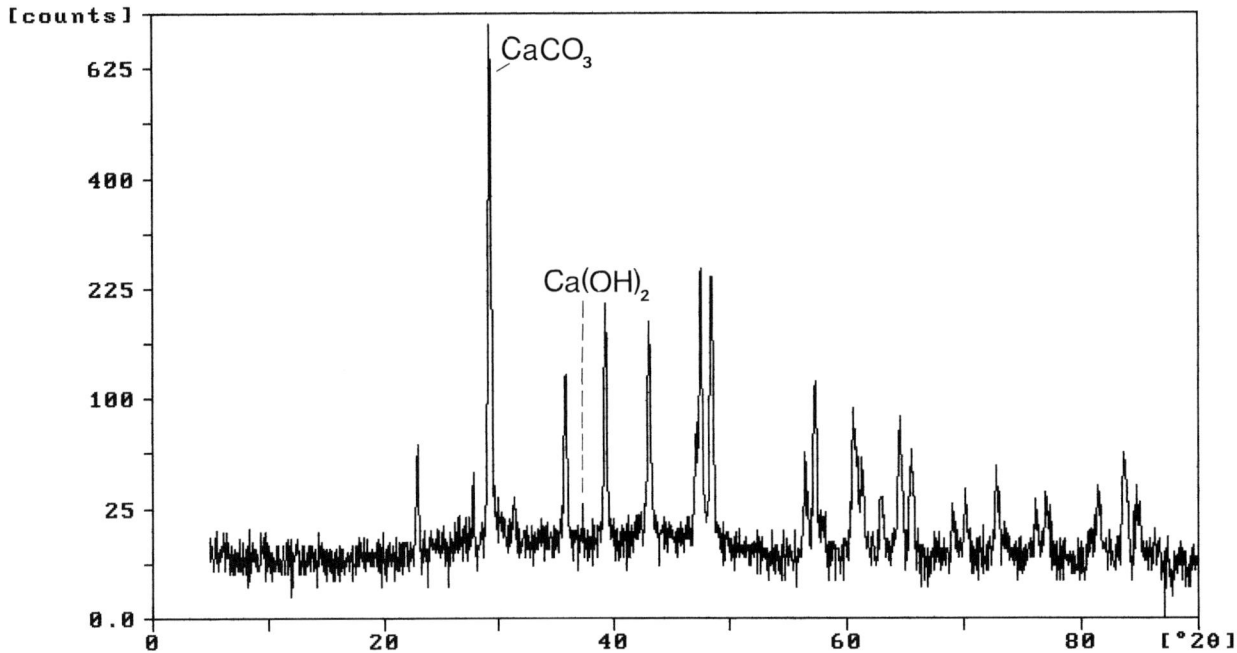

Fig. 18: X-ray diffractogram of Ca(Oh)$_2$ and CaCo$_3$ in the ashy deposits.

The results of the bulk chemical analysis of 4 tile samples and 1 kiln spacer produced at Taşkapı were compared to 17 samples of tiles or bricks made at Sagalassos (Fig. 14). The clay fabric used for bricks, tiles and water pipes at Sagalassos can be identified as the ophiolitic clays of the site of Sagalassos with, as the main clay mineral, smectite and smaller amounts of chlorite and illite. The feldspars in this fabric are mainly plagioclase and K-feldspar poor in Na. Large amounts of large, idiomorphic amphibole minerals (ferro-hornblende, ferro-richterite and ferro-pargasite, determined by XRD) and biotite crystals are present, together with small amounts of idiomorphic ferro-augite. Magnetite, ilmenite, chromite, hematite, diopside, apatite, perovskite and monazite are common minerals in these clays (Degryse et al. 2000). This fabric typically contains a high proportion of grog (>20%) (Degeest et al. 1997: fabric 3). The comparison indicates that the clay used at Taşkapı is somewhat poorer, more sandy and mainly less rich in calcium-oxides. Apparently, the same type of poor clay was also used to construct the arches and floors of the kiln itself (5 samples analysed).

However, a preliminary pedological and geological survey of the immediate vicinity of the tile kiln indicated that the clays of the slope into which the kiln was dug, and in the small circular valley in front of the kiln, are of very poor quality for ceramic production. 6 samples of the local clays were investigated mineralogically and chemically. In general, the content of clay minerals in the sediments and rocks in the valley of Taşkapı is very low with no deposits of clay. Less than 5% of the sediment belongs to the fraction smaller than 2 µm, while the fraction between 38 and 250 µm is dominant. The low content of clay minerals has a negative effect on the plasticity, and hence on the quality of these clays for ceramic production, especially in the forming process.

When we compare the chemical composition of the tiles produced at Taşkapı and of the kiln itself with the clay materials available locally, we see that their chemical signature does not correspond (Fig. 15). For the tiles and the kiln a Fe-rich illitic clay was used (seen in the total Fe- and K_2O-content). This is not the case with the clay material of Taşkapı, enriched in feldspars (seen in the CaO- and Na_2O-content and the low loss on ignition) and ophiolitic material (seen in the MgO-content), both present in the coarser fraction. It is necessary to stress that no real clay deposits are present in the valley of Taşkapı. Analyses were done on the fraction of clay material smaller than 250 µm, which still includes bedrock. The analyses indicate that neither the tiles produced at Taşkapı, nor the kiln structure were made from local clay material and suggest moreover that these clays are not suitable raw material for ceramic production of any kind. More research is therefore needed to locate the origin of the clay raw materials of this production unit. Water and fuel, the other two raw materials essential for ceramic production, would have been available in the area around the kiln.

As part of this project, the chemical composition of 13 sherds produced at Bağsaray was analysed and compared to Sagalassos red slip ware (Fig. 16). A couple of tableware sherds from Bağsaray were found in the ashy deposit in the combustion chambers. The clay used for the tableware of Sagalassos can be characterised as rich in chlorite and chlorite/smectite mixed layers with small amounts of illite and kaolinite (Ottenburgs et al. 1993). The comparison indicated that the clays are similar although the Bağsaray material contains less chlorite (less MgO) and is richer in calciumoxides.

Finally, samples of the ashy layer found on the floor of the combustion chamber were also examined and unexpectedly revealed evidence for a second artisanal process here. The ash deposit contained small fragments of tiles and kiln spacers, very small pieces of charcoal, small particles of limestone and sandstone, some of the latter in a partly molten condition, quicklime, slaked lime and fine grained calcite.

The fragments of limestone are small, angular, broken bits of a greyish colour, clearly affected by fire. Petrographical analysis indicated that this type of allochthonous limestone derives from the Lycian nappes of the western Taurus mountain chain (Paulissen et al. 1993: 230), also present around the valley of Taşkapı. Burning limestone at around 800° C produces CaO or quicklime, identified in the ashy deposit of the kiln (Fig. 17). With the addition of water the quicklime reacts to form Portlandite ($Ca(OH)_2$) or slaked lime. This chemical reaction was experimentally attested with a fraction of the ashy layer. Slaked lime was also detected on the XRD-diagram of the ashy deposit itself (Fig. 18). Portlandite reacts with atmospheric CO_2, to form $CaCO_3$, abundantly present in the ashy deposit (Fig. 18) (Adam 1994: 65-66; Viaene et al. 1997). In this case, the formation of the slaked lime and calcite most probably happened accidentally after the production unit was abandoned.

The presence of small fragments of tiles and kiln spacers in the ashy layer are clearly related to the local production of building materials. The charcoal, on the other hand, is a result of the firing process. During excavation, it was observed that more charcoal was concentrated in the upper part of the ashy deposit. This may be explained by the fact that quicklime oxidizes and thus causes charcoal to disintegrate, leaving only the upper horizon of the fuel more or less intact. Also, repeated firing of the kiln will cause the charcoal to oxidize and disintegrate further with every new firing. The bits of sandstone may have belonged to the kiln structure and were detached after exposure to high temperatures. XRD-analyses indicated that some fragments of sandstone were partly molten, showing lower intensities and a larger glass peak compared to non-molten fragments. Mineralogically, the sandstone consists mostly of quartz, albite and anorthite.

The larger part of the ashy deposit consisted, however, of limestone, quicklime, slaked lime and calcite fragments, which clearly provides evidence of lime burning. It appears that the kiln of Taşkapı was used simultaneously for the production of tiles and bricks and quicklime, which, after slaking, was mixed with an aggregate to produce lime mortar. The even mixture of tile and kiln spacer fragments and bits of limestone, quicklime, slaked lime and calcite, fallen through the vent holes into the combustion chambers, throughout the ashy deposit indicates that tiles and bricks were fired at the same time as lime was burned. Alternative firing of these products would have resulted in some kind of layering in the ashy deposit, which was not observed. In his overview of modern parallels, Adam (1994: 68) notes the practice of firing bricks and lime simultaneously in Tunisia (Kairouan, Nabeul). The stones are said to be stacked on an internal shelf, avoiding direct contact with the fire, and covered with bricks. Adam considered this combined effort to be a logical one, but knew of no example in documentary sources or in the archaeological record to illustrate the practice in antiquity. The type of fuel used at Taşkapı has not been identified yet. Adam (1994: 62-63, 68-69) mentions a variety of possibilities: pine-cones, olive kernels, cherry or plum stones, almond shells, various nuts, small bits of wood or brushwood and dried grass. The fuel had to provide an intense heat with a lot of flame. During firing, (partly) combusted fuel would be raked out from the combustion chambers and sieved to separate the charcoal, which could be further recycled, from the bits of stone that had fallen into the fire. In every observed case the firing was continued from a couple of days to a week.

5. CONCLUSION

Ceramic production was one of the traditional crafts in antiquity. Products of fired clay served a plethora of functions in nearly every aspect of daily life. Moreover, when we take into account the simple nature and the availability of the raw materials and the traditional level of technology involved, we can envisage that pottery production on a modest local or regional scale would fulfil most needs of local communities. As with everything in ancient times, what could be made locally was made locally. So it is deeply regrettable that this local dimension of pottery production remains nearly completely unknown to us, in the Roman East in general and especially in Asia Minor. If classical archaeology pays attention to the potter's craft, the more representative features such as sigillata and amphora are the usual favoured fields of study. Against this background, the interdisciplinary research conducted at Taşkapı aims to illustrate another dimension. This small-scale, short term and low budget project provided an insight into a nearly undocumented, but perhaps normal practice in antiquity. The local community at Taşkapı combined their efforts, practical experience and detailed knowledge of their region to set up a production unit where both tiles and bricks and lime were burned simultaneously, thus providing them with two very essential building materials at the same time. We consider this as an early Byzantine example from one particular region which, no doubt, forms part of a much wider and more ancient tradition.

Further archaeological research on the remains of the settlement and necropolis mentioned above would allow us to understand the functioning of this tile kiln within the local rural community. It will also enable us to study the importance of this rural economic system within the network of rural communities in the territory of ancient Sagalassos, and to evaluate the relation between these rural and urban ecologies.

In order to conserve this tile kiln, all the parties involved decided to backfill the remains by dumping river sand on a plastic gauze, and reconstructing the slope and road in its original state. A rubble wall was made at the highest point of the slope to avoid erosion.

6. ACKNOWLEDGEMENTS

This research is supported by the Belgian Programme on Interuniversity Poles of Attraction (IUAP 4/12) initiated by the Belgian State, Prime Minister's Office, Science Policy Programming. The text also presents the results of the concerted Action of the Flemish Government (GOA 97/2) and the Fund fur Scientific Research-Flanders (Belgium) (FWO) (G.2145.94). Scientific responsibility is assumed by its authors. Jeroen Poblome is Postdoctoral Fellow of the Fund for Scientific Research-Flanders (Belgium) (FWO).

7. REFERENCES

J. P. Adam (1994) *Roman Building Materials and Techniques*, London.

R. Degeest, R. Ottenburgs, W. Viaene, H. Kucha, D. Laduron, A. Bocquet and M. Waelkens (1997) Characterization of the common wares manufactured in Roman Sagalassos. An overview, in: M. Waelkens and J. Poblome (eds) *Sagalassos IV. Report on the Survey and Excavation Campaigns of 1994 and 1995 (Acta Archaeologica Lovaniensia Monographiae* 9) Leuven University Press: 519-531.

P. Degrijse, R. Degeest, J. Poblome, W. Viaene (†), R. Ottenburghs, H. Kucha and M. Waelkens (2000) Mineralogy and goechemistry of Roman common waves produced at Sagalas-

sos and their possible clay sources, in: M. Waelkens and L. Loots (eds) *Sagalassos V. Report on the Survey and Excavation Campaigns of 1996 and 1997 (Acta Archaelogica Lovaniensia Monographiae 10)* Leuven University Press. 709-720.

R. Ottenburgs, C. Jorissen and W. Viaene (1993) Study of the clays, in: M. Waelkens (ed.) *Sagalassos I. First General Report on the Survey (1986-1989) and Excavations (1990-1991) (Acta Archaeologica Lovaniensia Monographiae 5)* Leuven University Press: 163-169.

E. Paulissen, J. Poesen, G. Govers and J. De Ploey (1993) The physical environment at Sagalassos (Western Taurus, Turkey). A reconnaissance survey, in: M. Waelkens and J. Poblome (eds) *Sagalassos II. Report on the Third Excavation Campaign of 1992 (Acta Archaeologica Lovaniensia Monographiae 6)* Leuven University Press: 229-247.

J. Poblome (1999) *Sagalassos Red Slip Ware. Typology and Chronology* (*Studies in Eastern Mediterranean Archaeology* 2) Brepols publishers.

W. Viaene, M. Waelkens, R. Ottenburgs and K. Callebaut (1997) An archaeometric study of mortars used at Sagalassos, in: M. Waelkens and J. Poblome (eds) *Sagalassos IV. Report on the Survey and Excavation Campaigns of 1994 and 1995 (Acta Archaeologica Lovaniensia Monographiae 9)* Leuven University Press: 405-422.

M. Waelkens (1995) The 1993 survey in the district south and east of Sagalassos, in: M. Waelkens and J. Poblome (eds) *Sagalassos III. Report on the Fourth Excavation Campaign of 1993 (Acta Archaologica Lovaniensia Monographiae 7)* Leuven University Press: 11-22.

M. Waelkens, E. Paulissen, H. Vanhaverbeke, I. Öztürk, B. De Cupere, H.A. Ekinci, P.M. Vermeersch, J. Poblome and R. Degeest (1997) The 1994 and 1995 Surveys on the Territory of Sagalassos, in: M. Waelkens and J. Poblome (eds) *Sagalassos IV. Report on the Survey and Excavation Campaigns of 1994 and 1995 (Acta Archaeologica Lovaniensia Monographiae 9)* Leuven University Press: 11-102.

A CATALOGUE OF THE TILE STAMPS FOUND AT SAGALASSOS

Lieven LOOTS[1], Marc WAELKENS[1], Willy CLARYSSE[2], Jeroen POBLOME[1] and Gerhild HÜBNER[3]

1 - Department of Archaeology, KULeuven, Blijde Inkomststraat 21, B-3000 Leuven, Belgium
2 - Department of Ancient History, KULeuven, Blijde Inkomststraat 21, B-3000 Leuven, Belgium
3 - Titurelstraße 5, D 81925 München, Germany

INTRODUCTION

Although the prevalent building material at Sagalassos has always been the local limestone, fired brick made from the locally abundant ophiolitic clays (Degeest et al.1997: 525) became, under Roman influence, an important construction material from the second century AD onwards. On the other hand, the use of terracotta tiles was not due to Roman influence. Such tiles were already developed in the Greek world towards the end of the Geometric period (Martin 1965: 65 78) and were widely used at Sagalassos in pre-Roman times. The excavations at Sagalassos have revealed, so far, 50 stamped tiles (to these have been added 20 more stamps; see appendix). Catalogues of Roman brick and tile stamps found in Asia Minor are rare, which does not help a detailed study of this category of finds. A fairly extensive body of Hellenistic stamps from Pergamon has been published in the German excavation reports (Boehringer and Klauss 1937; Ziegenaus and DeLuca 1975; Pinkwart and Stammitz 1984). A small selection of stamps from Priene has also been published (von Gaertringen 1906: 177-179). There have also been papers written on early Byzantine stamps (e.g. Mango 1950). However, the Hellenistic stamps especially, which often bear royal names, differ so much from the tile stamps found at Sagalassos, that a valid comparison cannot be made. Early Byzantine stamps frequently carry Christian symbols or the names of Byzantine emperors. As such, they must also be distinguished from the stamps found at Sagalassos.

2. DISCUSSION

2.1. Typology of the carriers

The carriers on which the stamps have been found are, as far as they can be identified with certainty, exclusively roof tiles (27 *tegulae*, 11 *imbrices*, 12 fragments of an uncertain type). Of the ΕΛΑΙΟΥ stamp (see below 2.3) 11 examples are found on Corinthian *tegulae*, 11 on Laconian *imbrices*, while the tile type of 7 is not clear. The occurrence of the same stamp on both curved and flat tiles confirms that the old canonical tile system of Asia Minor (Åkerström 1966: fig. 64 n° 3) was still in use in Roman times. All ΕΥΡΙΚ stamps occur on Corinthian *tegulae*. The other stamps are found either on Corinthian *tegulae*, or on fragments of which the type of tile is not clear. Thus, at Sagalassos only roof tiles seem to have been stamped. It is generally acknowledged that in Greek architecture stamps mainly occur on tiles and only to a lesser extent on bricks (e.g. Martin 1965: 84). This is not surprising since Greek architects hardly made use of fired brick before the introduction of Roman building techniques (Martin 1965: 63). In Roman architecture stamped brick occurred more frequently (Adam 1984: 67), but even here, for instance in Roman Britain, stamping was more common on tiles, particularly *tegulae*, whereas larger bricks were more likely to be stamped than small *bessales* (Brodribb 1987: 123-125). So far, no stamped bricks have been found at Sagalassos.

2.2. Function of the stamps

The practice of stamping a tile or a brick could serve various purposes. The chief reason was certainly to advertise an identity (Brodribb 1987: 117). Thus, in the Greek world stamped tiles could identify the authority (for instance the *dèmos*, a king, or a private donor) financing the building, the building proper or the divinity to which it was consecrated, the city or its eponymous magistrates, and also the supplier, the contractor or the architect (Martin 1965: 84-86).

In Roman architecture tile or brick stamps originally only identified the supplier. However, from the second century

AD onwards, they also show a greater variety and can identify the owner of the clay beds, the manufacturer (for instance a military unit), the trader, the storage facility and the building itself. Others include consular dates and even acclamations (Bloch 1947; Adam 1984: 67).

The great variety of stamp types suggests that they could have served different purposes. Those identifying a building may have acted as an address label to set aside a particular section of a production for a specific building project. Stamps carrying the names of a building authority (*polis*, *dèmos*, king, private donor), or eponymous magistrate may also have been aimed at self-advertisement. On the other hand, both types of stamp also marked the tiles or bricks which carried them as official, religious or military property and may have been intended to diminish the risk of theft during storage (Brodribb 1987: 117). On many other tile or brick constructions, the names of the manufacturer or the supplier, the building contractor or the architect may have identified their owners for advertisement purposes (Brodribb 1987: 117).

Some scholars, however, propose more practical or even 'legal' explanations. Just as stone-carvers or quarrymen sometimes marked their ashlar blocks for payment, stamps would permit the reckoning of the number of bricks and tiles produced by a certain brickyard so that they could be checked off against the original contract between the builders and the managers of the brickyards (Aubert 1994: 232-233 with note 105). This may imply that all bricks and tiles had to be stamped. Yet, the fragmentary state of most buildings and the fact that surviving tiles could be recycled easily, makes it in most cases extremely difficult, if not impossible, to assess whether stamps were impressed on every tile or only on a selected few. The material from Roman Britain seems to suggest a frequent, although not a general stamping of tiles, whereas the practice was much less common on bricks, particularly those of smaller dimensions (Brodribb 1987: 117). McWhirr and Viner (1978: 363), while discussing bricks and tiles in Roman Britain, propose an interpretation which takes into account the fact that not all tiles were stamped, but which may not sufficiently explain their very frequent occurrence in some buildings (Brodribb 1987: 123-124). In their view, each stamped brick or tile may have indicated a certain number of objects produced and thus have been part of a process of storage or building up stocks. Finally, Aubert (1994: 234) suggested a possible legal purpose, according to which the stamps would have allowed customers to identify the producers of bricks and tiles of inferior quality and thus to start a civil law suit against them.

At Sagalassos it is certain that only some tiles and apparently none of the bricks were stamped. The tile stamps may have helped to identify the manufacturer or the donor of a batch of tiles, at least once a certain number of them were marked. Theoretically, this may still have enabled the brickmakers to receive the correct payment from their customers. For larger building projects, such as the Roman baths, the tiles may have had to be ordered from different manufacturers to meet the deadlines set by the builders. The fact that most tile stamps from Sagalassos were found in the baths (see catalogue), may at first sight seem to confirm this hypothesis. However, one should not forget that the building has been used and maintained for nearly five centuries. Many of the stamps therefore may not have been contemporary and many old tiles may have been re-used during later repairs or alterations (Brodribb 1987:124). If tiles from different manufacturers were mixed during a single building phase, it may have become quite difficult to differentiate them sufficiently with the help of the few stamped ones in order to calculate a correct payment. So, at least at Sagalassos, it seems safer to assume that the main purpose of the stamps was to identify the supplier or the building authority, as a commercial or political form of advertisement. The various stamps that have been found thus far fall nicely into these two categories. It is still possible that some of the material was dumped inside the ruins of the baths at a later date, that is after the earthquake which levelled the city around the middle of the seventh century AD. Yet, the lack of pot sherds in the Roman Bath deposits seems to imply that the ruins never became an important dumping area. Therefore, most of the tile fragments clearly belonged to the building itself.

2.3. The stamps

Eleven different groups of tile stamps can be identified. A survey of published tile stamps from major sites in Asia Minor in the *Supplementum Epigraphicum Graecum* and the *Bulletin Épigraphique* did not produce any exact parallels, suggesting that the stamps at Sagalassos were of local production. This is hardly surprising in a city which was a significant producer of fine table wares and of coarse pottery. Moreover, to import such quantities of tiles and bricks as were used in the local building industry over longer distances would have been excluded both for economic and practical reasons. Theoretically this does not mean that all bricks and tiles were produced in or near the city itself. Brick and tile kilns may have caused more ecological inconveniences than did pottery kilns (Adam 1984: 63-66). So some production sites may have been located in the open countryside, further away from the settlement, as is still the case with the modern tile and brick factories in the region. The urban periphery of the Roman empire was the site of many activities serving the needs of the cities. Tile and brick kilns, sometimes also intended for private use, could be found on many rural estates (Purcell 1996: 156, 160). The surveys on the territory of Sagalassos have made it clear that ceramic production in the area was not confined to the city's potters' quarter alone, but that it was a regional activity (Waelkens *et al.* 1997). A few years ago, an early Byzantine tile kiln was excavated near Taşkapı, a few kilometers to the west of the ancient city (Poblome *et al.* 2000). Recently, another tile kiln was discovered in the valley of Köyünü, a few kilometers to the south of Ağlasun. Yet, in the case of Sagalassos these kilns may have served primarily rural needs.

The excavated dumps in the potter's quarter of Sagalassos itself all contained a small amount of tile fragments. These dumps should be considered above all as depots from which misfired pottery was ground up to be re-used as a filler material. But there is at least one concentration of surface material in the potter's quarter which is mainly composed of tile fragments, suggesting a nearby production. Moreover, all the architectural ceramics analysed so far are composed of clays from this quarter.

Some stamps can be identified as representing a personal name, most likely in the genitive case with an understood Greek version of words such as *opus*, *officina* or *manu* (Brodribb 1987: 117). To this category belongs stamp cat. 48 which seems to include the name *Makedonikos* (Μακεδονικοῦ). Both Fraser and Matthews (1987, 1997) and Solin (1982) mention the occurrence of this name during the first and second centuries AD in Thasos, on Sicily, and in Rome. Similar names (Μακεδόνιος) which occur in the inscriptions of the city could also be related to the settlement of Macedonian veterans by the Seleucids during the Hellenistic period (Kosmetatou and Waelkens 1997; Vandorpe 2000). Stamp cat. 49 (ΔΗΜΕ?) may include an abbreviation of the common name Δημεας (Fraser and Matthews 1987: 124, 1997: 122; Osborne *et al.* 1994: 103-104). The stamps reading ΚΑΛΕΞΠΡ (cat. 35, 36, 37, 38) can be identified as the name Κ(λαύδιος) Ἀλέξ(ανδρος) πρ(εσβύτερος). The ligature of Π and Ρ undoubtedly refers to πρεσβύτερος, meaning 'the older' (Guarducci 1967: 404; Larfeld 1902: 534). Although the normal abbreviation of Klaudios would be Κλ, the limited space on a tile stamp may explain why only the kappa is present here. The same name does not appear in the inscriptions at Sagalassos, but Tiberii Claudii occur frequently (Devijver 1996), so Claudius Alexandros may have been a member or a freedman of one of these families. The name would certainly fit a factory owner. Makedonikos and Demeas could also represent makers and/or factory owners, but it is also possible that they were workmen (or even slaves) of an unknown owner. In the case of Makedonikos the name could refer to his provenance. The reading of stamps cat. 42 and 43 (Ρ.ΠΝ, both in retrograde) remains uncertain.

One stamp may suggest the existence of municipal tile and brick works at Sagalassos or identify official goods or a public building. Stamp cat. 47 reading ΠΟΛ may be short for πολέως, thus referring to the city (Martin 1965: 84; Orlandos 1966: 94; von Gaertringen 1906: 179 nr. 26. Municipal brickworks controlled and run by city authorities and mainly producing for municipal building projects are known elsewhere. Sometimes their products could also be sold privately (Peacock 1979: 8). Because of the context in which it was found (see below 2.4), this stamp could not be attributed to a specific building.

Stamp cat. 1 to 29 is difficult to understand. The stamp can be read in retrograde as ΕΛΑΙΟΥ in which Λ and Α are written in ligature. However, the shape of the ligature of Λ and Α has no direct parallels elsewhere and could, when turned upside down, also be thought of as a ligature of Χ and Α. Thus, turned upside down the ΕΛΑΙΟΥ stamp could also be read as ΕΧΑΙΟΥ, unless it is a mis-spelling for ΑΧΑΙΟΥ (genetive of Ἀχαιός) and refers to the provenance of the man, as in the case of Makedonikos. One should not forget either that the stamps were mostly written by workmen, who did not care or know about orthography. However, the reading ΕΧΑΙΟΥ is totally meaningless. It is not clear how the ΕΛΑΙΟΥ stamp may be explained. Because no less than 27 of the 29 stamps were found during the excavations of the Roman bath building (see below 2.4), where oil would have been needed in large quantities, there could be a connection with ἔλαιον ('oil') in the genitive. In that case, the stamp may have been intended to identify the building for which the tiles were made. However, this explanation seems rather far fetched. A second, better explanation may be that the stamp is short for ἐλαιού(ργιον) ('oil factory'). In that case, it may refer to a toponym, i.e. the name of an estate. We now know that there was in Roman antiquity a significant olive cultivation on the territory of Sagalassos (Waelkens *et al.* 1997).

In any case the stamps suggest at least three different groups of names: the city itself, factory owners with Roman citizenship, and owners, workmen or even slaves with Greek names.

The interpretation of stamps cat. 30 to 34 (ΕΥΡΙΚ) of which two different dies exist, of stamps cat. 39 to 41 (ΑΡΚΟΜΕΚΑ[...]) and of stamp cat. 50 (ΑΡΚΙ[...]) remain enigmatic. The knobs after the Ο and after the combined Μ and Ε of stamps cat. 39 to 41, and those after the Ρ and Κ of cat. 50 are, contrary to the knob of stamps cat. 42 and 43 (Ρ.ΠΝ), not part of the inscription, but the result of the technique used to attach the stamp to its handle. Wooden or terracotta taps piercing the die proper, were most probably inserted in handles of the same material. When these taps penetrated sufficiently deep in the die, the slight recesses in the surface of the die would result in this kind of knobs. The material of the original dies used at Sagalassos is uncertain.

Since the impressions are not really sharp or clean-cut, they were probably not metal so the most likely materials are wood or terracotta. However, impressions made by wooden dies often show clear signs of the grain (Brodribb 1987: 119). The absence of this, combined with the fact that many characters of the impressions are rather irregular, suggests that the Sagalassos dies were of clay.

Most, that is, 45 of the 50 stamps, are rectangular. Tile stamps of the Roman period could be rectangular, crescent-shaped or round (Adam: 1984: 67 fig. 146; Brodribb 1987: 116 fig. 55). At Sagalassos, only the shape of the *planta pedis* stamp (cat. 44, 45, 46) and the oval P.ΠN (cat. 42, 43) differ significantly from the other rectangular types. It is not clear if this is due to chronological or to other factors. The appearance of the *planta pedis* stamp on the tiles of Sagalassos is at least remarkable. Although this kind of stamp occurs on bricks and tiles from military contexts in the western empire (e.g. Neumann 1973), to our knowledge, they had not so far been identified on tiles in the eastern Mediterranean. *Planta pedis* stamps are fairly common on western, but quite rare on eastern sigillata. On eastern pottery they certainly do not date before the second quarter of the first century AD (Hayes 1997: 57). The *planta pedis* stamps found at Sagalassos carry the acclamation εὐτύχει which is fairly common for this kind of stamp (for a discussion see Zabehlicky-Scheffenegger 1995: 257). Still, it remains a mystery how it found its way onto the three tiles at Sagalassos. It may indicate that at Sagalassos there was sometimes a direct link between stamping pottery and stamping tiles, at least during the first centuries AD. However, none of the locally produced red slip ware was stamped and no (stamped) imported sigillata have been identified yet at Sagalassos.

2.4. Chronology of the stamps

The practice of stamping tiles at Sagalassos seems to have been rather exceptional. Unfortunately, the stratigraphical deposits in which stamped tiles have been found are not well defined (see below), and many of them may already have been recycled in antiquity. As a result, the origin, the chronological evolution and the abandoning of this practice cannot yet be determined. At present one can only shed some light on this tradition by placing it in the general context of the ceramic production in the Roman empire. As we have said, the practice of stamping tiles in the Greek East can be traced back from Classical to early Byzantine times. Rectangular stamps are common throughout this period, and this from the very beginning. During the Imperial period, particularly in the West, crescent-shaped or circular stamps also became popular, but during the later empire rectangular stamps reappeared again in large numbers (Adam 1984: 67). This means that the shape of our stamps can hardly be invoked as a feature with chronological value.

In the East, potters also stamped another type of product in a comparable and more or less systematic way – their tablewares or so-called 'eastern sigillata'. Apparently, only the potters of eastern sigillata A (ESA), eastern sigillata B (ESB) and, to a certain extent, eastern sigillata C (ESC) adopted the practice and applied it in a more or less regular way. For the other types of eastern sigillata, stamping is less common or even exceptional. This is also the case at Sagalassos, where the potters do not seem to have stamped their tableware (Sagalassos red slip ware or SRSW) in the same way. This may, however, be related to the fact that at Sagalassos the stratigraphical deposits which can be dated to the period when stamping table wares was fashionable remain rather restricted.

Pergamene sigillata seem to have been stamped from the third quarter of the first century BC. The appearance of Italian sigillata in the East may have invoked a more widespread use of the practice of stamping. Stamps occur shortly afterwards on ESA and ESB. Stamping of ESC continues but does not seem to have been as regular as it was for both other types of eastern sigillata. The potters of ESB were the first to abandon stamping their wares, towards the end of the third quarter of the first century AD. Within fifty years or so, that is, during the first half of the second century AD, the other types of eastern sigillata seem to have followed. The practice of stamping eastern table wares should be seen as a result of the far-reaching influence which Italian sigillata had on tableware throughout the Roman empire (Poblome *et al.* in press).

Thus, potters' stamps on eastern sigillata seem to have been mainly a first and early second century AD phenomenon. The practice originated on late Hellenistic Pergamene sigillata, but this tableware seems to have been traded only on a regional scale during this period. The morphology of some stamps, specifically the use of the *planta pedis* stamp, suggests that the tile-makers of Sagalassos followed the tradition of pottery stamping. However, the locally produced tableware seems not to have been stamped at all. Unfortunately, we have no indisputable chronological criteria to date the tile stamps of Sagalassos. If the practice of stamping tiles was influenced by that in pottery production, a first or second century AD date could be suggested for most of our stamps. In that case, the absence of stamps on the locally produced tableware would be even more striking. Indeed, all stamped tiles come from later destruction levels, most of them caused by an earthquake around the middle of the seventh century AD. It cannot be excluded and it is even likely that some of these tiles were re-used, and originated from older constructions. In the case of the Roman baths, where most of the stamped tiles were found (and possibly even those found elsewhere on the lower agora), such a hypothesis is even plausible because of the long period of use of this building and its many alterations. The present destruction levels, however, contain material from a final reconstruction dated to the sixth century AD, during which the excavated rooms, including their roofs, were largely rebuilt (Waelkens *et al.* 2000). So it seems rather unlikely that so many first or second century AD tiles would have survived so long, while contemporary stamped pottery has so far not turned up. The completion of the original construction of the baths can probably be dated to the second half of the second century AD, almost a generation after the disappearance of stamped terra sigillata, while most of the marble veneering, especially the pilaster capitals, seem to belong to the late third or fourth century AD suggesting an important remodelling of the interior layout during that period. So, the practice of stamping tiles at Sagalassos, except for the *planta pedis* stamps, should rather be linked to that of tile production elsewhere in Asia Minor, either in contemporary cities or in legionary camps, the material of which remains largely unpublished. Of the ΕΛΑΙΟΥ stamp, 32 out of 34 examples (including those found during 1999) can be connected with the Roman baths. The most plausible explanation is that the stamp belongs to the production of a batch of tiles for the reconstruction of the building during the early sixth century AD, or that it represents recycled material from a (slightly) older period. It seems unlikely that much older tiles would have survived in such large numbers as are implied by the amount of surviving material with the ΕΛΑΙΟΥ stamp. The letter types of its characters, as well as those of the other stamps from Sagalassos, are difficult to date. But, a date in the late Roman period, that is, from the early fourth until the sixth century AD, would correspond rather well with the lack of uniformity discernible in these stamps, most of which come from contexts which belong exactly to that period. The same features are also characteristic of contemporary inscriptions found elsewhere in Asia Minor (Roueché 1989: XXII).

Except for two examples, all of the ΕΛΑΙΟΥ stamps belong to the Roman baths. The first exception (cat. 27) was found in the excavations of the sixth century AD portico along the western edge of the lower agora, the second (cat. 15) in the excavations of the bouleuterion which during the fifth century AD was transformed into a church and remained in use until the middle of the seventh century AD (Waelkens *et al.* 2000). Because it was not found at any great distance, the first example may also belong to the Roman baths. Thus, most of the surviving ΕΛΑΙΟΥ stamped tiles seem to have been connected with the reconstruction of the bath building.

None of the other stamps found at Sagalassos seem to be linked to one specific building, although the two stamps reading Ρ.ΠΝ were also found in the Roman bath building. Since most of the stamps from Sagalassos were found in late Roman to early Byzantine destruction layers or fills, some even being found during cleaning activities before or after the excavations, further research is needed to define the local practice of tile stamping in more detail and to assess its implications for the building history of those monuments with which it can be firmly associated.

3. CATALOGUE

This catalogue contains all the stamps found since the start of the excavations in 1990, including the 1998 campaign. It describes the shape of the stamp and its characters, inventory numbers, the site from which they originate, the type of the carriers (see Martin 1965: 65-69), the preserved text and the dimensions of the stamp. This list is illustrated by drawings (cat. 44) or photographs of the stamps themselves. Ten different stamps have been identified so far. Three of these stamp groups can be subdivided by details, indicating that different dies were used during a certain period. Height and width are in centimeters.

1. Stamps bearing the inscription ΕΛΑΙΟΥ
This is the largest group, comprising 29 stamps. Eight different dies can be identified.

1.a. Rectangular field, stamp in retrograde, angular raised capitals, lambda and alpha in ligature, bottom of lambda and alpha, and that of omicron flat

1 SA95 RB 158
   Roman bath building
   Type of tile not clear
   ΕΛΑΙΟΥ
   h.: 3.4; pres. w.: 8.2

2 SA95 RB 137
   Roman bath building
   Type of tile not clear
   ΕΛΑ[ΙΟΥ]
   h.: 3.1; pres. w.: 6.3

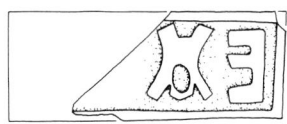

3 SA96 RB 126
   Roman bath building
   Laconian *imbrex*
   [Ε]ΛΑΙΟΥ
   pres. h.: 2.6; pres. w.: 5.3

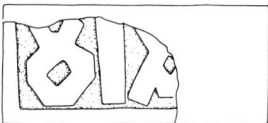

4 SA96 RB 254
Roman bath building
Corinthian *tegula*
ΕΛΑΙΟΥ
h.: 3.4; pres. w.: 7.8

5 SA96 RB 38
Roman bath building
Laconian *imbrex*
[Ε]ΛΑΙΟΥ
h.: 3.2 cm; pres. w.: 4.7

6 SA96 RB 43
Roman bath building
Laconian *tegula*
[Ε]ΛΑΙΟΥ
h.: 3.6 cm; pres. w.: 6.5

7 SA98 RB1-74
Roman bath building
Type of tile not clear
ΕΛΑΙΟΥ
h.: 3.7; w.: 8.8
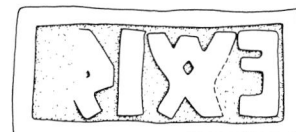

1.b. Rectangular field, stamp in retrograde, angular raised capitals, lambda and alpha in ligature, bottom of combined lambda and alpha, and that of omicron angular

8 SA95 RB 198
Roman bath building
Laconian *tegula*
ΕΛΑΙ[ΟΥ]
h.: 3.8; pres. w.: 6.2
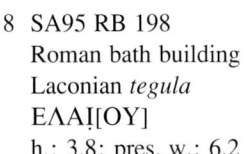

9 SA96 RB 125
Roman bath building
Type of tile not clear
ΕΛΑΙΟΥ
h.: 3; w.: 8.9
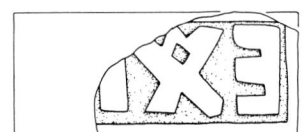

10 SA96 RB 117
Roman bath building
Corinthian *tegula*
ΕΛΑΙ[ΟΥ]
h.: 3.4; pres. w.: 4.8
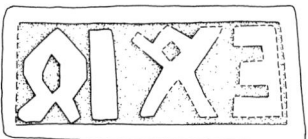

11 SA96 RB 187
Roman bath building
Corinthian *tegula*
ΕΛΑ[ΙΟΥ]
pres. h.: 3; pres. w.: 3.9
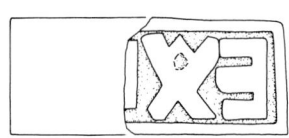

12 SA96 RB 88
Roman bath building
Corinthian *tegula*
[ΕΛΑΙ]ΟΥ
pres. h.: 2.9; pres. w.: 3.1
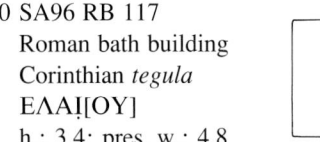

1.c. Rectangular field, stamp in retrograde, angular raised capitals, lambda and alpha in ligature, bottom of combined lambda and alpha flat, and that of omicron angular, right lower side of iota curved

13 SA98 RB1-43
Roman bath building
Laconian *imbrex*
ΕΛΑΙΟΥ
h.: 4; w.: 8.8

14 SA98 RB1-26
Roman bath building
Corinthian *tegula*
ΕΛΑΙΟΥ
h.: 3.6; pres. w.: 7.6
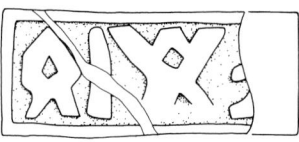

1.d. Rectangular field, stamp in retrograde, angular raised capitals, lambda and alpha in ligature, bottom of combined lambda and alpha angular, and that of omicron flat

15 SA98 B2-88
Bouleuterion
Type of tile not clear
[Ε]ΛΑΙΟΥ
h.: 3.6; pres. w.: 7.7
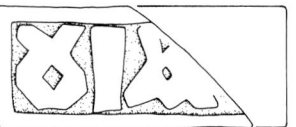

1.e. Rectangular field, stamp in retrograde, angular raised capitals, lambda and alfa in ligature, right lower side of iota curved, bottom of omikron flat

16 SA97 RB1-20
Roman bath building
Laconian *imbrex*
ΕΛΑΙΟΥ
h.: 3.6; w.: 8.4
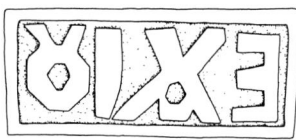

17 SA97 RB1-55
Roman bath building
Laconian *imbrex*
ΕΛΑΙΟΥ
h.: 3.5; pres. w.: 7.2

18 SA98 RB1-26
Roman bath building
Corinthian *tegula*
ΕΛΑΙ[ΟΥ]
h.: 4.2; pres. w.: 6.9
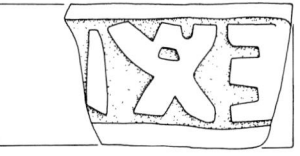

1.f. Rectangular field, stamp in retrograde, angular raised capitals, lambda and alpha in ligature, left lower side of iota curved, bottom of omicron flat

19 SA95 RB 95
Roman bath building
Type of tile not clear
[Ε]ΛΑΙΟΥ
h.: 3.2; pres. w.: 4
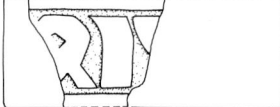

20 SA95 RB 170
Roman bath building
Type of tile not clear
ΕΛΑΙΟΥ
h.: 3.3; w.: 7.9
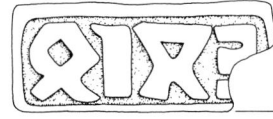

21 SA96 RB 53
Roman bath building
Laconian *imbrex*
[Ε]ΛΑΙΟΥ
h.: 3.3; pres. w.: 6.7

22 SA97 RB2-136
Roman bath building
Corinthian *tegula*
ΕΛΑΙΟΥ
h.: 3.4; pres. w.: 7.4

1.g. Rectangular field, stamp in retrograde, angular raised capitals, lambda and alpha in ligature, left lower side of iota curved, omicron curved

23 SA95 RB 76
Roman bath building
Corinthian *tegula*
[ΕΛΑ]ΙΟΥ
h.: 3.4; pres. w.: 4.5
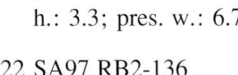

24 SA95 RB 129
Roman bath building
Laconian *imbrex*
[ΕΛΑ]ΙΟΥ
pres. h.: 2; pres. w.: 5.9

25 SA98 RB1-74
Roman bath building
Corinthian *tegula*
ΕΛΑΙΟΥ
h.: 3.7; w.: 8.7
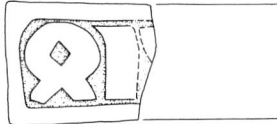

26 SA98 RB2-127
Roman bath building
Corinthian *tegula*
ΕΛΑΙΟΥ
h.: 3.8; pres. w.: 6.8
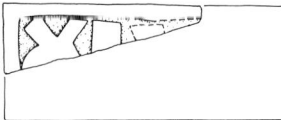

1.h. Rectangular field, angular incised capitals, lambda and alpha in ligature

27 SA95 AG 150
West portico of the lower agora
Laconian *imbrex*
ΕΛΑΙΟΥ
h.: 2.8; w.: 6.3
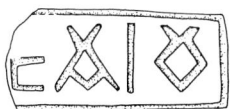

1.i. Fragmentary dies

28 SA96 RB 40
Roman bath building
Corinthian *tegula*
Rectangular field
  with raised capitals
Stamp in retrograde
ΕΛΑ[ΙΟΥ]
pres. h.: 3.1; pres. w.: 5.7

29 SA98 RB1-29
Roman bath building
Laconian *imbrex*
Rectangular field
  with raised capitals
Stamp in retrograde
ΕΛΑ[ΙΟΥ]
h.: 4.1; pres. w.: 5.6
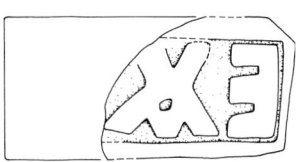

2. Stamps bearing the inscription ΕΥΡΙΚ
This group comprises five stamps. Two different dies can be identified. All stamps are rather undeep.

2.a. Rectangular field with raised capitals, stamp in retrograde

30 SA95 UA 336
Upper agora
Corinthian *tegula*
ΕΥΡΙΚ
h.: 4.1; pres. w.: 6.4

31 SA97 RB1-65
Roman bath building
Corinthian *tegula*
ΕΥΡΙΚ
h.: 4.3; w.: 6.6

32 SA97 B2-158
Bouleuterion
Corinthian *tegula*
ΕΥΡΙΚ
h.: 4.2; w.: 6.5
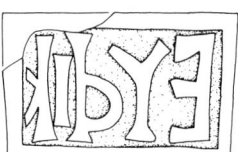

2.b. Rectangular field with raised capitals, stamp in retrograde, rho connected to top of field

33 SA96 RB 253
Roman bath building
Corinthian *tegula*
ΕΥΡΙΚ
h: 4.4; w.: 6.9

34 SA97 B2-5
Bouleuterion
Corinthian *tegula*
ΕΥΡΙΚ
h: 4.1; w: 6.8

3. Stamps bearing the inscription ΚΑΛΕΞΠΡ
This group comprises four stamps. Two different dies can be identified.
3.a. Kappa, alpha and lambda connected

35 SA96 RB 252 Rectangular field with raised capitals h.: 4.0
Roman bath building   ΚΑΛΕΞΠΡ   w.: 13.4
Corinthian *tegula*   E rounded, Π and Ρ in ligature

3.b. Kappa and alfa connected, lambda unconnected

36 SA95 RB 96   Rectangular field with raised capitals h.: 4.0
Roman bath building   ΚΑΛΕΞΠΡ   w.: 13.4
Corinthian *tegula*   E rounded, Π and Ρ in ligature

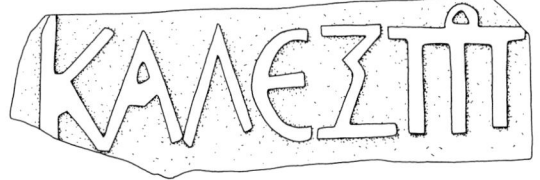

37 SA95 AG 223
Area of the Tiberian gateway
on the lower agora
Type of tile not clear
Rectangular field
   with raised capitals
E rounded
[Κ]ΑΛΕ[ΞΠΡ]
pres. h.: 4.3; pres. w.: 6.5

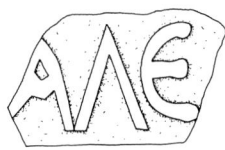

3.c. Fragmentary die

38 SA95 RB 157
Roman bath building
Type of tile not clear
Rectangular field
   with raised capitals
[ΚΑ]ΛΕΞΠΡ
E rounded, Π and Ρ in ligature
h.: 3.9; pres. w.: 8.5

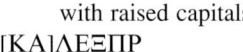

4. Stamps bearing the inscription ΑΡΚΟΜΕΚΑ[...]
This group comprises 3 stamps. Only one die can be identified. Small raised round knobs on the surface of the stamp indicate that the dies were most likely attached to a handle by means of wooden or terracotta taps.

39 SA97 S 28 (stray find) Rectangular field with raised capitals
Roman bath building   [...]ΚΟΜΕΚΑ[...]
Corinthian *tegula*   M and E in ligature
pres. h.: 2.5; pres. w.: 12.8

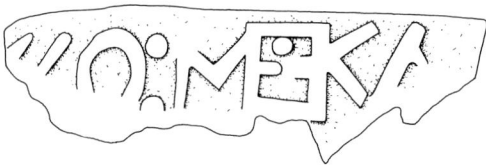

40 SA97 RB2-100
Roman bath building
Type of tile not clear
Rectangular field
   with raised capitals
[...]ΟΜΕΚ[...]
M and E in ligature
pres. h.: 2.8; pres. w.: 7.6

41 SA98 Y 8
Stray find
Corinthian *tegula*
Rectangular field
   with raised letters
ΑΡΚΟΜΕ[...]
A and Ρ in ligature,
 M and E in ligature
h.: 3.2; pres. w.: 10.6

5. Stamps bearing the inscription Ρ.ΠΝ
This group comprises 2 stamps. Only one die can be identified

42 SA95 RB 119
Roman bath building
Corinthian *tegula*
Oval field with raised capitals
Ρ.ΠΝ
Stamp in retrograde
h.: 3.6; w.: 6.4

43 SA97 RB1-59
Roman bath building
Corinthian *tegula*
Oval field with raised capitals
Ρ.ΠΝ
Stamp in retrograde
h.: 3.2; w.: 6.3

6. *Planta pedis* bearing the inscription ΕΥΤΥΧΕΙ
This group comprises 3 stamps. Only two of these have been drawn.

44 SA95 Y 11
Stray find
Type of tile not clear
planta pedis
ΕΥΤΥΧ[ΕΙ]
Stamp in retrograde
h.: 2.0 to 2.7; w.: 6.0

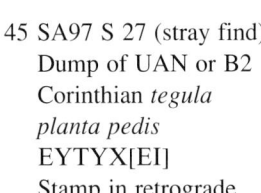

45 SA97 S 27 (stray find)
Dump of UAN or B2
Corinthian *tegula*
planta pedis
ΕΥΤΥΧ[ΕΙ]
Stamp in retrograde
h.: 2.4 to 3.2; w.: 7.0

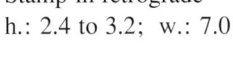

46 SA98 Y 5 (stray find)
Bouleuterion courtyard
Corinthian *tegula*
planta pedis
ΕΥΤΥΧ[ΕΙ]
Stamp in retrograde
h.: 2.3 to 3.2; w.: 6.6

7. Stamps bearing the inscription ΠΟΛ
This group comprises 1 stamp

47 SA97 RB1-43
Roman bath building
Corinthian *tegula*
Rectangular field
    with raised capitals
ΠΟΛ
h.: 2.6; w.: 4.6

8. Stamps bearing the inscription ΜΑΚΕΔΟΝΙΚΟΥ
This group comprises 1 stamp

48 SA95 AG 178
Area of the Tiberian gateway
    on the lower agora
Type of tile not clear
Rectangular field
with raised capitals
[Μ]ΑΚΕΔΟΝΙΚΟΥ
Δ upside down, N and I in ligature,
 K and O in ligature, Y upside down
h.: 2.5; pres. w.: 9.3

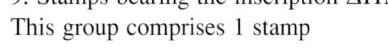

9. Stamps bearing the inscription ΔΗΜΕ (?)
This group comprises 1 stamp

49 SA96 H 33
NW Heroon
Corinthian *tegula*
Rectangular field
    with raised capitals
ΔΗΜΕ
H , M (?) and E in ligature
h.: 3.5; w.: 5.9

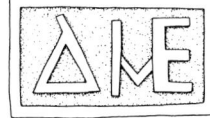

10. Stamps bearing the inscription ΑΡΚΙ[…]
This group comprises 1 stamp. Small raised round knobs on the surface of the stamp indicate that the die was most likely attached to its handle with wooden or terracotta taps.

50 SA98 RB2-197
Roman bath building
Type of tile not clear
Rectangular field
    with raised capitals
ΑΡΚΙ[…]
A and P connected
h.: 3.5; pres. w. 7.6

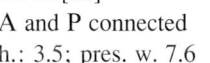

4. ACKNOWLEDGEMENTS

This research is supported by the Belgian Programme on Interuniversity Poles of Attraction (IUAP 4/12) initiated by the Belgian State, Prime Minister's Office, Science Policy Programming. The text also presents the results of the Concerted Action of the Flemish Government (GOA 97/2) and the Fund for Scientific Research-Flanders (Belgium) (FWO) (G.2145.94). Scientific responsibility is assumed by its authors. Lieven Loots is research assistant of the Fund for Scientific Research Flanders – Belgium (FWO). Jeroen Poblome is postdoctoral Fellow of the Fund for Scientific Research – Flanders (Belgium) (FWO). The authors wish to thank Mrs E. Mahy, Mr. P. Stuyven, T. Şen and S. Saral for their kind assistance in drawing, photographing and casting of the stamps.

5. APPENDIX: THE TILESTAMPS FOUND AT SAGALASSOS DURING 1999

5.1. Introduction

During the 1999 campaign at Sagalassos, 20 more tile stamps were unearthed. Most of them belong to the previously described categories, but a new type of stamp was also identified (cat. 70). Sixteen of the stamps were found in the Roman baths (RB1), one in the area to the east of the bouleuterion (B3) and one was a stray find. No more stamps were found in 1999 in the other sites where the previous ones had been found. Two stamps excavated in previous years were recorded. SA93 UA 60 (nr. 67) was found during the 1993 excavation of the upper agora and SA96 RB (nr. 69) was found during the 1996 excavations of the Roman bath building.

5.2. The stamps

Except for the previously unknown stamp cat. 70, the type of carrier, the reading and the find locations of the stamps found in 1999 do not differ from those that were known already. All the types of carriers that could be identified are either Corinthian *tegulae* or Laconian *imbrices* (7 Corinthian *tegulae*, 10 Laconian *imbrices*, 3 of which the identification is not clear). All ΕΛΑΙΟΥ stamps (cat. 51 to 65) were found in the Roman bath building. One new die could be identified (1.j., stamp cat. 65). Stamp cat. 68. reading ΑΡ[ΚΙ...] found in 1999 and stamp cat. 69 reading ΑṚΚ[...] found in 1996 come from the Roman bath building, as did the identical stamp cat. 50 found in 1998. Stamps cat. 66 and 67 (ΕΥṚΙΚ) were unearthed on the upper agora and immediately to the east of the bouleuterion respectively. Two (nrs 32 and 34) of 5 similar stamps that were excavated earlier were found in the bouleuterion, while cat. 30 was excavated on the upper agora, east of the bouleuterion. Two other stamps reading ΕΥΡΙΚ were found at the Roman baths (cat. 31 and 33).

No parallel has been found at Sagalassos for the form of the new stamp (cat. 70) which consists of two lines. The reading of the top line (ΑΡΚΟΜΕ) corresponds partially with the reading of the previously found stamps cat. 39, 40 and 41. Stamp cat. 50 and stamps cat. 68 and 69 unearthed in 1999 (ΑΡΚΙ[]) may also possibly even be considered a variant of this reading. The meaning of the first line remains enigmatic, while the meaning of the second line (ΑΤΜΑ) is not certain

5.3. Catalogue

1. ΕΛΑΙΟΥ

1.a. Rectangular field, stamp in retrograde, angular raised capitals, lambda and alpha in ligature, bottom of lambda and alpha, and that of omicron flat

51 SA99 RB1-060
Roman bath building
Corinthian *tegula*
ΕΛΑΙΟΥ
h.: 3.6; w.: 8.6

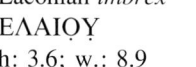

1.c. Rectangular field, stamp in retrograde, angular raised capitals, lambda and alpha in ligature, bottom of combined lambda and alpha flat, and that of omicron angular, right lower side of iota curved

52 SA99 RB1-121
Roman bath building
Corinthian *tegula*
ΕΛΑΙΟΥ
h.: 3.6; pres. w.: 9.4

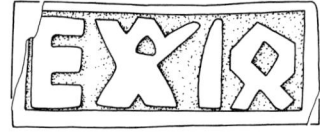

53 SA99 RB1-115
Roman bath building
Laconian *imbrex*
ΕΛΑΙΟΥ
h.: 3.7; pres. w.: 8.9

54 SA99 RB1-60
Roman bath building
Laconian *imbrex*
ΕΛΑΙΟΥ
h: 3.6; w.: 8.9

55 SA99 RB1-74
Roman bath building
Laconian *imbrex*
ΕΛΑΙΟΥ
h.: 3.8; w.: 8.8

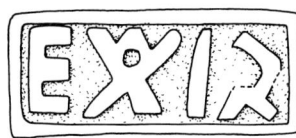

1.f. Rectangular field, stamp in retrograde, angular raised capitals, lambda and alpha in ligature, left lower side of iota curved, bottom of omicron flat

56 SA99 RB1-62
Roman bath building
Laconian *imbrex*
ΕΛΑΙΟΥ
h.: 3.7: w.: 8.5

1.g. Rectangular field, stamp in retrograde, angular raised capitals, lambda and alpha in ligature, left lower side of iota curved, omicron curved

57 SA99 RB1-99
Roman bath building
Corinthian *tegula*
ΕΛΑΙΟΥ
h.: 3.9; w.: 8.7

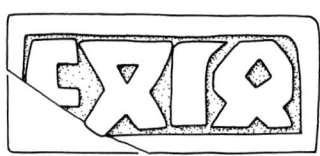

58 SA99 RB1-36
Roman bath building
Corinthian *tegula*
ΕḶΑΙΟΥ
h.: 3.7: pres. w.: 7.4

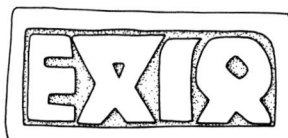

1.h. Rectangular field, angular incised capitals, lambda and alpha in ligature

59 SA99 RB1-36
Roman bath building
Laconian *imbrex*
ΕΛΑΙΟΥ
h.: 2.8; w.: 6.7

1.i. Fragmentary dies

60 SA99 RB1-60
Roman bath building
Laconian *imbrex*
ΕΛΑΙ[ΟΥ]
h.: 3.8; pres. w.: 7.2

61 SA99 RB1-60
Roman bath building
Laconian *imbrex*
ΕΛΑ[ΙΟΥ]
h.: 3.6; pres. w.: 4.8

62 SA99 RB1-62
Roman bath building
Laconian *imbrex*
ΕΛΑ[ΙΟΥ]
h.: 3.6; pres. w.: 5.2

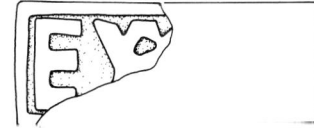

63 SA99 RB1-74
Roman bath building
Laconian *imbrex*
ΕΛΑΙΟΥ
pres. h.: 3.1; pres. w.: 8.5

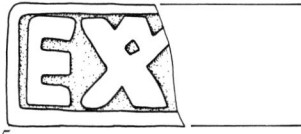

64 SA99 RB1-60
Roman bath building
Laconian *imbrex*
ΕΛΑ[ΙΟΥ]
h.: 3.9; pres. w.: 5.1

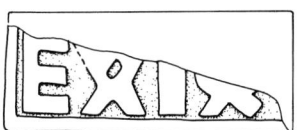

1.j. Rectangular field, stamp in retrograde, angular raised capitals, lambda and alpha in ligature, bottom of combined lambda and alpha, and that of omicron flat, left lower side of iota curved

65 SA99 RB1-37
Roman bath building
Type of tile not clear
ΕΛΑΙΟΥ
h.: 3.5; w.: 8.6

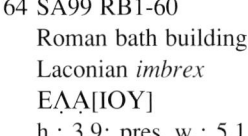

2 Stamps bearing the inscription EYPIK

2.b. Rectangular field with raised capitals, stamp in retrograde, rho connected to top of field

66 SA99 B3-57
Shops east of bouleuterion
Corinthian *tegula*
EYPIK
h.: 4.1; w.: 6.8

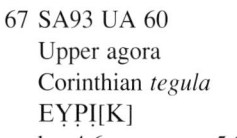

c. unidentifiable die

67 SA93 UA 60
Upper agora
Corinthian *tegula*
EYPI[K]
h.: 4.6; pres. w.: 5.9

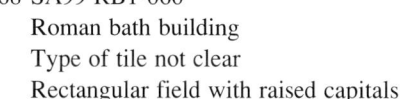

10. Stamps bearing the inscription APKI[...]

68 SA99 RB1-060
Roman bath building
Type of tile not clear
Rectangular field with raised capitals
AP[KI...]
A and P connected
h.: 3.5; pres. w.: 5.4

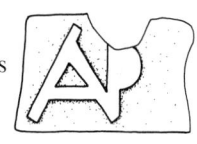

69 SA96 RB
Roman bath building
Type of tile not clear
Rectangular field
with raised capitals
APK[I...]
A and P connected
h.: 3.6; pres. w.: 9.1

11. APKOME/ATMA

70 SA99 Y 31
Stray find (possibly shops east of bouleuterion)
Corinthian *tegula*
Rectangular field
with incised capitals
APKOME/ATMA
Two lines
h.: 4.3; w.: 6.7

6. REFERENCES

J.P. Adam (1984) *La construction romaine. Matériaux et techniques*, Paris.

Å. Åkerström (1966) *Die architektonischen Terrakotten Kleinasiens* (Skriftner utgivna av Svenska institutet i Athen. In-4 11) Lund.

J.J. Aubert (1994) *Business Managers in Ancient Rome. A Social and Economic Study of Institores, 200 B.C. – A.D. 250*, Leiden – New York – Köln.

H. Bloch (1947) *I bolli laterizi e la storia edilizia di Roma*, Roma.

E. Boehringer and F. Klauss (1937) *Das Temenos für den Herrscherkult: Prinzessinen Palast (Altertümer von Pergamon* 9) Berlin.

G. Brodribb (1987) *Roman Brick and Tile*, Gloucester.

R. Degeest, R. Ottenburgs, W. Viaene, H. Kucha, D. Laduron, A. Bouquet and M. Waelkens (1997) Characterisation of the common wares manufactured in Roman Sagalassos. An overview, in: M. Waelkens and J. Poblome (eds) *Sagalassos IV. Report on the Survey and Excavation Campaigns of 1994 and 1995 (Acta Archaeologica Lovaniensia Monographiae* 9) Leuven University Press: 519-532.

H. Devijver (1996) Local elite, equestrians and senators: a social history of Roman Sagalassos, *Ancient Society* 27: 106-112.

P. M. Fraser and E. Matthews (1987) *A Lexicon of Greek Personal Names 1. The Aegean Islands, Cyprus, Cyrenaica*, Oxford.

P.M. Fraser and E. Matthews (1997) *A Lexicon of Greek Personal Names 3a. The Peleponnese, Western Greece, Sicily and Magna Graecia*, Oxford.

H. von Gaertringen (1906) *Inschriften von Priene*, Berlin.

M. Guarducci (1967) *Epigrafia Greca* 1, Roma.

R. Hayes (1997) *Handbook of Mediterranean Pottery*, London.

E. Kosmetatou and M. Waelkens (1997) The "Macedonian" shields of Sagalassos, in: M. Waelkens and J. Poblome (eds) *Sagalassos IV. Report on the Survey and Excavations Campaigns of 1994 and 1995 (Acta Archaeologica Lovaniensia Monographiae* 9) Leuven University Press: 277-292.

W. Larfeld (1902) *Handbuch der attischen Inschriften (Handbuch der griechischer Epigraphik 2. Die attischen Inschriften)* Leipzig.

C.A. Mango (1950) Byzantine brickstamps, *American Journal of Archaeology* 54: 19-27.

R. Martin (1965) *Manuel d'architecture grecque 1. Matériaux et techniques*, Paris.

A. McWhirr and D. Viner (1978) The production and distribution of tiles in Roman Britain with particular reference to the Cirencester region, *Britannia* 9: 359-377.

A. Neumann (1973) *Ziegel aus Vindobona (Der römische Limes in Österreich* 27), Wien.

A.K. Orlandos (1966) Les matériaux de construction et la technique architecturale des anciens grecs, Paris.

M.J. Osborne, S. G. Byrne and P.M. Fraser (1994) *A Lexicon of Greek Personal Names 2. Attica*, Oxford.

D. Peacock (1979) An ethnoarchaeological approach to the study of Roman bricks and tiles, in: A. McWhirr (ed.) *Roman Brick and Tile. Studies in Manufacture, Distribution and Use in the Western Empire (BAR International Series* 68) Oxford: 5-10.

D. Pinkwart and W. Stammitz (1984) *Peristylhäuser westlich der unteren Agora (Altertümer von Pergamon* 14) Berlin.

J. Poblome, H.A. Ekinci, I. Öztürk, P. Degryse, W. Viaene and M. Waelkens (1998) An early Byzantine tile kiln on the territory of Sagalassos, in: *XIX Kazı sonuçları toplantısı. 26-30 Mayıs 1997 Ankara II*: 507-522.

J. Poblome, H.A. Ekinci, I. Öztürk, , P. Degryse, W. Viaene (†) and M. Waelkens (2000) An early Byzantine tile kiln on the territory of Sagalassos, in: M. Waelkens and L. Loots (eds) *Sagalassos V. Report on the Survey and Excavation Campaigns of 1996 and 1997 (Acta Archaeologica Lovaniensia Monographiae* 11), Leuven University Press: 669-683.

J. Poblome, R. Brulet and O. Bounegru (in press) The origin of Terra Sigillata. Regionalism or integration, in *Rei Cretariae Romanae Fautorum. Acta* 36.

N. Purcell (1996) The Roman villa and the landscape of production, in: T.J. Cornell and K. Lomas (eds) *Urban Society in Roman Italy*, London: 151-179.

T. Rook (1979) Tiled roofs, in: A. McWhirr (ed.) *Roman Brick and Tile. Studies in Manufacture, Distribution and Use in the Western Empire (BAR International Series* 68) Oxford: 295-302.

C. Roueché (1989) *Aphrodisias in Late Antiquity*, London.

H. Solin (1982) *Die Griechische Personennamen in Rom. Ein Namenbuch* I, Berlin – New York.

K. Vandorpe (2000) Negotiator's laws from rebellious Sagalassos in an early Hellenistic inscription, in M. Waelkens and L. Loots (eds) *Sagalassos V. Report on the Survey and Excavation Campaigns of 1996 and 1997 (Acta Archaeologica Lovaniensia Monographiae* 11) Leuven University Press: 489-508.

M. Waelkens, E. Paulissen, H. Vanhaverbeke, I. Öztürk, B. De Cupere, H. A. Ekinci, P.M. Vermeersch, J. Poblome and R. Degeest (1997) The 1994 and 1995 surveys on the territory of Sagalassos, in: M. Waelkens and J. Poblome (eds) *Sagalassos IV. Report on the Survey and Excavation Campaigns of 1994 and 1995 (Acta Archaeologica Lovaniensia Monographiae* 9) Leuven, University Press: 11-102

M. Waelkens, J. Poblome, R. Degeest, L. Vandeput, L. Loots, E. Paulissen, P. Talloen, J. Van Den Bergh, V. Vanderginst, B. Arıkan, I. Vandamme, I. Akyel, F. Martens, M. Martens, I. Uytterhoeven, T. Debruyne, D. Depraetere, K. Baran, B. Vandaele, Z.Parras, S. Yıldırım, S. Bubel, H. Vanhaverbeke, C. Licoppe, F. Landuyt, T. Patricio, S. Ercan, K. Van Balen, E. Smits, F. Depuydt, L. Moens and P. De Paepe (2000). The 1996 and 1997 excavation seasons at Sagalassos, in: M. Waelkens and L. Loots (eds) *Sagalassos V. Report on the Survey and Excavation Campaigns of 1996 and 1997 (Acta Archaelogica Lovaniensia Monographiae* 10) Leuven University Press: 217-398.

S. Zabehlicky-Scheffenegger (1995) Die Italiener in Ephesos, in *Rei Cretariae Romanae Fautorum. Acta* 34, Alba Regia: 253-272.

O. Ziegenaus and G. De Luca (1975) *Das Asklepieon 2. Der nordliche Temenosbezirk und angrenzende Anlagen in Hellenistischer und Frühromischer Zeit (Altertümer von Pergamon* 11.2) Berlin.

MINIATURE JARS OF SAGALASSOS.
AN ANALYTICAL, QUANTITATIVE AND TYPOLOGICAL OVERVIEW OF A SERIES OF VERY SMALL POTTERY VESSELS FROM LATE ANTIQUITY

Roland DEGEEST[1], Patrick DEGRYSE[2], Raoul OTTENBURGS[2],
Willy VIAENE (†)[2] and Marc WAELKENS[1]

1 - Department of Archaeology, KULeuven, Blijde Inkomststraat 21, B-3000 Leuven, Belgium
2- Physico-Chemical Geology, Laboratory of Mineralogy, KULeuven, Celestijnenlaan 200C, B-3001 Heverlee, Belgium

1. INTRODUCTION

In antiquity, Sagalassos was for most of its known history a fairly important town in the mountainous region known as Pisidia. It straddled a then important north-south connection between the coastal plains of Pamphylia to the south and the central Anatolian plateau. Although historically attested since the fourth century BC, when Alexander the Great took the town by storm in 333 BC, as the second century AD historiographer Arrian recounts in his *Anabasis Alexandri* I.28, what remains today as archaeological fabric at the site is in essence Roman remodelling. The site was abandoned probably around or shortly after the middle of the seventh century of our era and subsequently was never permanently inhabited again. The situation encountered by later explorers is therefore that of the later phases of the occupation, modified by the damage caused by human and natural forces over the following centuries.

Since regular excavations under the direction of M. Waelkens of the Katholieke Universiteit Leuven started in 1990, their scope has gradually expanded (Waelkens 1993; Waelkens and Poblome 1993; Waelkens and Poblome 1997a). Among the many finds were large quantities of ceramics, indeed it was established even before the start of the excavations that Sagalassos had been a producer of what proved to be a distinctive kind of fine red slip ware (Poblome *et al.* 1993; Poblome 1995; Poblome 1999). Fine wares are only part of the ceramics spectrum, however. Large quantities of other wares, mainly of local origin, are also found. Among the latter are some groups of vessels that did not at first attract much attention, compared to the main groups, but that nevertheless are worthy of closer study.

One of those minor finds is a group of miniature vessels, which although relatively rare, attracted the attention of the excavation teams, because of their size and the fact that they were apparently different from the mainstream of Sagalassos sherds. For these reasons, we thought it useful to present them as a separate group.

Examples of the miniature jars were encountered first on one site within Sagalassos, the Doric Temple site, but turned up fairly frequently thereafter. Two different types could be discerned, which belonged to the same production. In our general overview of the common wares of Sagalassos, they are classified as types 7I100 and 7I110, which form fabric group 7 (Degeest 2000). To date 10 different fabric groups have been identified at Sagalassos. These have been classified macroscopically according to the simple but effective algorithm developed by Peacock (Peacock 1977; Fulford and Peacock 1984: 6-7) in the seventies for the excavations at Carthage. The primary classification system at Sagalassos is based on fabrics rather than on pottery types (Degeest 2000). The criteria used for fabric determination are the composition of inclusions, the size of inclusions, the colour of the matrix, hardness, feel and fracture. After macroscopic determination samples of the different ware fabric groups were analysed using chemical bulk analysis and mineralogical/optical methods. This allowed us to determine two things: first, whether the macroscopic classification was valid or not, and secondly, whether the differences would allow us to differentiate between local products and imported ones. It proved to be the case in every instance, although sometimes archaeological arguments had to be used as well to strengthen the case (Degeest 2000).

Since the fabric of the miniature jars is some kind of fine ware, a comparison between this fabric and the fabric of the known local production of fine ware, our fabric 1, was the obvious next step.

2. THE FABRIC OF THE MINIATURE JARS

The main characteristic of pottery in this fabric is the finely dispersed mica dusting of the exterior. Whereas the fine ware of Sagalassos has a clear red colour, usually Munsell colour 2.R 5/6 red, hence its name 'Sagalassos red slip ware', the miniature fabric is mostly rather more purplish. No inclusions are visible to the naked eye. The fracture is smooth to conchoidal. The fragments often have a harsh feel on a fresh break, while the surface feel is often soapy because of the micaceous surface finish. The fabric is hard. For a long time it proved impossible to collect sufficient samples to allow chemical or mineralogical analysis, because the recovered fragments were usually too small. The number of analyses conducted to date is still limited, but growing. The preliminary results are presented in this paper. Bulk chemical analysis results are shown in table 1 (n=4).

SiO_2	Al_2O_3	TOTFe	MnO	MgO	CaO	Na_2O	K_2O	TiO_2	P_2O_5	L.O.I.
51.19	21.72	9.96	0.20	4.41	5.70	0.85	3.06	0.91	0.12	1.31
48.15	20.51	8.67	0.15	3.39	6.10	0.66	3.09	0.88	0.19	7.49
50.83	21.48	10.43	0.22	4.77	5.35	0.77	3.13	0.91	0.13	1.34
53.17	20.54	8.76	0.19	3.96	5.44	0.98	3.15	0.89	0.15	2.07

Table 1: Bulk chemical analysis results of the minature jars

We can compare these values with the mean values obtained for the regular Sagalassos fine ware, the so-called fabric 1 in our classification (Table 2: n=128) (Degeest 2000):

SiO_2	Al_2O_3	TOTFe	MnO	MgO	CaO	Na_2O	K_2O	TiO_2	P_2O_5	L.O.I.
52.57	16.13	8.28	0.10	6.53	7.79	0.97	2.75	0.88	0.26	3.14

Table 2: Bulk chemical analysis results for fabric 1

From this we can determine that the miniature fabric has some similarities to the typical Sagalassos fabrics. Differences can be seen mainly in the Al_2O_3 content, which is higher for the miniature fabric, as is the generally more ferrous composition and the K_2O content. On the other hand, the MgO and CaO contents are lower. Based on the chemical bulk composition it seems likely that the fabric of our subject is of a different origin.

Mineralogical/optical analysis provided us with more detailed information. In all the investigated samples of ware group 7 we find a similar mineralogical content through the study of thin sections and X-ray diffraction (Fig. 1). All samples show a high quartz and Muscovite content.

Quartz is present as rounded crystals of maximum 400 μm diameter while Muscovite is present as small (sometimes weathered) elongated crystals of maximum 100 μm length. Plagioclase occurs as rounded crystals of maximum 200 μm diameter. Pyroxenes, amphiboles and opaque minerals are poorly represented in these samples and show as rounded, weathered crystals of maximum 50 μm diameter. The general texture in thin section of the samples of ware group 7 is that of small, rounded crystals of maximum 400 μm embedded in a fine, clay-rich matrix.

The mineralogy of these sherds, together with their chemical signature, does not correspond to any of the known possible clay resources for ceramic production in the area of Sagalassos, neither does it correspond to any other fabric found in the excavations conducted at Sagalassos.

We can therefore conclude that fabric 7 of the miniature jars is certainly not the same as the typical Sagalassos fabric 1 and is probably not a locally produced ceramic, but probably an imported one.

3. DESCRIPTION OF THE MINIATURE JARS

3.1. Type 7I100: a two-handled jar

This is a miniature jar with a wide, biconical body shape and a slightly flared neck with an everted plain rim (Fig.2, 4, cat. 1-21). The vessel is wheel-thrown. Two round or oval-sectioned handles are attached to the outer rim and to the widest part of the body. The bottom is flat and string-cut. The so-called mica dusting, which is too thin to be called a regular slip, is typical. This makes these sherds easily recognisable after cleaning, because it is not found on the normal Sagalassos products. The micaceous dusting is sometimes overlooked during the excavations, but the distinctive shape facilitates the identification. The height of the complete examples varies between 35 and 53 mm, sizes between 40 and 50 mm being the most common. The body shape can be described as biconical and of squarish proportions, since the height and maximum body diameter at the carination are the same or nearly the same. Body diameter at the carination varies between 30 and 52 mm. Rims are normally flared with a plain rounded shape. The external rim diameters vary between 30 and 50 mm, most being between 35 and 40 mm. Internal rim diameters vary between 22 and 40 mm, but most of them are between 24 and 28 mm wide. The base diameter varies between 13 and 31 mm, with a preponderant value of 16 mm.

3.2. Type 7I110: a miniature jug

The other main type of miniature pottery found at Sagalassos is shaped like a miniature jug (Figs 3,5, cat. 22-41). The body is pear-shaped with normally a small rounded disk base and a rounded thickened flared, often somewhat inverted, rim. The single handle is attached below the rim and to the widest part of the body. The section of this handle is usually round on the outside and a flattened oval on the inside. The height of the complete profiles varies between 52 and 60 mm. The rim diameters are between 18 and 23 mm with most in the 20-21 mm range. Base diameters vary more with a range from 14 to 21 mm, while the diameter of the vessels lies between 30 and 38 mm, with a preponderance of the 30-33 mm range.

4. THE STRATIGRAPHY OF THE MINIATURE VESSELS

The miniature vessels were recovered from a number of sites at Sagalassos. The locations do not give an accurate picture of the distribution of these ceramics at the site, because the actual excavations cover only a small part of the main centre of the ancient town. Table 3 provides an overview of the locations:

site	grid location (old system between brackets)	layer	type 7I100	type 7I110	fabric 7 sherds not readily attributable to one or the other type
Agora gate	5330/4775	layer 6		SA-95-AG-268-1	
Bouleuterion	5285/4970	layer 2	SA-96-B-233-1		
	5305/4980	layer 2	SA-95-B-95-1		
	5305/4980	layer 3C		SA-96-B-121-1	
Doric temple*	5265/4975 (X)	layer 2	SA-91-DT-266-1		
	5265/4975 (X)	layer 3	SA-91-DT-292-24		
	5270/4965+5270/4970 (V+VII)	layer 4		SA-92-DT-177-I	
	5270/4975 (IX)	layer 1	SA-91-DT-258-1	SA-91-DT-275-1	
	5270/4975 (IX)	layer 2	SA-91-DT-305-11 SA-91-DT-305-6	SA-91-DT-305-13	
	5270/4975 (IX)	layer 3	SA-91-DT-330-118	SA-91-DT-330-130	
	5270/4980-5265/4980 (XI-XII)	layer 3	SA-92-DT-32-166	SA-92-DT-32-165 SA-92-DT-32-167	
	5275/4980	cleaning			SA-97-DT-100
	5280/4970-5280/4975 (XIV-XV)	layer 4	SA-92-DT-228-1		
NW Heroon	5295/4995	layer 3	SA-94-H-141-1		
	5300/4990	layer 3	SA-96-H-49 (base, not drawn)		
Lower Agora	5325/4790	layer 3	SA-97-LA-100-1		
	5330/4790	layer 2			SA-97-LA-42
	5335/4795	layer 3	SA-97-LA-179 (base, not drawn		
	5360/4810 (XXVI)	layer 5	SA-93-LA-273-6		

site	grid location (old system between brackets)	layer	type 71100	type 71110	fabric 7 sherds not readily attributable to one or the other type
Roman Baths	5380/4800	layer 3	SA-96-RB-219-1		
Upper Agora	5315/4980 (LXVI-W1)	layer 2			SA-95-UA-322
	5315/4980 (LXVI-W1)	layer 4A		SA-95-UA-280	
	5320/4980 (LXVI-W)	layer 3		SA-94-UA-178-3	
	5320/4980 (LXVI-W)	layer 4		SA-94-UA-439-2	
	5325/4980 (LXVI)	layer 3			SA-94-UA-278
	5330/4980 (LXV)	layer 4	SA-94-UA-366-2	SA-94-UA-366-1	
	5330/4985 (LXXIV)	layer 3	SA-94-UA-65-5		
	5330/4985 (LXXIV)	layer 4			SA-94-UA-252
	5340/4975 (LIV-W)	layer 1			SA-94-UA-379
	5340/4980 (LXIII)	layer 1	SA-95-UA-209-1		
	5340/4985 (LXXII)	layer 2	SA-94-UA-135-1		
	5345/4980 (LXII)	layer 1			SA-95-UA-214
	5345/4985 (LXXI)	layer 5			SA-95-UA-139
	5345/4990 (LXXX)	layer 1			SA-95-UA-7
	5350/4985 (LXX)	layer 1			95-UA-87
	5350/4990 (LXXIX)	layer 2	SA-95-UA-45-14		
	5355/4980 (LX)	layer 3			SA-94-UA-233
	5355/4990 (LXXVIII)	layer 2		SA-95-UA-55-1 SA-95-UA-55-2	
	5355/4995 (LXXXVII)	layer 1		SA-95-UA-51-1	
	5355/4995 (LXXXVII)	layer 2	SA-95-UA-67-1		
	5365/4995 (LXXXV)	layer 3		SA-96-UA-110-1	
	tunnel	destruction layer		SA-96-UA-131-18	
Upper Agora North	5310/4980	layer 6A		SA-97-UAN-53-1	
	5310/4980	layer 6			SA-97-UAN-101
	5320/4985	layer 4SB	SA-97-UAN-178-1	SA-97-UAN-172-1	
	5325/4985 (LXXV-W)	layer 2S	SA-96-UAN-108-15		
	5330/4990	cleaning			SA-97-UAN-25
	5330/4995 (XCII)	layer 2N		SA-94-UAN-220-8	
	5340/4990	layer 7S			SA-96-UAN-119

* approximate grid positions only, as the original grids (Roman numerals) were not aligned to the new grid system, whereby the coordinates of each 5 x 5 m square are identified by the coordinates of its SE-corner (first coordinate = X, second coordinate = Y).

Table 3: Find locations of the miniature jars

The agora gate site is located adjacent to the southeast corner of the lower agora. It forms the entrance to a monumental street oriented north-south. Layer 6 in grid square 5330/4775 is described as a 0.55 to 0.80 m thick fill overlaying the old Imperial stairway. The pottery in it was dated to the first half of the sixth century (Waelkens *et al.* 1997b: 210).

The bouleuterion site is situated in the area between the Doric temple and the upper agora. Here miniature jars were excavated from layers 2 and 3C, where layer 2 is the destruction layer of the site, containing mainly late material, i.e. of sixth and early seventh century date, and layer 3C is the fill of a room-like construction (W2) to the north of the courtyard wall of the bouleuterion. The archaeological material dated mainly to the late period, i.e. late fifth to early seventh century.

A significant number of finds came from the Doric temple site to the east of the bouleuterion, both from inside the temple proper, and from the area to the west of it. Three main areas can be discerned. The interior of the temple (5280/4970-5280/4975) had type 7I100 in layer 4. The latter is dated to the end of the fifth and first half of the sixth century by its ceramics (Poblome 1999; Degeest 2000). The area to the west of the temple was divided by a late fortification wall in two sections. The north side (areas 5265/4975, 5270/4980, 5265/4980) had finds in layers 1, 2, and 3; datable by pottery to the sixth century (Degeest 2000; Poblome 1999). The area to the south of the fortification wall (areas 5270/4965-5270/4970) had fabric 7 in layer 4. In this case we see that both types are present in the same layers, which can be taken as an indication for their contemporaneity.

At the NW Heroon site to the northeast of the Doric temple, type 7I100 jars were found in layer 3, dated by the pottery to the first half of the sixth century (Waelkens *et al.* 1997b: 191-192).

The lower agora site provided us with another series of miniature jars. With the exception of one example from layer 5 inside a shop at the west side of the agora, all were found in the debris layers on the east side of the agora. The latter can be dated to the sixth century or later. The former is an artificial fill which contains material stemming in part from the sixth and seventh century (Degeest 2000; Poblome 1999; Waelkens *et al.* 1997b: 205).

The adjacent Roman baths site also produced evidence of the presence of fabric 7 miniature jars in layer 3 of area 5380/4800.

One of the more productive sites proved to be the upper agora and the Upper Agora North site. The upper agora was largely free from debris even before the start of the excavations. The only areas where an accumulation of archaeological layers could be found were situated at the north and west side of the agora. These layers are clearly related to the erosion and collapse of the buildings adjoining the agora. On the north side is a large ruin, which was possibly originally a Hellenistic market building (Waelkens *et al.* 1997b: 127), altered and partly rebuilt at various times in Roman Imperial times. During the late Imperial/early Byzantine period, i.e. sixth – seventh century, a number of small shops were built in it. After the partial collapse of the superstructure, the internal layers of fill eroded and covered the middle Antonine nymphaeum, which formed a transition to the agora proper. The same happened on the west side, where a chapel or small church was erected between the agora and the bouleuterion complex. Finds of miniature vessels were only made in the grid squares at the northern end of the agora, i.e. adjacent to the nymphaeum and the late shops. These layers contained mainly sixth- to seventh-century finds and their relation to the finds made in the remains of the building itself is evident. In this building we have a series of partly eroded levels, sometimes reaching considerable depths. If we look at the other ceramic material from these levels, it is clear that most of them contain mostly late, i.e. sixth to seventh century, pottery. This is for instance the case for the finds from layer 6/6A in the western end of the construction, and for level 2S in the northern part of the building and 2N (street to the north of the market building). Levels 4SB and layer 7S, both in the southern part of the building, were more problematic. Layer 4SB contained fine ware ceramics which indicated a date in the second half of the second century, and the proportion of the common wares in relation to these (Degeest 2000) added additional arguments to this dating. However, the layer on top of this was clearly dated to the sixth and seventh century. This therefore seems to indicate the presence of an intrusion, as there is absolutely no typological or fabric difference between these and the later vessels. The same argument probably applies to layer 7S.

5. COMPARATIVE MATERIAL

The miniature vessels that form the subject of this text are not the only vessels of extremely small size to be found at Sagalassos. Other, extremely rare finds appear of very small or even miniature vessels. One unique find was a small two-handled jar, excavated from a site to the west of the so-called library area east of the public centre of Sagalassos (SA-94-LW-177-1, (Fig. 5, cat. 42). However, there seems to be no direct relation to the miniature jars described here, as the vessel is of a different shape and is clearly made from the normal Sagalassos fine ware fabric 1. The body is cylindrical, and wider than it is high. It has a ring base rather than a flat or disk base. The neck is also cylindrical with a

Fig. 1: A thin section of fabric 7.

Fig. 2: A typical 7I100 miniature jar.

Fig. 3: A typical 7I110 miniature jar.

distinct triangular everted rim with a diameter of 24 mm. The total height is 46 mm for a maximum diameter of the body of 53 mm. Diameter of the base is 37 mm. The vessel is wheel-thrown and coated with slip on the outside in typical Sagalassos fashion. The two round-sectioned handles have flattened small disks on top of the attachments of the handle, both at the rim and at the lower shoulder. According to the fine ware that was found in the same stratigraphical context, this vessel could be dated between the second century and the first half of the fourth century.

Another sherd that may have some relation to our subject is SA-97-UAN-101-1 (Fig. 5, cat. 43). This is a rim sherd of a bowl-like ceramic element that has the same fabric and mica-dusted finish as the miniatures.

Outside Sagalassos the number of finds, at least of published ones, is very meagre indeed. However, a direct connection could be made with two unique finds at Saraçhane in Istanbul. Coincidentally, these finds are each a perfect parallel to the two types found in relative abundance at Sagalassos.

An example of identical shape and finish to our type 7I100 from the Saraçhane excavations in Istanbul is described by J.W. Hayes as belonging to his Mica-Dusted III ware, a red-brown ware with thin mica-dusting, which was apparently used for miniature vessels only. There is little doubt that this vessel is of the same type as the more numerous Sagalassian examples. However, the only dating that was provided was mid-Byzantine or earlier, since the sole find, namely BP 134, was found in context 1219, situated in narthex sector B in the former church of St. Polyeuktos (Harrison *et al.* 1986: 89). This context contained twelfth century and later material (Hayes 1992: 49, 221, fig. 18.7). The church itself was built by Anicia Juliana, probably in the years 524-527 (Harrison *et al.* 1986: 3).

Remarkably enough, the only jug of type 7I110 found its twin also in the Saraçhane excavations (Hayes 1992: 49, 221, fig. 18.8). The latter object, BP 346, was recovered from context 1065, situated outside the church in grid reference Y/16-17, a fill between a drain and a wall, containing pre-tenth century pottery and eleventh century coins (Harrison *et al.* 1986: 82).

6. CHRONOLOGY

If we consider the Sagalassian evidence a fairly clear picture emerges of a pottery type series, which can be dated at least from the beginning of the sixth to the first half of the seventh century AD. One has to take into account, however, that for the moment no later contexts have been found at Sagalassos. Based on the archaeological evidence is seems likely that the main distribution should be situated in the first half of the sixth century. Evidence from outside Sagalassos, *in casu* Saraçhane, is scant, but does not contradict this conclusion. It seems likely that we have there residual material, probably related to the original church building of Anicia Juliana, which is also dated to this period. No close relations to these miniature jars could be found in the earlier strata of Sagalassos, with the exception of a few individual pieces, which are most probably later intrusions.

7. FUNCTION OF THE MINIATURE VESSELS

As to the function of these curious vessels, no direct evidence could be found. One could imagine a votive offering of some kind, but this seems unlikely in view of the fact that there seems to be a distinct relation between commercial activity and the locations of the main finds. This in itself does not necessarily contradict a votive/religious purpose, as these were also the subject of trade, but there seems to be no direct link with the religious buildings in use at the time, that is, the churches. There were churches, both on the upper agora and the lower one, but the sum of the evidence is not associated with them. On the other hand, there is a distinct relationship between the miniature finds and the late shops, certainly on the upper agora/Upper Agora North sites, and possibly also on the lower agora/Roman baths sites. This could indicate a commercial use of these vessels. The question then remains whether the vessels themselves or their contents were the commodity. So far, no internal residue of any kind could be discerned macroscopically. On the other hand, the quality of the finish of these vessels makes it unlikely that they were a valuable trade object *in se*. But, the two sites where these vessels have been found, i.e. Sagalassos in southern Turkey and Istanbul in the northwest, lay far apart, which is perhaps an indication of a relatively valuable commodity. It seems therefore likely that some small-volume, high-value item was traded in these vessels.

8. CONCLUSIONS

Considering the available evidence we can say that the miniature vessels of Sagalassos, were in fact of two types, one a single-handled jug, the other a two-handled jar, which are found in the same time frame from the sixth to possibly the seventh century. The evidence indicates that the major distribution would be in the first half of the sixth century. They are certainly not of local origin and contained in all likelihood a valuable, small-volume substance, which was traded over large distances.

9. ACKNOWLEDGEMENTS

This research is supported by the Belgian Programme on Interuniversity Poles of Attraction (IUAP 4/12) initiated by the Belgian State, Prime Minister's Office, Science Policy Programming. The text also presents the results of the Concerted Action of the Flemish Government (GOA 97/2) and the Fund for Scientific Research-Flanders (Belgium) (FWO) (G.2145.94). Scientific responsibility is assumed by its authors.

10. CATALOGUE OF FINDS

10.1. Key

All measurements are in mm. Context numbers are integrated in the numbering system for the finds, where SA stands for Sagalassos, followed by the year, the site designation, the context number, and finally the find number. The elements of the system are separated by hyphens, since the site designation may be a combination of letters and numbers. The other elements are:

height: total height of the vessel when a complete profile is available.
fragm. height: height of the fragment when put in its normal position if the vessel was complete.
max. diam.: maximum diameter of the vessel if the complete profile can be reconstructed at this point.
rim. diam.: external rim diameter.
bot. diam.: diameter of the base.

10.2. Type 7I100

Site: Bouleuterion
1. SA-96-B-95-1, fragm. height: 47 mm, max. diam.: 41 mm, rim diam.: 40 mm. Nearly full profile remaining, only the bottom half of the body and one of the handles is missing. The remaining handle has a round section on the outside and a flat one on the inside.
2. SA-96-B-233-1, height: 53 mm, max. diam.: 52 mm, rim diam.: 50 mm, bot. diam.: 16 mm. Complete miniature jar with two handles. Handles have an oval section. The rim is horizontally flattened. The base is somewhat concave.

Site: Doric Temple
3. SA-91-DT-258-6, fragm. height: 15 mm, rim diam.: 40 mm. Rim fragment with typical mica dusting on the exterior.
4. SA-91-DT-266-1, height: 48 mm, max. diam.: 45 mm, rim diam.: 46 mm, bot. diam.: 24 mm. Complete profile of miniature jar with attachment of a vertical loop handle just below the rim and on the body, no slip, some micaceous inclusions.
5. SA-91-DT-292-24, fragm. height: 18 mm, bot. diam.: 16 mm. Fragment of flat base, light brown red fabric, mica dusted, wiped finish.
6. SA-91-DT-305-11, fragm. height: 11 mm, rim diam.: 40 mm. Rim fragment with micaceous fabric, wiped finish, handle attachment below the rim.
7. SA-91-DT-305-6, fragm. height: 17 mm, rim diam.: 40 mm. Rim fragment with micaceous fabric, no visible slip, light brown, fine finish. The partial handle shows a squarish section.
8. SA-91-DT-330-118, fragm. height: 19 mm, bot. diam.: 16 mm. Base fragment with many fine mica particles, exterior well finished, wiped, interior coarse.
9. SA-92-DT-32-166, fragm. height: 19 mm, bot. diam.: 20 mm. Flat base, handle attachment visible on body, micaceous surface, brown fabric.
10. SA-92-DT-228-1, fragm. height: 34 mm, max. diam.: 40 mm, bot. diam.: 18 mm. Only rim and handles missing, flat base.

Site: Heroon
11. SA-94-H-141-1, height: 40 mm, max. diam.: 32 mm, rim diam.: 35 mm, bot. diam.: 13 mm. Complete vessel, showing the typical mica dusting. The handles are round sectioned, and the base is slightly concave.

Site: Lower Agora
12. SA-93-LA-273-6, fragm. height: 33 mm, max. diam.: 38 mm, rim diam.: 43 mm. Nearly complete profile, only the bottom is missing.
13. SA-97-LA-100-1, height: 41 mm, max. diam.: 34 mm, rim diam.: 30 mm, bot. diam.: 22 mm. Nearly complete miniature jar, one handle missing. Although the typical micaceous fabric and finish are found, the handles are rectangular in section rather than the usual round one.

Site: Roman Baths
14. SA-96-RB-219-1, height: 45 mm, max. diam.: 39, rim diam.: 40 mm, bot. diam.: 20 mm. Nearly complete miniature jar, two-handled with one handle missing. The handles are rounded in section.

Site: Upper Agora
15. SA-94-UA-135-1, fragm. height: 31 mm, max. diam.: 36 mm, bot. diam.: 15 mm. Lower half of miniature jar.
16. SA-94-UA-366-2, fragm. height: 28 mm, max. diam.: 37 mm, bot. diam.: 16 mm. Three-quarters of the body of a two-handled miniature jar with a flat base and mica dusting.
17. SA-95-UA-45-14, fragm. height: 19 mm, bot. diam.: 18 mm. Lower half of miniature jar with flat base and irregular mica dusting.

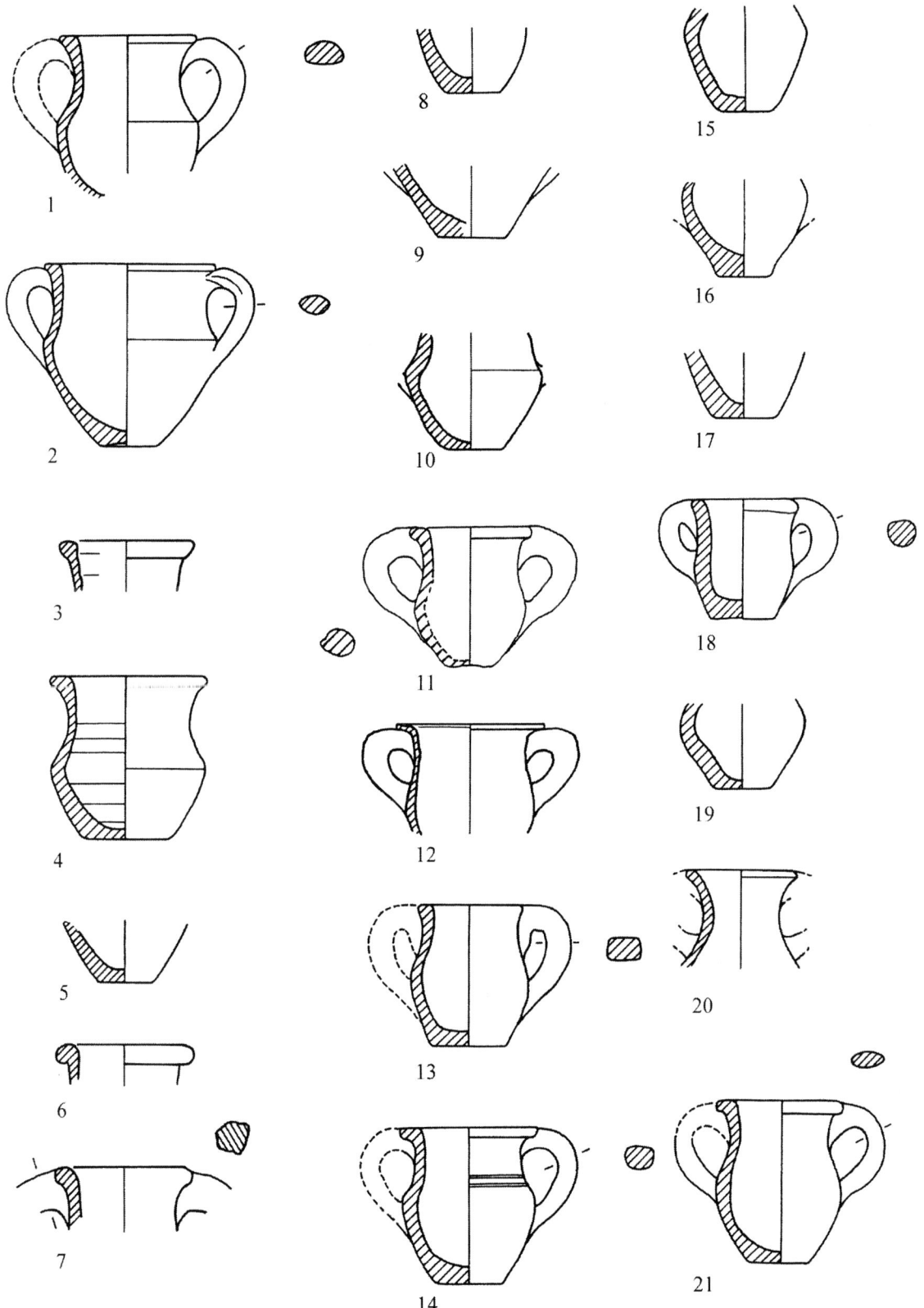

Fig. 4: Type 7I100 miniature jars.

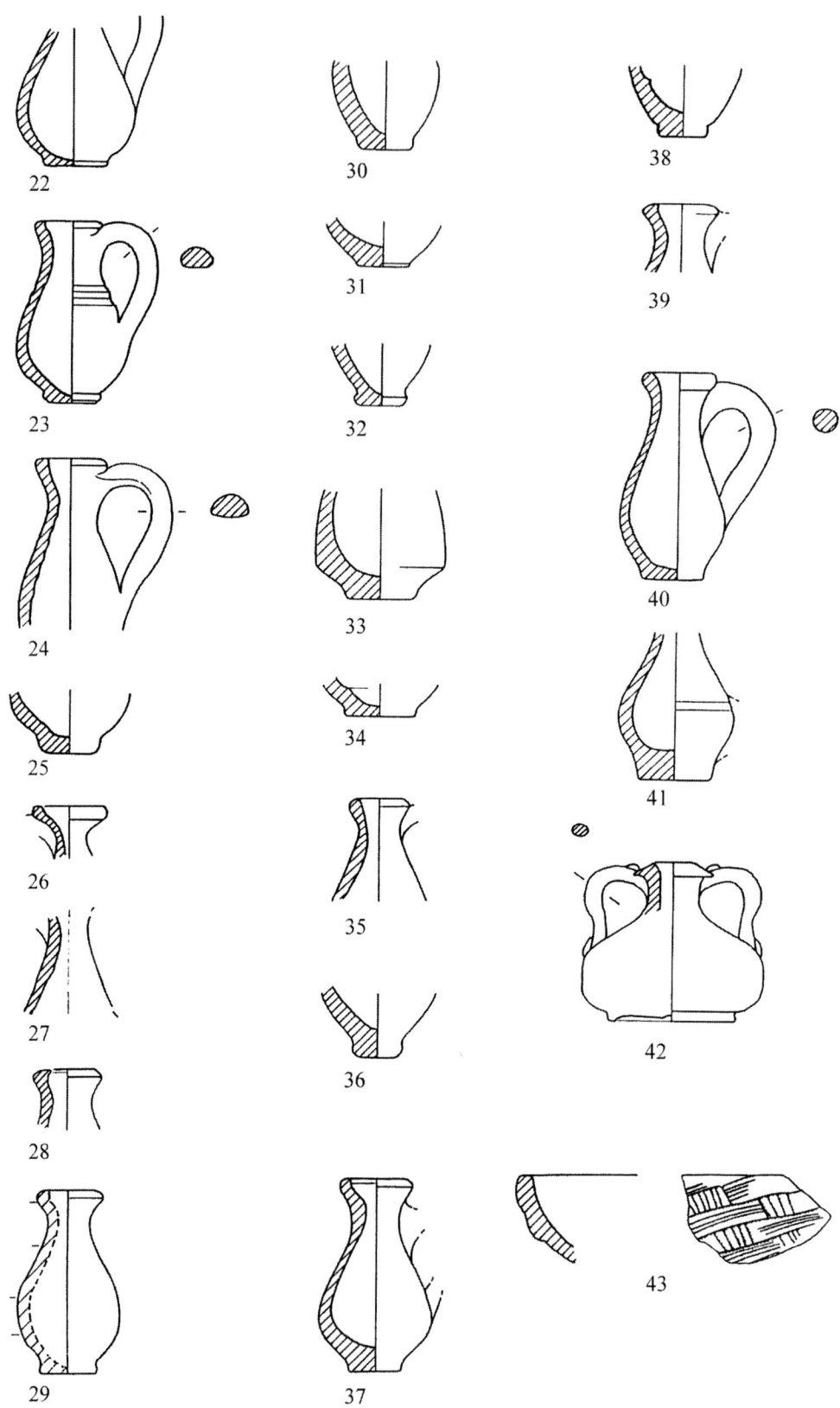

Fig. 5: Type 7I100 miniature jars and comparative material (cat. 42-43).

18. SA-95-UA-67-1, height: 35 mm, max. diam.: 30 mm, rim diam.: 32 mm, bot. diam.: 19 mm. Complete miniature jar with two handles of round section and a slightly concave base.
19. SA-95-UA-209-1, fragm. height: 25 mm, max. diam.: 37 mm, bot. diam.: 17 mm. Body of miniature jar with characteristic mica dusting. Attachments of two handles visible.

Site: Upper Agora North
20. SA-96-UAN-108-15, fragm. height: 29 mm, rim diam.: 33 mm. Neck and rim of miniature jar. Although the fabric and finish are typical, the attachment of the handles is somewhat higher on the body than usual.
21. SA-97-UAN-178-1, height: 47 mm, max. diam.: 38 mm, rim diam.: 38 mm, bot. diam.: 17 mm. Nearly complete vessel, only part of one handle missing. The handles have an oval section. Typical mica dusting and colouring of the fabric.

10.3 Type 7I110

Site: Agora Gate
22. SA-95-AG-268-1, fragm. height: 40 mm, max. diam.: 34 mm, bot. diam.: 18 mm. Body of miniature jug with partial round-sectioned handle, only the neck and rim are missing.

Site: Bouleuterion
23. SA-96-B-121-1, height: 52 mm, max. diam.: 33 mm, rim diam.: 19 mm, bot. diam.: 16 mm. Complete jug, with disk base and handle with rounded outside and flat inside. The finish is somewhat irregular.

Site: Doric Temple
24. SA-91-DT-275-1, fragm. height: 49 mm, max. diam.: 30 mm, rim diam.: 21 mm. Nearly complete profile of a miniature jar with single handle. The handle has a rounded outer section and a flat inner one.
25. SA-91-DT-305-13, fragm. height: 22 mm, max. diam.: 35 mm, bot. diam.: 17 mm. Complete flat base of miniature jug, wipe marks on interior of the body, smoothed, fairly worn exterior.
26. SA-91-DT-330-130, fragm. height: 17 mm, rim diam.: 20 mm. Complete neck of miniature jug, handle attachment visible, light brown micaceous slip, light brown fabric.
27. SA-92-DT-32-165, fragm. height: 26 mm. On this body fragment of a jug the attachment for a single vertical loop handle is visible, micaceous surface, brown fabric, abraded.
28. SA-92-DT-32-167, fragm. height: 16 mm, rim diam.: 21 mm. Complete rim of jug with attachment for a single vertical loop handle.
29. SA-92-DT-177-1, height: 52 mm, max. diam.: 30 mm, rim diam.: 20 mm, bot. diam.: 17 mm. Jug with single vertical handle. The handle has disappeared but the attachment traces remain on rim and body, fine micaceous inclusions in a light brown fabric. The rim is somewhat asymmetrical and higher on the side of the handle, disk base, no slip.

Site: Upper Agora
30. SA-94-UA-65-6, fragm. height: 26 mm, max. diam.: 31 mm, bot. diam.: 16 mm. Lower half of miniature jug with fine mica dusting and disk base.
31. SA-94-UA-178-3, fragm. height: 13 mm, bot. diam.: 16 mm. Part of lower body of miniature jug with only slightly pronounced disk base.
32. SA-94-UA-366-1, fragm. height: 18 mm, bot. diam.: 15 mm. Fragment of lower half of miniature jar with pronounced carinated disk base.
33. SA-94-UA-439-2, fragm. height: 32 mm, max. diam.: 38 mm, bot. diam.: 20 mm. lower part of miniature jug. The body shows a carination rather than the usual pear shaped curve. The vessel seems to have been slightly larger than the normal type, although it shows the characteristic fine mica dusting and finish.
34. SA-95-UA-51-1, fragm. height: 9 mm, bot. diam.: 21 mm. Lower body of miniature jar.
35. SA-95-UA-55-1, fragm. height: 31 mm, rim diam.: 18 mm. Top half of miniature jug with mica dusting. The handle attachment is visible below the flared thickened rim.
36. SA-95-UA-55-2, fragm. height: 18 mm, bot. diam.: 15 mm. Lower part of miniature jug, perhaps part of the previous one, as the finish is very similar. Disk base.
37. SA-96-UA-110-1, height: 55 mm, max. diam.: 33 mm, rim diam.: 22 mm, bot. diam.: 15 mm. Nearly complete miniature jar with single missing handle.
38. SA-96-UA-131-18, fragm. height: 42 mm, max. diam.: 33 mm, bot. diam.: 20 mm. Body of miniature jug with lower handle attachment visible on the widest part of the body.

Site: Upper Agora North
39. SA-94-UAN-220-8, fragm. height: 21 mm, max. diam.: 30 mm, bot. diam.: 14 mm. Lower half of a miniature mica-dusted jug.
40. SA-97-UAN-53-1, fragm. height: 20 mm, rim diam.: 23 mm. Rim and neck of miniature jug with single handle attachment visible below the rim.
41. SA-97-UAN-172-1, fragm. height: 60 mm, max. diam.: 30 mm, rim diam.: 21 mm, bot. diam.: 18 mm. Nearly complete miniature jug with round sectioned vertical loop handle and fine mica dusting.

11. REFERENCES

R. Degeest (2000) *The Common Wares of Roman Sagalassos* (*Studies in Eastern Mediterranean Archaeology* 3) Brepols publishers.

M. Fulford and D. Peacock (1984) *Excavations at Carthage: the British Mission I, 2. The Avenue du président Habib Bourguiba, Salammbo: the Pottery and Other Ceramic Objects from the Site*, Sheffield.

R. Harrison, M. Gill, M. Hendy, S. Hill, D. Brothwell and K. Kosswig (1986) *Excavations at Saraçhane in Istanbul 1. The Excavations, Structures, Architectural Decoration, Small Finds, Coins, Bones, and Molluscs*, Princeton – Washington, D.C. – Guildford.

J. Hayes (1992) *Excavations at Saraçhane in Istanbul 2. The Pottery*, Princeton – Washington D.C. – Oxford.

D. Peacock (1977) Ceramics in Roman and medieval archaeology, in: D. Peacock (ed.) *Pottery and Early Commerce. Characterization and Trade in Roman and Later Ceramics*, London – New York – San Francisco: 21-33.

J. Poblome, R. Degeest, M. Waelkens and E. Scheltens (1993) Ceramic studies. Sagalassos ware I. The fine ware, in: M. Waelkens (ed.) *Sagalassos I. First Report on the Survey (1986-1989) and Excavations (1990-1991)* (*Acta Archaeologica Lovaniensia Monographiae* 5) Leuven University Press: 113-130.

J. Poblome (1995) The archaeological process of dating Sagalassos red slip ware. An anatomy, in: M. Waelkens and J. Poblome (eds) *Sagalassos III. Report on the Fourth Excavation Campaign of 1993* (*Acta Archaeologica Lovaniensia Monographiae* 7) Leuven University Press: 177-184.

J. Poblome (1999) *Sagalassos Red Slip Ware. Typology and Chronology* (*Studies in Eastern Mediterranean Archaology* 2) Brepols publishers.

M. Waelkens (ed.) (1993) *Sagalassos I. First Report on the Survey (1986-1989) and Excavations (1990-1991)* (*Acta Archaeologica Lovaniensia Monographiae* 5) Leuven University Press.

M. Waelkens and J. Poblome (eds) (1993) *Sagalassos II. Report on the Third Excavation Campaign of 1992* (*Acta Archaeologica Lovaniensia Monographiae* 6) Leuven University Press.

M. Waelkens and J. Poblome (eds) (1995) *Sagalassos III. Report on the Fourth Excavation Campaign of 1993* (*Acta Archaeologica Lovaniensia Monographiae* 7) Leuven University Press.

M. Waelkens and J. Poblome (eds) (1997a) *Sagalassos IV. Report on the Survey and Excavation Campaigns of 1994 and 1995* (*Acta Archaeologica Lovaniensia Monographiae* 9) Leuven University Press.

M. Waelkens, P.M. Vermeersch, E. Paulissen, E. Owens, B. Arıkan, M. Martens, P. Talloen, L. Gijsen, L. Loots, C. Peleman, J. Poblome, R. Degeest, T. Patrício, S. Ercan and F. Depuydt (1997b) The 1994 and 1995 excavation seasons at Sagalassos, in: M. Waelkens and J. Poblome (eds) *Sagalassos IV. Report on the Survey and Excavation Campaigns of 1994 and 1995* (*Acta Archaeologica Lovaniensia Monographiae* 9) Leuven University Press: 103-216.

MINERALOGY AND GEOCHEMISTRY OF ROMAN COMMON WARES PRODUCED AT SAGALASSOS AND THEIR POSSIBLE CLAY SOURCES

Patrick DEGRYSE[1], Roland DEGEEST[2], Jeroen POBLOME[2], Willy VIAENE (†)[1],
Raoul OTTTENBURGS[1], Harry KUCHA[1] and Marc WAELKENS[2]

1 - Laboratory of Mineralogy, Physico-Chemical Geology, KULeuven, Celestijnenlaan 200C, B-3001 Heverlee, Belgium
2 - Department of Archaelogy, KULeuven, Blijde Inkomststraat 21, B-3000 Leuven, Belgium

1. INTRODUCTION

In 1986 a Belgian archaeological project started in the ancient town of Sagalassos and its territory (Waelkens 1992; Waelkens 1995). Among the most important finds was the discovery that Sagalassos was an important centre of pottery manufacture from at least the late Hellenistic period into early Byzantine times (Mitchell et al. 1989). A wealth of both table and common wares was produced in the local potters' quarter. This led to a concerted effort by archaeologists and geologists to trace the different stages of the manufacturing and distribution process, from raw materials to trade in the finished product. A series of papers on these subjects and on the typology of the ceramic products, among them two monographs, has already been published (Degeest and Waelkens 1993; Scheltens 1993; Poblome *et al.* 1993; Poblome 1996; Poblome 1999; Degeest 2000).

One of the first problems to be solved was the identification of the clay raw materials used for these ceramics. Ottenburgs *et al.* (1993a and 1993b) discovered that the clays found in the plain northwest of the village of Çanaklı were suitable for the production of the local tableware called Sagalassos red slip ware (fabric 1). This was based on a chemical and mineralogical correspondence between the clays and the ceramics. The same questions arose in the study of the common wares (fabric 2, 4 and 5) and the building ceramics (fabric 3). This paper discusses the origin of the clay raw materials used for the production of the common wares. Because the raw materials for the common wares are tempered, the mineralogical and geochemical study is more complex than for the tableware. The study of the building ceramics is still in progress. The classical approach of chemical comparison will be supplemented by the mineralogy of the raw materials and of the ceramics and the geochemistry of individual minerals in the determination of the raw materials used in the production of common wares at Sagalassos.

Based on a macroscopic fabric analysis the common and tablewares can be divided into ten fabric groups. These can be divided on archaeological grounds into locally made or imported wares (Poblome 1996; Degeest *et al.* 1997). The raw material research in this paper concerns some groups that are thought to be local. The studied groups are fabrics 2, 4 and 5. The groups not treated here are the tableware fabric 1 of Sagalassos, the building ceramics of group 3, the imported fine wares of groups 6, 7 and 8, and the common wares of groups 9 and 10. The latter are based on single sherd finds.

Ware fabric group 2 is mainly found from the fifth to the middle of the sixth century AD. This production is virtually limited to storage containers of medium to large size and basins, often *mortaria* of some kind. The main fabric colour is a homogeneous 5YR 6/6 reddish yellow on the Munsell Soil Colour Charts. The paste is sometimes powdery. Because of the inclusions the texture is rough and the fracture is hackly. The surface of these vessels is normally eroded. Large quantities, including rejects are found, sometimes even in the dumps.

Next to fabric 1, fabric 4 is the most commonly occurring in Sagalassos and is found in every chronological period. Consequently, the range of vessels is important. The essential types in this fabric can be classified under two headings: namely, cooking wares of all kinds and jar types, in this case the Sagalassian amphorae or their equivalents. This ware is predominant toward the end of Sagalassian ceramic production, i.e. the middle of the seventh century AD, and has by then replaced fabric 1 ware. The core colour varies between 2.5R 4/8 red and 5YR 5/6 yellowish red. Surfaces are between 2.5YR 5/8 red and 5YR 6/6 reddish yellow. The hardness can be described as hard to very hard. The feel is rough to harsh, sometimes powdery. The fracture is always hackly. The frequency of the inclusions is sparse to moderate. The inclusions are mostly dull white and dark red but very occasionally shiny yellow or shiny black. Surface treatment can be wiped or smooth.

Fabric 5 is mostly limited to the large dolia or storage vessels. Chronologically, this fabric is found throughout the Roman period, but more concentrated in the later phase, i.e. from the fifth to the seventh century AD. The ware has a distinctive reddish brown colour. The core normally is 2.5YR 5/6 red, while the surface is often 2.5YR 5/4 reddish brown. All vessels of this kind are shaped on a wheel-thrown base using handmade slabs. The neck and rim are usually also wheel-thrown.

2. MATERIALS AND METHODS

The availability of sources of clay is the most obvious factor favouring the development of pottery production. The minimum resources needed for pottery making are clay, water and fuel for firing. Temper is not as necessary since most naturally occurring clays contain some non-plastics. If the raw material is too plastic, the potter may need to add some non-plastics to improve workability, counteract shrinkage, facilitate drying and moderate the firing properties (Shepard 1956; Rye 1976).

With regard to the primary raw material for ceramic production, i.e. the clays, the area around Sagalassos was surveyed for likely clay sources and several promising sites were sampled. The ability of a population to exploit a material profitably is closely related to the expenditure of energy necessary for this exploitation (Jarman 1972). This in turn is closely related to the proximity of the source. Several authors (Jarman 1972; Higgs and Vita-Finzi 1972; Jarman et al. 1972) have developed the concept that an archaeological site occupies a position within an exploitable territory and has certain economic possibilities according to its location. How does this model apply to ceramic resources? Arnold (1985), using ethnological evidence, showed that the geodesic distance to clay resources is in the range of 1 to 50 km. The preferred territory of exploitation seems to occur within 1 km because most of the clay resources are at a distance of 1 km or less. Eighty-four percent are within 7 km and this probably represents the upper limit of the maximum range of profitable exploitation (Arnold 1985). The distances to temper resources are very similar. These range from less than 1 km to 25 km. The 1 km range is probably the preferred distance of exploitation. Ninety-seven percent of the sites obtain their temper within a radius of 7 to 9 km from the site of production, suggesting that this is the upper limit of the range of profitable temper exploitation (Arnold 1985). It should be noted that the actual walking distance is probably a more accurate measure because this includes some correction for different factors such as topography and more closely reflects energy costs. For example, in mountain areas more time is needed to traverse a certain geodesic distance than in a fluvial plain. The type of transportation available may also affect the distances for profitable exploitation. Transportation such as pack animals would reduce the overall energy cost by greatly increasing the amount of clay or temper obtained in one journey (Arnold 1985).

The different sites sampled around Sagalassos are indicated on Fig. 1. Three of the five sets of samples taken fall within the distance of 7 to 9 km proposed by Arnold (1985) as the upper limit for profitable raw material exploitation. The five sets are the following: a first set of samples was taken in 2 boreholes in the southeastern part of the potters' quarter of Sagalassos. The samples were taken at 0.5 m intervals. The upper layers to a maximum depth of 1.3 m contained limestone and pottery fragments, indicating disturbed layers. Below this is a layer of weathered red to green shales and red sticky clay (Ottenburgs et al. 1993a). These lower layers are residual material from the weathering of the ophiolitic bedrock found in this location. A second and third set of samples were taken from the weathered material of ophiolitic bedrock found outside Sagalassos in the villages of Başköy and Taşkapı (Fig. 1). In 1996, an early Byzantine tile kiln was excavated at Taşkapı (Poblome et al. 2000). In both sets the samples consist of weathered green to red shales with only a small amount of clayey material. A fourth set of samples was taken from two promising sites in the valley of Çanaklı (Fig. 1). Pottery was until recently locally produced in the village with this name. The village of Çanaklı is situated some 11 km to the southeast of Sagalassos. Nine clay samples were collected from the slopes in the immediate area around the village. They consisted of brown-yellow to dark red sedimentary-residual clays weathered from shales, with poor plasticity. Another site for sampling was closer to Sagalassos at about 8 km south of it, in the intramontane valley northwest of the village of Çanaklı which is full of lake-deposited clays. Previous research identified these clays as the raw materials used for the production of Sagalassos red slip wares (Viaene et al. 1995). Brown, green and red detrital clays with intercalated sandy material and some pebbles were collected from the plain. A fifth and last set of samples was taken from detrital clays present to the east of Sagalassos, in and around the valley of Köyünü and in the valleys of Ağlasun and Yazır (Fig. 1). Shortly before its complete

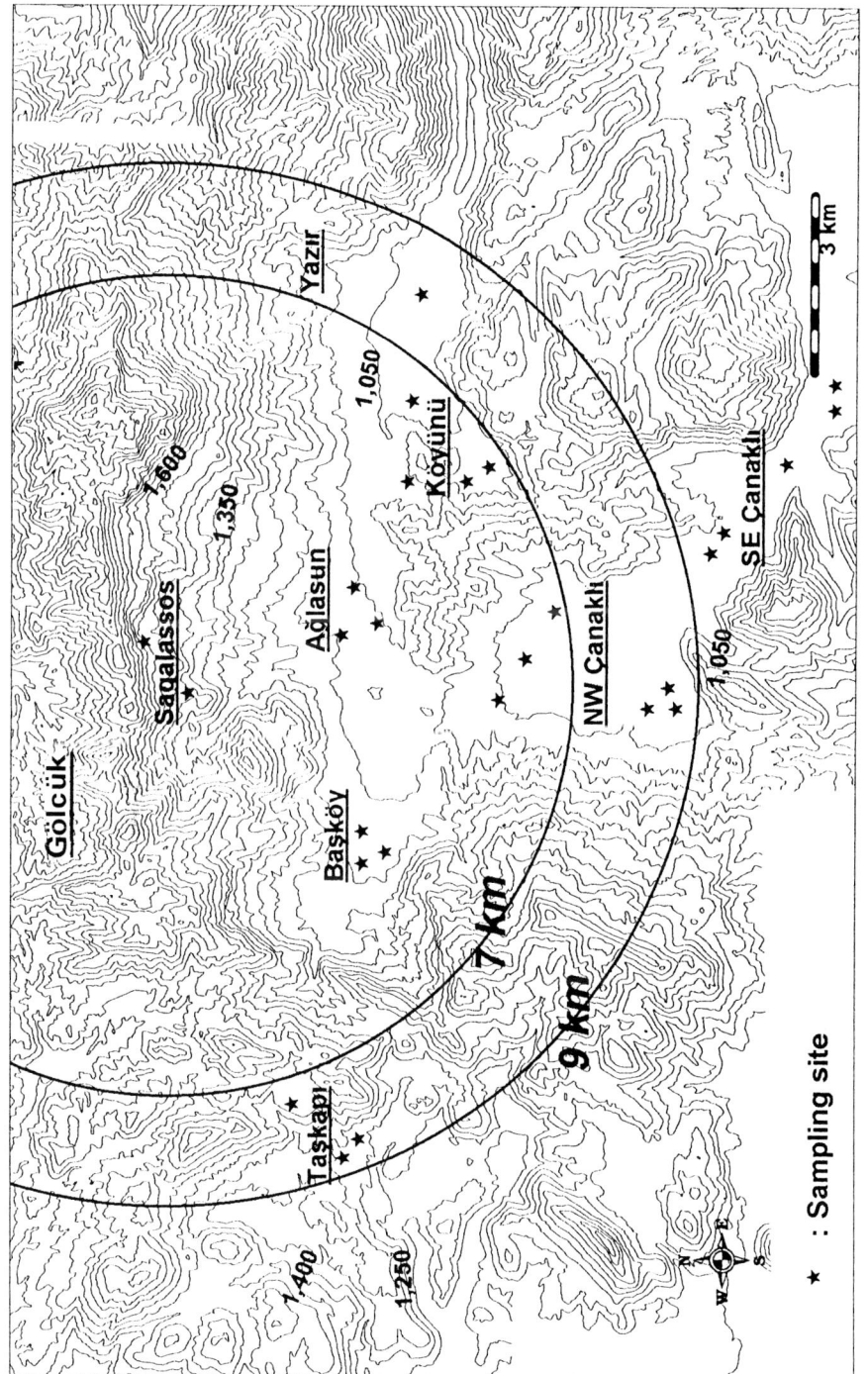

Fig. 1: Situation of Sagalassos and neighbouring villages; location of the possible sampled raw materials.

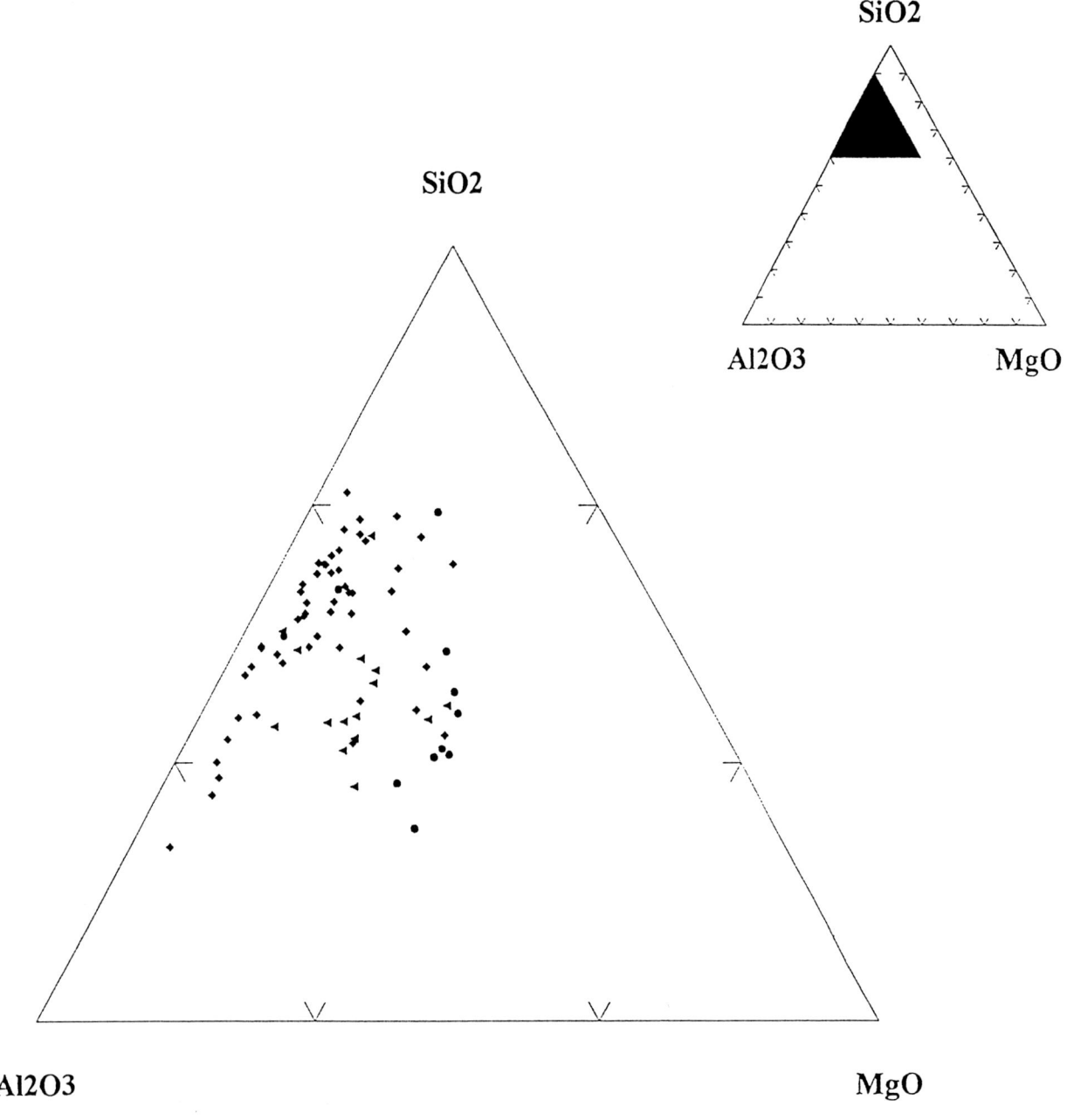

Fig. 2: Chemical signature of the Sagalassos common ware.
● Ware group 5
▲ Ware group 4
◆ Ware group 2

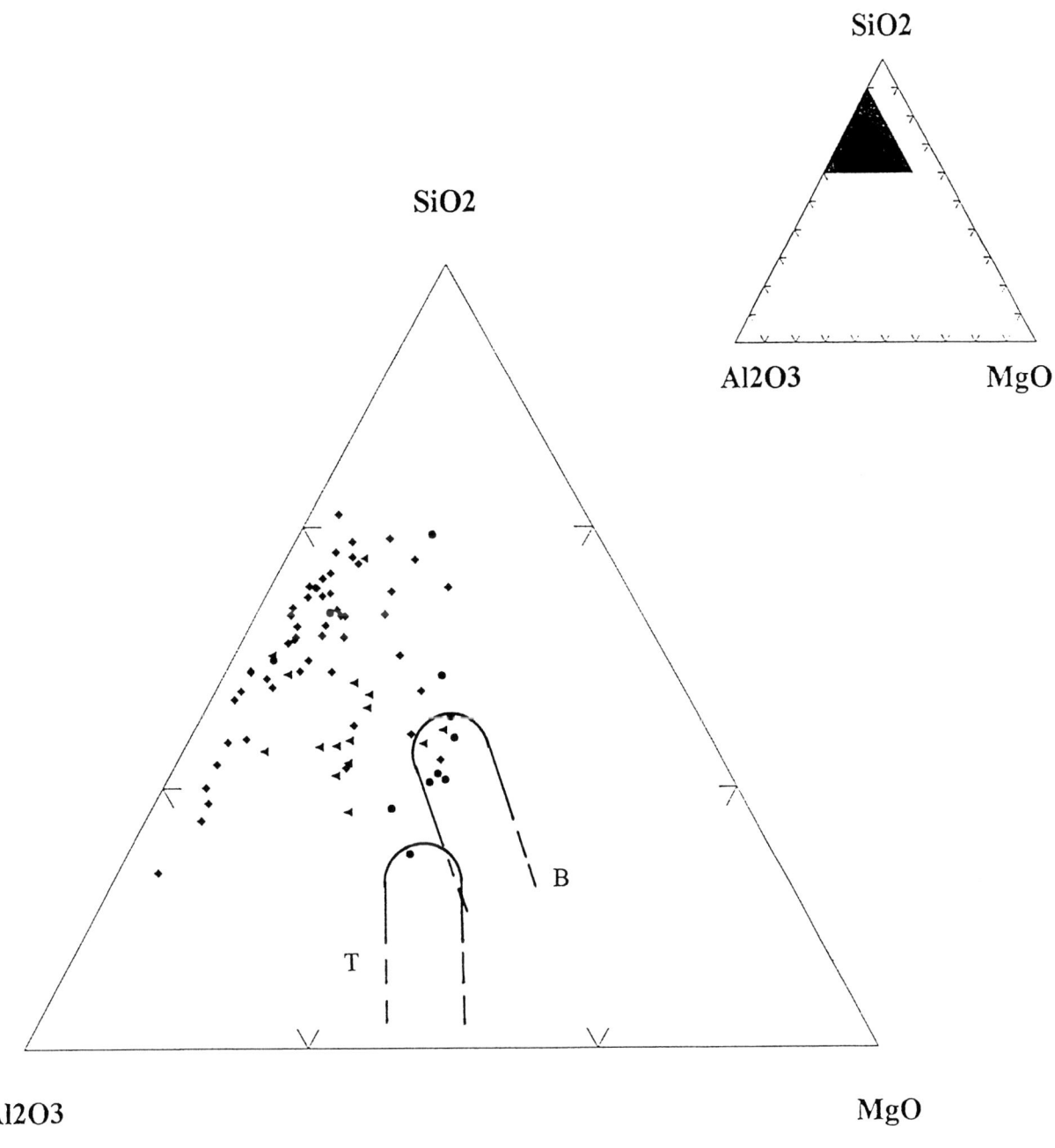

Fig. 3: Comparison between the chemistry of the clays of Başköy (B) and Taşkapı (T) and the common ware.

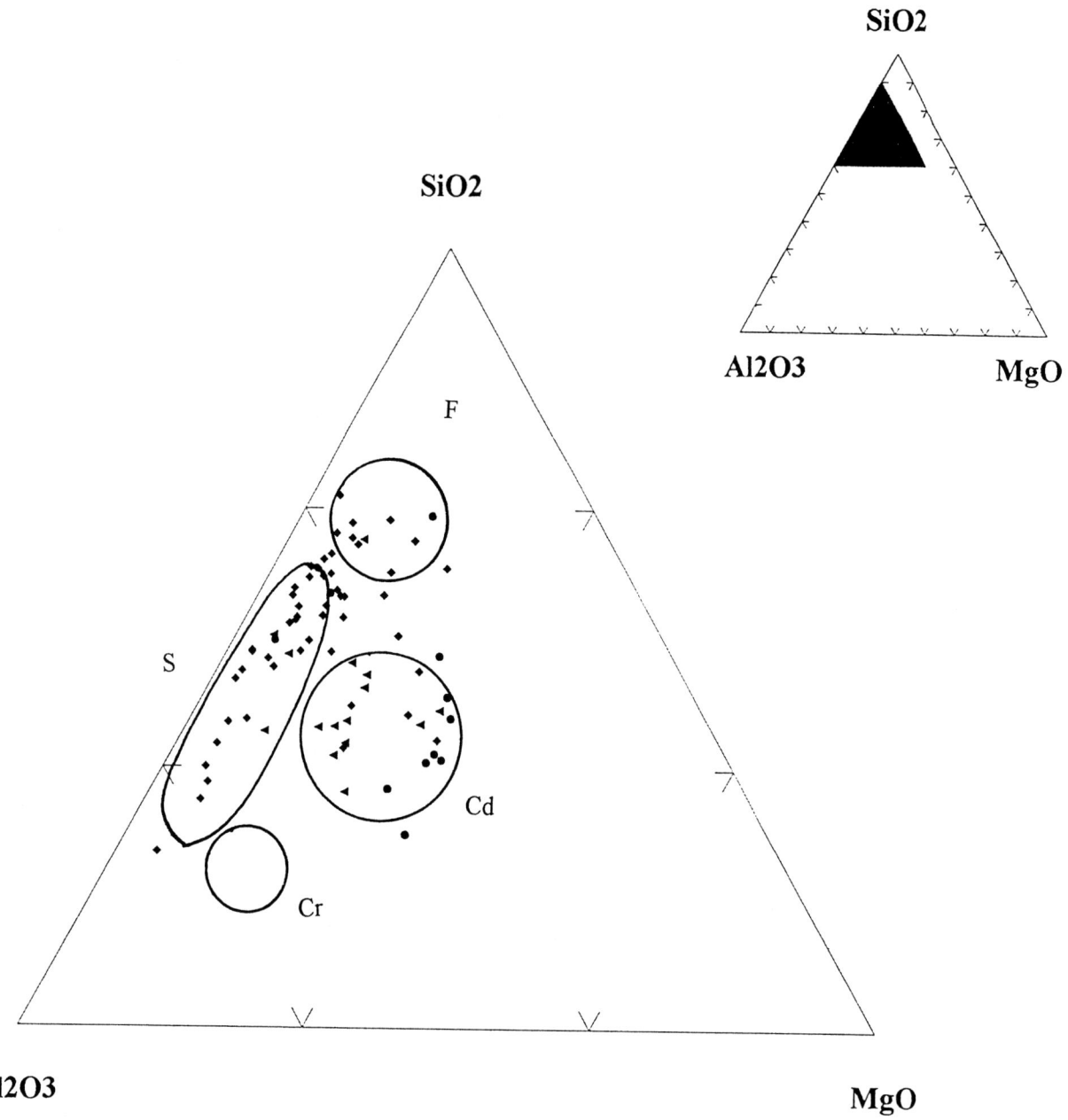

Fig. 4: Comparison between the chemistry of the clays from the site of Sagalassos (S), the clays from the flysch deposits at Köyünü (F) and the detrital (Cd) and sedimentary-residual (Cr) clays from Çanaklı.

destruction, the remains of a (pottery?) kiln were noted at Köyünü. The clays here are red to yellow detrital clays weathered from the flysch deposits in the area. They consist of clays from alluvial fans and terraces of a palaeo-river.

A total of 51 clay samples and 78 sherds has been analysed for their major elements (Table 1). When dry, the clay samples containing unweathered rock fragments were gently crushed and sieved to get rid of the fragments. The fraction smaller than 250 µm was used for analysis. A representative part of each sample was dissolved in a lithium metaborate flux, which was then dissolved in diluted HNO_3. Components of SiO_2, Al_2O_3, Fe_2O_3, MgO, CaO, P_2O_5 and TiO_2 were determined by AES. Na_2O and K_2O contents were measured from the same solution by means of AAS. For a valid comparison between clays and sherds, the chemical composition of the clays was recalculated by putting the sum of the non-volatile oxides equal to one hundred percent, since a large part of the volatile components of the clays disappear during firing and are no longer present in the resulting ceramics (Ottenburgs et al. 1993a). The mineralogical composition of the clays was determined by X-ray diffractometry (XRD). Operational parameters were as follows: Cu Ka radiation, graphite monochromator, 45 kV, 30 mA, automatic divergence slit, receiving slit of 0.1°. Optical analysis and quantitative image analysis was carried out with a Zeiss Axioskop optical microscope linked through a video camera to the image analysis system run by the Foster Findlay software package. Microprobe analysis were done at UCL (Louvain-la-Neuve, Prof. J. Naud) with a Cameca Camebax SX 50 microbeam electron microprobe with energy dispersive X-ray analysis system.

3. RESULTS OF THE MAIN ELEMENT ANALYSIS

A summary of the results is given in Table 1. With exception of the Loss On Ignition (LOI), all results are expressed as percentage weight of oxides. 78 sherds of Sagalassos common ware (groups 2, 4 and 5) were analysed. A ternary composition diagram of the common ware chemistry is given in Fig. 2. With this diagram the chemistry of the sherds can easily be compared with the chemistry of the possible raw materials, recalculated without the volatile components and LOI. An apparent (but not absolute) difference in MgO-content between the three different ware-groups (Fig. 2), could not be confirmed by the mineralogical data. Since no relevant geochemical separation could be made between the three waregroups, no distinction is made between them regarding the geochemical data. Fifty-one samples of clays taken from different locations (Fig. 1) are plotted in Figs 3 and 4 for a graphical comparison with the common wares.

In the different ternary diagrams we see that the chemical signature of the common ware does not correspond to the chemical signature of the clays from the villages of Başköy and Taşkapı (Fig. 3). Some samples of the clays correspond to some sherds of common ware, but this correspondence is always for different samples. In general, the clays of Taşkapı and Başköy have a low clay content (the Al_2O_3 content is low). Other differences with the common wares are the lower K_2O and Si_2O contents and the higher CaO content (possibly due to calcite veinlets present in the ophiolitic rocks). Hence, the correspondence can be regarded as coincidental and the clays of Taşkapı and Başköy are probably not the raw material for common ware production.

On the other hand, identical groups of sherds correspond with the chemical signatures of the clays from Sagalassos, Çanaklı and Köyünü/Ağlasun/Yazır (Fig. 4). The same sets of sherds always have the same chemical signature as a certain clay, either the clay from the site, the detrital clay from the northwest-Çanaklı plain or the clay weathered from the flysch in the Ağlasun-Köyünü-Yazır area. No sherds show a correspondence with the sedimentary-residual clays of southeast-Çanaklı. In addition, some sherds always fall between the chemical signatures of the ophiolitic clays of the potters' quarter at Sagalassos and the detrital clays of Çanaklı. Other sherds always fall between the chemical signature of the ophiolitic clays of the site and the clays weathered from the flysch. No sherds fall between the chemical signatures of the detrital clays of Çanaklı and the clays originating from the flysch. Hence, the common ware can be divided into three groups, each with their own geochemical signature. We have a group of sherds corresponding geochemically to the clays weathered from the flysch, a group of sherds corresponding to the detrital clays found near Çanaklı and a group of sherds corresponding to the ophiolitic clays of the site of Sagalassos. Moreover, we have two groups of sherds with a mixed chemical signature. All groups contain sherds of the three different waregroups.

From the chemical analysis, therefore, we have three clay raw materials that could have been used in the common wares. Further mineralogical study of the clays and the comparison of these data with the common wares enables a more conclusive identification of the use of these clays as a raw material and their relative importance in the production of the ceramics.

4. MINERALOGICAL ANALYSIS

The mineral content of the common ware and the clays was determined by XRD and by the study of thin sections. The ratios and percentages of the different minerals were determined visually and by image analysis.

4.1. Mineralogy of the non-clay materials in the common wares

The mineral content of each group of sherds with a typical chemical signature corresponding to a potential clay raw material was determined in a representative sample. For the group with the chemical signature of the clays weathered from the flysch the results of image analysis are given in Table 2, column 1. For quartz, large angular grains of 300 µm as well as small, rounded grains of 10 µm are found. For amphiboles and biotites large angular grains of 200 to 400 µm as well as small rounded (often heavily weathered) grains of 10 µm are found. The latter however are far more abundant than the amphiboles. The feldspars consist of K-feldspar and Ca-plagioclase, poor in Na. The rounded nodules in the sherds are probably balls (pebbles) of clay, formed during the preparation of the clay for shaping. Chert fragments and basalt clasts of up to 2 mm are also found, mostly as rounded grains. Magnetite, ilmenite, hematite, chromite, calcite, pyroxene and apatite are present in small amounts.

For the group with the chemical signature of the ophiolitic clays from the site of Sagalassos the results of image analysis are given in Table 2, column 2. For quartz, mostly large angular grains of up to 800 µm are found. Amphiboles and biotites are present in large amounts as idiomorphic crystals up to 800 µm. Entire biotite plates are preserved. The feldspar consists mainly of Ca-plagioclase with smaller amounts of K-feldspar. Chert fragments and basalt clasts present are large (up to 2 mm) and angular. Pyroxene, magnetite, ilmenite, chromite, hematite, calcite, apatite, diopside and perovskite were found in small amounts.

For the group with the chemical signature of the detrital clays from the northwest-Çanaklı plain the results of image analysis are given in Table 2, column 3. The grog consisting of crushed tableware is up to 2 mm. No grog of crushed common ware was observed. Large idiomorphic amphiboles, biotites and pyroxenes of up to 800 µm can be seen. Ca-plagioclase and K-feldspar as well as chert are present in large amounts. Quartz, magnetite, ilminite and diopside were found in small amounts.

The general characteristics of the minerals present in the sherds have also been studied. The amphiboles in the sherds are always the same, that is, ferro-hornblende, kaersutite and ferro-richterite. The amphiboles in sherds with a chemical signature comparable to the ophiolitic clays are always large and idiomorphic. In other sherds, smaller, rounded (weathered) crystals also occur. The same is true of the pyroxenes (always belonging to the augite/ferro-augite series) and the biotites in the sherds. The pyroxene/amphibole ratio is smaller in the sherds with the chemical signature of the ophiolitic clay than in sherds of a different signature. This is also true of the pyroxene/biotite ratio. The feldspars present in the sherds are plagioclases and Na-poor K-feldspars. In all sherds, apatite, magnetite, chromite and hematite are found, and occasionally perovskite, diopside and ilmenite. Clasts with a basaltic appearance are found in all sherds to some extent. They are similar to certain volcanic materials found near the Lake Gölcük, northwest of Sagalassos (Fig. 1). Their provenance however is uncertain. No limestone was added to the common wares. The calcite present in the sherds is due to the deposition of secondary $CaCO_3$ in the pores of the ceramics. The clay nodules in the sherds may represent the use and mixing of two different clay raw materials or may indicate a bad mixture of several layers from the same deposit. The chert fragments present in the sherds probably come from the silicified limestone present around the ophiolites. Fragments of this chert may be present through weathering and transport in the clays derived from the ophiolites. However, cherts were also found in the flysch deposits and in the clays derived from them. Their provenance thus remains unclear.

4.2. Clay sources

A general mineralogical characterisation was made of all the clays with a chemical signature similar to certain groups of common ware. For the ophiolitic clays from Sagalassos, the main clay mineral present is smectite with a smaller amount of chlorite and illite. The feldspars are mainly plagioclase and K-feldspar poor in Na. Large amounts of large, idiomorphic amphibole minerals (ferro-hornblende, ferro-richterite and ferro-pargasite, determined by XRD) and biotite crystals are present, together with small amounts of idiomorphic ferro-augite. Magnetite, ilmenite, chromite, hematite, diopside, apatite, perovskite and monazite are common.

For the clays from the flysch deposits in the area of Köyünü (Schrooten 1997), Ağlasun and Yazır, the main clay mineral is illite, with small amounts of smectite and kaolinite. Feldspars are mainly K-feldspar with lesser amounts of plagioclase. Rounded, small amphiboles and biotites are present in far smaller amounts than pyroxenes (small, rounded augite). Quartz is frequently found. Magnetite, chromite and ilmenite are minor or accessory minerals in these clays. It should be mentioned here that the flysch is in fact a weathering product of the ophiolitic sequences and the limestones in the area.

For the detrital clays from the Northwest-Çanaklı plain (Jorissen 1993; Ottenburgs et al. 1993a), the main clay minerals present are chlorite and mixed layers of chlorite/smectite with smaller amounts of illite and kaolinite. The feldspars are mainly plagioclases, with a smaller amount of K-feldspar. A large quartz fraction is present. Magnetite, hematite, calcite and dolomite are common minerals.

		n	SiO_2	Al_2O_3	Fe_2O_3	MnO	MgO	CaO	Na_2O	K_2O	TiO_2	P_2O_5	LOI
common ware	mean	78	58.24	17.04	7.15	0.13	2.92	4.91	1.15	2.85	0.85	0.34	3.75
	st.dev.		5.20	2.65	1.24	0.04	1.99	3.59	0.55	0.80	0.14	0.18	2.74
(LOI free bases)			60.92	17.82	7.48	0.14	3.05	5.14	1.20	2.98	0.89	0.36	-
ophiolitic clay	mean	7	54.62	17.99	6.18	0.18	2.45	4.24	1.96	3.98	0.81	0.22	6.18
	st.dev.		1.77	4.02	1.17	0.04	1.10	3.24	0.84	1.22	0.17	0.09	2.63
(LOI free bases)			58.93	19.41	6.67	0.19	2.64	4.57	2.11	4.29	0.87	0.24	-
Çanaklı clay													
detrital	mean	7	49.80	15.54	7.43	0.12	4.16	6.81	1.12	2.60	0.81	0.22	10.78
	st.dev.		2.87	1.98	0.49	0.02	1.16	2.27	0.61	0.66	0.03	0.07	2.47
(LOI free bases)			56.17	17.53	8.38	0.14	4.69	7.68	1.26	2.93	0.91	0.25	-
residual	mean	11	54.22	19.72	7.65	0.18	1.68	2.76	2.00	3.52	0.93	0.33	6.28
	st.dev.		2.90	2.28	1.58	0.03	0.93	2.09	0.50	0.74	0.11	0.24	1.56
(LOI free bases)			58.29	21.20	8.22	0.19	1.81	2.97	2.15	3.78	1.00	0.35	-
flysch clay	mean	8	58.70	14.20	6.28	0.16	2.41	4.59	1.73	2.96	0.71	0.18	7.37
	st.dev.		3.33	2.17	0.64	0.06	0.58	2.93	0.87	0.93	0.04	0.03	2.61
(LOI free bases)			63.81	15.44	6.83	0.17	2.62	4.99	1.88	3.22	0.77	0.20	-
Taşkapı clay	mean	6	48.88	14.04	6.85	0.14	5.20	14.28	2.05	0.88	0.54	1.66	4.74
	st.dev.		5.43	6.12	4.24	0.06	3.50	7.21	1.83	1.35	0.59	3.61	5.18
(LOI free bases)			51.67	14.84	7.24	0.15	5.50	15.09	2.17	0.93	0.57	1.75	-
Başköy clay	mean	12	48.67	10.36	6.64	0.13	6.82	11.12	2.01	1.26	0.62	0.40	11.25
	st.dev.		15.79	4.08	2.65	0.06	8.39	10.32	1.85	0.96	0.51	0.48	8.58
(LOI free bases)			55.24	11.76	7.54	0.15	7.74	12.62	2.28	1.43	0.70	0.45	-

Table 1: Analysis results for common ware and possible clay sources.

Mineral/phase	Estimated quantity (%)		
Signature	Flysch	Ophiolite	Northwest Çanaklı plain
porosity	25	15	15
	(% of temper)	(-): not present	
Feldspar	25	35	)
Quartz	5	5	)
Chert	15	5	in total 57
Basaltic clasts	14	15	)
Clay nodules	20	7	)
Grog	-	-	28
Biotite	1	7	2
Pyroxene	5	3	2
Amphibole	7	12	7
Opaque Minerals	3	5	2
Calcite	5	5	?
Apatite	<1	<1	-
Perovskite	-	<1	-

Table 2: Image analysis results for sherd 200 (ware group 4), having the chemical signature of the flysch deposits, for sherd 201 (ware group 5), having the chemical signature of the ophiolitic clay of the site and for sherd 62 (ware group 5), having the chemical signature of the detrital clays of Çanaklı. The % porosity is calculated on the total of the sherd and the total of temper minerals is taken as 100%.

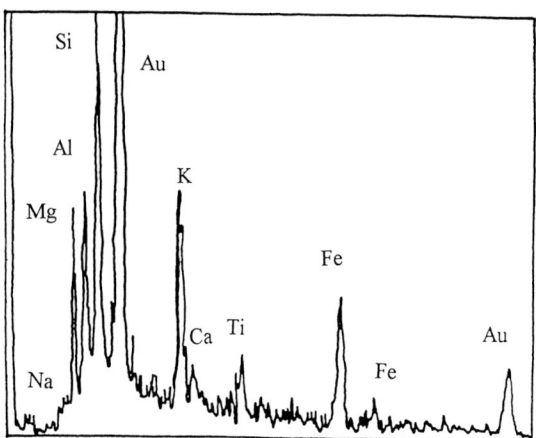

Fig. 5: Comparison between the chemistry of a biotite in common ware (sample Sag 200, ware group 4) and in the ophiolitic clay from the site of Sagalassos. (X-ray beam at 20 KeV.)
A: common ware (carbon coated); B: ophiolitic clay (gold coated)

Mineral		n	SiO_2	Al_2O_3	Fe_2O_3	MnO	MgO	CaO	Na_2O	K_2O	TiO_2
Amphibole	Mean	9	39.33	12.79	16.95	-	11.47	12.03	1.46	2.24	2.75
(Kaersutite)	St. Dev.		0.94	0.91	1.82	-	1.07	0.35	0.53	0.33	0.18
Biotite	Mean	6	42.92	18.36	14.67	0.34	10.63	0.58	0.18	7.73	3.39
	St. Dev.		9.07	6.36	5.42	0.43	7.59	0.6	0.13	2.72	1.84

Table 3: Microprobe analysis of amphiboles and biotites in Sagalassos common ware.

4.3. Geochemistry of the biotites and amphiboles

The chemical composition of the idiomorphic biotites in the sherds, with 4% of TiO_2 and no more than 0.5% CaO and 0.5% MnO, indicates an alkaline-peralkaline ophiolite as the parent-rock for the raw materials. The idiomorphic ferro-hornblende and ferro-richterite in the ceramics contains 2 to 3% of TiO_2 indicating an alkaline parent rock, such as the ophiolite from Sagalassos (Table 3). In addition, the amphiboles and biotites in the sherds and in the ophiolitic clays have an identical chemistry, as can be seen in Fig. 5. The same elements are present in the same proportions. The difference in background is due to the difference in coating of the samples.

5. DISCUSSION

If we compare the different possible clay resources with the different groups of common ware (based on their chemical signatures), we see that the mineralogy of a particular sherd corresponds to the mineralogy of the clay resource of which it has the chemical signature. In some cases, we are probably dealing with mixes of raw materials. Looking at the sherds with the chemical signature of the ophiolitic clay from Sagalassos, we observe a practically identical mineralogy with the clays: large idiomorphic biotites, large idiomorphic crystals of amphiboles and pyroxenes, the presence of apatite and perovskite, a low pyroxene/amphibole ratio (smaller than in other signatures) and a large proportion of plagioclase in the feldspar content. This similarity strongly supports the idea that clays from the site have been used in the production of Sagalassos common wares.

Looking at the sherds with the chemical signature of the clays derived from the flysch, we see certain mineralogical characteristics of the ophiolitic clays from the site, but also certain characteristics of the clays from the flysch taken at Köyünü, Yazır and Ağlasun. We observe a smaller proportion of plagioclase, a higher pyroxene/amphibole ratio and the presence of small, rounded (weathered) crystals of all minerals, together with large idiomorphic crystals of the same minerals. These features point to the mixing of these clay materials for the production of Sagalassos common wares.

Looking at the sherds with the chemical signature of the detrital clays from Çanaklı, we see all the mineralogical characteristics of the ophiolitic clays of Sagalassos with the addition of grog in the ceramics. This points to the use of the ophiolitic clays from the site with the addition of large amounts of grog from crushed Sagalassos red slip ware. The addition of a grog derived from the local tableware gave a result partially consonant with the chemical signature of the detrital clays from Çanaklı, from which the red slip wares were made (Ottenburgs et al. 1993a; Viaene et al. 1995).

The sherds with a mixed chemical signature can hence be formed through the greater or lesser addition of grog or of flysch clay as a temper. The addition of volcanic material as a temper has no clear effect on the chemical signatures, but such an effect cannot be ruled out. It could be the cause of small variations within the different groups of (mixed) chemical signatures. The absence of sherds with a chemical signature derived from a mixture of clay from the flysch and detrital clay from Çanaklı indicates that the ophiolitic clay of Sagalassos was used continuously throughout our period. This is confirmed by the mineralogy of the pottery. Also, the geochemistry of the large idiomorphic biotites and amphiboles in the sherds indicates an ophiolitic parent rock for these minerals, such as the ophiolite which forms the bedrock at Sagalassos.

Ware-groups 2 and 5 supply sherds corresponding to the chemical signatures and mineralogy of all three chemical/mineralogical groups. The ceramics of ware group 4 show only a small addition of grog in their chemical signature and mineralogy. So far no chronological patterns can be discerned in the use of different clays and tempers through the evolution of the common wares.

All these materials used for the production of common ware can be found close to the production site in the potters' quarter, situated immediately to the east of Sagalassos. This gives these sources a high economic value because of the low energy cost of exploitation and transportation. All the materials which have been proposed as clay sources of common ware fall mostly within the optimum distance for economically profitable exploitation as proposed by Arnold (1985).

6. CONCLUSION

A comparison of the chemical composition of Sagalassos common ware and its potential clay sources and of the mineralogy of these same materials permits us to conclude that the common ware was mainly produced from the residual clays derived from the weathered ophiolite found at the site of Sagalassos. Clay derived from the flysch deposits around Sagalassos and/or a grog of Sagalassos red slip ware and/or volcanic material has been added to temper the material. All the materials used as a resource for the common ware fall within the distance proposed by Arnold (1985) as a maximum for the exploitation of raw materials. The fact that the potters of Sagalassos continuously exploited raw material present in the potters' quarter itself for the production of their common wares also helps to explain why they never moved their activities closer to the detritic clays which they exploited for manufacturing tablewares. In fact, the quantities of clay used for the latter ware-type, mostly smaller pieces, must have been far surpassed by the amounts of clay needed for the medium to large sized coarse wares. The ophiolitic clay from the site of Sagalassos can be seen as the most important raw material for the production of Sagalassos common ware from its chemistry, the presence of large idiomorphic crystals of amphiboles and biotites with a defined composition and the presence of the same trace minerals (perovskite, apatite, diopside, chromite, magnetite, ilmenite, hematite). These features are observed in both the sherds and the clays at Sagalassos. The chemistry, the lack of large, well-preserved idiomorphic crystals, the depletion in loss of easily weathered minerals and the lack of several trace minerals all indicate that the clay derived from the flysch deposits sampled around Köyünü, Ağlasun and Yazır was used as a temper in some ceramics and not for the main raw material. The addition of grog derived from Sagalassos red slip ware can clearly be seen in the sherds with the geochemical signature of the detrital clays of Çanaklı. The addition of volcanic material resembling the volcanic material from Gölçük is also observed in several sherds. From this study, it is clear that mineralogical data from common and trace minerals such as amphiboles and biotites prove to be of great value in explaining geochemical data and more importantly in defining the provenance of clay raw materials for the production of ceramics in general.

7. ACKNOWLEDGEMENTS

This research is supported by the Belgian Programme on Interuniversitary Poles of Attraction (IUAP 4/12) initiated by the Belgian State, Prime Minister's Office, Science Policy Programming. This paper also presents the results of the Concerted Action of the Flemish Government (GOA 97/2) and the Fund for Scientific Research-Flanders (Belgium) (FWO) (G.2145.94). Scientific responsibility is assumed by the authors. J. Poblome is postdoctoral Fellow of the Fund for Scientific Research -Flanders (Belgium) (FWO). The authors sincerely thank S. Lens and D. Coetermans for the geochemical analysis, D. Steeno for the technical assistance and H. Nijs for the preparation of the thin sections.

8. REFERENCES

D. Arnold (1985) *Ceramic Theory and Cultural Process*, Cambridge.
R. Degeest (2000) *The Common Wares of Roman Sagalassos* (Studies in Eastern Mediterranean Archaeology 3) Brepols publishers.
R. Degeest and M. Waelkens (1993) Sagalassos ware II. The common ware, in: M. Waelkens (ed.) *Sagalassos I. First General Report on the Survey (1986-1989) and Excavations (1990- 1991)* (Acta Archaeologica Lovaniensia Monographiae 5) Leuven University Press: 131-152.
R. Degeest, R. Ottenburgs, W. Viaene, H. Kucha, D. Laduron, A. Bocquet and M. Waelkens (1997) Characterization of the common wares manufactured in Roman Sagalassos. An overview, in: M. Waelkens and J. Poblome (eds) *Sagalassos IV. Report on the Survey and Excavation Campaigns of 1994 and 1995* (Acta Archaeologica Lovaniensia Monographiae 9) Leuven University Press: 519-532.
E.S. Higgs and C. Vita-Finzi (1972) Prehistoric economies: a territorial approach, in: E. S. Higgs (ed.) *Papers in Economic Prehistory*, Cambridge: 27-46.
M.R. Jarman (1972) A territorial model for archaeology: a behavioural and geographical approach, in: D.L. Clarke (ed.) *Models in Archaeology*, London: 705-733.
M.R. Jarman, C. Vita-Finzi and E.S. Higgs (1972) Site catchment analysis in archaeology, in: P.J. Ucko, R. Tringham and G.W. Dymbleby (eds) *Man, Settlement and Urbanism*, Boston: 61-66.
C. Jorissen (1993) *Karakterisering van kleigrondstoffen nabij Sagalassos (Ağlasun, Zuid- Turkije) en hun relatie met archeologische keramiek*, Unpublished M.Sc. thesis, KULeuven.
H. Kucha (1995) *Ceramics of Sagalassos: their Mineralogy and Trace Element Chemistry*, Unpublished internal report.
S. Mitchell, M. Waelkens and E. Owens (1989) Ariassos and Sagalassos 1988, *Anatolian Studies* 39: 74-77.
R. Ottenburgs, C. Jorissen and W. Viaene (1993a) Sagalassos ware IV. Study of the clays, in: M. Waelkens (ed.) *Sagalassos I. First General Report on the Survey (1986-1989) and Excavations (1990-1991)* (Acta Archaeologica Lovaniensia Monographiae 5) Leuven University Press: 163- 169.
R. Ottenburgs, W. Viaene and C. Jorissen (1993b) Mineralogy and firing properties of clays at and near the archaeological site of Sagalassos, in: M. Waelkens and J. Poblome (eds) *Sagalassos II. Report on the Third Excavation Campaign of 1992* (Acta Archaeologica Lovaniensia Monographiae 6) Leuven University Press: 209-220.
J. Poblome, R. Degeest, M. Waelkens and E. Scheltens (1993) Sagalassos Ware I. The fine ware, in: M. Waelkens (ed) *Sagalassos I. First Report on the Survey and Excavations (1990-1931)* (Acta Archaeologica Lovaniensia Monographiae 5) Leuven University Press: 113-130.
J. Poblome (1996) Production and distribution of Sagalassos red slip ware. A dialogue with the Roman economy, in: M. Herfort-Koch, U. Mandel and U. Schädler (eds) *Hellenistische und kaiserzeitliche Keramik des östlichen Mittelmeergebietes*, Frankfurt am Main: 75-103.
J. Poblome (1999) *Sagalassos Red Slip Ware. Typology and Chronology* (Studies in Eastern Mediterranean Archaeology 2) Brepols publishers.
J. Poblome, H. A. Ekinci, I. Öztürk, P. Degrijse, W. Viaene (†) and M. Waelkens (2000) An early Byzantine tile and lime kiln in the territory of Sagalassos, in: M. Waelkens and L. Loots (eds) *Sagalassos V. Report on the Survey and Excavation Campaigns of 1996 and 1997 (Acta Archaeologica Lovaniensia Monographiae 11)* Leuven University Press 669-684.
O.S. Rye (1976) Keeping your temper under control: materials and the manufacture of Papuan pottery, *Archaeology and Physical Anthropology in Oceania* 11: 106-137.
E. Scheltens (1993) Some wheelmade lamps of Sagalassos. A preliminary note, in: M. Waelkens and J. Poblome (eds) *Sagalassos II. Report on the Third Excavation Campaign of 1992 (Acta Archaeologica Lovaniensia Monographiae 6)* Leuven University Press: 191-208.
P. Schrooten (1997) *Ofiolietgesteenten te Sagalassos (Turkije): voorkomen, alteratie, verwering en relatie met keramiek*, Unpublished M.Sc. thesis, KULeuven.
A.O. Shepard (1956) Ceramic technology, *Carnegie Institution of Washington Yearbook* 51: 263-266.
W. Viaene, J. Poblome, R. Ottenburghs, H. Kucha, J. Hertogen, C. Vynckier, M. Waelkens and D. Laduron (1995) Geochemical distribution of trace elements in Sagalassos red slip ware, in: M. Waelkens and J. Poblome (eds) *Sagalassos III. Report on the Fourth Excavation Campaign of 1993* (Acta Archaeologica Lovaniensia Monographiae 7) Leuven University Press: 245-254.
M. Waelkens (1992) Die neuen Forschungen (1985-1989) und die belgischen Ausgrabungen (1990-1991) in Sagalassos, in: E. Schwertheim (ed.) *Forschungen in Pisidien* (Asia Minor Studien 6) Münster: 43-60.
M. Waelkens (1995) Rise and fall of Sagalassos, *Archaeology* May/June 1995: 28-34.

PART VI

ENVIRONMENTAL STUDIES

TOWARDS A LAND EVALUATION OF THE TERRITORY OF ANCIENT SAGALASSOS

Kristien DONNERS[1], Marc WAELKENS[2], David CELIS[1], Kris NACKAERTS[1],
Jozef DECKERS[1], Marleen VERMOERE[3] and Hannelore VANHAVERBEKE[2]

1 - Institute for Land and Water Management, KULeuven, Vital Decosterstraat 102, B-3000 Leuven
2 - Department of Archaeology, KULeuven, Blijde Inkomststraat 21, B-3000 Leuven
3 - Laboratory of Plant Systematics, KULeuven, Kardinaal Mercierlaan 92, B-3001 Heverlee

1. INTRODUCTION

This study is integrated within the framework of a general interdisciplinary investigation of the territory of Sagalassos (Waelkens and the Sagalassos Team 1997) and intends to throw light on the agricultural situation in ancient times. In order to make an agricultural assessment of the area in the past, a thorough insight in the present situation is important. From the present setting an attempt is made to refer to the past. Field interpretation focussed on a selected pilot area, with the question of where, during Hellenistic-Roman times, fertile soils could have been located for the two most important types of land use: arable farming and forestry. In the knowledge that soils represent a unique source of information about the palaeo-environment, a particular attention was paid to the palaeo-soil scape. Soil information in combination with knowledge of climate, vegetation and geomorphology served as a base to estimate the potential crop production in antiquity.

2. MATERIALS AND METHODS

2.1. The setting

The study area covered some 5600 ha of land, located in between the villages of Başköy, Çanaklı, Yazır and Ağlasun. North of it graces the mountaintop of the Akdağ (2271 m), which forms part of the Western Taurus belt. Three valleys interrupt the hills, all located at a height of 1050 m: the valley of Ağlasun, the valley of Çanaklı and the valley of Köyünü. Köyünü, a small valley to the southeast of Ağlasun, where since 5 years clay has been quarried for the construction of a dam (further, this place is referred to as 'Quarry'), forms a unique location for investigating deep soil profile exposures.

2.2. The land use survey

Preliminary to the fieldwork following baseline information was compiled:

2.2.1. Maps

Existing geological maps (Poisson 1984; Schrooten 1997) of the region were consulted in order to obtain an overall idea of parent materials. Since the scale of the existing soil map of the area is too small (*Soil Map of the World*, scale 1/5.000.000, *FAO-Unesco* 1978 and *Soil map of Turkey*, scale 1/80.000, Oakes 1954), a more detailed soil map of the pilot zone was made during the survey.

2.2.2. Climatic data

Climatic data of the weather station of Isparta were used for the land evaluation in the study area because of its rather comparable agro-ecological setting. Figs 1 and 2 illustrate respectively the rainfall and the temperature regime. The area is characterised by a Xeric moisture regime (USDA 1998), characterised by a wet season in winter and spring and by a dry season during the summer.

Temperatures in Mediterranean Turkey show a linear decrease corresponding with the altitude. For the mean annual temperature this decrease is expressed by the following temperature-altitude (< 2000 m) relationship (Akman and Daget 1971; Paulissen et al. 1993):

$$T_m = 18.74 - 0.0059h \text{ (with } r^2 = 0.89);$$

in which: T_m = mean annual temperature in °C
h = altitude above sea level.

For Isparta (h = 1050m) the calculated mean annual temperature of 12.5 °C compares well with the measured value of 12 °C. In August the mean temperature is 22 °C, compared to 28 °C for Antalya. Minimum temperatures in January and February are below zero and possible frost periods may occur from October until April.

The standard method of FAO was used to calculate evapotranspiration (ETo) by making use of the formula of Penman-Monteith (Allen *et al.* 1998).

2.3. The soil survey

During the land use survey in August 1996, the soil profiles were investigated and described according to the *FAO Guidelines for Soil Profile Description* (*FAO* 1990). Special attention was paid to Munsell soil colour, soil texture and soil structure, stoniness, carbonate, manganese nodules, organic matter and phosphate content. Three representative soil profile pits were formally described and sampled for chemical and physical analysis. The soils were classified according to the FAO/Unesco legend of the *Soil Map of the World* (*FAO* 1990).

2.4. Laboratory procedures

The samples taken from the various profiles were subjected to the following types of analysis:

2.4.1. Granulometry

Following the Atterberg method, granulometry was determined in the following fractions: percentages of clay (< 2°μm), silt (2-50°μm) and sand (> 50°μm).

2.4.2. Hydro-physical analysis of undisturbed samples

- Water retention characteristic was analysed on sandbox for pF 0; 0.5; 1.0; 1.5; 2.0 and in Richardsplate for pF values of 2.3; 2.8; 3.4 and 4.2.
- Saturated hydraulic conductivity: by means of the ICW perimeter (in a closed system) (*ILRI* 1980).
- Total available soil moisture was calculated as the amount of water held between the field capacity (pF = 2.3) and the permanent wilting point (pF = 4.2), i.e. the water available for a crop in mm per meter soil depth. Furthermore bulk density (g/cm^3) and porosity (%) were also determined.

2.4.3. Chemical analysis included the following:

- The pH (soil reaction) was measured in water and in KCl (in a 1:2.5 soil-water extract)
- Amorphous oxides. The content of amorphous iron and aluminium oxides (in mg/100 g soil) was determined, since this content is a good indicator of the soils stocking capacity of phosphor in acid conditions.
- Cation Exchange Capacity (CEC) was measured in a 1 N ammonium acetate percolation at pH 7. The content of exchangeable basic cations Ca^{2+}, Mg^{2+}, Na^+ and K^+ was determined by atom absorption spectro-photometry.
- Base Saturation (BS) or the ratio of the sum of exchangeable cations to CEC in %.
- Electrical conductivity (mmhos/cm). The electrical conductivity was measured in a soil/water extract of 1:5.
- Free sulphate (mg/l) was measured with the "continuous flow system" on 1:5 soil-water solution
- Organic C matter. The organic matter content was determined by means of wet oxidation (K_2CrO_7) in acid condition (H_2SO_4) (Walkey-Black-method).
- The total nitrogen percentage was measured by titration (Kjeldahl-method).
- The total phosphorous content (in ppm) was measured after destruction by means of "inductive coupled plasma spectrophotometry".
- C/N ratio. The relation of the organic matter percentage to the total N-percentage results in the C/N ratio.

2.5. Selection of potential land use types and definition of their requirements in Hellenistic-Roman times

Compared with present day land evaluation, each scholar working in an archaeological perspective has to face two major problems. On the one hand one needs to find out which crops or tree species could be or were cultivated in the target area in antiquity. On the other hand one has to establish the specific requirements of each species that was grown at that time. However, data about the requirements of present day varieties may be a starting point.

2.5.1. Arable farming

Cereals

Theoretically, and if present-day distributions can be taken as a reference, the territory of Sagalassos could have incorporated stands of wild progenitors of several domesticated cereals.

Wild barley, *Hordeum spontaneum*, which does not tolerate extreme cold, and which is only occasionally found above 1500 m, has, apart from that, quite a wide ecological range. It occurs in southeastern Turkey, the hilly parts of Iraq and the slopes of the Zagros and in Iran, where it occurs as a weed. Scattered throughout the same area are also stands of wild barley in primary habitats. The wild barley found a.o. in western Anatolia occurs in secondary, disturbed habitats (Harlan and Zohary 1966: 1076-1077).

Two distinct eco-geographic races of wild einkorn are found nowadays: a small, usually one-seeded race (*Triticum boeoticum* sp. *aegilopoides* or *Triticum aegilopoides*) which is characteristic for the Balkans and western Anatolia; and a much larger two-seeded race (*Triticum boeoticum* sp. *thaoudar* or *T. thaoudar*) found in southern Turkey, Iraq and Iran. If we disregard regions where wild einkorn is found only as a weed of disturbed habitats, the evidence leads to the Taurus-Zagros arc, this time with Palestine omitted. Wild einkorn seems most at home in southeastern Turkey (Harlan and Zohary 1966: 1078).

Emmer is not a weedy plant and is rather demanding in its requirements. Two races occur in the wild, *Triticum dicoccoides*, which is confined to the Near Eastern 'arc' and *Triticum araraticum*, which has a more northeasterly distribution: it is spread over eastern Turkey, western Iran, northern Iraq and Soviet Transcaspia. It was the former which played a part in the origin of cultivated emmer (Harlan and Zohary 1966: 1079; Zohary 1989: 361-2).

Helbaek's analysis of the Hacılar botanical remains revealed domesticated emmer (*Triticum dicoccum*), wild einkorn (*Triticum boeoticum*), domesticated naked six-row barley (*Hordeum vulgare* var. *nudum*) and hulled two-row barley (*Hordeum distichon*) in the Aceramic Neolithic levels (Helbaek 1970: 189). The principal ceramic Neolithic and Chalcolithic food plants included umbellate goat-face grass (*Aegilops umbellulata*), which is a wild cereal-, wild einkorn, domesticated einkorn (*Triticum monococcum*), domesticated emmer, bread wheat (*Triticum aestivum*), hulled two-row and six-row barley and naked six-row barley (95% of all barley samples) (Helbaek 1970: 214). Among these Neolithic and Chalcolithic samples, barley constituted 45% of the plant remains and wheat 40% (Helbaek 1970: 196). The later appearance of hulled six-row barley (*Hordeum vulgare*) in the Early Chalcolithic is according to Helbaek probably linked with irrigation agriculture, as is the appearance of bread wheat (Helbaek 1970: 214-215, 218, 222).

Few plant remains were recovered during the other prehistoric excavation in the area, at Kuruçay. Botanical plant remains were only found in its Late Chalcolithic levels. The major cereals were emmer and hulled six-row barley (Nesbitt 1996: 90, 134-7).

Some of the cereals were thus possibly present in their wild form in the territory of Sagalassos (wild einkorn and possibly wild barley). Wild emmer occurs more to the east. The question whether it was in Southwestern Turkey that some of the domesticates originated, has to remain open. Recent genetic research seems to support a monophyletic origin for emmer, einkorn, lentil, chickpea and pea (Zohary 1989, 1996). Zohary concludes that the available data appear to support the hypothesis that the development of agriculture in Southwestern Asia was triggered in each crop by a single domestication event or at most by very few such events.

Soon after the first non-shattering and easily germinating cereals, pulses and flax appeared, their superior performance under cultivation became decisive, and there was no need for repeated domestication of the wild progenitors. Moreover, because this new system of crop cultivation expanded quite rapidly, there was little chance for agriculture to develop independently in different places (Zohary 1996: 156; Uerpmann 1996: 232). However, it remains an open question whether all these crops were taken into cultivation together in the same place, or whether different crops were domesticated in different places within Southwestern Asia (Zohary 1996: 156).

By Roman times, grain had become the main agricultural crop of Roman Anatolia as is attested in many literary sources (Sartre 1995: 272). Moreover, cereals also formed the largest part of the ancient diet, perhaps representing even 70-75% of it. Because of transport problems, certainly for inland sites, these cereals were almost entirely of local production (Foxhall and Forbes 1982; Jongman 1988: 78). However, this does not exclude the fact that in Anatolia grain was transported along the main roads as a tax contribution from inland communities to Rome, whereby transport costs could also be reckoned as part of the tax liability to others. The destination of this grain seems to have been the Roman army in the East (Mitchell 1993: 250-255).

During the Roman period four important groups of crops were cultivated: barley, wheat, rye and millet (White 1970). In general, the studied area certainly does not lend itself for rye (*Secale cereale*) production because of such constraints as water logging in wintertime and a long-lasting snow cover. Yet, around the middle of this century, rye was grown on poor, stony fields near Isparta (de Planhol 1958: 151). Soils, that were not suitable for barley and wheat, because of their low fertility, such as the eroded hills of Campania (Italy) for instance, sometimes were cultivated with millet (*Panicum miliaceum*) (Hyams 1976). This may also have been the case in parts of Anatolia. According to Galen people around Pergamon used low-grade cereals in place of wheat and barley, where the land or the climate was unfavourable to them. Even today, millet is grown abundantly in this region (Mitchell 1993: 168-169). The rich profiles in the study area around Sagalassos however, usually did not require such as second-class crops.

Most probably cereals formed also the most important part of the diet of Sagalassos' urban and rural population. A lot of these must have been eaten as bread which is still the case today, but boiled cereals (bulgur), at present very popular in the rural areas, particularly during the winter months (de Planhol 1958: 176-177), were prepared already in Roman times as well (Mitchell 1993: 168).

It is still extremely difficult to assess the exact size of Sagalassos' population. As the numbers of soldiers which the larger cities (Selge, Etenna, Termessos) during the fourth and third century BC could mobilise show, Pisidia was a substantial reservoir of population already in early Hellenistic times (Mitchell 1993: 71). During the Roman imperial period, the size and presumably the population of the cities of the eastern provinces was more differentiated than before. In the early imperial period one to two dozen cities may have crossed the 100,000 inhabitants threshold but even middle ranking cities did not show a preponderance in any of the eastern provinces (Woolf 1997: 5). Few cities of inland Anatolia will have contained more than 25,000 or 30,000 inhabitants, and most were much smaller, falling in a range between 5000 and 15,000 (Mitchell 1993: 187, 244). However, there also was an important rural population living in villages or isolated farmsteads. The surveys in the territory of Sagalassos have revealed that this certainly was also the case there and that the settlement pattern in Roman and early Byzantine times was even denser than it is today (Waelkens et al. 1997). This corresponds very well with the *Novellae* (24) of Justinian which mention, as late as even the sixth century AD, "large villages with many inhabitants" in Pisidia. It is known from Roman Egypt that some of its villages even approached the smaller metropolei as far as their population numbers were concerned (Woolf 1997: 5). So, throughout the classical period, there were certainly many mouth to feed in Sagalassos and in its territory. Except for some imported species of marine and fresh water fishes (Van Neer et al. 2000), most of this people's subsistence must have been produced locally.

The two main cereal types from antiquity, wheat and barley were certainly grown in the fertile Sagalassos area. This is shown by the fact that in 189 BC the Sagalassians were able to pay 40,000 measures of wheat and the same amount of barley to the troops of Cn. Manlius Vulso (Livy XXXVIII,15.9). There is no reason to assume that during the Roman period this production would have changed drastically. Recent palynological research in the area (Vermoere et al. 2000) indicates also an important cultivation of olives and walnuts in Roman times but the same pollen diagrams show that this cultivation was already widespread since the Hellenistic period. Moreover, one of the most important developments in Anatolia during the early imperial period seems to have been the enormous expansion of cereal agriculture. However, because of the presence of much spare land in the rural areas and a probable improvement of cultivation methods and grain types, an enlargement of the scale of cereal farming in many areas must not have caused necessarily a conflict with the cultivation of olives and walnuts or with pastoralism (Mitchell 1993: 241, 245, 257).

At Sagalassos, faunal remains indicate an increase in cattle throughout the Roman period (until ca. 400 AD). Many of these animals may have been kept as draught animals, for transportation purposes for instance (Waelkens and the Sagalassos team 1997). Therefore, their increase does not necessarily mean an expansion of farming. However de Planhol's study of our district, around the middle of this century, showed that the possibilities of cattle breeding were then closely linked to that of farming because of feeding problems (de Planhol 1958: 163).

In any case, the expansion of the city in the Roman period and its growing population must have required at least to some extent a growing agricultural output, and possibly also a better cereal production. On the other hand the palynological research mentioned above suggests, for imperial times a more varied type of farming, including a better developed cultivation of olives and walnuts. Despite these cultures, cereals remained certainly one of the main crops of the district. Ears of corn featuring on various third century AD coins of Sagalassos even document for that period the role which the city played in the *annona* (provisions) system of the Roman troops in the East (Waelkens 1993: 39; Weiss 1992: 159-163). Part of it, including the costs of the initial track of the transport, may have been sent as a tax contribution. The terms used in the Tiberian regulation for requisitioned transport from the territory of Sagalassos imply that already then the city had to support with wagons and pack animals official convoys crossing the Sagalassos territory (Mitchell 1993: 247). Yet, there is sufficient evidence that requisitioned grain for the army was also supplemented by grain purchased at official prices (Mitchell 1993: 251), so that its suppliers could also profit from their sales.

Normally, barley is most suitable to obtain high yields for Mediterranean conditions. In fact this crop is less demanding than wheat (Garnsey 1985). It was, however, bulkier and heavier and therefore more difficult to transport over long distances (Jongman 1988: 81). This explains why in the case of famine, wheat was the preferred crop to alleviate food shortages by means of long-distance transport (Rathbone 1983).

Both winter and summer barley (*Hordeum vulgare*) must probably have been grown by the farmers of Sagalassos. Columella (II 9, 16), who wrote towards the end of the Julio-Claudian period, mentioned a two-row variety of barley originating from Galatia. Because, under the Julio-Claudians, Sagalassos was still part of the *provincia Galatia* (Devijver and Waelkens to be published in Sagalassos VI), there is a fair chance that this variety was available there as well. It required however, the richest soils and had to be sown in cool conditions, during the months of March. According to the same author six-row barley was suitable for loose, very

	Class of Landuse assessment wheat (Triticum aestivium)				
Land characteristic	S1	S2	S3	N1	N2
Length of growing period (days)					
summerwheat	120-145				other values
winterwheat	180-250				other values
Climate					
1. Precipitation growing season (mm)	350-1250	250-1500	200-1750		other values
2. Monthly precipitation (mm)					
a) vegetative period	20-120	>12	>8		other values
b) florescence	30-120	>15	>10		other values
c) ripening	30-120	10-150			other values
3. Mean temperature (°C)					
a) vegetative period	6 to 18	4 to 24	2 to 28		other values
b) florescence	12 to 26	10 to 32	8 to 36		other values
c) ripening	14 to 30	12 to 36	10 to 42		other values
4. Mean min. T of coldest month (°C)	<8	>8	<13		
with certain mean max.T	if	if	if		other values
of coldest month (°C)	<21	<21	>21		
5. Light intensity	clear	clouded			other values
Topography					
Slope (%)	<8	<12	<16	16-20	other values
Soil					
Drainage (moisture)	b or c		b to d		other values
Texture	silty clay loam tot loam	clay to loamy sand	clay to		other values
Coarse fragments (%)	<15	<35	<55		other values
Soil depth (cm)	>50	>20	>10		other values
CaCO$_3$ (%)	<30	<40	<60		other values
Gypsum (%)	<5	<10	<20		other values
pH H$_2$O	6-7	5.5-8.5			
C.E.C. (meq/100 g clay)	>16				other values
Base saturation (%)	>50	>35			other values
Organic C (%)	>1	>0.5			other values
E.C. (dS/m)	<8	<12	<16	<24	other values

Table 1: Requirements of wheat (FAO-Ecocrop 1996; Sys 1985; Huajin 1993 and Deckers 1996).

Land characteristic	Class of Landuse assessment barley (Hordeum vulgare)				
	S1	S2	S3	N1	N2
Length of growing period (days)					
summer barley	90-130				other values
winter barley	180-240				other values
Climate					
1. Precipitation growing season (mm)	300-1100	200-1300	150-1500		other values
2. Monthly precipitation (mm)					
a) vegetative period	15-95	10-120	5-120		other values
b) florescence	20-95	10-120			other values
3. Mean temperature (°C)					
a) vegetative period	6 to 18	4 to 24	2 to 28		other values
b) florescence	12 to 26	10 to 32	8 to 36		other values
c) ripening	14 to 30	12 to 36	10 to 42		other values
4. Mean min. T of coldest month (°C)	<8	>8	<13		
with certain mean max.T	if	if	if		other values
of coldest month (°C)	<21	<21	>21		
5. Light intensity	clear	clouded			other values
Topography					
Slope (%)	<8	<12	<16	16-20	other values
Soil					
Drainage (moisture)	b or c		b to d		other values
Texture	silty clay loam tot loam	fine clay to loam to sandy loam	fine clay to loamy sand		other values
Coarse fragments (%)	<15	<35	<55		other values
Soil depth (cm)	>50	>20	>10		other values
CaCO3 (%)	<20	<40	<60		other values
Gypsum (%)	<5	<10	<20		other values
pH H2O	6,5 to 7,5	8 to 6			
C.E.C. (meq/100 g clay)	>16				other values
Base saturation (%)	>50	>35			other values
Organic C (%)	>0,8	>0.4			other values
E.C. (dS/m)	<12	<16	<20	<25	other value

Table 2: Requirements for barley (Hordeum vulgare) (Sys 1985 and FAO-Ecocrop 1996).

rich or lean, but dry soils, which however were weakened after cultivation (Columella II 9,14). In the 1940s still, barley was mainly grown in our district on the less manured fields further away from the settlements (de Planhol 1958: 151). Charred seeds from a Chalcolithic site in the western part of the Sagalassos territory, i.e. Kurna Hüyük near Burdur, that were examined at the request of the Sagalassos team and the Burdur Museum by M. Nesbitt contained already a number of barley grains (*Hordeum vulgare*). Current descriptions of the various crops are quantitatively summarised in Tables 1 and 2 (*FAO* 1996; Sys 1985).

Compared to wheat, barley is more resistant to cold, frost and high precipitation (Sys 1985). The soil fertility requirements are comparable with those of wheat (fine soil texture, high light intensity and high fertility) but the optimal pH is a little higher (namely 6.5-7.5 against 6-7 in the case of wheat) and the crop is even more resistant to salt (*FAO* 1996).

Bread wheat (*Triticum aestivum*) evolved through the hybridisation of emmer wheat (*Triticum dicoccum*) and of a wild grass. Bread wheat appears in the archaeo-botanical record from about 6500 BC onwards (Hyams 1976), some 1000 years later than the domestication of emmer, and at about the same time as that of *durum* wheat. But even in the second century BC some of the first domesticated wheat varieties such as 'einkorn' (*Triticum monococcum*) and emmer wheat (*Triticum dicoccum*) were still eaten by the country people around Pergamon during food shortages, because all high quality wheat was taken to the cities (Mitchell 1993: 169). Certain types of wheat (*Triticum durum* and *Triticum tugidum*) provided an excellent quality of bread (Jongman 1988: 82).

Both the winter and the summer variety of wheat must have been available to the farmers of Sagalassos. In the seventies of the nineteenth century goods, chiefly wheat, were exported in large quantities on camel back from Isparta to Antalya (Davis 1874: 152-53). Despite the fact that the transport costs made the price per kilo four times more expensive upon arrival than the normal price, this trade of Anatolian grain still remained profitable. The reason may have been that the production of the Pamphylian plain itself was not sufficient to allow the required export (Mitchell 1993: 247). According to Arab sources of the late tenth century AD, Antalya then was the centre of a cereal producing district (de Planhol 1958: 84). At the time of its conquest by Ottoman Turks in 1391 it had become a major centre for exporting Anatolian grain towards the Aegean islands (de Planhol 1958: 94). Thus the export of wheat from the Isparta district could already have started then. Grain transport from Isparta is also mentioned in the mid-seventeenth and again in the late eighteenth centuries (de Planhol 1958: 113-114, 124). In the 1940s the district around Isparta still possessed hundreds of camels as a relict from the old winter caravans (de Planhol 1958: 167). The caravans even transported grain from Isparta to Konya (de Planhol 1958: 175).

Growing wheat is only possible in the best fields. This explains why, around the middle of this century, Pisidian wheat (buğday) was mainly grown on the better manured fields, called 'buğdaylık', in the vicinity of agglomerations (de Planhol 1958: 148, 150). The crop requires a well drained soil which, throughout a longer period, is neither too dry neither too saturated. Moreover, the soil must be fertile, possess a fine texture and a high light intensity (*FAO* 1996). Roman authors (Columella II 4, 3-5 and 9; II 9, 3; Pliny *Naturalis Historia* XVIII 1, 63; XVIII 70, 101 and 103; Varro *RR* I 23) recommended to grow winter (*diligo*) and summer (*trimense*) bread wheat in the richest plains and slopes that were well exposed to the sun. Theoretically, the plain of Ağlasun and its northern slopes could have been a good environment for this crop. Another advantage, certainly for this district, was that wheat is very winter resistant and that it supports fairly high temperatures as well, be it only in a rather dry atmosphere.

Nowadays *Triticum durum* is the dominant cereal in the study area. As already mentioned, the Isparta district exported large quantities of wheat during the late nineteenth century but this could also have been the result of the fact that wheat was easier to transport over a longer distance (Rathbone 1983). It is however problematic to find out how the situation was in ancient times because it is impossible to distinguish cereals in pollen studies. Furthermore there are no other archaeobotanical data which can provide more information because (a) thus far almost no classical plant remains have been recovered from this or from adjacent areas and (b) only very few identifications of the ancient wheat have made use of modern rachis criteria (the grains of free-threshing wheat cannot be identified beyond a *durum/aestivum* distinction).

Legumes

Although animals, particularly cattle, pig, sheep/goat and chicken (Van Neer and De Cupere 1993: 234) formed an important source of proteins, they probably needed to be complemented by legumes. Even today, beans compose a major product in the area for subsistence and for commerce (de Planhol 1958: 152-153). Besides they also served as fodder and preserved the soil fertility by means of N-fixation and green manuring (White 1970).

Four types of legumes are cultivated in the Mediterranean since the Neolithic: pea (*Pisum sativum*), chickpea (*Cicer arietinum*), lentils (*Lens culinaris*) and maybe horsebean (*Vicia faba*).

The wild ancestor of the pea was either *Pisum elatius* or *Pisum humile*. *Elatius* peas are pan-Mediterranean in their distribution and grow as annual climbers in maquis formations. *Humile* peas are restricted to the Near East; they thrive in steppe-like habitats and also invade cultivated fields. Of the two wild types, *P. humile*, resembles more closely the cultivated crop. It is also a characteristic annual constituent of the oak-dominated park-forest formation in the Near Eastern arc, i.e. the same zone that also harbours the wild progenitors of emmer, einkorn and barley (Zohary 1989: 363).

The wild progenitor of the lentil, *Lens orientalis*, is distributed over the Near East and reaches even into Asia (Zohary 1989: 364).

The cultivated chickpea is derived from the wild *Cicer reticulatum*. It is also an element of the oak-dominated park-forest zone of the Near Eastern arc and is especially endemic to the middle segment of the crescent (Zohary 1989: 365).

At Aceramic Hacılar, domesticated lentil (*Lens esculenta*) was recovered (Helbaek 1970: 189). Carbonised plant remains from the Neolithic and Chalcolithic levels yielded lentil, purple pea (*Pisum elatius*) and bitter vetch (*Vicia ervilia*) (Helbaek 1970: 214). Helbaek does not think that purple pea was cultivated at Hacılar. It could have been collected in arable plots near water sources (1970: 227). Bitter vetch was probably a food plant in prehistoric times but may have been collected or even cultivated as fodder to be fed to the livestock kept in the villages during winter months. At Hacılar only one small deposit was recovered during the excavations, but stray seeds in most other samples show the plant to have occurred as a straggler throughout the whole occupation of the village (Helbaek 1970: 227-228). Lentil and pea are also attested at Late Chalcolithic Kuruçay (Nesbitt 1996: 90, 134-7).

The majority of the charred seeds from Chalcolithic Kurna Hüyük, identified by M. Nesbitt and M. Vermoere were composed of bitter vetch (*Vicia ervilia*). According to M. Nesbitt it was an important crop from the Neolithic period, when it already occurred at Hacılar, to the current day. M. Nesbitt kindly informed us that "today it is grown as a fodder crop for animals, but in the past bitter vetch was certainly an important food for humans as well".

Both pea and lentil could have been domesticated locally. Chickpea occurs in the wild more to the east. However, the same remark which has been made concerning the origin of cereals must be made here: it remains an open question whether all the crops were taken into cultivation together in the same place, and where this happened (Zohary 1996: 156).

Because lentils are not frost resistant (*FAO* 1996) it is unlikely that they could have been cultivated in most of the Sagalassian territory. Yet, in prehistoric times, they were grown in the plain of Burdur (Hacılar, Kuruçay). The most cold resistant crop of the remaining three is horsebean, followed by chickpeas and peas. On the other hand, the latter is less demanding than the other two as far as optimal growth temperatures are concerned. All three crops require a good precipitation, a good drainage and a high light intensity (Table 3). Only chickpeas also grow on rather dry soils. In the 1940s various types of beans and peas were cultivated in the area, depending on the soil texture and its moisture (de Planhol 1958: 152-153).

Forestry

The above-mentioned problems of selecting cultivated species for arable farming and of defining their requirements are less pronounced in the case of silviculture. The reason is that forestry species usually are more robust as far as the edaphological environment is concerned.

Previous research in the Sagalassos area has already revealed that during the Hellenistic and Roman periods, the city was still surrounded by a well forested environment alternating with open spots for farming or for pastoralism (Paulissen *et al.* 1993; Waelkens and the Sagalassos team 1997). According to palynological data, deciduous oak trees (mainly *Quercus cerris* and *Quercus infectoria*) must have been much more important constituents of the forests than they are now (Vermoere *et al.* 2000).

In antiquity, trees and wood certainly played a major role in a city's economy, although their expansion and exploitation may have undergone various changes throughout time. Heavy woodcutting and grazing can reduce forests to low-growing scrub communities, while abandoned fields may support changing vegetation sequences, eventually resulting in genuine forests (Rackham 1983: 290-337; Forbes 1996: 70). The territory of Sagalassos witnessed both developments during the historical period.

Whatever the situation at a certain moment was, there was no such thing as 'unused' land. Uncultivated mountain areas could be used for grazing and beekeeping whereas mountain grazing was also recognised as potential arable land (Forbes 1996: 77, 92-93). Wooded areas served many purposes. First of all timber played a major role in architecture (as a construction and roofing material), in agriculture (for the production of agricultural equipment) and even in industry (scaffolding, presses, supports) (Forbes 1996: 79-81). But even brushwood was exploited and "maintained" for the construction of sheep and goat folds, for basketry and especially as fuel for private and public

Land characteristic	Pea (Pisum sativum)					Chickpea (Cicer arietinum)					Tickpea (Vicia faba)				
	S1	S2	S3	N1	N2	S1	S2	S3	N1	N2	S1	S2	S3	N1	N2
Length of growing period (days)	60-140				o. v.	90-180				o. v.	100-150				o. v.
Climate															
1. Yearly precipitation (mm)	800-1200	350-2500			o. v.	600-1000	300-1800			o. v.	650-1000		250-2600		o. v.
2. Mean growth temperature (°C)	10 to 24	4 to 30	16 to 20	20 to 24	o. v.	15-29	5 to 35	20 to 24		o. v.	18-28		5 to 32		o. v.
3. Light intensity	clear	clouded			o. v.	clear	clouded			o. v.	clear	clouded			o. v.
Topography															
Slope (%)	< 8	8 to 16	16 to 20	20 to 24	o. v.	< 8	< 20	20 to 24		o. v.	< 8	8 to 16	16 to 20		o. v.
Soil															
Texture	fine clay - loamy sand	sand			o. v.	fine clay-loam	fine clay-sandy loam	sand		o. v.	fine clay-loam	fine clay-sandy loam	sand		o. v.
Soil depth (cm)	> 50	> 20	> 10		o. v.	> 50	> 20	> 10		o. v.	> 50	> 20	> 10		o. v.
CaCO$_3$ (%)	< 25	< 40	< 60		o. v.	< 30	< 60	< 75		o. v.	< 25	< 40	< 60		o. v.
Gypsum (%)	< 0.5	0.5-1	1 to 3		o. v.	< 3	< 10	< 15		o. v.	< 0.5	0.5-1	1 to 3		o. v.
pH H$_2$O	5.5-7	4.5-8.3			o. v.	6-8.5	4.7-9.5			o. v.	6 to 7	4.5-8.8			o. v.
E.C. (dS/m)	< 8	< 12	< 16	< 20	o. v.	< 12	< 16	< 20	< 24	o. v.	< 8	< 12	< 16	< 20	o. v.

Table 3: Requirements of legumes (FAO-Ecocrop 1996).

Land characteristic	Pinus nigra				Pinus brutia				Abies cilicica			
	S1	S2	S3	N	S1	S2	S3	N	S1	S2	S3	N
Heigth southern slope (m)	1150-1550	1100-1150 1550-1600	1000-1100 1600-1700	<1000 >1700	850-1150	800-850 1150-1200	700-800 1200-1300	<700 >1300	1450-1550 1550-1650	1150-1200 1950-2000	1350-1450 2000-2100	<1350 >1650
Heigth northern slope (m)	1250-1750	1200-1250 1750-1800	1100-1200 1800-1900	<1100 >1900	750-850	700-750 850-900	600-700 900-1000	<600 >1000	1200-1950	1150-1200 1950-2000	1050-1150 2000-2100	<1050 >2100
Gradient (°)	<40°			>40°	<30°			>30°	<45°			>45°
Substrate	limestone, flysch		others		limestone, flysch		others		limestone	others		others

Land characteristic	Cedrus libani				Juniperus excelsa and oxycedrus				Quercus calliprinos			
	S1	S2	S3	N	S1	S2	S3	N	S1	S2	S3	N
Heigth southern slope (m)	1150-1950	1100-1150 1950-2000	1000-1100 2000-2100	<1000 >2100	1250-2150	1200-1250 2150-2200	1100-1200 2200-2300	<1100 >2300	850-1150	800-850 1150-1200	700-800 1200-1300	<700 >1300
Heigth northern slope (m)	1050-1650	1000-1050 1650-1700	900-1000 1700-1800	<900 >1800	1150-1850	1100-1150 1850-1900	1000-1100 1900-2000	<1000 >2000	1250-1750	800-850 950-1000	700-800 1000-1100	<700 >1100
Gradient (°)	<30°			>30°	<40°			>40°	<35°			>35°
Substrate	limestone	others			all substrates				limestone	flysch	others	others

Land characteristic	Quercus cerris			
	S1	S2	S3	N
Heigth southern slope (m)	850-1150	800-850 1150-1200	700-800 1200-1300	<700 >1300
Heigth northern slope (m)	850-1350	800-850 1350-1400	700-800 1400-1500	<700 >1500
Gradient (°)	<35°			>35°
Substrate	limestone	flysch	others	others

Table 4: Requirements of tree species: Black pine (*Pinus nigra*), Calabrian pine (*Pinus brutia*), Cilician fir (*Abies cilicica*), Lebanon cedar (*Cedrus libani*), Grecian and Prickly juniper (*Juniperus excelsa and oxycedrus*), Kermes oak (*Quercus calliprinos*) and Turkish oak (*Quercus cerris*) (Mayer and Askoy 1986).

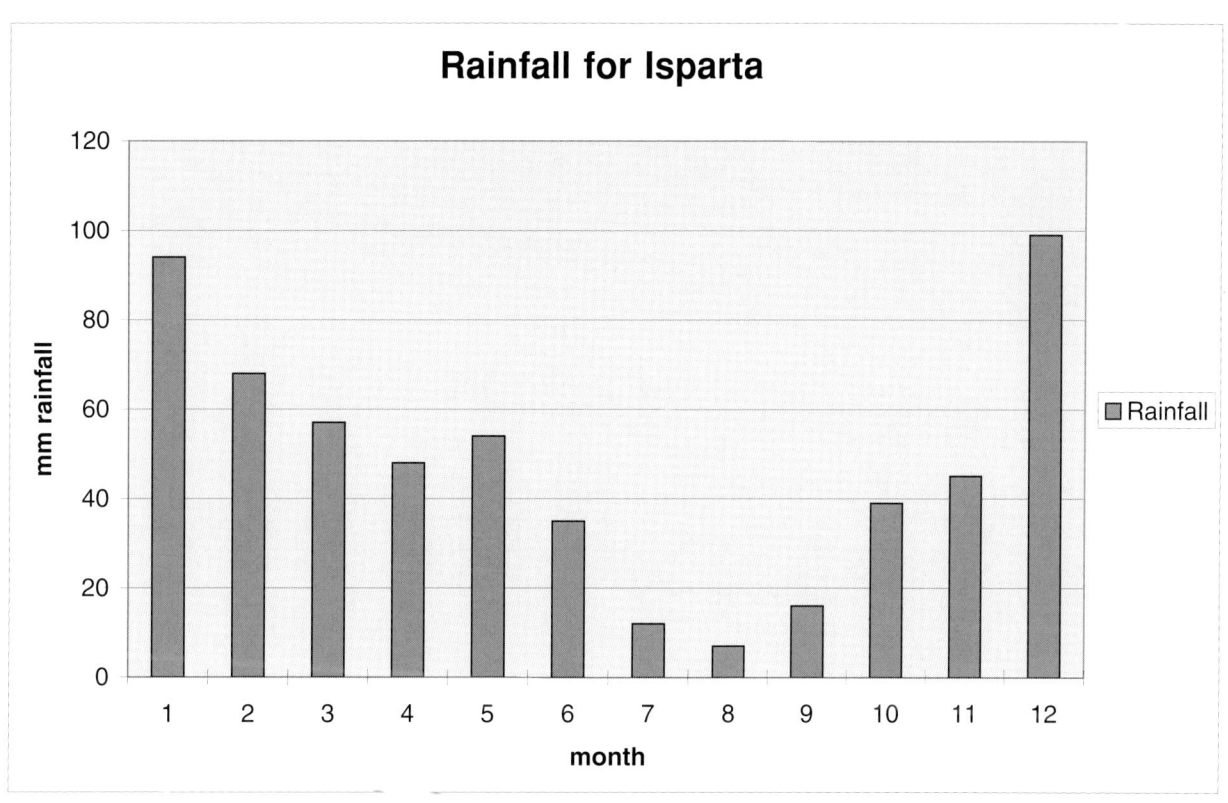

Fig. 1: Rainfall regime of Isparta.

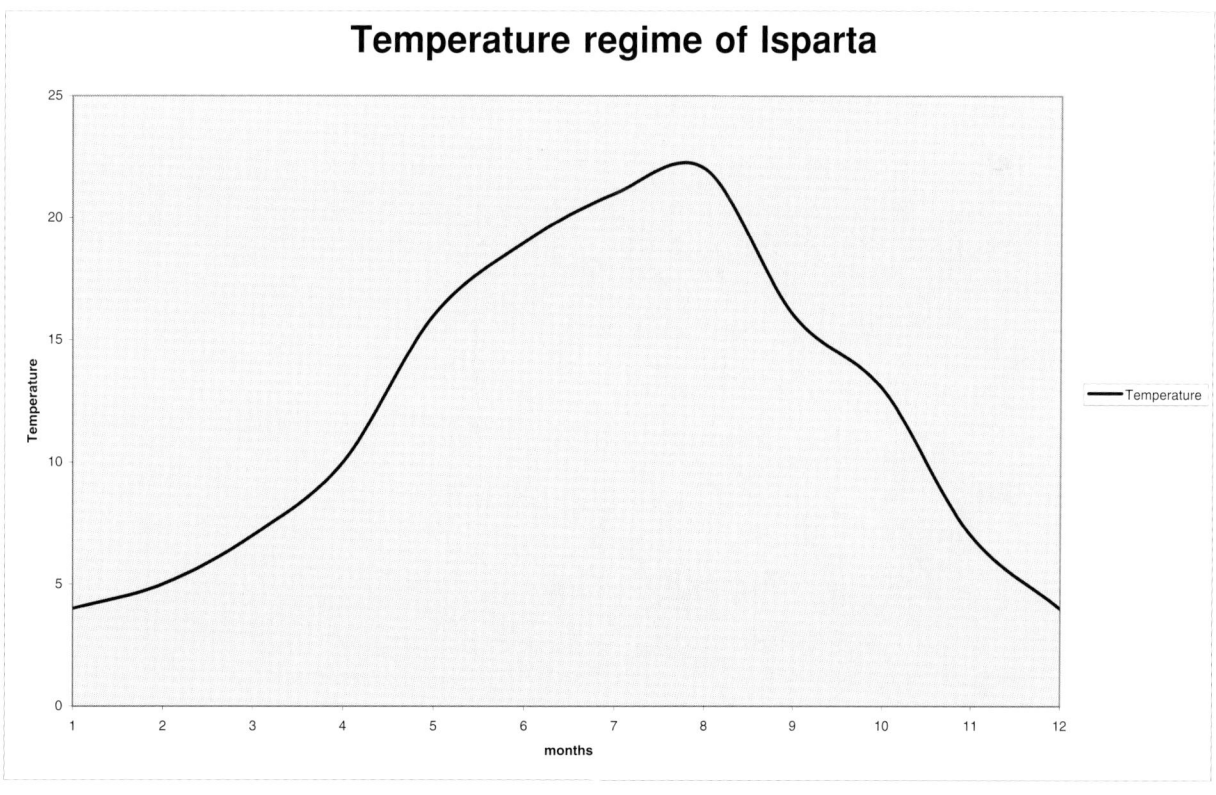

Fig. 2: Temperature regime of Isparta.

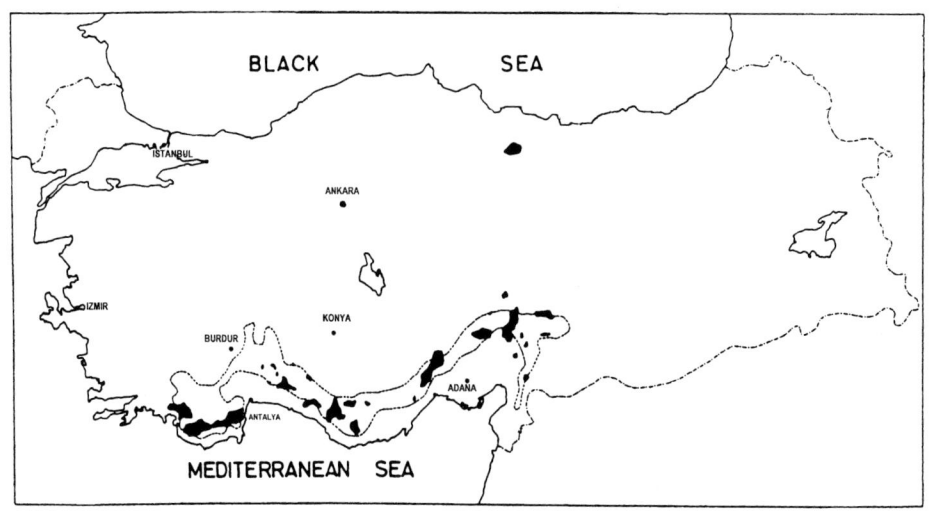
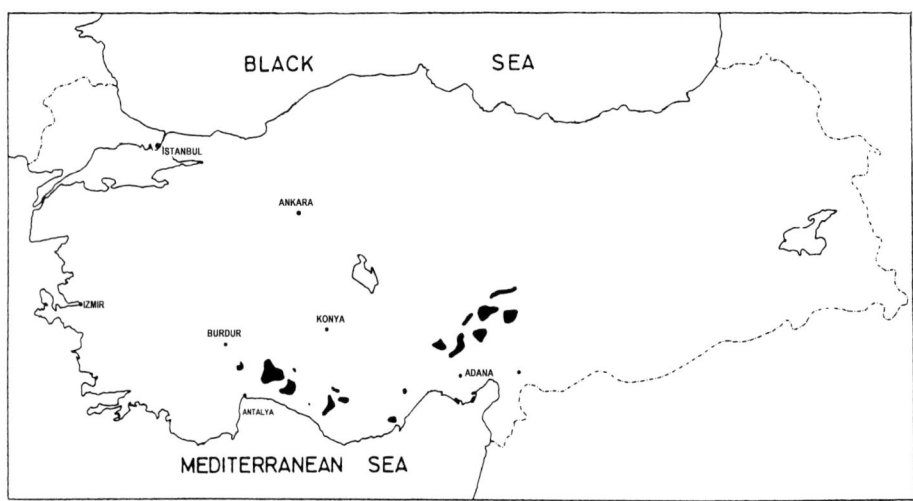
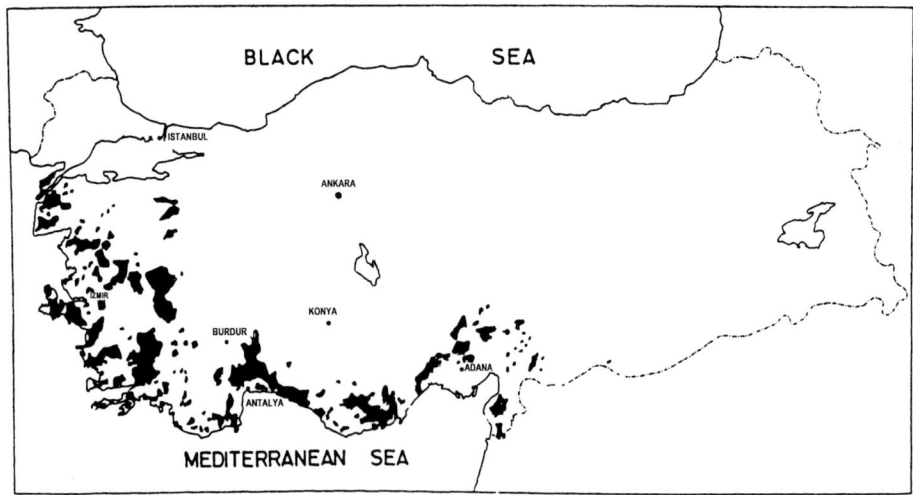

Fig. 3a: natural distribution area of Lebanon cedar (*Cedrus libani*).
3b: natural distribution area of Cilician fir (*Abies cilicia*).
3c: natural distribution area of Calabrian pine (*Pinus brutia*).

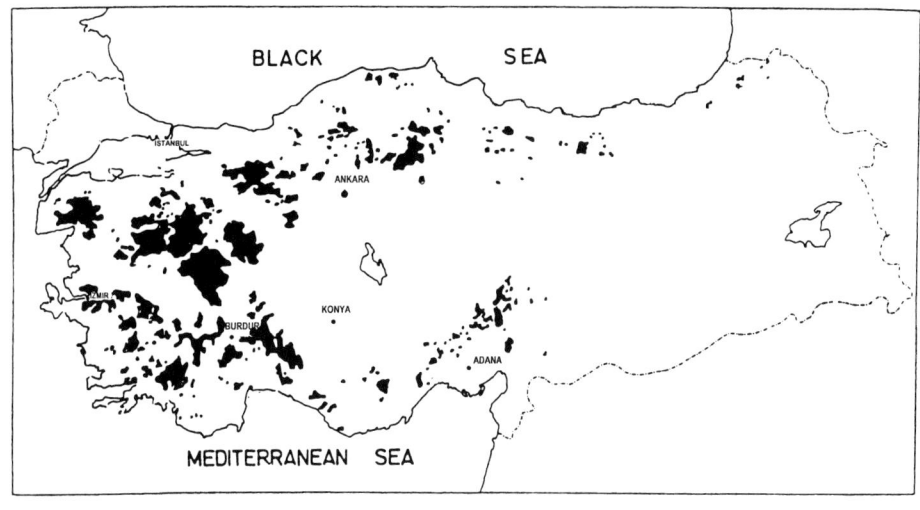
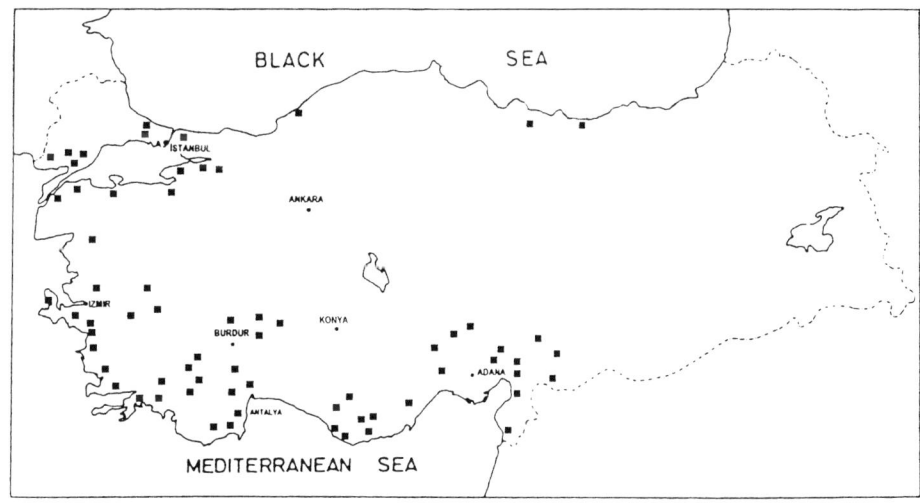
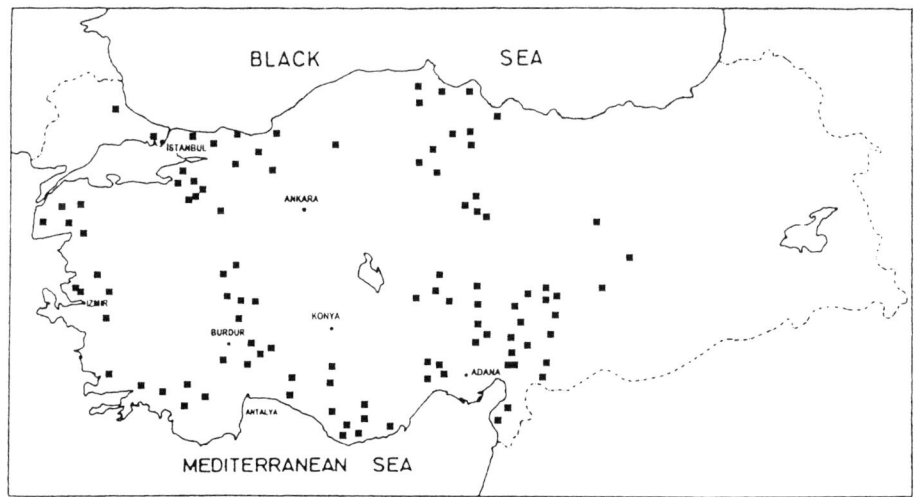

Fig. 3d: natural distribution area of Black pine (*Pinus nigra*).
  3e: natural distribution area of Kermes oak (*Quercus coccifera*).
  3f: natural distribution area of Turkish oak (*Quercus cerris*).

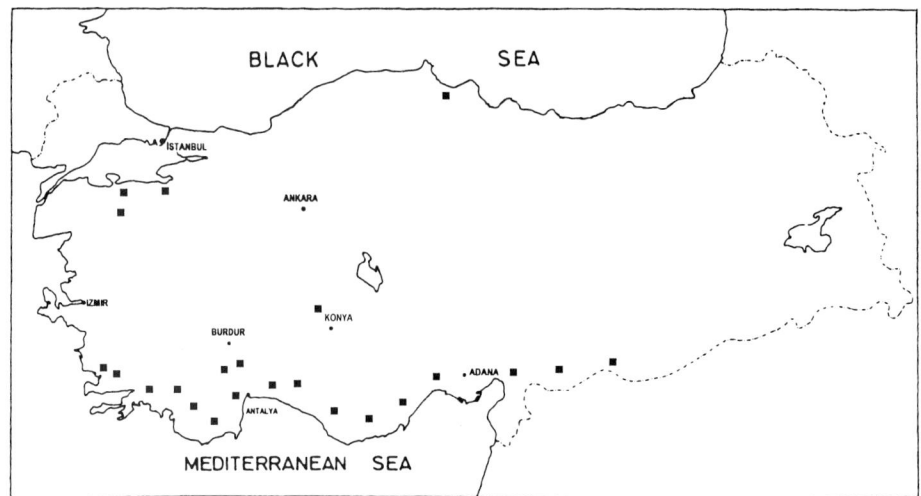

Fig. 3g: natural distribution area of *Styrax officinalis*.

Class	Suitability	Explanation
S 1	Highly suitable	Land having no significant limitations to sustained application of a given use, or only minor limitations that will not significantly reduce productivity or benefits and will not raise inputs above an acceptable level
S 2	Moderately suitable	Land having limitations which in aggregate are moderately severe for sustained application of a given use; the limitations will reduce productivity or benefits and increase required inputs in the extent that the overall advantage to be gained from the use, although still attractive, will be appreciable inferior to that expected on class S1 land
S 3	Marginally suitable	Land having limitations which in aggregate are severe for sustained application of a given use and will so reduce productivity or benefits, or increase required inputs, that this expenditure will be marginally justified
N 1	Currently not suitable	Land having limitations which may be surmountable in time but which cannot be corrected with existing knowledge at currently acceptable cost; the limitations are so severe as to preclude successful sustained use of the land in the given manner
N 2	Permanently not suitable	Land having limitations which appear so severe as to preclude any possibilities of successful use of the land in the given manner

Table 5: Land suitablility classes (*FAO* 1976).

Horizon	Summary description of soil profiles			Horizon	Soil characteristics		
	Site Landuse Topography Soil type	Profile 1 Bushland Slope (>15%) **CAMBISOL** under colluvium	Profile 2 Shrubs Slope (8-16%) **LUVISOL** under colluvium		Site Soil type	Profile 1 **CAMBISOL**	Profile 2 **LUVISOL**
A	Depth (cm) Texture Structure Colour (moist) Compaction Roots	115-159 Loam Crumb 10 YR 4/6 Weak Few	70-90 Silt-loam Massive 7.5 YR 4/3 Intermediate Common	A	% clay pH C.E.C. B.S. P-tot	23 8,4 29 90 555	22 8,1 30 85 821
E	Depth (cm) Texture Structure Colour (moist) Compaction Roots	N.A.	90-115 Sandy loam Massive 10 YR 4/4 Porous Few	E	% clay pH C.E.C. B.S. P-tot	N.A.	5 8,2 29 74 1020
Bw	Depth (cm) Texture Structure Colour Compaction Roots	159-213 Silt-loam Angular blocky 10 YR 3/4 Weak Few	N.A.	Bw	% clay pH C.E.C. B.S. P-tot	25 8,4 28 80 409	N.A.
Bt	Depth (cm) Texture Structure Colour Compaction Roots	N.A.	115-220 Loam Crumb 5 YR 4/6 Compact Common	Bt	% clay pH C.E.C. B.S. P-tot	N.A.	25 8,5 25 83 948
C	Depth (cm) Texture Structure Colour Compaction Roots	215-265 Silt-loam Granular 10 YR 6/6 Weak Few	220-... Silt-clay-loam Crumb 10 YR 5/8 No Few	C	% clay pH C.E.C. B.S. P-tot	23 8,3 28 92 367	28 8,3 26 97 1040

Table 6: Soil data of representative profiles.

N.A. = not available (or horizon not present)
pH = pH measured in water
C.E.C. = Cation exchange capacity
B.S. = Base saturation   P-tot = Total phosphor content

buildings (baths for instance), or as fuel for furnaces and kilns (Forbes 1996: 81-88). Many trees, for instance *Styrax* which made Pisidian Selge famous, could provide resin (Forbes 1996: 88-91). Finally, many slopes or valleys could also be turned into olive yards or orchards. In any case, arboriculture usually was a most labourious and time-consuming activity which involved many people (Foxhall 1996: 54-65). All these activities took also place around Hellenistic and Roman Sagalassos (Waelkens and the Sagalassos team 1997). The export of Pisidian timber, particularly towards Egypt, started already in antiquity and continued until recent times (Waelkens and the Sagalassos team 1997; de Planhol 1958: 92, 109-110, 124). In the 1940s Burdur was still a resin producing centre (de Planhol 1958: 125).

Deforestation of the mountain slopes around the site is a rather recent phenomenon, mainly due to overgrazing, but some 'native' species representing underbrush, are still present and well documented (Waelkens and the Sagalassos team 1997). Various surviving species are described below, requirements and habitats are given in respectively Table 4 and Fig. 3.

Cedrus libani (Lebanon cedar)
This species has as natural distribution area the mountains of Turkey, Lebanon and Israel and is considered as a transition type for the Mediterranean region and the continental inland (Vermoere 1996) (Fig. 3.a). Isolated stands of cedar still appear in the region of Sagalassos up to an altitude of 1500 m (Waelkens and the Sagalassos team 1997). A large stand of old cedar trees was observed to the south of Çanaklı on limestone slopes exposed to the north. Furthermore, degraded remnants of a former cedar forest were seen to the west of Alexander's hill. Together with *Abies cilicica* they dominated the highest forested zones (Paulissen *et al.* 1993). Pure cedar stands only grew on northern slopes, but because of the trees affection for light it grows better in the Taurus mountains on southern slopes, between 1100 and 2000 m (Mayer and Askoy 1986). However, on slopes steeper than 30° it is replaced by *Abies cilicica* (Mayer and Askoy 1986). As substrate the cedar prefers limestone or dolomite but it also thrives rather well on flysh.

Abies cilicica (Cilician fir)
The natural distribution area of this species is comparable to that of cedar (Paulissen *et al.* 1993) but it is more cold resistant and it can grow on steeper slopes as well (Fig. 3.b). East of the study area a natural forest of Cilician fir was found on a calcareous northern slope, which is the only parent material on which it grows successfully.

Pinus brutia (Calabrian pine)
Western Turkey forms a natural habitat for the Calabrian pine (Fig. 3.c). In the Western Taurus mountains this pine species dominates forests between 800 and 1200 m altitude (Paulissen *et al.* 1993). This Mediterranean tree thrives better on southern slopes than on the northern ones, where it performs best below the 900 m level. As substrates it prefers limestone, dolomite, marl, gabbro or flysh (Mayer and Askoy 1986).

Pinus nigra var. pallasiana (Black pine)
This variety of the black pine was growing originally along the Mediterranean coasts of Greece and Western Turkey (Fig. 3.d) and dominates forests in the Western Taurus between an altitude of 1200 to 1600 m (Paulissen *et al.* 1993). *Pinus nigra* is more cold-resistant than *Pinus brutia* and therefore can be found at a higher level on the northern slopes (1100 to 1800 m) than on southern ones (1000 to 1600 m) (Mayer and Askoy 1986). This variety endures a mean monthly temperature down to minus 3° C and prefers as substrates limestone, marl or flysh (Mayer and Askoy 1986).

Juniperus excelsa and Juniperus oxycedrus (resp. Grecian and prickly juniper)
Nowadays these juniper species determine the secondary woodland vegetation around Sagalassos between 1500 and 1800 m (Waelkens and the Sagalassos team 1997). They do not form homogeneous culmination stands but do grow in between *Pinus nigra*, *Abies cilicica* and *Cedrus libani* stands at altitudes between 1200 and 1800 m (Paulissen *et al.* 1993). Here *Juniperus excelsa* grows in the upper layer whereas *Juniperus oxycedrus* can be found as underbrush. Both can adapt to cold and heath, to wet and dry conditions. Because of their high resistance to cold they can grow higher on northern slopes (up to 2200 m compared to 1900 m on southern slopes) (Mayer and Askoy 1986). Concerning soil substrates, they are less exigent than the other mentioned tree species.

Quercus coccifera (Kermes oak)
The so-called kermes oak finds its natural habitat near the Mediterranean, i.e. in Spain, Northern Africa, Greece and Western Turkey (Fig. 3.e). Today, this evergreen oak dominates the secondary vegetation around Sagalassos up to an altitude of 1500 m (Waelkens and the Sagalassos team 1997). Originally it was part of the underbrush of *Pinus nigra* and *Pinus brutia*. As a Mediterranean species it is known to be temperature sensitive and needs a mean monthly temperature >0°C. Therefore it grows higher on southern (800-1200 m) than on northern slopes (800-1000 m). Substrates are preferably limestone and dolomite, though flysh, is also suitable (Mayer and Askoy 1986).

Quercus cerris (Turkish oak)
The Turkish oak was originally growing along the Mediterranean coasts of Italy, Greece and Turkey (Fig. 3.f). This

deciduous species is more cold resistant than kermes oak. This oak species often grows together with *Quercus infectoria* on shallow slopes, as was observed in a deciduous oak woodland in Kayaaltı (near Gravgaz). Sometimes deciduous oak shrubs can occur as underbrush in *Pinus nigra* forests (between 800 and 1200 m altitude). On northern slopes it is growing between 800 and 1400 m, on southern slopes between 800 and 1200 m altitude. Its substrate requirements are comparable with those of *Quercus coccifera* (Mayer and Askoy 1986).

Very few pure stands of deciduous oak can be observed in the area around Sagalassos. Isolated oak trees in and around the valley of Başköy witness of their former omnipresence in this area. Indeed, palynological research of several travertine profiles originating from this valley suggests that they were the main tree species of the woodland in this area around 9000 years BP (Vermoere 1996; Vermoere *et al.* 1999).

Styrax officinalis
Styrax is a broad-leaved tree from the *Styracaceae*. It grows naturally in Pamphylia and Cilicia along the Mediterranean coast, to the southeast of Sagalassos (Fig. 3.g). By making carves into the bark it is possible to extract a hard resin. In ancient times *Styrax* was an important economic product for the inhabitants of southern Turkey, especially at Pisidian Selge, because it was in demand to be used as incense, as perfume or for medical applications (Zedler 1954). The species has comparable requirements as those of *Quercus coccifera* and occurs in the Taurus mountains at the same altitudes (Zedler 1954). As this tree can grow on southern slopes to an altitude of 1200 m, theoretically it could have been an economical product of the inhabitants of Sagalassos. As already mentioned above, Burdur still exported resin during this century.

Other tree species such as *Acer monspessulanum*, *Ostrya carpinifolia*, *Pistacia terebinthus*, *Celtis australis* and *Fraxinus angustifolia* occur only sporadically in the remaining forests and woodlands.

2.6. Land evaluation and yield calculation

For land evaluation one can focus on present land performance. Frequently however, it should involve also a land use change analysis and the study of its effects (*FAO* 1976). In this study an actual land evaluation has been conceived as a starting point in order to arrive at a palaeo-land-use assessment. Characteristics (attributes of land which can be measured or estimated) concerning the climate, the soil and the topography of the study area and the requirements of the different selected types of land use, formed the scientific base for a land suitability classification.

Land suitability is the fitness of a given type of land for a specific use (Table 5). The focal point in the evaluation procedure is the moment where various data are brought together and compared, resulting in a suitability classification. This is the so-called matching process: land characteristics are tested against crop or tree requirements (*FAO* 1996). In line with data availability, a semi-quantitative method was opted for: the researcher determines the restrictive values by which land characteristics for a specific type of land use can be divided into five suitability groups.

Matching was done in different steps. First, all soil requirements (threshold values) were tested against soil data from described and analysed soil types. Next, the topography was introduced (with the help of the digitised topographical map, a map of slope percentages was made). In a final stage, use of a topographic Information System (IDRISI) (Clark Labs 1987) made it possible to model spatial soil and topographic data so as to produce suitability charts.

Potential yields of wheat (*Triticum aestivum*) and barley (*Hordeum vulgare*) were calculated by using the *FAO* Agro-ecological zoning model (*FAO* 1996).

3. RESULTS AND DISCUSSION

3.1. The reconstruction of palaeosol units

3.1.1. 'Palaeosol'

In general, the term 'palaeosol' is used to define the original state of soil profiles. A distinction is made for three profile situations: (1) soils of which the characteristics are in line with the present environmental situation i.e. the soil development can be explained without changes in climate, vegetation or human influence, etc.; (2) relic soils, where an environmental change is necessary to explain the soil characteristics which could not have been developed in present conditions; (3) buried soils, where an old profile is located at such a depth that biological activity can no longer influence them (Yaalon 1971). In this context, the definition of palaeosol is that of a relic soil. Buried profiles can also be called palaeosols but this is not a necessity (Yaalon 1971). Hand auguring and the study of recently exposed profiles allowed to identify various palaeosols.

3.1.2. Point observations

An evaluation of the measured characteristics of palaeosols resulted in a classification into different soil types and soil units. Soil units were grouped according to their geomorphologic affiliation into soil catenas, i.e. soil associations developed in the same parent material. Valley soils were

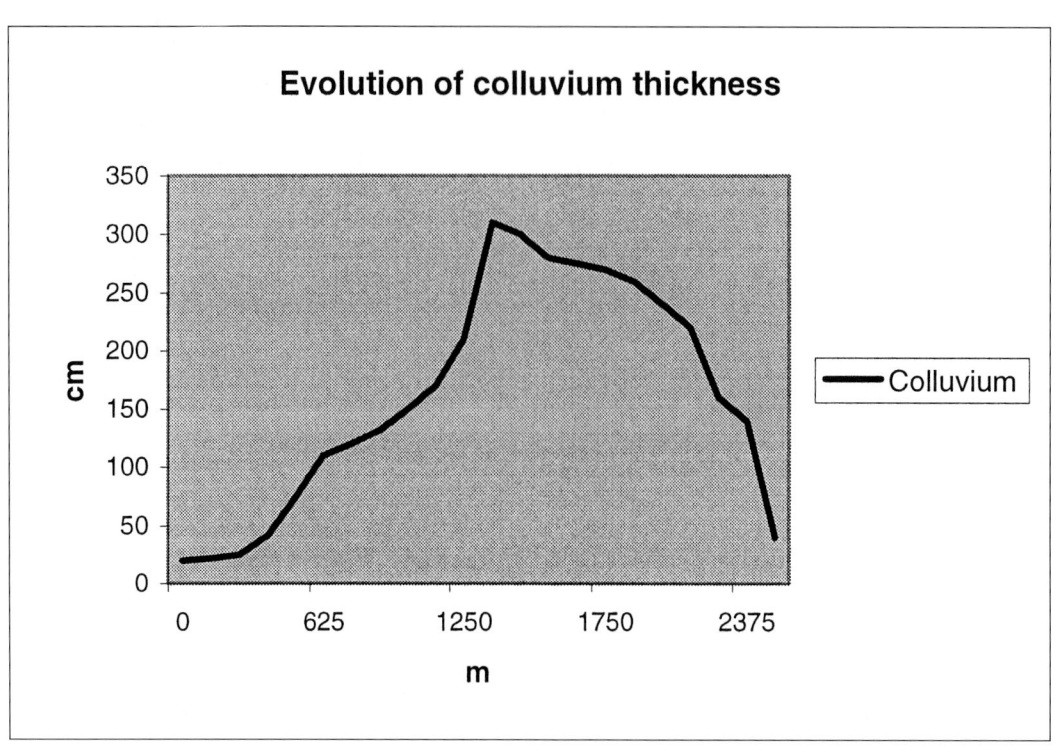

Fig. 4: Variation of colluvium thickness along the Köyünü transect.

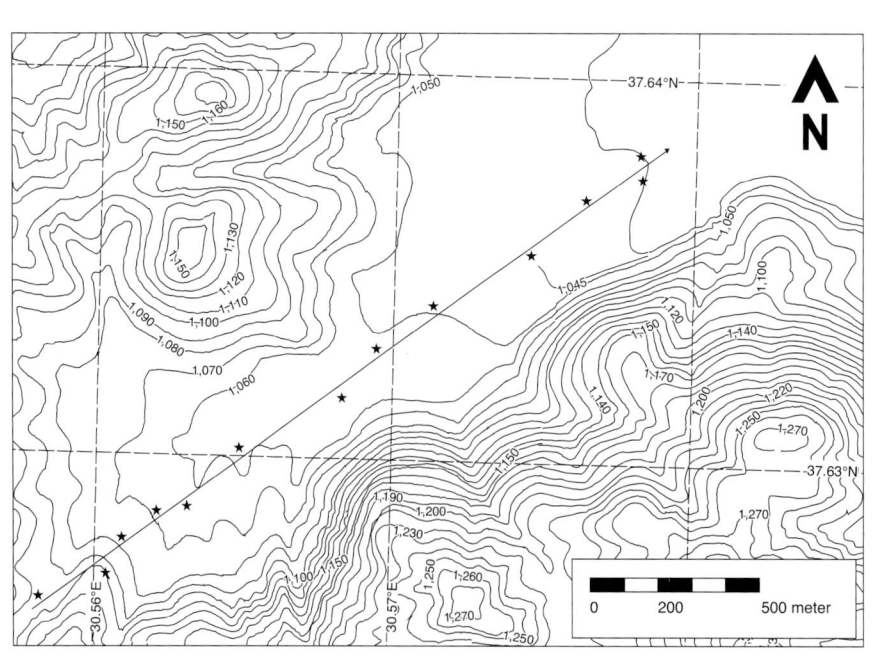

★ : Sampled points along the transect

Fig. 5: Transect in Köyünü.

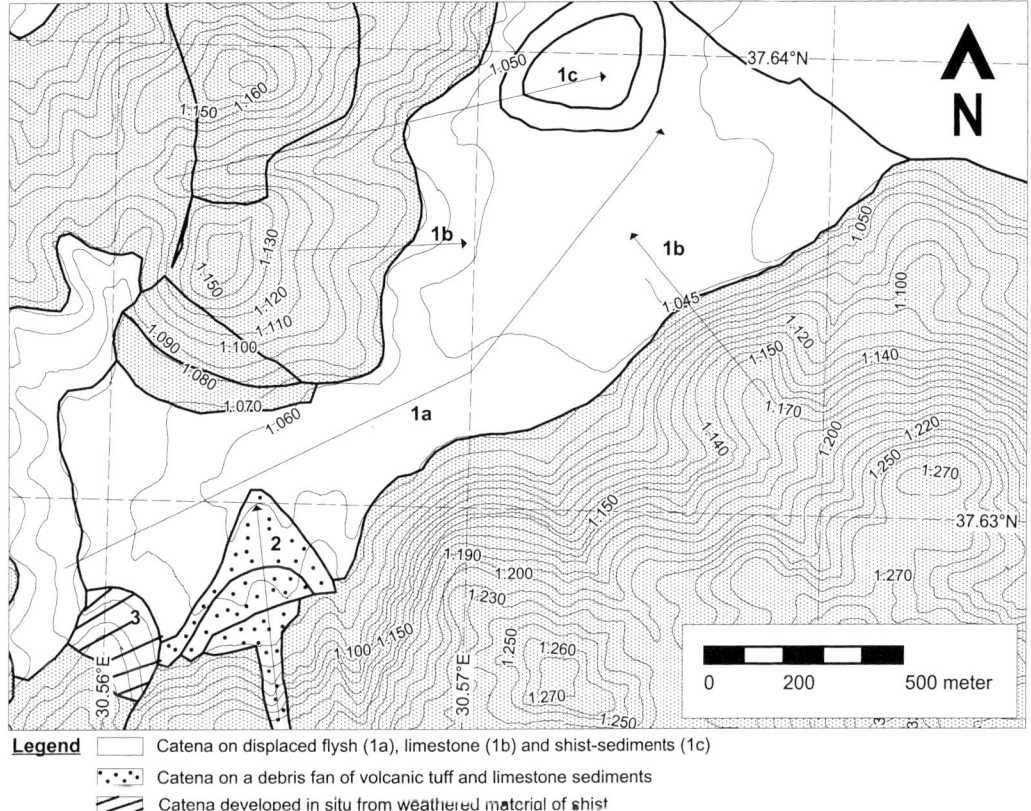

Legend
☐ Catena on displaced flysh (1a), limestone (1b) and shist-sediments (1c)
▨ Catena on a debris fan of volcanic tuff and limestone sediments
▧ Catena developed in situ from weathered material of shist

Fig. 6: Palaeosols distinguished in the three catenas

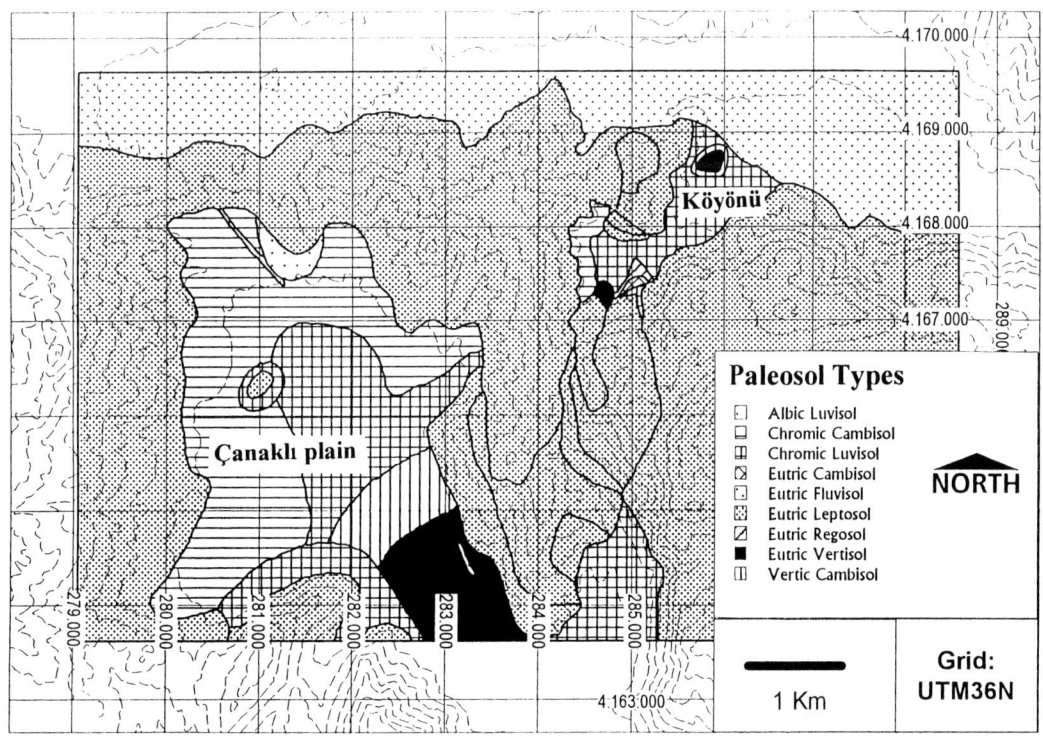

Fig. 7: Palaeosoil map of the study area.

studied, sampled and analysed in most detail because (1) they certainly represent the greatest part of potential ancient farming land and (2) on their fringes buried palaeosols are most common and therefore warrant a special attention in this study. Table 6 gives a summary of the soil profile description and analytical data for the most representative soil units. In the study area, three valleys can be distinguished were pilot studies were conducted: Köyünü (area of the Quarry), the valley of Çanaklı and the valley of Ağlasun.

In Köyünü (Quarry) the entire sampled surface is covered with recent erosion sediments, i.e. colluvial material, at some spots down to a depth of 3 meters. Fig. 4 illustrates the variation of the colluvium thickness along the transect (Fig. 5). These sediments are moderately to very stony and still in an initial stage of soil profile development. Consequently they are classified as Regosols (soils developed in unconsolidated material with a near absence of significant soil profile development) and to a lesser extent as Cambisols (soils with a weakly developing soil profile development, e.g. changes in texture or in structural development in the lower levels). The stoniness, the weak structure, the high erosion sensitivity and the low nutrient and water storage capacities of the Regosols, make them less fit for successful farming. The fact that in various spots, locally produced potsherds, dated to the first and second century AD were found in the lower levels of the colluvium, indicates that the original soils have to be located at a deeper level. These palaeosols could be distinguished in three catenas, shown in Fig. 6. Arrows indicate the assumed displacement of the mother sediment, the numbers identify the three different catenas under discussion: (1) a catena of palaeosols developed on allochtonous flysh, limestone and schist sediments (which is in this valley as well as in Çanaklı the dominant catena). This catena is dominated by Cambisols, Luvisols and Vertisols; (2) a catena in a debris fan of volcanic tuff and limestone sediments at the foot of an allochtonous limestone formation and containing Luvisols, Cambisols and Regosols and (3) a catena developed *in situ* from weathered material of a shist hill and containing buried Vertisols. Compared to the present-day soils at the surface (Cambisols and Regosols) these palaeosol units were more favourable for agricultural production.

In the valley of Çanaklı the soil catena is developed in allochtonous sediments and is dominated by Cambisol, Luvisols and Vertisols (compare the dominating catena in the Quarry). Furthermore a soil catena is developed in sediments of an old rivulet which is dominated by Fluvisols and Luvisols. In the studied catena of Ağlasun only Fluvisols were described. On steep slopes, landscape positions are mainly shallow and undeveloped soils occur that were described as Leptosols and Regosols. In what follows, a brief description will be given of the key components of the above mentioned soil systems, with a special attention to their archaeo-pedological aspects.

Cambisols

Cambisols are soils in an early stage of development (young sediment) or soils in which a specific factor is restricting the development, in this case the slope (up to 30%) and the colluvium cover. The presence of a Chromic Cambisol type can easily be verified by the brown colour of its soil surface, although part of the A and B-horizon are eroded. In the Köyünü valley this unit contained archaeological evidence of ancient farming activities: ruins of a farm, cisterns and a water pit. There was also a destroyed pottery kiln. Table 6 illustrates that the 20% clay jump between the two upper horizons is not reached to define it as a Luvisol. A comparison between the physical characteristics of colluvium and of buried soil layers indicates a compaction in the lower horizon. The most important chemical parameter is the pH, which is higher than 8 in every layer, and therefore basic. This can also be deduced from the base saturation and the high percentage of free carbonates. Free carbonate and nodules of $CaCO_3$ diminish indeed with depth. The fertility parameter CEC shows favourable values (CEC values higher than 20meq/100 g soil are considered as optimal (*FAO* 1983), values lower than 7 meq/100g soil cause serious restrictions (Buol *et al.* 1975)).

Luvisols

Luvisols characterised by a translocation of clay, an E-horizon out of which most of the clay has been eluviated, and a B_t-horizon, the layer in which the clay is accumulated. The results of the granulometry analysis clearly show the clay-jump (Table 6) between the E (5% clay) and the B_t- horizon (25% clay). The data of the physical analyses highlight the porosity of the E, the compactness of the B_t and the intermediate compaction of the A-horizon. The hypothesis of $CaCO_3$ illuviation can also be used to explain the high values of pH, of the content of free carbonates and of base saturation. Absence of salt problems (low EC) and high values of CEC indicate that these soils form a suitable location for arable farming. Values for total nitrogen, organic carbon and free sulphates were low which may be indicative for soil exhaustion as the result of ancient agriculture without good manuring.

Fluvisols

Their name refers to fluviatile, marine and lacustrine sediments which receive, or have received in a recent past, at regular intervals fresh materials through surface flooding. The former presence of a rivulet in the Çanaklı valley can be deduced from thin soil layers of different textures. No analyses however are available for this soil type.

Vertisols

Vertisols are well-developed soils, containing at least 30% of clay in all horizons, to a depth of at least 50 cm (Driessen and Dudal 1991). They occur mainly in depressions and level to undulating areas in climates with an alternation of distinct wet and dry seasons. Physical parameters form the main restriction for agriculture. In clayey sediments under a climate showing strong fluctuations in moisture and temperature, illite weathers to minerals of the smectite group, which have a high water storage capacity. This results in a vertic structure: prismatic elements that swell when wetted. Hence surface flooding is common during the rainy season. Shrinking occurs during drier periods so that structural elements break up and cracks are formed. Chemical characteristics are positive but not discussed in detail here, because it are mainly physical characteristics which are limiting productivity. Palaeosols of this type were present in the Çanaklı valley, where flooding still occurs at a much larger scale today.

Leptosols and Regosols

Both soil types are typical for eroding uplands and marked by the occurrence of unstable rocky slopes and outcrops of bedrock. When put under terraced agriculture, as frequently is done in the study area, today the erosion processes can be stabilised if properly managed. However, stoniness of the profiles is a major problem for productive agriculture. During the survey some field observations seem to indicate evidence of a climatic change. Traces of disappeared streams, like layered sediments, travertine or deep valleys may be signs of a drying trend in the climate. This is confirmed by occurrence of thick Mn-oxide nodules in the subsoil, which testify a lowering of the ground water table. Further research needs to be done for exact dating of these phenomena. There are however strong indications that a 'drying' period occurred in late Roman times (Waelkens and the Sagalassos team 1997).

3.1.3. Regional extrapolation (soil map)

Fig. 7 gives the soil map of the target area. In the valley of Köyünü as well as in the valley of Çanaklı a typical sequence of palaeosols occurs in the dominating catena (Fig. 8). From the flysh hills down to the lowlands soil profiles evolve according to the topo-sequence from upslope to valley bottom: Chromic Cambisol – Chromic Luvisol – Vertic Cambisol and Eutric Vertisol; all developed in allochtonous sediments. On smaller surfaces Eutric Vertisols (Quarry) and Albic Luvisols (valley of Çanaklı) also occur. They developed in autochtonous material. On a colluvial fan in the Quarry a sequence Chromic Luvisol – Eutric Cambisol – Eutric Regosol was found.

In the northwestern part of the Çanaklı valley, some soils could be classified as Eutric Fluvisols. Large pebbles present in the subsoil indicate that flow rates in ancient times were far more important than present-day discharges and point towards a rivulet. Comparable Fluvisols were encountered in the valley of Ağlasun, near the Ağlasun Çayı. Shallow Eutric Leptosols on remaining hill slopes are present.

From various analyses of the soil profiles, it became clear that in ancient times the largest part of the surface in the valleys consisted of fertile profiles, where no major constraints occurred to prevent a productive agriculture. Because of their high clay-content in the root zone, Luvisols and Fluvisols were very fertile. The steeper locations of Cambisols resulted in less clay-illuviation and consequently they had a lower, but still acceptable, productivity. Vertic Cambisols are characterised by the same fertility class, but they show a swell-shrink behaviour which may have caused problems. Swell shrink is even more pronounced in the case of completely developed Eutric Vertisols, which may lead to surface flooding during rainstorms and lead to crop yield reduction. Eutric Leptosols are rather infertile, due to limited soil depth and/or stoniness.

Because the material in the colluvial deposits dates to the post Roman period, there is a strong possibility that the valleys of Köyünü and of Çanaklı which at present are largely unfit for agriculture, in classical times could be used as mostly excellent farming land. The valley of Ağlasun was and still is very fit for such activities.

3.2. Climate

The main climatic restrictions of the high altitude in the Central Taurus mountains are frost in spring and drought during the summer. Compared to the Pamphylian plain the cold is more severe in the Isparta area, but the length of its frost season is shorter than that of Central Anatolia (plain of Konya) with its continental climate. Summer temperatures around Sagalassos are less extreme than those of Central Anatolia and Pamphylia so that there is less evaporation and drought stress. Moreover, there is also more summer precipitation. Because the growing season of most crops includes some or most of the summer months, climatic conditions theoretically are rather favourable for agriculture in the territory of Sagalassos. Most likely this climate was one of the reasons why Sagalassos was selected as a place to settle and why it could develop into an important city. The fertility of the plains and valleys around Sagalassos was already praised by Livy who described the area as "*uber fertilisque omni genere frugum*" (Livy XXXVIII.15.9).

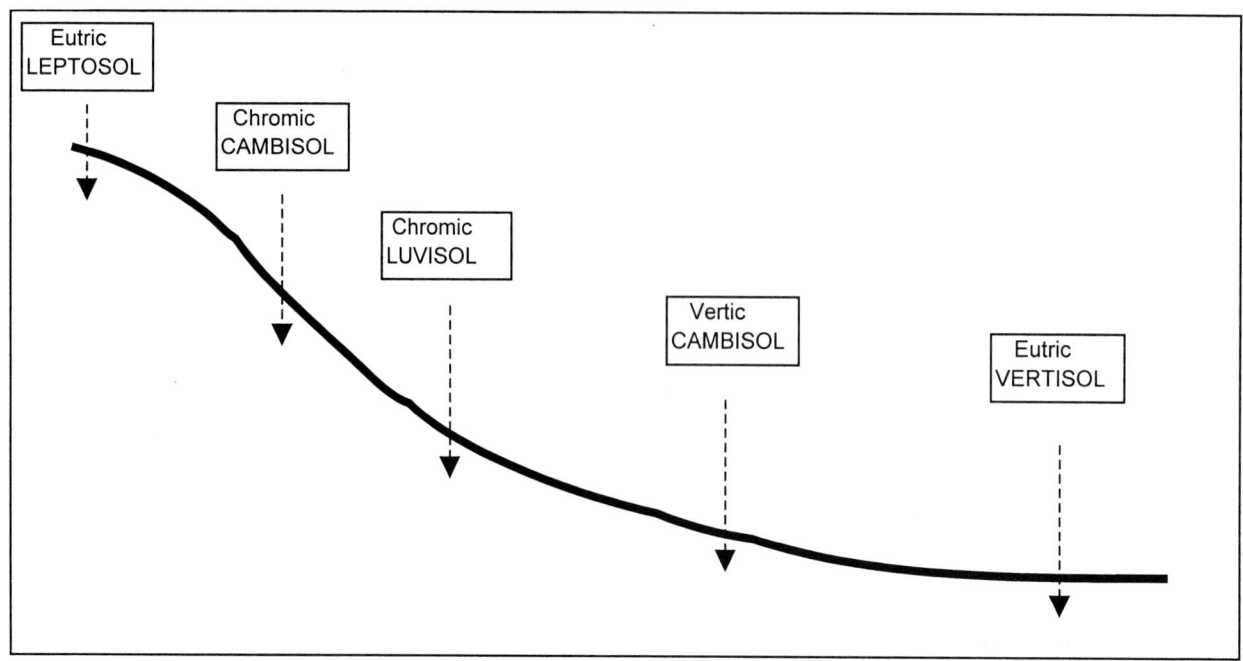

Fig. 8: Dominating catena.

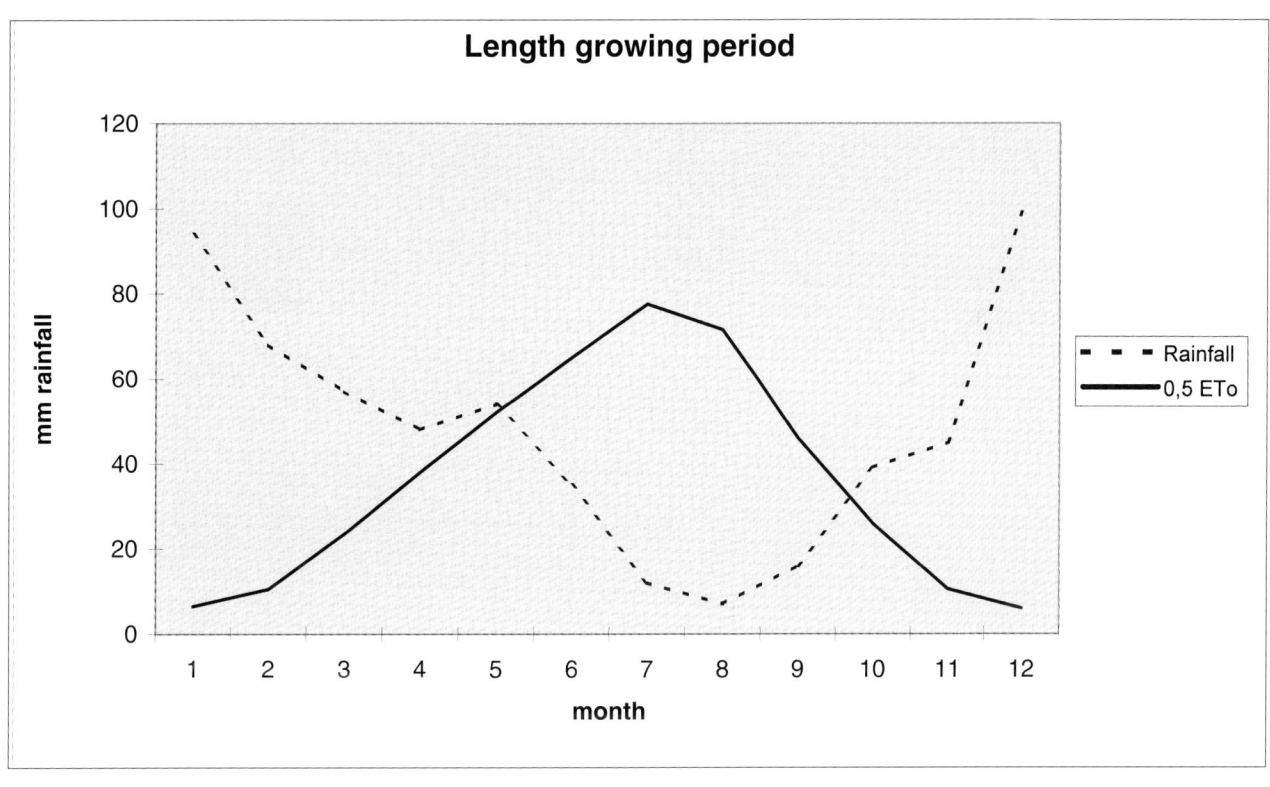

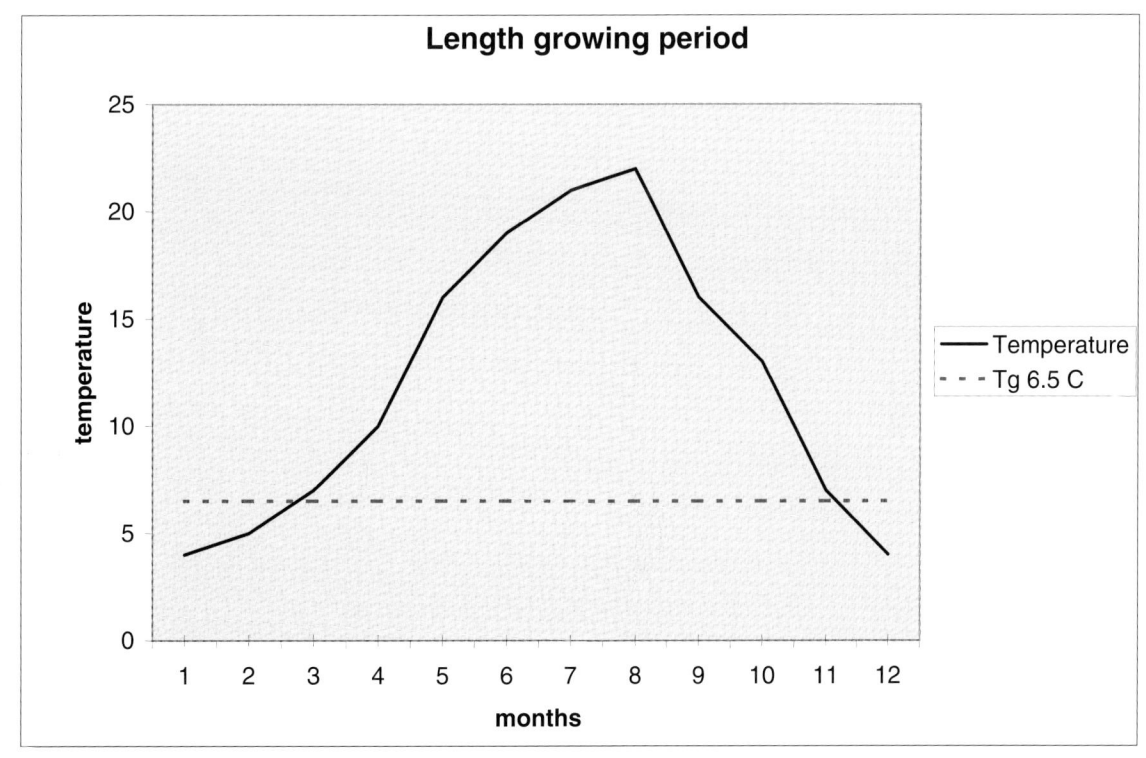

Fig.9: Determination of growing period.

Soil type	Soil parameters								
	moisture content (vol %)	texture	Soil depth (cm)	$CaCO_3$ (%)	pH (H_2O)	CEC (meq per 100 g clay)	Base saturation (%)	Organic C (%)	EC (dS/m)
Albic LUVISOL	19-25	silty loam		15	8.1-7.1	30	85	0,7	0,14
Chromic LUVISOL	20	sandy loam – loam		2	7-6.7	22-26	81-76	0,5	< 0.1
Chromic CAMBISOL	15	loam	100	17-15	8.4-8.3	29-23	90-100	0.5-0.2	0.13-0.16
Eutric CAMBISOL	/	silty loam	62	6	8	30	65	0,5	0,07
Vertic CAMBISOL	/	loam-sandy clay	150	11	7,9	28	70	0,5	0,14
Eutric REGOSOL	/	loam	>100	6	8	30	65	0,5	0,07
Eutric VERTISOL	/	clayey-sandy clay	<50	14	7.9-8.2	35-39	63-84	0.2-0.3	0.07-0.13

Table 7: Matching table for soil requirements.

Sowing date: 1 nov Yield date: 3 june
Length growth cycle (Ng) 215 days (= 7months + 3 days = 7.1 months)

Calculation of mean temperature (Tm) during growth cycle, from known mean temperatures from Isparta (Walter *et al.*, 1960 in Paulissen *et al.*, 1993)

  Tm = (7 + 4 + 4 + 5 + 7 + 10 + 16 + 0.1x19) / 7.1 = 7.7 °C

At this temperature, the maximum assimilation for winter wheat is 20 kg/ha/hour (Kassam *et al.*, 1982 in Driessen *et al.*, 1992)

Calculation of mean clouding fraction fO (fO = 1 – n/N) from known monthly means n/N   n/N = cloudity, n = hours sunshine/day; N = day length

  fO = 1 – [(0.32 + 0.35 + 0.29 + 0.38 + 0.35 + 0.69 + 0.49 + 0.1x0.56) / 7.1] = 0.59 %

Calculation of daily assimilation on a bright day (Bc) (data from Driessen *et al.*, 1982)

  Bc = (256 + 221 + 234 + 296 + 361 + 430 + 478 + 0.1x301) / 7.1 = 328 kg / ha / day

Calculation of daily assimilation on a coudy day (Bo) (data from Driessen *et al.*, 1982)

  Bo = (121 + 101 + 109 + 145 + 184 + 225 + 252 + 0.1x266) / 7.1 = 164 kg / ha / day

Calculation of total assimilation for winter wheat (Bgma)

  Bgma = (f0 x Bo) + (1 – f0) x Bc = 231 kg / ha / day

Calculation of the part of Bgma, lost by transpiration (Ct)

  Ct = 0.0108 x [0.044 + (0.0019 x Tg) + (0.001 x Tg2)] = 0.00128 kg / ha /dag

Calculation of potential netto dry matter production, in case of complete soil cover

  Bna = 0.36 x Bgma x Ng / (1 + 0.36 x Ct x Ng) = 16300 kg / ha

Calculation of yield for winter wheat, in absence of restrictions

  Bya = Bna x yield index (= 0.4 for wheat) = **6250 kg / ha**

Table 8: Calculation of possible yield for winter wheat (*Triticum aestivum*).

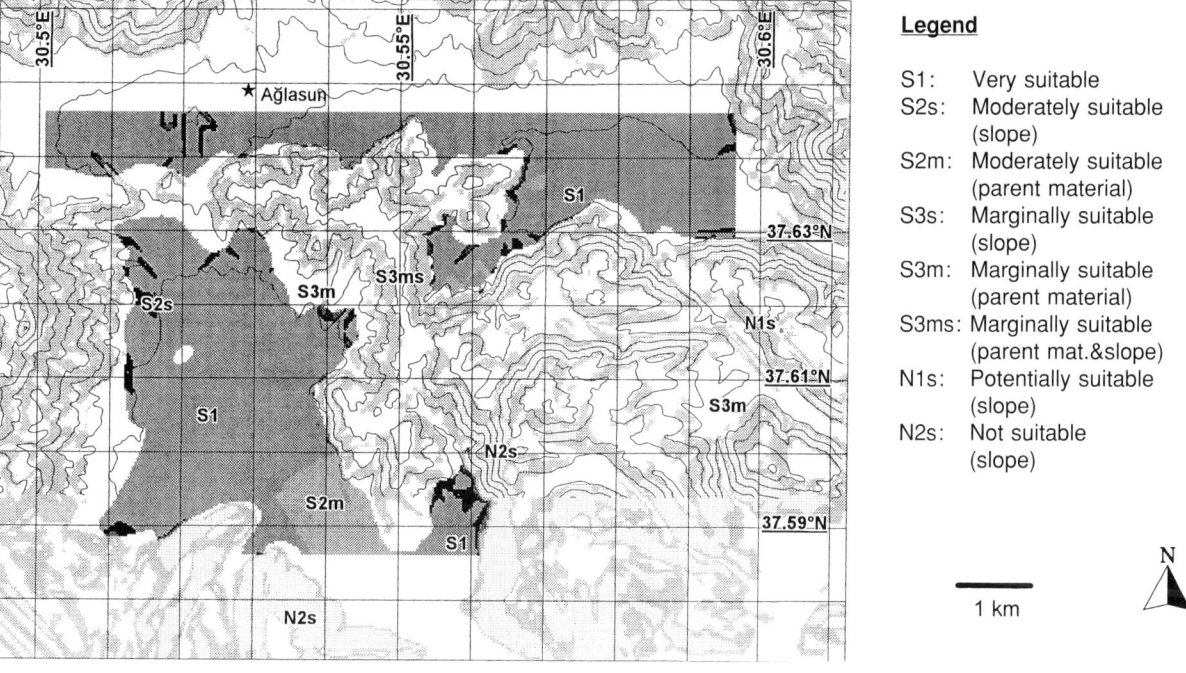

Fig. 10: Soil suitability map for *Triticum aestivum* and *Hordeum vulgare*.

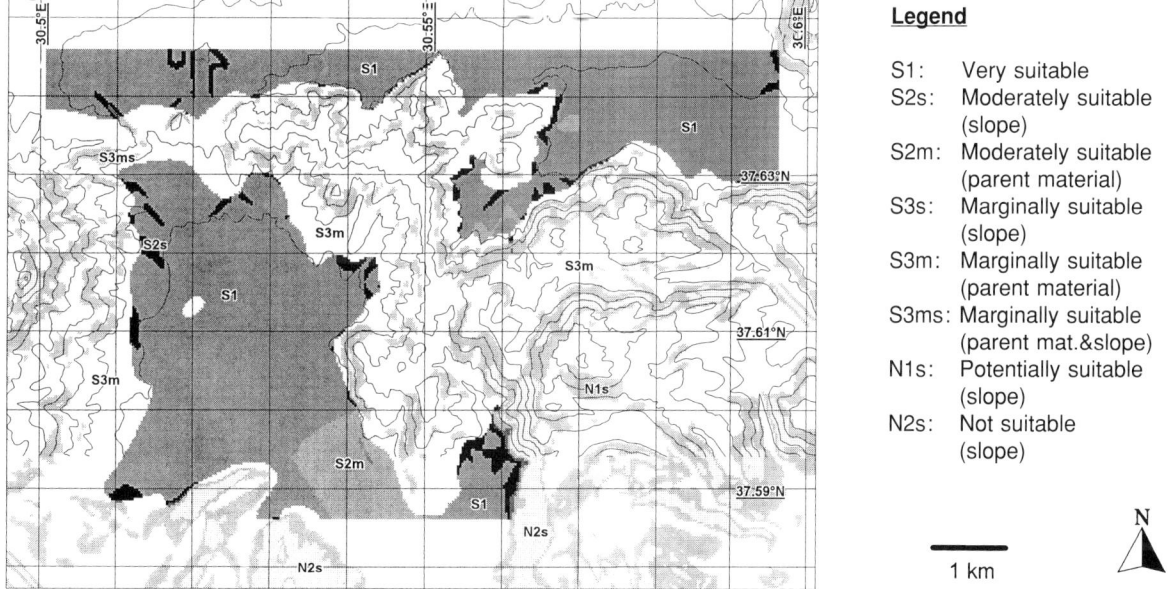

Fig. 11: Soil suitability map for *Pisum sativum* and *Vicia faba*.

Length of the growing period of Isparta

According to the FAO-Unesco system the length of the growing period (LGP) is defined as a continuous period within the year when precipitation exceeds half of the Penman evapotranspiration values (ETo) and as a additional period which is required to evaporate an assumed soil moisture reserve with mean daily temperatures exceeding 6.5 °C (*FAO* 1996). A combination of monthly ETo-values with rainfall data for Isparta resulted in LGP-diagrams (Fig. 9) showing that from mid May till mid October drought stress occurs. Hence, no rainfed agriculture is possible during this period. From the end of November throughout March temperatures (T_{mean} < 6.5 °C) are too low and hamper agricultural crop growth.

Summing up, the resulting growing period is rather short, and covers two periods: (1) from March till mid of May and (2) from mid October to the end of November, in all some 110 days. In order to overcome this problem people may have used cold resistant crops and/or irrigation during the strategic summer months. As a result, despite climatologically not unfavourable conditions, farming must have required irrigation during the summer months.

3.3. Vegetation: present land use

3.3.1. Arable farming at present

Because of water shortage, agricultural potential today is low in larger parts of the study area with the exception of the irrigated fields (the entire Ağlasun valley and the upper part of the valley of Çanaklı), where relatively good yields are obtained for the four basic crops of the region (winter cereals, sugar beets, maize and chickpeas). Poplars and fruit trees also are doing well. These zones could be indicative of the fertility and the potential farming activities in Hellenistic-Roman times. On the other hand on the stony, poorly developed and often shallow soils located on eroded landscape positions in the hills, yields nowadays are quite low. Today, farmers use the best fields for maize and sugar beets, while less demanding crops such as winter cereals and chickpeas are cultivated on less fertile parcels. When the snow starts melting and there is no longer any frost danger, the farmers plough their fields. Sequentially maize, chickpeas and sugar beets are sown. In May chemical fertilisers are applied and from June onwards irrigation becomes necessary to overcome water shortage. After harvesting which is done in August for chickpeas and in September for sugar beets and maize, organic manure is applied prior to ploughing. Parcels for winter wheat and barley undergo a similar treatment: ploughing and sowing is done in November, harvesting in June and July.

3.3.2. Forestry today

Most of the original coniferous forest on the slopes has disappeared (Waelkens and the Sagalassos team 1997; Schroyen *et al.* 2000) and has been replaced by a secondary woodland vegetation of oak shrub (*Quercus coccifera*) and to a smaller extent of deciduous oak (*Quercus cerris*). On the hilltops mainly juniper (*Juniperus excelsa* and *Juniperus oxycedrus*) is growing. During the last 15 years an extensive reforestation programme has been carried out. *Pinus brutia* and *Pinus nigra* have been planted mainly on flysh slopes, whereas *Cedrus libani* is suitable for reforestation of steep limestone slopes. This vast reforestation effort, combined with a ban on cutting specific trees by the provincial Forestry Service of Burdur, has been successful in decreasing the erosion risk over wide areas.

3.4. Land suitability maps for ancient times

At this stage in the land evaluation, the suitability zones for each land use type can be deduced as the result of a matching process. In this paper, the resulting maps are given for the most representative crops and trees. In the matching tables (Table 7) an easy update is possible in case more precise information becomes available, for example about climate, soils and crop requirements.

3.4.1. Wheat (*Triticum aestivum*)

A combination of the soil requirements for wheat (Table 1) and of the information which could be gathered for the palaeosols in the study area resulted in a soil suitability map (Fig. 10). By implementation of the hypothesis that a recent pH-increase occurred because of lime illuviation from colluvium, the values for pH(H_2O) of palaeo-sols were adjusted to those of recent Chromic Luvisol profiles, namely values between 6.5 and 7. The values of base saturation lowers then as well, but surely stays above 50%. Bread wheat develops optimally in the following situation (in case of no other restrictive parameters): pH-values between 6 and 7, a CEC > 16 meq/100g soil, a base saturation higher than 50%, an EC lower than 8 dS/m and a $CaCO_3$-content lower than 30%. A comparison of the optimal growth conditions of wheat with results of the chemical analysis of sampled profiles gave an optimal chemical suitability for all soils, except for Leptosols. Also physical soil parameters such as soil texture (silty, clayey loam to loam), soil depth (> 50 cm), stoniness (< 15% coarse fragments) and drainage scored favourably (suitability S_1) in all profiles, except in Leptosols, Eutric Regosols and Eutric Vertisols. Leptosols are too stony, too shallow and are excessively drained. The suitability class for this soil type is S_3 which means only marginally suitable. Eutric Regosols are moderately suitable (S_2) because of their sandy loam texture. For Eutric Vertisols is the fine clayey texture determining for the suitability class S_2. An overlay of the soil map with the topographical map during the matching process resulted in the final soil suitability map for wheat (Fig. 10), and shows that this crop could be cultivated in all three valleys under study.

3.4.2. Barley (*Hordeum vulgare*)

A comparison of the soil requirements for an optimal growth of barley (Table 2) with the results of chemical analysis of the sampled profiles gave an optimal suitability for all soils except for Leptosols. Also concerning the requirements of texture, soil depth, stoniness and drainage class an optimal suitability (S_1) was obtained for all profiles, except for Leptosols and Eutric Vertisols. The introduction of the topography into the matching process produced a final soil suitability map for barley (Fig. 10). It shows that the crop theoretically could grow in the same areas as those suitable for wheat.

3.4.3. Legumes

A study of the possibility to grow legumes revealed that the climate in the pilot area was too cold during the growth period of *Vicia faba* and of *Pisum sativum* (pea) and also that irrigation was required for an optimal harvest. Only chickpeas (*Cicer arietinum*) may have found a good environment for potential growth, which explains why they form still one of the four main crops in the area today (Figs 11 and 12).

3.4.4. Forestry

The higher hills with calcareous sediments (between 1100 and 1500 m) in the southeastern part of the study area form an excellent environment for *Pinus nigra*, *Cedrus libani*, *Abies cilicica* (only southern slopes), *Juniperus excelsa*, *Juniperus oxycedrus* and *Quercus cerris* (only northern slopes). They result in a S_1 classification. Most likely the hills of the study area were forested with an upper growth that was dominated by *Cedrus libani*, *Abies cilicica* and *Pinus nigra*, supplemented with *Juniperus excelsa*. The lower growth comprised *Juniperus oxycedrus* and *Quercus cerris*.

On the lower hills with flysh sediments (between 1050 and 1250 m) around the valley of Çanaklı, in the western part of the study area, *Pinus brutia*, *Quercus coccifera* and *Styrax officinalis* can grow in optimal conditions on the dominating hills with a southern exposure, up to a height of 1150 m (S_1). At a higher level *Pinus nigra*, *Juniperus excelsa* and *Juniperus oxycedrus* were better suited to the environment (S_1), while *Cedrus libani* and *Quercus cerris* were only moderately suited (S_2). The southern exposed flysh slopes were most probably forested with *Pinus brutia* up to an altitude of 1150 m (S_1). Higher in this area, *Pinus nigra*, *Juniperus excelsa* and *Juniperus oxycedrus* could also grow in optimal conditions (S_1), while *Cedrus libani* and *Quercus cerris* met only moderate conditions (S_2).

Between an altitude of 1150 and 1250 m, *Pinus nigra* may have dominated in the upper growth, complemented by *Cedrus libani* and *Juniperus excelsa*, while the undergrowth consisted of *Juniperus oxycedrus* and *Quercus cerris*.

Results of the matching process are presented in the soil suitability maps: Fig. 13 for *Cedrus libani*, Fig. 14 for *Abies Cilicica*, Fig. 15 for *Pinus brutia*, Fig. 16 for *Pinus nigra*, Fig. 17 for *Juniperus excelsa* and *Juniperus oxycedrus*, Fig. 18 for *Quercus coccifera* and Fig. 19 for *Quercus cerris*. However, more basic field measurements are required in order to arrive at more refined suitability assessment and at a calculation of the production capacity of the study area, for which detailed information concerning climatic conditions in classical times is still lacking.

3.5. Yield forecasting

Since winter wheat (*Triticum aestivum*) is nowadays the most important cereal in the area, first a potential yield of wheat was calculated for present climatic conditions, with the help of the *FAO Agro-ecological zoning model* (*FAO* 1996). Thus, if winter wheat is planted at the beginning of November (1/11), it has a normal growing period of 215 days, so that farmers can harvest early in June. For winter wheat therefore no irrigation is required because sufficient moisture is available throughout the growing period (Table 8).

In absence of other non-climatic limitations a maximum yield of 6250 kg/ha is theoretically possible. Compared to summer wheat, for which the potential yield is lower (calculation following the same method gave 6199 kg/ha) and for which irrigation is necessary because of summer drought, winter wheat is much more interesting for farming. This explains why it is the preferred cereal today. These simulated yield levels exceed farmer's yields by far. National statistics (based on information prepared by the State Institute of Statistics) report mean yields for wheat of 2010 kg/ha for the year 1992 as a national average, which is in line with average yield over the last ten years, namely 1967 kg/ha.

It is known from Livy that the farmers at Sagalassos also cultivated barley, at least during the second century BC. As mentioned above the soil suitability for this crop is the same as that for wheat. It could however have formed a better summer crop, since summer barley is more drought resistant than summer wheat. Today, yields for barley are in the same

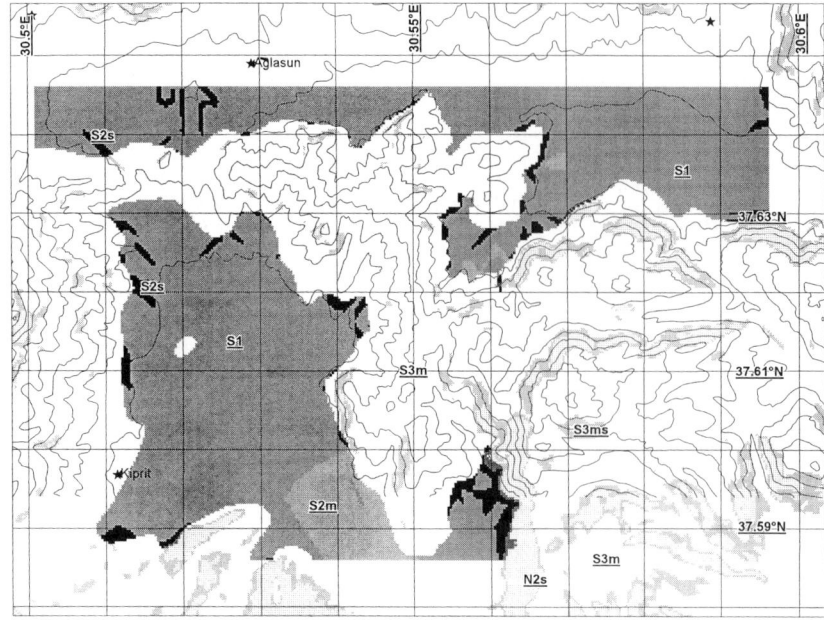

Fig. 12: Soil suitability map for *Cicer*.

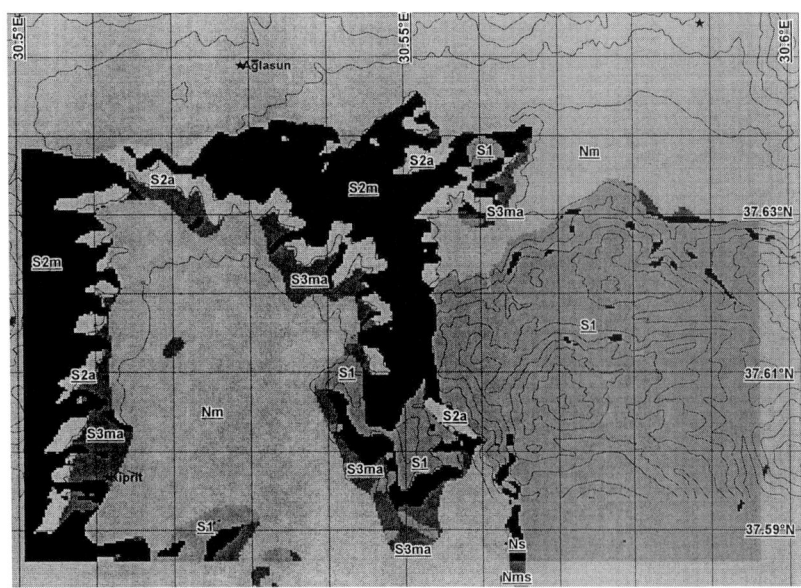

Fig. 13: Soil suitability map for *Cedrus libani*.

750

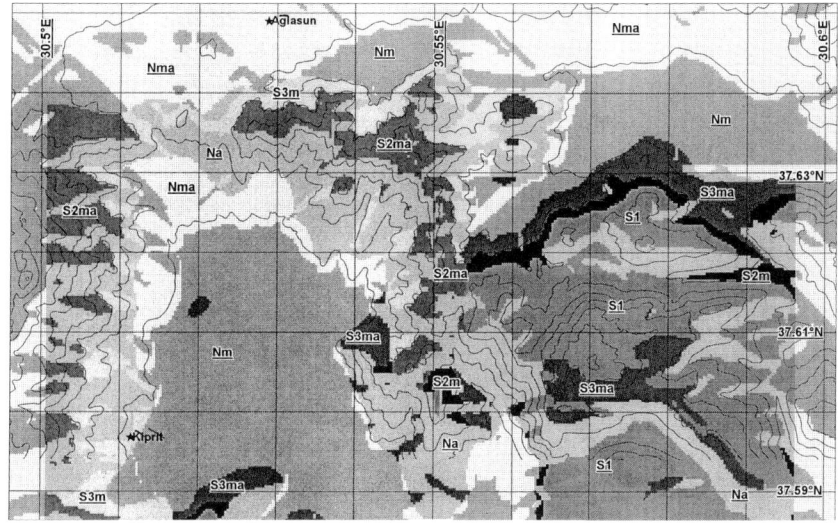

Fig. 14: Soil suitability map for *Abies cilicia*.

LEGEND

S1: Very suitable
S2m: Moderately suitable
 (parent material)
S2a: Moderately suitable
 (altitude)
S3ma: Moderately suitable
 (parent mat. & altitude)
Nma: Not suitable
 (parent mat. & altitude)
Nms: Not suitable
 (parent mat. & slope)
Nm: Not suitable
 (parent material)
Na: Not suitable
 (altitude)

1 km   N

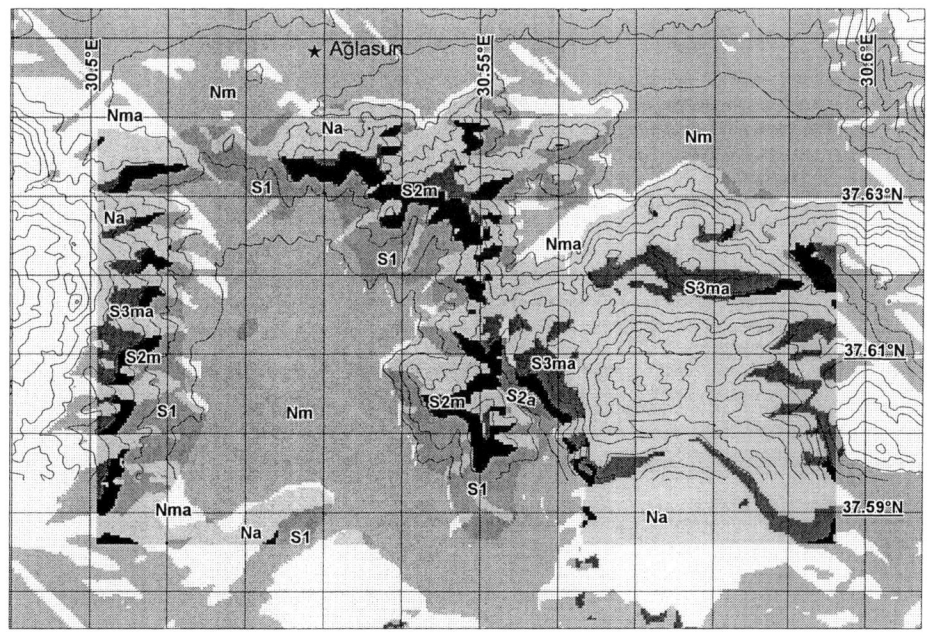

Fig. 15: Soil suitability map for *Pinus brutia*.

LEGEND

S1: Very suitable
S2m: Moderately suitable
 (parent material)
S2a: Moderately suitable
 (altitude)
S3ma: Moderately suitable
 (parent mat. & altitude)
Nma: Not suitable
 (parent mat. & altitude)
Nms: Not suitable
 (parent mat. & slope)
Nm: Not suitable
 (parent material)
Na: Not suitable
 (altitude)

1 km   N

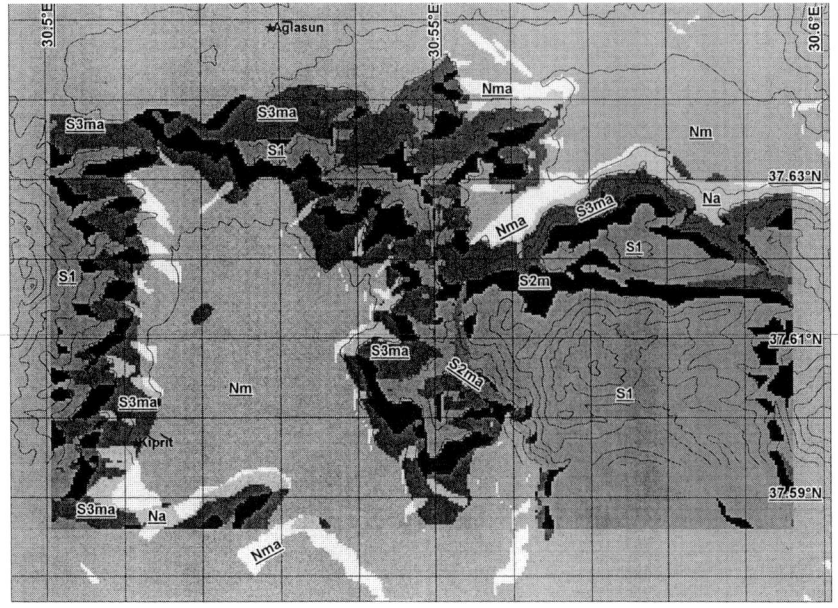

Fig. 16: Soil suitability map for *Pinus nigra*.

LEGEND

S1:   Very suitable
S2m: Moderately suitable
        (parent material)
S2a: Moderately suitable
        (altitude)
S3ma: Moderately suitable
        (parent mat. & altitude)
Nma: Not suitable
        (parent mat. & altitude)
Nms: Not suitable
        (parent mat. & slope)
Nm: Not suitable
        (parent material)
Na: Not suitable
        (altitude)

1 km

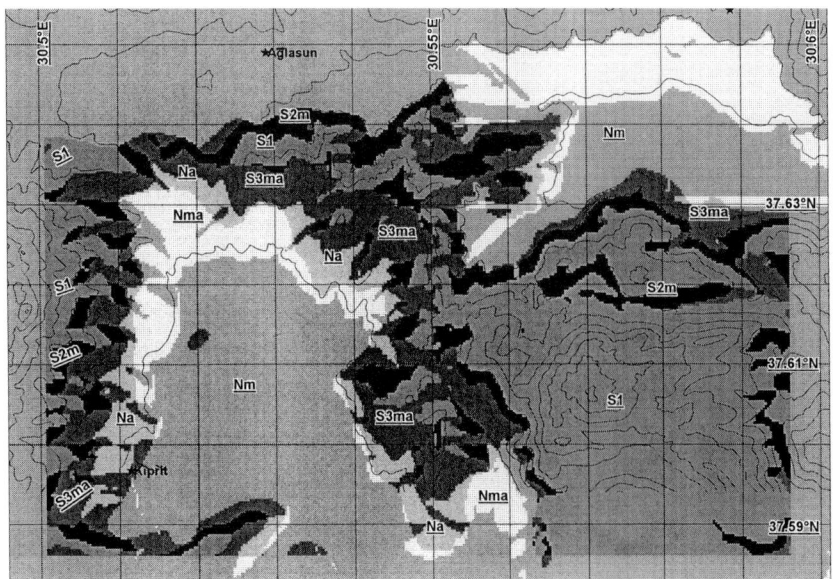

Fig. 17: Soil suitability map for *Juniperus excelsa* en *Juniperus oxycedrus*.

LEGEND

S1:   Very suitable
S2m: Moderately suitable
        (parent material)
S2a: Moderately suitable
        (altitude)
S3ma: Moderately suitable
        (parent mat. & altitude)
Nma: Not suitable
        (parent mat. & altitude)
Nms: Not suitable
        (parent mat. & slope)
Nm: Not suitable
        (parent material)
Na: Not suitable
        (altitude)

1 km

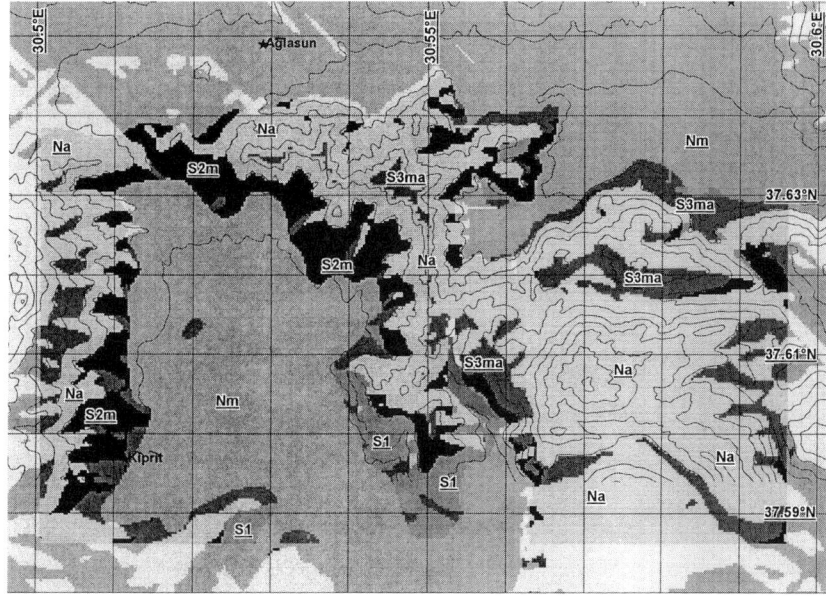

Fig. 18: Soil suitability map for *Quercus coccifera*.

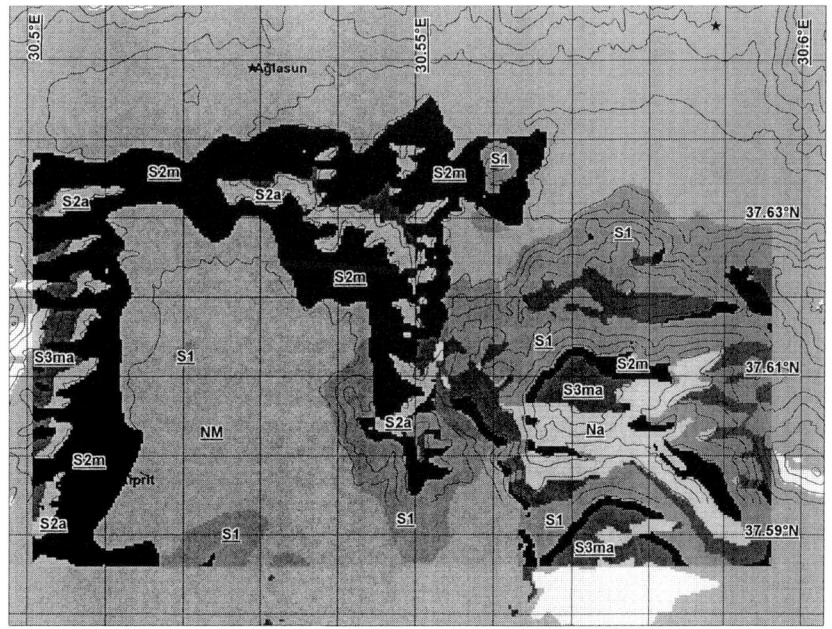

Fig. 19: Soil suitability map for *Quercus cerris*.

order of magnitude as those for wheat: a mean of 1996 kg/ha over the last ten years. The FAO model overestimates yields for the Sagalassos territory. Reasons for this discrepancy are that simulation models do not take local yield reduction factors such as sub-optimal farm management, soil constraints, climatic hazards, etc. into account. Model validation by using test fields is therefore necessary in the future to come to more reliable potential yield predictions.

Predictions for antiquity should also incorporate a study of past farming practices such as annual or biennial use of fields (see de Planhol 1958: 147, 172, 216, 219, 318). One should also try to figure out at what moment in the past farmers abandoned growing barley in favour of an almost exclusive cultivation of wheat. If this happened already in Roman times, the role of the city in the *annona* system and the better possibilities to transport wheat could have played a role. As mentioned above, the area exported wheat in Ottoman times as well.

4. GENERAL CONCLUSION

The soil scape of the pilot area can be summarised by the following soil sequences. In the Çanaklı catchment from mountain slope to valley bottom: Eutric Leptosol, Chromic Cambisols, Chromic Luvisol, buried coarse textured Fluvisol, Vertic Cambisol and Eutric Vertisol. In the Ağlasun valley, the lower part of the above mentioned soil sequence comprises also old terraces with Regosols and in the valley bottom Eutric Fluvisols.

The reason for the fundamental soil genetic difference between these two valley systems may be linked to the hydrological situation prevailing during ancient times. The Ağlasun river system is rather active, especially during wet years when plenty of well water surfaces near the limestone/flysh interface on the southern slopes of the Akdağ mountain. There are strong indications that this river system was even more active in the past (Waelkens and the Sagalassos team 1997). Therefore, regular surface flooding and therefore fluvic properties were to be expected for the Ağlasun valley. In the Çanaklı valley however, rivers are and likely were more ephemeral. They may temporarily flood the lake during the winter, but during the following summer the whole catchment drains slowly through dolines, which connect the catchment to a karst system. This semi-endoreic system inevitably leads to soils with vertic properties on the lower slopes and in the valley bottom of the Çanaklı depression. No saline soils were found which indicates that leaching by winter rains is sufficient to drain excess salts out of the watershed. It should be noted that in the western part of the Çanaklı valley a buried braided riverbed was found, with rather large pebbles interbedded with fine fluviatile material. Sherds from the Roman era may indicate that the river was more active then than it is at present.

Throughout the surveyed zone, most of the original soils have been buried since Roman times under meters thick colluvium, indicating that soil degradation became rather dramatic during the last millennia.

From the point of view of soil cover and from the matching process in the land evaluation exercise, it can be concluded that the soils of the lower reaches of the Akdağ and of the Ağlasun valley were best suited for agricultural production, this for several reasons: (1) the lowlands are and were more fertile; (2) the soils on the slopes are less shallow and less stony than in the upper reaches of the Çanaklı valley and (3) there was more water for irrigation purposes. A climate assessment confirmed that the major climatic restraints in the area are early frost and summer drought. Therefore the irrigation aspect of farming around ancient Sagalassos certainly warrants further attention in the future. Winter wheat seems to be the most suitable cereal, while barley has better cultivation changes as a summer crop.

The matching process applied to forestry showed that on the high limestone hills (between 1100 and 1500 m), in the southeastern part of the pilot zone, forests were most likely composed of *Cedrus libani*, *Abies cilicica* and *Pinus nigra* complemented by *Juniperis exelsa* in the upper tier, and *Juniperus oxycedrus* and *Quercus cerris* in the lower growth. On the lower flysh hills (between 1050 and 1250 m), around the valley of Çanaklı, most likely a forest of *Pinus brutia* occurred on the slopes exposed to the south with *Quercus coccifera* and perhaps *Styrax officinalis* in the lower tier. Between an altitude of 1150 and 1250 m, *Pinus nigra* dominated the upper growth, complemented by *Cedrus libani* and *Juniperus excelsa*. The undergrowth contained a shrub layer of *Juniperus oxycedrus* and of *Quercus cerris*.

A multidisciplinary approach to a land evaluation of the territory of ancient Sagalassos is a prerequisite for its successful implementation. Archaeologists can provide literary evidence concerning potential types of crops or trees. Moreover in the field, the interaction with the archaeologists can provide ready answers as to the age of specific soil layers. This information is of invaluable importance in order to suggest a relative dating of buried soil scapes. Information from palaeo-botanists, palynologists and zoologists can confirm the presence of specific crop/forest/animal species during the occupation of Sagalassos. The study and publication of some cores drilled in the marshes of Gravgaz during the 1997 and 1998 seasons will be of vital importance.

Very fruitful is also the interaction with geologists and geomorphologists, who provide a background on the physical framework into which soil scapes were eventually projected. With this information in mind, the decision was taken to map the soils by following an integrated toposequence approach. In this way, a maximum of soil variability could be captured with a minimum of soil profile pits and of auguring. This method also provides a key to generalise point observations into a regional changes.

5. ACKNOWLEDGEMENTS

This research is supported by the Belgian Programme of Interuniversitary Poles of Attraction initiated by the Belgian State, Prime Minister's Office, Science Policy Programming. (IUAP 4/12) The text also presents the results of the Concerted Action of the Flemish Government (GOA 97/2) and the Fund for Scientific Research-Flanders (Belgium) (FWO G.2145.94). Scientific responsibility is assumed by its authors.

6. REFERENCES

R. Allen, L. Pereira, D. Raes and M. Smith (1998) *Crop Evapo transpiration – Guidelines for Computing Crop Water Requirements. FAO Irrigation and Drainage Paper* N° 56. Rome.

Y. Akman and P. Daget (1971) Quelques aspects synoptiques des climats de la Turquie, *Bulletin de la Société Languedocienne de Géographie* 5: 269-300.

S. Buol, P. Sanchez, R. Cate and M. Grager (1975) Soil fertility capacity classification, in: P. Alvarado and E. Bornemisza (eds) *Soil Management in Tropical America*, Raleigh.

Clark Labs (1987) *IDRISI for Windows*, St. Worcester, V.S.

E. J. Davis (1874) *Anatolica*, London.

de Planhol X. (1958) *De la plaine pamphylienne aux lacs pisidiens. Nomadisme et vie paysanne (Bibliothèque archéologique et historique de l'Institut Français d' Archéologie d'Istanbul* III) Paris.

H. Devijver and M. Waelkens (forthcoming) Roman inscriptions from the sixth and seventh campaigns at Sagalassos, in: *Sagalassos VI*.

P. Driessen and R. Dudal (1991) *The Major Soils of the World*, Wageningen.

FAO (1996) *ECOCROP 1. The adaptability level of the FAO crop environmental requirements database*, Rome.

FAO-UNESCO (1978) *Soil Map of the World*. Edition 1/1978. Europe Page V-2, Rome.

FAO (1976) *A Framework For Land Evaluation (FAO Soils Bulletin* 32) Rome.

FAO (1983) *Guidelines: Land Evaluation for Rainfed Agriculture (FAO Soils Bulletin* 52) Rome.

FAO (1990) *Guidelines for Soil Description* (FAO) Rome.

FAO (1996) *Guidelines: Agro-ecological Zoning (FAO Soils Bulletin* 73) Rome.

L. Foxhall (1996) Feeling the earth move: cultivation techniques in steep slopes in classical antiquity, in: G. Shipley and J. Salmon (eds) *Human Landscapes in Classical Antiquity. Environment and Culture*, London-New York: 44-64.

L. Foxhall and H.A. Forbes (1982) Sitometria: the role of grain as a staple food in classical antiquity, *Chiron* 12: 41-90.

H. Forbes (1996) The uses of the uncultivated landscape in modern Greece: a pointer to the value of the wildness in antiquity?, in: G. Shipley and J. Salmon (eds) *Human Landscapes in Classical Antiquity. Environment and Culture*, London-New York: 68-97.

P.D.A. Garnsey (1985) Grain for Athens, in: P.A. Cartledge and F.D. Harvey (eds) *Crux. Essays Presented to G.E.M. de Ste. Croix on his 75th Birthday*, Exeter: 62-78.

J.R. Harlan and D. Zohary (1966) Distribution of Wild Wheats and Barley, *Science* 153, 1074- 1080.

H. Helbaek (1970), The plant husbandry of Hacılar, in J. Mellaart (ed.) *Excavations at Hacılar*, Edinburgh, 189-244.

E. Hyams (1976) *Soil and Civilization*, London.

ILRI (1980) *Drainage Principles and Applications III. Surveys and Investigation. Lecture Notes of the International Course on Land Drainage*, Wageningen.

W. Jongman (1988) *The Economy and Society of Pompeii*, Amsterdam.

P. Mayer and L. Askoy (1986) *Wälder der Turkei*, München.

S. Mitchell (1993) *Anatolia. Land, Men and Gods in Asia Minor. I. The Celts and the Impact of Roman Rule*, Oxford.

M. Nesbitt (1996) Chalcolithic crops from Kuruçay Höyük: An interim report, in R. Duru (ed.) *Kuruçay Höyük, II: 1978-1988 Kazilarının sonuçları Geç Kalkolitik ve İlk Tunç Çağı yerleşmeleri/Results of the Excavations 1978-1988. The Late Chalcolithic and Early Bronze Settlements*, Ankara, 134-137.

H. Oakes (1954) *The Soils of Turkey*, Ankara.

E. Paulissen, J. Poesen, G. Govers and J. De Ploey (1993) The physical environment at Sagalassos (Western Taurus, Turkey). A reconnaissance survey, in: M. Waelkens and J. Poblome (eds) *Sagalassos II. Report on the Third Excavation Campaign of 1992 (Acta Archaeologica Lovaniensia Monographiae 6)* Leuven University Press: 229-248.

A. Poisson (1984) Neogeen thrust belt in the W-Taurides, the imbricate systems of thrustsheets along a NNW-SSE transect, in: *The Geological Evolution of the Eastern Mediterranean (Special Publications of the Geological Society of London* 17): 225-254.

O. Rackham (1983) Observation on the historical ecology of Boeotia, *Abstracts of the British School at Athens* 78: 291-351.

D. Rathbone (1983) The grain trade and grain shortages in the Hellenistic East, in: P.D.A. Garnsey and C.R. Whittaker (1983) (eds) *Trade and Famine in Classical Antiquity*, Cambridge: 45-55.

M. Sartre (1995) *L' Asie Mineure et l' Anatolie d' Alexandre à Dioclétien. IVe siècle av. J.C./IIIe siècle ap. J.C.*, Paris.

P. Schrooten (1997) *Geologie van het gebied rond Sagalassos (Turkije) met nadruk op het voorkomen van ofiolieten*, unpublished M.Sc. thesis KULeuven.

C. Sys (1985) *Land Evaluation. Part* III, Gent.

K. Schroyen, M. Vermoere, I. Librecht, P. Degryse, P. Muchez, W. Viaene (†), E. Smets, E. Paulissen, E. Keppens and M. Waelkens (2000) Preliminary study of travertine deposits in the vicinity of Sagalassos: petrography, geochemistry, geomorphology and palynology, in: M.Waelkens and L. Loots (eds) *Sagalassos V. Report on the Survey and Excavation Campaigns of 1996 and 1997 (Acta Archaeologica Loveniensia Monographiae 10)*, Leuven University Press: 757-781.

H.P. Uerpmann (1996) Animal domestication – accident or intention?, in: D.R. Harris (ed.) *The Origins and Spread of Agriculture and Pastoralism in Eurasia*, London, 227-237.

USDA (1998) *Keys to Soil Taxonomy by Soil Survey Staff*, Washington.

W. Van Neer and B. De Cupere (1993) First archaeozoological results from the Hellenistic-Roman site of Sagalassos, in: M. Waelkens (ed.) *Sagalassos I. First general report on the survey (1986-1989) and the excavations (1990-1991)* (*Acta Archaeologica Lovaniensia Monographiae* 5) Leuven University Press: 225-235.

M. Vermoere (1996) *Palynologisch onderzoek van travertijnen uit Baskoy (nabij Sagalassos, Zuidwest Turkije)*, Unpublished M. Sc. thesis, KULeuven.

M. Vermoere, P. Degryse, L. Vanhecke, E. Smets, Ph. Muchez, E. Paulissen and M. Waelkens (1994) Pollen analysis of two travertine sections from Başköy (SW Turkey) and implicuations for environmental conditions during the Early Holocene, *Review of Palaeobotany and Palynology* 105:93-110.

M. Vermoere, M. Waelkens, H. Vanhaverbeke, I. Librecht, L. Vanhecke, E. Paulissen and E. Smets (2000) Late Holocene environmental change and the record of human impact at Gravgaz near Sagalassos, SW Turkey, Journal of Archaeological Science. 27 (7):571-595.

M. Waelkens (1993) Sagalassos. History and archaeology, in: M.Waelkens (ed.) *Sagalassos I. First General Report on the Survey (1986-1989) and Excavations (1990-1991)* (*Acta Archaeologica Lovaniensia Monographiae* 5) Leuven University Press: 37-82.

M. Waelkens, E. Paulissen, H. Vanhaverbeke, I. Öztürk, B. De Cupere, H.A. Ekinci, P.M. Vermeersch, J. Poblome and R. Degeest (1997) The 1994 and 1995 surveys on the territory of Sagalassos, in: M. Waelkens and J. Poblome (eds) *Sagalassos IV. Report on the Survey and Excavation Campaigns of 1994 and 1995 (Acta Archaeologica Lovaniensia Monographiae 9)* Leuven, University Press: 11-102.

M. Waelkens and the Sagalassos team (1997) Interdisciplinarity in classical archaeology. A case study: The Sagalassos Archaeological Research Project (southwest Turkey), in: M. Waelkens and J. Poblome (eds) *Sagalassos IV. Report on the survey and excavation campaigns of 1994 and 1995* (*Acta Archaeologica Lovaniensia Monographiae* 9) Leuven University Press: 225-252.

P. Weiss (1992) Pisidien: eine historische Landschaft im Lichte ihrer Munzprägung, in E. Schwertheim (ed.), *Forschungen in Pisidien* (*Asia Minor Studien* 6) Bonn: 143-166.

K. D. White (1970) *Roman Farming*, London – Southampton.

G. Woolf (1997) The Roman Urbanisation of the East, in: S. Alcock (ed.) *The Early Roman Empire in the East* (*Oxbow Monograph* 95) Oxford: 1-14.

D. H. Yaalon (1971) Soil forming processes in time and space, in D. H. Yaalon (ed.) *Palaeopedology. Origin, Nature and Dating of Palaeosols*, Jerusalem.

D. H. Yaalon (1995) *Soils in Mediterranean Region: What Makes them Different?*, Jerusalem.

D. Zohary (1989) Domestication of the southwestern Asian Neolithic crop assemblage of cereals, pulses, and flax: evidence from the living plants, in: D.R. Harris and G.C. Hillman (eds) *Foraging and Farming. The Evolution of Plant Exploitation*, London, 358-373.

D. Zohary (1996) The mode of domestication of the founder crops of SW Asian agriculture, in: D.R. Harris (ed.) *The Origins and Spread of Agriculture and Pastoralism in Eurasia*, London, 142-158.

J. Zedler (1954) *Grosses Vollständiges Universal-Lexikon*, Graz.

PRELIMINARY STUDY OF TRAVERTINE DEPOSITS IN THE VICINITY OF SAGALASSOS: PETROGRAPHY, GEOCHEMISTRY, GEOMORPHOLOGY AND PALYNOLOGY

Kristof SCHROYEN[1], Marleen VERMOERE[2], Ireen LIBRECHT[3], Patrick DEGRYSE[1], Philippe MUCHEZ[1], Willy VIAENE (†)[1], Erik SMETS[2], Etienne PAULISSEN[3], Eddy KEPPENS[4] and Marc WAELKENS[5]

1 - Laboratory of Mineralogy, Physico-Chemical Geology, KULeuven, Celestijnenlaan 200C, B-3001 Heverlee, Belgium
2 - Laboratory of Plant Systematics, KULeuven, Kardinaal Mercierlaan 92, B-3001 Heverlee, Belgium
3 - Geomorphology and Regional Geography, KULeuven, Redingenstraat 16, B-3000 Leuven, Belgium
4 - Faculty of Science, VUBrussel, Pleinlaan 2, B-1050 Brussel, Belgium
5 - Department of Archaeology, KULeuven, Blijde Inkomststraat 21, B-3000 Leuven, Belgium

1. INTRODUCTION

Fragments of travertines were first discovered as a filling material in walls at Sagalassos. The source deposits were found in the village of Başköy, which is situated 7 km to the southwest of the site.

Travertines are freshwater limestone deposits which form according to the following reactions:

$$H_2O + CO_2 \uparrow\downarrow H_2CO_3 + CaCO_3 \gtreqless Ca^{2+} + 2\,HCO_3^- \quad (1) \uparrow\downarrow H^+ + HCO_3^-$$

For calcium carbonates to precipitate, the precipitating water must lose CO_2. Because of the non-equilibrium between CO_2-saturated groundwater and CO_2 in the atmosphere, the loss of gas will occur automatically. Further loss is induced by: (a) turbulence of water near waterfalls and rapids, (b) a temperature rise of the water and (c) absorption of CO_2 by plants during photosynthesis. In addition to this *in situ* formation, deposits can also form as the result of the erosion of older travertines. These are the so-called detrital travertine deposits or chalk tuffs. Generally, travertine deposits are classified into three types, depending on their position (Folk *et al.* 1985). These types are: (a) pond travertines which form in quiet waters and are mainly organic in origin, (b) fall travertines which are precipitated inorganically in turbulent waters and (c) detrital travertines. The main aims of this paper are to investigate the chemistry of the recent travertine-producing waters at Başköy, the precipitation environment of the travertines and climatic variations which can possibly be deduced from palynological and stable isotope analysis.

2. GEOLOGICAL SETTING AND VEGETATION IN THE REGION

The region of Sagalassos and Başköy is characterized by three tectonostratigraphic units, separated by large thrust faults (Dilek and Rowland 1993). The first unit, the basement, is formed by autochthonous carbonate platforms: the Bey Dağları platform in the west and the Anamas-Aksesi in the east. They mainly consist of Mesozoic limestones on which Tertiary flysch is deposited. In late-Maastrichtian time, the Antalya and Alanya nappes thrusted over the platforms and formed the second tectonostratigraphic unit. A second tectonic phase occurred in mid-Tertiary time when the Lycian and Beyşehir-Hoyran-Hadım nappes were thrusted northwards onto the Bey Dağları and Anamas platforms respectively. These nappes consist of ophiolitic sequences which are structurally overlaid by allochthonous white limestones: the third unit (Fig. 1). Viaene *et al.* (1993) distinguished several types of allochthonous limestones in the area around Sagalassos, used as building stones:
- Peloidal wackestone to packstone with bioclasts.

- Mudstone, slighty enriched in organic matter.
- Bioclastic wackestone, partly dolomitized.
- Algal mudstone to packstone.
- Grainstone with pellets and some litho- and bioclasts.
- Mudstones with radiolaria, often silicified.

A very common feature of the allochthonous limestones is the numerous veins. These veins are the result of the various tectonic deformation stages. Autochthonous limestones are made up of bioclastic wackestone which is partly dolomitized and radiolarian mudstone to wackestone. Most of these limestones are partly or totally silicified. Groundwater saturated in carbonate, which creates the recent travertine deposition, flows through the allochthonous limestone units and probably through the autochthonous limestones.

From former palynological studies in southwest Turkey (van Zeist et al. 1975; Bottema and Woldring 1986, 1990) and from vegetation studies in southeast Turkey (Kürschner 1984), it is thought that the potential vegetation above an altitude of 1200 m in this region would be evergreen needle-leaved forests resistant to cold. *Cedrus libani, Abies cilicica* and *Pinus nigra* would be the dominant trees at this elevation. At lower altitudes, between 0 and 1200 m, mixed evergreen forests (broad-leaved and needle-leaved trees) would predominate. Nowadays, most of the forests have disappeared and regeneration of the former vegetation is hampered, mainly by the grazing and trampling effect of goats. Maquis of *Quercus coccifera* is predominant on the hills up to 1600 m. This tree species mostly appears as a creeping shrub and covers large areas. Also, there are many stands of juniper (*Juniperus excelsa* and *Juniperus oxycedrus*) on the limestone hills. These trees can withstand extreme climatological and environmental conditions. Both these secondary tree species can tolerate the destructive activities of the goats. At the highest elevations (above 2000 m) thorn-cushions are characteristic (Kürschner 1984). On the slopes around the ruins of Sagalassos, steppe plants of the genera *Verbascum, Euphorbia, Phlomis* and *Artemisia* have foliage adapted to the dryness and high temperatures of the summer time.

In the past, intensive deforestation in the region gave rise to all kinds of erosion processes (Waelkens et al. 1997). The wood of *Cedrus libani* was used for many purposes, not only because of its resistence to natural decaying processes and insect attacks, but also for its aromatic smell (Meiggs 1982). Nevertheless, some natural *Cedrus*-forests (e.g. in the valley of Çanaklı; northern slopes), forests of *Abies cilicica* and *Pinus nigra* (at Dereköy) and deciduous oak trees at a lower altitude are still reminiscent of the potential vegetation of the region. According to Meiggs (1982), the greatest damage to the forests in the Taurus range occurred over the last hundred years. In his work, the sharp decline of the Taurus forests is explained by two factors: firstly, there was an increasing conversion of large forest areas into agricultural and grazing land in the nineteenth century and, secondly, there were large demands for wood when the Suez Canal was built. It has never been estimated to what extent the forests of southwest Turkey were already depleted by the end of the Roman Empire.

In the last few decades, the Turkish authorities have realized that deforestation causes erosion on the slopes of the Taurus hills, and now the felling of trees is considered a crime. Forestry services have been founded for the organisation of massive replanting of forests.

3. MATERIALS AND METHODS

Samples were collected from the face of an abandoned waterfall at the village of Başköy and in an outcrop along the road from Ağlasun to Burdur (Figs 2 and 3). Two sections were made at a depth of 0.3 m to avoid recent surface contamination of the travertines. Samples were taken vertically every 10 cm to obtain a good comparison of travertine deposits through time. Recent travertines were sampled in brooks. Nearby allochthonous limestones were sampled to compare their stable isotopic composition with that of the travertines. The pH, conductivity, hardness and temperature of the brooks were measured to ascertain the precipitation conditions of recent travertines. These measurements were respectively performed with an Eijkelkamp18.37 pH-meter, a Consort K990 conductivity-meter, an Aquamerck® 1.11103 Carbonate Hardness Test and an alcohol thermometer.

Samples were examined by standard petrographic methods using polarized light, scanning electron microscopy (SEM) and cathodoluminescence. Chemical analyses were carried out by dissolving the travertine samples in 1N HCl and concentrations of the elements Ca, Fe, Mg, Mn, Zn, Sr, Na, Pb and K were measured on a Varian Techtron AA6 flame atomic absorption spectrometer. The insoluble residue (IR) was measured gravimetrically. Qualitative determinations of minerals in the insoluble residue of the travertine carbonates were performed on a Phillips TMPW3020 X-ray diffractometer, with Cu K_α radiation.

For the carbon and oxygen isotope analyses of the carbonates, the samples were reacted in a vacuum with 100% H_3PO_4 which releases CO_2. This gas was analysed with a mass spectrometer at the Vrije Universiteit Brussel (VUB). Isotope data are expressed as per mil (‰) deviation from the Pee Dee Belemnite (PDB) standard. Reproducibilities determined from replicate analyses were better than 0.1 ‰ for oxygen and better than 0.05 ‰ for carbon at 2 level. For the

Fig. 1: Geological map, showing the different tectonostratigraphic units (after Poisson *et al.* 1983).
- Unit 1: autochthonous limestone of the Bey Dağları platform (Cr).
- Unit 2: Late-Maastrichtian ophiolitic sequences (Ol grey). - Transgressive Tertiary flysch deposits (m_{2-1}).
- Unit 3: Ophiolitic sequences, Lycian nappe (Ol dark). - White limestones, Lycian nappe (Dd, E).
- Recent strata: Pliocene volcanism (v) and Quaternary alluvial deposits (clays and travertines, q).

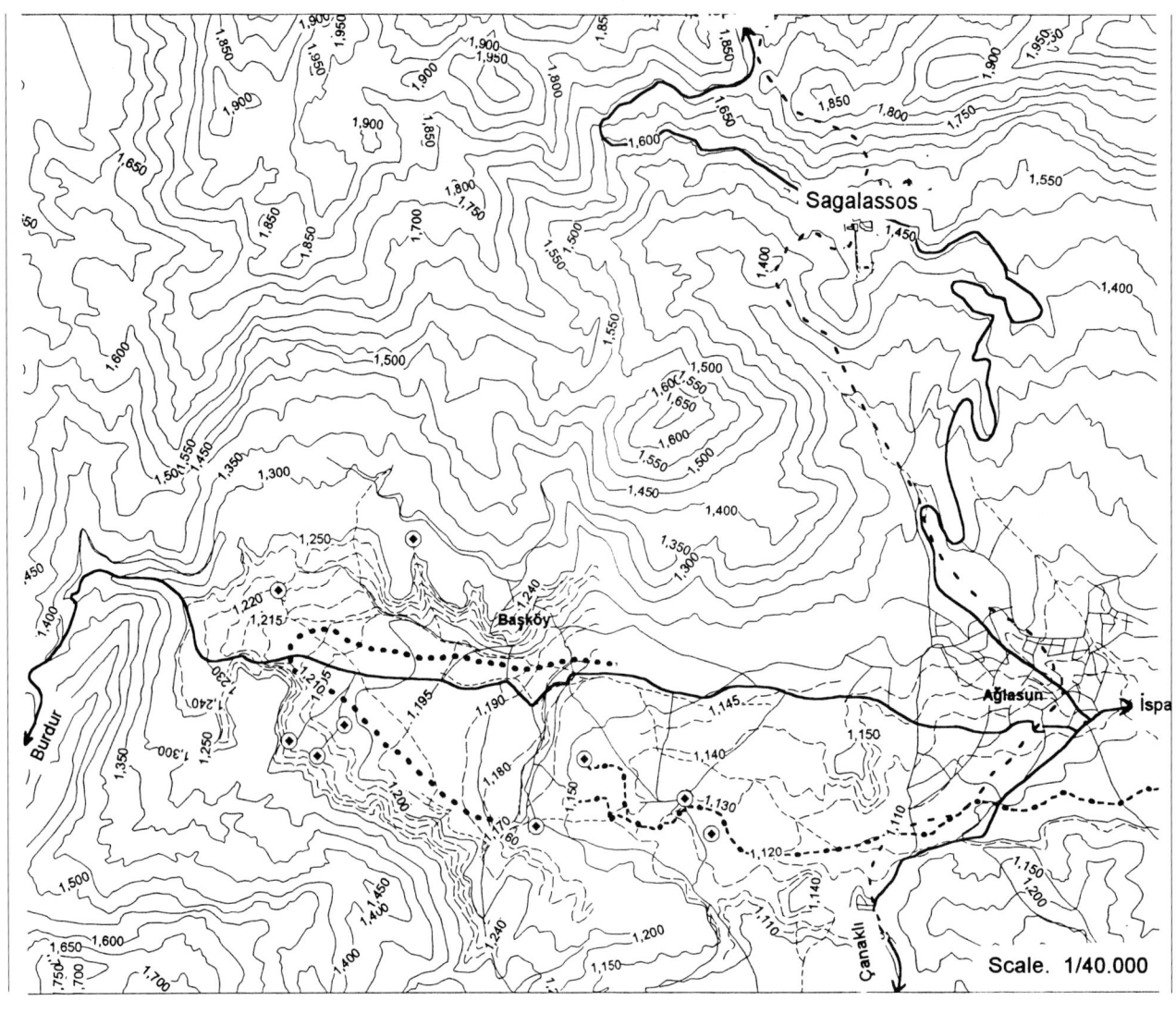

Fig. 2: Map showing the area of Sagalassos and Başköy.

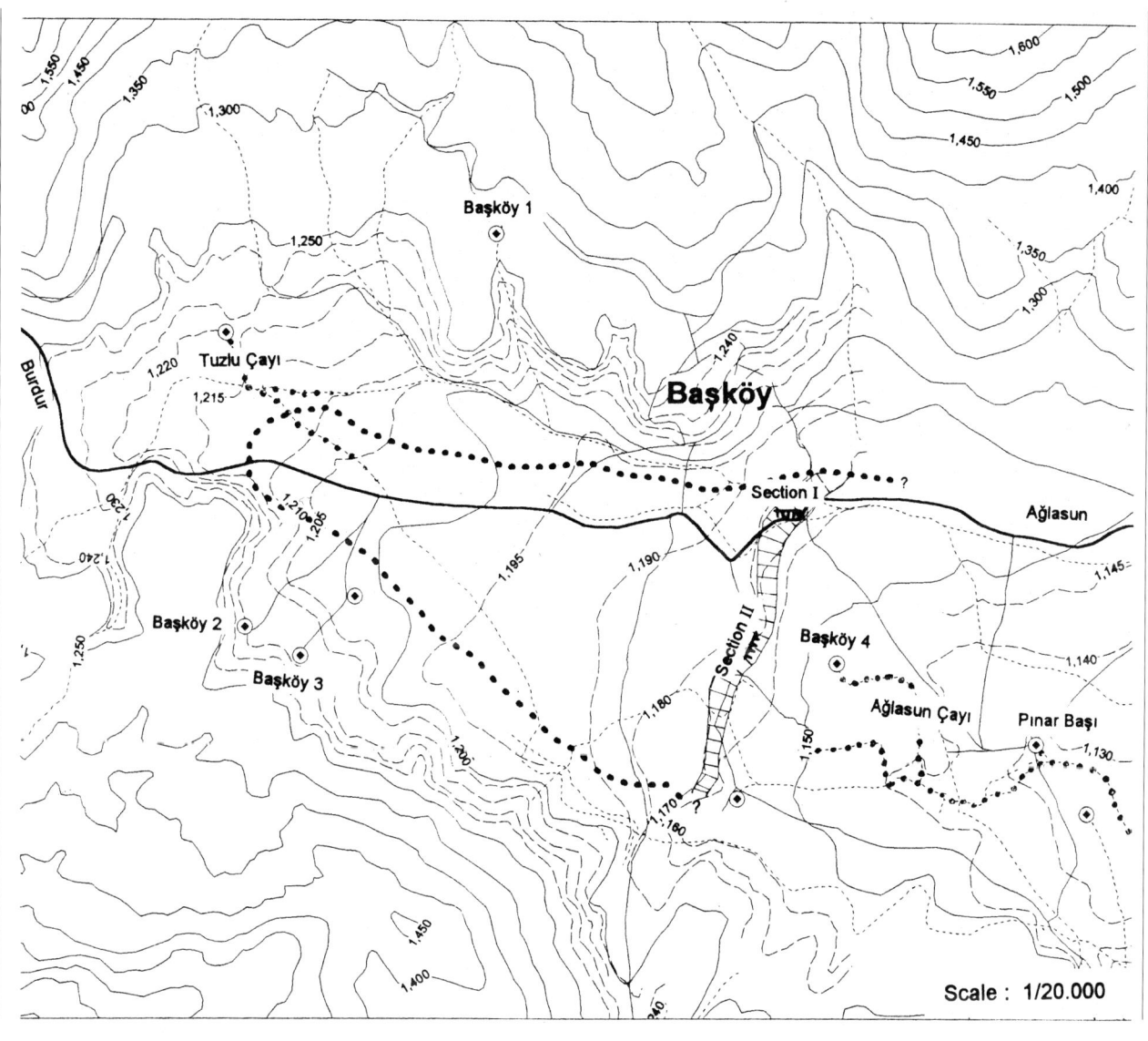

Fig. 3: Map showing the sampled travertine-forming (Tuzlu Çay) and non-travertine-forming waters (springs in Ağlasun/Sagalassos and Başköy 1-4) and the sampled sections.

Fig. 4: Photograph of section I.

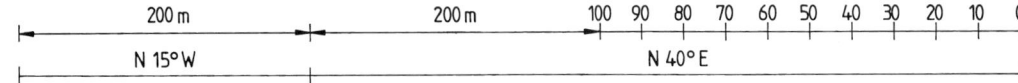

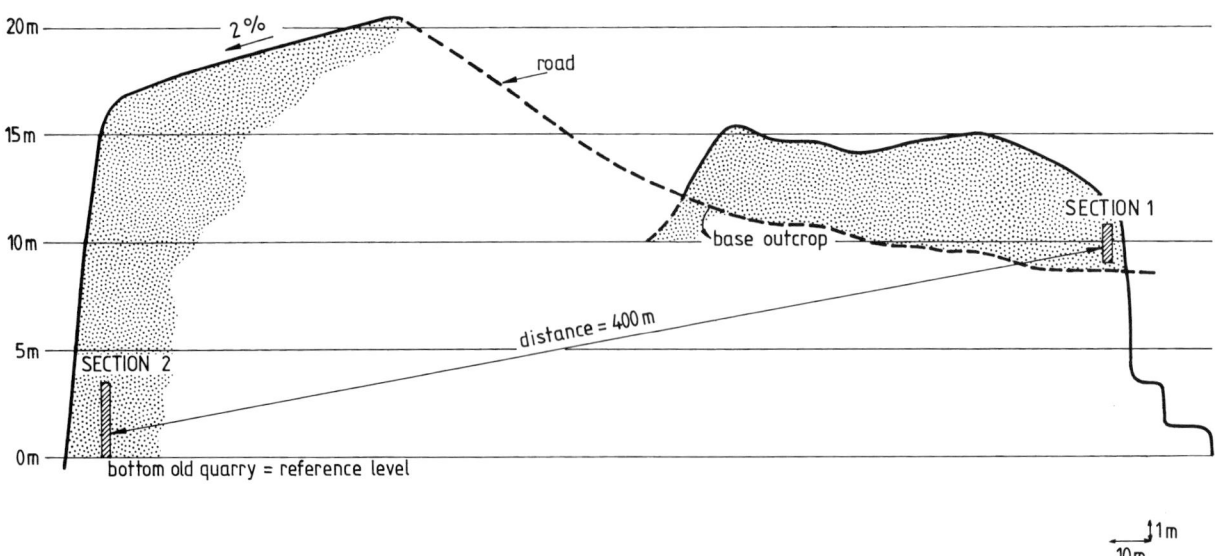

Fig. 5: Overview of section I along the road Ağlasun-Burdur (not to scale).

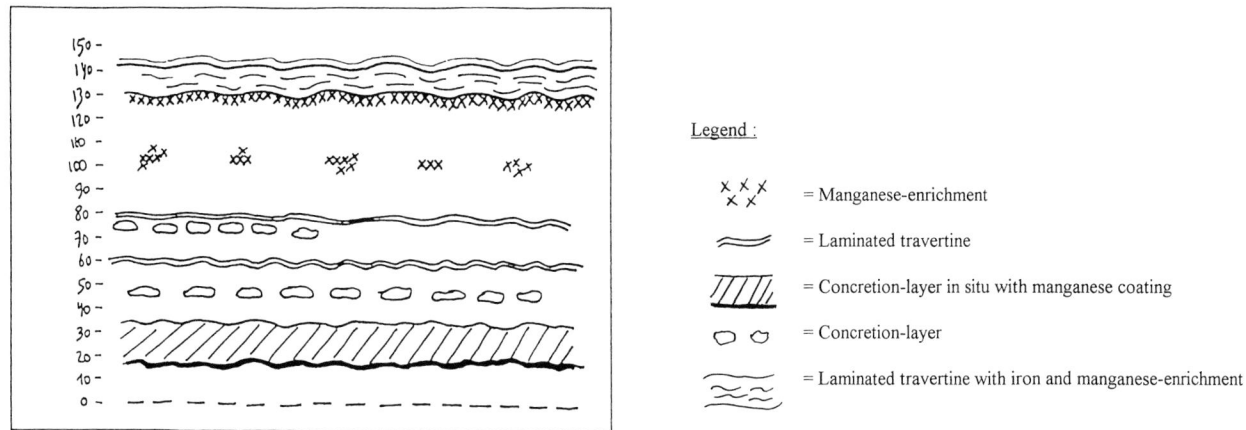

Fig. 6: Detailed view of the channel in the eastern part of section I.

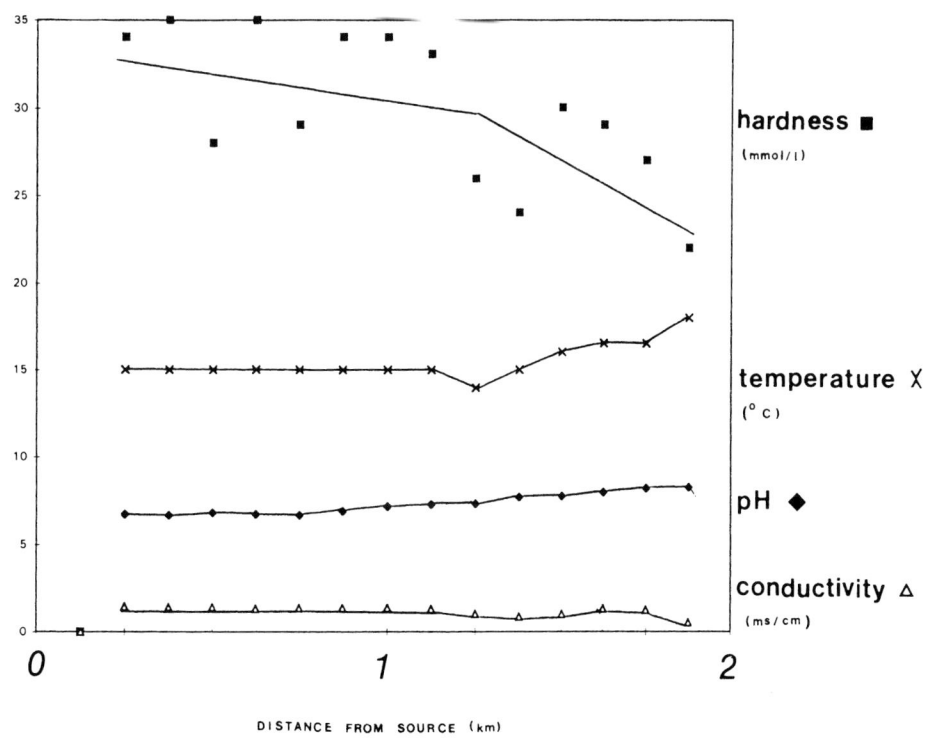

Fig.7 : Evolution of physical and chemical parameters as a function of the distance from the source of the Tuzlu Çay stream (travertine-forming water).

Fig. 8: Travertine precipitated on Chironomida-larvae.
Crossed polars.
Sample KS52-A1 (Scale bar is 2 mm).

Fig. 9: Acicular fabric in a recent travertine.
Crossed polars.
Sample KS57 (Scale bar is 2 mm).

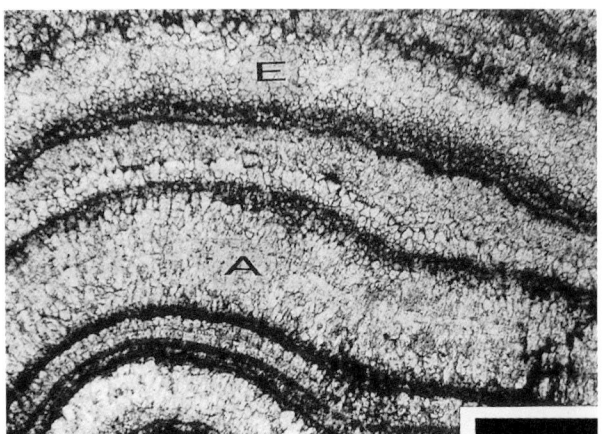

Fig. 10: Alternation of an acicular (A) and an equant (E) fabric in a recent laminated travertine.
Parallel polars.
Sample KS39C (Scale bar is 2mm).

analysis of water, CO_2 was added to the water in a vacuum. Equilibrium was reached after six hours under standard conditions. Subsequently, the CO_2 was extracted and analysed. In order to carry out palynological analyses, the travertine samples were prepared according to the procedure designed by Bastin (1978), who used the method for the extraction of pollen grains from stalagmites. 100 g of travertine is needed for the preparation of each sample. Such large quantities are required because of the low concentration of pollen grains in the relatively fast precipitation of travertines. Before the preparation of the travertine samples, a determined quantity of *Lycopodium*-spores was added to each sample before preparation to get an idea of the absolute pollen density (Stockmarr 1971). The procedure includes the following treatments of the samples:

1 – dissolution of the calcium carbonate by adding HCl 30%;
2 – boiling in a solution of NaOH 10% to dissolve the organic material;
3 – the floatation of the fossilized pollen grains out of the residue by adding a heavy liquid (Thoulet solution);
4 – dissolving the siliceous material by boiling the residue in HF 40%;
5 – dehydration with 99% acetic acid, followed by acetolysis with a solution of nine parts anhydric acetic acid and one part H_2SO_4;
6 – mounting the residue with the pollen grains in glycerine. Observations of pollen grains were made with a 'WILD Heerbrugg' microscope (400 x and 1000 x). Reference collections of the pollen types, present in Louvain-la-Neuve and in Groningen, and the pollen flora of Reille (1992, 1995) were used to determine the pollen grains.

4. GEOMORPHOLOGY AND TOPOGRAPHICAL POSITION OF THE TRAVERTINE DEPOSITS

The village of Başköy is situated at an elevation of 1200 to 1260 m, at the northern edge of a 1 km wide valley, which drains towards the east (by the upper course of the Ağlasun Çayı) and towards the southeast (Ağlasun Ovası). The village is situated nearly at the valley head, which is bounded by the Çatak Tepe (1969 m) to the north, the Balık Tepe (1500 m) and the Tavşankırı Tepe (1610 m) to the west and the Kosekoyağı Tepe (1790 m) and the Delikkaya Tepe (1791 m) to the south. Below Başköy, the valley floor is situated at 1150 m above sea level. It is used for agriculture and consequently liberally irrigated by a network of irrigation canals, fed by the water of different springs (see Fig. 3).

The travertine deposits studied and sampled are from two different places in a travertine terrace above the valley floor. The two sections (Figs 3 and 4) are situated in a topographical successive position. Section one is situated below and to the north of section 2.

The first section (Fig. 4) is in an outcrop along the road from Ağlasun to Burdur and was created by the construction of this road. The complete outcrop has a length (east – west) of ca. 50 m and a height of ca. 4 m. This deposit is a fall travertine, which has its origin in a northern side valley. The top of this travertine deposit is 30 m above the valley floor. There is a hiatus of nearly 5 m between the base of this outcrop and the top of the second section, described below. In the outcrop along the road, several layers and morphological units can be distinguished (Fig. 5). The eastern part of the outcrop consists of an incision or channel, filled with chalk tuffs (Fig. 6). In this part of the outcrop, a Roman potsherd was found. To the west of this channel, the travertine is more compact. Different layers, composed of alternating compact and looser material can be recognized. The top of the outcrop consists of colluvium, which contains travertine that is not *in situ*.

The second section is situated south of the first one, in a possibly abandoned travertine quarry. The travertine deposits are distinctly layered and slope down 5 to 8 degrees to the southeast (towards the present valley floor). The fall of these deposits and consequently of the former river at this place, is greater than the average fall of the valley towards the east which implies a steeper part of the valley or a water-fall. The outcrop consists of alternating compact and loose travertine layers. The base of this outcrop is situated at an elevation of 1171 m, or about 20 m above the valley floor. This second outcrop has a total height of ca. 5 m.

5. FIELD MEASUREMENTS

Conductivity, pH, hardness and temperature tests revealed a great difference between travertine- and non-travertine-forming waters (Table 1). The travertine-forming waters typically have: greater hardness, temperature and conductivity. This suggests a more prolonged interaction with the limestone aquifers and possibly a deeper circulation of the fluids. It is remarkable that within a distance of 1 km from the source, the characteristics of the water are completely different (Table 1). When the distance from the source increases, the following features are observed in the travertine-forming waters (Fig. 7):
- the pH increases due to the loss of CO_2;
- the hardness decreases due to the precipitation of $CaCO_3$;
- the conductivity decreases, suggesting a smaller amount of ions in the water;
- a temperature rise from the heat of the sun.

6. PETROGRAPHIC DESCRIPTIONS

6.1. Macroscopic fabrics

In the field, classification was made based on the macroscopic textures of the travertine deposits. Most deposits are formed by precipitation around plants. The geometry of these plants dictates the general appearance of the deposits. Recent travertines are mostly characterized by a laminated aspect, a texture also present in the palaeodeposits. In the sections investigated, conglomeratic layers can be observed. The latter contain abundant angular fragments of a different nature, which are cemented by carbonates. These layers are probably the result of infill of eroded fragments in a river channel and at the foot of waterfalls. In addition, two other texture types can be found in travertine deposits:
- Bubble-like structures which are carbonate deposits around Chironomida-larvae (Fig. 8, Thienemann 1954).
- 'Plate' travertine which consists of small spheres. This results in a porous but close fabric which explains the frequent use of this travertine as a building stone.

According to Folk *et al.* (1985), bubble-like structures can be classified as fall travertines, whereas plate travertines are placed in the pond travertine class.

6.2. Microscopic textures

6.2.1. Inorganic textures

The most abundant travertine texture is the acicular fabric (Fig. 9). This type of deposit consists of elongated carbonate crystals with a length up to 0.5 cm. They occur in layers around plants. In recent laminated travertines several layers of acicular crystals are recognized, alternating with an equant fabric (Fig. 10). This results in a concentric, laminated pattern. In addition to this lamination, there is also a micro-lamination which consists of thin layers of micritic crystals. Often, a lateral transition from acicular to equant fabric can be observed (Fig. 11). On small plant stalks (mosses), small equant crystals with a diameter of ca. 160 µm precipitate abundantly. During degradation of the stalks, many holes arise and the sparite crystals come apart (Fig. 12). This explains the lesser strength of this travertine type.

An acicular fabric is interpreted as the result of rapid loss of gas in turbulent environments (Gonzales *et al.* 1992), whereas a calm environment gives rise to equant fabrics. In turbulent environments there is a large number of crystal nuclei of $CaCO_3$ per unit of surface. The nuclei show a random orientation of their C-axis. Because growth along the C-axis is favoured in turbulent environments, the nuclei which do not have an orientation of their C-axes perpendicular to the surface of growth will not grow (Fig. 13, Gonzales *et al.* 1992). The change of turbulence also depends on the shape of the plants, which explains the transition from acicular to equant fabric. The lamination is the result of alternating periods of precipitation and non-deposition. The thickness and texture of the laminae depend on the type of the water flow (turbulent or quiet environments) and the duration of this flow. The micro-lamination is the result of the incorporation of dust or micrite particles on the surface of crystals during growth.

6.2.2. Organic fabrics

Plate travertines have a totally different fabric. The spheres are composed of a micritic nucleus which is surrounded by irregular concentric laminae (Fig. 14). The diameter of these spheres is ca. 1.5 mm. SEM revealed a dense concentration of filaments. These are hollow tubes having a diameter of ca. 10 µm (Fig. 15). With cathodoluminescence the plate travertines show a yellow to ochre colour. Also, the filaments may have been formed by carbonate precipitation around algae. The yellow to ochre luminescence of the plate travertines could be due to the incorporation of Mn^{2+} in the calcite lattice (Frank *et al.* 1982). The reducing conditions needed for the presence of Mn^{2+} are probably induced by organic activity. Generally, it is believed that plate travertines form by organic activity (photosynthesis) in quiet waters, and are therefore classified as pond travertines.

6.2.3. Weathering and early diagenesis

Corroded edges of acicular crystals are often recognized with SEM. The crystals become 'rounded' and the edges are covered by a micritic layer. Also, slat-like fibre crystals with a length of 20 µm and a width of 1 µm were observed (Fig. 16). It is thought that the slat-like crystals are the first indication of diagenesis (Jones and Kahle 1993). The rounded edges are the result of early weathering of calcite rhombohedra. By the differential weathering of carbonates because of differences in crystal fabrics and crystal defects a needle-like fabric is created in which the original lamination and micro-lamination is preserved (Fig. 17).

7. GEOCHEMICAL ANALYSIS

7.1. Major and trace-elements

Geochemical analyses have been performed on samples of the two sections and on recent samples for Fe, Mg, Ca, Mn, Zn, Sr, Na, Pb and K. The insoluble residue (IR) was also measured. To show mutual relationships the concentrations of the elements and the IR have been treated statistically, resulting in bivariant plots and correlation matrices (Fig. 18, Table 2).

Most travertines have a very low trace elements content and IR, except in section I (Fig. 18). This means that most travertines consist of pure calcite. In general, the investi-

Fig. 11: Lateral transition from an acicular (A) to an equant fabric round plant stalks.
Crossed polars.
Sample KS48B (Scale bar is 2 mm).

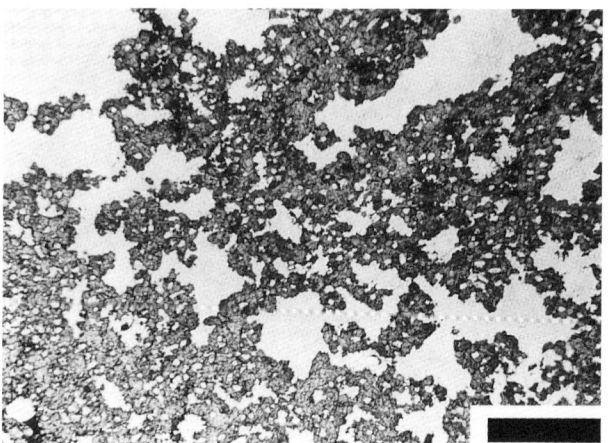

Fig. 12: Degradation of plant stalks results in a very porous fabric with reduced strength.
Crossed polars.
Sample of section II, nr. KSSA103 (Scale bar is 2 mm).

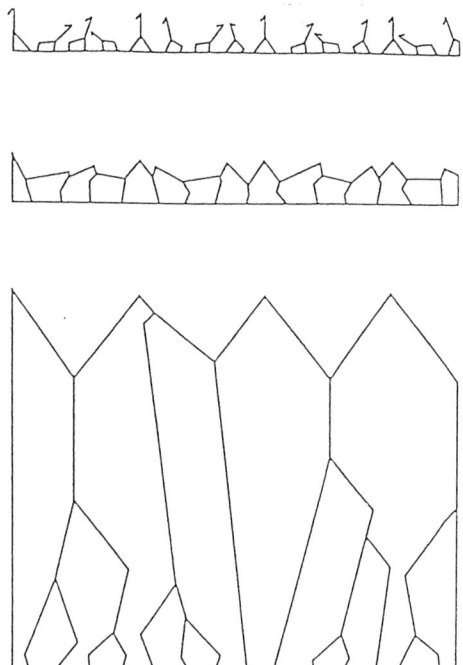

Fig. 13: Competitive growth of crystallites. Growth of crystal nuclei with their C-axes (indicated by arrows) perpendicular to the substrate is favoured (after Gonzales *et al.* 1992).

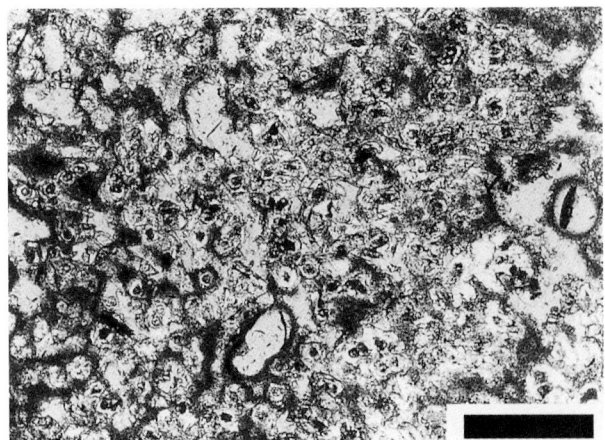

Fig. 14: Typical organic fabric in a plate travertine. Parallel polars. Sample KS11 (Scale bar is 750 µm.

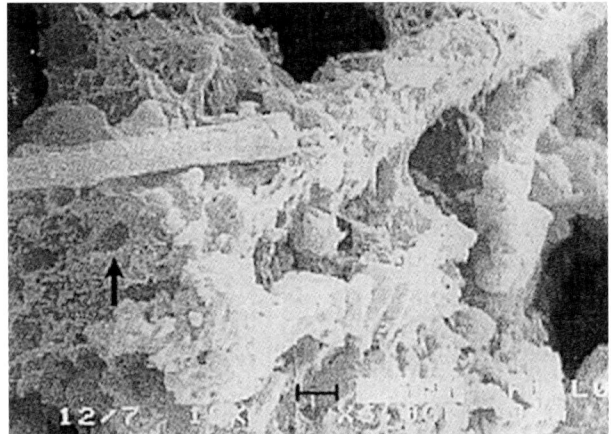

Fig. 15: Algal filaments: hollow tubes as seen by SEM. The cavity of the tube is indicated by an arrow. Sample KS90 (Scale bar is 10 µm).

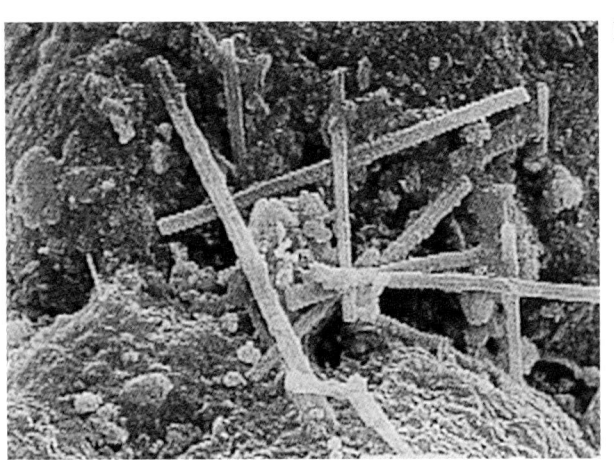

Fig. 16: Effect of the weathering and early diagenesis. Slat-like crystals. SEM-photograph of sample KS90 (Scale bar is 10 µm).

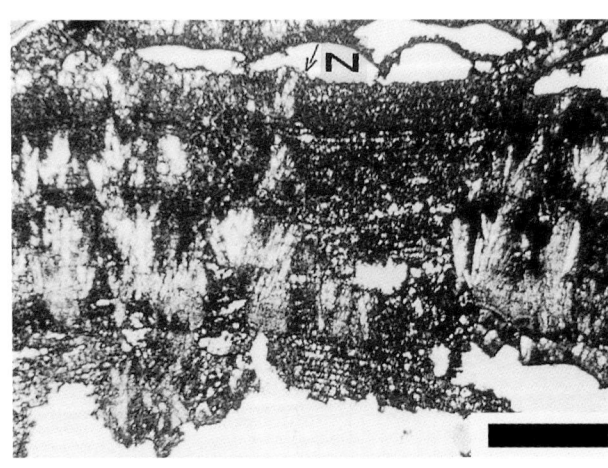

Fig. 17: Development of a needle-like fabric (N). The original microlamination of the travertine is still preserved. Parallel polars (Scale bar is 2 mm).

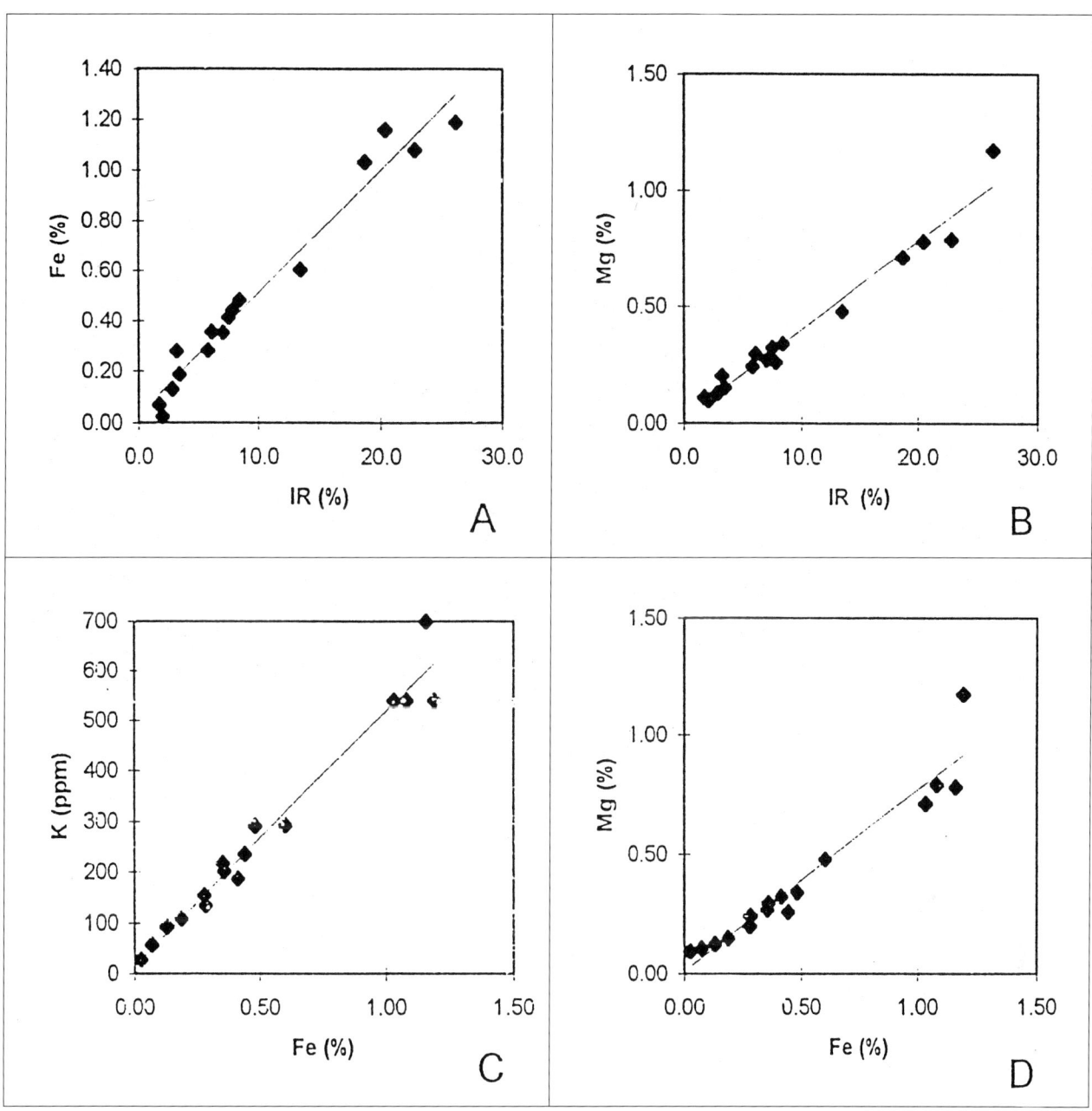

Fig. 18: Bivariant plots revealing a mutual relationship between the investigated trace-elements and the insoluble residue (IR).
A, B: Positive correlation of Fe and Mg with IR.
C, D: Positive correlation of Fe with Mg and K with Fe.

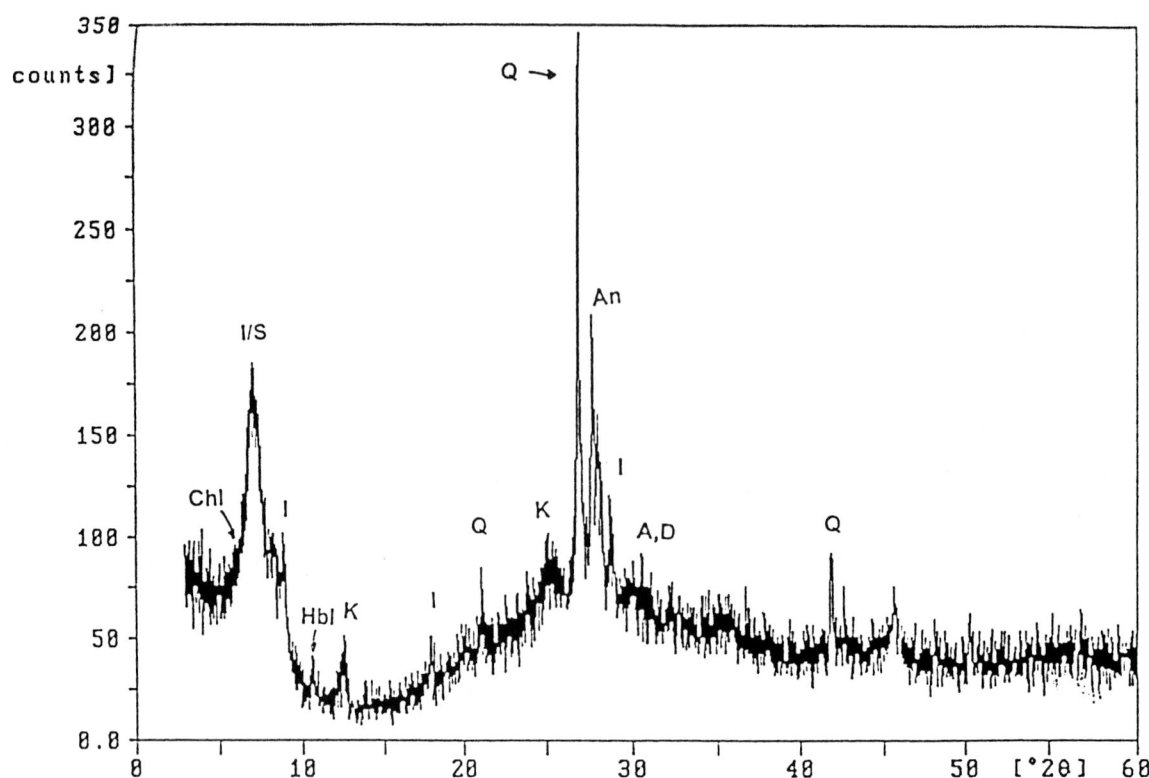

Fig. 19: X-ray diffractogram of the IR in travertines. Following peaks have been identified: A, D: augite, diopside; An: anorthite; Chl: chlorite; Hbl: hornblende; I: illite; I/S: mixed-layer illite/smectite; K: kaolinite; Q: quartz.

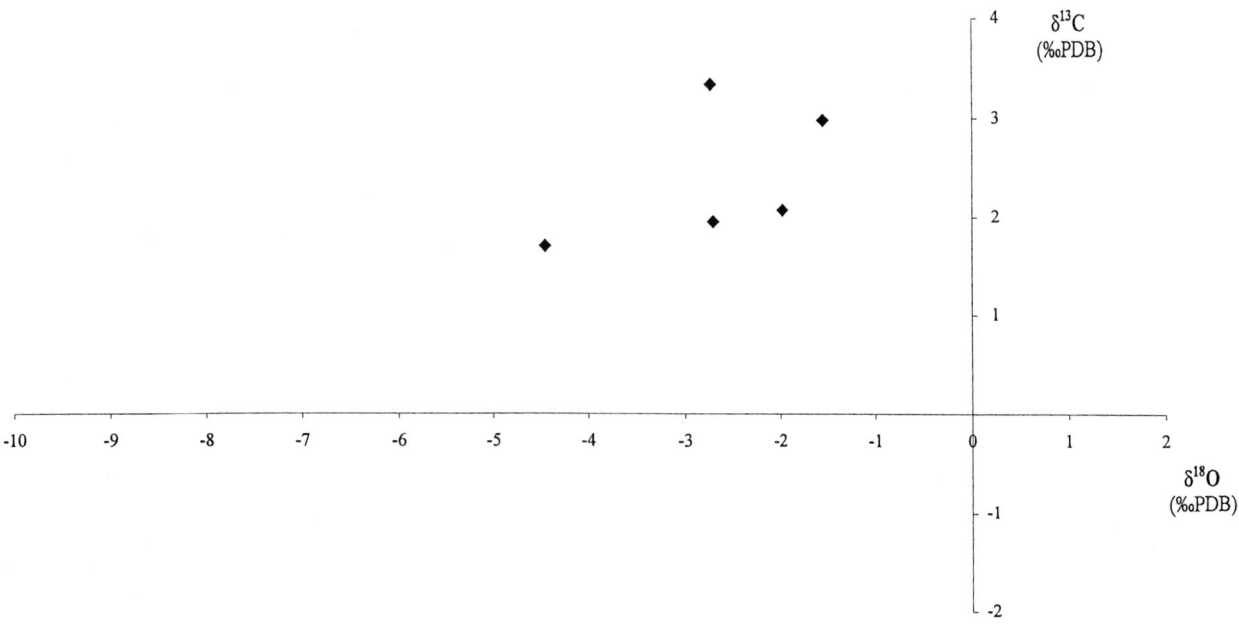

Fig. 20: ^{13}C versus ^{18}O for allochthonous limestones of the Lycian nappes.

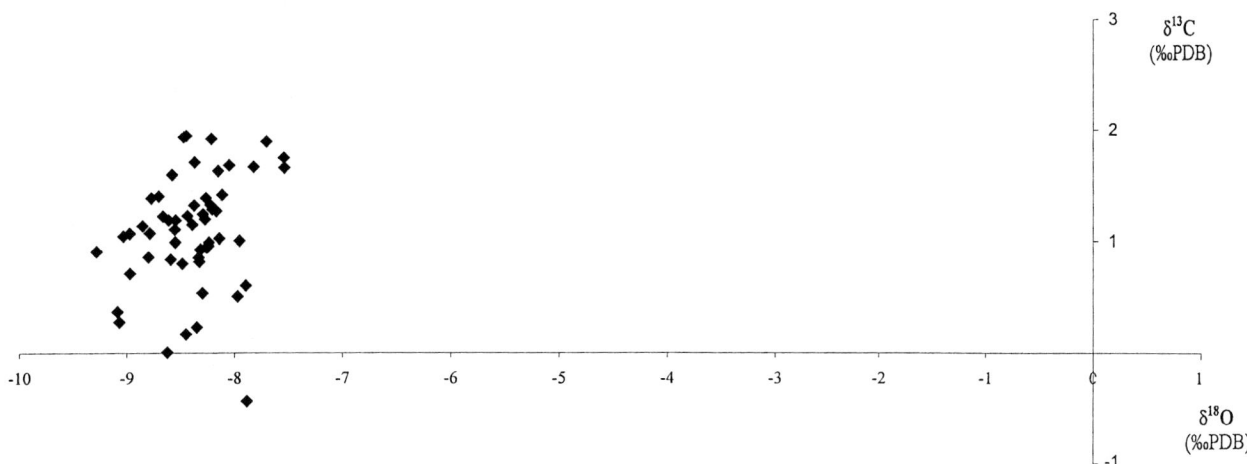

Fig. 21: ^{13}C- ^{18}O-diagram for travertine samples.

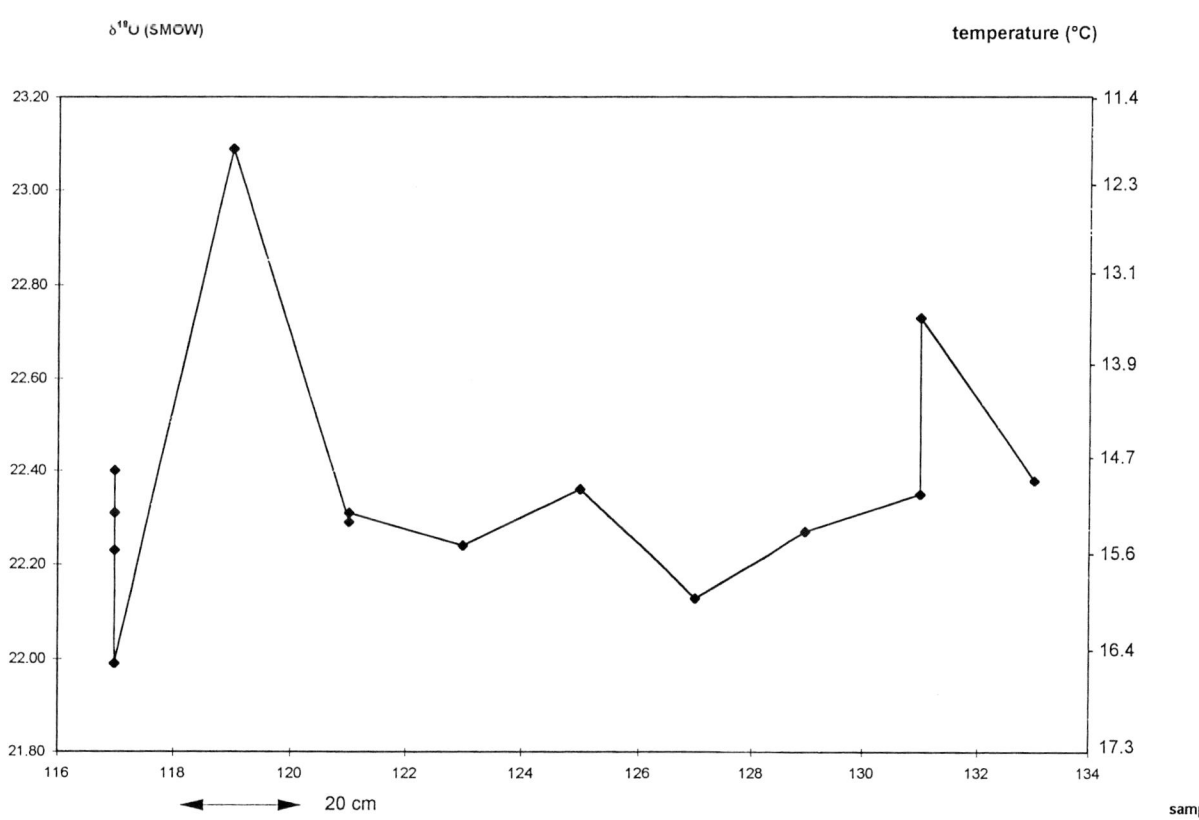

Fig. 22: ^{18}O (‰ SMOW) values and calculated temperatures in travertine deposits of section I.

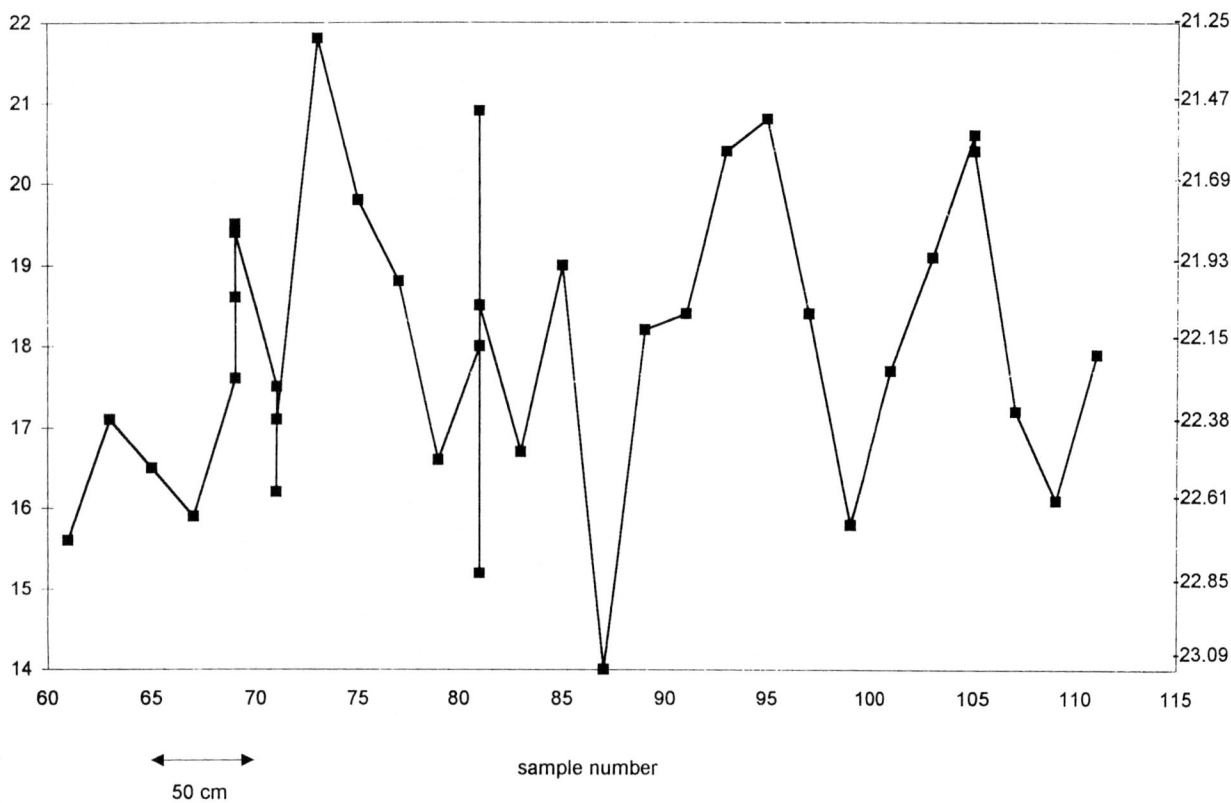

Fig. 23: ^{18}O (‰ SMOW) values and calculated temperatures in travertine deposits of section II. Notice the large variation of ^{18}O values in the different travertine types in one sample, indicating non-equilibrium precipitation and throwing doubt on the validity of the calculated temperatures.

A

distance (km)	pH	hardness (mmol/l)	conductivity (ms/cm)	temp. (°C)
0	6.74	34	1.44	15
	6.68	35	1.40	15
	6.82	28	1.40	15
	6.75	35	1.33	15
	6.70	29	1.36	15
	6.93	34	1.36	15
	7.18	34	1.36	15
	7.30	33	1.30	15
	7.35	26	1.03	14
	7.70	24	0.86	15
	7.74	30	1.00	16
	7.97	29	1.31	16.5
	8.18	27	1.24	16.5
1.50	8.25	22	0.52	18

B

location	pH	hardness (mmol/l)	conductivity (ms/cm)	temp. (°C)
Sagalassos	7.95	8.96	0.35	-
Sagalassos	7.78	15.96	0.63	-
Sagalassos	7.82	8.96	0.32	-
Sagalassos	7.82	5.88	0.29	-
Sagalassos	8.88	7.00	0.52	-
Ağlasun	7.26	3.92	0.52	-
Ağlasun	7.40	12.88	0.36	-
Başköy 1	7.66	8.96	0.28	10.00
Başköy 2	7.60	15.96	0.59	12.00
Başköy 3	7.25	17.82	0.79	13.00
Sagalassos	8.11	-	0.30	-
Sagalassos	8.05	-	0.30	-
Başköy 4	7.03	22.00	0.95	11.00

Table 1: Physical and chemical parameters of travertine-forming and non-travertine-forming waters.
A - Travertine forming stream: Tuzlu Çay. Evolution in function of distance to the source.
B - Non-travertine forming waters. Measurments at spring.

	%IR	%Fe	%Mg	ppm Mn	ppm Zn	ppm Sr	ppm Na	ppm Pb	ppm K
%IR									
%Fe	0.9831								
%Mg	0.9835	0.9631							
ppm Mn	0	0	-0.07						
ppm Zn	0.9371	0.9619	0.902	0.12063					
ppm Sr	0.049	0.119	0.1199	-0.2505	-0.014				
ppm Na	0.9327	0.9113	0.8934	-0.099	0.85921	-0.05			
ppm Pb	-0.109	-0.176	-0.118	0.14224	-0.14	-0.2445	-0.12993		
ppm K	0.9438	0.983	0.9133	-0.025	0.96129	0.10448	0.865774	-0.2371	

Table 2: Correlation matrix for the investigated chemical elements and the IR.

Fig. 24: Pollen diagram of section I.

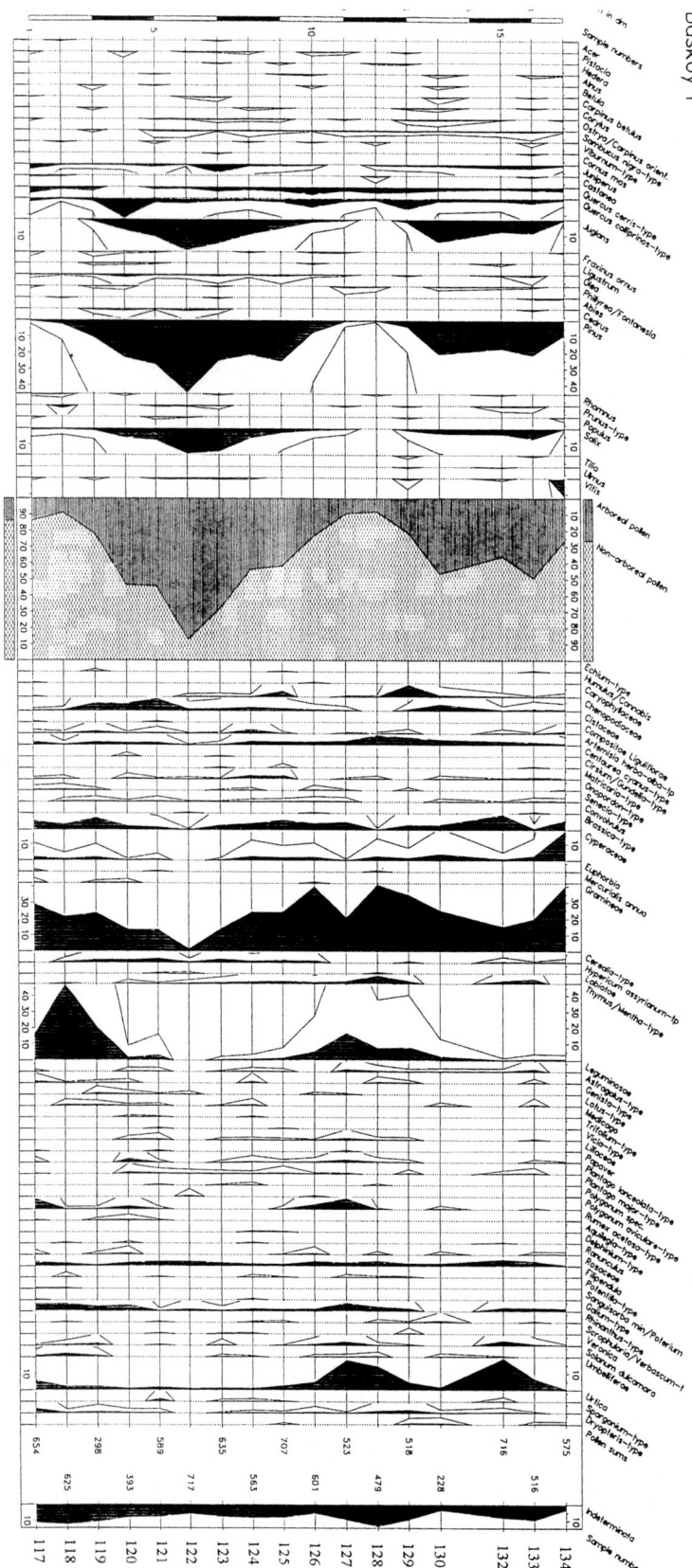

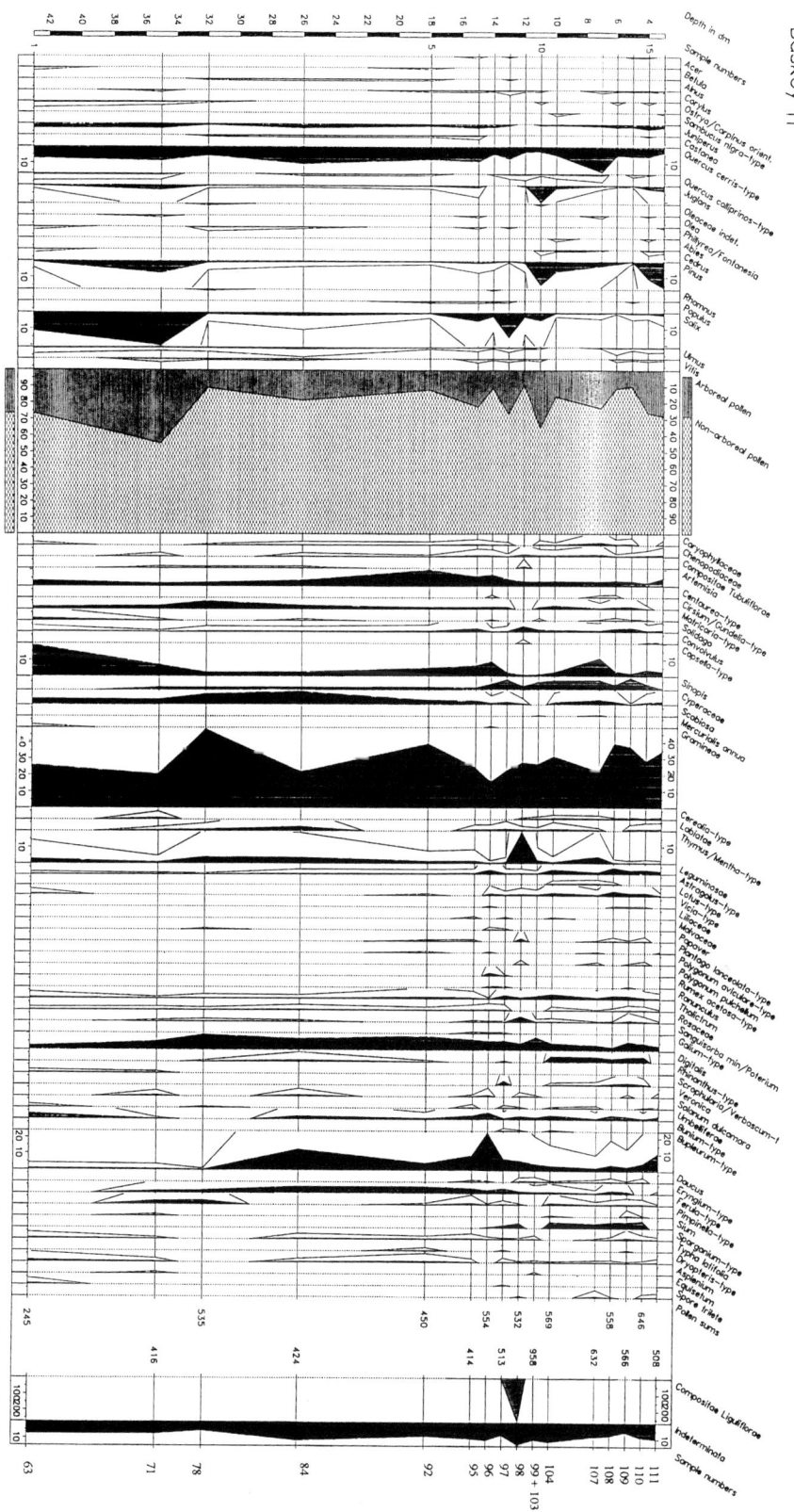

Fig. 25: Pollen diagram of section II.

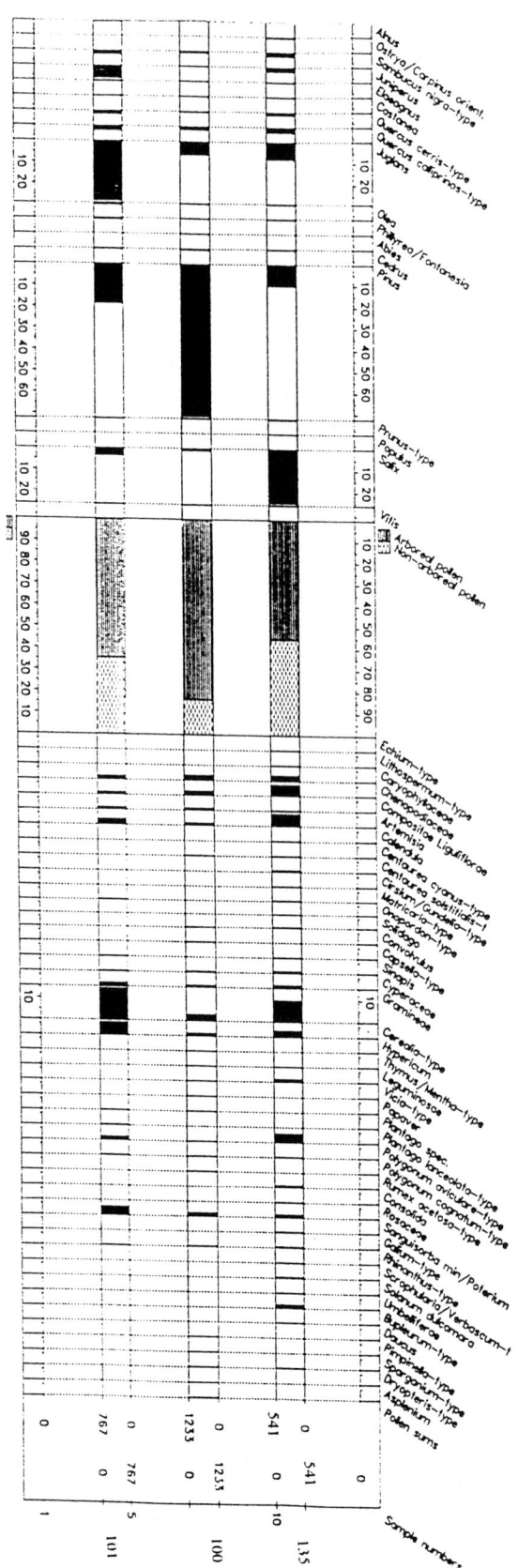

Fig. 26: Pollen diagram of recent travertines.

Section 1

SAMPLE	MORPHOLOGY	DETRITAL MATERIAL (% IR)	CLAYEY MATERIAL (ppm K)	AP-PERCENTAGE
SA-95-117	holes of plant stalks/unlayered	2.8	92	14.4
SA-95-118	holes of plant stalks/unlayered	1.7	57	8.8
SA-95-119	fine holes of plant stalks/unlayered/compact	2.0	28	22.4
SA-95-120	unlayered	20.4	700	53.7
SA-95-121	unlayered	no data	no data	54.4
SA-95-122	layered	8.4	292	87
SA-95-123	unlayered	18.7	540	68.3
SA-95-124	with 1 hole of a plant stalk/unlayered	22.8	540	44.1
SA-95-125	unlayered	13.5	293	42
SA-95-126	unlayered	7.5	188	23.7
SA-95-127	much little holes of plant stalks/unlayered	3.4	108	9.6
SA-95-128	unlayered	7.8	235	8.5
SA-95-129	unlayered	5.8	135	21.9
SA-95-130	layered	3.2	155	47.1
SA-95-132	unlayered	no data	no data	36.3
SA-95-133	layered	6.1	202	49.5
SA-95-134	holes of plant stalks/only a part of the sample is layered/compact	7.0	218	26.4

Section 2

SAMPLE	MORPHOLOGY	DETRITAL MATERIAL (% IR)	CLAYEY MATERIAL (ppm K)	AP-PERCENTAGE
SA-96-63	fine and big holes of plant stalks/unlayered	2.6	28	24.7
SA-96-71	fine and big holes of plant stalks/unlayered	2.8	35	41.8
SA-96-78	fine and big holes of plant stalks/unlayered	2.8	34	10.5
SA-96-84	fine and big holes of plant stalks/unlayered	0.2	27	16.7
SA-96-92	fine and big holes of plant stalks/unlayered	1.4	21	11.2
SA-96-95	fine holes of plant stalks	2.1	47	20.4
SA-96-96	fine and big holes of plant stalks	1.5	55	9.9
SA-96-97	fine holes of plant stalks/unlayered	1.3	40	25
SA-96-98	fine holes of plant stalks/unlayered	2.6	80	7.6
SA-96-99	fine and big holes of plant stalks	3.0	540	44.3
SA-96-103	fine holes of plant stalks/unlayered	2.4	48	20.5
SA-96-104	fine holes of plant stalks/compact	1.5	41	14.6
SA-96-107	big holes of plant stalks/unlayered	2.0	33	21.5
SA-96-108	fine holes of plant stalks/unlayered	2.8	51	10.5
SA-96-109	with 1 big, round hole of a plant stalk/unlayered	2.4	36	9.5
SA-96-110	unlayered	2.6	51	24
SA-96-111	fine holes of plant stalks	3.5	100	25.6

Table 3: Relationship between morphology, composition of the travertine samples and the arboreal pollen-percentage. The quantity of detrital material is expressed in weight % insoluble residu (IR). The amount of clayey material is correlated with element kalium (K), though K can also be a constituent of other, non-clayey materials.

	% IR	ppm K	AP-%
% IR			
ppm K	0.8638		
AP-%	0.6032	0.6736	

Table 4: Correlation diagram between the IR, K and the arboreal pollen-percentage. A rather good correlation can be observed.

gated elements are correlated with the IR. Therefore, these elements are not incorporated in the carbonate crystal lattice. The IR has further been investigated by optical microscopy (fraction > 38 µm) and by X-ray diffraction (fraction < 2 µm). The IR consists of angular fragments. It suggests a nearby source of these grains. However, some grains have rounded forms and are smaller, which could indicate a wind-blown transport. The following minerals have been identified by X-ray diffraction (Fig. 19) and binocular: illite $(K,Na)Al_2(AlSi_3O_{10})(OH)_2$ and smectite (variable composition); chlorite $(Mg,Fe)_3(Si, Al)_4O_{10}(OH)_2$; kaolinite $Al_2Si_2O_5(OH)_4$; quartz SiO_2; hornblende $(Ca,Na)_{2-3}(Mg,Fe,Al)_5Si_6(Si,Al)_2O_{22}(OH)_2$; augite $(Ca,Na)(Mg,Fe,Al)(Si,Al)_2O_6$; diopside $CaMgSi_2O_6$; magnetite Fe_3O_4; anorthite $CaAl_2Si_2O_8$; Fe- and Mn-oxides and -hydroxides.

Most of the elements analysed are incorporated in phyllosilicates (chlorite, illite and smectite which contain Fe, Mg, K and Na) or diopside (Ca, Mg) and augite (Ca, Mg, Fe, Na) or adsorbed on clay minerals (Fe, Mn, Zn). Zn can also be adsorbed on the surfaces of Fe- and Mn-oxides and -hydroxides. The mineral assemblage is characteristic of the topographically higher situated ophiolitic sequences and their weathering products. The ophiolitic sequence is part of the Lycian nappe.

7.2. Stable isotope geochemistry

The carbon isotopic composition of the travertines varies between -0.44‰ and +1.95‰ PDB. The $\delta^{13}C$ value of the allochthonous limestones is +1.70‰ to +3.34‰ PDB (Fig. 20). The oxygen isotopic values of the travertine samples lie between -9.38‰ and -7.54‰ PDB (Fig. 21), corresponding with values between +21.29‰ and +23.09‰ SMOW. In section I, one major maximum can be observed in the $\delta^{18}O$ values, i.e. in layer 119 (Fig. 22). A higher value is also present in one of the two analyses of layer 131. In section II, the $\delta^{18}O$ values show a very irregular pattern (Fig. 23). The average oxygen isotopic composition of the meteoric water analysed at Başköy is -8.5‰ SMOW.

The $\delta^{13}C$ values of +1.70‰ to +3.34‰ PDB of the allochthonous limestones indicate a marine signature (Hudson 1977). The $\delta^{13}C$ values of the travertines are comparable with those of the allochthonous limestones. This could be due to a buffering of the carbon isotopic composition of the water from which the travertines precipitated. However, the HCO_3^- (in the water) in carbon isotopic equilibrium with the atmosphere has also a $\delta^{13}C$ composition between +1‰ and +4‰ PDB (Cerling 1984). An organic origin of the carbon can be excluded since carbonates, which have incorporated a large amount of organic carbon, have much lower $\delta^{13}C$ values (Salomons et al. 1978).

The $\delta^{18}O$ values between +21.29‰ and +23.09‰ SMOW are in agreement with the general values of meteoric carbonate precipitates (Tucker and Wright 1990). Assuming equilibrium precipitation conditions, an idea of the possible precipitation temperatures of the travertines can be calculated from the $\delta^{18}O$ values of the travertines and from the oxygen isotopic composition of the actual meteoric water ($\delta^{18}O$ = -8.5‰ SMOW). The calculated temperatures vary between 12 °C and 19.5 °C (Figs 22 and 23) and are comparable to the temperatures of the waters from which recent travertines have precipitated (Table 1). However, it should be noted that the temperature variation measured in different types of carbonate textures in one sample can be as much as 6 °C (Fig. 23). The fact that, on the same level of deposition, the isotope values for different types of travertine differ widely indicates a non-equilibrium precipitation of these travertines. This makes a climatic interpretation of this type of travertine carbonates impossible. The same conclusion has been reached by Hendy (1971) and Schwarzc (1986).

8. PALYNOLOGY

Former palynological studies of cores originating from the sedimentary basin of Çanaklı did not give satisfactory results (Bottema and Woldring 1995). Pollen analysis of the travertine deposits of Başköy offers an alternative to this research.

8.1. Section I and section II

The results of the pollen analysis of the two sections are shown in two pollen diagrams (Fig. 24, Fig. 25). In section I, it is worth noting that an archaeologic red slip ware fragment of the type 1A100 was found, dating from the first to second century AD (Poblome 1999). When the pollen diagram of section I (Fig. 24) is considered, it is clear that *Pinus*, *Juglans* and *Salix* predominate in some samples. In other samples, pollen of the type *Mentha-Thymus* dominate. These pollen grains originate from *Mentha longifolia*, a plant growing near springs and in wet areas. The occurrence of the *Olea*-pollen type (up to 1.8%) is significant. Nowadays, no olives are cultivated in the region because of spring frosts. Based on pollen diagrams from cores around Beyşehir (van Zeist et al. 1975), *Olea* seems to have been an important tree in the Beyşehir Occupation Phase. Also, a piece of *Olea*-charcoal has been found in an iron slag sample of Sagalassos (Schoch 1995). It has even been suggested that climatological conditions could have been more favourable for cultivating olives during classical periods than nowadays (Roberts 1990). It is remarkable that *Quercus calliprinos* is well represented in the pollen diagram. This indicates that, at the time of the travertine deposition of section I, secondary vegetation formations had already replaced the conifer woods.

The decline of the percentage of total arboreal pollen in layer 127 and 128 could suggest a phase of deforestation. However, there are no indications that a secondary maquis-vegetation, represented by *Quercus calliprinos*, replaces the needle-leaved (*Pinus*) forests. The percentages of this pollen type do not suddenly increase. On the contrary, the pollen type *Mentha-Thymus* becomes more important in layer 127 and 128, suggesting that other factors caused the low percentages of arboreal pollen types. Therefore, it seems more likely that the pollen distribution in the section represent a cyclicity in the formation of the travertine: a lot of *Mentha*-pollen (suggesting precipitation during summer time), followed by huge amounts of *Juglans*-, *Salix*- and *Pinus*-pollen (suggesting travertine precipitation during spring time). A rapid formation of the travertine is reflected by the low concentration of pollen grains in the samples: between 44 and 1225 pollen per gram. For comparison, 1.5 million pollen per gram have been detected in clayey soil (Dimbleby 1957).

The pollen diagram of section II (Fig. 25) shows that *Quercus calliprinos*, *Juglans regia* and *Olea europaea* are poorly represented in the vegetation at the time of travertine deposition. Also, *Pinus*, *Cedrus libani* and *Abies cilicica* must have been nearly absent in the vegetation. On the other hand, deciduous oaktrees (*Quercus cerris/infectoria*) and junipers (*Juniperus*) play a more important role in the arboreal pollen types. Consequently, it can be assumed that the hills around the valley were more or less covered with deciduous oaktrees on the gentler slopes, and junipers on the steeper limestone slopes. Also, steppe plants such as *Artemisia* sp. and lots of grasses seem to have played an important role in the vegetation at the time of deposition of section II. Apparently, the vegetation around Başköy at this time was a forest-steppe.

Cyperaceae, *Typha* and *Sparganium*-pollen types indicate the presence of a marsh vegetation in the past, which has disappeared in the valley because of intense canalisation of the streams. Section II does not show any cycles. On the contrary, the pollen spectra, like the morphology and geochemistry of the travertine samples, do not show much variation over the section. This means that there were no great vegetation fluctuations while the travertine wall of about 5 m high was built up.

Pollen analysis of the different types of travertine samples through the two sections revealed a link between the arboreal pollen percentage (AP) and the geochemical composition of the samples. In general, it has been observed that travertine samples with a high content of detrital material contain a lot of arboreal pollen grains (Table 3, Table 4). These travertine samples were possibly deposited during spring time, when relatively large amounts of melt water could have eroded the hills. The high AP-percentages would then be explained by the fact that most tree species flower in this season and thus pollen grains of these trees are enclosed in the travertine that is deposited in the spring time.

In both sections, pollen of anthropogenic indicators, such as *Plantago lanceolata* (a plant common along roadsides and grazed places), *Sanguisorba minor* (also a characteristic plant species of grazed places) and the *Cerealia*-pollen type are poorly represented. This observation is in agreement with the opinion of Geurts (1976), who claims that human influences are not clear from pollen diagrams of travertine sections.

8.2. Recent travertine samples

Former research of recent pollen precipitation in southwest Turkey has been carried out by van Zeist *et al.* (1975) and Bottema and Woldring (1995), by analyses of moss cushions.

In this study, three recent travertine deposits were sampled. No vegetation study in the vicinity of the samples was carried out. The results of the pollen analysis of the modern travertine samples are shown in pollen spectra (Fig. 26). It is clear from these pollen spectra that the three different samples do not have the same pollen composition. This is clearly related to the fact that the vegetation composition is different in the different places where the travertine has been sampled. In addition, this phenomenon can be explained by differences in the periods of travertine precipitation (spring, summer). Indeed, according to Geurts (1976), pollen grains in travertine deposits originate mainly from the very local vegetation. Further, the pollen spectra reveal quite high percentages of arboreal pollen (*Pinus, Juglans* and *Salix*). This must be due to the presence of these tree species in the immediate vicinity of the travertine deposits. Pollen of the evergreen oaktree *Quercus calliprinos* is also well represented, indicating again secondary vegetation (maquis) at the hills around the valley. On the contrary, deciduous oaktrees (*Quercus infectoria/cerris*) are rather poorly represented. In the three travertine samples, low percentages of *Olea europaea*-pollen grains have been detected, although no olives are found in the immediate vicinity of Başköy. Pollen grains of this wind-pollinated tree must originate from more southerly regions (Bottema and Woldring 1990).

9. CONCLUSIONS

The travertine deposits studied are mainly precipitated inorganically from meteoric water. This results in typical crystal fabrics: acicular in a turbulent environment and equant in a quieter environment. Organic fabrics occur only in the southern part of the deposit and these are believed to have formed in a very quiet environment (ponds). Only a limited sampling of these deposits was done and further research is required.

From pollen analysis, we can deduce that the vegetation in the vicinity of Sagalassos evolved from an open forest-steppe (*Quercus, Juniperus* and *Artemisia*) to an open needle-leaved forest of *Pinus* on the mountain slopes, and stands of *Juglans* and *Salix* in the wet valley of Başköy. At this time, the landscape changed enormously and this is reflected, for example, in the pollen diagram of section I by the increase of *Quercus calliprinos*.

10. ACKNOWLEDGEMENTS

This research is supported by the Belgian Programme on Interuniversity Poles of Attraction (IUAP 4/12) initiated by the Belgian State, Prime Minister's Office, Science Policy Programming. The text also presents the results of the Conserted Action of the Flemish Government (GOA 97/2) and the Fund for Scientific Research-Flanders (Belgium) (FWO) (G.2145.94). Scientific responsibility is assumed by its authors. The authors sincerely thank Prof. Dr. S. Bottema and Prof. Dr. A. Munaut for their kind assistance in the palynological part of this study, Dr. P. Nielsen for practical information about isotopic analysis, S. Lens and D. Coetermans for the geochemical analysis, D. Steeno for the technical assistance and H. Nijs for the preparation of the thin sections.

11. REFERENCES

B. Bastin (1978) L'analyse pollinique des stalagmites: une nouvelle possibilité d'approche des fluctuations climatiques du Quaternaire, *Annales de la Société Géologique de Belgique* 101: 13-19.

S. Bottema and H. Woldring (1986) Late Quaternary vegetation and climate of Southwest Turkey. Part II, *Palaeohistoria* 26: 123-149.

S. Bottema and H. Woldring (1990) Anthropogenic indicators in the pollen record of the Eastern Mediterranean, in: S. Bottema, G. Entjes-Nieborg and W. van Zeist (eds) *Man's Role in the Shaping of the Eastern Mediterranean Landscape*, Rotterdam: 231-264.

S. Bottema and H. Woldring (1995) The environment of classical Sagalassos, in: M. Waelkens and J. Poblome (eds) *Sagalassos II. Report on the Third Excavation Campaign of 1992 (Acta Archaeologica Lovaniensia Monographiae* 7) Leuven University Press: 327-343.

T.E. Cerling (1984) The stable isotopic composition of modern soil carbonate and its relationship to climate, *Earth and Planetary Science Letters* 71: 229-240.

Y. Dilek and J.C. Rowland (1993) Evolution of a conjugate pair in Mesozoic southern Turkey, *Tectonics* 12/4: 954-970.

G.W. Dimblebey (1957) Pollen analysis of terrestrial soils, *New Phytologist* 56: 12-28.

R.L. Folk, H.S. Chafetz and P.A. Tiezzi (1985) Bizarre forms of depositional and diagenetic calcite in hot spring travertines, Central Italy: Schneiderman and Harris carbonate cements, *Society of Economic Paleontologists and Mineralogists Special Publication* 36: 349-369.

J.R. Frank, A.B. Carpenter and T.W. Oglesby (1982) Cathodoluminescence and composition of calcite cement in the Taum Sauk limestone (Upper Cambrian, Southeast Missouri), *Journal of Sedimentary. Petrology* 52: 631-638.

M.A. Geurts (1976) *Genèse et stratigraphie des travertins de fond de vallée en Belgique* (Acta Geographica Lovaniensia 16) Leuven.

L. Gonzales, S.J. Carpenter and K.C. Lohmann (1992) Inorganic calcite morphology: roles of fluid chemistry and fluid flow, *Journal of Sedimentary Geology* 62/3: 382-399.

C.H. Hendy (1971) The isotope geochemistry of speleothems I. The calculation of the effects of different modes of formation on the isotopic composition of speleothems and their applicability as palaeoclimatic indicators, *Geochimica Cosmochimica Acta* 35: 801-824.

J.D. Hudson (1977) Stable isotopes and limestone lithification, *Journal of Geological Society of London* 133: 637-660.

B. Jones and C.F. Kahle (1993) Morphology, relationship and origin of fiber and dendrite calcite crystals, *Journal of Sedimentary Petrology* 63/6: 1018-1031.

H. Kürschner (1984) *Der östliche Orta Toroslar (Mittlere Taurus) und angrenzende Gebiete* (Beihefte zum Tübinger Atlas des Vorderen Orients, Reihe A (Naturwiss.)15) Wiesbaden.

R. Meiggs (1982) *Trees and Timber in the Ancient Mediterranean World*, Oxford.

J. Poblome (1999) *Sagalassos Red Slip Ware. Typology and Chronology* (Studies in Eastern Mediterranean Archaeology 2) Brepols publishers.

M. Reille (1992) *Pollen et spores d'Europe et d'Afrique du Nord*, Marseille.

M. Reille (1995) *Pollen et spores d'Europe et d'Afrique du Nord. Supplément 1*, Marseille.

N. Roberts (1990) Human-induced landscape change in south and southwest Turkey during the Later Holocene, in: S. Bottema, G. Entjes-Nieborg and W. van Zeist (eds) *Man's Role in the Shaping of the Eastern Mediterranean Landscape*, Rotterdam: 53-64.

W. Salomons, A. Goudie, W.G. Mook (1978) Isotopic composition of calcrete deposits from Europe, *Earth Surface Processes* 3: 43-57.

W.H. Schoch (1995) Analyse von Holzkohlen in Schlacken von Sagalassos, in: M. Waelkens and J. Poblome (eds) *Sagalassos II. Report on the Third Excavation Campaign of 1992 (Acta Archaeologica Lovaniensia Monographiae* 7) Leuven University Press: 293-296.

J. Stockmarr (1971) Tablets with spores used in absolute pollen analysis, *Pollen et spores* 13/4: 615-621.

H.P. Schwarzc (1986) Geochronology and isotopic geochemistry of speleothems, in: P. Fritz and J.C. Jones (eds) *Handbook of Environmental Isotope Geochemistry* 2: 271-303.

A. Thienemann (1954) *Die Binnengewasser. Einzeldarstellungen aus der Limnologie und ihren Nachbargebieten: Chironomus, Leben, Verbreitung und wirtschafliche Bedeutung der Chironomiden*, Stuttgart: 50-53, 109-110, 154-163, 351-362.

M.E. Tucker and P.V. Wright (1990) *Carbonate Sedimentology*.

W. van Zeist, H. Woldring and D. Stapert (1975) Late Quaternary vegetation and climate of southwestern Turkey, *Palaeohistoria* 17: 53-143.

W. Viaene, R. Ottenburghs, Ph. Muchez and M. Waelkens (1993) The building stones of Sagalassos, in: M. Waelkens (ed.) *Sagalassos I. First General Report on the Survey (1986-1989) and Excavations (1990-1991)* (*Acta Archaeologica Lovaniensia Monographiae* 5) Leuven University Press: 85-92.

M. Waelkens, E. Paulissen, H. Vanhaverbeke, I. Öztürk, B. De Cupere, H.A. Ekinci, P.M. Vermeersch, J. Poblome and R. Degeest (1997) The 1994 and 1995 surveys on the territory of Sagalassos, in: M. Waelkens and J. Poblome (eds) *Sagalassos IV. Report on the Survey and Excavation Campaigns of 1994 and 1995* (*Acta Archaeologica Lovaniensia Monographiae* 9) Leuven University Press: 11-102.

M. Waelkens and the Sagalassos team (1997) Interdisciplinarity in classical archaeology. A case study: the Sagalassos Archaeological Research Project (Southwest Turkey), in: M. Waelkens and J. Poblome (eds) *Sagalassos IV. Report on the Survey and Excavation Campaigns of 1994 and 1995* (*Acta Archaeologica Lovaniensia Monographiae* 9) Leuven University Press: 225-252.

LIMESTONE PLATFORMS AROUND SAGALASSOS RESULTING FROM GIANT MASS MOVEMENTS

Gert VERSTRAETEN[1], Etienne PAULISSEN[2], Ireen LIBRECHT[2], and Marc WAELKENS[3]

1 - Laboratory for Experimental Geomorphology, KULeuven, Redingenstraat 16, B-3000 Leuven, Belgium
2 - Geomorphology and Regional Geography, KULeuven, Redingenstraat 16, B-3000 Leuven, Belgium
3 - Department of Archaeology, KULeuven, Blijde Inkomststraat 21, B-3000 Leuven, Belgium

1. INTRODUCTION

The archaeological site of Sagalassos is situated on the lower slopes of a limestone front. A first geomorphological approach to the area surrounding the site was made during a field survey in 1991 and 1992 (Paulissen *et al.* 1993). It was then concluded that the topography strongly resembled the lithology of the area. The steepest slopes are those of the limestone front of the Lycian nappe. The hilly topography downslope this front consists of autochthonous flysch deposits. In between these lies a small layer of allochthonous ophiolites. This generalised representation of the geomorphology does not include the massive limestone blocks lying at a lower level than the limestone front, forming a kind of plateau (Fig. 1). It was only mentioned that these could be the result of macro-slumping phenomena or that they could be 'klippen'. During a field survey in August 1995, these limestone blocks were further investigated in order to analyse their characteristics and discover their genesis. This article is a summary of the result of this survey which was the basis of a M.Sc. thesis (Verstraeten 1996).

2. TERMINOLOGY: 'KLIPPEN' VERSUS MASS MOVEMENT

A clear understanding of the terms used in this discussion is necessary both to define them and differentiate between them as both terms are sometimes applied to the same geomorphologic feature. The term 'klippen' especially has a far too wide definition (e.g. Tollman 1987). We suggest therefore a more carefully defined use of this term. We see a 'klippe' as a remnant of a once more extensive nappe resting on an alien footing or base but isolated on all sides from the nappe by erosion.

It should be clear then that what is called a 'klippe' has not undergone any displacement since the thrusting occurred. It is in no way a block which has become detached from the thrust front. The reason for the separation of the 'klippe' from the rest of the nappe has to be searched for in between them, not at the 'klippe' itself.

A mass movement is the downhill movement of surface materials (including solid rock) under the influence of gravity (Whittow 1984). So in this case a movement of material displaces rocks, for example, from their original position. The reason why the displaced mass is isolated from the rest of the rock has to be looked for at that point. In the literature it often occurs that material which has slid from a thrust front during the phase of thrusting are called sedimentary 'klippen'. We suggest that in those cases the term 'fossil' mass movements is adopted. This should make it clear that we consider a 'klippe' to be in no way a form of subaerial or submarine mass movement.

3. INVESTIGATION OF LIMESTONE BLOCKS

During the field campaign of 1995, we searched for limestone blocks over an area of ± 50 km^2, located them and measured some characteristics of them such as their internal structure, dimensions, degree of weathering, etc. Two areas have been investigated in more detail: the area around Başköy, a village a few kilometers west of Ağlasun and the area east of Sagalassos towards the Akdağ of Isparta-Ağlasun. Fig. 2 is a contour map of the area just east of the historical site with the studied limestone blocks marked.

3.1. Characteristics of the limestone blocks

Some giant limestone blocks show very specific characteristics, which can be seen on a DEM (Digital Elevation Model) of the same area as that of the contour map (Fig. 3). These blocks are lying at a lower level than the main limestone front: they are isolated phenomena which make a break in the topography, i.e. their faces are steeper than the surroundings and the ground between them and the main front is flatter. In the field we found that this flatter topography consists mainly of rock debris and sometimes finer, ophiolitic material while the steep front is built of the same limestone as the main front. Another important characteristic of these isolated blocks, which is not visible on the contour map or the DEM (Figs 2 and 3), is that most of them have a small anti-slope. This means that the surface of the limestone block has a slope opposite to that of the general slope of the topography. This is illustrated for limestone block 5 (Fig. 4). Finally, one can see that the limestone blocks are not all situated at the same distance from the main front nor are they lying at the same altitude.

Fig. 5 gives a good illustration of some of these details: one can see the position of limestone blocks 5, 6, 7 and 8, each one located at a different distance from the main limestone front and at a different altitude. The same picture shows very well the flatter topography between limestone blocks 6 and 7 and between limestone block 7 and the main limestone front (the afforested zone).

3.2. Interpretation of the limestone blocks as giant rock slides

The characteristics described above are also found where giant rock slumps occur, as is shown in Fig. 6. Because of the sliding of a rock mass, two cliffs, built up of the same material, come into existence: one of the displaced mass and the other where that material was during this displacement, it is common for rotation to occur so that an anti-slope is created. The depression created between the two cliffs may be filled with debris originating from the cliff above it. Such rotating slides often occur where horizontal, compact sedimentary rocks, such as limestone, are underlain by weaker rocks, such as mudstones, shales or clays (Strahler and Strahler 1992). It is typical of a rotational slide that the plane of failure should be curved (Selby 1993). Another characteristic of rotational slides is that the rock mass comes to rest close to its original position.

The situation at Sagalassos is more or less as presented in Fig. 6: compact limestone is underlain by weak clay-rich strata like ophiolites and flysch deposits. Based on all the characteristics, we interpret the different limestone blocks around Sagalassos as the result of giant mass movements, in particular giant rock slumps. The sliding surface is presumably to be found on top of the flysch deposits.

One of the limestone blocks that slid down the thrust front is block 3 or the 'block of the aqueducts' (Fig. 7), so-called because of the presence in its face of the remains of two rock-cut aqueducts, which may date back to the Hellenistic period (Owens 1995; Steegen 2000). It is located 1 km to the east of the site proper (number 3 on Figs 2 and 3). On the profile one can see that the sliding surface is located in the flysch deposits underlying the limestones (Fig. 8). One can also see that the block of the aqueducts has an anti-slope. This anti-slope, however, is only partially visible in the field (only 30 m in some places) because of the accumulation of a heterogeneous mix of very fine material (weathered reddish chertified limestone and ophiolite deposits), limestone debris and even small limestone blocks in the depression between the thrust front and the 'block of the aqueducts' (see below).

More evidence of macro-rotational sliding can be found at block 11. This area is characterised by large concentrations of solidified scree deposits with a clear stratification. This stratification inclines 15 to 20° to the north, thus creating an anti-slope (in strata, not in topography), since most of the other stratified calcretes around Sagalassos, like the present non-solidified scree-deposits (Librecht et al. 2000), have an inclination of 28 to 33° to the south. This difference in inclination can only be explained by assuming that the indurated scree-deposits rotated as they slid downwards. If one assumes that this scree was deposited at an angle of 28 to 33° (like the main screes today east of the city), a rotation of 45 to 50° may be suggested.

Limestone block 4 is a special case. This block is not (yet) isolated from the main limestone front, but appears in profile as a step in the topography (Fig. 9). We interpret this step as being the result of a limited rotational downward movement. The chertified limestone at the surface of the step dips 60° north, while the same limestone at the foot of the upper part of the main front, around 20 m higher, dips only 28° north. Therefore we assume a rotation of 32°.

Some limestone blocks are situated so far from the main front that their position cannot be explained only by a rotating slide. This is the case for blocks 7 and 8. We suggest that these limestone blocks did undergo a rotating slide off the main front, but that they moved translationally further downwards over a planar sliding surface. It is typical of rock block slides or translational slides that they can travel over large distances, without rotating (Strahler and Strahler 1992). In these cases, the sliding surface is planar. Fig. 10 is a profile through limestone blocks 6 and 7 which shows the translational slide of block 7. Afterwards, limestone block 6 has been displaced rotationally off limestone block 7.

Other examples of rock slumps are found in the Central

Fig. 1: A view along the Ağlasun Dağı and the Akdağ of Isparta-Ağlasun forming the limestone front north of the excavation site. Different limestone platforms can be observed at the base of the mountain range.

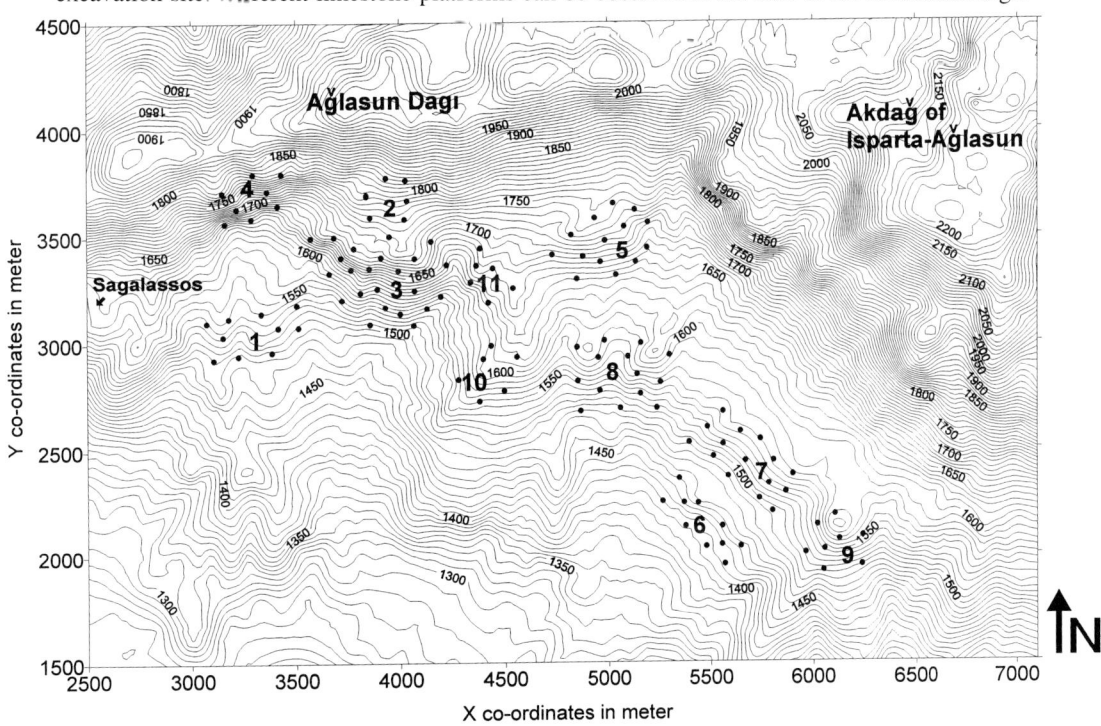

equidistance of the contour lines : 10 meter

•1• : some limestone massifs with their rank number

Fig. 2: A contour map of the area east of the excavation site to the Akdağ of Isparta-Ağlasun. Several limestone massifs are indicated.

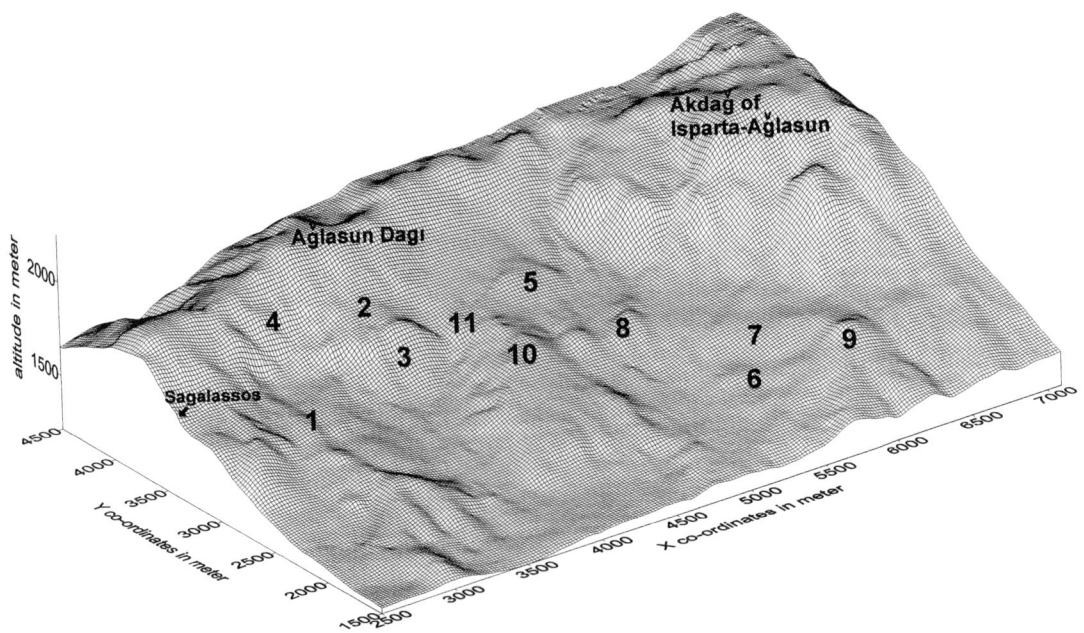

Fig. 3: A digital elevation model (DEM) of the same area as presented in Fig. 2 with the indication of limestone massifs.

Fig. 4: The top of limestone massif 5 clearly showing the topographic anti-slope: the general topography slopes down to the left in this picture.

Fig. 5: An overview over limestone massifs 5, 6, 7 and 8, and the mountain range of the Ağlasun Dağı, illustrating the major characteristics of these massifs.

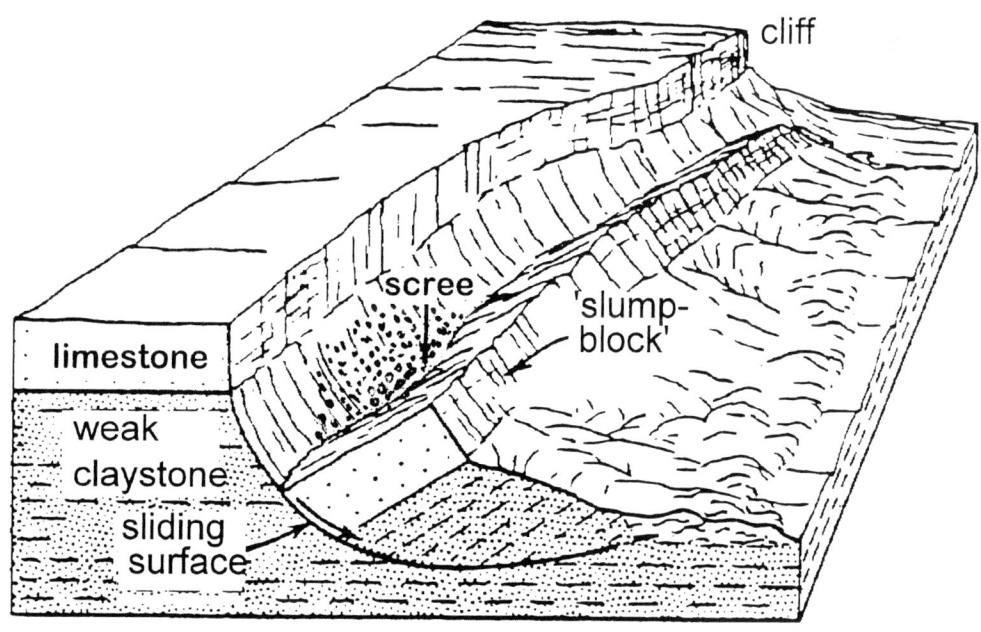

Fig. 6: Schematic representation of a rock slump (modified from Strahler *et al.* 1992).

Fig. 7: Massif 3 or the massif of the aqueducts: the steep, bare, rock front of the massif is in contrast with the gentle vegetated debris slopes above.

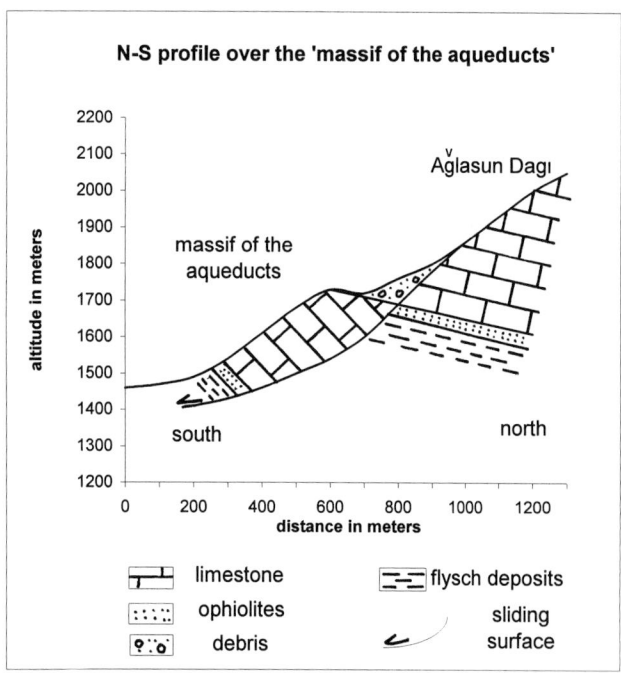

Fig. 8: A profile through massif 3 representing the rotational slide of the massif.

Sahara where thick and resistant sandstones underlain by thick layers of clay and siltstone slumped downwards off a 300 m high cliff, over a length of several kilometers (Grünert 1987). Near Villerville (Normandy) several slumps of compact chalk were detected with the sliding surface in the underlying marls, clays and sands (Flageollet and Helluin 1987). A typical rock block slide is the 'Gros Ventre Slide', Wyoming (USA) where a sandstone layer slid down over a layer of mudstone (Press and Siever 1986).

Another type of a rock mass slide has been observed in the area around Başköy (for its location see Fig. 11). Three huge limestone blocks are lying underneath the main limestone cliff. They show a slight anti-slope and are surrounded by ophiolitic material with a varying concentration of limestone debris. We interpret this morphology as a lateral spread of the limestone blocks due to a slide or flow of the underlying ophiolites (Fig. 12). The limestone blocks are dragged with the flowing ophiolites and are first rotated causing the anti-slope.

Lateral spreads are present where resistant rocks are underlain by weak rocks which are susceptible to liquefaction or becoming liquid (Selby 1993). In reality, these three rock mass movements are often present in one complex mass movement. Because of the liquefaction of the underlying weak rock, the resistant rock mass is dragged down and first undergoes a rotation followed by a translational movement, as is the case at Başköy. In this case, we can better speak of a lateral-sliding-flowing movement which focuses on the different processes involved in this movement. However, it is also possible that the movement starts with the sliding over a distinct plane of failure which evolves into a flowing movement because of changing pore pressures and granular temperatures (Iverson et al. 1997). Other examples of lateral spreading are found in the Central Sahara: thick layers of clay become liquid and take sandstone blocks with them in their downward movement (Grünert 1987). The mass movements at the Mackenröderspitze (Germany) are a good example of the coexistence of three types of movement in a complex lateral rock mass-sliding-flowing movement (Ackermann 1959). Other examples of lateral spreads are found in Calabria (Gulla and Sorisso-Valva 1985).

To the west of the site, in the valley leading towards the ancient pass to Isparta (Loots et al. 2000), more isolated limestone platforms can be observed. Since many of them are situated above one another and are surrounded by a mixture of ophiolites and limestone debris, it can be suggested that a complex lateral-sliding-flowing movement has also occurred here.

It was already noted that the former depression between limestone block 3 and the main front is filled up with debris, fine material and eight smaller limestone blocks or blocks (number 2 on Figs. 2 and 3). This is a very chaotic environment and the general setting of these limestone blocks (Fig. 13) indicates that they are involved in a sliding-flowing movement. Some blocks also indicate clear evidence of rotation.

The ancient site itself also comprises a complex of limestone platforms, e.g. the platform supporting the Tiberian gateway to the lower agora, that carrying the temple of Apollo Klarios, and that on which the temple of Antonius Pius was built. These may also be the result of rotational sliding. Even the conical hill to the south of Sagalassos on which Alexander the Great defeated the city in 333 BC, can be seen as a giant mass movement. Further investigation is, however, necessary.

3.3. Dimensions of the displaced blocks

The rock slumps discussed here are of an enormous size. They have a length of several hundreds of meters. We tried to estimate the volume of the slumped limestone blocks to get an idea of their dimensions. This was based on profiles, such as the one through the 'block of the aqueducts' (block 3) (Fig. 8), *in situ* observations and topographical information. Table 1 shows the estimated volumes of some displaced limestone blocks.

Situation	type of movement	limestone block	limestone volume in millions of m^3
Sagalassos East	rotational	1	19-23
Sagalassos East	rotational	3	30-40
Sagalassos East	rotational	4	19-23
Sagalassos East	rotational	5	22-28
Sagalassos East	rotational	6	1-2
Sagalassos East	rotational	7	7-13
Sagalassos East	rotational	9	4-8
Başköy	lateral spread	1	0.8
Başköy	lateral spread	2	0.2
Başköy	lateral spread	3	1.7

Table 1: volume of some displaced limestone blocks

These estimates are of course very rough since they are based on very little information. However, they give a good indication of the order of magnitude of the volumes dealt with. One must also realise that the volume of the ophiolites and flysch deposits, which were also displaced by the sliding of the limestone, were not taken into account.

In the literature, very little is known about the dimensions of mass movements. An example of a mass movement, generally described as a very big one, is the rockfall avalanche off Mount Huascarán in Peru, where 50 to 100 million m^3 of rock was displaced (Selby 1993). It should be clear then that the rock slumps east of Sagalassos are very large.

3.4. The age of the rock slumps

3.4.1. East of Sagalassos

It is always interesting to know when all these rock slides occurred. Did they occur during a single, short period under extreme conditions or were there more phases of instability? Did some of them occur when there was already significant human occupation of the area? These questions are very difficult to answer because of the huge problems that arise when trying to date sliding phenomena.

However, we tried to date the rock displacements relative to each other based on the total amount of debris that had accumulated between the slumped blocks and the limestone front of the Lycian nappes. The underlying idea was that the older the slumps are, the older the created depression is, and the longer the time available for the accumulation of debris in the depression and thus the greater the accumulation would be. We tried to calculate the amount of accumulated debris behind some limestone blocks that are lying next to each other. Based on the profiles we calculated the volume of debris accumulated behind some blocks over a unit of distance (m^3/m). The results for some blocks are listed below in Table 2.

limestone block	amount of debris in m^3/m
3	10,000
5	34,000
7	51,000
9	7,000

Table 2: Estimation of the amount of debris accumulated behind some limestone blocks over a unit of distance.

Although these figures are very rough estimates, it is clear that the amounts of accumulated debris in the depressions between the slumped limestone blocks and the limestone front, are quite substantially different from one another. It should be said that coarse and fine debris had accumulated behind blocks 5, 7 and 9, while behind block 3 (the aqueducts) some small limestone blocks had also slid down (blocks 2). The rate of debris accumulation therefore may be considered to be higher behind block 3 than behind the other blocks.

If the underlying hypothesis is correct, we might conclude that the rock slumps did not occur within the same period. A relative dating of the four blocks listed in Table 2 would then be that the movement of block 7 is the oldest one, followed respectively by those of blocks 5 and blocks 3 and 9. Limestone blocks that are situated above each other can be placed in a relative dating scheme in a different way (see 4).

The remains of aqueducts carved in the face of block 3 gives us an indication of the absolute age of the rock slumps. The block must have been displaced long before the construction of the aqueducts. Since they were built in late Hellenistic to Roman times, this gives a minimum age of 2100 years for the displacement of the limestone block. However, there may be some indication that limestone block 3 underwent a small displacement only recently, i.e. during the occupation of Sagalassos. At block 3, clear remains of at least 2 aqueducts have been found (Owens 1995). These were mapped during the field campaign of 1995 (Steegen et al. 2000). So far, the lower of these two aqueducts could not be discerned closer to the city, where there is only evidence of a single rock-cut channel. One thus might suppose that originally the lowest aqueduct in block 3 corresponded with the only channel observable more towards the west. A small downward movement of block 3, or of a part of this block, could then have lead to an interruption in the water supply system and hence a new aqueduct had to be carved. This new aqueduct would then have been the present upper one. Since its degree of weathering is slight, while that of the lower aqueduct and that of the conduit near the city are greater, this hypothesis may well turn out to be correct. However, before a conclusion can be proposed, an accurate dating of the aqueducts should be undertaken. In any case it has already been suggested that the two aqueducts in block 3 are of different dates (Owens 1995; Steegen et al. 2000).

3.4.2. At Başköy

Fig. 11 is a geomorphological interpretation of a small area near Başköy with the slide of the three limestone blocks (see also Fig. 12). There are some indications that these mass movements around Başköy are a very recent phenomenon. A local farmer explained that after a long period of stability, some 50 years ago, there was a slide of ophiolitic material from above the great cliff, resulting in a debris cone between the cliff and the limestone blocks. This created a hollow above the cliff. In this hollow, there is now a single tree, a *Salix*, about 40 to 50 years old, which might bear out the farmer's story. The movement above the cliff

Fig. 9: The top of limestone massif 4 makes a step in the topography. This step can be seen as a narrow vegetated zone contrasting with the bare rock faces above and beneath.

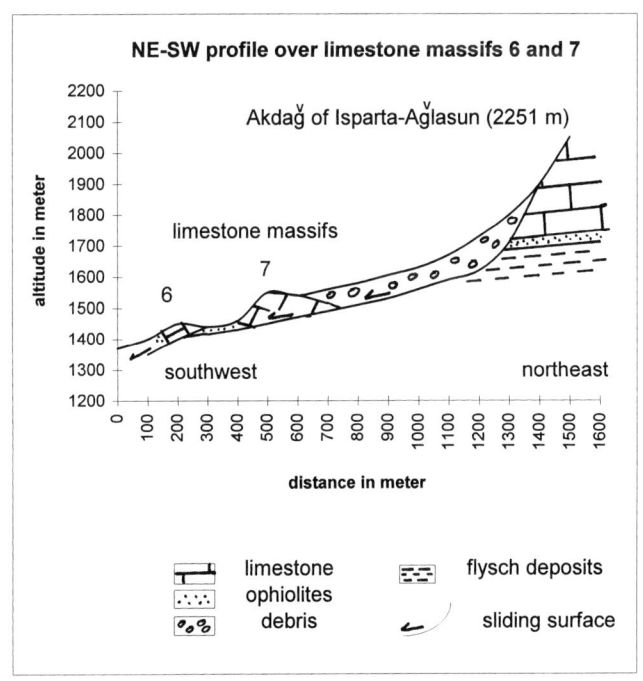

Fig. 10: A profile through limestone massifs 6 and 7 showing the sliding of these massifs.

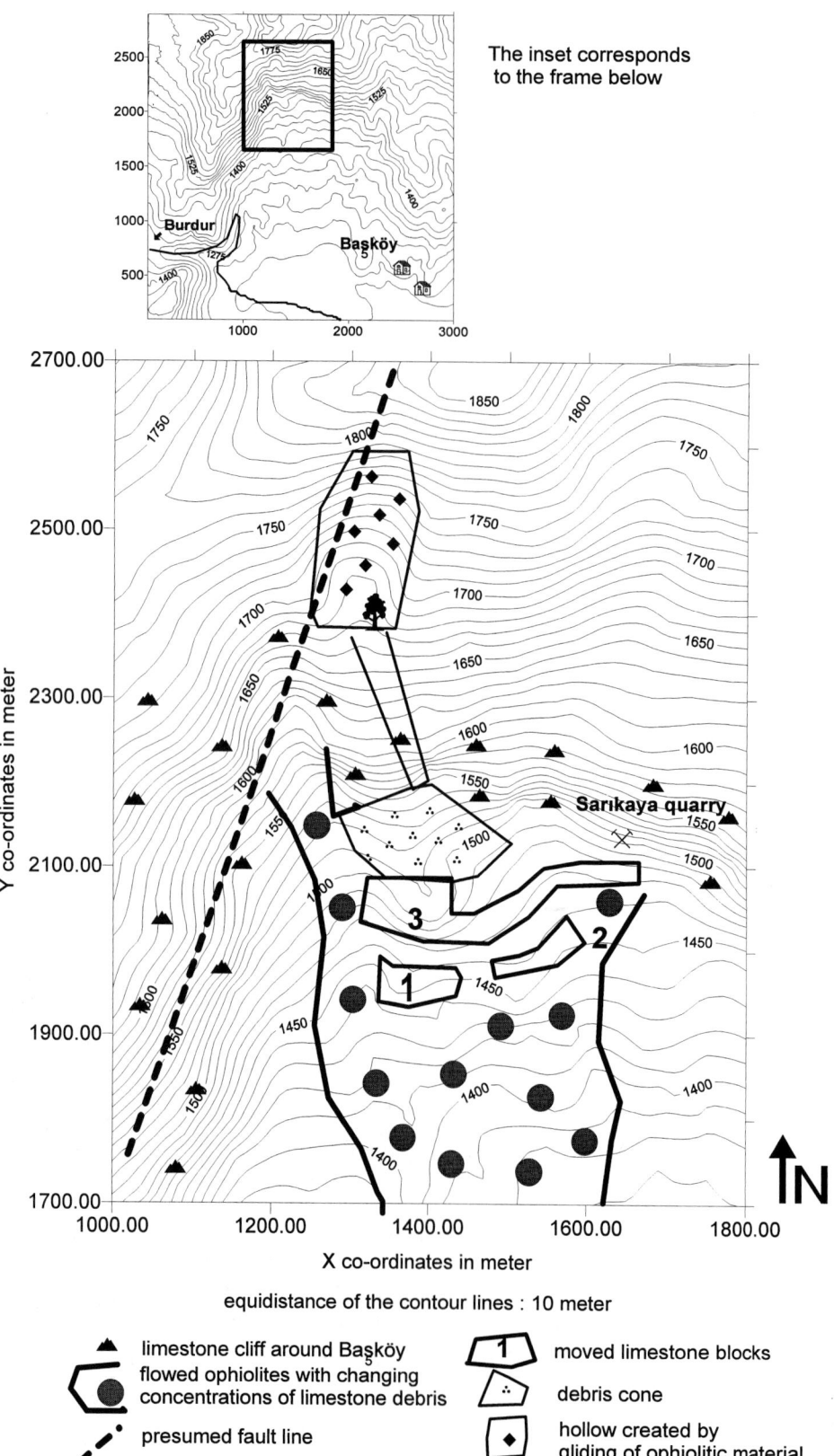

Fig. 11: Situation and geomorphic interpretation of the studied area near Başköy.

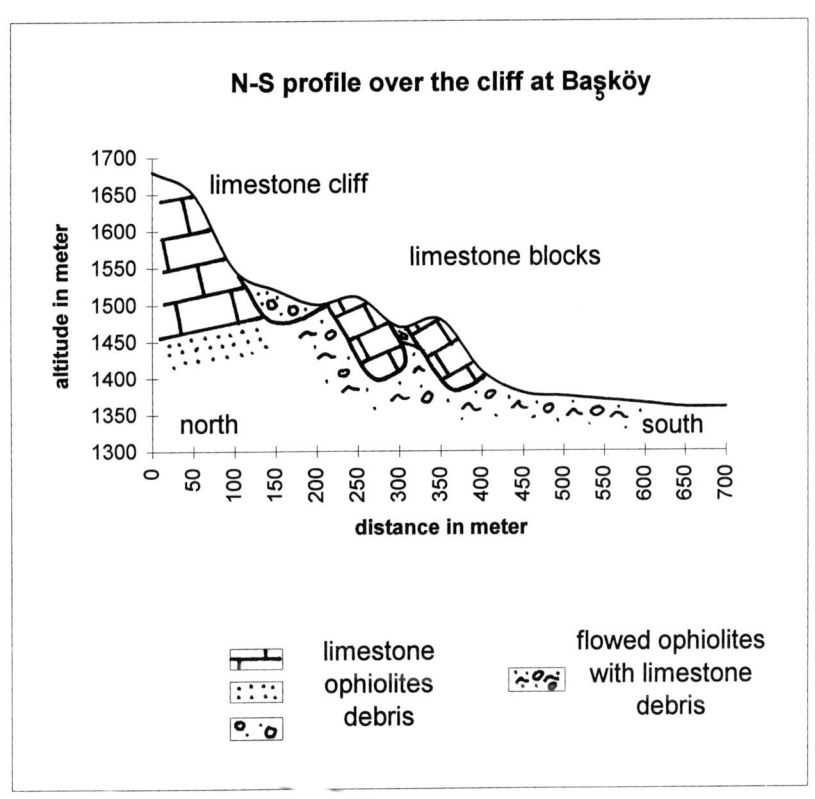

Fig. 12: The lateral-sliding-flowing movement of the limestone blocks at Başköy.

Fig. 13: Eight small limestone blocks that moved in a sliding-flowing movement in the depression behind massif 3.

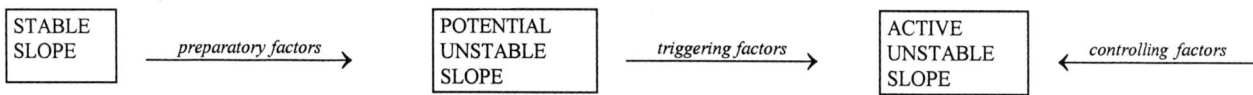

Fig. 14: Relation between the three categories of causes of mass movements (after Crozier 1986).

Fig. 15: Two vertical joints separating two limestone units from the rest of the cliff.

results from the instability of the slope above the cliff which in turn was probably due to the prior detachment of the three limestone blocks from the cliff. The two phenomena are thus connected and it is therefore not unrealistic to believe that the displacement of the three limestone blocks occurred in recent or at least historic times. Moreover, the faces of the limestone blocks and the cliff appear to be quite 'fresh', i.e. they do not yet show a black-grey patina and probably have not been exposed to the atmosphere for a very long period. The southern face of the most southerly limestone block however, has a clear patina: this face was in fact the face of the main cliff before the displacement of the blocks took place and has therefore been exposed to atmospheric weathering processes for a longer period. Since part of the cliff wall, which has become exposed by the loss of the limestone blocks, was already exploited as a quarry in Roman times, that is, the quarry of Sarıkaya (Waelkens et al. 1997), one can attribute a date of at least 2000 years to these mass movements.

3.5. The nature of the rock mass movements around Sagalassos

Since their plane of failure is situated very deep (more than 50 m in most cases), the rock mass movements around Sagalassos can be considered as deep-seated landslides (Petley 1996). The nature of these movements is not fully understood because of their scarcity and the difficulty of obtaining mechanical information from near the base of the movement. However, there seems to be more and more evidence that creeping movements in the order of centimeters to meters/year may suddenly change into a catastrophic failure, as was the case with the devastating 1963 Vaiont-landslide (Petley 1996). In experiments, Petley and Allison (1997) observed a transitional phase of behaviour in which creep will manifest itself at the base of a deep-seated landslide by the growth of microcracks. These microcracks may eventually coalesce to form a shear surface, which may then produce a sudden failure. After this sudden failure, the displaced mass comes to rest, but very slow creeping movements can occur again for a longer period as was, for example, observed by Ackermann (1959) in Germany.

We suggest that the large rock mass movements around Sagalassos presented a similar sequence to that sketched above: a longer period with very slow displacement rates preceded a major failure. Afterwards, slow movement can still occur, some of which may be going on even today. The history of block 3 as suggested above (see 3.4.1) might be an indication that there were distinct periods when slow movements alternated with sudden failures. There is a strong possibility that the sliding-flowing movement of the three limestone blocks near Başköy (see 3.4.2) is not yet completed. These movements may be of the order of cm/year or even less, but it would be interesting to follow up this site in the future in greater detail by means of total station mapping or GPS. Such a survey could also detect possible large movements still to come, as is being done in Calabria, for example (Gulla and Sorisso-Valva 1985), where the beginning of large lateral spreads is monitored by measuring the widening of tension cracks.

3.6. Other mass movements around Sagalassos

Besides the sliding of huge limestone masses, one can also observe some other types of mass movements in the area surrounding the site. In the first place, there are the numerous debris slopes resulting from rockfall processes and small debris flows. These debris slopes were further investigated and the results are presented by Librecht et al. 2000. It is often the case that, right at the point where a huge limestone mass slid down the cliff, there is an increased debris production. This can be explained by assuming that the sliding of the limestone mass makes the limestone along the sliding surface very brittle. Since the upper part of this surface becomes the new face, it is clear that the face becomes quite unstable and may produce further rockfalls.

4. GEOMORPHOLOGICAL EVOLUTION

An attempt has been made to place the different kinds of morphologies east of Sagalassos (i.e. the displaced limestone blocks, the debris flows and the debris accumulations) in a schematic evolutionary framework. The successive steps which can be distinguished in this scheme can be illustrated in an example, that is, the evolution which occurred near limestone blocks 6 and 7:

- rotational sliding of a limestone block (in this case block 7) off the major limestone face of the Lycian nappes (i.e. Akdağ of Isparta-Ağlasun or Ağlasun Dağı)
- debris accumulation in the depression which was developed by the rock slump (this process is still active today): formation of a rockfall talus
- further translational movement of the limestone block (7)
- large rockfalls, small slides and the development of a debris flow or block stream off the weakened face of the displaced limestone block (in this case also the sliding of block 6 off block 7)

Other limestone blocks have not (yet) completed this evolution. Block 3, for example, has only slid rotationally and there is a debris accumulation between the block and the Lycian front. This also supports the earlier conclusion that the displacement of block 7 must be older than that of block 3 and that, therefore, different periods of instability should be distinguished.

Sometimes, however, development went a step further. After a similar evolution had taken place for block 8, a new rotational sliding occurred, that of block 5, followed by a new debris accumulation. The same scheme therefore can repeat itself at the same place. This also makes it possible to propose a relative dating sequence to some displacement phenomena which are situated above one another.

Another slightly different scheme can be observed near blocks 10 and 11. After the slide of block 10, a rockfall talus developed. This scree deposit transformed into a hard calcrete, which in turn, also underwent a rotational downward movement (see above). Today, a non-indurated rockfall talus is situated north of the displaced calcrete (block 11).

5. CAUSES OF THE GIANT ROCK SLIDES

The causes of mass movements in general, as represented in Fig. 14, can be divided into three categories (Crozier 1986). Preparatory factors change a stable slope into a potentially unstable slope, whereas triggering factors make them actively unstable, i.e. the slopes are put into movement. Controlling factors have an influence on the shape, speed and duration of the movement. Often, these factors merge and a preparatory factor can become a controlling factor. Without being complete, a number of possible causes of giant rock slides in the surroundings of Sagalassos are given here.

5.1. Preparatory factors

Some preparatory factors which are important for Sagalassos are the topography and the presence of discontinuities.

5.1.1. Topography

Steep slopes and huge differences in altitude turn the area into a zone which is potentially unstable. This aspect of the topography is closely connected with the general tectonics of the district: it was only recently uplifted (Miocene, 10-15 million years ago, see Paulissen et al. 1993). Since the topography is the result of endogenous and exogenous processes, a new balance needs arrived at in response to recent endogenous activity. Tectonics also cause numerous faults and joints (see 5.1.2).

5.1.2. Discontinuities

There are different types of discontinuities in rocks that play a part in the stability of a slope: tectonic joints, faults, lithological boundaries and decompression joints (Hencher 1987). These play a very important part in the development of huge rock mass slidings (Zolotarev 1974).

The lithologic succession at Sagalassos – permeable limestone underlain by nearly impervious ophiolites and flysch deposits – does not contribute to the stability of the slopes (see also Fig. 6). The lithologic boundaries are an important frontier for groundwater movements. The layers dip to the north, i.e. into the slope. In our opinion, this is very favourable for the genesis of large, but occasional rock mass movements. However, when the layers dip away from the slopes, more, albeit smaller, rockfalls or slidings may be expected.

Discontinuities are zones of weakness where the resistance against sliding is low and where water infiltrates more easily to weaken the rocks through lubrication.

Joints separate the rock into smaller units. For giant rock mass movements, such as those around Sagalassos, the number of joints needs to be fairly low and the distance between them fairly high. This makes the displaced masses bigger. Near Başköy is a good example of two big vertical joints separating two limestone units from the rest of the cliff (Fig. 15). If the underlying clayey deposits started to slide, they could transport the limestone units further down. This would explain the movement of the three limestone blocks at Başköy (Fig. 12). If, however, more, but smaller joints exist, rather smaller rock fragments will be transported downwards, predominantly by rockfall processes. It is the presence or absence of zones with discontinuities that determines whether many units of limited dimensions or a few larger ones will become detached from the *in situ* rock mass (Zolotarev 1974).

Faults are also zones of weakness, even more than joints are: the surface of the fault has already served as a sliding surface. Because of this, it is smoother and exhibits an even lower resistance to sliding than joints do (Hencher 1987). Since faults are rarely close-spaced, they play a very important role in the development of giant rock slides. The majority of landslides after the 1993 Pyrgos earthquake in Western Greece thus occurred along fault scarps (Koukouvelas et al. 1996). Proximity to major faults also was a common feature of the landslides in the Mengen region in Northwest Turkey (Gokçeoğlu and Aksoy 1996). At Başköy, a number of faults in the sliding area can be observed. For example, the western wall of the hollow created above the cliff, is thought to be a fault plane (see also Fig. 11). To the east of Sagalassos, near the Akdağ of Isparta-Ağlasun, there are also some faults. Tectonic breccies, slickensides, smooth fault surfaces and the presence of a valley are all evidence. A large debris flow is also located on this spot. Block 8 has probably slid down from this direction. According to Yalçınkaya (1983), an approximately east-west trending subvertical tear fault is located on the prominent east-west running scarp in the topography. This tear fault is characterised by the occurrence of breccies several meters thick, that are oriented parallel to the topographic scarps. This may be a reason why so many massive sliding phenomena are observed in the area around Sagalassos and not in the larger surrounding area.

5.2. Triggering factors

Some triggering factors which could influence the occurrence of giant rock mass slides around Sagalassos are fluctuations in the groundwater level over a short period and earthquakes.

5.2.1. Groundwater level fluctuations over a short period
A sudden and quick rise in the groundwater level as the result of long and heavy rainfall or the rapid melting of snow, can cause a rapid decrease in rock mass strength. This plays an important role especially in rocks since groundwater is primarily present in their many discontinuities. Therefore, the rise of the groundwater level in a rock mass is many times higher than it is in soil material (Selby 1993). Because of higher groundwater levels, very high pore pressures can develop in the discontinuities (joints or faults). Two small rotational slides above the cliff near Başköy thus resulted from heavy rainfall which caused problems of water surplus in the surrounding area, for example, the flooding of streets at Isparta and a rise of the level of Lake Gölcük. According to a local farmer this would have happened in 1985 or 1986.

5.2.2. Earthquakes

Although mass movements caused by earthquakes are probably one of the most ignored denudation processes (Young and Young 1992), earthquakes play an important role in the genesis of the landscape in tectonically and seismically active areas. Often there is a relation between seismicity, mass movements and faults: seismicity will cause a reactivation of existing faults and the majority of landslides occurring during or shortly after an earthquake can be found in close proximity to these faults. Examples are found in Ecuador (Tibaldi *et al.* 1995), Greece (Koukouvelas *et al.* 1996) and Japan (Shiono *et al.* 1996). This clear relationship suggested that faults strongly amplified seismic waves (Shiono *et al.* 1996).

Keefer (1984) found some statistical relationship between the magnitude of an earthquake and the genesis of a mass movement. This relationship has been tested on the earthquake catalogue by Ergin *et al.* (1967) and led to the conclusion that there are dozens of earthquakes which could have caused mass movements around Sagalassos. The relationship could be completed by further data on ancient earthquakes, up to the tenth century, published by Guidoboni (1994). For the town of Sagalassos, Waelkens *et al.* (2000) suggest that at least four earthquakes struck the city respectively in the second half of the first century AD, the middle of the third century AD, the first quarter of the sixth century AD and around the middle of the seventh century AD. The latest of these earthquakes could have been so destructive that eventually the city was abandoned.

Although we do not have complete and correct data on the earthquakes, it should already be clear that there are fewer mass movements than earthquakes which could have caused them. So not every heavy earthquake had an influence on the geomorphology. Ota *et al.* (1997) came to a similar conclusion for many late Quaternary landslides in Papua New Guinea. One should remember in most cases that earthquakes are only a triggering factor: if the slope has not become potentially unstable as the result of other processes, an earthquake may have no effect on it.

6. CONCLUSIONS

This study was intended to provide an explanation for the existence of different limestone blocks, acting as platforms that are isolated from the limestone cliff of the Lycian nappes in the surroundings of Sagalassos.

An analysis of some characteristics of these limestone blocks and of some specific features of mass movements leads to the conclusion that most of the limestone blocks can be identified as giant rock mass slides, mostly with a rotational character. The dimensions of these sliding phenomena are in the order of some millions to a few tens of millions of m^3 of transported limestone. The site of Sagalassos proper was partly built on top of such platforms.

A geomorphological reconstruction of the landscape around Sagalassos was set up wherein one can distinguish different phases of landscape development. Based on debris accumulations it was postulated that the rock mass slides took place in different periods. Some of them seem to have occurred in historic times. One even may have damaged part of the late Hellenistic (to Roman Imperial) aqueduct, which consequently had to be recarved over a certain distance.

Finally some possible causes of the sliding phenomena were investigated. The lithologic succession and the presence of faults and major joints makes this area very susceptible to giant rock mass slides. Earthquakes could have initiated the slides although one should not conclude that every heavy earthquake had such an impact. But the potential force of some of these earthquakes is well illustrated by the fact that such a seismic event around the middle of the seventh century AD, seems to have eventually caused the complete abandonment of Sagalassos.

7. ACKNOWLEDGEMENTS

This research is supported by the Belgian Programme on Interuniversity Poles of Attraction (IUAP 4/12) initiated by the Belgian State, Prime Minister's Office, Science Policy Programming. The text also presents the results of the Concerted Action of the Flemish Government (GOA 97/2) and the Fund for Scientific Research-Flanders (Belgium) (FWO) (G.2145.94). Scientific responsibility is assumed by its authors. Gert Verstraeten is postdoctoral fellow of the Fund for Scientific Research Flanders (FWO).

8. REFERENCES

E. Ackermann (1959) Der Abtragungsmechanismus bei Massenverlagerungen an der Wellenkalk-Schichtstufe 1: Bewegingsarten der Massenverlagerungen und morphologische Formen, *Zeitschrift für Geomorphologie* 3/3: 193-226.

M.J. Crozier (1986) *Landslides, Causes, Consequences and Environment*, London.

K. Ergin, U. Güçlü and Z. Uz (1967) *A Catalogue of Earthquakes for Turkey and Surrounding Area, 11 AD to 1964 AD*, Istanbul.

J.C. Flageollet and E. Helluin (1987) Morphological investigations of the sliding areas along the coast of Pays d'Auge, near Villerville, Normandy, France, in: V. Gardiner (ed.) *International Geomorphology*, New York: 477-486.

C. Gökçeoğlu and H. Aksoy (1996) Landslide susceptibility mapping of the slopes in the residual soils of the Mengen region (Turkey) by deterministic stability analyses and image processing techniques, *Engineering Geology* 44/1-4: 147-161.

G. Gulla and M. Sorriso-Valva (1985) Deep-seated block slides and lateral spreads in Calabria, in: *International Symposium on Erosion, Debris Flows and Disaster Prevention, September 3-5, 1985, Tsukuba, Japan*: 311-316.

J. Grünert (1987) Landslides in the Central Sahara (South-West Libya and East Niger), in: V. Gardiner (ed.) *International Geomorphology*, New York: 487-498.

E. Guidoboni (1994) *Catalogue of Ancient Earthquakes in the Mediterranean Area up to the 10th Century*, Rome.

S.R. Hencher (1987) The implications of joints and structures for for slope stability, in: G.M. Andersen and R.S. Richards (eds) *Slope Stability, Geotechnical Engineering and Geomorphology*, Chichester: 187-230.

R.M. Iverson, M.E. Reid and R.G. Lahusen (1997) Debris flow mobilisation from landslides, *Annual Review of Earth and Planetary Sciences* 25: 85-138.

D.K. Keefer (1984) Landslides caused by earthquakes, *Geological Society of America, Bulletin* 95/4: 406-421.

I. Koukouvelas, A. Mpresiakas, E. Sokos and T. Doutsos (1996) The tectonic setting and earthquake ground hazards of the 1993 Pyrgos earthquake, Peloponnese, Greece, *Journal of the Geological Society* 153: 39-49.

I. Librecht, E. Paulissen, G. Verstraeten and M. Waelkens (2000) Implications of environmental changes on slope evolution nearby Sagalassos, in: M. Waelkens and L. Loots (eds) *Sagalassos V, Report on the Survey and the Excavation Campaigns of 1996 and 1997 (Acta Archaeologica Lovaniensia Monographiae 11)* Leuven University Press: 799-817.

L. Loots, M. Waelkens and F. Depuydt (2000) The city fortifications of Sagalassos from the Hellenistic to the late Roman period, in M. Waelkens and L. Loots (eds) *Sagalassos V. Report on the Survey and the Excavation Campaigns of 1996 and 1997 (Acta Archaeologica Lovaniensia Monographiae 11)* Leuven University Press: 595-634.

Y. Ota, J. C. Chappel, K. Berryman and Y. Okamoto (1997) Late Quaternary paleolandslides on the coral terraces of Huon peninsula, Papua New Guinea, *Geomorphology* 19/1-2: 55-76.

E. Owens (1995) The aquaducts of Sagalassos, in: M. Waelkens and J. Poblome (eds) *Sagalassos III. Report on the Fourth Excavation Campaign of 1993 (Acta Archaeologicavaniensia Monographiae 6)* Leuven University Press: 209-220.

E. Paulissen, J. Poesen, G. Govers and J. De Ploey (1993) The physical environment at Sagalassos (Western Taurus, Turkey). A reconnaissance survey, in: M. Waelkens and J. Poblome (eds) *Sagalassos II. Report on the Third Excavation Campaign of 1992 (Acta Archaeologica Lovaniensia Monographiae 6)* Leuven University Press: 229-248.

D. Petley (1996) The mechanics and landforms of deep-seated landslides, in: M.G. Anderson and S.M. Brooks (eds) *Advances in Hillslope Processes* 2, Chichester: 823-835.

D. Petley and R.J. Allison (1997) The mechanics of deep-seated landslides, *Earth Surface Processes and Landforms* 22/8: 747-758.

F. Press and R. Siever (1986) *Earth*, New York.

M.J. Selby (1993) *Hillslope Materials and Processes*, Oxford.

K. Shiono, K. Nakagawa, M. Mitamura, S. Masumoto and K. Irikura (1996) Focusing of seismic waves along the Uemachi fault: damage in the Osake area caused by the 1995 Hyogo Ken Nanbu earthquake and a subsurface geologic structure, *Journal of Physics of the Earth* 44/5: 591-599.

A. Steegen, K. Cauwenberghs, G. Govers, E. Owens and P. Desmet (1998) The water supply to Sagalassos, in: M. Waelkens and L. Loots (ed.) *Sagalassos V, Report on the Survey and the Excavation Campaigns of 1996 and 1997 (Acta Archaeologica Lovaniensia Monographiae 11)* Leuven University Press: 635-650.

A.H. Strahler and A.N. Strahler (1992) *Modern Physical Geography*, New York.

A. Tibaldi, L. Ferrari and G. Pasquarè (1995) Landslides triggered by earthquakes and their relations with faults and mountain slope geometry: an example from Ecuador, *Geomorphology* 11: 215-226.

A. Tollman (1987) Klippe, in: C.K. Seyfert (ed.) *The Encyclopaedia of Structural Geology and Plate Tectonics*, New York: 377-381.

G. Verstraeten (1996) *Verglijdingen van grote rotsmassa's rondom Sagalassos, Turkije*, Unpublished M.Sc. Dissertation, KULeuven.

M. Waelkens, E. Paulissen, H. Vanhaverbeke, I. Öztürk, B. De Cupere, H.A. Ekinci, P.M. Vermeersch, J. Poblome and R. Degeest (1997) The 1994 and 1995 surveys on the territory of Sagalassos, in: M. Waelkens and J. Poblome (eds), *Sagalassos IV. Report on the Survey and Excavation Campaigns of 1994 and 1995 (Acta Archaeologica Lovaniensia Monographiae 9)* Leuven University Press: 11-102.

M. Waelkens, M. Sintubin, Ph. Muchez and E. Paulissen (2000) Archaeological and geological evidences for a major earthquake at Sagalassos (SW Turkey) around the middle of the seventh century AD, in: W.J. Mcguire, D.R. Griffiths and I.S. Stewart (eds) *The Archaeologiy of Geological Catastrophes (Geological Society, Special Publication 171)* London:373-383.

J. Whittow (1984) *The Penguin Dictionary of Physical Geography*, London.

S. Yalçınkaya (1983) *Geological Map of Isparta, M25-d.1, scale 1/25.000*.

R. Young and A. Young (1992) *Sandstone Landforms (Springer Series in Physical Environment* 11) Berlin.

G.S. Zolotarev (1974) Geological regularities of the development of landslides and rockfalls as the basis for their study and prognosis, in: L. Calembert (ed.), *La géologie de l'ingenieur*, Liège: 211-235.

IMPLICATIONS OF ENVIRONMENTAL CHANGES ON SLOPE EVOLUTION NEAR SAGALASSOS

Ireen LIBRECHT[1], Etienne PAULISSEN[1], Gert VERSTRAETEN[2] and Marc WAELKENS[3]

1 - Geomorphology and Regional Geography, KULeuven, Redingenstraat 16, B-3000 Leuven, Belgium
2 - Laboratory for Experimental Geomorphology, KULeuven, Redingenstraat 16, B-3000 Leuven, Belgium
3 - Department of Archaeology, KULeuven, Blijde Inkomststraat 21, B-3000 Leuven, Belgium

1. INTRODUCTION

Two papers deal already with slopes and slope processes in the territory of Sagalassos. In 1993, Paulissen *et al.* presented a first outline of the physical environment of the site and its surroundings together with an overview of the present day geomorphological processes. In 1995, Poesen *et al.* analysed in more detail debris flows and water erosion hazards and some of their controlling factors. It became clear that the most active slopes are the sparsely vegetated ones (> 25°) above 1500 m a.s.l.

This paper focuses on the characteristics and the distribution of the actual slope deposits related to rapid mass movements and those of fossil slope deposits, mainly rockfall talus and debris mantled slopes. All these deposits seem to occur nearly exclusively on steep slopes related to the limestone substrate and to the areas of the limestone-ophiolite tectonic mélange between 1000 and 2000 m a.s.l. This paper also deals with areas where rock fragments are produced and with the further quantification of sediment fluxes.

Finally, this paper discusses the main apparent contradiction in the area between its alpine environment on mountain slopes with altitudes above a mere 1500-1600 m a.s.l. and its oro-mediterranean climate. This climate is characterised by 3 dry and warm months and by a cold and wet winter (Paulissen *et al.* 1993; Poesen *et al.* 1995). The alpine environment is characterised by a steppe vegetation and by processes such as the production of rock fragments and rapid mass movements.

Information presented in this paper was collected during different campaigns, but mainly during the field season of 1995, which resulted in a M.Sc. thesis (Librecht 1996).

2. GENERAL SETTING

The slopes under consideration are located in the close vicinity of Sagalassos and near the villages of Ağlasun and Çanaklı. The altitude of this area ranges between 1000 (Ağlasun and Çanaklı Ovası) and 2300 m a.s.l. (Akdağ of Isparta-Ağlasun).

The slopes can mainly be found on three types of lithology:
1 – *slopes on limestone formations*, mainly of Cretaceous age, forming the most prominent and steeper parts of the physical landscape. They are exposed throughout the area over the full range of altitudes. The limestone formations are both autochthonous and allochthonous in origin. The allochthonous limestone formations make up the major part of the Lycian nappes, which have arrived via major thrusts. The front of this nappe, mainly situated above 1600 m a.s.l. forms a huge limestone cliff dominating Sagalassos. It has been subject to massive rock glides (Verstraeten *et al.* 2000). This cliff has a general northeast-southwest orientation and is exposed towards the south and the southeast. Part of the city's rock-cut necropolis is carved in this front. The autochthonous limestone formations are situated to the southeast of the Lycian overthrusting front, in this area at an altitude mainly below 1600 m a.s.l. They mostly occur as limestone blocks. It has to be stressed that the weathering and erosion of the limestone formations is almost exclusively responsible for the production of the rock fragments which make up the fossil and the actual slope deposits at different altitudes.

2 – *slopes on flysch formations*, occurring at altitudes below 1600 m a.s.l. They form the lower and gentler reliefs creating a hilly topography. Nowadays, the flysch formations are clearly very prone to disintegrations by ravines and gullies. For this reason, large parts of the flysch area have been

reafforested by pine trees. Fossil slope deposits are rare on the flysch slopes and, if they are present, they are quite thin. Auger surveys indicate that huge quantities of the eroded flysch material are deposited in the valley bottoms, the basins and on the adjacent lower slopes. The study of the colluvial deposits originating from the flysch formations is not included in this paper.

3 – *slopes on ophiolitic deposits*, situated between the allochthonous limestone formations and the flysch deposits. The ophiolitic formations, with a significant clay component, have a reduced thickness. Since the ophiolitic formations are linked with the allochthonous limestone formations, they are exposed over the entire range of altitudes in the area. They also occur in the highest mountain areas in a tectonic mélange with the limestone formations, where, as will be shown later, the ophiolitic deposits are the source of specific slope processes and deposits.

In conclusion one can suggest that the slope deposits on the mountain slopes around Sagalassos are nearly exclusively confined to the limestone substrate and to the areas of the limestone-ophiolite tectonic mélange.

3. THE SCREE DEPOSITS NEAR SAGALASSOS

In this section the different types of scree deposit are described in relation to their environmental context. Observed actual processes are also mentioned.

A scree is defined as "an accumulation of fragmented rock waste below a cliff or rock face, formed as a result of disintegration, largely by mechanical weathering of a rock exposure"(Whittow 1984). If the rate of debris production exceeds the rate at which it can be removed, debris will accumulate at the base of the cliff as a scree or talus slope (Statham *et al.* 1986). Although it is not a necessary characteristic of scree, most of the scree deposits described in literature are clearly stratified, with beds parallel to the scree slope. In general, a 'scree' and a 'talus' are considered to be synonymous.

The most striking characteristic of a scree deposit is its association with a cliff, located higher up, that deposits its debris on the slope. At Sagalassos, the rock fragments composing scree deposits derive from limestone cliffs. On the south-facing slope of the Ağlasun Dağı above the city this cliff is as high as 300 m but most cliffs are only a few tens of metres high and less than 100 m wide.

Scree may take the morphological form of a sheet of debris or of a talus cone. A sheet of debris is formed where the debris has accumulated below a cliff, which has weathered more or less uniformly along its face. A talus cone is formed below a chute or gully through which descending debris is funnelled. Talus deposits may form any combination of slope and cone forms depending on the nature and the distribution of weathering and erosion processes along a cliff face, and on whether or not the pattern of joints in the cliff permits the development of chutes (Selby 1993).

The Neon library of Sagalassos is at present in such a 'debris-free' hollow at the base of a less fractured part of the cliff, in between two debris cones. If this location is more than a coincidence, it would suggest that there was already significant scree activity on the slopes during the second century AD when the Neon library was built (Waelkens *et al.* 1997). Other evidence, however, suggests a more forested environment during that period (Schroyen *et al.* 2000; Vermoere *et al.* 1999). But, the excavations of the area immediately to the west of the library revealed a scree deposit 3 m wide and ca. 1 m thick a few metres to the west of the building (layer 20c). This deposit was tentatively interpreted as an early second century AD artificial drainage ditch rather than a natural scree (Waelkens *et al.* 1997: 125). But even in this case, it means that there was already scree on the mountain slopes that could be exploited for its debris. At present a more recent scree surface west of the library is situated 3 m above the level of the mosaic floor (Waelkens *et al.* 1997).

White (1981) proposed a classification of talus which he distinguishes, according to the mode of arrival of the debris fragments on the scree, as rockfall talus, alluvial talus and avalanche talus, the rock fragments being respectively transported by gravity, debris flow and avalanches. Rockfall talus are widespread in the area and will be described below. Debris flows occur very frequently on talus slopes in the study area. If they are not the most important process in building the talus, they are mentioned here as a contributory factor in the building of a rockfall talus. If the debris flows are more prominent, the talus is called an alluvial talus. The alluvial talus is an accumulation of rocks of varied size or shape, carried by rain-wash or snow meltwater down a gully or couloir in a cliff face. The presence of water in the processes acting on these talus, means that the slopes are in general less steep than on pure rockfall talus, resulting in a shape between a fan and a cone. This type of talus occurs at the foot of the Akdağ of Isparta-Ağlasun (Fig. 1). The heterogeneous deposits characterising an alluvial talus are also recognisable in the section across the scree west of the Neon library of Sagalassos. This talus will be studied in another paper. Avalanche talus were observed around Sagalassos.

Research on the internal structure of some screes has shown that they are composed of different sedimentological units.

Fig. 1: Alluvial talus at the foot of the Akdağ of Isparta-Ağlasun.

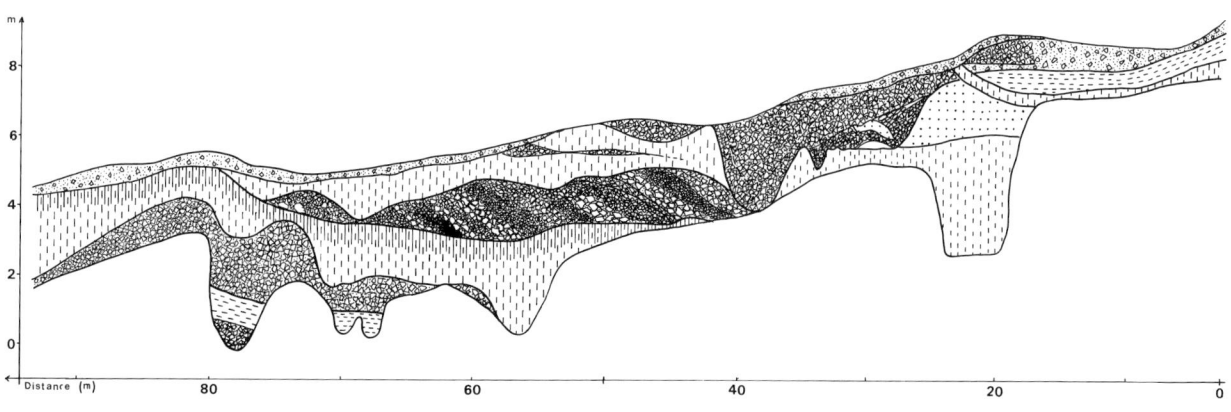

Fig. 2: Drawing of an exposure through a debris cone at the foot of the Zencirükin Tepe, showing the internal heterogeneity in fabrics in a visually homogeneous depositional landform.

Fig. 3: The active rockfall talus cones, 'the three ladies', at the base of the free face.

Fig. 4: Part of the talus sheet between the massif of the aqueducts and the Akdağ of Isparta-Ağlasun. Note the presence of recent debris flows.

This means that the landform is constructed discontinuously by different processes, which are limited in extent and in time. A section through a talus shows different fabrics (Fig. 2), such as:
- individual superficial grain movements at the surface, due to dry or wet sheet flows, creating fine laminations or beds
- distinct bedded units of limited width, created by channelled water
- unsorted mixed-size and matrix-supported masses of rock, created by debris flows

The most widespread type of slope deposit in the neighbourhood is the rockfall talus. This kind of accumulation unit is mainly the result of falling debris. As distinct from other accumulation forms caused by water or ice, such as alluvial fans or fluvioglacial deposits, the rockfall talus is mainly formed by stone chutes, nearly dry accumulations of debris that result in steep slopes and clast supported sediments.

Both rockfall talus cones and sheets occur near Sagalassos. The shape of the rockfall talus depends on the existing morphology in the debris delivery area, and more especially on the distance between the different debris feeding paths in the cliff. If the rockfall talus is fed via one channel, the contributing area is large and a talus cone will form. Talus cones occur for instance just east of the potters' quarter of Sagalassos where the 'Three Ladies' (Fig. 3) form three individual rockfall cones. They have covered or perhaps even destroyed a larger section of the late Hellenistic (to Roman Imperial) rock-cut eastern aqueduct(s). On the eastern part of the south facing slope of the Çalbalı Tepe, several channels are close to one another so that the contributing area for each of these channels is small. The individual cones merge together and form a straight slope in plan form (Fig. 4).

3.1. Active rockfall talus

In this paper rockfall talus are considered to be active when the upper part of their surface is still free from vegetation. It is known that talus surfaces are commonly diachronous, that means surfaces are older and less disturbed by recent events towards the base of the debris slope (Whitehouse and McSavenney 1983).

The rockfall talus illustrated in Figs 3 and 4 are still active nowadays. The talus cones of the 'Three Ladies' (Fig. 3) are situated at about 1600 m a.s.l. The apexes of these talus cones are still growing and now cover the channel of the upper rock-cut aqueduct, the best preserved aqueduct bringing water towards the city (Owens 1995: 92; Steegen et al. 2000). According to a detailed levelling by Steegen, the channel of this aqueduct is at an altitude of 1613 m a.s.l. This evidence indicates that the production of coarse debris from the fractured limestone substrate is still active on the 300 m high cliff.

The rockfall talus that covers nearly the entire slope over a lateral distance of about 1 km below the Çalbalı Tepe, between 1850 and 2050 m a.s.l., is also still active (Fig. 4). This talus slope with a concave profile covers nearly the total scarp and the limestone substrate is now only exposed at its very top. The limestone substrate is heavily fractured there and rock fragment production is high. This is evidenced by the presence of angular rock fragments situated very close to their source area as indicated by their imprint in the substrate. The colour differences between the fresh brownish surfaces on the one hand (colour of the matrix within the scree) and the somewhat older grey surfaces on the other hand also suggest an active debris production. The upper part of this scree slope is nearly rectilinear with an inclination of 33° and bears no vegetation cover. The gentler lower slope has a concave form with an average slope inclination of 28.5° and is completely overgrown by thorn clumps and some other shrubs. The vegetation limit on this slope is not considered to be a climatological vegetation limit since herbs and shrubs still grow higher on the mountain in such quantities as to allow sheep and goat herding on a seasonal basis (Beuls et al. 2000). We suggest that this vegetation line is local and that the growth of vegetation on the rectilinear slope is precluded by the intensity of accumulation of fresh scree deposits and by the reactivation of the slope, mainly by the debris flows which occur frequently. These flows are seen from a distance as patches with a brown colour on the whitish-grey scree surface (see Fig. 4). Because of a fine matrix within these flows, they are quickly covered by sparse vegetation but most of these flows are completely bare and therefore not more than a few years old. These debris flows are quite similar to the debris flows as described by Van Steijn (1989): they do not form continuous layers but are shaped in tongues with a limited extent; the upper part of the flow consists of a channel, flanked by two small levees. The most important argument to establish that these shapes are debris flows and not dry grain flows (Van Steijn et al. 1995) is that the deposits are rich in matrix but still clast supported. The debris particles are oriented parallel to the scree surface, there is no clear imbrication and the boundary with the underlying scree sediments is very clear. Since no vegetation is able to settle on the upper part of the scree, the reworking processes must be considerable. The frequency of erosive events (debris flows and shallow landslides) can be estimated by comparing the precipitation intensity data of Sagalassos with the critical intensity-duration figures for rainfall that can cause debris flows (Poesen et al. 1995). These calculations indicate that debris flows can be expected in the Sagalassos area at least once a year. Field observations confirm that debris flows occur in the area with a periodicity of a few years.

The vegetation limit, which fluctuates on the talus sheet in altitude between 1777 and 1828 m a.s.l., is still gradually pushed downhill as several small debris flows cover the upper part of the vegetation.

Active scree building resulting from production of scree material is common on fractured limestone cliffs at altitudes above 1800 m a.s.l., especially on the Akdağ.

Active production of scree material has also been recognised at an altitude of about 1600 m a.s.l. on the vertical cliffs in a former nivation niche on the north facing side of the Zencirükin Tepe (1666 m a.s.l.), which is visible from Sagalassos (Fig. 5) and which carries a Hellenistic watchtower (Loots et al. 2000).

Recent reworking and displacement of scree deposits is also apparent from the exposures in the trenches that were made in a rock shelter (cave 3) at the foot of the northern slope of Alexander's Hill, a hill littered with scree deposits (Waelkens et al. 1997: 108). The rock shelter is situated at an altitude of about 1450 m a.s.l. A trench (Waelkens et al. 1997: 109, fig. 8) reveals at a depth of 0.6 m a layer (layer 7) consisting of a very organic clay, some weathered limestone grit and fresh Roman archaeological materials. This layer is considered to have been the floor of the cave during most of the Holocene until at least the Roman occupation and it covers older rock fragments. Posterior to layer 7 there are two layers of limestone fragments (layer 6: 0.2 m thick; layer 4: 0.1 m thick), separated by a clay layer (layer 5) and capped by a compact layer of sheep and goat dung (layers 3 and 1, separated by a thin layer of limestone grit). A section parallel to the actual slope towards the inside of the rock shelter shows that all the layers, including the top of layer 7, dip towards the inside of the shelter. At least parts of the cryoclastic limestone fragments in the different layers are considered therefore to be reworked slope material that moved into the shelter from scree material outside in post-Roman times. This is also attested by the presence of very rolled ceramics in layers 6 to 1.

It can be concluded that the activity on scree slopes is twofold. Firstly, there is the pure scree building activity: rock fragments are produced from the substrate and added to the scree slope. Field observations suggest that the active scree building processes are limited to cliffs in the higher parts of the mountains above altitudes of 1500-1600 m a.s.l. The present degree of production of rock fragments and the accumulation of scree material in the mountains above Sagalassos is closely related to the degree of fracturing of the limestone formations on the cliff. In the study area the fracturing of the limestone, and hence the production of rock fragments, is quite different from place to place and ranges from very homogeneous to very fractured units with mean distances between fissures of less than 0.1 m. The most fractured zone is the eastern part of the Ağlasun Dağı between the 'block of the aqueducts' (block 3 in the study of Verstraeten et al. 2000) and the Akdağ of Isparta-Ağlasun at altitudes between 1800-2000 m a.s.l. (Fig. 6), just above the scree slope illustrated in Fig. 4. It is suggested that these heavily fractured limestone formations are located in a fault zone related to the fault lime indicated on fig. 7. The fracturing is possibly also induced by slumping processes of the limestone (Verstraeten et al. 2000). Contrary to this eastern part of the Ağlasun Dağı, the general fracturing of the limestone formations west of the 'block of the aqueducts' is very much less pronounced and the limestone front is still a free face with some incisions that deliver debris to scree cones (see Fig. 3).

Secondly, there are the bare screes that are no longer fed by rock fragments originating from a cliff, but whose surfaces are constantly reworked by processes active on the scree itself. The main processes are debris flows, such as mentioned above. The intermittent downslope movement of stones happens through a washing process, but also through disturbances by flocks of sheep and goats (Govers et al. 1997, 1998).

3.2. Fossil rockfall talus

The onset of the accumulation of the active rockfall talus described in section 3.1 is unknown and still has to be documented. There are also several fossil scree deposits throughout the area, not only in the mountains above Sagalassos but also at lower altitudes, as is shown by a number of examples. This list is not exhaustive.

A clearly-layered fossil scree deposit is exposed east of the aqueducts block and is located below the active rockfall talus of the Çalbalı Tepe (see 3.1). Although most of the layers are openworked, the entire scree is strongly consolidated with calcite, sometimes pure, sometimes together with a fine brown matrix. Once exposed, these screes are very difficult to break up with a hammer. In the present state of knowledge, we should consider these deposits as the oldest generation of scree deposits in the area. In some exposures, these scree deposits show a slope opposed to the general slope direction (Fig. 8), indicating that they have undergone an important rotation (slumping) after their formation and consolidation.

A number of exposures show thick brown to redbrown scree deposits, consisting of an alternation of layers of coarse and fine rock fragments. Some of the layers are encrusted by calcite. These calcretes often follow the original stratifica-

Fig. 5: Active rockfall talus on the north-facing side of the Zencirükin Tepe; visible from the site.

Fig. 6: Deeply fractured limestone delivering debris to the screes.

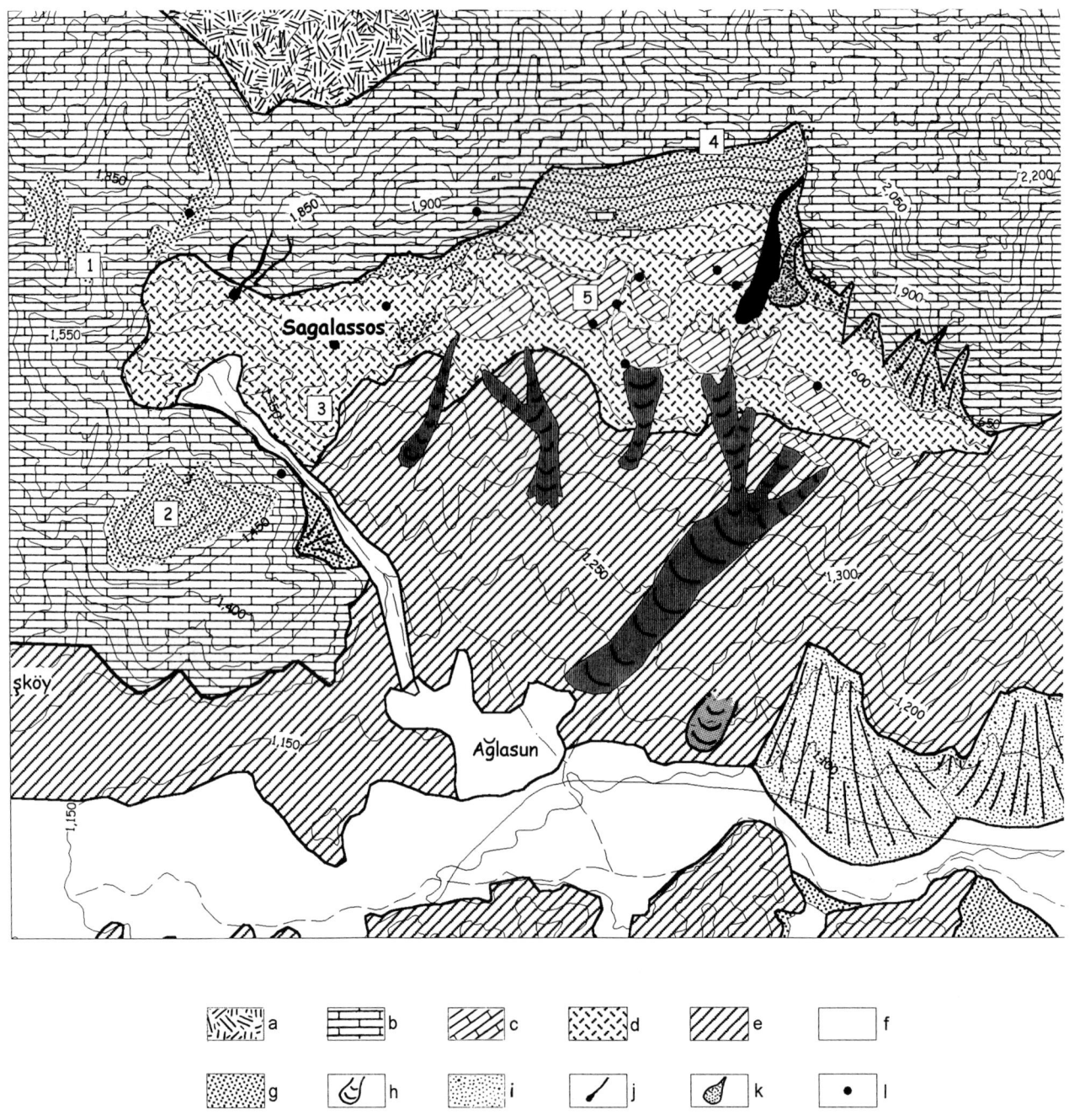

Fig. 7: Localisation of different types of slope deposits near Sagalassos in a geomorphological context. a. Volcanic deposits covering lower reliefs; b. Steep slopes on allochthonous limestone formations; c. Macroslumps; d: Gentle slopes on tectonic mélange; e. Gentle slopes on flysh deposits; f. Quaternary deposits in valley bottoms; g. Scree deposits and debris-mantled slopes; h. Block streams; i. Colluvial fans; j. Debris avalanches; k. Mudflow; l. Fossil scree deposits.

1 Place along the ancient road to Isparta, where the erosion rate was estimated; 2 Zencirükin Tepe, 1666 m.a.s.l.; 3 Alexander's Hill; 4 Çalbalı Tepe (2000 m.a.s.l.); 5 massif of the aqueducts.

Fig. 5: Active rockfall talus on the north-facing side of the Zencirükin Tepe; visible from the site.

Fig. 6: Deeply fractured limestone delivering debris to the screes.

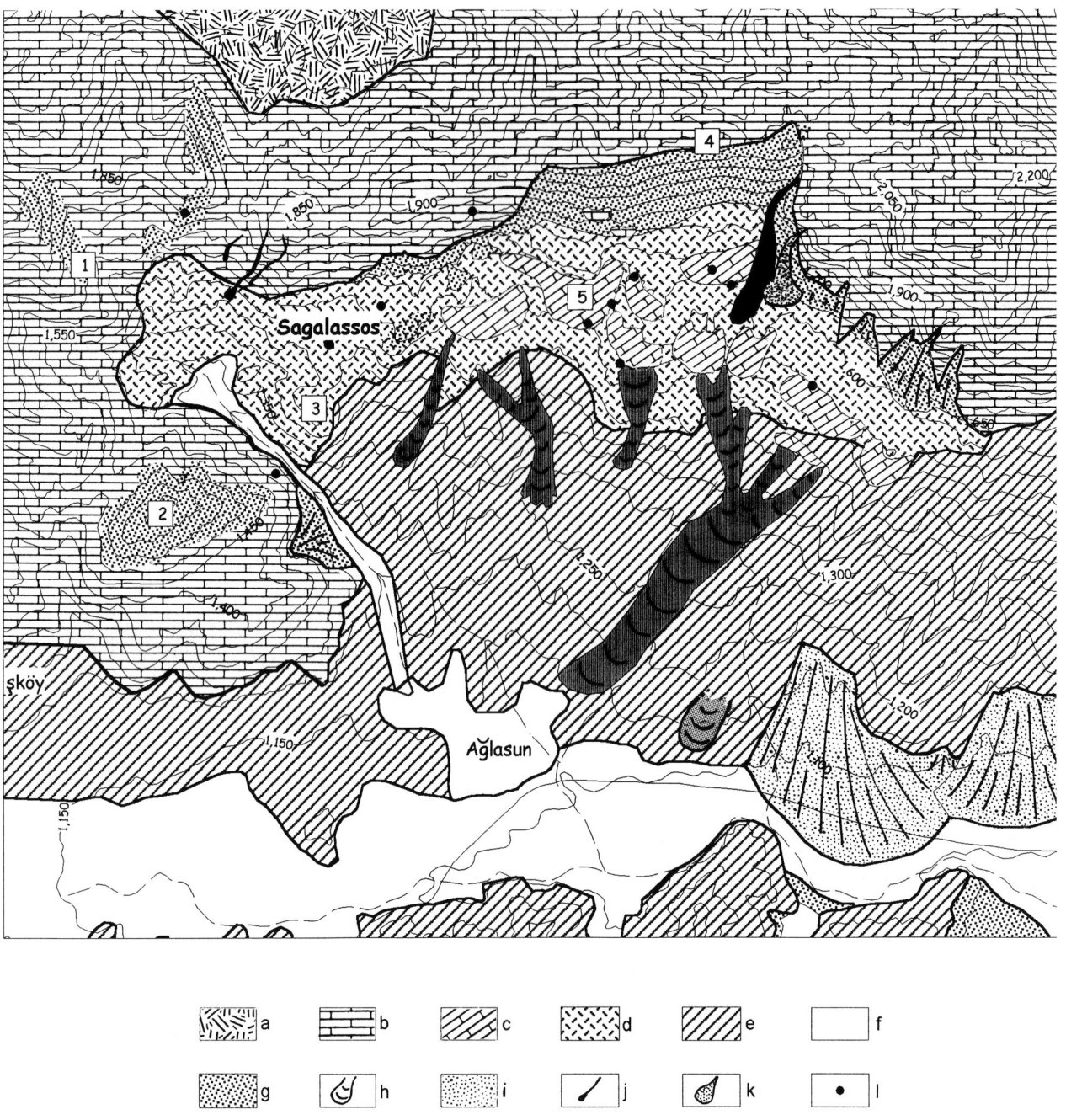

Fig. 7: Localisation of different types of slope deposits near Sagalassos in a geomorphological context. a. Volcanic deposits covering lower reliefs; b. Steep slopes on allochthonous limestone formations; c. Macroslumps; d: Gentle slopes on tectonic mélange; e. Gentle slopes on flysh deposits; f. Quaternary deposits in valley bottoms; g. Scree deposits and debris-mantled slopes; h. Block streams; i. Colluvial fans; j. Debris avalanches; k. Mudflow; l. Fossil scree deposits.

1 Place along the ancient road to Isparta, where the erosion rate was estimated; 2 Zencirükin Tepe, 1666 m.a.s.l.; 3 Alexander's Hill; 4 Çalbalı Tepe (2000 m.a.s.l.); 5 massif of the aqueducts.

Fig. 5: Active rockfall talus on the north-facing side of the Zencirükin Tepe; visible from the site.

Fig. 6: Deeply fractured limestone delivering debris to the screees.

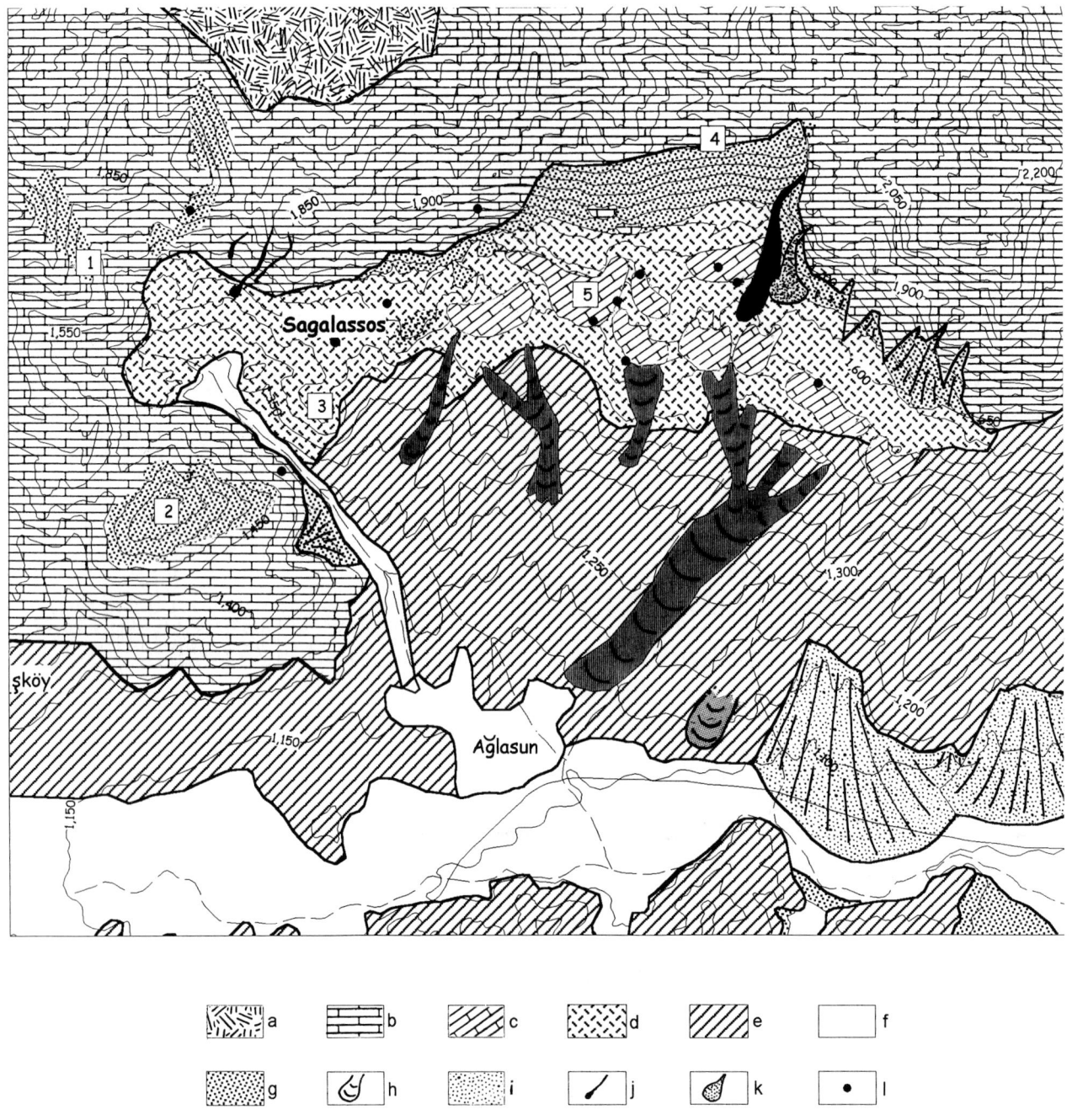

Fig. 7: Localisation of different types of slope deposits near Sagalassos in a geomorphological context. a. Volcanic deposits covering lower reliefs; b. Steep slopes on allochthonous limestone formations; c. Macroslumps; d: Gentle slopes on tectonic mélange; e. Gentle slopes on flysh deposits; f. Quaternary deposits in valley bottoms; g. Scree deposits and debris-mantled slopes; h. Block streams; i. Colluvial fans; j. Debris avalanches; k. Mudflow; I. Fossil scree deposits.
1 Place along the ancient road to Isparta, where the erosion rate was estimated; 2 Zencirükin Tepe, 1666 m.a.s.l.; 3 Alexander's Hill; 4 Çalbalı Tepe (2000 m.a.s.l.); 5 massif of the aqueducts.

Fig. 8: Fossil scree deposits with an inclination opposed to the general slope direction, indicating that they underwent a rotation (slumping) after their formation and consolidation.

Fig. 9: The Karain cave was formed by erosion and dissolution of already consolidated slope deposits.

Fig. 10: Debris avalanches west of Sagalassos as seen from the south.

Fig. 11: Mudflow originating at the western side of the Akdağ of Isparta-Ağlasun.

Fig. 12: Debris-mantled slope west of Sagalassos where the erosion rate was estimated.

tion, indicating that the calcrete formation is mainly due to a lateral supply of calcite. In a fresh exposure, these duricrusts are rather soft and easily break down under a hammer blow. They become very hard when exposed to the air.

An example of these brown scree deposits is found between the villages of Dereköy and Çamlıdere, on either side of the valley of the Ağlasun Çayı. The south facing scree was once fed by a limestone cliff at an elevation of 1550 m a.s.l. The screes reached as far as the bottom of valley of the Ağlasun Çayı at 1000 m a.s.l. and have been consolidated. Later, the Ağlasun Çayı has eroded a gorge through these screes and caves have been formed in them (Fig. 9). During the 1997 season a late Palaeolithic occupation of one of these caves (Karain) or the terrace in front of it (ca. 12,000 BP) was documented by Vermeersch et al. (2000). During springtime, water still flows through pipes coming from uphill which means that the process of calcrete formation is still going on. The steep scree slopes are nowadays covered with a natural pine forest (*Pinus brutia*) and by some other types of vegetation (Vermeersch et al. 2000). The surface of these slopes is often formed by a calcrete, which means that the loose part above this calcrete has been eroded away. The uncovered paths within this forest are the only spots where individual particles are eroded. The total erosion is evaluated as very low.

The cedar forest to the south of the village of Çanaklı is also located on consolidated screes, comparable to those around the Karain cave near Dereköy. This north-facing scree that could be traced up to an altitude of 1150 m a.s.l., derived from a 50 m high limestone cliff at an altitude not higher than 1350 to 1400 m a.s.l. In the cedar forest some areas are bare and some individual rock fragments are eroded and deposited behind the trunks. The present-day pine forest was only formed soon after 6000 BP (Waelkens and the Sagalassos team 1997).

Considerable rockfall talus deposits, redbrown in colour and with calcretes in several layers, are exposed along the road Ağlasun – Bucak on the west-facing slope of the Erendağı Tepe, to the west of Çanaklı. These talus have accumulated below a limestone cliff at an elevation of 1350 to 1450 m a.s.l. and reach as far as the valley bottom at 1000 m a.s.l. The vegetation on these slopes is heavily degraded due to grazing. Some erosion of individual rock fragments is observed along paths and in bare areas.

'Abris sous roches' are also formed in consolidated screes to the north of the 'tuğla fabrikası' (brick factory) to the east of Çanaklı. These talus deposits are located at an elevation of 1250 m a.s.l. and originate from a limestone cliff at 1400 m a.s.l. The consolidated screes belong to the source area of the more recent colluvial fan just north of the brick factory.

Similar brown talus slopes with calcretes are found in the mountains around Sagalassos on the south facing slopes of the Ağlasun Dağı:

1 – on the slopes above the potters' quarter (altitude over 1590 m a.s.l.)
2 – in the bottom of the Koyaklının Valley, to the west of the site, at an altitude of 1600 m a.s.l. (Fig. 6) This talus slope contains a huge quantity of brown silt filling the pores. It grades into the debris-covered slopes on the mountainsides in this area (see 7.1)
3 – in the valley of the Gürleyik Deresi, between Alexander's Hill and the Zencirükin Tepe, at an elevation of 1300 m a.s.l., on the north facing slope of the Zencirükin Tepe. In Hellenistic and Roman times this valley formed the main approach to the site of Sagalassos and contained a Roman necropolis.

This list of fossil talus slope deposits is sufficient to conclude that in the Sagalassos area there are different generations of talus slope deposits of so far unknown age. It is also clear that the altitudinal limit for active talus slope formation is higher up the mountains than the occurrence of fossil scree deposits, which still occur beneath the lowest limestone cliffs in the area, this means up to altitudes of about 1000 m a.s.l.

The sedimentary facies of Quaternary colluvial aprons above Lake Eğirdir (alt. 916 m and about 35 km. east of Sagalassos) have been studies recently in great detail by Nemec et al. (1999). These colluvial aprons are arrays of coalescent fans, up to 17-20m thick with depositional slopes of 30-40°. They are associated with the slopes of Mount Sivri and originate from an area with the highest parts at 1380 m (Nemec et al 1994, Fig. 1). Nemec et al. (1999) distinguish four lithostratigraphic units. The basal redbrown colluvium, colluvium A, is attributed mainly to rockfalls and cohesive debrisflows, with minor grainflows and sheetwash processes. It contains in the middle part interbeds of early Pleistocene tephra, with KAR isotopic dates of 1,50 $\pm$ 0.18 and 1.38 $\pm$ 0.13 Ma. The light-grey colluvium B consists of bedded gravel and its deposition is attributed to waterflow, rockfalls and cohesive debrisflows. Colluvium C, medium-grey in colour, consists mainly of stratified pebbly sands and its deposition is attributed to sheetwash processes accompanied by rockfalls and wet snowflows/slushflows). The youngest colluvium D is yellow-grey and consists of bedded, mainly pebbly and open-work gravel, whose deposition is attributed to dry grainflows, rockfalls and minor cohesive debrisflows. The latter is correlated with the Holocene stage of warm semi-arid climate. The modern climatic characteristics at Isparta (alt. 1050 m and situated 30 km west of Eğirdir) are: mean annual temperature: 12° C and mean annual precipitation:

628 mm, three months with the mean daily minimum temperature below 0°C and 5 months with absolute minimum temperature below 0°C (Paulissen *et al.* 1993).

4. DEBRIS AVALANCHE

Just west of the site, three debris avalanches are visible (Fig. 10). Avalanches are normally triggered by extreme rains or snowmelt which cause supersaturation of the soil, reduction of soil strength, failure and flow. It is remarkable that the avalanche paths that are visible on Fig. 10 start downslope of limestone outcrops, suggesting that the rock outcrops have acted as an (impermeable) catchment or as areas of accumulation of drifted snow, resulting in the irregular but considerable movement downhill. This runoff saturated the coarse debris further downslope, which eventually led to slope failure and avalanche formation.

The most important debris avalanche west of Sagalassos is 500 m long, and is located between 1680 m and 1400 m a.s.l. on slopes between 28 and 32°. This avalanche has a depth of 1.05 m and a total width of 10 m, including the parallel levees of debris that mark the path of the flow and terminate downslope in a small tongue.

Debris avalanches are highly destructive rapid mass movements, discontinuous through time, but following the same path. The progress of the longest avalanche has destroyed the old Roman road towards Isparta (still drawn by Lanckoronski 1893) as well as the three western aqueducts leading to Sagalassos (Owens 1995). At the crossing with the former road Sagalassos-Isparta (abandoned in 1962 and no longer maintained) this road is still intact, but traces of the avalanche path are still clearly visible at either side of the road. The general appearance of the debris avalanches to the west of Sagalassos, which is quite fresh, suggests a subrecent activity. The fact that the debris accumulation at the end of the avalanche path in the valley bottom is quite limited and that there are no soil horizons could indicate that the whole system is quite recent but the onset of it remains unknown.

5. BLOCK STREAMS

Block streams are long deposits of large isolated blocks mixed with fine materials that extend further downslope than across (White 1981). They can be situated in the bottom of existent valleys. Depths of block streams vary from a few metres to 10 m. The largest blocks (up to 10 m in section) are on the surface; finer debris is located below. In the neighbourhood of Sagalassos, four block streams were studied in more detail (see Fig. 7): one just east of the site (width: 250 m, slope gradient: 12°, length: 1 km, located between 1460 and 1287 m a.s.l.), one to the east of the road at present leading to the site (width: 100 m; slope gradient: 8.5°; length: 1 km, located between 1450 and 1300 m a.s.l.), one starting beneath a limestone block southeast of the aqueduct block (width: 100 m; slope gradient: 22°; length: 500 m, located between 1500 and 1350 m a.s.l.) and one starting in the tectonic mélange at the base of the Akdağ of Isparta – Ağlasun and reaching the north-eastern boundary of the village of Ağlasun (source area: 1450 m a.s.l., estimated width: more than 100 m, mean slope gradient: 9°, length: 2 km, located between 1450 and 1100 m a.s.l.). In one of the big rocks transported by the latter, a Roman Imperial tomb of the arcosolium type is carved *in situ*.

In contrast with the debris avalanches that derive from limestone scarps, the block streams originate from the tectonic mélange of limestone and ophiolitic formations. Two elements probably play a significant role in their genesis: the clay fraction within the ophiolitic formations and the presence in these areas of several springs wetting the top layers.

Owens (1995: 93) has observed previously that "both the channels of the upper and the middle (eastern) rock-cut aqueducts stop at the point where a major geological catastrophe brought about the collapse of a cliff face". We will detail the observations further. The point where the two rock-cut aqueducts disappear corresponds exactly with the contact of the limestone-ophiolitic formations, and the place where one of them re-emerges in the limestone cliff face corresponds again with the limit of the ophiolitic-limestone formations. The aqueduct has disappeared over a distance of 450 m, in a zone that corresponds exactly with the outcropping of the ophiolitic formations. In this zone, the ophiolitic deposits cannot be considered as deriving from a fall, but have to be considered as the substrate, from which a block stream may have started. The fact that on the surface of these deposits no trace at all of an aqueduct has been found (Owens 1995: 93) is indeed an argument to suggest that the catastrophe post-dates the construction of the canals (Verstraeten *et al.* 2000). Further research on the downslope deposits is necessary to look for evidence of the destruction of the aqueduct and to date the catastrophic event which caused it. When this disaster occurred, it cut off for ever the most important water supply of the city.

6. MUDFLOW

The most active mass movement nowadays is the mudflow at the western edge of the Akdağ of Isparta-Ağlasun. This mudflow is regularly active and changes in its configuration have been observed since 1993. The fanlike shape of the deposit at its outlet indicates that the material is deposited by a process induced by a considerable amount of water (Fig. 11). The actual mudflow dissects a much more extensive fossil mudflow.

7. DEBRIS-MANTLED SLOPES

7.1. Characteristics

On places where slope deposits occur and where there is no cliff as a source of debris, the normal slope cover on mountain slopes is a thin sheet or blanket of mostly matrix-supported rock fragments which reflect the configuration of the rock surface underneath. These slopes are called debris-mantled slopes (Church *et al.* 1979) or block slopes (White 1981).

In theory, this type of slope deposit can be considered as the normal slope cover in former periglacial areas, as was also the case here, at the end of the Last Glacial. If stabilised, the Holocene soil should develop on top. It is astonishing that until now such a succession has never been observed, but active debris-covered slopes have been identified. An example of an active debris-mantled slope is exposed in the Koyaklının Valley, to the west of the site, at an altitude above 1600 m a.s.l. (Fig. 6). This slope is one of the most active debris-covered slopes in the region: not only is the former slope material eroded, but in some areas fresh limestone fragments have already been produced out of the much fractured bedrock.

The middle western aqueduct of Roman Imperial date was also located on this slope, where it extended from the "three small lengths of once continuous rock-cut channel... and all traces of the aqueduct have disappeared for a distance of approximately 400 m" (Owens 1995: 97 and fig. 22). To the east of the rock-cut channel mentioned above, it is evident that for quite a long distance, the aqueduct was constructed on the debris-mantled slopes and its water carried in terracotta pipes. Here again, this can be considered as proof that not all slopes surrounding the Roman city were well forested and that some sections were already covered with debris.

7.2. Erosion rate

An estimation of the volumes of sediments eroded on debris-mantled slopes in the present environmental conditions has been made by assessing the volumes of sediment deposited on the caravan road from Ağlasun to Isparta which crosses this slope. Since the road was abandoned in 1962 (and since then no longer maintained), it has trapped sediment from the upper slopes (30°, length 270 m) over a time span of 33 years. The surveyed road section, which runs more or less on the contour line of 1552 m a.s.l. was characterised by a rather constant amount of accumulated eroded debris. Mean measured sediment volume on this active section amounts to 0.62 m^3/m. Assuming a mean bulk density of the debris of 1500 kg/m^3, this figure corresponds to 930 kg/m. Since the bulk density of limestone is 2500 kg/m^3, this corresponds to 0.372 m^3 accumulated limestone per meter in 33 years. One can calculate the mean surface decrease on the debris-covered slopes by spreading this volume over the slope above the section (270 m), and estimating that the loss from the surface is 41 mm in 1000 years.

Another way to estimate the amount of debris production is to calculate the volume of limestone that has disappeared on a section of the road indicated on the historical map of Lanckoronski (1893), to the east of the block slope. At present, considerable sections of the ancient road (indicated on the map by Lanckoronski (1893)) have completely disappeared. A reconstruction of the road surface was made based on one place where the passage was hewn out of the limestone bedrock. The volume of disappeared bedrock between the historical road surface and the present soil surface, was determined along a road section of 16.3 m long. Supposing that the ancient road was 3 m wide, 80 m^3/16.3 m of limestone had disappeared. If all this bedrock has disappeared during the last 100 years, since the publication of the historical map of Lanckoronski, this results in an erosion rate of 0.8 m^3/year or 0.05 m^3/m/year. The fact that Lanckoronski indicated the road sometimes as a dashed line suggests that the road was already seriously damaged when the map was drawn in 1884 or 1885. In that case, the erosion-rate is significantly lower and much more acceptable. Considering the accumulation measured on the caravan road from Ağlasun to Isparta (see above: 0.0112 m^3/m/year), the road indicated on Lanckoronski's historical map had been subjected to erosion for 700 years.

8. DISCUSSION

In the Sagalassos area, actual slope evolution on limestone formations varies as a function of the altitude. Scree slopes and debris-mantled slopes are nowadays forming at altitudes above 1500-1600 m a.s.l. and the slope processes that are suggested are similar to those suggested for periglacial environments. Slope activity consists not only of a reworking of the existing slope deposits, but also of slope building: new rock fragments are produced and added to the slope. The production of new rock fragments is quite significant above 1800 m a.s.l., but only in those areas where the limestone substrate is heavily fractured, for instance along fault zones. The only process that one can envisage as capable of dislodging the rock fragments is frost action: water freezes in the existing fine fissures; the fissures widen due to the expansion of the water and the rock fragments are finally dislodged from their original position and move down the cliff. At present, in more massive, less fractionated limestone formations, production of rock fragments is very limited or non-existent. In the very massive limestone formations, different types of solution phenomena ('rillen' and 'karren') are present.

The production of rock fragments on an active debris-covered slope located at an altitude of 1600 m a.s.l. was measured over a period of 33 years. The total mean measured sediment volume over a period of 33 years was estimated at 0.62 m^3/m, which corresponds with a surface loss of 41 millimetres in 1000 years. Poesen et al. (1995) report on their estimate of the total sediment transport over a longer distance along the same road. Their estimates are four times higher than ours. Steegen et al. (2000) have also estimated the erosion rate of the slope scarps by measuring the fills along four sections of the upper aqueduct to the east of Sagalassos. They calculated erosion rates between 1 and 31 mm per 1000 years. These results are of the same order of magnitude as the 41 mm per 1000 years arrived at here. Other measurements of the mechanical amount of surface lowering by debris production in a Mediterranean climate fluctuate between 10 and 30 mm in 1000 years (Saunders et al. 1983).

The scree slopes above 1500 m a.s.l. are nowadays undergoing modification mainly from debris flows, secondly from torrential downpours, from intermittent downslope movement of stones due to wash and frost action, and from the trampling of sheep and goats (Govers et al. 1997, 1998).

Below 1500-1600 m a.s.l., the scene changes dramatically and slope processes on the limestone formations are extremely limited. There is no production of rock fragments on limestone cliffs and also the actual reactivation of the talus slopes (see for example at Çanaklı) is very limited: debris flows are absent, although individual rock fragments are detached from bare patches and along paths on the screes, probably mainly as the result of trampling and overland flow.

In the following paragraphs, the climatological and environmental conditions of the mountains between 1000 and 2000 m a.s.l. are analysed in greater detail.

Climatological information for a north-south transect from Ağlasun over Sagalassos as far as the Çalbalı Tepe (a mountain range between Ağlasun and Isparta, also called the 'Ağlasun Dağı') is assembled in Table 1 (see also Paulissen et al. 1993 and Poesen et al. 1995). The climatological information is based on data from the weather station at Ağlasun (altitude 1150 m a.s.l. and only 3 km south of Sagalassos) and on estimations from the weather stations at Isparta (1050 m a.s.l., and 10 km to the north), at Burdur (1025 m a.s.l. and 21 km to the west-northwest) and at Aslanköy (1650 m a.s.l., situated at a comparable altitude, but only at 30 km from the Mediterranean, while Sagalassos is situated at 100 km from the Mediterranean).

	Ağlasun (1150 m)	Sagalassos (1550 m)	Çalbalı Tepe (2000 m)
Annual precipitation	884 mm	*990 mm*	*1090 mm*
Mean annual temperature	10.8 °C	*+/- 8.2 °C*	*+/- 5.6 °C*
Number of months with mean temperature above 10 °C	6 / 7	5	3
Mean temperature of the coldest month	2 °C	*-4 / -5 °C*	*< -4 / -5 °C*
Mean daily minimum	-2 / -3 °C	*-6 °C*	*-8 °C*
Number of very cold months (mean daily temperature < 0 °C)	0	2/3	3
Number of cold months (mean daily minimun temperature < 0 °C)	3	5	6
Number of months with frost	7	7	8

Table 1: Climatic data of Ağlasun, Sagalassos and the Çalbalı Tepe (Paulissen et al. 1993; Poesen et al. 1995). Estimated values are printed in italic and are also based on climatic data from the weather stations of Burdur and Isparta.

The climate of Ağlasun is characterised by a fairly short dry period in the summer (July until September) and by a (long) wet period (autumn, winter and spring), which is typical for the Mediterranean climate. Ağlasun receives most of its precipitation in December and January (Poesen et al. 1995: 350). As the area south of the Ağlasun Dağı experiences orographic rains, higher precipitation amounts are assumed for the mountain slopes. It is also assumed that during the winter months with mean monthly temperatures equal to 0 °C or less, 50% of the precipitation falls as snow (Poesen et al. 1995: 342). The data and estimations on Table 1 show that there are no climatological constraints for tree growth: precipitation is abundant, the dry period is short and at 2000 m a.s.l. one still can estimate three months with a mean monthly temperature above 10 °C (one month with a mean monthly temperature of 10 °C is accepted as the limit for tree growth). The climatological data fully confirm the vegetation studies that suggest evergreen needle-leaved forest as the natural vegetation of this area for altitudes between 1000 and 2000 m a.s.l. (Waelkens et al. 1997: 230). This vegetation would still cover the hillsides today if man had not interfered with nature. Sagalassos could then have been located in the midst of rather extensive forest (Waelkens et al. 1997: 232). The present vegetation on the slopes around and above Sagalassos is that of a degraded 'thorn-cushion' steppe, because of human impact, while at lower altitudes stands of kermes oak (*Quercus coccifera*) and of pine occur (Waelkens et al. 1997: 229). The data indicate a significant discrepancy between the actual and the potential vegetation in relation to the actual climate.

The climatological and environmental characteristics of the area need therefore to be related to the observations on slope processes and deposits described above.

It thus appears that frost (Table 1) is a very important characteristic of the present climate. This is expressed by the number of months with frost, of cold and of very cold months at different altitudes. It is to be expected that in this oro-mediterranean climate the number of frost cycles in the air will be high, especially on the higher slopes (50-100 frost cycles per year?). The number of actual frost-thaw cycles in the ground is unknown. A comparison of the field data on present day slope evolution and environment with the information on the intensity and distribution of frost relative to altitude, suggests that from a climatological point of view, frost is nowadays the main agent in producing rock fragments in areas with an already heavily fissured limestone substrate. The number of very cold months (mean daily temperature < 0 °C) seems to be especially important in this respect, confirming the fact that at lower altitudes, such as at Ağlasun with an estimated 3 cold months and 7 months with frost, the production of rock fragments cannot be observed.

It is assumed that it is not so much the present climate as such, but rather the interaction of its cold elements with the degraded environment, which determines the present slope evolution. The present day environment in the mountains, a degraded thorn-cushion steppe, is indeed at odds with the present-day climate, for which coniferous woods would be the natural vegetation. Without human impact, the soil would have been better protected by the natural vegetation against the influence of the cold elements of the current climate. As the natural vegetation was progressively degraded by human impact, the soil surface became gradually more bare. So the existing climate could induce processes typical of an alpine environment, such as frost weathering and a series of processes of rapid mass movement: scree formation, debris flows, debris avalanches, and eventually rock flows. The reactivation of the slope deposits inhibits the recovery of vegetation, and decreases the biomass, thus increasing the instability. It is important to stress that solifluction phenomena have not been observed.

To evaluate the relative importance of the environmental degradation or the oro-mediterranean climate on frost activity and rapid mass movements, it would be necessary to study these phenomena in a nearby forest on limestone and above 1500 m a.s.l. and to compare them with the observations made around Sagalassos.

It is therefore assumed that the present slope evolution in the mountains above Sagalassos is a response to the deforestation and the further degradation of the natural vegetation and that it reaches its climax under the present very degraded steppe vegetation. As once vital elements for the town, such as the aqueducts and a road coming from the northwest, are out of use now as the result of frost action and of processes and deposits of rapid mass movements, one can venture to infer that most of the cold-related slope processes reported in this paper are posterior to the abandonment of Sagalassos around the middle of the seventh century AD (Waelkens et al. 2000). If the slopes were already partly bare and degraded in Roman times as is suggested by some evidence, the inhabitants of Sagalassos would have had to clear and repair their mountain roads regularly in order not to become isolated. The aqueducts would also need a regular clearing of rock fragments, or local repairs because of debris flows, debris avalanches or frost damage, in order to ensure a good water supply to the city.

More research is needed to ascertain the initiation of the contemporaneous slope processes (such as scree building, debris flows, debris avalanches and block streams) as a function of the local history of deforestation and afforestation of the slopes. This history may be complicated (Waelkens and the Sagalassos Team 1997). Palynological studies in southwestern Turkey (Bottema et al. 1990; Van Zeist et al. 1991; Vermoere et al. 2000) show the effects of forest-clearing in +/- 3000 BP and of a massive reafforestation phase starting in the early Byzantine period. The hypothesis by Owens (1995: 93) that the final destruction of the main eastern aqueduct was caused by a mass movement, deserves further detailed investigation from a geomorphological point of view. It is indeed possible that it was a rapid mass movement (a block stream?) which affected the aqueduct.

The presence of fossil scree deposits in the Sagalassos area is not unique for the Mediterranean area: they have been described in Corsica (Conchon 1975), Southern Italy (Bernini et al. 1978), Sardinia (Ozer et al. 1981), Crete (Poser et al. 1957) and Greece (Hagedorn 1977). In mid-latitudes these features are commonly interpreted as reflecting intense frost wedging of exposed rock surfaces. In Europe these accumulations are known to occur in most of the upland massifs and low mountain ranges. In the European geomorphic literature, most of these deposits are interpreted as periglacial features. This interpretation is challenged by French (1996: 236): since there is no proof that these deposits form only under periglacial conditions, they are of limited use in Pleistocene periglacial reconstruction.

The observations made around Sagalassos clearly indicate that nowadays accumulations of angular boulders and coarse debris are also forming in an oro-mediterranean climate, at least where the vegetation is markedly degraded by human impact. For the interpretation of fossil scree deposits in this area, and possibly also in many other mountains, it is inadequate to compare past and present environments, as many of the latter are strongly affected by man. Fossil screes are formed in an environment where, apart from local elements, the type of vegetation was a response to the existing climate. For the mountains around Sagalassos one can suggest that scree development requires a steppe-like vegetation. One possible palaeo-environment for the formation of talus and debris-covered slopes could be the open forest-steppe that covered the area during a period of the Last Glacial, when temperatures dropped considerably (a depression of 6-8 °C or even 5-10 °C in the mean annual temperature – see Waelkens and the Sagalassos Team 1997: 230). The distribution of fossil debris-covered slopes and fossil scree deposits are considered to be good geomorphological arguments for suggesting former cold climatic conditions for this part of the Taurus mountains and for altitudes as low as 1000 m a.s.l. It is however difficult to get more detailed information on former palaeo-climates from the stratified slope deposits as such, as their formation is not restricted to a single, clearly delimited environment and as the individual properties of the deposits are not diagnostic.

The different generations of fossil scree deposits around Sagalassos suggest that scree formation was not a continuous process throughout time, but that there existed periods of more intense scree formation alternating with periods of much less activity. Research on the stratigraphical and sedimentological characteristics of the fossil scree deposits is under way in order to detail their characteristics and age. The study of the calcretes within the different generations of talus slope deposits could contribute significantly to a palaeo-climatological reconstruction.

9. CONCLUSION

Near Sagalassos, scree slopes, debris avalanches, block streams, debris-covered slopes and mudflows are common geomorphological features. Research focussing on the characteristics and the distribution of the present and fossil slope deposits near the ancient city revealed that all these deposits seem to occur nearly exclusively on steep slopes related to the limestone substrate and to the areas of the limestone-ophiolite tectonic mélange between 1000 and 2000 m a.s.l.

Rapid mass movements such as debris avalanches, block streams and mudflows destroyed the old Roman road towards Isparta and the aqueducts supplying Sagalassos. The present activity on scree slopes is twofold. On one hand there is the pure scree-building activity that is closely related to the degree of fracturing of the limestone. On the other hand there are mass movements that are reworking the scree deposits. Throughout the area, fossil scree deposits of different generations also occur, not only in the mountains above Sagalassos, but also at lower latitudes. It is clear that the altitudinal limit for active talus slope formation is located higher up the mountains than the occurrence of fossil scree deposits, which still occur beneath the lowest limestone cliffs in the area, that is up to altitudes of about 1000 m a.s.l. The present production of rock fragments was measured on a debris-covered slope at an altitude of 1600 m a.s.l. Here, it results in a denudation of the limestone slopes of 41 mm per 1000 years. One can conclude that frost is nowadays the main agent in producing rock fragments in areas with an already heavily fissured limestone substrate.

It is assumed that it is not the present, oro-mediterranean climate as such, but the interactions of the coldest elements of this climate with the present degraded environment, which determine the present slope evolution. The present environment in the mountains, a degraded thorn-cushion steppe, is at odds with the present climate, in which coniferous woods would be the natural vegetation. It is therefore assumed that the present slope evolution in the mountains above Sagalassos is a response to the deforestation and the further degradation of the natural vegetation and that it reaches its climax under the present very degraded steppe vegetation. The fact that once vital elements for the town, such as the aqueducts and a road coming from the northwest, are out of use today due to frost action and to processes and deposits of rapid mass movements permits us to deduce that most of the cold-related slope processes reported in this paper are posterior to the abandonment of Sagalassos around the middle of the seventh century AD.

On the other hand, the fossil scree deposits were formed in a natural environment, not influenced by man, where the type of vegetation was a response to the existing climate. Suggesting that scree development requires at least a steppe-like vegetation, one possible palaeo-environment for the formation of talus and debris mantled slopes could have been the open forest-steppe that covered the area during a period of the Last Glacial. The distribution of fossil debris-covered slopes and fossil scree deposits are considered to be good geomorphological arguments to suggest former cold climatic conditions for this part of the Taurus mountains and at altitudes as low as 1000 m a.s.l. Anyhow, different generations of fossil scree deposits around Sagalassos suggest that scree formation was not a continuous process through time, but that there existed periods with a more intense scree formation alternating with periods of much less activity. It is clear that the town must have developed during one of the latter periods.

10. ACKNOWLEDGEMENTS

This research is supported by the Belgian Programme on Interuniversity Poles of Attraction (IUAP 4/12) initiated by the Belgian State, Prime Minister's Office, Science Policy Programming. The text also presents the results of the Concerted Action of the Flemish Government (GOA 97/2) and the Fund for Scientific Research-Flanders (Belgium) (FWO) (G.2145.94). Scientific responsibility is assumed by its authors. Gert Verstraeten is research assistant of the Fund for Scientific Research Flanders – Belgium (F.W.O.).

11. REFERENCES

M. Bernini, A. Carton, D. Castaldini, M. Cremaschi (1978) Segnalazione di un depositi di versante di tipo Grèzes litées a sud di M. Prampa, *Gruppo di Studio del Quaternario Panado* 4: 153-162.

I. Beuls, B. De Cupere, M. Vermoere, L. Vanhecke, H. Doutrelepont, L. Vrydaghs, I. Librecht and M. Waelkens (2000) Modern sheep and goat herding near Sagalassos and its relevance to the reconstruction of pastoral practices in Roman times, in: M; Waelkens and L. Loots (eds) *Sagalassos V. Report on the Survey and Excavations Campaigns of 1996 and 1997 (Acta Archaeologica Lovaniensia Monographiae* 11) Leuven University Press 847-861.

S. Bottema and H. Woldring (1990) Anthropogenic indicators in the pollen record of the eastern Mediterranean, in: S. Bottema, G. Entjes-Nieborg and W. Van Zeist (eds) *Man's Role in the Shaping of the Eastern Mediterranean Landscape*, Rotterdam - Brookfield: 231-264.

M. Church, R.F. Stock and J.M. Ryder (1979) Contemporary sedimentary environments on Baffin Island, N.W.T., Canada: debris slope accumulations, *Arctic and Alpine Research* 11: 371-402.

O. Conchon (1975) *Les formations quaternaires de type continentale en Corse orientale*. Thèse de doctorat, Paris.

P. Degryse, R. Degeest, J. Poblome, W. Viaene, R. Ottenburgs, H. Kucha and M. Waelkens (2000) Mineralogy and goechemistry of Roman common wares produced at Sagalassos and their possible clay resources: in: M. Waelkens and L. Loots (eds) *Sagalassos V. Report on the Survey and Excavations Campaigns of 1996 and 1997 (Acta Archaeologica Lovaniensia Monographiae* 11) Leuven, University Press 709-722.

B. Francou (1988) Eboulis stratifiés dans les Hautes Andes Centrales du Pérou, *Zeitschrift für Geomorphologie*: 32: 47-76.

H.M. French (1996) *The Periglacial Environment,* Harlow.

G. Govers, J. Poesen and S. Mertens (1997) Transport of rock fragments by animal trampling on scree slopes: experimental results and J. Poblome (eds) *Sagalassos IV. Report on the Survey and Excavation Campaigns of 1994 and 1995 (Acta Archaeologica Lovaniensia Monographiae* 9) Leuven University Press: 541-551.

G. Govers and J. Poesen (1998) Field experiments on the transport of rock fragments by animal trampling on scree slopes, *Geomorphology* 23: 193-203.

J. Hagedorn (1977) Probleme der periglazialen Höhenstufung in Griechenland, *Abhandlungen der Akademie der Wissenschaften in Göttongen, Mathematisch-Physikalische Klasse, Dritte Folge* 31: 233-237.

C. Lanckoronski (1893) *Les villes de la Pamphylie et de la Pisidie 2. La Pisidie*, Paris.

I. Librecht (1996) *Bijdrage tot de studie van hellingsafzettingen rondom Sagalassos* (Turkije) Unpublished M.Sc.thesis, KULeuven.

L. Loots, M. Waelkens and F. Depuydt (2000) The city fortifications of Sagalassos from the Hellenistic to the late Roman period, in: M. Waelkens and L. Loots (eds) *Sagalassos V. Report on the Survey and Excavations Campaigns of 1996 and 1997 (Acta Archaeologica Lovaniensia Monographiae* 11) Leuven University Press 595-634.

W. Nemec and N. Kazanci (1999) Quaternary colluvium in west-central Anatolia: sedimentary facies and paleoclimatic significance, *Sedimentology* 46: 139-170.

E. Owens (1995) The acqueducts of Sagalassos, in: M. Waelkens and J. Poblome (eds) *Sagalassos III Report on the Fourth Excavation Campaign of 1993 (Acta Archaeologica Lovaniensia Monographiae 7)* Leuven, University Press: 209-220.

A. Ozer and A. Ulzega (1981) Sur la répartition des éboulis en Sardaigne, *Biuletyn Peryglacjalny* 28: 259-265.

E. Paulissen, J. Poesen, G. Govers and J. De Ploey (1993) The physical environment at Sagalassos (Western Taurus, Turkey) A reconaissance survey, in: M. Waelkens and J. Poblome (eds) *Sagalassos II. Report on the Third Excavation Campaign of 1992) (Acta Archaeologica Lovaniensia Monographiae 6)* Leuven University Press: 229-247.

J. Poesen, G. Govers, E. Paulissen and K. Vandaele (1995) A geomorphological evaluation of erosion risk at Sagalassos, in: M. Waelkens and J. Poblome (eds) *Sagalassos III. Report on the Fourth Excavation Campaign of 1993 (Aca Archaeologica Lovaniensia Monographiae 7)* Leuven University Press: 341-355.

H. Poser (1957) Klimamorphologische Probeme auf Kreta, *Zeitschrift für Geomorphologie. Neue Folge* 1: 113-142.

I. Saunders and A. Young (1983) Rates of surface processes on slopes, slope retreatand denudation, *Earth Surface Processes and Landforms* 8: 473-501.

K. Schroyen, M. Vermoere, I. Librecht, P. Degryse, Ph. Muchez,

W. Viaene, E. Smets, E. Paulissen, E. Keppens and M. Waelkens (2000) Preliminary study of travertine deposits in the vicinity of Sagalassos: petrography, geochemistry, geomorphology and palynology, in: M. Waelkens and L. Loots (eds) *Sagalassos V. Report on the Survey and Excavations Campaigns of 1996 and 1997) (Acta Archeaologica Lovaniensia Monographiae* 10) Leuven University Press 757-781.

M.J. Selby (1993) *Hillslope Materials and Processes*, Oxford.

I. Statham and S.C. Francis (1986) The influence of scree accumulation and weathering, in: A.D. Abrahams (ed.) *Hillslope Processes*, Boston: 245-267.

A. Steegen, K. Cauwenberghs, G. Govers, M. Waelkens, E.J. Owens and Ph. Desmet (2000) The water supply to Sagalassos, in: M. Waelkens and L. Loots (eds) *Sagalassos V. Report on the Survey and Excavations Campaigns of 1996 and 1997 (Acta Archaeologica Lovaniensia Monographiae* 11) Leuven University Press 635-650.

H. Van Steijn (1989) Puinstromen, *Koninklijk Nederlands Aardrijkskundig Genootschap Geografisch Tijdschrift* 23: 119-128.

H. Van Steijn, P. Bertran, N. Francou, B. Hetu and J.P. Texier (1995) Models for the genetic and environmental interpretation of stratified slope deposits - a review, *Permafrost and Periglacial Processes* 6: 125-146.

W. Van Zeist and S. Bottema (1991) *Late Quaternary Vegetation of the Near East (Beihefte zum Tübinger Atlas der vorderen Orients, Reihe A,* 18) Wiesbaden.

P.M. Vermeersch, I. Oztürk, H.A. Ekinci, P. Degryse, B. De Cupere, J. Poblome, W. Viaene and M. Waelkens (2000) Late Paleolithic at the Dereköy Karain cave, in: M. Waelkens and L. Loots (eds) *Sagalassos V. Report on the Survey and Excavations Campaigns of 1996 and 1997 (Acta Archaeologica Lovaniensia Monographiae* 11) Leuven University Press 451-462.

M. Vermoere, P. Degryse, L. Vanhecke, Ph. Muchez, E. Paulissen, E. Smets and M. Waelkens (1999) Pollen Analysis of two travertine sections in Başköy (southwest Turkey): implications for environmental conditions during the early Holocene, *Review of Palaeobotany and Palynology* 105: 93-110.

M. Vermoere, M. Waelkens, H. Vanhaverbeke, I. Librecht, L. Vanhecke, E. Paulissen, E. Smets (2000) Late Holocene environmental change and the record of human impact at Gravgaz near Sagalassos, Southwest Turkey, *Journal of Archaeological Sciences* 27: 571-595.

G. Verstraeten, E. Paulissen, I. Librecht and M. Waelkens (2000) Limestone platforms around Sagalassos resulting from giants mass movements, in: M. Waelkens and L. Loots (eds) *Sagalassos V. Report on the Survey and Excavations Campaigns of 1996 and 1997 (Acta Archaeologica Lovaniensia Monographiae* 11) Leuven University Press 777-792.

M. Waelkens, P.M. Vermeersch, E. Paulissen, E. Owens, B. Arıkan, M. Martens, P. Talloen, L. Gijsen, L. Loots, Ch. Peleman, J. Poblome, R. Degeest, T. Patricio, S. Ercan, F. Depuydt (1997) The 1994 and 1995 excavation seasons at Sagalasso, in: M. Waelkens and J. Poblome (eds) Sagalassos IV. Report on the Survey and Excavation Campaigns of 1994 and 1995 (Acta Archaeologica Lovaniensia Monographiae 9) Leuven University Press: 103-216.

M. Waelkens and the Sagalassos Team (1997) Interdisciplinary in classical archaeology. A case study: the Sagalassos Archaeological Research Project (Southwest Turkey), in: M. Waelkens and J. Poblome (eds) *Sagalasos IV. Report on the Survey and Excavation Campaigns of 1994 and 1995 (Acta Archaeologica Lovaniensia Monographiae* 9) Leuven University Press: 225-252.

M. Waelkens, E. Paulissen, M. Vermoere, P. Degryse, D. Celis, K. Schroyen, B. De Cupere, I. Librecht, K. Nackaerts, H. Vanhaverbeke, W. Viaene, Ph. Muchez, R. Ottenburgs, J. Deckers, W. Van Neer, E. Smets, G. Govers, G. Verstraeten, A. Steegen and K. Cauwenberghs (1999) Man and environment in the territory of Sagalassos, a classical city in SW Turkey, *Quaternary Science Reviews* 18: 697-709.

M. Waelkens, M. Sintubin, Ph. Muchez and E. Paulissen (2000) Archaeological geolomorphological and geological evidences for a major earthquake at Sagalassos (SW Turkey) around the middle of the seventh century A.D., in: W.J. McGuire, D.R. Griffits and I. S. Stewart (eds) *The Archaeology of Geological Catastrophies (Geological Sociaty Special Publication* 171) London: 373-383.

S.E. White (1981) Alpine mass movement forms (non-catastrophic): classification, description and significance, *Arctic and Alpine Research* 13: 127-137.

I.E. Whitehouse and M.J. McSavenney (1983) Diachronous talus surfaces in the southern Alps, New Zealand, and their implications to talus accumulation, *Arctic and Alpine Research* 15: 53-64.

J. Whittow (1984) *The Penguin Dicitionary of Physical Geography*, Londen.

PART VII

ANTHROPOLOGICAL AND ARCHAEOZOOLOGICAL STUDIES

DNA ANALYSIS OF ARCHAELOGICAL HUMAN REMAINS FROM SAGALASSOS

Els JEHAES[1], Marc WAELKENS[2], Ann MUYLDERMANS[3], Jean-Jacques CASSIMAN[1], Elisabeth SMITS[4], Jeroen POBLOME[2], Paul LAMBRECHTS[3] and Ronny DECORTE[1]

1 - Center for Human Genetics, KULeuven, Campus Gasthuisberg, Herestraat 49, 3000 Leuven
2 - Department of Archaeology, KULeuven, Blijde Inkomststraat 21, 3000 Leuven
3 - School of Dentistry, KULeuven, U.Z. St. Rafaël, Capucijnenvoer 7, 3000 Leuven
4 - University of Amsterdam, Amsterdams Archeologisch Instituut (AAC) Nieuwe Prinsengracht 130, 1018 VZ Amsterdam, The Netherlands

SUMMARY

Deoxyribonucleic acid (DNA) was isolated from human skeletal remains (bone and tooth samples) of the archaeological site of Sagalassos. The hypervariable D-loop of mitochondrial DNA could be amplified and sequenced. Evidence is provided that authentic mtDNA sequence information could be obtained from the ancient bone and tooth samples of Sagalassos, though not for all 24 excavated skeletons. No identical D-loop sequences were obtained which suggests a non-maternal relationship. All obtained mitochondrial D-loop sequences, except two, fit into one of the five lineage groups distinguished in 821 individuals from European and Middle Eastern populations (Richards *et al*. 1996: 185-203).

1. INTRODUCTION

The first indication that molecular genetic information might persist in ancient materials was the demonstration that peptidebonds could last up to 10^8 years in fossil shells and bones (Weiner *et al*. 1976: 2541-2545). These findings inspired the hope that genetic information could be retrieved from amino acid sequences in ancient remains. With the development of the polymerase chain reaction (PCR), it became possible to analyse DNA from ancient sources (Pääbo *et al*. 1988: 9775-9787). Recently, it has been shown that mitochondrial DNA (mtDNA) analysis can be performed successfully on human remains up to 12,000 years old (Hagelberg *et al*. 1989: 485) and even on a skeleton from a Neanderthaler (Krings *et al*. 1997: 19-30). The genetic information obtained can support phylogenetic and anthropological findings like kinship, migration of ancient populations, taxonomic relationships and the genetic origin of modern populations. This new area has, therefore, been called "molecular archaeology" (Pääbo *et al*. 1989: 9709-9712).

A serious concern pertinent to the study of ancient DNA (aDNa) is the occurrence of post-mortem oxidative processes that damage the DNA in archaeological specimens (Rogan and Salvo 1990: 195-214). Moreover, only trace amounts of DNA are found amidst a vast excess of other DNA, mainly from bacterial origin. The PCR technique is an ideal tool to amplify a small number of intact molecules from a vast excess of damaged molecules. The main problem, however, encountered in using PCR to amplify DNA sequences from ancient human specimens, is the risk of contamination with small amounts of exogenous DNA either from modern DNA or from previous amplifications. During the procedure of prelevation of the skeletons and DNA analysis of the archaeological remains, contamination must be controlled in order to prove the authenticity of the obtained genetic information.

Nucleotide sequences provide the highest possible resolution to examine molecular evolution in populations. The study of genealogical relationships between individuals within a species requires rapidly evolving, non-recombining sequences such as those found in maternally inherited mtDNA (Orrego and King 1990: 416-426). MtDNA accumulates base changes at a rate 5-10 times that of nuclear DNA and the 1.1 kb non-coding D-loop is the fastest-changing segment (Aquadro and Greenberg 1983: 287-312). Within the D-loop, most polymorphic nucleotide sites are concentrated in two hypervariable regions (HVR1 and HVR2). Another advantage of mtDNA is that it exists in numerous copies per cell (Bogenhagen and Clayton 1974: 7991-7995) and as a result are more likely to survive the post-mortem degradation of nucleic acids after death than single-copy nuclear sequences.

This study describes the first results obtained from the mtDNA analysis on teeth and bone samples of 24 excavated skeletons from the archaeological site of Sagalassos excavated from 1994 till 1997. This allowed us to address questions such as possible maternal relatedness between the excavated individuals and the phylogenetic placement of the ancient mitotypes into known European and non-European haplogroups.

2. MATERIALS AND METHODS

2.1. Excavation of the skeletons

During four excavations seasons (1994-1997) human remains have been found on the slope along the western side of the lower agora (Fig. 1). In Roman Imperial times, this area had been occupied by a portico, originally constructed during the second half of the first century AD, but later rebuilt, reusing most of the original building elements, after the 518 AD earthquake. When around the middle of the seventh century AD, a massive earthquake levelled the whole city, which shortly afterwards seems to have been abandoned in favour of Ağlasun, located 7 kilometres to the south, the last phase of the west portico collapsed as well. Its ruins got partially mixed with that of a church into which the former Apollo Klarios temple, located at a terrace above the west portico had been transformed.

In the mean time, the 1998 and 1999 excavation campaigns have revealed that even before this final seismic catastrophe of the mid seventh century AD, a Christian necropolis had already been laid out in the area between the back wall of the west portico and the church. After this catastrophic event, the tumble of all structures covering the western edge of the Lower Agora was never removed. On the contrary, inhumation burials serving the last inhabitants of Sagalassos continued to be arranged here. Stratigraphical evidence has shown that these burials must have belonged to the second half of the seventh century AD (Waelkens *et al.* 1997; Waelkens *et al.* 2000).

From 1994 to 1997, a total of 23 burial sites, including two double graves have been recovered here. In 1994, three burial sites were excavated, in 1995 fourteen, in 1996 five and in 1997 only one. Physical anthropological research revealed sex and age of the excavated skeletons (Table 1; E. Smits personal communication). Eleven skeletons belonged to adults, predominantly in their twenties. The other skeletons belonged to children of about two years old. Neither sex nor age of the deceased represent the normal average of an urban population. As a result, a catastrophic event may have been responsible for the deaths. Yet, this event seems not to have been linked directly to the earthquake itself, since no fractures have been noticed on the corpses.

These human remains clearly belong to one homogeneous group considering the similarities in the way they have been buried. In other words, this cemetery was in use during one specific period in the history of the town Sagalassos. All individuals were placed in a pit lying on their back, in an outstretched position, many times with the arms folded across the chest. The position of infants and juveniles are less clear. Burials 6 and 16 (Fig. 2) were double graves where an infant was found between the legs of an adult. Sometimes, pieces of jewellery (rings, earrings, bracelets, cross-shaped pendents) were present, indicating that the deceased were dressed when they were buried. Around most of the incubations, traces of a stone or brick/tile alignment were found. They were, mainly left *in situ* around the upper (western) part of the burial site. The eastern extremity, lower down the slope, in many cases had gone as the result of slope erosion. In some cases, even the feet of the deceased had disappeared this way. The graves were probably covered by stone blocks of which some were found still *in situ*. Since none of the tombs intersect with other burial sites, these stone covers may have been visible at the surface, or they may have been some kind of simple grave marker. No clear indications of the use of coffins were found (e.g. the presence of iron nails in the corners of the grave). In addition to the skeletons no specific grave goods were found, except for some coins found in three of the tombs. However, it is not certain that they really belonged to the burials, since the state of the latter cannot exclude that they are to be considered as intrusive material resulting from later slope movements. As is normal in seventh century AD contexts at Sagalassos, these coins range in date from the fourth to the early seventh century AD (Waelkens *et al.* 1997: 212).

2.2. Prevention of contamination

DNA isolation, PCR and post-PCR analysis were carried out in three separate rooms with dedicated laboratory equipment (e.g. centrifuges, pipette set, laboratory coat) which was only used for samples containing low amounts of DNA. All work was done in a (laminar flow) cabinet equipped with a UV light to decontaminate the work area after use. The use of sterile pipette tips with a cotton plug prevented any contamination with aerosols containing DNA or PCR products. Samples were always handled with sterile forceps. Disposable gloves and a mouth shield were used to avoid contamination by skin cells, sweat or saliva and were changed regularly to avoid cross sample contamination.

In order to minimise contamination by surface cells through handling, biological samples were 'cleaned' before DNA extraction. The external layer of the bone samples was removed with sterile drills. For DNA extraction of teeth only the internal dental pulp was taken after drilling a hole in the tooth by a dentist.

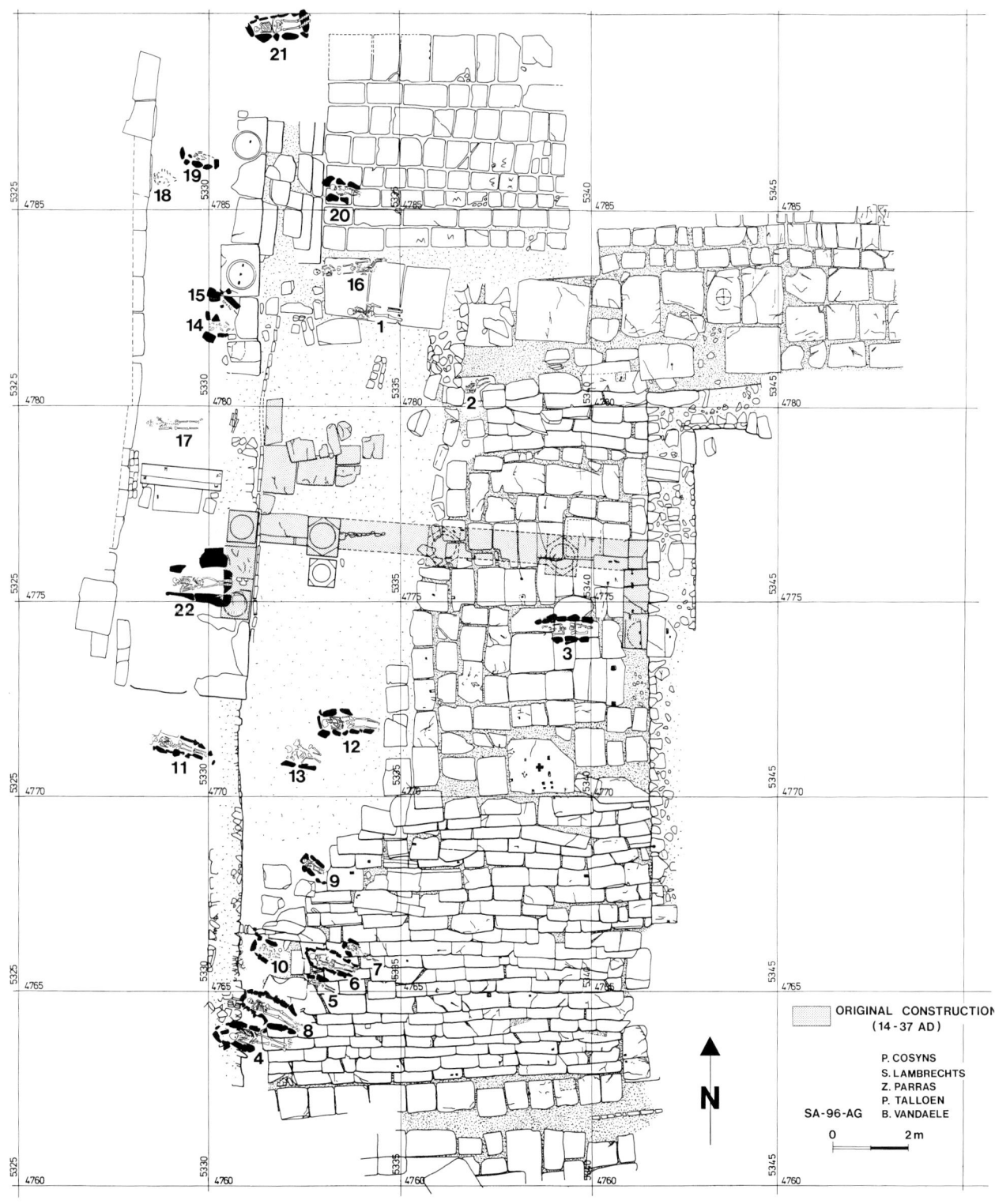

AGORA GATE

Fig. 1: Map with the localization of the burial sites on top of the stairway from sixth century AD (Lower Agora) (From P. Cosyns, S. Lambrechts, Z. Parras, P. Talloen, B. Vandaele).

Fig. 2: Double grave 16: an infant was found between the legs of an adult.

The reagents were made DNA-free by autoclaving and microfiltration. In addition, blank extraction and PCR controls (no biological sample added) were taken through the entire procedure in order to detect possible contamination of reagents or glassware. When the blank control was positive after PCR, the results were rejected.

2.3. Extraction of DNA from bones and teeth

DNA was extracted from the milled bones by a silica-based method (Höss and Pääbo 1993: 3913-3914). In brief, 0.5 g of bone powder was incubated at 60° C overnight in lysis solution containing 10 M guanidinium thiocyanate, 0.1 M Tris-HCl (pH 6.4), 0.02 M EDTA and 1.3% Triton X-100. The released DNA was captured by silica particles and the silica pellet was washed several times. The DNA was eluted in 120 µl TE buffer, containing 0.1 mM EDTA and 10 mM Tris-HCl (pH 8.3).

The DNA extraction method used for a tooth has been described by Hagelberg et al. (1994: 25-26). Dental pulp was incubated overnight at 37° C in a lysis buffer containing 0.5 mM EDTA, 50 mM Tris-HCl (pH 8.0), 0.5% SDS and 200 mg/ml proteinase K. This was followed by extraction with phenol/chloroform and finally concentration of the DNA by microfiltration. DNA was recovered from the filter in 100 µl TE buffer.

2.4. Amplification and analysis of the D-loop

Because of the relative high risk for contamination with a double PCR, a single 'hot-start' PCR (Ruano et al. 1992: 266-274) was developed to amplify two overlapping fragments (between 242 and 330 bp) for each of the two hypervariable regions of the mtDNA D-loop directly in 45 cycles using AmpliTaq 'Gold' DNA-polymerase (Perkin Elmer). High concentrations of bovine serum albumin (1 mg/ml) and Taq DNA-polymerase (5 U) were used to overcome the effect of PCR inhibitors of unknown origin which could be present in the DNA extracts of the ancient bones. The reaction contained further 0.4 µM primers (Decorte et al. 1996: 17-20), 0.2 mM of dNTP, 1x PCR buffer, 2.5 mM $MgCl_2$ and 10% of DNA extract.

The PCR products were directly sequenced with the Sanger dideoxy chain termination method (Sanger et al. 1977: 5463-5467) and analysed on the A.L.F. DNA sequencer.

2.5. Quantitation of the number of amplifiable molecules

In order to evaluate the authenticity of the obtained sequences for aDNA the number of template molecules must be determined. It is useful in the evaluation of the role of contaminating contemporary molecules and PCR errors in amplifications from aDNA (Handt et al. 1996: 368-376).

A competitive PCR assay was developed in order to quantitate the number of amplifiable molecules. An internal standard of 258 bp was constructed, encompassing positions 16290 to 16547 in the first hypervariable region of the human mtDNA D-loop with a deletion of 10 bp between bases 16311 to 16320 (Förster 1994: 18-20). This molecule was cloned into a plasmid vector and the concentration of the purified construct was determined. In order to determine the approximate number of template molecules in an extract, a 'hot-start' PCR as described in 2.4 was performed with six consecutive dilution steps of the standard (from an estimated number of 250 down to 5 construct copies), to which a constant amount of extract had been added. In order to quantify template molecules of different lengths, two primer sets were chosen to determine the amount of 131 and 258 bp PCR amplifiable fragments. Amplification products were analysed on the automated A.L.F. DNA sequencer.

2.6. Analysis of X-Y homologous gene amelogenin

Amplification of part of the X-Y homologous amelogenin gene with a single primer pair generates a 106 bp and 112 bp PCR products respectively from the X and Y chromosome. PCR conditions and primer pairs have been described by Sullivan et al. (1993: 100-119). The fluorescence-tagged PCR products were analysed on the A.L.F. DNA sequencer.

2.7. Criteria for the authenticity of ancient DNA sequences

It is necessary to use criteria that have to be fulfilled before a mtDNA sequence can be regarded as authentically ancient:
1. Mock extractions and PCR blanks must be negative.
2. Concordance of the results must exist in multiple *independent* extractions from each sample and from at least one other piece of the same skeleton.
3. PCR reactions have to start from 50-100 template molecules.
4. An inverse dependence of the amplification efficiency on the size of the segment to be amplified must exists in the aDNA extracts.
5. No concordance should exist with the mtDNA sequence of the experimenter or with the sequences of people who have handled the remains on the archaeological field.
6. The sequence should make phylogenetic sense: the obtained aDNA sequence must fit in the known mtDNA sequence databank of the population group to which the skeletons belong.

3. RESULTS

3.1. Mitochondrial DNA analysis of the human remains

Table 1 gives an overview of the 24 excavated skeletons

available for DNA analysis, together with the investigated bone and tooth samples for each skeleton. From each individual at least two, mostly three or more independent samples of the skeleton were analysed. For the bone samples, different extractions (with different batches of extraction buffers on different dates) of the same bone were performed if enough material was present.

The results of the mtDNA analysis on the ancient samples of Sagalassos can be divided into four groups. The division into four groups was done on the basis of the fulfilment of the criteria formulated in order to proof the authenticity of the obtained sequences.

Group A: Authentic results could not be determined due to insufficient material from the skeletons
To this group belong skeleton numbers SA95AG260a, SA95AG285, SA95AG328, and SA96 5330-4785/78. As seen in table 1 these skeletons were from children of two years old or younger. The available bone samples for DNA analyses were too small. Therefore, only one tooth sample from each skeleton could be analysed which is not enough to fulfil the criteria for concordance of the results in at least two independent samples of the skeleton.

Group B: No authentic results could be obtained due to contamination or too few start templates for PCR
To group B belong SA94AG70, SA94AG103, SA95AG334, SA95AG326, SA95AG240, SA95AG310, SA96AG36. In these skeletons no authentic sequences could be obtained. In different aDNA extracts of the skeletons too few templates for PCR of the 131 and 258 bp fragment were present (<100 molecules) so that the role of PCR errors or DNA damage can not be excluded in the final PCR product pool. Especially in SA94AG70, aDNA extracts showed a non-inverse relationship between the amplification efficiency and the length of the amplification products (data not shown). Ambiguous sequences were obtained, caused by contamination by the experimenter, the dentist who extracted the pulp or the archaeologists or most often from an unknown source. Partial mtDNA sequences were amplified probably due to DNA fragmentation. In the few DNA extracts which yielded a full unambiguous mtDNA sequence, the result could not be confirmed in other independent DNA extracts of the same skeleton.

Group C: Potential authentic results
To group C belong SA95AG249, SA94AG119, SA95AG260b (radius), SA95AG367 and SA95AG356. In these skeletons, mtDNA results were obtained with potential authentic results. Difficulties were obtained in explicit confirmation of the results in the same bone sample or between the different samples of a skeleton. The common mtDNA sequence was very often seen with a background of a contaminated sequence of the experimenter, an archaeologist or most often from an unknown source. Degradation of the aDNA was another explanation. Concerning SA95AG260b, the results of the fibula, the two ribs and the molar can be classified under group B. The DNA extracts of the radius, however, showed a potential authentic sequence for HVR1. It is not clear if the radius came from the skeleton of the child or the adult, although the physical measures fit more with a skeleton of an adult. For HVR2 only partial sequences were obtained which could not be confirmed. This was also observed in SA95AG356 and SA95AG367.

Group D: Authentic mtDNA results
Reliable authentic aDNA sequences were obtained for the skeletons SA95AG243, SA96 5325-4775/23, SA96 5330-4785/120, SA97LA5325/4795-145, SA95AG278, SA96 5325-4785/45, SA95AG341 and SA95AG90. The sequences from these eight skeletons fulfilled all criteria to consider the results as genuinely authentic.

In summary, we were able to obtain authentic mtDNA sequences for eight skeletons (group D). In these skeletons concordance of the results was observed in the same sample and between different samples (at least two) of the skeleton. This concordance was however not the case for the five skeletons belonging to group C although potential authentic results could be obtained for HVR1 and often for HVR2 also. The mtDNA sequences found in the thirteen skeletons are summarised in table 2. For the remaining eleven skeletons no authentic results could be obtained.

3.2. Possible maternal relationships in the skeletons

Comparison of the obtained mtDNA sequences in the skeletons (Table 2), revealed no identical sequences which suggests a non-maternal relationship between the buried individuals. Concerning the two double graves, the remains of the skeleton of the child of grave 6 were not suitable for mtDNA analysis but for the skeletons of grave 16 potential authentic results could be obtained for HVR1. Except for position 16146, the mtDNA sequence for HVR1 of the adult differs from that of the child at one position (16304). Definitive exclusion of a maternal relationship on the basis of one difference is however questionable. Because of the presence of mutational hotspots in mtDNA and the existence of heteroplasmy (Parson et al. 1997: 363-368), it might be possible that the skeletons of grave 16 are maternally related. HVR2 could give further exclusion of maternal relationship. The same reasoning can be applied for mtDNA sequences of SA94AG119 and SA95AG243, SA95AG260b radius and SA95AG367 (for the latter also no results for HVR2 were obtained). Systematic prelevation of new samples of these skeletons and further mtDNA analysis might give more information.

Grave°	Identification number of the skeleton	Sex*	Age (years)*	Tissue sample available for DNA analysis
1	SA94AG70	M	16-18	sternum, fibula, rib, two molars
2	SA94AG119	?	0.6-1.5	clavicula, two ribs, two milk teeth
3	SA94AG103	F	18-19	radius, two ribs, two molars
4	SA95AG90	M	22-24	two ribs, premolar, fibula
5	SA95AG240	?	2-3	tibia, two ribs, milk tooth
6	SA95AG260a	?	2	pelvis, two ribs, milk tooth
6	SA95AG260b	F	21-23	fibula, two ribs, radius?, two molars
7	SA95AG249	?	1.5-2.5	humerus, two ribs
9	SA95AG243	?	2-3	tibia, two ribs, two milk teeth
10	SA95AG310	?	1.5	ulna, two ribs, milk tooth
11	SA95AG341	F?	25-35	fibula, rib, two molars
12	SA95AG278	F	35-50	ulna, rib, two molars
13	SA95AG285	?	1-1.5	radius, two ribs, milk tooth
14	SA95AG326	?	4	humerus, rib, milk tooth
15	SA95AG328	?	1-1.5	clavicula, two ribs, milk tooth
16	SA95AG367	?	4	humerus, rib, two milk teeth
16	SA95AG356	M	66-75	two ribs, premolar
17	SA95AG334	?	12-15	radius, rib, two molars
18	SA96AG36	?	1.5	tibia, two milk teeth
19	SA96 5325-4785/45	?	1.5-2	rib, two diaphysis, molaris, milk tooth
20	SA96 5330-4785/78	?	1.5	rib, milk tooth
21	SA96 5330-4785/120	F	16-18	phalanx, rib, molar
22	SA96 5325-4775/23	M	40-50	phalanx, molar
23	SA97LA5325/4795-145	F	21-33	three unknown bone fragments, three molars

Table 1: Overview of the excavated skeletons available for
DNA analysis and the investigated samples.

° Number of the grave refers to figure 1
* Sex and estimated age were determined by anthropological investigation (E. Smits personal communication); for infant skeletons morphometric analysis of the gender is impossible.
Note: Grave 8 (SA95AG350) was not available for DNA analysis.

		% of A73G
European populations	British (Piercy et al. 1993: 85-90)	45
	Belgian (unpublished results)	55
	French (Jorde et al. 1995: 523-538)	40
	Bulgarian (Calafell et al. 1996: 35-49)	70
Turkey	Turkish (Calafell et al. 1996: 35-49)	62
	ancient (this study)	66
non-European populations	Central American (Batista et al. 1995: 921-929)	63
	African (Vigilant et al. 1991: 1503-1507)	100
	Chinese (personal communication)	100
	Japanese (Horai et al. 1996: 579-590)	95

Table 3: Distribution of A73G in European and non-European populations.

REFERENCE*	16092	16126	16129	16146	16153	16163	16168	16183	16186	16188	16189	16192	16193.1	16223	16224	16249	16256	16258	16270	16278	16291	16294	16296	16304	16311	16319	16320	16323	16325	16343	73	150	195	199	204	247	250	263	285	309.1	315.1	haplogroup
	T	T	G	A	C	A	C	C	T	C	C	T	-	C	T	T	C	A	C	C	C	C	C	T	T	G	C	T	T	A	A	C	T	T	T	G	T	A	C	-	-	
SA95AG90	*	*	*	*	*	*	*	*	*	*	*	*	*	*	*	*	*	*	*	*	*	*	*	*	C	*	*	*	*	*	G	*	*	*	*	A	*	*	*	*	C	group 4
SA95AG243	*	*	*	*	*	*	*	*	*	*	*	*	*	*	C	*	*	*	*	*	*	*	*	*	C	*	*	*	*	G	G	T	*	*	*	*	*	G	*	C	C	group 4
SA95AG278	C	C	*	*	*	*	T	*	*	*	*	T	*	*	C	*	*	*	*	*	*	*	*	*	*	*	*	*	*	G	G	T	*	*	*	*	*	G	*	C	C	group 2b
SA95AG341	C	*	*	A	*	A	*	*	*	*	*	*	*	*	*	*	*	*	*	*	*	*	*	*	C	*	*	*	*	*	G	*	*	*	C	*	*	G	*	*	C	group 2b
SA96 5325-4775/23	*	*	A	*	*	*	*	*	*	*	*	*	*	T	*	*	*	*	*	T	*	T	*	*	C	*	*	C	*	G	*	T	*	*	C	*	*	G	*	*	C	group 3a
SA96 5325-4785/45	*	*	*	*	*	*	*	C	*	T	*	C	*	*	*	C	*	*	*	*	*	*	*	*	*	*	T	C	*	G	*	*	*	*	*	*	*	G	T	*	C	group 1
SA96 5330-4785/120	*	*	*	*	G	*	*	*	*	*	*	T	*	*	*	*	T	*	*	*	T	*	*	*	*	*	*	*	*	*	*	*	*	*	*	*	*	G	*	*	C	group 5
SA97 LA6325/4976-145	*	*	*	*	*	*	*	*	*	*	*	*	*	*	*	*	T	*	*	*	*	T	*	*	*	*	T	*	*	G	G	*	C	*	*	*	*	G	*	*	C	group 1
SA94AG119	*	*	*	*	*	*	*	*	*	*	*	*	*	*	*	*	*	*	*	*	*	*	*	*	*	*	*	*	*	*	*	*	*	*	*	*	*	G	*	*	C	group 1
SA95AG249	*	*	*	*	G	*	T	*	*	T	*	*	*	*	*	*	*	*	*	T	*	T	*	*	*	*	*	*	*	*	*	*	*	*	*	*	*	*	*	*	C	group 2b
SA95AG260B radius	C	C	*	*	G	*	*	*	*	T	*	*	*	*	*	*	*	*	*	*	*	T	C	*	*	*	*	*	*	*	?	?	?	?	?	?	?	?	?	?	?	group 2b
SA95AG356	C	?	*	**A/G**	*	*	*	*	*	*	*	*	*	*	*	*	*	*	*	*	*	*	*	C	*	*	*	*	*	*	?	?	?	?	?	?	?	G	?	?	?	group 2b
SA95AG367	C	*	*	*	G	*	*	*	*	*	*	*	*	*	*	*	*	*	*	*	*	T	*	*	*	*	*	*	*	*	?	?	?	?	?	?	?	G	?	?	?	group 2b

Table 2: D-loop sequences of the ancient remains of Sagalassos and the division into haplogroups of Richards et al. (1996: 185-203)

Note: HVR1 is from position 16070 to 16370; HVR2 is from position 60 to 370. The mtDNA D-loop sequences of the skeletons belonging to group D are marked in bold. In SA95AG356 nucleotide site 16146 in HVR1 could not be determined. In the two identical sequences in rib 1 and rib 2 this nucleotide showed an adenine and a guanine. The other contaminated sequences in rib 1 and rib 2 showed a G at position 16146. Whether this double peak at 16146 in the consensus sequence is derived from contamination (most probably) or heteroplasmy can not be distinguished by cloning of the PCR products. Also amplification of smaller PCR fragments (<150 bp) could not give a solution for this ambiguous position.
* Reference is according to Anderson et al. (1981: 547-465).

3.3. Genetic sex determination.

Amplification via PCR of the X-Y amelogenin homologous gene has been proposed as a valid alternative for gender determination to the morphometric analysis, especially in case of infant remains or heavily damaged skeletons where morphological sex determination is not possible. It is also interesting to compare the genetic results with the results of morphometric evaluations performed on the same specimens.

Each aDNA extract was subjected to this sex determination PCR. Only in three skeletons, [SA95AG278, SA95AG243 and SA95AG260b (radius)] repeatedly the same gender was determined in the aDNA. In concordance with the morphometric analysis, genetic sex determination revealed that skeleton SA95AG260b (radius) and SA95AG278 were female individuals. The infant remains of SA95AG243 showed to be female after amplification of the X-Y amelogenin gene.

The remaining nine skeletons that yielded authentic or potential authentic mtDNA results, were mostly negative in PCR; sometimes female and male results were obtained in the different samples.

3.4. Phylogenetic analysis of the mtDNA results of the human remains

As mentioned in table 2, all obtained mitochondrial D-loop sequences, except for two (SA95AG278 and SA96 5330-4785/120) fit into one of the five lineage groups distinguished in 821 individuals from European and Middle Eastern populations (Richards et al. 1996: 185-203). The mtDNA sequence of SA95AG249, SA94AG119 and SA96 5325-4785/45 belong to group 1 (all derivatives of the Anderson sequence (Anderson et. al. 1981) with an adenine at site 73 in HVR2), known as the biggest lineage group and the youngest corresponding to the population expansion linked to climate improvements following the end of the Last Ice Age. The D-loop sequence of SA95AG249 corresponds to the Anderson sequence, which is the most frequent in all European populations but absent in the contemporary population of the Middle East. The presence of the Anderson sequence in the ancient population of Sagalassos supports the hypothesis that its origin is in the Middle East (Richards et al. 1996: 185-203). Haplogroup 2 to 5 contain all sequences carrying a guanine at site 73 in HVR2 (Richards et al. 1996: 185-203). These lineages have a much older common mtDNA ancestor than the subset of individuals with A at 73. The ancient mitotypes are most probably remnants of the pre-glacial population (Wilkinson-Herbots et al. 1996: 499-508). The sequences of SA95AG341, SA95AG260b (radius), SA95AG367, SA95AG356 fit into lineage 2b, characterised by transitions at site 16126 and 16294. This subgroup of lineage 2 occurs at a low frequency in the Middle East. However, the ancestral state of lineage 2 (transition at 16126 unaccompanied) is only found in the Middle East. One aDNA sequence of SA96 5325-4775/23 belongs to group 3a, characterised by transitions at site 16223 and 16129, which is also found in the Middle East and known as the most ancient Caucasian-specific lineage. It encompasses most of the extant mtDNA variation in Asia and Africa. Two mtDNA sequences of SA95AG243 and SA95AG90 fit into lineage 4 (transition at site 16224 and 16311) which has not yet been described outside Europe and the age of this lineage corresponds to lineage 1. Finally, one mtDNA sequence of SA97 5325/4795-145 fits into lineage 5 (transition at 16270), also not yet described outside Europe. It is hypothesised that lineage 4 and 5 had Middle Eastern origins. These haplogroups are however not found in contemporary populations in the Middle East and might suggest that they are now very rare or extinct. The finding of mtDNA sequences of these lineage groups in the ancient population of Sagalassos supports the hypothesis that they originated in the Middle East regions and that Europe was colonised from the Middle East through Turkey. Lineage 2b, 3a and 5 are probably the lineages brought into Europe during the early Upper Palaeolithic colonisation by anatomically modern humans (non-expanding).

Two mtDNA sequences of SA95AG278 and SA96 5330-4785/120 do not fit in any of the four lineages of the European and Middle Eastern mtDNA gene pool carrying a G at site 73.

Since position 73 in HVR2 is of special importance for the genetic origin of European populations, this position was further analysed in the samples of the skeletons where no authentic results were obtained. A primer set (L21-M13 together with H118-BIO) was designed in order to amplify a short fragment of 116 bp. In concordance with the quantitation results of the number of amplifiable molecules for PCR, reliable results could only obtained for SA96LA36, SA95AG240 and SA95AG285. The majority of the aDNA extracts in the different samples of these skeletons revealed an A at site 73 (some extracts yielded a mixture of A and G). The three skeletons (SA95AG260b radius, SA95AG367, SA95AG356) of group C which yielded no consensus sequence for HVR2, revealed a G at site 73 which is in concordance with the haplogroup to which they belong. For the remaining skeletons, no consensus results could be obtained for the different aDNA extracts. As a result, in the ancient population of Sagalassos, five skeletons of the analysed 15 skeletons for site 73 carried an A while the majority, 10 skeletons (66%) carried a G at site 73. A comparison of this result with the observed distribution of A73G in European and non-European populations (Table 3), revealed that the Turks take an intermediate position in the gradient of 90-100% G at site 73 in Asia and Africa to 40% in the French population. Noticable is that the distribution of A73G in the ancient population of Sagalassos is very similar to the distribution observed in the mtDNA study of the 25 modern Turks by Calafell et al. (1996: 35-49).

4. DISCUSSION

We have provided evidence that authentic mtDNA sequence information can be obtained from ancient human remains at Sagalassos, although not for all excavated skeletons. From a total of 24 excavated skeletons, the mtDNA sequence of eight skeletons (33%) was scientifically solid and fulfilled all criteria for authenticity. The aDNA extracts of five other skeletons (21%) revealed potential authentic (did not fulfil all criteria) and in another seven skeletons (29%) the amplification of authentic D-loop sequences was not successful due to contamination or to too few templates for PCR. For the remaining four skeletons (17%) the available samples for DNA analysis were too small. Contamination in the field was observed in the mtDNA analysis of the skeletons of Sagalassos. It is remarkable that the excavated skeletons of the last two campaigns (grave 18 untill 23) which were prelevated with precautions (protective umbrellas, mouth masks, gloves) gave better authentic results than the others which were prelevated without precautions.

The skeletons that were amenable to authentic analysis showed a non-maternal relationship although some individuals differed only at one nucleotide position, which is not sufficient to definitively exclude maternal relationship.

Although the study of nuclear DNA is problematic in ancient remains, it was possible to determine the sex of certain skeletons with a highly sensitive PCR. The analysis of the X-Y homologous amelogenin gene was done on all the aDNA extracts but with repeated success only on the samples of three skeletons. In view of the low amount of mtDNA (an average 100 to 200 mtDNA molecules/10 μl extract) observed in the aDNA extracts of the remains of Sagalassos (±1000 mtDNA copies corresponds to one or two copies of nuclear DNA) the analysis of nuclear DNA will indeed be problematic. The hot climate in Sagalassos might explain that quantitation of the amplifiable mtDNA molecules in authentic aDNA extracts of the bone samples revealed on average not more than 100 to 200 copies mtDNA. Compared with the DNA extracts of the Tyrolean Ice man of 5,200 years old, which contained ±1000 molecules/ml of extract of the 103 bp-fragment (Handt et al. 1996: 368-376), the amounts of mtDNA molecules found in the remains of Sagalassos are low. Most degradation processes are promoted by high temperatures. Heat-induced DNA degradation involves deamination of cytosine residues, destruction of deoxyribose residues and hydrolytic cleavage of pyrimidine glycosyl bonds (Lindahl and Nyberg 1972: 3610-3618). They also proceed at physiological temperatures, though at greatly reduced rates.

Finally, we investigated the place of the ancient mitotypes of the population of Sagalassos into the known haplogroups of European and non-European populations. All obtained mitochondrial D-loop sequences, except two, fit into one of the five lineage groups distinguished in 821 individuals from European and Middle Eastern populations. It can be hypothesised that these two sequences are typical ancient and that they disappeared in the present population.

We investigated the distribution of A73G in the ancient population of Sagalassos and compared it with the distribution of 25 modern Turks investigated by Calafell et al. (1996: 35-49). Anatolia is often called 'the cradle of civilisation' as it has been the homeland of a variety of tribes and populations since 6500 BC. The languages spoken were diverse and largely unrelated. Around 1100 AD, with the invasion of the Turkmen nomads, part of the original population of Anatolia descending from ancient civilisations, adopted the Turkish language. Although some Turkish contemporary population samples have been used in mtDNA analyses of population studies, it is not known how great the impact of the Turkish nomads on the genetic background of the original population has been. An additional problem is the fact that it can not be excluded that the contemporary population of Turkey is not suitable because of recent admixture, caused by people who came from the former Ottoman provinces and settled more recently in Turkey. However, a preliminary comparison of the genome diversity of the ancient population with that of modern people of Anatolia offers the opportunity to trace the genetic affinity between the ancient and the contemporary population and place the former in a wider ethnic context. At first sight, the results from our study could suggest that the genetic impact of the Turkmen nomads on the 25 modern Turks from Calafell's study would have been rather small. This tentative conclusion is based on the similar distribution of A73G in the ancient population of Sagalassos and in the small sample of the modern Turkish population from the study of Calafell et al. (1996: 35-49). The 15 skeletons, in which it was possible to analyse nucleotide position 73, yielded a percentage of A73G of 66%. This percentage can however further change when more skeletons can be analysed for mtDNA.

However, one should remain very cautious with such preliminary conclusions. In fact, another reason which might prevent a definitive conclusion concerning the genetic influence of the Turkmen nomads on Calafell's population, is the fact that a profound study of the mtDNA diversity of different population groups of Anatolia and of Central Asia is still missing. Moreover, it should also be noticed that only mtDNA, which is exclusively maternally transmitted, has been investigated. It can be hypothesised that the invading Turkmen were mainly composed of men. In that case as well no contribution of mtDNA information from these Turkmen nomads will be seen, although their impact on nuclear DNA would be present. In order to trace this, highly polymorphic microsatellite loci on the Y chromosome should be analysed. However, the very small amounts of nuclear DNA in the samples of Sagalassos exclude at the present time the possibility of obtaining this Y chromosomal information.

5 ACKNOWLEDGEMENTS

This text presents the results of the Belgian Programme on Interuniversitary Poles of Attraction initiated by the Belgian State, Prime Minister's Office, Science Policy Programming (IUAP 4/12). This research was also made possible thanks to an FWO-Vlaanderen research grant (FWO/G.0215.96, FWO/G.0241.98 and G.0408.00) and to a GOA-programme (97/2). Scientific responsibility is assumed by its authors.

6. REFERENCES

S. Anderson, A.T. Bankier, B.G. Barrell, M.H.L. de Bruijn, A.R. Coulson, J. Drouin, I.C. Eperon, D.P. Nierlich, B.A. Roe, F. Sanger, P.H. Schreier, A.J.H. Smith, R. Staden and I.G. Young (1981) Sequence and organisation of the human mitochondrial genome, *Nature* 290: 457-465.

C.F. Aquadro and B.D. Greenberg (1983) Human mitochondrial DNA variation and evolution: analysis of nucleotide sequences from seven individuals, *Genetics* 103: 287-312.

D. Bogenhagen and D.A. Clayton (1974) The number of mtDNA genomes in mouse L and human Hela-cells, *Journal of Biological Chemistry* 249: 7991-7995.

F. Calafell, P. Underhill, A. Tolun, D. Angelicheva and L. Kalaydjieva (1996) From Asia to Europe: mitochondrial DNA sequence variability in Bulgarians and Turks, *Annals of Human Genetics* 60: 35-49.

R. Decorte, E. Jehaes, F.X. Xiao, and J.J. Cassiman (1996) Genetic analysis of single hair shafts by automated sequence analysis of the mitochondrial D-loop region, *Advances in Forensic Haemogenetics* 6: 17-20.

E. Förster (1994) An improved general method to generate internal standards for competitive PCR, *BioTechniques* 16:18-20.

E. Hagelberg, B. Sykes and R. Hedges (1989) Ancient bone amplified, *Nature* 342, 485.

E. Hagelberg, S. Quevedo, D. Turbon and J.B. Clegg (1994) DNA from ancient Islanders, *Nature* 369: 25-26.

O. Handt, M. Krings, R.H. Ward and S. Pääbo (1996) The retrieval of ancient DNA sequences, *American Journal of Human Genetics* 59: 368-376.

M. Höss and S. Pääbo (1993) DNA extraction from Pleistocene bones by a silica-based purification method, *Nucleic Acids Research* 21: 3913-3914.

M. Krings, A. Stone, R.W. Schmitz, H. Krainitzki, M. Stoneking and S. Pääbo (1997) Neanderthal DNA sequence and the origin of modern humans, *Cell* 90: 19-30.

T. Lindahl and B. Nyberg (1972) Rate of depurination of native deoxyribonucleic acid, *Biochemistry* 11: 3610-3618.

C. Orrego and M.C. King (1990) Determination of familial relationships, in M.A. Innis, D.H. Gelfand, J.J. Sninsky and T.J. White (eds) *PCR Protocols: A Guide to Methods and Applications*, San Diego: 416-426.

S. Pääbo, J.A. Gifford and A.C. Wilson (1988) Mitochondrial DNA sequences from a 7000-year old brain, *Nucleic Acids Research* 16: 9775-9787.

S. Pääbo, R.G. Higuchi and A.C. Wilson (1989) Ancient DNA and the polymerase chain reaction. The emerging field of molecular archaeology, *Yearbook of Biological Chemistry* 264: 9709-9712.

T.J. Parson, D.S. Muniec, K. Sullivan, N. Woodyatt, R. Alliston-Greiner, M.R. Wilson, D.L. Beery, K.A. Holland, V.W. Weedn, P. Gill and M.M. Holland (1997) A high observed substitution rate in the human mitochondrial control region, *Nature Genetics*: 363-368.

M. Richards, H. Côrte-Real, P. Forster, V. Macauley, H. Wilkinson-Herbots, A. Demaine, S. Papiha, R. Hedges, H.-J. Bandelt and B. Sykes (1996) Palaeolithic and Neolithic lineages in the European mitochondrial gene pool, *American Journal of Human Genetics* 56: 185-203.

P.K. Rogan and J.J. Salvo (1990) Study of nucleic acids isolated from ancient remains, *Yearbook of Physical Anthropology* 33: 195-214.

G. Ruano, E.M. Pagliaro, T.R. Schwartz, K. Lamy, D. Messina, R.E. Gaensslen and L. Lee (1992) Heat-Soaked PCR: An efficient method for DNA amplification with applications to forensic analysis, *BioTechniques* 13: 266-274.

F. Sanger, S. Nicklen and A.R. Coulson (1977) DNA sequencing with chain-terminating inhibitors, *Proceedings of the National Academy of Sciences U.S.A.* 74: 5463-5467.

K.M. Sullivan, A. Mannuci, C.P. Kimpton and P. Gill (1993) A rapid and quantitative DNA sex test: Fluorescence-based PCR analysis of X-Y homologous gene amelogenin, *BioTechniques* 15:100-119.

M. Waelkens, E. Paulissen, H. Vanhaverbeke, I. Öztürk, B. De Cupere, H.A. Ekinci, P.M. Vermeersch, J. Poblome and R. Degeest (1997) The 1994 and 1995 excavation seasons at Sagalassos, in: M. Waelkens and J. Poblome (eds) *Sagalassos IV. Report on the Survey and the Excavation Campaigns of 1994 and 1995 (Acta Archaeologica Lovaniensia Monographiae 9)* Leuven University Press: 103-216.

M. Waelkens, J. Poblome, R. Degeest, L. Vandeput, L. Loots, E. Paulissen, P. Talloen, J. Vanden Bergh, V. Vanderginst, B. Arıkan, I. Van Damme, I. Akyel, F. Martens, M. Martens, I. Uytterhoeven, T. Debruyne, D. Depraetere, K. Baran, B. Van Daele, Z. Parras, Ş. Yıldırım, Sh. Bubel, H. Vanhaverbeke, C. Licoppe, F. Landuyt, T. Patrício, S. Ercan, K. Van Baelen, E. Smits, F. Depuydt, L. Moens and P. De Paepe (2000). The 1996 and 1997 excavation seasons at Sagalassos, in: M. Waelkens and L. Loots (eds) *Sagalassos V. Report on the Survey and Excavation Campaigns of 1996 and 1997 (Acta Archaeologica Lovaniensia Monographiae* 11) Leuven University Press 217-388.

S. Weiner, H.A. Lowenstam and L. Hood (1976) Characterization of 80-million-year-old mollusk shell proteins, *Proceeding of the National Academy of Sciences U.S.A.* 73: 2541-2545.

H. Wilkinson-Herbots, B. Richards, P. Forster and B.C. Sykes (1996) Site 73 in hypervariable region II of the human mitochondrial genome and the origin of European populations, *Annual of Human Genetics* 60: 499-508.

RESULTS OF THE 1996 SURVEY OF THE FISH FAUNA OF THE AKSU RIVER AND SOME LAKES IN SOUTHWESTERN ANATOLIA, AND THE IMPLICATIONS FOR TRADE AT SAGALASSOS

Wim VAN NEER[1], Ruud WILDEKAMP[1], Fahrettin KÜÇÜK[2], Mustafa ÜNLÜSAYIN[2], Marc WAELKENS[3] and Etienne PAULISSEN[4]

1 - Royal Museum of Central Africa, B-3080 Tervuren, Belgium
2 - Eğirdir Fisheries Faculty, Süleyman Demirel University, 32500 Eğirdir, Turkey
3 - Department of Archaeology, KULeuven, Blijde Inkomststraat 21, B-3000 Leuven, Belgium
4 - Physical and Regional Geography, KULeuven, Redingenstraat 16B, B-3000 Leuven, Belgium

1. INTRODUCTION

Fish remains have been discovered both by hand-collecting and by sieving since the beginning of the excavations at Sagalassos in 1991. The bones retrieved during the 1991-1994 excavations come from contexts dating between the Augustan period and early Byzantine times and show that fish was imported from various regions (Van Neer *et al.* 1997). Most of the remains are from Anatolian freshwater species but marine fish and exotic freshwater species have been found as well. The marine fish comprise mainly scombrids: little tunny (*Euthynnus alletteratus*), bullet tuna (*Auxis rochei*), bonito (*Sarda sarda*), and chub mackerel (*Scomber japonicus*). In addition, a few bones were found of grouper (*Epinephelus* sp.), pilchard (*Sardina pilchardus*) and an unidentified *Clupeidae* (herrings and sardines). Three of these marine taxa live exclusively in the Mediterranean, whereas the others occur in both the Mediterranean and the Black Sea. It is assumed, because of the relative proximity of the site to the Mediterranean and the existence of good roads in that direction, that all the marine fish was imported from the southern coast. In fact, from 6 BC onward, a new road, called the *via Sebaste*, linked the newly founded Augustan colonies in Pisidia and Lycaonia with one another and to the Pamphylian ports (Mitchell 1993: 76-77 map 5). A Tiberian regulation for requisitioned transport from the territory of Sagalassos shows that the city controlled about 42 km of this road (Mitchell 1976). A fish trade along this road is understandable, since fish was not commonly available everywhere in the ancient world, and was a 'cash crop' for the people who caught and sold it (Gallant 1985). *Garum* or fish sauce especially was traded over long distances and created a very competitive market. Pompeii, for example, which produced and exported *garum*, also imported fish sauce from Spain (Laurence 1994: 64). But fresh fish from coastal areas, lakes or rivers must also have provided a much appreciated additional income (Sartre 1995: 275). As the distance from Sagalassos to the southern coast is approximately 110 km, the fish must have been imported in preserved form. Salted, sun-dried or smoked fish was also brought into Sagalassos from even more distant areas. This is indicated by the finds of the catfish *Clarias* sp. and of Tilapiini. Both are typical African taxa, the distribution of which extends however into the Levant. It is unclear for the moment whether these fish were imported from the Nile or from the Syro-Palestinian area. The import of these exotic freshwater fish, as well as of the marine species, is attested over a period of six centuries. Throughout this period, however, Anatolian freshwater species formed the major part of the consumed fish. Cyprinids are the most common family, among which wild carp (*Cyprinus carpio*) predominate, followed by bream (*Abramis brama*), *Leuciscus* sp. and *Vimba vimba*. In antiquity, wild carp were famous for their great reproductive capacities and popular for their fleshy palates that were esteemed as a great delicacy (Thompson 1947: 135-136). At Sagalassos, wild carp was also the most frequently consumed fish. Other freshwater species found so far are the European catfish (*Silurus glanis*) and pike (*Esox lucius*). The European catfish was also known in antiquity from certain Greek rivers. According to ancient sources, the female was better eating than the male, and it was also reported that this fish was peculiarly sensitive to thunder. Its gigantic size was often exaggerated (Thompson 1947: 43-48). Pike is not so frequently mentioned by ancient authors. Ausonius (*Mos.* 120), however, despised it as a fish for the greasy cookshop (Thompson 1947: 151-152). In addition there is evidence at Sagalassos for a sturgeon species (Acipenseridae), a marine fish which travels up rivers for spawning. All the aforementioned species are indigenous to Turkey but their precise geographic distribution is unclear from the available literature. Since these data are vital for the understanding of the former trade routes it was decided to search for additional Turkish literature and to start fieldwork.

The major commercial relationships of Sagalassos were to the south of the site as is evidenced by archaeological data. Coins from Sagalassos comprise issues from major contemporary cities in Pisidia (Termessos, Cremna, Selge, Baris) and Pamphylia (Side, Perge, Attaleia and Aspendos). After the Sagalassian issues, most city coins found during the excavations were minted at Perge suggesting that this town became the major port for export and import (Scheers 1993a, 1993b, 1995). The Sagalassian red slip ware, occurring in more southerly situated towns and settlements, also bears witness to this trade (Poblome 1999; Waelkens and the Sagalassos team 1997). With the foregoing in mind, it was supposed that most of the freshwater fish would have been derived from the Aksu river (ancient Kestros) and its tributaries, although the existing data in the ichthyological literature did not always support such a hypothesis. During the Roman period, the Aksu canyon must have formed the eastern boundary of the territory of Sagalassos (Waelkens *et al.* 1997). The river Kestros is even represented on the city's coinage (Levante 1994: 1773, 1863). The available distribution maps in general ichthyological textbooks (Maitland 1978; Banarescu *et al.* 1971) and certain revisions (e.g. Ladiges 1960) seemed to indicate that species such as *Abramis brama* or *Esox lucius* occur only in the northern part of Turkey at a distance which may seem too great to make easy and regular import by land acceptable. It should be taken into account, however, that the modern freshwater fish fauna of Turkey is only partially known and insufficiently documented in the international literature. Several regional surveys published in Turkish and other languages have not always found their way to the general scientific community. As an example, the more southerly finds of *Esox lucius* published by Kosswig (1969) were neglected in these general books on fish. *Abramis brama* was found at Sagalassos but also at Pergamon in a late Hellenistic-Roman context (Boessneck and von den Driesch 1985), outside its commonly accepted distribution range. When previously dealing with these conflicting data (Van Neer *et al.* 1997) it was reasoned that additional sampling would be necessary to elucidate further the present-day distribution patterns of the species encountered at Sagalassos. The possibility could not be ruled out *a priori* that certain species occurred in the southern catchment area of Sagalassos. For these reasons, the Aksu basin was chosen as a first major area for the sampling of present-day fish.

2. MATERIAL AND METHODS

The survey took place between 28 July and 9 August 1996. Sampling was carried out at 60 localities (Fig. 1) the coordinates of which were recorded by a handheld GPS (Magellan GPS Satellite Navigator) with an estimated precision of 100 m (Table 1). Sampling concentrated on the Aksu river and its tributaries, but in addition a survey was carried out around lakes Gölcük, Eğirdir and Beyşehir. Lakes Burdur, Salda, Karataş, Söğüt and Gölhisar were also sampled in order to verify the status of *Aphanius* species which are possibly threatened with extinction (Wildekamp and Valkenburg 1994; Wildekamp *et al.* 1999).

The gear used for sampling comprised electric fishing equipment, seines with a mesh size of 7 mm, castnets, driftnets, handnets, fishtraps and rod and line. In addition to the material that was sampled by our own team, we also noted the species that were captured by local fishermen. A selection of the fish was preserved in formalin and is presently kept at the Fisheries Faculty in Eğirdir. A sub-sample was taken to Belgium for further study and has been registered in the Tervuren Museum as collection number MRAC 96053. A total of 56 fish belonging to 12 species have been prepared as skeletons. These specimens were identified, photographed, measured and filleted in the field and were brought in salted form to the laboratory for further preparation of their skeletons. This material (Tervuren Museum register number MRAC 96054) comprises mainly commercially important food fishes and has been added to the reference collection that is used for the identification of fish remains.

In addition to the data gathered during the 1996 fieldwork, some results are included of the surveys previously conducted in the Aksu basin by one of us (Küçük 1997).

The nomenclature used in this paper follows the latest revisions published by Kottelat (1997) and Bogutskaya (1997).

3. RESULTS

Table 2 lists the fish species that were collected at the different localities. Localities where no fish were found have been omitted from this table, namely Gürleyük Deresi near Çukur Pınarı and Güneyce both on the Isparta Çayı (17 and 18), the Ağlasun Çayı at Ağlasun (21), the Eren river at Yazıköy (31), a channel fed by the Senirkent river (38),

Üstünler junction at the southwest side of Beyşehir lake (44), two localities at Eğirdir near the outlet of the port (49 and 50), the Sarıtaş channel near Söğüt (57) and Kırkpınar source (58).

Larger species from lake Beyşehir were only observed on the market and comprised *Leuciscus lepidus*, *Cyprinus carpio* and the introduced *Sander lucioperca*, *Tinca tinca* and *Carassius carassius*. The main commercial species from Eğirdir lake seen on the market were the introduced *Sander lucioperca*, as well as *Cyprinus carpio* and small numbers of *Vimba vimba*. Our methods captured mainly smaller species such as *Aphanius anatoliae anatoliae*, *Barbatula angorae* and juvenile Cyprinids. In addition, we found *Gambusia affinis* and *Knipowitschia caucasica* at many localities in and around the lake.

4. DISCUSSION

4.1. General observations

The most important affluents in the upper part of the modern drainage basin of the river Aksu are the Ağlasun Çayı, the Isparta Çayı, and the Kovada Çayı which is connected with the Kovada lake. As is the case in general for the Mediterranean rivers, the discharges of the river Aksu are highly seasonal, with considerable flow during the rain-rich winter season and low discharge during the rainless summer season. The Aksu is a permanent river with a limited base flow from spring waters, mainly of karstic origin, during summer time. The volume and duration of discharge is significantly increased during the spring season with the meltwaters of the thick snow cover in the high mountains. Table 3 gives some information for the year 1996 on discharges, water breadth and average velocity for the Upper Aksu river, measured near Asağı Gökdere just before the Isparta Çayı river mouth. We have to take into account that the discharge data for summer and autumn are significantly reduced because of irrigation and that, during winter and spring, there is a small reduction in the discharge because water from the Ağlasun Çayı is diverted into the Çanaklı Basin. The Ağlasun Çayı is a permanent river with, under natural conditions, probably the highest base flow as it is fed by several important karstic springs around Başköy and Ağlasun/Sagalassos. In Hellenistic and Roman times it seems to have formed a more important river system that was perhaps greatly reduced by drought or other natural causes during the early Byzantine period (Waelkens und das Sagalassos-Team 2000; Waelkens *et al.* 1999; Waelkens and the Sagalassos Team 1997). It is possible that the Kestros river depicted on Sagalassos' city coins referred to this larger predecessor of the Ağlasun Çayı. The lower course of this river, downstream from Dereköy, is nowadays dry in summer as all its waters are used for irrigation. The discharge of the Isparta Çayı is also very seasonal, with today only a very limited flow in summer. But, in antiquity, this river was considered to be wide enough to form the eastern boundary of Sagalassos' territory (Waelkens *et al.* 1997).

The most striking observation during our survey was the relatively low species diversity and the low densities of fish in the Aksu river and its tributaries. As fishing pressure is low in the riverine habitats we believe that this result is mainly related to the poor nutrient content of the waters and to the low temperatures. In the upper reaches of the system (Ağlasun Çayı and Isparta Çayı, north of locality 19) almost no fish were found. These fast running waters are suitable for salmonids but, unlike the upper reaches of the Köprü Çayı, there were no river trout (*Salmo trutta macrostigma*). The only fish that were encountered were rainbow trout (*Oncorhynchus mykiss*), a species that was introduced in ponds for fish farming. Recently, trout farms have become an important economic activity in the district. In less than ten years, more than twenty such farms have been established in the Başköy and Ağlasun valleys, which cater for the tourist hotels from Antalya to Alanya. The specimens found in the rivers may represent individuals that escaped from fish farms but given the occurrence of small specimens it seems that self-reproducing populations already exist as well. A few kilometers east of Sagalassos the Ağlasun river now seasonally dries out as a result of the diversion of waters for irrigation, but in ancient times the numerous karstic springs in the area must have guaranteed a permanent flow. Nevertheless, the maximum sustained ichthyofauna would probably have remained limited. Judging indeed from comparison with similar habitats, the only important food fish that may have populated these upper reaches would have been the barbel *Capoeta Antalyensis*. Cyprinids and Cobitidae of small size may have occurred as well but their nutritional value for man was probably limited.

In the middle reaches of the Aksu river (between localities 19 and 11) the greatest densities of fish are found in the dam lakes Karacaören I and II. Here, slow running or stagnant water is available in which introduced species such as common carp (*Cyprinus carpio* f. *domestica*) and pike-perch (*Sander lucioperca*) are common, along with the autochthonous *Vimba vimba*. Large cyprinids such as *Capoeta Antalyensis* and *Capoeta capoeta* seem to be rare. To what extent this is due to *Sander lucioperca* is unclear since there are no ichthyological data prior to the introduction of this predator. The remaining part of the ichthyofauna comprises mainly small species of Cyprinidae and Cobitidae (*Cobitis simplicispinna* and *Barbatula angorae*). Locally, killifish (*Aphanius*) are found in places usually with abundant aquatic vegetation. Nowadays, such environments mainly occur in backwaters and in artificial canals used for irrigation where the survival of *Aphanius* is threatened by competition with *Gambusia affinis*, a Poeciliidae introduced for mosquito control. In any case, the killifish cannot have been important as food as they are too small. As a conclusion, it is difficult to estimate the original densities of the larger cyprinids in the middle Aksu, and their possible importance as a food resource in the past, because of the incalculable effect of damming and the introduction of species in the fauna currently found.

The lower reaches of the Aksu (south of locality 11) afford not only freshwater species but also euryhaline marine species. Mullet (Mugilidae), shad (*Alosa fallax*), seabream (Sparidae; *Sparus aurata* and *Diplodus annularis*) and sea bass (*Dicentrarchus punctatus* and *D. labrax*) are commonly found in the rivermouths. We were informed that *Dicentrarchus* migrates inland as far as Güloluk (locality 11). The inland migration of eels (*Anguilla anguilla*) reaches just south of the Karacaören II dam (locality 14) which was operational in 1991. The eel specimens that we collected north of Karacaören I at Asağı Gökdere (locality 19) and at Yazılı canyon (locality 24) were large specimens which must have reached the area prior to the construction of the dams. Typical freshwater inhabitants of the lower reaches of the Aksu river are *Vimba vimba*, *Capoeta capoeta*, *Salarias fluviatilis*, *Pseudophoxinus antalyae* and an undiscribed species of *Alburnus*.

Of the lakes north of Sagalassos covered by our survey so far, only Eğirdir lake has been properly sampled. The original fauna, prior to the introduction of pike-perch in 1955, comprised about 10 species (Kosswig 1954; Campbell 1992). Of the autochthonous inhabitants of the lake only carp and *Vimba vimba* seem to have survived the introduction of *Sander lucioperca*. Two fish species that would have been big enough to make them attractive food fishes, *Capoeta pestai* and *Pseudophoxinus handlirschi*, were no longer found in the lake, but it is possible that small populations still survive in the rivers entering the lake.

The 1996 survey around lake Beyşehir was carried out at a few localities only and a visit to the markets at Beyşehir town demonstrated that carp and pike-perch were the predominant food species. A few *Leuciscus lepidus* specimens were available but they were all of small size. Interviews showed that many of the species recorded in the past (Kosswig 1954; Ladiges 1960; Erdemli 1982) have almost, or perhaps completely, disappeared. This is especially the case for *Alburnus akili*, whereas *Chondrostoma beysehirense*, *Pseudophoxinus anatolicus* and *Capoeta pestai* were said to occur seasonally in small numbers. The chances of finding signs of these species are greatest during the spawning season when they are found inshore, and this is when the next fieldwork is planned. In an attempt to reduce the damage brought about by the introduction of pike-perch, additional species have been introduced. We noticed tench (*Tinca tinca*) and Crucian carp (*Carassius carassius*), but no evidence was found for *Abramis brama* mentioned by Gersar (1995).

Lake Gölcük is a volcanic lake 7 kilometers northwest of Sagalassos as the crow flies. Despite the fact that this lake was most probably not part of the territory of Sagalassos (Waelkens *et al.* 1997), the volcanic sediment around it was used by the Sagalassians as a temper in both their mortars (Viaene *et al.* 1997; Callebaut *et al.* 2000) and their coarse pottery (Degryse *et al.* 2000). A mountain pass, already used in antiquity (Loots *et al.* 2000), provides an easy route to the lake so the possible import of fish from there would not have posed any problem. Present-day catches in lake Gölcük comprise mainly carp and pike-perch and the smaller cyprinid *Alburnus chalcoides* which is used as bait. During our survey we noticed that dramatic changes have occurred in the habitat from excessive pumping of water, recreation and pollution. This has resulted in the disappearance of much of the aquatic vegetation and the extinction of *Aphanius anatoliae splendens* and *Hemigrammocapoeta kemali*, two species which one of us (RW) still observed in 1989. The pike-perch is certainly introduced but, because of the absence of records, it is unclear whether the carp belongs to the original fauna. Carp was mentioned by Ladiges (1960) from Lake Gölcük but Geldiay and Balık (1996: 243) consider that in this area the species was introduced. This seems to be confirmed by the first description of the lake's ichthyofauna by Kosswig and Sözer (1945) who mentioned only *Anatolichthys splendens* (synonymised with *Aphanius anatoliae splendens*) and *Hemigrammocapoeta kemali*.

Given the low densities of fish in the rivers and the abundance of them in lakes, it will be worth investigating the lakes in more detail in the future. Through interviews and investigation of the DSİ (Devlet Su İşleri) archives, an attempt will be made to document the original ichthyofauna and the subsequent introductions.

Pseudorasbora parva and *Knipowitschia caucasica* are new species for Anatolia but their presence is believed to be a fairly recent phenomenon probably due to unintentional introduction. Since these facts have no archaeological relevance, the detailed description of the two species and the possible modes of dispersal will be dealt with in detail elsewhere (Wildekamp *et al.* 1997; Van Neer *et al.* 1999).

4.2. Archaeological implications

In the following paragraphs we concentrate on the fish taxa that have been thus far identified from the site of Sagalassos. The carp *Cyprinus carpio* occurs in the Aksu basin in

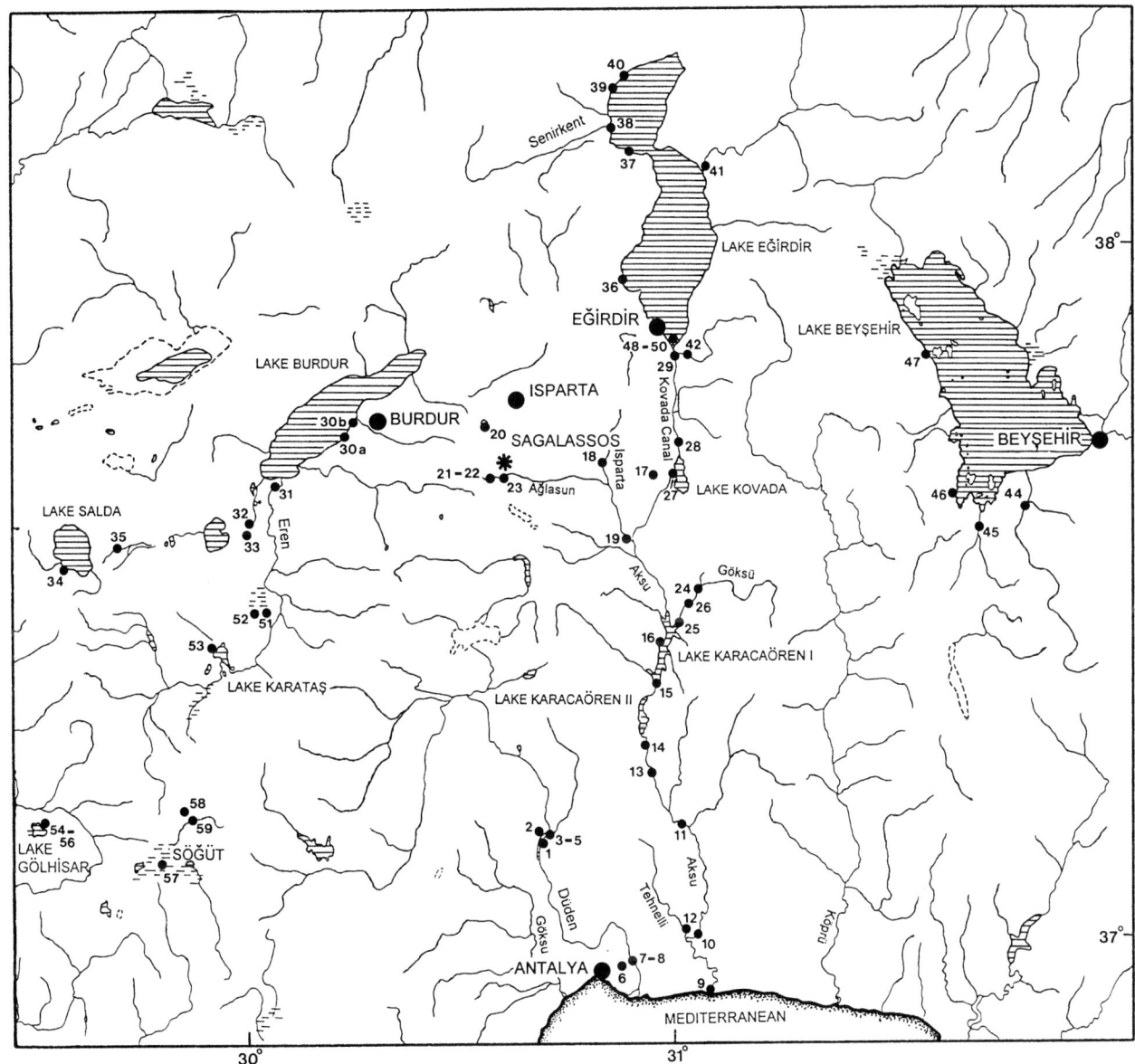

Fig. 1: Localities where fish sampling was conducted in summer 1996.

1	Kırkgöz, pools and channels	37°05'31"N/30°34'51"E	28/7/1996
2	Kırkgöz, lakelet near source	37°06'25"N/30°35'00"E	28/7/1996
3	Kırkgöz, channel area	37°06'18"N/30°35'29"E	28/7/1996
4	Kırkgöz, channel area, near pumping station	37°06'18"N/30°35'29"E	28/7/1996
5	Kırkgöz, channel area	37°06'09"N/30°35'25"E	28/7/1996
6	Topçular, channel connected to Düden	36°53'59"N/30°45'39"E	28/7/1996
7	Düden, bridge	36°54'17"N/30°46'46"E	28/7/1996
8	channel parallel with Düden	36°54'17"N/30°46'46"E	28/7/1996
9	Kundu Köyü, Aksu mouth	36°51'05"N/30°56'17"E	28/7/1996
10	Aksu köprüsü (Aksu bay)	36°56'52"N/30°53'46"E	29/7/1996
11	Güloluk, DSI regulator	37°06'10"N/30°52'25"E	29/7/1996
12	Tehnelli river	36°56'27"N/30°52'21"E	29/7/1996
13	Karaöz, Aksu river	37°14'20"N/30°47'41"E	30/7/1996
14	south of Karacaören II dam, near end pipeline	37°15'33"N/30°47'17"E	30/7/1996
15	Kargı (Karacaören I)	37°19'40"N/30°49'00"E	30/7/1996
16	Karacaören I	37°23'17"N/30°49'49"E	31/7/1996
17	Gürleyük Deresi- Çukur (Isparta)	37°38'51"N/30°48'21"E	31/7/1996
18	Isparta river, near spring	37°29'26"N/30°42'41"E	31/7/1996
19	Asağı Gökdere, Aksu river	37°32'43"N/30°46'59"E	31/7/1996
20	Gölcük lake	37°43'55"N/30°29'54"E	1/8/1996
21	Ağlasun river	37°38'30"N/30°31'27"E	1/8/1996
22	Ağlasun river	37°38'32"N/30°31'25"E	1/8/1996
23	Ağlasun river	37°38'35"N/30°32'21"E	1/8/1996
24	Yazılı canyon, Göksu river	37°27'41"N/30°54'34"E	2/8/1996
25	Çandır, outlet of Göksu in Karacaören	37°27'00"N/30°52'36"E	2/8/1996
26	Çandır, Göksu river near trout farm	37°26'43"N/30°54'09"E	2/8/1996
27	Kovada lake, southern outlet to Aksu	37°38'55"N/30°52'14"E	2/8/1996
28	Yukarı Gökdere köprüsu (Kovada canal)	37°41'53"N/30°52'35"E	2/8/1996
29	Eğirdir, Kovada canal	37°50'25"N/30°51'53"E	2/8/1996
30	Burdur lake between Çendik and Burdur	37°41'15"N/30°10'56"E 37°44'34"N/30°14'47"E	3/8/1996
31	Yazıköy, Eren river	37°38'15"N/30°05'25"E	3/8/1996
32	Düger, behind mosque	37°34'50"N/30°01'36"E	3/8/1996
33	Düger, near source (Pınargözü)	37°34'23"N/30°01'21"E	3/8/1996
34	Salda lake	37°31'43"N/29°39'25"E	3/8/1996
35	Karapınar-Yeşilova	37°32'53"N/29°46'17"E	3/8/1996
36	Eğirdir lake at Bedre DSİ station	37°56'26"N/30°46'23"E	4/8/1996
37	Kayaağzı, source	38°08'14"N/30°46'15"E	4/8/1996
38	channel fed by Senırkent river	38°10'08"N/30°43'25"E	4/8/1996
39	Gençali, channel to Eğirdir lake	38°12'40"N/30°45'14"E	4/8/1996
40	Taşkesti, in lake Eğirdir	38°15'07"N/30°47'00"E	4/8/1996
41	Karaot fishing ground	38°07'58"N/30°54'33"E	4/8/1996
42	Köprüçay – Aksu Kanalı	37°50'36"N/30°53'19"E	4/8/1996
43	Beyşehir, market		5/8/1996
44	Üstünler	37°37'09"N/31°35'19"E	5/8/1996
45	Soğuksu köprüsü	37°32'25"N/31°21'43"E	5/8/1996
46	Beyşehir lake, near well	37°35'56"N/31°26'43"E	5/8/1996
47	Beyşehir lake, close to Gedikli	37°50'29"N/31°21'58"E	5/8/1996
48	Eğirdir lake, near Eğirdir	37°50'46"N/30°53'12"E	7/8/1996
49	Eğirdir lake, near outlet port at institute	37°50'35"N/30°51'50"E	7/8/1996
50	Eğirdir lake, near outlet port at Eğirdir	37°52'29"N/30°51'33"E	7/8/1996
51	Pınarbaşı (Burdur)	37°27'12"N/30°03'25"E	9/8/1996
52	Pınarbaşı, irrigation channel	37°27'22"N/30°01'33"E	9/8/1996
53	Karataş lake, Bahçeözü	37°23'29"N/29°57'45"E	9/8/1996
54	channel near Gölhisar	37°07'24"N/29°36'24"E	9/8/1996
55	Gölhisar, bay	37°07'40"N/29°36'03"E	9/8/1996
56	river to Gölhisar lake	37°09'00"N/29°36'44"E	9/8/1996
57	Saritaş channel near Söğüt	37°03'21"N/29°47'18"E	9/8/1996
58	Kırkpınar, main spring	37°08'45"N/29°54'24"E	9/8/1996
59	Kırkpınar, channel	37°08'23"N/29°55'38"E	9/8/1996
60	Eğirdir lake, east side		4/8/1996

Table 1: The 1996 sampling localities and their coordinates.

Locality	Anguilla anguilla	Oncorhynchus mykiss	Capoeta antalyensis	Carassius carassius	Alburnus chalcoides	Alburnus sp.	Cyprinus carpio	Gobio gobio microlepidotus	Leuciscus borysthenicus	Leuciscus lepidus	Pseudophoxinus anatolicus	Pseudophoxinus antalyae	Pseudophoxinus maendri	Pseudophoxinus sp.	Pseudorasbora parva	Tinca tinca	Vimba vimba	Chondrostoma sp.	Cobitis simplicispinna	Cobitis sp.	Barbatula angorae	Barbatula lendli	Clarias gariepinus	Aphanius anatoliae anatoliae	A. anatoliae sureyanus	Aphanius mento	Gambusia affinis	Mugil cephalus	Mugil auratus	Sander lucioperca	Tilapiini	Salarias fluviatilis	Knipowitschia caucasica	Gobiidae indet.
Aksu basin																																		
9/ Kundu Köyü, Aksu mouth	-	-	-	-	-	-	-	-	-	-	-	-	-	-	-	x	-	-	-	-	-	-	-	-	-	-	-	x	x	-	-	-	-	x
10/ Aksu köprüsü (Aksu bay)	-	-	x	-	-	-	-	-	-	-	-	-	-	-	-	x	-	-	-	-	-	-	-	-	-	-	-	x	x	x	-	-	x	-
11/ Güloluk, DSİ regulator	x	-	x	-	-	x	-	-	-	-	x	-	-	x	-	x	-	-	-	-	x	-	-	-	-	-	x	-	x	-	-	-	x	-
12/ Tehnelli river	x	-	x	-	-	-	-	-	-	-	-	-	-	-	-	x	-	-	-	-	-	-	-	-	-	-	-	-	-	x	-	-	-	-
13/ Karaöz, Aksu river	-	-	x	-	-	-	-	-	-	-	x	-	x	-	-	-	-	-	-	-	x	-	-	-	-	-	x	-	-	-	-	-	-	-
14/ south of Karacaören II dam, near end pipeline	x	-	x	-	-	-	-	-	-	-	-	-	-	-	-	x	-	-	-	-	x	-	-	-	-	-	x	-	-	-	-	-	-	-
15/ Kargı (Karacaören I)	-	-	x	-	-	-	-	-	-	-	-	-	-	-	x	x	-	-	-	-	-	-	-	-	-	-	-	-	-	-	-	-	-	-
16/ Karacaören I	-	-	-	-	-	x	-	-	-	-	-	-	-	-	-	x	-	-	-	-	-	-	-	-	-	-	-	-	-	x	-	-	-	-
19/ Asağı Gökdere, Aksu river	x	-	x	-	-	-	-	-	-	-	-	-	-	-	-	-	-	-	-	-	x	-	-	-	-	-	-	-	-	-	-	-	-	-
21-23/ Ağlasun river	-	x	-	-	-	-	-	-	-	-	-	-	-	-	-	-	-	-	-	-	-	-	-	-	-	-	-	-	-	-	-	-	-	-
24/ Yazılı canyon, Göksu river	x	x	x	-	-	-	-	-	-	-	-	-	-	-	-	-	-	-	-	-	-	-	-	-	-	-	-	-	-	-	-	-	-	-
25/ Çandır, outlet of Göksu in Karacaören	-	-	-	-	-	x	-	-	-	-	-	-	-	-	-	-	-	-	-	-	-	-	-	-	-	-	-	-	-	-	-	-	-	-
26/ Çandır, Göksu river near trout farm	-	x	x	-	-	-	-	-	-	-	-	-	-	-	-	-	-	-	-	-	-	-	-	-	-	-	-	-	-	-	-	-	-	-
Eğirdir and Kovada area																																		
27/ Kovada lake, southern outlet to Aksu	-	-	-	-	-	x	-	-	-	-	-	-	-	-	-	-	-	-	-	-	-	-	-	-	-	-	x	-	-	x	-	-	-	-
28/ Yukarı Gökdere köprüsü (Kovada canal)	-	-	-	-	-	x	-	-	-	-	-	-	-	-	-	-	-	x	-	-	-	-	-	x	-	-	-	-	-	-	-	-	x	-
29/ Eğirdir, Kovada canal	-	-	-	-	-	-	-	-	-	-	-	-	-	-	-	-	-	x	-	-	-	-	-	x	-	-	-	-	-	-	-	-	x	-
36/ Eğirdir lake at Bedre DSİ station	-	-	-	-	-	-	-	-	-	-	-	-	-	-	-	-	-	-	-	-	-	-	-	x	-	-	-	-	-	-	-	-	-	-
37/ Kayaağzı, source	-	-	-	-	-	-	-	-	-	-	-	-	-	-	-	-	-	-	-	-	-	-	-	x	-	-	-	-	-	-	-	-	-	-
39/ Gençali, channel to Eğirdir lake	-	-	-	-	-	-	-	-	-	-	-	-	-	-	-	-	-	-	-	-	-	-	-	x	-	-	-	-	-	-	-	-	x	-
40/ Taşkesti, in lake Eğirdir	-	-	-	-	-	-	-	-	-	-	-	-	-	-	-	-	-	-	-	-	-	-	-	x	-	-	-	-	-	-	-	-	x	-
41/ Karaot fishing ground	-	-	-	-	-	-	-	-	-	-	x	-	-	-	-	-	-	x	-	-	x	-	-	x	-	-	-	-	-	-	-	-	x	-
42/ Köprüçay – Aksu canal	-	-	-	-	-	-	-	-	-	-	-	-	-	-	-	-	-	-	-	-	-	-	-	-	-	-	-	-	-	-	-	-	x	-
48/ Eğirdir lake, near Eğirdir	-	-	-	-	-	-	-	-	-	-	-	-	-	-	-	-	-	x	-	-	-	-	-	-	-	-	-	-	-	-	-	-	-	-
60/ Eğirdir lake, east side	-	-	-	-	-	x	-	-	-	-	-	-	-	-	-	-	-	-	-	-	-	-	-	-	-	-	-	-	-	-	-	-	-	-
Beyşehir area																																		
43/ Beyşehir, market	-	-	x	-	x	-	x	-	x	-	-	-	-	-	-	x	-	-	-	-	-	-	-	-	-	-	-	-	-	x	-	-	-	-
45/ Soğuksu köprüsü	-	-	-	-	-	-	x	-	x	-	-	-	-	x	-	-	-	-	-	-	x	-	-	x	-	-	-	-	-	-	-	-	-	-
46/ Beyşehir lake, near well	-	-	-	-	-	-	-	-	-	-	-	-	-	-	-	-	-	-	-	-	-	-	-	x	-	-	-	-	-	-	-	-	-	-
47/ Beyşehir lake, close to Gedikli	-	-	-	-	-	-	-	-	-	-	-	-	-	-	-	-	-	-	-	-	-	-	-	x	-	-	-	-	-	-	-	-	-	-
Düden basin																																		
1/ Kırkgöz, pools and channels	-	-	-	-	-	-	-	-	-	-	-	-	-	-	-	-	-	-	-	-	-	-	-	-	-	-	x	x	-	-	-	-	-	-
2/ Kırkgöz, lakelet near source	-	-	-	-	-	-	-	-	-	-	x	-	-	-	-	-	-	-	-	-	-	-	-	-	-	-	x	x	-	-	-	-	-	-
3-5/ Kırkgöz, channel area	-	-	-	-	-	-	-	-	-	-	x	-	-	-	-	-	-	-	-	-	-	-	-	-	-	-	x	-	-	-	-	-	-	-
6/ Topçular, channel connected to Düden	-	-	-	-	-	-	-	-	-	-	x	-	-	-	-	-	-	-	-	-	-	-	-	-	-	-	x	-	-	-	-	-	-	-
7/ Düden, bridge	-	-	-	-	-	-	-	-	-	-	x	-	-	-	-	-	-	-	-	-	-	-	-	-	-	-	x	x	-	-	-	-	-	-
8/ channel parallel with Düden	-	-	-	-	-	-	-	-	-	-	x	-	-	-	-	-	-	-	-	-	-	-	-	-	-	-	-	-	-	-	-	-	-	-
Burdur																																		
30/ Burdur lake between Çendik and Burdur	-	-	-	-	-	-	-	-	-	-	-	-	-	-	-	-	-	-	-	-	-	-	-	-	x	-	-	-	-	-	-	-	-	-
32/ Düger, behind mosque	-	-	-	-	-	-	-	-	-	-	x	-	-	-	-	-	-	-	x	-	-	-	-	-	x	-	-	-	-	-	-	-	-	-
33/ Düger, near source (Pınargözü)	-	-	-	-	-	-	-	-	-	-	x	-	-	-	-	-	-	-	x	x	x	-	-	-	x	-	-	-	-	-	-	-	-	-
51/ Pınarbaşı (Burdur)	-	-	-	-	-	-	-	-	-	-	-	-	-	-	-	-	-	-	-	-	-	-	-	-	-	-	-	-	-	-	x	-	-	-
52/ Pınarbaşı, irrigation channel	-	-	-	-	-	-	-	-	-	-	-	-	-	-	-	-	-	-	x	-	x	x	-	-	x	-	-	-	-	-	-	-	-	-
other basins																																		
20/ Gölcük lake	-	-	-	x	-	x	-	-	-	-	-	-	-	-	-	-	-	-	-	-	-	-	-	-	-	-	x	-	-	-	-	-	-	-
34/ Salda lake	-	-	-	-	-	-	-	-	-	-	x	-	-	x	-	x	-	x	-	-	x	-	-	-	-	-	-	-	-	-	-	-	-	-
35/ Karapınar-Yeşilova	-	-	-	-	-	-	-	-	-	-	x	-	-	-	-	-	-	-	-	-	-	-	-	-	-	-	-	-	-	-	-	-	-	-
53/ Karataş lake, Bahçeözü	-	-	-	-	x	x	-	-	-	-	-	-	-	-	-	-	-	-	-	-	-	-	-	-	-	-	x	-	-	x	-	-	-	-
54/ channel near Gölhisar	-	-	-	-	-	-	-	-	-	-	-	-	-	-	-	-	-	-	-	-	-	-	-	-	-	-	x	-	-	-	-	-	-	-
55/ Gölhisar, bay	-	-	-	-	-	-	-	x	-	-	-	-	-	-	-	-	-	-	-	-	-	-	-	-	-	-	x	-	-	-	-	-	-	-
56/ river to Gölhisar lake	-	-	-	-	-	-	-	x	-	-	-	-	-	-	-	-	-	-	-	-	-	-	-	-	-	-	-	-	-	-	-	-	-	-
59/ Kırkpınar, channel	-	-	-	-	-	-	-	-	-	-	-	-	-	-	-	-	-	-	x	-	x	x	-	-	x	-	-	-	-	-	-	-	-	-

Table 2: Fish species identified on each locality

	water width (m)	average velocity (m/s)	average discharge (m³/s)
September- November	15.25	0.47	1.5
December-February	20.58	0.75	6.4
March-May	41.33	1.28	20.9
June-August	10.5	0.46	1.6
Average pH	8.2		
Average conductivity	347µohmSiemens		
Average water hardness (French scale)	18.5F		

Table 3: Hydrological parameters of the Aksu river at Asağı Gökdere measured in 1996.

	Eğirdir	Kundu
L.Lat.	50-58	40-55
L.trans.	9-10/4-5	9-11/5
D	III-9	III-8-9
A	III-16-19	II-III-17-19
P	I-13-15	I-15-17
operculum rays	16-18	15-18
pharyngeal teeth	5-5	5-5

Table 4a: Comparison of the meristic characters of *Vimba vimba* from Eğirdir lake and from the Aksu river at Kundu.

Eğirdir Lake				
	n	average (x± sx)	sd	min-max
standard length/total length	5	3.63±0.06	0.14	3.46-3.83
standard length/head length	5	4.13±0.02	0.04	4.09-4.18
total length/head length	5	1.17±0.03	0.08	1.12-1.28
head length/eye diameter	5	4.50±0.16	0.37	4.22-5.11
head length/nose length	5	3.00±0.09	0.2	2.87-3.28
head length/caudal height	5	2.68±0.06	0.14	2.53-2.88
predorsal length/postdorsal length	5	1.33±0.04	0.09	1.24-1.42
preventral/prepectoral length	5	1.93±0.02	0.03	1.89-1.97
Kundu village (Aksu river)				
	n	average (x± sx)	sd	min-max
standard length/total length	7	3.81±0.09	0.24	3.55-4.06
standard length/head length	7	3.87±0.06	0.17	3.71-4.17
total length/head length	7	1.03±0.01	0.03	1.00-1.08
head length/eye diameter	7	4.31±0.15	0.39	3.71-4.87
head length/nose length	7	3.05±0.07	0.19	2.89-3.36
head length/caudal height	7	2.84±0.05	0.11	2.70-2.99
predorsal length/postdorsal length	7	1.33±0.04	0.11	1.13-1.42
preventral/prepectoral length	7	1.86±0.02	0.05	1.81-1.92

Table 4b: Comparison of the morphometric characters of *Vimba vimba* from Eğirdir lake and from the Aksu river at Kundu.

the artificial dam-lakes at Karacaören. These bodies of water meet the ecological requirements of carp, that is, slow running or stagnant water with abundant aquatic vegetation and a fine substrate. The species was also found in the southern outlet of the Kovada canal to the Kovada dam lake. With the information thus far available we are unable to establish how the carp reached the lakes. Introduction by man seems the most likely explanation for the Karacaören lakes, but for the Kovada lake a natural colonisation may have occurred from Eğirdir lake after the digging of the Kovada canal and the construction of the Kovada dam in 1955. Attempts have been made at least since the late 1980s to increase production by introducing domestic carp. Both the scaled morph and the mirror carp were introduced, but no specimens were seen of the latter. For the Kovada lake, introduction of mirror carp would have happened from 1984 onwards, but, according to the interviews made, these have never been abundant. According to information from the Kepez fishery station (Dr. Yılmaz Emre personal communication) introduction of mirror and scaled carp occurred mainly from 1988 onward in small dam-lakes used for irrigation along the Aksu. All the aforementioned information strongly suggests that the occurrence of carp in the Aksu basin is a recent phenomenon. No trace whatsoever has been found of the wild rheophilic form. The two rivers near Sagalassos (Ağlasun Çayı and Isparta Çayı) with their swift running water, low nutrient content and poor aquatic vegetation can certainly be excluded as possible habitats for this species. The localities closest to the site where carp are found today are lake Gölcük and lakes Eğirdir and Beyşehir. The species is considered indigenous to these last two lakes although interbreeding with the domestic form seems to have occurred judging from the rather increased body depth of the fish. For lake Gölcük we have some doubts for the moment concerning the carp's status. As we have said above, Ladiges (1960) lists *Cyprinus carpio* from lake Gölcük, but Geldiay and Balık (1996: 243) consider that this lake is outside the natural distribution area of the wild carp. This is also suggested by the article of Kosswig and Sözer (1945) who mention only *Aphanius anatoliae splendens* and *Hemigrammocapoeta kemali*. If carp were present in lake Gölcük in classical times, this body of water would have been the nearest locality where they could be caught and transported to Sagalassos. Given the proximity to the site, i.e. entailing a walk of a mere 5 to 6 hours, it would not have been necessary to preserve the fish to assure fresh delivery. The carp is a very resistant species which can survive primitive conditions of transport (Balon 1974). The origin of the carp found at Sagalassos needs to be further elucidated. A comparison of the growth rate of the Sagalassos carp to those of present-day specimens from the different lakes and rivers north of Sagalassos would probably not afford useful data. It would be wrong to assume that the growth rates of present-day carp in the several basins would be comparable to those in the past. Growth rate depends on temperature, food availability, population density and fishing pressure. The major drawbacks are probably that modern fishing pressure is higher than in the past and, more importantly, that species interactions have dramatically altered as a result of the introduction of pike-perch (*Sander lucioperca*). As a possible strategy for the future we suggest a physico-chemical analysis of the carp bones from Sagalassos and a comparison of these data with those obtained on water samples and modern carp skeletons from the different bodies of water. This might give us an indication of the possible role of lake Gölcük in former carp fishing. Since Gölcük is the only volcanic lake in the area its water must have a characteristic chemical composition which is also likely to be reflected in the skeleton of its fish.

According to the distribution maps published by Maitland (1978: 108) and Banarescu et al. (1971), pike (*Esox lucius*) only occur in the northernmost part of Turkey. However, the species had also been reported previously from more southerly localities. It was found in lakes Eber and Akşehir, in the sources of the Büyük Menderes near Işıklı, and in small rivers flowing into the Seyhan river (Kosswig 1969), localities which were also mentioned by Geldiay and Balık (1996: 229). Because of these southerly finds it seemed worth checking whether the present-day distribution extended even further to the south. It became clear, however, during our survey that the Ağlasun Çayı and Isparta Çayı are not suitable waters for pike and that, moreover, the species is totally lacking from the rest of the Aksu basin. It must be accepted that this species was imported to Sagalassos from the north. During the next survey we will attempt to find the locality closest to Sagalassos. The ancient name for the Aksu, and perhaps even the Ağlasun Çayı, was 'Kestros' according to local coinage from Sagalassos (see above) and this name has been linked in the literature to two fish species. It has been suggested that 'Kestros' may have been derived from κέστρα, perhaps meaning pike (Tischler 1977: 78). κέστρα was, however, the Attic name for σφύραινα or σφῦρα which stands for spet, a long pike-like fish, sometimes mistaken for the pike proper (Thomson 1947: 108, 256-257). One of the Greek names for grey mullet is κεστρεύς which is also reminiscent of the ancient name of the Aksu. If the Aksu were indeed named after a fish, it is more likely that it would refer to grey mullet since this species is abundant in the relatively wide, estuarine part of the river.

Vimba vimba has been reported in the early 1960s from lakes and the lower reaches of rivers in northern Turkey and was, in addition, found in the Eğirdir lake (Geldiay and Kosswig 1949; Ladiges 1960; Akşıray 1961). More recent data indicate that the species is also present in the Aksu river and the Kovada lake (Balık 1980). Küçük and Ikiz

(1993) mention the species from the following localities in the Aksu basin: Aşağı Gökdere, Kargı Boğazı and Kundu Köyü. Also, during the 1996 survey, *Vimba vimba* was found in many localities along the Aksu. The presence of the species at these sites along the Aksu all date from the 1980s and 1990s and it should therefore be ascertained that their distribution is natural and not a result of recent human impact. Since 1955, the Kovada canal has connected the Eğirdir lake with lake Kovada which has an overflow to the Aksu. This canal may have allowed the original population of Eğirdir lake to expand to the south and to further colonise the lower reaches of the Aksu. The populations from Eğirdir lake and from the Aksu river currently differ in several striking criteria. The colour pattern as well as the number of scales in the lateral line and the number of anal and pectoral fin-rays show differences (Table 4). The divergent colours may possibly be seen as a result of the differences between a lacustrine and riverine environment, although it is not clear how quickly such adaptations would appear. The striking differences in the number of scales and fin-rays, on the contrary, are significant in regard to the time elapsed since the river and lake populations came into existence. The connection by the Kovada canal is only about 40 years old which is considered too short a period for the divergence observed in the scales and fin-rays. Populations of cyprinids such as *Barbus macrops* in the Central Sahara and in western Africa, which have been isolated from each other for at least 4000 years, differ only slightly in the scale counts (Lévêque 1989). Another argument also favours a natural, riverine *Vimba vimba* population in the Aksu basin of Turkey. The species was also found in the Köprü Çayı, a river east of the Aksu basin that was never connected to the Eğirdir lake (Küçük 1997). The foregoing arguments allow us to conclude that the natural distribution of *Vimba vimba* includes the Eğirdir lake as well as the Aksu (and Köprü), but is not yet clear from which source the Sagalassians obtained their supply of this fish.

The archaeological material of *Leuciscus* sp. that is so far available from Sagalassos is not enough to permit a species identification. The genus was not encountered during our survey in the Aksu basin and its occurrence in that river is not attested by the available literature (Ladiges 1960; Geldiay and Balık 1996: 280-287). From lake Beyşehir *Leuciscus lepidus* was collected which is one of the few species that have not yet disappeared because of the introduction of pike-perch, although the capture of large specimens has become a rare event. *Leuciscus borysthenicus* was found during the survey in lakes Karataş and Gölhisar. The distribution of this species extends further west where it occurs amongst others in the Büyük Menderes (Geldiay and Balık 1996: 284-285). It is also found in the northeastern part of Turkey. The locality closest to Sagalassos where *Leuciscus cephalus* has been reported is lake Gölhisar, near the ancient site of Cibyra. It occurs also in the Büyük Menderes (the ancient Maeander which has its main source near Dinar (Apamea) ca. 50 km northwest of Sagalassos), the Gediz (Hermos river) and the Küçük Menderes or Kaystros river (Geldiay and Balık 1996: 282).

The bream *Abramis brama* is usually considered as essentially a European species with only a restricted distribution in the northwestern part of Turkey in the region around the Sea of Marmara and in the rivers flowing into the eastern part of the Black Sea (Ladiges 1960; Maitland 1978: 162). It has not been encountered during our survey or previous fieldwork in the Aksu basin (Küçük and Ikiz 1993) and it was never mentioned from Lakes Gölcük or Eğirdir. Bream was recently reported from Lake Beyşehir (Gersar 1995). It was not mentioned from that lake, however, in previous literature (Ladiges 1960; Geldiay and Balık 1996: 247). For the moment we are inclined to consider this record as a misidentification since we were unable to find bream and since our local informants around lake Beyşehir did not know this species either. The possibility may not be ruled out, however, that at some stage this species was introduced as an experiment. The tench (*Tinca tinca*) and Crucian carp (*Carassius carassius*) are other species that were recently introduced in attempt to raise the lake's fish production again after the fatal introduction of pike-perch. More data are needed to elucidate further the status of bream in Lake Beyşehir. Records of the DSİ (Devlet Su İşleri) will be checked for possible documentation on the introduction of the species and additional interviews with older fishermen are planned for the next campaign. The information available thus far seems to indicate that *Abramis brama* must have been imported to Sagalassos from a great distance certainly necessitating some form of curing of the fish prior to transport. Bream is a rather fatty species which is today commonly smoked in Europe.

Distribution maps indicate *Silurus glanis* over almost the entire Turkish territory (Maitland 1978: 180; Geldiay and Balık 1996: 400). It is unlikely, however, that this species has ever occurred in the upper reaches of rivers. The European catfish prefers large bodies of water (rivers and lakes) but seems to avoid shallow, swift running rivers. The need of the larger catfish for deep water during spawning was mentioned by Aristotle (*H.A.* 568 or 22). A reconstruction of the precise natural distribution is hampered by the fact that the species is sensitive to habitat destruction and to overfishing because of its slow reproduction. *Silurus glanis* does not occur in the Aksu today and it is rather unlikely that the river was ever inhabited by this species. The Aksu river is shallow and lacks the deep troughs which these fish seek during the day. The catfish is presently found to the north and the west of Sagalassos in large streams such as the Sakarya (Sangarios river) and the Büyük Menderes

(Maeander river). The presence of this species at the site indicates that it must have been imported from a considerable distance. During the Roman period, the Sangarios was famous for its fish (Pliny, *Naturalis Historiae* XXXIX, 18,8). Sagalassos was connected over Apamea (Dinar) with the Maeander valley, and from there also with Synnada and Dokimeion from where the Sangarios river system in Galatia could be reached. Trade relations with western and central Anatolia are already documented in two ways. Firstly, the city imported marble from those areas, i.e. from the quarries and workshops of Dokimeion and Aphrodisias (Moens *et al.* 1997). Secondly, the locally produced Sagalassos red slip ware was exported both to the north and to the west (Poblome 1999).

It was argued in a previous article (Van Neer *et al.* 1997) that the *Clarias* remains found at Sagalassos must represent fish imported from the Nile or from the Syro-Palestinian area. This hypothesis is not contradicted by the present finds of *Clarias gariepinus* in the Aksu basin. We found this catfish at Güloluk just south of Catalar and it is mentioned in the literature from Kundu Köyü (Küçük and Ikiz 1993) and from the Tehnelli river, which is a branch of the Aksu (Balık 1988: 174). The catfish in the Aksu basin appear to have been introduced (Balık 1988 and personal communication) although it is not specified where the stock originated. In Turkey, the species occurs naturally in the Asi Nehri (Orontes river) and in the Ceyhan (Pyramos river) which was traditionally considered the western limit of the spread of this African fish in the Near East (Kosswig 1969). Balık (1988) reports, however, that he found the species also in Silifke (ancient Seleukeia on the Kalykadnos).

5. CONCLUSIONS

The survey, that was undertaken for a better documentation of the geographical distribution of the freshwater fish fauna near and south of Sagalassos, showed that the Aksu river system is relatively poor in both number of species and number of fish. Except for the artificial canals and damlakes, rather low densities of fishes were observed which is probably related to the poor nutrient content of the water. Although the reconstruction of the original fish fauna is hampered by the effects of introductions, the building of dams, and the changing water regimes of rivers due to excessive pumping for irrigation, it is possible to make inferences about the former fishing grounds from which the Sagalassians were supplied. Our survey, and data from the literature also, demonstrate that, of all freshwater fish species thus far identified at Sagalassos, only *Vimba vimba* may possibly have come from the Aksu river. All the other species namely carp, bream, *Leuciscus* sp., pike and European catfish seem to have been imported from localities north or west of the site. Further fieldwork will be undertaken to reconstruct the distribution of these fish. Establishing the precise origin of the carp, which was the most frequently consumed fish at Sagalassos, will be a priority. For the other species, it is clear already at this stage of the research that their origin must be located much farther to the north or the west and this in spite of the fact that the archaeological data indicate that commercial relationships were directed more intensely to the regions south of Sagalassos.

As we have said, only *Vimba vimba* provides possible evidence of fish derived from the Aksu, although additional archaeozoological material may provide evidence for the import of fish from that basin. The Aksu river holds good food fish such as the *Capoeta* species (maximum size 40 cm). The original fauna of both Lake Beyşehir and Lake Eğirdir included several important food fish in the recent past, some of which were endemic and, therefore, possible ideal indicators of former trade. This is the case for *Alburnus akili* typical of Lake Beyşehir and for *Pseudophoxinus handlirschi* found exclusively in Lake Eğirdir. *Capoeta pestai* is only found in the latter two lakes. All these fish belong to the Cyprinidae which are the best represented fish family at Sagalassos. The identification of cyprinid species from archaeozoological material is, however, possible from a few diagnostic bones only. As more fish remains become available, the chances of finding additional species may increase and, thus, further elucidate past trade relationships.

6. ACKNOWLEDGEMENTS

This research is supported by the Belgian Programme on Interuniversity Poles of Attraction (IUAP 4/12) initiated by the Belgian State, Prime Minister's Office, Science Policy Programming. The text also presents the results of the Concerted Action of the Flemish Government (GOA 97/2) and the Fund for Scientific Research-Flanders (Belgium) (FWO) (G.2145.94). Fieldwork in summer 1996 was sponsored by the Fund of Scientific Research-Flanders (Belgium) (project G.0215.96). We also thank Prof. Dr. Aksoylar (Eğirdir) for his encouragement and for logistic support. Prof. Peter Miller (Bristol) kindly identified the gobies for us. Scientific responsibility is assumed by the authors.

7. REFERENCES

F. Akşıray (1961) About sudak (*Lucioperca sandra* Cuv. Val.) introduced into some of the lakes of Turkey, *General Fisheries Council for the Mediterranean. Proceedings and Technical Papers* 6: 335-343.

S. Balık (1980) *Güney Anadolu Bölgesi içsularında yaşayan tatlısu balıkların sistematik ve zoocoğrafik yönden araştırılması*, Doçentlik Tezi, Izmir.

S. Balık (1988) Türkiye'nin Akdeniz Bölgesi içsu balıkları üzerinde sistematik ve zoocoğrafik araştırmalar, *Doğa Tu Zooloji D.* 12/2:156-179.

E.K. Balon (1974) *Domestication of the carp Cyprinus carpio L* (*Royal Ontario Museum Life Sciences Miscellaneous Publication*) Toronto.

P. Banarescu, M. Blanc, J.L. Gaudet and J.C. Hureau (1971) *European Inland Water Fish. A Multilingual Catalogue*, London.

J. Boessneck and A. von den Driesch (1985) *Knochenfunde aus Zisternen in Pergamon*, München.

N.G. Bogutzkaya (1997) Contribution to the knowledge of leuciscine fishes of Asia Minor 2. An annotated check-list of leuciscine fishes (Leuciscinae, Cyprinidae) of Turkey with descriptions of a new species and two new subspecies, *Mitteilungen aus den Hamburgischen Zoologischen Museum und Institut* 94: 161-186.

K. Callebaut, W. Viaene, M. Waelkens, R. Ottenburgs and J. Naud (2000) Provenance and characterization of raw materials for lime mortars used at Sagalassos with special reference to the volcanic rocks, in M. Waelkens and L. Loots (eds) *Sagalassos V. Report on the Survey and Excavation Campaigns of 1996 and 1997* (*Acta Archaeologica Lovaniensia Monographiae* 11) Leuven University Press: 651-668.

R.N.B. Campbell (1992) Food of an introduced population of pikeperch, *Stizostedion lucioperca* L., in Lake Eğirdir, Turkey, *Aquaculture and Fisheries Management* 23: 71-85.

P. Degryse, R. Degeest, J. Poblome, W. Viaene, R. Ottenburgs, H. Kucha and M. Waelkens (2000) Mineralogy and geochemistry of Roman common wares produced at Sagalassos and their possible clay sources, in M. Waelkens and L. Loots (eds) *Sagalassos V. Report on the Survey and Excavation Campaigns of 1996 and 1997* (*Acta Archaeologica Lovaniensia Monographiae* 11) Leuven University Press: 709-722.

Ü. Erdemli (1982) Beyşehir gölü balıkları, *Bulletin of Selçuk University, Faculty of Sciences* 2 (Biology): 131-142.

T.W. Gallant (1985) *A Fisherman's Tale: an Analysis of the Potential Productivity of Fishing in the Ancient World* (*Miscellanea Graeca* 7) Gent.

R. Geldiay and C. Kosswig (1949) *Eğridir gölü balıkları* (Istanbul Üniv. Fen Fak. Dergisi 3).

R. Geldiay and S. Balık (1996) *Türkiye tatlısu balıkları* (*Ege Üniversitesi Basımevı*) Bornova, Izmir.

Gersar (1995) *Analysis of the Hydrological Balance of the Lakes in the Isparta Region* (*Ministry of Agriculture and Rural Affairs, Republic of Turkey/Ministère de l'Agriculture et de la Pêche, République Française*).

C. Kosswig and F. Sözer (1945) Nouveaux Cyprinodontidae de l'Anatolie centrale, *Revue de la Faculté des Sciences de l'Université d'Istanbul* 10/2: 77-83.

C. Kosswig (1954) Türkiye tatlısu balıkları zoocoğrafyası, *Istanbul Üniversitesi Fakültesi Hidrobiologi Araştırma Enstitüsü Yayınlarından A* 2/1: 3-20.

C. Kosswig (1969) New contributions to the zoogeography of fresh water fish of Asia Minor, based on collections made between 1964-1967, *Israel Journal of Zoology* 18: 249-254.

M. Kottelat (1997) *European Freshwater Fishes*, Slovak Academic Press.

F. Küçük (1997) *Antalya körfezine Dökülen Akarsuların Balık Faunası ve Bazi Ekologik Parametreleri üzerine Bir Araştırma SDÜ* (*Fen Bilimleri Enstitüsü Dok. Tezi* 1285) Isparta.

F. Küçük and R. Ikiz (1993) Aksu Çayı ve Kollarında (Antalya) bulunan balık türlerinin saptaması, *Turkish Journal of Zoology* 17: 427-443.

W. Ladiges (1960) Süßwasserfische der Türkei 1. Teil Cyprinidae, *Mitteilungen des Hamburgischen Zoologisches Museum und Institut* 58: 105-150.

R. Laurence (1994) *Roman Pompeii. Space and Society*, London – New York.

E. Levante (1994) *Sylloge Nummorum Graecorum. France 3. Cabinet des médailles. Pamphylie – Pisidie – Lycaonie – Galatie*, Zurich.

C. Lévêque (1989) Remarques taxinomiques sur quelques petits *Barbus* (Pisces, Cyprinidae) d'Afrique de l'ouest (première partie), *Cybium* 13: 165-180.

L. Loots, M. Waelkens and F. Depuydt (2000) The city fortifications of Sagalassos from the Hellenistic to the late Roman period, in M. Waelkens and L. Loots (eds) *Sagalassos V. Report on the Survey and Excavation Campaigns of 1996 and 1997* (*Acta Archaeologica Lovaniensia Monographiae* 11) Leuven University Press: 595-634.

P.S. Maitland (1978) *Elseviers gids van de zoetwatervissen*, Amsterdam-Brussel.

S. Mitchell (1976) Requisitioned transport in the Roman empire, *Journal of Roman Studies* 66: 106-131.

S. Mitchell (1993) *Anatolia. Land, Men, and Gods in Asia Minor. Volume I. The Celts in Anatolia and the Impact of Roman Rule*, Oxford.

L. Moens, P. De Paepe and M. Waelkens (1997) An archaeometric study of the provenance of white marble sculptures from an Augustan Heroon and a middle Antonine nymphaeum at Sagalassos (Southwest Turkey), in: M. Waelkens and J. Poblome (eds) *Sagalassos IV. Report on the Survey and Excavation Campaigns of 1994 and 1995* (*Acta Archaeologica Lovaniensia Monographiae* 9) Leuven University Press: 367-384.

J. Poblome (1999) *Sagalassos Red Slip Ware. Typology and Chronology* (*Studies in Eastern Mediterranean Archaeology* 2) Brepols publishers.

M. Sartre (1995) *L'Asie Mineure et l'Anatolie d'Alexandre à Dioclétien; IVe siècle av. J.-C./IIIe siècle ap. J.-C.*, Paris.

S. Scheers (1993a) Catalogue of the coins found during the years 1990 and 1991, in: M. Waelkens (ed.) *Sagalassos I. First General Report on the Survey (1986-1989) and Excavations (1990-1991)* (*Acta Archaeologica Lovaniensia Monographiae* 5) Leuven University Press: 197- 205.

S. Scheers (1993b) Catalogue of the coins found in 1992, in: M. Waelkens and J. Poblome (eds) *Sagalassos II. Report on the Third Excavation Campaign of 1992* (*Acta Archaeologica Lovaniensia Monographiae* 6) Leuven University Press: 249-260.

S. Scheers (1995) Catalogue of the coins found in 1993, in: M. Waelkens and J. Poblome (eds) *Sagalassos III. Report on the Fourth Excavation Campaign of 1993* (*Acta Archaeologica Lovaniensia Monographiae* 7) Leuven University Press: 307-317.

J. Tischler (1977) *Kleinasiatische Hydronomie. Semantische und morphologische Analyse der griechischen Gewässernamen*, Wiesbaden.

D'A.W. Thompson (1947) *A Glossary of Greek Fishes*, London.

W. Van Neer, B. De Cupere and M. Waelkens (1997) Remains of local and imported fish at the ancient site of Sagalassos (Burdur prov., Turkey), in: M. Waelkens and J. Poblome (eds) *Sagalassos IV. Report on the Survey and Excavation Campaigns of 1994 and 1995* (*Acta Archaeologica Lovaniensia Monographiae* 9) Leuven University Press: 571-586.

W. Van Neer, R.H. Wildekamp, F. Küçük, M. Ünlüsayın (1999) First inland records of the Euryhaline Goby *Knipowitschia Caucasica* from lakes in Anatolia. *Journal of fish biology* 54: 1334-1337.

W. Viaene, M. Waelkens, R. Ottenburgs and K. Callebaut (1997) An archaeometric study of mortars used at Sagalassos, in: M. Waelkens and J. Poblome (ed.) *Sagalassos IV. Report on the Survey and Excavation Campaigns of 1994 and 1995* (*Acta Archaeologica Lovaniensia Monographiae* 9) Leuven University Press: 405-422.

M. Waelkens, E. Paulissen, H. Vanhaverbeke, I. Öztürk, B. De Cupere, H.A. Ekinci, P.M. Vermeersch, J. Poblome and R. Degeest (1997). The 1994 and 1995 surveys on the territory of Sagalassos, in: M. Waelkens and J. Poblome (eds) *Sagalassos IV. Report on the Survey and Excavation Campaigns of 1994 and 1995* (*Acta Archaeologica Lovaniensia Monographiae* 9) Leuven University Press: 11-102.

M. Waelkens and the Sagalassos-team (1997) Interdisciplinarity in classical archaeology. A case study: the Sagalassos Archaeological Research Project (southwest Turkey), in: M. Waelkens and J. Poblome (eds) *Sagalassos IV. Report on the Survey and Excavation Campaigns of 1994 and 1995* (*Acta Archaeologica Lovaniensia Monographiae* 9) Leuven University Press: 225-252.

M. Waelkens, E. Paulissen, M. Vermoere, P. Degryse, D. Celis, K. Schroyen, B. De Cupere, I. Librecht, K. Nackaerts, H. Vanhaverbeke, W. Viaene, Ph. Muchez, R. Ottenburgs, J. Deckers, W. Van Neer, E. Smets, G. Govers, G. Verstraeten, A. Steegen and K. Cauwenberghs (2000). Man and environment in the territory of Sagalassos, a classical city in SW Turkey, *Quarternary Science Reviews,* 18 (4-5):697-709.

M. Waelkens und das Sagalassos-Team (2000) Sagalassos und sein Territorium. Eine interdisziplinäre Methodologie zur historischen Geographie einer kleinasiatischen Metropole, in K. Belke, F. Hild, J. Koder and P. Soustal (eds) *Byzans als Raum. Zu Methoden und Inhalten der historischen Geographie des östlichen Mittelmeerraumes, Veröffenslichungen der Kommission für die Tabula Imperii Byzantini,* Wien, 261-288.

R.H. Wildekamp and K. Valkenburg (1994) Notizen über Zahnkarpfen-Lebensräume in Anatolien, *Die Aquarien und Terrarien Zeitschrift* 47/7: 447-453.

R.H. Wildekamp, F. Küçük, M. Ünlüsayın and W. Van Neer (2000) The genus *Aphanius* Nardo 1827 (Pisces: Cyprinodontidae) and its species in Turkey, with remarks on systematics, *Turkish Journal of Zoology* 23: 23-44.

R.H. Wildekamp, W. Van Neer, F. Küçük and M. Ünlüsayin (1997) First record of the eastern Asiatic gobionid fish *Pseudorasbora parva* from the Asiatic part of Turkey, *Journal of Fish Biology* 51: 858-861.

MODERN SHEEP AND GOAT HERDING NEAR SAGALASSOS AND ITS RELEVANCE TO THE RECONSTRUCTION OF PASTORAL PRACTICES IN ROMAN TIMES

Ingrid BEULS[1], Bea DE CUPERE[1], Marleen VERMOERE[2], Leo VANHECKE[3],
Hugues DOUTRELEPONT[1], Luc VRYDAGHS[1], Ireen LIBRECHT[4] and Marc WAELKENS[5]

1 - Royal Museum of Central Africa, Leuvensesteenweg 13, B-3080 Tervuren, Belgium
2 - Laboratory of Plant Systematics, KULeuven, Kardinaal Mercierlaan 92, B-3001 Heverlee, Belgium
3 - National Garden of Belgium, Domein van Bouchout, 1860 Meise, Belgium
4 - Geomorphology and Regional Geography, KULeuven, Redingenstraat 16, B-3000 Leuven, Belgium
5 - Department of Archaeology, KULeuven, Blijde Inkomststraat 21, B-3000 Leuven, Belgium

1. INTRODUCTION

Since 1991, a year after the start of excavations at Sagalassos, more than 200,000 faunal remains have been studied. This material, dating from the first century BC to the seventh century AD, has yielded information on the historical subsistence patterns, the animal husbandry practices, the former environment, the bone-working industry and possible trade-routes (De Cupere 1993; De Cupere et al. 1993; Degeest et al. 1993; Van Neer and De Cupere 1993; De Cupere et al. 1995; Van Neer et al. 1997; De Cupere and Waelkens 1998). The species composition of the excavated faunal assemblages indicate that wild animals were of minor importance in the food provisioning of Sagalassos. Subsistence was mainly based on domestic species (cattle, sheep, goats, pigs and chickens), the relative importance of which changed through time. During the first and last centuries of the period under consideration (first century BC to seventh century AD) sheep and goats were more commonly slaughtered. During the intermediate period of greater stability and prosperity of the city, beef consumption increased (De Cupere and Waelkens 1998). However, since meat formed only a small proportion of the diet of most people in Roman antiquity, this increase in beef consumption was most probably mainly a result of expanding farming activities wherein more cattle were needed as draught animals for ploughing and transport (for example, during the harvest season). In fact, ovicaprines, especially sheep, and people compete in a sense for the same resources. The number of sheep thus could only be increased if the extent of cereal agriculture were reduced, since sheep farming was an extensive activity (Jongman 1988: 161). At Sagalassos, the relative importance of ovicaprines, expressed as a percentage of the number of domestic mammal remains, ranges from 20 to 58 % depending on the period considered. The sheep/goat ratio varies between 0.11 and 0.74.

Historical sources (White 1970; Toynbee 1973; Frayn 1979; Frayn 1984; Whittaker 1988; Jongman 1988: 159-161) mention the importance of sheep and goats as an economic asset in Greece and Italy during the Hellenistic and Roman periods. It is generally assumed that in antiquity sheep were bred mainly for wool used for the manufacturing of, among other things, clothes and blankets. At Sagalassos a local inscription notes the activity of a corporation of textile dyers during the second half of the second century AD or shortly after (Lanckoronski 1892: 225 no. 195; Devijver 1996: 117-119; Waelkens et al. 1999) indicating the importance of sheep during that period. However, according to a study carried out in 1947-1950 in Pisidia and Pamphylia, wool production was then only a secondary activity. In antiquity, sheep would mainly have been kept for meat and milk production (de Planhol 1958: 163). Other sources also mention milk, processed further into cheese or yoghurt, and meat as being the main products derived from sheep and goats in antiquity (Zeuner 1963; White 1970; Toynbee 1973; Frayn 1979; Frayn 1984; Signe and Skydsgaard 1992). Other less important products were the skin and hair (Zeuner 1963; White 1970; Toynbee 1973; Signe and Skydsgaard 1992). Ovicaprine manure was also used. As White (1970) noted, the main source of manure available to a Roman farmer was the stall-fed sheep and cattle.

Their manure was used fresh to fertilise the meadows or was allowed to rot for use as a fertiliser for cereal crops. Besides the gathering of manure from pens, direct fertilising occurred when ovicaprines were allowed to graze on the fields. This might happen in winter when extra food such as roots and silage were supplied, or in spring and summer when the animals grazed between the growing crops, feeding on their side-shoots, or grazed on the stubble left after harvesting (White 1970). Although these practices are documented for Roman farmers in Italy only, it is likely that, insofar as they are not a common Mediterranean practice, some of the Roman agricultural techniques were also imported into Asia Minor through Romanization and possibly into the territory of Sagalassos (Ramsay and Anderson 1941; Levick 1967; Mitchell 1995). In fact, Sagalassos was surrounded by several Roman colonies (Antioch ad Pisidiam, Cremna, Conana, Parlais, Olbasa) and had a common boundary with one (Cremna). The number of colonists established by Augustus in these foundations is estimated at ca. 8500 without counting their families. Many of them came from Northern Italy, Cisalpine Gaul and Campania (Sartre 1995: 211) and thus could have brought with them western farming or herding practices.

Given the importance of ovicaprines at Sagalassos (De Cupere and Waelkens 1998), a more detailed study of their former use and management was started. Herds of ovicaprines are still a common feature in the landscape around the small city of Ağlasun and the ruins of Sagalassos. Modern material, as a point of reference for the archaeological remains, can thus easily be obtained.

In this article, possible methods of reconstructing ancient subsistence and live-stock management practices will be discussed. The results of a preliminary study on present-day traditional herding of sheep and goats, conducted in June 1996, are presented.

2. RECONSTRUCTING ANCIENT PASTORAL HUSBANDRY PRACTICES

2.1. Age at death and season of slaughtering

Information on ancient subsistence and the use of animal resources can be obtained through the establishment of slaughtering ages and the season of death of the animals. In the archaeozoological work thus far carried out at Sagalassos, only the relative age at death of ovicaprines could be determined. These ages were established by the degree of tooth wear in the excavated lower jaws, using the method described by Grant (1982). This method, however, yielded little information on seasonal slaughtering patterns, probably because of the relatively old age of most individuals (De Cupere 1993; Van Neer and De Cupere 1993; De Cupere and Waelkens 1998).

The analysis of incremental bands in tooth cementum may help to refine the results. The technique was developed and has been used successfully in wildlife studies to determine the age at death of modern mammals (Reimers and Nordby 1968; McCutchen 1969; Turner 1977; Wigal and Chapman 1983; Heggeberget 1984; Kay and Cant, 1988). Cementum is an avascular, bone-like connective tissue surrounding the roots of teeth. It is deposited appositionally throughout the life of an individual or until the tooth falls out (Hillson 1990). The alternating opaque and translucent bands observed under transmitted, polarized light correspond to periods of slow and fast growth.

The age at death of the animal can be determined by counting the number of incremental bands, taking into account the eruption age of the tooth. In archaeological studies, the technique was refined to determine seasonal patterns in the use of animals (Bourque et al. 1978; Lieberman et al. 1990; Pike-Tay 1991; Lieberman and Meadow 1992; Lieberman 1994; Burke and Castanet 1995). Burke and Castanet (1995) obtained information on the seasonal use of Upper Paleolithic sites in the southwest of France through the analysis of cementum lines in the wild horse (*Equus caballus*). Lieberman et al. (1990) gained information on seasonal occupations of several sites in the Levant by growth ring analysis in *Gazella gazella* teeth. In these studies, the season of death was determined by studying the appearance and width of the outermost incremental band in the cementum (Grue and Jensen 1979; Lieberman and Meadow 1992; Lieberman 1993; Lieberman 1994).

The interpretation of growth rings is hampered, however, by an incomplete knowledge of the factors playing a role in their formation. Primary factors would be a difference in the relative mineralization of the cementum and a variation in its collagen fibre orientation. The variation of these primary causal factors, in turn, depend on the seasonal variation in the food availability, on a change in biomechanical stresses due to the seasonal variation in physical characteristics of the food and, possibly, on the occurrence of hormonal changes (Klevezal and Kleinenberg 1967; Pike-Tay 1991; Lieberman 1993; Lieberman 1994; Burke and Castanet 1995). The slaughtering age and season of death of archaeological animals can therefore only be determined successfully if a modern comparative sample is studied of the same species originating from the same environment.

2.2. The diet

Another promising tool in the reconstruction of the management of sheep and goat herds, is the analysis of past diets by dental microwear studies.

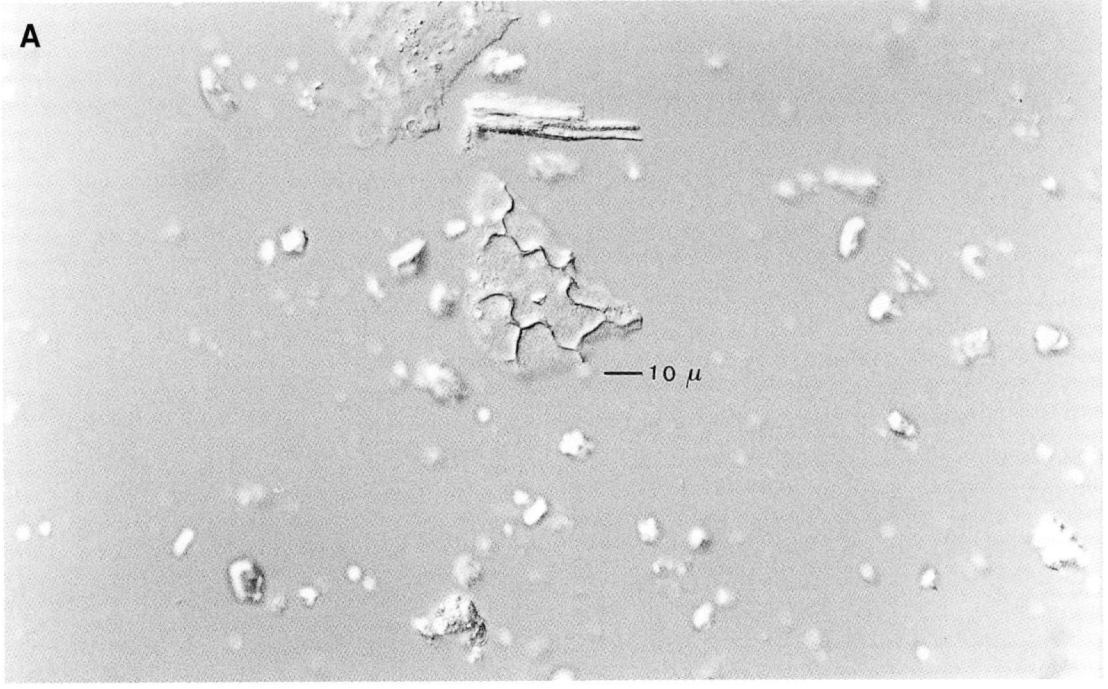
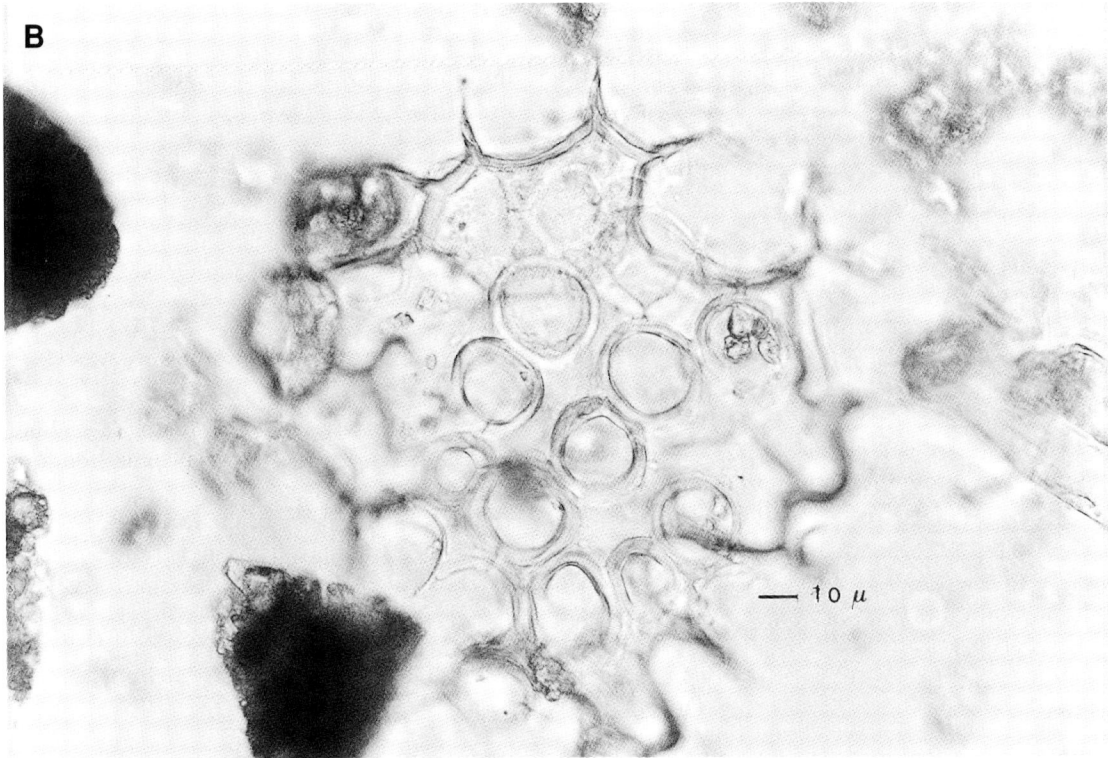

Fig. 1: Modern phytoliths of *Carduus pycnocephalus* (A) and *Crepis foetida* (B), 2 Asteraceae species consumed by goats and sheep, respectively (magnification, x 400).

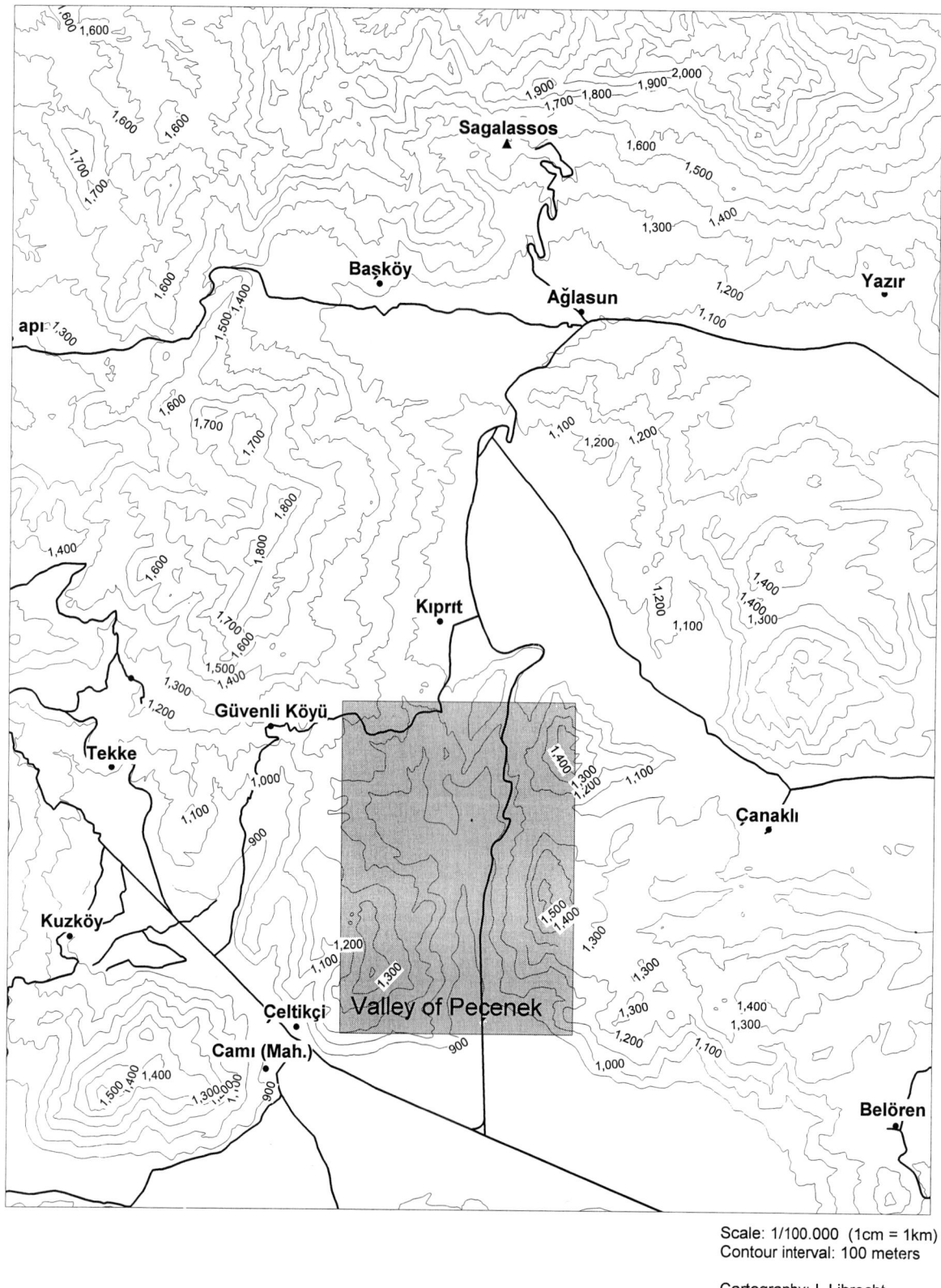

Fig. 2: Map of the area with contourlines. The Peçenek valley is indicated in grey.

Fig. 3: Some aspects of the vegetation in the Peçenek valley.

Fig. 4: A goat of the Kıl Keçi breed.

Fig.5: A sheep of the Karagöz breed.

Register number	Species	Breed	Sex	Age
96-055-M0001	Goat	Kıl Keçi	f	5 yr
96-055-M0002	Goat	Kıl Keçi	f	5 yr
96-055-M0003	Goat	Kıl Keçi	f	5 yr
96-055-M0004	Goat	Kıl Keçi	f	5 yr
96-055-M0005	Goat	Kıl Keçi	f	5 yr
96-055-M0006	Goat	Kıl Keçi	f	4-5 mo
96-055-M0007	Goat	Kıl Keçi	m	4-5 mo
96-055-M0008	Goat	Kıl Keçi	m	4-5 mo
96-055-M0009	Goat	Kıl Keçi	m	4-5 mo
96-055-M0010	Goat	Kıl Keçi	f	4-5 mo
96-055-M0011	Sheep	Karagöz	f	2 yr
96-055-M0012	Sheep	Karagöz	f	1 yr
96-055-M0013	Sheep	Karagöz	f	3 yr
96-055-M0014	Sheep	Karagöz	f	3 yr
96-055-M0015	Sheep	Karagöz	f	4 yr
96-055-M0016	Sheep	Karagöz	f	3 yr
96-055-M0017	Sheep	Karagöz	f	4 yr
96-055-M0018	Sheep	Karagöz	f	1 yr
96-055-M0019	Sheep	Karagöz	f	4 yr
96-055-M0020	Sheep	Karagöz	f	2 yr

Table 2: Sex, breed and age of sheep and goats selected for study (m=male, f=female, yr=year, mo=month).

Fig. 3: Some aspects of the vegetation in the Peçenek valley.

Fig. 4: A goat of the Kıl Keçi breed.

Fig.5: A sheep of the Karagöz breed.

Register number	Species	Breed	Sex	Age
96-055-M0001	Goat	Kıl Keçi	f	5 yr
96-055-M0002	Goat	Kıl Keçi	f	5 yr
96-055-M0003	Goat	Kıl Keçi	f	5 yr
96-055-M0004	Goat	Kıl Keçi	f	5 yr
96-055-M0005	Goat	Kıl Keçi	f	5 yr
96-055-M0006	Goat	Kıl Keçi	f	4-5 mo
96-055-M0007	Goat	Kıl Keçi	m	4-5 mo
96-055-M0008	Goat	Kıl Keçi	m	4-5 mo
96-055-M0009	Goat	Kıl Keçi	m	4-5 mo
96-055-M0010	Goat	Kıl Keçi	f	4-5 mo
96-055-M0011	Sheep	Karagöz	f	2 yr
96-055-M0012	Sheep	Karagöz	f	1 yr
96-055-M0013	Sheep	Karagöz	f	3 yr
96-055-M0014	Sheep	Karagöz	f	3 yr
96-055-M0015	Sheep	Karagöz	f	4 yr
96-055-M0016	Sheep	Karagöz	f	3 yr
96-055-M0017	Sheep	Karagöz	f	4 yr
96-055-M0018	Sheep	Karagöz	f	1 yr
96-055-M0019	Sheep	Karagöz	f	4 yr
96-055-M0020	Sheep	Karagöz	f	2 yr

Table 2: Sex, breed and age of sheep and goats selected for study (m=male, f=female, yr=year, mo=month).

Fig. 3: Some aspects of the vegetation in the Peçenek valley.

Fig. 4: A goat of the Kıl Keçi breed.

Fig.5: A sheep of the Karagöz breed.

Register number	Species	Breed	Sex	Age
96-055-M0001	Goat	Kıl Keçi	f	5 yr
96-055-M0002	Goat	Kıl Keçi	f	5 yr
96-055-M0003	Goat	Kıl Keçi	f	5 yr
96-055-M0004	Goat	Kıl Keçi	f	5 yr
96-055-M0005	Goat	Kıl Keçi	f	5 yr
96-055-M0006	Goat	Kıl Keçi	f	4-5 mo
96-055-M0007	Goat	Kıl Keçi	m	4-5 mo
96-055-M0008	Goat	Kıl Keçi	m	4-5 mo
96-055-M0009	Goat	Kıl Keçi	m	4-5 mo
96-055-M0010	Goat	Kıl Keçi	f	4-5 mo
96-055-M0011	Sheep	Karagöz	f	2 yr
96-055-M0012	Sheep	Karagöz	f	1 yr
96-055-M0013	Sheep	Karagöz	f	3 yr
96-055-M0014	Sheep	Karagöz	f	3 yr
96-055-M0015	Sheep	Karagöz	f	4 yr
96-055-M0016	Sheep	Karagöz	f	3 yr
96-055-M0017	Sheep	Karagöz	f	4 yr
96-055-M0018	Sheep	Karagöz	f	1 yr
96-055-M0019	Sheep	Karagöz	f	4 yr
96-055-M0020	Sheep	Karagöz	f	2 yr

Table 2: Sex, breed and age of sheep and goats selected for study (m=male, f=female, yr=year, mo=month).

	Goat	Sheep
Grasses		
Poaceae		
Cynodon dactylon (L.) Pers.	x	x
Melica ciliata L.		x
Phleum montanum C. Koch subsp. *serrulatum* (Boiss.) M. Dogan	x	
Phleum subulatum (Savi) Aschers. et Graebn.		x
Herbs		
Apiaceae		
Echinophora sibthorpiana Guss.		x
Asteraceae		
Asteraceae sp.	x	
Anthemis pseudocotula Boiss.		x
Carduus nutans L.	x	
Carduus pycnocephalus L.	x	
Crepis foetida L.		x
Echinops viscosus DC.	x	
Hieracium L. sp.	x	
Boraginaceae		
Echium italicum L.	x	x
Brassicaceae		
Alyssum strigosum Banks and Sol.	x	
Sisymbrium L. sp.	x	
Caryophyllaceae		
Velezia rigida L.	x	
Convolvulaceae		
Convolvulus arvensis L.	x	
Convolvulus cantabricae L.		x
Fabaceae		
Medicago praecox DC.		x
Medicago cfr. *sativa* L.	x	
Vicia villosa Roth.	x	
Geraniaceae		
Erodium ciconium (L.) L'Hérit.		x
Hypericaceae		
Hypericum triquetrifolium Turra		x
Lamiaceae		
Ballota cfr. *macrodonta* Boiss. and Bal.	x	
Origanum onites L.		x
Salvia sclarea L.	x	
Satureja cuneifolia Ten.		x
Teucrium L. sp.		x
Malvaceae		
Malva neglecta Wallr.		x
Plantaginaceae		
Plantago L. sp.		x
Polygonaceae		
Atraphaxis billardieri Jaub. and Spach		
Scrophulariaceae		
Scrophularia L. sp.		
Trees and Shrubs		
Cupressaceae		
Juniperus excelsa Bieb.	x	
Fabaceae		
Quercus coccifera L.	x	x
Moraceae		
Morus alba L.	x	
Oleaceae		
Phyllyrea latifolia L.	x	x
Rhamnaceae		
Paliurus spina-christi Miller	x	
Rosaceae		
Crataegus aronia (L.° Bosc. var. *minuta* Browicz	x	

Table 1: Botanical composition of the diet of sheep and goats (17-20/06/1996).

In Hellenistic-Roman times a number of different systems of ovicaprine husbandry existed, ranging from nomadic to sedentary systems with or without seasonal movements (White 1970; Frayn 1979; Frayn 1984; Whittaker 1988). The same systems still existed in Pisidia around 1947-1950 (de Planhol 1958). The diet of the animals could vary from fresh pasture or fodder to the stubble of recently harvested fields (White 1970; Whittaker 1988; Skydsgaard 1988).

Since stomach contents are very rarely retrieved in archaeological excavations, information on former diets have to be derived from dental studies (Teaford 1991; Teaford 1994). Teeth, thanks to their durability, are mostly well represented among faunal remains. In attempts to reconstruct past diets researchers, after studying tooth shape and wear facets, eventually discovered the potential of microscopic defects, known as dental microwear, found on the surfaces of teeth (Healy et al. 1967; Nolan and Black 1970; Teaford 1988; Teaford 1991; Teaford 1994). It is generally accepted that the observed wear pattern reflects the food intake of the week prior to the death of an animal ('last supper effect') (Walker and Teaford 1989). Dental microwear has proved its potential for the reconstruction of ancient diets in studies on humans and primates (Teaford and Walker 1984; Ryan and Johanson 1989; Bullington 1991; Lalueza et al. 1996; Teaford et al. 1996; Ungar and Teaford 1996). The method has also been applied to studies of several carnivore and ruminant species (Solounias et al. 1988; van Valkenburgh et al. 1990; Strait 1993; Solounias and Hayek 1993; Mainland 1994).

These studies demonstrate that dietary reconstructions can be made by establishing an unambiguous relationship between the diet and dental microwear present on the surfaces of teeth. To ascertain the deductive value of dental microwear, factors causing or influencing dental microwear were studied (Walker and Teaford 1989). The physical properties of the food (e.g. opal phytoliths, hardness of the food, the presence of exogenous grit) are considered as primary causal factors (Wallace 1974; Walker et al. 1978; Peters 1982; Ungar 1994; Ungar et al. 1995; Lalueza et al. 1996; Teaford and Lytle 1996). Other primary factors considered are the magnitude and direction of chewing and the structural organisation of prisms and crystallites in the tooth enamel (Gordon 1982; Gordon 1984b; Gordon 1984c; Maas 1991). The age of the animal and the season of food intake would influence the microwear pattern to a lesser degree (Gordon 1982; Gordon 1984a; Teaford and Robinson 1989; Bullington 1991). From the foregoing it is clear that dietary reconstructions of archaeological specimens are only feasible when existing relationships between diets and microwear patterns in extant, related species are studied simultaneously.

Walker and Teaford (1989) stressed that microwear studies should not be used alone in dietary reconstructions because of the multitude of factors influencing dental microwear. It was therefore decided to explore the possibilities of phytoliths as an aid to the interpretation of observed microwear patterns at Sagalassos. Phytoliths are microscopic particles, produced mainly in the leaves of some plant families such as the *Poaceae*, *Cyperaceae* and *Equisetaceae* (Fig. 1). Although the chemical composition of these elements can vary, phytoliths are commonly constituted of opal and calcium oxalate crystals. Since these crystals can scratch enamel, phytoliths are believed to be one of the major factors responsible for the production of dental microwear (Baker et al. 1959; Bullington 1991). Morphological features of phytoliths are often diagnostic at family level (Twiss et al. 1969; Twiss 1992). Sometimes the morphology, morphometrical characteristics and frequencies in a context permit phytolith identification to genus (Doutrelepont et al. 1996) and species level (Rosen 1996). In archaeological excavations phytoliths have thus far been retrieved from sediments (Piperno 1988), organic charred crusts of pottery sherds (Doutrelepont et al. 1996), from human coprolites, from the rumen of sheep and from excavated teeth. In the latter case, phytoliths were found impregnated in the buccal or lingual surfaces of the tooth or incorporated in the dental calculus (Baker et al. 1961; Armitage 1975; Bryant and Williams-Dean 1976; Ciochon et al. 1990; Bullington 1991; Lalueza-Fox et al. 1994; Lalueza-Fox et al. 1996).

2.3. Distinguishing sheep from goat teeth

Dental microwear and growth ring analyses of the Sagalassos material are carried out on the first and second lower molars, according to standards described in the literature (Lieberman 1994; Mainland 1994; Teaford 1991; Teaford 1994). It is vital that teeth are identified to species level prior to analysis. This distinction cannot be made reliably using the mandibulae from which the teeth are extracted (Boessneck et al. 1964). The macroscopic morphological differences described for lower teeth by Payne (1985) cannot be used either, since they are only applicable on deciduous teeth and unworn first molars.

The identification of isolated teeth of adult sheep and goats would be possible, with a statistical certainty of 95 %, using the ultrastructural features of the enamel. The applied technique is based on a visualisation of the ultrastructural prism packing pattern of the tooth enamel, followed by a determination of metrical parameters that are compared statistically (Grine et al. 1986; Grine et al. 1987).

An alternative method for distinguishing between archaeological sheep and goat teeth, could be the use of carbon iso-

topes. Stable isotopes of carbon extracted from bone or teeth are often used to reconstruct palaeodiets in archaeological studies (van der Merwe and Vogel 1978; Ambrose 1986; Lynott *et al.* 1986; Ambrose and DeNiro 1986; Lubell *et al.* 1994). The stable ratio of carbon isotopes ($\delta^{13}C/^{12}C$) allowed Vogel (1978) to distinguish between grazing and browsing ungulates in South Africa. This distinction was based on the differential carbon isotope ratios of the tropical South African grasses with a preponderant C4 photosynthesis, that differ from those in shrubs and trees following the C3 photosynthesis. It remains to be verified, however, if grasses in the environment around Sagalassos follow a different photosynthetic pathway from the shrubs and trees in the same environment, which might result in different carbon isotope ratios between grazing sheep and browsing goats.

3. PRESENT-DAY TRADITIONAL HERDING AT SAGALASSOS

3.1. The grazing area

In June 1996, a first field study was conducted in the valley of Peçenek near Celtikçi (37°32' N 30°31' E). This valley is located approximately 11 km south of Sagalassos (Fig. 2). The Peçenek valley is situated at an elevation of 900 to 1000 m above sea level. In the month of June the average temperature is 25°C. Sheep and goats were tended in the same area, which is characterised by a mixed vegetation of dispersed, isolated low shrubs and deteriorating herbs and grasses (Fig. 3).

3.2. Traditional management of ovicaprine herds

3.2.1. The goat herd

A herd of goats from the 'Kıl Keçi' breed (Fig. 4), consisting of 125 adults (120 females, 5 males) and 120 kids, was observed on two consecutive days (17-18 June 1996). Kıl Keçi is the general Turkish name for the hair goat. Other current Turkish names for this breed are Adı Keçi or Kara Keçi. English names are the Turkish native or the Anatolian Black (Mason 1966). Together with the Angora goat, the hair goat is the most common breed kept in Turkey. The Angora goats are mainly kept for the production of hair while the hair goats are mainly raised to produce meat and milk. In 1983 there were about 13 million hair goats in Turkey which were mainly found in the mountainous regions of the Mediterranean, the Aegean and the southeastern part of Anatolia (Mason 1966; Yalçın 1979; Yalçın 1986). According to de Planhol (1958) the Angora goat became more and more predominant in the plain of Isparta, located to the north of Sagalassos during the years of his survey (1947-1950). However, most goats in the Pisidia district then belonged to the white 'Malta' breed or to the yellowish 'Syrian' breed which was an excellent milk producer (de Planhol 1958: 165).

According to the shepherds, grazing of the goat herd began at dawn. The observations started at 8 am. On the first day, animals were observed until 5.30 pm, while on the second day observations stopped at noon. Adult goats and kids were kept in separate grazing areas (the mountain slope and valley respectively) to ensure the retention of sufficient milk for human use. After a grazing period of a few hours, the kids were driven to a water reservoir to drink for half an hour. At this time of the year kids were still allowed to suckle from their mothers after the latter had been milked by the shepherds. According to the shepherds, each goat produced about 200 to 300 grams of milk daily. After a resting period at noontime, the goats started feeding again at 1 pm. In the afternoon, the adult animals drank at the water reservoir and were then allowed to graze freely for the rest of the day at higher altitudes. The shepherds informed us about food supplements given to the animals. Salt was provided on a daily basis throughout the year while straw, oil-cake and grain were given as a supplement during winter. At 7 pm, the goats were driven back to the camp to spend the night in the pen. The observed herd was kept in the Peçenek region during the months of June and July, when the area was rented from the local municipality. During the rest of the year, the shepherd tended his goat flock north of the small Peçenek valley, higher up in the mountains. According to the shepherd, conception in the flock normally takes place in September and October, with kids being born in February and March. In general, one kid is born to each female. Products derived from the goat flock are milk, processed further into cheese and sold at local markets. The fleece of the animals is cut each year in August. The goats studied by de Planhol in the late 1940s had their coats cut in the middle of June for the young animals of one year of age (cebis), or towards the end of July for the other animals. The present-day practice still seems largely to correspond with this (de Planhol 1958: 165). Every animal is said to produce about 200 grams of hair which is used for the production of kilims, tent-cloth, sacks, etc. The manure of the goats, produced overnight in the pen, is gathered each morning and stored. Afterwards, it is sold as a fertiliser and used in the intense agricultural industry in the region of Antalya.

3.2.2. The sheep herd

A sheep flock was observed on the eighteenth and twentieth of June (from 12 am to 8 pm and from 8.30 am until noon, respectively).

The shepherd distinguished four types of sheep. The majority was said to belong to the 'Karagöz' type (Fig. 5) while the other 3 types ('Tırp', 'Mandak' and 'Çapar') occurred in smaller numbers. Cross-breeds were also present (e.g. 'Mandak' x 'Karagöz').

The fatness of the tail, the colour of the legs and the colour and texture of the fleece were used as distinguishing features. From these four sheep 'breeds' only the name 'Karagöz' could be linked to a breed discussed in the literature. According to Mason (1966) and Yalçın (1979) 'Karagöz' sheep are one of the two possible types of the 'Karayaka' breed of sheep, commonly found in Northern Anatolia (Turkey). The 'Karagöz' type has a white fleece and black eyes while the 'Çakrak' type has a white fleece but black legs and a completely black head (Mason 1966; Yalçın 1979). However, the 'Karagöz' as described by Mason (1966) and Yalçın (1979; 1986) has a thin tail and a wool patch on the forehead. The sheep called 'Karagöz' in the studied area were semi-fat to fat-tailed and did not have a wool patch. According to Mason (1966) and Yalçın (1979; 1986) sheep breeds commonly found in the area of Ağlasun and the territory of Sagalassos are the 'White Karaman' and 'Daglıç' breeds. The type called 'Karagöz' in our study area shows the greatest resemblance to the 'White Karaman' breed. According to de Planhol, in 1947-1950, all the sheep of Pisidia and Pamphylia would have belonged either to the 'Daglıç' or to the 'Karaman' breeds. In his description, both flocks have a fat tail. The 'Daglıç' breed is described as having black or brown heads and legs and as having a flat tail, while the 'Karaman' breed was characterised by an S-tail. The former were famous for their meat, while the latter produced better milk (de Planhol 1958: 165). The other three types of sheep mentioned by the shepherd ('Tırp', 'Mandak' and 'Çapar') could not be identified (Mason 1966; Yalçın 1979 and 1986).

The observed flock of sheep consisted of adult animals only (150 ewes and 6 rams). The lambs, born in October, had already been sold in May. In general, each ewe was said to give birth to one lamb, although twin lambs had occasionally occurred. According to the shepherd, some ewes were able to produce lambs twice a year. The sheep started feeding at dawn. During the field survey they grazed the flanks of the valley and high up in the mountains. They were said to graze in the Peçenek valley most of the year. Only during the summer months (July and August) was the flock moved to Celtikçi, situated southwest of Peçenek, where it was allowed to graze the stubble of recently harvested fields. Around 10 am, the animals were driven back to the shepherds' camp and received their daily supplement of salt. During winter, sheep received food supplements in the form of oil-cake, straw, grain, bran and barley. After the supply of salt, the sheep were watered near the camp and then allowed to graze in the valley. To avoid the hottest period of the day the animals rested in the shade from 11 am until 5 pm. Afterwards, they continued feeding until dark. During nighttime, the sheep were shut inside the pen.

The shepherd informed us that the animals were shorn in the first weeks of June. The average production of wool per sheep was 1.5 to 2 kg.

This represents a good production since in 1954-1955 the estimated average wool production of sheep breeds other than Merino or crossbreds was 1.13 kg per head of greasy wool and 0.56 kg clean wool (Jongman 1988: 161). At the time of de Planhol's survey in the area (1947-1950) sheep were also shorn early in the summer, producing a rather coarse wool called 'yapak yünü'. However, in the plain of Tefenni, to the southwest of Sagalassos, and in some semi-arid parts of the Pamphylian plain, sheep were also shorn a second time during the autumn, producing a much finer wool called 'güz yünü' (de Planhol 1958: 163).

3.3. Dietary composition

During the field work, the plant species consumed by sheep and goats were noted and/or collected. The amount of each plant species taken up by sheep and goats was not quantified in detail. The collected plants were identified with the *Flora of Turkey* (Davis 1965-1988) and by comparison with the reference collection at the herbarium of the National Garden of Belgium (Meise). A list of plant taxa consumed by the observed sheep and goats is given in Table 1. Not all collected plants could be identified to species level, because of the absence of fruits or flowers or because they were damaged by grazing.

Both sheep and goats consumed grasses, herbs and shrub or tree species. The total number of plant species consumed by the ovicaprines was 39, representing 22 different plant families. Sheep and goats, considered separately, showed only a small difference in the total number of species consumed. The goats were seen eating a total of 22 different species, representing 14 different plant families, while the sheep ate 20 different plant species representing 15 plant families. The 22 different plant species eaten by goats included 2 grass species, 14 herb species and 6 tree or shrub species. The sheep, on the other hand, consumed 3 species of grasses, 15 species of herbs and 2 species of trees or shrubs. From the visual observations and the species of food plants collected, we can conclude that both sheep and goats consumed a wide variety of species (14 and 15 different plant families by goats and sheep respectively).

Although no precise quantification was carried out of the dietary preferences of sheep and goats, it was noted that the goats showed a definite preference towards the leaves of one shrub/tree species (*Quercus coccifera*). *Juniperus excelsa* was also highly appreciated when available. The observation of a high variability in consumption combined with a high selectivity, has been made for several goat breeds in different regions around the world, from rangelands in the Southern highlands of Scotland (Bullock 1985), to African rangelands in Kenya and Malawi (Rutagwenda *et al.* 1990; Becker and Lohrmann 1992), to pastures in Malaysia (Van Mele and Anthonysamy 1994; Van Mele *et al.* 1994b) and semi-arid shrublands in Mexico (Ramirez *et al.* 1990). The preference of goats for shrub/tree species, as noted in our study, was also seen in goats grazing on a semi-arid temperate rangeland in Central Mexico (Ricardi and Shimada 1992), although only in summer. These authors observed seasonal variations in the dietary preferences of goats with a preference for shrubs in summer and for grasses in spring. Two goat breeds grazing on rangelands in southern Italy showed a preferential consumption of herbs in summer and of grasses in winter (Fedele *et al.* 1993). Thus, in general, goats can be considered to be mixed feeding opportunists, selecting the foods with highest nutritive value (Lu 1988).

The sheep at Peçenek, on the contrary, beside consuming leaves of *Quercus coccifera* with a high preference, showed a high selectivity towards small herbs and grasses. In a number of studies on the dietary preferences of sheep it was observed that these ruminants graze more on grasses than do goats (Bullock 1985; Rutagwenda *et al.* 1990).

The preference of sheep as well as goats for the leaves of several plant species can be possibly explained by the high protein content of the leaves compared to other plant parts (Church 1979). Because of this high protein content, the leaves can be considered as a highly nutritious food element (Church 1979).

Four plant species were common to the diets of both sheep and goats. Of these, one belonged to the grasses (*Cynodon dactylon*, Poaceae), one was a herb species belonging to the Boraginaceae (*Echium italicum*) and two species were shrubs (*Phyllirea latifolia*, Oleaceae, *Quercus coccifera*, Fagaceae). A low to intermediate dietary overlap was observed in ovicaprines from southern Scotland (Bullock 1985) and Kenya (Rutagwenda *et al.* 1990).

Environmental studies conducted on the territory of Sagalassos indicate that during the Roman period the mountains around the site were probably characterised by an alternation of woods and open spaces (Bottema and Woldring 1995; Waelkens *et al.* 1999). *Quercus* as well as *Juniperus* may therefore have been available for consumption by ovicaprines. Since similar food plants were possibly available in the past a comparison of teeth from recent sheep and goats with teeth from archaeological animals is valid in our dental microwear and cementum line studies.

3.4. The comparative ovicaprine material

After the observation of the sheep and goats, ten specimens of each herd were selected for study. Detailed information on the breeds, sex and age of these animals is listed in Table 2. For both species it was attempted to obtain animals of different age classes and sex, but ultimately we depended heavily on the goodwill of the shepherds selling the animals.

Ten goats of the studied herd were slaughtered on the nineteenth of June in the village of Ağlasun by a local butcher. Heads, a sample of the contents of each stomach and each rectum were taken for further study. The ten selected sheep were slaughtered on the twenty-first of June by the same butcher and similar samples were taken. Sheep and goat heads were defleshed in water of approximately 100°C and then cleaned thoroughly by maceration. After cleaning, the skulls were transported to Belgium where they are preserved in the collection of the Royal Museum of Central Africa at Tervuren (register numbers: 96055M01-M20).

3.5. Summary and conclusions

The methods have been presented that will be used in the attempt to reconstruct pastoral husbandry practices in the territory of Sagalassos during the Roman period. After the identification of excavated sheep and goat teeth using the method described by Grine *et al.* (1986) or using isotopes, we will attempt to determine the absolute age and season of death by cementum line analysis. The results will be used to establish possible differential uses of old and young animals and to determine seasonal patterns of slaughtering. Dental microwear, aided by a study on plant phytoliths extracted from teeth, will be carried out to reconstruct the former diet of sheep and goats. Modern sheep and goats from the Sagalassos area are used as a reference for the archaeological material.

The results of the first study of modern sheep and goat flocks in the territory of Sagalassos, conducted in June 1996, are presented. A flock of sheep and one of goats were each observed for 2 days and dietary preferences were noted. Both animal species showed a wide variety in their dietary choice, with sheep consuming 20 different plant species and goats eating 22 different species. Despite the apparent wide range of food plants, a high preference for certain species and plant parts was observed. Goats showed a particular preference for the leaves of *Quercus coccifera*. *Juniperus excelsa* was also preferentially selected. Sheep preferred mainly small herbs and the leaves of *Quercus coccifera*. The lack of a thorough quantification of the dietary intake precluded a statistical approach in the comparison of food preferences and the possible relation to dental microwear patterns. During future field surveys we will therefore try to adopt a quantitative method based on visual observations of sheep and goat herds (Van Mele and Anthonysamy 1994; Van Mele *et al.* 1994a, Van Mele *et al.* 1994b).

Interviews with the shepherds indicated that several practices described in ancient texts are still in use today in the territory of Sagalassos. This is the case for seasonal movements and the use of manure as fertiliser. From reconstructions of the former environment in the territory of Sagalassos it is also evident that the vegetation in Roman times possibly included the main food plants eaten by sheep and goats today. Although, because of the absence of hair and wool remains, the ovicaprid material of Sagalassos did not permit an identification of the type of breeds present, we have no reason to assume that, in a similar environment, the dietary habits of former breeds would be any different from that of the present-day animals.

Molars of modern sheep and goats are currently under study in order to establish a correlation between dental microwear patterns and diet. These data will be used to make inferences about the diet of archaeological specimens. Results will be presented in following volumes of this series.

4. ACKNOWLEDGEMENTS

This research is supported by the Belgian Programme on Interuniversity Poles of Attraction initiated by the Belgian State, Prime Minister's Office, Science Policy Programming. The text also presents the results of the Concerted Action of the Flemish Government (GOA 97/2) and the Fund for Scientific Research-Flanders (Belgium) (FWO) (G.2145.9). Scientific responsibility is assumed by its authors. The authors would like to thank Wim Van Neer for critically reading draft versions of this paper.

5. REFERENCES

S.H. Ambrose (1986) Stable carbon and nitrogen isotope analysis of human and animal diet in Africa, *Journal of Human Evolution* 15: 707-731.

S.H. Ambrose and M.J. DeNiro (1986) The isotopic ecology of East African mammals, *Oecologia* 69: 395-406.

P.L. Armitage (1975) The extraction and identification of opal phytoliths from the teeth of ungulates, *Journal of Archaeological Science* 2: 187-197.

G. Baker, L.H.P. Jones and I.D. Wardrop (1959) Cause of wear in sheep's teeth, *Nature* 184: 1583-1584.

G. Baker, L.H.P. Jones and I.D. Wardrop (1961) Opal phytoliths and mineral particles in the rumen of the sheep, *Australian Journal of Agricultural Research* 12: 462-471.

K. Becker and J. Lohrmann (1992) Feed selection by goats on tropical semi-humid rangeland, *Small Ruminant Research* 8: 285-298.

J. Boessneck, H.H. Müller and M. Teichert (1964) Osteologische Unterscheidungsmerkmale zwischen Schaf (*Ovis aries* L.) und Ziege (*Capra hircus* L.), *Kühn-Archiv* 78/1: 1-129.

S. Bottema and H. Woldring (1995) The environment of classical Sagalassos: a palynological investigation, in: M. Waelkens and J. Poblome (eds) *Sagalassos III. Report on the Fourth Excavation Campaign of 1993* (Acta Archaeologica Lovaniensia Monographiae 7) Leuven University Press: 327-340.

B.J. Bourque, K. Morris and A. Spiess (1978) Determining the season of death of mammal teeth from archeological sites: a new sectioning technique, *Science* 199/3: 530-531.

V.M. Bryant Jr. and G. Williams-Dean (1976) The coprolithes of man, in: B. Fagan (ed.) *Avenues to Antiquity*, San Francisco: 257-266.

J. Bullington (1991) Deciduous dental microwear of prehistoric juveniles from the Lower Illinois River Valley, *American Journal of Physical Anthropology* 84: 59-73.

D.J. Bullock (1985) Annual diets of hill sheep and feral goats in southern Scotland, *Journal of Applied Ecology* 22: 423-433.

A. Burke and J. Castanet (1995) Histological observations of cementum growth in horse teeth and their application to archaeology, *Journal of Archaeological Science* 22: 479-493.

D.C. Church (1979) Chapter 11: Taste, appetite and regulation of energy balance and control of food intake, in: D.C. Church (ed.) *Digestive Physiology and Nutrition of Ruminants 2: Nutrition*, Oxford: 281-320.

R. Ciochon, D.R. Piperno and R.G. Thompson (1990) Opal phytoliths found on the teeth of the extinct ape *Gigantopithecus blacki*: implications for paleodietary studies, *Proceedings of the National Academy of Science USA* 87: 8120-8124.

P.H. Davis (1965-1988) *Flora of Turkey and the East Aegean Islands I-II*, Edinburgh.

B. De Cupere (1993) Faunal remains at Sagalassos: preliminary results of the archaeozoological analysis, in: *IX. Arkeometri Sonuçlari Toplantisi 24-28 May 1993, Ankara*: 225-235.

B. De Cupere, W. Van Neer and A. Lentacker (1993) Some aspects of the bone-working industry in Roman Sagalassos, in: M. Waelkens and J. Poblome (eds) *Sagalassos II. Report on the Third Excavation Campaign of 1992* (Acta Archaeologica Lovaniensia Monographiae 6) Leuven University Press: 269-278.

B. De Cupere, A. Lentacker and M. Waelkens (1995) Sieving experiments in the lower agora and their implications for the interpretation of archaeozoological data from Sagalassos, in: M. Waelkens and J. Poblome (eds) *Sagalassos III. Report on the Fourth Excavation Campaign of 1993* (Acta Archaeologica Lovaniensia Monographiae 7) Leuven University Press: 367-377.

B. De Cupere and M. Waelkens (1998) The antique site of Sagalassos (Burdur province, Turkey): Faunal results from the 1990-1994 excavation seasons, in: H. Buitenhuis, L. Bartosiewicz and A.M. Choyke (eds), *Archaeozoology of the Near East* III (*Proceedings of the Third International Symposium on the Archaeozoology of Southwestern Asia and Adjacent Areas*), Leiden – Groningen: 276-284.

R. Degeest, J. Poblome and B. De Cupere (1993) A preliminary report on the excavations at site W, 1992. Sagalassos ware and faunal remains, in: M. Waelkens and J. Poblome (ed.) *Sagalassos II. Report on the Third Excavation Campaign of 1992* (Acta Archaeologica Lovaniensia Monographiae 6), Leuven University Press: 125-139.

X. de Planhol (1958) *De la plaine pamphyliennes aux lacs pisidiens. Nomadisme et vie paysanne* (Bibliothèque archéologique et historique de l'Institut Français d'Archéologie d'Istanbul 3), Paris.

H. Devijver (1996) Local elites, equestrians and senators: A social history of Roman Sagalassos, *Ancient Society* 27: 106-162.

H. Doutrelepont, L. Vrydaghs, E. De Langhe, B. Janssens, R. Swennen, C.H. Mbida and P. de Maret (1996) Banana in Africa, in: A. Pinilla, M.J. Machado and J.J. Treserras (eds) *First European Meeting on Phytolith Research*, Madrid: 27.

V. Fedele, M. Pizzillo, S. Claps, P. Morand-Fehr and R. Rubino (1993) Grazing behavior and diet selection of goats on native pasture in Southern Italy, *Small Ruminant Research* 11: 305-322.

J.M. Frayn (1979) *Subsistence Farming in Roman Italy*, Centaur Press Limited: 168.

J.M. Frayn (1984) Sheep-rearing and the wool trade in Italy during the Roman period, in: F. Cairns and R. Seager, *ARCA: Classical and Medieval Texts, Papers and Monographs*, Trowbridge – Wiltshire: 208.

K.D. Gordon (1982) A study of microwear on chimpanzee molars: implications for dental microwear analysis, *American Journal of Physical Anthropology* 59: 195-215.

K.D. Gordon (1984a) Hominoid dental microwear: Complications in the use of microwear analysis to detect diet, *Journal of Dental Research* 63/8: 1043-1046.

K.D. Gordon (1984b) The assessment of jaw movement direction from dental microwear, *American Journal of Physical Anthropology* 63: 77-84.

K.D. Gordon (1984c) Orientation of occlusal contacts in the chimpanzee, *Pan troglodytes verus*, deduced from scanning electron microscopic analysis of dental microwear patterns, *Archives of Oral Biology* 29/10: 783-787.

A. Grant (1982) The use of tooth wear as a guide to the age of domestic ungulates, in: B. Wilson, C. Grigson and S. Payne (eds) *Ageing and Sexing Animal Bones from Archaeological Sites* (*BAR British Series* 109): 191-126.

F.E. Grine, G. Fosse, D.W. Krause and W.L. Jungers (1986) Analysis of enamel ultrastructure in archaeology: the identification of *Ovis aries* and *Capra hircus* dental remains, *Journal of Archaeological Science* 13: 579-595.

F.E. Grine, D.W. Krause, G. Fosse and W.L. Jungers (1987) Analysis of individual, intraspecific and interspecific variability in quantitative parameters of caprine tooth enamel structure, *Acta Odontologica Scandinavica* 45: 1-23.

H. Grue and B. Jensen (1979) Incremental lines in tooth cementum, *Danish Review of Game Biology* 11: 3-48.

W.B. Healy, T.W. Cutress and C. Michie (1967) Wear of sheep's teeth. IV. Reduction of soil ingestion and tooth wear by supplementary feeding, *New Zealand Journal of Agricultural Research* 10: 201-209.

T.M. Heggeberget (1984) Age determination in the European otter *Lutra lutra lutra*, *Zeitschrift für Saugetierkunde* 49/5: 299-305.

S. Hillson (1990) *Teeth (Cambridge Manuals in Archaeology)*.

W. Jongman (1988) *The Economy and Society of Pompei*, Amsterdam.

R.F. Kay, D.T. Rasmussen and K.C. Beard (1984) Cementum annulus counts provide a means for age determination in *Macaca mulatta* (Primates, Anthropoidea), *Folia Primatologica* 42: 85-95.

R.F. Kay and J.G.H. Cant (1988) Age assessment using cementum annulus counts and toothwear in a free-ranging population of *Macaca mulatta*, *American Journal of Primatology* 15: 1-16.

G.A. Klevezal and S.E. Kleinenberg (1967) *Age Determination of Mammals from Annual Layers in Teeth and Bones* (Academy of Sciences of the USSR. Severtsov Institute of Animal Morphology) Moskva: 6-41.

C. Lalueza, A. Pérez-Pérez and D. Turbon (1996) Dietary inferences through buccal microwear analysis of Middle and Upper Pleistocene human fossils, *American Journal of Physical Anthropology* 100: 367-387.

C. Lalueza-Fox, A. Pérez-Pérez and J. Juan (1994) Dietary information through the examination of plant phytoliths on the enamel surface of human dentition, *Journal of Archaeological Science* 21: 29-34.

C. Lalueza Fox, J. Juan and R.M. Albert (1996) Phytolith analysis on dental calculus, enamel surface and burial soil: information about diet and paleoenvironment, *American Journal of Physical Anthropology* 101: 101-113.

K. Lanckoronski (1892) *Städte Pamphyliens und Pisidiens II. Pisidien*, Wien-Prag-Leipzig.

B. Levick (1967) *Roman Colonies in Southern Asia Minor*, Oxford.

D.E. Lieberman, T.W. Deacon and R.H. Meadow (1990) Computer image enhancement and analysis of cementum increments as applied to teeth of *Gazella gazella*, *Journal of Archaeological Science* 17: 519-533.

D.E. Lieberman and R.H. Meadow (1992) The biology of cementum increments (with an archaeological application), *Mammal Review* 22/2: 57-77.

D.E. Lieberman (1993) Life history variables preserved in dental cementum microstructure, *Science Reprint Series* 261: 1162-1164.

D.E. Lieberman (1994) The biological basis for seasonal increments in dental cementum and their application to archaeological research, *Journal of Archaeological Science* 21: 525-539.

C.D. Lu (1988) Grazing behavior and diet selection of goats, *Small Ruminant Research* 1: 205-216.

D. Lubell, M. Jackes, H. Schwarcz, M. Knyf and C. Meiklejohn (1994) The Mesolithic-Neolithic transition in Portugal: Isotopic and dental evidence of diet, *Journal of Archaeological Science* 21: 201-216.

M.J. Lynott, T.W. Boutton, J.E. Price and D.E. Nelson (1986) Stable carbon isotopic evidence for maize agriculture in southeast Missouri and northeast Arkansas, *American Antiquity* 51/1: 51-65.

M.C. Maas (1991) Enamel structure and microwear: an experimental study of the response of enamel to shearing force, *American Journal of Physical Anthropology* 85: 31-49.

I.L. Mainland (1994) *An Evaluation of the Potential of Dental Microwear Analysis for Reconstructing the Diet of Domesticated Sheep (Ovis aries) and Goats (Capra hircus) within an Archaeological Context*, Ph.D dissertation.

I.L. Mason (1966) Sheep breeds of the Mediterranean, *Food and Agriculture Organization of the United Nations (FAO)-Commonwealth Agricultural Bureaux*: 133-184.

H.E. McCutchen (1969) Age determination of pronghorns by the incisor cementum, *Journal of Wildlife Management* 33/1: 172-175.

N.J. van der Merwe and J.C. Vogel (1978) 13C content of human collagen as a measure of prehistoric diet in woodland North America, *Nature* 276: 815-816.

S. Mitchell (1995) *Anatolia: Land, Men and Gods in Asia Minor I. The Celts and the Impact of Roman Rule*, Oxford.

T. Nolan and W.J.M. Black (1970) Effect of stocking rate on tooth wear in ewes, *International Journal of Agricultural Research* 9: 187-196.

S. Payne (1985) Morphological distinctions between the mandibular teeth of young sheep, *Ovis*, and goats, *Capra*, *Journal of Archaeological Science* 12: 139-147.

C.R. Peters (1982) Electron-optical microscopic study of incipient dental microdamage from experimental seed and bone crushing, *American Journal of Physical Anthropology* 57: 283-301.

A. Pike-Tay (1991) l'Analyse du cement dentaire chez les cerfs: l'application en prehistoire, *Paléo* 3: 149-166.

D.R. Piperno (1988) *Phytolith analysis. An Archaeological and Geological Perspective*.

R.G. Ramirez, A. Rodriguez, L.A. Tagle, A.C. Del Valle and J. Gonzalez (1990) Nutrient content and intake of forage grazed by range goats in northeastern Mexico, *Small Ruminant Research* 3: 435-448.

W.N. Ramsay and J.G.C. Anderson (1941) *The Social Basis of Roman Power in Asia Minor*, Aberdeen.

E. Reimers and F. Nordby (1968) Relationship between age and tooth cementum layers in Norwegian reindeer, *Journal of Wildlife Management* 32/4: 957-961.

C. Ricardi and A. Shimada (1992) A note on diet selection by goats on a semi-arid temperate rangeland throughout the year, *Applied Animal Behaviour Science* 33: 239-247.

A.M. Rosen (1996) Phytolith evidence for mousterian plant exploitation at Tor Faraj, Jordan, in: A. Pinilla, M.J. Muchedo and J.J. Tresserras (eds) *First European Meeting on Phytolith Research, 23-26 September*, Madrid.

T. Rutagwenda, M. Lechner-Doll, H.J. Schwartz, W. Schultka and W. von Engelhardt (1990) Dietary preference and degradability of forage on a semiarid thornbush savannah by indigenous ruminants, camels and donkeys, *Animal Feed Science and Technology* 31: 179-192.

M.S. Ryan and D.C. Johanson (1989) Anterior dental microwear in *Australopithecus afarensis*: comparisons with human and non-human primates, *Journal of Human Evolution* 18: 235-268.

M.S. Sartre (1995) *L'Asie Mineure et l'Anatolie d'Alexandre à Dioclétien: IVe siècle av. J.C./ IIIe siècle ap. J.C.*, Paris.

I. Signe and J.E. Skydsgaard (1992) *Ancient Greek Agriculture: An Introduction*, London – New York.

J.E. Skydsgaard (1988) Transhumance in ancient Greece, in: C.R. Whittaker (ed.) *Pastoral Economies in Classical Antiquity. Supplementary Volume 14 (The Cambridge Philological Society)*: 75-86.

N. Solounias, M. Teaford and A. Walker (1988) Interpreting the diet of extinct ruminants: the case of a non-browsing giraffid, *Paleobiology* 14/3: 287-300.

N. Solounias and L.A.C. Hayek (1993) New methods of tooth microwear analysis and application to dietary determination of two extinct antelopes, *Journal of Zoology* 229: 421-445.

S.G. Strait (1993) Molar microwear in extant small-bodied faunivorous mammals: an analysis of feature density and pit frequency, *American Journal of Physical Anthropology* 92: 63-79.

M.F. Teaford and A. Walker (1984) Quantitative differences in dental microwear between primate species with different diets and a comment on the presumed diet of *Sivapithecus*, *American Journal of Physical Anthropology* 64: 191-200.

M.F. Teaford (1988) A review of dental microwear and diet in modern mammals, *Scanning Microscopy* 2/2: 1149-1166.

M.F. Teaford and J.G. Robinson (1989) Seasonal or ecological differences in diet and molar microwear in *Cebus nigrivittatus*, *American Journal of Physical Anthropology* 80: 391-401.

M.F. Teaford and K.E. Glander (1991) Dental microwear in live, wild-trapped Alouatta palliata from Costa Rica, *American Journal of Physical Anthropology* 85: 313-319.

M.F. Teaford (1994) Dental microwear and dental function, *Evolutionary Anthropology*: 17-30.

M.F. Teaford and J.D. Lytle (1996) Brief communication: diet-induced changes in rates of human tooth microwear: a case study involving stone-ground maize. *American Journal of Physical Anthropology* 100: 143-147.

M.F. Teaford, M.C. Maas and E.L. Simons (1996) Dental microwear and microstructure in Early Oligocene primates from the Fayum, Egypt: implications for diet, *American Journal of Physical Anthropology* 101: 527-543.

J.M.C. Toynbee (1973) Animals in Roman life and art, in: H.H. Scullard (ed.) *Aspects of Greek and Roman Life*, London.

J.C. Turner (1977) Cemental annulations as an age criterion in North American sheep, *Journal of Wildlife Management* 41/2: 211-217.

P.C. Twiss, E. Suess and R.M. Smith (1969) Morphological classification of grass phytoliths, *Soil Science Society of America, Proceedings* 33: 109-115.

P.C. Twiss (1992) Predicted world distribution of C3 and C4 grass phytoliths, in: G. Rapp Jr. and S.C. Mulholland (eds) *Phytolith Systematics: Emerging Issues, Advances in Archaeological and Museum Science* 1, New York – London: 113-128.

P.S. Ungar (1994) Incisor microwear of Sumatran primates, *American Journal of Physical Anthropology* 94: 339-363.

P.S. Ungar, M.F. Teaford, K.E. Glander and R.F. Pastor (1995) Dust accumulation in the canopy: a potential cause of dental microwear in primates, *American Journal of Physical Anthropology* 97: 93-99.

P.S. Ungar and M.F. Teaford (1996) Preliminary examination of non-occlusal dental microwear in Anthropoids: implications for the study of fossil primates, *American Journal of Physical Anthropology* 100: 101-113.

W. Van Neer and B. De Cupere (1993) First archaeozoological results from the Hellenistic-Roman site of Sagalassos, in: M. Waelkens and J. Poblome (eds) *Sagalassos I. First General Report on the Survey (1986-1989) and Excavations (1990-1991) (Acta Archaeologica Lovaniensia Monographiae* 5) Leuven University Press: 225-238.

W. Van Neer, B. De Cupere and M. Waelkens (1997) Remains of local and imported fish at the ancient site of Sagalassos (Burdur Prov., Turkey), in: M. Waelkens and J. Poblome (eds) *Sagalassos IV. Report on the Survey and Excavation Campaigns of 1994 and 1995 (Acta Archaeologica Lovaniensia Monographiae* 9) Leuven University Press: 571-586.

P. Van Mele and S. Anthonysamy (1994) How goats exploit available resources, *Third Symposium of Applied Biology, 28-29 May*: 7-9.

P. Van Mele, M.P. Davis and R.A. Halim (1994a) A fast method to estimate quality and quantity of pasture intake by grazing animals, *Second Symposium on Sheep Production in Malaysia*, Serdang: 105-106.

P. Van Mele, S. Anthonysamy, C. Symoens and H. Beeckman (1994b) Feeding time and botanical composition of diets selected by indigenous goats on native pastures in Malaysia, *Pertanika Journal of Tropical Agricultural Science* 17/3: 229-237.

B. van Valkenburgh, M.F. Teaford and A. Walker (1990) Molar microwear and diet in large carnivores: inferences concerning diet in the sabretooth cat, *Smilodon fatalis*, *Journal of Zoology* 222: 319-340.

J.C. Vogel (1978) Isotopic assessment of the dietary habits of ungulates, *South African Journal of Science* 74: 298-301.

M. Waelkens, E. Paulissen, M. Vermoere, P. Degryse, D. Celis, K. Schroyen, B. De Cupere, I. Librecht, K. Nackaerts, H. Vanhaverbeke, W. Viaene, Ph. Muchez, R. Ottenburgs, J. Deckers, W. Van Neer, E. Smets, G. Govers, G. Verstraeten, A. Steegen and K. Cauwenberghs (1999). Man and environment in the territory of Sagalassos, a classical city in SW Turkey, *Quarternary Science Reviews* 18(4-5), 297-709.

A. Walker, H.N. Hoeck and L. Perçz (1978) Microwear of mammalian teeth as an indicator of diet, *Science* 201: 908-910.

A. Walker and M. Teaford (1989) Inferences from quantitative analysis of dental microwear, *Folia Primatologica* 53: 177-189.

J.A. Wallace (1974) Approximal grooving of teeth, *American Journal of Physical Anthropology* 40: 385-390.

C.R. Whittaker (1988) *Pastoral Economies in Classical Antiquity (The Cambridge Philological Society Supplementary Vol. 14)*.

K.D. White (1970) Roman farming, in: H.H. Sculland (ed.) *Aspects of Greek and Roman Life*, London – Southampton.

R.A. Wigal and J.A. Chapman (1983) Age determination, reproduction and mortality of the gray fox (*Urocyon cinereoargenteus*) in Maryland, USA, *Zeitschrift für Saugetierkunde* 48/4: 226-245.

B.C. Yalçın (1979) The sheep breeds of Afghanistan, Iran and Turkey, *Food and Agriculture Organization of the United Nations, FAO/UNEP Project FP/1108-76-02(833)*.

B.C. Yalçın (1986) Sheep and goats in Turkey, *Food and Agriculture Organization of the United Nations (FAO)*.

F.E. Zeuner (1963) *A History of Domesticated Animals*, London.

AN EXPERIMENTAL APPROACH TO UNDERSTANDING THE BONE WORKING INDUSTRY AT ROMAN SAGALASSOS

Zissis PARRAS

3376 Colonial Dr., Mississauga ON, L5L 5C6 Canada

1. INTRODUCTION

This paper is a summary of the author's master's thesis which was completed in 1996 at the Katholieke Universiteit Leuven, where worked bone objects that have been discovered during the previous campaigns from the site of Sagalassos were reproduced. This summary also includes first hand observations made by the author of the aforementioned bone objects. The experiment represents only one possible way in which these bone objects may have been manufactured, but in the author's opinion the simplest method is usually the best method, as is the case with this experiment.

The bone artifacts from Sagalassos have already been reviewed by Van Neer and De Cupere 1993 (see also De Cupere et al. 1993). The majority of artifacts consist of hairpins, pins, needles and spoons and have been collected from most areas on the site but the greatest concentrations come from the Neon Library, the late Hellenistic fountain house and the Doric temple excavation sites (De Cupere et al. 1993).

The objectives of this report are to document the way in which the experiment was carried out and its conclusions. This report will also compare these conclusions with data collected from observations made during the 1996 campaign on artifacts from the site.

2. MATERIAL

Most of the identifiable worked bone material comes from cattle (99%) and of that total amount, 53.3% has been identified as metapodials. For this experiment 22 cattle metapodials were used because they are the most represented raw material (De Cupere et al. 1993). The cattle bones were provided by the Laboratory of Osteology of the Royal Museum for Central Africa at Tervuren (Belgium). They were acquired from a slaughter-house at Anderlecht.

3. TOOLS USED

From the British Isles to the Middle East, including Sagalassos, worked bone artifacts have been found, but as yet none of the bone-workers' tools nor the workshops have ever been identified (Boon 1974; Clason 1980; De Cupere et al. 1993; Sackett 1992; Wapnish 1991). Fortunately, markings on unfinished worked bone give an indication of the tools that could have been used to make them (De Cupere et al. 1993). These may represent saw marks, knife marks, chisel marks, polish marks, incision marks and grooves (Al Walda 1978; De Cupere et al. 1993; Reese 1988; Wapnish 1991). Crabtree (1985) suggests that various markings, which are obviously not related to butchery, such as incised lines, shave markings and surface polish are almost always related to bone working. In addition to the above-mentioned tools there also seems to be evidence for broad chisels used for splitting, gouges, centre bits and compasses (Carmelez 1982; Reese 1988; Wapnish 1991). Some other tools which could have been used for polishing and smoothing such as rubbing stones, pumice, sand with leather and fish skins have also been noted (Carmelez 1982; Reese 1988; Wapnish 1991). From the tools already mentioned it seems as though the bone worker used many more than merely saws, knives and files and there would have been subtle differences in the tools of bone-workers in different regions.

For this experiment the following tools were used (from top to bottom in Fig. 1): 1 steel hack-saw with many blades (10 teeth per cm); 2 fine files (one flat file and one half round file); 1 flat coarse file; 1 steel knife (used for carving); 1 butter knife with sharpened end; 1 small chisel and 1 clamp (not shown).

One other bone-working tool that may be used but is not mentioned above is the lathe. Lathes, or some other mechanism used to turn bones, have been identified as tools for bone-workers (Wilson 1976; Al Walda 1978; MacGregor 1989; Wapnish 1991). The bone-worker's lathe would probably have been similar to the carpenter's lathe. A lathe was not used in the experiment for the simple reason that one was made by the author but it did not function properly in the manufacture of the replicas. As will be discussed later in the discussion, the results of the experiment were not affected by the lack of a lathe.

When reducing the bone wedges with a knife or draw knife, the piece must be held in a clamp or a vice. While working the bones during the experiment, they were placed in a metal vice and small grip marks became imprinted on the bones from the vice. When a later stage of the bone working was reached, the small marks were removed by filing. The ancient clamp may have been made of wood and would not have left marks on the bone. None of these clamp marks have been observed on the Sagalassos material or on any published evidence.

The tools used were all modern tools made of good quality steel. The Roman tool equivalents would probably have been made of iron. Iron tools were not used in the experiment because iron saws and knives are not made very often and are very difficult to obtain. Substituting iron for steel would not have made any significant difference in this experiment.

4. EXPERIMENT

It must be emphasised that in this experiment the parameters reflect the reproduction of artifacts found at Sagalassos, and one important consideration has been omitted -that is, the customer. The bone-worker's most important concern along with the above criteria would have been the destined user of the finished product. This would certainly have influenced the selection of raw materials, the time of preparation and the tools used.

There were essentially two steps involved in the experiment. The first was the processing of the raw material into suitable blanks and the second was shaping the blanks into reproductions of the artifacts found at the site.

4.1. Preparation of raw material

The first step in preparing the metapodials was to remove the fur, muscles and tendons and to separate the phalanges from the metapodials. This was done with the aid of a sharp knife, which took approximately 5-10 minutes per bone. Throughout the cleaning, the knife needed to be re-sharpened for each metapodial. Cleaning continued until the bone shaft (diaphysis) was exposed and the ends of the bones (epiphyses) were also cleaned thoroughly. The bones were cleaned sufficiently thoroughly to allow anatomical measurements to be made. The measurements taken were in accordance with the manual *A Guide to the Measurement of Animal Bones from Archaeological Sites* (von den Driesch 1976). One point to consider is that the bone-worker would not have needed to clean the ends of the bone because they would have been sawn off, which would have decreased the amount of time needed to prepare the bone. After the measurements were taken, the epiphyses were sawn off. The next stage of the preparation was to remove the fat, marrow and odour from the bones which was achieved by two different methods. One method is maceration, which was used for half the bones. The second method is boiling, which was used for the other half of the bones.

4.1.1. Maceration

The first method was to allow the bones to soak in water at room temperature until the grease and fat disappeared. Half of the assemblage (11 bones), made up of metacarpus and metatarsus bones, were cleaned by this method. The bones were soaked for approximately 17 weeks. This method requires little effort but is time-consuming. The water was regularly changed once a week to help remove the grease from the bones. When the grease had been removed, the bones were rinsed with warm water. The climate in southern Turkey is much warmer in summer than it is in Belgium. If the bones had been allowed to soak outside in the high temperatures and in direct sunlight during the summer, the maceration process may have taken less than half the time. During the winter in Sagalassos the temperatures are colder, therefore maceration would be most efficient during the summer.

4.1.2. Boiling

The second method involved boiling the other eleven bones to remove the grease and marrow. The bones were placed in boiling water for approximately 20 minutes. Because bone "loses much of its organic matter in cooking, only fresh bone is really suitable for working." (Krzyszkowska 1990: 25). The bones were boiled just long enough to remove the grease and fat, so that they would still retain their strength. After boiling they were also scraped with a knife to remove any remaining muscles and tendons. This took 2-3 minutes per bone. When removing muscles and tendons after the bone had been boiled, the knife was used as a scraper and did not have to be sharpened at all. This allowed the bones to be cleaned quickly and more completely.

Another method, which was not employed in this experiment, is to remove the epiphyses, extract the marrow, then allow the bones to soak in cold water for approximately two to three days to allow the blood to leach out. At this stage the bones should be boiled in water for 1.5 hours and finally rinsed with hot water (Nieuwenburg 1984). According to Ulbricht (1984), ancient peoples boiled bones for bone-working, as this seems to be a more efficient and quicker way to prepare them. Boiling is quicker but requires fuel to burn and cooking ware in which to boil the bones. Macerating requires only water and containers to leave the bones in. A full-time bone-worker may have employed both methods to prepare his material.

4.2. Preparation of bone before working

All of the bones were soaked in water to soften them before working. Soaking for at least 48 hours was necessary, as soaking for any less time meant the bones were still too brittle to work. Some of the bones, which had been left out of the water for more than three days, broke during the working process and when some of these same bones fell on the cement floor, they shattered. The bones soaked for over 48 hours remained very malleable, and suffered no damage when dropped.

4.3. Methods used to work bone

From the 22 bones that were prepared, only those which were long enough to make hair pins and thick enough to make spoons were selected. After the shaft had soaked in water for enough time, the bone's length and thickness was considered to see what could be made. Because the bone objects found at Sagalassos were pins, needles, hairpins, and spoons, these were the objects that were made.

4.3.1. Pins, hairpins and needles

For pins, hairpins and needles the shafts were sawn lengthwise into quarters, producing wedge-shaped pieces (Fig. 2). One shaft yielded some 7 or 8 pieces, and from these pieces the long thin ones were selected for pins and needles and the long thick ones for hairpins. The bone was then placed in the vice and the knife was used to reduce the size by shaving. Because the bone had been soaked for a sufficient amount of time, the shavings were removed very easily. When the bone was left out of the water for more than 24 hours, removing shavings was more difficult. Also, when the bone had been softened, the knife did not need to be sharpened as often. The bone was regularly rotated lengthwise and reduced until the piece took on a conical shape.

Once the bone was the correct shape and thickness, the files were used instead of the knife for further shaping. The coarse flat file was used first by placing it in the vice with its teeth uppermost. The bone was held in the operator's right hand and pushed across the upturned teeth of the file in a continuously rotating movement. This method worked very well with the left hand applying pressure on the bone, while the right hand guided the piece across the file, reducing the bone quickly and evenly. After every 10 to 15 movements across the file, work was stopped while the bone dust was blown out of the file teeth because the build-up of dust reduced the efficiency of the file.

Any decorative motifs were prepared during this stage using the coarse flat file. The head of the pin was prepared by leaving approximately 1 to 2 cm on the top of the cone unfiled and this was rounded by holding the opposite end of the bone and moving it in a rotating manner.

The coarse file was no longer needed when the bone had been rounded to the desired thickness, made into a conical shape, with a defined head and the knife marks and the saw marks erased. The finer flat file was placed in the vice and was used to remove the marks left from the coarse file. The bone was moved across the fine file in the same manner as described above for the coarse file. The file was fine enough to polish the surface of the bone, so no other polishing was required. The head was rounded and shaped during this stage. Hutchinson et al. (1988) suggest that during this stage the object could be waxed or oiled to give a high polish.

After the piece was polished, the final stage was the addition of any desired decoration to the bone. Any incised marks or grooves can be easily made by moving the bone across the corner of the fine flat file or the half-round file placed in the vice. The bone could be rotated across the file to create an even circular groove around it. The eye of the needle was also made in this final stage. The eye was made with a hand-driven drill.

4.3.2. Spoons

Spoons have to be made from bones that are long, straight and thick. They were probably made from radio-ulnas and metapodials (De Cupere et al. 1993). In this experiment, spoons were made from metacarpus and metatarsus bones that were the appropriate size and thickness. De Cupere et al. (1993) suggest that one spoon could be made from one long bone and the rest of the bone could be sectioned into wedges for making other bone objects. During the manufacturing process, it was found that up to three spoons could be made from the same metapodial (Fig. 3).

The first step in spoon manufacture was to section the bone into appropriately sized wedges. If the bone that was selected was thick enough for only one spoon, the remainder of the bone was made into wedge-shaped pieces to make pins and hairpins out of (Fig. 4). The posterior surface of the bone was sawn off to make one relatively broad and flat

Fig.1: Bone working tools.

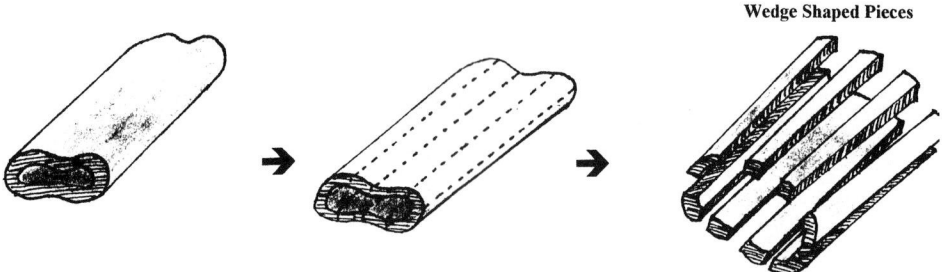

Fig.2: Sectioning of the shaft for pins, hair pins and needles.

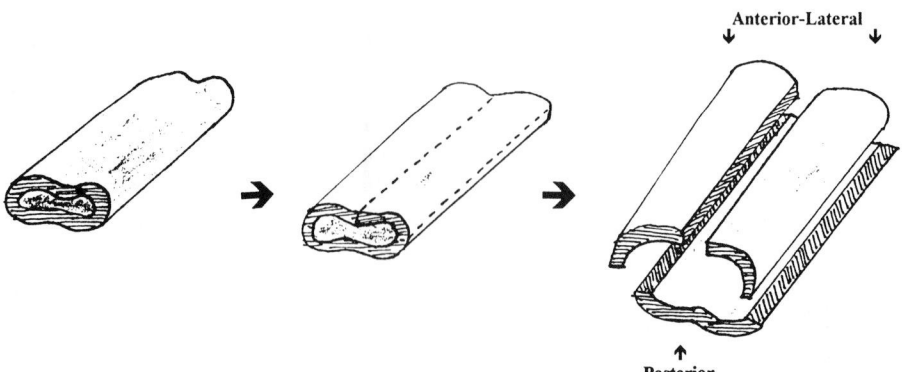

Fig.3: Sectioning of shaft for three spoons.

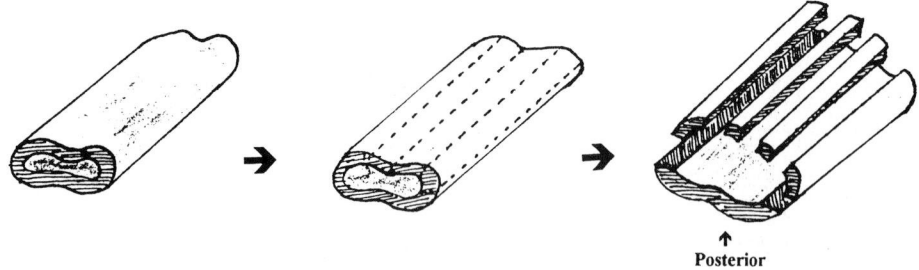

Fig. 4: Sectioning of the shaft for spoons, pins, hair-pins and needles.

Fig. 5: Finished pins, hair-pins and needles.

Fig. 6: Finished spoons showing underside.

Fig .7: Finished spoons showing open bowl side.

Fig. 8: Knife refuse.

Fig. 9: Spoon refuse.

Fig. 10: Chisel refuse from spoon bowl.

piece. Because the external surface of the bone is already naturally rounded, it served as the back part of the bowl of the spoon. To make three spoons from one bone, the posterior side should be sectioned as described above, but the anterior section should be sawn longitudinally into two sections. An outline of the spoon shape was then drawn on the outer surface of the bone segment and the spoon shape was sawn out while it was held in the vice.

The spoon blanks were rounded and smoothed with a knife and a coarse flat file. As with making the hairpins, the spoon was placed in the vice and the knife used to shave off pieces of bone. Then the coarse flat file was placed in the vice and the spoon blank was moved across the file in the same manner as with the needles, pins and hairpins.

The spoon blank was placed within the vice and the bowl of the spoon was carved out with the chisel. The spoon blank was then held in the left hand and smoothed with the sharpened butter knife held in the right hand. The butter knife removed most of the ridges from the bowl and smoothed it. The knife itself left small grooves in the bowl but they were polished out in the next stage.

The finishing stage was where the spoon was smoothed with the fine flat file. The file was again placed in the vice.

Decoration was added to the spoons in the same way as with the pins and hairpins using the edge of the flat file. The insides of the bowls were polished with the aid of some fine beach sand and a pair of leather gloves. The spoon was held in the palm of the left hand with the bowl facing up and a small amount of sand was placed in the bowl. The right hand gloved thumb rubbed the sand round the inside of the bowl in a circular motion. This procedure took approximately 10 minutes for each spoon. This smoothed the bowl and took out most of the grooves left by the butter knife.

5. FINISHED PIECES AND TIME TAKEN

The pins, hairpins and needles that were completed are shown in Fig. 5 and their relevant data listed in Table 1. In Fig. 5 the second needle from the bottom was intended for a pin but it broke during manufacture and so was finished as a needle. The bone-worker would have probably encountered similar situations and would have also improvised. The three finished spoons (Table 2) were all made from one metatarsal bone. Each stage of the spoons was completed before proceeding to the next stage. Throughout the experiment, the author was improving as a bone-worker (Figs 6 and 7).

#	Object	Bone	SL	OL	Time
1	Pin	B1	99	88	2h
2	Hairpin	B1	99	97	2h30min
3	Hair pin	B2	112	110	2h
4	Needle	B11	150	76	1h30min
5	Pin	B11	150	129	3h
6	Needle	B2	112	79	1h
7	Pin	B11	150	144	4h30min

Table 1: Objects made in order as they appear in Fig. 5 from top to bottom. All objects were made from bones that were boiled. The number identifies the source bone, SL (Shaft Length) identifies the length of the shaft of bone and OL (Object Length) identifies the length of each finished object. The time states the total approximate time taken to complete each object from the cleaning of the bone to carving. Alle measurements are in millimeters and all times are rounded off to hours and minutes.

#	Object	Bone	SL	OL	Time
1	Spoon	M10	140	132	2h 27 min
2	Spoon	M10	140	134	2h 17 min
3	Spoon	M10	140	133	2h 37 min

Table 2: Spoons that were made from the same bone prepared by maceration. The headings are the same as in Table 1.

6. REFUSE

One aspect of this experiment is the refuse produced that gives evidence of the bone-working process. The type of refuse found at Sagalassos was mostly unfinished pieces, bone rings, wedges and epiphyses. The refuse resulting from the experiment included this type of refuse as well as some additional smaller refuse. This refuse includes knife shavings, chisel flakes, bone dust and many small pieces of bone (Figs 8-10).

A key to the identification of a bone workshop at Sagalassos, or at any other site, is to look at the refuse rather than the finished pieces. Finished pieces are usually removed from the work area and used by the customer and so cannot be used to identify the work shop. Bone dust from saws and files is very difficult to find, but the larger bone pieces and even the knife and chisel debris can be found, with the aid of a small screen if preservation conditions are optimal.

Of the worked bone refuse from Sagalassos, an interesting part of the material was rings of bone. There were 46 rings of bone out of 1042 total cattle bones, or 4.4% (De Cupere et al. 1993). These were short cylindrical pieces from the shaft of the bone, usually removed from the distal or proximal ends to obtain the desired length for the artifacts. This suggests that the bone worker already had an idea of what was going to be made even before dividing the shaft into wedge shaped blanks. In contrast, during the experiment, rings were not produced because, when sectioning the shaft, the primary aim was to remove as many long bone wedges as possible. Only when work on one of the wedges began would each be shortened to the desired length, thus not producing a ring but a small length of bone usually 10-15 mm in length. Rings were removed from the shafts by ancient bone workers possibly because there was a standard length for certain objects like pins and hairpins. Thus, removing a bone ring from a shaft would make all the subsequent bone wedges the same length as a type of 'mass production' of objects. The end result of the experiment was that the artifacts produced were identical to the Sagalassos material but the refuse was of a different nature, indicating that refuse at any site may take many forms.

6.1. Saw marks

In the experiment only one saw was used for all the cutting. From the saw marks on the modern bones, it looks as if the same saw produced two different sizes of marks, one smaller than the other. The amount of force needed to cut the piece of bone is important when examining saw marks. When sawing a long piece of bone, long powerful strokes are needed, but when cutting smaller pieces a shorter and gentler stroke is needed to cut the bone properly and it can thus seem as though two different saws have been used. The average number of saw marks on the ends of the bone wedges, from the experiment, was 12.75 per cm compared to 12.5 per cm from Sagalassos bone wedges. The average number of saw marks on the long sides of the bone wedges was 5.5 per cm compared to 5.8 per cm from Sagalassos bone wedges. From this evidence it is clear that the same saw used with varying force can produce different size cut marks. It is therefore possible that the bone-workers at Sagalassos may have used only one type of saw.

7. DISCUSSION

Because it is not permitted to remove artifacts from Turkey, the author had only photographs to refer to when making the replicas. It was not until the experiment had ended that the author was able to visit Sagalassos and examine the original bone-working refuse first hand. Since no tools relating to bone-working have as yet been found at Sagalassos, no comparison of tools is possible and only the finished pieces and the refuse will be examined.

Of the finished pieces from Sagalassos, it is apparent that most have been made without the use of a lathe. Although they are very straight, they are not perfectly straight, as one would expect if a lathe had been used. Also, the heads of the pins and hairpins are not perfect spheres, as would be produced on a lathe. It seems that the simple pins and hairpins were 'mass produced' and fit a number of general shapes and sizes. The bone objects show the same imperfections as the ones that were manufactured during the experiment. There were a small number of finished objects that were definitely made using a lathe and some of these show signs of an all round higher degree of skill and care.

The chisel marks from an unfinished spoon appear to have been made beginning at the handle and moving towards the centre of the bowl and from the lip of the spoon to the centre. These marks suggest that the spoon could have been held in the hand and the chisel pushed with the other hand and used as a carving tool, or it could perhaps have been held in a vice. This method is essentially the same as that used in the experiment. This way the carver has much better control of the carving tool and can make a strong lip on the spoon.

Looking closely at the unfinished objects, it is possible to see file marks, smoothing out the bone's rough shape, overlying knife marks which were used to give the bone its general shape. This technique is the same as that used by the author in the experiment and verifies that the method used in the experiment is similar to that used by the ancient bone-workers. A very fine polish was observed on the shaft of the hairpins, but this polish was probably not produced by the bone-worker but rather from everyday use. The heads of the pins do not have this polish. Adding the decoration was the final stage in the manufacture of any bone artifact. The decoration for some of the pieces in the experiment was achieved by adding grooves to the piece. There are two ways in which these grooves were made: by making small 'cuts' into the hairpin with the saw blade or by using the corner of a fine flat file. These two methods can be distinguished by the shape of the grooves. The saw leaves a U-shape and the file leaves a V-shape. This method was also observed on the various artifacts from Sagalassos. Decoration made by knives, centre bits, and drills have also been observed on the Sagalassos material.

From a series of unfinished pins that were examined, it was obvious that the way the heads were made is the same way as those of the pins in the experiment. The wedges would be prepared by saw and knife and then the file would be used to make the shape of the head. Also, a series of unfinished pins are all broken in the same way at the same place, which clearly shows that they must have been held in a vice or clamp in order for the break to be the same on each.

8. CONCLUSION

From this experiment a number of points regarding bone-working at Sagalassos have been determined. The replicas of the spoons, pins, hairpins and needles that were made indicate a plausible ancient manufacturing technique. The different types of saw marks indicate the possibility that only one saw is needed for bone-working, even though two different sizes of saw marks are found on the unfinished bones.

The examination of the refuse from bone-working has shown three important points. Firstly, it shows the particular shapes of refuse produced from the manufacture of spoons, pins, hairpins and needles. Secondly, because the refuse produced by the experiment is comparable to that found at Sagalassos, the methods of production are probably similar. Thirdly, in being able to determine what the refuse from specific tools (knife and chisel) looks like, archaeologists in the future may be better able to identify the remains of bone-worker's workshops.

An interesting point to consider is that most of the hairpins from the Sagalassos assemblage are not of a very good quality. Many of them were made crudely and apparently quickly. The bone-worker was a highly skilled individual who possibly 'mass-produced' large quantities of 'rough' looking hairpins and other objects for most of his customers but may have taken greater time and effort to manufacture more personalised objects for wealthy customers.

The bone-worker was probably a specialist who used common tools but in specialised forms (e.g. a small saw and a fine file). A bone specialist was responsible for the large quantities of worked bone objects, but there may have also been other individuals who made the odd hairpin or needle when needed. It would be possible to distinguish between the specialist's products and the ones made by the common person by the workmanship, but also the location and the amount of refuse at the work area would distinguish the work of the specialist from that of a common person. A daily bone industry would have produced a large quantity of debris and the occasional bone-worker would have produced very little.

As more of the site of Sagalassos is excavated and greater attention is given to the industrial sectors and the living quarters, more information will be gained about the local economy of the town and how the bone-worker contributed to it. This experiment has provided a basis from which archaeologists can now recognise many more aspects of the bone-worker's craft and the bone artifacts.

9. ACKNOWLEDGEMENTS

This research is supported by the Belgian Programme on Interuniversity Poles of Attraction (IUAP 4/12) initiated by the Belgian State, Prime Minister's Office, Science Policy Programming. The text also presents the results of the Concerted Action of the Flemish Government (GOA 97/2) and the Fund for Scientific Research-Flanders (Belgium) (FWO) (G.2145.94). Scientific responsibility is assumed by the author.

I also would like to thank a few people who throughout my research and experimentation were invaluable; Dr. Wim Van Neer whose guidance and direction was greatly appreciated, Philippe Charlier who assisted me with preparing the bones, Dr. Bea De Cupere, Dr. An Lentacker, Dr. Joann McDaniel and Dr. Jeroen Poblome who helped me with my research, the Osteology Laboratory of the Royal Museum of Central Africa in Tervuren, Dr. Dirk Huyge, Dr. Charles Frank Herman, Prof. Dr. Etienne Paulissen and the facilities at the Earth Sciences Building of KUL, Shawn Bubel and Julie Van Den Bergh for helping with translating some texts, Dr. Lutgarde Vandeput for providing me with maps of Sagalassos, Prof. Dr. Marc Waelkens for allowing me the opportunity of examining the worked bone artefacts, the depot personnel at Sagalassos, Dr. David S. Reese for sending me some articles on bone-working and my wife Aida whose constant support and love were indispensable.

10. REFERENCES

H.M. Al Walda (1978) Bone objects from the excavations at Petra, Jordan, *Institute of Archaeology Bulletin* 15.

G.C. Boon (1974) *Silchester: The Roman town of Calleva*, London.

J.C. Carmelez (1982) *Artisanat Gallo-Romain: Le travail de l'os et de la Corne*, Bavay.

A.T. Clason (1980) Worked bone and antler objects from Dorestad, Hoogstraat I, in: W.J.H.Verwers and W.A. van Es (eds) *Excavations at Dorestad 1 The Harbour: Hoogstraat (Kromme Rijn Projekt* I. *Nederlandse Oudheden* 9), Amersfoort.

P. Crabtree (1985) West Stow the Angle-Saxon village, *East Anglian Archaeology* 1/24: 1-186.

B. De Cupere, W. Van Neer and A. Lentacker (1993) Some aspects of the bone-working industry in Roman Sagalassos, in: M. Waelkens and J. Poblome (eds) *Sagalassos II. Report on the Third Excavation Campaign of 1992 (Acta Archaeologica Lovaniensia Monographiae* 6) Leuven University Press: 269-278.

V.J. Hutchinson and D.S. Reese (1988) Worked bone industry at Carthage, in: J.H. Humphrey (ed.) *The Circus and a Byzantine Cemetery at Carthage* 1/2, Ann Arbor: 549-594.

O. Krzyszkowska (1990) *Ivory and Related Materials: An Illustrated Guide (Bulletin Supplement* 59).

A.G. MacGregor (1989) Bone antler and horn industries in the urban context, in: D. Serjeantson and T. Waldron (eds) *Diet and Crafts in Towns: The Evidence of Animal Remains from the Roman to the Post-Medieval Periods (BAR British Series* 199): 107- 128.

A. Nieuwenburg (1984) *Beenbewerken. Het maken van sieraden en gebruiksvoorwerpen*, de Bilt.

D.S. Reese (1988)- Iron age bone working in the Mediterranean basin, *American Journal of Archaeology* 92/2: 276.

L.H. Sackett (1992) Objects in bone and bone working, in: L.H. Sackett (ed.) *Knossos from Greek City to Roman Colony: Excavations at the Unexplored Mansion II (The British School of Archaeology at Athens)*: 379-389.

W. Van Neer and B. De Cupere (1993) First archaeozoological results from the Hellenistic-Roman site of Sagalassos, in: M. Waelkens (ed.) *Sagalassos I. First General Report on the Survey (1986-1989) and Excavations (1990-1991) (Acta Archaeologica Lovaniensia Monographiae* 5) Leuven University Press: 225-238.

A. von den Driesch (1976) *A Guide to the Measurement of Animal Bones from Archaeological Sites (Peabody Museum Bulletins* 1).

P. Wapnish (1991) Beauty and utility in bone: new light on bone crafting, *Biblical Archaeological Review* 27/4 July/August: 54-57.

D.M. Wilson (1976) Craft and industry, in: D. M. Wilson (ed.) *The Archaeology of Anglo-Saxon England*, Cambridge: 253-281.

PRINTED ON PERMANENT PAPER • IMPRIME SUR PAPIER PERMANENT • GEDRUKT OP DUURZAAM PAPIER - ISO 9706
ORIENTALISTE, KLEIN DALENSTRAAT 42, B-3020 HERENT